Morocco

THE ROUGH GUIDE

There are more than one hundred and fifty Rough Guide titles
covering destinations from Amsterdam to Zimbabwe

Forthcoming travel titles include
Beijing • Cape Town • Croatia • Ecuador • Switzerland

Rough Guide Reference Series
Classical Music • Drum 'n' Bass • English Football • European Football
House • The Internet • Jazz • Music USA • Opera • Reggae
Rock Music • Techno • World Music

Rough Guide Phrasebooks
Czech • Dutch • Egyptian Arabic • European Languages • French
German • Greek • Hindi & Urdu • Hungarian • Indonesian
Italian • Japanese • Mandarin Chinese • Mexican Spanish • Polish
Portuguese • Russian • Spanish • Swahili • Thai • Turkish • Vietnamese

Rough Guides on the Internet
http://www.roughguides.com

ROUGH GUIDE CREDITS

THIS EDITION
Text editors Orla Duane and Mark Ellingham
Proofreading Elaine Pollard
Typesetting Helen Ostick
Maps Mick Bohoslawec

Series editor Mark Ellingham
Editorial Martin Dunford, Jonathan Buckley, Samantha Cook, Jo Mead, Kate Berens, Amanda Tomlin, Ann-Marie Shaw, Paul Gray, Sarah Dallas, Chris Schüler, Caroline Osborne, Helena Smith, Kieran Falconer, Judith Bamber, Olivia Eccleshall, Orla Duane, Ruth Blackmore, Sophie Martin (UK); Andrew Rosenberg (US)

Production Susanne Hillen, Andy Hilliard, Judy Pang, Link Hall, Nicola Williamson, Helen Ostick, James Morris
Cartography Melissa Flack, Maxine Burke, Nichola Goodliffe
Picture research Eleanor Hill
Online editors Alan Spicer, Kate Hands (UK); Geronimo Madrid (US)
Finance John Fisher, Celia Crowley, Neeta Mistry
Marketing & Publicity Richard Trillo, Simon Carloss, Niki Smith (UK); Jean-Marie Kelly, SoRelle Braun (US)
Administration Tania Hummel, Alexander Mark Rogers

ACKNOWLEDGEMENTS

The main **researchers** for this fifth edition of *The Rough Guide to Morocco* were Don Grisbrook, Daniel Jacobs, and, in the Atlas Mountains, Hamish Brown. Hamish also provided many of the **photos**, as did long-term contributor Dan Eitzen, along with his fellow Agadir-based photographer, D. Britel.

The researchers on this edition would like to thank the following, Laghmir Abdelmoula; Annie Austin of CLM; Tony Andrews; Ali El Kasmi and Hassan Benlamlih of the Moroccan Tourist Board

in London; Stephen Brown; Robin Cluley; Don Cruckshank; Bert Flint; Najim Lahcen; Annie Lambton; Kristy Larson; Roger Mimó; Sabir Mohammed; Samir Mustapha; Nioua Noureddine; Cherie Nutting; Andrew Rosenberg, Benzianme Saïd; Jill Swift; Badi Taoufik; Ian Twilley; and Jasper Winn.

We would also like to thank all the **readers** who wrote in with updates and comments – for the roll of honour, see "Readers' Letters", following.

PUBLISHING INFORMATION

This fifth edition published July 1998 by Rough Guides Ltd, 62-70 Shorts Gardens, London WC2H 9AB. Reprinted in April 1999 and in February 2000. Previous editions 1985, 1987, 1990, 1993.
Distributed by the Penguin Group:
Penguin Books Ltd, 27 Wrights Lane, London W8 5TZ
Penguin Books USA Inc., 375 Hudson Street, New York 10014, USA
Penguin Books Australia Ltd, 487 Maroondah Highway, PO Box 257, Ringwood, Victoria 3134, Australia
Penguin Books Canada Ltd, 10 Alcorn Avenue, Toronto, Ontario, Canada M4V 1E4
Penguin Books (NZ) Ltd, 182–190 Wairau Road, Auckland 10, New Zealand
Typeset in Linotron Univers and Century Old Style to an original design by Andrew Oliver.
Printed in England by Clays Ltd, St Ives PLC
Illustrations in Part One and Part Three by Edward Briant.

Illustrations on p.1 and p.519 by Henry Iles.
© Mark Ellingham, Shaun McVeigh and Don Grisbrook 1998.
No part of this book may be reproduced in any form without permission from the publisher except for the quotation of brief passages in reviews.
640pp – Includes index
A catalogue record for this book is available from the British Library
ISBN 1-85828-169-5

Morocco

THE ROUGH GUIDE

written and researched by

Mark Ellingham, Don Grisbrook
and Shaun McVeigh

Contributors

Hamish Brown, Dan Eitzen, Daniel Jacobs,
Jon Marks, Margaret Hubbard, Peter Morris,
Chris Overington and David Muddyman

THE ROUGH GUIDES

THE ROUGH GUIDES

TRAVEL GUIDES • PHRASEBOOKS • MUSIC AND REFERENCE GUIDES

 We set out to do something different when the first Rough Guide was published in 1982. Mark Ellingham, just out of university, was travelling in Greece. He brought along the popular guides of the day, but found they were all lacking in some way. They were either strong on ruins and museums but went on for pages without mentioning a beach or taverna. Or they were so conscious of the need to save money that they lost sight of Greece's cultural and historical significance. Also, none of the books told him anything about Greece's contemporary life – its politics, its culture, its people, and how they lived.

So with no job in prospect, Mark decided to write his own guidebook, one which aimed to provide practical information that was second to none, detailing the best beaches and the hottest clubs and restaurants, while also giving hard-hitting accounts of every sight, both famous and obscure, and providing up-to-the-minute information on contemporary culture. It was a guide that encouraged independent travellers to find the best of Greece, and was a great success, getting shortlisted for the Thomas Cook travel guide award,

and encouraging Mark, along with three friends, to expand the series.

The Rough Guide list grew rapidly and the letters flooded in, indicating a much broader readership than had been anticipated, but one which uniformly appreciated the Rough Guide mix of practical detail and humour, irreverence and enthusiasm. Things haven't changed. The same four friends who began the series are still the caretakers of the Rough Guide mission today: to provide the most reliable, up-to-date and entertaining information to independent-minded travellers of all ages, on all budgets.

We now publish 100 titles and have offices in London and New York. The travel guides are written and researched by a dedicated team of more than 100 authors, based in Britain, Europe, the USA and Australia. We have also created a unique series of phrasebooks to accompany the travel guides, along with an acclaimed set of music reference books, and a best-selling pocket guide to the Internet and World Wide Web. We also publish comprehensive travel information on our Web site:

http://www.roughguides.com

HELP US UPDATE

We've gone to a lot of effort to ensure that this new edition of *The Rough Guide to Morocco* is accurate and up to date. However, things change – places get "discovered", opening hours are notoriously fickle, restaurants and rooms raise prices or lower standards, extra buses are laid on or off. If you feel we've got it wrong or left something out, we'd like to know, and if you can remember the address, the price, the time, the phone number, so much the better.

We'll credit all contributions, and send a copy of the next edition (or any other Rough Guide if you prefer) for the best letters. Please mark letters: "Rough Guide Morocco Update" and send to:
Rough Guides, 62–70 Shorts Gardens, London WC2H 9AB, or Rough Guides, 375 Hudson St, 9th floor, New York NY 10014. Or send email to: mail@roughguides.co.uk
Online updates about this book can be found on Rough Guides' Web site at http://www.roughguides.com

Hamish Brown is a mountain writer, guide and photographer, who has spent much of the past two decades walking and climbing in Morocco's Atlas Mountains.

Mark Ellingham originated the *Rough Guide* series and now spends most time working on the online development of the books.

Dan Eitzen is an American writer, walker, and photographer, based in Agadir.

Don Grisbrook discovered *Rough Guides* when on the verge of retirement – and has injected the series with his extraordinary research skills ever since. He makes several trips to Morocco each year.

Margaret Hubbard wrote the section "From A Woman's Perspective" in "Basics". She works in further education in Edinburgh.

Daniel Jacobs has contributed to many *Rough Guides*, and is author of the forthcoming title on *Israel and the Palestinian Territories*.

Jon Marks covers North Africa for the *Middle East Economic Digest*. He wrote the section on recent history and politics.

Shaun McVeigh co-wrote the first edition of this book and has since moved on from travel writing to the mysteries of jurisprudence, which he teaches in Brisbane, Australia.

Peter Morris works in banking, currently. He is author of *The Rough Guide to Tunisia* and wrote the section on Islam for this book.

David Muddyman wrote the piece on music in "Contexts". He is a London-based musician, playing mainly with the group Loop Guru.

Chris Overington is a naturalist and writer. He contributed the "Wildlife" overview and birdwatching feature-boxes.

As ever, research on this edition of *The Rough Guide to Morocco* has been helped enormously by readers who wrote in with comments, changes and discoveries. The letters we receive about Morocco are consistently the best of all those sent to Rough Guides – detailed, wonderfully generous in their sharing of knowledge and experiences.

A **thousand thanks** to the following:

Liz Agostino; Petra Ahrens; Dr. and Mrs C.I. Aitchison; S.D. Allan; Geoff Allen; Lilla Amirante; Tamara Atkinson; Gary Baker; Dave Banks; Sean Beattie; Francine Becker; Keren Beckermann; Karl Beenhey; Kirsty Bell; B. Berman; M de Bièvre; Rev. Richard Blakeway-Philips; Joy Bodine; Daniel Borden; G.D. Bowen; Susan & John Bowman; J.M. Bradshaw; El Ouarzazi Brahim; Roxanne Brame; Rob Bregoff; David Brien; Laurence Brook; Dr. A.R. Brown; Janet Brown; Justin Bryan; Dianne Budd; Nicholas Butcher; Lisa Byfield; Liz Campbell; Joseph Capute; Lisa Cardus; Nicholas Carpluk; Fatima Casewit; Colin J. Caulfield; Barry J. Charman; Jonathan Clarke; D.R. Cluely; John Cochrane; Dr Matthew Cock; Nick Cockcroft; Isobel Coleman; Sarah Condie; Barrie Cooper; John Cooper; R. deP. Daubeny; Mark Davis; Lesley Delacourt; E. Denys; Jean-François Deperetti; Tom Dixon; Maurice Dobie; Carol Donaldson; Marie Donn; Sally and Stuart Dunsmore; D. Durham; Jonathan & Sally Easterbrooke; Paul Emmerson; Mark Ensleigh; Denise Entin; S. Entwistle; Nicholas Farbridge; Jason Fargo; Brian & Gina Field; Kathleen Fleming; Lucia Gallagher; Susanne Gänsicke; Peter Gardiner; Ian Gardner; John Garratt; Carrie Gibson; Ralph Gilchrist; Nathan P. Gillet; Linda Glennie; Victoria Gosling; Brooke Graham; Camilla Gray; Douglas Gray; Chris Green; Rachel Grimshaw; Peter Guilliatt; Sue Hall; Viv Harrison; Michael Hastik; Barry Hawkins; Stephen Hayward; Catherine J.D. Heriot; Suzy Herring; Peter Heyn; Yasuko Higuchi; S. Hillier; Kirsten Hively; Terry Hodgkinson; Ernest Hole; Charles S. Holmes; Gavin Hookway; Kimberly Horelick; Jamie Hughes; Janet Huige-Lees; Suzan Inceer; Sue Inone; Louise James; Stephen Jarvis; Isabel & David Jordan; Aaron Karsh; Aengus Kelly; Bill Kelly; John Kelly; Fran King; Brian & Lesley Knox; Oren Kosansky; Johan Lagae; Chi Lam; Cathy Lee; Doris K. Lenart; Dot Lewis; Irene Paul Lombardo; G. Lovick; G. Luginbuhl; Daniel Luskin; Monica Mackaness; Paul Makkar; Bostjan Malovsh; Jo Manson; Warren Marsh; Lee Marshall; David Martin; Tony Masters; Andrew Matheson; Sarah Maul; Alycen C. McAuley; Alice McQuillin; C. McPetrie; Linda Anne Mead; Rosemary Mead; Ziad Mehdi; George & Gloria Melhuish; Aderdour M'hammed; Christine & Laurence Monkhauser; Gavin Mooney; John Mooney; Daniel Morgan; Sue Morris; K.W. Morrow; Harry Mount; Allen & Lynne Mulder; Joelle Nadle; Peter Newman; Ken Nicholson; Danial Nord; Per Nyberg; Colleen O'Conell; Doug Oldfield; Ahmed Oubana; Kerry Parkin; Wendy Parry; Piergiorgio Pascali; Carolyn Payne; Agnieska Pinowska; Alex Pointon; Steve & Zena Polin; Jonathan Pope; Susan Pot; Neil Poulter; Tessa Pye; Pat Rathbon; M.J. Rayward; L. Rex; Carol & David Roberts; Andrea Robinson; Richard de Rothschild; Ellen Rombouts; Frank Schaer; Nick Scrannage; Jonathan Sear; Paul Seggery; Brenda Senecal; El Houssin Serrab; Andrea Shallcross; Jeffrey Sherwin; Fran Siegel; Simon Skerrit; Mandy Skinner; Jacqueline Sluis; Ken Smith; Dan Staff; Sam Stephenson; Jake Stevens; Ann & Mark Stevenson; Ben Stewart; Renae Stewart; Peter Stock; Lucille Strachan; Kim Stringer; Kate de Syllas; Wymon Symes; Kate Taylor; Matthew Teller; Louis Tham; David Thornton; Tom Tolk; Liana Tomchesson; Richard Tookey; David Traham; Sabine Van Cauwenberge; Richard Vasey; Phil Veal; M. van Rees Vellinga; Veeke Verstraete; Blake Vonder Haar; Bruno de Wachter; Mary Wall; Andrew Wallace; Mike Walsh; Anne Wareham; M.C. Warnotte; Jon Wayth; R.J. Weetch; Mark Whatmore; Barbara Williams; Emyr Williams; Sarah Wood; Andrew Wolff; David Young; and Alberto Zezza.

See Routes map on p xii-xiii for more detail

MOROCCO

CONTENTS

Introduction xi

• CHAPTER 4: THE WEST COAST: FROM RABAT TO ESSAOUIRA 246–318

• CHAPTER 5: MARRAKESH 319–357

• CHAPTER 6: THE HIGH ATLAS 358–391

• CHAPTER 7: THE GREAT SOUTHERN OASIS ROUTES 392–447

PART THREE CONTEXTS 519

LIST OF MAPS

MAP SYMBOLS

—•— Railway	⚪ Hill	ⓘ Tourist office
═══ Motorway	▲ Peak	✉ Post office
─── Road	⋀⋀ Mountains	Stadium
----- Track/trail	∴ Ruins	Building
– – – Ferry route	⚶ Viewpoint	Church
─── Waterway	⚲ Lighthouse	Christian Cemetery
— — — Chapter division boundary	⚱ Waterfall	Muslim Cemetery
—••— International borders	★ Bus/taxi stop	Jewish Cemetery
♦ Points of interest	⊙ Hotel	Park
☾ Mosque	Δ Campsite	Beach
⌂ Cave		

INTRODUCTION

For Westerners, **Morocco** holds an immediate and enduring fascination. Though just an hour's ride on the ferry from Spain, it seems at once very far from Europe, with a culture – Islamic and deeply traditional – that is almost wholly unfamiliar. Throughout the country, despite the years of French and Spanish colonial rule and the presence of modern and cosmopolitan cities like Rabat or Casablanca, a more distant past constantly makes its presence felt. **Fes**, perhaps the most beautiful of all Arab cities, maintains a life still rooted in medieval times, when a Moroccan empire stretched from Senegal to northern Spain; while in the mountains of the **Atlas** and the **Rif**, it is still possible to draw up tribal maps of the Berber population. As a backdrop to all this, the country's physical make-up is also extraordinary: from a Mediterranean coast, through four mountain ranges, to the empty sand and scrub of the Sahara.

All of which makes **travel** here an intense and rewarding – if not always easy – experience. Certainly, there can be problems in coming to terms with your privileged position as tourist in a nation that, for the most part, would regard such activities as those of another world. And the northern cities especially have a reputation for hustlers: self-appointed guides whose eagerness to offer their services – and whose attitude to tourists as being a justifiable source of income (and to women as something much worse) – can be hard to deal with. If you find this to be too much of a struggle, then it would probably be better to keep to low-key resorts like Essaouira or Asilah, or to the more cosmopolitan holiday destination of Agadir, built very much in the image of its Spanish counterparts, or even a packaged sightseeing tour.

But you'd miss a lot that way. Morocco is at its best well away from such trappings. A week's hiking in the Atlas; a journey through the southern oases or into the pre-Sahara; or leisured strolls around Tangier, Fes or Marrakesh – once you adapt to a different way of life, all your time will be well spent. And it is difficult for any traveller to go for long without running into Morocco's equally powerful tradition of hospitality, generosity and openness. This is a country people return to again and again.

Regions

Geographically, the country divides into five basic zones: the **coast**, Mediterranean and Atlantic; the great cities of the **plains**; the **Rif** and **Atlas** mountains; and the oases and desert of the **pre-** and fully-fledged **Sahara**. With two or three weeks – even two or three months – you can't expect to cover all of this, though it's easy enough (and highly recommended) to take in something of each aspect.

You are unlikely to miss the **mountains**, in any case. The three ranges of the Atlas, with the Rif a kind of extension in the north, cut right across the interior – physical and historical barriers, and inhabited for the most part by the indigenous Moroccan **Berbers**. Contrary to general preconceptions, it is actually the Berbers who make up most of the population; only around ten percent of Moroccans are "pure" Arabs, although with the shift to the industrialized cities, such distinctions are becoming less and less significant.

A more current distinction, perhaps, is the legacy of Morocco's colonial occupation over the fifty-odd years before it reasserted its independence in 1956. The colonized country was divided into **Spanish** and **French** zones – the former contained Tetouan and the Rif, the Mediterranean and the northern Atlantic coasts, and parts of the Western Sahara; the latter comprised the plains and the main cities (Fes, Marrakesh,

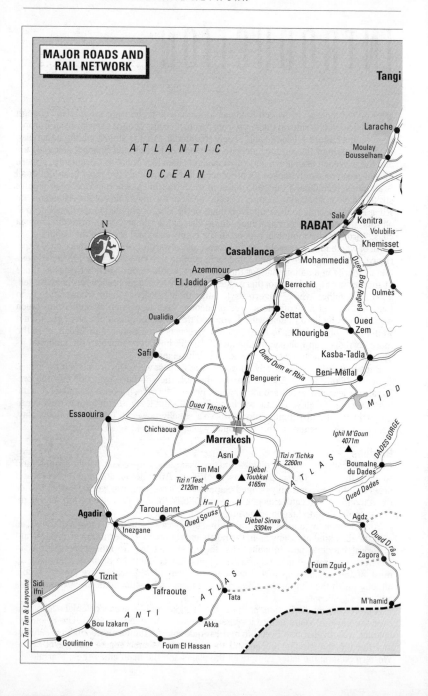

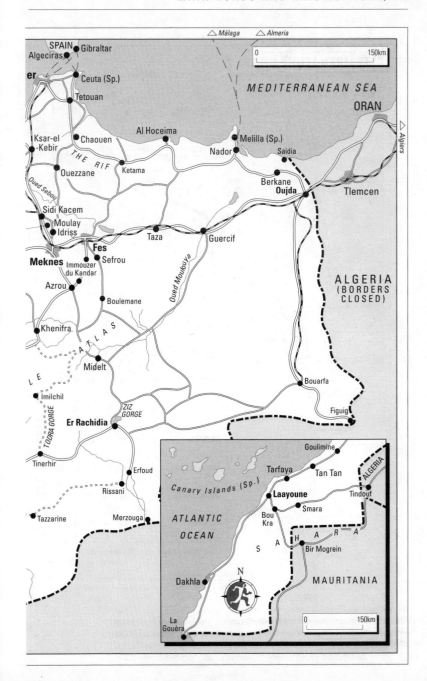

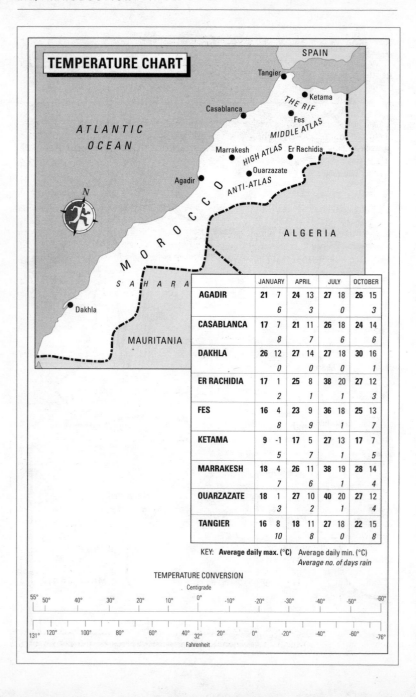

TEMPERATURE CHART

SPAIN

Tangier

Ketama

THE RIF

Casablanca

Fes

MIDDLE ATLAS

ATLANTIC OCEAN

Marrakesh

HIGH ATLAS

Er Rachidia

Ouarzazate

Agadir

ANTI-ATLAS

N

M O R O C C O

ALGERIA

S A H A R A

Dakhla

MAURITANIA

	JANUARY	APRIL	JULY	OCTOBER
AGADIR	21 7	24 13	27 18	26 15
	6	3	0	3
CASABLANCA	17 7	21 11	26 18	24 14
	8	7	6	6
DAKHLA	26 12	27 14	27 18	30 16
	0	0	0	1
ER RACHIDIA	17 1	25 8	38 20	27 12
	2	1	1	3
FES	16 4	23 9	36 18	25 13
	8	9	1	7
KETAMA	9 -1	17 5	27 13	17 7
	5	7	1	5
MARRAKESH	18 4	26 11	38 19	28 14
	7	6	1	4
OUARZAZATE	18 1	27 10	40 20	27 12
	3	2	1	4
TANGIER	16 8	18 11	27 18	22 15
	10	8	0	8

KEY: **Average daily max. (°C)**   Average daily min. (°C)
Average no. of days rain

TEMPERATURE CONVERSION

Centigrade

55° 50°   40°   30°   20°   10°   0°   -10°   -20°   -30°   -40°   -50°   -60°

131° 120°   100°   80°   60°   40° 32° 20°   0°   -20°   -40°   -60°   -76°

Fahrenheit

Casablanca and Rabat), as well as the Atlas. It was the French, who ruled their "protectorate" more closely, who had the most lasting effect on Moroccan culture, Europeanizing the cities to a strong degree and firmly imposing their language, which is spoken today by all educated Moroccans (after Moroccan Arabic or the three local Berber languages).

Highlights

The attractions of the individual regions are discussed in the chapter introductions. Broadly speaking, **the coast** is best enjoyed in the north at **Tangier**, beautiful and still shaped by its old "international" port status, **Asilah** and **Larache**; in the south at **El Jadida**; at **Essaouira**, perhaps the most easy-going resort; or at remote **Sidi Ifni**. **Agadir**, the main package tour resort, is less worthwhile – but a functional enough base for exploration.

Inland, where the real interest of Morocco lies, the outstanding cities are **Fes** and **Marrakesh**. The great imperial capitals of the country's various dynasties, they are almost unique in the Arab world for the chance they offer to witness some city life that, in patterns and appearance, remains in large part medieval. For monuments, Fes is the highlight, though Marrakesh, the "beginning of the south", is for most visitors the more enjoyable and exciting.

Travel in the **south** – roughly beyond a line drawn between Casablanca and Meknes – is, on the whole, easier and more relaxing than in the sometimes frenetic north. This is certainly true of the **mountain ranges**. The **Rif**, which can feel disturbingly anarchic, is really for hardened travellers; only **Chaouen**, on its periphery, could be counted a "holiday spot". But the **Atlas ranges** (Middle, High and Anti-) are beautiful and accessible.

Hiking in the **High Atlas**, especially around North Africa's highest peak, **Djebel Toubkal**, is in fact something of a growth industry. Even if you are no more than a casual walker, it is worth considering, with summer treks possible at all levels of experience and altitude. And, despite inroads made by commercialization, it remains essentially "undiscovered" – like the Alps must have been in the last century.

Equally exploratory in mood are the great **southern routes** beyond – and across – the Atlas, amid the **oases** of the pre-Sahara. Major routes here can be travelled by bus; minor ones by rented car or local taxi; the really remote ones by four-wheel-drive vehicles or by getting lifts on local *camions* (lorries), sharing space with the market produce and livestock.

The oases, around **Tinerhir**, **Zagora** and **Erfoud**, or (for the committed) **Tata** or **Figuig**, are classic images of the Arab world, vast palmeries stretching into desert horizons. Equally memorable is the architecture that they share with the Atlas – bizarre and fabulous mud (or pisé) **kasbahs** and **ksour**, with Gothic-looking turrets and multi-patterned walls.

Climate

As far as the **climate** goes, it would be better to visit the south – or at least the desert routes – outside **midsummer**, when for most of the day it's far too hot for casual exploration, especially if you're dependent on public transport. But July and August, the hottest months, can be wonderful on the coast and in the mountains; there are no set rules.

Spring, which comes late by European standards (around April to May), is perhaps the best overall time, with a summer climate in the south and in the mountains, and water warm enough to swim in on both the Mediterranean and Atlantic coasts. **Winter** can be perfect by day in the south, though be warned that desert nights can get very cold – a major consideration if you're staying in the cheaper hotels, which rarely have heating. If you're planning to **hike** in the **mountains**, it's best to keep to the months from April to October unless you have some experience of snow conditions.

Weather conditions apart, the **Islamic religious calendar**, and its related festivals, will have the most seasonal effect on your travel. The most important factor is **Ramadan**, the month of daytime fasting; this can be a problem for transport, and especially hiking, though the festive evenings do much to compensate. See "Festivals" in the *Basics* section following for details of its timing, as well as that of other festivals.

PART ONE

THE

BASICS

You tell me you are going to Fes.
Now, if you say you are going to Fes,
that means you are not going.
But I happen to know that you are going to Fes.
Why have you lied to me, you who are my friend?

Moroccan saying quoted in Paul Bowles' *The Spider's House*

GETTING THERE FROM BRITAIN AND IRELAND

The simplest way to get to Morocco is, of course, to fly. There are flights from Britain direct to Tangier, Agadir, Casablanca and Marrakesh, and connections at Casablanca to other Moroccan airports. Alternatively, you can travel overland (or fly) to France, Spain or Gibraltar and pick up a ferry from there. All-in package deals are worth considering too, either for specialist holidays or off-season bargains.

FLIGHTS FROM BRITAIN

Flying to Morocco from Britain, you have the choice between **flights direct to Morocco** – scheduled or on charters – or **flying to Spain** and making your way on from there by ferry. At the time of writing, charter flights to Morocco are in short supply – and most are valid for just one or two weeks. With a **scheduled flight** (which will tend to be cheaper if booked two weeks in advance) you can stay for up to three months and fly to one airport and back from another.

SCHEDULED FLIGHTS

Royal Air Maroc fly more or less daily from London Heathrow to Agadir, Casablanca, Marrakesh and Tangier, and once or twice a week to Ouarzazate; add-on flights from UK regional airports are available. Fares ex-London cost from £210 for Tangier, from £240 for Casablanca and from £280 for Agadir and Marrakesh, dependent on season; flight times are around three hours (five hours for a flight via Casablanca). For details,

contact *Royal Air Maroc*, 205 Regent St, London WIR 8PE (☎0171/439 4361 or 439 8854).

The only other scheduled airline with direct flights from Britain to Morocco are **GB Airways**, who fly from London Heathrow to Casablanca (four days a week), Marrakesh (twice a week) and Tangier (once a week). Again, add-on flights are available from UK regional airports and fares ex-London £200–300 return. For details, contact *British Airways* (☎0345/222111).

Another alternative is to fly via Paris, which has many more connections with Morocco. **Royal Air Maroc** has daily flights from Paris to Agadir, Casablanca, Marrakesh and Tangier, and up to six flights a week to Fes and Oujda. **Air France** has daily flights to Casablanca, up to five flights a week to Agadir, up to four a week to Marrakesh and up to two a week to Fes and Oujda. For schedules and fares, which can again include an add-on flight from various regional UK airports, contact *Royal Air Maroc* (see above) or *Air France*, Colet Court, 100 Hammersmith Road, London W6 7JP (☎0181/759 2311).

CHARTER FLIGHTS

The main Moroccan destinations for British-run charter flights are **Tangier** in the north and **Agadir** in the south, although a few operators also offer **Marrakesh**. The cheapest flights are invariably from London but there are also direct charter flights from Manchester, Birmingham, Newcastle and Glasgow. If you're lucky, outside peak periods (July & Aug, Christmas/New Year and Easter), you might find return flights to Tangier or Agadir for as low as £100–150 return. In peak season you should expect to pay £220–260 return – and you may well have problems finding a seat.

Looking for a charter fare, it is worth keeping an eye out for full **package holidays**, which may work out little more expensive than a flight-only option. See pp.6–7 for details of tour operators.

VIA SPAIN

Charter flights are usually easier to come by to **Spain** than to Morocco, especially if you want to travel from one of the smaller regional British airports. Fares can drop as low as £75–100 return to Málaga or Almería – the best destinations for travelling on to Morocco.

If you get a flight to **Málaga**, you've a choice of onward travel to Morocco: a ferry direct to **Melilla** or a bus trip down to **Algeciras** and the crossings to Ceuta or Tangier. Málaga to Algeciras is a simple journey by bus (there's no direct train). From the airport, take the train into Málaga (20–30min; service starts at 7.30am), and then a bus from the terminal opposite; the journey takes 3–5 hours depending on traffic.

If you fly to **Almería**, you'll want to make use of the direct ferry to Melilla.

For **more on the crossings**, see "Ferry Routes and Agents" on p.8.

VIA GIBRALTAR/LA LINEA

Gibraltar is another possible starting point for travelling on to Morocco. Scheduled return flights from London on *GB Airways* (handled by British Airways – see previous page) go for around £175 low season, £230 high season, and there are charter flights from major regional British airports. From Gibraltar, there are **ferries** direct to Tangier twice a week, or you can take a local bus to pick up a hydrofoil from La Linea (the town just over the border from Gibraltar) or the ferry from Algeciras, half an hour round the bay (again, see the "Ferry Routes and Agents" box on p.8). There are also flights from Gibraltar on *GB*

FLIGHT SOURCES AND AGENTS

The best **sources for finding a flight from Britain** are the classified advertisements in the travel section of *The Sunday Times* newspaper or (for London) *Time Out*. A reputable flight-only agent is *Flightbookers* (☎0171/757 2000). High-street travel agents are also worth a look for deals on package holidays and charter flights.

Among specialist **agents**, *Alecos Tours* (3a Camden Rd, London NW1 9LG; ☎0171/267 2092) offer **discount "SGIT" fares** on scheduled flights to Morocco. *STA Travel* (Priory House, 6 Wrights Lane, London W8 6TA; ☎0171/361 6100) and *Campus Travel* (52 Grosvenor Gardens, London SW1W 0AG; ☎0171/730 3402) both cater for **student/youth** needs but have a competitive range of fares open to all. Both have offices on campuses throughout Britain and Campus operate in Ireland.

Morocco specialists like *CLM* and *Moroccan Travel Bureau* will all book flight-only holidays, too; see the box on p.6 for their addresses and phone numbers.

Airways to Tangier, Casablanca and Marrakesh, though at £65–150, adding on the cost of these to a flight from Britain to Gibraltar makes little sense.

If you plan to **overnight** in Gibraltar, beware that hotel rooms start at £50 a double – and there is no youth hostel or campsite.

FLIGHTS FROM IRELAND

Charter flights direct from Ireland to Morocco are operated by *Sunway Travel*, Blackrock, Dublin 6 (☎01/288 6828). These apart, the cheapest access is either to pay a tag-on fare for a **transit via London or Paris**, or to travel **via Spain** – Málaga (see above) being the obvious airport choice.

For **student/youth** deals, contact *USIT*, who have branches throughout Ireland, including Aston Quay, O'Connell Bridge, Dublin 2 (☎01/6778117) and Fountain Centre, 13b College St, Belfast, BT1 6ET (☎01232/324073).

BY TRAIN

London to Morocco by train and ferry takes the best part of three days, but it's a great trip if you have the time to stop en route and take in something of France and Spain. Paris, the Pyrenees, Madrid, Córdoba and Granada all lie pretty much on the route. Unless you are under 26 (the age qualification for discount BIJ tickets or rail passes), however, you will probably end up paying a higher fare than for a flight.

Train departures are from London's **Victoria Railway Station** (Victoria tube). For schedules and information contact ☎0171/ 922 9875.

TICKETS

Standard rail tickets from London to Casablanca, inclusive of the ferries en route, cost around £320 return. They are available from any *British Rail* travel office, or from *Thomas Cook* and other major travel agents.

BIJ youth tickets – available to anyone under 26 years – discount standard rail fares by 20–35 percent, with a return ticket to Casablanca going for £265. The tickets allow any number of stopovers along a pre-specified route and can be used on all standard European trains (some express services have a surcharge). The period of validity is six months if they have a Moroccan end-destination, two months with a European end-destination.

In Britain, BIJ tickets are marketed as Eurotrain by *Campus Travel* (see box opposite) and are available from any youth/student travel agency.

THE INTERRAIL PASS

Morocco is covered by the European under-26 **InterRail pass** (£275) which buys one month's unlimited travel on trains in Morocco and most of Europe, along with half-price fares on most ferries (including those from Algeciras to Tangier).

Hidden costs are supplements on express trains and fifty percent of the fares on the channel ferries and between the British station you set out from/return to. The pass is available through youth/student travel agencies or from any major British Rail station or travel office. For further information, or in case of difficulty, ring ☎0171/834 2345).

BY COACH

There are regular **coach services from London to Morocco**, via the ferry at Algeciras. Be warned, though, that it is a 50-hour journey to Tangier and another 8 to 12 hours to Marrakesh or Agadir – quite an endurance test.

The coaches are operated jointly by the British and Spanish companies, **Eurolines** and **Iberbus**. The main route (four departures a week, year round) is to Tangier, Rabat, Casablanca, Marrakesh, Tiznit and finally Agadir. The other route (twice a week, year round) runs through Fes, Meknes and Nador to Oujda. Fares from London range from £193 to £236 return, according to destination and season; there are no student/youth reductions on these routes.

For details contact *Eurolines* (4 Cardiff Road, Luton, Beds LU1 1PP; ☎01582/404511) or *Campus Travel* (see box opposite) **Departures** are from London's **Victoria Coach Station** which is served by *National Express* coaches from throughout the UK and by Victoria train station (British Rail and Tube).

DRIVING OR HITCHING

If you plan to **drive down to Morocco through Spain and France**, you'll be well advised to set aside a minimum of four days for the journey. The buses detailed above cover the route to Algeciras in 48 hours but they are more or less nonstop, with two drivers and just a few short meal breaks.

There are **car ferries** across to Morocco from Spain at **Almería and Málaga** (to Melilla) and at

Algeciras (to Ceuta or Tangier). Ferries also sail from **Sète** in France to Tangier (year round) and Nador (June–Sept). Once again, see the box on "Ferry Routes and Agents"on p.8.

DRIVING ROUTES

Heading through France for the ferries from Spain, there is much to be said for getting off at least some of the main routes. However, if time is all important, the most direct **route** is:

London – Dover/Folkestone (channel ferry to Calais/Boulogne); Calais/Boulogne – Paris – Tours – Poitiers – Bordeaux – Bayonne; San Sebastian – Madrid – Jaen/Córdoba; then Jaen – **Almería**, Córdoba – **Malaga**, or Córdoba – **Algeciras**.

At quite a significant extra expense, it is possible to cut off the French section of the route by using the **car ferry from Plymouth** or **Portsmouth** to **Santander** in northern Spain. This runs twice weekly, March to November, from Plymouth and once weekly, December to February, from Portsmouth. The ferry spends a few days in dry dock whilst based at Portsmouth; for further information phone ☎0990/360360.

VEHICLE RED TAPE

Driving to (and within) Morocco you must take out **Green Card Insurance**; some insurance companies don't cover Morocco, so you may need to shop around; it speeds things up if the reference to Morocco is prominent and in French.

Entering Morocco, you will need to present the card, along with your vehicle registration document – which must be in your name or accompanied by a letter from the registered owner. **Caravans** need temporary importation documents, which are obtainable at the frontier for no charge.

Entering Morocco through the Spanish enclaves of Ceuta or Melilla (the most economic crossings for vehicles), try to avoid, if possible, arriving at the weekend. If there are any problems, you may well be sent back to Ceuta or Melilla to wait until the Monday to sort them out. Some visitors choose to tip at the frontier, leaving a note in their passport to get them through more quickly.

European, Australasian and North American **driving licences** are recognized and valid in Morocco, though an **International Driving Licence**, with its French translations (available from the AA or equivalent motoring organizations) is a worthwhile investment. The **minimum age**

UK SPECIALIST AND PACKAGE OPERATORS

Morocco is covered by a variety of UK travel agents and operators, offering everything from straight **package holidays**, through mountain **trekking** or **desert overland "exploration" safaris** in customized trucks and landrovers, to **tailor-made itineraries**, with flights, car rental and hotels booked to your specifications.

MOROCCO SPECIALISTS

Best of Morocco, Seend Park, Seend, Wilts SN12 6NZ (☎01380/828533). *One of the best Moroccan specialists, with accommodation in quality hotels and upmarket 'designer' trekking. Knowledgeable about alternatives to the traditional tourist traps. Currently represented in Morocco by Max Lawrence, Menara Tours, Marrkesh (see Marrakesh listings).*

CLM ("Morocco Made to Measure"), 69 Knightsbridge, London SW1X 7RA (☎0171/235 0123). *This reliable and highly flexible agency, run by the redoubtable Annie Austin, will arrange flights and tailor holidays from a wealth of personal knowledge. Accommodation on offer ranges from the country's top hotels, through individual gems like the Villa Maroc in Essaouira, to more modest, out of the way auberges.*

Moroccan Travel Bureau, 304 Old Brompton Rd, London SW5 9JF (☎0171/373 4411). *A range of holidays concentrating on budget-priced flight and accommodation packages in main cities and resorts.*

TREKKING TOURS

Most trekking companies run High Atlas tours in spring, summer and autumn, which are fine for the averagely fit walker and require no actual climbing. In winter these are areas for experienced hikers only, and south-facing areas such as the Djebel Sarhro, Anti-Atlas (Tafraoute region) and Djebel Sirwa are offered instead.

AMIS (Atlas Mountain Information Services), 26 Kircaldy Road, Burntisland, Fife KY3 9HQ (☎01592/873546). *This small agency is run by Hamish Brown, who wrote the High Atlas chapter in this book. He leads pre-arranged treks and climbing trips (summer/winter) in most Atlas areas, and occasional bird/flower tours.*

Exodus Expeditions, 9 Weir Rd, London SW12 0LT (☎0181/673 0859; reservations 675 550). *Two- and three-week High Atlas, Anti-Atlas and Djebel Sarhro treks. Highlight is the three-week Atlas Grand Traverse, a crossing of the Middle and High Atlas ranges (summer only). Also two-week truck tours and one-week mountain-bike trips. Recently introduced is the one-week ascent of Djebel Toubkal (April–Oct). Exodus have an office in Sydney, Australia and agents in New Zealand, Canada (in Toronto, serving USA as well) and in five western European countries (Norway, Denmark, Belgium, Switzerland and Italy).*

Explore Worldwide, 1 Frederick St, Aldershot, Hants (☎01252/319448). *An imaginative range of treks include fifteen days in the High Atlas or Djebel Sarhro. Also desert and Imperial City truck tours. Agents in Canada and USA (listed in brochure).*

Sherpa Expeditions, 131a Heston Rd, Hounslow, Middlesex TW5 0RD (☎0181/577 2717). *Choice of four fifteen-day tours in the High Atlas (Toubkal area and little-explored Mgoun Massif), and Djebel Sarhro. Sherpa have agents in Canada, New Zealand, Australia, USA and the Netherlands.*

Worldwide Journeys, 8 Comeragh Rd, London W14 9HP (☎0171/381 8638). *Fairly upmarket operator which runs High Atlas and Djebel Sarhro treks, plus desert safaris as part of tailor-made itineraries.*

---

for driving in Morocco is 21 years. For further details, see "Driving", p.33.

HITCHING

Hitching down to Morocco through France and Spain, it's best to buy a bus ticket to cover the first part of the journey. You will, in any case, have to pay for a channel ferry ticket, and buses from London to inland French cities don't add significantly to that; for example London to Rouen is £49 return, and to Tours is £88 return. Further details from *Eurolines* (see previous page). You could easily spend a lot of time – and money – hitching out of London or the channel ports.

The worst place of all to hitch is Paris; people can wait days on the roads out of the city – don't

OVERLAND EXPEDITION TOURS

Discover, Timbers, Oxted Rd, Godstone, Surrey RH9 8AD (☎01883/744392).*Discover run three or four Morocco tours each year, taking in some Atlas trekking and overland transit down to Zagora and the desert. They have (very beautifully) restored an old Kasbah above Imlil as an expedition base and field study centre.*

Dragoman Overland Expeditions, 63 Camp Green, Kenton Road, Debenham, Stowmarket, Suffolk IP14 6LA (☎01728/861133). *Trips from 3 to 36 weeks overlanding through Morocco to West and East Africa.*

Encounter Overland, 267 Old Brompton Rd, London SW5 9JA (☎0171/370 6845). *Fifteen-day tour of Morocco including Fes, High Atlas, Todra Gorge, Meski, Zagora and Marrakesh; starts and ends in Casablanca.*

Guerba, Wessex House, 40 Station Road, Westbury, Wiltshire BA13 3JN (☎01373/826611). *Two-week tours in customized trucks: Morocco Deserts and Mountains (June –Sept); Trekking in the High Atlas (July–Aug); and Imperial Cities (Oct–May). Active agents in New Zealand, Australia, Canada and USA..*

Headwater Holidays, 146 London Road, Northwich, Cheshire CW9 5HH (☎01606/48699). *Easy walking trips based on Marrakesh and Ouarzazate oriented to local culture and nature. October to April; 11 nights.*

Steppes East, Castle Eaton, Cricklade, Wiltshire, SN6 6JU (☎01285/810267). *A few set itineraries eg Call of the Coast: Essaouira, Immouzer des Ida Outanane and Taroudannt. Worth sending for the current brochure.*

Top Deck, Tours 131/135 Earls Court Road, London SW5 9RH (☎0171/ 244 8641). *Coach camping tours of Morocco; 36 days London to London. The double-decker buses have been pensioned off, but the tours are still a perennial favourite with Australians in Europe. Age limits: 18–38.*

Travel Bag Adventures, 15 Turk Street, Alton, Hampshire GU34 1AG (☎01420/541007). *Small*
groups off the beaten track, around Taroudannt or based at Merzouga. 9–14 days.

BIRD-WATCHING TOURS

Birdquest, Two Jays, Kemple End, Stonyhurst, Lancashire BB7 9QY (☎10254/826317). *Upmarket bird-watching with winter and spring tours visiting the classic (birding) sites from Larache to Erfoud and staying in the best hotels.*

Naturetrek, Chautara, Bighton, Hants SO24 9RB (☎01962/733051). *Two trips a year: High Atlas – birds and flowers (end of May: 2 weeks) and Southern Morocco – birds (winter: 1 week).*

MAINSTREAM TOUR OPERATORS

The advantage of mainstream operators rests in getting a good-value deal on flight plus resort accommodation; some can offer excellent rates, too, on stays at top hotels like the *Mamounia* in Marrakesh, *El Minzah* in Tangier, or *Palais Jamai* in Fes. The best of the operators (some of the majors dropped Morocco from their schedules during the Gulf War, and have not restarted) include:

Abercrombie & Kent (☎0171/730 9600). *Major hotels and "Morocco à la carte". Upmarket.*

British Airways (☎01293/723100). *Newly introduced City breaks to Marrakesh (3,4 and 7 nights). 3-, 4- and 5-star hotels.*

Cadogan Travel (☎01703/332551). *Tangier, Marrakesh, Agadir. Modest/upmarket.*

CV Travel (☎0171 591 2810). *Upmarket and often extraordinary villa rentals.*

Hayes & Jarvis (☎0181/748 5050 or 0088). *Marrakesh, Taroudannt and Agadir; southern and "Imperial City" tours. Recommended by several readers. Modest.*

Prestige (☎01425/480400). *Marrakesh and Agadir. Modest.*

Saga (☎0800/414383). *No packages, but happy to book flights and hotels – for over 50s. Modest.*

Travelscene (☎0181/427 4445). *Marrakesh and Casablanca. Modest.*

---

try it! Once south of Paris, getting rides becomes a little easier but the position deteriorates again as you cross the border into Spain – and Madrid is another terrible city for hitchers. In fact, once at Madrid, you'll probably save money cutting your losses and saving on accommodation by taking the night train down to Algeciras (about 2000ptas, £12/$18). Harassment is also especial-

ly overt in southern Spain and hitching there is not recommended for women travelling alone.

Hitching back from Morocco, starting at the car ferry in **Ceuta** is by far your best bet. It's quite possible you'll get a lift the whole way back to Britain from there. Other useful points to ask around are the **campsites** at **Fes**, **Meknes** and **Martil** (near Tetouan), all traditional last stops.

FERRY ROUTES AND AGENTS

All ferry **frequencies** are given below for summer (in general, mid-June to early September) and winter (mid-September to mid-June). **Fares** quoted are for a **regular adult single**; children (up to 12 years) normally pay half fare. For detailed schedules and prices, contact the UK agent, **Southern Ferries**, 179 Piccadilly, London W1V 9DB (☎0171/491 4968, fax 0171/491 3502), who handle most of the services detailed below.

ALGECIRAS

Ferries detailed below are operated in Spain by **Transmediterranea** *(☎66.52.00) and* **Isnasa** *(☎65.20.00); in Morocco by* **Limadet** *and* **Comarit**. *In Algeciras,* **tickets** *can be bought from any travel agent (there are dozens along the seafront and on the approach roads to the town) or at the port gates. Ticket prices are standard, wherever you buy them.*

● **Algeciras–Tangier ferry** Up to 20 crossings daily in summer; up to 10 crossings daily in winter. Passenger £20/$32, medium car from £64/$102 motorbike/bicycle £18/$29. 2hr 30min.

● **Algeciras–Ceuta ferry** 14–15 crossings daily in summer; 8–9 crossings daily in winter. Passenger £8.90/$14.25, medium car from £23.50/$37.50; 1hr 30min. A new, faster ferry, the *Albayzin* operates 4 crossings daily mid-October to end of April. Passenger £14.50/$23, medium car £40.50/$65; 1hr.

● **Algeciras–Tangier hydrofoil (passenger only)** 2 crossings daily in summer; 1 daily in winter, weather permitting. Passenger £14.50/$23; 1hr.

● **Algeciras–Ceuta hydrofoil (passenger only)** 4–8 crossings daily, weather permitting, year round. Passenger £14.50/$23; 30min.

● **Algeciras–Ceuta catamaran (passenger only)** 5 crossings daily in summer only, weather permitting. Operated by *Isnasa*.

TARIFA

● **Tarifa–Tangier ferry** 1 crossing each morning except Sunday. Passenger £16/$25.50; car £50/$80. Operated by *Transtour*. 1 hr. (There is no longer a hydrofoil service from Tarifa).

GIBRALTAR

● **Gibraltar–Tangier ferry** Early morning on Monday and Wednesday and early evening on Friday. Passenger £19/$30.50; car £45.40/$72.60. Gibraltar agent is *TourAfrica*, International Commercial Centre, Casemates Square (☎77666); alternatively book at *Bland Travel*, Cloister Building, Irish Town (☎76155) who also sell trips to Tangier. 2hr.

LA LINEA

● **La Linea–Tangier hydrofoil** One crossing daily in summer. 1 hr.

MALAGA/ALMERÍA

● **Málaga–Melilla ferry** Daily crossing Monday to Saturday at midday; in summer additional crossing Sunday late evening. Passenger £17/$27; car £43.40/$69.40 (a little cheaper in winter). Operated by *Transmediterranea*, Estacíon Maritima, Local E–1 (☎222 4391). 7hr 30min.

● **Almería–Melilla ferry** In winter midday crossings Tuesday to Saturday and late evening crossing Sunday; in summer 1–2 crossings daily mid-evening, late afternoon or overnight depending on the day of the week. Fares as from Málaga (see above). Operated by *Transmediterranea*, 19 Parque Nicolás Salmerón (☎23.61.55). 6hr 30min.

SÈTE

Bookings well in advance are essential for Sète ferries. The French agent is **SNCM**, *12 Rue Godot de Mauroy, Paris 75009 (☎91.56.36.66) or 4 Quai d'Alger, Sète 34202 (☎67.74.93.05); in Morocco, book tickets through* **COMANAV** *offices in Tangier, Casablanca, Marrakesh or Agadir (see local "Listings" sections in the main guide).*

● **Sète–Tangier ferry** The ferry *Marrakesh* runs every four days (except in February when it is out of service for maintenance) leaving Sète at 7pm, arriving Tangier 9am two days later. Passengers from £160/$256 to £390/$624 depending on accommodation (interior 4 berth/exterior 1 berth); price includes meals. Car from £190/$304 to £330/$528; motorbike from £70/$112 to £105/$168; cycle £70/$112. 38hr. From mid-July to mid-October, the *Marrakesh* is supplemented by the ferry *Ambassador* which runs 24hr behind the *Marrakesh*.

● **Sète–Nador ferry** The new ferry *Beauport* runs from Sète to Beni-Enzar, north of Nador and alongside the Moroccan/Melilla frontier, once every four days from mid-June to end September. Fares as for Sète-Tangier, above.

FERRIES TO MOROCCO

Crossing to Morocco by **ferry** – sailing from Europe to Africa – is the most satisfying (and apt) way to arrive in the country. From Spain the trip is just a couple of hours by ferry – or half an hour on the (passenger-only) hydrofoils.

ROUTES

Routes are covered in the box opposite. Your main choice is in deciding which port to head for. Most overland travellers cross (and services are most frequent) on the routes from Algeciras to Ceuta (a Spanish enclave) and Tangier. **Ceuta** is the cheaper crossing – with considerable savings for cars – but for pedestrians it is time-consuming, as you need to get a bus to the Moroccan border and another from there to the rather intimidating town of Tetouan. **Tangier** is a little easier to get to grips with and is better placed for public transport on into Morocco, being located at the beginning of the railway line.

Among alternatives, the crossings from **Málaga** and **Almería** to **Melilla**, another Spanish enclave, are most useful for drivers heading for Fes and southern Morocco, while the ferry from **Sète** in southern France to Tangier offers a convenient (if expensive) short cut, avoiding Spain entirely. For passengers, the **hydrofoils** from Algeciras to Ceuta and Tangier, and the new link from La Linea (on the border with Gibraltar) to Tangier, cut time off a journey.

Note that the **ferries to Ceuta, Tangier and Melilla** are **booked solid** for 3–5 days from the beginning of August, and **from those ports** during the last 3–5 days of August: the holiday month for Moroccans working in Northern Europe. Ferries are also packed out at either end of the **Easter** (Semana Santa) week holiday.

RED TAPE

It's important to note that for **all ferries from Spain to Morocco** (excepting Ceuta/Melilla) you must collect an exit visa (in Algeciras from a lone official in a passport kiosk) before boarding. Then, once on board, you have to complete a **disembarkation form** and have your **passport stamped** at the ship's purser's office. Announcements to this effect are not always made in English, but if you don't have a stamp, you'll have to wait until everyone else has cleared frontier and customs controls before being attended to.

Returning from Morocco to Spain, you need to collect an embarkation form and departure card and have these stamped by the port police prior to boarding your ferry.

GETTING THERE FROM NORTH AMERICA

Although there are direct flights from New York and Montréal to Casablanca, most North Americans travel to Morocco via Europe. Flights across the Atlantic to London, Paris or Madrid can be purchased with an add-on connection to a number of Moroccan destinations. Alternatively, if time is not your main concern, you could fly to Europe and travel overland through Spain and cross over to Morocco on the ferry (see "Getting There From Britain and Ireland", p.3).

DIRECT FROM THE USA

Royal Air Maroc (RAM), the Moroccan national airline, operates direct flights to Casablanca from New York and Montréal. Tickets can be bought in conjunction with one or more add-on flights to other Moroccan airports, or, if you are embarking on a trip across North Africa, with flights east to Tunisia or Egypt. Alternatives to the *RAM* routes include flights on **British Airways**, **Air France**, **KLM** and **Iberia**. These offer a number of Moroccan destinations – Tangier, Casablanca, Agadir and Marrakesh are the most common – routed through the airlines' respective hubs of London, Paris, Amsterdam and Madrid.

Student/youth discount fares are not particularly promising for direct flights, though

Council, STA, and **Nouvelles Frontières** (see boxes for addresses) may turn up the occasional budget fare to Casablanca. All three of these agencies, however, are likely to come up with much better deals on **flights to London, Paris or Madrid**. Given that the cheapest and most frequent flights to Morocco are from France, *Nouvelles Frontières* should probably be your first call if you are planning to holiday purely in Morocco. They should be able to fix up a low-cost add-on fare to one or other of the Moroccan airports. Note that although *Council, STA, CIEE* and *Nouvelles Frontières* specialize in the student/youth market, they offer **low-cost fares to all travellers** – irrespective of age or student status.

Discounted tickets aside, your best bet will probably be an **Apex** (Advance Purchase Excursion) ticket, although this carries certain restrictions: you'll most likely have to book – and pay – up to 45 days before departure, be restricted as to the time you spend abroad (minimum seven days, maximum stay three months, must include a Saturday night etc) and pay heavy surcharges if you want to change your schedule.

If you decide to make your own way to **Morocco via Britain**, you have a wide range of flights to London to choose from. Contact the **discount travel agents** in the box opposite and check Sunday travel supplements of the major newspapers. For **London-only flights**, *Virgin Atlantic* offer good service and value with 45-day advance r/t APEX fares from New York $625/$475 (high/low), Miami $715/$555 and LA $892/$532. *Delta* offer competitive r/t APEX fares from Chicago to London for $777/$418. In addition *Virgin* run fairly regular special limited offers with fares as low as $238 (from New York) or $368 (from LA). And, at the time of writing, *Delta* have a special limited Chicago–London fare of $348.

All prices quoted exclude taxes and are subject to availability and change.

EAST COAST

The US division of *Royal Air Maroc* operates three flights a week from **New York to Casablanca** (flight time 6hr 40min). Departures

DISCOUNT AGENTS, CONSOLIDATORS AND TRAVEL CLUBS

Council Travel, Head Office, 205 E 42nd St, New York, NY 10017 (☎800/226-8624; 888/COUNCIL; 212/822-2700); Other offices at: 530 Bush St, Suite 700, San Francisco, CA 94108 (☎415/421-3473); 10904 Lindbrook Drive, Los Angeles 90024 (☎310 208 3551); 1138 13th St, Boulder, CO 80302 (☎303/447-8101); 3300 M St NW, 2nd Floor, Washington, DC 20007(☎202/337-6464); 1153 N Dearborn St, Chicago, IL 60610 (☎312/951-0585); 273 Newbury St, Boston, MA 02116 (☎617/266-1926) etc. *Nationwide US organization. Mostly, but by no means exclusively, specializes in student travel.*

New Frontiers/Nouvelles Frontières, 12 E 33rd St, New York, NY 10016 (☎800/366-6387; 212/779-0600); 1001 Sherbrook East, Suite 720, Montréal, PQ H2L 1L3 (☎514/526-8444). *French discount travel firm. Other branches in LA, San Francisco and Quebec City.*

STA Travel, 10 Downing St, New York, NY 10014 (☎800/777-0112; 212/627-3111); 7202 Melrose Ave, Los Angeles, CA 90046 (☎213/934-8722); 51 Grant Ave, San Francisco, CA 94108 (☎415/391-8407); 297 Newbury St, Boston, MA 02115 (☎617/266-6014); 429 S Dearborn St, Chicago, IL 60605 (☎312/786 9050); 3730 Walnut St, Philadelphia, PA 19104 (☎215/382-2928); 317 14th Ave SE, Minneapolis, MN 55414 (☎612/615-1800) etc. *Worldwide specialists in independent travel.*

Travac, 989 6th Ave, New York NY 10018 (☎800/872-8800). Also in Orlando. *Consolidator and charter broker.*

Travel Avenue, 10 S Riverside, Suite 1404, Chicago, IL 60606 (☎800/333-3335). *Discount travel agent.*

Travel Cuts, 187 College St, Toronto, ON M5T 1P7 (☎800/667-2887; 888/238-2887 from US; 416/979-2406). 180 MacEwan Student Centre, University of Calgary, Calgary, AB T2N 1N4 (☎403/282-7687); 12304 Jasper Av, Edmonton, AB T5N 3K5 (☎403/488-8487); 1613 Rue St Denis, Montréal, PQ H2X 3K3 (☎514/843-8511); 555 W 8th Ave, Vancouver, BC V5Z 1C6 (☎888/ FLY CUTS; 604/822-6890); University Centre, University of Manitoba, Winnipeg MB R3T 2N2 (☎204/269-9530) etc. *Canadian student travel organization.*

Unitravel, 1177 N Warson Rd, St Louis, MO 63132 (☎800/325-2222). *Consolidator.*

from New York are on Tuesdays, Thursdays and Saturdays. Their most economical mid-week APEX return fares (requiring 14-day advance purchase) are $593 (low season); $653 (shoulder); $825 (high). Weekend flights are around $60 extra. Their high season is from June 1 to August 31; low season September 1 to March 21; shoulder season March 22 to May 31 and over the Christmas period.

For anyone under 24, *RAM* issue a **youthpass**, which frees you from APEX restrictions, but is significantly higher than the APEX fare.

At certain times of year, you may find direct **charter flights** to Morocco from the East Coast. Check the Sunday travel section of the *New York Times* and phone around. One company always worth a call for charters is *Access International* (☎1-800/333-7280).

The major European carriers, *British Airways, Air France, Iberia* and *KLM* have **scheduled flights to Morocco via Europe**. *British Airways* fly via London to Casablanca and Marrakesh. *Air France* fly to Casablanca, Marrakesh and Agadir via Paris. *Iberia* fly to Casablanca and Tangiers via Madrid. *KLM* fly via Amsterdam to Casablanca and Tangiers. APEX return fares from New York run from $765/1075 (low/high) to Tangier; $765/1095 to Marrakesh; $810/1140 to Agadir.

TOLL-FREE AIRLINE NUMBERS

American Airlines ☎800/433-7300
British Airways ☎800/247-9297 (US); 800/668-1059 (Canada)
Continental ☎800/231-0856
Delta ☎800/241-4141
Air France ☎800/237-2747 (US); 800/667-2747 (Canada)
Iberia ☎800/772-4642 (US); 800/423-7421 (Canada)
KLM ☎800/374-7747 (US); 800/361-5073 (Canada)
Royal Air Maroc ☎800/892-6726 (US); 800/361-7508 (Canada)
Virgin Atlantic ☎800/862-8621

SPECIALIST TOUR OPERATORS

All prices quoted below exclude taxes and are subject to change; return flights are quoted from New York.

Adventure Center 1311 63rd Street, Suite 200. Emeryville, CA 94608 ☎1-800/227 8747. *Budget adventure travel.*

Backroads 801 Cedar St, Berkeley, CA 94710-1800 ☎1-800/462-2848. *10-day mountain-biking, walking & camel-riding adventure holiday. From $2995 (land only).*

Crystal Cruises 2121 Avenue of the Stars, Los Angeles, CA 90067 ☎1-310/785-9300. *'Morrocan Nights' 10-day cruise from Barcelona to Lisbon. From $3375 (+ $185 port charges + $799 air add-on).*

Escapade Tours 9W Office Center, 2200 Fletcher Ave, Fort Lee, NJ 07024 ☎1-201/346-9061. *Extensive Moroccan programmes range from city stays through Imperial City and Kasbah tours to 4x4 Sahran adventures. One of the most experienced Moroccan specialists in the US.*

Heritage Tours 57 W59th St, Suite 6G, New York, NY 10025 ☎1-212/749-1339. *Customized tours and packages exploring the 2,500 year Jewish experience and the tradition of Muslim/Jewish coexistence in Morocco.*

Homeric Tours 55 E59th St, New York, NY 10022 ☎1-800/223-5570; 212/753-1100. *Several Morocco packages. 8-day Marrakesh & Agadir Super Winter Specials from $849 (land/air); 8-day Morocco Golf Deluxe from $1599 (land/air) etc.*

Le Soleil Tours 50 E42nd St, Suite 2001, New York, NY 10017 ☎1-800/225-4723; 212/687-2600. *Packages and customized tours.*

Maupintour, 1515 St. Andrews Drive, Lawrence KS 66047 ☎1-800/255-6162. *'Moroccan Treasures'. Fully escorted 15-day package from $3800 (land/air).*

Morocco Travel International 5146 Leesburgh Pike, Alexandria, VA 22302 ☎1-800/428-5550. *Customized tours and packages. 7-day Imperial Cities tour to Fes, Meknes, Casablanca, Rabat & Marrakesh from $1399 (land/air).*

Mountain Travel-Sobek 6420 Fairmount Av, El Cerrito, CA 94530 ☎1-888/MT SOBEK (687-6235). *Winter Camel Trek (14 days $2990 land only); Summer Atlas Mountains Trek (14 days $2490 land only).*

Overseas Adventure Travel 625 Mount Auburn St, Cambridge, MA 02138 ☎1-800/221-0814; 617/876-0533. *15-day 'Morocco Sahara Odyssey' includes a tour of the Imperial Cities and a trip to the desert. From $2990 (land/air).*

Questers Worldwide Nature Tours 381 Park Av. South, New York, NY 10016 ☎1-800/468-8668. *15-day Natural History tours of Morocco. $3210 (land only).*

Safaricentre 3201 N. Sepulveda Bd, Manhattan Beach, CA 90266 ☎1-800/223-6046. *Adventure and nature tours. Camel safaris, mountain trails etc. 15-day 'Highlights of Morocco' from $750 (land only).*

Saga Holidays 222 Berkeley St, Boston, MA 02116 ☎1-800/343-0273. *Specialists in group travel for the over 50's. 21-night tour of Morocco, Spain and Portugal (6 days in Morocco) from $2499 (land/air).*

Wilderness Travel 801 Allston Way, Berkeley, CA 94710 ☎1-800/368-2794; 510/548-0420. *'High Atlas Trek' 15 days from $1995 (land only). 'Camels to Casbahs' 15 days from $2395 (land only).*

WEST COAST

Scheduled flights to Morocco via Europe from LA or San Francisco cost around $400 more than the New York fares. That's approximately $1000 (low-season) or $1225 (high season).

Check also the travel pages in the *LA Times* or the *San Francisco Chronicle* – either of which may produce the occasional charter or a good deal to London, Paris or Madrid.

MIDWEST

Once again, it is worth spending a Sunday checking the **travel sections** of major newspapers, which can reveal a range of special offers to Europe. On the whole, the cheaper flights involve transiting via New York with an add-on fare of $250. This amounts to a cost of around $850 (low season) or $1075 (high season).

DIRECT FROM CANADA

Royal Air Maroc (☎514/285-1435) have three weekly flights **from Montréal to Casablanca** via New York, on Tuesday, Thursday and Saturday, with a flight time of 9 hours 40 minutes. They currently offer a Super Apex 7-day advance midweek fare of Can$690/820 (low/high season). From Vancouver their Apex fares are Can$1206/1616 (low/high). Weekend supplements range from Can$40 to Can$80.

Other airlines with scheduled flights to **Casablanca via Europe** are *KLM* and *Air France*, flying from Toronto, Montréal or Vancouver. Shopping round the **travel agencies**, you may be able to get better prices. Good sources include *Travel CUTS* (known as *Voyages CUTS* in Québec) and *Nouvelles Frontières*. See boxes for addresses.

VIA BRITAIN

If you decide to **transit via Britain**, there is quite a wide range of travel routes available – see the previous section "Getting there from Britain and Ireland". Note that, if you intend to travel by **train**, the *EurRail* pass (available in various permutations for one or two months of travel in Europe – full details from any travel agent) does

not cover travel in Morocco, although it will get you down to the ferries at Algeciras in Spain.

The **InterRail pass**, which *does* cover Morocco, is in theory only available to people resident in Europe for six months – though in practice travel agents aren't always too fussy about the regulation.

PACKAGE TOURS

For ease and convenience, **package tours** make a lot of sense: you get to see the country without worrying too much about the hassles of getting to and from. Among available tours, some cover Morocco exclusively, others in combination with Spain and Portugal, or beyond.

See boxed listings opposite for recommended North American agencies and check also the **UK specialist tours** detailed on pp.6–7; many of these are sold by American travel agents, and if you contact the UK companies direct, they will put you in touch with their North American agent.

GETTING THERE FROM AUSTRALIA & NEW ZEALAND

Although there are no direct flights from Australasia to Morocco it is possible to get there with a minimum of hassle. The most "direct route" is with Alitalia to Casablanca via Bangkok and Rome from Sydney and Auckland. Most Australasian travellers, however, make their way to Morocco via London,

with tag-on flight or overland transport to Tangier or Agadir – although more time-consuming this can be a cheaper option if funds are tight (see "Getting there from Britain and Ireland, p.3"). Given the high cost of flights from Australasia a "round the world" (RTW) fare can also be worth considering.

Airfares vary throughout the year with low season to Europe from mid January to the end of February and October to the end of November; high season mid May to the end of August and December to mid January; shoulder seasons cover the rest of the year. Seat availability on most international flights out of Australia and New Zealand is often limited so it's best to book several weeks ahead.

Tickets purchased direct from the airlines tend to be expensive, with published fares (from eastern cities/Auckland) listed at A$2399/NZ$2699 (low season) and A$2999/NZ$3399 (high season). Travel agents offer better deals on fares and have the latest information on special offers. *Flight Centres* and *STA* (which offer fare reductions for ISIC card holders and under 26s) generally offer the lowest fares.

AIRLINES

Alitalia Australia ☎02/9247 9133; New Zealand ☎09/379 4457. *Weekly scheduled service – and three times a week with a transfer or stopover in Rome – to Casablanca via Bangkok from Sydney and other major Australasian cities (code-share with Qantas).*

Air France Australia ☎02/9321 1000; New Zealand ☎09/303 3521. *Daily to Casablanca via Paris and Singapore. Teams up with Qantas for links from major Australasian cities.*

Britannia Airways Australia ☎02/9251 1299 No NZ office. *Several flights per month to London, during their charter season from Nov-March, via Bangkok and Abu Dhabi from Sydney, Brisbane, Cairns and Auckland.*

British Airways Australia ☎02/9258 3300; New Zealand ☎09/356 8690. *Code share with Qantas to offer their 'Global Explorer' round-the-world ticket*

Garuda Indonesia Australia ☎02/9334 9944 or 1800 800 873; New Zealand ☎09/366 1855. *Several flights a week to London via either a transfer or stopover in Jakarta/Denpasar from major Australasian cities.*

KLM Australia ☎02/9231 6333 or 1800/505 747. *Two flights a week to Casablanca via Amsterdam and Singapore from Sydney and via either Sydney and Singapore and Amsterdam or LA and Amsterdam from Auckland*

Malaysia Airlines Australia ☎13 2627 New Zealand ☎09/373 2741. *Twice weekly flights to Madrid and Paris via Kuala Lumpur from major Australasian cities.*

Philippine Airlines, Australia ☎02/9262 3333. No NZ office. *Three flights a week to London via either a transfer or stopover in Manila from major Australian cities.*

Qantas Australia ☎13 1211; New Zealand ☎09/357 8900 or 0800/808 767. *Code share with British Airways to offer their 'Global Explorer' round-the-world ticket*

Royal Brunei Airlines Australia ☎02/9223 1566 No NZ office. *Three flights a week to London from Sydney, Brisbane and Cairns via a transfer or stopover in Brunei.*

Singapore Airlines Australia ☎13 1011 New Zealand ☎09/379 3209. *Several flights a week to Paris and Madrid via a transfer in Singapore from major Australasian cities.*

Thai Airways Australia ☎13 1960 New Zealand ☎09/377 3886. *Several flights a week to Paris and Madrid from Sydney, Brisbane, Cairns,*

From **Australia**, *Alitalia* have a scheduled service to Casablanca via Bangkok and Rome once a week for A$1780-2280, but if you don't mind going a little out of the way, *Air France* and *KLM* can also get you there via a transfer in their home cities for A$1999-2499. Fares from major eastern

DISCOUNT TRAVEL AGENTS

Anywhere Travel, 345 Anzac Parade, Kingsford, Sydney (☎02/9663 0411).

Brisbane Discount Travel, 260 Queen St, Brisbane (☎07/3229 9211).

Budget Travel, 16 Fort St, Auckland, plus branches around the city (☎09/366 0061 or 0800/808 040).

Destinations Unlimited, 3 Milford Rd, Auckland (☎09/373 4033).

Flight Centres Australia: 82 Elizabeth St, Sydney, plus branches nationwide (☎13 1600). New Zealand: 205 Queen St, Auckland (☎09/309 6171), plus branches nationwide.

Northern Gateway, 22 Cavenagh St, Darwin (☎08/8941 1394).

STA Travel, Australia: 702 Harris St, Ultimo, Sydney; 256 Flinders St, Melbourne; other offices in state capitals and major universities (nearest branch ☎13 1776, fastfare telesales ☎1300/360 960). New Zealand: 10 High St, Auckland (☎09/309 0458, fastfare telesales ☎09/366 6673), plus branches in Wellington, Christchurch, Dunedin, Palmerston North, Hamilton and at major universities. *www.statravelaus.com.au* email: *traveller@statravelaus.com.au*

Thomas Cook, Australia: 175 Pitt St, Sydney; 257 Collins St, Melbourne; plus branches in other state capitals (local branch ☎13 1771, Thomas Cook Direct telesales ☎1800/063 913); New Zealand: 96 Anzac Ave, Auckland (☎09/379 3920).

Tymtro Travel, Level 8, 130 Pitt St, Sydney (☎02/9223 2211 or 1300 652 969).

SPECIALIST AGENTS

If you are interested in organized adventure holidays in Morocco, or have a limited amount of time, a number of specialist agents can assist with travel arrangements.

Adventure Travel Shop, 164 Parnell Rd, Parnell ☎09/377 5770. *All travel arrangements and a wide selection of adventure tours in Morocco.*

Adventure Specialists, 69 Liverpool St, Sydney (☎02/9261 2927). *Overland and adventure tour agent for a variety of adventure wholsalers.*

Adventure World, 73 Walker St, North Sydney (☎02/9956 7766 or 1800/221 931), plus branches in Brisbane and Perth; 101 Great South Rd, Remuera, Auckland (☎09/524 5118). *Accommodation, treks, discount airfares and tours through the Anti Atlas.*

Africa Travel Centre, 456 Kent St, Sydney (☎02/9267 3048 or 1800/622 984); 21 Remuera Rd, Auckland (☎09/520 2000). *Specialists in camping holidays in Morocco.*

IB Tours, 1/47 New Canterbury Road, Petersham, Sydney (☎02/9560 6932). *3-5 star accommodation and individually tailored holidays in Morocco.*

Ibertours, 84 William St, Melbourne (☎03/9670 8388 or 1800/500 016). *Escorted small group and private tours in Morocco.*

Peregrine, 258 Lonsdale St, Melbourne ☎03/9663 8611), plus offices in Brisbane, Sydney, Adelaide and Perth. *Small group hiking and archeological trips with an emphasis on local contact.*

Top Deck Adventure, 8th Fl, 350 Kent St, Sydney (☎02/9299 8844). *Agents for Exodus's biking and trekking expeditions (see UK Specialist Operators box on p.6).*

cities are common rated, from Perth and Darwin are usually between $100-200 less.

From **New Zealand**, *Qantas-Alitalia* fly from Auckland via Sydney and Rome while *KLM* can take you via Amsterdam and either Asia or the US, both cost around NZ$2199-2999

To European gateways you'll find the cheapest fares are to **London** with *Britannia* (A$1280-1800/NZ$1460-2130 during their Nov–March charter season) while *Royal Brunei, Philippine Airlines* and *Garuda* all start around A$1499/NZ$1800. *Malaysia Airlines, Thai Airways*, and *Singapore Airlines* all fly to **Paris** and **Madrid** for around A$1899–2510/NZ$2199-2999 from where you can continue on to Morocco.

There are several **RTW fares** that take in Casablanca, with the cheapest offered by *Qantas-Air France* allowing a limited number of stops in each direction for around A$1599/NZ$1999. More flexibility is possible with *ANZ-KLM-Northwest* "World Navigator" and *Alitalia* (in combination with a variety of other carriers), both of which run from A$2399/NZ$2699. *Qantas-British Airways* "Global Explorer" runs from A$2499/NZ$2899 but allows up to 6 stopovers world wide, open jaw travel, some backtracking and extensive network of routes and destinations.

RED TAPE AND EXTENDED STAYS

If you hold a full passport from Britain, Ireland, Australia, New Zealand, the Scandinavian countries or North America, you require no visa to enter Morocco for up to ninety days. Among European nations, only Dutch, Belgian and Luxembourg citizens need visas – imposed in response to restrictions placed on visiting Moroccans. When **entering the country**, formalities are fairly straightforward, though you will have to fill in a form stating personal details, purpose of visit and your **profession**. In recent years, Moroccan authorities have shown an occasional reluctance to allow in those who categorize themselves as "journalist"; an alternative profession on the form might be wise.

Note that items such as **electronic equipment and video cameras** are entered on your passport. If you lose them during your visit, they will be assumed "sold" when you come to leave and (unless you have police documentation of theft) you will have to pay 100 percent duty. All goods on your passport should be "cleared" when leaving to prevent problems on future trips.

CHILDREN AND PASSPORTS

Parents travelling with children should note that photographs of the children must be affixed to the passports of each parent. If this is not done, it is possible that you will be refused entry to Morocco. This is not just a piece of paper bureaucracy: families are regularly refused entry for failing to comply.

VISA EXTENSIONS

To **extend your stay** in Morocco you should – officially – apply to the *Bureau des Étrangers* in the nearest main town for a residence permit (see below). This is, however, a very complicated procedure and it is usually possible to get round the bureaucracy by simply leaving the country for a brief time when your three months are up. If you decide to do this – and it is not foolproof – it is best to make a trip of at least a few days outside Morocco. Spain is the obvious choice and some people just go to the enclave of Ceuta; the more cautious re-enter the country at a different post. If you are very unlucky, you may be turned back and asked to obtain a **re-entry visa** prior to your return. These can be obtained from any Moroccan consulate abroad (see opposite).

OFFICIAL BUSINESS

Extending a stay officially involves opening a bank account in Morocco (a couple of days' procedure in itself) and obtaining an *Attestation de Résidence* from your hotel, campsite or landlord. You will need a minimum of 14,000dh

المملكة المغربية
الأمن الوطني

Date ....

Entry Entree الدخول ....
الاسم العائلي

1 NOM
NAME (En caractères d'imprimerie
please print)
الاسم ما قبل الزواج
NOM DE JEUNE FILLE
MAIDEN NAME
الاسم الشخصي
PRÉNOMS
GIVEN NAMES

2 DATE DE NAISSANCE
DATE OF BIRTH
محل الازدياد
1 LIEU DE NAISSANCE
PLACE OF BIRTH

4 NATIONALITE
NATIONALITY
المهنة
5 PROFESSION
OCCUPATION
قادم من (العنوان)
6 VENANT DE (adresse)
COMING FROM (Address)

7 PASSEPORT N°   délivré à   le
PASSPORT N°   issued at   on
قصد (العنوان)
8 ALLANT a (adresse)
GOING TO (Address)

Réservé a l'Administration   مصلحة الإدارة

MOROCCAN CONSULATES ABROAD

Australia: *Consulate:* 11 West Street, North Sydney ☎02/9957 6717.

Britain: 49 Queens Gate Gardens, London SW7 (☎071/581 5001).

Canada: *Embassy*: 38 Range Rd, Ottawa K1N 8J4 (☎613/236-7391); *Consulate*: 1010 Sherbrook W, Montreal, Quebec H3A 2R7 (☎514/288–8750).

Denmark: Oregarrds Allé 19, 2900 Hellerup, Copenhagen (☎62.45.11).

Netherlands: Oranje Nassaulaan 1-1075, Amsterdam (☎736-215).

New Zealand: No consulate. Contact the Australian office.

Spain: *Embassy*: Serrano 179, Madrid (☎458.0950). *Consulates*: Rambla de Catalunya 78, Barcelona (☎32.99.66); Av. de Andalucia 63, Málaga (☎952/329962); Av. de Francisco 4, Algeciras (☎67.36.98).

Sweden: Kungsholmstorg 16, Stockholm (☎54.43.83).

USA: *Embassy*: 1601 21st St NW, Washington DC 20009 (☎202/462-7979). *Consulate*: 10 E 40th St, 24th Floor, New York, NY 10016 (212/758-2625).

(£1100/$1750) deposited in your bank account before making an application.

Once you have got through these two stages, you need to go to the **Bureau des Étrangers** equipped with: your passport; seven passport photos; two copies of the *Attestation de Résidence*; two copies of your bank statement (*Compte de Banque*); and a 60dh stamp (available from any *Tabac*). If the police are not too busy they'll give you a form to fill out in duplicate and, some weeks later, you should receive a plastic-coated permit with your photo laminated in.

For anyone contemplating this labyrinthine operation, the *Bureau des Étrangers* in **Agadir** is perhaps the simplest place to approach, since a number of expatriates live in the city and banking facilities there (try the Banque Populaire) are fairly efficient. The *Bureau* is located behind the fire station on Rue du 18 Novembre.

COSTS AND MONEY

For visitors, Morocco is inexpensive and in most respects excellent value, with costs for food, accommodation and travel low by European or North American standards. If you stay in the cheaper hotels (or camp out), eat local food, and share expenses and rooms with another person, £80 (US$125) a week would be enough to survive on. On £110–140 ($175–225) you could live pretty well, while with £325–425 ($525–680) a week split between two people you would be approaching luxury.

SOME BASIC COSTS

Accommodation costs range from £4/$6.50 a night for a double room in a basic, unclassified "local" hotel to £75/$120 a night in the country's half-dozen top-range luxury palaces. On a limited budget, you can expect to get a decent double room in a two- or three-star hotel for around £15–25/$25–40 a night, while the occasional splurge in a four-star hotel, with a swimming pool, will set you back around £25–45/$40–72 for a double, depending on season and location.

The price of a **meal** reflects a similar span. The basic Moroccan staple of soup (usually the bean-based *harira*), *brochettes* (small kebabs) or *tajine* (casserole) can be had in a local café for around £1.75/$2.80. More substantial Moroccan meals can be had for around £3.75/$6 and European-style meals in restaurants from around £7.50/$12; it's worth bearing in mind that comparable meals in a hotel can cost twice as much. **Drinks** are really the only things that compare unfavourably with European or American prices: a bottle of Moroccan wine costs upwards of £4.50/$7.25 and a can of local beer about 90p/$1.45 in the shops, or £2.50/$4 in hotel bars and discos.

Beyond accommodation and food, your major outlay will be for **transport** – expensive if you're hiring a car (£220/$350 a week plus petrol), but very reasonable if you use the local trains, buses and shared taxis. The 475km trip from Fes to Marrakesh, for instance, costs around £12/$19.25 by bus, or £17.50/$28 for a place in a faster shared taxi.

REGIONAL VARIATIONS

To some extent, all of these costs are affected by **where you are and when**. Inevitably, larger **cities** and **resorts** (Agadir especially) prove more expensive, with bottom-line hotel prices from around £7.50/$12 a night for a double. In **remote parts** of the country, too, where all goods have to be brought in from some distance and where transport (often only lorries or landrovers) has to be negotiated, prices can be steep. This is particularly true of the popular trekking region of Djebel Toubkal in the High Atlas.

HIDDEN COSTS

Hidden costs in Morocco are twofold. The most obvious, perhaps, is that you'll almost certainly end up buying a few things. Moroccan **crafts** are very much a part of the fabric of the towns and cities, with their labyrinthine areas of *souks* (markets). Rugs, blankets, leather and jewellery are all outstanding – and few travellers leave without at least one of these items.

A harder aspect to come to terms with is that you'll be confronting real **poverty**. As a tourist, you're not going to solve any problems, but with a labourer's wages at little more than 5 dirhams (40p/65¢) an hour, and an unemployment rate in excess of 25 percent, even a small **tip** to a guide

can make a lot of difference to individual family life. For Moroccans, giving money and goods is a natural function – and a requirement of Islam. For tourists, rich by definition, local poverty demands at least some response. Do not, however, dispense money indiscriminately to **children**, which simply promotes a dependence on begging.

CURRENCY

Morocco's basic unit of **currency** is the **dirham** (dh). The dirham is not quoted on international money markets, a rate being set instead by the Moroccan government. The present rates are approximately **£1=13.5dh, US$1=8.5dh;** as with all currencies, there are fluctuations – in recent years the pound and dollar have bought up to 15.75dh and 10.5dh, respectively.

The dirham is divided into 100 **centimes** (5-, 10-, 20- and 50-centime coins are in circulation), and you may find prices written or expressed in centimes rather than dirhams. Confusingly, centimes may also be referred to as *francs* or, in former Spanish zones of the country, as *pesetas*. You may also hear prices quoted in **rials**, or *reales*. In most parts of the country a dirham is considered to be 20 *rials*, though in Tangier and the Rif there are just 2 *rials* to the dirham. These are forms of expression only: there are no actual physical Moroccan *rials*, *francs* or *pesetas*.

It is possible to buy a small amount of dirhams at the bank exchange desks in the Algeciras ferry terminal or at banks in Gibraltar, but the currency is not easily exchangeable outside Morocco, and there are, in any case, regulations against taking it out of the country. When you're nearing the end of your stay, it's best to get down to as little Moroccan money as possible. To change money back from dirhams, you may be asked to produce bank exchange receipts – and you can change back only fifty percent of sums detailed on these.

At Moroccan banks, you'll be offered re-exchange into French francs only.

CARRYING YOUR MONEY

Arriving in Morocco it is useful to have at least two days' survival money in **cash**, especially as you cannot always count on airport banks/*bureau de change* offices being open. English pounds, US dollars, French francs or Spanish pesetas are easy to exchange, at banks, hotels and tourist shops; note, however, that both **Irish currency and banknotes** and also **Scottish banknotes** are not recognized or accepted in Moroccan banks. The rest of your money should, ideally, be spread around different forms – Eurocheques, travellers' cheques or Girocheques and plastic – for the sake of security.

Travellers' cheques and cash are easily exchanged at most Moroccan banks, and at the more upmarket hotels, travel agencies and tourist shops; a surcharge of around 5dh per cheque is levied; when cashing travellers' cheques, you may be asked to provide evidence of their original purchase – the offical record of their numbers (against loss) will usually suffice, but don't let the bank keep it! **Eurocheques** can be cashed at larger banks, though a higher commission – averaging out at around 5 percent – is charged; the limit on each cheque encashment is currently 2000dh (£148/$237). Better value, on the whole, are **International Girocheques** (available through European post offices), which can be changed at any sizeable Moroccan post office.

VISA and **Access/Mastercard** can also be used to obtain cash at some banks (see below), as well as in payment at the more upmarket hotels, restaurants and shops, and for car rental. It's wise to make sure your card is in good condition, as banks will refuse cash advances if machines reject the card.

BANKS AND EXCHANGE

For exchange purposes, by far the most useful and efficient chain of banks is the **BMCE** (*Banque Marocaine du Commerce Exterieur*). There is at least one *BMCE* in all major cities and they are dotted about in smaller towns (see listings in the text of the guide). Their *bureaux de change* (usually located in a separate office to the main bank) are open every weekday from 8am to 8pm and sometimes on Saturdays and Sundays, but with

more limited hours. They handle travellers' cheques and Eurocheques, and give cash advances on VISA and Access, as well as currency exchange.

The **Banque Credit du Maroc** also handle VISA, as does the generally efficient **Citibank**. Most other banks don't tend to have facilities for credit card transactions, despite the stickers in their windows, though they will exchange cash, Eurocheques and travellers' cheques. If you are travelling in the south, the **Banque Populaire** alone is usually the only choice outside the main towns – and its smaller branches offer limited facilities (no VISA/Acess advances).

Standard banking hours are Monday to Friday, 8.30am to 11.30am and 3pm to 4.30pm in winter; in summer and during Ramadan (see "Festivals" on p.47) from 8.30am to 2pm. In major resorts there is usually one or more bank that keeps extended hours on *bureau de change* transactions to meet tourist demand.

In most **exchange transactions**, customers fill in forms at one desk, then join a second queue for the cashier. Cheque/cash transactions usually get dealt with in 10 to 15 minutes, but it's wise to allow up to an hour if you need to draw cash on a credit card.

ATMs (cashpoints/cash dispensers) are to be found outside more and more banks in the bigger towns, but they are often out of service.

AMERICAN EXPRESS

American Express is represented by the *Voyages Schwartz* agencies in Tangier, Casablanca and Marrakesh. Their agency in Rabat is at present closed, though it is scheduled to reopen in the *Hyatt Regency* hotel. At all these offices, not every American Express service is available. *Voyages Schwartz* can cash and issue Amex travellers' cheques, and hold clients' mail, but they cannot cash personal cheques or receive wired money. Addresses are:

● Tangier: *Voyages Schwartz*, 54 Bd. Pasteur (☎09/93.34.59)

● Casablanca: *Voyages Schwartz*, 112 Rue Prince Moulay Abdallah (☎02/22.29.47).

● Marrakesh: *Voyages Schwartz*, Immeuble Moutoukil, 1 Rue Maruitania (☎04/43.66.00).

Most **offices are open** Monday to Friday 8.30am to 12.30pm and 3pm to 6pm, though banking services are sometimes mornings only.

EMERGENCY CASH

Despite travellers' tales, very few people lose (or are conned out of) all their money in Morocco – but it does happen. Access to an **emergency source** of money – whether it be a credit card or an arrangement with your bank or family to wire you money after a phone call – is reassuring and may prove invaluable.

As a last resort, your **consulate** is duty-bound to offer some assistance – though this will rarely go as far as lending you the money to continue a holiday, or even to fly home unless you accept "repatriation". For addresses, see p.29.

HEALTH AND INSURANCE

For minor health complaints, a visit to a *pharmacie* is likely to be sufficient. Moroccan pharmacists are well trained and dispense a wide range of drugs, including many available only on prescription in Europe or North America. If pharmacists feel you need a full diagnosis, they can recommend a doctor – sometimes working on the premises. Addresses of English- and French-speaking doctors can also be obtained from consulates and large hotels.

If you need **hospital treatment**, contact your consulate at once and follow their advice. If you are near a major city, reasonable treatment may be available locally. Morocco, however, is no country in which to fall seriously ill.

INOCULATIONS

There are no **inoculations** officially required of travellers, although you should always be up-to-date with polio and tetanus. **Typhoid** and **cholera** are widespread, so a jab against these is worthwhile, too – although some doctors doubt the effectiveness of the cholera jab. Some doctors also advise inoculation against **hepatitis B**, following the recent introduction of effective vaccines. A course of **malaria pills** (preferably weekly *Chloroquin* tablets) is recommended if you intend to travel in the south.

If you haven't had a typhoid jab then buy some *Intétrix* capsules (available from any pharmacy in Morocco). These are excellent anti-bacterial medication – useful for diarrhoea as well as typhoid prevention – and some doctors consider them more effective than inoculation. They are certainly valuable if you are travelling for any length of time in the south.

WATER AND HEALTH HAZARDS

The **tap water** in northern Morocco is generally safe to drink (in Chaouen, for example, it is pumped straight from a well), though in the south it's best to stick to bottled mineral water.

A more serious problem in the south is that many of the **river valleys and oases** are said to be infected with **bilharzia**, so avoidance of all contact with slow-flowing rivers and oasis water is a wise precaution. Care should be taken, too, in drinking water from **mountain streams**. In areas where there is livestock upstream **giardiasis** may be prevalent. Using water purification tablets and boiling any drinking or cooking water would be sensible.

DIARRHOEA

At some stage in your Moroccan travels, it is likely that you will get **diarrhoea**. As a first stage of treatment it's best simply to adapt your diet. Yoghurt is an effective stomach settler and cactus fruit (widely available in summer) are good, too.

Steer clear of other fruit and keep up your body fluids by drinking up to a couple of litres of bottled water and/or tea daily.

If this course doesn't shake it off in a couple of days, you could obtain **carbosylate capsules** (eg *Carbosylane*) from a chemist, or, if you have an "enteric" type attack (with cramps, for example), **Imodium**. It is important, especially for children, not to exceed the suggested doses; *Imodium* is a morphine-related drug.

OTHER HAZARDS

There are few natural hazards in northern Morocco, whose wildlife is not far different from that of Mediterranean Europe. If you venture into the Sahara, however, be aware of the very real dangers of a bite from a **snake, palm rat** or **scorpion**. Several of the Saharan snakes are deadly, as is the palm rat. Bites should be treated as medical emergencies.

Certain scorpions (for instance, a black one with a fat tail and thin claws known *as Androctonus Mauretanicus*), are very dangerous; their sting can be fatal if not treated. Avoid going barefoot or in flip-flops in the bush, or turning over stones. In the desert, shake out your shoes before putting them on in the morning.

A much more common problem for travellers is **heatstroke**. Make sure you are adequately protected against the sun, or you will be extremely vulnerable to attacks – resulting, most commonly, in headaches and nausea.

AIDS

Moroccan cities such as Tangier and Marrakesh have a long-time reputation as gay resorts – diminished these days, but still evident. There is very little awareness of AIDS (or *SIDA*, as it is called in French), although the Moroccan Health Ministry has been represented at recent AIDS conferences. At present, official statistics of AIDS sufferers in Morocco are very low but if the European experience is anything to go by, the reality is likely to be much higher – and rising.

As throughout the world, the need for extreme caution, and safe sex, cannot be overstressed.

INSURANCE

Travel insurance can buy you peace of mind as well as save you money. Before you purchase any insurance, however, check what you have already. North Americans, in particular, may find themselves covered for medical expenses and possibly loss of valuables, while abroad, as part of a family or student policy. Some credit cards, too, now offer insurance benefits if you use them to pay for your holiday tickets.

If you are travelling for any real length of time, however, you are likely to find a **specific travel insurance policy** reassuring. Most such policies are pretty comprehensive, anticipating everything from charter companies going bankrupt to delayed (as well as lost) baggage, by way of sundry illnesses and accidents. **Premiums**, however, vary considerably, and it's worth a few phonecalls to see what's on offer.

This applies particularly to **North Americans**, who, if transiting via Britain, might consider buying a policy from a British travel agency. British policies tend to be cheaper than American ones, and routinely cover thefts – which are often excluded from the more health-based American policies. Some of the best American **premiums** are to be had through student/youth travel agencies – STA policies, for example, come with or without medical coverage. Rates are: up to 7 days $45/$35 (with/without medical cover); 8-15 days $60/$45; 1 month $110/$85; 45 days $140/$115; 2 months $165/$135; then $50/$35 each additional month.

Most North American travel policies apply only to items lost, stolen or damaged while in the cus-

---

TRAVEL INSURANCE COMPANIES

NORTH AMERICA

Access America	☎1-800/284-8300
Carefree Travel Insurance	☎1-800/323-3149
Desjardins Travel Insurance	
Canada only,	☎1-800/463-7830
STA Travel	☎1-800/777-0112
Travel Guard	☎1-800/826-1300
Travel Insurance Services	☎1-800/937-1387

AUSTRALIA AND NEW ZEALAND

Cover More, 9/32 Walker St, North Sydney (☎02/9202 8000 or 1800/251 881).

Ready Plan, 141 Walker St, Dandenong, Melbourne (☎03/9791 5077 or 1800/337 462); 10/ 63 Albert St, Auckland (☎09/379 3208).

tody of an identifiable, responsible third party – hotel porter, airline, luggage consignment, etc. Even in these cases you will have to contact the local police within a certain time limit to have a complete report made out so that your insurer can process the claim.

REIMBURSEMENT

All insurance policies work by **reimbursing you** once you return home, so be sure to keep all your receipts from doctors and pharmacists. Any thefts should be reported immediately to the nearest police station and a police report obtained; no report, no refund.

If you have had to undergo serious medical treatment, and incur major hospital bills, contact your consulate. They will normally be able to arrange for an insurance company, or possibly relatives, to cover the fees, pending a claim.

INFORMATION, MAPS AND TREKKING GUIDES

Besides this book, the most readily available (and obvious) sources of information on Morocco are the national tourist board (ONMT), which has offices in around 25 Moroccan cities and towns. In addition, there are local tourist information offices known as Syndicats d'Initiatives. There are also – and this is a very mixed blessing – local, often self-appointed guides (for more on which see p.26).

TOURIST OFFICES

The **ONMT** maintains general information offices in several European capitals (see box), where you can pick up a number of pamphlets on the main Moroccan cities and resorts, and a few items on cultural themes.

ONMT OFFICES ABROAD

Australia c/o Moroccan Consulate, 11 West St North, Sydney NSW 2060 (☎02/22 49 99).

Britain 205 Regent St, London W1R 7DE (☎071/437 0073).

Canada 2001 Rue Université (Suite 1460), Montréal, Québec (☎514/84 228 111).

Spain C/Quintana 2 (2°e), Madrid (☎01/542 7431).

Sweden Sturegatan 16, Stockholm 11436 (☎08/66 19 504).

USA 20 E 46th St (Suite 1201), New York, NY10017 (☎212/557-2520); 421 North Rodeo Drive, Beverly Hills, Los Angeles, CA 90210 (☎271-8939); Florida, PO Box 2263, Lake Brune, Florida.

In Morocco itself, you'll find an **ONMT** office or **Syndicat** bureau in all towns of any size or interest – often both; their addresses are detailed in the relevant sections of the guide. Occasionally, these offices can supply you with particular local information sheets and they can of course try to help out with specific questions. But don't expect too much from them; their main function, from their point of view, is to gather statistics and to put you in touch with an officially recognized guide (for more on which, read on).

ROAD MAPS

The **maps of Moroccan towns** in this book are pretty functional. Local commercial ones exist but add little to those we've printed; the most authoritative local series, the **Plan-Guides** published by *Éditions Gauthey*, look impressive but are next to useless in trying to find your way round the twists and turns of a Medina.

What you will probably want to buy, though, is a good **road map**. The best are those published by Michelin (1:1,000,000; sheet 969; generally the most accurate), *Kummerley & Frey* (1:1,000,000), and the local *Marcus Carte Routière* (1:1,000,000, with Middle and High Atlas inserts at 1:500,000). The latter is readily available in Morocco.

Note that maps (or guidebooks) which do not show the **former Spanish Sahara (Western Sahara)** as Moroccan territory are liable to confiscation. Even maps showing a reduced-scale version of the territory are frowned upon.

TREKKING MAPS AND GUIDES

At present, the vital **topographical maps** needed by trekkers, climbers, skiers, etc (1: 50,000 and 1: 100,000) are very difficult to find in Morocco. You have to go in person to the *Division de la Cartographie*, 31 Av. Moulay El Hassan (☎07/76 51 92), show your passport, and submit an order which is then available for collection several days later – if the request is approved. The only exceptions are the maps of Toubkal (both scales) which will be served over the counter. These are also sporadically available at the *Hôtel Ali*, Marrakesh, or in Imlil, the trailhead for treks in the area. However, if you are planning to go trekking, it is best to try and get maps through a **specialist map outlet** before you leave (see box below). Look for 1:100,000 (and if you're lucky 1:50,000) maps of the Atlas and other mountain areas. *Stanfords* do a good pack of colour photocopies.

In addition to the official Moroccan survey maps, **Atlas Maps** (see box) produce very useful, photocopied **map-guides** to the Asni-Toubkal,

Western High Atlas (Taroudannt) and Sirwa (Taliouine), Anti-Atlas (Tafraoute), Aklim (Igherm) and Djebel Bou Iblane/Bou Naceur (Middle Atlas) areas. Written by our High Atlas contributor, Hamish Brown, these are useful complements to the coverage in this guide.

Also worth acquiring is an **ONMT pamphlet** entitled *La Grande Traversée des Atlas Marocains*, or *GTAM* – the promotional acronym with which the ONMT is now actively promoting trekking. At present this pamphlet is published in French only (an English version is said to be on the way), but even if your French is patchy the details and tarifs for local trekking guides, and contacts for specialized agencies and four-wheel-drive hire, might be useful. It is available through ONMT outlets in Morocco – and abroad.

More **detailed trekking guidebooks** are also available in both English and French. The most useful are Michael Peyron's *Grand Atlas Traverse* (West Col, UK; 2 vols; £11.95 each), Robin Collomb's *Atlas Mountains* (West Col, UK: £10.95) and Karl Smith's *Atlas Mountains: A Walker's Guide* (Cicerone Press, UK; £9.95). New from West Col, and in English, is a map guide to the Mgoun Massif (£8.95) at 1:100,000, which is useful for a wide region, second only to Toubkal in popularity. In Morocco, Rabat has some good bookshops. In Marrakesh, there are two out towards the far end of Av. Mohammed V; the one furthest out, on the left, has the best selection of titles. Guidebooks are also on sale at the CAF refuge at Oukaïmeden.

If you can get to London en route, you might also want to consult some of the Expedition Reports at the **Royal Geographical Society** (1 Kensington Gore, London SW7 2AR); the RGS's **Expeditionary Advisory Centre** (☎0171/589 5466 or 581 2057) will help locate relevant material, maps and reports.

SPECIALIST MAP SHOPS

The following stock topographical maps – and trekking guides – for Morocco.

Stanfords, 12–14 Long Acre, London WC2E 9LP (☎0171/836 1321). Callers and mail order. Stanfords have two smaller outlets in central London (callers only): British Airways building, 156 Regent Street, W1R 5TA, and Campus Travel, 52 Grosvenor Gardens, SW1W 0AG.

The Map Shop, 15 High St, Upton-upon-Severn, Worcs WR8 0HJ (☎01684/593146). Callers/mail order.

Atlas Maps, 26 Kirkcaldy Road, Burntisland, Fife KY3 9HQ, Scotland; (sae with all correspondence; closed Feb–May). Mail order only.

MOROCCO ON THE INTERNET

The Internet has come to Morocco and is fully operational. There are scores of Web sites (both in English and French) run from within and without the country, more than 20 local ISPs, and even a scattering of cybercafés in the major cities.

NEWS GROUPS

The following newsgroups are good for reading and posting travel and cultural questions, and for discussions about Morocco.

rec.travel.africa

soc.culture.maghreb

soc.culture.berber

An excellent **Morocco FAQ** compiled from Morocco postings on rec.travel is maintained by Jey Burrows on a number of Web sites, including: *www.geocities.com/TheTropics/4896/ morocco.html*
This contains a multitude of links across the Web and should be your first port of call.

WEB SITES

Al Akhawayn University
www.alakhawayn.ma/
The Ifrane International University Web site has details on their language and other courses and an excellent "resource" section covering Web sites

Arab.net
www.arab.net/morocco
Arab.net includes a range of info on Moroccan government, culture, history, etc.

Barbarity
www.maroc.net/barraka/
Barbarity is an adventurous record label, mixing Moroccan singers and rhythms in a dance context.

City.net: Morocco
www.city.net/countries/morocco/

City.net's Web indexes usually unearth the interesting new sites. This one was a bit lacking at time of writing but may well improve.

Channel#Maroc
www.mines.u-nancy.fr/~mhamdi/maroc. html
IRC (chat) channel, used mainly by Moroccans living abroad. Multilingual discussions take place.

Discover
www.discover.ltd.uk/net/morocco/
Homepage of the adventure tour company, including notes from its High Atlas kasbah field centre.

Hotels on the Net
www.city.net/countries/morocco/
Links to Moroccan hotel Web sites.

La Maison du Maroc
www.maroc.net/kiosque/
A "kiosque" of local press, including daily news from Radio Casablanca in Real Audio.

Marrakesh Express
uslink.net/ddavis/meintr.html
This US-based Moroccan carpet store has a gallery of photos, plus illuminating text on weaving techniques. And if you're thinking of buying in Morocco, you might do well to check prices here before leaving.

Maroc Hebdo
www.maroc-hebdo.press.ma/
French-language weekly magazine covering political and economic issues.

Sephardic-Moroccan Page
www.geocities.com/CapitolHill/1717/
From Moroccan synagogues around the world to music and cooking. There is more on Sephardic Moroccan music (including sound samples) at
Sylvain's Web Page:
www.geocities.com/Paris/6256/judeo.htm

Tamazight
www.physics.mcgill.ca/~karim/tamazight/
Explore the world of Tamazight Berber culture.

US Consular Travel Advisory
http://travel.state.gov/morocco.html
A fairly cautionary warning sheet on matters such as crime and health, as well as more mundane details.

CYBERCAFÉS

If you have a web-based account, you can pick up mail from cybercafés abroad. The best current directory of Moroccan cybercafés is to be found on the Al Akhawayn University "resources' page (see opposite site). Current addresses include:

Agadir: *Internet Cybercafe*, Gallerie Inbiaat, Av. Hassan II (near the Clinique des Spécialités).

Casablanca: *CyberClub*, 63 Bd.Moulay Youssef, Residence Adriana (☎02/29.34.50).

Rabat: *Interplanet*, Av. de la Victoire, 6 Rue Ibn Al Yasmine (☎07/68.22.33).

Tangier: *Mamnet*, 53 Av. Prince Moulay Abdellah.

Tetouan: *Cyber Space*, 68 Bd. Mohammed V (☎09/70.49.87; email *info@cybermania.net.ma*).

INTERNET CONNECTIONS (ISPs)

The following ISPs (the Al Akhawayn resource pages – see opposite – have full lists) have English-speaking staff and have been personally recommended.

Cybermania
www.cybermania.net.ma (☎09/70.49.87).

MTDS
www.mtds.net.ma (☎07.67.48.61).

GUIDES, HUSTLERS, CON MEN AND KIDS

The question of whether to employ a guide will be one of your first (and most frequent) decisions in Morocco. With tourism so important a part of the economy, guiding has become quite a business – especially in the major cities of Fes and Marrakesh. In addition to the guides authorized by the local Délégation du Tourisme, there are scores of young Moroccans offering their services to show you round the *souks* (markets) and sights. These "unofficial guides" are not, strictly speaking, legal, and there are occasional crackdowns by the police on offenders. However, they remain very much a factor (and bane) of tourist life.

With all guides, official or otherwise, it is important to establish at the outset what you want to see. You may well find it useful to agree an itinerary – perhaps showing your guide the points you want to visit on the maps in this book. Do not be pushed into a tour of the craft stores – where your guide will be looking for commission on purchases – or you will see nothing else. If you do want to visit shops, make it clear what kind of goods you are interested in seeing, and equally clear that you do not want to purchase on an initial visit.

OFFICIAL GUIDES

Official guides, engaged through tourist offices (or some of the larger hotels) are paid at a fixed rate of 100dh (£8/$12.50) for a half day. The rate is for the guide's time, and can be shared by a group of people – though the latter would be expected to make some additional tip.

> **FRIENDSHIPS** Following clampdowns on "unofficial guides", there are laws in effect that can make relationships with Moroccans problematic. In theory, any Moroccan – without a guide's permit – seen "accompanying" a tourist can be arrested and imprisoned. In practice this is rarely enforced but friendships, especially with young Moroccans in tourist cities like Tangier, Agadir or Marrakesh, should be discreet. On the whole, once invited to a home, and having met a family, you are unlikely to encounter problems, and your hosts will deal effectively with any enquiries from curious local policemen.

Taking an introductory tour of a new city with an official guide can be a useful exercise in orientation – especially in the vast Medinas (old quarters) of Fes and Marrakesh. Your guide may well be an interesting and entertaining presence, too. Some are highly knowledgeable. There is an advantage also in that, if you are accompanied by an official guide, you won't be approached or hassled by any of their (sometimes less than reputable) unauthorized equivalents.

Official guides can identify themselves by a large, brass "sheriff's badge".

UNOFFICIAL GUIDES AND HUSTLERS

Unofficial guides will approach you in the streets of any sizeable town, offering to find you a hotel, show you the sights, or perhaps, if you look a likely customer, sell you some *kif* (hashish). You will need to develop a strategy to deal with these approaches, otherwise you are unlikely to enjoy urban Morocco.

The most important point to realize is that there are **good** and **bad guides**. Some are genuine students, who may want to earn a small fee, but may equally be interested (as so many claim) in practising their English. Others are out-and-out hustlers, preying on first-visit innocence and paranoia. Your task is to distinguish between offers, to accept (perhaps limited) services from those who seem friendly and enjoyable company, and to deal as humanly as possible with approaches you wish to decline. Politeness is essential, or you'll find things unpleasant, and silence is taken as rudeness; mutual preservation of **dignity** is important.

In general, there is little harm in agreeing to let a guide show you to a **hotel**, though it is best to know which you want to go to – check our listings before arrival. Equally, letting someone guide you to a **café** or **restaurant** won't increase the price of a meal (although waiters will generally make a small tip to the guide).

Offers of a **tour of the town**, however, you may want to avoid. To do so, it is a golden rule to look as if you know where you are going. Never admit to this being your first visit to Morocco. If you feel confident enough, say that you have visited the town before and that you are glad to be back. You will be on your way to setting the parameters of discussion. The most exploitative

ATTITUDES AND BEHAVIOUR

If you want to get the most from a trip to Morocco, it is vital not to start assuming anyone who approaches or talks to you is a hustler. Too many tourists do, and end up making little contact with what must be one of the most hospitable peoples in the world.

Behaviour and attitude are equally important on your part. If some Moroccans treat tourists with contempt, and exploit them as a simple resource, it has much to do with the way the latter behave. It helps everyone if you can avoid **rudeness** or aggressive behaviour in response to insistent offers from guides. And be aware, too, of the importance of **dress**: shorts are acceptable only on the beach, in resorts; shirts (for both sexes) should cover your arms. Note how the locals dress – and not how other tourists choose to.

Photography needs to be undertaken with care. If you are obviously taking a photograph of someone, ask their permission – especially in the more remote, rural regions where you can cause genuine offence. On a more positive front, taking a photograph of someone you've struck up a friendship with and sending it on to them, or exchanging photographs, is often greatly appreciated. In fact, while in Morocco, you may be surprised to find yourself dragged off by new friends or acquaintances to a street or studio photographer for a photo session. This is quite common practice and has no untoward ends.

When **invited to a home**, you normally take your shoes off before entering the reception rooms. It is customary to take a gift: sweet pastries or tea and sugar are always acceptable, and you might even take meat (by arrangement) to a poorer home. (See also note on "Eating Moroccan style" on p.43).

---

guides will probably drop you to look elsewhere. If you are unsure of a guide, suggest taking a mint tea together in a café. Don't make any agreement to employ him prior to this, or any suggestion of an agreement. In addition, never allow yourself to be bullied into going with someone with whom you don't feel at ease – there is no shortage of candidates. And if you feel genuinely threatened or harassed, don't hesitate to threaten or indeed to go to the police: hustlers tend to vanish fast at the prospect of police involvement.

Recently, the civil police have adopted a navy blue uniform to differentiate them from khaki-clad soldiers; and there is now talk of appointing trained tourist police (see p.28).

If you do decide to hire an unofficial guide, be sure to **fix the rate**, as well as the **itinerary**, in advance. You should make it clear that you know the official rates for guides and should agree on these as a maximum. Many unofficial guides will attempt to charge a rate per person.

CON MEN AND SCAMS

Hustlers and con men are a distinct minority in Morocco, as anywhere else. Arriving in one of the main hustler cities – Tangier, Fes or Marrakesh – you will, on your first day, encounter just about all those available. On the second and subsequent days, they'll know your face and approaches will notably drop off. However, forewarned is forearmed, **so a few notes on the most common scams**:

● As stressed in the introduction, all guides have an interest in getting you into craft shops, where they can earn commission of 30 to 50 percent. Even if you say you're not interested, they may suggest taking tea with a cousin who owns a shop. Don't be afraid to keep to your agreed itinerary; keep moving and show interest in the next place on the agreed itinerary.

● A favourite line is that there is a Berber market taking place – and this is the only day of the week to see it. This is rarely true. You will probably visit everyday shops and *souks*.

● Some of the more exploitative hustlers will guide you into the Medinas, then, when you have no idea where you are, charge a large fee to take you back out and to your hotel. If this happens to you, don't be afraid to appeal to people in the street; your hustler will not want attention.

● A few tales are told each year of people approaching visitors with a letter or package to mail to the USA or Europe when you leave Morocco. Never agree to this; you may be involving yourself in a drugs plant.

● Many more hustlers will simply use the excuse of a letter ("Could you help translate or write one?") as a means of attaching themselves to you; it's best to decline assistance.

● On the trains, especially at Tangier, hustlers sometimes pose as porters or railway staff, demanding an extortionate fee for carrying baggage or payment of supplements. Genuine rail staff wear beige overalls and have ID cards, which, if suspicious, you should ask to see.

● Drivers should beware of hitchhiking-hustlers, who spend all day hitching between a pair of towns and can get highly obnoxious in their demands for money when you approach one or other destination.

● In the south, be wary of offers to meet "Blue Men" (desert Touareg nomads) in the "desert". The "nomads" are almost invariably rogues.

● In a number of towns, con-men have been posing as students, working alone or in couples, befriending tourists, and then, after a day or two, telling some sad tale about needing money for getting a passport off a corrupt official, or to look after sick relatives, or some such. You may feel a little foolish if you give money and then meet six other travellers with identical tales to tell.

● Heading for the beach, especially in Tangier, leave most of your money back at your hotel. Thefts and pickpocketing are common and on the increase, particularly in the Medinas and by juveniles; mugging is rare but alas on the increase, especially in Tangier and Marrakesh.

DEALING WITH CHILDREN

In the countryside, and especially along the major southern routes, you will find fewer hustlers and guides, but many more children, eager in their demands for a dirham, *un cadeau* (present) or *un stylo* (a pen/pencil).

Working out your own strategy is all part of the game, but, whatever else you do, be sure to keep a good humour: smile and laugh, or kids can make your life hell. Faced with **begging from children**, we strongly recommend not obliging, as this ties them to a begging mentality.

SECURITY, THE POLICE AND CONSULATES

Keeping your luggage and money secure is an important consideration in Morocco. For all the tales, the situation is probably no worse than in Spain or Italy, but it is obviously unwise to carry large sums of cash or valuables on your person – especially in the main tourist cities like Fes, Marrakesh and Tangier.

Hotels, generally, are secure and useful for depositing money before setting out to explore; larger ones will keep valuables at reception. **Campsites** are considerably less secure, and

many campers advise using a **money belt** – to be worn even while sleeping. If you do decide on a money belt (and many people spend time quite happily without!), leather or cotton materials are preferable to nylon, which can irritate in the heat.

If you are **driving**, it almost goes without saying, you should not leave anything you cannot afford to lose visible or accessible in your car.

THE POLICE

There are two main types of Moroccan **police**: the *Gendarmerie* (who wear grey uniforms and man the checkpoints on main roads, at junctions and the entry to towns), and the *Police (Sûreté)*, who now appear in navy blue (to differentiate from the military) or in plain clothes. Either force may demand to see your passport (and driving papers); the carrying of ID cards (and/or passports) is obligatory.

The **Gendarmes** have jurisdiction outside built-up areas, but you will find their prominent headquarters in, or on the edge of, most towns; they are generally better educated and more polite than the police. You can report any kind of crime to them – or turn to them if you need help.

The **Police** are of little help to visitors, being more concerned with public order and petty crime

FOREIGN EMBASSIES AND CONSULATES IN MOROCCO

Canada *Embassy*: 13 bis Rue Jaâar As-Saddik, Agdal, Rabat (☎07/67.28.80).

Denmark *Embassy*: 4 Rue de Khémisset, Rabat (☎07/76.92.93). *Consulates*: 150 Bd. Rahal El Meskini, Casablanca (☎02/31.44.91); 3 Rue Henri Regnault (4th floor), Tangier (☎09/93.81.83).

Netherlands *Embassy*: 40 Rue de Tunis (☎07/335.12). *Consulates*: Immeuble Miramonte, 47 Av. Hassan II, Tangier (☎09/93.12.45).

Norway *Embassy*: 9 Rue de Khenifra, Agdal (☎07/76.40.84 or 76.40.85). *Consulates*: 3 Rue Henri Regnault, Tangier (☎09/93.36.33); Sogep-ONP, Immeuble A, Agadir (☎08/82.17.01).

Sweden *Embassy*: 159 Av. John Kennedy, Souissi, Rabat (☎07/75.93.13). *Consulates*: 3 Rue du Lt. Sylvestre, Casablanca (☎02/30.46.48); 3 Rue de l'Entraide, Agadir (☎08/82.30.48).

United Kingdom *Embassy*: 17 Bd. Saomaât Hassan, Rabat (☎07/72.09.05). *Consulates*: 9 Rue Amerique du Sud, Tangier (☎09/93.58.95 or 09/93.58.97); 60 Bd. d'Anfa, Casablanca (☎02/22.16.53); Honorary Consul, c/o Agadir Beach Club Hotel, Chemin du Oued Souss, Agadir (☎08/84.43.43).

USA *Embassy*: 2 Av. de Marrakech, Rabat (☎07/62..22.65). *Consulates*: 8 Bd. Moulay Youssef, Casablanca (☎02/22.41.49).

Irish, Australian and **New Zealand citizens** can use UK consular facilities while in Morocco.

---

in the towns. However, there is talk of appointing tourist police in cities such as Marrakesh and Fes.

If you do need to **report a theft**, try to take along a fluent French-speaker, if your French is not too hot. You may only be given a scrap of paper with an official stamp to show your insurance company, who then have to apply themselves to a particular police station for a report (in Arabic). If you cannot prove that a theft has taken place, the police may decline to make any report, especially if the theft is of money only. They will always give you a report, however, if you have lost any official document (passport, driving licence, etc).

The **police emergency number** is ☎19.

GETTING AROUND

Moroccan public transport is, on the whole, pretty good. There is an efficient rail network linking the main towns of the north, the coast and Marrakesh, and elsewhere you can travel easily enough by bus or collective taxi. In the mountains and over the more remote desert routes, where roads are often just dirt tracks or pistes, locals maintain a network of market-day lorries – uncomfortable but fun. And for trekkers, the Atlas mountains, in particular, are crossed by a series of beautiful trails, some easy enough to follow by yourself, others best trekked with a guide and mule.

Renting a car can be a good idea, at least for a part of your trip, opening up routes that are time-consuming or difficult on local transport. Most major companies allow you to rent a car in one city and return it to another.

FLIGHTS

Royal Air Maroc (*RAM*) operate **domestic flights** between all the major cities. If you're very pressed for time, you might want to use the service between **Tangier** and **Marrakesh**; this would cost around £50/$80, well above the bus and train fares but – at two hours, as opposed to nearly thirteen hours – saves considerable effort. For anyone intrepid enough to explore the **Deep South** of the country, flights can also be worthwhile – for example, returning from the southernmost visitable towns of Ad Dakhla or Laayoune.

Details of *RAM* flights, and addresses of the company's local offices, are given in the main part of the guide and the "Travel Details" at the end of chapters. Remember that you must always confirm flights at a *RAM* office 72 hours before departure. Student and under-26 youth **discounts** of 25 percent are available on all *RAM* domestic flights but only if the ticket is bought in advance from one of their offices.

There are now **Regional Air Lines** operating in, and from, **Morocco**. At the moment, they fly to/from Agadir, Marrakesh, Tangier, Fes and Oujda. To be added shortly are Tetouan, Ouarzazate, Laayoune – and Málaga and Las Palmas. For Details and reservations contact Aéroport Mohammed V, Nouasser, Casablanca (☎02/53.80.80; Mon–Sat 8.30am–7pm; Sun 10am–7pm).

TRAINS

Trains cover a limited network of routes, but for travel between the major cities they are easily the best option – reliable, comfortable, efficient and fairly fast.

The **communications map** at the beginning of this book shows all the train routes in the country, and schedules are listed in the "Travel Details" at the end of each chapter. These change very little from year to year, but it's wise to check times in advance at stations. **Timetables**, printed by ONCF, the national railway company, are sporadically available at major train stations and tourist offices.

There are two **classes** of tickets – first and second. **Costs** for a second-class ticket are comparable to what you'd pay for buses; on certain "express" services, which are first and second class only, they are around thirty percent higher. In addition, there are **couchettes** (50dh extra) available on the Tangier–Marrakesh and Tangier–Oujda night trains; these are worth the money for the sake of security, as passengers are locked into a carriage with a guard.

Most of the **stations** are located reasonably close to the modern city centres, in the French-built quarters – the *villes nouvelles*. They generally have **left luggage** depots, though these accept only luggage that can be locked (effectively excluding rucksacks). An alternative is usually provided by nearby cafés, who will look after your luggage for a small tip.

GRANDS TAXIS

Collective **grands taxis** are one of the best features of Moroccan transport. They operate on a wide variety of routes, are much quicker than buses (often quicker than trains, too), and fares are very reasonable. They are also a good way of meeting people and having impromptu Arabic lessons.

The taxis are usually big Peugeot or Mercedes cars carrying six passengers (Peugeots have a slightly less cramped seating arrangement). Most business is along specific routes, and the most popular routes have more or less continuous departures throughout the day. Consequently, you don't have to worry about timetables. You just show up at the terminal (locations are detailed, city by city, in the guide) and ask for a *place* to a specific destination. As soon as six (or, if you're willing to pay extra, four or five) people are assembled, the taxi sets off.

Most of the *grands taxis* run over a fairly short route, from one large town to the next. If you want to travel further, you will have to change taxis from time to time. Some routes are covered routinely in **stages** (eg Agadir–Taroudannt, or Agadir–Taliouine) and on others taxi drivers will generally assist you in finding a connecting taxi and in settling the fare with the driver.

On established routes *grands taxis* keep to fixed **fares** for each passenger. Before leaving, ask at your hotel (or around the terminal) what that price is – or, as a general guideline, consult the "Fares" box opposite.

If you want to take a **non-standard route**, or an excursion, it is possible to pay for a whole *grand taxi* (*une course*) for yourself or a group. But you'll often have to bargain hard before you get down to a realistic price. Hotels can sometimes be useful in helping to "charter" taxis.

BUSES

Bus travel is marginally cheaper than taking a *grand taxi*, and there are far more **regular routes**. Travelling on public transport for any length of time in Morocco, you are likely to make considerable use of the various networks.

Where you can take a *grand taxi* rather than a bus, however, do so. The difference in **fare** is small, and all except the express buses are very much slower and less comfortable than *grands taxis*. Bus legroom is extremely limited and long journeys can be torture for anyone approaching six feet or more in height. In summer, it can be worthwhile taking **night buses** on the longer journeys. Though still not very comfortable, many long-distance buses run at night and they are both quicker and cooler.

CTM AND PRIVATE LINES

There are a variety of bus services and companies. In all sizeable towns, you will generally find both CTM (the national company) and a number of other companies, privately owned and operated.

The **CTM buses** are faster and more reliable, with numbered seats and fixed departure schedules. Their services are often referred to as the *rapide*, and buses come equipped with videos on the longer routes. Some of the **larger private company** buses, such as *SATAS* (which operates widely in the south) are of a similar standard. By contrast, many other of the private companies are tiny outfits, with a single bus which leaves only when the driver considers it sufficiently full.

In some of the larger cities – Rabat and Marrakesh, for example – CTM and the private companies share a single **terminal**, often positioned on the edge of town. You can find out the most useful departure times and routes by asking round at the various windows. In other cities, there might be two or more separate terminals (these are detailed in the guide) and possibly no choice of companies on a particular route.

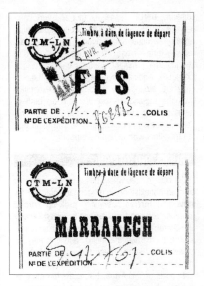

Bus stations tend to have place names on destination boards and indicators in Arabic only – and so you may have to ask around for the appropriate window. On the more popular trips (and especially with CTM services, which are often just once a day in the south), it is worth trying to buy **tickets in advance**; this may not always be possible on smaller private-line services, but it's worth enquiring about.

You can sometimes experience problems getting tickets at **small towns** along major routes, where buses often arrive and leave already full. It's usually possible to get round this problem by taking a local bus or a *grand taxi* for the next section of the trip (until the bus you want empties a little), or by waiting for a bus that actually starts from the town you're in. Overall, the best policy is simply to arrive early in the day (ideally 5.30–6am) at a bus station.

On private-line buses, you generally have to pay for your **baggage** to be loaded onto the roof (and taken off). Moroccans pay just a small tip for this but tourists are expected to pay 2–3dh (some porters ask as much as 15dh for a rucksack!). If you are asked for more than 2–3dh, try to resist. On CTM buses your luggage is weighed and you are issued with a receipt (again about 3dh).

ONCF BUSES

An additional service, on certain major routes, are the **Supratour express buses** run by the train company, **ONCF**. These are fast and very comfortable, connecting Tetouan, Nador, Essaouira, Agadir, Laayoune, Smara and Dakhla to the main railway lines from, respectively, Tnine Sidi Lyamani (near Asilah), Taourirt and Marrakesh (Essaouira, Agadir, Laayoune, Smara and Dakhla). They are around fifty percent more expensive than the regular buses and compare, both in terms of time and cost, with the *grands taxis*. Reserve seats in advance and bear in mind that rail travellers with tickets have priority.

TRUCKS AND HITCHING

In the countryside, where buses may be sporadic or even nonexistent, it is standard practice for **vans** and **lorries** (*camions*), **pick-up trucks** (*camionettes*) and **transit-vans** (*transits*) to carry and charge passengers. You may be asked to pay a little more than the locals, and you may be expected to bargain over the price – but it's straightforward enough.

In parts of the **Atlas**, the locals run more or less scheduled truck or transit services, generally to coincide with the pattern of local *souks*. If you plan on traversing any of the more ambitious Atlas pistes, you'll probably be dependent on these vehicles, unless you walk.

HITCHING

Hitching is not very big in Morocco. Most people, if they own any form of transport at all, have mopeds – which are said to outnumber cars by something like five hundred to one. However, it is often easy to get rides from other **tourists**, particularly if you ask around at the campsites, and for **women travellers** this can be an effective and positive option for getting round – or at least a useful respite from the generally male preserves of buses and *grands taxis*.

Out on the road, it's inevitably a different matter – and hitching is definitely not advisable for women travelling alone. Hitchers should not be surprised to be asked to **pay for a ride** if picked up by country Moroccans. Local rides can operate in much the same way as truck taxis (see above).

CAR RENTAL

Car rental is expensive, from around £200/$320 per week or £35/$56 a day for a basic car with unlimited mileage. Petrol prices are high, too (see opposite). However, having a car does pays obvious dividends if you are pushed for time, allowing you

POLICE CHECKS ON TRAVEL
Police checks take place on travellers throughout the country. They come in three forms. One is a check on local transport; European cars, or hire cars, are usually waved through. The second is a routine but simple passport check – most often polite and friendly, with the only delay due to a desire to relieve boredom with a chat.

The third is more prolonged and involves being stopped by police stationed at more or less permanent points on the roads, who will conduct a fairly detailed inquisition into all non-resident travellers. There is a considerable amount of form-filling and delay. In the Deep South these checks may be conducted by the military rather than by the police.

In the **Rif mountains**, especially in the *cannabis* region near Ketama, you may also come across police checks – concerned, obviously enough, with just the one substance.

to explore unusual routes and take in much more in a lot less time. This is especially true in the **south**, where getting around can be quite an effort if you have to rely on local buses. Driving yourself also gives a certain sense of invulnerability, if Morocco's hustling ways are a bit too much for you.

Many visitors choose to hire a car in Casablanca, Marrakesh or Agadir, expressly for the southern routes. If you're organized, however, it usually works out cheaper to **arrange car rental in advance** through the travel agent who arranges your flight. If you have problems, try one of the UK Morocco specialists detailed on p.6.

Details of **car rental companies in Morocco** are given where relevant in city listings in the guide. The best-value places are mostly in Casablanca and Agadir. Deals to go for are unlimited mileage and daily/weekly rates; paying by the kilometre invariably works out more expensive. The cheapest car on offer is usually a **Renault 4** – well designed for unsurfaced piste roads, with its high suspension and sturdy frame. If you can't or don't want to drive, car hire companies can usually arrange a **driver** for around 100dh (£8/$12.50) a day, plus meals and accommodation.

Before making a booking, be sure to find out if you can pick the car up in one city and return it to another. Most companies will allow this. Check also, if booking in Morocco, whether you will be charged extra for payment with a credit card; there is often a (negotiable) six percent fee for this. Before setting out, make sure the car comes with spare tyre, tool kit and full documentation – including insurance cover, which is compulsory issue with all rentals.

DRIVING

There are few real problems driving in Morocco, but be aware that accident rates are high – in large part because much of the population is not yet tuned in to looking out for motorized vehicles. You should treat all pedestrians with the suspicion that they will cross in front of you, and all cyclists with the idea that they may well swerve into the middle of the road.

Daytime driving can, with the caveats stated above, be as good as anywhere. Good road surfaces, long straight roads, and little traffic between inhabited areas allow for high average speeds. The official speed limit outside towns is 100km per hour, which is difficult to keep down to in desert areas, where perceptions of speed change. On certain roads the speed limit can be as low as 40km per hour. (There is an on-the-spot fine of 30dh for each offence.) The French rule of giving priority to traffic from the right is observed at roundabouts and junctions.

Be very wary about driving after dark. It is legal to drive without lights at up to 20km per hour, which allows all cyclists and mopeds to wander at will; donkeys, goats and sheep do not carry lights, either.

By law, drivers and passengers are required to wear seatbelts. Almost no one does, but if you're stopped by the police, you may have a small fine or *cadeau* (present) extracted.

PISTE DRIVING

On the pistes (rough, unpaved tracks in the mountains or desert), there are special problems. Here you do need a good deal of driving and mechanical confidence – and if you don't feel your car's up to it, don't drive on these routes. Obviously, a 4x4 vehicle, albeit expensive, is best suited to the pistes, but the cheaper Renault 4L is still a sturdy favourite with old hands. On mountain roads, beware of gravel, which can be a real danger on the frequent hairpin bends and, in spring, flash-floods caused by melting snow.

EQUIPMENT

Whether you hire a car or drive your own, always make sure you're carrying a spare tyre in good

---

**DRIVING REQUIREMENTS –
AND MINIMUM AGE**

Note that the **minimum age** for driving in Morocco is 21 years.

You must **carry your driving licence and passport** at all times. International Driving Licences are useful, but not mandatory.

You **drive on the right**.

---

condition (plus a jack and tools). Flat tyres occur very frequently, even on fairly major roads, and you can often be in for a long wait until someone drives along with a possible replacement.

Carrying an emergency windscreen is also useful, especially if you are driving your own car for a long period of time. There are lots of loose stones on the hard shoulders of single-lane roads and they can fly all over the place.

If you're not mechanically minded, make sure to bring a car maintenance manual with you – a useful item, too, for anyone planning to rent a vehicle.

PETROL/GAS AND BREAKDOWNS

Petrol/gas stations are to be found in towns of any size but can be few and far between in rural areas: always fill your tank to the limit. Premium is the standard brand for cars; lead-free is available at larger stations, including most of the Afriquia branches. Prices are pretty much in line with Western Europe, at 7.52dh (Western Sahara 4.92dh) a litre of 4-star (super) petrol and 4.52dh (Western Sahara 2.92dh) of diesel (gasoil). Petrol costs for a Renault 4 work out at around 5dh for every 10km.

Moroccan mechanics are usually excellent at coping with breakdowns and all medium-sized towns have garages (most with an extensive range of spare parts for Renaults and other French cars). But be aware that if you break down miles from anywhere you'll probably end up paying a fortune to get a lorry to tow you back.

If you are driving your own vehicle, there is also the problem of having to re-export any car that you bring into the country (even a wreck). You can't just write off a car: you'll have to take it out of Morocco with you.

VEHICLE INSURANCE

Insurance must by law be sold along with all rental agreements. Driving your own vehicle, you

MOTORBIKING IN MOROCCO

Each year an increasing number of **motorbikers** travel to Morocco and find that it has all the major attractions sought by the enthusiast. Surfaced roads over the Atlas are easy to navigate – although most are only one lorry wide and bends are likely to be gravelly. The shoulder on either side is used by whichever approaching vehicle is the smaller – and this is usually the motor cycle. Read the comments on driving on p.33, too, particularly in relation to the absence of lights at night.

RENTING A MOTORBIKE – AND PAPERWORK

There is a fair bit of bureaucracy involved in taking a motorbike to Morocco. One way of getting around the hassles is to **rent a motorbike** there. The Paris-based company *Sport Adventure* (☎331/142 09 97 73) offers local bikes for rent and also runs some organized tours. Alternatively, the British company, *Dust Trails* (☎01985/841184) will ship you and your bike to Spain for the border crossing, eg Ceuta, Melilla, and then offer advice and a choice of tours.

If you take your own motorbike, you will need **special insurance**. Most companies, especially those based outside Europe, will not cover motorcycling as part of a holiday overseas, particularly when off-road riding is contemplated or inevitable (as it often is in Morocco). You will have to shop around and remember to take the policy with you, together with your bike registration certificate, biker's licence and international licence.

Even large insurance companies cannot give clear answers about **'green cards'** for motorcycling in Morocco and cannot understand that you

may encounter up to a dozen police roadblocks a day where the first language is Arabic, the second French and the third Baksheesh. For 'green card' queries in Britain, contact Green Card Bureau, 152 Silbury Boulevard, Milton Keynes MK9 1NB (☎01908/830 001). In Morocco, the contact is Bureau Central Morocain, Stes d'Assurances, 154 Bd. D'Anfa, Casablanca (☎02/30.18.57 or 58).

When entering Morocco, try to arrive as early in the day as possible. If you are a lone traveller and speak neither Arabic nor French, you may be left queuing until those without queries have been dealt with. If the office then closes, you may have to return the next morning. In these circumstances, it might be worth investing in a tout who, for a fee, will take your papers to a friendly officer.

SPARES AND CLOTHING

Don't take a model of bike likely to be unfamiliar in Morocco. Previous bikers recommend that you take all cables and levers, inner tubes, puncture repair kit, tyre levers, pump, fuses, plugs, chain, washable air filter, cable ties, good tape and tool kit. For riding off-road, take knobbly tyres and rim locks, brush guards, metal number plate and bashplate. In winter, take tough fabric outer clothing. In summer, carry lighter-weight clothing, wool pullovers and waterproofs. Drying out leathers takes a long time.

For further information, see Chris Scott's *The Adventure Motorbiking Handbook* (Compass Star Publications, £13.99), which claims to be 'the first world guide to overlanding on two wheels'!

---

should obtain green card cover from your insurers; this is now valid in Morocco. If you don't have it on arrival, you can buy *Assurance Frontière* for around £25/$40 a month, at any frontier post except for Figuig (the southern entry point from Algeria); to renew it, the main AF office is at 197 Av. Hassan II, Casablanca (☎276.142).

PARKING: GARDIENS AND HOTELS

In almost every town of at least moderate size, you will find a *gardien de voitures* makes an appearance. *Gardiens* are often licensed by local authorities to look after cars, claiming a few dirhams by way of parking fees. Red and white striped curbs (sidewalks) mean 'no parking'.

Most of the larger hotels in the ville nouvelle quarters of cities have parking space (and occasionally garaging) available.

CYCLING

Biking – and particularly **mountain biking** – is becoming an increasingly popular pursuit for Western travellers to Morocco. The country's regular roads are well maintained and by European standards very quiet, while the extensive network of **pistes** – dirt tracks – makes for exciting mountain bike terrain, leading you into areas otherwise accessible only to trekkers or four-wheel drive expeditions.

The biggest negative factor is the pest of **local kids** in the countryside, who for some reason have developed a fondness for the sport of **throwing stones** at cyclists. You need to keep your wits about you, wherever you cycle, and your eyes wide open. The heat and the long stretches of dead straight road across arid, featureless plains – the main routes to (or beyond) the mountain ranges – can all too easily drain your energy. Additionally, public **water** is very rare – there are very few roadside watering places such as are found in Europe – and towns and villages are often a long way apart.

Regular roads – locals refer to surfaced roads as *goudronné* or *revêtue* – are generally well-surfaced but narrow and you will often have to get off the tarmac to make way for traffic. Beware also of open land-drains close to the roadsides, and loose gravel on the bends.

Cycling on the **pistes**, mountain bikes come into their own with their "tractor" tyres and wide, stabilizing handlebars. There are few pistes that could be recommended on a regular tourer. By contrast, some intrepid mountain bikers cover footpaths in the High Atlas, though for the less than super-fit this is extremely heavy going. Better, on the whole, to stick to established pistes – many of which are covered by local trucks, which you can pay for a ride if your legs (or your bike) give out.

GETTING YOUR BIKE TO MOROCCO

Most **airlines** – even charters – carry bikes free of charge, so long as they don't push your baggage allowance over the weight limit. When buying a ticket, register your intention of taking your bike and check out the airline's conditions. They will generally require you to invert the handlebars, remove the pedals, and deflate the tyres; some (like *KLM*) provide/sell a cardboard **box** to enclose the bike, as protection for other passengers' luggage as much as for the bike; you are, however, unlikely to be offered a box for the return journey. A useful alternative, offering little protection but at least ensuring nothing gets lost, is to customize an industrial nylon sack, adding a drawstring at the neck.

If you plan to fly to Spain and cross over **by ferry to Morocco**, things couldn't be simpler. You ride on with the motor vehicles (thus avoiding the long queues of foot passengers) and the bike is secure during the voyage. At the time of writing, there's a small charge for bikes on the ferries from Algeciras to Ceuta and Tangier, but not on the crossings from Málaga or Almería to Melilla.

CYCLES AND LOCAL TRANSPORT

Cycling around Morocco, you can make use of local transport to supplement your own wheels. **Buses** will generally carry cycles on the roof. CTM usually charge around 10dh per bike – make sure you get a ticket. On other lines it's very much up to you to negotiate with the driver and/or baggage porter (who will expect at least 5dh at each end – don't pay both ends in advance!). If you're riding, and exhausted, you can usually flag down private-line buses (but not usually CTM services) on the road.

Some **grands taxis** also agree to carry cycles, if they have space on a rack. The fare will be about the same as for a place in the taxi: again, you may well have to bargain! In mountain/desert areas, you can have your bike carried with you on **truck or transit services** (see p.32). Prices for this are highly negotiable, but should not exceed your own passenger fare.

Cycles are carried on **trains** for a modest handling fee, though it's not really worth the hassle. Bikes have to be registered in advance as baggage and they won't necessarily travel on the same train as you (though they will usually turn up within a day!).

ACCOMMODATION

Accommodation doesn't present any special problems. The cheaper **hotels** will almost always let you keep your bike in your room – and others will find a disused basement or office for storage. It is almost essential to do this, as much to deter unwelcome tampering as theft, especially if you have a curiosity-inviting mountain bike. At **campsites**, there's usually a guardian on hand to keep an eye on your bike, or stow it away in his chalet.

ROUTES
Rewarding areas for biking must include:

● **Tizi n'Test** (High Atlas): **Asni to Ijoukak**, and an excursion to Tin Mal.

● **Asni to Setti Fatma** (High Atlas: Ourika Valley) and beyond if you have a mountain bike.

● **Western** (well-watered) **side of the Middle Atlas**.

In summer, at least, it wouldn't be a good idea to go much **beyond the Atlas**, though given cooler winter temperatures **southern oasis routes** – like **Ouarzazate to Zagora** or **Ouarzazate to Tinerhir** – and the **desert routes** down to **Er Rachidia**, **Erfoud** and **Rissani** – could be rewarding.

REPAIRS

Most towns reveal a wealth of **general repair shops** in their Medina quarters, well used to servicing local bikes and mopeds. Though they are most unlikely to have the correct spare parts for your make of bike, they can usually sort out some kind of temporary solution.

It is worth bringing with you **spare spokes** (and tool), plus **brake blocks** and **cable**, as the mountain descents can take it out on a bike.

Tyres and **tubes** can generally be found for tourers, though if you have anything fancy, best bring at least one spare, too.

Obviously, before setting out, you should make sure that your brakes are in good order, renew bearings, etc, and ensure that you have decent quality (and condition) tyres.

PROBLEMS AND REWARDS

All over Morocco, and particularly in rural areas, there are stray, wild and semi-cared-for **dogs**. A cyclist pedalling past with feet and wheels spinning seems to send at least half of them into a frenzied state. Normally, cycling like the clappers is the best defence, but on steep ascents and off-road this isn't always possible. In these situations, keep the bike between you and the dog, and use your pump or a shower from your water bottle as defence. If you do get bitten, a rabies inoculation is advisable.

Another factor to be prepared for is your susceptibility to unwanted attentions of locals. Small **children** will often stand in the road to hinder your progress, or even chase after you in gangs. This is normally good-natured but it can become intimidating if they start throwing stones. Your attitude is important: be friendly, smile, and maintain strong eye contact. On no account attempt to mete out your own discipline. Small children always have big brothers.

Lastly, the dreaded **hustlers** – for more on whom see p.26. As a cyclist you will avoid the customary hassle at ports and train stations but you are vulnerable to motorbike hustlers who pull alongside tourists in Fes and Marrakesh. Some of these characters can be pretty unpleasant if you decline their services of guiding you to hotels.

So – as one correspondent put it – after all these warnings, and the extra expense and hassle, **is it worth cycling in Morocco**? His answer was a definite yes: "I felt an extra intimacy with the country by staying close to it, rather than viewing it from car or bus windows. And I experienced unrivalled generosity, from cups of tea offered by policemen at roadside checkpoints to a full-blown breakfast banquet from a farming family whose dog had savaged my leg. People went out of their way to give me advice, food, drink and lifts, and not once did I feel seriously threatened. Lastly, the exhilaration I felt on some of the mountain descents, above all the Tizi n'Test in the High Atlas, will remain with me forever. I was not an experienced cycle tourer when I arrived in Morocco, but the grandeur of the scenery helped carry me over the passes."

FURTHER INFORMATION

For a fact sheet on conditions for cyclists in Morocco and some suggested routes, it's worth contacting the British **Cycle Touring Club**, Cotterell House, 69 Meadrow, Godalming, Surrey GU7 3HS (☎01483/417217). The club also arranges good-value **insurance**, etc, for members.

Inspiration for mountain bikers can be found in Nick Crane's book, **Atlas Biker** (Oxford Illustrated Press, £12.95; UK), an adventurous account of a traverse of the High Atlas on – or at times carrying – mountain bikes. For general advice on equipment and clothing, **Bicycle Expeditions** by Paul Vickers (available from the Expedition Advisory Service, Royal Geographical Society, Kensington Gore, London SW7 2AR, UK) is useful.

TREKKING

Trekking is one of the very best things Morocco has to offer. In the High Atlas, the country boasts one of the most rewarding mountain ranges in the world – and one of the least spoilt. If you are used to the Pyrenees or Alps, here you will feel you are moving a century or so back in time.

A number of **long-distance Atlas routes** can be followed – even a "Grand Traverse" of the full range. Most people, however, limit themselves to **shorter treks** round the **Djebel Toubkal** area (best in spring or autumn; conditions can be treacherous in winter). Other promising areas include the **Djebel Sirwa**, **Western High Atlas**, or in winter the **Djebel Sarhro** and **Tafraoute** region of the Anti-Atlas. The **Middle Atlas** has much attractive walking too, from such places as **Tazzeka** (Taza), the **Djebel Iblane** range, **Kerrouchen** and **Azrou**.

Each of these areas is featured in some detail in this guide. For further information, check the **trekking books** detailed on p.23. And if you haven't had much experience or feel a little daunted by the lack of organized facilities, try one of the **specialist trekking companies** offering Moroccan trips (see box on p.6).

For general **trekking practicalities**, see the Toubkal section (Chapter Six). For details of survey-style **maps**, see p.23.

GETTING AROUND CITIES

You'll spend most time exploring Moroccan cities on foot. The alleys of the old Medina quarters, where the sights and *souks* are to be found, will rarely accommodate more than a donkey. In the newer quarters, you may want to make use of city taxis and occasionally a bus. In the new city quarters, you should be aware that pedestrian crossings don't count for very much, except perhaps at junctions 'controlled' by traffic lights. And even then, cycles and mopeds pay scant attention to traffic lights showing red.

Petits taxis, usually Fiats or Simcas, carry up to three passengers and (unlike *grands taxis*) are limited to trips within city limits. Officially, all of them should have meters, but in practice you're unlikely to find one that works (at least for tourists) outside Rabat or Fes. It is then a matter of bargaining for a price – either before you get in (wise to start off with) or by simply presenting the regular fare when you get out. If you are a lone passenger, your taxi driver may pick up one or two additional passengers en route, each of whom will pay the full fare for their journey, as of course will you. This is standard practice.

Fares vary enormously (in Marrakesh and Agadir, demands can often be excessive), though everywhere it depends to a large extent on what you look like, how you act, and where you're going. Don't be afraid to use *petits taxis* or to argue with the driver if you feel you're being unreasonably overcharged. After 8pm, standard fares rise by 50 percent.

ACCOMMODATION

Hotels in Morocco are cheap, good value, and usually pretty easy to find. There can be a shortage of places in the major cities and resorts (Tangier, Fes, Marrakesh and Agadir) in August, and in Rabat or Casablanca when there's a big conference on. Other times, you should be able to pick from a wide range.

The most important distinction among Moroccan hotels is between **classified hotels** (which are given star-ratings by the tourist board) and **unclassified hotels** (which are not). The latter tend to be cheap places, with few facilities, in the old Medina quarters. For any level of comfort, you'll want a classified hotel.

If you're on a limited budget, a good course is to **alternate between the extremes**, spending most nights in basic Medina hotels but going for the occasional blast of grandeur. At any rate don't limit yourself to the middle categories – these are mostly dull, and staying all the time in the *villes nouvelles* will cut you off from the most interesting aspects of traditional Moroccan life.

CLASSIFIED HOTELS

Classified (classé) hotels are almost always in a town's **ville nouvelle** – the "new" or administrative quarters, built by the French and usually set slightly apart from the old Medina quarters.

HOTEL PRICE CODES AND STAR RATINGS

Hotels are no longer obliged to charge according to the official star-ratings (from 1* to 5* luxury), as had long been the custom. Nevertheless, **prices** continue to reflect the star-ratings acquired. The basis of our own **hotel price codes**, set out below and keyed throughout the guide, is the price currently quoted for the cheapest double room in high season (June–September) – and is thus more reliable than quoting notional prices according to star-rating.

Note that cheaper prices in the lower categories are generally for rooms with just a wash-basin – you always pay extra for **en-suite** shower and WC– and that double rooms can generally be converted into **triples/family rooms**, with extra beds, for a modest extra charge. Note also that the prices quoted by all hotels are subject to various local and regional **taxes**, which can add 15 to 20 percent to the bill.

Our code	Classification	Single room price	Double room price
ⓤ	Unclassified	25–60dh	50–99dh
①	1*A/1*B	60–105dh	100–149dh
②	2*B/2*A	105–145dh	150–199dh
③	3*B/3*A	145–225dh	200–299dh
④	4*B/4*A	225–400dh	300–599dh
⑤	5*luxury	Upwards of 400dh	Upwards of 600dh

Since 1993, classified hotels have been allowed, regardless of **star-rating**, to set their own prices – and to vary these according to season and depending on demand. Nevertheless, prices generally reflect the star-rating (see box above) and both prices and ratings should be on display at reception and behind the bedroom door. If in doubt about value for money, don't hesitate to ask to see the room in question; indeed, you will normally be invited to do so.

At the bottom end of the scale – a **one-star hotel** – a basic double room with a washbasin will cost around £9.50/$14; with a shower and WC around £12/$17.50. Moving into **two- and three-star hotels**, you will be paying around £22.50/$36 for a double with shower and WC, at the top end of the scale. You get a fair bit more comfort for your money and there are a scattering of elegant, old hotels in these categories – places which used to be *the* grand hotel in town but have since declined.

For European/American standards of comfort, you need to look, on the whole, at **four-star hotels**. These are used by most foreign tour operators and charge around £25–40/$40–72 for a double. If you can afford the upper end of this scale, you'll be moving into real style, with rooms looking out onto palm-shaded pools and gardens – at their best in buildings that have been converted from old palace residences. But even here, you are advised to check what's on offer. The plumbing, heating and lighting are sometimes

unreliable; restaurants are often closed and swimming pools empty. Many of these hotels were state-owned and are now being privatized which has recently led to some improvements.

Hotels accorded the **five-star-luxury rating** more or less guarantee style, either in a historic conversion (the most famous of which are the *Hotel Mamounia* in Marrakesh and the *Palais Jamai* in Fes) or in a modern building with a splendid pool and all the international creature comforts.

UNCLASSIFIED HOTELS

Unclassified (*non-classé*) hotels are mainly to be found in the older, Arab-built parts of cities – the **Medinas** – and are almost always the cheapest accommodation options. They offer the additional advantage of being at the heart of things: where you'll want to spend most of your time, and where all the sights and markets are concentrated. The disadvantages are that the Medinas can at first appear daunting – with their mazes of narrow lanes and blind alleys – and that the hotels themselves can be, at worst, dirty flea traps with tiny, windowless cells and half-washed sheets. At their best, they're fine: traditional "caravanserai" buildings with whitewashed rooms round a central patio.

One other minus-point for unclassified Medina hotels is that they often have a problem with **water**. Most of the Medinas remain substantially unmodernized, and in the hotels hot showers

HAMMAMS

The absence of hot showers in some of the cheaper Medina hotels is not such a disaster. Throughout all the Medina quarters, you'll find local **hammams** – steam baths where you can go in and sweat for as long as you like, get scrubbed down and rigorously massaged, and douse yourself with endless buckets of hot and cold water. Those for women are particularly welcoming and turn out to be a highlight for many women travellers.

Several *hammams* are detailed in the text, but the best way of finding one is always to ask at the hotel where you're staying. You will often, in fact, need to be led to a *hammam*, since they are usually unmarked and very hard to find. In some towns, you find a separate *hammam* for women and men; at others the same establishment offers different hours for each sex – usually 9am–7pm for women, 7pm–1am (and sometimes 5–9am) for men.

For both sexes, there's more **modesty** than you might perhaps expect: it's customary for men (always) and women (generally) to bathe in **swimming costume**, and men will undress facing the wall. Women may be surprised to find their Moroccan counterparts completely shaven and may (in good humour) be offered this service; there's no embarrassment in declining.

As part of the Islamic tradition of cleanliness and ablutions, *hammams* sometimes have a **religious element**, and you may not be welcome (or allowed in) to those built alongside mosques, particularly on Thursday evenings, before the main weekly service on Friday. On the whole, though, there are no restrictions against *Nisara* ("Nazarenes", or Christians).

Finally, don't forget to bring your own **soap**, **shampoo and towels** along to *hammams*; the latter are rented but can be a bit dubious. Locals often bring a **plastic mat** to sit on, too, as the floors can get a bit clogged. These can be bought easily enough in any town.

---

are a rarity and the squat toilets sometimes pretty disgusting. On the plus side, there is usually a steam bath or *hammam* (see box) nearby.

Unclassified hotel **rates** fluctuate widely, depending on place, season and, above all, demand. The cost of a double room in high season ranges from 50dh (£3.70/$5.90) to 100dh (£7.40/$11.80) Single occupancy costs from 25dh (£1.85/$3) upwards.

YOUTH HOSTELS

Morocco has expanded its **youth hostel** organization in recent years, and there are now eleven *Auberges de Jeunesse* scattered round the country. Most are clean and reasonably well run, and charges are a modest 15–25dh (£1.10–1.85/$1.80–2.95) per person, per night. The hostels are located at Asni (High Atlas), Azrou (Middle Atlas), Casablanca, Chaouen, Fes, Laayoune, Marrakesh, Meknes, Oujda, Rabat and Tangier. Addresses and details are given for all of these in the relevant sections of the guide. One general attraction is the opportunity for meeting other travellers, including Moroccans on holiday.

REFUGES AND GÎTES D'ÉTAPES

In the **Djebel Toubkal** area of the High Atlas mountains, the French-run *Club Alpin Français*

(*CAF*) maintain five huts, or **refuges**, equipped for trekkers. These provide dormitory beds for 10–15dh (75p–£1.10/$1.20–1.75) per person and sometimes meals and/or cooking facilities. They are detailed in the relevant sections.

Also in trekking areas, a number of locals offer rooms in their houses: an informal scheme which the Moroccan tourist authorities have begun promoting as **gîtes d'étape**. Lists of these *gîtes* are to be found in the pamphlet *La Grande Traversée des Atlas Marocains* (see p.23). Current charges are set at 10dh (75p/$1.20) per person, per night, for "*non-classé*; 30dh (£2.25/$3.60) per person, per night, for "*2e-classé*; breakfast is charged at 12dh and an evening meal at 30dh.

CAMPSITES

Campsites are to be found at intervals along most of the developed Moroccan coast and in most towns or cities of any size. They are inexpensive and often quite informal and makeshift, advertised from season to season on roadside signs. Most sites are very cheap, at around 8dh (60p/$0.95) per person, plus a similar charge for a motorcaravan or campervan; they usually have basic (and sometimes very basic) washing and toilet facilities. A few more upmarket places, in Meknes or Fes, for example, offer swimming pools and better facilities at around double the cost – sometimes more. Details and addresses are given in relevant sections of the guide.

Note that campsites don't tend to provide much **security**, and you should never leave valuables unattended. Camping **outside official sites**, this obviously applies even more, and if you want to do this, it's wise to ask at a house if you can pitch your tent alongside – you'll usually get a hospitable response. If you're trekking in the Atlas, it is often possible to pay someone to act as a *gardien* for your tent.

EATING AND DRINKING

Like accommodation, food in Morocco falls into two basic categories: ordinary Moroccan meals served in the Medina cafés (or bought from stalls), and French-influenced tourist menus in most of the hotels and *ville nouvelle* restaurants. There are exceptions – cheap local cafés in the new cities and occasional palace-style places in the Medina. Whatever your budget, don't be afraid to try both options. The Medina places are mostly cleaner than they look and their food is usually fresh and tasty.

BASIC CAFÉ FOOD

Basic Moroccan meals generally centre on a thick, very filling soup – most often the spicy, bean-based **harira** (which is a meal in itself, and eaten as such to break the Ramadan fast). To this you might add a plateful of **kebabs** (either *brochettes*, *shish kebabs* or *kefta*, made from minced meat) and perhaps a **salad** (often very finely chopped), and maybe some **dates** bought at a market stall.

Alternatively, you could go for a **tajine**, which is essentially a stew, steam-cooked slowly in an earthenware dish, with a conical earthenware 'lid', over a charcoal fire. Classic *tajines* include lamb/mutton with prunes and almonds, or chicken with olives and lemon – or, less often, fish and vegetables. Mopped up with bread, a *tajine* can be unbelievably delicious. An alternative, which is very popular, is *kefta* – this time in the shape of meatballs, cooked *tajine*-style with an egg.

Kebabs or a *tajine* would in all likelihood set you back little more than 20dh (£1.50/$2.40) at one of the hole-in-the-wall places in the Medina, with their two or three tables. You are not expected to bargain for cooked food, but prices can be lower in such places if you enquire how much things cost before you start eating. There is often no menu – or a board written in Arabic only.

If you're looking for **breakfast or a snack**, you can buy a half-**baguette** – plus butter and jam, cheese or eggs, if you want – from many bread or grocery stores, and take it into a café to order a coffee.

RESTAURANT MEALS

More expensive dishes, available in some of the Medina cafés as well as in the dearer restaurants, include **fish**, particularly on the coast, and **chicken** *(poulet)*, either spit-roasted *(rôti)* or with lemon and olives *(poulet aux olives et citron)*.

You will sometimes find **pastilla**, too, a succulent pigeon (in cheaper versions chicken may be used) pie, prepared with filo pastry coated with sugar and cinnamon; it is a particular speciality of Fes.

And, of course, there is **couscous**, perhaps the most famous Moroccan dish, based on a

VEGETARIAN/VEGAN OPTIONS

Moroccan cuisine presents distinctly limited options for vegetarians – a preference which will meet with little comprehension on your travels. *Tajines* can be requested without meat (and, with some difficulty, without meat stock), but beyond these vegetarian casseroles, and ubiquitous omelettes and sandwiches, the menus don't present very obvious choices. *Harira* (vegetable broth) may or may not be made with meat stock, while most foods are cooked in animal fats.

It's possible, however, to maintain a balanced and reasonably interesting diet, so long as you're not too strict, and are prepared for a few problems outside the cities. If you're vegan, however, you will really need to come equipped and do a fair bit of cooking for yourself.

Provisions that most vegetarians will feel grateful to have brought include yeast extract, peanut butter, veggie pâtés/spreads, and stock cubes – which you can present to cafés for preparing your *tajine*. You might also take along a small gas stove and pan – gas is cheap and readily available, and in the cheaper hotels a lot of Moroccan people cook in their rooms.

Locally, there are plenty of beans, grains, seeds and pulses available, basic cheeses, excellent yoghurts, and a great selection of fruit and nuts; dates, figs, almonds and pistachio nuts can all enliven dishes. In the countryside, you may find fresh fruit and vegetables hard to obtain except during the weekly *souk*, but you can often buy from locals, who grow a small stock on their terraces.

In cafés and restaurants, asking for a dish *sans viande ou poisson* (without meat or fish) can still result in your being served chicken or lamb, so you'll need to take the trouble to explain matters very clearly. It often helps to talk of being a vegetarian in terms of religious restrictions or rules: concepts that Moroccans are themselves familiar with.

The most difficult situations are those in which you are invited to eat at someone's house – a common occurrence in the countryside. You may find people give you meat when you have specifically asked for vegetables because they think you can't afford it: a scenario in which you might decide that it's more important not to offend someone showing you kindness than to be dogmatic about your own principles. Picking out vegetables from a meat *tajine* won't offend your hosts; declining the dish altogether, on the other hand, may well end up with the mother/sister/wife in the kitchen getting the flack.

---

huge bowl of steamed semolina piled high with vegetables and mutton, chicken, or occasionally fish. *Couscous*, however, tends to be disappointing. There is no real tradition of going out to eat in Morocco, and this is a dish that's traditionally prepared at home for a special occasion (on Friday, the holy day, in richer households; perhaps for a festival in poorer ones). As a general rule, you'll need to give two or three hours' notice for it to be cooked in a restaurant. In the home, remember that every Moroccan's mother cooks the finest *couscous* in the kingdom!

At festivals, which are always good for interesting food, and at the most expensive tourist restaurants, you may also come across **mechoui** – a whole sheep roasted on a spit.

To supplement these standard offerings, most tourist restaurants add a few **French dishes** – steak, liver, various fish and fowl, etc – and the ubiquitous **salade marocaine**, actually very different from the Moroccan idea of salad, since it's based on a few tomatoes, cucumbers and other greens. Together with a dessert consisting either of fruit or pastry, these meals usually come to around 75–100dh (£5.60–7.45/$8.95–11.95) per person.

CAKES, DESSERTS AND FRUIT

Cakes and desserts are available in some Moroccan café-restaurants, though you'll find them more often at pastry shops or street stalls. They can be excellent. The most common are sugar-coated pastries filled with a kind of marzipan; there are infinite variations, like *m'hencha* (almond-filled pastry coils which sometimes appear covered in honey) and *cornes de gazelles* (cornets of pastry filled with cream).

Yoghurt (*yaourt*) is also delicious, and Morocco is surprisingly rich in seasonal **fruits**. In addition to the various kinds of **dates** – sold all year but at their best fresh from the October harvests – there are grapes, melons, strawberries, peaches and figs, all advisably washed before eaten. Or for a real thirst-quencher (and a good cure for a bad stomach), you can have quantities of **prickly pear**, cactus fruit, peeled for you in the street for a couple of dirhams.

A GLOSSARY OF MOROCCAN FOOD

*Note that where food/dishes are commonly available in all kinds of restaurants, both **French** and **Arabic** words are given; in Arabic words, the letters printed in **bold italics** should be stressed.*

BASICS

Pain	*l-khobz*	Bread	Sauce	*l-merga*	Sauce
Oeufs	*l-bayd*	Eggs	Sucre	*soukar* (*sanida*	Sugar
Poissons	*l-hout*	Fish		is granulated	
Viande	*l-hem*	Meat		sugar; *soukar*,	
Huile	*zit*	Oil		lump sugar)	
Poivre	*lebzar*	Pepper	Légumes	*l-khoudra*	Vegetables
Salade	*shalada*	Salad	Vinaigre	*l-khel*	Vinegar
Sel	*l-melha*	Salt			

SOUPS, SALADS AND VEGETABLES

–	*Harira*	Spicy bean soup	Frites	*l'batata*	Fried potatoes
Potage	–	Thick soup	Tomates	*matecha*	Tomatoes
Bouillon	–	Thin soup	Épinards	*salk*	Spinach
Salade Marocaine	–	Mixed salad	Oignons	*l-basla*	Onions

MAIN DISHES

Tajine de viande	*l-hem*	Meat stew
Tajine des poissons	*l-hout*	Fish stew
Couscous (aux sept légumes)	*Couscous bidaoui*	Couscous (with seven vegetables)
Poulet aux olives et citron	–	Chicken with olives and lemon
–	*Djaja mahamara*	Chicken stuffed with almonds, semolina and raisins
Boulettes de viande	*kefta*	Meatballs
Bifteck	*l-habra*	Steak
Agneau	*Mechoui*	Roast lamb
Pastilla	*B'stilla*	Pigeon pie

MEAT, POULTRY AND FISH

Poulet	*djaj*	Chicken	Sardines	*sardile*	Sardines
Pigeon	*lehmama*	Pigeon	Merlan	*l-mirla*	Whiting
Lapin	*qniya*	Rabbit	Crevettes	–	Shrimps
Mouton	*l-houli*	Mutton	Langouste	–	Lobster

TEA AND OTHER DRINKS

The national drink is **thé à la menthe** – green tea ("Whisky Marocain" as locals boast) flavoured with sprigs of mint (*naanaa* in Arabic: the gift of Allah) and sweetened with a minimum of four cubes of sugar per cup. It tastes a little sickly at first but is worth getting used to – perfect in the summer heat and a ritual if you're invited into anyone's home or if you're doing any serious bargaining in a shop. In cafés, it is usually cheaper to ask for a pot (*une théière*) for two or three people.

In winter, Moroccans often add *chiba* (Arabic for wormwood or *absinthe*) to mint tea to 'keep out the cold'. You can also occasionally get red or **amber** tea – more expensive and rarely available, but delicious when you can find it – and tea with **aniseed** (*anis*) and **verbena** (*verveine*).

"English style" tea is usually referred to as *thé Lipton* – after the ubiquitous brand of teabags.

SWEETS AND FRUITS

Cornes de gazelles	kab l-ghzal	Marzipan-filled pastry horns	Bananes	banane	Bananas
–	m'hencha	Coiled, almond-filled pastry	Fraises	l-fraise	Strawberries
			Cerises	hblmluk	Cherries
			Pêches	l-khoukh	Peaches
Briouats au miel	–	Similar – but covered in honey	Oranges	limoune	Oranges
			Melon	l-battikh	Melon
			Pasteque	dellah	Watermelon
–	fekkas	Sweet aniseed biscuits	Raisins	la'anb	Grapes
			Pommes	tufaah	Apples
Fromage	ejben	Cheese	Abricots	mishmash	Apricots
Dattes	tmer	Dates	Figues de Bsarbarie	Kermus d'ensarrah (or Takanareete)	Cactus fruit (prickly pear)
Figues	kermous	Figs			
Amandes	louze	Almonds			

DRINKS

Eau (Minerale)	agua, l-ma (mazdini)	Water (Mineral)	Bière	birra	Beer
			Vin	sh-rab	Wine
Thé (à la menthe)	atay (deeyal naanaa)	Tea (Mint)	Café (au lait)	qahwa (bi lahlib)	Coffee (with milk)

SOME ARABIC PHRASES

What do you have . . .	**Ashnoo kane** . . .	Without meat	Ble l-hem
. . . to eat?	. . . f'l-makla?	This is not what I asked for!	Hedee meshee heea li tlubt!
. . . to drink?	. . . f'l-mucharoubat?		
What is this?	Shnoo hada?	This is not fresh/clean!	Hedee meshee treea/n'qeea!
Can you give me. . .	Ateenee . . .		
. . . a knife/fork/ spoon	. . . moos/forsheta/ malka?	This is (not) good!	Hedee (meshee) mezyena!
. . . a plate/glass/ napkin?	. . . t'b-sil/kess/ l-fota?	The bill, please.	L'h'seb minfadlik.
		Please write it down.	Minfadlik, k'tib'h.
Less/without sugar	Shweeya/ble soukar		

EATING MOROCCAN STYLE

Eating in local cafés, or if **invited to a home**, you may find yourself using your hands rather than a knife and fork. Muslims eat only with the **right hand** (the left is used for the toilet), and you should do likewise. Hold the bread between the fingers and use your thumb as a scoop; it's often easier to discard the soft centre of the bread and to use the crust only – as you will see many Moroccans do. Eating from a **communal plate** at someone's home, it is polite to take only what is immediately in front of you, unless specifically offered a piece of meat by the host.

Also common at cafés and street stalls are a range of wonderful fresh-squeezed **juices**: jus d'orange (if you don't want sugar, remember to say so!), jus d'amande ('almond milk'), jus des bananes and jus de pomme (apple); the last two are milk-based and served chilled. Leben – soured milk – is often sold at train and bus stations and does wonders for an upset stomach.

Other **soft drinks** inevitably include Coke, Fanta and other fizzy lemonades – all pretty inex-pensive and sold in large bottles. **Mineral water**, which is a worthwhile investment throughout the country, is usually referred to by brand name, ubiquitously the still Sidi Harazem or Sidi Ali (some people claim to be able to tell one from the other), or the naturally sparkling Oulmès.

Coffee (café) is best in French-style cafés – either noir (black), cassé (with a drop of milk), or au lait (made with milk). Instant coffee is known, like tea, after its brand – in this case Nescafé.

EAU MINERALE NATURELLE

sidi harazem

Lastly, do not take risks with **milk**: buy it fresh and drink it fresh. If it smells remotely off, don't touch it.

WINE AND BEER

As an Islamic nation, Morocco gives **drinking alcohol** a low profile. It is, in fact, not generally possible to buy any alcohol at all in the Medinas, and for beer or wine you always have to go to a tourist restaurant or hotel, or a bar in the *ville nouvelle*. Outside of tourist hotels, **bars** – which are often called **brasseries**, though they serve no food – are very much **all-male preserves**, in which women travellers may feel uneasy.

On the drinks front, Moroccan **wines** can be palatable enough, if a little heavy for drinking without a meal. The best to be found is the pinkish red *Clairet de Meknès*, made purposefully light in French claret style. Other varieties worth trying include the strong red *Cabernet*, the rosé *Gris de Boulaoune* and the dry, white *Spécial Coquillages*.

Those Moroccans who drink in bars tend to stick to **beer**, usually the local *Stork* or *Flag*, which are about 50 percent cheaper than imported European brands.

KIF (HASHISH)

The smoking of **kif** (hashish, *chocolaté*) has for a long time been a regular pastime of Moroccans and tourists alike. Indeed, in the 1960s and 1970s (or further back, in the 1930s), its ready availability, good quality and low cost made *kif* a major tourist attraction. It is, however, illegal, or, as the ONMT puts it:

Tourists coming to Morocco are warned that the first article in the Dahir of April 24th 1954 prohibits

the POSSESSION, the OFFER, the DISTRIBUTION, the PURCHASE, the SALE and the TRANSPORTATION as well as the EXPORTATION of CANNABIS IN WHATEVER FORM. The Dahir allows for a penalty of IMPRISONMENT from three months to five years and a fine of 2400 to 240,000 dirhams, or only one of these. Moreover the law court may ordain the SEIZURE of the means of transport and the things used to cover up the smuggling as well as the toxic products themselves.

In practice, there is no real effort to stop Moroccans from using *kif*, but as a tourist you are rather more vulnerable. Not so much because of the **police**, as because of the **dealers**. Many have developed aggressive tactics, selling people hash (or, occasionally, even planting it) and then returning or sending friends to threaten to turn you in to the police (or even doing so). Either way, it can all become pretty paranoiac and unpleasant – and large fines (plus prison sentences for substantial amounts) do get levied.

What can you do to avoid all this? Most obviously, keep well clear – above all, of the *kif*-growing areas of the **Rif mountains** and the processing centre in **Ketama** – and always reply to hustlers by saying you don't smoke. If you *are* going to indulge, don't buy anything in the first few days (definitely not in Tangier and Tetouan), and only smoke* where you feel thoroughly confident and in control. Above all, however, **do not try to take any out** of the country, even to Spain (where attitudes to possession are relaxed but there's nearly always a prison sentence for importing).

If you do get in trouble there are **consulates** for most nationalities in Rabat/Casablanca and, to a lesser extent, in Tangier (see lists on p.29). All of the consulates are notoriously unsympathetic to drug offenders – the British one in Rabat has an old French poster on the wall, "*Le kif détruit l'esprit*" – but they can help with technical problems and find you legal representation.

---

*Kif is not necessarily smoked – a traditional Moroccan speciality is *majoun*, a kind of fudge made with the pounded flowers and seeds of the plant. As James Jackson wrote in his *An Account of the Empire of Morocco, 1814*, "a piece of this as big as a walnut will for a time entirely deprive a man of all reason and intellect". It is also reputed to be a good stomach settler.

COMMUNICATIONS: POST, PHONES AND THE MEDIA

MAIL AND POSTE RESTANTE

Letters between Moroccan and Western Europe generally take around a week to ten days, around two weeks for North America or Australasia. There are postboxes at every post office (**PTT** aka *La Poste*) and on the wayside; they seem to get emptied fairly efficiently, even in out-of-the-way places.

Stamps can sometimes be bought alongside postcards, or from any *Tabac*, as well as at the *PTT*, where there may be a dedicated window or counter (labelled *timbres*).

At the *PTT*, there is a separate window for **parcels**, where the officials will want to examine the goods you are sending. Always take them unwrapped; alongside the parcels counter, there is usually someone (on a franchise) to supply wrapping paper, string and all the trimmings, or wrap your parcel, if you want.

Post office hours are Monday to Friday, 8am to noon and 3 to 6pm in winter, 8am to 3pm in summer; closed Saturday and Sunday.

POSTE RESTANTE

Receiving letters **poste restante** can be a bit of a lottery, as Moroccan post office workers don't always file letters under the name you might expect. Ask for all your initials to be checked (including *M* for Ms, etc), and, if you're half-expecting anything, suggest other letters as well.

To pick up your mail you need your passport. To have mail sent to you, it should be addressed (preferably with your surname underlined) to

Poste Restante at the *PTT Centrale* of any major city (Marrakesh is notoriously inefficient).

Alternatives to sending *poste restante* to post offices are to pick a big **hotel** (anything with three or more stars should be reliable) or have things sent **c/o American Express** – represented in Morocco by *Voyages Schwartz* in Tangier, Casablanca and Marrakesh (see p.19, for addresses).

PHONES

The **public telephone section** is usually housed in a city's main post office (*PTT Centrale*), though it often has a separate entrance and stays open longer hours – 24 hours a day in some of the main cities. Since **international direct dialling** reached Morocco it's been possible to place calls with little problem, and in most major towns you can also make international calls from centrally placed **phone boxes** (*cabines*). In large cities you can now use local phonecards in some *cabines*; they are usually on sale at a nearby kiosk, or less reliably, from a hovering phonecard tout. Alternatively, you can **make calls through a hotel**. Even fairly small places will normally do this; however, be sure to ask in advance both of possible surcharges and the chargeable rate.

To **make a call from a cabine**, you place the phonecard – or coins – into the slot on the phoneset and then dial. Using coins, a few dirhams are enough for a call within Morocco; for international calls you need at least four of the larger 5dh coins for Europe and eight or more for North America or Australia.

Recently, **teleboutiques** have appeared in most towns and villages of any size. They are staffed but most have card-operated phones – for which you buy a phonecard from the boutique. Some boutiques will send a fax for you – and, by arrangement, receive one for you. A few also have a photocopier, but they are not well maintained and you may have to visit several boutiques to find one which works.

Note that international calls are charged for each **three-minute period**. If you go one second over, you're charged for the next period. If phoning from a *PTT*, you can request the operator to cut you off after a three-minute period.

In the Western Sahara, there are neither *cabines* nor *teleboutiques* and you must go to the *PTT* to make a call.

MOROCCAN CALLS AND NUMBERS

The Moroccan phone system has recently been rationalized, with all numbers prefixed by one of eight **area zones**:

02 Casablanca	03 Settat
04 Marrakesh	05 Fes
06 Oujda	07 Rabat
08 Laayoune	09 Tangier

To call a number in another zone, you use the prefix; if you are calling from within the same zone, you omit it. The full number will always have **eight digits** (including the zone prefix), unless it's incredibly out-of-the-way, in which case it may still just have a village name and **two-digit** number, which you have to dial through the operator.

When dialling, the **ringing tone** consists of one-and-a-half-second bursts of tone, separated by a three-and-a-half-second silence. The **engaged tone** is similar to the one used in Britain. A series of rapid pips may also be heard, indicating that your call is being connected.

If you want to phone the **Spanish conclaves** in Morocco, dial 00 3456 for **Ceuta** and 00 3452 for **Mellilla**; to call from Spain or Melilla to Ceuta you just dial 956 and from Spain or Ceuta to Mellilla dial 952.

INTERNATIONAL CALLS

For an **international call**, dial **00** and wait for a musical-sounding dialling tone, which is the signal that you can put in an international call. Now dial the **country code**:

Australia 61	Britain 44
Canada 1	Netherlands 31
New Zealand 64	Spain 34
USA 1	

Then dial the **individual number**, leaving out the initial 0 of its local code (USA and Canada have no initial 0; for Spain omit the 9).

PHONING MOROCCO FROM ABROAD,

Phoning Morocco from abroad, you dial the international code (00 from Britain, Ireland, Netherlands and New Zealand; 0011 from Australia; and 011 from USA and Canada), then the country code (212) and the full eight-digit number (omitting the initial zero of the zone code).

If you are successfully connected you will hear the local tones for your number. If not, you will hear either a busy signal, a recording in Arabic and then French informing that lines are "saturated", or silence. Persevere: it may well take three or four attempts to get through.

The **rate for international calls** is currently around 12dh (off peak) and 18dh (90p and £1.35) a minute to Britain and Western Europe; between 24dh (off peak) and 60dh (US$2.90 and 7.25) a minute to the USA and Canada. A good policy is to phone someone briefly and get them to ring you back. Actual reverse charge (collect) calls are hard to arrange.

THE MEDIA

A selection of British and French **newspapers** and the *International Herald Tribune* are available in all the main cities. *The Guardian* (printed in Frankfurt or Roubaix) and *Le Monde* are the most common.

If you take a short-wave radio, you can pick up the **BBC World Service**, which is broadcast on various frequencies through the day, from 6am to midnight local time. The most consistent evening reception is generally on 9.41 and 5.975 MHz (31.88m and 50.21m bands); full programme listings are available from the BBC or the British Council in Rabat. You can also pick up the **Voice of America**.

Some of the pricier hotels these days can receive **satellite TV** – CNN, the French TV5, and occasionally the UK Sky channel. In the north of the country you can also get Spanish TV stations and, in Tangier, the English-language **Gibraltar** TV and radio broadcasts.

Morocco's own two TV channels broadcast in Arabic, but include some French programmes – and news bulletins in Arabic, French, Spanish and, more recently, Berber.

THE MOROCCAN PRESS

The **Moroccan press** encompasses a reasonable range of papers, published in French and Arabic. Of the **French-language** papers, the most accessible is the official – and somewhat rigorously pro-government – French-language daily, *Le Matin du Sahara* (circulation 70,000). Others include *L'Opinion* (conservative opposition) and *Al-Bayannne* (communist).

In **Arabic**, there are *Al Alam* (circ. 50,000), which is supportive of the Istiqlal party, and *Al Muharnir* (circ. 17,000), which supports the socialist USFP party. There is also a fundamentalist paper, *Al Djemaa* (circ. 3000).

FESTIVALS: RAMADAN, HOLIDAYS AND MOUSSEMS

If the popular image of Islam is somewhat puritanical and ascetic, Morocco's festivals – the *moussems* and *amouggars* – do their best to contradict it. The country abounds in holidays and festivals of all kinds, both national and local, and coming across one can be the most enjoyable experience of travel in Morocco – with the chance to witness music and dance, as well as special regional foods and market *souks*.

Perhaps surprisingly, there are rewards, too, in coinciding with one of the major Islamic celebrations – above all Ramadan, when all Muslims (which in effect means all Moroccans) observe a total fast from sunrise to sunset for a month. This can pose some problems for travelling but the celebratory evenings are again good times to hear music and to share in hospitality.

RAMADAN

Ramadan, in its observance, parallels the traditional Christian Lent. The ninth month of the Islamic calendar, it commemorates the time in which the Koran was revealed to Muhammad. In contrast to the Christian West, the Muslim world observes the fast rigorously – indeed Moroccans are forbidden by law from "public disrespect" of the fast, and a few are jailed for this each year.

The Ramadan fast involves abstention from food, drink, smoking and sex during daylight hours throughout the month. With most local cafés and restaurants closing during the day, and people getting on edge towards the month's end, it is in some respects an unsatisfactory time to travel: efficiency drops, drivers fall asleep at the wheel (hence airline pilots are excused fasting), and guides and muleteers are unwilling to go off on treks.

But there is compensation in witnessing and becoming absorbed into the pattern of the fast. At sunset, signalled by the sounding of a siren and the lighting of lamps on the minarets, an amazing calm and sense of wellbeing fall on the streets, as everyone drinks a bowl of *harira* and possibly a glass of milk, and maybe eats dates. You will also see almsgiving (*zakat*) extended to offering *harira* to the poor and homeless.

After breaking their fast, everyone – in the cities at least – gets down to a night of celebration and **entertainment**. This takes different forms. If you can spend some time in Marrakesh during the month, you'll find the Djemaa El Fna square there at its most active, with troupes of musicians, dancers and acrobats coming into the city for the occasion. In Rabat and Fes, there seem to be continuous promenades, with cafés and stalls staying open up to 3am. Urban cafés provide venues for live music and singing, too, and in the southern towns and Berber villages, you will often come across the ritualized *ahouaches* and *haidus* – circular, trance-like dances often involving whole communities.

If you are a **non-Muslim** outsider you are not expected to observe Ramadan, but it is good to be sensitive about breaking the fast (particularly smoking) in public. In fact, the best way to experience Ramadan – and to benefit from its naturally purifying rhythms – is to enter into it. You may lack the faith to go without an occasional glass of water, and you'll probably have breakfast later than sunrise, but it is worth an attempt.

OTHER ISLAMIC HOLIDAYS

At the end of Ramadan comes the feast of **Aïd Es Seghir**, a climax to the festivities in Marrakesh, though observed more privately in most communities. Equally important to the Muslim calendar is **Aïd El Kebir**, which celebrates the willingness of Abraham to obey God and to sacrifice Isaac. The Aïd El Kebir is followed, about three weeks later, by **Moharem**, the Muslim new year.

RAMADAN AND ISLAMIC HOLIDAYS

Islamic religious holidays are calculated on the **lunar calendar**, so their dates rotate throughout the seasons (as does Ramadan's). Exact dates in the lunar calendar are impossible to predict – they are set by the Islamic authorities in Fes – but approximate dates for the next two cycles are:

Ramadan	20 Dec 1998	9 Dec 1999
Aïd Es Seghir	18 Jan 1999	7 Jan 2000
Aïd El Kebir	27 March 1999	16 March 2000
Moharem	22 May 1999	11 May 2000
Mouloud	5 July 1999	24 June 2000

FÊTES NATIONALES

Secular **fêtes nationales**, all celebrated to some extent, are tied to Western calendar dates:

January 1	New Year's Day
March 3	Feast of the Throne
May 1	Labour Day
May 23	Fête Nationale
July 9	King's Birthday and Youth Day
August 14	Allegiance Day
November 6	Green March
November 18	Independence Day

The **Feast of the Throne** is the largest secular holiday, a colourful affair, celebrated throughout Morocco, over two to three days, with fireworks, parades, and music.

Both *aïds* are traditional family gatherings. At the Aïd El Kebir every household that can afford it will slaughter a sheep. You see them tethered everywhere, often on rooftops, for weeks prior to the event; after the feast, their skins are to be seen, being cured on the streets. Note that, on both *aïd* days, shops and restaurants close and buses don't run; on the following day, all transport is packed, as people return to the cities from their family homes.

The fourth main religious holiday is the **Mouloud**, the Prophet's birthday. This is widely observed, with a large number of *moussems* (see next column) timed to take place in the weeks around it.

PUBLIC HOLIDAYS

Nowadays each of the big **religious feasts** is usually marked by **two days off**. These are announced or ratified by the king, each time, on TV and radio the preceding day.

On these public holidays, and on the secular *fêtes nationales* (see box above), all **banks**, **post offices** and most **shops** are closed; **transport** is reduced, too, but never stops completely.

MOUSSEMS AND AMMOUGARS

Moussems – or *ammougars* – are held in honour of saints or *marabouts*. They are basically local, and predominantly rural, affairs. Besides the Aïd Es Seghir and Aïd El Kebir, however, they form the main religious and social celebrations of the year for most Moroccans, especially for the country Berbers.

Some of the smaller *moussems* amount to no more than a market day with religious overtones; others are essentially harvest festivals, celebrating a pause in agricultural labour after a crop has been successfully brought in. A number, however, have developed into substantial occasions – akin to Spanish fiestas – and a few have acquired national significance. If you are lucky enough to be here for one of the major events, you'll get the chance to witness Moroccan popular culture at its richest, with horse-riding, music, singing and dancing, and of course eating and drinking.

AIMS AND FUNCTIONS

The ostensible aim of the *moussem* is religious: to obtain blessing, or *baraka*, from the saint and/or to thank God for the harvest. But the social and cultural dimensions are equally important. *Moussems* provide an opportunity for country people to escape the monotony of their hard working lives in several days of festivities. They may provide the year's single opportunity for friends or families from different villages to meet. Harvest and farming problems are discussed, as well as family matters – marriage in particular – as people get the chance to sing, dance, eat and pray together.

Music and singing are always major components of a *moussem* and locals will often bring tape recorders to provide sounds for the rest of the year. The different religious brotherhoods, some of whom may be present at larger *moussems*, each have their own distinct styles of music, dancing and dress.

Moussems also operate as **fairs**, or markets, with artisans offering their produce to a wider market than is available at the weekly *souk*. Buyers in turn can inform themselves about new products and regional price differences, as the *moussem* attracts people from a much wider area than the *souk*. There is a welcome injection of cash into the local economy, too, with traders and entertainers doing good business, and householders renting out rooms.

At the **spiritual level**, people seek to improve their standing with God through prayer, as well as the less orthodox channels of popular belief. Central to this is *baraka*, good fortune, which can be obtained by intercession of the saint. Financial contributions are made and these are used to buy a gift, or *hedia*, usually a large carpet, which is then taken in procession to the saint's tomb; it is deposited there for the local *shereefian* families, the descendants of the saint, to dispose of as they wish. Country people may seek to obtain *baraka* by attaching a garment or tissue to the saint's tomb and leaving it overnight to take home after the festival.

The procession which takes the gift to the tomb is the high point of the more **religious moussems**, such as that of **Moulay Idriss**, where an enormous carpet is carried above the heads of the religious **brotherhoods**. Each of these brotherhoods will be playing its own music, hypnotic in its rhythms; spectators and participants may go into trance, giving themselves up to the music. If you witness such events, it is best to keep a low profile (and certainly don't take photographs); the presence of foreigners or non-

Muslims at these times is sometimes considered to impede trance.

Release through trance probably has a therapeutic aspect, and indeed some *moussems* are specifically concerned with **cures** of physical and psychiatric disorders. The saint's tomb is usually located near a freshwater spring, and the cure can simply be bathing in and drinking the water. Those suffering from physical ailments may also be treated at the *moussem* with herbal remedies, or by recitation of verses from the Koran. Koranic verses may also be written and placed in tiny receptacles fastened near the affected parts. The whole is reminiscent of the popular remedies found at European pilgrimage centres like Lourdes.

PRACTICALITIES

There are enormous numbers of *moussems*. An idea of quite how many can be gathered from the frequency with which, travelling about the countryside, you see *koubbas* – the square, white-domed buildings covering a saint's tomb. Each of these is a potential focal point of a *moussem*, and any one region or town may have twenty to thirty separate annual *moussems*. Establishing when they take place, however, can be difficult for outsiders; most local people find out by word of mouth at the weekly *souks*.

Many *moussems* are held around religious occasions such as the **Mouloud**, which change date each year according to the lunar calendar (see box opposite). Others, concerned with celebrating the **harvest**, have their date decided at a local level according to when the harvest is ready. *Moussems* of this type are obviously more difficult to plan a visit around than those which occur at points in the Islamic year. **August** and **September** are the most promising months overall, with dozens of *moussems* held after the grain harvest when there is a lull in the agricultural year before sowing starts prior to the first rains in October or November.

The **lists** overleaf give an approximate idea (sometimes an exact one) of when the *moussems* are, but you will generally need to ask at a local level for information. Sometimes tourist offices may be able to help, though often not.

The **accommodation** situation will depend on whether the *moussem* is in the town or countryside. In the country, the simplest solution is to take a tent and camp – there is no real objection to anyone

MOULOUD MOUSSEMS

Meknes: Ben Aissa Moussem

The largest of all the *moussems*, this includes a spectacular **fantasia** (a charge of horses with riders firing guns at full gallop) if weather conditions permit, held near Place El Hedim. With this, the enormous conical tents, and crowds of country people in white djellabahs, beneath the city walls, it has the appearance of a medieval tournament. At least, that is, until you see the adjoining fairground, which is itself fun, with its illusionists and riders of death.

In the past, this *moussem* was the principal gathering of the **Aissoua** brotherhood, and the occasion for them to display their extraordinary powers of endurance under trance – cutting themselves with daggers, swallowing glass and the like. Their activities today are more subdued, though they still include going into trance, and of course playing music. Their focus is the *marabout* tomb of Ben Aissa, near the road in from Rabat.

Accommodation in Meknes is a problem at this time unless you arrive two or three days in advance. However, you could quite easily visit on a day-trip from Fes.

Salé: Wax Candle *Moussem*

As the name suggests, this festival centres on a procession of wax candles – enormous lantern-like creations, carried from Bab El Rih to the Grand Mosque on the eve of the *Mouloud*. The candle bearers (a hereditary position) are followed by various brotherhoods, dancing and playing music.

The **procession** starts about 3pm and goes on for three or four hours; the best place to see it is at Bab Bou Hadja, where the candles are presented to local dignitaries.

OTHER POPULAR MOUSSEMS

May	**Moulay Bousselham**. *Moussem of Sidi Ahmed Ben Mansour*.
June	**Goulimine**. Traditionally a camel traders' fair, elements of which remain.
	Tan Tan. *Moussem of Sidi Mohammed Ma El Ainin*. Large-scale religious and commercial *moussem*. Saharan "Guedra" dance may be seen performed.
July	**Tetouan**. *Moussem of Moulay Abdessalem*. A very religious, traditional occasion with a big turnout of local tribesmen. Impressive location on a flat mountain top south of the town.
August	**Setti Fatma**. Large and popular *moussem* in the Ourika valley, southeast of Marrakesh.
	El Jadida. *Moussem of Moulay Abdallah*. Located about 9km west of the city at a village named after the saint. Features displays of horse-riding, or *fantasias*.
	Tiznit. *Moussem of Sidi Ahmed ou Moussa*. Primarily religious.
September	**Chaouen**. *Moussem of Sidi Allal Al Hadh*. Located in the hills out of the town.
	Moulay Idriss Zerhoun. *Moussem of Moulay Idriss*. The largest religious *moussem*, but visitable only for the day as a non-Muslim. Impressive display by brotherhoods, and a highly charged procession of gifts to the saint's tomb. Also a large *fantasia* above the town.
	Imilchil. *Marriage Moussem*. Set in the heart of the Atlas mountains, this is the most celebrated Berber *moussem* – traditionally the occasion of all marriages in the region, though today also a tourist event. In fact there now seem to be two *moussems*, with one laid on specifically for package tours from Marrakesh and Agadir; the real event is held in the last week in September or the first in October.
	Fes. *Moussem of Moulay Idriss II*. The largest of the *moussems* held inside a major city, and involving a long procession to the saint's tomb. The Medina is packed out, however, and you will have a better view if you stand at Dar Batha or Place Boujeloud before the procession enters the Medina proper.

camping wherever they please during a *moussem*. In small towns there may be hotels – and locals will rent out rooms in their houses. **Food** is never a problem, with dozens of traders setting up stalls, though it is perhaps best to stick to the grills, as stalls may not have access to running water for cleaning.

HARVEST MOUSSEMS			
February	Tafraoute (almonds)	July	Sefrou (cherries)
March	Beni Mellal (cotton)	July	Al Hoceima (sea produce)
April	Immouzer des Ida Outanane (honey)	August	Immouzer du Kandar (apples/pears)
May	Berkane (clementines) El Kelâa des Mgouna (roses)	November	Erfoud (dates) Rhafsaï (olives)

SPORTS AND ACTIVITIES

Morocco is doing much to keep up with the increasing interest in activity and sporting holidays. In addition to its magnificent trekking opportunities (for information on which see p.36), the country offers impressive golf and tennis facilities, a couple of ski resorts (plus some adventurous off-piste skiing) and excellent fishing. The national sporting obsession, however, is football; enthusiasts can join in any number of beach kick-about games, or watch local league and cup matches.

FOOTBALL

Football is important in Morocco and the country is a growing force. The national team qualified for the **World Cup** finals in 1986 (when they reached the quarter finals), 1994, and most recently, France 1998, and are important participants in the annual **African Nations Cup** championship.

Moroccan clubs play at the top level in the various African club tournaments too, and at home compete in an annual **league** and the (knock-out) **Throne Cup**. For a long time there was just one full-time professional team, **FAR** (the army), but the 1990s saw the introduction of sponsorship and other semi-professional sides, the best of which are **WIDAD** and **RAJA**, the two big Casablanca teams, **MAS** from Fes and **KAC** from Kenitra. There's consequently a fairly high standard in the league these days, although the top players continue to be enticed by big clubs and big money in France, Belgium, Spain and Britain.

One negative factor about Moroccan league games is a tendency towards defensive play – the points system gives two points for a draw and three for a win. But there is always the potential for displays of individual dynamism and inspiration – a parallel, so Moroccans would have it, with the Brazilian style of play.

Brazilian comparisons could certainly be made with the social background of Moroccan football, players developing their game in unstructured **kick-arounds** on the beach, street or patches of wasteland. The lack of a team strip in these games (and hence easy recognition of team mates) discourages long balls and intricate passing, and encourages individual possession and quick one-twos. The same conditions produced Pelé and Maradona.

SKIING

Morocco isn't immediately thought of as a skiing destination, but the High Atlas mountains are reliably snow-covered from late January to early April, and occasionally the Middle Atlas, too, has sufficient snows for the sport.

In the High Atlas, the main resort is **Oukaïmeden**, two hours' drive from Marrakesh. It is quiet, well appointed and inexpensive, with pleasant chalet hotels, seven piste runs, a ski lift, local instructors, and equipment for hire. In the Middle Atlas, **Mischliffen** – a volcanic crater – has rather more limited facilities, with three lifts, a shorter and unreliable season, and very old-fashioned equipment rental. A third prospective ski centre is the high-altitude resort of **Bou Iblane** in the Anti-Atlas, which offers little more than an approach road (not always covered by the snowplough) and a single ski lift.

Off-piste skiing is increasingly popular in the High Atlas, in particular around the famed **Toubkal massif**, where groups often combine skiing with mountaineering to the summits. At present, in the absence of organized facilities, this is an area best left to those with considerable experience and expertise.

RIDING

The established base for **riding holidays** is *La Roseraie* hotel at **Ouirgane** on the Tizi n'Test road. The hotel runs trekking tours into the **High Atlas**, offering anything from one-day excursions to extended trips staying at villages en route Yous should bring your own helmet. Stays or packages can be arranged through most of the Moroccan specialist agents detailed in pp.6–7.

You might also want to visit the **Haras de Meknes** (see p.172), Morocco's largest National Stud Farm, where you can both exercise and ride the horses.

FISHING

French visitors to Morocco have long appreciated the possibilities for fishing. The country offers an immense Atlantic (and small Mediterranean) **coastline**, with opportunities to arrange boat trips at Safi, Essaouira, Moulay Bousselham (near Asilah), and elsewhere.

Inland, the **Middle Atlas** shelters beautiful **lakes** and **rivers**, many of them well stocked with trout. Good bases could include **Azrou** (near the Aghmas lakes), **Ifrane** (near Zerrrouka), **Khenifra** (the Oum Er Rbia River) and **Ouirgane** (the Nfis River). Pike are also to be found in some Middle Atlas lakes (such as Aguelmame Azizgza, near Khenifra), and a few of the huge artificial *barrages*, like **Bin El Ouidaine** (near Beni Mellal), are said to contain enormous bass.

For the really determined and adventurous, the most exciting Moroccan fishing is along the coast of the **Western Sahara**, where catches weigh in regularly at 20–30 kilos. The regional capital of Laayoune is the only feasible base at present, unless you're totally self-reliant.

For all fishing in the country, you need to take your own **equipment**. For coarse or fly fishing you need a **permit** from the *Administration des Eaux et Fôrets* (11 Rue Revoil, Rabat). For trout fishing, you are limited to the hours between 6am and noon; the season starts on March 31.

WATER SPORTS AND SWIMMING

Agadir has **sailing, yachting, windsurfing** and **diving** on offer, with Tarhazoute, just north of the resort, developing a growing reputation among **windsurfers**. The biggest **surfing and windsurfing** destination, however, is **Essaouira**, more or less west of Marrakesh, which draws European devotees of the sport all year round.

Here – and indeed anywhere on the Atlantic coast – surfers and **swimmers** alike should beware of strong undertows. The Atlantic can be very exposed, with crashing waves, and you'll often see Moroccan bathers venturing rather timidly into the water in formation.

Inland, most towns of any size have a municipal **swimming pool** – they're always very cheap and addresses are given in the guide. In the south, you'll be dependent on campsite pools or on those at the luxury hotels (who often allow outsiders to swim, either for a charge or if you buy drinks or a meal).

GOLF AND TENNIS

The British opened a golf course in Tangier as far back as 1917 – a rather more refined alternative to their then-favoured sport of pig-sticking. Today the country has an international-level course at **Rabat** (*Royal Dar-Es-Salam Royal Golf*), further 18-hole courses at **Mohammedia** (*Royal Golf*), **Marrakesh** (*Palmeraie Golf; Royal Golf*), **Tangier** (*Royal Country Club*), **El Jadida** (*Royal Golf*); and nine-hole courses at **Casablanca** (*Royal Anfa*), **Agadir** (*Royal Golf; Dunes Golf Club*), **Fes** (*Royal Golf*), **Cabo Negro** (*Royal Golf*), **Beni Slimane** (*Royal Golf*), **Ouarzazate** (*Royal Golf*), and **Meknes** (*Royal Golf* – actually within the confines of the Royal Palace gardens).

For a **golf-centred holiday** package, or details (and photos) of the courses, consult the golf brochure issued by *Best of Morocco* (☎01380/828533). *Cadogan Travel* (☎01703/332 551) also arrange golfing holidays.

Tennis courts are to be found at most four-star and five-star hotels, especially in Agadir (which now has a total of over 120 courts) and Marrakesh. Tennis equipment can often be loaned from hotels but it is not often up to much and you'd be advised to take rackets and balls.

SOUKS AND MOROCCAN CRAFTS

Souks – markets – are a major feature of Moroccan life, and among the country's greatest attractions. They are to be found everywhere: each town has its special *souk* quarter, large cities like Fes and Marrakesh have labyrinths of individual *souks* (each filling a street or square and devoted to one particular craft), and in the countryside there is a moveable network, shifting between the various villages of a region.

SOUK DAYS

Some of the villages, or areas between villages, are in fact named after **their market days**, so it's easy to see when they're held.

The *souk* days are:

Souk El Had – Sunday (literally, "first market")
Souk El Tnine – Monday market
Souk El Tleta – Tuesday market
Souk El Arba – Wednesday market
Souk El Khamees – Thursday market
Souk Es Sebt – Saturday market

There are no village markets on **Friday** (*El Djemaa* – the "assembly", when the main prayers are held in the mosques), and even in the cities, *souks* are largely closed on Friday mornings and very subdued for the rest of the day.

In general, village *souks* begin on the afternoon preceding the *souk* day, as people travel from all over the region; those who live nearer set out early in the morning of the *souk* day. As a consequence, the *souk* itself is usually over by noon and people disperse in the afternoon. You should therefore arrange to arrive by mid-morning at the latest.

CRAFT TRADITIONS

Moroccan **craft**, or *artesanie*, traditions are still highly active, and even goods mass-produced for tourists are surprisingly untacky. To find pieces of real quality, however, is not that easy – some crafts have become dulled by centuries of repetition and others have been corrupted by modern techniques and chemical dyes.

In general, if you're planning on buying anything, it's always worth getting as close to the source of the goods as possible, and to steer clear

of the main tourist centres. **Fes** might have the richest traditions, but you can often find better work at much cheaper prices elsewhere; **Tangier** and **Agadir**, neither of which has imaginative workshops of their own, are generally poor bets. As stressed throughout the guide, the best way to get an idea of standards and quality is to visit the various **traditional crafts museums** spread round the country: there are good ones in Fes, Meknes, Tangier, Rabat and Marrakesh.

CARPETS, RUGS AND BLANKETS

Moroccan **carpets** are not cheap – you can pay £1000/$1600 and more for the finer Arab designs in Fes or Rabat. However, it is possible to find **rugs** or **kellims** (which are woven rather than knotted) at more reasonable prices, with a range of strong, well-designed weaves from £30–50 ($50–80).

Most of these kellims will be of Berber origin and the most interesting ones usually come from the High and Middle Atlas; if you're looking seriously, try to get to the town *souk* in **Midelt** or the weekly markets in **Azrou** and other villages around **Marrakesh**. The chain of *Maison Berbère* shops in Ouarzazate, Tinerhir and Rissani are good hunting grounds, too.

On a simpler and cheaper level, the **Berber blankets** (*foutahs*, or *couvertures*) are imaginative, and often very striking with bands of reds

and blacks; for these, **Tetouan** and **Chaouen**, on the edge of the Rif, are promising.

JEWELLERY

Silver jewellery went into decline with the loss to Israel of Morocco's Jewish population, the country's traditional workers in precious metals and crafts in general; in the **south**, however, you can pick up some fabulous Berber necklaces and bracelets, always very chunky, and charactersied by bold combinations of semiprecious (and sometimes plastic) stones and beads. There are particularly good jewellery *souks* in Essaouira, Marrakesh and Tiznit.

SEMIPRECIOUS STONES

You'll see a variety of semiprecious stones on sale throughout Morocco, and in the High Atlas they are often aggressively hawked on the roadsides. If you're lucky enough to be offered genuine **amethyst** or **quartz**, prices can be bargained to very tempting levels. Be warned, however, that all that glitters is not necessarily the real thing. Too often, if you wet the stone and rub, you'll find traces of dye on your fingers . . .

WOOD AND POTTERY

Marquetry is one of the few crafts where you'll see genuinely old pieces – inlaid tables and shelves – though the most easily exportable objects are boxes and chess sets, beautifully inlaid in *thuya* and cedar woods in **Essaouira**.

Pottery on the whole is disappointing, though the blue-and-white designs of **Fes** and the multi-coloured pots of **Chaouen** (both produced largely for the tourist trade) are highly attractive. The essentially domestic pottery of **Safi** – Morocco's major pottery centre – is worth a look, too, with its crude but effective plates and garden pots. Best of all, perhaps, are the works produced by the Oulja pottery at **Salé**, near Rabat.

CLOTHING AND LEATHER

Moroccan clothes are easy to purchase, and though Westerners – men at least – who try to imitate Moroccan styles by wearing the cotton or wool *djellaba* (a kind of cloak) tend to look a little silly, there are some highly desirable items. Some of the cloth is exquisite in itself, and walking down the dyers' *souks* is an inspiration.

Leather is also excellent, and here you can buy and wear goods with perhaps greater confidence. The classic Moroccan shoes are *babouches*, open at the heel, immensely comfortable, and produced in yellow (the usual colour), white, red (for women) and occasionally grey or (for the truly fetishistic) black; a good pair – and quality varies enormously – can cost £6–15 ($10–25). Marrakesh and Tafraoute are especially good for *babouches*.

BARGAINING

Whatever you buy, and wherever you buy it, you will want (and be expected) to **bargain**. There are no hard and fast rules – it is really a question of paying what something is worth to you – but there are a few general points to keep in mind.

First, **bargaining is entirely natural** in Morocco. If you ask the price in a market, the answer, as likely as not, will come in one breath – "Twenty; how much will you pay?"

Second, don't pay any attention to **initial prices**. These are simply a device to test the limits of a particular deal or situation. Don't think, for example, in terms of paying one-third of the asking price (as some guides suggest) – it might well turn out to be a tenth or even a twentieth. Equally, though, it might not – some sellers actually start near the price they have in mind and will bustle you out of their shop for offering an "insulting" price. Don't feel intimidated by either tactic; if you return the following day for some coveted item, you will most likely be welcomed as an old friend. Take your chances!

Third, **don't ever let a figure pass your lips** that you aren't prepared to pay – nor start bargaining for something you have absolutely no intention of buying – there's no better way to create bad feelings.

Fourth, **take your time**. If the deal is a serious one (for a rug, say), you'll probably want to sit down over tea with the vendor, and for two cups you'll talk about anything but the rug and the price. If negotiations do not seem to be going well, it often helps to have a friend on hand who seems a little less interested in the purchase than you – as they may well become, given the protracted experiences involved . . .

The final and most golden rule of them all is never to go shopping with a **guide** or a hustler, even "just to look" – the pressures will be either too great or it'll be too boring, depending on how long you've been in the country and how you've learned to cope with these people.

In the villages – and with beach traders – you might find **bartering goods** to be more satisfactory than bargaining over a price. This way you know the value of what you're offering better than your partner (though he'll have a pretty good idea), and in a sense you're giving a fairer exchange. Items particularly sought after are training shoes (even if they're well worn), printed T-shirts (rock designs – especially Prince – are favourites), football shirts (British or American) and other sports clothes, basic medicines (in country areas), and Western department-store clothes (*Marks & Spencer* has particularly good currency).

An approximate idea of what you should be paying for handicrafts can be gained from checking the **fixed prices** in the state- or co-operative-run *Ensembles Artisanals*. Even here, though, there is sometimes room for bargaining as prices are slightly higher than elsewhere.

MOSQUES AND MONUMENTS

Without a doubt, one of the major disappointments of travelling in Morocco is not being allowed into its mosques – as is permitted in many other Muslim countries. In Morocco, all non-Muslims are excluded and the rule is strictly observed.

However, there is much architecture to be admired in the form of *medersas* – medieval "colleges" attached as teaching institutions to urban mosques – and in the numerous, elaborately decorated gateways (*babs*) to be found in any well-preserved city walls. Cities also reveal some beautiful *fondouks* – caravanersais – and the occasional palace. There is a scattering of remains, too, from Morocco's ancient civilizations under Roman and even Phoenician rule.

Most public monuments, including *medersas*, museums and archaeological sites, levy a standard 10dh admission fee and open Tuesday to Sunday (closed Mondays) from 9am to noon and 3 to 6pm.

MOSQUES AND KOUBBAS

The only "mosques" that non-Muslims *are* allowed to visit are the ruined Almohad structure of **Tin Mal** in the High Atlas, the courtyard of the sanctuary

mosque of Moulay Ismail in **Meknes**, the sanctuary of Mohammed V in **Rabat**, the Bou Inania *medersa* in **Fes** and the new Grand Mosquée Hassan II in **Casablanca**. Elsewhere, you'll have to be content with an occasional glimpse through open doors, and even in this you should be sensitive: people don't seem to mind tourists peering into the Kairaouine Mosque in Fes (the country's most important religious building), but in the country you should never approach a shrine too closely.

This rule applies equally to the numerous domed and whitewashed **koubbas** – the tombs of *marabouts*, or local saints – and the "monastic" **zaouias** of the various Sufi brotherhoods. It is a good idea, too, to avoid walking through **graveyards**, as these also are regarded as sacred places.

OTHER ISLAMIC MONUMENTS

As some compensation, many of the most beautiful and architecturally interesting of Morocco's monuments are open to view – the great imperial gateways, or *babs*, of the main cities, for example, and, of course, the **minarets** (towers from which the call to prayer is made) attached to the mosques.

Of buildings that can be visited, highlights must include the **Berber Kasbahs** (fortified castle residences) of the south; a series of city **palaces** and **mansions** – many of them converted into hotels, restaurants or craft shops – in Fes and Marrakesh; and the intricate **medersas** of Fes, Meknes, Salé, and Marrakesh.

The **medersas**, many of them dating from the thirteenth and fourteenth centuries, are perhaps the most startling – and certainly the most "monumental" – of all Moroccan buildings, each displaying elaborate decoration and designs in stucco (gypsum or plaster), cedar and tile mosaics (known in Morocco as *zellij*). Originally, these buildings served as religious universities or student residences for a neighbouring mosque school, but by the turn of the century they had largely fallen into decay and disuse. Today, they have almost all become secularized. Their role is discussed in the chapter on **Fes**, which is where you'll find the richest and most varied examples.

ANCIENT REMAINS

Unlike Tunisia and Algeria, Morocco never saw extensive **Roman** colonization – and indeed, the south of the country remained unconquered by any outside force until the French invasion of the 1920s. Ancient sites are, therefore, limited. The most interesting, and really the only one worth going out of your way to visit, is **Volubilis**, close to Meknes. For enthusiasts, **Lixus** (near Larache) is worthwhile, and there are good bronze collections and statuary at **Rabat**.

A number of **prehistoric sites**, with well-preserved **rock paintings** (*gravures rupestres* in French), survive in the south of the country, though most are extremely difficult to reach – and to find. The most rewarding and easily accessible ones are around **Oukaïmeden**, near Marrakesh. More significant, but remote, sites are scattered among the hills near the desert town of **Foum El Hassan**.

FROM A WOMAN'S PERSPECTIVE

Margaret Hubbard spent one month travelling on her own around Morocco:

I knew that there were likely to be difficulties in travelling as a woman alone around Morocco. I'd been warned by numerous sources (this book's previous edition included) about hustling and harassment and I was already well aware of the constraints imposed on women travellers within Islamic cultures. But above and beyond this, I knew I'd be fascinated by the country. I had picked up a smattering of Arabic and the impetus to study Islamic religion and culture during trips to Damascus and Amman (both times with a male companion). Also, I already had enough experience of travelling alone to know that I could live with myself should I meet up with no one else.

So, a little apprehensive, but very much more determined and excited, I arrived in Tangier, took the first train out to Casablanca, and found a room for the night. It was not until I emerged the next morning into the bright daylight of Casablanca that I experienced my first reaction to Morocco.

BEGINNINGS

Nothing could have prepared me for it. Almost instantly, I was assailed by a barrage of: "*Voulez-vous coucher avec moi?*" "*Avez-vous jamais fait l'amour au Maroc?*" "*Venez avec moi, madame*" "*Viens, m'selle*". Whatever I had to say was ignored at will, and wherever I went, I felt that I was being constantly scrutinized by men.

Fighting off the panic, I headed for the bus station, where, after a lot of frantic rushing to and fro (I couldn't decipher the Arabic signs) I climbed onto a bus for Marrakesh.

Marrakesh proved to me that I was right in coming to Morocco. It wasn't that the harassment was any less – in fact, it was almost as constant as in Tangier. But wandering through the Djemaa

El Fna (the main square and centre of all life in Marrakesh), among the snake charmers, kebab vendors, water sellers, and merchants of everything from false teeth to handwoven rugs, I became ensnared to such an extent that my response to the men who approached me was no longer one of fear but irrelevance.

There was too much to be learned to shut out contact with people, and I heard myself utter, as if it were the most normal reply in the world: "*Non, monsieur, je ne veux pas coucher avec vous, mais pouvez-vous me dire pourquoi ils vendent* false teeth/*combien d'années il faut pour faire des tapis à main. . . ?*" That first night, I returned to my room at 2am more alive than I had felt for months.

STRATEGIES

I'd also stumbled upon a possible strategy for pre-empting, perhaps even preventing, harassment. Moroccan hustlers know a lot about tourists and have reason to expect one of two reactions from them: fear or a sort of resigned acceptance.

What they don't expect is for you to move quickly through the opening gambits and launch into conversation about Moroccan life. Using a mixture of French and Arabic, I developed the persona of a "serious woman" and, from Marrakesh to Figuig, discussed the politics of the Maghreb, maternity rights, housing costs, or the Koran with almost anyone who wanted my attention.

It became exhausting, but any attempt at more desultory chat was treated as an open invitation and seemed to make any harassment more determined. That isn't to say that it's impossible to have a more relaxed relationship with Moroccan men – I made good friends on two occasions with Arab men and I'm still corresponding with one of them. But I think this was made easier by my defining the terms of our friendship fairly early on in the conversation. (As a general rule, whenever I arranged to meet up with someone I didn't know very well, I chose well-lit public places. I was also careful about my clothes – I found it really did help to look as inconspicuous as possible, and I almost always wore loose-fitting blouses, longish skirts, and, occasionally, also a head scarf.)

CONTACT: THE HAMMAM

After exploring Marrakesh for five days, I took a bus out over the Atlas mountain range to Zagora. The journey took twelve hours and the bus was hot and cramped, but wedged between a group of Moroccan mothers, jostling their babies on my lap and sharing whatever food and drink was going around, I felt reassured, more a participant than an outsider.

This was also one of the few occasions that I'd had any sort of meaningful contact with Moroccan women. For the most part, women tend to have a low profile in public, moving in very separate spheres from the tourists.

For me, the most likely meeting place was the *hammam*, or steam bath, which I habitually sought out in each stopping place. Apart from the undoubted pleasures of plentiful hot water, these became a place of refuge for me. It was a relief to be surrounded by women, and to be an object of curiosity without any element of threat. Any ideas about Western status I might have had were lost in the face of explaining in French, Arabic, and sign language to an old Moroccan woman with 24 grandchildren the sexual practices and methods of contraception used in the West. "Is it true that women are opened up by machine?" is a question that worries me still.

FESTIVITIES

I arrived in Zagora on the last night of the festival of the king's birthday. It was pure chance. The town was packed with Moroccans who had

travelled in from nearby oases. Oddly, though, I met just one other tourist – a German man. We were both swept along, as insignificant as any other single people in the crowd, dancing and singing in time to the echoing African sounds.

At the main event of the night, the crowd was divided by a long rope with women on one side and men on the other, with only the German and me standing side by side. I felt overwhelmed with a feeling of excitement and wellbeing, simply because I was there.

INTO THE DESERT

From Zagora I headed for Figuig and the desert, stopping overnight en route in Tinerhir. It's possible that I chose a bad hotel for that stop, but it was about the worst night that I had spent in the entire trip. The men in and around the hotel jeered, even spat, at me when I politely refused to accompany them, and throughout the night I had men banging on the door shutters of my room. For twelve hours I stood guard, tense, afraid, and stifled by the locked-in heat of that dismal hotel room. I escaped on the first bus out*.

Further south I met up with a Danish man in a Land Rover and travelled on with him to spend four days in the desert. It was a simple business arrangement – he wanted someone to look after the van while he slept and I wanted someone to look out for me while I slept. I can find no terms that will sufficiently describe the effect the desert had on me. It was awesome and inspiring and it silenced me. I also found that the more recent preoccupations that I had about my life, work, and relationships had entirely slipped from my mind. Yet strangely, I could recall with absolute clarity images from over ten years ago. I remain convinced that the desert, with its simplicity, its expansiveness, and its power changed me in some way.

At Figuig I parted company with the Dane and made it in various stages to Fes. I tended to find myself becoming dissatisfied after travelling for a while with a male companion. This was not because I didn't enjoy the company, which was, more often than not, a luxury for me, but I used to feel cheated that I was no longer at the forefront and that any contact with Moroccans would have to be made through him. This is often the case in Islamic countries, where any approaches or offers of hospitality are proffered man to man, with the woman treated more or less as an appendage. I was prepared to go on alone however uncomfortable it might become, so long as I was treated as a person in my own right.

JOGGING

In Fes I discovered yet another, perhaps even more effective, strategy for changing my status with Moroccan men. I am a runner and compete regularly in marathons, and I'm used to keeping up with my training in almost any conditions. Up until Fes, I'd held back, uncertain as to the effect of dashing out of a hotel in only a tracksuit bottom and a T-shirt. My usual outfit, the long skirt and blouse, was hardly suitable for the exercise I had in mind. After seriously considering confining myself to laps around the hotel bedroom, I recovered my sanity and my sense of adventure, changed my clothes, and set off.

The harassment and the hustling all melted away. I found that the Moroccans have such a high regard for sport that the very men who had hassled me in the morning were looking on with a respectful interest, offering encouragement and advice as I hurtled by in the cool of the evening. From then on, I became known as "the runner" and was left more or less in peace for the rest of my stay.

After this, I made it a rule to train in all the villages and towns I stayed in on my way back to Tangier. Now when I run, I conjure up the image of pacing out of Chaouen towards the shrine on the hillside, keeping time with the chants of the *muezzin* at dawn.

RETURN TO TANGIER

Returning to Tangier, I felt as far removed as it is possible to feel from the apprehensive new arrival of the month before. I felt less intimidated and more stoic about my status as an inferior and an outsider, and I had long since come to accept that I was a source of income to many people whose options for earning money are severely limited.

Walking out of the bus station, I was surrounded by a group of hustlers. I listened in silence and then said, in the fairly decent Arabic that I had picked up along the journey from Figuig to Fes, that I had been in the Sahara and hadn't got lost so I didn't think I needed a guide in Tangier, and furthermore, that I had talked with some Touaregs in Zagora who told me that it is a lie that Moroccans buy their women with camels; would they please excuse me, I had arrangements?

I spent the next few days wandering freely around the town, totally immersed in plotting how to return.

Editor's note: Individual experiences of Moroccan towns obviously differ enormously. A correspondent wrote in to say that, although she agreed with the tenor of this piece, she had spent a lot of time in Tinerhir and in her experience it was the friendliest town she has visited in the country .

DIRECTORY

ADDRESSES Arabic names – *Derb, Zankat*, etc – are gradually replacing French ones. The main street or square of any town, though, is still invariably *Avenue* or *Place* Hassan II (the present king) or Mohammed V (his father). Older street signs are usually in French and Arabic lettering; new ones are often Arabic only.

ANIMAL WELFARE Animals – and especially pack animals – have a tough life in Morocco. The

Society for the Protection of Animals in North Africa (SPANA) works throughout North Africa to improve conditions, replacing painful, old-style bits on donkeys and horses, employing vets, and runing animal clinics and refuges. They have centres in Rabat, Marrakesh, Meknes, Khémisset, Khenifra, Midelt and Tangier – all of which can be contacted or visited if you are interested or are concerned about animals you've come across. The best initial contact address in Morocco is SPANA's administrative office in Temara (☎07/74.72.09), 14km south of Rabat. The Society also has a British office at 15 Buckingham Gate, London SW1E 6LB (☎0171/828 0997) which can provide you with details of the Moroccan centres listed above.

CONSULATES AND EMBASSIES are in Rabat, Tangier, Agadir and Casablanca; see p.29 for lists.

CONTRACEPTIVES Somewhat poor quality and unreliable condoms (*préservatifs*) can be bought in most chemists, and so can the pill (officially by prescription, but this isn't essential). If you're suffering from diarrhoea, the pill (or any other drug) may not be in your system long enough to be absorbed, and consequently may become ineffective.

CULTURAL SOCIETIES OVERSEAS Anyone interested in Morocco is recommended to join the **Society for Moroccan Studies** (c/o School of African and Oriental Studies, Thornhaugh St, Russell Square, London WC1H 0XG); the society publishes an interesting bi-annual journal and hosts a series of lectures. Also of interest, for British residents, is the older-established **British Moroccan Society** (c/o Embassy of Morocco, 49 Queens Gate Gdns, London SW7 5NE), which organizes various Moroccan-orientated events and discussions, usually in London.

CUSTOMS ALLOWANCES You're allowed to bring a litre of spirits into Morocco, which is well worth doing. Up to 200 cigarettes are also permitted, which saves money on American brands.

ELECTRICAL VOLTAGE Most of the country runs on 220v but some towns still have 110v sockets and it's not uncommon to have both in the same building. Note that electric shavers work okay but heat-producing items like hairdryers need converters to function properly.

GAY ATTITUDES Male homosexuality is common in Morocco, although attitudes towards it are a little schizophrenic. No Moroccan will declare himself gay – which has connotations of femininity and weakness; the idea of being a passive partner is virtually taboo, while a dominant partner may well not consider himself to be indulging in a homosexual act. Private realities, however, are rather different from public show. (On which subject, note that Moroccan men often walk hand-in-hand in public – a habit which has nothing to do with homosexuality and is simply a sign of friendship).

If you are visiting Morocco specifically as a "gay destination" be warned that the legendary Joe Orton days of Tangier – and Marrakesh – as gay resorts are long gone. Gay sex is, of course, still available, and men travelling alone or together may be propositioned. But attitudes are tending increasingly towards hustling and exploitation on all sides. Gay sex is, in addition, officially illegal under Moroccan law. Article 489 of the Moroccan penal code prohibits any "shameless or unnatural act" with a person of the same sex and allows for imprisonment of six months to three years, plus a fine. There are also various provisions in the penal code for more serious offences, with correspondingly higher penalties in cases involving, for example, corruption of minors.

As emphasized under "Health and Insurance", p.20, AIDS is a real threat in Morocco, despite a lack of reported cases. There is some awareness of AIDS among Moroccans but most are steadfast in seeing it as a "disease for foreigners" and the concept, let alone practice, of "safe sex" is yet to emerge.

There is no public perception of lesbianism.

HOSPITAL EMERGENCIES ☎15.

LAUNDRIES in the larger towns will take in clothes and wash them overnight, but you'll usually find it easier to ask at hotels – even basic places will be able to offer the service.

LEFT LUGGAGE You can deposit baggage at most train stations, but it will have to be locked/padlocked; if you are catching a late train, make sure that the office will be open on your return. There are similar facilities at the main bus stations, CTM offices and ferry stations (Tangier, Ceuta, Melilla).

OPENING HOURS follow a reasonably consistent pattern: **tourist sights** (Tues–Sun 9am–noon & 3–6pm); **banks** (Mon–Fri 8.15–11.30am & 2.15–4.30pm); **shops** (Mon–Sat 8.30am–noon & 2–6.30pm); **offices** (Mon–Thurs 8.30am–noon & 2.30–6.30pm; Fri 8.30–11.30am & 3–6.30pm).

TAMPONS can be bought at general stores, not pharmacies, in most Moroccan cities. Don't expect to find them in country or mountain areas.

TIME Morocco keeps Greenwich Mean Time the whole year. It is therefore one hour (two hours in summertime) behind Spain – something to keep in mind when catching ferries. Remember that Ceuta and Melilla keep Spanish time.

TIPPING You're expected to tip – among others – waiters in cafés (1dh per person) and restaurants (5dh or so); museum and monument curators (3dh); *gardiens de voitures* (4–5dh; see p.34); petrol pump attendants (2–3dh); and bus porters (3–4dh; see p.31).

WORK Your only chance of paid work in Morocco is **teaching English**. For information, try the following schools: *The British Council* (6 Av. Moulay Youssef, Rabat; or 10 Spring Gdns, London SW1; ☎0171/930 8466), *The American Language Centre* (1 Place de la Fraternité, Casablanca; also in Rabat, Kenitra, Tangier, Tetouan, Meknes, Fes and Marrakesh) or *The American School* (Rue Al Amir Abdelkader, Agdal, Rabat; also in Casablanca and Tangier). Reasonable spoken French is normally required by all of these.

WORK CAMPS If you are interested in taking part in a work camp, a number of possibilities exist. The *United Nations Association* (UK head office: 3 Whitehall Court, London SW1; ☎0171/930 2931) recruit international teams to work on manual and community projects for two or three weeks in the summer; applicants pay their own travel costs but are provided with accommodation. Alternatively, there are three Moroccan organisations: *Les Amis des Chantiers Inter-nationaux de Meknes* (PO Box 8, Meknes), whose projects generally involve agricultural or construction work around Meknes – three weeks in July and August, accommodation and food pro-

vided; *Chanteuse Jeunesse Maroc* (PO Box 566, Rabat), who offer some inspired work camps – recently, creating green spaces at Asilah, and constructing lanes and alleyways in shanty towns near Mohammedia; or *Pensés et Chantiers* (26 Rue de Pakistan, BP 1423, Rabat), involving community schemes – painting, restoration and gardening. Most of the work camps are open to all-comers over 17 years of age; travel costs have to be paid by the participant, but you generally receive free accommodation (take a sleeping bag) and meals.

USEFUL THINGS TO BRING

● **Alarm clock**. Vital for early-morning buses.

● **Bartering gifts**. If you want to bargain for handicrafts, bring things to barter with (see p.54); hiking in the Atlas, spare gear is always appreciated by local guides.

● **Camping gear**. If you are planning on a lot of camping, a sleeping bag and foam pad are invaluable, but it is worth considering whether you will make enough use of campsites to justify the weight, as hotels are remarkably cheap. A good compromise is to pack a **sheet sleeping bag** – reassuring in those hotels that don't relentlessly pursue cleanliness awards.
Camping gas is widely available in larger towns (but not *Epigas*).

● **Clothes**. Keep both practicality and sensitivity in mind. As emphasized in the piece "From a Woman's Perspective", Morocco is a deeply conservative nation: the more modest your dress the less hassle you will attract.

On the practicalities front, keep in mind that the mountain areas and Sahara alike can get distinctly **chilly** at night, even in spring and autumn. A warm sweater, or even lightweight track suit, is invaluable. So, too, in winter and spring, is some kind of waterproof clothing and a solid pair of shoes: mountain storms (and resulting flash floods) are commonplace and wandering round a muddy Medina in sodden sandals is

a miserable experience. For advice on **trekking gear**, see Chapter Six.

● **Film**. Kodak and Fuji film is available in most towns and major resorts, but it's relatively expensive and may well be pretty old stock. It's best to bring adequate supplies. For photography in the Medinas – all dark alleyways and hidden corners – fast film (400–800 ASA) is useful. If you're looking for good landscape photographs, especially in the south, slow film (and/or early rising) is a must. See also notes on behaviour (p.27).

● **Medicines**. Salt tablets, some insect repellent, water purifying tablets, anti-diarrhoea tablets, aspirin and plasters are all useful. You may also find yourself dispensing them to locals, especially in mountain areas, where they are in very short supply.

● **Plug**. If you like your water to fill a basin, it is worth packing an omnisize plug: few hotels (even relatively upmarket ones) supply such equipment or replace it when it disappears.

● **Toiletries** and (rough!) **toilet paper** (*papier hygénique*) are easy enough to obtain in all but the most remote parts of the country. Despite this, many hotels fail to supply it.

● **Towels** Some hotels do not provide towels and you will certainly need one if you are hostelling or camping.

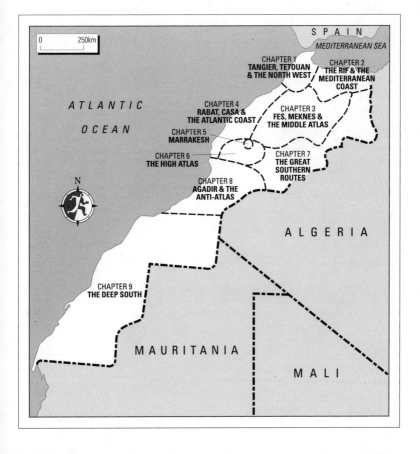

The map shows chapter divisions of Morocco:

- **CHAPTER 1** TANGIER, TETOUAN & THE NORTH WEST
- **CHAPTER 2** THE RIF & THE MEDITERRANEAN COAST
- **CHAPTER 3** FES, MEKNES & THE MIDDLE ATLAS
- **CHAPTER 4** RABAT, CASA & THE ATLANTIC COAST
- **CHAPTER 5** MARRAKESH
- **CHAPTER 6** THE HIGH ATLAS
- **CHAPTER 7** THE GREAT SOUTHERN ROUTES
- **CHAPTER 8** AGADIR & THE ANTI-ATLAS
- **CHAPTER 9** THE DEEP SOUTH

SPAIN

MEDITERRANEAN SEA

ATLANTIC OCEAN

ALGERIA

MAURITANIA

MALI

N

0   250km

CHAPTER ONE

TANGIER, TETOUAN AND THE NORTHWEST

The northwest can be an intense introduction to Morocco. Its two chief cities, Tangier and Tetouan, are the country's blackspots for hustlers and unofficial guides (police crackdowns notwithstanding) preying on first-time travellers. However, once clear of the port or bus stations, and having set your bags down in a hotel, it doesn't take long to get the measure of the cities – and to begin to enjoy the experience. **Tangier**, hybridized and slightly seedy from its long European contact, has a culture distinct from any other Moroccan city, and a setting and skyline the equal of any Mediterranean resort. Difficult it may be, but it is compelling, too, in its age-old role as meeting point of Europe and Africa. **Tetouan**, in the shadow of the wild Rif mountains, feels more Moroccan – its Medina a glorious labyrinth, dotted with squares, *souks* and buildings from its fifteenth-century founding by Muslim refugees from Spanish Andalucia.

Moving on from either city, the most popular destination is the mountain town of **Chaouen** – a small-scale and enjoyably laid-back place to come to terms with being in Morocco. It is most easily reached via Tetouan. Heading south from Tangier – which is the terminus for the railway lines to Fes, Rabat, Casablanca and Marrakesh – the best places to get acclimatized are the seaside resorts of Asilah and Larache. **Asilah** is a low-key, though growing tourist resort, and in August (most years) hosts an **International Festival**, northern Morocco's major cultural event of the year. **Larache** is less well known and perhaps more enjoyable, with its relaxed feel, fine beach and proximity to the ancient Carthaginian-Roman site of **Lixus**.

International zones – and language

Northern Morocco has an especially quirky **colonial history**, having been divided into three separate zones. Tetouan was the administrative capital of the **Spanish zone**, which encompassed Chaouen (and the Rif) and spread south through Asilah and Larache – itself a provincial centre. The **French zone** began at Souk El Arba du Rharb, the edge of rich agricultural plains sprawling south towards the French Protectorate's capital, Rabat. **Tangier**, meanwhile, experienced **"International Rule"** under a group of European legations.

One modern consequence of this past is that, although French is the official second **language** (after Arabic) throughout Morocco, most adults in the northwest are equally, or more, fluent in **Spanish** – a basic knowledge of which can prove extremely useful. Adding to and perpetuating the colonial legacy is the fact that Spanish TV and radio can be received (and attracts enthusiastic audiences) throughout much of northern Morocco.

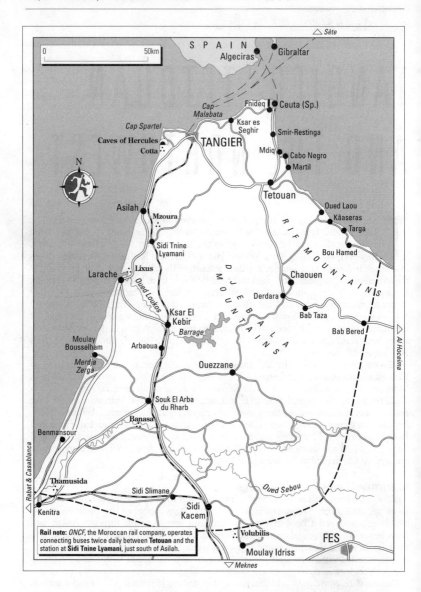

Rail note: ONCF, the Moroccan rail company, operates connecting buses twice daily between Tetouan and the station at Sidi Tnine Lyamani, just south of Asilah.

TANGIER AND THE COAST

Tangier has an international airport (at Boukhalef) and ferry connections with Algeciras, Gibraltar and the French port of Sète. Unless you are bringing a car over from Spain, it's a better point of arrival than Ceuta: both for the town's own attractions, and for the convenience in moving straight on into Morocco. Asilah is a mere forty minutes' ride on the train; Meknes, Fes, Rabat and Casablanca are all comfortably reached within the day, while if you are in a hurry to get south, there is a night train for Marrakesh.

The **coast** detailed in this section is the **Atlantic** stretch south towards Rabat. **Asilah**, on the train line, is the easiest destination; **Larache** can be reached by bus or *grand taxi* only, either from Tangier or (simpler) from Asilah. A more distinctively Moroccan resort is **Moulay Bousselham**, south of Larache and accessible by bus or *grand taxi* via Ksar El Kebir or Souk El Arba du Rharb.

Tangier (Tanja, Tanger)

For the first half of this century **TANGIER** was one of the stylish resorts of the Mediterranean – an "International City" with its own laws and administration, plus an eclectic community of exiles, expatriates and refugees. It was home, at various times, to Spanish and Central European refugees; to Moroccan nationalists; and – drawn by loose tax laws and free-port status – to over seventy banks and 4000 companies, many of them dealing in currency transactions forbidden in their own countries. Writers also were attracted to the city: the American novelist Paul Bowles has lived in Tangier since the war, William Burroughs spent most of the 1950s here, and most of the Beats – Jack Kerouac, Allen Ginsberg, Brion Gysin and the rest – passed through. Tangier was also the world's first and most famous gay resort, a role it maintains to a smaller degree.

When Moroccan independence was gained in 1956, however, Tangier's special status was removed. Almost overnight, the finance and banking businesses shifted their operations to Spain and Switzerland. The expatriate communities* dwindled, too, as the new national government imposed bureaucratic controls and instituted a "clean-up" of the city. Brothels – previously numbering almost a hundred – were banned, and in the early 1960s "The Great Scandal" erupted, sparked by a handful of pedophile convictions and escalating into a wholesale closure of the once outrageous gay bars.

These ghosts have left a slight air of decay about the city, still tangible in the older hotels and bars, despite a recent flurry of development and, especially, apartment building. There seems, too, a somewhat uncertain overall identity: a city that seems halfway to becoming a mainstream tourist resort – and an increasingly popular destination for holidaying Moroccans – yet which still retains hints of its dubious past amid the shambling 1930s architecture and style. It is, as already noted, a tricky place for first-time arrivals – hustling and mugging stories here should not be underestimated and the characters you run into at the port are as objectionable as any you'll find in Morocco – but once you get the hang of it, Tangier is lively and very likeable, highly individual and with an enduring eccentricity.

Orientation

After the initial confusion of an unfamiliar Arab city, Tangier is surprisingly easy to find your way around. As with all the larger Moroccan cities, it's made up of two parts: the **Medina**, the original Moroccan town, and the **Ville Nouvelle**, built by its several European colonizers. Inside the Medina, a classic web of alleyways and stepped passages, is the old fortified quarter of the **Kasbah**, with the former Sultanate's palace at its centre.

Together with the **beach** and the seafront **Avenue d'Espagne**, the easiest reference points are the city's three main squares – the Grand Socco, Petit Socco and Place de France.

*At the international zone's peak in the early 1950s, Tangier's foreign communities numbered 60,000 – nearly half the then-population. Today there are under 2000 (including 800 Spanish, 600 French, and 150 Britons and Americans) in a city population of 425,000.

POINTS OF ARRIVAL AND CITY TRANSPORT

BY FERRY

Disembarking by ferry at Tangier can be a slow process, with long queues for passport control and customs: be prepared. Most importantly, make sure that you have your **passport stamped** (and departure card collected) while *on board the ferry*; announcements to this effect are not always made in English, so make your way to the purser's office during the journey. If you miss out on this, you'll be left until last by the officials in Tangier. If you arrive on the **hydrofoil** things are a little easier, as they dock by their own individual passport office.

Once ashore, and through customs, ferry arrivals pass into the **ferry terminal building**. There's a **bureau de change** here and outside the building is a branch of the Banque Populaire; both sell dirhams at regular rates and accept most currencies, travellers' cheques and eurocheques. There is also a *Trans-Med* shipping office just outside the port gates, which changes currency and travellers' cheques, and sells ferry tickets for the return journey. (For credit card exchange or a cash dispenser you need a bank in the city proper – see p.87).

Also within the ferry terminal building is an **ONCF** railways office; it's worth queueing immediately here for train tickets if you're going straight on. Currently there is just one train a day (the 4.25pm to Asilah, Rabat and Casablanca; change at Sidi Slimane for Meknes and Fes) from the adjacent port train station, the Gare du Port. All other trains (see p.88) leave from the town station, the Gare de Ville, a five-minute walk along the waterfront.

Nearby the Gare du Port – and still inside the port enclosure – there are ranks for **grands and petits taxis** (see below for practicalities); they are best engaged here, before you get outside the enclosure to the hustle (and hustlers) around the port gates. Just outside the gates you also find **CTM buses**, to Tetouan, Fes and elsewhere; it's a lot easier to catch them here than at the main bus station, or *gare routière* (see p.88).

BY AIR

Tangier's **airport** is 15km outside the city. If you arrive on a package tour you'll be met by a hotel shuttle (try to get a transfer with your ticket, if you're on flight only). If you're on your own, either bargain with the **taxi** drivers, who *should* charge 60–70dh for up to six passengers (get a group together before leaving the terminal building, or they will charge each person 60–70dh), or walk the two kilometres to the main road, where you can pick up the #17 or #70 **buses** to the Grand Socco (see "Orientation", opposite).

There are two **banks** at the airport which are usually open to meet incoming flights; one – or sometimes both – of them will cash travellers' cheques or eurocheques. There is no cash dispenser.

CITY TAXIS AND BUSES

Grands taxis (large cream/beige Mercedes) are permitted to carry up to six passengers. The price for a ride should be fixed in advance – 10dh per person is standard for any trip within the city, including tip. Small blue/green **petits taxis** (which carry just three passengers) can be flagged down around the town. Most of these are metered – standard rate for a city trip is 5dh per person. On the streets you can **hail a taxi**, whether it has passengers or not; if it is going in your direction it will generally take you. If you join a taxi with passengers, you pay the full fare, as if it were empty. Both *grand* and *petit taxi* rates increase by fifty percent **after 8pm**.

Minibuses operated by *Bourghaz* run to a number of useful destinations – including the bus station and Cap Spartel; there is a stop just outside the port gates. Regular bus services (*Tingis* or *Raihini*) serve mainly the city suburbs.

For details on the bus and taxi terminals for journeys out of Tangier, see "Leaving Tangier", on pp.88–89.

STREET NAME CHANGES

Spanish colonial names are still in use alongside their Arabicized successors. In addition, both *Rue* and *Calle* are sometimes replaced by *Zankat*, and *Avenue* and *Boulevard* by *Charih*.

Local maps tend to use the new Arabic versions, though not all of the street signs have been changed. In the text and maps of this guide, we have used new names only when firmly established. Among the main street-name changes, note:

Main squares
Place de France – Place de Faro
Grand Socco – Place du 9 Avril 1947
Petit Socco – Place Souk Dakhil

Ville Nouvelle
Avenue Louis (sic) van Beethoven –
   Avenue Yacoub El Mansour
Rue Dante – Rue El Farabi
Rue Dickens – Rue Ibn Albanna
Rue Goya – Rue du Prince Moulay
   Abdallah
Rue de la Liberté – Rue El Houria
Rue Murillo – Rue Ahmed Chaouki

Rue de la Plage – Rue Salah Eddine
   El Ayoubi
Rue Rembrandt – Rue El Jaba
   El Quatania
Rue Sanlucar – Rue El Moutanabi
Rue Shakespeare – Rue Mohammed
   Tazi

Medina
Rue des Chrétiens – Rue des
   Almouahidines
Rue de la Marine – Rue Djemaa Kebir
Rue des Postes – Rue Mokhtar
   Ahardane

Place de France is a conventional, French-looking square at the heart of the Ville Nouvelle, flanked by elegant cafés and a **terrace-belvedere** looking out over the straits to Spain (Tarifa is usually visible). From here, **Boulevard Pasteur** (the main city street) leads off past an ONMT **tourist office**, a couple of blocks up, towards the main *PTT* (post office).

In the other direction from Place de France, **Rue de la Liberté** runs down to the **Grand Socco**, an amorphous open space in front of the Medina. The north side of the square opens onto the Medina's principal street, **Rue Es Siaghin**, which culminates in the **Petit Socco**, a tiny square of old cafés and cheap hotels.

Guides and hustlers

At time of writing, the police have cracked down on Tangier's unofficial **"guides"** – or hustlers – but if police activities slacken, be warned. Hustlers can be incredibly persistent around the port entrance. They will tell you some fairly amazing tales: the hotels

HOTEL KEY: TANGIER MAIN MAP

A   Pension Atou
B   Pension Talavera
C   Pension Miami
D   Pension Majestic
E   Hôtel Valencia
F   Pension Mendes
G   Hôtel Biarritz
H   Hôtel El Muniria
I   Hôtel Ibn Batouta
J   Hôtel Magellan
K   Hôtel Marco Polo
L   Hôtel El Djenina
M   Auberge de Jeunesse/Youth Hostel

N   Hôtel Bristol
O   Pension Omar Khayam
P   Hôtel Rif
Q   Hôtel Miramar
R   Hôtel El Minzah
S   Hôtel Lutetia
T   Hôtel de Paris
U   Rembrandt Hôtel
V   Tanjah Flandria Hôtel
W   Hôtel Chellah
X   Pension Hollande

Off map:
Hôtel Solazur

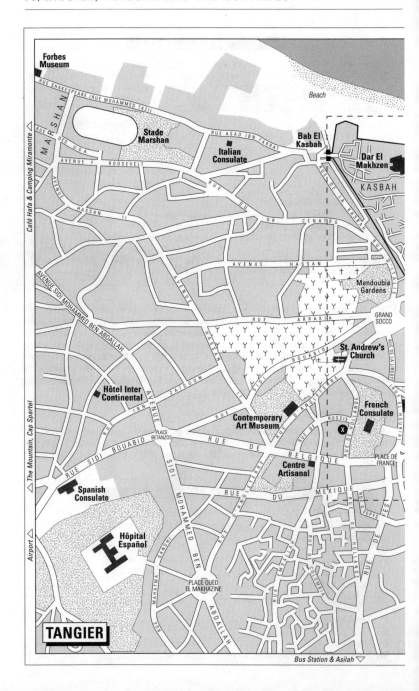

Forbes Museum

RUE SHAKESPEARE (RUE MOHAMMED TAZI)

Beach

MARSHAN

RUE DES U.S.A.

Stade Marshan

RUE ASAD IBN FARRAT

Bab El Kasbah

Dar El Makhzen

AVENUE F   ROOSEVELT

Italian Consulate

KASBAH

RUE DU

HASSAN II

Café Hafa & Camping Miramonte

DR.   CENAIRO

RUE DE LA KASBAH

RUE D'ITALIE

AVENUE   HASSAN I

AVENUE SIDI MOHAMMED BEN ABDALLAH

AVENUE HASSAN

Mendoubia Gardens

GRAND SOCCO

RUE   ARRAKIA

HASSAN II

SIDI BOUABID

St. Andrew's Church

RUE DE LA LIBERTÉ

Hôtel Inter Continental

IBN ZAIDOUN

AVENUE

Contemporary Art Museum

RUE D'ANGLETERRE

RUE DE   HOLLANDE

French Consulate

RUE EL HOURIA

The Mountain, Cap Spartel

PLACE BETANZOS

RUE   DE   RUSSIE

X

RUE DE   BELGIQUE

PLACE DE FRANCE

SIDI MOHAMMED BEN

Centre Artisanal

RUE DE   MEXIQUE

RUE DE FÈS

Airport

Spanish Consulate

RUE SIDI BOUABID

RUE   DU

RUE   D'ANGLETERRE

RUE DE PEPYS

Hôpital Español

RUE MAHATMA GANDHI

RUE   HASSANIA

RUE DE HOLLANDE

RUE DE COLUMBIA

PLACE OUED EL MAKHAZINE

MOHAMMED BEN ABDALLAH

TANGIER

Bus Station & Asilah ▽

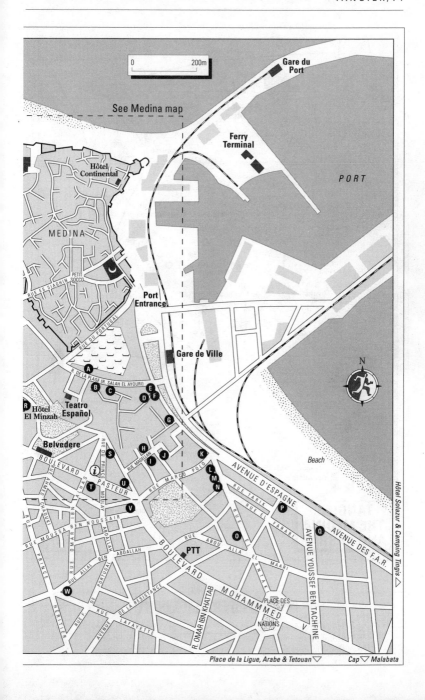

Gare du
Port

Ferry
Terminal

P O R T

See Medina map

Hôtel
Continental

MEDINA

PETIT
SOCCO

RUE ES SIAGHIN

RUE DU PORTUGAL

Port
Entrance

Gare de Ville

R DE LA PLAGE (R. SALAH EL AYOURI)

Ⓐ
Ⓑ Ⓒ Ⓔ
Ⓓ Ⓕ

Ⓡ Hôtel   Teatro
El Minzah Español

Ⓖ

Belvedere

Ⓗ
Ⓢ   Ⓘ Ⓙ   Ⓚ

BOULEVARD

ⓘ   Ⓛ
Ⓜ
Ⓣ
Ⓥ

Beach

N

RUE DU PRINCE MOULAY

PASTEUR

RUE MAGELLAN

RUE MARCO POLO

AVENUE D'ESPAGNE

RUE TARIK

RUE E. FARABI

Ⓟ

RUE MOUSSA BEN NOUSSAIR

RUE OMAR IBN ABDALLAH

Ⓞ

RUE ABOU ALLA EL MAARI

AVENUE DES F.A.R.
Ⓠ

AVENUE YOUSSEF BEN TACHFINE

RUE PRINCE

RUE ATLAL BEN ABDALLAH

AIMED CHAQUIR

RUE DE PORTUGAL

BOULEVARD   MOHAMMED   V

PTT

R. OMAR IBN KHATTAB

RUE DE LA RESISTANCE

RUE ANTAKI

PLACE DES
NATIONS

Ⓦ

RUE HERITIER

AVENUE LAFAYETTE

0   200m

Hôtel Solazur & Camping Tingis ▽

Place de la Ligue, Arabe & Tetouan▽   *Cap*▽ *Malabata*

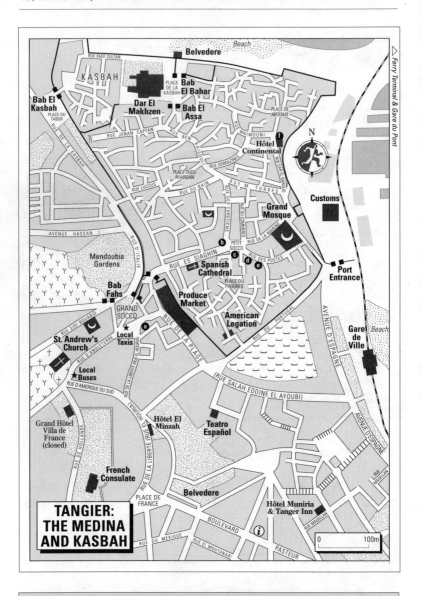

TANGIER: THE MEDINA AND KASBAH

TANGIER MEDINA

a Hôtel Grand Socco
b Hôtel Mauretania
c Pension Fuentes
d Pension Palace
e Hôtel Mamora
f Hôtel Continental

are full, the Medina is dangerous, the trains and buses are on strike. Don't take too much of this at face value, and don't feel in any way duty bound to employ anyone's services – you don't need a guide in Tangier.

Accommodation

Tangier has dozens of **hotels and pensions**, and finding a room is rarely much of a problem: if the first place you try is full, ask them to phone and reserve you a place elsewhere – most will be happy to do so. The city does, however, get crowded during July and August, when many Moroccan families holiday here, or spend a few days en route to and from Europe. Unclassified hotels hike up their prices at this time of year, and if you want an inexpensive room you'll often do best by going for one of the officially classified hotels.

Of the **hotels** listed below, a few of the three- and four-star places are detailed simply because they are regular package choices (which you may be booked into); the rest, however, are all to some extent recommended. As always, there is a choice between the **Medina** or **Ville Nouvelle**. If it's your first time in Tangier, you will probably prefer the easier, more familiar feel (and greater comforts) of the Ville Nouvelle places.

Seafront hotels

All the places below are along or just off the seafront **Avenue d'Espagne** and its continuation **Av. des F.A.R.** (Av. des Forces Armées Royales); the name change takes place, it seems, after the *Hôtel Rif*, though maps differ. Several hotels are on Rue Magellan, which is easy to miss: it zigzags up from the seafront alongside the *Hôtel Biarritz* towards Bd. Pasteur in the Ville Nouvelle. A number of others are on Rue Salah

---

HOTEL PRICE CODES AND STAR RATINGS

Hotels are no longer obliged to charge according to the official star-ratings (from 1* to 5* luxury), as had long been the custom. Nevertheless, **prices** continue to reflect the star-ratings acquired. The basis of our own **hotel price codes**, set out below and keyed throughout the guide, is the price currently quoted for the cheapest double room in high season (June–September) – and is thus more reliable than quoting notional prices according to star-rating.

Note that cheaper prices in the lower categories are generally for rooms with just a washbasin – you always pay extra for **en-suite** shower and WC – and that double rooms can generally be converted into **triples/family rooms**, with extra beds, for a modest extra charge. Note also that the prices quoted by all hotels are subject to various local and regional **taxes**, which can add 15 to 20 percent to the bill.

Our code	Classification	Single room price	Double room price
ⓤ	Unclassified	25–60dh	50–99dh
①	1*A/1*B	60–105dh	100–149dh
②	2*B/2*A	105–145dh	150–199dh
③	3*B/3*A	145–225dh	200–299dh
④	4*B/4*A	225–400dh	300–599dh
⑤	5*luxury	Upwards of 400dh	Upwards of 600dh

TELEPHONE CODES

All telephone numbers in the Tangier/Tetouan region are prefixed 09. When making a call within the region you omit this prefix. For more explanation of phone codes and making calls within (or to) Morocco, see pp.45–46.

Eddine El Ayoubi (aka Rue de la Plage), which runs uphill from the town train station to the Grand Socco and is lined with small pensions.

On the whole, the seafront places get pricier and fancier as you move around the bay away from the port. All those listed below, however, are within walkable distance of the port and train stations, though you may prefer to take a *petit taxi* for the further ones.

CHEAP

Pension Atou [A], 45 Rue Salah Eddine El Ayoubi (☎09/63.63.33). Halfway up the street, on the right, this is one of the friendliest places on this pension-packed street. It's basic, with shared bathrooms, but it's clean and there's a great rooftop terrace looking out onto the Jewish cemetery and the port. ①

Hôtel Biarritz [G], 102–104 Av. d'Espagne (☎09/93.24.73). Old hotel with fading charm, renovated of late, with all rooms en suite, and a decent restaurant below. ①

Hôtel El Muniria [H], 1 Rue Magellan (☎09/93.53.37). Old-established hotel, owned until recently by an Englishman and still in good shape, and good value; its late-night bar (the *Tanger-Inn*) can be amusing, too. Burroughs, Kerouac and Ginsberg all stayed here when they first came to Tangier, Burroughs writing *The Naked Lunch* in room 9. ①

Hôtel Ibn Batouta [I], 8 Rue Magellan (☎09/94.72.12). Another pleasant, well-run pension, just across the street from the *El Muniria*; some rooms en suite. ①

Hôtel Magellan [J], 16 Rue Magellan (☎09/93.87.26). Well kept, inexpensive pension, with fine views from the front rooms upstairs, and fitful hot showers. ①

Pension Majestic [D], 33 Rue Ibn Zohr (☎09/93.72.46). A popular, good-value pension, attracting a young clientele. Look out for its blue and white building just uphill from the prominent *Hôtel-Restaurant L'Marsa* (whose own accommodation is less recommendable). ①

Pension Mendes [F], 80 Av. d'Espagne (☎09/93.31.59). Another popular pension, again near the *Hôtel-Restaurant L'Marsa*; look for the 1920s Spanish tiles depicting Don Quijote by the door. Toilets and showers on corridor. Pavement café below. ①

Pension Miami [C] and **Pension Talavera [B]**, 126 and 124 Rue Salah Eddine El Ayoubi (☎09/93.29.00 and ☎09/93.14.17). These two adjoining pensions are beautifully tiled old Spanish townhouses, said to be a hundred years old; the *Miami* was built for a Jewish-Spanish family. Both have pleasant rooms and bathrooms on each corridor. ①

Pension Omar Khayam [O], 28 Rue El Antaki (☎09/94.33.93). A charming Andalucian, two-storey, white-and-pink building, some distance uphill from the *Hôtel Bristol*. Quiet and comfortable, with some rooms en suite. ①

Youth Hostel (Auberge de Jeunesse) [M], 8 Rue El Antaki (☎09/94.61.27). A newish hostel – clean, central (it's just by the Hôtel El Djenina), and well run. Open 8–10am, noon–3pm & 6–10.30pm (midnight in summer). ①

MODERATE

Hôtel Bristol [N], 14 Rue El Antaki (☎09/94.29.14). This well-managed hotel, 100m uphill from the beach, is a good bet, with en-suite baths, plus a bar and restaurant (you may be obliged to have half board in midsummer). ②

Hôtel El Djenina [L], 8 Rue El Antaki (☎09/94.22.44). A bit drab, and overpriced in summer, though well maintained, with hot baths in all rooms. ③

Hôtel Marco Polo [K], corner of Av. d'Espagne/Rue El Antaki (☎09/94.11.24). Comfortable German-run hotel, with a fair restaurant-bar. Try for a front room overlooking the beach. ②

Hôtel Miramar [Q], 168 Av. des F.A.R. (☎09/94.17.15). By far the best budget hotel on the seafront – old and a little shabby (it's very 1930s) but friendly, with a popular restaurant and bar, big rooms and hot showers en suite. ②

Hôtel Valencia [E], 72 Av. d'Espagne (☎09/93.07.70). A decent hotel in a useful situation – almost opposite the city train station – but a bit overpriced for what's on offer. ③

EXPENSIVE

Hôtel Rif [P], 152 Av. des F.A.R. (☎09/94.17.31). This long-established upmarket beach hotel is now looking a touch old-fashioned, and its restaurant can have off days. However, it's comfortable, if sometimes noisy, and prices are negotiable out of season or for long stays. ④

Hôtel Solazur [off map], Av. des F.A.R. – on the next block after Av. Yacoub El Mansour (☎09/94.01.64). This is arguably the best of the upmarket beach hotels and was requisitioned by the late Malcolm Forbes for his seventieth birthday bash (see p.81); his balloon still floats in the foyer. Apparently Forbes's guests complained of the lack of air conditioning, to which he retorted "What did they expect me to do – build them a hotel?". Well, quite. ⑤

Central Ville Nouvelle hotels

Most of these recommendations are within a few blocks of Place de France/Place de Faro and the central Boulevard Pasteur; coming up from the port, if you've got much luggage, a taxi could be a useful investment.

CHEAP

Pension Hollande [X], 139 Rue de Hollande (☎09/93.78.38). A big airy house, shaded by trees, behind the French Consulate; simple rooms but a nice place and good value. ①

Hôtel de Paris [T], 42 Bd. Pasteur (☎09/93.18.77). A pleasant, functional hotel right at the heart of things, opposite the tourist office. ①

MODERATE

Hôtel Chellah [W], 47–49 Rue Allal Ben Abdallah (☎09/94.33.88). Regular tour group hotel, with a small pool and garden, and its own club on the beach, El Cavabo. It is a bit isolated, however, being some way from both the beach and Bd. Pasteur. ④

Hôtel Lutetia [S], 3 Rue du Prince Moulay Abdallah (☎09/93.18.66). This has seen better days but it is excellent value for its two-star category and well located – a block below Bd. Pasteur. It has a range of rooms, with and without private bath, and a bar, too. ②

EXPENSIVE

Hôtel El Minzah [R], 85 Rue El Houria (aka Rue de la Liberté) (☎09/93.58.85). Built in 1931 by one Lord Bute, this remains Tangier's finest hotel, with a wonderful garden, a pool overlooking the sea and town, and an elegant (if pricey) bar. Past guests have included Cecil Beaton and Mick Jagger (not together). ⑤

Rembrandt Hôtel [U], angle of Bd. Pasteur/Bd. Mohammed V (☎09/93.78.70). Another large package tour hotel, though with more style than most (the decor is unregenerated 1940s), plus a pool, restaurant and good views of the port. ④

Tanjah Flandria Hôtel [V], 6 Bd. Mohammed V (☎09/93.32.79). Slightly superior modern package tour hotel, with a pool on the roof, disco and sauna. ⑤

Note: The old Grand Hôtel Villa de France on Rue de Hollande is, at present, closed. It was once among the country's most elegant hotels – Matisse stayed in, and painted the view from, room 35 – but it fell on hard times in the late 1980s and it is in the process of a "redevelopment" that looks like stripping away all its historic interest.

Medina hotels

With the exception of the *Continental* and the *Mamora,* these listings – the best of the thirty-five Medina hotels – are unclassified and fairly basic; they are safe enough, though, so long as you have the initial confidence for the area, and have distinct character. To reach the Medina from the port or train station, there's a choice of routes: either up Rue du Portugal to the Grand Socco, or up the steps behind the port entrance, round to the Grand Mosque and the junction of Rue des Postes/Rue Dar El Baroud. If you're unsure of yourself – and the Medina can be intimidating if this is your first visit to Morocco – it's best to take a *petit taxi.*

All map references following refer to the Medina map on p.72.

CHEAP

Pension Fuentes [C], 9 Petit Socco, at the heart of the Medina (☎09/93.46.69). A scruffy but friendly little place, above a lively café in the heart of the Medina. It was one of the first hotels in

Tangier, boasting Camille Saint-Saens among its nineteenth-century residents, though there's little residual glamour. ⑩

Hôtel Grand Socco [a], Grand Socco (☎09/93.19.46). Not the most salubrious rooms but an interesting location, poised on the edge of the Medina, and extremely easy to find; there are a number of large rooms that offer good value for three to five people. ⑩

Hôtel Mauretania [b], 2 Rue des Chrétiens – aka Rue des Almouahidines, just off the Petit Socco (☎09/93.46.77). Cold showers, but otherwise fairly well kept, and cheap. ⑩

Pension Palace [d], 2 Rue des Postes (☎09/93.61.28). A touch of past splendours – balconies and a central court with fountain – led Bertolucci to shoot here in his film of Paul Bowles's novel, *The Sheltering Sky*. Rooms are quite pleasant, including a few en suite. ⑩

MODERATE

Hôtel Continental [f], 36 Rue Dar El Baroud (☎09/93.10.24). This is by far the best choice in the Medina. Founded in 1865, it was once the most fashionable hotel in Tangier, and had Queen Victoria's son Alfred as its first official guest. It is well run (the staff, Abdessalam and Tifou, are institutions), and it still has style, with a grand piano and huge parrot cage in the hall and a beautiful terrace overlooking the port – and it was another of Bertolucci's locations for *The Sheltering Sky*. To reach the hotel, either take a taxi from the port entrance, or walk up to the Petit Socco and take Rue de la Marine to the left of Rue des Postes; follow this around past the Grand Mosque and a terrace, and you'll come to the hotel gates. As the hotel is offered by several package companies, bookings are strongly recommended; ask for rooms 108 or 208, which are a *fin-de-siècle* treat – or, if they're gone, for any first- or second-floor seafront room; "back" rooms are not so good. ③

Hôtel Mamora [e], 19 Rue des Postes (☎09/93.41.05). If the Continental is full, you might want to try this classified hotel, close by the Petit Socco. It is no great shakes but offers a bit more security and comfort than the cheapies above and stands right at the heart of the Medina. ②

Campsites

Tangier's campsites are sited well outside the city, and worth considering mainly if you are travelling in a campervan or with a caravan; for those with a tent, security is not great, and costs (especially if you have no transport) the equal of a budget hotel; another factor to beware is the uncertainty over water in summer. It might be better to consider going on to Asilah (see p.91), if you want to camp by the sea, and the campsites there are an easy walk from the train station. Anyway, in the Tangier area, choices are:

Camping Miramonte – aka **Camping Marshan** (☎09/93.71.33). The closest and most popular campsite, 3km from the centre, with reasonable facilities, a restaurant, and a swimming pool. The beach is 1km away, and the nearest stretch has a summer café; there's also a pleasant family restaurant and motel in the woods above, also called the *Miramonte*. The campsite itself is a bit tricky to find, due to lack of signs. Driving, leave the city on the road to the west of the Kasbah; on public transport, take bus #2, # 21, or preferably #1 from the local bus station near the Grand Socco.

Camping Tingis (☎09/94.01.91). This large complex is 6km east of the city, out towards Cap Malabata (see p.91), beside the Oued Moghoga lagoon. The site is well-equipped with bungalows, shops and swimming pool but it is plagued by mosquitoes; again it's a 1km walk from the beach – though this, with the nearby woods, is highly unsafe at night. To get there, take bus #11 from the Grand Socco. Open summer only.

Camping Ashakar (☎09/93.38.40). This new beach campsite, carved out from the old *Robinson Plage Camping*, is 16km from town, and 5km south of the Cap Spartel lighthouse, close to the Caves of Hercules (see p.90). It's a pleasant, well-wooded site with showers, café, restaurant and shop. An unnumbered bus (ask for Ashakar) runs from the local bus station by the Grand Socco but this is really a site for those with transport.

The beach and Ville Nouvelle

Tangier's interest and attraction lies in the city as a whole: its café life, beach, and the tumbling streets of the Medina. The handful of "monuments", with the notable exception of the Dar El Makhzen palace, are best viewed as adding direction to your wanderings, rather than as unmissable sights.

The town beach

It was the beach and mild climate which drew in Tangier's first expatriates, the Victorian British, who used to amuse themselves with afternoon rides along the sands and weekends of "pig-sticking" in the wooded hills behind. Today's pleasures come a little more packaged on the **town beach**, with camel rides, pedalos, windsurfing, and a string of club-like beach bars. It's no Acapulco, nor even an Agadir, but by day the sands are diverting and fun, with Moroccans entertaining themselves in acrobatics and football.

It is easier, safer and some say compulsory to change in a cabin, so when you arrive at the beach you might like to attach yourself to one of the **beach bars**, most of which offer showers and deck chairs, as well as food and drink. Some of these are institutions, like *Emma's BBC Bar* (still serving up English breakfasts), *The Sun Beach*, where Tennessee Williams wrote a first draft of *Cat on a Hot Tin Roof*, and *The Windmill*, where Joe Orton knocked about. One of the most pleasant is *Chez Miami*, with its gardens to laze around in, but the scenes change each year, so look around and take your pick. All are open in summer only.

By day, it more or less goes without saying, don't leave anything on the beach unattended. By night, limit your exploration to the beach bars (a few of which offer evening cabarets – if Arabic Country & Western appeals), as the beach itself becomes a dangerous venue for rough trade.

The Grand Socco and Place de France

The **Grand Socco** is the obvious place to start a ramble around the town. Its name, like so many in Tangier, is a French–Spanish hybrid, proclaiming its origins as the main market square. The markets have long gone, but the square remains a meeting place and its cafés are good points to sit around and absorb the city's life. The Grand Socco's official but little-used name, **Place du 9 avril 1947**, commemorates the visit of Sultan Mohammed V to the city on that date – an occasion when, for the first time and at some personal risk, he identified himself with the struggle for Moroccan independence.

A memorial to this event (in Arabic) is to be found amid the luxuriant **Mendoubia Gardens**, flanking the square. These enclose the former offices of the Mendoub – the Sultan's representative during the international years – which are nowadays used for registering weddings. The gardens, a welcome shade from the midday sun, are open daily except Sundays; besides the memorial and some old cannons, they include a spectacular banyan tree, said to be 800 years old.

The old **markets** of the Grand Socco were moved out in the 1970s, onto the Rue de Portugal (running down to the port) and to some cramped terraces beside the Rue d'Angleterre, southwest of the square. More interesting, however, is the little **Fondouk Market**, which is to be found by following **Rue de la Liberté** from the Grand Socco towards Place de France, then turning left down a series of steps, past the *El Minzah* hotel. The stalls here offer everything from pottery to spectacle repairs, from fruit and vegetables to junk.

Over in the **Place de France**, the cafés are the main attraction – and at their best in the late afternoon and early evening, when an interesting mix of local and expatriate regulars turn out to watch and be watched. The seats to choose are outside the *Café Paris*, a legendary rendezvous throughout the years of the International Zone. During World War II, this was notorious as a centre of deal making and intrigue between agents from Britain, America, Germany, Italy and Japan; later the emphasis shifted to Morocco's own politics: the first nationalist paper, *La Voix du Maroc*, surfaced at the café, and the nationalist leader Allal El Fassi, exiled in Tangier from the French-occupied zone, set up his Istiqlal party headquarters nearby.

Saint Andrew's church and the Modern Art museum

Just south of the Grand Socco, on Rue d'Angleterre, is the nineteenth-century Anglican church of **Saint Andrew**, one of the city's odder sights in its fusion of Moorish decoration and English country churchyard. The congregation has fallen to around twenty but the church is still used for a Sunday morning service (11am). Other days, the caretaker, Mustapha Cherqui, is generally around to show off the church, whose interior is notable for its rendition of the Lord's Prayer in Arabic script around the chancel arch.

In the graveyard, among the laments of early deaths from malaria, you come upon the tomb of **Walter Harris** (see "Contexts"), the most brilliant of the chroniclers of "Old Morocco" in the closing decades of the nineteenth century and the beginning of the twentieth. Other graves reveal epitaphs to **Caid Sir Harry Maclean**, the Scottish military adviser to Sultan Moulay Abd El Aziz at the turn of the century; to **Dean** of *Dean's Bar* ("Missed by all and sundry"), a bit of a legend himself from the 1940s and 50s; and to a number of allied aircrew who died over the straits in the last days of World War II. Inside the church another eccentric Briton, **Emily Keane**, is commemorated. A contemporary of Harris, she lived a very different life, marrying in 1873 the Shereef of Ouezzane – at the time one of the most holy towns of the country (see p.123).

A little further down the Rue d'Angleterre is a large white-walled villa, formerly the British Consulate and now the **Musée d'Art Contemporain de la Ville de Tanger** (daily except Tues 9am–noon & 3–6pm; 10dh). Devoted exclusively to contemporary Moroccan artists, it often has interesting exhibitions.

The American Legation and Spanish Theatre

If you follow Rue de la Plage out of the Grand Socco, then turn left down towards the port on the Rue du Portugal, you come to a small gate in the Medina wall on the left, opposite the Jewish Cemetery. Just through the gate is the **Old American Legation** (open Mon, Wed & Thurs 10am–1pm & 3–5pm; free; other times by appointment, ☎09/93.53.17), a former palace given to the US government by the Sultan Moulay Slimane, and preserved today as an American Historic Landmark. Morocco was the first overseas power to recognize an independent United States and this was the first American ambassadorial residence, established in 1777. A fascinating three-storey palace, bridging an alleyway (the Rue d'Amerique) below, it houses excellent historical exhibits on the city's history – including the correspondence between Sultan Moulay Ben Abdallah and George Washington – and has displays of paintings by, in the main, Moroccan-resident American artists.

Over to the southeast of the Grand Socco, off the Rue de la Plage, is another interesting relic of Tangier's international past, the **Gran Teatro Cervantes** – the old Spanish theatre. Located on a side street still labelled in Spanish as Calle Esperanza Orellana (the wife of its architect), it is an unmistakeable buiding, with its tiled, Art Deco front. It is due to be restored – it stands much as it must have done in its heyday with its glass dome, stage and balcony intact – and meanwhile remains closed to visitors, unless you're lucky enough to meet a caretaker or workman on the site.

The Medina

The Grand Socco offers the most straightforward **approach to the Medina**. The arch at the northwest corner of the square opens onto Rue d'Italie, which becomes Rue de la Kasbah, the northern entrance to the Kasbah quarter. To the right, there is an opening onto Rue Es Siaghin, off which are most of the *souks* (markets) and at the end of which is the Petit Socco, the Medina's principal landmark and little square. An alternative approach to the Medina is from the seafront: follow the steps up, walk round by the Grand Mosque, and Rue des Postes (aka Rue Mokhtar Ahardane) will lead you into the Petit Socco.

Rue Es Siaghin

Rue Es Siaghin – Silversmiths' Street – was Tangier's main thoroughfare into the 1930s, and remains an active one today, with a series of fruit, grain and cloth markets opening off to its sides. Halfway along from the Grand Socco (on the right), locked and decaying, is the old **Spanish Cathedral** and **Mission**; behind this building was formerly the **Mellah**, or Jewish quarter, centred around Rue des Synagogues. Moroccan Jews traditionally controlled the silver and jewellery trade – the "Siaghin" of the street name – but few remain in Tangier, having left at Moroccan independence in 1956 for Gibraltar, France and Israel. The street itself has long been taken over by tourist stalls.

The Petit Socco

The **Petit Socco** or Socco Chico (Little Market) seems too small ever to have served such a purpose. Old photographs, in fact, show it almost twice its present size: it was only at the turn of the century that the hotels and cafés were built. These, however, give the place its atmosphere: seedy and slightly conspiratorial, and the location for many of the Moroccan stories of Mohammed Mrabet (see "Contexts").

In the heyday of the "International City", with easily exploited Arab and Spanish sexuality a major attraction, it was in the alleys behind the Socco that the straight and boy brothels were concentrated. William Burroughs used to hang out around the square: "I get averages of ten very attractive propositions a day," he wrote to Alan Ginsberg, ". . . no stasis horrors here." The Socco cafés (the *Central* was the prime Beat location) lost much of their allure at independence, when the sale of alcohol was banned in the Medina, but they remain diverting places to sit around, people watch, talk and get some measure of the town.

Towards the Kasbah

It is beyond the Petit Socco that the Medina proper seems to start, "its topography", to quote Paul Bowles, "rich in prototypal dream scenes: covered streets like corridors with doors opening into rooms on either side, hidden terraces high above the sea, streets consisting only of steps, dark impasses, small squares built on sloping terrain so that they looked like ballet sets designed in false perspective, with alleys leading off in several directions; as well as the classical dream equipment of tunnels, ramparts, ruins, dungeons and cliffs".

Walking up from the Petit Socco, you can follow **Rue des Chrétiens** (aka Rue des Almouahidines) and its continuation **Rue Ben Raisuli** and emerge, with luck, around the lower gate to the Kasbah. Heading past the Socco towards the sea walls are two small streets straddled by the Grand Mosque. If you want to get out and down to the beach, follow **Rue des Postes** and you'll hit the flight of steps (known as the "American Steps") down to the port. If you feel like wandering, take the other one, **Rue de la Marine**, which curls into **Rue Dar El Baroud** and the entrance to the old *Hôtel Continental* – another fine place to sit and drink tea. From here it's relatively simple to find your way across to the square below the Kasbah Gate.

The **Grand Mosque** itself is screened from public view – and, as throughout Morocco, entrance is strictly forbidden to non-Muslims. Enlarged in the early nineteenth century, the mosque was originally built on the site of a church by the Sultan Moulay Ismail in celebration of the return of Tangier to Moroccan control in 1685. Prior to this, the city had seen some two centuries of European rule: it was first conquered by the Portuguese in the aftermath of the Moors' expulsion from Andalucia and the Algarve, and in 1663 it passed to the British as part of the dowry of Catherine of Braganza, bride to Charles II.

It was the British – in just 22 years of occupation – who destroyed the city's medieval fortifications, including a great upper castle which covered the entire site of the present-day Kasbah. Under virtually constant siege, they found it an expensive and unrewarding possession: "an excrescence of the earth", according to Samuel Pepys, who oversaw the garrison's withdrawal, shocked at the women of the town ("generally whores") and at the governor ("with his whores at the little bathing house which he has furnished with jade a-purpose for that use"). Dining alone with the chaplain, Pepys had "a great deal of discourse upon the viciousness of this place and its being time for God Almighty to destroy it".

The Kasbah and beyond

The **Kasbah**, walled off from the Medina on the highest rise of the coast, has been the palace and administrative quarter since Roman times. It is a strange, somewhat sparse area of walled compounds, occasional colonnades, and a number of luxurious villas built in the 1920s, when this became one of the Mediterranean's most chic residential sites. Richard Hughes, author of *A High Wind in Jamaica* (and of a book of Moroccan tales), was the first European to take a house here – his address fabulously titled "Numéro Zero, La Kasbah, Tangier". Among those who followed was the eccentric Woolworth's heiress, Barbara Hutton, who reputedly outbid General Franco for her palace. Her parties were legendary – including a ball where thirty Reguibat racing camels and their drivers were brought 1000 miles from the Sahara to form a guard of honour.

Local guides point with some pride to these locations, but the main point of interest here is the former **Sultanate Palace**, or **Dar El Makhzen**, now converted to an excellent **museum of crafts and antiquities** (open daily except Sun, 9am–3.30pm in summer; 9am–noon & 3–6pm in winter; 10dh). It stands near the main gateway to the Medina, the **Bab El Assa**, to the rear of a formal court, or *mechouar*, where the town's pashas held public audience and gave judgement well into the present century. The entrance to the palace, a modest-looking porch, is in the left-hand corner of the court as you enter from the Medina – scores of children will probably direct you.

Just before the entrance to the palace, you pass (on your left) the ramshackle club-house of the *Orquesta Andalusi de Tanger*, a fine group of musicians who play Andalous music with a lot of swing. If they're around practising, they'll probably invite you in to watch them play.

The Dar El Makhzen and Café Detroit

The **Dar El Makhzen** – built, like the Grand Mosque, by Moulay Ismail – last saw royal use in 1912, with the residence of the Sultan Moulay Hafid, who was exiled to Tangier after his forced abdication by the French. The extraordinary negotiations which then took place are chronicled in Walter Harris's *Morocco That Was*. According to Harris, the ex-Sultan found the building "uncomfortable, out-of-date, and out-of-repair . . . and by no means a satisfactory place of residence, for it was not easy to install 168 people within its crumbling walls with any comfort or pleasure". Most of this extended entourage seem to have been members of the royal harem and well able to defend their limited privileges. Moulay Hafid himself ended up with "only a couple of very shabby rooms over the entrance", where he apologetically received visitors and played bridge with a small circle of Americans and Europeans.

The ramparts at Asilah

Larache: Spanish Mauresque buildings

Tangier beach and port

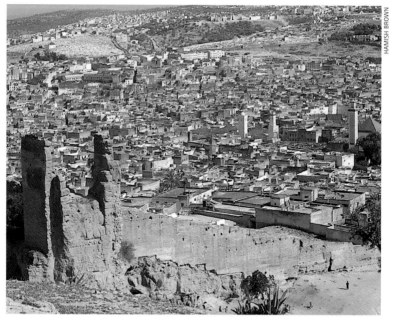

A view of Fes from the Merenid tombs

Fes tanneries

Meknes

> ## GARDENS ON THE MOUNTAIN
>
> The two most prestigious addresses in Tangier are **La Marshan**, the area west of the Forbes Museum, and **La Montagne**, the 'Mountain' behind the Spanish Consulate, on the inland route to Cap Spartel (see p.90). The Mountain, less imposing than its name suggests, was a rebel base against the British and Portuguese occupations of Tangier, but is now thoroughly tamed. Its cork and pine woods shield two vast royal palaces: one, built by the Victorian British consul Sir John Hay, which was (until her recent death), the residence of King Hassan's mother; the other, heavily guarded, among the numerous retreats of the Saudi royal family. It is also peppered with villas, many of which have beautiful gardens with stunning views of the bay, and several of which are owned by expats who are prepared to show serious garden lovers around. One such is Anne Lambton, Villa Palma, La Vielle Montagne (☎09/93.13.93), who asks only for a donation to SPANA, the animal welfare charity. Like many who live on the Mountain, Anne is an artist and occasionally exhibits at the Tanjah Flandria Art Gallery (see p.86).
>
> To reach La Montagne you'll need to drive or take a taxi. From Place de France take Rue Belgique to its end, where it becomes the Rue de la Montagne and begins winding its way up. If you want to make a day-trip of it, you can continue, over the mountain, towards the Caves of Hercules (see "Around Tangier", p.89).

re Forbes's unrivalled collections of toy soldiers – a series of battle tableaux includ-
the 1578 *Battle of the Three Kings* at Ksar El Kebir (in which virtually the entire
tuguese nobility was killed or imprisoned) and the 1975 *Marche Verte* (when 350,000
rmed Moroccans, led by King Hassan, "reclaimed" the former Spanish Sahara). At
e of writing, the collections have been put up for sale by the Forbes estate, so the
re of the museum – which also has a fascinating display of wartime propaganda
ers, along with numerous photos of Forbes's beloved motorbikes and hot-air bal-
s – is uncertain. If it remains open, you should be able to visit the gorgeous **palace**
ens, and possibly part of Forbes's private wing which includes an extraordinary
te gym and "Throne Room".

e Mohammed Tazi (Rue Shakespeare) runs on west from the museum, past sev-
further palaces (one of them housing the Italian Consulate), before reaching,
d 1km from the Forbes Museum, the cliff-top **Café Hafa**, overlooking the straits,
ts tables shaded by shrubs and trees. Serving up coffee, mint tea, sandwiches and
this is just the place to spend the late afternoon.

ou were to continue past the Café Hafa for a further 1km, you would reach the
ampsite, Camping Miramonte, and a track down to the **Jews' Beach** – so called
ts role as the landing stage for Spanish Jews fleeing the Inquisition. There is a
t little **beach café** open here in summer.

g, drinking and nightlife

r is not really a night-time city, and if you're looking for international resort-style
or the Tangier of sin-city legend, you'll be disappointed. There are nevertheless
d generally inexpensive **restaurants**, a fair scattering of **bars** and **discos**, and
ities for films and the occasional concert.

rants

most Moroccan cities, the cheapest places to eat are in the **Medina**, though
alcoholic drinks are not served in this quarter. For fancier meals – and drinks
eed to try the **Ville Nouvelle** or the **seafront**; for late-night snacks, several of

Bou Inania medersa, Fes

Barbary apes near Azrou

Roman mosaic at Volubilis

Cascades d'Ouzoud

Royal palace gate, Fes

Mohammed V Mausoleum, Rabat

View of Rabat from Salé

However out of date and uncomfortable the palace may have been, it is by no
a poor example of Moroccan craftsmanship and architecture. The design is cer
two interior courtyards, each with rich arabesques, painted wooden ceilings a
ble fountains. Some of the flanking columns are of Roman origin, particularly
ed to the small display of **mosaics and finds from Volubilis** (see Chapte
The main part of the museum, however, is devoted to **Moroccan arts**, laid o
ing to region and including an exceptional collection of ceramics from Mekne

At the entrance to the main part of the palace is the **Bit El Mal**, the old tre
adjoining is a small private **mosque**, near to which is the entrance to the
shrub-lined palace **gardens**, shaded by jacaranda trees. If you leave this w
come out by the stairway to the **Café Détroit**, set up in the early 1960s by
Brion Gysin. Gysin created the place partly as a venue for the Master M
Jajouka, drummers and pipe-players from a village in the foothills of
achieved cult fame through an LP recorded by his friend, Rolling Stone Bri
group resurfaced on the Stones' 1990 *Steel Wheels* album and these days
at festivals in the US and Europe. The café itself is now a rather shabb
though worth the price of a mint tea for the views. Its main entrance i
Sultan, the street running alongside the outer walls of the Kasbah.

The Forbes Museum, Café Hafa and Jews' Beach

Leaving the Medina by the Kasbah gate, a ten- to fifteen-minute walk
the quarter known as *la marshan*, an exclusive residential quarter with
villas, consulates and royal properties. The finest of the residences
Mendoub on Rue Mohammed Tazi (aka Rue Shakespeare), Tange
the millionaire publisher Malcolm Forbes (see below), until his death
sequently opened as the **Forbes Museum**. The main displays he

---

MALCOLM FORBES: TANGIER'S LAST TYCO

The American publishing tycoon, **Malcolm Forbes** bought the **Pal**
(see above) in 1970. His reason, ostensibly at least, was the acquis
launching and publishing an Arab-language version of *Forbes Maga*
aires' journal". For the next two decades, until his death in 1990, he
to the city, and it was at the Tangier palace that he decided to host
agance, his **seventieth birthday party**, in 1989.

This was the grandest social occasion Tangier had seen since the
heiress Barbara Hutton (see opposite), whose scale and spectacle
intended to emulate and exceed. Spending an estimated $2.5m, he
Elizabeth Taylor as co-host and chartered a 747, a DC–8 and Conco
world's rich and famous from New York and London. The party e
equally imperial scale, including 600 drummers, acrobats and dan
cavalry charge which ends with the firing of muskets into the air
men.

In the media, Malcolm's party was a mixed public relations exe
sip press feeling qualms about such a display of American aff
Morocco, and, despite Liz Taylor's presence at Forbes's side, us
to hint at the tycoon's sexual preferences (a story that broke
death). However, Forbes most likely considered the party a
included not just the celebrity rich – Gianni Agnelli, Robert M
Henry Kissinger – but half a dozen US state governors and th
idents of scores of multinational corporations likely to adverti
course, it was tax deductible.

the cafés around the Grand Socco stay open all night. All of our **"out of town"** recommendations will require use of a car.

Restaurants below are rated as: **cheap** (£2–5/$3–8 a head); **moderate** (£5–10/$8–16); and **expensive** (over £10/$16).

MEDINA

Restaurant Ahlen, 8 Rue des Postes (aka Rue Mokhtar Ahardane). Simple but well-cooked food – roast chicken, grilled beef, *harira* soup – and a warm welcome. Cheap.

Restaurant Andaluz, 7 Rue de Commerce. The best of the cafés on this street – the first alley to the left off Rue de la Marine (the street running from the Petit Socco to the Grand Mosque). With a trio of tables, it is about as simple as it's possible to be – and excellent, serving impeccably fried swordfish and grilled *brochettes*. Cheap.

Chez Hammadi, 2 Rue d'Italie. This is actually just outside the west wall of the Medina: a rather kitsch salon, where traditional Moroccan dishes are served to entertainment from a worthwhile band of Andalucian musicians. Moderate.

Grèce Restaurant, 21 Rue de Commerce. This is a rival and neighbour to the *Andaluz* – and to be honest there's little to choose between them. Moroccan dishes – not Greek as the name might suggest. Cheap.

Restaurant Ibn Batouta, Rue es Siaghin. Small, unpretentious restaurant on the main street of the Medina, not far from the Petit Socco. Cheap.

Restaurant Marhaba, 67 Palais Ahannar, off Rue de la Kasbah (inside the Kasbah Gate, take the first small alley to the left). A splendid old palace, stacked with antiques, and with good music and food. Moderate.

Ray Charley, Place Petit Socco. A good little café serving big portions of egg, tomato and chips. (Very) cheap.

Sandwich Salam, 1 Place Petit Socco (at the bottom end of the square). Upstairs café snackbar that's clean and friendly. Cheap.

VILLE NOUVELLE

Restaurant Africa, 83 Rue Salah Eddine El Ayoubi (aka Rue de la Plage). Best of the many restaurants on this street, which leads down from the Grand Socco. It's at the bottom of the hill, opposite *Hôtel Valencia*. It was a Spanish town house and a tiled Goya of the Duchess of Alba still looks down on proceedings. Regular Moroccan dishes, well prepared, and there's beer and wine. Moderate.

Restaurant Agadir, 21 Rue Prince Heritier, off Place de France. This small and friendly restaurant, run by a Tafraouti, with accomplished French and Moroccan cooking, is a personal favourite. Moderate.

Casa d'Italia, in the Palais Moulay Hafid – follow Rue d'Italie north of the grand Socco and it's on the left. Owned by the Italian state, this is a bit of a treat – the best Italian food you'll find in Morocco, let alone Tangier. Expensive and reservations advisable.

Las Conchas, Rue Ahmed Chaouki. Good French menu, though the chef who made its name has defected to the *Osso Buco* (see below). Moderate.

Restaurant Le Coeur de Tanger, 1 Rue Annoual, off Place de France (it's above the *Café Paris*, though the entrance is on a side street). Moroccan dishes served in some style. Moderate to expensive.

El Dorado, 21 Rue Allal Ben Abdallah, by the *Hôtel Chellah*. Dependable Jewish-Moroccan/Spanish cooking; try the fish dishes. Moderate.

Guitta's, 110 Sidi Bouabid, near the modern Hassan II Mosque on Place de Koweit (closed Mon). This is a little hard to find, and its dismal exterior offers little promise. However, this is a relic of old Tangier and a favourite of the expats, redolent of the 1950s International Zone. An Italian family serves up simple European dishes – and Sunday roasts. Moderate.

El Korsan, in the *Hôtel El Minzah*, 85 Rue de la Liberté (☎09/93.58.85). The hotel's Moroccan restaurant has a reputation as one of the country's best, serving authentic and traditional specialities to the accompaniment of a group of musicians. However, it has the occasional lapse and if you want classic Moroccan cooking you may feel your money is better spent at *Raihani's* (see overleaf). Expensive.

Restaurant Number One, 1 Bd. Mohammed V, across the side street from the *Hôtel Rembrandt*. A restaurant and cocktail bar which attracts a business crowd at lunchtime and tends to be fairly quiet in the evenings. French-Moroccan menu. Good cooking. Expensive.

Restaurant Osso Buco, on the ground floor of the *Maroc Hôtel*, 1 Rue du Prince Moulay Abdallah. Excellent Italian dishes from an extensive menu, presided over by an Englishwoman. Moderate.

Restaurant Pagode, just off Rue Prince Héritier, facing the *Carousel Bar*. The best Chinese food in Tangier, though the service is pretty joyless. Expensive.

Restaurant Raihani, 10 Rue Ahmed Chaouki – a side street opposite the terrace-belvedere on Bd. Pasteur (☎09/93.48.66). This is an excellent restaurant, serving traditional Moroccan food – it's worth at least one meal here for the superb *couscous* and *pastilla* (pigeon pie) – as well as a decent French-based menu. Moderate.

Restaurant Romero, 12 Rue du Prince Moulay Abdallah – off Bd. Pasteur (☎09/93.22.77). Spanish fish and seafood. Not as good as it was, following a change of ownership, but it's an attractive place and still worth a try. Moderate.

Restaurant San Remo, 15 Rue Ahmed Chaouki – see *Raihani's* above. Credible, good-value Italian cooking, and with a cheaper pizzeria across the road. Moderate.

Rubis Grill, 3 Rue Ibn Rochd, off Av. Prince Moulay Abdallah. Long established, serving Spanish and other European dishes; the candle-lit hacienda decor is a bit over the top, but the food and service is exemplary.

SEAFRONT

Restaurant Bab Al Maghreb, 30 Av. d'Espagne, facing the town train station. The best restaurant along this rather elegant footage which featured at the beginning and end of Bertolucci's *The Sheltering Sky*. Moderate.

Hôtel Biarritz, 102–104 Av. d'Espagne. One of the nicer hotel restaurants, with old-style service and a limited but reliable menu. Moderate.

Emma's BBC Bar, on the beach facing the *Hôtel Miramar*. The only one of the beach-cafés where food is a significant attraction. Open summer only – and until late. Moderate.

L'Marsa, Av. d'Espagne. Superb pizzas and spaghetti, with home-made ice cream to follow, served (slowly!) on a roof terrace, open-air patio or inside. Moderate.

Hôtel Marco Polo, corner of Av. d'Espagne/Rue El Antaki. Restaurant is on the first floor and top floors, with views of the bay. Limited menu, but generous helpings. Cheerful and swift service. Moderate.

Restaurant Mendes, 80 Av. d'Espagne. Pavement restaurant under awnings which specializes in grills. Friendly and value for money. Moderate.

Hôtel Miramar, 168 Av. d'Espagne. There are good value set meals in this popular and often very crowded hotel restaurant. Moderate.

Restaurant-Bar La Paix, 66 Av. d'Espagne, at the junction with Rue Salah Eddine El Ayoubi. More of a bar than a restaurant, but if that's what you're after you can eat on the first floor and watch the action. Cheap.

OUT OF TOWN

Chez Abdou, 17km out of town, on the coastroad leading south towards Asilah, in the so-called Fôret Diplomatique. Recommended for seafood. Expensive.

Club Le Mirage, near the Caves of Hercules (see p.89) in the area known as Ashakar, 5km south of the Cap Spartel lighthouse. The old, friendly hotel here, with its camel rides and resident apes, has been replaced by an international-style restaurant. But the food is still pretty good and the views fabulous. Moderate to Expensive.

Le Riad Restaurant, 7km along the Malabata road, amid the trees to the right of the road. A pleasant lunchtime stop. Moderate.

Cafés

Like all Moroccan towns, Tangier has many cafés, each with its particular clientele and daily rhythm, some good for breakfast, others popular late-morning or evening. Following are a few long-standing favourites.

Café Atlas, by the *Hôtel Rembrandt*. Open until midnight and often beyond, this is a good fallback for late-night snacks.

Pâtisserie Florence, corner of Rue Lafayette and Rue du Portugal, near *Hôtel Chellah*. Less of a café than a shop – serving fine European and Moroccan pastries and cakes.

Café Hafa, Marshan – past the stadium and near the Forbes Museum. This cliff-top café is a perfect late afternoon local to gaze across the straits and write your postcards. Coffee, mint tea, sandwiches and cakes to sustain you.

L'Marsa, 92 Av. d'Espagne. Recommended opposite for its pizzas, this serves equally delicious croissants, *pains chocolats* and cakes for breakfast or tea.

Café Metropole, 27 Bd. Pasteur – next to the synagogue. This serves the best *café-au-lait* in town and pastries can be bought across the road at *Patisserie Le Petit Prince* and consumed at your table.

Café Paris, Place de France. Tangier's most famous café, from its conspiratorial past, is a little dull these days, though still an institution for expats.

Pâtisserie Rahmouni, 35 Rue du Prince Moulay Abdallah. The rival to *Florence* for the best pastries and cakes in town.

Bars

Tangier **bars** are much depleted from past glories. The legendary *Parade* died with its owner in 1987, and most of those that do survive have fallen into a not very interesting seediness. The better options remaining are to be found in or alongside the older hotels, supplemented in summer by the beach bars, which stay open till 1am or so (though take care in this area after dark). Possibilities include:

Caid's Bar in the *Hôtel Minzah*, 85 Rue de la Liberté. Long the chi-chi place to meet – ritzy decor and very pricey drinks. Over the bar is a grand painting of Caid Harry Aubrey Maclean, former Commander in Chief of the Sultan's army (see p.78).

Carousel Bar, opposite the Chinese Restaurant, *Le Pagode*, off Rue Prince Heritier. Comfortable British-run wine bar.

Hôtel Chellah, Rue Allal Ben Abdallah. Lively, with music some evenings, and a sporadic happy hour from 6–7pm.

Dean's Bar, Rue d'Amerique du Sud. The closest bar to the Medina – a tiny shop-room that was once the haunt of people like Tennessee Williams, Francis Bacon and Ian Fleming. It is now frequented more or less exclusively by Moroccans and tourists are not really welcomed.

Chez Miami – aka Miami Beach, on the beach – nearest Rue Salah Eddine Al Ayoubi turning. The liveliest of the beach bars and one of the most easily accessible, too.

Hôtel Marco Polo, Av. d'Espagne. The ground floor is popular with tourists, especially hard-drinking Scandinavians and Germans getting through its range of European beers.

Negresco – aka English Bar, 14 Rue du Mexique. A small, somewhat down-at-heel bar serving draught beer and tapas, alongside the *Restaurant Negresco*.

Le Pub, 4 Rue Sorolla – behind the *Hôtel Tanjah Flandria*, off Bd. Mohammed V. British-run pub, with hunting scenes on the walls and bar food. Open 9pm–1am.

Tanger Inn, 16 Rue Magellan – below the *Hôtel Muniria*. Deadpan imitation of a Brighton pub, circa 1955, with the (British) Queen's portrait on the wall. One of Tangier's last surviving International Zone relics. Open 9pm–2am.

Discos and clubs

The principal area for **discos** is a grid of streets off Place de France, in particular Rue Sanlucar (aka Zankat Moutanabi) and Rue Méxique, and Rue du Prince Moulay Abdallah (off Bd. Pasteur). Drinks are two or three times regular bar prices and take care if leaving late at night as the streets are none too safe hereabouts; the best idea is to tip the doorman 5dh to call you up a taxi.

Borsalino, 30 Rue du Prince Moulay Abdalah. A small and usually quite lively disco, with a mixed crowd, screened by the doorman.

Morocco Palace, Rue du Prince Moulay Abdallah. A clear winner among Tangier's nightspots, this strange, sometimes slightly manic, place puts on traditional Moroccan music and dance (plus a couple of Egyptian belly-dancing sets) each night from around 9pm until 4am. Customers are predominantly Moroccan and expect – and get – a good show.

Radio Club, Rue du Prince Moulay Abdallah. Attractively sleazy club which sometimes puts on Moroccan bands.

Regine Club, Rue El Mansour Dahbi (opposite the Roxy Cinema). Mainstream disco, larger and a little cheaper than most. Open from 10pm.

Scott's, Rue El Moutanabi (aka Rue Sanlucar). Traditionally (though not exclusively) a gay disco, this is worth a look if only for its very particular choice of paintings – Berber boys in Highland military uniform. It's usually very quiet until after midnight.

Concerts, art and films

Music concerts – traditional and popular – are sporadic events in Tangier. The old Spanish bullring, out near the bus station in the Ville Nouvelle, has had a major refurbishment as an open-air concert hall, so it might be worth asking about events there. Cultural events are also hosted by the **Old American Legation** (see p.78) and the **Institut Français de Tangier**.

You can pick up a programme for Institut Français events from the Galerie Delacroix, 86 Rue de la Liberté, where there is usually an interesting exhibition by contemporary artists. Two other **galleries** are also worth a look for work by local artists: the Tanjah Flandria Art Gallery, Rue Ibn Rochd, and the Volubilis Art Gallery, 6 Sidi Boukouja (in the Kasbah).

There are a dozen or so **cinemas** scattered about the Ville Nouvelle, in the grid around Boulevard Pasteur. Films are frequently shown in their original language, with Arabic subtitles, though some are dubbed into French. The Cinéma Rif on the Grand Socco shows an exclusive and entertaining diet of Indian and Kung Fu films.

More upmarket are the Cinéma Flandria, Rue Ibn Rochd, and the two-screen cinema in the *Istiraha* tourist complex, opposite the old *Grand Hôtel Villa de France* on Rue de Hollande.

Shops and stalls

Many of the Tangier **market stalls and stores** are eminently avoidable, geared to selling tourist goods that wouldn't pass muster elsewhere. But a few are worthwhile, unique, or both; a half-hour preliminary browse at the more "fixed price" outlets on Boulevard Pasteur is useful for establishing roughly what you should pay for things.

Crafts and antiques

Ensemble Artisanal, Rue Belgique (left-hand side, going up from Place de France). Modern Moroccan crafts are displayed in this small government-run store, as in other major cities. They are rarely the best or the cheapest available but prices are (more or less) fixed, so this can be a useful first call to get an idea of quality and costs before bargaining elsewhere. Trouble is, it keeps very unpredictable hours.

Perfumerie Madini, 14 Rue Sebou, in the Medina; from the Petit Socco take the alley between the *Tingis* and *Centrale* cafés, which leads into Rue Sebou, and look for the shop on your left. Madini makes inspired copies of brand-name perfumes from natural oils, which he sells at a fraction of the "real" price, as well as musk and traditional fragrances. Given a couple of days and a sample, he will reproduce any scent you like. Closed 1–4pm and Friday.

Bazaar Tindouf, 64 Rue de la Liberté, opposite the *Hôtel El Minzah*. One of the better quality junkantique shops, with a good array of cushion-carpets and old postcards. Bargaining is difficult but essential.

Rue Touahin – first right off Rue Saighin, entering the Medina from the Grand Socco. This line of jewellery stalls may turn up something appealing, though don't take silver, gold or most stones at face value: judge on aesthetics.

Volubilis Boutique, 15 Place Petit Socco. A more than usually interesting mix of traditional Moroccan and Western fashion.

Fruit and vegetables

There are fruit and vegetable stalls in a couple of central lcoations. One is at the bottom of the **steps beyond the Hôtel El Minzah**. Another is the **Fes Market**, between Rue de Fes and Rue de Hollande in the Ville Nouvelle, where you can also buy groceries.

Listings

Airlines *GB Airways,* 83 Rue Houria aka Rue de Liberté (☎09/93.52.11 or 93.58.77) have flights to Casablanca, Marrakesh, Gibraltar and London, and handle British Airways business (they are a *BA* subsidiary). For domestic flights (and some international destinations) contact *Royal Air Maroc* at 1 Place de France (☎09/93.47.22). For flights to Spain (cheapest departures are from the Spanish enclave of Melilla – over to the east, see Chapter Two) try *Iberia* at 35 Bd. Pasteur (☎09/93.61.77). Three other airline offices are to be found at 7 Rue du Mexique: *Air France* (☎09/93.64.77), *KLM* (☎09/93.89.26) and *Lufthansa* (☎09/93.13.27). Tangier's airport is called *Boukhalef* (information: ☎09/93.51.29)

American Express Represented by *Voyages Schwartz,* 52 Bd. Pasteur (☎09/93.34.59). Open Mon–Fri 9am–12.30pm and 3–7pm, Sat 9am–12.30pm.

Animal welfare The local SPANA (Society for the Protection of Animals Abroad) representative is Mr Abdelkadar Haskouri, 35 Rue Sidi Bouabid, look for the small blue door (☎09/93.88.37).

Banks Most are grouped along Bd. Pasteur/Bd. Mohammed V. The *BMCE bureau de change* on Bd. Pasteur is the most efficient, changing cash and travellers' cheques, and handling cash advances on Visa and Mastercard; daily 9am–12.30pm and 3–7pm and there is an ATM cash dispenser outside. The *SGMB* at 58 Bd. Mohammed V (opposite the main post office) takes some bank cheques backed by credit cards. *Crédit du Maroc,* Bd. Pasteur, also handles Visa transactions.

Beer and wine is sold by supermarkets in the Ville Nouvelle.

Books The long-established *Librairie des Colonnes* at 54 Bd. Pasteur (Mon–Fri 9.30am–1pm & 2–7pm; Sat 9.30am–noon) has a fair selection of English-language books, including some of Paul Bowles's Moroccan translations.

Car parking The *Hôtel Tanjah Flandria* (labelled on the main plan) has an underground garage open to non-residents (10dh for 24hr).

Car rental Most of the big companies have offices along Bd. Pasteur/Bd. Mohammed V. The include: *Avis,* 54 Bd. Pasteur (☎09/93.30.31); *Europcar/InterRent,* 87 Bd. Mohammed V (☎09/94.19.38); *Hertz,* 36 Bd. Mohammed V (☎09/93.33.22); and *Tourist Cars,* 84 Bd. Mohammed V (☎09/93.54.93). Also centrally located are *Budget,* 7 Rue du Prince Molay Abdallah (☎09/93.79.94). *Avis, Europcar/InterRent* and *Hertz* also have desks at the airport. A local agency, offering a more personal service is *Harris Rent-a-Car,* 1 Rue Zerktouni, off Bd. Mohammed V (☎09/94.21.58).

Car repairs Most repairs can be undertaken – or arranged – by Garage Lafayette, 27 Rue Mohammed Abdou (☎09/93.28.87).

Consulates include: **Britain,** 41 Bd. Mohammed V – 7th floor (☎09/94.15.57; summer: Mon–Thur 8am–2pm, Fri 8am–1pm; winter: Mon–Thur 8am–12.30pm & 2–5.30pm, Fri 8am–1pm); **Denmark,** 3 Rue Ibn Rochd (☎09/93.81.83); **France,** Place de France (☎09/93.20.39); **Italy,** 37 Rue Asad Ibn Farrat (☎09/93.76.47); **Portugal,** 9 Place des Nations (☎09/93.17.08); **Spain,** Rue Sidi Bouadid (☎09/93.56.25); and **Sweden,** 31 Rue Prince Héritier (☎09/93.87.30); Despite the presence of the old American Legation, there is no **USA** consulate and the nearest USA diplomatic representation is in Rabat.

Ferry companies You can buy ferry tickets from any travel agent (see our recommendations overleaf) but, in case you need them, here are the offices of ferry companies sailing from Tangier (with destinations served after their phone numbers): *Comanov,* 43 Av. Abou Alla El Maari (☎09/93.26.49; Algeciras); *Comarit,* 7 Rue du Mexique (☎09/93.12.20; Algeciras); *Intercona,* 31 Av. de la Resistance (☎09/93.48.83; Algeciras); *Limadet/Transmediterranea* 13 Rue du Prince Moulay Abdallah (☎09/93.36.26; Algeciras); *Transtour,* 4 Rue Jabha Al Ouatania (☎09/93.40.04; Tarifa/Gibraltar).

Newspapers English-language newspapers are sold outside the post office, in various stores along Bd. Pasteur, and by vendors around the *Café Paris.*

Pharmacies There are several English-speaking pharmacies in the Place de France (try the Pharmacie de Paris, opposite the *Café Paris*) and along Bd. Pasteur. A roster of all-night and weekend pharmacies is displayed in every *pharmacie* window. Pharmacists are happy to recommend local doctors.

Photographic developing Studio Farah, opposite the *Hôtel El Minzah* on Rue de la Liberté, offers a good quality one-hour service for Kodak film; Studio Flash, further down Rue de la Liberté on the same side as the *Minzah*, does the same for Fuji film.

Police Main station is on Rue Ibn Toumert. Emergency ☎19.

Post, Phones, *Poste Restante* All available at the main *PTT*, 33 Bd. Mohammed V; open Mon–Sat 8.30am–12.15am & 2.30–6.45pm; phone section is open 24hr. As Tangier has direct dialling you can phone (internationally) from any phone box or from one of the new *teleboutiques* – look out for their blue and white lettering and logos.

Tourist office There's an ONMT office at 29 Bd. Pasteur (☎09/93.82.39), just down from Place de France and open (in theory) Mon–Sat 8am–2pm. It is in fact open very erratically, and to be honest it doesn't have a lot to offer in any case, save a few leaflets.

Travel agencies There are many travel agents, particularly along the seafront; they handle ferry and flight bookings and most will advise on – and book – travel and hotels in Morocco. Three reliable agents are: *Voyages Marco Polo*, 72 Av. d'Espagne – by the *Hôtel Valencia* (☎09/93.43.45); *Transalpino Maroc*, 100 Av. d'Espagne (☎09/93.25.94); and *Koutoubia*, 112 bis Av. d'Espagne (☎09/93.55.40).

Around Tangier: capes, caves and coast

The **Bay of Tangier** curves around to a pair of capes – Malabata to the east, Spartel to the west. Either makes a pleasant detour or afternoon's trip, if you have a day to fill waiting for a ferry or flight.

LEAVING TANGIER

Travelling on **into Morocco** from Tangier is simplest either by **train** (the lines run to Meknes/Fes/Oujda or to Rabat/Casablanca/Marrakesh; all trains stop at Asilah en route), or, if you are heading east to Tetouan, by **bus** or shared **grand taxi**. Leaving the country, **ferries** run to Algeciras, Tarifa, Gibraltar and Sète (France).

TRAINS

There are two stations: the **Gare du Port** (by the port) and **Gare de Ville** (400 metres along the seafront from the port). At present the 4.25pm train (Rabat/Casablanca; connection at Sidi Slimane for Meknes/Fes) is the only departure from the Port station (it calls at the Ville station ten minutes later). All other departures are from the Ville station only. There is a **baggage consigne** at the Ville train station, but it will accept locked luggage only; cafés across the road will also look after bags for a small fee.

If you **arrive in Tangier by ferry and plan to travel straight on**, the **4.25pm train** is likely to be the most convenient departure. If you want to travel at night, however, there is an **10pm night train to Marrakesh** (arriving 7.30am). If you take this, try to book a couchette, available as a supplement, which gives you a guaranteed booking and a separate carriage with an attendant – useful for baggage security. You're given bedding but should take your own toilet paper.

Note: Beware of hustlers on the train saying you need to change at Asilah: you don't. It's a ruse to sell you carpets in their shop while you wait for the next train.

BUSES AND GRANDS TAXIS

A few CTM buses leave from the port entrance (for example, to Tetouan), but most **long-distance buses** start out from the **gare routière**, 2km from the centre of town, by the large, modern 'Syrian mosque', Sahat Al Jamai Al Arabia. This is reached by following Rue de Fes to the Rue de Lisbonne roundabout (where the road to the airport separates from that to Tetouan) but it's a long walk so get a *petit taxi* (12dh). Useful departures include **Tetouan** and **Chaouen** (the latter doesn't involve a change of bus,

West: the Caves of Hercules and "Atlantic Beach"

The **Caves of Hercules** (Grottes d'Hercule) are something of a symbol for Tangier, with its strange sea window, shaped like a map of Africa. The name, like Hercules' legendary founding of Tangier, is purely fanciful, but the caves, 16km outside the city and above the "Atlantic Beach", make an attractive excursion, together with the minor Roman site of Cotta. If you feel like staying for a few days by the sea, the beach can be an attractive base, too; outside of July and August only stray groups of visitors share the long surf beaches. Take care with currents, however, which can be very dangerous even near the shore.

If you have your own transport, you can head out to the caves via La Montagne (see below) and make a round trip by continuing along the S701 and then taking either the minor S702 or the faster P2 back to Tangier. If you don't, the cheapest access is a local **bus** (unnumbered but with a placard reading Ashakar – in Arabic – in its window) which runs throughout the day from the local bus station near the Grand Socco; this takes the S702 out of Tangier, turns onto the S701 and runs past *Camping Ashakar*, close by the caves, then carries on 5km to the Cap Spartel lighthouse. An alternative is to charter a **grand taxi** (from the Grand Socco or by the port gates); this should cost around 120dh for the return trip – for which price most drivers can be persuaded to drop you in the morning and pick you up late afternoon; you should, obviously enough, pay at the end.

though you stop in Tetouan for 20 min; don't pay extra to hustlers there who might just suggest your ticket includes only a "reservation fare" for the Chaouen stage!).

There are **grands taxis** leaving through the day to **Tetouan**, again from the gare routière by the Syrian Mosque. To get a place in a taxi, just announce yourself to the driver at the head of the rank. You will then be crammed (with five other passengers) into the car. The cost is only slightly more than going by bus and journey time is considerably less. Taxis can also be chartered here for expeditions further afield, direct to **Chaouen** or **Asilah** for example, and work out relatively economical shared between a group. On your own, heading for Chaouen, it's a lot cheaper to get a bus on from Tetouan. The cost of a place to Tetouan is a standard tariff (currently 20dh); all other destinations are negotiable.

For destinations in the immediate **vicinity of Tangier**, such as the Caves of Hercules or Cap Malabata, you need to negotiate a *grand taxi* at the rank on the Grand Socco.

FERRIES AND HYDROFOILS

Although **ferries** invariably depart an hour or so late, you should **check in** at the port at least one hour before official sailing time to get through the chaos of official business. At the ferry terminal, you have to get an embarkation card and departure card from the *depart* desk of the ferry companies, then you must take this, along with your passport, to the police *visa de passeport* desk on the same floor (opposite the bar), and have your passport stamped before going through customs to the boat. Arrive later than an hour before official departure time and you may find the visa police have knocked off – which means waiting for the next ferry. **Hydrofoils** have a separate *visa de passeport* desk and departures are normally on time.

Two **periods to avoid** the ferries from Tangier are the end of the **Easter week** (Semana Santa) holiday, and the **last week of August**, when the ferries can be full for days on end with Moroccan workers returning to northern Europe.

Details of **ferry/hydrofoil routes** are to be found in the "Basics" section of this book (see p.8). **Tickets and timetables** can be obtained from any travel agent in Tangier or from the ferry company's agents (see our 'Listings').

Cap Spartel and the Caves

The most interesting route to the caves and Cap Spartel runs around and above the coast via the quarter known as La Montagne (see box on p.82). Following this road, you'll reach, around 14km out of Tangier, a short turnoff to the lighthouse at **Cap Spartel** – a dramatic and fertile point, known to the Greeks and Romans as the "Cape of the Vines". The lighthouse, which you can visit and climb, was built in 1864 by Sultan Mohammed III, who then persuaded Britain, France, Italy and Spain to pay for its maintenance; they did, until Moroccan independence in 1956.

To the south of Cap Spartel begins the vast and wild "Atlantic Beach", known locally as **Robinson Plage**. It is broken only by a rocky spit – 5km from the Cape – and then rambles off for as far as you can see. On the spit are located the **Caves of Hercules**. Natural formations, occupied in prehistoric times, they are most striking for a man-made addition – thousands of disc-shaped erosions created by centuries of quarrying for millstones. There were still Moors cutting stones here for a living until the 1920s, but by that time their place was beginning to be taken by professional guides and discreet sex hustlers; it must have made an exotic brothel. Today, there's a standard admission charge of 2.5dh (9am–sunset), though you're unlikely to get away without a guide, too, whose descriptive abilities tend to be somewhat dwarfed by the utter obviousness of all there is to see ("wet cave", "dark cave", "sea", etc). In midsummer there are usually a couple of stalls nearby, serving grilled fish caught on the rocks below.

Ancient Cotta

Five minutes' walk past the caves, a track turns inland from the beach and leads you to the rather scant ruins of **Ancient Cotta**, a small Roman town, founded in the second century AD and occupied for 200 years or so. Like Lixus to the south (see p.99), the town produced *garum* (a kind of anchovy paste) for export. Parts of the factory, and of a temple and baths complex, can be made out, while nearby have been found the ruins of several Roman farms which cultivated olives for oil. Even before the Romans, and certainly afterwards, this was a well-populated and prosperous area.

The most remarkable feature, these days, is the modern factory plant you see just beyond the site, with its tall, thin red-and-white chimneys discharging hot air and flames. This is the point where the **double pipeline**, carrying natural gas from Algeria across Morocco, goes under the straits of Gibraltar to Spain. The 45km submarine section was a unique challenge, given that the strait has a rocky, mountainous seabed, and strong currents, often in three layers, with the top and bottom flowing in one direction, the middle in the opposite direction. Inspired by its success, and perhaps by the Channel Tunnel between Britain and France, Spain and Morocco agreed, in February 1996, to build a rail tunnel along much the same course. The project, costed at £2.5bn ($4bn), is still very much at planning stage but if funds materialize, it is planned to have trains running by 2010.

Between the gas plant and Ancient Cotta a Saudi prince has built a **royal palace**; if you are lucky you will see one of his servants rolling out a carpet across the beach to the water's edge for a royal party to bathe.

Accommodation

Close by the caves, on the same rocky spit, are two **hotels**, the *Hôtel Robinson* (☎09/93.87.65; ④), a pleasant old-established place, and the *Club Le Mirage* (☎09/93.33.32; ⑤), an upmarket cliff-top complex with swimming pool and satellite TV, which has replaced the old *Mirage* restaurant. On the wooded, landward side of the hotels there is also a **campsite**, *Camping Ashakar* (see p.76).

East: Cap Malabata and Ksar es Seghir

The best beaches in the immediate vicinity of Tangier are to be found at **Cap Malabata**, where much wealthy villa development has been taking place. Beyond here, **Ksar Es Seghir** offers a pleasant day by the sea, or a stop on the coast road to Ceuta, if you have your own transport to get there.

Cap Malabata and Villa Harris

The bay east of Tangier is flanked by a gritty strip of beach and a chain of elderly villas and new apartment blocks until you reach the "complexe touristique" of **Cap Malabata**. This has a couple of hotels, intermittently open, and the *Club Aquarius* (℡09/94.60.13), an outpost of the *Club Méditerranée*, which, unusually, is prepared to take guests without an advance reservation, if it has vacancies. Its buildings encompass the splendid turn-of-the-century **Villa Harris** and its gardens, built by the writer Walter Harris (see "Contexts") and given by him to the people of Tangier. Harris's wife decently cited his obsession with the garden (rather than his predilection for boys) in her case for divorce. If you're interested in visiting the villa and gardens, you may be able to talk your way in at the gates, even if you're not staying at the Club.

You can get to Cap Malabata on bus #11 from the local bus station near the Grand Socco, or by *petit taxi*, but once **around the cape** the buses give out (save for a single daily bus from Tangier to Ksar Es Seghir), along with the hotels and villas. There is in fact virtually no development the whole way down the coast to Ceuta: just a road winding through the hills above enticing stretches of beach.

Ksar es Seghir and Djebel Moussa

KSAR ES SEGHIR is quite a reward at the end of this road: a relaxed and picturesque little fishing port with a friendly café-restaurant on a terrace above the sea. The village attracts a fair number of Moroccan beach campers in summer but few Europeans. There are usually **rooms** for rent if you ask around.

From Ksar es Seghir the road to Fnideq climbs around the windy **Djebel Moussa** – the mountain which, with Gibraltar, forms the so-called Pillars of Hercules, gateway to the Classical world. Mythologies aside, the twin pillars effect remarkable thermal currents, speeding passage for **migratory birds** at this, the shortest crossing between Africa and Europe. A spring or autumn visit should ensure sightings, as up to 200 species make their way across the Strait.

Asilah

The first town downcoast of Tangier – and first stop on the train line – **ASILAH** is one of the most elegant of the old Portuguese Atlantic ports, ranking with El Jadida and Essaouira to the south of Casablanca. First impressions are of wonderful square stone ramparts, flanked by palms, and an outstanding beach – an immense sweep of sand stretching to the north halfway to Tangier. Further exploration reveals the Medina, which is one of the most attractive in the country, colourwashed at every turn, and with a series of murals painted for the town's International Festival. In addition, the town itself is small, easy to manage, and exceptionally clean – perhaps due in part to the fact that the country's ex-Minister of Culture (currently Moroccan Ambassador to the US) has a residence here.

The former minister was closely involved in the **International Festival**, a month-long event, held annually until 1994, and sporadically since, encompassing art exhibitions and a series of performances – ranging from Lebanese singers to European jazz,

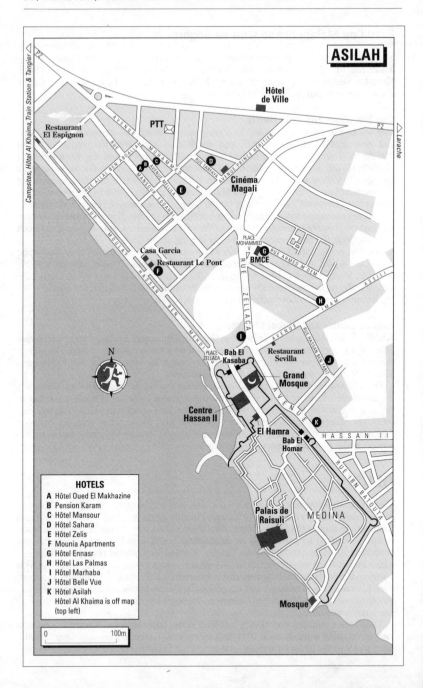

ASILAH

Campsites, Hôtel Al Khaima, Train Station & Tangier

P2

Larache

Hôtel
de Ville

PTT

Restaurant
El Espignon

AVENUE MOHAMMED

RUE ALLAL BEN ABDALLAH

RUE TARFAYA

AVENUE PRINCE HÉRITIER

D

A B
AVENUE MELILIA

E

Cinéma
Magali

MANSOUR EDDAHBI

RUE MOULAY

Casa Garcia

Restaurant Le Pont
F

HASSAN BEN MEHDI

PLACE
MOHAMMED
V

RUE ZELLACA

BMCE
G

RUE AHMED M DEM

ASSILI

H

IMAM

I

AVENUE

RUE HASSAN BEN TABIT

PLACE
ZELLACA

Bab El
Kasaba

Restaurant
Sevilla

J

Grand
Mosque

AVENUE

Centre
Hassan II

El Hamra

Bab El
Homar

K

HASSAN II

RUE IBN BATOUTA

Palais de
Raisuli

MEDINA

Mosque

N

HOTELS
A Hôtel Oued El Makhazine
B Pension Karam
C Hôtel Mansour
D Hôtel Sahara
E Hôtel Zelis
F Mounia Apartments
G Hôtel Ennasr
H Hôtel Las Palmas
I Hôtel Marhaba
J Hôtel Belle Vue
K Hôtel Asilah
  Hôtel Al Khaima is off map
  (top left)

0   100m

Moroccan folk musicians to American university choirs. When the fetival takes place (normally in August), it is followed by a three-day **horse fair**, with a *fantasia* (cavalry charge with muskets) display on each of the days.

Arriving and accommodation

The **train station** is 2km north of the town; there is occasionally a taxi to meet arrivals but don't count on it. It's an easy enough walk into town, so long as you're not weighed down with bags. Arriving by **grand taxi** (1hr from Tangier), or by **bus**, you're dropped in or around **Place Mohammed V**, a small square at the edge of the Medina, a short walk from the ramparts and a prominent gate, **Bab El Kasaba**.

Hotels

Asilah can be packed during its festival but at other times, even high season, there's usually space to be found in the dozen or so pensions and hotels.

CHEAP

Hôtel Asilah [**K**], 79 Av. Hassan II (☎09/91.72.86). A decent cheapie, with recently refurbished rooms that open out onto a terrace above the ramparts, overlooking the daily vegetable market. Usually closed out of season. ①

Hôtel Belle Vue [**J**], Rue Hassan Ben Tabit (☎09/91.77.47). A new hotel with some bizarre decor. Very reasonably priced, with breakfast included. ①

Hôtel Ennasr [**E**], 3 Rue Ahmed M'dem (☎09/41.73.85). Rooms around a courtyard; plain but clean. The sign is small – look for it on the right-hand side of the street, behind a row of banks, walking from Place Mohammed V. ①

Hôtel Marhaba [**I**], 9 Rue Zellaca (☎09/91.71.44). A friendly place, close by the town gate; small, simple rooms but good value for your money. ①

Hôtel Sahara [**D**], 9 Rue Tarfaya (☎09/91.71.85). A little way from the action, behind the *Cinéma Magali*, but quiet and comfortable. Showers are charged extra. ①

MODERATE

Pension Karam [**B**], 39 Rue Mansour Eddahbi (☎09/91.71.80). A small pension close by the seafront promenade (and behind the more prominent *Hôtel Oued El Makhazine*). Rooms are simple and beds hospital style but there's a nice feel about the place. ②

Hôtel Las Palmas [**H**], 7 Rue Imam Assili (☎09/91.76.94). Another newish hotel – comfortable and good value. ②

Hôtel Mansour [**C**], 49 Av. Mohammed V (☎09/91.73.90). This is probably the best mid-range hotel in Asilah: a well-run little place with clean, modern rooms (all with showers, most with toilets). ③

Hôtel Oued El Makhazine [**A**], Av. Melilla (☎09/91.70.90). A pleasant and comfortable hotel, close to the seafront, and with a new swimming pool. It has a bar, too, so depending on your sensitivities you may find it either lively or noisy. ②

EXPENSIVE

Hôtel Al Khaima [**off map**], Route de Tanger – 1km north of town on the Tangier road (☎09/91.74.28). This modern, comfortable hotel is built around a pool and has had some very positive reports in recent months. It has a pleasant bar, open to all-comers, which can be a little noisy in high season. ④

Mounia Apartments [**F**], 14 Rue Moulay Hassan Ben Mehdi (☎09/91.74.97). A range of apartments, with kitchenettes, located by the *Restaurant Casa Garcia* on the promenade. The owner has other apartments and studios elsewhere. ④

Hôtel Zelis [**E**], 10 Rue Mansour Eddahbi (☎09/91.70.29). Opened in 1995, this is a good-looking, very comfortable hotel, which perhaps has a slight edge over the *Al Khaima*. ④

Campsites

Camping Echrigui (☎09/91.71.82). This is the closest – and probably the best – of a string of camp-sites south of the train station. Located about 400m from the town, it is well maintained, with thatched 'bungalows' as well as pitches for tents, and has hot showers, a small shop and a cafeteria. Open all year.

The town

Before the tourists and the International Festival, Asilah was just a small fishing port, quietly stagnating after the indifference of Spanish colonial administration. Whitewashed and cleaned up, it now has a prosperous feeling to it – the Grand Mosque, for example, has been rebuilt and doubled in size and a marina complex is planned.

The ramparts and Medina

The Medina's circuit of **towers and ramparts** – built by the Portuguese military architect Botacca in the sixteenth century – are pleasant to wander around. They include two main gates: **Bab El Homar**, on Avenue Hassan II, and **Bab El Kasaba**. If you enter by the latter, you pass the **Grand Mosque** and the **Centre Hassan II des Rencontres Internationales**, a venue and accommodation centre for the festival, with a cool open courtyard.

Further on is a small square overlooked by the "red tower", **El Hamra**. This is used for exhibitions, particularly during the festival. Turn right past here, along a tiny network of streets, and down towards the platform overlooking the sea, and you'll come upon at least a half-dozen **murals** painted (and subsequently repainted) during the festivals; they form an intriguing mix of fantasy-representational art and geometric designs. In turn, these offset the whitewashed walls of the houses, with their doors and windows picked out in cool pastel shades. It's quite an entrancing quarter.

Palais de Raisuli

The town's focal sight – stretching over the sea at the heart of the Medina – is the **Palais de Raisuli**, built in 1909 with forced tribal labour by one Er Raisuli, a local bandit. One of the strangest figures to emerge from what was an almost routinely bizarre period of Moroccan government, he began his career as a cattle rustler, achieved notoriety with a series of kidnappings and ransoms (including the British writer Walter Harris and a Greek-American millionaire, Perdicaris, who was bailed out by Teddy Roosevelt), and was eventually appointed governor over practically all the tribes of northwest Morocco. Harris described his captivity in *Morocco That Was* as an "anxious time", made more so by being confined in a small room with a headless corpse. Despite this, captor and captive formed a friendship, Harris finding Raisuli a "mysterious personage, half-saint, half-blackguard", and often entertaining him later in Tangier.

Another British writer, Rosita Forbes, visited Raisuli at his palace in 1924, later writing his biography. She described the rooms, today mostly bare, as hung with rugs "of violent colours, embroidered with tinsel", their walls lined with cushions stuffed with small potatoes. The decoration seems logical enough – the palace today still looks more like a glittering Hollywood set than anything real. The great reception room, a long glass terrace above the sea, even has dialogue to match: Raisuli told Forbes that he made murderers walk to their death from its windows – a ninety-foot drop to the rocks. One man, he said, had turned back to him, saying, "Thy justice is great, Sidi, but these stones are more merciful".

The palace overhangs the sea ramparts towards the far end of the Medina (away from the beach). It is not officially open to visitors but if you're interested – and the interior is worth seeing – knock or enlist the help of a local and you may strike lucky with the caretaker. If you are really determined you could visit the Hôtel de Ville (the town-hall) beforehand and ask them to give you a note in Arabic for the caretaker.

The **Hôtel de Ville** is to be found inland on the Tangier-Rabat road as it bypasses Asilah. Nearby is a modern, massive **monument** commemorating the passage of Mohammed V on his way to Tangier in April 1947, when he identified himself with the struggle for Moroccan independence.

There's a Djebali villagers' **market**, at its liveliest on Thursday and Sunday, held on the far side of the Tangier–Rabat road.

The beaches

As with Tangier, the **beach** is the main focus of life. The most popular stretches are to the north of the town, past the building works for the new marina complex and out towards the campsites. For more isolated strands, walk south, past the Medina ramparts, for about fifteen minutes.

Restaurants, cafés, discos and baths

The town's most prominent **restaurants** are *El Oceano* (aka *Casa Pepe*) and *Al Kasaba,* facing each other in the Place Zellaca, just outside the ramparts. Both have outdoor tables and Spanish-style fried fish; *La Alcazaba* scores for its site, with tables shaded by palms, across the road, and a roof terrace overlooking the ramparts and harbour; *El Oceano* has, alas, acquired a microwave. Further north along the seafront are a couple of similar restaurants, *Casa Gracia* and *El Espignon*, again specializing in fish and seafood, and, between the two, the popular *Café-Restaurant Le Pont*.

In the town 'proper' the *Restaurant Ifrane*, on Place Mohammed V, and the *Restaurant Sevilla*, near the *Hôtel Las Palmas* at 18 Ave. Imam Assili, both serve generous helpings of Spanish style dishes; the *Ifrane* also has the distinction of table flowers fashioned from old plastic bags.

Asilah's other diversions include a couple of lively **cafés**, *Café Haddou*, by the *Hôtel Asilah*, and *Café Salam*, further along Av. Hassan II as it turns inland. Neither café has a sign but anyone will direct you. In summer, there are **discos** at the *Hôtel Al Khaima* and at several of the campsites. Much further afield, and calling for transport, are the *Club Solitaire* and the *Atlantis* nightclub, beyond the last campsite north of town, towards the Mohammed V bridge.

Finally, ask directions to the town's small **hammam**, tucked down an alleyway in the north of the Medina. Unusually, the keeper charges Westerners a group rate and gives you the place to yourselves.

Mzoura

If you have an interest in ancient sites, you might devote a half-day to explore the prehistoric **stone circle of Mzoura**, south of Asilah. The site, whose name means "Holy Place" in Arabic, originally comprised a tumulus, assumed to be the tomb of some early Mauritanian king, enclosed by an elliptical circle of some 167 standing stones. It was excavated in 1935 and the mound is now reduced to a series of watery hollows. To the north of the circle, there still stands a tall, upright stone known as El Uted, where, legend has it, Sebastian, the young king of Portugal, picnicked on his way from Asilah, where he had landed, to his death the following day at the cataclysmic Battle of the Three Kings at Ksar El Kebir (see p.100). There is a model of Mzoura, pre-excavation, in the archaeological museum in Tetouan.

To reach Mzoura, follow the P2 south of Asilah for 16km, then turn left along the P37 towards Tetouan. After crossing the railway line, and 4km from the junction with the P2, turn left by the *Somepi* petrol station and onto a side road signposted El Yamini (aka

---

ROADSIDE BIRD-WATCHING: TANGIER TO LARACHE

When travelling between Tangier and Larache, there are interesting bird habitats to be seen on both sides of the road.

A few kilometres **north of Asilah**, the dry flatlands attract wintering **great bustards** and large numbers of **common cranes**, and you're also likely to see **callandra** and **crested larks**. Hereabouts, too, and particularly between Asilah and Larache, there are wetlands and salt pans which attract the **water pipit**, **black-winged stilt**, and **greater flamingo**.

To the southeast of Larache, and accessible by car, are the **Loukos wetlands**. These marshes and pools are said to be the best spot in Morocco for spotting the **little bustard** and in winter there are four species of rails to look out for – moorhen, coot, crested coot, and purple gallinule. Amongst other birds recorded here are the squacco heron, white stork, glossy ibis, and greater flamingo. Birdwatching historians might like to note that it was close to here, around the confluence of the Oued Loukous and its tributary, the Oued El Makhazine, that the **Battle of the Three Kings** (see p.100) was fought.

A little further south of Larache is the major bird habitat in this part of Morocco, Merdja Zerga, the **Moulay Boussleham lagoon**; see p.101.

Tnine Sidi Lyamani). From here the site is 5km northeast, across a confusing network of sandy tracks; it would be wise to enlist a guide at El Yamini.

Larache

LARACHE is a relaxed, easy-going resort, its summer visitors primarily Moroccan tourists. In consequence it is one of the best towns of the north in which to spend a few days by the sea: the local beach to the north is superb and for once is very mixed, with as many women around as men – a reassuring feeling for women travellers looking for a low-key spot to bathe. Nearby, too, are the ruins of **ancient Lixus**, legendary site of the Gardens of the Hesperides.

Physically, the town looks like an amalgam of Tangier and Tetouan – an attractive place, if not spectacularly so. It was the main port of the northern Spanish zone and – though the central Plaza de España has since become Place de la Libération – still bears much of its former stamp. There are faded old Spanish hotels, Spanish-run restaurants and Spanish bars, even an active Spanish cathedral for the small colony who still work at the docks. In its heyday it was quite a metropolis, publishing its own Spanish newspaper and journal, and drawing a cosmopolitan population that included the French writer Jean Genet; Genet spent the last decade of his life here and is buried in the old Spanish cemetery.

Before its colonization in 1911, Larache was a small trading port, its activities limited by dangerous offshore sand bars. Without these, it might have rivalled Tangier, for it is better positioned as a trade route to Fes. Instead, it eked out a living by building pirate ships made of wood from the nearby Forest of Mamora for the "Barbary Corsairs" of Salé and Rabat. There had been an earlier period of Spanish occupation in the seventeenth century, before it was reclaimed and repopulated by Moulay Ismail.

Accommodation

Larache has some decent accommodation but there's not a lot of choice. In summer, you'd be well advised to book ahead.

CHEAP

Pension Amal [F], 10 Rue Abdallah Ben Yasin (☎09/91.27.88). Clean, quiet and friendly, this is signposted – off to the left down an alleyway – on the street from the bus station to the Place de la Libération. There is a *hammam* just down the street. ①

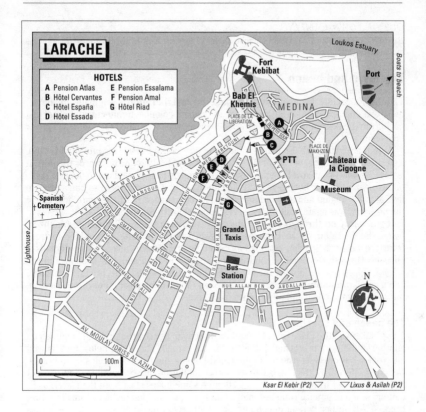

LARACHE

HOTELS
A Pension Atlas   E Pension Essalama
B Hôtel Cervantes F Pension Amal
C Hôtel España   G Hôtel Riad
D Hôtel Essada

Ksar El Kebir (P2) ▽   ▽*Lixus & Asilah (P2)*

Hôtel Atlas [E], 154 Rue 2 Mars (☎09/91.20.14). The only hotel worth recommending in the tiny Medina – the nearby *Victoria* and *Al Watan* are pretty grim. The *Atlas*, by contrast, is pleasant, if basic. To reach it, enter the Medina through Bab El Khemis, turn right immediately and walk the full length of Rue du Petit Souk; the hotel is on the left at the far corner of the *souk*. ①

Hôtel Cervantes [B], 3 Rue Tarik Ibnou Ziad, off Place de la Libération (☎09/91.08.74). A downbeat old hotel that's listed here only as a fallback. ①

Hôtel España [C], Place de la Libération/entrance at 6 Av. Hassan II (☎09/91.31.95). The Grand Hotel in Spanish days – much decayed but retaining a touch (and no more!) of elegance. It has a range of rooms (with and without bathrooms) and prices. ①

Pension Essalama [E], 50 Av. Moulay Mohammed Ben Abdallah (☎09/91.01.92). Similar credits for this welcoming and refurbished hotel – though the plumbing's still a bit whiffy. ①

Hôtel Saada [A], 16 Av. Moulay Mohammed Ben Abdallah (☎09/91.36.41). Basic but cheap and clean hotel on the street from the bus station to the Place de la Libération. ①

EXPENSIVE

Hôtel Riad [G], Av. Moulay Mohammed Ben Abdallah (☎09/91.26.26). The town's grand hotel – it was the former mansion of the Duchesse de Guise, mother of the current pretender to the French throne – has had a recent overhaul by the Kasbah Tours chain and justifies a bit of a splurge. Most of the big airy rooms overlook the extensive gardens, which include tennis courts and a swimming pool, with water more often than not. There's a restaurant-bar indoors and another bar, the *Princess*, at the bottom of the garden; both are open to non-residents. ④

Hostal-Camping Flora, 3km from Larache on the P2 towards Ksar El Kebir (☎09/91.22.50). This modest little hotel has a camping patch beside it, shaded and secure. It also has a restaurant. ①

The town and beach

The town's circular main square, the **Place de la Libération** – originally, of course, the Plaza de España – is a striking piece of Spanish colonial architecture. It is set just back from the sea and a straightforward 400-metre walk from the bus station and *grand taxi* stand.

A high archway, **Bab El Khemis**, at the centre of the *place* leads into the **Medina**, a surprisingly compact wedge of alleys and stairways leading down towards the port. It is now the poorest area of Larache – better-off families have moved out to the new parts of town, leaving their houses here to the elderly – but it doesn't seem so bad a place to live, artfully shaded and airy in its design. The colonnaded market square, just inside the archway, was again built by the seventeenth-century Spanish.

If you carry on through the Medina, you can reach the small Place de Makhzen, below the **Château de la Cigogne** (Stork's Castle), a hulking, three-sided fortress from the original Spanish occupation. Standing back from here, to the right, is a Hispano-Moorish-Deco palace, built by the Spanish in 1915 and now used as a music school. Opposite, overlooking the Oued Loukos and across to Lixus, is a fine esplanade and a small **museum**, converted from a prison (and complete with dungeon), containing a few Roman coins and other relics from Lixus.

The beach and coastline

If you walk from the Place de la Libération, directly to the seafront, you find yourself on another and longer promenade, Avenue Moulay Ismail. The shore below here is wild and rocky, but cross its estuary of the Oued Loukos and there are miles of fine sandy **beach** sheltered by trees and flanked by a handful of café-restaurants. You can get there by bus (#4 from the port, every 20min – some buses start from the *place*), a circuitous seven-kilometre route, or, more fun, from the port in a flotilla of small **fishing boats** (5–15dh per person depending on whether you haggle!) which shuttle across from the base of a flight of stone steps and help you out in the shallows on the other side. From the *place*, the quickest route down to the **port** is along the promenade and under the crumbling ruins of the **Fort Kebibat** (Little Domes), built by Portuguese merchants in the sixteenth century.

In summer, an oddity on the beach is the variety of foreign languages you hear – yet with so few foreigners around. The explanation is the number of migrant families, scattered about Europe, who return to the town for the holiday. As well as communities in Barcelona, Naples and Paris, Larache accounts for most of the Moroccan community in London, and on the beach you're likely to come upon kids with disarming English accents. Almost all of the London Moroccans come from the Bayswater area.

For an alternative walk, head southwest of the town, **along the cliffs** towards the jail and the **lighthouse**. Before you reach the jail, you will pass the neglected Spanish Christian cemetery where **Jean Genet** is buried; the gravestone, regularly whitewashed, is marked by a small handwritten card.

Eating and drinking

Meals in Larache, except at the Medina cafés, or the sardine grills down by the port, remain resolutely Spanish. The cheapest cafés are in the Place de la Libération around Bab El Khemis, the entrance archway of the Medina. The *Restaurant Sekala*, here, serves fine paella, fish and chicken *tajine*.

A little more upmarket, and worth trying for seafood, are *Restaurant Larache* at 18 Av. Moulay Mohammed Ben Abdallah, next door to the *Hôtel Saada*, and the *Estrella del Mar* at 68 Av. Mohammed Zerktouni (the other end from Place de la Libération). Take a look, too, at the *Lixus*, a grand old restaurant on Place de la Libération/Av. Mohammed Zerktouni, and, a little further afield, *Restaurant Al Khozama* at 114 Av. Mohammed V.

For **drinks**, the choice is between the *Hôtel Riad* bars and the downmarket *Bar Hillal*, near the *Hôtel Saada*, where you can play pinball and video games with the locals; the latter looks a dive but is friendly enough – and prices are half those in the *Riad*.

Ancient Lixus

Ancient Lixus is one of the oldest – and most continuously – inhabited sites in Morocco. It had been settled in prehistoric times, long before the arrival of Phoenician colonists around 1000 BC, under whom it is thought to have become the first trading post of North Africa. Later, it was in turn an important Carthaginian and Roman city, and was deserted only in the fifth century AD, two hundred years after Diocletian had withdrawn the empire's patronage. There are remains of a church from this period, and Arabic coins have also been found.

As an archeological site, then, Lixus is certainly significant, and its legendary associations with Hercules (see box below), are rich soil for the imagination. It has to be said, though, that the visible ruins are not especially impressive, and only around a quarter of the site has ever been excavated. Even so, if you're spending any amount of time in Larache, or passing through by car, the Lixus ruins are good for an hour or two's exploration. They lie upon and below the summit of a low hill on the far side of the estuary, at the crossroads of the main Larache–Tangier road and the narrow lane to Larache beach. It's a four- to five-kilometre walk to the ruins from either the beach or town, or you can use the bus which runs between the two; alternatively, for about 75dh you could charter one of the boats to row you over from Larache, wait an hour or so, and then row you back to the town or beach. The site is not effectively enclosed, so there are no real opening hours.

The site
The site's **Lower Town**, spreading back from the modern road, consists largely of the ruins of factories for the production of salt – still being panned nearby – and, as at Cotta, anchovy-paste *garum*. The factories seem to have been developed in the early years of the first century AD by the Carthaginians, and they remained in operation until the Roman withdrawal.

LIXUS AND HERCULES

The **legendary associations** of Lixus – and the site's mystique – centre on the Labours of Hercules. For here, on an island in the estuary, Pliny and Strabo record reports of the palace of the "Libyan" (by which they meant African) King Antaeus. Behind the palace stretched the **Garden of the Hesperides**, to which Hercules, as his penultimate labour, was dispatched.

In the object of Hercules' quest – the **Golden Apples** – it is not difficult to imagine the tangerines of northern Morocco, raised to mythic status by travellers' tales. The site, too, seems to offer reinforcement to conjectures of a mythic pre-Phoenician past. Megalithic stones have been found on the Acropolis – they may have been linked astronomically with those of Mzoura (see p.95) – and the site was known to the Phoenicians as Makom Shemesh (City of the Sun).

A track, some 100m down the road to Tangier, leads up to the Acropolis (upper town), passing on its way eight rows of the Roman **theatre** and **amphitheatre**, unusually combined into a single structure. Its deep, circular arena was adapted for circus games and the gladiatorial slaughter of animals. Morocco, which Herodotus knew as "the wild-beast country", was the major source for these Roman *venationes*, and local colonists must have grown rich from the trade. Amid **baths** built into the side of the theatre, a mosaic remains *in situ*, depicting Neptune and the Oceans.

Climbing above the baths and theatre, you pass through ramparts to the main enceinte (fortifications) of the **Acropolis** – a somewhat confused network of walls and foundations – and **temple sanctuaries**, including an early **Christian basilica** and a number of **pre-Roman buildings**. The most considerable of the sanctuaries, with their underground cisterns and porticoed priests' quarters, were apparently rebuilt in the first century AD, but even then retained Phoenician elements in their design.

Heading south towards Fes or Rabat

Heading **south from Larache**, the main road and most of the buses bypass **Ksar El Kebir** on their way towards Meknes, Fes or Kenitra/Rabat. You'll probably do likewise, though the town does have one of the largest weekly markets in the region (on Sundays). Just past here, you cross the old border between Spanish and French colonial zones. Beyond, Roman enthusiasts may want to explore the minor sites at **Banasa** and **Thamusida**, while **bird-watchers** should head for the lagoon and local bathing resort of **Moulay Boussleham**.

Ksar El Kebir

As its name – in Arabic, "the Great Enclosure" – suggests, **KSAR EL KEBIR** was once a place of some importance. Founded in the eleventh century, it became an early Arab power base and was enlarged and endowed by both Almohads and Merenids, and perennially coveted by the Spanish and Portuguese of Asilah and Larache. It was close by here that, in 1578, the Portuguese fought the disastrous **Battle of the Three Kings**, the most dramatic and disastrous in their nation's history – a crusading expedition which saw the death or capture of virtually the entire nobility; for the Moroccans it resulted in the fortuitous accession to power of Ahmed El Mansour, the greatest of all Merenid sultans.

The town fell into decline in the seventeenth century, after a local chief incurred the wrath of Moulay Ismail, causing him to destroy the walls. Neglect followed, although its fortunes revived to some extent under the Spanish protectorate, when it served as a major barracks.

Practicalities
The **Sunday souk** is held right by the bus and *grand taxi* terminals. On any morning of the week, however, there are lively **souks** around the main **kissaria** (covered market) of the old town – in the quarter known as *Bab El Oued* (the Gate of the River). There is also an active **tannery** on the south side of the Medina and a handful of minor Islamic monuments scattered about. It doesn't amount to much, but if you've time to spare you might get a local to show you around – especially the *souks*.

If you want to stay, the new *Hôtel Ksar Alyamama*, 8 Av. Hassan II (☎09/90.79.60; ②) is good value. The other possibility is the *Café-Hôtel Andaluz* (①), but it's decidedly down at heel. For **meals**, the *Café-Restaurant Manar*, on the central square with the fountain, is popular and good.

Arbaoua and Souk El Arba du Rharb

Beyond Ksar El Kebir, a decaying customs post at **ARBAOUA** marks the old colonial frontier between the Spanish and French zones. There is a row of worthwhile **pottery stalls** at the border post, while close by, on the wooded hill, is a group of French-built hunting lodges and a **hotel**, the *Hostellerie Route de France* (no phone at present; ②), which does good French meals. There used to be a campsite in the woods here, but it has closed down.

South again, **SOUK EL ARBA DU RHARB** is the first settlement of any size, though it is little more than its name suggests (Wednesday Market of the Plain), a roadside sprawl of market stalls, with some grill-cafés and a few **hotels**. The best of these is the *Gharb Hôtel* (☎07/90.02.42; ②), recently refurbished; opposite is the older *Hôtel Souss* (☎07/90.22.87; ①), with small rooms above a restaurant. On the Tangier side of town is the *Grand Hôtel* (☎07/90.20.20; ①), with a bar on the ground floor. The town is not a very compelling place to stay, though you may want to head here for transport connections to Ouezzane (a standard *grand taxi* run, or infrequent buses) or Moulay Bousselham (regular *grands taxis* take 20 minutes; buses, if they stop at all villages en route, up to two hours!).

Moulay Bousselham

MOULAY BOUSSELHAM is a very low-key resort, popular almost exclusively with Moroccans. It comprises little more than a single street, crowded with grill-cafés and sloping down to the sea at the side of a broad lagoon and wetland area, known as **Merdja Zerga**. This is one of northern Morocco's prime **bird-watching** locations (see below), and any foreign visitor will be enouraged to see the lagoon's flamingo and other bird colonies in one of the locals' fishing boats. The **beach** itself is sheltered by cliffs – rare along the Atlantic – and has an abrupt drop-off, which creates a continual thrash

---

WETLAND WILDLIFE: MERDJA ZERGA

Adjoining the Moulay Bousselham lagoon is a large wetland area – recently given protected wildlife status – known as **Merdja Zerga** ('Blue Lake'). This open barren space is used for grazing by nomadic herds of sheep, cattle and goats, while around the periphery are lines of dwarf palm and the giant succulent agave.

This diversity of habitat, and the huge extent of the site, ensures rewarding **bird-watching** at all times of year. There are large numbers of waders, including a large colony of flamingoes, plus little winged plovers, black-winged stilts and black-tailed godwits. These can be seen most easily by taking a boat trip – though at 120dh an hour this can be expensive, and make sure that you arrange to set off at least an hour before high tide or you will run aground a tantalizing distance from the birds.

For serious bird-watchers, it is the **gulls and terns** that roost on the central islands which are worthy of the closest inspection, as among the flocks of lesser black-backed gull and black tern, it is possible to find rarer species such as **Caspian tern**. However, the campsite at Moulay Bousselham is probably the best place in Morocco to see pairs of North African **marsh owl** which usually appear hunting over the adjacent grassland ten to fifteen minutes after sunset, and the same vantage point is also a good spot for seeing **Barbary partidge**. One bird you'll certainly see wintering here, usually around cattle (and sometimes sitting on their backs), is the **cattle egret**.

The *Café Milano* in Moulay Bousselham keeps a **bird log** and will put you in touch with a local bird guide if you wish. For rarity-spotters, the grail is the slender-billed curlew, an endangered species, spotted once or twice in recent years; it is smaller than the European curlew with distinct spade-like markings on its flanks.

of breaking waves. While a lot of fun for swimming, the currents can be highly dangerous and the beach is strictly patrolled by lifeguards. Take care.

For Moroccans, the village is part summer resort, part pilgrimage centre. The saint from which the village takes its name, the **Marabout Moulay Bousselham**, was a tenth-century Egyptian, whose remains are housed in a *koubba* prominently positioned above the settlement. In July this sees one of the largest **moussems** – or religious festivals – in the region.

Accommodation and food

Most Moroccan visitors to Moulay Bousselham stay at the lagoon **campsite**, which is beautifully positioned but is very run-down and plagued by mosquitoes; it is open in summer only. If you don't want to camp, the alternatives are limited to two small hotels, or, if you ask around, **rooms** above the cafés.

The best of the **accommodation** is the *Villanora* (☎07/43.20.17; ③), a family-run villa overlooking the beach and the Atlantic rollers. It's 2km out of town but an attractive place, with English owners, Alan Gabriel and his sister Jean Oliver, who are knowledgable on local birdlife and in summer have exhibitions of Moroccan art.

The *Hôtel Le Lagon* (☎07/43.26.03; ②), on the main street, gets mixed reports, as the management seems to change regularly, always promising improvements. On the plus side, it does have the only **bar** in the place.

Any of the **grill-cafés** will fix you a mixed platter of fish – served in copious quantity and at very reasonable prices. For more of a **restaurant** meal, *L'Océan* and *La Jeunesse*, both on the main street, are good bets.

Moulay Bousselham has a **post office** and a **teleboutique** but no bank.

Banasa and Thamusida

This pair of minor Roman sites is really of specialist interest – and for those with transport. **Banasa** lies south of Souk El Arba, and **Thamusida** just west of the main P2 road to Kenitra.

Banasa

BANASA was settled from around 250BC, but later enlarged by Octavian (the future Emperor Augustus) as a colony for veterans. It was linked by both land and water with Lixus (see p.99) and prospered into the second and third centuries AD, the period from which most of the visible ruins date. Within the traces of the city walls, the central feature is a forum, around which stood the capitol, a basilica (or law courts) and municipal buildings. In the town, among the houses and shops, were two public baths.

The custodian, who lives nearby, will probably notice your arrival and add a little life to the stones. He can point out a few mosaics, though most, he claims, have been removed to museums.

The site is easy to find. Leave Souk El Arba by the main road (P2) to Kenitra, then, just after Souk Tleta, turn left onto a minor road, crossing the Oued Sebou by a bridge. After 2km you reach a T-junction with the S210: turn left and, after another 2km, look for a track on the left (better signposted coming the other way, from Mechra Ben Ksiri). This leads to the ruins, which are overlooked by a *koubba* dedicated to Sidi Ali Boujnoun.

Thamusida

THAMUSIDA is more or less contemporary with Banasa, some 45km to the north. A Roman camp and small town, it was occupied from around 200BC, fortified fifty years later, and abandoned by 250AD, after fire damage. You can trace the walls of the camp and barracks, and make out a temple and baths, though the site as a whole is less extensive – and less interesting than Banasa; its setting, however, closer to the Oued Sebou, is impressive.

There are two possible **approaches** to the site, which is quite tricky to find. Neither approach is signposted and both are along tracks impassable in wet weather. The **first** approaches the site from the east. Leave the Souk El Arba road 13km north of Kenitra by a petrol station on the right-hand side and near a few houses known as Souk El Khemis. After a couple of kilometres, the track splits three ways: follow the central track. The **second**, possibly easier to find, approaches from the southwest. Continue on the P2, under the railway bridge, and 8km from Kenitra turn right along a track signposted Nkhakhsa (2476); there is a level crossing and then the village of Ahmed Taleb. Once again, the track divides several times.

In both cases, look (and ask) for a prominent *koubba*, dedicated to Sidi Ali Ben Ahmed, and a favourite picnic spot for locals. The site lies between this *koubba* and the river.

CEUTA, TETOUAN AND CHAOUEN

The Spanish enclave of **Ceuta** is a slightly frustrating port of entry. Although in Africa, you are not yet in Morocco, and you must make your way to the border at Fnideq, then on from there to **Tetouan**, the first Moroccan town. It can be a time-consuming business. However, if you are making for **Chaouen**, Tetouan has the advantage of regular bus connections.

The Mediterranean coast between **Fnideq** and **Martil**, Tetouan's home beach, has been developed over the past ten years, its sands colonized by large hotels, a golf course, a couple of marinas and a clutch of tourist complexes (including a *Club Med* at Smir). **Mdiq** and **Martil** are the only resorts here with much charm, though **Oued Laou**, in the shadow of the Rif, remains a "travellers' resort", with basic facilities. All are easily reached from Tetouan.

Ceuta (Sebta)

A Spanish enclave since the sixteenth century, **CEUTA** (Sebta in Arabic) is a curious political anomaly. Along with Melilla, east along the coast, it was retained by Spain after Moroccan independence in 1956 and today functions largely as a military base, its economy bolstered by a limited duty-free status. It is something of an embarassment for the Spanish government, in the light of its own claims to Gibraltar, visible just a few sea miles across the straits. They would find it hard politically to return the colony to Morocco, and, in many ways, nobody is much interested in their so doing. Large numbers of Moroccans live and/or work in Ceuta; the local police and taxi drivers are fluent in both Spanish and Arabic; and both pesetas and dirhams are used and accepted in shops and restaurants.

Note that Ceuta works to Spanish time, which is usually one or two hours different from Morocco. When **phoning Ceuta** from Morocco (or anywhere else outside Spain), you must prefix phone numbers with the international code (☎0034). Dialling numbers within Ceuta, omit the local code (☎56).

The Town

Ceuta has a long and eventful history, with occupation by Phoenicians, Romans, Visigoths and Byzantines, prior to the Moors, who from the eighth century onwards

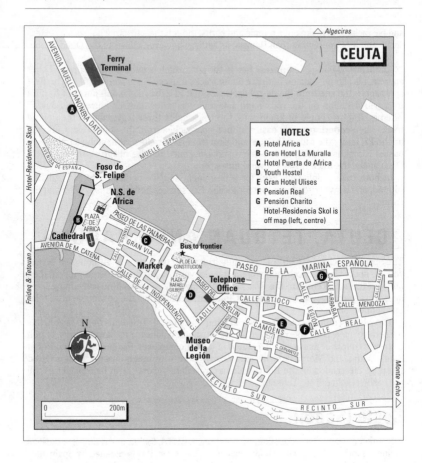

used it as a springboard for invasions of Andalucia. The Europeans only regained pre-eminence in the fifteenth century, with Portugal first taking control, and ownership passing to Spain in 1580. In 1936, the port and airstrip were used by Franco, then commanding the Spanish army garrison at Tetouan, to launch his revolt against the Spanish Republic, igniting the Spanish Civil War.

All of this notwithstanding, there's not a great deal to see – or to do. The town is modern, functional and provincial in the dullest Spanish manner, and its most attractive part is within a couple of hundred metres of the ferry dock, where the **Plaza de Africa** is flanked by a pair of Baroque churches, **Nossa Senhora de Africa** (Our Lady of Africa) and the **Cathedral**. Bordering the square, to the west, is the **Foso de San Felipe**, a walled moat that is all that survives of the town's fortress.

Over to the east of the Plaza de Africa, an oldish quarter rambles up from the end of the long **Paseo del Revellin**. To the south, the **Museo de la Legión** (Mon–Fri 10am–2pm, Sat 10am–2pm & 4–6pm; closed Sun), on the Paseo de Colón, offers an intriguing glimpse of Spanish-African military history, crammed with uniforms, weapons and paraphernalia of the infamous Spanish Foreign Legion.

BORDER TRADE: PEOPLE AND DRUGS

Until recently, the economies on both sides of the border seemed to benefit from the enclave, spurred by Ceuta's duty-free status, but there has been growing political friction of late, aggravated by Spain's membership of the European Union (EU). The border here is the frontier between Africa and Europe and the EU is increasingly concerned about traffic in drugs and illegal immigrants, financing a £15m ($22m) hi-tech "wall" with closed circuit TV and sensors along the eight-kilometre boundary.

The money to be made from outflanking these defences has attracted equally hi-tech smugglers, trading in hash, hard drugs, disadvantaged Moroccans, and refugees from as far south as Liberia and Rwanda. The refugees are sent over to Spain nightly, often in small boats unsuited to the short but difficult crossing. Hundreds have drowned, hundreds more are arrested as soon as they land. However, many immigrants make it, either slipping away into Spain, or claiming statelessness, hence making it impossible for the Spanish authorities to return them to Morocco.

The Moroccan government, keen to gain some form of member status in the EU itself, has made efforts to stamp out the trade in both people and drugs. In the past few years, numbers of customs and police officers have been arrested and jailed. The trade, however, continues little affected.

If you walk to the end of the Paseo del Revellin, you can continue along a circuit of the peninsula, which is known as **Monte Acho**, in little over an hour. As the buildings, three to a dozen blocks in width, gradually disappear from view, the land swells into a rounded, pine-covered slope, offering fine views out to the Rock of Gibraltar. Around midway, signs direct you to the **Ermida de San Antonio**, an old convent rebuilt during the 1960s and dominated by a monument to Franco.

And that's about it, as far as diversions go. The local authorities plan to create a town beach, but at present there are no sands to speak of – locals go by bus to **Playa Benzou**, 6km out of town on the northern coast of the peninsula. The duty-free status of the port draws many of the Tangier expatriates on day-trips to buy cheap spirits, and Spanish day-trippers to buy radios and cameras, but neither are very compelling pursuits for casual visitors. If you do want a cheap bottle for Moroccan travels, stop at the *Dumaya* or *Spar* supermarkets opposite the *Mobil* petrol station on Av. Muelle Canonera Dato, by the port, or the *Roma* supermarket on Paseo del Revellin.

Practicalities

There are two **tourist offices** in Ceuta: one at the exit from the ferry terminal and the other a breeze-block box near the local bus terminal at the start of Paseo del Revellin. For more detailed information – or ferry tickets – you will do better at the *Flandria* **travel agency** at Calle de la Indepencia 1 (☎56/51.20.74).

Accommodation

If you plan to stay overnight in Ceuta, be warned that it can be hard to find a room – and not cheap when you do; with its large garrison and its consumer goods, the town has a constant flow of Spanish families. Accommodation problems are compounded at **festival times**, the main events being Carnival (February), Holy Week, the Fiesta de Nuestra Señora de Monte Carmel (July 16), and the Fiesta de Nuestra Señora de Africa on August 5.

Most of the dozen or so hotels and *hostales*, and cheaper *pensiones*, *casas de huespedes* and *fondas* are to be found along the main thoroughfare, Paseo del Revellin, or its extensions, Calle Camoens and Calle Real. Some of the cheaper places are, as on the Spanish mainland, easy to miss, distinguished only by their blue and white signs (H for Hostal; P for Pension; CH for Casa de Huespedes; F for Fonda). There is at present no town **campsite** – ignore signs for *Camping Marguerita*, which has been closed for some time.

CHEAP

Pensión Charito [G], Calle Arrabal 5 (☎56/51.39.82). The best and most welcoming of a number of small, cheap lodgings in this area (ask to be directed elsewhere if it is full). Cold showers. Double rooms 1500–2000ptas.

Youth Hostel (Pousada de Juventud) [D], Plaza Rafael Gilbert 27. Centrally placed: take the steps up from Paseo de Revellin, past the Gran Muralla Chinese restaurant, and turn right at the top. Dormitory beds and rooms for two to six people, but open in July and August only. IYHFA cards are advisable. 1700ptas per person.

MODERATE

Hotel Africa [A], 9 Avda. Muelle Canonero Dato (☎56/50.94.67). A comfortable, air-conditioned three-star hotel, sited right opposite the ferry terminal. Doubles 7000–8500ptas.

Gran Hotel Ulises [E], Calle Camoens 5 (☎56/51.45.40). An old and respectable four-star business hotel on a rather busy street. Doubles 7500ptas.

Pensión Real [F], Calle Real 1 (☎56/51.14.49). A shift upmarket but this is a pleasant, comfortable little pensión. Doubles 4000ptas.

Hotel-Residencia Skol [off map], Avda. Reyes Catolicos 6 (☎56/50.47.18). A quiet two-star hotel, 1km uphill from the centre – off our map to the west. Doubles 5000ptas.

EXPENSIVE

Gran Hotel La Muralla [B], Plaza de Africa 15 (☎56/51.49.40). Ceuta's characterful old *parador* remains the prime choice if you can afford it. 12,500ptas.

Hotel Puerta de Africa [C], Gran Via 2 (☎56/51.71.91). A new four-star hotel with a gleaming white atrium and quite luxurious rooms. Doubles 10,000ptas.

Eating and drinking

Ceuta's main concentration of restaurants is around the Plaza de la Constitucion. Promsing options include:

SPANISH/SEAFOOD

Club Nautico, Calle Edrissis (☎56/51.44.00). A small fish restaurant, just off Paseo de las Palmeras and overlooking the fishing harbour. Open 1–4pm and 7pm till late. Moderate.

Restaurante Marina, on a side street between the Paseo del Revellin and Paseo de la Marina Española. Good place for coffee and *tostadas* to start the day, or for full meals later on. Moderate to expensive.

Marisqueria Silva, Calle Real 87. A tiny restaurant (it's actually squeezed between nos 85 and 87) with fish and seafood specialities. Moderate to expensive.

Restaurant La Torre, in the *Hotel La Muralla*, Plaza de Africa (☎56/51.49.40). Generally reckoned to be the best restaurant in town, serving Andalucian classics. Expensive.

CHINESE

China Town, Marina Club (☎56/50.90.53). A new, cheerful and busy Chinese restaurant by the ferry terminal. Cheap to moderate.

Gran Muralla, Plaza de la Constitución 4 (☎56/51.76.25). A popular, long-established Chinese restaurant with extensive menu and sweeping views over the harbour. It's located up the steps from the square and near the youth hostel. Moderate.

ITALIAN

Café Pizzeria Roma, at the junction of Calle Arrabal and Paseo de la Marina Española. A friendly pizza/pasta place. Cheap to moderate.

Ferries

Leaving Ceuta **by ferry** for Algeciras, you can normally turn up at the port, buy tickets, and board a ferry within a couple of hours. The two periods to avoid, as at Tangier, are the end of the **Easter week** (Semana Santa) holiday and the **last week of August**, when the ferries can be full for days on end with Moroccan workers and their families returning to northern Europe.

If you plan to use the quicker **hydrofoil service** to Algeciras, it's best to book the previous day – though you should be OK outside the high season; details and tickets are available from the agents at Avenida Muelle Caõnero Dato 6 (☎56/51.60.41), by the ferry terminal.

For details of ferry services, see p.8. Be aware that all arrivals from Ceuta need to go through customs at Algeciras – and drug suspects are very thoroughly searched.

ENTERING MOROCCO FROM CEUTA: FNIDEQ

Since the Algeciras–Ceuta ferries and hydrofoils are quicker than those to Tangier (and the ferries significantly cheaper for cars or motorbikes), Ceuta is a popular **point of entry**. Coming over on a first visit to Morocco, however, try to arrive early in the day so that you have plenty of time to move on to Tetouan – and possibly beyond. There is no customs/passport check at the port. You don't officially enter Morocco until the border at **FNIDEQ**, 3km out of town. This can be reached by local bus from the centre of Ceuta (turn left as you come off the ferry or hydrofoil and it is about 800m away, in Plaza de la Constitución).

At **the border**, formalities are brief on the **Spanish side** (at least, if you are leaving Spain: searches are common for those coming back – and there are long tailbacks of cars on Sunday evenings). On the **Moroccan side**, they are often convoluted and time-consuming, especially for drivers. What you need to obtain to get across is a registration form (yellow or photocopied white) for yourself, and, if you have a car, an additional green form; these are available – if you ask for them – from the security *chefs* outside the frontier post. The car form requires inconvenient details such as chassis number and date of registration. If you despair of getting a form and having it processed, you can always enlist an official porter (they have badges – ask to see them) for a 10dh tip; don't get hooked up with an unofficial tout if you can avoid it. The whole business can take ten minutes on a good day, an hour or two on a bad one.

Once across and into Morocco proper, the easiest transport is a shared **grand taxi** to **Tetouan** (20dh per person) or **Chaouen** (60dh per person); buses also run infrequently to Tetouan. There are **exchange facilities**, including *BMCE* and *Banque Populaire* bank offices, which accept cash and travellers' cheques, at the frontier.

Drivers should note that **petrol/gas** in Ceuta is about 40 percent cheaper than in Morocco, so stock up as best you can.

Tetouan

If you're a first-time visitor to Morocco, coming from Ceuta, **TETOUAN** will be your introductory experience to a Moroccan city: a disadvantage that you'll quickly be made aware of. The Medina here seems – initially – overwhelming and totally unfamiliar, and the hustlers, often dealing large quantities of *kif* from the nearby Rif mountains, have the worst reputation in Morocco. On the positive side, the city boasts a new university, albeit based at Martil, 11km to the east, on the coast, so people you meet are just as likely to be genuine students. Nonetheless, you do need to keep your wits about you for the first few hours, especially at the bus station where pickpockets and con men await.

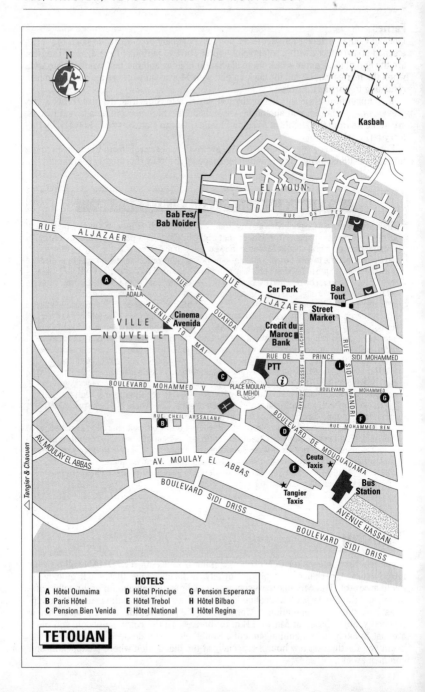

N

Kasbah

EL AYOUN

RUE DE FES

Bab Fes/
Bab Noider

RUE   ALJAZAER

RUE EL OUAHDA

RUE

ALJAZAER

Car Park

Bab
Tout

Street
Market

PL. AL
ADALA

AVENUE 10 MAI

Cinema
Avenida

Credit du
Maroc
Bank

RUE SIDI MOHAMMED

VILLE
NOUVELLE

RUE DE   PRINCE

PTT

AVENUE YOUSSEF BEN TACHFINE

RUE SIDI MANDRI

BOULEVARD   MOHAMMED V

PLACE MOULAY
EL MEHDI

BOULEVARD   MOHAMMED   V

BOULEVARD MOHAMMED V

RUE CHKIL ARSSALANE

BOULEVARD DE MOUQUAUAMA

RUE MOHAMMED BEN

AV. MOULAY EL ABBAS

Ceuta
Taxis

Bus
Station

AV. MOULAY. EL ABBAS

BOULEVARD SIDI DRISS

Tangier
Taxis

AVENUE HASSAN

Tangier & Chaouen

BOULEVARD
SIDI DRISS

HOTELS

A Hôtel Oumaima   D Hôtel Principe   G Pension Esperanza
B Paris Hôtel   E Hôtel Trebol   H Hôtel Bilbao
C Pension Bien Venida F Hôtel National   I Hôtel Regina

TETOUAN

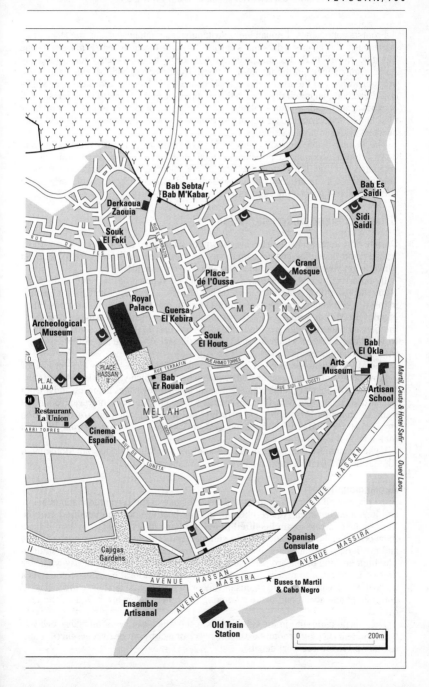

Bab Sebta/
Bab M'Kabar

Bab Es
Saidi

Derkaoua
Zaouia

Sidi
Saidi

Souk
El Foki

RUE ELJARIZIN

RUE DE FES

Grand
Mosque

Place
de l'Oussa

Royal
Palace

Guersa
El Kebira

M E D I N A

Archeological
Museum

Souk
El Houts

Bab
El Okla

RUE TERRAFIN

Arts
Museum

RUE AHMED TORRES

PLACE
HASSAN II

Bab
Er Rouah

RUE SIDI EL YOUSTI

Artisan
School

PL. AL
JALA

MELLAH

Restaurant
La Union

ARBI TORRES

Cinema
Español

RUE DE LA LUNETA

AVENUE HASSAN II

Martil, Ceuta & Hotel Safir

Oued Laou

Spanish
Consulate

AVENUE MASSIRA

Cajigas
Gardens

AVENUE HASSAN II

AVENUE MASSIRA

★ Buses to Martil
& Cabo Negro

Ensemble
Artisanal

Old Train
Station

0   200m

From its approaches, Tetouan looks strikingly beautiful, poised atop the slope of an enormous valley against a dark mass of rock. Its name (pronounced *Tet-tá-wan*) means "open your eyes" in Berber, an apparent reference to the town's hasty construction by Andalucian refugees in the fifteenth century. The refugees, both Muslims and Jews, brought with them the most refined sophistication of Moorish Andalucia – an aristocratic tradition that is still reflected in the architecture of the Medina. Their houses, full of extravagant detail, are quite unlike those of other Moroccan towns; indeed, with their tiled lintels and wrought-iron balconies, they seem much more akin to the old Arab quarters of Córdoba and Seville.

The Spanish connection was reinforced by colonization in the early years of this century, Tetouan becoming a provincial capital of the Spanish northern protectorate, encompassing the Rif Mountains. Spanish is still the second language of older Tetouanis and there are many other reminders of mainland Spain, particularly in the cuisine and in *el paseo* – the summer evening stroll.

Orientation and accommodation

Despite first impressions (particularly if you arrive at the chaotic bus station with its "guides" and "students" laying claim to new arrivals), Tetouan is not too hard a city in which to get your bearings – or to find your own way around.

If you arrive by bus, or by *grand taxi*, you'll find yourself on the edge of the **Ville Nouvelle** – slightly left of centre near the bottom of our town map. Built by the Spanish in the 1920s, this quarter of town follows a straightforward grid. At its centre is **Place Moulay El Mehdi**, with the *PTT* (post/telephone office) and main banks. From there the pedestrianized Boulevard Mohammed V runs east **to Place Hassan II** and the **Royal Palace**, beyond which lies the Medina, still partially walled and entered through the Bab Rouah gateway.

The **Medina** is not as large as it appears and, by day at least, you won't get lost for long without coming to an outer wall or gate – beyond which you can loop back to the Ville Nouvelle. Specific points of interest are detailed in the pages following and are not too hard to find on your own. If this is your first foray into Morocco, however, you might want to consider arranging an **official guide** at the helpful **tourist office** (☎09/96.19.16; Mon–Fri 8.30am–noon & 2.30–6.30pm), a few metres from Place El Mehdi at 30 Bd. Mohammed V.

If you run into trouble, the main **police station** is on Rue de Prince Sidi Mohammed (the former Bd. General Franco – as some signs still proclaim).

Accommodation

Try to ignore all offers from touts and head for one of the recommendations below and keyed on our map. You're likely to get the best deal at the **classified hotels**. Most of the thirty-or-so **unclassified pensions** (including the few we've listed) raise their prices well above basic rates in summer and offer little security against touts and hustlers; some, also, are distinctly seedy, frequented by dealers and prostitutes. The high pension prices are partly because newly arrived tourists will pay whatever they're asked but also reflect demand. With its excellent local beaches, Tetouan is a popular Moroccan resort and rooms in July or August can be in short supply. If at all possible, phone ahead and make a booking. All hotels below are keyed on the map overpage.

There is no **campsite** in the city. The nearest – which can be useful fallbacks if you have problems finding a room – are on the beach or nearby on the river at **Martil**, 11km out (see p.115 for transport details).

CHEAP

Pension Bien Venida [C], Av. 10 Mai – just off Place Moulay El Mehdi (no phone). You could do worse than this central pension but it's best considered a fallback. ①

Hôtel Bilbao [H], 7 Bd. Mohammed V (☎09/96.79.39). This is one of the cheapest unclassified pensions but centrally placed and reasonably clean, with cold showers in the rooms. ①

Pension Esperanza [G], 11 Bd. Mohammed V (no phone). Located on the third floor, above the BCM bank, this is another decent cheap, unclassified pension. ①

Hôtel National [F], 8 Rue Mohammed Ben Larbi Torres (☎09/96.32.90). Reasonable, old-fashioned hotel with a patio bar and restaurant; some of the rooms are a shade musty but most have bath or shower. The hotel sometimes insists on full board in midsummer. ①

Hôtel Principe [D], 20 Av. Youssef Ben Tachfine (no phone). A decent cheapie with comfortable rooms, some of them with (functioning) showers. Sited midway up from the bus station to the main *place* of the Ville Nouvelle, just off the pedestrianized strip of Bd. Mohammed V. Has a ground-floor café for breakfast and snacks. ①

Hôtel Trebol [E], 3 Av. Yacoub El Mansour (☎09/96.20.93). Right behind the bus station so very noisy if you get a room at the front; still, it's safe, clean, and has showers in all rooms. ①

MODERATE

Paris Hôtel [B], 11 Rue Chkil Arssalane (☎09/96.67.50). An adequate if rather drab hotel in a central (and sometimes noisy) location. Still, it's clean and prices are reasonable. ②

Hôtel Oumaima [A], Av. 10 Mai (☎09/96.34.73). Central, clean and functional, offering decent value for money. There's a ground floor café for breakfast. ②

Hôtel Regina [I], 8 Rue Sidi Mandri (☎09/96.21.13). An adequate small hotel with en-suite rooms (though erratic hot water). ①

EXPENSIVE

Hôtel Safir, Rue Kennedy/Route de Ceuta (☎09/96.70.44). Package tour hotel, 3km out from the city centre on the Ceuta road. Comfortable – with a pool, restaurant and nightclub – but hardly worth the extra money and out of town inconvenience. ④

Note: the **Hôtel Dersa** – which used to be the city's best hotel – is not recommended, having dropped all three stars and become a seedy den of dealers and prostitutes.

The Medina

Tetouan has been occupied twice by the Spanish. It was seized, briefly, as a supposed threat to Ceuta, from 1859 to 1862, a period which saw the Medina converted to a town of almost European appearance, complete with street lighting. Then in 1913 a more serious, colonial occupation began. Tetouan served first as a military garrison for the subjugation of the Rif, later as the capital of the **Spanish Protectorate Zone**. As such it almost doubled in size to handle the region's trade and administration, and it was here, in 1936, that General Franco issued his proclamation of uprising against the Spanish Republican government, beginning the Spanish Civil War.

For Tetouan's Moroccan population, there was little progress during the Spanish colonial period. "Native tradition" was respected to the extent of leaving the Medina intact, and even restoring its finer mansions, but Spanish administration retained a purely military character and only a handful of schools was opened throughout the entire zone. This legacy had effects well beyond independence in 1956, and the town, alongside its Rif hinterland, adapted with difficulty to the new nation, dominated by the old French zone. It was at the centre of anti-government rioting as recently as 1984.

Place Hassan II and the Mellah

To explore Tetouan, the place to start is **Place Hassan II**, the old meeting place and former market square. Completely remodelled in 1988, this is a squeaky-clean public square, with a shiny pavement of Islamic motifs, minaret-like floodlights at each corner and a brand-new Royal Palace – replacing the old Spanish consulate and incorporating parts of a nineteenth-century Caliphal Palace that stood beside it.

The usual approach to the Medina is through **Bab Er Rouah** (Gate of the Winds), the archway just south of the Royal Palace. The lane on the right, just before the archway, opens on to Rue Al Qods, the main street of the **Mellah**, the old Jewish quarter. This was created as late as 1807, when the Jews were moved from an area around the Grand Mosque. Very few of the population remain today, although if you ask around someone will point out the old synagogues, the oldest of which, the eighteenth-century **Yitzhak Benoualid**, remains in use.

Into the Medina: the souks

Entering the Medina proper, at Bab Er Rouah, you find yourself on **Rue Terrafin**, a relatively wide lane which (with its continuations) cuts straight across to the east gate, Bab El Okla. Along the way a series of alleys give access to most of the town's food and craft *souks*. The **Souk El Houts**, a small shaded square directly behind the grounds of the Royal Palace, is one of the most active: devoted to fish in the mornings, meat in the afternoons, and with an all-day smattering of local pottery stalls.

From the north side of the Souk El Houts, two lanes wind up through a mass of alleys, *souks* and passageways towards Bab Sebta. Following the one on the right (east) for about twenty metres you'll see an opening to another small square. This is the **Guersa El Kebira**, essentially a cloth and textile *souk*, where a number of stalls sell the town's highly characteristic *foutahs* – strong and brilliantly striped lengths of rug-like cotton, worn as a cloak and skirt by the Djebali and Riffian women.

Leaving the Guersa at its top right-hand corner, you should emerge more or less on **Place de l'Oussa**, another beautiful little square, easily recognized by an ornate, tiled fountain and trellis of vines. Along one of its sides is an imposing nineteenth-century **Xharia**, or almshouse; on another is an *artesania* shop, elegantly tiled and with good views over the quarter from its roof.

Beyond the square, still heading up towards Bab Sebta, are most of the specific **craft souks** – among them copper and brass workers, renowned makers of *babouches* (pointed leather slippers), and carpenters specializing in elaborately carved and painted wood. Most of the shops along the central lane here – **Rue El Jarrazin** – focus on the tourist trade, but this goes much less for the *souks* themselves.

So, too, with the nearby *souks* around **Rue de Fes**, which is reached most easily by following the lane beside the Royal Palace from Place Hassan II. This is the main thoroughfare of a much more mundane area selling ordinary everyday goods, with the occasional villagers' **Joutia**, or flea market. At its main intersection – just to the right as you come out on to the lane up from Place Hassan II – is **Souk El Foki**, once the town's main business sector, though it's little more than a wide alleyway. Following this past a small perfume *souk* and two sizeable mosques, you meet up with Rue El Jarrazin just below **Bab Sebta** (also known as Bab M'Kabar).

Walk out this way, passing (on your left) the superb portal of the **Derkaoua Zaouia** (no admission to non-Muslims), headquarters of the local Derkaoua brotherhood, and you enter a huge **cemetery**, in use since at least the fifteenth century and containing unusually elaborate Andalucian tombs. Fridays excluded, non-Muslims are tolerated in most Moroccan cemeteries, and walking here you get illuminating views over the Medina and across the valley to the Rif.

Had you proceeded along the newly re-roofed main drag of Rue Terrafin/Rue Ahmed Torres/Rue Sidi El Yousti, you would have reached the eastern edge of the Medina at **Bab El Okla**. The quarter to the north of here, below the Grand Mosque, was the Medina's most exclusive residential area and contains some of its finest mansions.

Walking towards the gate you see signs for a *Palais*, one of the best of the buildings, but converted into a carpet and crafts warehouse aimed at tourists.

The Museum of Moroccan Arts and the Crafts School

Considerably more authentic, and an interesting comparison for quality, is the **Museum of Moroccan Arts** (*Musée d'Art Marocain*), whose entrance is just outside Bab El Okla. A former arms bastion, the museum has one of the more impressive collections around of traditional crafts and ethnographic objects. Take a look particularly at the *zellij* – enamelled tile mosaics – and then cross the road to the **Crafts School** (*École des Métiers*), where you can see craftsmen working at new designs in the old ways, essentially unmodified since the fourteenth century. Perhaps owing to its Andalucian heritage, Tetouan actually has a slightly different *zellij* technique to other Moroccan cities – the tiles are cut before rather than after being fired. A slightly easier process, it is frowned upon by the craftsmen of Fes, whose own pieces are more brittle but brighter in colour and closer fitting.

Both school and museum are – in theory – open 8.30am–noon and 2.30–6.30pm Mon–Fri, though the hours are often changed (they are displayed on the clockfaces outside), and the school is often closed (for most of August, for example).

The Centre Artisanal and Archaeological Museum

Outside the Medina the most interesting sight is the **Centre Artisanal** on the main road below the town. The regular exhibits on the ground floor are well worth a check if you're planning to make purchases in the *souks* and want to assess prices and quality first. But where it scores most highly is in the displays of craftworking. Go up the stairs, at either the front or back of the main building, and you come to a fascinating array of carpet and embroidery workshops, while outside the building there are metalwork, basketry and musical instrument artisans at work.

If time needs filling, there is also a pleasant, if rather unmemorable, **Archaeological Museum** (same hours as Museum of Moroccan Arts, above). This was assembled during the Spanish protectorate, so it features exhibits from throughout their zone, including rock carvings from the Western Sahara. Highlights, as so often in North Africa, are the Roman mosaics, mostly gathered from Lixus and the oft-plundered Volubilis. Other than these, the most interesting exhibits are concerned with the stone circle at Mzoura (see p.95), including a model and aerial photos.

Eating, entertainment and practicalities

Tetouan is a fairly small city but it offers a good spread of restaurants, some (generally dive-like) bars, a scattering of cinemas, and the chance to catch one of the best music groups in the country.

Eating

As ever, the cheapest food is to be found in the **Medina**, particularly the stalls inside Bab Er Rouah and along Rue de la Luneta in the old Mellah quarter. For variety, try one of the many places on or around Bd. Mohammed V or Rue Mohammed Ben Larbi Torres in the **Ville Nouvelle**. Good choices include:

RESTAURANTS

Restaurant Granada, at the junction of Bd. Mohammed V and Place Al Jala. Spotless and cheap café-restaurant with the usual soups and *tajines*, and above average *couscous*.

Restaurant La Union (formerly known as *Restaurant Moderno*), 1 Pasaje Achaach, off Rue Mohammed Ben Larbi Torres – to find it, go through the arcades opposite Cinema Español.

Excellent budget meals from an extensive menu – and with fast, friendly service. No aolcohol. Open 9am–9pm daily.

Restaurant Restinga, 21 Bd. Mohammed V – almost opposite the tourist office. Eat indoors or in a courtyard at this very pleasant restaurant that's been serving *tajine, couscous* and fried fish twelve hours a day (11.30am–11.30pm) since 1968. Beer available with meals.

Restaurant Café Saigon, 2 Rue Mohammed Ben Larbi Torres. Mainstream Spanish-Moroccan cooking, despite the name. But it's a popular place, and does a good paella. Open daily 6am–midnight.

CAFÉS AND SNACK BARS

Pic-Nic Cafétérie Hamburger, 6 Av. 10 Mai. A lively snack bar for breakfast and snacks. Open 8am–10pm.

Cafétérie Pâtisserie Smir, 17 Bd. Mohammed V. Rich gateaux, sweets and soft drinks. Open 6am–11pm.

Music

The Orquesta Andalusi de Tetouan is one of the best-known groups playing Moroccan-Andalucian music, a seductive style awash with oriental strings. It was founded, and is still conducted, by Abdessadaq Chekana, and his brother Abdellah leads on lute. They often play in Tetouan and you may be able to catch them locally at an official reception, or at a wedding or festival; ask at the tourist office, who may be able to help.

The orchestra has recorded with Spanish flamenco singer Juan Peña Lebrijano and has toured with British composer Michael Nyman (best known for his soundtracks for Peter Greenaway's films – and for *The Piano*). Despite such collaborations, none of them reads music; everything is committed to memory.

Cinema

Two good cinemas are the *Avenida*, on Place Al Adala (off Av. 10 Mai) and the *Monumental*, near the *Hôtel Principe* (keyed D on our map). The *Español*, near the *Restaurant La Union*, has an exclusive diet of kung fu and Indian epics.

Markets

There is a regular **street market** by Bab Tout, spilling out of the gates and along Rue Aljazaer. This is well worth a stroll and is only a couple of blocks north of Bd. Mohammed V.

Leaving Tetouan: transport links

From the main **bus station** there are regular departures to Chaouen, Meknes, Fes and Tangier; ask around for times at the various windows, as both CTM and private companies operate on all of these routes (if it's convenient, best take the CTM*)*. Beware of con men at the station. Tales abound of youths posing as bus officials and demanding "supplements" or "booking fees" on top of your ticket – often on the bus itself; resist and, if needs be, appeal to your fellow passengers.

Tangier/Ceuta

Heading for **Tangier** or **Ceuta** it's easiest to travel by **grand taxi**; these are routine runs – just go along to the ranks (see map) and get a place (currently 30dh and 20dh, respectively); it's also possible to negotiate a price for **Chaouen** (around 250dh – for up to six passengers). Ceuta taxis (or buses) will drop you at the border; once there, you can walk across and pick up a Spanish bus for the 3km into town.

Martil and the beaches

For the **beaches** at Martil and Mdiq – all easy day-trips – buses leave frequently through the day in summer from behind the ornate, old train station on the road to Ceuta, or from the bus station in winter. For **Oued Laou**, there are two buses daily from the main station (7am and 5pm), or – considerably easier – you can share a *grand taxi* (from the Oued Laou road junction).

Train connections

If you prefer to travel by **train**, an **ONCF office** (☎09/96.75.59) on Av. 10 Mai, opposite the Hôtel Oumaima, sells through tickets to Fes, Rabat, Marrakesh, etc, including a connecting bus service (currently leaving at 8.45am and 4pm) to the station of TNINE SIDI LYAMANI, just south of Asilah. The bus (usually *Supratours*) leaves from outside the ONCF office in Tetouan.

The Tetouan beaches: Mdiq to Oued Laou

Despite the numbers of tourists passing through, Tetouan is above all a resort for Moroccans, rich and poor alike – a character very much in evidence on the extensive beaches to the east of the town. Throughout the summer whole villages of family tents appear at **Martil**, **Mdiq** and, particularly, around **Restinga-Smir,** further north. At **Oued Laou**, 40km southeast of Tetouan, there's a younger and slightly alternative atmosphere with summer colonies of German, French and, to a lesser extent, British and American travellers.

West: Martil and Mdiq

MARTIL, essentially Tetouan's city beach, was its port as well until the river between the two silted up. From the fifteenth to eighteenth centuries, it maintained an active corsair fleet, twice provoking Spanish raids to block the harbour. Today it is a small semi-active fishing village with a slightly ramshackle appearance, owing to unmade roads and the rows of tourist huts along the seafront. The beach, stretching all the way around to the headland of Cabo Negro, is superb – a stretch of fine, yellow sand that is long enough (at 8km!) to remain uncrowded, despite its summer popularity and colonization by *Club Med* and other tourist complexes.

There are various options for accommodation. For a simple pension **room**, try the *Residence Restinga* (☎09/97.95.27; ②) at 59 Av. de la Mer or the *Hôtel Nuzha* (☎09/97.92.32; ②) at 9 Rue Miramar. Somewhat more expensive, but good value for money, is the *Hôtel Étoile de la Mer* (☎09/96.92.76; ③), on the seafront by the *grands taxis* stand; known locally as the *Nejuna El Bahr*, it has a popular café and restaurant. The *Restaurant Rio Martil*, opposite, competes with good seafood meals.

Of the two **campsites**, *Camping Martil*, set just back from the beach, is friendly and cheap, though not a place to leave bags unattended. *Camping Oued El Maleh* is further out to the north (signposted from town), reached along a river bed. It's a dusty site but safe enough and has some shade and a useful shop; the beach is just 200m away, through a wood.

Mdiq

MDIQ is a lovely coastal village and fishing port, which can be approached via Martil or direct from Tetouan (18km on the P28). Though it is getting a little overdeveloped, its beach is superb and there are some nice places to stay. The best of the cheaper options is the seafront *Hôtel Playa* (☎09/97.51.66; ②), which has a bar and a good restaurant. Nearby, but at the other extreme, is a major resort hotel, the *Golden Beach* (☎09/97.50.97; ④). There is no campsite.

Restinga-Smir and Fnideq

RESTINGA-SMIR is more a collective name for a length of beach than for an actual place or village: an attractive strip of the Mediterranean, but a little too dominated by package hotels and "holiday villages". Nevertheless, many Moroccan families still camp in the woods between here and Fnideq. The rather spartan but inexpensive *Al Fraja* **campsite**, here, opposite the *El Andalouz* tourist complex and 15km from Fnideq, makes a good first or last stop in the country in summer; in winter it's open but deserted and possibly not so secure.

In addition, there are several **hotels** in **FNIDEQ**, just 2km from the Ceuta border. The best of these is the *Hôtel Ceuta* (☎09/97.61.40; ②), on the main drag, Avenue Mohammed V. Fnideq, however, has little to recommend it, except a busy market for cheap Spanish goods; Moroccans from Tetouan and even Tangier come here regularly for household items and clothes.

Southeast: in the shadow of the Rif

Southeast of Tetouan the coastline is almost immediately distinct. For a few kilometres, the road (S608) follows the sea and the still more or less continuous beach, dotted in summer with communities of tents. But very soon it begins to climb into the foothills of the Rif, a first taste of the crazily zigzagging Moroccan mountain roads, though in this case always with the sea down below, and including the occasional swoop down to cross the estuary of a mountain stream, dry in summer but often destructive in winter – watch out for diversions around broken bridges. Alongside the beach, near Cap Mazari, is the nicely shaded *Camping Azla* (14km from Tetouan) with a small café/shop.

Tetouan is connected to Oued Laou by local **bus** (#9) and **grand taxi**.

Oued Laou

When you finally emerge at **OUED LAOU** (44km from Tetouan), you're unlikely to want to return too immediately. A stay, in any case, is a positive option. Oued Laou is not an especially pretty place – Riffian villages tend to look spread out and lack any core. However, it has a terrific, near-deserted beach, which extends for miles on each side, particularly to the southeast, where the river has created a wide, fertile bay down to Kâaseras, 8km distant. Equally important, Oued Laou is a very easy-going sort of place and one of the best parts of the Rif to meet and talk with local people. Hustlers have nothing to hustle except *kif* and rooms, and aren't too bothered about either; having come out here, off the tourist track, it is assumed that you're not completely innocent.

There are two small **hotels** and a campsite. The *Hôtel-Restaurant Oued Laou* (①) is open all year round and has hot showers in winter; the *Hôtel-Restaurant Laayoune* (⑩) opens from mid-June to mid-September only and has no showers. They are to be found one block from the beach on Boulevard Massira. If they are full, or if you want to pay a bit less, they'll find you **rooms** elsewhere – everyone knows everyone here. *Camping Oued Laou* (☎09/99.39.95; open year round), alongside the muncipal building, is a secure site, a hundred metres back from the beach. There's a small restaurant and shops nearby and a mosque with an unusual octagonal minaret. On Saturdays, there is a **souk**, held 3km inland of the beachside settlement, which draws in villagers from all over the valley; look for the terracotta pottery, fired locally.

East: Kâaseras, El Jebha and the roads to Chaouen

Heading east from Oued Laou is quite complicated without your own transport. The coast road is now paved all the way to **El Jebha** (see below), but just one bus a day, leaving Tetouan at 7am, travels the full six-hour-plus, 137km, route, via Oued Laou, Kâaseras, Targha and Bou Hamed.

It's little problem to get a taxi as far as **KÂASERAS**, however, just twenty minutes from Oued Laou – and in similar mould. A tiny resort, it is geared towards Moroccans camping on the beach, though there are usually a few rooms to be had, if you ask around. If you are heading from Oued Laou to Chaouen, it's possible to drive (or get a bus connection) via Kâaseras, and continue along the minor road (8304) up the Oued Laou valley – which includes some impressive gorge sections. At present, a bus from Kâaseras leaves for Chaouen at 6am, and returns in the afternoon, leaving Chaouen at 5pm.

It's also possible to keep to the coast and make a circuit to Chaouen via **BOU HAMED** (38km from Oued Laou) or, further on, via **EL JEBHA** (93km from Oued Laou). Bou Hamed is a largish village on a broad alluvial plain. The road from here into the Rif calls for a Renault 4L or better still a 4x4. The Rif road (8310) from El Jebha is easier and shorter but El Jebha itself is not the most appealing of destinations – a shabby sort of place, with little beyond a lighthouse and a few fishermen's cottages.

Chaouen (Chefchaouen, Xaouen)

Shut in by a fold of mountains, **CHAOUEN** becomes visible only once you have arrived – a dramatic approach to a town which, until the arrival of Spanish troops in 1920, had been visited by just three Europeans. Two of these were missionary explorers: Charles de Foucauld, a Frenchman who spent just an hour in the town, disguised as a rabbi, in 1883, and William Summers, an American who was poisoned by the townsfolk here in 1892. The third, in 1889, was the British journalist Walter Harris (see "Contexts"), whose main impulse, as described in his book, *Land of an African Sultan*, was "the very fact that there existed within thirty hours' ride of Tangier a city in which it was considered an utter impossibility for a Christian to enter".

This impossibility – and Harris very nearly lost his life when the town was alerted to the presence of "a Christian dog" – had its origins in the foundation of the town in 1471. The region hereabouts was already sacred to Muslims due to the presence of the tomb of Moulay Abdessalam Ben Mchich – patron saint of the Djebali tribesmen and one of the "four poles of Islam" – and over the centuries acquired a considerable reputation for pilgrimage and *marabouts* – "saints", believed to hold supernatural powers. The town was actually established by one of Moulay Abdessalam's *shereefian* (descendant of the Prophet) followers, Moulay Rachid, as a secret base from which to attack the Portuguese in Ceuta and Ksar es Seghir. In the ensuing decades, as the population was boosted by Muslim and Jewish refugees from Spain, Chaouen grew increasingly anti-European and autonomous. For a time, it was the centre of a semi-independent Emirate, exerting control over much of the northwest, in alliance with the Wattasid sultans of Fes. Later, however, it became an almost completely isolated backwater. When the Spanish arrived in 1920, they were astonished to find the Jews here speaking, and in some cases writing, medieval Castilian – a language extinct in Spain for nearly four hundred years.

These days, Chaouen is well established on the excursion routes and indeed becoming a little over-concerned with tourism. There are the inevitable *souks* and stalls for the tour groups and a major hotel disfigures the twin peaks (*ech-Chaoua*: the horns) from which the town takes its name. But local attitudes towards tourists, and to the predominantly backpacking travellers who stop over, are generally relaxed, the Medina pensions are among the friendliest and cheapest around, and to stay here a few days and walk in the hills remains one of the best possible introductions to Morocco.

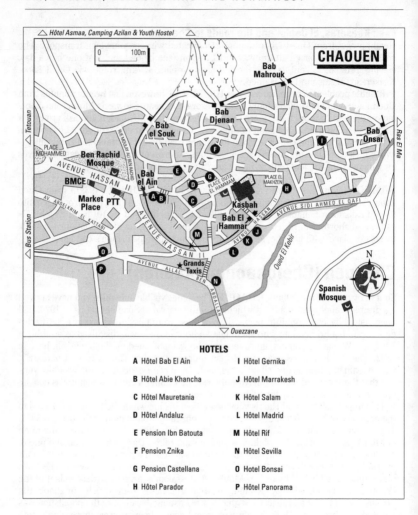

Orientation and accommodation

With a population of around 36,000 – a tenth of Tetouan's – Chaouen is more like a large village in size and feel, and confusing only on arrival. **Buses** drop you at the new *gare routière*, 20–30 minutes' walk from the town centre; **grands taxis** from Tetouan and Ouezzane drop much more centrally, close to the *Hôtel Sevilla*. The marketplace and a straggle of modern buildings are to be found in the Ville Nouvelle alongside Av. Hassan II, which is dominated by the Ben Rachid mosque. You'll find a *PTT* and three **banks** here, all of which change money and travellers' cheques.

To reach the Medina, walk up across the marketplace to the tiny arched entrance, **Bab El Ain**, just beyond the prominent *Hôtel Magou*. Through the gate a clearly dominant lane winds up through the town to the main square, **Place Outa El Hammam** (flanked by the gardens and ruined towers of the **Kasbah**) and, beyond, to a second, smaller square, **Place El Makhzen**.

Both along and just off this main route in the Medina are a number of small, **pensions**, most of them converted from private houses. These are the places to stay for anyone wanting to meet and mix with fellow travellers – rooms can be a bit cell-like, but most are exceptionally clean and remarkably inexpensive. For more comfort (and less "community life"), several of the **classified hotels** in the Ville Nouvelle are good value, too, and there's also an old Spanish parador in the heart of the Medina.

Medina

All the recommendations below are grouped close together in the Medina and – with the exception of the four-star *Hôtel Parador* – all charge much the same prices: a very modest 60–100dh for a double room.

CHEAP

Pension Abie Khancha [B], 75 Rue Lalla El Hora (☎09/98.68.79). An excellent new pension, 30m up on the right from the Bab El Ain. A converted house, it has an open courtyard, salon and a high terrace. ⑩

Hôtel Andaluz [D], 1 Rue Hauta (☎09/98.60.34). Small, basic pension, whose rooms face an inner courtyard – not too airy, but otherwise OK, and with a friendly management. It is signposted off to the left at the near end of Place Outa El Hammam. ⑩

Hôtel Bab El Ain [A], 77 Rue Lalla El Hora (☎09/98.69.35). A well-maintained modern conversion, just inside the Bab El Ain on the right. It charges a bit more than most of the pensions but the rooms are comfortable. ①

Pension La Castellana [G], 4 Rue Bouhali (☎09/98.62.95). Just to the left at the near end of Place Outa El Hammam – follow the signs. Aficionados return loyally to the *Castellana* each year, creating a distinctly laid-back and youthful atmosphere; others take one look at the poky rooms and leave. The key is the manager, Abdeslam, who has introduced new hot showers and arranges communal meals and excursions on request. In addition, there is a *hammam* right next door, open for men until noon and women after noon. ⑩

Hostal Gernika [I], 49 Onsar (☎09/98.74.34). This excellent new conversion of an old house by a Spanish woman owner deserves a look. It's in the higher quarter of the Medina, going up towards Bab Onsar. Includes some en-suite rooms. ①

Pension Ibn Batouta [E], Rue Abie Khancha (☎09/98.60.44). One of the quietest of the pensions, with less feel of a "travellers' hangout"; located in an alley to the left, about 70m along from Bab El Ain, beyond the *Restaurant El Baraka*. Cold showers only. ⑩

Hôtel Mauretania [C], 20 Hadi Alami (☎09/98.61.84). For the participatory: communal dormitories, as well as individual rooms, and awash with rock music most hours. Located down a maze of alleys to the southeast of Place Outa El Hammam. ⑩

Pension Znika [F], Rue Znika (☎09/98.66.24). Another new, excellent-value pension, with welcoming management, and plans to add a café-restaurant on its panoramic terrace. ⑩

EXPENSIVE

Hôtel Parador de Chaouen [H], Place El Makhzen (☎09/98.61.36). The former Spanish "grand hotel", once part of the parador chain, recently reconstructed for the package trade. The bar and swimming pool help justify the expense and there are stunning views from the terrace. However, if you're only having an occasional splurge, this isn't special enough. ④

Ville Nouvelle

There is more comfort in the Ville Nouvelle's purpose-built hotels and a few of them have the character to match the Medina pensions. None is far from the Medina, except for the hilltop *Hôtel Asmaa*.

CHEAP TO MODERATE

Hôtel Bonsai (O), 12 Rue Sidi Srif (☎09/98.69.80). A pleasant new hotel in a converted house, with scented orange trees in the garden. Three-en suite rooms, six with common facilities, and sporadic hot water. ⑩

Hôtel Madrid (L), Av. Hassan II (☎09/98.69.82). Another new hotel, tastefully decorated, and with a fine panoramic rooftop breakfast terrace. Fitful hot water ②; or en suite ③

Hôtel Marrakesh (J), Av. Hassan II (☎09/98.71.13). A bright, modern hotel, opened in 1992. Small but comfortable rooms, some en suite. Plus a decent restaurant. ①

Hôtel Panorama (P), 33 Rue Moulay Abderrahmane Chrif. Formerly a pleasant hotel, with great views, but closed as of Spring 1998.

Hôtel Rif (M), 29 Av. Hassan II (☎09/98.69.82). Attracts a mainly youthful clientele, with its well-stocked sound system, bar, restaurant, en-suite rooms, and low rates for long stays. Opinions differ on the management; women travelling alone have, in years past, written to caution others not to stay here. Many travellers rate it a favourite, however. ①

Hôtel Salam (K), 39 Av. Hassan II (☎09/98.62.39). Just below Bab El Hamman and long a favourite with individuals and groups. Back rooms and a shady roof terrace overlook the valley. Meals are served in a salon or on the terrace, which can get a bit crowded with groups at times. Overall, highly recommended. ⑩

Hôtel Sevilla (N), Av. Allal Ben Abdellah (☎09/98.72.85). A little out of the way, and quite a climb from the Medina, but a well-run place with good rooms – most en suite. ①

EXPENSIVE

Hôtel Asmaa (off map), (☎09/98.71.58). An ugly modern building on the site of an old fort, half an hour's walk above the town. The views of the town and valley, and a swimming pool (50dh for non-residents), are its best features. Comfortable rooms geared for package trade but not a very welcoming place. ④

The campsite and youth hostel

Camping Azilan (off map), (☎09/98.69.79). Chaouen's **campsite** is on the hill above the town, by the *Hôtel Asmaa* (see above), whose signs you can follow along the road; on foot, there is a short-cut through the cemetery. It is shaded and inexpensive, with a café and small shop, but can be crowded in summer, and with pensions so cheap it hardly seems worth the 2km-climb.

Youth Hostel Auberge de Jeunesse (off map), (☎09/98.60.31). Adjoining the campsite but closed as of Spring 1998.

The town and river

Like Tetouan, Chaouen's architecture has a strong Andalucian character: less elaborate (and less grand), perhaps, but often equally inventive. It is a town of extraordinary light and colour, its whitewash tinted with blue and edged by soft, golden, stone walls – and it is a place which, for all its present popularity, still seems redolent of the years of isolation. The roofs of its houses, tiled and with eaves, are an obvious physical assertion, in contrast to the flat ones found everywhere else in Morocco. But it is something you can sense about life in general here, even about the people themselves – inbred over many generations.

The souks and Mellah

Since the Medina is so small, it is more than ever a place to explore at random: the things which draw your attention are not so much "sights" as unexpected strands of detail. At some point, though, head for the two main squares, and for the **souks** – just below Place Outa El Hammam.

There are basic town *souks* held on Mondays and Thursdays in the market square, so these, to some degree, have been set up for, or at least geared to, the tourist industry. But both the quality and variety are surprising. When the Spanish arrived – just seven decades ago – Chaouen craftsmen were still working leather in the manner of twelfth-century Córdoba, tanning with bark, and hammering silver to old Andalucian designs. Although you won't see any of this today, the town's carpet and weaving workshops remain active and many of their designs unchanged. Vendors are well used to haggling with travellers, and if you're staying for a few days, prices can fall dramatically.

It's interesting, too, to observe the contrasts in feel between the main, Arab part of Chaouen and the still modestly populated Jewish quarter of the **Mellah**. This is to be found behind the jewellers' *souk*, between the Bab El Ain and the Kasbah.

Place Outa El Hammam and the Kasbah

The elongated **Place Outa El Hammam** is where most of the town's evening life takes place. It's a pretty square, with its cafés overhung by upper rooms (some the preserve of *kif* smokers), though by day, alas, it's virtually obscured by massed ranks of tour buses. On one side of the square is the town's **Kasbah**, a quiet ruin with shady gardens, and a little museum of crafts and old photos (Mon–Sat 9am–1pm & 3–7pm; 10dh). The Kasbah was built, like so many others in northern Morocco, by Moulay Ismail. Inside, and immediately to the right, in the first of its compounds, are the old town prison cells, where Abd El Krim (see p.128) was imprisoned after his surrender in nearby Targuist in 1926. Five years earlier, he had himself driven the Spanish from the town, a retreat which saw the loss of several thousands of their troops.

The *place* was once the main market square, and off to its sides are a number of small **fondouks**; one of the more visible is at the beginning of the lane opposite the Kasbah. The local Djebala tribesmen, who form most of the town's population, have a particular tradition of homosexuality, and there were boy markets held here until as recently as 1937, when they were officially banned by the Spanish administration.

Place El Makhzen and Ras El Ma

Place El Makhzen – the old "government square" – is in some ways a continuation of the marketplace, an elegant clearing with an old fountain, and pottery stalls set up for the package tourists.

If you leave the Medina at this point, it's possible to follow **the river**, the Oued El Kebir, around the outside of the walls, with Bab Onsar up to your left. Here, past a couple of traditional flour-mills, you reach **Ras El Ma** (the water-head), a small, seasonal cascade in the mountainside with water so clear and cold that, in the local phrase, "it knocks your teeth out to drink it". It has long been a favourite picnic spot – and is to an extent a holy place, due to the nearby *marabout*'s tomb of Sidi Abdallah Habti.

Over to the southeast of the town, an enjoyable walk is to the ruined "**Spanish Mosque**". Set on a hilltop, its interior is covered in graffiti, but nevertheless it gives a good sense of the layout of a mosque – normally off-limits in Morocco. Nobody seems to mind you looking around.

Up into the hills

Further afield, a good **day's hike** is to head east, up over the mountains behind Chaouen. As you look at the "two horns" from town, there is a path winding along the side of the mountain on your left. A four-hour (or more) hike will take you up to the other side, where a vast valley opens up, and if you walk further, you'll see the sea. The valley, as even casual exploration will show, is full of small farms cultivating *kif* – as they have done for years. Walking here, you may occasionally be stopped by the military, who are cracking down on foreign involvement in the crop. For more ambitious hikes – and there are some wonderful paths in the area – ask at the pensions about hiring a **guide**. Someone knowledgeable can usually be found to accompany you, for around 50 to 100dh a day; the harder the climb, the more it costs!

CHAOUEN'S HAMMAMS

The uncertain showers in some of the pensions are mitigated by the ease of visiting the local **hammams**. The town, unusually, has separate *hammams* for men and women. The male one is next door to the *Pension Castellana*, off Place Outa El Hammam; the one for women, which is older and much more elaborate, is in the quarter of the *souks* – ask someone to show you the way because it totally defies written directions.

In recent years, entrance to the *hammams* for tourists has been limited, and sometimes refused unless you have a group and book the *hammam* together. Ask your pension/hotel for advice, or for someone to accompany you.

Restaurants and cafés

Compared with the hotels, Chaouen is not overstocked with **restaurants**. Which is not to say there aren't some good choices to search out, most of them in the back streets of the Medina. Worthwhile possibilities include:

Medina

Restaurant Ali Baba, Place Outa El Hammam. Best of the café-restaurants around the square but recommended more for the location than the food.

Restaurant Assada, on a nameless lane just north of Bab El Ain, opposite the *Hôtel Bab El Ain*. A tiny, three-table joint, very friendly, and with fine *tajines*.

Restaurant El Baraka, near *Pension Andaluz*. This is a great little place: a beautiful 150-year-old house, built for a judge, sensitively converted; the food's good, too.

Restaurant Marbella, opposite the fountain on the square between the pensions *Valencia* and *Cordoba* (neither of which we list – ask for Rue Granada). Good simple dishes.

Restaurant Tissemlal, again near the *Pension Valencia* (see above). For our money, the best restaurant in the Medina: a beautifully decorated old house with imaginative French-Moroccan menus. There are a few rooms here, too, if you take a liking to the place.

Ville Nouvelle

Restaurant Ben Rachid and **Restaurant Zouar**, Rue Moulay Ali Ben Rachid – up from the Bab El Ain. Two decent small places with inexpensive, simple menus. Given the choice, the *Ben Rachid* seems more popular with the locals than the *Zouar*.

Restaurant Nakhlil, Av. Hassan II. A modest place, popular with locals.

Practicalities and transport

As noted, Chaouen has most facilities you need, including a post office and banks in the Ville Nouvelle. Its biggest drawback is an edge-of-town bus station – and buses that all too frequently arrive full, with no space for extras.

Swimming

The *Hôtel Parador de Chaouen* has a small pool, open to non-residents for 25dh a day, and there's a larger one at the *Hôtel Asmaa*, which charges 50dh a day.

Alternatively, you can join the locals, by sharing a taxi to a **pool** in the Oued El Hipe a few kilometres downstream – an excellent alternative for which any of the pension staff will give you the details.

Festivals

As the centre of so much *maraboutism*, Chaouen and its neighbouring villages have a particularly large number of **moussems**. The big events are those in Moulay Abdessalam

Ben Mchich (40km away: usually in May) and Sidi Allal El Hadj (August 9). There are dozens of others, however – ask around and you should come upon something.

Buses and grands taxis

As noted, the new **gare routière** is a 20–30 minute walk (or a taxi ride) southwest from the town centre, and problems are compounded in that CTM and most other lines start their Chaouen routes elsewhere so that buses can (despite promises) arrive full, with no available space. The best advice is to visit the bus station the evening before you plan to leave and, if possible, book a ticket in advance.

Fes is the most difficult place to get to and you may have to settle for a bus to Meknes and change there, or alternatively take a local bus or *grand taxi* to Ouezzane, which has a lot more bus and *grand taxi* traffic (including regular *grand taxi* runs to Fes). If all else fails, you could always backtrack to Tetouan by bus or *grand taxi* and travel on from there. Availability tends to be better on the routes to Tetouan, or on the daily departures to the border at Fnideq, to the coast at Oued Laou, and east to Al Hoceima and beyond.

For the more affluent, or anyone who can get a group of people together, **grands taxis** can be **chartered** – a stylish way to travel to Tangier or to Fes. The cost for either trip should be around 450dh, for up to six passengers.

Ouezzane (Wazzan)

OUEZZANE, like Chaouen, has a fine, mountainous site, looping around an outreach of the Djebala mountains. It stands virtually at the edge of the Rif and formed the old traditional border between the *Bled es-Makhzen* (the governed territories) and the *Bled es-Siba* (those of the lawless tribes). As such, the town was an important power base, and particularly so under the last nineteenth-century sultans, when its local sheikhs became among the most powerful in Morocco.

The Ouezzani

The sheikhs – the *Ouezzani* – were the spiritual leaders of the influential **Tabiya brotherhood**. They were *shereefs* (descendants of the Prophet) and came in a direct line from the Idrissids, the first and founding dynasty of Morocco. This, however, seems to have given them little significance until the eighteenth century, when Moulay Abdallah es-Shereef established a *zaouia* (religious cult centre) at Ouezzane. It acquired a huge following, becoming one of the great places of pilgrimage and an inviolable sanctuary.

Unlike Chaouen, the town that grew up around this centre was not itself sacred, but until the turn of this century Jews and Christians were allowed to take only temporary residence in one of the *fondouks* set aside for this purpose. Walter Harris, who became a close friend of the Ouezzani *shereefs* in the late nineteenth century, found the town "the most fanatical that Europeans may visit" and the *zaouia* a virtually autonomous religious court. Strange to relate, however, an Englishwoman, Emily Keane, married in 1877 the principal *shereef*, Si Abdesslem, whom she had met while out riding. For several decades she lived in the town, openly as a Christian, dispensing medical care to the locals. Her *Life Story*, published in 1911 after her husband's death, ends with the balanced summing up: "I do not advise anyone to follow in my footsteps, at the same time I have not a single regret." She is commemorated in the Anglican church in Tangier.

The Zaouia, town and souks

The **Zaouia**, distinguished by an unusual octagonal minaret, is the most striking building in the town, and though the Tabiya brotherhood now maintain their main base elsewhere, it continues to function and is the site of a lively spring **moussem**, or pilgrimage festival. (As in the rest of Morocco, entrance to the *zaouia* area is forbidden to non-Muslims.)

The older quarters of Ouezzane – many of their buildings tiled, gabled and sporting elaborate doors – enclose and rise above the *zaouia*, newer suburbs sprawling into the hills on each side.There is a grandeur in the site though, with the *zouia* off limits, little of specific interest.

The main **souks** climb up from an archway on the main square, Place de l'Indépendance, behind the *Grand Hôtel*. Ouezzane has a local reputation for its woollen rugs – most evident in the weavers' *souk*, around Place Rouida near the top end of the town. Also rewarding is the metalworkers' *souk*, a covered lane under the Mosque of Moulay Abdallah Shereef; to find it, ask directions for the pleasant (and adjacent) *Café Bellevue*. The town also has a couple of *Centres Artesanal* – one facing Place de l'Indépendance, the other on Av. Hassan II.

There is a large **Thursday souk** on the Place de l'Indépendance.

Accommodation and transport

Few tourists stay in Ouezzane, as it is only a couple of hours out of Chaouen, but there are worse places to be stranded. The bus and *grand taxi* terminal is about 50m below the **Place de l'Indépendance**, where you'll also find three basic **hotels**, the *Marhaba*, *Horloge* and *El Elam* (all ⑩). There is little to choose between them though all are preferable to the *Grand Hôtel* just off the square. There is a **hammam** on Av. Mohammed V and grill-cafés on the square.

Buses

Ouezzane provides a useful link if you're travelling by public **transport** (bus or *grand taxi*) between **Chaouen and the Atlantic coast**, or vice versa, or if you're moving on to Meknes or Fes (there are regular *grand taxi* runs to both). There are a fair number of **buses** also to Meknes and Fes, but if you're stopping or staying, buy onward tickets in advance; as with Chaouen it's not unusual for them to arrive and leave full.

travel details

Trains

Four or five trains a day leave Tangier, all running through either **Sidi Kacem** or **Sidi Slimane**, where you may need to get a connection to the Meknes/Fes/Oujda or Rabat/Casablanca/Marrakesh lines. There is a **night train** to Marrakesh, which currently leaves at 10.15pm, arriving 8.20am.

Journey times from Tangier are approximately:

Asilah (50 mins).

Sidi Kacem (2hr 25min).

Sidi Slimane (2hr 20min).

Meknes (4hr)

Fes (5hr)

Taza (8hr)

Oujda (11hr)

Rabat (5hr)

Note: ONCF runs connecting Supratour coaches to/from **Tetouan** from/to Sidi Tnine Lyamani, near **Asilah**.

Buses

From Tangier CTM to Casablanca, via Kenitra and Rabat (5 daily; 7hr); to Fes direct (1 daily; 6hr); to Fes via Tetouan (1 daily; 7hr) and to Tetouan (10 daily; 1hr). Other lines to Asilah (9 daily; 1hr). Laroche (6 daily; 1hr 40min); to Tetouan (18 daily; 1hr 15min); Rabat, via Kenitra (8 daily; 5hr); to Meknes (8 daily; 7hr); and to Fes (4 daily; 8hr).

From Asilah Larache (5 daily; 1hr).

From Larache Ksar El Kebir (3 daily; 40min); Souk El Arba (5; 1hr); Rabat (4; 3hr 30min); Meknes (2; 5hr 30min).

From Souk El Arba Moulay Bousselham (5 daily; 35min); Ouezzane (3; 1hr 30min).

From Ouezzane Meknes (2 daily; 4hr); Fes (2; 5hr 30min); Chaouen (4; 1hr 20min).

From Tetouan CTM to Casablanca (3 daily; 7hr); to Chaouen (up to 6 daily; 1hr 30min); to Nador, via Al Hoceima (2 daily; 9hr 30min); to Fes, via Ouezzane (2 daily; 5hr); and to Tangier (10 daily; 1hr). Other lines to Tangier (18 daily; 1hr 15min); to Chaouen (10 daily, 2hr); to Fnideq (24 daily; 30min); and to Oued Laon (2 daily; 2hr).

From Chaouen CTM to Casablanca (1 daily; 8hr). Other lines to Tetouan (10 daily; 3hr); Ketama/Al Hoceima (2 ; 5hr/8hr); Meknes (1 daily; 5hr 30min); Fes (2 daily; 7hr); El Jebha (2 a week; 7hr).

Grands Taxis

From Tangier Regularly to Tetouan (1hr); less frequently to Larache, Rabat, and occasionally Fes.

From Ouezzane Regularly to Souk El Arba (1hr) and Chaouen (1hr 15min).

From Tetouan Regularly to Tangier (1hr), Oued Laou (1hr 20min) and Fnideq (Ceuta border) (20min).

From Souk El Arba Regularly to Moulay Bousselham (30min) and Larache (50min).

Ferries

See p.8 for details of ferries, hydrofoils and catamarans from Tangier and Ceuta.

Flights

From Tangier In summer, daily (except Sunday) flights on **RAM** to Casablanca and from there to Agadir (six days a week), to Fes (five days a week), to Marrakesh (six days a week), to Ouarzazate (three days a week) and to Oujda (four days a week). In addition, there are direct flights to Agadir (two days a week) and to Al Hoceima (two days a week). In winter, daily (except Sunday) flights on *RAM* to Casablanca and from there to Agadir (six days a week), to Marrakesh (four days a week), Ouarzazate (two days a week). In addition, there are direct flights to Agadir (one day a week) and to Fes (one day a week).

International flights on **RAM**, in summer, to Amsterdam (five days a week), to Barcelona (one day a week), to Brussels (four days a week), to Copenhagen (one day a week), to Frankfurt (one day a week), to London (five days a week), to Madrid (five days a week) and to Paris (one day a week). In winter, to Amsterdam (two days a week), to Barcelona (one day a week), to Brussels (one day a week), to Frankfurt (one day a week), to London (two days a week), to Madrid (five days a week) and to Paris (one day a week).

From Tetouan In summer, three flights a week on **RAM** to Casablanca and from there to Agadir (three days a week), to Marrakesh (two days a week), and to Ouarzazate (two days a week). In addition, there are direct flights to Al Hoceima (one day a week) and to Rabat (one day a week). In winter, two flights a week on *RAM* to Casablanca and from there to Agadir (two days a week), to Marrakesh (two days a week), and to Ouarzazate (two days a week). In addition, there are direct flights to Al Hoceima (two days a week).

CHAPTER TWO

THE MEDITERRANEAN COAST AND THE RIF

Morocco's **Mediterrannean coast** extends for nearly 500km – from the Spanish conclave of Ceuta east to Saïdia on the Algerian border. The westerly reaches around Tetouan, described in the previous chapter (see pp.115–117), shelter the only established resorts. Beyond Tetouan you enter the shadow of the Rif mountains, which restrict access to the sea to a very few points. Such beaches as there are here

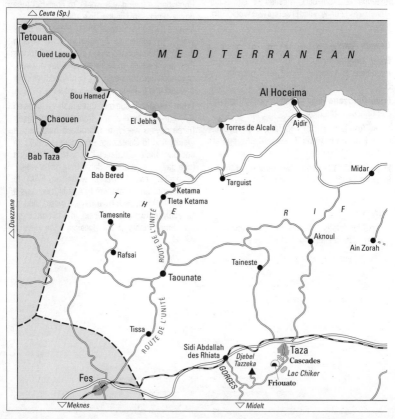

TELEPHONE CODES

Telephone numbers in the Mediterranean Coast and Rif area are prefixed by 06; those in the Taza area 05 and those in the Al Hoceima area 09. When making a call within the region you omit this prefix. For more explanation of phone codes and making calls within (or to) Morocco, see pp.45–46.

---

remain almost entirely undeveloped and for a seaside stop you really need to head east to the fishing harbour and small-time resort of **Al Hoceima**, or to **Saïdia**, beach playground for the city of **Oujda**, at the end of the road. Neither is much visited by foreigners, particularly since the closure of the Moroccan/Algerian frontier, though if you're making a loop east, you'll find Oujda a pleasant, relaxed city, with a scenic side-trip through the **Zegzel** gorges, and further gorges, cutting into the Middle Atlas, at Taza, on the Fes-Oujda road.

Between Al Hoceima and Oujda is a second Spanish conclave, **Melilla**, which with its flights and ferries to Málaga and Almería on "the mainland" sees a fair bit of traffic. These transport links aside, though, Melilla is scarcely worth a trip in itself, other than for bird-watchers, who will find the dunes and lagoons spreading around nearby **Nador** among the richest sites in Morocco.

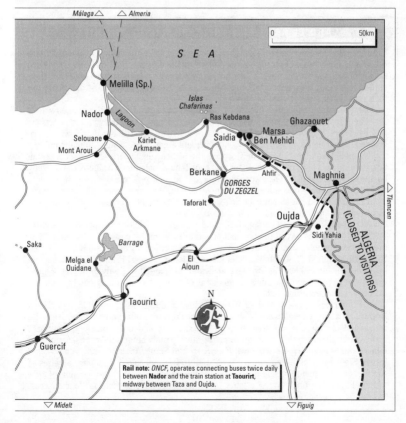

Rail note: ONCF, operates connecting buses twice daily between **Nador** and the train station at **Taourirt**, midway between Taza and Oujda.

The **Rif Mountains** themselves are even less on the tourist trail than the coast – and with some reason. This is wild, isolated country, and always has been, with a tradition of dissent from central government and little relationship with the authorities. A vast, limestone mass, over 300km long and up to 2500m in height, the Rif is in fact the natural boundary between Europe and Africa, and with the Sahara it cuts off central Morocco from Algeria and the rest of the Maghreb. In the past this was a powerful barrier – it took the first recorded European traveller three months to travel from Al Hoceima to Melilla – and even today there is no other part of Morocco where you feel so completely incidental to ordinary local life. That is, unless you happen to be involved in smuggling. For the Riffian economy, these days, is based very largely on cannabis, and the sale of its dried leaves to smoke as **kif** or of its resin, compressed into browny-black blocks, to eat as **hashish**. Even where uncultivated, the plants grow wild around the stony slopes, and with prices bringing growers five times that of other cereal crops, it is not surprising that it has taken over so much of the farmland. The cultivation itself is legal, but Moroccan laws forbid its sale, purchase and even possession outside the region (see p.44). These laws are enforced on occasion with some vigour, so don't be seduced by the locals: police roadblocks are frequent, informers common. Cannabis in the Rif is big business and not for casual visitors to get mixed up in; there are Europeans and Americans enough already in jail in Morocco.

ABD EL KRIM AND THE REPUBLIC OF THE RIF

Until the establishment of the Spanish protectorate in 1912, the **tribes of the Rif** existed outside government control – a northern heartland of the *Bled Es-Siba*. They were subdued temporarily by *harkas*, the burning-raids with which sultans asserted their authority, and for a longer period under Moulay Ismail; but for the most part, bore out their own name of *Imazighen*, or "Free Ones".

Closed to outside influence, the tribes developed an isolated and self-contained way of life. The Riffian soil, stony and infertile, produced constant problems with food supplies, and it was only through a complex system of alliances (*liffs*) that outright wars were avoided. Blood feuds, however, were endemic, and a major contributor to maintaining a viably small population. Unique in Morocco, the Riffian villages are scattered communities, their houses hedged and set apart, and each family maintained a pillbox tower to spy on and fight off enemies. They were different, too, in their religion: the *salat*, the prayers said five times daily – one of the central tenets of Islam – was not observed. *Djinns*, supernatural spirits from pagan nature cults, were widely accredited, and great reliance was placed on the intercession of local *marabouts*.

It was an unlikely ground for significant and organized rebellion, yet for over five years (1921–27) the tribes forced the Spanish to withdraw from the mountains. Several times they defeated whole Spanish armies, first and most memorably at **Annual** in 1921 (see History in "Contexts"), which with later disasters led to General Primo de Rivera becoming – with the king's blessing – the virtual dictator of Spain. It was only through the intervention of France, and the joint commitment of nearly half a million troops, that the Europeans won eventual victory.

In the intervening years, **Abd El Krim**, the leader of the revolt, was able to declare a **Republic of the Rif** and to establish much of the apparatus of a modern state. Well educated, and confident of the Rif's mineral reserves, he and his brother, Mohammed, manipulated the *liff* system to forge an extraordinary unity among the tribes, negotiated mining rights in return for arms with Germany and South America, and even set up a Riffian State Bank. Still more impressive, the brothers managed to impose a series of social reforms – including the destruction of family pillboxes and the banning of *kif* – which allowed the operation of a fairly broad administrative system. In their success,

If you want a look at some dramatic Riffian scenery, however, there's nothing to stop you taking a bus, or driving the roads between Chaouen (see Chapter One) and Fes, via **Ketama**, or Al Hoceima or Nador and Taza, via **Aknoul**. Drivers uneasy about the whole business of the Rif – there are incidents of *kif* being pressed for sale upon tourists driving these parts – might prefer to keep to the main roads, routing from Taza to Melilla via **Taourirt**.

On top of the Rif: the road from Chaouen to Ketama and Al Hoceima

There are very few journeys in Morocco as spectacular as that from **Chaouen** (see p.117) **to Al Hoceima**. The road literally – and perversely – follows the backbone of the Western Rif, the highest peaks in the north of the country. You can look down on one side to the Mediterranean coast, and on the other across the southern range; "big mountains and more big mountains" – as Paul Bowles put it in a wonderful travel piece, "The Rif, to Music", in *Their Heads are Green* – "mountains covered with olive trees, with oak trees, with bushes, and finally with giant cedars".

however, was the inevitability of defeat. It was the first nationalist movement in colonial North Africa, and although the Spanish were ready to quit the zone in 1925, it was politically impossible that the French would allow them to do so.

Defeat for the Riffians – and the capture of Abd El Krim at Targuist – brought a virtual halt to social progress and reform. **The Spanish** took over the administration en bloc, governing through local *caids* (district administrators), and although they exploited some mineral deposits there was no road-building programme nor any of the other "civilizing benefits" introduced in the French zone. There were, however, two important changes: migration of labour (particularly to French Algeria) replaced the blood feud as a form of population control, and the Riffian warriors were recruited into Spain's own armies. The latter had immense consequences, allowing General Franco to build up a power base in Morocco. It was with **Riffian troops** that he invaded Andalucia in 1936, and it was probably their contribution which ensured the fascist victory in the Spanish Civil War.

Abd El Krim was a powerful inspiration to later nationalists, and the Riffians themselves played an important guerrilla role in the 1955–56 **struggle for independence**. When, in April 1957, the Spanish finally surrendered their protectorate, however, the Berber/Spanish-speaking tribes found themselves largely excluded from government. Administrators were imposed on them from Fes and Casablanca, and in October 1958, the Rif's most important tribe, the Beni Urriaguel, rose in open **rebellion**. The mutiny was soon put down, but necessitated the landing at Al Hoceima of then-Crown Prince Hassan and some two-thirds of the Moroccan army.

Forty years later, the Rif is still perhaps the most unstable part of Morocco, remaining conscious of its under-representation in government and its underdevelopment, despite substantial school-building programmes, improved road communications and a large, new, agricultural project in the plains south of Nador and Al Hoceima. Labour **emigration**, too, remains high – with Western Europe replacing Algeria as the main market – and (as in the rest of Morocco) there is widespread resentment at the difficulty of obtaining a passport and then a visa for this outlet. With the growth of more sophisticated government systems, further tribal dissidence now seems unlikely, though there were riots in the Riffian towns of Nador, Al Hoceima and Tetouan as recently as 1984.

This is not a route to be undertaken by inexperienced drivers; although in good condition, it seems constructed entirely of zigzags and hairpin turns.

Bab Taza, Bab Berred and Ketama

BAB TAZA, 23km out of Chaouen, is the first village of any size – an attractive place surrounded by rolling, green, flower-strewn countryside and outcrops of claret thyme. It has a Wednesday *souk* and a café. Ten kilometres further on is CHEFERAT, a small hamlet with a noted spring and a small waterfall which rushes under the road. Like Bab Taza, it has no hotel, though there are two cafés, one on the roadside serving grilled *brochettes*.

Once beyond Bab Taza, you wind around the tops of ridges, sheer drops on either side to gorges and isolated valleys. **BAB BERRED**, a smallish market village and former Spanish administrative centre, has a reasonable pension, the *Tizirane* (①), near the *grand taxi* stand. The village also signals the real beginning of *kif* country – it is surrounded, in fact, by the plants – and at Ketama, 30km to the east, you arrive at the epicentre.

KETAMA, even in transit, is an initiation because absolutely everybody seems to be involved in "Business". If you get off the bus, you will immediately be offered hash – and few locals will believe that you are here for any other purpose. Which, really, is fair enough. Anywhere in Morocco, if people introduce themselves as "from Ketama", there is no ambiguity about what they are offering. Small-time dealers or growers here may invite you to stay at their farms – not to be recommended, even if you've got an insa-

---

THE TRADITIONS OF KIF . . .

Smoking *kif* or consuming hashish is an age-old tradition in the Rif and northern Morocco. Its effects were enthusiastically described by James Grey Jackson in *An Account of the Empire of Marocco* , published in 1809:

The plant called Hashisha is the African hemp plant; it grows in all the gardens and is reared in the plains of Marocco for the manufacture of string, but in most parts of the country it is cultivated for the extraordinary and pleasing voluptuous vacuity of mind which it produces in those who smoke it; unlike the intoxication from wine, a fascinating stupour pervades the mind, and the dreams are agreeable. The kief, *which is the flower and seeds of the plant, is the strongest, and a pipe of it half the size of a common English tobacco pipe, is sufficient to intoxicate. The infatuation of those who use it is such that they cannot exist without it.*

The Kief is usually pounded, and mixed with an invigorating confection which is sold at an enormous price; a piece of this as big as a walnut will for a time entirely deprive a man of all reason and intellect: they prefer it to opium from the voluptuous sensations which it never fails to produce. Wine or brandy, they say, does not stand in competition with it.

The Habisha, *or leaves of the plant, are dried and cut like tobacco, and are smoked in very small pipes; but when the person wishes to indulge in the sensual stupour it occasions, he smokes the Hashisha pure, and in less than half an hour it operates: the person under its influence is said to experience pleasing images: he fancies himself in company with beautiful women; he dreams that he is an emperor, or a* bashaw, *and that the world is at his nod. There are other plants which possess a similar exhilarating quality, amongst which is a species of the Palma Christi, the nuts of which, mixed with any kind of food, affect a person for three hours, and then pass off. These they often use when they wish to discover the mind of a person, or what occupies his thoughts.*

. . . AND THE MODERN INDUSTRY

Although many of the Riffian tribes in the mountains had always smoked *kif*, it was the Spanish who really encouraged its cultivation – probably as an effort to keep the

tiable appetite and curiosity for *kif* production travellers tend to leave parted from their money and possessions, sometimes at knife-point. The only **hotel** on the Ketama road is the old Spanish *parador*, the *Hôtel Tidighine* (☎09/81.30.16; ③), where once upon a time tourists stayed to ski or hunt wild boar on **Djebel Tidirhine**. Buses drop you outside its doors but it's been best avoided for the last thirty or so years. The main village of Ketama is, in fact, 8km down the road to Fes at **TLETA KETAMA** but there is no accommodation there, nor any reason to stay.

Roads to the coast lead off 23km before and 12km beyond Ketama, cutting through the mountains to EL JEBHA (see p.117). This is a memorable trip but there are much better resorts at Torres de Alcala and Kalah Iris, accessible from the next junction (see overleaf).

Continuing east from Ketama, with the cedar forests giving way to barren, stony slopes, you reach the town of **TARGUIST**, Abd El Krim's HQ and last stronghold (see box on pp.128–129) and the site of his surrender to the French. Paul Bowles described the place, almost forty years ago, in "The Rif, to Music", as "a monstrous excrescence with long dirty streets, the wind blowing along them, whipping clouds of dust and filth against the face, stinging the skin". It has not improved and, despite a trio of **pensions** (all ①), would be a perverse place to stay. It does, however, have a lively **Saturday souk**, which draws villagers from the dozens of tiny communities in the neighbouring hills.

Back on the main road, 1km beyond the junction to Targuist and alongside the Shell petrol station, there is a good, modest **restaurant**, the *Targuist*, favoured by long-distance buses.

---

peace. This situation was apparently accepted when Mohammed V came to power, though the reasons for his doing so are obscure. There is a story, probably apocryphal, that when he visited Ketama in 1957, he accepted a bouquet of cannabis as a symbolic gift.

Whatever, Ketama continued to supply the bulk of the country's cannabis, and in the early 1970s it became the centre of a significant drug industry, exporting to Europe and America. This sudden growth was accounted for by the introduction, by an American dealer, of simpler techniques for producing hash resin. Overnight, the Riffians had access to a compact and easily exportable product, as well as a burgeoning world market for dope. Inevitably, big business was quick to follow and a quarter of a century on, Morocco is reckoned the world's leading producer of cannabis, supplying over half of Europe's demand, and contributing an estimated US$2bn (£1.2bn) to the Moroccan economy. Even bigger money, however, is made by the dealers – mainly British, Dutch, Spanish, and Italians – who organize the shipments and sell the hash on the streets at prices fifty times higher than those paid to the Riffian growers.

The Moroccan authorities are caught between a rock and a hard place over the cannabis industry. They are pressured by Western European governments – and the UN – to take action against growers and dealers, and given their aspirations to join the EU, have made efforts to co-operate. But the cultivation and sale of cannabis are important items in the local economy. Short of radically diversifying the agriculture of the Rif, and paying large subsidies to the local farms, little can be done to limit the cultivation. Hassan II actually announced such a scheme as long ago as 1994, promising to devote US$2.2 billion to the economy of the Rif in a programme developed with the European Union.

The EU, thus far, has come up with grants of around £50m to improve the north's infrastructure, but with an estimated 60,000 hectares of land devoted to cannabis, there is an awful long way to go. Meantime, recent summers, blessed with rains as well as sun, have seen record-breaking harvests . . .

Torres de Alcala and Kalah Iris

A pair of temptingly low-key beach resorts, **Torres de Alcala** and **Kalah Iris** can be reached by a road (signposted Beni Boufrah and Torres de Alcala) 5km west of Targuist. They can be reached by *grand taxi* from Targuist or Al Hoceima, or by a daily bus; the bus leaves Targuist at 6am, arrives at Torres de Alcala at 7.30am and Al Hoceima at 9am, then turns round from Al Hoceima at 3pm, arriving at Torres de Alcala at 4.30pm and Targuist at 6pm.

Torres de Alcala

TORRES DE ALCALA is a simple, whitewashed hamlet, 250m from a small, pebbly beach. Cliffs frame its beach and on the western headland is a deserted fort, probably Spanish, with stunning views along the Mediterranean coast. It's a perfect resort-in-embryo, with – as yet – no hotel. In summer there are a few rooms available for rent and rough camping behind the small café on the beach. Other than that, there's just a bakery and the smallest of shops.

Along a rocky cliff-path, 5km to the east, are the **ruins of Badis**, which from the fourteenth to the early sixteenth century was the main port of Fes, and used for trade with the Western Mediterranean states, in particular Venice. A once-considerable caravan route ran across the Rif, following the course of the modern S302 road, the so-called Route de l'Unité (see below)

Offshore from Badis is a small island, the **Peñon de Velez de la Gomera**, which – like the islands off Al Hoceima, and Chafarinas further east – remains Spanish territory. It was this that caused the port's decline. The Spaniards occupied it in 1508, then in 1522 it passed to the Turks, who used it as a base for raids along the Spanish coast. Philip II of Spain tried to regain it, failed to do so, but destroyed Badis in the process. Subsequently, the island was used by Turkish and other pirates before, in this century, the Spanish took possession, using it until recent years as a penitentiary.

Kalah Iris

At **KALAH IRIS**, 4km east of Torres de Alcala, along a paved road, there's a longer beach, with a natural breakwater, formed by a sandspit which runs out to one of two islets in the bay. There is no village as such here but a few facilities: a good **campsite** (open year round, and with twenty brick **bungalows**, sleeping up to six people, for rent), a restaurant, café, and a shop with fresh food. It is not totally undiscovered, with excursions being offered to European holidaymakers in Al Hoceima, but it's still a delightful spot.

The Route de L'Unité: Ketama to Fes

At the end of the Spanish Protectorate in 1957, there was no north–south route across the Rif, a marked symbol both of its isolation and of the separateness of the old French and Spanish zones. It was in order to counteract these aspects – and to provide working contact between the Riffian tribes and the French-colonized Moroccans – that the **Route de l'Unité** was planned, cutting right across the range from Ketama south to Fes.

The Route, completed in 1963, was built with volunteer labour from all over the country – Hassan II himself worked on it at the outset. It was the brainchild of Mehdi Ben Barka, first President of the National Assembly and the most outstanding figure of the nationalist Left before his exile and subsequent "disappearance" in Paris in 1965. Ben Barka's volunteers, 15,000-strong for much of the project, formed a kind of labour university, working through the mornings and attending lectures in the afternoons.

Today the Route de l'Unité sees little traffic – travelling from Fes to Al Hoceima, it's quicker to go via Taza; from Fes to Tetouan, via Ouezzane. Nevertheless, it's an impressive and very beautiful road, certainly as dramatic an approach to Fes as you could hope for.

Taounate and Tissa

Going by bus, the village which most tempts a halt is **TAOUNATE**. The largest community along the Route, it stands on a hill above the valley of the Oued Ouerrha. If you can make it for the huge **Friday market** here, you should be able to get a lift out to any number of villages in the region. If you choose to stay overnight, there's quite a pleasant little hotel, the *Entente* (☎05/68.82.91; ⑩), halfway down the hill on the left-hand side, with panoramic views. There are also a couple of cafés in the village.

Continuing south along the Route, there is a turning, 33km from Taounate, to **TISSA**, announced by a sign at the entrance to the village as the "Berceau des Chevaux". Here, in late September/early October, horses and riders from the region gather to compete at the annual **horsefair**. The climax are the competitive **fantasias** judged on speed, discipline and dress. Elsewhere, *fantasias* – traditional cavalry charges culminating in firing of muskets in the air – are put on largely for tourists but these are the real thing, for aficonados.

West of Taounate

To the west of Taounate lies **RAFSAÏ**, the last village of the Rif to be overrun by the Spanish, and the site of a December **Olive Festival**. Until recently this was reached by taking the S304 towards the village of Fes El Bali – as marked on most maps – but this road has been diverted due to construction of a new reservoir, the Barrage Al Wahda (see below). If you are into scenic roads and have transport, you might consider taking a forty-kilometre dirt road out from here to the **Djebel Lalla Outka**, the peak reputed to offer the best view of the whole Rif range. The road is reasonable as far as the village of TAMESNITE, but thereafter is very rough piste – accessible only in summer.

FES EL BALI is, since 1997, to be found only on the maps. The Oued Ouerrha has been dammed at MJARA, 20km downstream of the old village, and when the waters rise to flood the broad valley, the **Barrage Al Wahda** will form a lake 34km long, second in Africa only to Aswan. If all goes to plan, it will irrigate a further 200,000 hectares of the **Gharb** coastal plain and protect it from floodwaters, as well as adding ten percent to the national electricity grid.

East: Aknoul

Going **east from Taounate**, an attractive though less spectacular route heads through cork and holm oak forests towards the scattered and rather grim village of **AKNOUL**. From here you can pick up a bus or *grand taxi* down to Taza, or sporadic buses over to Nador or Al Hoceima.

Taza and the Djebel Tazzeka

TAZA was once a place of great importance: the capital of Morocco for periods of the Almohad, Merenid and Alaouite dynasties, and controlling the Taza Gap, the only practicable pass from the east. It forms a wide passage between the Rif and Middle Atlas and was the route to central power taken by Moulay Idriss and the first Moroccan Arabs, as well as the Almohads and Merenids, both of whom successfully invaded Fes from Taza. Each of these dynasties fortified and endowed the city but as a defensive position it was never very effective: the local Zenatta tribe were always willing to join an attack by outsiders and, in the nineteenth century, they managed to overrun Taza completely, with centralized control returning only with the French occupation of 1914.

Modern Taza seems little haunted by this past, its monuments sparse and mostly inaccessible to non-Muslims. It is, however, a pleasant market town – an easy place to get acclimatized if you have arrived in Morocco at Melilla – and its Medina is saved from anonymity by a magnificent hilltop terrace site, flanked by crumbling Almohad walls. In addition, there is a considerable attraction in the surrounding countryside – the national park of **Djebel Tazzeka**, with its circuit of waterfalls, caves and schist gorges.

Orientation and practicalities

Taza splits into two parts, the **Medina** and the French-built **Ville Nouvelle**, distinct quarters separated by 2km of road. The Ville Nouvelle was an important military garrison in the Riffian war and retains much of the barrack-grid character. Its focal point, **Place de l'Indépendance**, actually serves a population of 70,000, but it's so quiet you'd hardly know it.

A shuttle bus runs between **Place de l'Indépendance** and **Place Moulay Hassan**, on the northern edge of the Medina. The train station and adjacent bus and *grands taxis* terminals are at the north end of the Ville Nouvelle, 2km from Place de l'Indépendance. *Petits taxis* are available for rides between the stations, Ville Nouvelle and Medina.

Accommodation

Taza doesn't have a great choice of accommodation – and there's no longer a campsite – but you should find a room any time of year. If you're not too fussy about comfort, Place de l'Indépendance is the best location, with a scattering of cafés and restaurants nearby.

CHEAP

Grand Hôtel du Dauphiné [A], Place de l'Indépendance (☎05/67.35.67). An old Art Deco hotel, once grand as the name proclaims, though now somewhat down-at-heel. Nonetheless, the rooms are decent-sized and it's reasonable value for money. ①

Hôtel de l'Étoile [F], Rue Bab El Guebour – just south of Place Moulay Hassan (☎05/67.01.79). This is a bargain cheapie: twelve rooms off a tiled courtyard, managed for twenty years or more by a grande dame. There are no showers but a *hammam* is nearby , as are several eating places. ①

Hôtel de la Gare [D], Av. Prince Sidi Mohammed – opposite the train station (☎05/67.24.48). If you have to get a dawn bus across the Rif, or to Nador, this is a convenient location – though it's a long haul to the Medina. The rooms, off a small courtyard with a banana tree, have been overhauled recently and a few now have shower and toilet. Others have none – and there's no communal shower. ①

Hôtel Guillaume Tell [C], Place de l'Indépéndance (☎05/67.23.47). More or less opposite the *Dauphiné*, this fifth-floor lodging house is the cheapest in town – and a tad grim, with its garage-style doors, outside stairs and cold showers. It was here that Paul Bowles, "feverish and depressed", ended his adventures in search of the music of the Rif. ①

Hôtel de la Poste [B], on Av. Moulay Youssef – just off Place de l'Indépendance (☎05/67.25.89). Located above the CTM bus office, this has small, quite comfortable rooms, but unreliable plumbing – and no showers. ①

MODERATE

Hôtel Friouato [E] (☎05/67.25.93). A rather charmless concrete outpost, set in its own grounds amid the scrubland between the Ville Nouvelle and Medina. Still, there's a functional swimming pool, a bar, and reasonable restaurant. ③

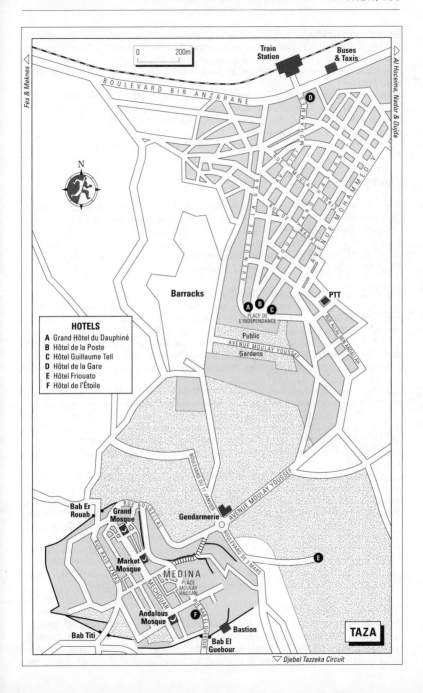

HOTELS

A Grand Hôtel du Dauphiné
B Hôtel de la Poste
C Hôtel Guillaume Tell
D Hôtel de la Gare
E Hôtel Friouato
F Hôtel de l'Étoile

Eating and drinking

As noted, most of the **cafés and restaurants** are to be found around **Place de l'Indépendance**. The *Restaurant Majestic*, at 26 Bd. Mohammed V, is a good choice here, as is the nicely named *Restaurant Youm-Youm* around the corner from the *Hôtel de la Poste*.

Down by the **train station**, you can eat reasonably well at the Café de la Roche, opposite the *Hôtel de la Gare*, while up at the **Medina** there are a couple of decent eateries on and around Place Moulay Hassan; try the one over the Cinema Friouato, or the other above the *Laiterie Aharrache*.

As noted above, there's a **bar** – and a passable restaurant – at the rather forlorn *Hôtel Friouato*.

The Medina

Buses from Place de l'Indépendance run up to the **Place Moulay Hassan**, a busy little square overlooking the Ville Nouvelle. The **Medina**, to the west of the square, is a compact, modernized quarter – easy enough to navigate, though you may need to ask directions for the few scattered sites. The quarter spreads out from a long main street, called the **Mechouar** on its initial stretch and changing name to Rue Koubet and Rue Cherkiyne as it approaches the **Grand Mosque**.

The Andalous Mosque and Palais Bou Hamra

From Place Moulay Hassan, look for a passageway between the square and the *Hôtel de l'Etoile*. This runs west to the **Andalous Mosque**, the largest building in the southern section of the Medina – though its courtyards are characteristically well concealed from public view. Close by the mosque, just west of the *Mechouar*, is the Merenid-era **Bou Abul Hassan Medersa**. An inconspicuous building, it is usually kept locked; if you can locate the *gardien*, there are rewards to be had in a classic court and beautiful *mihrab*.

To the rear of the Andalous Mosque is the **Palais Bou Hamra**, the largely ruined residence of Bou Hamra, the *Rogui* or pretender to the throne, in the early years of this century. There is little to see today, but for a decade or so this was a power base controlling much of eastern Morocco. Like most protagonists of the immediate pre-colonial period, Bou Hamra was an extraordinary figure: a former forger, conjurer and saint, who claimed to be the legitimate Shereefian heir and had himself proclaimed Sultan at Taza in 1902.

The name *Bou Hamra* – "man on the she-donkey" – recalled his means of travel round the countryside, where he won his followers by performing "miracles". One of these involved talking to the dead, which he perfected by the timely burying of a disciple, who would then communicate through a concealed straw; the pronouncements over, Bou Hamra flattened the straw with his foot (presumably not part of the original deal) and allowed the amazed villagers to dig up the by-then-dead witness.

Bou Hamra's own death – after his capture by Sultan Moulay Hafid – was no less melodramatic. He was brought to Fes in a small cage on the back of a camel, fed to the court lions (who refused to eat him), and was eventually shot and burned. Both Gavin Maxwell and Walter Harris give graphic accounts (see "Books" in Contexts).

The souks and Grand Mosque

Taza's **souks** branch off to either side of the main street (by now Rue Koubet), midway between the Andalous and Grand Mosques. Since there are few and sporadic tourists, these are very much working markets, free of the artificial "craft" goods so often found. In fact, one of the most memorable is a *souk* for used European clothing – a frequent feature of country and provincial markets, the more fortunate dealers having gained access to the supplies of international charities. The **granary** and the covered stalls of the **kissaria** are also worth a look, in the shadow of the **Market Mosque** (Djemaa Es Souk).

Taza's **Grand Mosque** is historically one of the most interesting buildings in the country, though, like that of the Andalous, it is so discreetly screened that it's difficult for non-Muslims to gain any glimpse of the interior. Even the outside is elusive: shielded by a net of buildings, you have to walk up towards Bab Er Rih for a reasonable impression of its ground plan. Founded by the Almohad sultan Abd El Moumen, it is probably the oldest Almohad structure in existence, predating even the partially ruined mosque at Tin Mal (see Chapter Five), with which it shares most stylistic features.

Bab Er Rih and the bastions

Above the Medina, at **Bab Er Rih** (Gate of the Winds), it is possible to get some feeling for Taza's historic and strategic significance. You can see up the valley towards the Taza Gap: the Djebel Tazzeka and the Middle Atlas on one side, and the reddish earth of the Rif behind on the other. The only drawback to this vantage point is the smell of garbage thrown down the hillside below.

The actual gate now leads nowhere and looks somewhat lost below the road, but it is Almohad in origin and design. So, too, is most of the circuit of walls, which you can follow round by way of a **bastion** (added by Moulay Ismail, in Spanish style) back to Place Moulay Hassan.

On from Taza: routes and transport

Taza is quite a transport junction, with good connections west to Fes, east to Oujda and north to Nador and Al Hoceima.

For **Fes** there's a wide choice of options. *Grands taxis* run throughout the day (just ask and wait for a place) from by the train station, arriving in Fes at Bab Ftouh (where you'll need to pick up a city taxi or bus to get to the hotels at Bab Boujeloud or the Ville Nouvelle). Fes is also served by four daily trains, plus a number of buses. **Oujda** is easiest reached by train – a quick route across the eastern steppes, through Guercif and Taourirt (see p.139).

For the **Rif**, most buses leave very early in the morning. There are currently two to **Nador** (at 4.30am and 5am): one going via **Aknoul**, the other over a new and more direct road to the east of Taourirt (on the P1). There are also one or two buses each morning to **Al Hoceima**, via Aknoul. From Aknoul you can catch sporadic, local buses across the southern slopes of the Rif to Taounate on the Route de l'Unité.

All the **buses** leave from by the train station – whatever anyone may tell you about stops in the Ville Nouvelle!

The Djebel Tazzeka ... and beyond

A loop of some 123km around Taza, the **Cirque du Djebel Tazzeka** is really a car-driver's route, with its succession of mountain views, marking a transition between the Rif and Middle Atlas. However, it has a specific "sight" in the immense **Friouato Cave** (*Gouffre du Friouato*), 22km from Taza, and the whole route is fertile ground for bird-watching and other wildlife (see box overleaf). If you don't have transport, you could negotiate a *grand taxi* in Taza (at the rank by the train station) to take you the cave and back, either waiting while you visit or picking you up later in the day; obviously, you'll want to pay at the end of the trip.

WILDLIFE IN THE DJEBEL TAZZEKA

The **Djebel Tazzeka National Park** is one of northern Morocco's most rewarding wildlife sites, positioned, as it is, at the point where the Rif merges with the Middle Atlas. The range's lower slopes are covered in cork oak, the prime commercial crop of this area, and interspersed with areas of mixed woodland containing holm oak, the pink-flowered cistus and the more familiar bracken.

These woodland glades are frequented by a myriad of **butterflies** from late May onwards; common varieties include knapweed, ark green fritillaries and Barbary skippers. The forest floor also provides an ideal habitat for **birds** such as the multicoloured hoopoe, with its identifying crest, and the trees abound with the calls of wood pigeon, nuthatch, short-toed treecreeper and various titmice. The roadside telegraph lines also provide attractive hunting perches for such brightly coloured inhabitants as rollers and shrikes, both woodchat and great grey, who swoop on passing insects and lizards with almost gluttonous frequency.

The cirque – and the Friouato cave

The **Cirque du Djebel Tazzeka road** starts out curline around below Taza's Medina before climbing to a narrow valley of almond and cherry orchards. About 10km out of Taza you reach the **Cascades de Ras El Oued**, a series of small waterfalls reduced to a trickle in the dry summer months. Beyond this point, you loop up towards the first pass (at 1198m) and emerge onto a large plateau. Here, in exceptional years, the **Dayat Chiker** appears as a broad, shallow lake. More often than not, though, it is just a fertile saucer, planted with cereals; geographers will recognize its formation as a classic limestone *polje*.

At this point, the road divides; to reach the Friouato cave, take the right fork. After 4km, midway along the polje, you'll pass a sign to the **Gouffre du Friouato**, 500m to the right of the road. The cave complex, explored down to 180m, is said to be the deepest in North Africa, and it feels it, entered through a huge 'pot', over 30m wide, with wall-clinging steps down. The complex has hardly been developed but there is a small café and a *gardien*/guide is usually at hand; he will sell you a map of the system, or for 75dh per head will accompany visitors. Sturdy shoes and warm clothing are essential, as is a torch if you're doing it alone.

Beyond Friouato, the cirque route runs through the dark schist **gorges of the Oued Zireg**. At Bab Bouidir, 8.5km from Friouato, there is an office (sporadically open) for the **Tazzeka National Park** (see box above); more or less alongside, a small café and campsite operates most summers.

The most dramatic and scenic stretch of the cirque is undoubtedly the **ascent of the Djebel** itself. This is passable by car in dry weather but very dangerous at other times: a very rough, seven-kilometre road cuts its way up some 15km beyond Friouato, leading to a TV broadcasting tower near the summit. The view from the top, encased in forests of cedars, stretches to the Rif, to the mountains around Fes and to much of the eastern Middle Atlas.

Completing the cirque, you can rejoin the Fes–Taza road at SIDI ABDALLAH DES RHIATA.

A route to Midelt

For anyone with sturdy transport (a Renault 4L should do the job), there is an adventurous route **through the Middle Atlas to Midelt**. The start of this is the left fork at the beginning of the Chiker plateau described above; it is paved road as far as MEGHRAOUA, where a dirt road (very rough) takes over to TALZEMT, eventually joining the P20 to Midelt at ENJIL DES IKHATARN.

Taza to Oujda

The route from **Taza to Oujda** is as bare as it looks on the map: a semi-desert plain, broken by little more than the odd roadside town. Nonetheless, if you've got time to spare, and transport, there are a trio of recommendable detours.

Msoun and Guercif

MSOUN, 29km east of Taza, and 3km north of the main road, is the first point of interest. The village, inhabited by a hundred or so members of the semi-nomadic Haoura tribe, is built within a **Kasbah**, dating to the reign of Moulay Ismail (1672–1727) which is still turreted and complete on three sides. You can view its original rainwater cistern and grain silos, alongside the settlement's shop, post office and mosque. Visitors are a curiosity here and you're likely to be guided around and possibly taken off to meet the *mukhtar* (headman).

Back on the main road, just opposite the track to Msoun, is the *Motel La Kasbah* (①), a friendly place for a meal or overnight stop.

Guercif, Gouttitir, and the Cascades

At the agricultural centre of **GUERCIF**, at 37km from Taza, is another small **hotel**, the *Hôtel Howary* (☎05/67.50.62; ⑩); it's a modest, recently built place with a reasonable restaurant at street level. Midway between here and Taourirt, you might consider a brief detour from the main road, off to the left, to the hamlet of **GOUTTITIR**. Signposted "Thermal Spring", this comprises a few buildings set around a **hot spring**, in a rocky, steep-sided gully, whose waters are pumped up to supply a *hammam* (used by men during the day; women after dusk). There are very basic **rooms** (no beds!) and **meals** to be had nearby at the *Café Sidi Chaffi*.

There's another possible detour: north of the road, 12km on from the Gouttitir turning, are the **Bou Mazouz Cascades**. These can be reached by turning left (north) for 9km along the road to the MELGA EL OUIDANE barrage. In contrast to the barren landscape either side of the main Taza road, this takes you past orange and olive orchards watered by the Oued Za. Look for a small mosque, with prominent loudspeaker, on the right; leave the road at this point and follow a rough track to the waterfalls; you can swim in a natural pool here, and camp beside it if you want.

Taourirt

TAOURIRT, the largest town along the route, was the crossroads between the old north–south caravan route linking Melilla and the ancient kingdom of Sijilmassa (see p.443), as well as the Taza corridor between Morocco and Algeria. The presence of the army (who occupy the old Kasbah) and of prominent radio aerials confirms its continuing strategic importance, and for travellers it is a useful train and road junction, with buses north to Nador connecting reasonably well with train arrivals from Oujda or Fes. The town itself is of little interest, however, save for its large **Sunday souk**. There are two **hotels**, much the better of which is the *El Mansour* (☎06/69.40.03; ⑩), with a good café, just off the roundabout in the middle of the town.

Al Hoceima

Coming from the Rif, **AL HOCEIMA** can be a bit of a shock. It may not be quite the "exclusive international resort" the tourist board claim, but it is truly Mediterranean and has developed enough to have little in common with the farming hamlets and tribal markets of the mountains around.

▽ Camping Plage El Jemil & Ajdir/ all routes

HOTEL KEY

A	Hôtel Florido	H	Hôtel National
B	Hôtel Afriquia	I	Karim Hôtel
C	Hôtel Casablanca	J	Hôtel Maghreb El Jadida
D	Hôtel Assalam	K	Hôtel Al Khouzama
E	Hôtel Oriente	L	Hôtel Marrakesh
F	Hôtel de Station	M	Hôtel Quemado
G	Hôtel Rif	N	Hôtel Mohammed V

If you're travelling through the Rif, you will probably want to stop here and rest a couple of days – maybe for longer. It is a relaxing place, with none of the hassle of Tangier or Fes or Tetouan, and the cafés and streets full of people going about their business or pleasure. In late spring, or September, when the beaches are quiet, it's near idyllic. In midsummer, though, be warned that the town and its beaches get pretty crowded under the weight of Moroccan families and French and German tourists, and rooms can be difficult to find. It is, after all, a small town and not geared to tourism on the scale of, say, Tangier or Agadir.

The Town

Al Hoceima's compact size is one of its charms. It has wide boulevards, fringed with occasional palms on familiar Spanish lines, and yet, at every turn, you can see either the wooded hills behind the town, or the sea.

From some vantage points, you also get a view of the **Peñon de Alhucemas**, another of the Spanish-owned islands off this coast (and another former penitentiary), over in the bay to the east of town. It's a pretty focal point, topped with sugar-white houses, a church and tower. The Spanish took it in 1673 and have held it ever since – a perennial source of dispute between Morocco and Spain. Some Moroccan patriots refer to it as the *Ile de N'Kor*, after the Oued Nekor, which flows into the bay.

There seems, however, no lobby for a change of name for Al Hoceima itself, which was developed by the Spanish after their counter-offensive in the Rif in 1925 (see pp.128–9), and was known by them as **Villa Sanjuro**. The name commemorated the Spanish General José Sanjuro, who landed in the bay, under the cover of Spanish and French warships, with an expeditonary force – and it is still occasionally used for the old part of town around the Place du Rif. Coincidentally, it was at Al Hoceima, too, that the then Crown Prince Hassan led Moroccan forces to quell the Riffians' revolt in 1958, following independence.

Names aside, the Spanish left little to distinguish their occupation. The only notable architectural feature is the **Spanish College**, the *Missión Cultural Española Marruecos*, which, until 1956, was their provincial headquarters. It is the custard cream and chocolate building, with blue and white *azulejos* tiles, on the north edge of town, beyond the main square, Place Massira.

Beaches

Swimming – and walking in the olive-groved hills if you want a change – is the main attraction of Al Hoceima. If you wake early enough it is worth going down to **Plage Quemado**, the town beach, to watch the *lamparo* fishermen coming in; they work at night using acetylene lamps to attract and dazzle the fish.

Besides Quemado, there is a less crowded beach at **Asfiha**, a kilometre west of town, along the Ajdir road (a cheap *petit taxi* ride, if you don't fancy walking). This stretches right round the bay to Djebel Hadid, the headland to the east.

There are further beaches at Torres de Alcala and Kalah Iris (see p.132), which, although 60km away, are nevertheless thought of as Al Hoceima beaches. They can be reached along a minor inland road by bus or *grand taxi*.

Practicalities

Until the 1950s, Al Hoceima consisted of just a small fishing port to the north of the bay, and a fringe of white houses atop the barren cliffs to the south. At the heart of this older quarter is the **Place du Rif**, enclosed by café-restaurants and pensions, and the terminal for CTM and private-line buses.

The newer part of town, with its neat grid of boulevards, occupies the land sloping down to the cliffs above the town beach, **Plage Quemado** – between the harbour and the original village. If this quarter can be said to have a heart, it is the **Place Massira**, a squeaky-clean square on the cliff top, at the top end of **Av. Mohammed V**, the principal boulevard.

There is a helpful **tourist office** on Av. Tariq Ibn Ziad, beyond the Provincial offices and the police headquarters.

Accommodation

Most of the cheaper pensions are grouped in and around the Place du Rif; they are reasonable, if basic; there are also a couple of more upmarket options.

CHEAP

Hôtel Afriquia [B], 20 Rue Al Alaouiyine (☎09/98.30.65). An old pension with clean, bright rooms, and cold showers on the corridor. It's just off the Place du Rif, so reasonably quiet. ⓪

Hôtel Assalam [D], 10 Place du Rif (☎09/98.14.13). A larger pension than most, with a café and summer restaurant on the ground floor. Some rooms have (cold) showers. ⓪

Hôtel Casablanca [C], 20 Rue Imzouren (☎09/98.30.79). Pricier than most of the other pensions around, but with little to justify the extra; it's best seen as a fallback. ⓪

Hôtel Florido [A], 40 Place du Rif (☎09/98.22.35). The top budget choice: an ornate Spanish building, with a lively café (decorated with Abd El Krim's truncated Star of David emblem) open all hours. Best rooms overlook the square; cold showers on the corridor. ⓪

Hôtel Marrakesh [L], 2 Rue Abdallah Hammou (☎09/98.30.25). A one-star hotel, showing its age, but the rooms are all en suite, the showers have reliable hot water, and, all in all, it's pretty good value for money. ①

Hôtel Oriente [E], Place du Rif (☎09/98.22.46). A clean, comfortable cheapie – if you can get a room with external windows. There's a café alongside for breakfast. ⓪

Hôtel Rif [G], 13 Rue Moulay Youssef (☎09/98.22.68). Another largish pension, away from the Place du Rif, in the jewellers' quarter. Simple rooms with cold showers on the corridor. ⓪

Hôtel de Station [F], Place du Rif (☎09/98.30.96). Clean rooms, with showers, and cheaper prices than any of the above. Probably a second choice after the *Florido*. ⓪

MODERATE TO EXPENSIVE

Karim Hôtel [I], 27 Av. Hassan II (☎09/98.21.84). An old but reasonably comfortable hotel, with en-suite rooms, a restaurant and a bar (which can be noisy). It is near the covered market – but a long way from the beach. ②

Hôtel Al Khouzama [K], Rue Al Andalous (☎09/98.56.69). A new (1995) hotel, with modern en-suite rooms. ②

Hôtel Maghreb El Jadida [J], 56 Av. Mohammed V (☎09/98.25.04). The best upmarket choice: a central hotel, with a top-floor restaurant and bar. ③

Hôtel Mohammed V [N], Place Massira (☎09/98.22.33). The old state-run grand hotel, privatized and re-opened in 1995. It's pricey but could be surprisingly good value for money if you get a few people together to share one of the bungalows. ④

Hôtel National [H], 23 Rue de Tetouan (☎09/98.26.81). A central location, close to buses in Place du Rif, ensures the popularity of this rather standard hotel. Nonetheless, it's a useful stop in that it accepts credit cards and will change money. ②

Hôtel Quemado [M], Plage de Quemado (☎09/98.33.14). Four ugly barrack blocks on the beach constitute this package hotel, whose main compensation is the seaview rooms. It is used by German and French tour groups in summer and in winter by Spanish ones on weekend breaks, so book in. Includes a bar, restaurant and disco. ③

CAMPSITES

There are two campsites, very different from each other:

Camping Plage El Jamil (aka Camping Cala Bonita), 500m east of town along the Ajdir road (☎09/98.40.26). A small, friendly site backing onto a stony beach, where pedalos and water ski-ing are on offer (to all comers); there is also a small café, a bar, restaurant, and shops. Open year-round.

Club Mediterranée, 10km out of town, past Ajdir, off the Ketama–Nador road (☎09/98.20.20). The largest *Club* in Morocco, with space for 1250 campers, sleeping two to a straw-roofed, concrete-based hut. Extensive facilities. Very French atmosphere. You generally have to book ahead, and for at least a week, through the *Club* office in Casablanca (☎02/31.19.06) or London (☎0171/581 1161). Open mid-June to mid-September.

Note that *Camping Plage Kalah Iris*, listed in some guides under Al Hoceima, is actually 60km west, near Torres de Alcala (see p.132).

Restaurants and nightlife

Al Hoceima has some reasonable places to eat, though not much else in the way of nightlife, beyond the *Jupiter* **disco** at the main beach, or discreet **bars** on the top floors of the hotels *Quemado* and *El Maghreb El Jadida*.

The best of the **café-restaurants** include:

Café Agadir, corner of Av. Abdelkrim Kattabi and Rue Idriss I. Good for breakfast and daytime snacks.

Restaurant Al Hoceima, Place du Rif. Reliable and inexpensive fare – mainly *brochettes* and *tajines*.

Snack Assada, 24 Av. Hassan II. A small place but with a wide-ranging menu. Modest prices and open late.

Restaurant La Belle Vue, Av. Mohammed V – on the right at the bottom end. A café all year – with snacks available – and a fully fledged restaurant each summer. Great views.

Hôtel-Restaurant Florido, 40 Place du Rif. The hotel's café-restaurant is a lively place to sit around of an evening, and the food's reasonable, too.

Café Hyatt Regency, Av. Mohammed V – just above the *Belle Vue*. Despite the name, this is a regular café unconnected with corporate chains. It's not quite as good as the *Belle Vue*, but it shares the fine views.

Hôtel-Restaurant Maghreb El Jadida, 56 Av. Mohammed V. You can eat – and drink beer and wine – in this top-floor restaurant.

Restaurant de Paris, 211 Av. Mohammed V (on the first floor). Good-value meals, though opening hours are at the whim of Ahmed, the cosmopolitan owner.

Transport

As in the rest of the Rif, most **buses** leave Al Hoceima early – to Taza at 4am; to Fes (via the Route de l'Unité), Chaouen and Tetouan slightly later; there are six buses a day to Nador, some of which continue to the Melilla border.

If you need to get anywhere in a hurry, there are also plenty of **grands taxis**, negotiable even for Rabat and Casablanca. It should be possible to find fellow passengers to share the expense of a taxi to Chaouen, Fes or the Melilla border.

The local **airport**, *Aeroport Charif Al Idriss*, is 17km east of Al Hoceima on the Nador road (P39), just before the village of Imzouen. It caters largely for charter flights from France and Germany – used as much by Moroccan workers as tourists – although *RAM* have a couple of flights each week to Casablanca and to Amsterdam and Brussels in summer.

There is a good **tourist office** on Av. Tariq Ibn Ziad, north-west of Place Massira.

East to Nador and Melilla

There is little of apparent interest to slow your progress over the 164km stretch of the P39 from **Al Hoceima to Nador**. For anyone who has read about the events of the Rif War, however, the names of the villages will be familiar. This was the territory of Abd El Krim's first, dramatic rising – the so-called **Rout of Annoual** – of July–August 1921. In those two months, the Spanish were forced back to Melilla, losing over 18,000 of their troops along the way.

Al Hoceima to Selouane

The road from Al Hoceima climbs inland alongside the Oued Nekor, crossing a high pass before arriving at **KASSITA** (43km), and the friendly *Hôtel-Restaurant Andalous* (☎06/36.47.06; ⓪). Here you can take the S312 south to Taza, via Aknoul. Heading east towards Nador, if you drive into the hills north of the road, at MIDAR or DRIOUCH, there is still the occasional lookout post and barracks remain to be seen from the Rif War.

At **MONT ARAOUI**, where the road crosses the Oued Moulouya, there is a large and wonderful **Sunday souk**, with storytellers, dentists and a sort of roulette wheel ("spin the live rat in the pail"). There are several café-restaurants and a spotless **hotel**, the *Hassan* (☎06/36.23.92; ②), with TVs in each room and showers on the corridors.

SELOUANE, 9km further east (and 11km short of Nador), stands at a rather complex junction of the roads to Al Hoceima and Oujda. It hosts a Saturday *souk* but is worth a short visit on any day of the week. There is an interesting **Kasbah**, built by Moulay Ismail, used as a base by the bizarre pretender to the throne, Bou Hamra (see p.136), and now adapted as a storehouse. But the main reason to stop is for a **meal** at the *Restaurant Brabo*, 110 Av. Mohammed V (☎06/60.90.33; closed Sun evening and all day Mon; accepts credit cards), the best **place to eat** in this entire chapter. A superlative restaurant, run by a Belgian chef (it is named after the Brabo Fountain in Antwerp) and his Moroccan wife, it is the only restaurant for hundreds of miles around that can boast a *Collier d'Or* from the *Gastronomique Internationale*. Phone ahead and splash out.

South to Guercif

The road **south to Guercif** (S333), heading off 8km west of Mont Araoui, is narrow and paved. It makes an interesting alternative to Taza or Oujda, with its vistas of palms and scrub, and the occasional wandering camel.

Nador

Entering or leaving Morocco at the Spanish enclave of Melilla you will have to pass through **NADOR**. If you're a bird-watcher, the marshes and dunes of Kariet Arkmane and Ras El Ma, 30–40km east of the town, may well entice a stay of several days (see box on p.147). If not, you will probably want to move straight out and on. Nador itself, fringed by a shallow lagoon, is earmarked as a centre for economic development and has little to offer conventional tourists.

When the Spanish left in 1957, Nador was just an ordinary Riffian village, given work and some impetus by the port of Melilla. Its later choice as a provincial capital was perhaps unfortunate. There was little to do for the local university students, while the iron foundry proposed to fuel the Rif's mining industry, never materialized: two reasons that explain why the 1984 riots started in this town.

The past decade saw some attempt to address these problems, along with much new building, but the effective closure of the Algerian border has hit loal business and tourism. A success story, however, is the MAROST fish farm, whose tower is visible across the lagoon. Set up in the 1980s, this specialises in sea perch, dorado, shrimps and oysters, which are mainly exported to France and Italy. It employs over 250 people, including a number of technicians engaged on research projects, whom you may well run across in the local restaurants.

Orientation and transport

The bulk of Nador lies between the **Selouane–Melilla road** (P39), to the west, and the **lagoon** of **Sebgha bou Areq** (or Mar Chica – "small sea"), to the east.

Driving in from Selouane, turn right at the first sign to "Centre Ville" and you'll find yourself at the **Municipalité** and the landmark *Hôtel Ryad*. From there, **Av.**

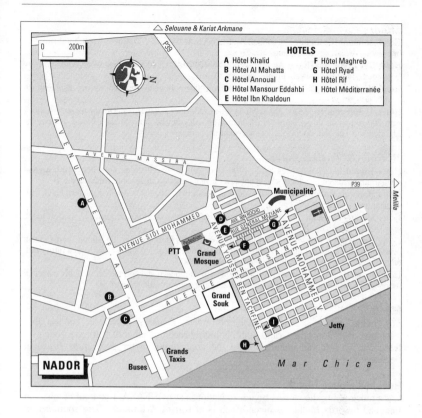

△ *Selouane & Kariat Arkmane*

HOTELS

A Hôtel Khalid
B Hôtel Al Mahatta
C Hôtel Annoual
D Hôtel Mansour Eddahbi
E Hôtel Ibn Khaldoun
F Hôtel Maghreb
G Hôtel Ryad
H Hôtel Rif
I Hôtel Méditerranée

0   200m

△ *Melilla*

Municipalité

AV. IBN ROCHD
RUE GENERAL MEZIANE

PTT

Grand Mosque

Pedestrian

Grand Souk

Jetty

Grands Taxis

NADOR

Buses

M a r   C h i c a

Mohammed V, with its palms and orange trees, runs down to a little jetty on the lagoon corniche. Parallel, and to the south, **Av. Youssef Ibn Tachfine** runs past the **Grand Mosque** with its tall, thin minaret down to the *Hôtel Rif* on the corniche. Halfway down, it is bisected by **Av. Hassan II**, where you will find the two-storey **Grand Souk**.

If you're arriving by **bus** or **grand taxi**, you'll likely be dropped at the ranks nearby the Grand Souk on the town's third main avenue, **Av. des F.A.R**; these terminals include connections to the Melilla border. CTM and SATAS buses use a terminal, across the avenue from the *Hôtel Ryad* on Rue General Meziane.

Leaving Nador, if you are heading for Tetouan or Chaouen, it's best to break the trip in Al Hoceima (3hr 30min): from there, either town is still an eight-hours-plus journey. If you are heading for **Fes**, **Taza** or **Oujda**, the best course is to take the Supratours buses run by **ONCF**, the rail company, to **Taourirt**, on the Fes–Oujda train line. They leave from outside the ONCF office on Av. Sidi Mohammed.

Details of the **Nador–Sète ferry** are to be found on p.8; the boats leave from Beni-Enzar, the Moroccan side of the Melilla border.

Accommodation

There is a wide choice of **hotels**, many of them built in the more optimistic climate of the late 1980s/early 1990s; the following is just a selection.

CHEAP

Hôtel Annoual [C], 16 Rue No. 20 – off Av. des F.A.R. (☎06/60.27.77). Cheap 1-star hotel, near the bus station, with a restaurant and café. ①

Hôtel Ibn Khaldoun [E], 91 Av. Ibn Rochd (☎06/60.70.42). A reasonable pension, with some en-suite rooms, and hot showers in the evenings. ①

Hôtel Maghreb [F], 72 Av. Youssef Ben Tachfine (☎06/60.46.64). Good-value cheapie that tends to be full. ①

Hôtel Al Mahatta [B], 38 Av. Abbas Mohammed Akkad (☎06/60.27.77). The town's largest hotel, with 200 rooms on three floors, which before the Algerian border was closed used to cater for Algerian and Tunisian visitors. A decent restaurant is open all day. ①

MODERATE TO EXPENSIVE

Hôtel Khalid [A], 129 Av. des F.A.R. (☎06/60.67.26). An excellent, modern hotel, with a good restaurant, managed by a local who spent several years in Holland; accepts credit cards. ②

Hôtel Mansour Eddahbi [D], 105 Rue de Marrakesh (☎06/60.65.83). Another modern hotel, with a restaurant and bar. ②

Hôtel Méditerranée [I], 2/4 Av. Youssef Ibn Tachfine (☎06/60.64.95). Reasonable, modest hotel, opposite the prominent *Hôtel Rif*. ②

Hôtel Rif [H], Av. Youssef Ibn Tachfine (☎06/60.47.73). An outpost of the *Maroc-Tourist* chain, overlooking the lagoon. Equipped with a swimming pool, restaurant and bar, but with a rather sad, empty air about proceedings. It is due for privatization. ④

Hôtel Ryad [G], Av. Mohammed V (☎06/60.77.15). A modern and spectacular wedding-cake of a hotel, with air-conditioning, restaurant, two bars , and underground car park. ④

Meals

For **meals**, beside the hotel-restaurants above, *Romero's*, 48/50 Av. Youssef Ben Tachfine, overloking the Grand Souk, is highly recommended. If you have your own transport, you should definitely take the opportunity to try *Restaurant Brabo* at Selouane (see p.144).

Beaches around Nador

For a quick swim, the closest **beach** to Nador is at BOUKANA, 10km out of town, on the road towards Melilla. A nicer beach is at **Kariet Arkmane**, 25km southeast of Nador, at the end of the lagoon (see below), which in summer becomes a popular camp-ground for Moroccan families.

Moroccans also set up camp at the beaches to the northwest of Nador, beyond BOUGHAFAR (30km northwest), and at the **Cap des Trois Forches**, the cape 35km north of Nador on the continuation of the Melilla road. There are no official campsites at either resort but you'd have no problem in joining the locals.

The coast east to Ras-El-Ma

The coast to the east of Nador has some of the most interesting **wildlife** sites in Morocco (see box opposite), and good beaches in addition. To get the most out of this area, a car would be a great help. However, you can make use of the *grands taxis*, or the daily bus from Nador (which runs along road 8101 to Kariet Arkmane and Ras-El-Ma, then turns round and heads back to town).

Kariet Arkmane

The village of **KARIET ARKMANE**, 30km from Nador, gives access to a sand and shell-packed **road along the spit of the lagoon**. This is a desolate area but pic-turesque in its own way, with saltmarshes that provide manifold attractions for bird-watchers. The road out follows the edge of the lagoon from Kariet, passing an old

---

BIRDS AND DUNES: EAST OF NADOR

The coast east of Nador (described opposite) offers compelling sites for bird-watching – and plant wildlife – with a series of highly frequented freshwater and saline sites.

At **KARIET ARKMANE** a path leads out, opposite the village mosque, past salt pans and a pumping station (right-hand side) to an **extensive area of salt marsh**. This is covered by the fleshy-stemmed **marsh glasswort** or *salicornia*: a characteristic "salt plant" or *halophyte*, it can survive the saline conditions through the use of glands which excrete the salt. The **insect life** of the salt marsh is abundant, including damselflies, brightly coloured grasshoppers and various ants and sand spiders. The **birds** are even more impressive, with black-winged stilt, greater flamingo, coot, great-crested grebe, and various gulls and terns wheeling overhead.

Further along the coast, a walk east of the resort of **RAS-EL-MAR** demonstrates the means by which plants invade **sand dunes**: a sequential colonization is known as "**succession**", where one plant community gradually cedes to the next as a result of its own alteration of the environment. Typical early colonizers are marram grass and sea couch, which are eventually ousted by sea holly and sea spurge and finally by large, "woodier" species such as pistacihu, juniper and cistus *sp*. Whole sequences can be seen occurring over time along the beach. The area attracts a variety of interesting **sea birds** as well, including the internationally rare **Audouin's gull** (thought to breed on the adjacent offshore Chafarinas Islands – see below). Other more familiar birds include dunlin, Kentish plover and oystercatcher.

Even further along the coast is the freshwater lagoon system which marks the mouth of the **OUED MOULOUYA**. The lagoons here are separated from the sea by a remarkable series of sand spits, no more than fifty metres across, and the **birdlife** is outstanding. Secluded among the reedbeds, it is possible to locate grey heron, white stork and little egret while the water's surface is constantly patrolled by the ever-alert black terns and kingfishers. Other varieties which you should manage to spot, wading in the shallows, are redshank, spotted redshank (in summer) and black-tailed godwit.

The Spanish-owned **Islas Chafarinas**, incidentally, are another important wildlife site, which Spanish ecologists are attempting to have declared a nature park. The three small islets support the Mediterranean's largest seabird colonies, and are home to the only known pair of **monk seals** surviving anywhere in Spanish waters. These are strictly protected as only about 500 pairs exist in the world.

Spanish lookout post en route to a shell-beach – a popular weekend spot with Spaniards from Melilla – before giving out at a tiny fishing village. On the beach, 1km beyond Kariet, is a **campsite**, *Camping Karia Plage*, and a ribbon of easy and relaxed café–restaurants and holiday homes.

Ras-El-Ma and the Oued Mouloya

The road **east of Kariet** is a pleasant drive, too, twisting into the hills, never far from the sea, and eventually bringing you to **RAS-EL-MA** (or Ras Kebdana, as it is also known), 70km from Nador – and closer to Saïdia and Berkane (see p.153). Facing another of Spain's offshore island possessions on this coast, the three tiny **Islas Chafarinas**, this is a mix of resort and fishing village, with a good **beach**, a smattering of cafés and street vendors, and a year-round **campsite**, *Camping Ras El Ma*, which has a small shop. Beyond the resort, dunes run virtually undisturbed to the Algerian border.

If you have your own transport, you could complete a loop back towards Nador from Ras-El-Ma, trailing the **Oued Moulouya** on road 8100 – or take the road across the river (once the border between the French and Spanish Protectorates) to the beaches around Saïdia (see p.153).

THE NADOR-MELILLA BORDER

On a good day you can cross the **Nador–Melilla border** in ten or fifteen minutes. At other times, you may need considerable time and patience. During the summer it's often extremely crowded, with Moroccans returning from (or going to) jobs in Europe, as well as travellers off the ferry. If you want to avoid the queues, it is a good idea to spend a couple of hours in Melilla after arriving off a ferry, to let the main traffic get through. Or travel on the next morning: Melilla is worth a stay.

If you are **driving**, be aware that smuggling goes on at the border, with periodic police crackdowns; in recent years, trading has included both drugs and people, with Moroccans (and sub-Saharan Africans) attempting to cross illegally into mainland Spain. Driving at night, keep an eye out for road checks – not always well lit but usually accompanied by tyre-puncturing blockades.

Hire cars, incidentally, are not allowed across the border, so if you want to take a day-trip to Melilla from Morocco, you'll have to use public transport.

GETTING TO THE BORDER

From Nador, there is a local bus and numerous *grands taxis* to the border post at **Beni Enzar**. Delays at the post are mainly on the Moroccan side, where officials can take a while collecting passports, passing them round and eventually stamping them. Leave up to two hours if you have a ferry connection to make.

From Melilla to **Beni Enzar** (and vice versa), there are buses to and from the Plaza de España (every 15min; takes 20min).

CURRENCY EXCHANGE

The frontier **currency exchange**, on both sides, is for cash only. However, you can use dirhams and pesetas quite widely in Melilla and Nador, and banks in both towns have exchange facilities between the two currencies.

Melilla (Mlilya)

There ought to be an eccentric appeal to Spanish-occupied **MELILLA**, and in part there is: if you're curious what provincial Spanish towns looked like in the late 1950s, there is no better place to come to find out. More conventional tourist pleasures are to be found, too, in an exploration of the walled old town, **Medina Sidonia**, with its stunning views out across the Mediterranean.

Together with Ceuta, Melilla is the last of Spain's Moroccan enclaves on Moroccan soil – a former penal colony which saw its most prosperous days under the Protectorate, when it was the main port for the Riffian mining industry. Since Moroccan independence in 1956, the city's population has halved to a little over 60,000, split two-to-one between Christians and Muslims, along with 3000 Jews and a few hundred Indian Hindus. Many of the Christians are gypsies, who, like the other communities, are reasonably well integrated, despite an episode of rioting in 1986, after the enactment of Spain's first real "Aliens Law" threatened to deprive certain Muslim families of their residence rights. There were further riots in 1996, when 400 Spanish Foreign Legionnaires, a tough bunch posted here by the Madrid authorities out of harm's way, went on the rampage after one of their number had been killed in a bar brawl.

Notwithstanding, Melilla is no "little Spain", for all its reputation on the Spanish mainland as traditional and right wing; and like Ceuta it actually wants – and has for a decade been promised – autonomous status: a plea which seems permanently lost in the Madrid government in-tray, for fear of offending Morocco. Meanwhile, the mainstay of the economy, as at Ceuta, remains the double anomaly of an army garrison plus the duty-free status of the port.

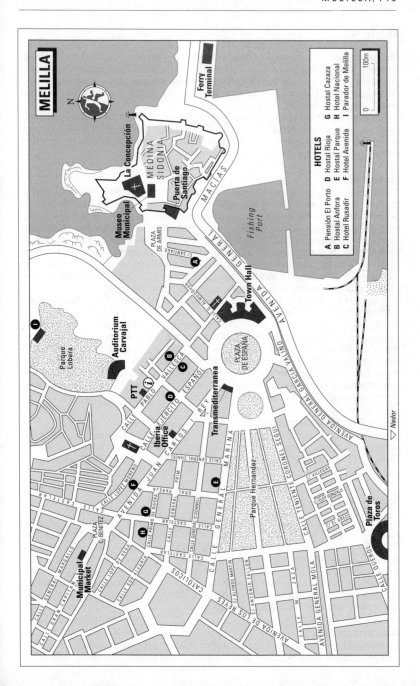

The Town

Melilla centres on the **Plaza de España**, overlooking the port, and the **Avenida Juan Carlos I Rey**, leading inland off it. This is the most animated part of town, especially during the evening *paseo*, when everyone promenades up and down, or strolls through the neighbouring **Parque Hernandez**, which on the town's numerous festival days hosts a fairground late into the night.

To the northeast, occupying a walled promontory, and adjacent to the ferry terminal, is the old part of town, **Medina Sidonia**. It is here that you should head, if you have time to fill waiting for a ferry – or you want to avoid queueing at the border after disembarking (see box on the Nador-Melilla border, p.148).

Medina Sidonia

Until the beginning of this century, the walled "Old Town" of **Medina Sidonia**, wedged in above the port, was all there was of Melilla. The enclave's security was always vulnerable, and at various periods of expansionist Moroccan rule – it was blockaded throughout the reign of Moulay Ismail – the Spanish population was limited to their fortress promontory and its sea approaches. The settlement was founded in 1497, a kind of epilogue to the expulsion of the Moors from Spain after the fall of Granada in 1492. The quarter's streets suggest the Andalucian Medinas of Tetouan or Chaouen, though inside, the design is much more formal; it was in fact laid out along the lines of a Castilian fort, following a major earthquake in the sixteenth century.

Steps near the fishing port lead up to the quarter's main square, **Plaza Maestranza**, entered by the Gothic **Puerta de Santiago**, a gate flanked by a chapel to Saint James the Apostle – known to Spaniards as *Matamoros*, "the Moor-Slayer". Beyond the square, which is in the throes of restoration, you come to an old barracks and armoury, and, if you follow the fortifications round from here, you'll come to a small fort, below which is the church of **La Concepción**, crowded with baroque decoration, including a revered statue of *Nuestra Señora de Victoria* (Our Lady of Victory), the city's patroness. A small **Museo Municipal** (Mon–Sat 10am–1pm & 5–7pm; free), nearby, houses a miscellany of historical documents, coins and ceramics.

The new town: Modernista

In the new town, many of the buildings around the **Plaza de España** were designed by **Enrique Nieto**, a *modernista* contemporary of the renowned Catalan architect, Gaudí. His 1930s tile and stucco facades are a quiet delight of the New Town, though, sadly, many of them are masked by the rows of duty-free shops.

Practicalities

Like Ceuta, Melilla is not that easy a place to stay; rooms tend to be in short supply – and are expensive by Moroccan standards. If you have problems, the **tourist office** (Mon–Fri 9am–2pm, Sat 10am–noon) in the Edificio de Correos, c/Pablo Vallesca, next to the *PTT* (post office), might be able to suggest alternatives. If possible, it's worth booking ahead.

There are a number of **banks** on or near Avda. Juan Carlos I Rey which will change cheques, sterling, dollars or dirhams. *Banco Central* is at c/Ejercito Español 1 and *Banco de España* is on the Plaza de España itself.

Accommodation

As noted above, rooms are quite pricey, with most budget hotels charging 5000–8000ptas for a double, more in high season (July–August). Still, you're unlikely to

PHONES AND CLOCKS

Phoning Melilla from Morocco, you must prefix phone numbers with the international and local codes (☎0034-52). To **phone Morocco from Melilla**, you need to dial ☎07, wait for a tone, then dial ☎212, followed by the local code and number. [Note: ☎07 will change to ☎00 by 1999].

Note also that Melilla works to **Spanish time**, which is usually one or two hours different from Moroccan time.

be staying more than a night. Note that the signposted campsite, on the Nador road at the edge of town, has been closed in recent years.

CHEAP

Pensión El Porto [A], c/Santiago 1 (☎68.12.70). A modern place, run by a Moroccan, this is the only real cheapie in town, with rooms from 2000ptas.

Hostal-Residencia Rioja [D], c/Ejercito Español 10 (☎68.27.09). Old but good value, with friendly and helpful staff. All rooms are en suite. Doubles from 3800ptas.

MODERATE

Hostal-Residencia Anfora [B], c/Pablo Vallesca 8 (☎68.33.40). A 2-star hotel, with some air-conditioned rooms. Has a bar and café and a top-floor restaurant with great views. Doubles from 8000ptas.

Hotel Avenida [F], Avda. Juan Carlos I Rey 24 (☎68.49.49). An old-style hotel above the China Town bazaar. It hardly merits its three stars but the rooms are all en suite. Doubles from 7500ptas.

Hostal-Residencia Cazaza [G], Avda. Primo de Rivera 6 (☎68.46.48). This is a fair walk from the centre, and the rooms are a little sombre, but it's a friendly, well-maintained place, with a small café on the ground floor for breakfast. Doubles from 5000ptas.

Hotel Nacional [H], Avda. Primo de Rivera 10 (☎68.45.40). Located just beyond the *Cazaza*, and with a slight edge over it in comfort. Doubles from 6000ptas.

Hostal-Residencia Parque [E], Avda. Generál Marina 15 (☎68.21.43). The location – opposite the park – is the best thing about this hotel. Rooms are very average. Nonetheless, it's a popular choice, invariably full. Doubles from 5500ptas.

EXPENSIVE

Parador de Melilla [I], Avda. de Candido Lobera – overlooking the Parque Lobera (☎68.49.40). The best upmarket choice: nothing much to look at, but with fine views over the town, and a swimming pool. Doubles from 14,000ptas.

Hotel Rusadir [C], c/Pablo Vallesca 5 (☎68.12.40). Melilla's top-range hotel is comfortable enough but lacks character or indeed anything much to justify its price – there's not even a pool. Doubles start at a hefty 16,000ptas.

Restaurants and bars

The nicest place to eat in Melilla is Medina Sidonia, for its stunning views and traditional surroundings. However, the main concentration of restaurants and tapas bars lies in the area east of Avda. Juan Carlos I Rey, between the Plaza de España and the Municipal Market.

MEDINA SIDONIA

La Muralla, c/Fiorentina 1 – in the southern corner of the ramparts. A good-looking restaurant, unbeatable for its position, and the cooking's good, too. Moderate to pricey.

Casa El Marco (aka Meson de la Tortilla), c/San Miguel 2. Closed for restoration at last look but worth checking to see if it has reopened. It boasted homely cooking and ambience.

NEW TOWN

Anthony Pizza Factory, c/Teniente Segui 18 – opposite the Parque Hernandez. Quick dishes and takeaways at modest prices. Open afternoons and evenings; closed Mon.

Bodegas Madrid, c/Castelar – on the left going up towards the market. This café-bar with wine-barrel tables serves drinks and snacks, and is one of the livelier night-time hangouts.

Bar El Moderno, c/Castelar – near *Bodegas Madrid*. Drinks and seafood tapas. Open late.

London Pub, c/Castelar – at the Parque Hernandez end. British-style pub.

La Pergola, Avda. Generál Macias, alongside the fishing port. A popular, youthful snack bar.

Caftería La Toga, Plaza Don Pedro de Estopiñan – just inland from the *Pension El Porto*. More of a pâtisserie than a café but good for a breakfast of hot chocolate and *churros*.

Restaurante Willy, just off c/Castelar – opposite *Bar Moderno*. Pizzas and pastas.

Ferries and flights

Ferries run three to five times a week between Melilla and **Málaga** and **Almería** (see p.9). Making advance bookings is critical in August – with waits of up to three days possible if you just turn up for a boat – and the period at the end of Semana Santa (Easter week) is also best avoided. For information and tickets, contact Transmediterrane*a*, Plaza de España 6 (☎68.12.45; Mon–Fri 9am–noon & 2–6pm; Sat 9am–noon).

Alternatively, for much the same cost, there are *Iberia* **flights** to **Málaga** (45min); up to eight a day in season, three to five daily out of season. Again, reserve ahead of time if possible, and be warned that flights don't leave in bad weather. The *Iberia* office is at the corner of Avda. Juan Carlos I Rey and c/Candido Lobera (☎68.24.34 or 68.15.07; Mon–Fri 9am–noon & 2–6pm). To call the **airport** direct, phone ☎68.99.47 or ☎68.99.48.

A helpful **travel agency** for information and reservations is *Andalucia Travel*, c/Teniente Segui 10, facing the Parque Hernandez (☎67.07.30; Mon–Fri 9am–noon & 2–6pm; Sat 9am–noon).

The Zegzel gorge, Berkane and Saïdia

The **route east from Nador to Oujda** is fast, efficient and well served by both buses and *grands taxis*. It holds little of interest along the way, but if you've got the time (or ideally a car), there's an attractive detour around Berkane into the **Zegzel gorge**, a dark limestone fault in the Beni Snassen mountains – the last outcrops of the Rif. And on the coast there is the considerable attraction of **Saïdia**, one of the country's most pleasant and relaxed seaside resorts.

The gorge route

The **Oued Zegzel** is a tributary of the Moulouya, which as it runs south of Berkane has carved out a fertile shaft of mountain valleys. These for centuries marked the limits of the Shereefian empire.

The route through these valleys is easily accessible today but still forbiddingly steep: virtually all traffic goes anti-clockwise (down) from Berkane to Taforalt, taking the P27 out of town and, after 10km, turning south onto the S403, climbing up to Taforalt, 10km from the turn-off. If you've got a car, this is the route to follow. If you're using public transport, stay on the bus to Berkane, where you can get a seat in a *grand taxi* to Taforalt and there negotiate another one back, this time via the gorge road. Neither is an expensive operation because the routes are used by locals as well as tourists.

Taforalt, the Grotte du Chameau and the gorge

TAFORALT is a quiet mountain village, active (or as active as it ever gets) only for the **Wednesday souk**. It does, though, have a reliable supply of *grands taxis*, and you should be able to move on rapidly towards the Zegzel gorge; before settling on a price, get the driver to agree to stop en route at the Chameau cave.

This – the **Grotte du Chameau** – is 10km from Taforalt, a cavern of vast stalactites, one of which is remarkably camel-like in shape (hence the name). The cave, with various tunnels leading off, is completely uncommercialized and it is not always open (you will need to locate the *gardien* to unlock the entrance); a torch is also essential. Near the entrance to the cave is a hot stream, which locals use for bathing.

The Zegzel gorge, or rather **gorges**, begin about a kilometre beyond the cave, scrupulously terraced and cultivated with all kinds of citrus and fruit trees. As the road crisscrosses the riverbed, they progressively narrow, drawing your eye to the cedars and dwarf oaks at the summit, until you eventually emerge (22km from Taforalt) on to the Berkane plain.

Berkane

BERKANE is a strategic little market town, French-built and prosperous, set amid an extensive region of orchards and vineyards. If you stay, you're likely to be the only European in the town – in consequence there are no hustlers and people may even buy *you* a coffee. Good eating places are to be found in the long, unpaved street running uphill from Av. Hassan II, along with lots of very dark, tented *souks*. Best of the four small **hotels** is the *Ennajah* (☎06/61.29.14; ⑩), on the corner of Bd. Hassan II and Bd. Moulay Youssef, uphill from the bus station; this also has a good restaurant, the owner having worked some time in Belgium.

Moving on from Berkane is straightforward, with frequent buses and *grands taxis* both to Oujda and Saïdia.

Saïdia

Sited almost on the Algerian border, **SAÏDIA** used to seem a good choice for staying put for a few days. A very low-key resort, rambling back from the sea in the shadow of an old and still occupied nineteenth-century Kasbah, it is fronted by one of the best beaches on the Mediterranean – an immense, sandy strand, stretching west to face the tiny Chafarinas islands at Ras-El-Ma (see p.147), and east, across the Oued Kiss, towards Algeria. In better times, it was a very relaxed place, Moroccans and Algerians mixing together by the seaside. These days, however, with what amounts to civil war in Algeria, there's a definite tension, signalled by a strong military presence guarding the beach and river bank.

If you stay here, you're likely to be a rare foreign visitor, though you might find the occasional European bird-watcher in residence. Saïdia has rewarding bird sites in the marshes and woodland stretching behind the beach towards the Oued Moulouya (see box on p.147).

Saïdia really only comes into its own in July and August, when many Moroccan families camp by the beach, and two small hotels open their doors. These are the *Hannour* (☎06/62.51.15; ③) and the *Paco* (☎06/62.51.10; ②); either should be reserved in advance, if possible. Other months, the resort is near deserted. There is also a **campsite**, *Camping El Mansour*, on the road in from Ras El Mar and the Oued Moulouya. The liveliest of the **café-restaurants** are by the market, past the Kasbah. At night, the *Hôtel Hannour* is the centre of life, with its **bar**, restaurant and occasional entertainment.

There are regular **buses** and **grands taxis** between Saïdia and Oujda.

A NOTE ON ALGERIA

It scarcely needs saying but Algeria is effectively off-limits to all foreign visitors. Since the nullified elections in 1993, over 40,000 people have been killed in attacks and reprisals by Islamic fundamentalists and the army. Foreigners, as well as Algerian intellectuals, journalists, and musicians, have been particular targets. Although it is still possible to obtain entry visas for Algeria, and (sometimes) to cross at Oujda, entering the country for the foreseeable future is extremely unwise.

Oujda

Open and easy-going, with a large and active university, **OUJDA** has that rare quality in Moroccan cities – nobody makes demands on your instinct for self-preservation. After the Rif, it is a surprise, too, to see women in public again, and to re-enter a Gallic atmosphere – as you move out of what used to be Spanish Morocco into the old French Protectorate zone. Morocco's easternmost town, Oujda was the capital of French *Maroc Orient* and an important trading centre. It remains today a lively and relatively prosperous place, strikingly modern by Moroccan standards, and with a population approaching half a million.

With its strategic location at the crossroads of eastern and southern routes across Morocco-Algeria, Oujda, like Taza, was always vulnerable to invasion and has frequently been the focus of territorial claims. In the thirteenth and fourteenth centuries, there were periods of occupation by the Algerian Ziyanids of Tlemcen, and from 1727 until the early nineteenth century Oujda was under Turkish rule – the only town in present-day Morocco to have been part of the Ottoman Empire. Following the French defeat of the Ottomans in Algeria, France twice occupied the town, prior to its incorporation within the Moroccan Protectorate in 1912: an early and prolonged association, which remains tangible in the streets and attitudes.

In recent years, the town's proximity to the Algerian border and distance from the government in Rabat led to a reputation for dissidence and unrest. This was particularly evident during the Algerian border war in the early 1960s, and again, in the 1980s, in a series of student strikes. Just as important, however, was the restoration of Moroccan-Algerian relations in 1988, when for a time the city became truely pan-Maghrebi, with Algerians coming in to shop, and Moroccans sharing in some of the cultural dynamism of neighbouring Oran, the home of *Raï* music. Alas, this is all in the past now, following Algeria's descent into civil war, and the closure of the border.

Orientation and accommodation

Oujda consists of the usual **Medina** and **Ville Nouvelle**, the latter highly linear in its layout, having started out as a military camp. The Medina, walled on three sides, lies right in the heart of town, with **Place du 16 Août**, the town's main square, at its northwest corner. Around this square are grouped the Hôtel de Ville, the **post office**, several **banks**, and a **tourist office** (open daily 8am–noon & 2.30–6.30pm).

Arriving at the **train station** you are in easy walking distance of the centre. The new **bus station**, which handles virtually all services, CTM and private, is more of a walk (or an inexpensive *petit taxi* ride), 500m southwest of the train station, across the Oued Nachef. The **airport**, *Les Angads*, is 15km north, off the P27; in town, *RAM* has an office alongside the *Hôtel Oujda* on Bd. Mohammed V (☎06/68.39.63).

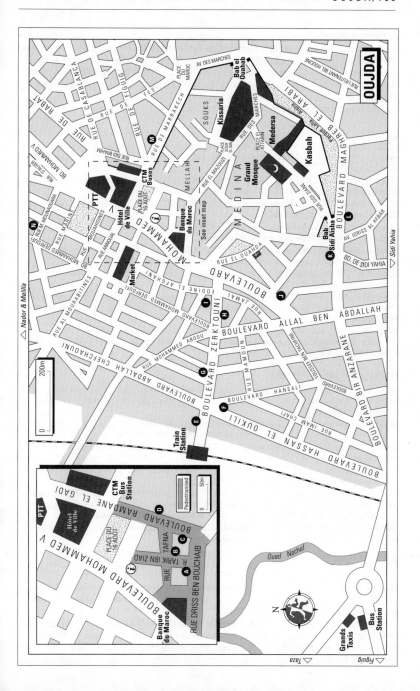

Accommodation

There are a number of **unclassified hotels** in the **Medina**; many are poor value, but the better choices are detailed below. Around the **Ville Nouvelle** are a range of much better, classified hotels, many of them built in the early 1990s. Booking ahead is a good idea during holiday periods, when many Moroccan migrant workers return home to their families.

The closest **campsite** is in Saïdia (see p.153).

CHEAP

Hôtel Afrah [B], 15 Rue Tafna (☎06/68.65.33). A modern hotel, opened in 1991, with neat decor and a fine view across the Medina from its rooftop café. Comfortable, if small, en-suite rooms, heated in winter. ①

Hôtel Angad [C], Bd. Ramdane El Gadi (☎06/69.14.52). Another newish hotel, on a pedestrianized street just inside the Medina. En-suite rooms and a breakfast café. ①

Hôtel 16 Août [M], 128 Rue de Marrakech (☎06/68.41.97). Best of the unclassified hotels, with clean rooms and hot showers. ⑩

Chic Hôtel [D], 34 Bd. Ramdane El Gadi (☎06/69.05.66). The name's a bit optimistic but this is yet another early 90s hotel, pleasant and well-maintained. ⑩

Hôtel Lutetia [F], 44 Bd. Hassan Loukili (☎06/68.33.65). An old hotel that looks its age, but respectable enough and conveniently positioned right by the train station. ①

Hôtel Riad [K], Av. Idriss Al Akbar (☎06/68.83.53). Another 1991-vintage hotel. Good value, with a café and friendly bar. ②

Royal Hôtel [H], 13 Bd. Zerktouni (☎06/68.22.84). Another old hotel but a much better option with clean rooms with hot showers, and a secure garage. Next door, the *Café Les Pyramides* provides breakfast. ①

Hôtel Simon [A], corner of Rue Tariq Ibn Ziad and Idriss Ben Bouchaib (☎06/68.63.03). Located just inside the Medina, this was the first European-style hotel in Oujda – opened in 1910. It remains a nice, firendly place, with a restaurant and bar. ①

MODERATE TO EXPENSIVE

Hôtel des Lilas [I], Rue Jamal Eddine El Afghani (☎06/68.08.40). A decent, modern hotel – with a restaurant but no bar. It has a number of luxury suites, which are often offered at more or less normal room rates. ④

Hôtel El Mamounia [N], Rue Madina El Mounaouara (☎06/69.00.72). This is a good value-for-money choice: central, comfortable, well-maintained, and with a restaurant. ②

Hôtel Al Manar [G], 50 Bd. Zerktouni (☎06/69.70.37). A smart, modest establishment, opened in 1992 and wearing well. ③

Hôtel Al Massira [L], Bd. Maghreb El Arabi (☎06/68.53.02). Comfortable, modern hotel, with a pool and tennis court, in a pleasant part of town. ③

Moussafir Hôtel [E], Bd. Abdallah Chefchaouni/Place de la Gare (☎06/68.82.02). One of the elegant "blue and white" chain of hotels, to be found by major rail stations. It has a restaurant, bar, swimming pool, TVs in all rooms, and at 300dh for a double, is pretty good value. ③

Hôtel Oujda [J], Bd. Mohammed V (☎06/68.44.82). An old-established landmark hotel, undistinguished but with a popular bar and a small swimming pool. ④

The Town

Oujda's **Medina** is largely a French reconstruction – obvious by the ease with which you can find your way around. Unusually, though, it has retained much of the city's commercial functions and has an enjoyably active air.

Entering from **Bab El Ouahab**, the principal gate, you'll be struck by the amazing variety of food – both on café and market stalls – and it's well worth a look for this alone. Olives are Oujda specialities, and especially wonderful if you're about after the September harvest. In the old days, more or less up until the French occupation, Bab

El Ouahab was the gate where the heads of criminals were displayed. In the evenings it is still a square where storytellers and musicians come to entertain, an increasing rarity in post-independence Morocco.

Exploring the quarter, a good route to follow from the gate is straight down the main street towards **Place El Attarin**, flanked by a *kissaria* (covered market) and a grand *fondouk*. At the far end of the *souks* you come upon **Souk El Ma**, the irrigation *souk*, where the supply of water used to be regulated and sold by the hour. Walking on from here, you'll arrive back at Place du 16 Août.

Running along the outside of the Medina walls, the **Parc Lalla Aisha** is a pleasant area to seek midday shade. Following it round to the west takes you to the Bab Sidi Aisha, from which Rue El Ouahda runs north to the old French **Cathedrale Saint Louis**. This is an evocative place. Its present congregation (mass is held on Sat 6.30pm and Sun 9am) numbers about ten, the fonts are dry, and the statue niches empty, but there is a beautiful chapel; for admission, ring at the door of the presbytery at the back, on Rue d'Azila.

Eating and drinking

Oujda has a strong cultural life and is one of the most enjoyable Moroccan cities to while away an evening. Hustlers don't really feature here and the bars and restaurants are sociable and open places.

Restaurants
The focus of evening activity is **Bab El Ouahab**, around which you can get all kinds of grilled food from stalls. On the other side of the Medina, too, there are plenty of good eating places on, or just off, **Bd. Zerktouni**.

In the **Ville Nouvelle**, in addition to the hotel restaurants mentioned opposite, recommended restaurants include:

Restaurant aux Delices (aka **Dauphin**), Bd. Mohammed Derfoufi, near the Mamounia hotel. Good for quick dishes – *brochettes*, pizzas, etc.

Brasserie Restaurant de France, Bd. Mohammed V. One of the fancier places in town, with a nightclub attached. Offers a mix of French and Moroccan dishes, well prepared, though at quite a price.

Iris Sandwich, Av. Idriss Al Akbar – near the *Al Massira* and *Riad* hotels. A good cheapie.

Restaurant Marius, Rue Mouahidines – between Bd. Mohammed V and Bd. Mohammed Derfoufi. An established restaurant, with dependable French and Moroccan cooking. Expect to pay around 100dh a head.

Restaurant Tourisme – one of several small café-restaurants on the pedestrianized streets south of Place du 16 Août. A friendly place with a small menu of staples, all well prepared.

Bars
Most of the town's bars are to be found in the **hotels**. Good bets include those in the *Moussafir*, the *Riad*, and the *Simon*. A lively local place is: **Bar Restaurant du Palais**, Bd. Mohammed Derfoufi.

Sidi Yahia

SIDI YAHIA, 6km south of Oujda, is a rather unimpressive little oasis for most of the year, with a "cascade" that is switched on at weekends. However, it's a place of some veneration, housing as it does the tomb of the *marabout* **Sidi Yahia**, a holy man identified by local tradition with John the Baptist. Nobody is quite sure where the saint is buried – several of the cafés stake an optimistic claim – but at the **moussems** held here in August and September almost every shrub and tree in the oasis is festooned with little pieces of cloth, a ritual as lavish and extraordinary as anything in the Mediterranean church.

South to Figuig

In past years, before the eruption of civil war in Algeria, there was a well-established travel route from Oujda, south to the ancient **date palm oasis of Figuig**, and across from there into the Algerian Sahara. This is no longer a possibility. However, those into isolated journeys might still want to consider the route from **Oujda** to **Figuig** – and on from there to the southern Moroccan oasis town of **Er Rachidia** (see Chapter Seven).

If you're on for the trip, be warned it's a long, hot haul: 369km from Oujda to Figuig, and a further 393km to Er Rachidia. You can travel by bus (there is usually a 6am departure from Oujda, arriving at Figuig around 1pm; later departures will subject you to the full heat of the day), or, if you have transport, you can drive: the road is paved all the way. There is also a weekly passenger train from Oujda to Bouarfa (leaving Oujda Saturday evening, and returning from Bouarfa on the Sunday morning), near Figuig.

Whichever way you travel, expect to explain yourself at a number of military checkpoints: this is a sensitive border area.

The route

En route between Oujda and Figuig there are just a few roadside settlements and mining towns – for coal, copper, manganese and zinc. If you are driving, **AÏT BENI-MATHAR**, 83km from Oujda, is a good point to break the journey: the village has a group of Kasbahs, an important (and ancient) **Monday souk**, and some grill-cafés. About 4km to its west is a small oasis, **Ras El Aïn**, with a (highly seasonal) waterfall.

Another possible stop could be **TENDRARA**, 198km from Oujda, a larger settlement with an important **Thursday souk**; it has a traditional marketplace in the centre and sheep and goats coralled on the outskirts. Again, there are grill-cafés.

At 241km, you reach **BOUARFA**, the region's administrative centre and transport hub, with buses to Er Rachidia (as well as Figuig and Oujda), and a couple of hotels. For details of **Bourfa, Figuig, and the route to Er Rachidia**, see p.446.

travel details

Trains

From Taza 4 trains daily to Oujda (3hr 15min–3hr 35min), and in the other direction to Fes (2hr) and Meknes (3hr 15min–3hr 45min).

From Oujda 4 trains daily to Taza (3hr 15min–3hr 40min), Fes (5hr 15min–5hr 40min) and Meknes (6hr 30min–7hr 25min). Also, on Saturday night, there are passenger seats on a freight train to Bouarfa, it returns the following morning.

Note: ONCF runs connecting *Supratour* coaches to/from Nador from/to Taourirt, midway between Taza and Oujda.

Buses

From Al Hoceima CTM to Nador (2 daily; 3hr); and to Tetouan (2 daily; 5hr 30min). Other lines to Nador (2 daily; 3hr 30min); and to Fes (1 daily; 7hr).

From Berkane to Oujda (6 daily; 1hr); and to Saïdia (4 daily; 1 hr).

From Nador CTM to Casablanca (1 daily; 11hr 45min); to Oujda (4 daily; 2hr 30min); to Tetouan (2 daily; 9hr 30min); to Tangier via Fes (1 daily; 12hr) and to Al Hoceima (2 daily; 3hr 30min).

From Oujda CTM to Casablanca via Rabat (1 daily; 11hr 30min); to Fes (1 daily; 6hr 30min); and to Nador (4 daily; 2hr 30min). Other lines to Saïdia (6 daily, 1hr); to Figuig (3 daily ; 7hr); and to Midelt (1 daily; 13hr).

From Taza CTM to Casablanca, via Fes, Meknes and Rabat (1 daily; 7hr 30min).

Grands Taxis

From Al Hoceima Regularly to Nador (3hr). Infrequently to Fes and Taza.

From Nador Regularly to Oujda (2hr 30min) and Al Hoceima (3hr).

From Oujda Regularly to Saïdia (50min) and Taza (2hr 30min).

From Taza Regularly to Fes (1hr 30min) and Oujda (2hr 30min). Occasionally to Al Hoceima.

Flights

From Al Hoceima In summer, three flights a week on **RAM** to Casablanca, two direct and one via Tangier; two days a week to Agadir, to Marrakesh and to Ouarzazate (all via Casablanca). In addition, there are direct flights to Tangier (two days a week), to Tetouan (one day a week), to Amsterdam (five days a week) and to Brussels (one day a week). In winter, two flights a week on *RAM* to Casablanca and one flight a week to Tetouan; two days a week to Agadir, to Marrakesh and to Ouarzazate (all via Casablanca). In addition, there is one direct flight a week to Amsterdam.

From Melilla On **Iberia**: to Málaga (at least five flights daily; 45min); to Almería (daily in mornings; 40min); Granada (two flights weekly; 50min); to Madrid (daily flights in mornings, via Málaga; 3hr).

From Oujda In summer, daily (except Sunday) flights on **RAM** to Casablanca and from there to Agadir (five days a week) and to Tangier (five days a week). In addition, there are direct flights to Amsterdam (four days a week), to Brussels (one day a week) and to Paris (two days a week). In winter, daily (except Sunday) flights on *RAM* to Casablanca and from there to Agadir (five days a week), to Marrakesh (two days a week) and to Tangier (four days a week). In addtion, there are direct flights to Amsterdam (two days a week), to Brussels (one day a week) and to Paris (two days a week).

Ferries

For details of ferry routes, see p.8.

CHAPTER THREE

MEKNES, FES AND THE MIDDLE ATLAS

T he undoubted highlight of this chapter is Fes. The imperial capital of the Merenid, Wattasid and Alaouite dynasties, the city has for the past ten centuries stood at the heart of Moroccan history – and for five of these it was one of the major intellectual and cultural centres of the West, rivalling the great university cities of Europe. It is today unique in the Arab world, preserving the appearance and much of the life of a medieval Islamic city. In terms of monuments, it has as much as the other Moroccan imperial capitals together, while the city's *souks*, extending for over a mile, maintain the whole tradition of urban crafts.

In all of this – and equally in the everyday aspects of the city's life – there is enormous fascination and, for the outsider, a real feeling of privilege. But inevitably, it is at a cost. Declared a historical monument by its French colonizers, and subsequently deprived of its political and cultural significance, Fes today retains its beauty but is in evident decline. Its university faculties have been dispersed around the country, with the most important departments in Rabat; the Fassi business elite have mostly left for Casablanca; and, for survival, the city depends increasingly on the tourist trade. Nonetheless, two or three days here is an absolute must for any visit to Morocco.

Meknes, like Fes (and Rabat and Marrakesh) an imperial city, sees comparatively few visitors, despite being an easy and convenient stopover en route by train from Tangier or Rabat, or by bus from Chaouen. The megalomaniac creation of Moulay Ismail, the most tyrannical of all Moroccan sultans, it is once again a city of lost ages, its enduring impression being that of an endless series of walls. But Meknes is also an important modern market centre and its *souks*, though smaller and less secretive than those of Fes, are almost as varied and generally more authentic. There are, too, the local attractions of **Volubilis**, the best preserved of the country's Roman sites, and the hilltop town of **Moulay Idriss**, home to the most important Islamic shrine in Morocco.

South of the two imperial cities stretch the cedar-covered slopes of the **Middle Atlas**, which in turn gradually give way to the High Atlas. Across and around this region, often beautiful and for the most part remote, there are two main routes. The most popular, a day's journey by bus, skirts the range beyond the market town of **Azrou** to emerge via **Beni Mellal** at Marrakesh. The second climbs southeastward from Azrou towards **Midelt**, an excellent carpet centre, before passing through great gorges to Er Rachidia and the vast date palm oasis of Tafilalt – the beginning of a tremendous southern circuit (see Chapter Seven). A third and distinctly adventurous route runs between these two, leaving the main Azrou–Marrakesh highway at **El Ksiba** and following a series of pistes (dirt roads) directly **across the Atlas** to Tinerhir (again, see Chapter Seven). You can take the latter route if you have a 4x4 – or by getting lifts over the various stages in local Berber lorries,

If you're travelling one of the main highways, and you've got the time, the Middle Atlas has considerable attractions of its own. Close to Fes, **Immouzer** and **Ifrane** are popular summer resorts, their air and waters a cool escape from the city. The Berber market town of **Azrou** is host to a great **Tuesday souk** and surrounded by pine forests and mountain lakes. And off the Marrakesh road, near Beni Mellal, are the **Cascades d'Ouzoud** – waterfalls which crash down from the mountains, even in midsummer, and beside which you can swim, camp and hike.

Meknes

Cut in two by the wide river valley of the Oued Boufekrane, **MEKNES** is a sprawling, prosperous provincial city. Monuments from its past – dominated by the extraordinary creations of Moulay Ismail (for more on whom, see p.169) – justify a day's rambling exploration, as do the varied and busy *souks* of its Medina. In addition, the Ville Nouvelle is pleasant and easy to handle, and there is the appeal of Roman Volubilis, within easy short bus or taxi distance.

To get the most out of the city's monuments and the atmosphere of the Medina and *souks*, it's best to visit before heading to Fes. Getting a grasp of Meknes prepares you a little for the drama of Fes, and it certainly helps give an idea of quality (and prices) for crafts shopping; visited second, it is inevitably a little disappointing by comparison.

Orientation and accommodation

Meknes is simpler than it looks on the map. Its **Ville Nouvelle** (aka in Arabic, *Hamriya*) stretches along a slope above the east bank of the river, radiating from an impressive public square, the **Place Administrative** – a stretch of garden and a foun-

---

HOTEL PRICE CODES AND STAR RATINGS

Hotels are no longer obliged to charge according to the official star-ratings (from 1* to 5* luxury), as had long been the custom. Nevertheless, **prices** continue to reflect the star-ratings acquired. The basis of our own **hotel price codes**, set out below and keyed throughout the guide, is the price currently quoted for the cheapest double room in high season (June–September) – and is thus more reliable than quoting notional prices according to star-rating.

Note that cheaper prices in the lower categories are generally for rooms with just a wash-basin – you always pay extra for **en-suite** shower and WC – and that double rooms can generally be converted into **triples/family rooms**, with extra beds, for a modest extra charge. Note also that the prices quoted by all hotels are subject to various local and regional **taxes**, which can add 15 to 20 percent to the bill.

Our code	Classification	Single room price	Double room price
⓪	Unclassified	25–60dh	50–99dh
①	1*A/1*B	60–105dh	100–149dh
②	2*B/2*A	105–145dh	150–199dh
③	3*B/3*A	145–225dh	200–299dh
④	4*B/4*A	225–400dh	300–599dh
⑤	5*luxury	Upwards of 400dh	Upwards of 600dh

TELEPHONE CODES

All telephone numbers in the Meknes/Fes region are prefixed **05**. When making a call within the region you omit this prefix. For more explanation of phone codes and making calls within (or to) Morocco, see pp.45–46.

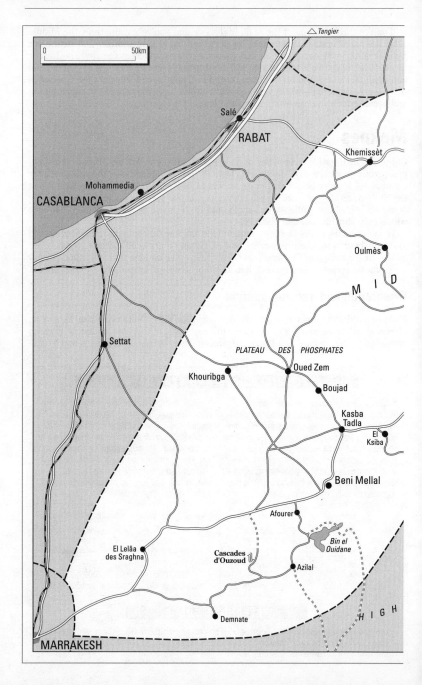

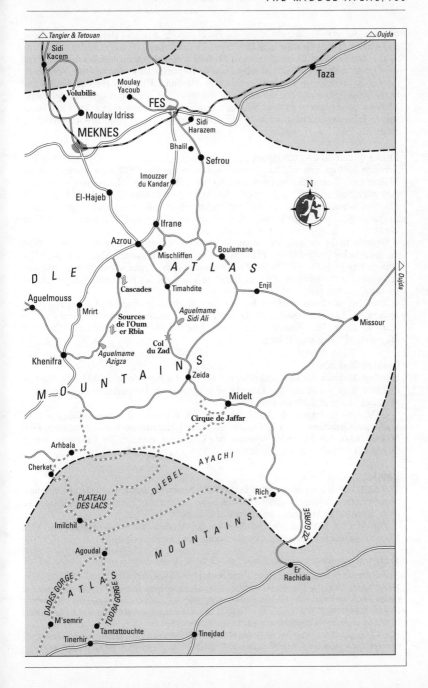

tain, flanked by the main post office, the Hôtel de Ville, a helpful Délégué du Tourisme, and a block of flats on stilts built in 1953 by Le Corbusier.

The **Medina** and its neighbouring **Mellah** (the old Jewish quarters) occupy the west bank, with the walls of Moulay Ismail's **Imperial City** edging away, seemingly forever, to their south. The focal point of the Medina is **Place El Hedim**, remodelled in the 1990s into a vast pedestrian plaza with fountains, decorated arcades and shops. This is a good place to fix your bearings: downhill, *petits taxis*, *grands taxis* and buses run to local destinations, while uphill buses #5, #7 and #9 head towards the Ville Nouvelle.

Points of arrival and transport

Arriving by **bus** you will be dropped either at the old **CTM bus station** on Av. Mohammed V, near the junction with Av. des F.A.R. in the Ville Nouvelle, or at the new main **bus station** on the north side of the New Mellah, just outside the Bab El Khemis. When leaving, you'll find that the bus station destinations indicators are in Arabic only; if you have problems, you can ask at the small one-man information kiosk.

Grands taxis use terminals alongside the new bus station or across the road from the local buses parked below Place El Hedim (see above) in the Medina, and on Rue Ghana, alongside the *PTT* in the Ville Nouvelle. There's also a **taxi** rank (*grands* and *petits taxis*) at the junction of Av. Mohammed V and Av. des F.A.R. which is convenient for the CTM bus station or hotels in that area.

There are two **train stations**, both in the Ville Nouvelle on the east bank. The **main station** is a kilometre away from the central area; a smaller, more convenient one, the **Gare El Amir Abdelkader**, is a couple of blocks from the centre (behind the *Hôtel Majestic*); all trains stop at both.

Leaving Meknes

Leaving Meknes for **Fes**, you have the choice of either taking a CTM bus, train or, quickest of all, *grand taxi*; the latter leave Meknes from alongside the bus station and set down in Fes at the train station.

CTM have at least daily departures, too, for **Rissani** (via Azrou, Midelt and Er Rachidia), **Casablanca** (via Khémisset and Rabat) **Marrakesh** (via Khenifra and Beni Mellal), **Taza** (via Fes) and **Tetouan** (via Chaouen). Heading for **Chaouen**, check times, and try to buy a ticket in advance.

Hotels

Meknes's hotels are concentrated in the **Ville Nouvelle**, and if you want any comfort, or proximity to bars and restaurants, this is the place to stay. It's only a ten-minute walk from there to the **Medina**, monuments and *souks*.

The Medina hotels are keyed A–F on the **Medina map** (see p.168); the Ville Nouvelle hotels are keyed G–M on the **main map** (see overleaf).

MEDINA HOTELS
These are all un-starred cheapies – and with pretty basic facilities.

Hôtel Agadir [C], Rue Dar Smen (☎05/53.01.41). Clean, friendly and with a bit of character, but rooms small and basic – and there are no showers. ①

Maroc Hôtel [A], 7 Rue Rouamzine (☎05/53.00.75). Pleasant, cleanest and quietist of Medina hotels; some rooms look onto a courtyard; cold showers. ①

Hôtel Meknes [E], 35 Rue Dar Smen (no phone). Undistinguished and not as friendly as most; it's between *Hôtel Nouveau* and *Hôtel Regina*, and possibly best as a fall-back if both are full. ①

Hôtel Nouveau [F], 65 Rue Dar Smen (☎05/53.31.39). Opposite the Banque Populaire. Helpful, warm reception, basic facilities – and claims (despite name) to be the first hotel in the Medina. ①

Hôtel de Paris [B], 58 Rue Rouamzine, (no phone). Up from the *Maroc Hôtel* and on the opposite side of the street; it's an older hotel, without showers, but there's a *hammam* nearby. ①

Hôtel Regina [D], 19 Rue Dar Smen (☎05/53.02.80). Gloomy and not too clean, with cold showers – but it's the cheapest hereabouts and central. ①

VILLE NOUVELLE HOTELS

Note that there are several prominent hotels in the Ville Nouvelle which are basically brothels – or unsuitable for one reason or another. Aim for those listed below and, even then, check tactfully before registering.

CHEAP

Auberge de Jeunesse (Youth Hostel) [B], Av. Okba Ibn Nafi, near the grand *Hôtel Transatlantique* (☎05/52.46.98). It's 1.5km from the train station; take bus #15. A well-maintained and friendly hostel with rooms around a courtyard. It's open all year: 8–10am, noon–3pm & 6–10pm (midnight in summer).

Hôtel Bordeaux [M], 64 Av. de la Gare (☎05/52.25.63). Near the main train station. There is no obvious sign and it stands off the road, but it is well worth the search; it is alongside the *Volvo* garage and opposite an old CTM garage. Friendly and a good atmosphere. Shady garden. ①

Hôtel du Marché [C], 1 Rue Abou Hassan M'Rini, on the corner with Av. Hassan II (no phone). This has seen better days but it's a better cheapie than the Medina places and has a handy *petit taxi* rank right outside the door. ①

Hôtel Touring [G], 34 Av. Allal Ben Abdallah (☎05/52.23.51). Central and quite congenial, though the facilities are pretty average and the showers aren't always hot. You pay a little more for en-suite facilities. ①

MODERATE

Hôtel Majestic [H], 19 Av. Mohammed V (☎05/52.20.35). An old, but comfortable hotel, with friendly management and clean, balconied rooms. Recently a terrace has been created for alfresco breakfasts. Some rooms are en suite; all in all, probably the best mid-priced choice in the Ville Nouvelle – and convenient for the El Amir Abdelkader train station. ②–③

Hôtel de Nice [E], 10 Rue Accra (☎05/52.03.18). A reasonable old hotel with helpful management; there's a bar, but the restaurant is now closed. Good value for money. ③

Hôtel Ouislane [I], 54 Av. Allal Ben Abdallah (☎05/52.17.43). This is a failsafe if nothing else is available – a basic, old hotel, overpriced for the (poor) facilities on offer. ②

Hôtel Palace [F], 11 Rue Ghana (☎05/51.12.60). A better choice, with respectable rooms and a reasonable bar. En-suite rooms cost more. ②–③

Rif Hôtel [D], Rue Accra (☎05/52.25.91). An upmarket 1950s hotel, bang in the centre, used by tour groups. It has a bar, good restaurant and a small swiming pool. ④

EXPENSIVE

Hôtel Akouas [L], 27 Rue Emir Abdelkader (☎05/51.59.67). This new, central hotel is a good choice – and not to be confused with the adjacent *Hôtel Excelsior*. There's a lively night-life hereabouts – and the *Akouas* has its own nightclub – but the rooms are quiet. ④

Hôtel Bab Mansour [K], 38 Rue Emir Abdelkader (☎05/52.52.39). Another modern hotel, opposite the *Akouas*, which recommends itself as the choice 'pour hommes d'affaires'. It has a covered garage, a bar, a nightclub and a restaurant that touts its fish specialities. ④

Hôtel Transatlantique [A], Rue El Marinyen (☎05/52.50.51). Meknes's luxury hotel has lovely gardens, stunning views, and a good-sized swimming pool. Nevertheless, it's not in the *Palais Jamai* nor *La Mamounia* class, despite the price which, for a double room, is nearly 1000dh. ⑤

Hôtel Volubilis [J], 45 Av. des F.A.R. (☎05/52.50.82). One of the older hotels in this quarter; it's still good, but it's on a noisy junction, not helped by the busy bar next door. ④

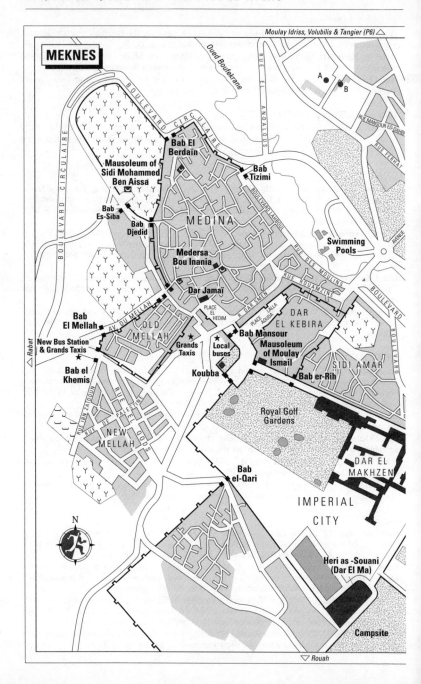

MEKNES

Moulay Idriss, Volubilis & Tangier (P6) △

Oued Boufekrane

RUE EL ANDALOUS

RUE MANSOUR ED-DAHBI

A

B

RUE FERHAT

BOULEVARD CIRCULAIRE

BOULEVARD CIRCULAIRE

Bab El Berdaïn

Mausoleum of Sidi Mohammed Ben Aissa

Bab Tizimi

Bab Es-Siba

Bab Djedid

MEDINA

BOULEVARD LAHBOUL

Swimming Pools

AVENUE

Medersa Bou Inania

RUE DES MOULINS

RUE ROUAMZINE

Dar Jamaï

PLACE EL HEDIM

R. DAR SMEN

PLACE LALLA AOUDA

RUE LALLA

DAR EL KEBIRA

BOULEVARD

Bab El Mellah

AV. DU MELLAH

OLD MELLAH

New Bus Station & Grands Taxis ★

Grands Taxis ★

Bab Mansour

Local buses ★

Mausoleum of Moulay Ismail

SIDI AMAR

Bab el Khemis

RUE IBN ZAIDOUN

RUE DE PALESTINE

Koubba ◆

Bab er-Rih

△ Rabat

NEW MELLAH

RUE DE PALESTINE OODS

Royal Golf Gardens

DAR EL MAKHZEN

Bab el-Qari

IMPERIAL CITY

N

Heri as-Souani (Dar El Ma)

Campsite

▽ Rouah

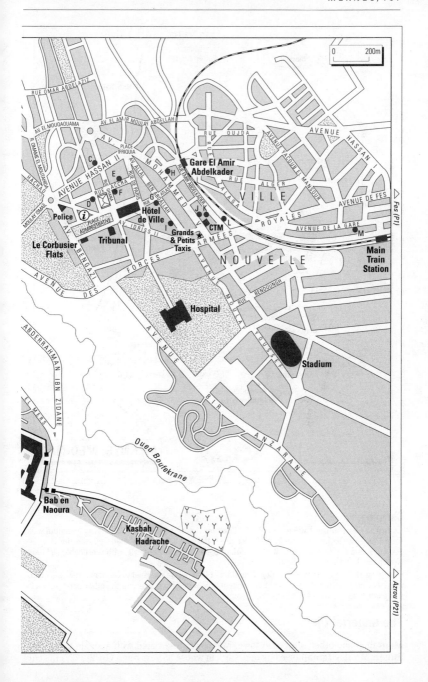

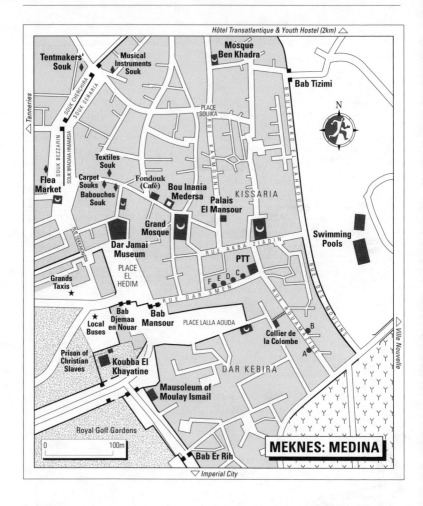

Hôtel Transatlantique & Youth Hostel (2km)

MEKNES: MEDINA

Camping

Camping Caravaning International, aka *Camping Aguedal* (☎05/55.18.28).A twenty-minute walk from Place El Hedim (or a 10dh *petit taxi* ride), the city campsite is sited opposite the Heri as-Souani. It is a pleasant, shaded site (*aguedal*, or *agdal*, means "garden"), with reasonable facilities. Not cheap, but a superb position.

Camping Belle-Vue (☎05/54.41.68). This site is 14km out on the road to Moulay Idriss. It's not as good as *Camping Aguedal* and is not convenient unless you have a car; on the other hand, buses to and from Moulay Idriss will drop or pick you up.

The Imperial City

More than any other Moroccan town, Meknes is associated with a single figure, the **Sultan Moulay Ismail** (see box opposite), in whose 55-year reign (1672–1727) the city

THE SULTAN MOULAY ISMAIL (1672–1727)

"The Sultan Moulay Ismail," wrote his chronicler, Ezziani, "loved Mequinez, and he would have liked never to leave it." But leave it he did, ceaselessly campaigning against the rebel Berber chiefs of the south, and the Europeans entrenched in Tangier, Asilah and Larache, until the entire country – for the first time in five centuries – lay completely under government control. His reign saw the creation of Morocco's strongest ever – and most coherent – army, which included a crack Negro guard, the Abid regiment, and, it is reckoned, a garrison force of one in twenty of the male population. The period was, in a very real sense, Morocco's last golden age, though the ruthless centralization of all decisions, and the fear with which the sultan reigned, led, perhaps inevitably, to a subsequent slide into anarchy and weak, inward-looking rule.

Ismail's achievements were matched by his tyrannies, which, even by the standards of the time – and contemporary Europeans were burning their enemies and torturing them on the rack – were judged extreme. His reign began with the display at Fes of 400 heads, most of them of captured chiefs, and over the next five decades, apart from battles, it is estimated that he was responsible for over 30,000 deaths. Many of these killings were quite arbitrary. Mounting a horse, Ismail might slash the head off the eunuch holding his stirrup; inspecting the work on his buildings, he would carry a weighted lance, with which to batter skulls in order to "encourage" the others. "My subjects are like rats in a basket," he used to say, "and if I do not keep shaking the basket they will gnaw their way through."

Throughout Morocco, the sultan was a tireless builder, constructing towns and ports, and a multitude of defensive Kasbahs, palaces and bridges. By far his greatest efforts, however, were directed at Meknes, where he sustained an obsessive building programme, often acting as architect and sometimes even working alongside the slaves and labourers. Ironically, in Meknes itself, the passing of time has not been easy on his constructions. Built mainly in *tabia*, a mixture of earth and lime, they were severely damaged by a hurricane even in his lifetime, and thereafter, with subsequent Alaouite sultans shifting their capitals back to Fes and Marrakesh, were left to decay. Walter Harris, writing only 150 years after Ismail's death, found Meknes "a city of the dead . . . strewn with marble columns, and surrounded by great masses of ruin". In recent years, however, the city authorities have set about restoring the main monuments with some energy.

was built up from a provincial centre to a spectacular capital with twenty gates, over fifty palaces and some fifteen miles of exterior walls.

The principal remains of Ismail's creation – the **Ville Imperiale** of palaces and gardens, barracks, granaries and stables – sprawl below the Medina, amid a confusingly maniac array of walled enclosures. If you intend to take in everything, it's a long morning's walk. Starting out from the Ville Nouvelle, make your way down to the main street at the southern edge of the Medina (**Rue Rouamzine/Rue Dar Smen**), and along to **Place El Hedim** and its immense gateway, **Bab Mansour**. There are usually **guides** hanging around here if you want to use one; you don't need to, but if you can find someone entertaining, he'll probably elaborate on the story of the walls with some superbly convoluted local legend.

Bab Mansour and around

Place El Hedim ("square of demolition and renewal") immediately recalls the reign of Moulay Ismail. Originally, it formed the western corner of the Medina, but the sultan demolished the houses here in order to form a grand approach to his palace quarter, the *Dar Kebira*. He used it, too, as a depot for marble columns and other construction material he had gathered from sites and cities throughout Morocco, including Roman Volubilis.

The centrepiece of the city's whole ensemble of walls and gateways is the great **Bab Mansour**, startlingly rich in its ceremonial intent, and almost perfectly preserved. Its name comes from its architect – one of a number of Christian renegades who converted to Islam and rose to high position at Ismail's court; there is a tale that when the sultan inspected the gate, he asked El Mansour whether he could do better – a classic catch-22, whose response ("yes") led to immediate and enraged execution. The story may be apocryphal, however, for the gate was actually completed under Ismail's son, Moulay Abdallah.

Whatever, the gate is the finest in Meknes and an interesting adaptation of the classic Almohad design, flanked by unusual inset and fairly squat bastions, which are purely decorative, their marble columns having been brought here from Volubilis. The decorative patterns on both gate and bastions are basically elaborations of the *darj w ktarf* (a cheek-and-shoulder pattern, begun by the Almohads), the space between each motif filled out with a brilliant array of *zellij* created by a layer of cut-away black tiles, just like the ornamental inscription above, which extols the triumph of Ismail and, even more, that of Abdallah, adding that no gate in Damascus or Alexandria is its equal. Alongside Bab Mansour is a smaller gateway in the same style, **Bab Djemaa en Nouar**.

Nowadays, traffic passes through neither of these gates, and indeed the inside of Bab Mansour is now used as an arts and crafts gallery, sometimes displaying work from the *Ensemble Artisanal* (see p.174). Passing through the smaller gate to the left of Bab Mansour, as you face it, and then through a further gap beyond, you will find yourself in an open square, on the right of which is the green-tiled **Koubba El Khayatine** (9am–noon and 3–5.30pm). This was once a reception hall for ambassadors to the imperial court. Beyond it, a stairway descends into a vast series of subterranean vaults, known in popular tradition as the **Prison of Christian Slaves**. This was probably, in fact, a storehouse or granary, although there were certainly several thousand Christian captives at Ismail's court. Most were captured by the Sallee Rovers (see p.252) and brought here as slave labour for the interminable construction projects; reputedly any of them who died while at work were simply buried in the walls they were building.

Ahead of the *koubba*, set within the long wall and at right angles to it, are three modest **gates**. The one in the centre is generally closed and is at all times flanked by soldiers from the royal guard; within, landscaped across a lake and the sunken garden of Ismail's last and finest palace, are the **Royal Golf Gardens** – private and generally *interdit*. The gate on the left opens on to an apparently endless corridor of walls and, a few metres down, the entrance to the **Mausoleum of Moulay Ismail**.

The Mausoleum

Together with the tomb of Mohammed V in Rabat, and the Medersa Bou Inania in Fes, **Moulay Ismail's Mausoleum** (9am–12.30pm and 3pm–sunset, but closed Friday afternoons for non-Muslims) is the only active Moroccan shrine that non-Muslims may visit. Modest dress, for both women and men, is required.

The mausoleum has been a point of reverence since Ismail's death (it was constructed in his own lifetime) and continues in high esteem. This may be puzzling to Westerners, given the tales of the ruler's excesses, but in Morocco he is remembered for his achievements: bringing peace and prosperity after a period of anarchy, and driving out the Spanish from Larache and the British from Tangier. His extreme observance of orthodox Islamic form and ritual also conferred a kind of magic on him, as, of course, does his part in the foundation of the ruling Alaouite dynasty. Although technically the dynasty began with his brother, Moulay Rachid, Ismail is generally regarded as the founder.

Entering the mausoleum, you are allowed to approach the **sanctuary** in which the sultan is buried – though you cannot go beyond this annexe. Decorated in bright *zellij* and spiralling stuccowork, it is a fine, if unspectacular, series of courts and chambers.

But what is most interesting, perhaps, is that the shrine was thoroughly renovated in the 1950s at the expense of Mohammed V, and also that the sarcophagus is still the object of veneration. You will almost invariably see country people here, especially women, seeking *baraka* (charismatic blessing) and intercession from the saintly sultan's remains.

The Dar El Makhzen and Heri as-Souani

Past the mausoleum, a gate to your left gives access to the dilapidated quarter of **Dar El Kebira**, Ismail's great palace complex. The imperial structures – the legendary fifty palaces – can still be made out between and above the houses here: ogre-like creations, whose scale is hard to believe. They were completed in 1677 and dedicated at an astonishing midnight celebration, when, the chronicles record, the sultan personally slaughtered a wolf so that its head might be displayed at the centre of the gateway.

In the grandeur of the plan there is sometimes claimed a conscious echo of Versailles – its contemporary rival – though, in fact, it was another decade until the first reports of the French building reached the imperial court. When they did, Ismail was certainly interested, and in 1699 he even sent an ambassador to Paris with the task of negotiating the addition of Louis XIV's daughter, Princess Conti, to his harem. He returned without success.

On the opposite side of the long-walled corridor, beyond the Royal Golf Gardens, more immense buildings are spread out, making up Ismail's last great palace, the **Dar El Makhzen**. Unlike the Kebira, which was broken up by Moulay Abdallah in 1733, this is still a minor royal residence – though Hassan II rarely visits Meknes. The most you can get are a few brief glimpses over the heads of the guards posted by occasional gates in the crumbling, twenty-foot-high wall.

The corridor itself, which eventually turns a corner to bring you out by the campsite and the Heri as-Souani, may perhaps be the **"strangee"** which eighteenth-century travellers recorded. A mile-long terrace wall, shaded with vines, it was a favourite drive of the sultan, who, according to several sources, was driven around in a bizarre chariot drawn by his women or eunuchs.

At the corridor's end is the chief sight of the Imperial City, the **Heri as-Souani** (or Dar El-Ma), which is often introduced by local guides as "Ismail's stables" (9am-noon and 3-6pm). The stables, in fact, are further south, and the startling series of high vaulted chambers to be seen here were again a series of storerooms and granaries, filled with provisions for siege or drought. A twenty-minute walk from Bab Mansour, they give a powerful impression of the complexity of seventeenth-century Moroccan engineering. Ismail's palaces each had underground plumbing (well in advance of Europe), and here you find a remarkable system, with chain-bucket wells built between each of the storerooms. One on the right, near the back, has been restored; there are lights you can switch on for a closer look.

Equally worthwhile is the view from the **roof** of the as-Souani, approached through the second entrance on the right. From the roof garden, which in summer has a café, you can gaze out over the Dar El Makhzen and the wonderfully still **Agdal Basin** – built as an irrigation reservoir and pleasure lake which now has a Geneva-style *jet d'eau* and beside which people picnic and wash their cars.

Over to the southwest, in the distance, you can make out another seventeenth-century royal palace, the **Dar al-Baida** (the "White House"), now a military academy, and beyond it, the **Rouah**, or stables (see below).

The Rouah

The ramshackle ruins of Moulay Ismail's stables, the **Rouah**, are a thirty-minute walk from the Heri as-Souani. They are officially closed to visitors – and unless you've a

HORSES AND MULES

THE HARAS DE MEKNES

The **Haras de Meknes** is the largest national stud-farm in Morocco. It is located in the Zitoun quarter on the southwest edge of town, near the military academy and the Rouah – the old imperial stables (see below). Take the road to Azrou or the bus #14 or #16 from the Ville Nouvelle and get off near the science and arts faculties of the university.

If you are interested, it's well worth an informal visit or, if you are knowledgeable and qualified, you can take out temporary membership of the club and help to exercise the horses (☎05/53.97.53: 100dh). On a short visit, you can see the *Première Ecurie,* the first stable to the left of the entrance. Here you will see valuable stallions of Arab and/or Berber stock. The cousins of such horses can be seen at riding stables around the world; and, in Morocco, they can, of course, be seen at any *fantasia* the length and breadth of the land.

SPANA

The British charity, **SPANA,** (Society for the Protection of Animals Abroad) is active in Meknes and you can visit their small centre on Rue de Laine, which runs from Bab El Qari (☎05/53.32.94); you will recognize the street by the wool traders (*laine* is wool). SPANA is at no. 72 on the left. Visitors are welcome by arrangement, morning or afternoon.

In the morning, staff visit local markets and treat donkeys and mules on the spot; in the afternoon, the centre is open to treat all manner of animals brought by their owners. As in other towns, strays are collected and taken to the abattoir where owners can recover them and SPANA can treat them. If uncollected, they are given to the local zoo.

Fafaite Mohamed at the centre is keen on improving the footwear of the beasts of burden. Makeshift 'shoes' made of old car tyres are not good for the animals and he is encouraging blacksmiths through the *Meknes Association of Blacksmiths*, which is working nationally.

serious interest, not especially worthwhile. If you are committed, though, there is usually a *gardien* with keys, if you turn up and ask around. To find the site, follow the road diagonally behind *Camping Aguedal* and Heri as-Souani for half a kilometre; when you reach a junction, turn right and you arrive at the **Djemaa Rouah** (Stable Mosque), a large, heavily restored building preceded by a well-kept gravel courtyard. Walk round behind the mosque and you will see the **stables** off to your right – a massive complex perhaps twice as large as the as-Souani.

In contemporary accounts the Rouah was often singled out as the greatest feature of all Ismail's building projects: some three miles in length, traversed by a long canal, with flooring built over vaults used for storing grain, and space for over 12,000 horses. Today, the province of a few scrambling goats, it's a conclusive ruin – piles of rubble and *zellij* tiles lining the walls and high arched aisles of crumbling pisé extending out in each direction. As such, it perhaps recalls more than anything else in Meknes the scale and madness of Moulay Ismail's vision.

The Medina

The Medina, although taking much of its present form and size under Moulay Ismail, bears less of his stamp. Its main sights, in addition to the extensive **souks**, are a Merenid *medersa* or "college" – the **Bou Inania** – and a nineteenth-century palace museum, the **Dar Jamai**; both are rewarding and easy to find.

The Dar Jamai

The **Dar Jamai** (9am–noon and 3–6pm, closed Tues) stands at the back of Place El Hedim, from which it is reached down a stairway. One of the best examples of a late nineteenth-century Moroccan palace, it was built in 1882 by the same family of viziers (high government officials) who put up the Palais Jamai in Fes. After 1912, it was used as a military hospital, becoming the Museum of Moroccan Art in 1920. The Andalucian Garden, with its cypress and fruit trees, and attendant birds, has been preserved.

The museum is one of the best in Morocco. Its exhibits, some of which have been incorporated to recreate reception rooms, are predominantly of the same age, though some of the pieces of **Fes** and **Meknes pottery** date back more or less to Ismail's reign. These ceramics, elaborate polychrome designs from Meknes and strong blue and white patterns from Fes, make for an interesting comparison, and the superiority of Fes's handicrafts tradition is evident. The best display, however, is of **Middle Atlas carpets**, and in particular the bold geometric designs of the Beni Mguild tribe.

The souks

To reach the *souks* from Place El Hedim, follow the lane immediately behind the Dar Jamai. You will come out in the middle of the Medina's major market street; on your right, leading to the Grand Mosque and Bou Inania Medersa, is **Souk Es Sebbat**; on your left is **Souk en Nejjarin**.

Turning first to the left, you enter an area of textile stalls, which later give way to the carpenters' (*nejjarin*) workshops from which the *souk* takes its name. Shortly after this, you pass a mosque on your left, beyond which is an entrance to a parallel arcade. The **carpet market**, or **Souk Joutiya as-Zerabi**, is just off here to the left. Quality can be very high (and prices, too), though without the constant stream of tourists of Fes or Marrakesh, dealers are much more willing to bargain. Don't be afraid to start too low.

Out at the end of Souk en Nejjarin you come to another *souk*, the **Bezzarin**, which runs up at right angles to the Nejjarin, on either side of the city wall. This looks an unpromsing, run-down neighbourhood, but if you follow the outer side of the wall, you'll come across an interesting assortment of craftsworkers, grouped together in their own trading guilds and often with an old *fondouk* or warehouse to the front of them. As you proceed, there are **basketmakers**, **ironsmiths** and **saddlers**, while near **Bab El Djedid**, at the top, you'll find **tent makers** and a couple of **musical instrument workshops**.

Had you turned right beyond the Dar Jamai, onto **Souk Es Sebbat**, you would have entered a classier section of the market – starting off with the *babouche* vendors, and then moving on to the fancier goods aimed at tourists near the *medersa*, finally exiting into the covered **kissaria**, dominated by caftan sellers. From here it is easy enough to find your way to the Bou Inania Medersa, whose imposing portal is visible on the left-hand side of the street. If you want a tea break before doing that, there's a nineteenth-century **fondouk** a short way back, which now doubles as a café and carpet/crafts emporium – look for its open courtyard. Meknes mint, incidentally, is reputed to be the best in Morocco.

Bou Inania Medersa

The **Bou Inania Medersa** (daily 9am–noon and 3–6pm) was built around 1340–50, and is thus more or less contemporary with the great *medersa*s of Fes. It takes its name from the notorious Sultan Abou Inan (see p.199), though it was actually founded by his predecessor, Abou El Hassan, the great Merenid builder of the Chellah in Rabat.

A modest and functional building, the *medersa* follows the plan of Hassan's other principal works in Rabat (the Chellah *zaouia* and Salé *medersa*), in that it has a single

courtyard opening on to a narrow **prayer hall**, and is encircled on each floor by the students' **cells**, with exquisite screens in carved cedar. It has a much lighter feel to it than the Salé *medersa*, and in its balance of wood, stucco and *zellij* achieves a remarkable combination of intricacy – no area is left uncovered – and restraint. Architecturally, the most unusual feature is a ribbed dome over the **entrance hall**, an impressive piece of craftsmanship which extends right out into the *souk*.

From **the roof**, to which there's usually access, you can look out (and you feel as if you could climb across) to the tiled pyramids of the **Grand Mosque;** you can just catch a glimpse of the interior. The *souk* is mainly obscured from view, but you can get a good, general panorama of the town and the mosques of each quarter. Inlaid with bands of green tiles, the minarets of these distinctive mosques are unique to Meknes; those of Fes or Marrakesh tend to be more elaborate and multicoloured.

North from Bou Inania

North of the *medersa* and Grand Mosque, the Medina is for the most part residential, dotted with the occasional fruit and vegetable market, or (up past the mosque of Ben Khadra) a carpenters' *souk*, for the supply of wood. If you continue this way, you'll eventually come out in a long, open square which culminates in the monumental **Bab El Berdaïn** (The Gate of the Saddlers). This was another of Ismail's creations, and echoes, in a much more rugged and genuinely defensive structure, the central section of Bab Mansour.

Outside, the city walls continue to extend up along the main road to Rabat, and past – about 1500m out, near the new bus station – the **Bab El Khemis** (or Bab Lakhmis), another very fine gate with a frieze containing a monumental inscription etched in black tiles on the brickwork. Between the two gates, inside the wall on your left, you will catch occasional glimpses of an enormous **cemetery** – almost half the size of the Medina in extent. Non-Muslims are not permitted to enter this enclosure, near the centre of which lies the *zaouia* and shrine of one of the country's most famous and curious saints, **Sidi Ben Aissa**.

Reputedly a contemporary of Moulay Ismail, Ben Aissa conferred on his followers the power to eat anything, even poison or broken glass, without suffering any ill effects. His cult, the *Aissaoua*, became one of the most important in Morocco, and certainly the most violent and fanatical. Until prohibited by the French, some 50,000 devotees regu-

---

ARTS AND CRAFTS

The **Ensemble Artisanal** (Mon–Sat, school hours; ☎05/05.08.08) is housed in a prominent, reddish building above and beyond the local bus and taxi park below Place El Hedim. It is large and trains apprentices, but despite the presence of a branch of the **Banque Populaire**, there is little to buy. There is a lot to be seen, however, including the work of the young people making **zellij** tiles. The building also houses several active co-operatives, including **La Cooperative Feminine de Ceramique**.

The **Village des Potiers** is in the valley of the Oued Boufekrane which divides the Ville Nouvelle from the Medina. It's to the north, between Bab El Berdaïn and the *Hôtel Transatlantique*; if in doubt and/or taking a *petit taxi*, ask for Farharine. It's just about worth a visit but, if Safi is on your itenerary, you can give the Meknes' potteries a miss.

The **Music Conservatoire** of Meknes is the impressive French-style building near Place Ifriquia, between Av. Mohammed V and Av. Allal Ben Abdallah. Here the students study and play classical Arab-Andalucian music, together with *Milhum* and, less so, *Gharnati*. The Conservatoire gives occasional concerts. The **Institut Français**, Place Farhat Hachad (☎05/52.40.71), also has a programme of music and other cultural activities and a popular student café.

larly attended the saint's annual *moussem* on the eve of Mouloud. Entering into a trance, they were known to pierce their tongues and cheeks with daggers, eat serpents and scorpions, or devour live sheep and goats. The only other confraternity to approach such frenzy was the *Hamadcha* of Moulay Idriss, whose rites included cutting each other's heads with hatchets and tossing heavy stones or cannonballs into the air, allowing them to fall down on their skulls. Both cults continue to hold *moussem*s, though successive Moroccan governments have effectively outlawed their more extreme activities.

Restaurants, bars and nightlife

Meknes is a small town compared with Fes or even Tangier. In the Ville Nouvelle, most of the action is within a few blocks of the central Place Administrative. From here, a fifteen-minute walk or 10dh *petit taxi* will take you to the Medina, where all you need is on either side of the dog-leg Rue Rouamazine/Rue Dar Smen leading to the Bab Mansour and Place El Hedim.

Cafés and restaurants

As ever, you have a choice of locations: the **Medina**, where most places are basic café-grills, or the **Ville Nouvelle**, where you'll find a dozen or so restaurants, mostly serving French-style menus. Good choices include:

MEDINA

Collier de la Colombe, 67 Rue Driba (☎05/52.50.41). A new restaurant in the ornate mansion of 'Sultan' Lakhal, a non-Alaouite pretender to the throne on the death of Monlay Youssef in 1927. Night and day, the views across the valley to the Ville Nouvelle are stunning. The à la carte menu is international and the cuisine is outstanding; main course around 65dh which, with the trimmings, means you can eat well for about 100dh. To find it, enter Place Lalla Aouda and walk diagonally across the *place*; follow the signs along the side street; the restaurant is 100m on the left.

Restaurant Economique, 123 Rue Dar Smen, opposite Bab Mansour and alongside *Restaurant Bab Mansour*, both are good café-restaurants, the *Economique* being marginally better.

Heri as-Souani. There is a café in the rooftop garden of the Heri as-Souani (see p.171) which looks down onto the campsite and the Agdal Basin – and beyond that to the Djebel Zerhoun. Perfect at sunset for courting couples and others.

Restaurant Zitouna, 44 Rue Djemaa Zitouna (☎05/53.02.81). Long-standing traditional restaurant with class and long-established dishes; there's a set menu for around 100dh which puts it on a par with the *Collier de la Colombe*, its new rival. It can be approached from Bab Tizimi or Rue Dar Smen. If in doubt, ask – it is not very easy to find.

VILLE NOUVELLE

Café-Restaurant Campriuus, corner of Rue Charif Idrissi and Rue Omar Ibn El Ass and across the street from the *Renault* garage. Limited traditional menu; you can eat well for 60dh.

La Coupole, corner of Av. Hassan II and Rue du Ghana. Popular with the locals. Reasonably priced Moroccan and European dishes: set menu from 70dh. There's a bar and a noisy nightclub.

Le Dauphin, 5 Av. Mohammed V, although the entrance is down the side street, Rue El Leanissa. Managed by the Hôtel Bab Mansour, this is an old-fashioned French place with reliable cooking and a reputation for seafood. There's a plat du jour for 60dh.

Restaurant Diafa, 12 Rue Badr El Kobra. This building looks like it's a private house but the cooking is extremely good and reasonably priced.

Restaurant Pizza Fongue, 8 Rue Accra, alongside to the *Hôtel de Nice*. Limited menu, beyond the pizzas, but reasonable value.

Pizzeria Le Four, 1 Rue Atlas – near the *Hôtel Majestic*, off Av. Mohammed V. The interior, mock Italian-Tudor, is a shade gloomy, but the food, vaguely Italian, is good value. Licensed.

Free Time, 2 Av. Mohammad V. A run-of-the-mill, hamburger joint, but good value and friendly.

Rôtisserie Restaurant Karam, 2 Rue Ghana, off Av. Mohammed V. Small, intimate: grills and *tajines*. More a café than a rôtisserie, which stays open until 11pm for a late night snack.

Pizzeria La Mamma, 7 Rue de Paris. Opposite the *Restaurant Novelty* near the pedestrianized length of street. Yet another pizzeria, but above average.

Restaurant Marhaba, 23 Av. Mohammed V, down a passage near the *Empire* cinema; not to be confused with the café *Glacier Marhaba* which fronts Av. Mohammed V. A functional eating place with soup, *brochettes* and lamb *tajine* – and popular with *les Meknassi*. It closes at 8pm in winter and 9pm in summer. Cheap.

Annexe Métropole, 11 Rue Charif Idrissi, behind the *Métropole* proper which is at 12 Av. Hassan II. Excellent cooking and well worth the little extra. There are two set menus, the cheaper being 80dh. Licensed.

Restaurant Mo-Dinero, one block northeast of the main post office in the Ville Nouvelle. Well-prepared chicken kebabs, pizzas and salads. Moderate.

Restaurant Montana, 4 Rue Atlas – opposite *Le Four* (above). There is a bar on the ground floor; upstairs is a restaurant decorated to imitate a tent. Limited menu – and not so good as it used to be, these days. Moderate.

Restaurant Novelty, 12 rue de Paris, opposite *La Mamma* (above). The restaurant is open in the evenings only; alongside is an all-day bar. Good value plat du jour 50dh.

Café Opéra, 7 Av. Mohammed V, near the *Hôtel Majestic*. A blend of café and pâtisserie which attracts a young crowd. Like the *Café Métropole* in Tangier, it stays open daytime during Ramadan and, like the *Métropole*, there's a small synagogue nearby.

Crémerie/Pâtisserie du Palmier, 53 Av. des F.A.R. Another excellent pâtisserie, located next door to the *Hôtel Excelsior*.

Bars

There are bars in many of the Ville Nouvelle hotels, most of which are quite lively of an evening; for a sedate drink, the *Hôtel Transatlantique* would be your best bet. In addition, the following can be worth a try:

Club de Nuit, near the *Hôtel Excelsior*, on Av. des F.A.R. Remember bars with swing doors and sawdust on the floors? This will take you back. Noisy and mixed.

Bar Continental, by the *Hôtel Continental*, on the opposite side of Av. des F.A.R.

Cabaret Oriental, Av. Hassan II. Occasionally hosts bands into the small hours.

Volubilis Nightclub, behind the *Hôtel Volubilis* on a side street and opposite the *Hôtel Guillaume Tell*. Worth checking out.

Listings

Banks are concentrated around Place Administrative, and along Av. Mohammed V (the *Crédit du Maroc* is at no. 33) and Av. des F.A.R. (*BMCE* at no. 98). In the Medina, the *Banque Populaire* on Rue Dar Smen, near Bab Mansour, has exchange facilities. The *Hôtel Rif* will exchange cash outside banking hours.

Bookshop *Top Notch* is an English Bookshop, run by an American at 28 Rue Emir Abdeldader; worth browsing.

Car rental Try either *Zeit*, 4 Rue Anserabi (☎05/52.59.18), or *Stop Car*, 3 Rue Essaoira (☎05/52.50.61). None of the major companies has offices in Meknes.

Car repairs Renault garages are to be found on Rue Charif Idrissi and out on the Route de Fes. For VW try *Maroc-France*, Av. Hassan II (☎05/52.28.58); for Opel, Central Garage, 7 Rue de Nice (☎05/52.15.10).

Chemist/pharmacist Pharmacie Central, Av. Mohammed V (☎05/52.11.81; open daily). Pharmacie d'urgence de nuit, next to the *Hôtel de Ville* on Place Administrative (☎05/52.33.75; open 8.30pm–8.30am).

Cinemas Central ones include the Camera (Kung Fu and crime*)*, on Place Ifriquia, and Régine, (Karate and Indian), near the *Hôtel Bab Mansour*.

Festivals The city's *Ben Aïssa Moussem* (aka *Moussem Cheikh El Kamal*) is one of the country's most impressive. Also worth planning for are the *Beni Rached Moussem* (seven days after Mouloud; at the village of Beni Rached, out of town on the Moulay Idriss road) and the *Moulay Idriss Moussem* (at Moulay Idriss, second week of August).

Hammam If you're staying in the Medina, the *Maroc Hôtel* should be able to steer you towards a *hammam*; in the Ville Nouvelle, you'll find a good one, *Hammam Al Hadika*, off Av. Hassan II, at 4 Rue Patrice Lumumba, with separate sections for women and men (both 7am–9pm).

Laundry and Dry Cleaning *Atlas Pressing*, 26 Av. Allal Ben Abdallah, opposite Collège Allal Ben Abdallah.

Post Office The *PTT* is just off Place de France (summer Mon–Fri 8am–2pm; winter 8.30am–noon and 2.30–6pm); the **telephone** section stays open until 9pm, but there are public callboxes by the entrance and many *téléboutiques* on Av. Mohammed V.

Police The local HQ is at the bottom end of Place Administrative, near the junction of Av. Hassan II and Av. Moulay Ismail (☎19).

Royal Air Maroc have an office at 7 Av. Mohammed V (☎05/52.09.63); the nearest airport is at Saïs, south of Fes.

Swimming Pools There are two public pools down by the river Oued Boufekrane, reached along a lane from Bd. El Haboul or from the intersection of Av. Hassan II and Av. Moulay Ismail. The first you encounter is very cheap; a little further down there's another – classier, less crowded, and three or four times the price. The pool at the *Hôtel Rif* is open to non-residents for a 30dh day-fee.

Traffic If you're driving, it's worth noting that traffic on Av. Mohammed and Av. Allal Ben Abdallah is one way, circulating anticlockwise.

Volubilis and Moulay Idriss

An easy excursion from Meknes, **Volubilis** and **Moulay Idriss** embody much of Morocco's early history: Volubilis as its Roman provincial capital, Moulay Idriss in the creation of the country's first Arab dynasty. Their sites stand 4km apart, at either side of a deep and very fertile valley, about 30km north of Meknes.

Transport and accommodation

You can take in both sites on a leisurely day-trip from Meknes. **Grands taxis** make regular runs to **Moulay Idriss** (10dh a place) from near the new bus station by Bab El Khemis in the Medina and from near the French Cultural Centre just off Av. Hassan II in the Ville Nouvelle. For **Volubilis**, you can take a Ouezzane bus and ask to be set down by the site (which is a 500m walk downhill from the P28 road), or you could charter a *grand taxi*. The whole taxi (*un course*) costs around 50dh, which can be split between up to six passengers; if you pay a little more, the taxi driver will wait at Volubilis and take you on to Moulay Idriss, where you can look round at leisure and then get a regular place in a *grand taxi* back to Meknes. You could also walk between Volubilis and Moulay Idriss, which are only around 4km apart.

Non-Muslims are not permitted to stay overnight in the town of Moulay Idriss – the only place in Morocco to keep this religious prohibition. However, there is a hotel and a campsite near Volubilis. The **hotel**, the *Volubilis Inn* (☎05/54.44.05; ④), is 1km from Volubilis (which it overlooks), and 3km from Moulay Idriss. It's luxurious and the views are dramatic, but it is expensive and, without transport, inconvenient – although a minibus (*navette*) will pick you up in Meknes or Fes by prior arrangement. The **campsite**, *Camping Belle-Vue,* aka *Camping Zerhoun* (☎05/54.41.68), is located 11km along the direct road from Volubilis to Meknes; it is a shaded site with a small café and a few rooms to let. Note that roads around this area are somewhat confusing; for the campsite, it's easiest to ask directions to the nearby *Refuge Zerhoun*.

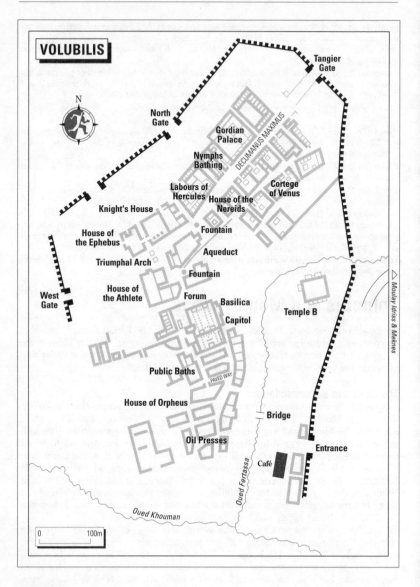

Volubilis

A striking site, visible for miles from the various bends in the approach road, **VOLU-BILIS** occupies the ledge of a long, high plateau. Below its walls, towards Moulay Idriss, stretches a rich river valley; beyond lie dark, outlying ridges of the Zerhoun mountains. The drama of this scene – and the scope of the ruins – may well seem familiar. It was the key location for Martin Scorsese's film, *The Last Temptation of Christ*.

Some history

Except for a small trading post on the island off Essaouira, Volubilis was the Roman Empire's most remote and far-flung base. The imperial roads stopped here, having reached across France and Spain and then down from Tangier, and despite successive emperors' dreams of "penetrating the Atlas", the southern Berber tribes were never effectively subdued.

Direct Roman rule here, in fact, lasted little over two centuries – the garrison withdrew early, in 285AD, to ease pressure elsewhere. But the town must have taken much of its present form well before the official annexation of North African Mauretania by Emperor Claudius in 45AD. Tablets found on the site, inscribed in Punic, show a significant Carthaginian trading presence in the third century BC, and prior to colonization it was the western capital of a heavily Romanized, but semi-autonomous, Berber kingdom, which reached into northern Algeria and Tunisia. After the Romans left, Volubilis saw very gradual change. Latin was still spoken in the seventh century by the local population of Berbers, Greeks, Syrians and Jews; Christian churches survived until the coming of Islam; and the city itself remained alive and active well into the eighteenth century, when its marble was carried away by slaves for the building of Moulay Ismail's Meknes.

What you see today, well excavated and maintained, are largely the ruins of second- and third-century AD buildings – impressive and affluent creations from its period as a colonial provincial capital. The land around here is some of the most fertile in North Africa, and the city exported wheat and olives in considerable quantities to Rome, as it did wild animals from the surrounding hills. Roman games, memorable for the sheer scale of their slaughter (9000 beasts were killed for the dedication of Rome's Colosseum alone), could not have happened without the African provinces, and Volubilis was a chief source of their lions. Within just two hundred years, along with Barbary bears and elephants, they became virtually extinct.

The site

Open daily, 9am–sunset; 20dh admission.

The entrance to the site is through a minor gate in the city wall, built along with a number of outer camps in 168AD, following a prolonged series of Berber insurrections. Just inside are the **ticket office**, and the cool *Café Oualili*, named after the Arabic for oleander; pre-Roman Volubilis was called Oulili, a corruption of oualili. Here there is a small, open-air **museum**, with remains of many altars and other sculptural fragments. From time to time, funds permitting, there are further excavations and discoveries – and attempts at the restoration of the fallen structures.

The best of the finds made here – which include a superb collection of bronzes – have all been taken to the Rabat museum which, for that alone, is worth a serious visit. Volubilis, however, has retained *in situ* the great majority of its **mosaics**, some thirty or so in a good state of preservation. You leave with a real sense of Roman city life and its provincial prosperity, while in the layout of the site it is not hard to recognize the essentials of a medieval Arab town.

Following the path up from the museum and across a bridge over the Fertassa stream, you come out on a mixed area of housing and industry, each of its buildings containing the clear remains of at least one **olive press**. The extent and number of these presses, built into even the grandest mansions, reflect the olive's absolute importance to the city and indicate perhaps why Volubilis remained unchanged for so long after the Romans' departure. A significant proportion of its 20,000 population must have been involved in some capacity in the oil's production and export.

Somewhat isolated in this suburban quarter is the **House of Orpheus**, an enormous complex of rooms just beside the start of a paved way. Although substantially in ruins, it offers a strong impression of its former luxury – an opulent mansion for perhaps one of the town's richest merchants. It is divided into two main sections – public and private – each with its separate entrance and interior court. The private rooms, which you come to first, are grouped around a small patio which is decorated with a more or less intact **dolphin mosaic**. You can also make out the furnace and heating system (just by the entrance), the kitchen with its niche for the household gods, and the **baths** – an extensive system of hot, cold and steam rooms.

The house's public apartments, a little further inside, are dominated by a large **atrium**, half reception hall, half central court, and again preserving a very fine mosaic, **The Chariot of Amphitrite drawn by a Seahorse**. The best example here, however, and the mosaic from which the house takes its name, is that of the **Orpheus Myth**, located to the south in a room which was probably the *tablinium*, or archives.

Above the Orpheus House, a broad, paved street leads up towards the main group of public buildings – the Capitol and Basilica, whose sand-coloured ruins dominate the site. Taking the approach on the left, you pass first through the remains of the city's main **Public Baths**. Restored by the Emperor Gallienus in the second century AD, these are clearly monumental in their intent, though sadly the mosaics are only fragmentary. The arrangement of the **Forum** is typical of a major Roman town: built on the highest rise of the city and flanked by a triumphal arch, market, capitol and basilica.

The **Capitol**, the smaller and lower of the two main buildings, has been dated from inscriptions to 217AD – a time at which this whole public nucleus seems to have been rebuilt by the African-born Severian emperors. Adjoined by small forum **baths**, it is an essentially simple building, with a porticoed court giving access to a small temple and altar. Its dedication – standard throughout the Roman world – was to the official state cult of Capitoline Jove, Juno and Minerva. The large five-aisled **Basilica** to its side served as the courthouse, while immediately across the forum were the small court and stalls of the central **market**.

The **Triumphal Arch**, right in the middle of the town, had no particular purpose other than creating a ceremonial function for the principal street, the Decumanus Maximus – on whose side it is more substantially ornamented. Erected in honour of the Severian emperor, Caracalla, its inscription records that it was originally surmounted by a bronze chariot. This, and the nymphs which once shot water into its basins below, are gone, though with its tall Corinthian columns (of imported marble), it is still an impressive monument. The medallions on either side, heavily eroded, presumably depict Caracalla and his mother, Julia Donna, who is also named in the inscription.

MANSIONS AND MOSAICS

The finest of Volubilis's mansions – and its mosaics – line the **Decumanus Maximus**, fronted in traditional Roman and Italian fashion by the shops built in tiny cubicles. Before you reach this point, however, take a look at the remains of an **aqueduct** and **fountains** across from the triumphal arch; these once supplied yet another complex of public baths. Opposite them is a small group of **houses**, mostly ruined but retaining an impressive **Mosaic of an Athlete** or "chariot jumper" – depicted receiving the winner's cup for a *desultor* race, a display of great skill which entailed leaping on and off a horse in full gallop.

First of the Decumanus Maximus mansions, the **House of the Ephebus** takes its name from the bronze of a youth found in its ruins (and today displayed in Rabat). In general plan it is very similar to the House of Orpheus, once again containing an olive press in its rear section, though this building is on a far grander scale – almost twice the size of the other – with pictorial mosaics in most of its public rooms and an ornamental pool in its central court. Finest of the mosaics is a representation of **Bacchus**

Being Drawn in a Chariot by Panthers – a suitable scene for the *cenacula*, or banquet hall, in which it is placed.

Separated from the Ephebus House by a narrow lane is a mosaic-less mansion, known after its facade as the **House of Columns**, and adjoining this, the **Knight's House** with an incomplete mosaic of **Dionysos Discovering Ariadne** asleep on the beach at Naxos; both houses are themselves largely ruined. More illuminating is the large mansion which begins the next block, similar again in its plan, but featuring a very complete mosaic of the **Labours of Hercules**. Almost comic caricatures, these give a good idea of typical provincial Roman mosaics – immediate contrasts to the stylish **Orpheus and Bacchus** and **Nymphs Bathing** of the second house down.

Beyond this area, approaching the partially reconstructed **Tangier Gate**, stands the **Palace of the Gordians**, former residence of the procurators who administered the city and the province. Despite its size, however, even with a huge **bath house** and pooled courtyards, it is an unmemorable ruin. Stripped of most of its columns, and lacking any mosaics, its grandeur and scale may have made it an all too obvious target for Ismail's building mania. Indeed, how much of Volubilis remained standing before his reign began is an open question; Walter Harris, writing at the turn of the twentieth century, found the road between here and Meknes littered with ancient marbles, left as they fell following the announcement of the sultan's death.

Back on the Decumanus, cross to the other side of the road and walk down a block to a smaller lane below the street. Here, in the third house you come to, is the most exceptional ensemble of mosaics of the entire site – the **Cortege of Venus**. You cannot enter the house but most of the fine mosaics can be seen by walking round the outside of the ruins. If you imagine walking into the main section of the house, a central court is preceded by a paved vestibule and opens on to another, smaller patio, around which are grouped the main reception halls (and mosaics). From the entrance, the **baths** are off to the left, flanked by the private quarters, while immediately around the central court is a small group of mosaics, including an odd, very worn representation of a **Chariot Race** – with birds instead of horses.

The villa's most outstanding mosaics lie beyond, in the "public" sections. On the left, in the corner, is a geometrical design, with medallions of **Bacchus Surrounded by the Four Seasons**; off to the right are **Diana Bathing** (and surprised by the huntsman Actaeon) and the **Abduction of Hylas by Nymphs**. Each of these scenes – especially the last two – is superbly handled in stylized but very fluid animation. They date, like that of the **Nereids** (two houses further down), from the late second or early third century AD, and were obviously a serious commission. It is not known for whom this house was built, but its owner must have been among the city's most successful patrons; here were found the bronze busts of Cato and Juba II which are now the centrepiece of Rabat's museum.

Leaving the site by a path below the forum, you pass close by the ruins of a **temple** on the opposite side of the stream. This was dedicated by the Romans to Saturn, but seems to have previously involved the worship of a Carthaginian god; several hundred votive offerings were discovered during its excavation.

Moulay Idriss

MOULAY IDRISS takes its name from its founder, Morocco's most venerated saint and the creator of its first Arab dynasty. His tomb and *zaouia* lie right at the heart of the town, the reason for its sacred status and the object of constant pilgrimage – and an important summer **moussem**, held in the second week of August. For non-Muslims, barred from the shrines, there is little specific that can be seen, and nothing that may be visited, but wandering the hilly lanes with their delightful window-views, or just sitting in a café absorbing the holiday-pilgrim atmosphere, is pleasant enough.

MOULAY IDRISS AND THE FOUNDATION OF MOROCCO

Moulay Idriss El Akhbar (The Elder) was a great-grandson of the Prophet Muhammad; his grandparents were Muhammad's daughter Fatima, and cousin and first follower, Ali. Heir to the Caliphate in Damascus, he fled to Morocco around 787, following the Ommayad victory in the great civil war which split the Muslim world into Shia and Sunni sects.

In Volubilis, then still the main centre of the north, Idriss seems to have been welcomed as an *imam* (a spiritual and political leader), and within five years had succeeded in carving out a considerable kingdom. At this new town site, more easily defended than Volubilis, he built his capital, and he also began the construction of Fes, later continued and considerably extended by his son Idriss II, that city's patron saint. News of his growing power, however, filtered back to the East, and in 792, the Ommayads had Idriss poisoned, doubtless assuming that his kingdom would likewise disappear.

In this they were mistaken. Idriss had instilled with the faith of Islam the region's previously pagan (and sometimes Christian or Jewish) Berber tribes and had been joined in this prototypical Moroccan state by increasing numbers of Arab Shiites loyal to the succession of his *Alid* line. After his assassination, Rashid, the servant who had travelled with Idriss to Morocco, took over as regent until 807, when the founder's son, Idriss II, was old enough to assume the throne.

As you approach the town, locals will point out that the town looks like a Bactrian camel, with the shrine and *zaouia* as the saddle between the two humps.

The Town

Arriving in Moulay Idriss, you find yourself below an enlongated *place* near the base of the town; above you, almost directly ahead, stand the green-tiled pyramids of the shrine and *zaouia*, on either side of which rise the two conical quarters of Khiber and Tasga.

The **souks**, such as they are, line the streets of the Khiber (the taller hill) above the *zaouia*. They offer a variety of religious artefacts for Muslim visitors, especially plain white candles for the shrines, together with excellent local nougat – which is produced and sold here in great quantities – and, in autumn, *arbutus* (strawberry tree) berries.

Moulay Idriss' shrine and zaouia, rebuilt by Moulay Ismail, stands cordoned off from the street by a low, wooden bar placed to keep out Christians and beasts of burden. To get a true sense of it, you have to climb up towards one of the vantage points near the pinnacle of each quarter – ideally, the **Terrasse Sidi Abdallah El Hajjam** right above the Khiber. It's not easy to find your way up through the winding streets (most end in abrupt blind alleys), and, unless you're into the challenge of it all, you'd do better to enlist the help of a young guide down in the *place*.

As you climb to the terrace, he will probably point out the unusual modern minaret of the **Idriss Medersa**, now a Koranic school. The *Medersa* was built with materials taken from Volubilis; the modern cylindrical minaret was built in 1939 by a *hadji* on his return from Mecca where he had seen such for the first time. A *surah* (chapter) from the Koran is inscribed in Kufic script in green mosaics.

There are several grill cafés on the elongated square. For more substantial fare, there is the *Restaurant Dar Diaf*, near the shrine, and the cheaper *Restaurant Baraka*, a small white building, near the *fantasia* ground on the way into the town.

Moving on from Meknes

Heading **north** from Meknes, towards Larache, Tangier or Chaouen, Volubilis (see preceding pages) provides by far the most interesting excursion; heading **east to Fes,** there is little to delay you on the hour-long journey. Covered below are the routes **west to Rabat** and **south to Azrou**, both of which offer a few points of interest along the way. For details on the trains, buses and *grands taxis* from Meknes, see p.164.

West to Rabat: Khémisset and Lake Roumi

The road **west of Meknes** (P1) is a pleasant drive, running at first through a rich, cultivated landscape, then cutting across low, forested hills, with lavender (planted for scent) on the lower slopes. Above a bend in the road, 30km from Meknes, is a model village (labelled "Village Pilote" on the *Michelin* map) built in 1965 as the first of a planned rehousing programme.

KHÉMISSET, 46km from Meknes, is a small market town, created by the French to encourage settlement of the scattered Zemmour Berbers of the region. It hosts a Tuesday *souk* which is known for its carpets and wood carvings, and has a pleasant **hotel**, the *Diouri* (☎05/55.26.45; ② en-suite ③), on the eastern outskirts of town. Driving from Meknes to Rabat, the hotel is about midway, and its restaurant makes a good stop for lunch. If you want just a quick snack, try the *Café Yasmina* next door.

If you're in no hurry, a diversion to the **Dayet Er Roumi** – Lake Roumi – is highly recommended. This lies 15km southwest of Khémisset, just off the S106, and it's a gorgeous place: shimmering water, lots of birdsong, woodsmoke from the fires of shepherds – every inch the pastoral idyll. From April to October, a **campsite** (☎07/55.29.77; 15dh per person and per tent) and **café** operate by the water's edge, and rent out pedalos to while away the afternoon. Swimming here is also fine, and you can fish, if you come equipped with a permit (see p.52).

To reach the café and campsite, you need to turn left, off the S106, on a rough road by a cactus field with five trees; the signposted road to the lake, 1500m beyond, leads only to a group of lakeside houses. If you don't have a car, it's possible to charter a *grand taxi* at Khémisset.

South to Azrou: Agouraï, El Hajeb and the Paysage d'Ito

South of Meknes is one of Morocco's few remaining **wine-growing areas**. Under French rule, Morocco and Algeria produced up to a third of the table wine consumed in France – and had some respectable vintages. Since independence, inevitably, the profile and marketplace dropped, as, alas, has the quality, which is very hit-and-miss.

Nonetheless, some decent reds – marketed as *Toulal* – are produced at **AÏT-SOUALA**, on the minor S3065 road, west of the main Azrou road, and if you're curious, the vineyards can be visited. Continuing along the 3065 brings you out at the **Kasbah** of **AGOURAÏ**, built by Moulay Ismail and now enclosing a small Berber village. It's an interesting spot, with water sluicing down the main street, and a buzzing Thursday **souk**. There is a café but no rooms or meals to be had.

Back on the main road to Azrou, the P21, the cultivation changes to wheat, planted in the *poljes* or depressions of this classic *karst* countryside. The small town of **El HAJEB** ("eyebrow" in Arabic) occupies a high, cliffside site, alongside a ruined nineteenth-century fort. It has a Monday **souk**, a bank and several cafés.

Just south of the town, the road divides, with a minor route, the S309, leading through cedar forests to Ifrane (see p.225). The P21 to Azrou, though, is the road to take, for after 18km (17km north of Azrou) you reach the remarkable **Paysage d'Ito** – a natural roadside balcony on the edge of a volcanic plateau, with a really stunning panorama, stretching for perhaps seventy kilometres. The landscape is wonderfully bizarre, with outcrops of extinct volcanoes, and was used as the backdrop for many of the early science fiction films of the 1950s and 1960s.

Nearby is the *Auberge d'Ito* (☎05 – connection through the *poste* Azrou). You can no longer sleep here, nor eat, unless you order in advance. But you can drink – and you won't be the only one. Be warned, however, that it's a little rough.

Fes (Fez)

The history of Fes is composed of wars and murders, triumphs of arts and sciences, and a good deal of imagination.

Walter Harris: *Land of an African Sultan*

The most ancient of the Imperial Capitals, and the most complete medieval city of the Arab world, **FES** is a place that stimulates your senses, with haunting and beautiful sounds, infinite visual details and unfiltered odours. More than any other city in Morocco, it seems to exist suspended in time somewhere between the Middle Ages and the modern world. As with other Moroccan cities, it has a French-built Ville Nouvelle – familiar and modern in appearance and urban life – but some 200,000 of Fes's half-million inhabitants continue to live in the extraordinary Medina-city of **Fes El Bali** – which owes little to the West besides its electricity and its tourists.

As a spectacle, this is unmissable, and it's difficult to imagine a city whose external forms (all you can really hope to penetrate) could be so constant a source of interest. But stay in Fes a few days and it's equally hard to avoid the paradox of the place. Like much of "traditional" Morocco, the city was "saved" and then re-created by the French – under the auspices of General Lyautey, the Protectorate's first Resident-General. Lyautey took the philanthropic and startling move of declaring the city a historical monument; philanthropic because he was certainly saving Fes El Bali from destruction (albeit from less benevolent Frenchmen), and startling because until then many Moroccans were under the impression that Fes was still a living city – the Imperial Capital of the Moroccan empire rather than a preservable part of the nation's heritage. In fact, this paternalistic protection conveniently helped to disguise the dismantling of the old culture. By building a new European city nearby – the Ville Nouvelle – and then transferring Fes's economic and political functions to Rabat and the west coast, Lyautey ensured the city's eclipse along with its preservation.

To appreciate the significance of this demise, you only have to look at the Arab chronicles or old histories of Morocco, every one of which takes Fes as its central focus. The city had dominated Moroccan trade, culture and religious life – and usually its politics, too – since the end of the tenth century. It was closely and symbolically linked with the birth of an "Arabic" Moroccan state due to their mutual foundation by Moulay Idriss I, and was regarded, after Mecca and Medina, as one of the holiest cities of the Islamic world. Medieval European travellers wrote of it with a mixture of awe and respect – as a "citadel of fanaticism" and yet the most advanced seat of learning in mathematics, philosophy and medicine.

The decline of the city notwithstanding, **Fassis** – the people of Fes – have a reputation throughout Morocco as successful and sophisticated. Just as the city is situated at the centre of the country, so are its inhabitants placed at the heart of government, and most government ministries are headed by Fassis. What is undeniable is that they have the most developed Moroccan city culture, with an intellectual tradition, and their own cuisine (sadly not at its best in the modern city restaurants), dress and way of life.

The development of Fes

When the city's founder, Moulay Idriss I, died in 792, Fes was little more than a village on the east bank of the river. It was his son, **Idriss II**, who really began the city's development, at the beginning of the ninth century, by making it his capital and allowing in refugees from

Andalucian Córdoba and from Kairouan in Tunisia – at the time, the two most important cities of western Islam. The impact on Fes of these refugees was immediate and lasting: they established separate, walled towns (still distinct quarters today) on either riverbank, and provided the superior craftsmanship and mercantile experience for Fes's industrial and commercial growth. It was at this time, too, that the city gained its intellectual reputation. The tenth-century Pope Silvester II studied here at the Kairouine University, and from this source he is said to have introduced Arabic mathematics to Europe.

The seat of government – and impetus of patronage – shifted south to Marrakesh under the Berber dynasties of the **Almoravides** (1068–1145) and **Almohads** (1145–1250). But with the conquest of Fes by the **Merenids** in 1248, and their subsequent consolidation of power across Morocco, the city regained its pre-eminence and moved into something of a "golden age". Alongside the old Medina, the Merenids built a massive royal city – **Fes El Djedid**, literally "Fes the New" – which reflected both the wealth and confidence of their rule. They enlarged and decorated the Kairaouine mosque, added a network of *fondouks* (inns) for the burgeoning commercial activity, and greatly developed the Kairaouine University – building the series of magnificent **medersas**, or colleges, to accommodate its students. Once again this expansion was based on an influx of refugees, this time from the Spanish reconquest of Andalucia, and it helped to establish the city's reputation as "the Baghdad of the West".

It is essentially Merenid Fes which you witness today in the form of the city and its monuments. From the fall of the dynasty in the mid-sixteenth century, there was decline as both Fes and Morocco itself became isolated from the main currents of Western culture. The new rulers – the **Saadians** – in any case preferred Marrakesh, and although Fes re-emerged as the capital under the **Alaouites,** it had begun to lose its international stature. Moulay Ismail, whose hatred of the Fassis was legendary, almost managed to tax the city out of existence, and the principal building concerns of his successors lay in restoring and enlarging the vast domains of the royal palace.

Under **French colonial rule,** there were positive achievements in the preservation of the old city and relative prosperity of the Ville Nouvelle, but little actual progress. As a thoroughly conservative and bourgeois city, Fes became merely provincial. Even so, it remained a symbol of Moroccan pride and aspirations, playing a crucial role in the **struggle for independence**. The nationalist factions came together in Fes in 1943 to form the unified independence party: **Istiqlal**; an event recorded in Arabic on a tablet outside the *Hôtel Batha*, on Place de l'Istiqlal. And later, in 1955, the subsequent events in Fes were marvellously brought to life in Paul Bowles's novel *The Spider's House*.

Since **independence** in 1956, the city's position has been less than happy. The first sultan, Mohammed V, retained the French capital of Rabat, and with this signalled the final decline of the Fassi political and financial elites. In 1956, too, the city lost most of its Jewish community to France and Israel. In their place, the Medina population now has a predominance of first-generation rural migrants, often poorly housed in mansions designed for single families but now accommodating four or five, while the city as a whole is increasingly dependent on handicrafts and the tourist trade. If UNESCO had not moved in with its Cultural Heritage plan for the city's preservation, it seems likely that its physical collapse would have become even more widespread.

Socially, too, the city has had major problems. It was a focus of the riots of December 1990, in which the disaffected urban poor and the students vented their frustrations on government buildings, and burnt out the luxury *Hôtel des Merenides*, above the Medina, though without attacking any tourists.

Orientation, maps and guides

Even if you'd felt you were getting accustomed to Moroccan cities, Fes is likely to prove bewildering. The basic layout is simple enough, with a Moroccan **Medina** and French-

POINTS OF ARRIVAL/DEPARTURE

● **By train**. The train station (☎05/62.50.01) is in the Ville Nouvelle, ten minutes' walk from the concentration of hotels around Place Mohammed V. If you prefer to stay in Fes El Bali, either take a *petit taxi*, bus #10 or #47 to Bab Boujeloud; or bus #19 or #29 to Bab Er Rsif south of the Kairouine Mosque; if you walk to Av. Hassan II, you can pick up the #9 bus to Dar Batha (pronounced *dar ba-t-ha*). From the train station, the #10 bus passes the main bus station and the #16 bus runs to the airport. Other buses from the train station run to outlying suburbs which are unlikely to interest you.

Beware of **unofficial taxi drivers** who wait at the station and charge very unofficial rates for the trip into town; the standard fare for Bab Boujeloud should be no more than 6dh per person. Be prepared, too, for hustlers: Fes rivals Tangier and Marrakesh in this respect, and the station is, as everywhere, a prime target.

Leaving Fes, if heading for Nador/Melilla, note that ONCF run connecting buses from Taorirt on the Oujda line; you can buy tickets straight through.

● **By bus**. Coming in by bus can be confusing, since there are terminals in both the Ville Nouvelle and by the various gates to the Medina. However, coming from most destinations, you will more than likely arrive at the main **bus station** (☎05/63.60.32) just north of Bab Mahrouk, between Kasbah Cherada and Borj Nord (see fes El Bali map) or at the CTM bus station (☎05/73.29.84) on Av. Mohammed V in the Ville Nouvelle (see Ville Nouvelle map). The main bus station is new and, as in Meknes, the destinations indicator is in Arabic only. You may have to ask around or at the several *guichets,* or ticket windows.

The main exception is if you're coming from, or departing for, **Taza and the east**, for which buses use a terminal by the Medina's southeast gate, **Bab Ftouh**. Note also that convenient **night buses** cover routes to the south – to Marrakesh and Rissani, for example.

● **Grands taxis**, like buses, tend to operate in and out of **Place Baghdadi**, though they're tucked around the corner, downhill from Bab Boujeloud. Exceptions are those from/for **Immouzer, Ifrane, Azrou** and **Marrakesh** which use a rank 100m west of Place de l'Atlas (see Ville Nouvelle map) and from/for **Sefrou**, which use a rank 100m down southeast of Place de la Résistance (aka La Fiat). *Grands taxis* based at **Bab Ftouh** run to and from **Sidi Harazem, Taza, Taounate** and other points east and north of Fes.

● **By air**. Fes Saiss, Fes's tiny **airport** is 15km south of the city, off the P24 to Immouzer (☎05/62.47.12); it is easiest reached by *grand taxi* (30dh for the taxi; 5dh a place). There are various internal flight services; direct flights to Er Rachidia (summer and winter) and Tangier (winter only). Otherwise, other destinations in Morocco are via Casablanca (summer flights 6 days a week; winter flights 5 days a week). There are also direct flights

---

built **Ville Nouvelle**, but here the Medina comprises two separate cities: **Fes El Bali** (Old Fes), down in the pear-shaped bowl of the Sebou valley, and **Fes El Djedid** (New Fes), established on the edge of the valley during the thirteenth century.

Fes El Djedid, dominated by a vast enclosure of royal palaces and gardens, is relatively straightforward. **Fes El Bali**, however, where you'll want to spend most of your time, is an incredibly intricate web of lanes, blind alleys and *souks*. It takes two or three days before you even start to feel confident in where you're going, and on an initial visit you may well want to pay for a guide (see opposite) to show you the main sights and layout. The learning process is not helped, either, by the fact that most of the street-signs are in Arabic only.

Maps

The **maps** in this guide are as functional as any available. Overpage is a plan of the Ville Nouvelle, showing the outline of Fes El Djedid and edge of Fes El Bali; on the following pages is a general plan of Fes El Bali (with enlargements of the Bab Boujeloud area

to Paris and Marseille (summer and winter) and to Lyon (summer only). Details and tickets from the *RAM* office at 54 Av. Hassan II (☎05/62.55.16, open Mon–Fri, 8.30am–12.15pm and 2.30–7pm; Sat, 8.30am–12.15pm and 3–6pm.

● **Driving**. Be prepared for "motorbike guides" – Morocco's most annoying hustlers – who haunt the approach roads to Fes, attach themselves to tourist cars and insist on escorting you to a hotel. They can be deeply unpleasant and are not best countered by aggression; on the whole, it's easier just to tell them where you're going (book your hotel in advance) and give them a small tip on arrival. Make it clear you do not want a subsequent tour of the city.

PETITS TAXIS AND CITY BUSES

● **Petits taxis** in Fes generally use their meters, so they're very good value; after 9.30pm, there's a fifty-percent surcharge on top of the meter price.
Useful *petit taxi* ranks include:

Place Mohammed V (Ville Nouvelle).
Main *PTT* on Av. Hassan II (Ville Nouvelle).
Place des Alaouites (Fes El Djedid).
Place Baghdadi (north of Bab Boujeloud, Fes El Bali).
Dar Batha (south of Bab Boujeloud, Fes El Bali).
Bab Guissa (north gate, by Palais Jamai, Fes El Bali).
Bab Er Rsif (central gate, south of the Kairaouine Mosque, Fes El Bali).
Bab Ftouh (southeast gate, Fes El Bali).

● **City buses** Useful city bus routes are detailed, where relevant, in the text. As a general guide these are the ones you're most likely to want to use:

#2: Av. Mohammed V to Bab Semarine (by Av. Hassan II and Place des Alaouites).
#3: Place de la Résistance (aka La Fiat) to Bab Ftouh.
#9: Route de Sefrou to Dar Batha (by Av. Hassan II); see above.
#12: Bab Boujeloud to Bab Ftouh.
#17: Place Jbari (just west of Place de Florence) to Ain Chkeff for the campsite (see p.196).
#27: Dar Batha to Bab Er Rsif, south of the Kairouine Mosque.
#28: Place de la Résistance (aka La Fiat) to Sidi Harazem.

Note: These **numbers are marked on the sides** of the buses; there are completely different numbers on the backs!

on p.193 and the Kairaouine Mosque area on p.203). An additional map of Fes El Djedid is on p.212. Inevitably, all maps of Fes El Bali – including our own – are heavily simplified: more than any other Medina in Morocco, the old city is composed of an impenetrable maze of lanes and blind alleys, whose precise orientation and localized names do not exactly lend themselves to cartography.

Guides

A half-day tour from an **official guide** is a useful introduction to Fes El Bali; the fee is 100dh for a half day, no matter how many people are in your group. Official guides can identify themselves by round gold medallions and can be engaged at the *Délégation de Tourisme* (☎05/62.62.97; Mon–Fri 8.30am–noon and 2.30–6.30pm: Sat 8.30am–noon); the ONMT, in Immeuble Bennani on Place de la Résistance (aka La Fiat); or outside the more upmarket hotels, or at the youth hostel.

Guides who tout their services are likely to be **unofficial** and technically illegal. This doesn't necessarily mean they're to be avoided – some who are genuine students (as all

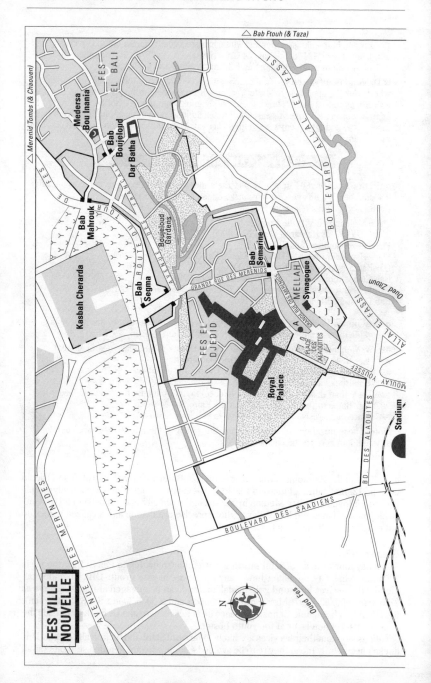

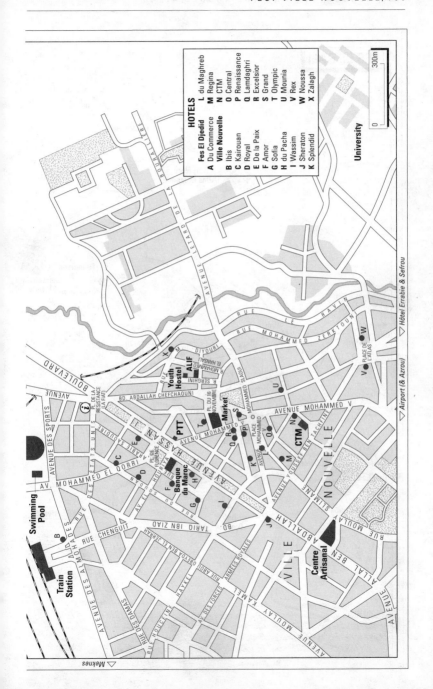

HOTELS

Fes El Djedid
A Du Commerce

Ville Nouvelle
B Ibis
C Kairouan
D Royal
E De la Paix
F Amor
G Sofia
H du Pacha
I Wassim
J Sheraton
K Splendid
L du Maghreb
M Regina
N CTM
O Central
P Renaissance
Q Lamdaghri
R Excelsior
S Grand
T Olympic
U Mounia
V Rex
W Noussa
X Zalagh

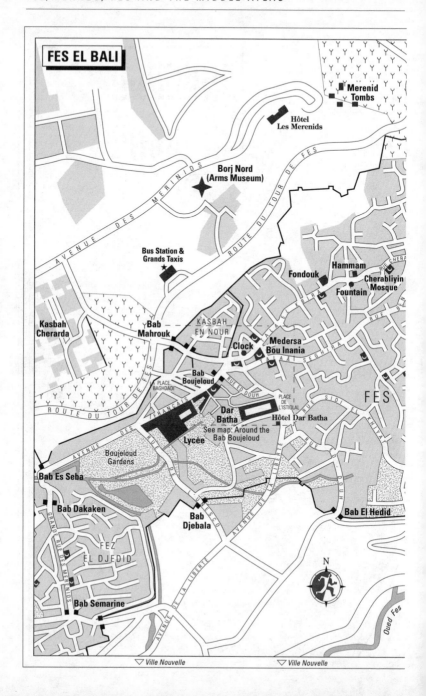

FES EL BALI

Merenid Tombs

Hôtel Les Merenids

Borj Nord (Arms Museum)

Bus Station & Grands Taxis

Fondouk

Hammam

Cherabliyin Mosque

Fountain

Kasbah Cherarda

Bab Mahrouk

KASBAH EN NOUR

Clock

Medersa Bou Inania

Bab Boujeloud

PLACE BAGHDADI

Dar Batha

PLACE DE L'ISTIQLAL

Hôtel Dar Batha

FES

See map: Around the Bab Boujeloud

Lycée

Boujeloud Gardens

Bab Es Seba

Bab Dakaken

Bab Djebala

Bab El Hedid

FEZ EL DJEDID

Bab Semarine

N

△ *Ville Nouvelle*   △ *Ville Nouvelle*

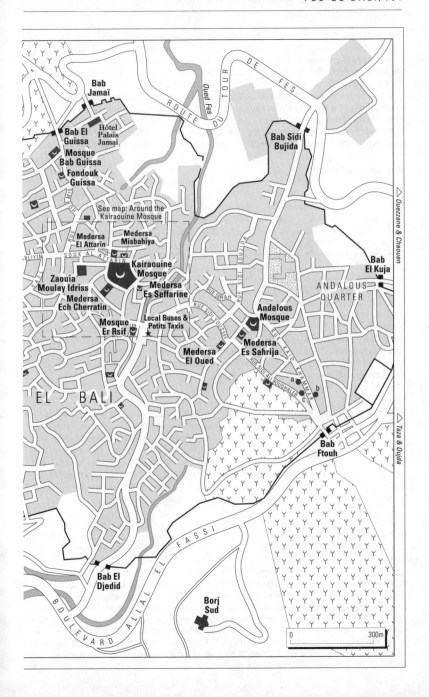

guides claim to be) can be excellent. But you have to choose carefully, ideally drinking a tea together before settling a rate or declaring interest. An unpleasant trick, employed by the more disreputable, is to take you into Fes El Bali and, once you're disorientated, maybe with dusk descending, demand rather more than the agreed fee to take you back to your hotel. Don't allow yourself to be intimidated.

Whether you get an official or unofficial guide, it's essential to work out in advance the **main points you want to see**: a useful exercise would be to mark them on the map of Fes El Bali in this book and show this to your guide. At all events, make it clear that you're not interested in **shopping** (unless that's all you want to do). For some hints on shopping on your own – which tends to be cheaper and more fun – see "Shopping for Crafts" on p.218.

Accommodation

Staying in Fes, you have the usual choice between comfort (and reliable water supply) in the modern **Ville Nouvelle** hotels, or lack of facilities in the basic, unclassified Medina hotels in **Fes El Bali** and **Fes El Djedid**. There is often a shortage of hotel space in all categories, so be prepared for higher than usual prices and – if possible – phone ahead to book a room.

If you are not overly concerned about the size and cleanliness of your room – or if you can afford one at the upmarket *Hôtel Batha* or *Hôtel Palais Jamai* – then **Fes El Bali/Fes El Djedid** is definitely the place to be. You will be at the heart of the city's *souks* and traditional life, well placed to explore the monuments, and witness to the amazing sounds of the early morning calls of muezzins from the hundreds of mosques.

Most visitors to Fes, however, are likely to be more comfortable in the **Ville Nouvelle**, where there is a wide choice of classified hotels – most of them adequate if unexciting – and a youth hostel. A few of the better hotels here have swimming pools, which can be worth a bit of a splurge in midsummer, when the heat of the plateau can be overwhelming. The Ville Nouvelle hotels also offer advantages in their proximity to restaurants and bars, and to the train station.

Fes El Bali

With two notable exceptions – the upmarket *Hôtel Batha* and *Palais Jamai* – all of the hotels in Fes El Bali are basic, unclassified *pensions*, most of which could do with more regular cleaning and plumbing. Some are also overpriced, charging the equivalent of one-star prices when they can get away with it in the summer months. However, so long as your expectations are modest, they're adequate – and the group around Bab Boujeloud are in a great position, poised for exploration of the old city's sights and *souks*. The problem of water – or, rather, lack of it – in many of these cheap hotels can be overcome by taking a steam bath in one of the nearby *hammams*.

BAB BOUJELOUD HOTELS

Bab Boujeloud is the western gateway to Fes El Bali and offers pedestrian access to Fes El Djedid. In the nearby **Place de l'Istiqlal** there are bus and *petit taxi* ranks for getting to and from the Ville Nouvelle.

The hotels listed below are keyed on the map of the Bab Boujeloud area, opposite.

Hôtel Erraha [B], Place Boujeloud (☎05/63.32.26). The cheapest place around and, for the price, reasonable enough. A useful fall-back if the *Hôtel Kaskade* is full – as it often is. ①

Hôtel de Jardin Public [A], signposted down a short lane by the Boujeloud Mosque (☎05/63.30.86). A popular Boujeloud choice (though it gets mixed reports from readers). Rooms are mainly grouped around a courtyard, although a few have external windows. Cold showers. ①

Hôtel Kaskade [E], 26 Rue Serajine (☎05/63.84.42). This is by the best Boujeloud cheapie by some way – an old building which incorporates a useful public *hammam*. Small, clean rooms – and most have windows. Hot showers. Helpful staff. ①

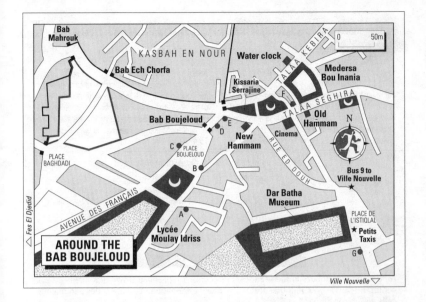

Around the Bab Boujeloud

Hôtel Lamrani [**F**], Talâa Seghira (☎05/63.44.11). Friendly with small, but acceptable, rooms – most with double beds. Opposite the old *hammam* – see below. ⑨

Hôtel Mouritania [**D**], 20 Rue Serajine (☎05/63.35.18). Okay fall-back next door to the *Hôtel Kaskade*. Wash-basins in rooms; hot showers on corridor. ⑨

Hôtel National [**C**], Place Boujeloud (☎05/63.32.48). The sign is in Arabic – it's opposite the *Hôtel Erraha*. A basic but cheerful place with a pleasant terrace. Tepid showers. ⑨

Through Bab Boujeloud, on the Talâa Seghira, are two **hammams**, known as the new and the old; these are open to foreigners, though it is best, especially for women, to ask someone at your hotel to escort you. Hours for women are noon–9pm at the new *hammam*; take a towel, shampoo and swimsuit.

BAB FTOUH HOTELS

An alternative trio of cheap, unclassified hotels is to be found by **Bab Ftouh** – a gate at the southeast corner of the Fes El Bali map; this is an untouristed area and all of the hotels listed are used more or less exclusively by Moroccans; they are keyed on the map (a–c). *Grands taxis* to Sidi Harazem, Taounate and other points east and north of Fes leave from Bab Ftouh – as do some buses to Taza and Al Hoceima.

Hôtel El Andalous [**a**], 31 Rue Kaid Khammer (☎05/64.82.62). Simple and tranquil; cold showers – but there's a *hammam* close by. ⑨

Hôtel Bahia, [**b**], Rue Sidi Ali Boughaleb (☎05/63.64.41). Borderline; no showers – and understandably the cheaper of the trio. ⑨

Hôtel Moulay Idriss, [**c**], 2 Rue Kaid Khammer (no phone). Well kept; only Arabic spoken. ⑨

UPMARKET OPTIONS IN FES EL BALI

Staying in style in Fes El Bali is the best of both worlds, but unfortunately it doesn't come cheap. The three places below are all labelled on our main Fes El Bali map.

Hôtel Palais Jamai, Bab Guissa – the north gate. (☎05/63.43.31). Alongside the *Mamounia* in Marrakesh, this is the most famous and historic hotel in Morocco, and its site above the Medina justifies its reputation – if not its prices. Its appeal is partly the building and gardens – the basis of

HOTEL PRICE CODES AND STAR RATINGS

Hotels are no longer obliged to charge according to the official star-ratings (from 1* to 5* luxury), as had long been the custom. Nevertheless, **prices** continue to reflect the star-ratings acquired. The basis of our own **hotel price codes**, set out below and keyed throughout the guide, is the price currently quoted for the cheapest double room in high season (June–September) – and is thus more reliable than quoting notional prices according to star-rating.

Note that cheaper prices in the lower categories are generally for rooms with just a wash-basin – you always pay extra for **en suite** shower and wc – and that double rooms can generally be converted into **triples/family rooms**, with extra beds, for a modest extra charge. Note also that the prices quoted by all hotels are subject to various local and regional **taxes**, which can add 15 to 20 percent to the bill.

Our code	Classification	Single room price	Double room price
⓪	Unclassified	25–60dh	50–99dh
①	1*A/1*B	60–105dh	100–149dh
②	2*B/2*A	105–145dh	150–199dh
③	3*B/3*A	145–225dh	200–299dh
④	4*B/4*A	225–400dh	300–599dh
⑤	5*luxury	Upwards of 400dh	Upwards of 600dh

TELEPHONE CODES

All telephone numbers in the Meknes/Fes region are prefixed **05**. When making a call within the region you omit this prefix. For more explanation of phone codes and making calls within (or to) Morocco, see p.45–46.

which is a nineteenth-century vizier's palace (see p.209) – and partly its position, poised just above Fes El Bali, with panoramic views (and sounds) of the city below. The hotel, in addition, has a rare literary fame, as one of the principal settings for Paul Bowles's novel, *The Spider's House*. Sadly, you do have to pay for the experience and the service and maintenance aren't always what you might expect of a five-star palace. If you book independently expect to pay upwards of £85/$127.50 per night for a basic double and £125/$187.50 for views over the Medina; it's a staggering £350/$525 if you want one of the original (and admittedly breathtaking) palace suites in the old part of the hotel. Rates may be a little lower as part of a package through one of the specialist travel agents (see "Getting There" in the Basics section of this guide). ⑤

Hôtel Batha [G], Place de l'Istiqlal (☎05/63.64.42). This upmarket hotel, located near the Dar Batha museum, should be one to recommend highly. However, the management has been very poor in recent years; we've had several reports of individual reservations not being honoured (the hotel is much used by tour groups),so if you book, be sure to phone again and reconfirm. If you do get a room, reception is curt and will only accept payment in cash. ④

Hôtel Les Merenides, Bordj Nord – on the road above Fes El Bali, (☎05/64.52.26). This was one of the city's prestige hotels until the Fes riots of 1990, when it was left burnt out by the mobs. Restored to its former glory, it has all the comforts, and wonderful views. However, it is isolated from the city, a bit soulless, and for our money very much a second choice to the *Palais Jamai* (whose prices it matches). ⑤

Fes El Djedid

Hotels in Fes El Djedid are in theory a good alternative to those around Bab Boujeloud: they are within a ten to fifteen-minute walk of Fes El Bali, and less frequented by tourists (and hustlers). However, the two most central places – the *Hôtel du Parc* and *Hôtel Moulay Al Cherif*, both on Grand Rue des Merenides – are both pretty squalid. This leaves only:

Hôtel du Commerce [keyed **A** on Ville Nouvelle map], Place des Alaouites (☎05/62.22.31). This is a nice place, owned for decades by a Jewish family; it is old but comfortable and friendly, with a lively café at street level. Its location on Place des Alaouites – facing the golden doors of the royal palace – is actually a little closer to the Ville Nouvelle than to Fes El Bali. ⓪

The Ville Nouvelle

As rooms can be tricky to obtain in Fes, we have listed most of the Ville Nouvelle hotels below – both the good and not so good; keyed letters refer to the map on pp.188–189.

YOUTH HOSTEL

Auberge de Jeunesse [keyed by name], 18 Rue Abdeslam Seghrini (☎05/62.40.85). One of the best of the Moroccan youth hostels; easy-going and friendly. It's in a quiet backwater of the Ville Nouvelle, but near the *Arabic Language Institute*, if you want to learn colloquial Moroccan Arabic, and the *Hôtel Zalagh*, who will usually allow non-residents to swim in their pool for a small fee. STOP PRESS: CLOSED FOR RESTORATION IN SPRING 1998. ①

CHEAP

Hôtel Amor [F], 31 Rue Arabie Saoudite, ex-Rue du Pakistan, (☎05/62.27.24). One block from Av. Hassan II, behind the *Banque du Maroc*. Attractive tiled frontage; bar and restaurant and reasonable accommodation. ①

Hôtel Central [O], 50 Rue du Nador, aka Brahim Roudani (☎05/62.23.33). Popular and often full. Like the CTM (below), it is convenient for early morning CTM buses – or late evening arrivals. ①

Hôtel CTM [N], Rue Ksar El Kebir/Av. Mohammed V (☎05/62.28.11). A pleasant 1930s building, with decent-sized rooms. There are showers in most rooms, toilets on the corridor. Reasonable value and popular; book early in high season. ①

Hôtel Errabie [off map], 1 Rue de Tangier (☎05/64.01.00). Just off the bottom, southern edge of the map – on the Route de Sefrou. A modern, well-built complex on the corner of a major junction, with three petrol stations. Café, pâtisserie, boulangerie, small swimming pool and hotel – simply but well finished, all rooms en suite. Easy parking. ②

Hôtel Excelsior [R], Av. Mohammed V /Rue Larbi El Kaghat (☎05/62.56.02). A fall-back cheapie – spartan, with hot water in winter only, not too clean, and a noisy location. Bad luck! ①

Hôtel Kairouan [C], 84 Rue de Soudan (☎05/62.35.90). A well-kept hotel with large rooms (all with showers) but in a rather no-man's land site between the train station and town centre. ①

Hôtel Lamdaghri [Q], Rue Abbas Msaadi (☎05/62.03.10). Big rooms with showers; restaurant on first floor and lively bar next door. It has seen better days, but it's well placed at the centre of the Ville Nouvelle and reasonable value. ①

Hôtel du Maghreb [L], 25 Av. Mohammed Es Slaoui (☎05/62.59.99). One of the cheaper hotels in the Ville Nouvelle; basic but clean. Reception is on the first floor, at the top of the stairs. ①

Hôtel Olympic [T], on a small side street off Av. Mohammed V, facing one side of the covered market (☎05/62.24.03). Clean, reliable and functional; some rooms en suite; reasonable restaurant. Used by young tour groups. ②

Hôtel du Pacha [H], 32 Av. Hassan II (☎05/65.22.90). An old-style downmarket hotel, catering mainly to Moroccans. Another fall-back alternative. ①

Hôtel Regina [M], 21 Rue du 16 Novembre, aka Rue Ghassan Kandani (☎05/62.24.27). This is a very ordinary, somewhat downbeat place; toilets and cold showers in rooms. ①

Hôtel Renaissance [P], 29 Rue Abdelkarim El Kattabi (☎05/62.21.93). Despite a rather gloomy entrance, a friendly and clean billet in a central position – and very cheap. ①

Hôtel Rex [V], 32 Place de l'Atlas (☎05/64.21.33). A bit out of the way – 1km from the centre of the Ville Nouvelle – but well maintained and very good value. There's a café on the ground floor. ①

Hôtel Royal [D], 36 Rue de Soudan (☎05/62.46.56). In no-man's land, near the *Hôtel Kairouan* and marginally better. All rooms have toilets and some dearer ones have showers also. ①

MODERATE

Grand Hôtel [S], Bd. Abdallah Chefchaouni (☎05/62.55.11). Old colonial hotel, recently restored and opposite the sunken gardens on Place Mohammed V. Prices vary according to season. ②–③

Ibis Hôtel [B], Place de la Gare/Av. des Almohades (☎05/65.19.02). One of a tasteful, modern chain of hotels (formerly called *Moussafir*) built beside train stations; this one, like its partners, has pleasant rooms, a restaurant, bar and small swimming pool. ③

Hôtel Mounia [U], 60 Rue Asilah (☎05/62.48.38). Modern hotel (central heating, TV in rooms) with friendly management. Restaurant and popular bar which can be noisy at times. Convenient for CTM bus station and Ville Nouvelle restaurants. ③

Hôtel Nouzha [W], 7 rue Hassan Dkhissi, just off Place d'Atlas (☎05/64.00.02). Splendid new hotel, with mosaic tilework, rich carpeting and natural wood. In an off-centre district, untouched by tourists, but only 15-20min walk from the centre of the Ville Nouvelle. ③

Hôtel de la Paix [E], 44 Av. Hassan II (☎05/62.68.80). An old-established tour group hotel, well worth a call. Recently refurbished, it has a bar and a reasonable restaurant, *Le Nautilus*. ③

Splendid Hôtel [K], 9 Rue Abdelkrim El Kattabi (☎05/62.67.70). An efficient modern hotel with a good restaurant, bar and small swimming pool; it attracts mainly tour groups and is not always interested in individual bookings. ③

EXPENSIVE

Sheraton Fes Hôtel [J], Av. des F.A.R. (☎05/93.09.09). The former *Hôtel de Fes* is now a link in the *Sheraton* chain. It is a large and not tremendously distinguished tour group hotel, on the fringe of the Ville Nouvelle; prices double in high season. Useful features include a branch of the *BMCE* bank and a *cyber-café* which are open to non-residents. ⑤

Hôtel Sofia [G], 3 Rue Arabie Saoudite, ex-Rue du Pakistan (☎05/62.42.65). Modern chain hotel with pool and the works, frequented almost exclusively by tour groups; bar and nightclub open to non-residents. ④

Hôtel Wassim [I], Rue du Liban – off Av. Hassan II, one block down from Av. des F.A.R. (☎05/65.49.39). A promising recent (1995) arrival, built on local initiative, with two restaurants and luxurious, fully equipped rooms. ⑤

Hôtel Zalagh [X], 10 Rue Mohammed Diouri (☎05/62.55.31). An old state-chain hotel, recently privatized and tastefully renovated; it attracts quite a chic clientele and even the tour groups are select. The swimming pool is open to non-residents, but expensive at 65dh. On the other hand, the fine views across to Fes El Djedid are anyone's for the cost of an orange juice. ⑤

Camping

The **old Fes campsite** in the **Ville Nouvelle** closed in 1989 – although it is still marked on many maps of the city (including the current *ONMT* pamphlet). The nearest site is thus:

Camping Diamant Vert (☎05/60.83.69), Aïn Chkeff – 6km south of the city. Although well out of town, this is a pleasant and shady site, with its own swimming pool, restaurant, café, playground and Barbary apes. Staying here also gives easy access to the neighbouring **Reda leisure complex** which includes a swimming pool, sports facilities, peacocks, two restaurants (*Étoile de Fes* and *Pizzeria La Source*) disco/nightclub often with a live band, and the four-star *Hôtel Reda* (☎05/60.09.78). It's really an option for those with transport, though bus #17 from Place Jbari just west of Place Florence in Fes Ville Nouvelle runs past the campsite.

Fes El Bali

With its mosques, *medersas* and *fondouks*, combined with a mile-long network of *souks*, there are enough "sights" in **Fes El Bali** to fill three or four days just trying to locate them. And even then, you'd still be unlikely to stumble across some of them except by chance or through the whim of a guide. In this – the apparently wilful secretiveness – lies part of the fascination, and there is much to be said for Paul Bowles's somewhat lofty advice to "lose oneself in the crowd – to be pulled along by it – not knowing where to and for how long . . . to see beauty where it is least likely to appear". If you do the same, be prepared to really get lost. However, despite what hustlers may tell you, the Medina is not a dangerous place, and you can always ask a boy to lead you out towards one of its landmarks: Bab Boujeloud, Talâa Kebira, the Kairaouine Mosque, Bab Er Rsif or Bab Ftouh.

Making your own way in purposeful quest for the *souks* and monuments, you should be able to find everything detailed in the following pages – with a little patience. As a prelude it's not a bad idea to head up to the **Merenid tombs** on the rim of the valley (see box pp.198–199), where you can get a spectacular overview of the city and try to make out its shape. For a break or escape from the intensity of the Medina, head to the **Boujeloud Gardens** (officially retitled "Jardins de la Marche Verte"; open 9am–6pm), a real haven and with a pleasant open-air café, to the west of Bab Boujeloud.

There are four principal entrances and exits to Fes El Bali:

● **Bab Boujeloud**. The western gate, easily identified by its bright polychrome decoration and the hotels and cafés grouped on either side.

● **Bab Er Rsif**. A central gate, by the square (and car park) beside the Mosque Er Rsif, this is a convenient entrance, just a few blocks below the Kairaouine Mosque. Bus #19 and bus #29 run between the square and the train station, by way of Av. Mohammed V in the Ville Nouvelle. Bus #27 runs between the square and Dar Batha.

● **Bab Ftouh**. The southeast gate at the bottom of the Andalous quarter, with cemeteries extending to the south. Bus #18 runs between here and Place de l'Istiqlal (near Bab Boujeloud) and there is also a *petit taxi* rank.

● **Bab Guissa**. The north gate, up at the top of the city by the *Hôtel Palais Jamai*: a convenient point to enter (or leave) the city from (or heading to) the Merenid tombs. *Petits taxis* are available by the gate.

Into the Medina: Bab Boujeloud and Dar Batha

The area around **Bab Boujeloud** is today the principal entrance to Fes El Bali: a place with a great concentration of cafés, stalls and activity where people come to talk and stare. Provincial buses leave throughout the day from **Place Baghdadi** (just west of the gate), while in the early evening there are occasional entertainers and a flea market spreading out towards the old *Mechouar* (the former assembly point and government square) and to **Bab El Mahrouk**, an exit onto the road to the Merenid tombs.

This focus and importance is all comparatively recent, since it was only at the end of the last century that the walls were joined up between Fes El Bali and Fes El Djedid and the subsequently enclosed area was developed. Nearly all the buildings here date from this period, including those of the elegant **Dar Batha** palace, designed for the reception of foreign ambassadors and now a **Museum of Moroccan Arts and Crafts**. Bab Boujeloud itself is comparatively modern, too, constructed only in 1913. Its tiled facades are blue (the traditional colour of Fes) on the outside, facing the ramparts, and green (the colour of Islam) on the interior, facing into the Medina.

DAR BATHA

The **Dar Batha** (open daily, except Tues 8.30am–noon and 2.30–6pm; 10dh) is worth a visit just for its courtyards and gardens, which offer useful respite from the general exhaustion of the Medina. The museum entrance is 30m up the narrow lane separating it from the *Hôtel Batha*.

The art and crafts collections concentrate on local artesan traditions. There are examples of **carved wood,** much of it rescued from the Misbahiya and other *medersas;* another room of **Middle Atlas carpets**; and examples of **zellij-work**, **calligraphy** and **embroidery**.

Above all, it is the **pottery** rooms which stand out. The pieces, dating from the sixteenth century to the 1930s, are beautiful and show the preservation of technique long after the end of any form of innovation. This timeless quality is constantly asserted as you wander around Fes. There is no concept here of the "antique" – something is either new or it is old, and if the latter, its age could be anything from thirty years to three centuries.

This timeless quality is occasionally reinforced at the museum itself when the work of local co-operatives is displayed for sale.

INTO THE MEDINA: THE TALÂA SEGHIRA AND TALÂA KEBIRA

Until you get a grasp of Fes El Bali, it's useful to stick with **Bab Boujeloud** as a point of entry and reference. With its polychrome tiled facades, it is a pretty unmistakeable landmark, and once inside, things are initially straightforward. You will find yourself in

THE MERENID TOMBS AND A VIEW OF FES

A crumbling and fairly obscure group of ruins, the **Merenid tombs** are not of great interest in themselves. People no longer know which of the dynasty's sultans had them erected and there is not a trace remaining of the "beautiful white marbles' vividly coloured epitaphs" which so struck Leo Africanus in his sixteenth-century description of Fes. Poised at the city's skyline, however, they are a picturesque focus and a superb vantage point. All round you are spread the Muslim cemeteries which ring the hills on each side of the city, while looking down you can delineate the more prominent among Fes's reputed 365 mosque minarets.

Getting up to the tombs is no problem. You can walk it in about twenty minutes from Bab Boujeloud, or take a taxi (around 10dh from the Ville Nouvelle). From the Boujeloud area, leave by **Bab El Mahrouk**, below the new bus station, and once outside the walls, turn immediately to the right. After a while you come to a network of paths, climbing up towards the stolid fortress of **Borj Nord**. Despite its French garrison-like appearance, this and its southern counterpart across the valley were actually built in the late sixteenth century by the Saadians. The dynasty's only endowment to the city, they were used to *control* the Fassis rather than to *defend* them. Carefully maintained, the Borj now houses the country's **arms museum** – daggers encrusted with stones and an interminable display of row upon row of muskets, most of them confiscated from the Riffians in the 1958 rebellion. Pride of place is given to a cannon 5m long and weighing 12 tons, said to be used during the Battle of the Three Kings (see p.100). Opening hours are as for Dar Batha (see p.197).

Clambering across the hillside from Borj Nord – or following (by road) Route du Tour du Fes past *Hôtel des Merenides* – you soon emerge at **the tombs** and an expectant cluster of guides. Wandering round here, you will probably be standing on the city's original

a small square (see map on p.193), flanked by the *Hôtel Kaskade* (on your right) and with a couple of minarets almost directly ahead. Just beyond the *Hôtel Kaskade,* the square splits into two main lanes, traversed by dozens of alleys but running parallel for much of the Medina's length.

The lower (right-hand) fork is the **Talâa Seghira** (also known, in its French translation, as Rue du Petit Talâa), a street which begins with a handful of small foodstalls where you can buy chunks of *pastilla,* the great Fassi delicacy of pigeon pie; further down, the lane, renamed Rue Ben Safi, has little of specific interest until it loops up to rejoin the upper lane at the Souk El Attarin.

The upper lane, **Talâa Kebira** (aka Rue du Grand Talâa), through an arched gateway labelled "Kissariat Serrajine", is the major artery of the Medina, and with its continuations runs right through to the Kairaouine Mosque. For virtually its whole length it is lined with shops and stalls, and, about a hundred metres down, it is host to the most brilliant of all the city's monuments, the **Medersa Bou Inania**. You can see the entrance to this *medersa*, down a step on your right, just before you come to a whitewashed arch-bridge over the road.

● **Access** Bus #18 from the Ville Nouvelle has a stop more or less outside Dar Batha in Place de l'Istiqlal, two minutes' walk below Bab Boujeloud. Here, and around the gate, you'll be pestered with offers of a **guide**. If you don't want one, be firm and explain that you're only going down to Bou Inania – which will probably be your first move anyway. Most hustlers give up after about fifty metres or so. To get a **petit taxi** in the Bab Boujeloud area, walk up to Place Baghdad by the Boujeloud bus terminal.

The Bou Inania medersa and clock

If there is just one building you actively seek out in Fes – or, not to put too fine a point on it, in Morocco – it should be the **Medersa Bou Inania**. The most elaborate, extrav-

foundations, before its rapid expansion under Moulay Idriss II. But it is **the view** across the deep pear-shaped bowl of the valley below which holds everyone's attention – Fes El Bali neatly wedged within it, white and diamond shaped, and buzzing with activity.

Immediately below is Adourat El Kairaouine, or the Kairaouine quarter: the main stretch of the Medina, where Idriss settled the first Tunisian refugees. At its heart, towards the river, stands the green-tiled courtyard of the **Kairaouine Mosque**, the country's most important religious building, preceded and partially screened by its two minarets. The main one has a dome on top and is whitewashed, which is an unusual Moroccan (though characteristically Tunisian) design; the slightly lower one to its right (square, with a narrower upper floor) is *Borj en Naffara* (The Trumpeter's Tower), from which the beginning and end of Ramadan are proclaimed. Over to the right of this, and very easily recognized, are the tall pyramid-shaped roof and slender, decoratively faced minaret of the city's second great religious building, the **Zaouia of Moulay Idriss II**.

The **Andalous quarter**, the other area settled by ninth-century refugees, lies some way over to the left of this trio of minarets – divided from the Kairaouine by the appropriately named **Bou Khareb** (The River Carrying Garbage), whose path is marked out by a series of minarets. **Djemma El Andalous**, the principal mosque of this quarter, is distinguished by a massive, tile-porched, monumental gateway, behind which you can make out the roofs enclosing its great courtyard.

Orientation aside, there is a definite magic if you're up here in the early evening or, best of all, at dawn. The sounds of the city, the stillness and the contained disorder below all seem to make manifest the mystical significance which Islam places on urban life as the most perfect expression of culture and society.

From the tombs you can enter Fes El Bali either through **Bab Guissa** (which brings you out at the Souk El Attarin), or by returning to **Bab Boujeloud**. There is a *petit taxi* stand by Bab Guissa.

---

agant and beautiful of all Merenid monuments, it comes close to perfection in every aspect of its construction – its dark cedar is fabulously carved, the *zellij* tilework classic, and the stucco a revelation.

In addition, the *medersa* is the city's only building still in religious use that non-Muslims are permitted to enter. Non-believers cannot, of course, enter the prayer hall – which is divided from the main body of the *medersa* by a small canal – but are allowed to sit in a corner of the marble courtyard and gaze across to it. The **admission hours** are daily 8am–noon and 2–6pm (Fri 3–6pm); occasionally tourists may be asked to leave at other times of prayer and as with all the Fes *medersas*, there is a standard 10dh admission fee.

Set somewhat apart from the other *medersas* of Fes, the Bou Inania was the last and grandest built by a Merenid sultan. It shares its name with the one in Meknes, which was completed (though not initiated) by the same patron, **Sultan Abou Inan** (1351–58). But the Fes version is infinitely more splendid. Its cost alone was legendary, and Abou Inan is said to have thrown the accounts into the river on its completion, claiming that "a thing of beauty is beyond reckoning".

At first glance, Abou Inan doesn't seem the kind of sultan to have wanted a *medersa* – his mania for building aside, he was most noted for having 325 sons in ten years, deposing his father, and committing unusually atrocious murders. The *Ulema*, the religious leaders of the Kairaouine Mosque, certainly thought him an unlikely candidate and advised him to build his *medersa* on the city's garbage dump, on the basis that piety and good works can cure anything. Whether it was this, or merely the desire for a lasting monument, which inspired him, he set up the *medersa* as a rival to the Kairaouine itself, and for a while it became the most important religious building in the city. A long campaign to have the announcement of the time of prayer transferred here failed in the face of the Kairaouine's powerful opposition; but the *medersa* was granted the status of a Grand Mosque – unique in Morocco – and retains the right to say the Friday *khotbeh* prayer.

THE MEDERSA

The basic **layout** of the *medersa* is quite simple – a single large courtyard flanked by two sizeable halls and opening onto an oratory – and is essentially the same design as that of the wealthier Fassi mansions. For its effect it relies on the mass of decoration and the light and space held within. You enter the **courtyard** – the *medersa*'s outstanding feature – through a stalactite-domed entrance chamber, a feature adapted from Andalucian architecture.

Off to each side of the courtyard are stairs to the upper storey, lined with student cells, and to the roof. Depending on the progress of restoration work, you may or may not be able to go up; if you can, head straight for the roof to get an excellent (and very useful) overview of this part of the city. The cells, as is usual in *medersa*s, are bare and monkish except for their windows and decorated ceilings.

In the courtyard, the **decoration**, startlingly well-preserved, covers every possible surface. Perhaps most striking in terms of craftsmanship are the wood carving and joinery, an unrivalled example of the Moorish art of *laceria*, "the carpentry of knots". Cedar beams ring three sides of the courtyard and the elegant black Kufic script rings all four sides, dividing the *zellij* (ceramic tilework) from the stucco, thus adding a further dimension; unusually, it is largely a list of the properties whose incomes were given as an endowment, rather than the standard Koranic inscriptions. Abou Inan, too, is bountifully praised amid the inscriptions, and on the foundation stone he is credited with the title *caliph*, an emotive claim to leadership of the Islamic world pursued by none of his successors.

THE WATER CLOCK, LATRINES AND ABLUTIONS

More or less opposite the *medersa,* just across the Talâa Kebira, Bou Inania's property continues with an extraordinary **water clock**, built above the stalls in the road (but at time of writing removed for research and possible restoration). An enduring curiosity, this consists of a row of thirteen windows and platforms, seven of which retain their

---

THE FUNCTION OF MEDERSAS

Medersas – student colleges and residence halls – were by no means unique to Fes and, in fact, originated in Khorassan in eastern Iran, gradually spreading west through Baghdad and Cairo where the *Al Azhar Medersa* was founded in 972 and became the most important teaching institution in the Muslim world. They seem to have reached Morocco under the Almohads, though the earliest ones still surviving in Fes are Merenid, dating from the early fourteenth century.

The word *medersa* means "place of study", and there may have been lectures delivered in some of the prayer halls. In general, however, the *medersa*s served as little more than dormitories, providing room and board to poor (male) students from the countryside and hence allowing them to attend lessons at the mosques. In Fes, where students might attend the Kairaouine University for ten years or more, rooms were always in great demand and "key money" was often paid by the new occupant. Although *medersa*s had largely disappeared from most of the Islamic world by the late Middle Ages, the majority of those in Fes remained in use right up into the 1950s. Since then, restoration work, partly funded by UNESCO, has made them more accessible, though several, which have now been restored, are once again accommodating students. This means that visitors are sometimes welcome only at certain times; as restoration continues, accessibility is impossible to forecast.

original brass bowls. Nobody has been able to discover exactly how it functioned, though a contemporary account detailed how at every hour one of its windows would open, dropping a weight down into the respective bowl.

Clocks had great religious significance during the Middle Ages in establishing the time of prayer, and it seems probable that this one was bought by Abou Inan as part of his campaign to assert the *medersa*'s pre-eminence; there are accounts of similar constructions in Tlemcen, just across the border in Algeria. As to its destruction, Fassi conspiracy tales are classically involved – most of them revolve round the miscarriage of a Jewess passing below at the time of its striking and a Jewish sorcerer casting the evil eye on the whole device. The building to which the clock is fixed, which was, in fact, once owned by a rabbi, is popularly known as "The House of the Magician".

Completing the *medersa* complex, and immediately adjacent to the clock, are the original **latrines and ablutions** (*wudu*) built for Friday worshippers. These have recently been closed, though it is possible that this will be temporary. Predating their use in the West by some four centuries, the "Turkish-style" toilets here were at last look very functional, flushed by quantities of running water. If they have re-opened – and you're male – take a look inside at the large central patio with its ablutions pool and unexpectedly rich stucco ceiling.

Further down Talâa Kebira

Making your way down the **Talâa Kebira** – a straightforward route to follow – you will eventually emerge at the labryrinth of lanes round the Kairaouine Mosque and Zaouia Moulay Idriss II. It's interesting less for any specific "sights" than for the general accumulated stimuli to your senses. The diarist Anaïs Nin expressed her reaction in terms of odours: ". . . of excrement, saffron, leather being cured, sandalwood, olive oil being fried, nut oil so strong at first that you cannot swallow". To which might be added sound – the shouts of muleteers (*balak!* means "look out!"), mantric cries from the beggars, the bells of water vendors – and, above all, the sight of the people, seen in shafts of light filtered through the rush roofings which cover much of the Talâa's length.

Along the first (upward) stretch watch out for a very large **fondouk** on your left, just after a row of blacksmiths' shops, about 300m beyond the Medersa Bou Inania. This was originally a **Merenid prison**, fitted out with solid colonnades and arches; it is now home to people selling butter and honey out of large vats.

Before the advent in Morocco of French-style cafés, at the beginning of this century, the *fondouk*s – or *caravanserai*s as they're called in the East – formed the heart of social life outside the home. They provided rooms for traders and richer students, and frequently became centres of vice, intrigue and entertainment. There were once some two hundred in Fes El Bali, but although many still survive, often with beautiful fourteenth- and fifteenth-century decorations, they tend now to serve as small factories or warehouses. Another *fondouk*, about 100m further down, is today used for curing animal skins (and smells awful).

RUE ECH CHERABLIYIN

A little way down from this latter *fondouk*, the street changes name – to **Rue ech Cherabliyin** – and, past the oldest **hammam** (men only) still in use in Fes, you find yourself in a district of **leather stalls and shoemakers**. The Fassi *babouches*, leather slippers, are reputed by Fassis to be the best in the country – although this is hotly disputed by Tafraoute in the South. Here, in Fes and unusually, you'll find sophisticated-looking grey and black pairs in addition to the classic yellow and white. If you want to buy a good pair, you'll have to spend some time examining the different qualities; for the best, be prepared to bargain hard until you're down to around 150dh.

The **Cherabliyin** (Slippermakers') **mosque**, in the midst of the quarter, was endowed by the Merenid sultan, Abou El Hassan, builder of the Chellah complex in

Rabat. It has been substantially restored, though the minaret is original. If you've gazed at the Koutoubia in Marrakesh, or the great Almohad monuments of Rabat, you'll recognize the familiar *darj w ktarf* motifs of its decoration.

SOUK EL ATTARIN

Continuing, Rue Ech Cherabliyin is flanked by a forgettable sequence of handicraft shops before reaching, at the bottom of the hill, an arched gateway marked **Souk El Attarin** – the "Souk of the Spice Vendors". This was the formal heart of the old city, and its richest and most sophisticated shopping district. It was traditionally around the grand mosque of a city that the most expensive commodities were sold and kept, and, approaching the Kairaouine, this pattern is more or less maintained. Spices themselves are still sold here, as well as Egyptian and Japanese imports, while in the web of little squares off to the left, you'll find all kinds of manufactured goods.

There are a few small cafés inside the spice *souk*, and on the main street is the **Dar Saada**, a nineteenth-century mansion now housing an expensive carpet shop and restaurant; you can look in or drink a cup of tea feeling only moderate pressure to buy something. Just beyond the Dar Saada, this time on the right of the street, is the principal **kissaria**, or covered market, again dominated by textiles and modern goods; totally rebuilt after a fire in the 1950s, it lacks any particular character.

● **Access.** Reaching the end of Souk El Attarin you come to a **crossroads of lanes** lying slightly askew from the direction of the street. On your right (and ahead of you) are the walls of the **Kairaouine Mosque;** to your left, and entered a few yards up the lane, is the magnificent **Attarin medersa** (see p.204). First, however, it seems logical to take a look at the area below the Souk El Attarin – dominated, as it has been for five centuries, by the **shrine and zaouia of Moulay Idriss II,** the city's patron saint.

The Zaouia of Moulay Idriss II and around

The principal landmark to the south of the Souk El Attarin is the **Zaouia Moulay Idriss II**, one of the holiest buildings in the city. Although enclosed by a highly confusing web of lanes, it is not difficult to find: take the first lane to the right – Rue Mjadliyin – as soon as you have passed through the arch into the Attarin and you will find yourself in front of a wooden bar which marks the beginning of its *horm*, or sanctuary precinct. Until the French occupation of the city in 1911, this was as far as Christians, Jews or mules, could go, and beyond it any Muslim had the right to claim asylum from prosecution or arrest. These days non-Muslims are allowed to walk round the outside of the *zaouia*, and although you are not permitted to enter, it is possible to get a glimpse inside the shrine and even see the saint's tomb.

Passing to the right of the bar, and making your way round a narrow alleyway, you emerge on the far side of the *zaouia* at the **women's entrance.** Looking in from the doorway, the **tomb** of Moulay Idriss II is over on the left, and a scene of intense and apparently high-baroque devotion is usually going on all round it. The women, who are Idriss's principal devotees, burn candles and incense here and then proceed around the corner of the precinct to touch, or make offerings at, a round brass grille which opens directly onto the tomb. A curious feature, common to many *zaouias* but rarely within view, are the numerous European clocks – prestigious gifts and very popular in the last century, when many Fassi merchant families had them shipped over from Manchester (their main export base for the cotton trade).

There is no particular evidence that Moulay Idriss II was a very saintly *marabout*, but as the effective founder of Fes and the son of the founder of the Moroccan state, he obviously has considerable *baraka*, the magical blessing which Moroccans invoke. Originally it was assumed that Idriss, like his father, had been buried near Volubilis, but in 1308 an incorrupted body was found on this spot and the cult was launched. Presumably, it was an immediate success, since in addition to his role as the city's patron saint, Idriss has an impressive roster of supplicants. This is the place to visit for poor strangers arriving in the city, for boys before being circumcised, and for women wanting to facilitate childbirth; also, for some unexplained reason, Idriss is a national protector of sweetmeat vendors. The shrine itself was rebuilt in the eighteenth century by Sultan Moulay Ismail – his only act of pious endowment in this city.

PLACE EN NEJJARIN

Standing at the women's entrance to the *zaouia,* you'll see a lane off to the left – **Rue du Bab Moulay Ismail** – full of stalls selling candles and silverware for devotional offerings. If you follow this lane round to the wooden bar, go under the bar (turning to the right), and then, keeping to your left, you should come out in the picturesque square of **Place en Nejjarin** (Carpenters' Square).

Here is the very imposing **Nejjarin Fondouk**, built in the early eighteenth century along with a beautiful canopied fountain on one side of the square. Despite its poor condition, the *fondouk* was in use until a few years ago as a hostel for students at the nearby Kariaouine university. It has now been restored, but its future has not yet been decided – an exhibition centre for local artists' work has been mooted.

In the alleys that lead off the square, you'll find the **Nejjarin souk**, easiest located by the sounds and smells of the carpenters chiselling away at sweet-smelling cedar wood. They produce mainly stools and tables – three-legged so they don't wobble on uneven ground – along with various implements for winding yarn, wooden boxes for storage and coffins. If there's a wedding coming up, you may see them making special ornamented tables, with edges, used for parading the bride and groom at shoulder level

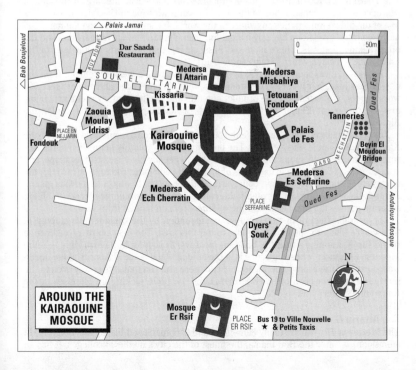

– a Fassi custom. Parallel to this lane is a **metalworkers' souk**, where the men hammer patterns onto large iron tubs and implements.

To return to the Souk El Attarin, turn left at the point where you entered the Place en Nejjarin.

SOUK EL HENNA

A similar arrangement of buildings characterizes the **Souk El Henna**, a quiet, tree-shaded square adjoining what was once the largest madhouse in the Merenid empire – an imposing building now in use as a storehouse. The stalls here continue to sell henna and the usual cosmetics (kohl, antimony, etc); on one side of the square there is a huge pair of scales used for weighing the larger deliveries. In addition several outlets here offer the more esoteric ingredients required for medical cures, aphrodisiacs and magical spells. If you get talking to the stallkeepers, you'll be shown an amazing collection of plant and animal (often insect) derivatives.

Pottery stalls are gradually encroaching on this traditional pharmacological business. Cheap but often striking in design, the pieces include Fassi pots, which are usually blue and white or very simple black on earthenware; and others from Safi, the pottery most commonly exported from Morocco, distinguished by heavy green or blue glazes; and Salé, often elaborate modern designs on a white glaze.

To get down to the square, take the lane to the right immediately in front of the entrance arch to Souk El Attarin.

The Kairaouine Mosque

The **Djemaa El Kairaouine** – the Kairaouine Mosque – was the largest mosque in Morocco until the construction of the new Hassan II Mosque in Casablanca – and it is one of the oldest universities anywhere in the world. It remains today the fountainhead of the country's religious life, governing, for example, the timings of Ramadan and the other Islamic festivals. There is an old Fassi saying that all roads in Fes lead to the Kairaouine – a claim which retains some truth.

The mosque was founded in 857 by a Tunisian woman, a wealthy refugee from the city of Kairouan, but its present dimensions, with sixteen aisles and room for 20,000 worshippers, are essentially the product of tenth- and twelfth-century reconstructions: first by the great Caliph of Cordoba, Abd Er Rahman III, and later under the Almoravids.

For non-Muslims, who cannot enter the mosque's courts and prayer halls, the Kairaouine is a rather elusive sight. The building is so thoroughly enmeshed in the surrounding houses and shops that it is impossible to get any clear sense of its shape, and at most you can get only partial views of it from the adjoining rooftops or through the four great entrances to its main courtyard. Nobody seems to object to tourists gaping through the gates, though inevitably the centrepieces that would give order to all the separate parts – the main aisle and the *mihrab* – remain hidden from view.

The overall effect of this obscurity is compounded by the considerable amount of time you're likely to spend getting lost round this area. The best **point of reference** round the Kairaouine – and the building most worth visiting in its own right – is the Medersa El Attarin, whose entrance is at the far end of the Souk El Attarin, at the northwest corner of the Kairaouine Mosque. From here you can make your way around the mosque to a succession of other *medersas* and *fondouks*, picking up glimpses of the Kairaouine's interior as you go.

The Attarin Medersa

The **Medersa El Attarin** (daily 8am–noon and 2–6pm, closed Friday mornings; 10dh admission) is, after the Bou Inania, the finest of the city's medieval colleges. It has an incredible profusion and variety of patterning – equally startling in the *zellij,* wood and stucco. Remarkably, each aspect of the decoration seems accomplished with an apparent ease, and the building's elegant proportions are never under threat of being overwhelmed.

The *medersa* was completed in 1325 by the Merenid sultan, Abou Said, and is thus one of the earliest in Fes. Interestingly, its general lightness of feel is achieved by the relatively simple device of using pairs of symmetrical arches to join the pillars to a single weight-bearing lintel – a design repeated in the upper storeys and mirrored in the courtyard basin. The later Merenid design, as employed in the Bou Inania, was to have much heavier lintels (the timbers above the doors and windows) supported by shorter projecting beams; this produces a more solid, step-like effect, losing the Attarin's fluid movement.

The basic ground plan, however, is more or less standard: an entrance hall opening onto a courtyard with a fountain, off which to the left are the latrines, and directly ahead the prayer hall. On your way in, stop a while in the **entrance hall,** whose *zellij* decoration is perhaps the most complex in Fes. A circular pattern, based on an interlace of pentagons and five-pointed stars, this perfectly demonstrates the intricate science – and the philosophy – employed by the craftsmen. As Titus Burckhardt explains (in his *Moorish Art in Spain*), this lies in direct opposition to the Western arts of pictorial representation:

> . . . with its rhythmic repetitions, [it] does not seek to capture the eye to lead it into an imagined world, but, on the contrary, liberates it from all the pre-occupations of the mind. It does not transmit specific ideas, but a state of being, which is at once repose and inner rhythm.

Burckhardt also notes that the way the patterns radiate from a single point serves as a pure simile for the belief in the oneness of God, manifested as the centre of every form or being.

In the **courtyard** you'll notice a change in the *zellij* base to a combination of eight- and ten-pointed stars. This probably signifies the hand of a different *maallem* (master craftsman), most of whom had a single mathematical base which they worked and reworked with infinite variation on all commissions. In comparison with these outer rooms, the actual **prayer hall** is very bare and meditative, focusing on its *mihrab* (or prayer niche) flanked by marble pillars and lit by a series of small *zellij*-glass windows.

If you are allowed to go up the stairs in the entrance hall, do so. Around the second floor are **cells** for over sixty students, and these operated as an annexe to the Kairaouine University until the 1950s. Budgett Meakin (in 1899) estimated that there were some 1500 students in the city's various *medersas* – a figure which may have been overestimated since it was based not on an actual count of the students themselves but on how many loaves of bread were prepared for them each day. Non-Muslims were not allowed into the *medersas* until the French undertook their repair at the beginning of the protectorate, and were banned again (this time by the colonial authorities) when the Kairaouine students became active in the struggle for independence.

VIEWS OF THE KAIRAOUINE

From the roof of the Attarin Medersa (not always open to visitors) you can get one of the most complete views possible of the **Kairaouine Mosque**.

Looking out across the mosque's green roof tiles three **minarets** are visible. The square one on the left belongs to the Zaouia Moulay Idriss. To its right are the Kairaouine's Burj an-Naffara (Trumpeter's Tower) and original minaret. The latter, slightly thinner in its silhouette than usual – most minarets are built to an exact 5 : 1 (width : height) ratio – is the oldest Islamic monument in the city, built in the year 956. Below it, you can also make out a considerable section of the central courtyard of the mosque – the **sahn**.

For a closer glimpse of the *sahn* at ground level, the best vantage point is the Bab El Wad gate: 20m down from the Attarin entrance (turn left as you step out, then immediately left again). At the end of the courtyard, a pair of magnificent pavilions are visible – the last additions to the structure of the mosque, added by the Saadians in the sixteenth century. They are modelled on the Court of the Lions in Granada's Alhambra palace, and were perhaps constructed by Spanish Muslim craftsmen.

Around the Kairaouine and Place Seffarine

There is a further new angle on to the *sahn* of the Kairaouine from the **Bab Medersa**, a gate near the end of this first stretch of the mosque wall. Opposite, as you'd expect, is another college – the semi-derelict **Misbahiya Medersa** which is currently closed for renovation. It has some fine details, though much of its best wood carving is now displayed at the Dar Batha museum. The elegant central basin was brought over by the Saadians from Almería in Spain; the marble floor in which it is set level came from Italy. Surprisingly large, with courtyards (and two latrines/ablutions) at each corner, it was built a couple of years before Bou Inania, again by the Merenid sultan, Abou El Hassan.

THE TETOUANI FONDOUK AND PALAIS DE FES

Moving on around the corner of the Kairaouine, you pass the **Tetouani** (or *Istroihani*) **fondouk**, a well-preserved Merenid building where the traders from Tetouan used to stay. Now partially occupied by a carpet store, you can look inside without any obligation and you'll probably be shown the huge, ancient door lock which draws across its gateway.

A few doors down, past another, much smaller *fondouk,* is the so-called **Palais de Fes**, a grand nineteenth-century mansion converted into a fine carpet shop and a splendid restaurant, somewhat ambiguously said to be 'dans un cadre du 14e siècle'. You can walk in and look round without pressure to buy, and if you ask you'll be allowed up to the **roof** to get a different view of the Kairaouine and an interesting exercise in orientation concerning the immediate area. There is a café on the roof, which will serve tea and pastries outside meal times – highly recommended.

PLACE SEFFARINE AND THE KAIRAOUINE LIBRARY

Another gate to the Kairaouine, essentially of Almoravid construction, stands right opposite the Palais de Fes; it is one of the ten which are opened only for Friday prayers. Alongside, notice the cedar panelling, placed to guide the blind towards the mosque.

If you follow this round, through a tight-wedged alley, you soon emerge into a very distinctive open square, metalworkers hammering away on each of its sides, surrounded by immense iron and copper cauldrons and pans for weddings and festivals. This is **Place Seffarin** – almost wilfully picturesque, with its faience fountain and gnarled old fig trees.

On the near side of the square a tall and very simple entrance in the whitewashed walls leads into the **Kairaouine Library**, again a building frustratingly denied to non-Muslims. Established by the Kairouan refugees in the ninth century, and bolstered by virtually the entire contents of Córdoba's medieval library, it once held the greatest collection of Islamic, mathematical and scholarly books outside Baghdad. Amazingly, and somewhat pointedly marking Fes's decline, much of the library was lost or dissipated in the seventeenth century. Now restored and in use, it is one of the most important in the Arab world.

The **university** here has had its function largely usurped by the modern departments established around Fes El Djedid and the Ville Nouvelle, and dispersed throughout Morocco. However, until recent decades it was the only source of Moroccan higher education. Entirely traditional in character, studies comprised courses on Koranic law, astrology, mathematics, logic, rhetoric and poetry – very much as the medieval universities of Europe. Teaching was informal, with professors gathering a group of students round them in a corner of the mosque, the students contriving to absorb and memorize the body of the professors' knowledge. It was, of course, an entirely male preserve.

A good spot to get your bearings, Place Seffarine offers a number of possible routes. You can continue round the mosque by taking the first lane to the right as you enter the square – **Sma't El Adoul** (The Street of the Notaries). The notaries, professional scribes, are sadly out of business, but before looping back to reach the Attarin *medersa*, you will be able to peek through a number of gates revealing the Kairaouine's rush-matted and round-arched interior. If you don't take this turning but continue straight ahead, you enter an area of *souks* specializing in **gold and silver jewellery** and used metal goods – a magnificent range of **pewter teapots** among them. As this road begins to veer left down the hill, a right turn will lead you up to the **Cherratin Medersa** (and eventually to Zaouia Moulay Idriss).

First, though, it is worth taking a look at the **Seffarine Medersa**, right on Place Seffarine.

THE MEDERSA ES SEFFARINE

The **Medersa Es Seffarine** (same hours as Attarin) is the earliest of these Fes colleges. Its entrance is fairly inconspicuous, and you might need it pointed out to you: leaving the Seffarine square at the bottom left-hand corner you follow a short lane down to the left and then briefly to the right – the door (studded and with an overhanging portico) is on your left; it now houses some students and is generally closed to the public, but it's always worth asking.

Built around 1285 – twenty years before the Attarin, 42 before the Bou Inania – the Seffarine is unlike all the other *medersas* in that it takes the exact form of a traditional Fassi house, with an arched balcony above its courtyard and still with suggestions of former grandeur in the lofty prayer hall. Elsewhere, the wandering vine and delicate ablutions pool give it a domestic air; in the far left-hand corner are wash basins and latrines.

Next door are two newer *medersas* housing students from the Lycée.

THE MEDERSA ECH CHERRATIN

Very different from the Seffarin, and indeed all the previous *medersas*, the **Medersa Ech Cherratin** (see directions from Place Seffarine, above) dates from 1670 and the reign of Moulay Rachid, founder of the Alaouite dynasty.

The whole design represents a shift in scope and wealth – to an essentially functional style, with student cells grouped round three corner courtyards and latrines/ablutions round the fourth.

The craftsmanship here represents a significant decline, though there is some impressive woodwork around the individual courtyards. It is interesting, too, in a general way as a rare surviving building from this period.

This *medersa* is being restored and more students continue to live there; it is generally open to the public.

● **Access.** Continuing down the lane **beyond the entrance to the Medersa Es Seffarine**, swinging down the hill to the right, you reach **Rue des Teinturiers** (The Dyers' *Souk*: see the following section) and a **bridge** over the Oued Fes, below which you can leave the Medina by the *place* beside the **Mosque Er Rsif.**

South of the Kairaouine: the dyers' souk and tanneries

If you're beginning to find the medieval prettiness of the central *souks* and *medersas* slightly unreal, then this region, just below the Kairaouine, should provide the antidote.

That's because the dyers' and tanners' *souks* – basis of the city's commercial wealth from the tenth to the nineteenth century – represent the nauseating underside of everything you've seen until now.

THE DYERS' SOUK

The **dyers' street** – **Souk Sabbighin** (or Rue des Teinturiers, in French) – is directly below the Seffarine Medersa. Continue down past the *medersa* to your left, and then turn right immediately before the bridge ahead.

The *souk* is short and very weird, draped with fantastically coloured yarn and cloth drying in the heat. Below, workers in grey, chimney-sweep-looking clothes toil over ancient cauldrons of multicoloured dyes. The atmosphere is thick and mysterious, and not a little disconcerting so close to one of the city's main entrances.

● **Access.** At the end of the dyers' souk you come to a second bridge, the humpbacked **Qantrat Sidi El Aouad** – almost disguised by the shops built on and around it. Walking across, you'll find yourself in the **Andalous quarter** (see p.210), and if you follow the main lane up to the left, Rue Sidi Youssef, you'll come out at the Andalous Mosque. Staying on the Kairaouine side of the river and taking the lane down to your right at the end of the *souk,* you should emerge at the open **square by the Rsif Mosque**; from here, if you want to return to the Ville Nouvelle, you can get a bus #19, #29 or #45 – or a *petit taxi.*

THE TANNERIES

For the tanneries quarter – the **Souk Dabbaghin** – return to Place Seffarine and take the right-hand lane at the top of the square (the second lane on your left if you're coming from the Palais de Fes). This lane is known as **Darb Mechattin** (Combmakers' Lane), and runs more or less parallel to the river for 150m or so, eventually reaching a fork. The right-hand branch goes down to the river and **Beyin El Moudoun Bridge** – another approach to the Andalous Mosque. The left branch winds up amid a maze of eighteenth-century streets for another 150 to 200m until you see the tanneries on your right; it sounds a convoluted route but is in fact a well-trodden one.

The most physically striking sight in Fes, the **tanneries** are constantly being visited by groups of tourists, with whom you could discreetly tag along for a while if you get lost. Otherwise, follow your nose or accept a guide up from the Place Seffarine. The best time to visit is in the morning, when there is most activity. You will be asked to pay a small fee – 10dh is usual – to one of the local *gardiens.*

There is a compulsive fascination about the tanneries. Cascades of water pour through holes that were once the windows of houses; hundreds of skins lie spread out to dry on the rooftops; while amid the vats of dye and pigeon dung (used to treat the leather) an unbelievably gothic fantasy is enacted. The rotation of colours in the enormous honeycombed vats follows a traditional sequence – yellow (saffron), red (poppy), blue (indigo), green (mint) and black (antimony) – though vegetable dyes have mostly been replaced by chemicals, with worrying effects on the health of the workers involved.

This innovation and the occasional rinsing machine aside, there can have been little change here since the sixteenth century, when Fes took over from Còrdoba as the pre-eminent city of leather production. As befits such an ancient system, the ownership is also intricately feudal: the foremen run a hereditary guild and the workers pass down their specific jobs from generation to generation.

The processes can best be seen from surrounding terrace rooftops, where you'll be directed along with the other tourists. There is, oddly enough, a kind of sensuous beauty about it – for all the stench and voyeurism involved. Sniffing the mint that you are handed as you enter (to alleviate the nausea) and looking across at the others doing the same, however, there could hardly be a more pointed exercise in the nature of comparative wealth. Like it or not, this is tourism at its most extreme.

North to Bab Guissa and the Palais Jamai

This region – **north from Souk El Attarin** towards Bab Guissa and the Palais Jamai Hôtel – is something of a tailpiece to the Kairaouine quarter of Fes El Bali. It is not a route which many tourists take, scattered as it is with curiosities rather than monuments, but in this itself there's a distinct attraction. Additionally, leaving the city at Bab Guissa you can walk out and round to the **Merenid Tombs**, a beautiful walk as the sun is going down on the city.

A ROUTE TO BAB GUISSA – AND THE JEWELLERS' SOUK

From **Souk El Attarin,** there are dozens of lanes climbing up in the general direction of Bab Guissa, many of them blind alleys which send you scuttling back to retrace your steps. One of the more interesting and unproblematic approaches is to take the first lane to your left just inside the entrance arch to the *souk* (that is, about 15m before you come to the *Dar Saada* palace restaurant). Following this as directly as you can, you will soon emerge at the **Joutia**, the ancient fish and salt market.

Spreading out above here is the **Sagha** – the **jewellers' quarter** – which curves round to the right into a small square flanked by the eighteenth-century **Fondouk Sagha** and a small fountain. The *fondouk* is now used as a wool storehouse, but you can wander in to take a look at the elegant cedar woodwork and (heavily restored) stucco.

Back at the main lane – Place Sagha and its *fondouk* are about 20m off to the right – you pass a series of small café-restaurants and a cinema near **Place Achabin**, the herbalists' square, where remedies and charms are still sold. The **café-restaurants** in this area are among the best value in Fes El Bali, serving good solid meals, and many double as pâtisseries, good for a mint tea or some fresh orange while rambling round the Attarin/Kairaouine area. Most of them are located in Rue Hormis.

Beyond Place Achabin, the road continues uphill, through an area filled with carpenters' workshops, towards Bab Guissa. On your way, look out for the **Fondouk Guissa** – or *Fondouk El Ihoudi* (The Jews' Fondouk) – on the left-hand side of the road. This dates back to the thirteenth century and was at the centre of the city's Jewish community until their removal to the Mellah in Fes El Djedid. It is used today for the sorting and storing of skins brought up from the tanneries: not a building for the queasy.

BAB GUISSA AND THE HÔTEL PALAIS JAMAI

The **Bab Guissa** and **Mosque Bab Guissa**, at the top of the hill, are of little interest, rebuilt in the nineteenth century to replace a string of predecessors which had occupied this site for 800 years.

A quick right just before the gate, however, takes you up to the **Hôtel Palais Jamai** – a building whose luxury comes as quite a shock after a day's rambling through the Medina below. It was built towards the end of the last century by the Jamai brothers, viziers to Sultan Moulay Hassan and, in effect, the most powerful men in the country. Fabulously rapacious, the brothers eventually fell from power amid spectacular intrigues at the accession of Abdul Aziz in 1894. Walter Harris records the full story in *Morocco That Was*, dwelling in great detail on the brothers' ignominious fate – "perhaps the blackest page of Moulay Abdul Aziz's reign".

They were sent in fetters to Tetouan, and confined, chained and fettered, in a dungeon. In the course of time – and how long those ten years must have been – Hadj Amaati (The Elder) died. The governor of Tetouan was afraid to bury the body, lest he should be accused of having allowed his prisoner to escape. He wrote to the court for instructions. It was summer, and even the dungeon was hot. The answer did not come for eleven days, and all that time Si Mohammed remained chained to his brother's corpse! The brother survived. In 1908 he was released after fourteen years of incarceration, a hopeless, broken, ruined man. Everything he had possessed had been confiscated, his wives and children had died; the result of want and persecution. He emerged from his dark dungeon nearly blind, and lame from the cruel fetters he had worn. In his days of power he had been cruel, it is said – but what a price he paid!

For an overt and dramatic contrast to this tale, wander into the hotel for a drink. Ask to do so on the terrace beside the old palace, now dwarfed by a huge modern extension. An hour in the gardens here, with their box-hedge courtyards and fountains, really does merit the bar prices (and there's an excellent Moroccan restaurant, in a beautiful old salon, if you can afford a splurge). The palace quarters themselves are used as special suites and conference rooms, but if they're unoccupied you may be able to look round one or two – ask at reception if a porter can show you the "Royal Suites"; a tip will be expected.

● **Access.** From **Bab Guissa** you can take a shortcut across through the hill cemetery to the Merenid tombs, or you can follow the road up and around. At **Bab Ferdaous**, just outside the *Palais Jamai*, there's a *petit taxi* stand, and from here **bus #10** runs to the train station in the Ville Nouvelle.

The Andalous Quarter

Coming across the **Bou Khareb** River from the Kairaouine to the **Andalous bank** is not quite the adventure it once was. For the first three centuries of their existence, the two quarters were entirely separate walled cities and the intense rivalry between them often resulted in factional strife. The rivalry still lingers enough to give each a distinct identity, though since the thirteenth century this has been a somewhat one-sided affair: as the Fassis tell it, the Andalucians are known for the beauty of their women and the bravery of their soldiers, while the Kairaouinis have always had the money.

Whatever the reasons, the most famous Andalucian scholars and craftsmen have nearly all lived and worked on the other side of the river and as a result the atmosphere has a somewhat provincial character. Monuments are few and comparatively modest, and the streets are quieter and predominantly residential. As such, it can be a pleasant quarter to spend the early evening – and to get caught up in the ordinary, daily life of Fes El Bali. Street trading here (and in the southern quarters of the Kairouine side, too) tends to revolve round daily necessities, providing a link between the "medieval" town and continuing urban life. And your relationship with the city changes alongside, as you cease for a while to be a consuming tourist – a factor reflected also in the near-total absence of "guides" and hustlers.

There are four principal **approaches to the quarter**, all providing more or less direct access to the area round the Andalous Mosque.

● **Cross the river at the El Aouad Bridge**. From here, take **Rue Sidi Youssef** up the hill to the right, and keep going straight to the top, where you'll come into line with the minaret of the Andalous Mosque. At this point, veer left, and you will see (on your right) the elaborate facade of the **Sahrija Medersa.**

● **Cross the river to the north, near the tanneries, on the Bein El Moudoun Bridge** (The Bridge Between the Cities). Then follow the main street, **Rue Seftah,** all the way up the hill as it winds round to the Andalous Mosque.

● **Start at the square by Mosque Er Rsif**. From here you can get to **Rue Sidi Youssef** by going through the gate opposite the mosque entrance, then taking a first left by the first mosque (Sidi Lemlili) you come to, followed by a right turn up the hill. The square can be reached (somewhat circuitously) from the area around the Kairaouine Mosque, or you can get a **bus** to it (#19, #29 or #45) from the Ville Nouvelle.

● **Start at Bab Ftouh, at the bottom of the quarter**, and head north to the Andalous Mosque. **Bus #3** runs to Bab Ftouh from Place de la Résistance (aka La Fiat) and **bus #12** connects Bab Boujeloud with Bab Ftouh. Bab Ftouh is connected by **bus #18** to the Place de l'Istiqlal, by the Dar Batha; a handy point from which to leave Fes El Bali.

THE SAHRIJA MEDERSA AND ANDALOUS MOSQUE

If you are seeking direction for your wanderings in the Andalous Quarter, the **Medersa Es Sahrija** is the quarter's most interesting monument and is generally rated the third finest *medersa* in the city, after the Attarin and Bou Inania. Anywhere else but Fes it would be a major sight, though here, perhaps because of the more accessible monuments, it fails to stand out as much as it should.

Still, it is currently undergoing restoration, and there's a considerable range and variety of original decoration. The *zellij* is among the oldest in the country, while the wood carving harkens back to Almohad and Almoravid motifs with its palmettes and pine cones. Built around 1321 by Sultan Abou El Hassan, it is slightly earlier than the Attarin and a more or less exact contemporary of the *medersa* in Meknes – which it in many ways resembles. Some students live here, but access is welcomed.

There is frustratingly little to be seen of the nearby **Andalous Mosque**, other than its monumental entrance gates, as it is built right at the highest point of the valley. Like the Kairaouine, it was founded in the late ninth century and saw considerable enlargements under the Almoravids and Merenids. The Sahrija Medersa originally served as a dormitory annexe for those studying at the mosque's library and under its individual professors.

A last Medersa, the **Sebbayin**, or **Medersa El Oued**, is located just southwest of the Sahrija. It, too, was once an Andalous Mosque student annexe, and it remains in use, as a residence for Lycée students.

TOWARDS BAB FTOUH AND THE POTTERS' QUARTER

South from the Andalous Mosque – out towards **Bab Ftouh** – you emerge into a kind of flea market: clothes sellers at first, then all variety of household and general goods and odds and ends. At the top of the hill, on the edge of a cemetery area, there are often entertainers – clowns, storytellers, the occasional musician, all performing to large audiences.

This region of the city, a strange no-man's land of **cemeteries** and run-down houses, was once a leper colony, and traditionally a quarter of necromancers, thieves, madmen and saints. At its heart, close by Bab Ftouh, is the whitewashed **koubba of Sidi Harazem**, a twelfth-century mystic who has been adopted as the patron saint of students and the mentally ill. The saint's *moussem*, held in the spring, is one of the city's most colourful; in past centuries it was often the cue for riots and popular insurrections. The **potters' quarter** used to be located by Bab Ftouh, though they have recently been moved out to Ain Nokbi, some two kilometres along the Taza road. You will see the columns of black smoke and the buildings of the *Complexe Ceramique du Maroc* down to the left of the road. If you're interested in the techniques – the moulding, drying and decorating of the pots and tiles – it's possible to look around the workshops. Although the quarter is new, the designs and workmanship remain traditional.

● **Access.** At **Bab Ftouh** you can pick up a *petit taxi* to any part of town (the route up to the Merenid tombs is good for its views), or you can catch bus #18 back to the Ville Nouvelle.

Fes El Djedid

Unlike Fes El Bali, whose development and growth seems to have been almost organic, **Fes El Djedid** – "Fes the New" – was an entirely planned city, built by the Merenids at the beginning of their rule, as both a practical and symbolic seat of government. The work was begun around 1273 by the dynasty's second ruling sultan, Abou Youssef, and in a maniac feat of building was completed within three years. The capital for much of its construction came from taxes levied on the Meknes olive presses; the Jews were also taxed to build a new grand mosque; and the labour, at least in part, was supplied by Spanish Christian slaves.

The site which the Merenids chose for their city lies some distance from Fes El Bali. In the chronicles this is presented as a strategic move for the defence of the city, though it is hard to escape the conclusion that its main function was as a defence of the new dynasty against the Fassis themselves. It was not an extension for the people, in any real sense, being occupied largely by the **Dar El Makhzen,** a vast royal palace, and by a series of army garrisons. With the addition of the **Mellah** – the Jewish ghetto – at the beginning of the fourteenth century, this process was continued. Forced out of Fes El Bali following one of the periodic pogroms, the Jews could provide an extra barrier (and scapegoat) between the sultan and his Muslim faithful, as well as a useful and close to hand source of income.

Over the centuries, Fes El Djedid's fortunes have generally followed those of the city as a whole. It was extremely prosperous under the Merenids and Wattasids, fell into decline under the Saadians, lapsed into virtual ruin during Moulay Ismail's long reign in Meknes, but revived with the commercial expansion of the nineteenth century – at which point the walls between the old and new cities were finally joined.

At the close of the nineteenth century, the *Encyclopedia Britannica* noted of Fes that: "The Jews suffer great persecutions and many indignities, but many of them continue to amass money."

Events this century, largely generated by the French Protectorate, have left Fes El Djedid greatly changed and somewhat moribund. As a "government city", it had no obvious role after the transfer of power to Rabat – a vacuum which the French filled by establishing a huge *quartier reservé* (red-light district) in the area around the Grand Mosque. This can have done little for the city's identity, but it was not so radical or disastrous as the immediate aftermath of independence in 1956. Concerned about their future status, and with their position made untenable by the Arab-Israeli war, virtually all of the Mellah's 17,000 **Jewish population** emigrated to Israel, Paris or Casablanca; today only a few Jewish families remain in the Mellah, though there is still a small community in the Ville Nouvelle.

The *Jewish Community Centre* (☎05/62.24.46) is opposite the copse which faces the *Splendid Hôtel*; the current president of the community is Dr Guigui (☎05/62.30.39). With his help, or that of others at the centre, you could learn more about the community – or about the old synagogues in Fes El Djedid (see pp.214–215).

Generally speaking, Moroccan Jews are well thought of and, at any one time, several hold high office in the government. Similarly, Moroccan Jews who play leading roles in Israel are noted with pride. At the same time, however, it was reported that recently a Fes hotel turned Israeli tourists away; we have omitted it from our list.

● **Access.** You can reach Fes El Djedid in a ten-minute walk from **Bab Boujeloud** (the route outlined below), or from the Ville Nouvelle by walking up or taking a **bus** (#2 from Place de la Résistance, aka La Fiat)) to **Place des Alaouites** and **Bab Semarine** beside the Mellah.

West from Boujeloud

Walking down to Fes El Djedid from **Bab Boujeloud** involves a shift in scale. Gone are the labyrinthine alleyways and *souks* of the Medina, to be replaced by a massive expanse of walls. Within them, to your left, are a series of gardens: the private **Jardins Beida**, behind the Lycée, and then the public **Jardins de Boujeloud** with their pools diverted from the Oued Fes. The latter have an entrance towards the end of the long Av. des Français, and are a vital lung for the old city. If everything gets too much, wander in, lounge about on the grass, and spend an hour or two at the tranquil **café**, by an old waterwheel, at their west corner.

THE PETIT MECHOUAR

Moving on, near the end of the gardens, you pass through twin arches to reach a kind of square, the **Petit Mechouar**, which was once the focus of city life and still sees the occcasional juggler or storyteller during Ramadan evenings. To its left, entered through another double archway, begins the main street of Fes El Djedid proper – the **Grande Rue.**

To the right is the monumental **Bab Dekakin** (Gate of the Benches), a Merenid structure which was, until King Hassan realigned the site in 1967–71, the main approach to the Royal Palace and Fes El Bali. It was on this gate that the Infante Ferdinand of Portugal was hanged, head down, for four days in 1437. He had been captured in an unsuccessful raid on Tangier and his country had failed to raise the ransom required. As a further, salutary warning, when his corpse was taken down from the Bab, it was stuffed and displayed beside the gate, where it remained for the next three decades.

THE VIEUX MECHOUAR

Through the three great arches you will find yourself in another, much larger courtyard, the **Vieux Mechouar**. Laid out in the eighteenth century, this is flanked along the whole of one side by the Makina, an Italian-built arms factory, which is today partially occupied by a rug factory and various local clubs.

A smaller gate, the nineteenth-century **Bab As Smen**, stands at the far end of the court, forcing you into an immediate turn as you leave the city through the Merenid outer gateway of **Bab Segma**, whose twin octagonal towers slightly resemble the contemporary Chellah in Rabat.

If you are walking to the **Merenid tombs** from here, you can either turn sharp right (and scramble up the hillside, after the Borj Nord, or go straight ahead along the longer Route du Tour de Fes. The latter route takes you past the huge **Kasbah Cherada**, a fort built by Sultan Moulay Rashid in 1670 to house – and keep at a distance – the Berber tribes of his garrison. The partially walled compound is now the site of a hospital, a school and an annexe of the Kairaouine University.

QUARTIER MOULAY ABDALLAH AND THE SOUKS
Back at the Petit Mechouar – and before turning through the double arch onto the Grande Rue de Fes El Djedid – a smaller gateway leads off to the right at the bottom of the square. This gives entrance to the old *quartier reservé* of **Moulay Abdallah**, where the French built cafés, dance halls and brothels. The prostitutes were mostly young Berber girls, drawn by a rare chance of quick money, and usually returning to their villages when they had earned enough to marry or keep their families. The quarter today has a slightly solemn, empty feel about it, with the main street twisting down to Fes El Djedid's **Great Mosque**.

Through the main gateway, the **Grand Rue** zigzags slightly before leading straight down to the Mellah. There are **souks**, mainly for textiles and produce, along the way but nothing very much to detain you too long. Just by the entrance, though, immediately to the left after you go through the arch, a narrow **lane** curves off into an attractive little area on the periphery of the Boujeloud gardens. There's an old **water wheel** here which used to supply the gardens, and the small café (mentioned above) in the gardens nearby. On the way down, you pass a handful of stalls; among them are, traditionally, the *kif* and *sebsi* (kif pipe) vendors.

The Mellah and Royal Palace

With fewer than a dozen Jewish families still remaining, the **Mellah** is a rather melancholic place, largely resettled by poor Muslim emigrants from the countryside. The quarter's name – *mellah*, "salt" in Arabic – came to be used for Jewish ghettos throughout Morocco, though it was originally applied only to this one in Fes. In derivation it seems to be a reference to the job given to the Fassi Jews of salting the heads of criminals before they were hung on the gates.

The enclosed and partly protected position of the Mellah represents fairly accurately the Moroccan Jews' historically ambivalent position. Arriving for the most part with compatriot Muslim refugees from Spain and Portugal, they were never fully accepted into the nation's life. Nor, however, were they quite the rejected people of other Arab countries. Inside the Mellah they were under the direct protection of the sultan (or the local *caid*) and maintained their own laws and governors.

Whether the creation of a ghetto ensured the actual need for one is, of course, debatable. Certainly, it was greatly to the benefit of the reigning sultan, who could both depend on Jewish loyalties and manipulate the international trade and finance which came increasingly to be dominated by them in the nineteenth century. For all this importance to the sultan, however, even the richest Jews had to lead extremely circumscribed lives. In Fes before the French Protectorate, no Jew was allowed to ride or even to wear shoes outside the Mellah, and they were severely restricted in their travels elsewhere.

HOUSES, SYNAGOGUES AND CEMETERIES
Since the end of the Protectorate, when many of the poorer Jews here left to take up an equally ambivalent place at the bottom of Israeli society (though this time above the

---

THE EVENING ROOST AT FES

The evening roost at Fes makes a spectacular sight. The performance begins with the frenzied activities of the resident starlings (including spotless starlings) but these are soon eclipsed by the overhead passage of dozens of little egret, gracefully returning to their roost sites in the Middle Atlas and environs. The skies soon appear to swarm with the appearance of literally thousands of alpine swift, wheeling on crescent-shaped wings in search of insects for their young in nests in the city walls. To complete the spectacle, it is worth casting an eye along the rooftop silhouette as the light begins to fade. With a little perseverence it is possible to locate the characteristic body profiles of white stork on their rooftop nests along the perimeter walls which line Fes El Djedid.

Arabs), memories of their presence have faded rapidly. What still remain are their eighteenth- and nineteenth-century **houses** – immediately and conspicuously un-Arabic, with their tiny windows and elaborate ironwork. Cramped even closer together than the houses in Fes El Bali, they are interestingly designed if you are offered a look inside.

The **Hebrew Cemetery** is easy to find; it lies to the east of the Place des Alaouites, on the edge of the Mellah overlooking the valley of the Oued Zitoun (see Fes El Djedid map). It is open every day, except Saturday, from 7am to sunset. The small iron gate faces the car park, between the *Garage Sahar* and the start of the flea market on the side street.

The neat, white, rounded gravestones extend to the horizon. Those nearest to the Mellah are the grandest; they are the tombs of Grand Rabbis – two or three of which are venerated as 'saints' and the object of regular pilgrimages. Interspersed, are the small, pitiful tombs of those who died young.

At the far end, with an entrance from the cemetery and another from the Mellah, is the **Habanim Synagogue**, built in 1928 and in regular use for services and as a religious school until quite recently. It is now, with help from American Jewry, being developed as a museum; it will complement the existing Casablanca museum of Judaica. To date, pride of place in the Habanim Synagogue is a three-hundred-year-old Torah; there are also a series of photographs providing glimpses of everyday life in the Mellah since the arrival of the camera.

During opening hours, there is always someone to show you round the cemetery and synagogue. Your guide should be able to direct you to the other synagogues on, or just off, the Grande Rue des Mereinides. The oldest is the seventeenth century **Ibn Danan Synagogue** now closed and empty; it is hoped that UNESCO monies may help with its restoration. Others, nearly as old, but smaller, include the **El Fassayine Synagogue**, now a martial arts club, and the **Synagogue Mansano**.

THE ROYAL PALACE

At the far end of the Mellah's main street – Grand Rue des Merenides (or Grand Rue de Mellah) – you come into **Place des Alaouites**, fronted by the new ceremonial gateway to the **Royal Palace**. The palace, which has been constantly rebuilt and expanded over the centuries, is one of the most sumptuous complexes in Morocco, set amid vast gardens, with numerous pavilions and guest wings.

In the 1970s, it was sometimes possible to gain a permit to visit part of the palace grounds, which were described in Christopher Kininmonth's *Traveller's Guide* as "the finest single sight Morocco has to offer . . . many acres in size and of a beauty to take the breath away". Today, the palace complex is strictly off limits to all except official guests, though it is reputedly little used by Hassan II, the present king, who divides most of his time between his palaces in Ifrane, Rabat and Marrakesh.

Food and drink

By day at least, there's little to keep you in the **Ville Nouvelle**, the new city established by Lyautey at the beginning of the Protectorate. Unlike Casa or Rabat, where the French adapted Moroccan forms to create their own showplaces, this is a pretty lacklustre European grid. The Ville Nouvelle is, however, home to most of the faculties of the city's university, and is very much the city's business and commercial centre. If you want to talk with Fassis on a basis other than that of guide to tourist, you'll stand the most chance in the cafés here, and it's more likely that the students you meet are exactly that. The quarter is also the centre for most of the city's restaurants, cafés, bars, bookshops and other facilities.

Fes El Bali and **Fes El Djedid** are quieter at night, except during Ramadan (when shops and stalls stay open till two or three in the morning). They have, as with all Medina quarters throughout Morocco, no bars, and with the exception of a few "Palace-Restaurants", many of which are open for lunch only and cater mainly for tour groups, their eating places are on the basic side.

Eating and drinking in the Ville Nouvelle

The Ville Nouvelle has quite a selection of restaurants, though few go any way towards justifying the city's reputation as home of the country's finest cuisine. Cafés, at least, are plentiful – and there are a few bars.

RESTAURANTS

The better possibilities, include:

Pizzeria Assouan, 4 Av. Allal Ben Abdallah. A pizzeria that serves everything from *couscous* to pizza and pasta. Helpings are generous and prices reasonable. The café of the same name round the corner on Av. Hassan II is also good – but more expensive and best reserved for a special occasion.

Restaurant Chamonix, 5 Rue Moukhtar Soussi, off Av. Mohammed V, behind the *Grand Hôtel*. A reliable restaurant serving Moroccan and European dishes; set menu for 45dh. Attracts a younger crowd and, in summer, stays open late.

Restaurant La Cheminée, 6 Av Lalla Asma (aka Rue Chenguit) on the right on the way to the train station. Small and friendly licensed restaurant, medium prices. Open noon–3pm and 7–11pm, closed Sun in low season.

Cracos and **Venesia**, on Av. El Housia, formerly Av. de France, round the corner from the *Hôtel Amor*; these are rival quick-food outlets. Aficionados argue that the Cracos' pommes frites are better and it also incorporates the *Pâtisserie Salon de Thé Florence*: the perfect fuel stop. As for the *Venesia*, there are grilled sausages, fish and *kefta* with a range of salads.

Fish Friture, 138 Bd. Mohammed V, at the far end of a short passage way off the main street. Fish dishes are the main stay, but there is much else on offer. Courteous and quick.

Restaurant Marrakesh, 11 Rue Abes Tazi (between *Hôtel Mounia* and CTM *bus station*). Small, but good and cheap with a limited menu.

Café Restaurant La Noblesse, 16 Place 16 Novembre, across the car park at the back of the covered market. New, it started Chinese as *Le Mandarin*, but quickly reverted to local cuisine – as yet untested, but it's a useful place for a restaurant.

Pizzeria Oliverdi, on Rue Moukhtar Soussi, opposite the *Restaurant Chamonix*, with a range of good pizzas and pasta dishes. Small and popular; it often spills out onto the pavement.

Chez Vittoria, 21 Rue du Nador, aka Brahim Roudani, almost opposite the *Hôtel Central*; reliable and value for money – but not very exciting.

Zagora Restaurant, 5 Bd. Mohammed V. French and Moroccan dishes; large portions are value for money; service cheerful and helpful.

CAFÉS AND BARS

Cafés and **pâtisseries** are scattered throughout the Ville Nouvelle, with some of the most popular around Place Mohammed V – the *Café de la Renaissance* here was an old Foreign Legion hangout – and along Av. Mohammed Es Slaoui, Av. Hassan II and Bd. Mohammed V. One of the most popular of these, boasting excellent crois-sants (and very clean toilets), is the *Café Floria*, beside the *PTT* on Av. Hassan II. Another very pleasant café is located in the sunken park alongside Bd. Mohammed V.

For **bars**, you have to look a little harder. There are a couple along the Av. Es Slaoui (the *Es Saada* here is usually lively) and some might enjoy the seedy but cheap *Dalilla* at 17 Bd. Mohammed V whose upstairs bar is a place for serious Moroccan drinking; another quite amusing bar, with 1960s decor, is just opposite the Municipal Market on Bd. Mohammed V. Beyond these, you're down to the handful of **hotel bars**: in the *Moussafir*, *Mounia*, *Lamdaghri*, *Splendid* and *Grand*, and the upmarket and rather dull *Sheraton Fes* and *Sofia*.

Eating and drinking in Fes El Bali

Fes El Bali has possibilities for budget meals and, at greater cost, for sampling (rela-tively) traditional cuisine in some splendid old palaces. **Fes El Djedid** also has some basic café-restaurants, though none worth specially recommending.

BUDGET MEALS

The two main areas for **budget eating** in Fes El Bali are around Bab Boujeloud – try the *Restaurant Bouayad* below the *Hôtel Kaskade* – and along Rue Hormis, (which runs up from Souk El Attarin towards Bab Guissa in the north and has some good hole-in-the-wall places). Other cheapish café-restaurants are to be found near Bab Ftouh.

If your money doesn't allow a full meal, you can get a range of **snacks** around Bab Boujeloud, including delicious chunks of *pastilla* from the stalls near the beginning of Talâa Seghira.

FANCIER MEALS

For a Fassi banquet, in an appropriate palace setting, most restaurants charge around 150–200dh a head. Some places, particularly those in the heart of Fes El Bali, serve lunch only because, even in daylight, they are difficult to find. If you're interested, phone ahead for a table at one or other of the following:

Restaurant Al Fassia, in the *Hôtel Palais Jamai*, Bab Guissa (☎05/63.43.31). A distinguished Moroccan cuisine restaurant, with a terrace overlooking the Medina. There are few more stylish ways to spend an evening, but count on at least 250dh each, and considerably more if you go for the full courses. The hotel also has a fine French restaurant, *La Djenina*.

Palais de Fes, 16 Rue Boutouil Kairaouine (☎05/63.47.07), above a rather good carpet bazaar. This caters largely for tour groups but the rooftop setting is as enjoyable as any in the city. The building is located by the Kairaouine Mosque and labelled on our map on p.203. Open at lunchtime only.

Restaurant Al Firdaous, 10 Rue Jenjifour, Bab Guissa – just down from the *Hôtel Palais Jamai* (☎05/63.43.43). A rich merchant's house of the 1920s, decked out to look like a tent. Meals, with music and belly dancing, from 150dh. Open noon–3pm and 8.30–11.30pm.

Palais des Merinides (☎05/63.40.28), near the Cherabliyin Mosque, 650m from Bab Boujeloud. Compared with *Palais de Fes*, the decor is not so grand, but the menu at 250dh is as good; lunch and dinner.

Restaurant Les Remparts, 2 Arset Jiar, Bab Guissa – 50m from the *Hôtel Palais Jamai* (☎05/63.74.15). A new restaurant in a renovated, beautiful mansion. Meals run at around 400dh a head, including folklore shows. Quality of both food and shows is variable.

Dar Saada, 21 Souk El Attarin (☎05/63.73.70). Wonderful *pastilla* or (ordered a day in advance) *mechoui*. Portions are vast and two people can do well by ordering one main dish and a plate of veg-etables. Located in the Souk El Attarin, in another century-old palace (see p.202), and labelled on our map on p.203. The fine decor was renewed after a disastrous fire in 1972. Lunches only.

SHOPPING FOR CRAFTS

Fes has a rightful reputation as the centre of Moroccan traditional crafts but if you're buying rather than looking, bear in mind that it also sees more tourists than any of its rivals, except perhaps Marrakesh. Rugs and carpets, however much you bargain, will probably be cheaper in Meknes, Midelt or Azrou; and although the brass, leather and cloth here are the best you'll find, you will need plenty of energy, a good sense of humour and a lot of patience to get them at a reasonable price. Fassi dealers are expert hagglers – making you feel like an idiot for suggesting a ludicrously low price, jumping up out of their seats to make to push you out of the shop, or lulling you with mint tea and elaborate displays.

All of this can be fun, but you do need a certain confidence and to have some idea of what you're buying and how much you should be paying for it. For some guidelines on **quality**, take a look at the historic pieces in the **Dar Batha** museum – keeping in mind, of course, that exhibits here are the best available. If you want to check on the prices of more modest and modern artefacts, have a browse through the various shops along Av. Mohammed V in the **Ville Nouvelle**, which tend to have fairly fixed prices (and are easy to leave!), and, especially, at the government-run and strictly fixed-price Centre Artisanal, out past the *Sheraton Fes Hôtel* and on the left-hand side of Av. Allal Ben Abdallah. It's not the best in the country – the one in Marrakesh leaves it standing – but it's worth a visit, time permitting.

Listings

Animal Welfare The American Fondouk is a free veterinary hospital on the left of Bd. Allal El Fassi, the broad avenue which links the Ville Nouvelle with Bab El Djedid and Bab Ftouh. It was established in 1927 and the present buildings were erected in memory of Rosalie Bull by her mother in 1931. You can visit Mon–Fri, 7–11am, to see the work with the animals. Ring the bell and wait.

Arabic Language Institute in Fes (ALIF) is at 2 Rue Ahmed Hiba (☎05/62.48.50) near the Youth Hostel and the *Hôtel Zalagh*. This American initiative offers a range of courses and the possibility of private/specialized lessons. There are three-week (60hr) and six-week (120hr) Colloquial Moroccan Arabic courses or, if you prefer, comparable courses in Modern Standard Arabic.

Banks Most of the banks are grouped along Bd. Mohammed V. As always, the *BMCE* (on Place Mohammed V) is best for exchange and handles VISA/Access transactions, as well as travellers' cheques. Others include: *Banque Populaire* (Av. Mohammed V; quick service for currency and travellers' cheques), *Crédit du Maroc* (Av. Mohammed V; also handles VISA) *SGMB* (at the intersection of Rue de la Liberté and Rue Soudan; again, handles *VISA*). *Crédit du Maroc* also has a branch in Fes El Bali (currency exchange only), in the street above the Medersa ech-Cherratin. Outside banking hours, most of the four- or five-star hotels will change money and cheques.

Books The English Bookshop, 68 Av. Hassan II (by Place de la Résistance, aka La Fiat), has a great selection of English novels, stocked for the city's students, and a fair number of North African writers (☎05/62.08.42; open Mon–Fri, 9am–12.30pm and 3–7pm). The Librairie du Centre, 134 Bd. Mohammed V (near the post office), is also worth trying.

Car rental Fes has quite a number of rental companies, though none are as cheap as the best deals in Casa. Call around the following, which all allow return delivery to a different centre: *Avis*, 23 Rue de la Liberté (☎05/62.67.48); *Budget*, corner of 55 Rue Bahrein and Av. Hassan II (☎05/62.09.19) and alongside *Hôtel Palais Jamai*, Bab Guissa (☎05/63.43.31); *Europcar/InterRent*, 45 Av. Hassan II (☎05/62.65.45); *Hertz*, Bd. Lalla Maryem, 1 Kissariat de la Foire (☎05/62.28.12); *Tourvilles*, 15 Rue Houmam Fetouaki, off Bd. Mohammed V (☎05/62.66.35); and *Zeit*, 35 Av. Mohammed Es Slaoui (☎05/62.55.10). *Avis*, *Budget*, *Europcar/InterRent* and *Hertz* have desks at the airport. *Safloc*, a new hire company has a desk inside the *Sheraton*.

Car repairs Mécanique Générale, 22 Av. Cameroun, in the Ville Nouvelle, is highly recommended, with excellent mechanics and fair prices. Try also Source Pièce Auto, 50 Rue Zambia, again in the Ville Nouvelle, for parts and advice; Auto Maroc, Av. Mohammed V (☎05/62.34.35) for Fiat repairs; and the garage on Rue Soudan (☎05/62.22.32) for Renault repairs.

Chemist/pharmacist There are numerous pharmacies throughout the Ville Nouvelle. The Pharmacie du Municipalité, just up from Place de la Résistance, on Av. Abdelkrim El Kattabi, stays open all night.

Cinemas Several in the Ville Nouvelle, show foreign films – mainly dubbed into French. The one by Bab Boujeloud is entertaining, showing an Indian and a Kung Fu film each day.

Festivals and cultural events Since 1995, Fes has hosted a **Festival of World Sacred Music** (usually around the end of May), which has developed into the country's most interesting and inspiring cultural festival. Recent years have seen Sufi chanters from Azerbaijan, dervishes from Konya, a Javanese gamelan, a Byzantine choir from Greece, and a Jewish pastor. Concerts take place at the Batha Museum and Bab Maqina, and sometimes further afield, such as amid the ruins of Volubilis. Major local festivals are the students' *Moussem of Sidi Harazem* (held outside the city at Sidi Harazem – see below – at the end of April) and the *Moulay Idriss II Moussem* (held in the city, in September). There are other *moussems* held locally – ask at the tourist office for details – and some good events a little further out, like the *Fête des Cerises* at Sefrou (see p.220) in June, and the *Fête du Cheval* at Tissa (see p.133) in September.

Cultural events in the city are relatively frequent, both Moroccan- and French-sponsored. Again, ask for details at the tourist office, or at the Institut Français (☎05/62.39.21) on Rue Loukili, off Rue des Etats-Unis. A Son et Lumiére show is presented from mid-Feb to mid-Nov; daily except Sat; Feb, Mar, Oct and Nov at 8pm; Apr, May and Jun at 9pm; Jul, Aug and Sep at 9.30pm; the show lasts 45min and costs 200dh. The audience views the show from the Borj Sud, which is south of Bd. Allal El Fassi, the broad avenue which links the Ville Nouvelle with Bab El Djedid and Bab Ftouh, between which a track leads uphill alongside the Bab Ftouh cemetery (see Fes El Bali map). Information and reservations ☎05/62.93.60.

Filling stations Several are to be found on the Place de l'Atlas, near the beginning of the road to Sefrou/Midelt.

TWO NEARBY SPAS: MOULAY YACOUB AND SIDI HARAZEM

The spa villages of **Moulay Yacoub** and **Sidi Harazem**, respectively 20km northwest and 15km southeast of Fes, are largely medicinal centres, offering – as for many centuries past – cures for the afflicted. They are local rather than tourist attractions, but Moulay Yacoub, in particular, makes a pleasant day-trip for a swim and hot bath. Either site can be reached by *grand taxi* from Bab Boujeloud or the main bus station to Moulay Yacoub (6 to 8dh) and from Bab Ftouh to Sidi Harazem (5 to 7dh). Bus #28 runs from Place de la Résistance (aka La Fiat) to Sidi Harazem.

MOULAY YACOUB

The trip to **MOULAY YACOUB** takes you across pleasant, rolling countryside, with wonderful views south across the plain of Saïss, with the Middle Atlas beyond. The village itself tumbles down a steep hillside, with a swimming pool and large *hammam* (with separate sections for women and men) around midway down. At the foot of the hill, in the "basin", are new and more scientific thermal baths used for serious medical treatment. Cars and taxis park at the top of the village, leaving you to descend flights of steps, flanked with some attractive little restaurants and cafés.

The spa has three unclassified **hotels** – the best of which by far is the *Hôtel Lamrani* (☎05/69.40.21; ⑩); it's open year round and has recently been renovated. There are also numerous rooms to let in private houses – and you won't lack for offers.

SIDI HARAZEM

The eucalyptus-covered shrine of **SIDI HARAZEM** was established by Sultan Moulay Er-Rachid in the seventeenth century, though the centre owes its current fame to its best-selling mineral water. The oasis is today heavily orientated towards its health industry; the old thermal baths tend to be crowded and the swimming pool is only full in summer (8.50dh). The main point of a visit, for those not seeking a cure, would be for the April *moussem* – one of the Fes region's biggest.

There is a state-run **hotel**, the *Sidi Harazem* (☎05/69.00.57; ③), near the thermal baths and swimming pool; both its accommodation and restaurant are pricey and, for a worthwhile snack, you would be better advised to walk the 600m to the grill complex beyond the hotel; look for the charcoal smoke and smell the *brochettes*.

Laundry and dry-cleaning Pressing Dallas, 4 Rue Zerktouni near *Hôtel Mounia* (☎05/65.07.39).

Newspapers British papers and the *International Herald Tribune* are sold at the boutique in the *Hôtel de Fes*; at a newsstand at the foot of Rue Abdelkrim El Khattabi, one block from Place Mohammed V; and another good newsstand on nearby Rue de Edouard Escalier, facing the space used as a car park.

Photographic The boutique at the Hôtel de Fes does good-quality film/photo work.

Police *Commissariat Central* is on Av. Mohammed V; ☎19.

Post office The main *PTT* is on the corner of Bd. Mohammed V/Av. Hassan II in the Ville Nouvelle (open summer 8am–2pm; winter 8.30am–noon and 2.30–6pm); the **poste restante** section inside the main building; the **phones section** (open until 9pm) has a separate side entrance when the rest is closed.

Religious services There is an English-speaking service at 10am on Sunday in the Protestant Church, 100m southeast of the Place de la Résistance, aka La Fiat.

Royal Air Maroc has an office at 54 Av. Hassan II in the ville nouvelle. The Fes airport is 15km south of the city at Saïs.

Swimming pools There is a **Municipal Pool** (open mid-June to mid-Sept) on Av. des Sports, just west of the train station. The upmarket *Hôtel Zalagh* (see p.196) has an open air pool, but at 65dh for non-residents, this is a little pricey.

Tourist office The main office is on Place de la Résistance, aka La Fiat (see p.187).

THE MIDDLE ATLAS

Heading south from Fes, most people take a bus straight to either **Marrakesh** or to **Er Rachidia**, the start of the great desert and *ksour* routes. Both journeys, however, involve at least ten to twelve hours of continuous travel, which, in the summer at least, is reason enough to stop off along the way.

The second, stronger reason, if you have the time (or, ideally, a car), is to get off the main routes and up into the mountains. Covered in forests of oak, cork and giant cedar, the **Middle Atlas** is a beautiful and relatively little-visited region. The brown-black tents of nomadic Berber encampments immediately establish a shift from the European north, the plateaux are pockmarked by dark volcanic lakes, and, at **Ouzoud** and **Oum Er Rbia**, there are some magnificent waterfalls. If you just want a day-trip from Fes, the Middle Atlas is most easily accessible at **Sefrou**, a relaxed market town, 28km southeast of Fes.

On the practical front, **bus** travellers may find a few problems stopping en route between Fes and Marrakesh, as many of the buses arrive and depart full. However, by taking the occasional *grand taxi*, or stopping for a night to catch a dawn bus, you shouldn't find yourself stuck for long. Along the Fes–Azrou–Midelt–Er Rachidia route, buses are no problem.

Sefrou and around

SEFROU, 30km south of Fes, is a very ancient walled town at the foothills of the Middle Atlas. The first stop on the caravan routes to the Tafilalet, it marked, until the Protectorate, the mountain limits of the *Bled El Makhzen* – the governed lands. It actually predates Fes as a city and might well have grown into a regional or Imperial Capital, if Moulay Idriss I and II had not acted differently. Into the 1950s, at least a third of the then 18,000 population were Jews; there seems to have been a Jewish-Berber population here long before the coming of Islam and, although most of them subsequently converted, a large number of Jews from the south again settled in the town under the Merenids. Today, sadly, only a handful of Jews remain.

From Fes, the town can be reached in an hour by **bus** or **grand taxi**; the latter leave from just below Place de la Résistance (aka La Fiat) in the Ville Nouvelle. In summer it makes a cool day-trip, as it is situated some 2900ft above sea level; in winter, it can often

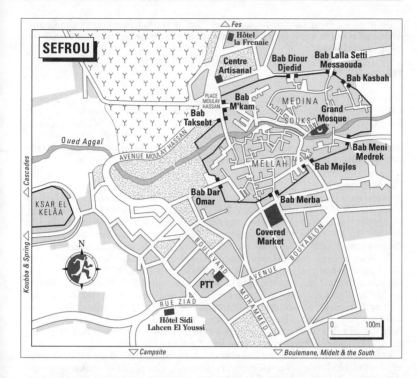

be covered in snow; it is a relaxed place which sees few tourists (or hustlers). The only times that the town draws crowds are during the annual **Fête des Cerises**, a cherry festival in June, usually the last weekend, with the crowning of the Cherry Queen on Saturday evening and, before and after, various music, folklore and sports events; and during the August **Moussem of Sidi Lahcen El Youssi**, a seventeenth-century saint from neighbouring Azzaba, 13km to the east of Sefrou – his *zaouia* and tomb are to be found in the Medina on the north bank of the Oued Aggaï.

Accommodation and other practicalities

Following the closure of the old *Hôtel des Cerises*, which stands empty on the bend of Bd. Mohammed V, the choice is between two hotels. The *Hôtel Sidi Lakcen El Youssi* (☎05.68.34.28; ②) has an alpine chalet feel, a restaurant (no liquor licence at present), and a swimming pool – sometimes full of water. Its rival, *Hôtel La Frenaie* (☎05/66.00.30; ⑩), is on the left as you enter Sefrou from Fes. It was originally run by a Frenchman, but now it is in Moroccan hands; recently renovated to a good standard, it has a snack bar and pool table on the ground floor which attracts a young crowd. Alternatively, a couple of kilometres to the west of town, there is a **campsite** (☎05/67.33.40), with a swimming pool and (cold) showers.

For **food and drink**, in addition to the hotels, you could try the *Café- Restaurant Oumnia*, on Bd. Mohammed V, for inexpensive meals.

Note that there is often **no water** in Sefrou from 6pm to 6am, so if you want a shower, arrive early! Note also that the town's two **banks** are not very wised up to cashing cheques, though they have no problems with cash exchange.

Between the *Hôtel La Frenaie* and Place Moulay Hassan (see below), the **Centre Artisanal** is worth a visit for its wood carvings and carpets which you can usually see being created by hand.

The Town

Although Sefrou is not a large place – the population today is only 40,000 – its layout is a little confusing. If you are coming in by bus or *grand taxi*, you are usually dropped in the recently landscaped **Place Moulay Hassan**, off which is **Bab M'kam**, the main entrance to the Medina. Beyond the *place*, the road and some of the buses continue round a loop above the town and valley, crossing the **Oued Aggaï** and straightening out onto **Bd. Mohammed V**, the principal street of the modest Ville Nouvelle.

The Medina

In many ways it's a pity that Sefrou is so close to Fes, in comparison with which its Medina inevitably feels rather low-key. It is, however, on its own modest scale, equally well-preserved, and the untouristy atmosphere makes it a very pleasant place to explore. The **Thursday souk**, for example, remains very much a local affair, drawing Berbers from neighbouring villages to sell their garden produce and buy basic goods.

Enclosed by its nineteenth-century ramparts and split in two by the river, the Medina isn't difficult to find your way around. Coming from the *PTT* on Bd. Mohammed V, you can take a shortcut down on the right of the road by way of **Bab Merba**, straight into the Mellah; if you were then to turn to the left, this would eventually lead you to Place Moulay Hassan by way of the small **Mosque Adloun** and the nearby **Hammam Adloun** with its unique chimney. You would arrive on the new, small *place* through the new, small **Bab Taksebt**. The most straightforward approach, though, is through **Bab M'Kram,** the old main gate on the *place* – on your left as you face the walls.

Entering at Bab M'Kram, you find yourself on the main street of the old Arab town, which winds clockwise down to the river, passing through a region of **souks**, to emerge at the **Grand Mosque**. The *souks* include some impressive ironwork stalls and, reflecting the traditional Jewish heritage, a number of silversmiths.

The Mellah

The **Mellah**, a dark, cramped conglomeration of tall, shuttered houses and tunnel-like streets, lies across the river from the Grand Mosque. It is today occupied largely by Muslims, though many of Sefrou's Jews only left for Israel after the June 1967 Six-Day War, and the quarter still seems distinct.

Over the years of the French Protectorate, the Sefrou Jewish community had become quite well off, owning good agricultural land in the environs. But when most of the houses here were built, in the mid-nineteenth century, the people's living conditions must have been pretty miserable. Edith Wharton, visiting in 1917, found "ragged figures . . . in black gabardines and skull-caps" living one family to a room in most of the mansions, and the alleys were lit even at midday by oil lamps. "No wonder," she concluded rather sanctimoniously, "[that] the babies of the Moroccan ghettoes are nursed on date-brandy, and their elders doze away to death under its consoling spell."

From the Mellah, you can return, still clockwise, to the *place* by way of the Mosque Adloun (see above).

Into the hills

High enough into the Middle Atlas to avoid the dry summer heat, Sefrou is a place where you might actually want to do some walking. There are dozens of **springs** in the hills above the town and, for part of the year, active waterfalls.

For a relatively easy target, take the road up behind the post office, which will divide into a fork after about a kilometre. The right branch goes up past the campsite; the left leads to a small, deserted, French military post, known as the **Prioux**, and to the **koubba** of one Sidi Bou Ali Serghin. The views from around here are exciting: in winter, the snow-capped Mischliffen; in summer, the cedars and holm oaks cresting the ridges to infinity.

Another good walk is to go up in the hills above the **Oued Aggaï**, a path followed by **Rue de la Kelâa** (just before the bridge, approaching from the post office direction). There are gorges, coves and waterfalls in this direction (for which you may want to engage a local guide).

Bhalil

BHALIL, 7km northwest of Sefrou (signposted off the Fes road), claims pre-Islamic Christian origins and, more visibly, retains a number of troglodyte (cave) dwellings. If you have a car, this is worth a brief detour on your way from Fes; it is signposted to the right 5km before Sefrou. The **cave houses** are to the rear of the village, reached by a dirt road; ask directions to Mohammed Chraibi (BP 42, Bhalil), the official guide, who will show you his own cave home.

The village itself – or at least the old part of it – is charming, its whitewhased houses tumbling down a hillside, and connected by innumerable bridges.

South and east of Sefrou

South and east of Sefrou are some of the most attractive swathes of the Middle Atlas: dense, wooded mountains, with great scope for hiking or piste driving, and not a hint of tourism. Immediately south of the town is the Massif du Kandar, which loops round to Imouzzer du Kandar. To the east, further afield, are the Bou Iblane mountains – an exploration of which could be combined by drivers with the Djebel Tazzeka circuit, near Taza (see p.137).

If you are simply intending to head south from Sefrou, there is a daily bus to **Midelt**, via the quiet roadside town of **Boulemane**, but none to Ifrane or Azrou on the Fes–Marrakesh road. To cross over to this route on local transport, it would be simplest to return to Fes. Boulemane itself can be worth a stop for its Sunday *souk* which serves a wide and diverse area.

The Massif du Kandar

The P4620 route over the Massif du Kandar leaves the P20 Sefrou–Midelt road 14km south of Sefrou. It has some rough stretches of track but is passable in summer with a Renault 4; in winter, you need to check conditions locally. For those without transport, it would be possible to charter a *grand taxi* in Sefrou (or, travelling west–east, in Immouzer du Kandar) for the 34km route.

Shortly after the piste turns off from the Sefrou–Midelt road, it begins to climb up into the hills around the **Djebel Abad** (1768m). If you reckon your car can make it – or you feel like walking – you can follow a rocky 4km track almost to the summit of the mountain; this leads off, to the right of the road, 10km down the P4620, coming from the Sefrou direction.

The Djebel Bou Iblane

East of Sefrou – and southeast of Fes – is a huge area of high country, culminating in the two mountains of **Djebel Bou Iblane** (3190m) and **Djebel Bou Nacceur** (3340m). It is an extraordinarily varied landscape: the northern aspects rise from the cedar forests, while the south is stark and waterless, although demarcated by the great Oued

Moulouya. The whole area is sparsely populated, and trekkers are almost unknown, yet it's rewarding and has relatively easy access. From either Sefrou or Fes, you could arrange a *grand taxi* to take you to the centre of the range – dropping you either at the forestry hut of **Tafferte** or at the largely abandoned ski resort under Djebel Bou Iblane where the local *caid* has an office; he is responsible for this great empty quarter.

From here, a web of pistes radiate throughout the area, and a circular trek with a mule would be memorable.

Grands taxis run to **Skoura** (on P4653) and **Immouzer des Marmoucha** (on P4656) giving access from the east.

Imouzzer du Kandar, Ifrane and Mischliffen

The first hills you see of the Middle Atlas, heading directly south from the plains around Fes, seem strangely un-Moroccan. At the "hill station" resort of **Ifrane**, where the French colonial chiefs retreated from the heat, the king now has an important summer palace, and at **Mischliffen** there's a ski centre. The road up to these two resorts is almost ceremonial, like the avenues leading to airports in the Third World. En route, and a little more mundane, is another small French-built hill station, **Immouzer du Kandar**, and, in the wet season, a gorgeous freshwater lake, the **Dayet Aaoua**.

Imouzzer du Kandar

IMOUZZER DU KANDAR, 78km south of Fes, is a one-road, one-square kind of place, where Fassis come up to swim, picnic and spend a few days. There are a handful of hotels if you feel like doing the same, and some good restaurants, too: it's a relaxed place, with a pleasant atmosphere.

A small Monday **souk** is held within the ruined Kasbah, and a **festival**, the *Fête des Pommes*, takes place in August, with a number of music and dance events. The municipal **swimming pool**, near the centre, is open from mid-June to mid-September and filled, like everything here, with natural spa water.

Accommodation and meals

Currently there are four **hotels** in Immouzer – all classified; a further three hotels are closed for restoration – or forever – and the campsite has disappeared. The remaining options comprise:

Hôtel Chahzazed, 2 Place du Marché (☎05/66.30.12). On the main road, opposite the square; a new hotel which is open all year – reservations advisable in summer. Comfortable rooms and a reasonable restaurant. ③

Hôtel La Chambotte (☎05/66.33.73). A small French-style *auberge*, across the road from the *Hôtel Royal*. The showers are hot and there's central heating when called for; open in summer and at holiday time. Small restaurant. ②

Hôtel Royal, Bd. Mohammed V (☎05/66.30.80). Central hotel with a reliable restaurant, but facing a small lake now permanently devoid of water and waterfowl. ③

Hôtel des Truites (☎05/66.30.02), on the left of the road in from Fes. The best choice: a delightful place with a bar and (unpredictable) restaurant. Great views back towards Fes. ②

Around the town centre, there are several decent **restaurants** with near identical menus; as ever, the busier are the best.

Dayet Aaoua

A good excursion from Immouzer, or an alternative place to break the journey south, is the lake of **Dayet Aaoua**; it is sited just to the left of the P24, 9km south of Immouzer. You can camp round the lakeside, but note that like other lakes in the Ifrane area,

Aaoua is often dry – due to the prevalence of limestone and sometimes to climatic changes. On the other hand, when it is full of water, it has a rewarding **birdlife habitat** – see the box feature overpage.

The P24 continues past the lake to Ifrane, climbing through ever more dense shafts of forest. If you are driving, it's possible to reach Ifrane by a longer and more scenic route, following a piste (P4627) up behind the Dayet Aaoua, then looping to the right, past another (often dry) lake, **Dayet Hachlef**, on piste P3325, before joining the last section of the road in from Boulemane (P21).

Ifrane

IFRANE was created in 1929 as a self-conscious *"poche de France"*, and its pseudo-Alpine villas and broad suburban streets have a distinctly peculiar feel in their Moroccan setting. After independence, they were absorbed by Moroccan government ministries and the wealthier bourgeoisie, and in recent years they have been granted additional prestige by the addition of a **Royal Palace**, whose characteristic green tiles (a royal prerogative) can be seen high above the trees on the descent into the valley.

Ifrane is also the site of another royal initiative. On 16 January, 1995, King Hassan inaugurated the **Al Akhawayn** University; the buildings of which can be seen on your right as you enter Ifrane from the north. The name of this institute of higher education, Al Akhawayn ('brothers' in Arabic), registers it as being the brainchild and beneficiary of the Moroccan king and his 'brother' King Fahd of Saudi Arabia; it has also been funded by the United States and, to a lesser extent, by the British Council. The undergraduate and postgraduate curricula are modelled on the American system of higher education and the language of instruction is English. Inevitably, many of the staff are, as yet, American, but it is impolitic to refer to it, as some do, as an American university.

King Hassan is keen to underpin this novel creation with the religious and cultural values of Christianity and Judaism as well as of Islam; it is dedicated to 'practical tolerance between faiths'; there are a mosque, church and synagogue on the campus to provide, as the king put it, 'a meeting place for the sons of Abraham' – a concept endorsed by the Prince of Wales when he visited Ifrane on 28 February, 1996.

You can visit the university campus, preferably on a weekday afternoon when the students are about. Dominated by chalet-style buildings, with cream walls and russet-tiled roofs, mirroring those in Ifrane, its architect was Michel Pinseau, who designed the great showpiece *Mosquée Hassan II* in Casablanca. Inevitably, there have been criticisms of the new university. The car park, crowded with expensive models, confirms the view that it is an elite initiative – restricted to those who can pay. There is also something of an anti-French feel; Moroccan academics are trying to escape the French educational strait-jacket and have begun to 'arabize' science teaching in the established universities.

As befits a royal resort and aspiring academia, **Ifrane town** is quite impressive in itself – squeaky clean, brilliantly lit by streetlamps and iluminated globes, and with a steady growth of new, costly houses. Not surprisingly, it is expensive (for accommodation, meals and even provisions in the shops) and somewhat lacking in the human touch. A policeman is on permanent duty to stop anyone posing for photographs on the resort's landmark **stone lion** – carved apparently by an Italian prisoner of war – and when the court is in residence in summer, security is very tight.

Nonetheless, a walk by the river, below the royal palace, is pleasant, as is the cool summer air, and the excellent municipal swimming pool.

BIRDLIFE IN THE DAYET, AAOUA AND MIDDLE ATLAS LAKES

Like other freshwater lakes in the Middle Atlas, **Dayet Aaoua**, has, when it's full, a good mosaic of habitat types and supports a wide variety of animals. Green frogs take refuge from the summer drought within the lake's protective shallows, and a multitude of dragonflies and damselflies patrol the water's surface in their resplendent red, blues and greens.

The **birdlife** is similarly diverse, attracting all kinds of waders and wildfowl. Waders include black-winged stilt, green sandpiper, redshank and **avocet** (one of Morocco's most elegant birds), and the deeper waters provide food for flocks of grebes (great-crested, black-necked and little varieties), and in the spring the magnificent **crested coot** (which has spectacular bright red knobs on either side of its white facial shield, when in breeding condition). The reedbeds provide cover for **grey heron** and **cattle egret** and ring out with the sound of hidden **reed-** and **fan-tailed warbler**.

The water's edge is traced by passage grey and yellow wagtails and in the summer the skies are filled with migrating swallows and martins – the sand martin especially. This abundance of life proves an irresistible draw for resident and migrant birds of prey and Aaoua offers regular sightings of the acrobatic **red kite** circling overhead. You may also see flocks of collared pratincole, whose darting flight is spectacular, and quartering overhead, the characteristic form of **Montagu's harrier**, ever alert for any unsuspecting duck on the lake below.

If the lake is dry, you will find, in the words of John Keats, that 'the sedge has withered from the lake and no birds sing'. But remember that there are still birds to be seen alongside – or close to – the 17km stretch of the P24 between Ifrand and Azrou. Here you will find the endemic Levaillant's green **woodpecker, firecrest**, short toed **tree creeper** and local variants of the **jay** and **blue tit**.

White storks, **ravens** and a colony of **lesser kestrels** have been recorded in the low hills behind the *Hôtel Panorama* in Azrou (see p.228).

GOURAUD'S CEDAR

Eight kilometres from Azrou, and marked on the Michelin map, is the legendary **Cèdre Gouraud**. This is well signposted from the main road and your arrival at the Gouraud cedar, amongst others of much the same calibre, is confirmed by a sign nailed to the tree. It's reputed to be at least 800 years old, 130ft high and its girth around 25ft. Its history is a mystery. Colonel Gouraud was Lyautey's second in command from 1912 to 1914 and, indeed, some say that Lyautey's cedar is nearby. Why two soldiers should lend their names to trees is not clear, 'confusion worse confounded' by a recent authority which says that Gouraud's cedar was felled at the turn of the century, when it was at least 980 years old. Maybe the sign is moved from tree to tree, possibly by the **Barbary apes** which you will see hereabouts (see box p.230). They are no friend of the cedar; they hungrily gnaw the buds or tear off strips of the bark.

Another enemy is the **processionary caterpillar** which eats the foliage. In spring, they live in a colony – in a white shroud-like 'tent' – to protect themselves from daytime feathered predators. At night, they come out and eat the neighbouring foliage. When that is gone, one of their number is sent to find more foliage elsewhere. On its return, the colony sets off in a procession, head-to-tail, and spins a new 'tent' for daytime security. Naturally, highly televisual, as in David Attenborough's *The Private Life of Plants*.

A local qualified guide, who could help with the trip to the Gouraud Cedar, and elsewhere, is Kallal Mohamed, 27 Rue Sidi Rachid, Sabbab, Azrou (☎05/56.19.49).

Practicalities

Accommodation is expensive and not always easy to obtain at the three hotels:
Hôtel Mischliffen (☎05/56.66.07) outside the town, with superb views and facilities – for which you pay dearly. ⑤

Hôtel Perce-Neige, Rue des Asphodelles (☎05/56.63.50). A small family hotel, recently refurbished and re-opened – with a modest restaurant. ④

Hôtel les Tilleuls (☎05/56.66.58). Another recently restored hotel, and good value with en-suite facilities throughout. A restaurant and, it is claimed, three bars. Enthusiastic management. ③

However, there is a municipal **campsite** (☎05/56.61.56), out on the road to Meknes, open all year, with a little shop and swimming pool open in summer.

As for other details, the *Restaurant de la Rose* does decent, modest-priced set **meals**; **CTM** buses operate from outside the former *Grand Hôtel; grands taxis* and other **buses** run from the stands on the left of the road out to the campsite and Meknes.

The Mischliffen

The Mischliffen is simply a shallow bowl in the mountains – the crater of an extinct volcano – enclosed on all sides by cedar forests. There's no village here and few buildings, and it's of interest, really, mainly for the skiing.

In the skiing season (Jan–March: but snow cover is often patchy) there are taxis from Ifrane up to its **refuge-club** (restaurant and bar, but no accommodation) and to the rather ancient **ski lifts**. You can **rent ski equipment** in Ifrane at the *Café-Restaurant Chamonix*, though like the ski lifts, it is about thirty years old.

Azrou

AZROU, the first real town of the Middle Atlas, stands at a major junction of routes – north to Meknes and Fes, south to Khenifra and Midelt. As might be expected, it's an important market centre (the main *souk* is held on Tuesday), and it has long held a strategic role in controlling the mountain Berbers. Moulay Ismail built a Kasbah here, the remains of which still survive, while more recently the French established the prestigious **Collège Berbère** – part of their attempt to split the country's Berbers from the urban Arabs.

The *collège*, now the Lycée Tarik Ibn Ziad, and still a dominant building in the town, provided many of the Protectorate's interpreters, local administrators and military officers, but in spite of its ban on using Arabic and any manifestation of Islam, the policy was a failure. Azrou graduates played a significant role in the nationalist movement – and were uniquely placed to do so, as a new French-created elite. Since independence, however, their influence has been slight outside of the army, many Berber student activists of the 1950s and 1960s having followed Mehdi Ben Barka's ill-fated socialist UNEP party (see History in "Contexts").

The town and its souk

Arriving in the town, you immediately notice a massive outcrop of rock – the *azrou* ("rock" in Berber) from which the town takes its name. Adjoining it is the main square, **Place Mohammed V**, with an impressive new Grand Mosque, as yet unfinished. On the other side of the rock is a public swimming pool, which in summer is almost reason enough to stop over in town.

The most compelling reason for a visit to Azrou, however, is provided by its **Tuesday souk**, which draws Berbers from all the surrounding mountain villages. It is held a little above the main part of town – just follow the crowds up to the quarter across the valley. The fruit and vegetable stalls sprinkled all over this area seem at first to be all there is; look further, though, and you'll see a stretch of wasteland – often with a few musicians and storytellers performing – beyond which is a smaller section for carpets, textiles and general goods. The **carpet stalls**, not particularly geared towards tourists, can turn up some beautiful items; reasonably priced if not exactly bargains.

For a further selection of rugs and carpets take a look at the **Coopérative Artisanale** (Mon–Fri 8.30am–noon and 2.30–6pm), on the Khenifra road; this has seen

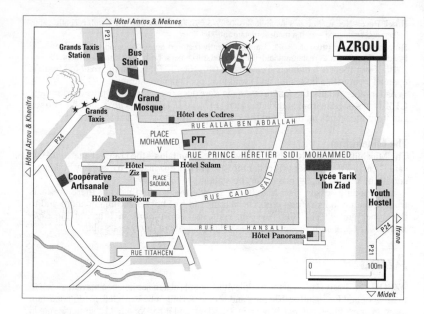

△ Hôtel Amros & Meknes

AZROU

Grands Taxis Station

Bus Station

Grand Mosque

Grands Taxis

Hôtel des Cedres

RUE ALLAL BEN ABDALLAH

PLACE MOHAMMED V

PTT

RUE PRINCE HÉRETIER SIDI MOHAMMED

Hôtel Ziz

Hôtel Salam

Coopérative Artisanale

PLACE SAOUIKA

Lycée Tarik Ibn Ziad

Youth Hostel

Hôtel Beauséjour

RUE CAID SAID

RUE EL HANSALI

Hôtel Panorama

RUE TITAHCEN

△ Hôtel Azrou & Khenifra

▷ Ifrane

0   100m

▽ Midelt

better days – it's a bit sleepy compared with other co-operatives – but some decent modern rugs, plus stone and cedar carvings, are still produced. Also worth an hour or so are some of the permanent stalls near the new bus station and in the old quarter of town off **Place Saouika** (aka Place Moulay Hachem Ben Salah). Most of the rugs you are shown have bright, geometric designs, based on the traditional patterns of the Beni M'Guild tribe.

There is little else to do in the town, though you can spend most of the day climbing through the hills roundabout – there are many seasonal springs – or wandering down to the river, which is reputedly well stocked with trout. Further afield – see the box feature overpage – there are also extensive cedar forests.

Rooms and food

Bear in mind that, in winter particularly, the nights are cold and that central heating is to be found only in the dearer (and more distant) **hotels**. Choices include:

Hôtel Amros, 3km out on the Meknes road (☎05/56.36.63). An upmarket hotel for which you will need a *petit taxi*. According to season, there is a nightclub/disco, and a swimming pool and tennis. There's a restaurant and bar but, for really serious drinkers, there's the neighbouring auberge. ④

Hôtel Azrou, Route du Khenifra (☎05/56.21.16). One kilometre out on the Khenifra road – downhill to the southwest of Place Mohammed V. Reasonable rooms, a restaurant and bar. ①

Hôtel Beauséjour, 45 Place Saouika (no phone). One of the cheapest hotels in town; central, fine roof terrace, but cold showers. The next door café, with the same management, is good for breakfast and snacks. ①

Hôtel des Cèdres, Place Mohammed V (☎05/56.23.26). The best of the cheap hotels, with a long balcony overlooking the square. Separate facilities, but hot water. There have been mixed reports about the restaurant, but you can check it – and the others around the *place* – before deciding. ①

Hôtel Panorama, Rue El Hansali (☎05/56.20.10). A short walk from the town centre; good views and birdlife in woods behind. But ownership has changed and standards fallen. Some rooms en suite; hot water and central heating. ③

Hôtel Salam, off Place Saouika (☎05/56.25.62). Central and best of the downmarket accommodation, but cold showers. *Café Salam* is next door and good. ①

Hôtel Ziz, 83 Place Saouika (☎05/56.23.62). Not too impressive – and cold showers. Best as a reserve if other cheapies are full and better than the nearby *Hôtel Atlas*. ①

Auberge de Jeunesse (Youth Hostel), Route de Midelt-Ifrane (☎05/56.37.33). On the outskirts of town, about 1km from the place and before the road forks to Midelt/Er Rachidia (P21) and to Ifrane/Fes (P24). Friendly and well-run.

As for **food**, in addition to the hotels above, there is a fine, unnamed *café-pâtisserie* on the corner of the main square, with great coffee and croissants. Towards the bus station, there are also various inexpensive grills and foodstalls.

Two **banks** (*BMCE* and *Banque Populaire*) are located in Place Mohammed V.

Buses and grands taxis

The new **bus station** is beyond the unfinished Grand Mosque; the **grand taxi** station is beyond the roundabout on the road out to Meknes (P21), but taxis for Aïn Leuh are by the Grand Mosque on the road out to Khenifra.

There are one or two **buses** a day to Midelt and to Beni Mellal. If you want to get to Er Rachidia and Rissani, and there is no direct bus, take the Midelt bus and change there. Similarly, to reach Marrakesh, you may have to change at Beni Mellal. One bus a day goes direct to Marrakesh, but it often arrives full and you should try to book the day before; even then, a place is not guaranteed. It's not usually a problem to get a bus to Fes or, less frequently, to Meknes.

Grands taxis have regular runs to Ifrane and Fes, and sporadic (but possible) ones for Khenifra. *Grands taxis* also run to Aïn Leuh fairly frequently; if you can get a group together it helps – and can ensure a full taxi if you all return to Azrou.

Aïn Leuh and the waterfalls of Oum Er Rbia

South of Azrou lies some of the most remote and beautiful country of the Middle Atlas: a region of cedar forests, limestone plateaus and *polje* lakes, that is home to some superb wildlife (see box overleaf), including Barbary apes.

It makes rewarding countryside for a few days' exploration, either by car or on foot. At the heart of the region – an obvious focus for a trip – are the **waterfalls of Oum Er Rbia**, the source of Morocco's largest river. If you don't have transport, you can get a daily **bus** from Azrou to **Aïn Leuh**, 30km along the route (and with some minor falls of its own), or, if you have the money, or get a group together, you could always charter a **grand taxi** from Azrou.

Aïn Leuh

AÏN LEUH (17km from Azrou along the main Khenifra road, then 13km up the S303) is a large Berber village, typical of the Middle Atlas, with its flat-roofed houses tiered above the valley. As at Azrou, there are ruins of a Kasbah built by Moulay Ismail; and in the hills behind the town there are **springs** and a more or less year-round waterfall.

Aïn Leuh's **souk** is held on Wednesday (a good day to hitch), though it can extend a day in either direction. It is the weekly gathering point of the **Beni M'Guild** tribe – still semi-nomadic in this region, and to be seen camping out beside their flocks in heavy, dark tents. As a colonial *zone d'insécurité*, this part of the Atlas was relatively undisturbed by French settlers, and the traditional balance between pasture and forest has remained largely intact.

The Oum Er Rbia sources and Aguelmane Azigza

The road to the **Oum Er Rbia waterfalls** begins just south of Aïn Leuh and is sign-posted "Aguelmane Azigza/Khenifra". It has recently been paved along its entire course, and several new bridges have been constructed over the Rbia. In winter, however, it can still get waterlogged and impassable, so ask about conditions in Azrou or Khenifra before setting out. For the most part it runs through mountain forest, where you're almost certain to come across apes.

About 20km south of Aïn Leuh, to the left of the road, there's a small lake, **Lac Ouiouane**, adjoining a couple of farms and a large *maison forestière*. A stretch of more open country, with grazing sheep and odd pitched-roof farmsteads, leads to the descent to the Oum Er Rbia valley. The road twists down, bends through a side valley and round to a concrete bridge over the Rbia, with a small parking area by the river. (Coming from the south, the descent to the Oum Er Rbia is unmistakeable – around 45km from Khenifra).

Guides will offer their services here for the **walk to the falls** but they are unnecessary as a clear path leads up to the gorge – a ten- to fifteen-minute walk. At the end of the path is a small waterfall, down petrified limestone deposits. All the water comes out in forty or more springs (sources), a little further down the gorge. Many have rough café-shelters built beside them, along the river edge.

The natural basin below the falls seems like a tempting place to swim, though beware that the currents here are extremely strong; there are smaller pools nearby. The water, full of salts, is not drinkable.

Aguelmane Azigza and beyond

On past the bridges, the main road heads off to the west, crossed by a confusing array of pistes. After 18km, a turnoff on the left leads to the **Aguelmane Azigza**, a dark and very deep lake, secluded among the cedar trees. You can camp and swim here, as many Moroccans do. There's also a **lodge-café**, relatively new, though closed up, for some reason, recently.

Azigza has terrific **wildlife**. The wooded slopes of the lake throng with insect life, including the brilliant red and black grasshopper and the beautiful small Amanda's blue butterfly, while the forest provides nesting and feeding areas for woodland finches and titmice, including the elusive hawfinch with its diagnostic heavy bill. There's more

---

BARBARY APES AND OTHER CEDAR FOREST WILDLIFE

The **cedar forests** which lie to the **south of Azrou** are a unique habitat in Morocco, their verdant atmosphere contrasting starkly with the surrounding aridity and barrenness of the Middle Atlas range. They shelter several troupes of **Barbary apes**, a glimpse of which is one of the wildlife highlights of a visit to Morocco. They can be found feeding along the forest margins – sometimes on the outskirts of Azrou itself – but they are shy animals and any excessive intrusion is likely to be met with a retreat to the lofty sanctuary of the treetops.

Almost as exhilarating is the forest **birdlife**, whose possibilities include the two species of Moroccan woodpecker, the pied and red great spotted and green and yellow Levaillant's varieties. Other overhead highlights include the splendid **booted eagle**, often seen soaring on outstretched wings in an attempt to evade the unwanted attentions of resident ravens. Kestrels nest in the Oum Er Rbia gorge, near the falls (see below) in spring.

The cedars also provide shelter for a vibrant carpet of flowers – pink peonies, scarlet dianthus, blue germander, golden compositae and a variety of orchids – which makes an ideal haven for a host of **butterflies** (from April onwards), among them the brilliant sulphur cleopatra, large tortoiseshell and cardinal.

See also Aguelmane Azigza, above.

birdlife in the waters, too, including diving duck (mainly grebes and coot) and marbled teal in autumn and winter.

From the Azigza turnoff, it's a further 24km to Khenifra. Alternatively, for the exploration-minded, the P3404 piste (poor but being improved) leads off east into the Djebel Irhoud mountains to ITZER and, finally, ZEIDA on the P21 (see below). A rather better road, the P3485, which is being surfaced, runs off from this to join the P21 at KIA AÏT OUTFELLA, just south of the Col du Zad.

South to Midelt and Er Rachidia

If you're travelling the southern circuits of the *ksour* and Kasbahs of the south, you're almost certain to take this route in one direction or the other. It's 125km from **Azrou to Midelt** and a further 154km to **Er Rachidia** – quite feasible distances for a single bus trip or a day's driving, but more satisfying taken in a couple of stages. You cross passes over both Middle and High Atlas ranges, catch a first glimpse of the south's fabulous *pisé* architecture and end up in the desert.

Azrou to Midelt

Climbing up from Azrou, the Midelt road (P21) follows a magnificent stretch of the Middle Atlas, winding through the forests to emerge at the **valley of the Oued Gigou**, the view ahead taking in some of the range's highest peaks. By bus you have little alternative but to head straight to Midelt, reached in around two hours, via the market village of TIMADHITE (large **Thursday souk**). With a car, there are two very brief and worthwhile detours.

The first of these comes 52km from Azrou, as the road levels out on a strange volcanic plateau littered with dark pumice rock. A turnoff here, to the left, (and where persistent 'guides' hang out) is signposted to **Aguelmane Sidi Ali**, the largest of many mountain lakes formed in the extinct craters of this region. It's only a kilometre from the road: long, still and eerily beautiful. Besides an occasional shepherd's tent and flock, there is unlikely to be anything or anyone in sight; if you can improvise a fishing rod, there are reputed to be plenty of trout, pike and perch.

The other point where you might want to leave the road is 24km further down, past the Col du Zad, a 2178m pass across the Middle Atlas. Superb trekking country lies west of the col, leading to the Oued Sefrou (a north-south piste goes via Kerrouchen and its marvellous cedar forests, another haunt of Barbary apes). South of the col, a road leads right in for 6km to the small village of ITZER, whose **market** is one of the most important in the region. Held on Mondays and Thursdays, it can be a good source of Berber rugs and carpets.

Back on the main road, you pass road junctions near BOULÔJUL (where the P20 from Boulemane joins) and ZEIDA (the P33 from Khenifra). A little beyond the lat-

---

BIRDLIFE AROUND ZEÏDA

Thirty kilometres north of Midelt and within 15km of Zeïda is a stony desert area renowned for the elusive **Dupont's Lark**. Other species to be found on the vast, open scrubby plain are the **Red-rumped Wheatear, Thick-brilled Lark, Lesser Short-toed Lark** and **Trumpeter Finch**. East and west of the P21 between kilometre posts 27 and 28 are recommended.

North of Zeïda, the aqueduct, parallel with the road, has **Rock Sparrows** and **Spotless Starlings.**

ter is a small, but good tourist complex, the *Centre Timnay*, including a shop, café-restaurant and a clean **campsite**. The owner, Aït Lemkaden Driss, hopes to develop this as a base for **landrover and walking expeditions** in the region.

Midelt

At **MIDELT**, approached through a bleak plain of scrub and desert, you have left the Middle Atlas behind. Suddenly, through the haze, appear the much greater peaks of the High Atlas, which rise sheer behind the town to a massive range, the **Djebel Ayachi**, at over 3700m. The drama of this site, tremendous in the clear, cool evenings, is the most compelling reason to stop over, for the town itself initially looks very drab – one street with a couple of cafés and hotels and a small *souk*. In fact, it's a pleasant place to stay – partly because so few people do, partly because it's the first place where you become aware of the more relaxed (and predominantly Berber) atmosphere of the south. Indeed, there is the hint of a frontier town, a sense reinforced by the derelict mines at Mibladene and Aouli, northeast of Midelt, in the nearby gorge of Oued Moulouya (see box on p.234).

Midelt is so far inland that the microclimate is one of extremes: bitterly cold in winter and oppressively hot in summer. One of the best times to visit is in the autumn, particularly at the start of October when there is a modest apple festival – and, year round, the best time to be here is for the huge **Sunday souk**, which spreads back along the road towards Azrou.

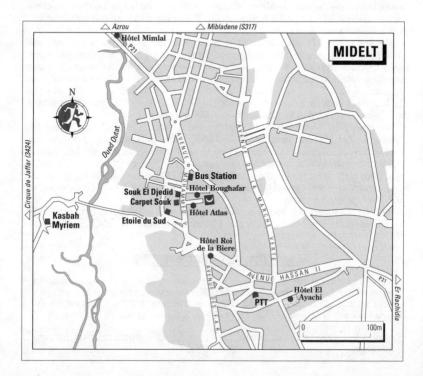

The Town: carpet shopping

The most interesting section of town, meriting at least a stop between buses, is the area around the old *souk* – **Souk Djedid**, behind the stalls facing the bus station. Just to the south of the main *souk*, which is a daily fruit and vegetable market, is an arcaded **carpet souk**, its wares slung out in rotation in the sunlight (for natural bleaching) and piled up in bewildering layers of pattern and colour in the various shops to the rear. This is a relaxed place for shopping and the rugs are superb – mostly local, geometric designs from tribes of the Middle Atlas. Ask to see the "antique" ones, few of which will be more than ten or twenty years old, but they are usually the most idiosyncratic and inventive. Good examples can also be seen at the **Étoile du Sud** carpet shop, just south of the *souk*, behind the *Hôtel Occidental*.

More carpets – and traditional-styled blankets and textiles – can be seen or bought at the **Atelier de Tissage**, part of a convent run by a group of Franciscan nuns. It is located just off to the left on the road to **Tattiouine** (signposted Cirque Jaffar from the town centre and over the Oued Outat to the west). Many of the nuns have been living here for years, and will quite happily talk about their time in Morocco.

At the moment, there are six nuns (three French, two Spanish and one Polish) and they also run a clinic and a small hospital, as part of the convent. The complex is known, locally, and inevitably, as *Kasbah Myriem* (☎05/58.24.43); the *atelier* is open every day, except Fridays and Sundays and the whole of August. The nuns welcome visitors who wish to join them in celebrating Mass on Tuesday evenings.

If you follow the Tattiouine road a few kilometres further, you find yourself in countryside very different from that around Midelt, with eagles soaring above the hills and mule tracks leading down to the valleys, and an occasional Kasbah. For more on this area – and the Cirque du Jaffar beyond – see p.235.

Practicalities

Midelt has a reasonable spread of accommodation but many of the **hotels** are often full by mid-afternoon, at busy tourist times of year, so arrive early or make a reservation by phone the day before.

HOTELS

Hôtel Atlas, [a] 3 Rue Mohammed Amraoui (☎05/58.29.38). A spotless new pension; family run and serving a good breakfast. Small; arrive early or book in advance. Showers cost extra. ①

Hôtel Boughafar [b] 7 Av. Mohammed V (☎05/58.30.99). A reasonable little place opened in 1995; rooms are okay, with toilets and hot showers on the landing; there are great views from the roof terrace; and a restaurant. It's also handy for the bus station. ①

Hôtel El Ayachi [d], Rue Agadir: follow the signs (☎05/58.21.61). The town's only upmarket hotel, favoured by tour groups and often block booked. Despite a 1990 *International Gastronomy Award*, still on proud display, the restaurant and service are not terribly brilliant but, with captive diners, the management doesn't appear too troubled. ③

Hôtel Mimlal [e], Route de Meknes (☎05/58.22.66). 250m from the bus station, on the right beyond the bridge over the Oued Outat. Simple, newish hotel with hot showers in rooms and toilets on the corridor. Given notice, the restaurant serves a menu du jour for 40/50dh. ①

Hôtel Roi de la Bière [c], corner of Av. Hassan II and Av. des F.A.R. (☎05/58.26.75). Cheap and rudimentary. Some rooms have showers albeit cold – but the welcome is warm. ①

At time of writing, neither the **Hôtel Occidental** nor the **Hôtel Zohors** is recommended. There are small **hammams** in the town for men and women – ask directions.

CAMPING

You can **camp** in the grounds of the *Hôtel El Ayachi*, as long as you take meals there or, better still (if you have, or can arrange transport) you can camp at the *Centre Timnay*, 30km northwest of Midelt on the road P21 to Azrou (see p.232).

MIBLADENE AND AOULI: MOROCCAN KLONDIKE

Less than an hour's drive from Midelt, on the banks of the **Oued Moulouya** where it emerges from its spectacular gorge, is the deserted mining settlement of **Aouli**. You can reach it by car from Midelt, first along the S317, past **Mibladene** (11km from Midelt) and then, by the 3419, to Aouli (25 km).

Once past Mibladene (appropriately 'our mother earth' in Berber) where there are modest excavations still being worked, the road deteriorates and drops into the gorge which is exciting enough in itself. Soon, you reach the apocalyptic mining ruins on both sides of the river. Here, from the turn of the century, and long before then on a more modest scale, the locals mined **lead**, which contained **silver**. In 1979, around 3000 still worked here but, by the mid-1980s, all had gone.

You don't have to be an industrial archeologist to be impressed by the tunnels, aqueducts, aerial ropeways, barrack-like living quarters and, above all, buildings pressed high against the cliff face resembling a Tibetan monastery. There are tracks cut into the sides of the gorge, first used by mules and than a mineral-line railway passing through tunnels. Everywhere there is rusting ironmongery.

Beyond Aouli, a rough track continues downstream to **Ksabi** and from there you can complete the circuit, by the S329 and P21 to Midelt. But this calls for a Renault 4 or 4 x 4, particularly in bad weather. Otherwise you must return the way you came.

At the outset, the exit from Midelt is not easy to find because it is not signposted. Leave by the straight, narrow road opposite the *Hôtel Zahors*, and alongside the Banque Populaire, on Avenue Mohammed V.

MEALS

For **meals**, try *Café-Restaurant Fes*, signposted on Rue des Esserghin, which does a very generous *menu du jour* (they like advance warning). Other decent restaurants include the *Restaurant Essaada*, opposite the bus station, the *Brasserie Chez Aziz*, on the Er Rachidia road, and *Café-Restaurant Le Sapin*, on Av. Moulay Abdallah, by a small park where the locals play *boules* on warm evenings.

DJEBEL AYACHI AND TOUNFITE

Djebel Ayachi can be climbed from Midelt, either returning to the town, or as part of a through-trek to Tounfite. From Midelt, a taxi or pick-up can be arranged to the springs 2km beyond Tattiouine, and the long **Ikkis valley** followed, with a bivouac at its head (the col at the end leads to the Cirque du Jaffar). An easy ascent leads to the many summits of this huge range, which was long thought to be the highest in Morocco (it is 3700m – compared to Toubkal at 4167m). A descent south to the Oued Taarart valley brings you to several villages and a Wednesday truck out to Tounfite.

At TOUNFITE, rooms are available and buses and taxis link it with Boumia (with a Thursday *souk*), Zeïda and Midelt. The village also gives access to the Djebel Masker (3265m), – a long day's climb, rising from cedar forests. Ayachi and Masker are long wave-crests, seen from a distance they appear to curve over the horizon such is the scale.

SERIOUS EXPEDITIONS

From Tounfite, an interesting piste runs west, between the Toujjet and Oujoud peaks to the head of the Melwiya plains and Arghbala, beyond which lies the main piste across the Central Atlas via Imilchil. South of Djebel Masker lies a chaos of spectacular peaks, little visited. The only information in English at present is in Peyron's *Grand Atlas Traverse* guide, which details the whole zone between Midelt and the Toubkal massif.

The Cirque Jaffar, Djebel Ayachi and beyond

The classic route around Midelt is the **Cirque Jaffar**, a very poor piste, practicable only in dry weather, which leaves the Midelt–Tattiouine road to edge its way through a kind of hollow in the foothills of the **Djebel Ayachi** (see below). This runs round the *cirque*, then loops back to the Midelt–Azrou road after 34km (turn right, on to the 3426, near the *Maison Forestière de Mitkane*); it is only 79km in all back to Midelt, though it takes a good half a day to get around.

Across the Atlas

Renault 4s make it over the Atlas from Midelt to Tinerhir in summer, though it's a lot easier with four-wheel-drive vehicles; everyone needs a pick and spade for the occasional very rough detour (beware of scorpions, by the way, when shifting rocks), as well as some warm clothes and a tent for sleeping out at night (Atlas nights are cold). If you don't have a vehicle, you can use Berber lorries over the various stages, which provide a kind of bus service most days. Travelling this way, you should reckon on up to three days for the journey to Imilchil (though you might make it in one), and a similar number from there down to the Todra Gorge and Tinerhir (see p.426).

South towards Er Rachidia

There's less adventure in continuing **south from Midelt to Er Rachidia,** though the route is a striking one, marking the transition to the south and the desert. The area was long notorious for raids upon caravans and travellers carried out by the Aït Haddidou, a nomadic Berber tribe, fear of whom led the main spring along this route to be known as *Ain Khrob ou Hrob* – "Drink and Flee". The tribe were pacified with great difficulty by the French, as late as the 1930s, and in consequence, the traditional *ksour* (fortified villages) are often shadowed by old Foreign Legion posts.

The Tizi n'Talrhmeht and Rich

Around 30km south of Midelt, you cross one of the lower passes of the High Atlas, the **Tizi n'Talrhmeht** (Pass of the She-Camel), before descending to what is essentially a desert plain. At AÏT MESSAOUD, just beyond the pass, there's a distinctly Beau Geste-like Foreign Legion fort, and a few kilometres further down, you come across the first southern *ksar*, AÏT KHERROU, a river oasis at the entrance to a small gorge. After this, the *ksour* begin to dot the landscape as the road follows the path of the great Ziz river.

The main settlement in these parts is **RICH**, a market town and administrative centre, approached from the main road (P21) along a rather bizarre red-washed esplanade. Enclosed by palms watered by a *seguia* or *khettara* (irrigation channel) from the Oued Ziz, the town developed around a *ksar* and was an important fort during the Protectorate. It still has shades of *Beau Geste* about it, as well as a lively Sunday **souk**, at the entrance to which are two cheap **hotels**, the *Salama* (☎05/58.93.43; ①) which has a small café, and the marginally preferable *Al Massira* (☎05/58.93.40; ①), which has hot showers, a restaurant and views from its roof terrace.

Over the Atlas from Rich

West of Rich, the Atlas mountains stretch desolately into the distance, skirted by a road up behind the town which trails the last section of the Oued Ziz. The road begins as the P3442 and is surfaced as far as AMOUGUER, where the rough P3443 piste takes over **to Imilchil**, by way of OUTERBATE and SOUNTAT: a wonderful trip through great gorges, valleys and passes.

The route is passable (just) in a Renault 4, though only in the dry summer months, and it can also be travelled in stages by **Berber lorries** (*camionettes*), paying as you go. Going on the lorries, the most promising day to set out from Rich is Friday, when you might get a ride the whole way to Imilchil, for its Saturday *souk*; make enquiries at the Rich hotels.

The Ziz Gorge

The scenic highlight of the regular Midelt–Er Rachidia route are the dramatic **Ziz Gorges**, tremendous erosions of rock which carve a passage through the Atlas. The route follows the Ziz valley from AÏT KROJMANE (7km from Rich) onwards, just past the *Ziz* ("gazelle" in Berber) filling station. About 20km from Rich, you will see, down on the right between the road and the river, a cluster of modern buildings, signposted **Hammat Moulay Ali Cherif.** This is a small, but well-known, spa with outdoor hot springs (over 100°F), rich in magnesium and sulphates, and said to cure rheumatic disorders. You will see the afflicted hopefuls in the nearby thickets from which steam rises. Men and women bathe on alternate days. There is a café and some primitive rooms to rent.

A further 5km on, you enter the gorges proper, around 25km from Rich, shortly after the **Tunnel du Légionnaire**, built by the French in 1930 to open up the route to the south, and still guarded by drowsy soldiers. The gorges are truly majestic, especially in late afternoon, cut by great swathes of sunlight, and the incredible mountain landscape is accompanied by sudden vistas of brilliant green oasis and red-brown *ksour*.

You emerge from the gorges near the vast **Barrage Hassan Addakhil**, built in 1971 to irrigate the valley of the Tafilalt beyond, and to supply electricity for ER RACHIDIA. The dam also regulates the flow of the Oued Ziz, preventing the serious flooding which occurred frequently before it was built, as witnessed by the deserted *ksour* in the gorges above and below the lake.

Azrou to Kasba Tadla

The **main route from Azrou to Marrakesh** – the P24 – skirts well clear of the Atlas ranges, its interest lying in the subtle changes of land, cultivation and architecture on the plains as you move into the south. The towns along the way are hot, dusty, functional market centres, unlikely to tempt you to linger. However, once again, contact with the Middle Atlas is close at hand, if you leave the main road and take to the pistes. A great network of them spreads out behind the small town of **El Ksiba**, itself 8km off the P24 but easily hitched to from the turnoff or reached by bus from Kasba Tadla.

Khenifra

With long-distance buses regularly passing through **KHENIFRA**, you're unlikely to get stranded there and it's equally difficult to imagine any other reason to linger. The old market town – now a provincial centre – stands on the west bank of the **Oued Oum Rbia**. Moulay Ismail built a Kasbah here, replaced by Moha ou Hammon at the close of the nineteenth century, the walls of which still stand alongside the humpback bridge built by Moulay Ismail. But the once clear, fast flowing river is filthy, and the modern quarters, bisected by the main road (P24) from Fes to Marrakesh, not much more enticing. Wide avenues and dull buildings come to life, from an outsider's perspective, only at the weekly Sunday *souk* or the Saturday afternoon rug auction put on by Berber women just across the new bridge near the bus station.

Historically, the town's chief claim to fame is as a focus of resistance, as the fiefdom of one Moha ou Hammou, in the early years of the Protectorate. The French suffered one of their worst military defeats here, losing 600 men when they took the town in 1914. There's an impressive **monument** recording this event – 7km south of Khenifra on the left-hand side of the P24 going towards Marrakesh. The town also played an important part in the struggle for independence which climaxed on August 20, 1955.

Gavin Maxwell in his book *Lords of the Atlas* records that Gilbert Grandval, Resident General, returned from Paris to Rabat "at 2am on the 20th, and at 7am the Director of the Interior, General Leblanc, telephoned to him with the opening words, 'It is war.' Massive rioting had broken out at Khenifra, and the General asked authorisation to use aircraft. The Medina was surrounded by troops, but mounted tribesmen were visible on all the ridges that could be seen from the town. Grandval gave his authorisation, but on the condition that use of aircraft should be limited to low flying dispersal of tribal cavalry, and that no shot be fired or bomb dropped. This was only the beginning..."

Practicalities

If you're following this chapter in reverse (from Marrakesh) note that you can approach the Cascades of Oum Er Rbia (see p.230) from Khenifra. If you've just done this, or plan to do so, you might want to use the town's **hotels**, the better among which are:

Hôtel Arego, near the bus station (☎05/58.64.87). Clean and simple, with separate facilities. It's on the main road and the rear rooms are quieter.

Hôtel de France, near the barracks: Quartier des F.A.R. (☎05/58.61.14). Large, en-suite rooms, but the showers are cold. The restaurant is excellent – and better than the hotel. ①

Hôtel Hammou Zayani, on the hill overlooking the 'new' town (☎05/58.60.70). Top choice for comfort, with a swimming pool. ④

Hôtel Mlilia, near the bus station. (☎05/38.46.09). Opened in 1995; quite pleasant and again with a reasonable restaurant. ①

SOUTH OF BENI MELLAL: ATLAS HIKES AND PISTES

The Middle Atlas to the south and southeast of Beni Mellal is ideal hiking and landrover expedition territory. Below are suggestions for four- or five-day expeditions in the region; they are impracticable in winter.

Djebel Tassemit (2248m) towers like a high wall behind Beni Mellal. Despite its height, it is a relatively easy climb, by way of Aïn Asserdoun and the ruined Kasbah de ras El Aïn, to the south of town. **Djebel R'Nim** (2411m) and **Djebel Tazerkount** (1730m) continue the wall to the southwest. For the energetic, they are not hard to climb, but two lower tracks cut between them from north to south. One of these runs southeast from Beni Mellal itself, and then swings southwest to **Ouaouizarht**, at the top end of the Bin El Ouidane lake (see p.242). The other runs south from **Oulad M'Barek** on the P24 and then swings southeast to Ouaouizarht.

South of Bin El Ouidane, the lower slopes of the High Atlas are appealing. A track from Ouaouizarht skirts the lake until it strikes southeast through forests towards Tilouggite (it is by this stage an extremely rough track, practicable only by jeep or lorry). This winds through the mountains for some 70km before reaching ZAOUIA AHANESAL, passing en route ZAOUIA TEMGA (40km), which faces the soaring limestone sculpture of *La Cathédrale des Rochers*. The road on to Zaouia Ahanesal is unbelievably tortuous but reasonably surfaced. It would be possible to cover this route in stages, using local Berber lorries or jeeps.

MAPS AND ASSISTANCE

If you haven't obtained a large-scale survey **map** (see p.23: AMIS/Atlas maps may help), a good substitute is the Michelin map, which has an insert covering this area at 1:600,000.

If you want **assistance**, two mountain guides are available in Beni Mellal or Azilal. Contact either: **Serrab El Housseine** (21 Bloc I Foughol, Av. Hassan II, Beni Mellal; (☎03/48.73.26), who will accompany groups or, if you wish, just help you plan routes; or **Mohammed Achari** (Imelghas, Aït Bou Goumez, Azilal), who will guide groups in the Irhil M'Goun and also has mules for hire. Both charge around 200–300dh a day. More expensive landrover expeditions are arranged by **Imilchil Voyages**, 416 Bd. Mohammed V, Beni Mellal (☎03/48.90.60).

Hôtel Najah, on the main road (P24) Av. Zerktouni (☎05/58.83.31). Another modern place with comfortable en-suite rooms – and satellite TV in every room. Café, restaurant and pâtisserie. ③
Hôtel Rif, near the bus station (☎05/58.60.30). Basic, but clean. Squat toilets. ①
Hôtel Sahara, 3 Av. Bir Anzarane (☎05/38.53.18). On the west bank, over the bridge nearest to the bus station; cheap, but satisfactory. ⑩

Oulmès

Northwest of Khenifra, a road leads through the Djebel Mouchchene, a forested out-crop of the Middle Atlas, towards Rabat. This is an attractive route through countryside cut by rivers and ravines, and with wild boar in the hills. There is a major **souk** at the crossroads settlement of AGUELMOUSS each Saturday.

Midway along the route is the small town of **OULMES** and – some 4km distant – the spa-hamlet of **OULMÈS-TARMILATE**, home of Morocco's most popular fizzy mineral water. The spa makes a good stop, if you can afford the *Hôtel les Thermes* (☎07/55.22.93; ③; closed July and Aug). Below the hotel you can walk down to a spring known as **Lalla Haya**, where Oulmès water cascades out from the rocks.

El Ksiba, Arhbala and across the Atlas

EL KSIBA is a sizeable and busy Berber village with a **Sunday souk**, enclosed by apri-cot, olive and orange groves. It has one **bank**, *Credit Agricole,* and one small **hotel**, the *Henri IV* (☎03/41.50.02; ①), on a loop road which bypasses the main part of the village; this is still a pleasant place, in a pleasant setting, but not as welcoming as it used to be. There is also a summer **campsite**, *Camping Taghbalout*, 2 km beyond the village, and others hidden in the wooded Atlas slopes, along the Arhbala road.

South of the town, a reasonable piste (P1909, then P1901) heads off into the Atlas, **towards Imilchil and the Plateau of the Lacs** (see the map and route details on p.429). This is more or less practicable by Renault 4, weather permitting. If you are relying on local transport, you should be able to get a bus or lorry along the surfaced road to the mar-ket village of AGHBALA (or ARHBALA). Local lorries shuttle passengers to Imilchil via CHERKET and TASSENT; connections are easiest early in the morning on Wednesday, when Arhbala has its *souk,* or on Thursday, the day before the *souk* at Imilchil.

Another, recently improved road, the P1805, leads southwest from the P1909 to the reservoir of **Bin El Ouidane** (see overleaf), via BEN CHERROU, TAGUELFT (very basic hotel) and OUAOUIAZARHT (Wednesday souk; and decent rooms and meals at *Hôtel Tizi Ghnim*, ☎03/44.21.15; ⑩). The road is wonderful, running across rugged, sparsely vegetated countryside, over several 1500m passes.

East of Taguelft a piste makes an incredible journey to reach ANERGUI in the Melloul gorges; only to be tackled by 4 x 4 vehicles. The easier approach to Anergui is via a new up-valley piste from TILOUGGUITE.

Kasba Tadla

KASBA TADLA was created by Moulay Ismail, and takes its name from a fortress he built here, strategically positioned beside the Oum Er Rbia river. It remains a military town, and is scarcely a place to linger. However, if you have a car, or are between buses, you might as well take the odd hour to look round. The **Kasbah** is only a few blocks from the bus station; it's a massive, crumbling quarter, whose palace and mosque are now derelict, their shells occupied by small farmholdings and cottages. The town has a sizeable **souk** on Mondays.

For anyone stranded, there are two cheap and very basic **hotels** near the bus station: the *Hôtel Atlas*, 46 Bd. El Majjata Obad (☎03/41.87.31; ⑩), and, round the corner, the

---

OLIVE OIL

On the main road (P24) near El Ksiba, and particularly either side of **Tirhboula** (45km from Beni Mellal), you will see plastic bottles hanging from roadside trees to advertise the availability of **olive oil** crushed from local olives in the adjacent domestic presses. Whether or not you have a passion for cooking, or drenching your salads with olive oil, it's well worth a stop in early autumn to see the presses at work. You'll be welcome to visit – and to buy.

When **ripe**, the black olives can contain up to 60 percent of oil. Some of them are harvested **unripe** or green and then pickled in salt. Both ripe and unripe olives are normally bitter; this can be corrected by soaking them first in an alkaline solution.

Hôtel des Alliés at 38 Av. Mohammed V (☎03/41.81.72; ①). The only other option is the *Hôtel Bellevue* (☎03/41.81.72; ④), out at the Kasba Tadla turn-off on the Khenifra–Beni Mellal road; it is modern and uninspiring, but functional enough.

Eating in Kasba Tadla is not very exciting; the better choices are the *Salem,* opposite the *Hôtel Alliés,* and the *Oum Rbia,* on the way into town – and still listed by the Beni Mellal tourist office as a hotel. Don't be surprised to find the cafés have sawdust and wood chippings on the floor – more wild west than military. The restaurant at the *Hôtel Bellevue* is dear and, according to reception, the food is 'poor'.

Besides pinball and pool, the only other **entertainment** is the *Cinema Chantecler.* Once again, the only **bank** is the *Credit Agricole.*

The most remarkable feature of the town is the four tall, square pillars at the Kasba Tadla turn-off; this is a memorial to the French soldiers killed hereabouts from 1912 to 1933. Understandably, it is not as well preserved as the monument outside Khenifra which celebrates Moroccan resistance to the French in 1914. Nevertheless, the Kasba Tadla **monument** affords a fine view of the *bidonville* by the river and the town beyond.

Beni Mellal

BENI MELLAL is one of Morocco's fastest-growing towns, with a population of some 250,000. It has few specific sights – and few tourists – and makes an easy, restful stop en route to Marrakesh. As a market centre for the broad, prosperous flatlands to the north, it hosts a large **Tuesday souk** – good for woollen blankets, which feature unusual Berber designs. Olives are grown on the lower slopes of the Djebel Tassemit and the plain is well-known for its oranges. It is also important for its transport links, with a regular bus towards the wonderful Cascades d'Ouzoud (see p.241).

As far as sights go, the town's **Kasbah** in the old Medina, yet another of Moulay Ismail's endowments, has been often restored and is of no great interest. Time would be better spent walking up to the smaller, ruined **Kasbah de Ras El Aïn**, set above gardens and from which local jokers say you can see the sea on a clear day, and to the spring of **Aïn Asserdoun**, to the south of town. The latter (signposted on a Circuit Touristique from town which peters out thereafter) is especially pleasant, feeding a series of artificial falls (Moroccans love waterfalls) amid well-tended gardens.

Practicalities

The main road from Fes to Marrakesh (once the P24) now skirts the northern suburbs of Beni Mellal as the P24a and, as so often, the **bus station** has been implanted here; to reach the centre from here you may want to get a *petit taxi* to save a long uphill walk. The old Fes–Marrakesh road still runs through the core of the town, as the **Av. Mohammed V**, and midway along there are brief views of the plain to the north and glimpses to the south of the cream-and-white arcaded **Place de la Libération**, focus of the old **Medina**

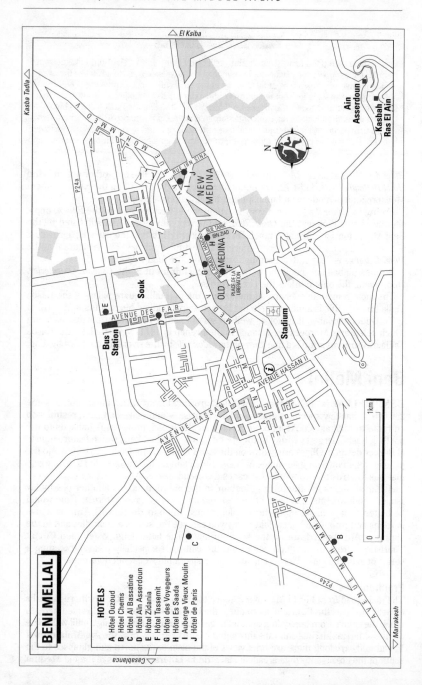

BENI MELLAL

HOTELS
A Hôtel Ouzoud
B Hôtel Chems
C Hôtel Al Bassatine
D Hôtel Aïn Asserdoun
E Hôtel Zidania
F Hôtel Tassemit
G Hôtel des Voyageurs
H Hôtel Es Saada
I Auberge Vieux Moulin
J Hôtel de Paris

quarter, which climbs up the lower slopes of the Djebel Tassemit. The **Ville Nouvelle** sprawls down onto the plain to the south, towards, and now beyond, the ring road.

HOTELS

There are twenty or so **hotels** scattered in and around the town, many built in the 1990s. The pick of them are:

Hôtel Aïn Asserdoun [D], Av. des F.A.R. (☎03/48.34.93). New, with a small restaurant and comfortable accommodation; popular with Moroccans passing through or visiting for sports fixtures. ③

Hôtel Al Bassatine, [C] Ouled Hamdane, Route de Fkih Ben Salah (☎03/48.22.47). On the northwest edge of town, alongside the orange and olive groves. Comfortable rooms and the best restaurant in the neighbourhood (but no alchohol). ④

Hôtel Chems [B], (03/48.34.60). One of two hotels out on the original Marrakesh road built for groups on escorted seven-day Imperial Cities tours; individual travellers are likely to find the reception unhelpful. ④

Hôtel Ouzoud [A], (☎03/48.37.52). This looks indistinguishable from the nearby *Hôtel Chems*, but the welcome is warmer and the service better; good restaurant, bar and swimming pool. ④

Hôtel de Paris [J], Hay Ibn Sina, New Medina (☎03/48.22.45). 1950s style place, fifteen minutes from the town centre; the restaurant is good, even if the accommodation is rather drab. ①

Hôtel Es Saada [H], 129 Rue Tarik Ibn Ziad (☎03/48.29.91). Helpful management; recently renovated; hot showers – and a *hammam* on the ground floor. A useful contact point for the local guide Serrab El Housseine (see box on p.237). ①

Hôtel Tassemit [F], Rue Ahmed El Hansali (☎03/42.13.13). A modern hotel deep in the old Medina, but easy to find if you follow the several signs. Some rooms en suite. ⑩

Auberge Vieux Moulin [I], Av. Mohammed V (☎03/48.27.88). This old-style French hotel, with rooms off a wide central corridor is still under French management, but has lost much of its charm of late. A reasonable fall-back, nonetheless. ①

Hôtel des Voyageurs [G], Av. Mohammed V (☎03/48.24.72). The best of the cheapies (though cold showers only). It backs on to the old Medina and from the rooftop terrace there are stunning views of the plain to the north. ⑩

Hôtel Zidania [E], Av. des F.A.R. (☎03/48.18.98). The best – and cheapest – of a trio of hotels facing the bus station. All rooms en suite. ②

OTHER FACILITIES

For **meals**, in addition to those in the hotels above, the *Restaurant Dounia Day* on Av. Mohammed V is excellent value. Next door to it is the *Café Basma*, which is a good spot for coffee and watching the world go by.

There are several **banks** around town and there is a branch of the *BMCE* at the bus station. The helpful **tourist office** is on the first floor of the **Immeuble Chichaoui** on Av. Hassan II (☎03/48.78.29; open Mon–Fri 8.30am–noon and 2.30–6.30 pm; in summer, 7am–2pm). For details of local guides – and adventure tours – into the Atlas from Beni Mellal, see the box on p.237.

Oulad Nemâ: a Saturday souk

If you're in Beni Mellal on a Saturday, it's worth a trip to what is traditionally the Middle Atlas's largest weekly **market**, held 35km southwest of the town at **SOUK SEBT DES OULAD NEMÂA**. There are regular buses.

The Cascades d'Ouzoud

The **Cascades d'Ouzoud** are a fairly long detour from the Beni Mellal–Marrakesh road – taking at least half a day's journey to reach if you're going by local bus and taxi. However, there are few places in Morocco so enjoyable and easy-going as these falls, with their seasonal campsites, and in midsummer it's incredible to encounter the cool air here, with the water crashing down onto a great drop of rocks amid thickets of lush green trees and vegetation. If you want to view the falls at their best, it is better to go in March, but you'll find the "resort" side of things pretty much closed down.

Getting to Ouzoud is simplest from Beni Mellal; there's a regular bus to Azilal (a winding 63km), where you can usually get a place in a *grand taxi* to the falls (10dh a place or 50dh for the *taxi*). There is also a bus twice a day from Marrakesh along the S508 road, which passes by Azilal. Getting back to Azilal is generally no problem, with *grands taxis* regularly shuttling from the falls. Better still, if you can arrange to fill a *grand taxi* from Beni Mellal to the falls it will cost you 55/60dh a place.

Bin El Ouidane and Azilal

On the way from Beni Mellal to Azilal, the road climbs almost straight up from the plain, zigzagging through the hills and crossing the immense **Bin El Ouidane reservoir**. This was one of the earliest (1948–55) and most ambitious of the country's irrigation schemes and has changed much of the land around Beni Mellal – formerly as dry and barren as the phosphate plains to the northwest. It also supplies much of central Morocco's electricity.

There's a small **hotel** beside the barrage, the *Auberge du Lac* (☎03/44.24.65; ②), which offers the choice of rooms in its main building, or camping by the river downstream of the dam. It has a bar, a restaurant, boats for hire, and fishing; swimming is prohibited. In winter, be warned, it is very cold up here – and, although the hotel has hot water, it has no room heating.

AZILAL, 27km further on, has the feel of a small village, with a garrison, banks, a Thursday *souk* and transport links; but it is now a provincial capital which explains a lot of new housing and an active **tourist office**, Rue Tarik Ibn Ziad (☎03/45.83.34), which will help you to contact mountain guides for expeditions south of here. One such is Rachid Boutafala, B.P. 58, Azilal (☎03/45.87.84). He speaks French, Spanish and a little Dutch (his wife is Flemish). He knows best the Bou Goumez Valley, Oued Tessaout and Irhil M'Goun (see opposite).

If by any chance you find yourself stranded here, there is a recently enlarged **hotel**, the *Tanoute* (☎03/45.87.78; ① without shower, ② with shower), on the road in from Beni Mellal. The hotel **restaurant** is closed, but the nearby *Café-Restaurant Tissir* is recommended.

Buses from Azilal to Marrakesh run twice daily, currently at 7am and 2pm.

The Cascades

The **Cascades d'Ouzoud** are a popular place to camp in the summer, with both Moroccan and foreign tourists attracted by the falls and cool, high air, though they are, as yet, refreshingly uncommercialized. At the road head, there is a seasonal **restaurant-hotel**, variously called *Mohammed's* or *Dar Essalam* (☎03/45.96.57; ⑩). This has an open courtyard, with an orange tree, off which are some large dormitory rooms. They are often used by *Club Med* groups, though individuals are welcome; in summer, it is wise to book ahead.

Alongside the hotel is a **campsite**, shaded by fruit trees and bordered by a stream, which also has a few rooms; it is run by a Berber, T'Hami Abassi, who cooks good meals on request. Several further **cafés** are located on terraces along the way down to the falls, and most offer camping for a few tents, either for a small fee, or free if you eat at them during your stay. They tend to have a youthful, international clientele.

From the campsites, paths wind down to the valley and the great basins below the **cascades**. You can swim in one of these – a fabulous natural pool – and might spot the occasional Barbary ape under the oak and pomegranate trees. Your best chance of a sighting is at daybreak or an hour or so before dusk, when they come out to drink in the river. On the lip of the falls, (best reached from T'Hami Abassi's campsite) there are some little sheds containing small, ancient **watermills**, some of which were still in use until quite recently. The river is diverted through them, before plunging over the edge; worn grindstones litter the edge of the abyss.

A memorable short hike is to go beyond the lower pools to the so-called 'Mexican village' (although some local guides prefer 'Berber village'), a fascinating place connected by semi-underground passages. To get there, follow the path down to the lower pools and you will see a path climbing up on the left, past a farmhouse and up to the top of the plain. Follow this path west. The village is sited on the slopes of the wooded hills, about 1km along the path which drops to a stream before climbing up to the houses.

On from Ouzoud

Continuing to Marrakesh from Ouzoud on local transport, it's easiest to backtrack to Azilal, picking up a bus there to Beni Mellal or (if you time it right) direct to Marrakesh. If you are driving, however, you could head down to KHEMIS-DES-OULAD on the Beni Mellal–Marrakesh road (P24); 17km of this 51km route is poor piste, passable only in dry weather.

Bou Goumez valley and Irhil M'Goun

A **dirt track southeast of Azilal** leads to the village of AÏT MEHAMMED and from there into the **Bou Goumez valley**, a popular trekking/climbing base. **Irhil M'Goun** (4068m) is the highest in Morocco outside the Toubkal massif. The area has some astonishing gorges. It is possible to trek south through the mountains to exit via El Kelaa de M'Gouna.

From Azilal you can get a taxi up to Aït Mehammed, from whence lorries or landrover taxis run on Wednesday, Friday and Sunday to **TABANT/SOUK EL HAD**, the administrative centre of the Bou Goumez, which has a large Sunday *souk*. Alternatively, you could make a two-day trek from Aït Mehammed with an overnight stop at the pretty hamlet of **SREMPT** (Sabre Brahim offers rooms) and the crossing of the **Tizi n'Aït Ourit** (2606m) with its vast view of the mountain ranges. Another possible approach is via Demnate (see overleaf) from where trucks go on to the road-end at **Imi n'Wakka** (Tabat n'Tirsal) under the bulk of Djebel Rhat. There is a spectacular trek of several days down the Bou Willi valley to connect with the Bou Goumez. On the **Tizi n'Tirghyst** (2390m) are prehistoric rock-carved pictures.

A longer circuit goes round the west flank of **Djebel Rhab** (3797m) and **Djebel Tignousti** (3820m) to reach the **Oued Tessaout** which is followed to its head under Irhil M'Goun whence the Bou Goumez can be regained. East from the Bou Goumez is the seasonal lake of **Izoughar**, dominated by Djebel Azourki and other big hills. A *tizi* leads to Arouadane and the Zaouia Ahanesal area of spectacular gorges. **Agoudim**, a village of remarkable architecture has several *gîtes* (1km south of Zaouia Ahanesal) as has **Taghia** which faces the finest gorge and cliff scenery in the country, a rock-climbers' playground of Dolomitic scope. There are many other treks, peaks, climbs and gorges of note, well-covered in Peyron (see p.23), and making use of local experts is highly recommended.

Several of the Bou Goumez valley villages have *gîte* accommodation, meals and mule hire (see lists in the ONMT Atlas guide). Mohammed Achari (Imelghas, Aït Bou Goumez, Bureau Tabant, par Azilal) is a mountain guide of wide experience who has helped many British parties.

Azilal to Marrakesh: Demnate

Having come as far as Azilal and the cascades, it is easier to continue along the S508 road to Marrakesh rather than try and cut back on to the main road from Beni Mellal. It is in any case the more interesting route.

Demnate

You'll probably have to change buses along the way at **DEMNATE**, a walled market town, with a Glaoui-era Kasbah, an old Mellah (half the population were Jews until the 1950s), and a **Sunday souk**. The *souk* is by far the largest in the region and an interesting, unaffected event worth trying to coincide with. It is held just outside the ramparts, the stalls spreading out into the town streets with their used clothes and other goods, together with enormous stacks of fresh produce.

The surrounding area is well-known for its **olives** and attractive glazed **pottery** which is made at out-of-town Bourghrat – also worth a visit. Another trip, if you have time and transport, is to follow the road up above the town to a curious-looking natural bridge – **Imi n'Ifri** (around 6.5km from Demnate). It spans a yawning gorge, the result of the partial collapse of an underground cave system. Those of a vertiginous disposition should stay away from the edge. There's a seasonal restaurant and you can sit outside and watch the iridescent crows and little swifts, with their white rumps and square tails, ever-wheeling in pursuit of insects; it's also a good spot to look for *sib sib* (ground squirrels – see p.490) playing on the roadside walls above the gorge. Close by is a series of springs, which account for the Demnate valley's prosperous and intense cultivation, this is the site of a large *moussem* held two weeks after the Aïd El Kebir.

Demnate is barely touristed and makes for a relaxed stopover: the *Hôtel Ouzoud* (☎04/45.60.87; ①) on the main street is cheap and cheerful; mountain guides hang out here or at the nearby *Café Agadir*. On the main street there's a *Banque Populaire* and *PTT*.

Demnate to Marrakesh

The land between Demnate and Marrakesh is generally poor and rocky, distinguished only by sporadic clusters of farmhouses or shepherds' huts. If you take the bus, it might follow either of the routes to Marrakesh – via Tamelelt (where you rejoin the P24) or a perfectly well-paved road via Tazzerte and Sidi Rahhal.

Given the choice, go for the latter. An old Glaoui village, **TAZZERTE** has four crumbling Kasbahs, off the road, from which the clan (see Telouet, p.384) used to control the region and the caravan routes to the north. There is a small Monday market held here, and a larger one on Fridays at Sidi Rahhal, 7km further down.

SIDI RAHHAL, named after a fifteenth-century *marabout*, is also a point of significant local pilgrimage and host to a small, but important, *mousssem* held at the time of Aïd El Kebir. The saint, in whose honour the festivities take place, has an unusual Judeo-Muslim tradition, and a multitude of stories told about him. All are timeless in their evocations of magic and legend. The most popular ones recount how he had the power to conduct himself and other creatures through the air – a "talent" which led to a minor incident involving the Koutoubia minaret in Marrakesh, whose upper storey one of his followers is supposed to have knocked down with his knee. His favours are sought by the mentally ill and their families.

Coming into Marrakesh from either Demnate or Beni Mellal, you skirt part of the huge **palmery** which encloses the northern walls of the city. Arriving by bus, you will almost certainly find yourself at the main **bus station** by Bab Doukkala – a ten-minute walk from the centre of Gueliz (or the Ville Nouvelle), or twenty minutes (or an 8–10dh taxi ride) from Place Djemaa El Fna and the Medina.

travel details

Trains

Fes–Meknes 8 daily in each direction (40min–1hr 5min: average 55min).

Fes–Rabat/Casablanca 8 daily. Rabat Ville (3hr 35min–4hr 45min: average 3hr 50min); Casa Voyageurs (6 trains: 4hr 30min–5hr 5min: average 4hr 55min; Casa Port (2 trains: 4hr 35min–4hr 45min; all via Meknes, Kenitra: average 3hr 15min) and Salé Ville (average 3hr 45min).

Fes–Taza/Oujda 3 daily (1hr 55min–2hr 25min/5hr 20min–6hr 5min).

Fes–Tangier 4 daily via Meknes, all changing at Sidi Kacem or Sidi Slimane and stopping at Asilah (5hr) and Tangier (5hr 45min).

Fes–Marrakesh 4 daily (average 8hr) via Meknes and Casa Voyageurs.

Buses

From Meknes CTM to Rissani (1 daily; 8hr 30min). Other lines, Fes (8 CTM daily and others hourly 7am-7pm; 50min); Larache/Tangier (3 CTM and 3 others daily; 5hr 30min/7hr); Rabat/Casablanca (9 CTM and 9 others daily; 4hr/5hr 30min); Chaouen/Tetouan (2 daily; 5hr 30min/7hr); Chaouen (1 daily; 5hr 30min); Ouezzane (2 daily; 4hr); Ifrane/Azrou (2 CTM and 2 others daily; 1hr/1hr 30min); Midelt/Er Rachidia (2 CTM daily; 5hr 30min/8hr 30 min) and CTM daily carries on to Rissani (10hr 30min); Beni Mellal/Marrakesh (1 CTM daily; 6hr/9hr).

From Fes CTM to Beni Mellal (1 daily; 5hr 30min); to Casablanca (8 daily; 5hr 15min); to Marrakesh (2 daily; 9hr); to Oujda (1 daily; 6hr 30min); to Tangier (2 daily; 5hr 45min) and to Tetouan; 5hr 20min). Other lines, Chaouen (2 daily; 5hr); Mdiq (1 daily; 5hr); Larache/Tangier (2 CTM and 4 others daily; 4hr 30min/6hr); Rabat/Casablanca (8 CTM and 17 others daily; 5hr 30min/7hr); Taza (2 CTM and 7 others daily; 2hr 30min) and 2 CTM daily carry on to Oujda (7hr 30min); Sefrou 17 daily; 1hr 30min); Immouzer/Ifrane (1 CTM and 12 others daily; 1hr/1hr 30min/2hr) and 1 CTM carries on to Midelt/Er Rachidia (5hr 30min/8hr 30min); Beni Mellal/Marrakesh (2 CTM and 2 others daily; 7hr/10hr); Agadir (1 CTM daily; 12hr30min).

From Sefrou Boulemane/Midelt (2 daily 2hr/5hr).

From Azrou Ifrane/Immouzer (4 daily; 1hr/1hr 30min); Midelt/Er Rachidia (5; 2hr/5hr); Khenifra/Kasba Tadla/Beni Mellal/Marrakesh (3; 3hr/4hr/4hr 30min/7hr).

From Midelt Er Rachidia (2; 3hr), Oujda (1; 13hr).

From Kasbah Tadla El Ksiba (3 daily; 20min); Beni Mellal (4; 1hr).

From Beni Mellal Demnate (4 daily; 3hr); Marrakesh (6; 6hr).

Grands Taxis

From Meknes Regularly to Fes (40min) and Volubilis/Moulay Idriss (35min).

From Fes Regularly to Meknes, Sefrou (1hr), Immouzer/Ifrane (40min/1hr) and Taza (1hr 15min).

Other **local and Middle Atlas** routes are specified in the text.

Flights

From Fes in *summer*, flights on **RAM** direct to Casablanca (6 days a week); and to Er Rachidia (2 days a week), and on **RAM**, via Casablanca, to Agadir (4 days a week); to Laayoune (3 days a week); to Marrakesh (4 days a week); to Rabat (5 days a week); to Tangier (4 days a week); and to London (5 days a week). In *winter*, flights on **RAM** direct to Casablanca (5 days a week); to Er Rachidia (2 days a week); to Rabat (1 day a week); and to Tangier (1 day a week); and on **RAM** via Casablanca, to Agadir (4 days a week); to Laayoune (3 days a week); to Marrakesh (3 days a week); to Rabat (5 days a week); to Tangier (2 days a week); and to London (4 days a week).

CHAPTER FOUR

THE WEST COAST: FROM RABAT TO ESSAOUIRA

This chapter takes in almost five hundred kilometres of Atlantic coastline, from Kenitra in the north to Essaouira in the south, and ranges through long stretches of scarcely developed lagoons and sands to Morocco's urban heartland. This latter comprises the cities of **Rabat** and **Casablanca** – the respective seats of government and of industry and commerce – and the neighbouring towns of **Kenitra, Salé** (alongside Rabat) and **Mohammedia** (alongside Casablanca). Together, these have a population of around five million – close on a fifth of the country's total. It is an astonishingly recent growth along what was, until the French Protectorate, a neglected strip of coast. At the turn of this century, Rabat was a straggling port with a population of 30,000 (today it is 900,000), while Casablanca (modern population 3,500,000), had just 20,000 inhabitants. In Morocco now, the bulk of new investment is in the Casablanca and Kenitra areas – and around **Settat**, 68km from Casablanca, on the road to Marrakesh.

Inevitably, it is French and post-colonial influences that are dominant in the main coastal cities. Don't go to **Casa** – as Casablanca is popularly known – expecting some exotic movie location; it is a modern city that looks very much like Marseilles. **Rabat**, too, which the French developed as a capital in place of the old imperial centres of Fes and Marrakesh, looks markedly European, with its cafés and boulevards, though it also has some of Morocco's finest and oldest monuments, dating from the Almohad and Merenid dynasties. If you're on a first trip to Morocco, Rabat is an ideal place to get to grips with the country. Its westernized streets make an easy cultural shift and it is an excellent transport hub, well connected by train with Tangier, Fes and Marrakesh. Casa is maybe more interesting after you've spent a while in the country, when you'll appreciate both its differences and its fundamentally Moroccan character.

South along the coast, populations and towns thin out, as the road skirts a series of beaches and dunes, with the odd detour inland when cliffs take hold. **El Jadida**, established as a beach resort by the French, now fulfils the same function for middle class Casablanca. **Oualidia**, to its south, has a similar, though rather more relaxed and small-scale style. **Safi**, between Oualidia and Essaouira, is a predominantly industrial town, but a friendly place, with some excellent beaches nearby.

Finally, there is **Essaouira**, which is also easily accessible from Marrakesh, and is a long-established backpackers' resort, and more recently a major centre for windsurfers. For most independent travellers, it is Morocco's coastal highlight, blending as it does a slightly alternative feel with the air of a traditional provincial town.

Kenitra and the coast to Rabat

Travelling to Rabat from Tangier or Fes, you will bypass the stretch of coast around **Kenitra** – which for the most part is no great loss. Kenitra is a dull, scruffy little town, as is its beach and port at **Mehdiya**. Further south, however, there are pleasant detours (if you have transport) to the **Plage des Nations** – Rabat's local beach resort – and to the botanical extravagance of the **Jardins Exotiques**; if you're dependent on buses, these can be visited as a day-trip from the capital. **Bird-watchers** may also want to explore the **Lac de Sidi Bourhaba**, near Mehdiya, which has protected status due to its notable birds of prey.

Kenitra and Mehdiya

KENITRA was established by the French as Port Lyautey – named after the Resident General – with the intention of channelling trade from Fes and Meknes. It never quite took off, however, losing out in industry and port activities to Casablanca, despite the rich farming areas of its hinterland. It has a population today of around 300,000, employed mainly in paper mills and a fish cannery. Until recently, additional income was provided by a large naval and military base, shared with the US, but the Americans left after the Gulf War, and the Moroccans have scaled down their own operations. A rather sad array of bars, pizza joints and discos struggle along in their wake.

Orientation is straightforward, with a long main street, **Av. Mohammed V/Av. Mohammed Diouri** – running from the main train station (at one end of town) to the bus station (at the other) by way of the central **Place Administrative**. It is about fifteen minutes' walk from the square to either bus or main train station, known as *Gare de Ville* or simply as Kenitra to differentiate it from the smaller station known as Kenitra Medina which, coming from Tangier or Fes/Meknes, is always the first stop.

The town has a dozen or so **hotels** and a good campsite:

Hôtel Ambassy, 20 Av. Hassan II (☎07/37.99.78). Comfortable and central; there is a bar and billiards. The restaurant, *Le Turbot*, is not as good as the accommodation; better to eat elsewhere. The *Café Restaurant Ouazzani* next door is recommended. ③

Hôtel du Commerce, small hotel near the *Hôtel de Ville* (☎07/37.16.03). Simple, but adequate, rooms with separate facilities on the corridor. Clean, but overpriced. ①

Hôtel d'Europe, 63 Av. Mohammed Diouri (☎07/37.14.50). An older hotel, opposite the *Hôtel La Rotonde*. En-suite rooms are dearer than those with separate facilities. Value for money. ②①

Hôtel Mamora, top end of Av. Hassan II, across the Place Administrative from the Hôtel de Ville (☎07/37.13.10). Comfortable, with en-suite facilities, swimming pool and reasonable restaurant, albeit with limited menu. ③

Hôtel de la Poste, 307 Av. Mohammed V (☎07/37.99.82). Basic and cheap – but with hot showers in most rooms. Good value. ①

Hôtel La Rotonde, 60 Av. Mohammed Diouri (☎07/37.14.01). Friendly, with recently restored decor and a good restaurant. Well placed for the remaining night-life. ③

Hôtel Safir, on the Place Administrative (☎07/37.19.21). Top of the market, with swimming pool *et al*, but business types prefer the *Hôtel Mamora* across the way. Ask for room at the back, overlooking the pool. ④

Camping La Chenaie, on the edge of town (☎07/36.30.01). As you approach from Rabat look for signs to the left to the *Complexe Touristique*. There's tennis, swimming pool and new football stadium. The campsite is good, inexpensive and secure.

If you're looking for **nightlife**, try the area around the triangular garden, at the junction of Av. Mohammed V, Av. Mohammed Diouri and the pedestrianized Rue Reine Elizabeth. Look for *Mama's Club*, *Le Village* night club/discotheque, *Big Boy* and *007*. Don't expect too much.

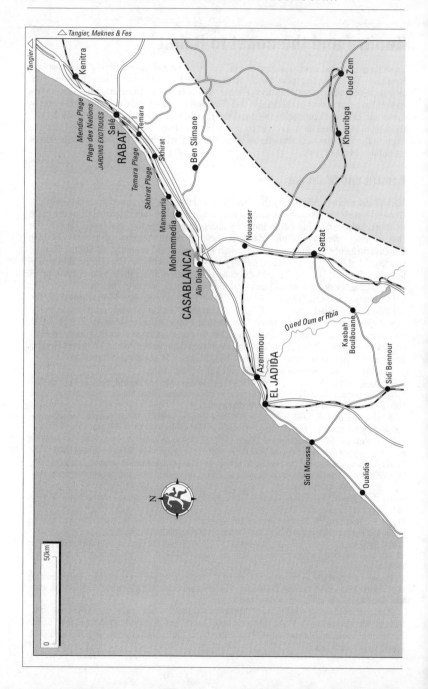

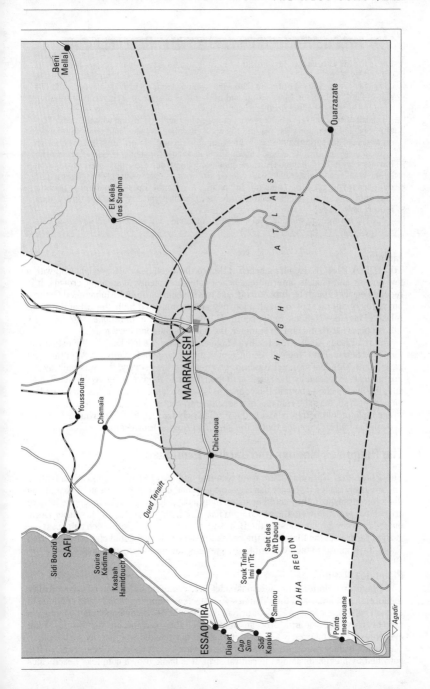

BIRD-WATCHING AT LAC DU SIDI BOURHABA

Lac de Sidi Bourhaba, just inland from Mehdiya, is a long, narrow freshwater lake, divided by a central causeway. The best viewing points for its rich birdlife are on the causeway, where the ever-present damselflies and dragonflies provide a spectacular display of flight and colour. Marsh frogs and Berber toad also make their vocal contribution from the sanctuary of the northern reedbeds.

The **birdlife** of Sidi Bourhaba is outstanding. The reedbeds throng with the calls of flitting reed and melodious warbler and the open stretches of water hold good numbers of crested coot (in spring) and marbled teal (in autumn and winter). It is, however, for its birds of prey that the site is best known. Circling almost constantly overhead are **marsh harriers**, with their characteristic low quartering flight, and these are joined on occasion by the smaller and whiter black-shouldered **kite** with its diagnostic black shoulders (and red eyes if you get close enough!). In winter, look for the **European hobby, greater flamingo** and, at any time, **wading godwits**. At sunset you may also see the **African marsh owl**.

In early spring, you will find wild crocuses, marigolds and white broom.

Mehdiya

MEHDIYA PLAGE, Kenitra's beach, 11km to the west, is a dull, greyish strip with a few houses and chalets, intermittent beach cafés and plenty of summer crowds. It is reached easily enough by *grand taxi* (these leave Kenitra from Av. Mohammed Diouri), but if you're after a spot to break a journey and swim, you'd be better off at the more relaxed Plage des Nations, to the south. The only **hotel**, the *Atlantique* (☎07/38.81.16; ③), is open year round and, in summer, the bar puts on good local music.

The road from Kenitra to Mehdiya Plage runs along the left bank of the estuary of the Oued Sebou. First, you will see on your right the large **fish cannery**. After this, you pass below Mehdiya's ruined **Kasbah.** Overlooking the estuary, this was built by the Portuguese, extended by the Spanish, demolished and then restored by Moulay Ismail and, finally, knocked about in the course of US troop landings in the last war (see box on p.288); it shelters the remains of a seventeenth-century governor's palace.

A couple of kilometres inland is the birdlife-rich **Lac de Sidi Bourhaba** (see box above), flanked by a *koubba* that is the site of an August **moussem**.

The Plage des Nations and Jardins Exotiques

The **Plage des Nations** (22km from Kenitra) and **Jardins Exotiques** (6km further on) are easily visited if you are driving the coast road between Kenitra and Rabat. If you don't have transport, they could be taken in as a day-trip from Rabat. In summer, there are regular *grands taxis* to the beach from Rabat's satellite town of Salé, as well as a local bus (#28; every 20min from the the Bab Khemis terminal in Salé), which runs past the gardens and on to the turn-off to the beach. Alternatively, you could charter a taxi from Rabat (or Kenitra) to take you out to the gardens and/or beach, and back.

Plage des Nations

The **Plage des Nations**, or Sidi Bouknadel as it's sometimes known, was named after the foreign diplomats and their families who started swimming there – and continue to do so. Unlike the capital's Kasbah or Salé beaches, it has a cosmopolitan feel and is a rare beach where young Moroccan women feel able to come out for the day. With everyone here to take a day's holiday, it's also a very relaxed and friendly sort of place. The beach itself is excellent, with big, exciting waves – but dangerous currents, so it is patrolled by lifeguards along the central strip. It is flanked by a couple of beach cafés and the modern and recently enlarged *Hôtel Firdaous* (☎07/82.21.31; ④), which has a swimming pool open to all for a small charge, plus a snack bar and two restaurants.

The beach lies 2km off the P2 coast raod, reached along an asphalted track. On the main road, directly opposite the turn-off, is an old mansion recently opened as the **Museé Dar Beghazi** , after its enterprising Fassi owner (☎07/82.21.78; open Mon–Sat; 50dh). This has a fine collection of carpets, woodwork, armour, jewellery – and a coach.

If you take the #28 bus from Salé to Plage des Nations, be aware that it turns round a couple of kilometres before the beach turn-off, just after the village of BOUKNADEL. Most passengers get out here and head left for the beach: a forty-minute walk along a path that heads off diagonally towards the sea, past market gardens, round some woods and then joins the final stretch of the asphalt road.

Jardins Exotiques

The **Jardins Exotiques** were laid out by one M. François in the early 1950s, in what contemporary French guidebooks called "une manière remarquable". They fell into something of a decline in the 1980s but have recently been taken over by the Ministry of the Interior, whose gardeners have been assiduously renovating the various original creations. If you can visit the gardens in spring or early summer, they are a delight.

Entering the gardens (open daily 9am–6pm; 10dh admission), you find yourself directed across a series of precarious bamboo bridges and dot-directed routes through a sequence of regional creations. There is a **Brazilian rain forest**, dense with water and orchids; a formal **Japanese garden**; and then suddenly a great shaft of **French Polynesia**, with rickety summerhouses set amid long pools, turtles paddling past, palm trees all round and flashes of bright-red flowers. The last of the series, returning to a more local level, is an **Andalucian garden** with a fine collection of Moroccan plants.

The gardens, in addition, have a little **zoo**, with five Barbary apes from the Middle Atlas, and a rather half-hearted children's playground. There is, as yet, no café.

Rabat

Capital of the nation since independence – and, before that, from 1912 to 1956, of the French Protectorate – **RABAT** is in many ways the city you'd expect: elegant in its spacious European grid, slightly self-conscious in its civilized modern ways, and, as an administrative centre, a little bit dull. If you arrive during Ramadan, you'll find the main avenues and boulevards an astonishing night-long promenade – at other times, it's hard to find a café open past ten at night. Rabat, as they tell you in Casa, is *provincial*.

None of this makes any difference to the considerable historic and architectural interest in the city – and across the estuary in Salé – which include some of the finest and oldest Arab monuments in the country, dating from the Almohad and Merenid dynasties. You can spend an enjoyable few days looking round these, and out on the local beaches, and there is a major plus in that, unlike Fes or Marrakesh, you can get round the place quite happily without a guide, and talk in cafés with people who do not depend on tourist money.

Some history

Rabat's **monuments** punctuate the span of Moroccan history. The plains inland, designated *Maroc Utile* by the French, have been occupied and cultivated since Paleolithic times, and there were Neolithic settlements on the coast south of Rabat, notably at present-day Temara and Skhirat.

Both Phoenicians and Carthaginians established trading posts on modern-day Rabat's estuary site. The earliest known settlement, *Sala*, occupied the citadel known today as **Chellah**. Here, after the demise of the Carthaginians, the **Romans** created their southernmost colony. It lasted well beyond the breakup of the empire in Africa and eventually formed the basis of an independent Berber state, which reached its peak of influence in the eighth century, developing a code of government inspired by the Koran but adapted to Berber customs and needs. It represented a challenge to the Islamic orthodoxy of the **Arab** rulers of the interior, however, and to stamp out the heresy, a *ribat* – the fortified monastery from which the city takes its name – was founded on the site of the present-day Kasbah.

The *ribat's* activities led to Chellah's decline – a process hastened in the eleventh century by the founding of a new town, **Salé**, across the estuary. But with the arrival of the **Almohads** in the twelfth century, the Rabat Kasbah was rebuilt and a city again took shape around it. The Almohad fort, renamed **Ribat El Fathi** (Stronghold of Victory), served as a launching point for the dynasty's campaigns in Spain, which by 1170 had returned virtually all of Andalucia to Muslim rule.

Under the Almohad Caliph **Yacoub El Mansour,** a new Imperial Capital was created. Its legacy includes the superb **Oudaïa Gate** of the Kasbah, **Bab Er Rouah** at the southwest edge of town, and the early stages of the **Hassan Mosque.** Until recent years, this was the largest ever undertaken in Morocco and its minaret, standing high above the river, is still the city's great landmark. Mansour also erected over five kilometres of fortifications – but neither his vision nor his success in maintaining a Spanish empire was to be lasting. He left the Hassan Mosque unfinished, and only in the last sixty years has the city expanded to fill his dark circuit of *pisé* walls.

After Mansour's death, Rabat's significance was dwarfed by the imperial cities of Fes, Meknes and Marrakesh, and the city fell into neglect. Sacked by the Portuguese, it was little more than a village when, as New Salé, it was resettled by seventeenth-century Andalucian refugees. In this revived form, however, it entered into an extraordinary period of international piracy and local autonomy. Its corsair fleets, the **Sallee Rovers,** specialized in the plunder of merchant ships returning to Europe from West Africa and the Spanish Americas, but on occasion raided as far afield as Plymouth and the Irish coast – Daniel Defoe's Robinson Crusoe began his captivity "carry'd prisoner into Sallee, a Moorish port".

The Andalucians, owing no loyalty to the Moorish sultans and practically impregnable within their Kasbah perched high on a rocky bluff above the river, established their own pirate state, the **Republic of the Bou Regreg**. They rebuilt the Medina below the Kasbah in a style reminiscent of their homes in Spanish Badajoz, dealt in arms with the English and French, and even accepted European consuls, before the town finally reverted to government control under Moulay Rashid, and his successor, Moulay Ismail. Unofficial piracy continued until 1829 when Austria took revenge for the loss of a ship by shelling Rabat and other coastal towns. From then until the French creation of a capital, Rabat-Salé was very much a backwater.

Arrival, orientation and hotels

With its **Medina** and **Ville Nouvelle** bounded by the river and Almohad walls, central Rabat never feels like a big city, and indeed all the city's points of interest are within easy walking distance. Our **maps** (a general one is on pp.254–255; an enlargement of the Kasbah des Oudaïas appears on p.260; and Salé is covered in a separate map on p.271) are adequate for most purposes.

Accommodation

Hotel space can be tight in midsummer, and especially in July, when budget-priced rooms, in particular, are at a premium. It's best, if at all possible, to make an advance

POINTS OF ARRIVAL

BY TRAIN

By far the easiest way to arrive. The **Rabat Ville** station (don't get off at Rabat Salé, across the estuary in Salé, nor at Rabat Agdal, serving the southern suburbs of Rabat) is at the heart of the Ville Nouvelle, with many hotels within a few minutes' walk. On the concourse, there is a *BMCE* branch, a *Budget* car rental desk (07/70.57.89) and a Tourisme kiosk which can help with train times but little else.

BY BUS

The main bus terminal is located in Place Zerktouni – 3km out from the centre by the road junction for Casa and Beni Mellal. To get into town from here (or vice versa), you'll have to take a local bus (#30 and others stop along Bd. Hassan II by the Hôtel Majestic) or compete for a *petit taxi* (6dh or so – usually metered – for up to three people). Easier, if you are coming by bus from the north, is to get off in **Salé** (see p.270) and take a *grand taxi* from there into Rabat; the distance is no greater than staying on the bus until the main bus terminal and then returning to the town centre by local bus or *petit taxi*. Experienced travellers, with little or no luggage, advocate splitting the difference by asking the bus driver to stop on the dual carriageway between the Kasbah des Oudaïas and the Medina, and then walking through the latter to Bd. Hassan II and the Ville Nouvelle.

BY GRAND TAXI

Grands taxis for non-local destinations operate from outside the main bus station (see above). Those from/to Casa cost only a couple of dirhams more than the bus and leave more or less continuously through the day. *Grands taxis* to Skhirat, Bouknadel and other local destinations leave from the lengthy and chaotic stands on Bd. Hassan II, such as those at Bab El Djedid or near the old *Hôtel Beauregreg*.

BY AIR

From the **Mohammed V Airport** (out beyond Casablanca), **buses** run to the square outside the Hôtel Terminus (by the train station); journey time is approximately 90 minutes. Departures **to the airport** from Rabat are (currently) at 6.25am, 9.50am, 10.20am and 3pm; tickets are sold at a kiosk by the departure point (open 8.30am–noon and 2.30–6.30pm). In both directions, specify *le prochain depart* (the next service). **Grands taxis** are an expensive alternative (400dh), unless you can split the fare; the airport is also connected by **train** with Casablanca Voyageurs and Casablanca Port (see p.282). With a dozen trains a day between the airport and Casablanca and good connections with Rabat, the bus is now little used and consequently runs less frequently – and may be discontinued.

CITY BUSES AND TAXIS

Local bus services radiate out from Bd. Hassan II. Buses #1, #2 and #4 run from here (via Av. Allal Ben Abdallah) to Bab Zaer and close to Chellah; #6 and #12 cross the bridge to Salé; and #17 heads south to Temara Beach.

Petits and **grands taxis** can be found on Bd. Hassan II and by the train station. Note that *petits taxis* are not allowed to run between Rabat and Salé.

reservation by phone. A couple of cheapies aside, all of the better hotels are to be found in the Ville Nouvelle – the modern quarters of the city – and there is little to gain here from staying in the Medina, which is in any case only a stroll across the boulevard.

The nearest **campsite** is across the river at **Salé**; it has recently been revamped and is pleasant and well equipped.

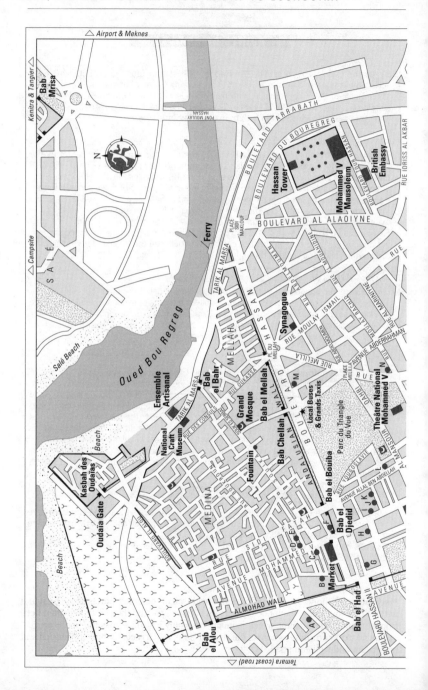

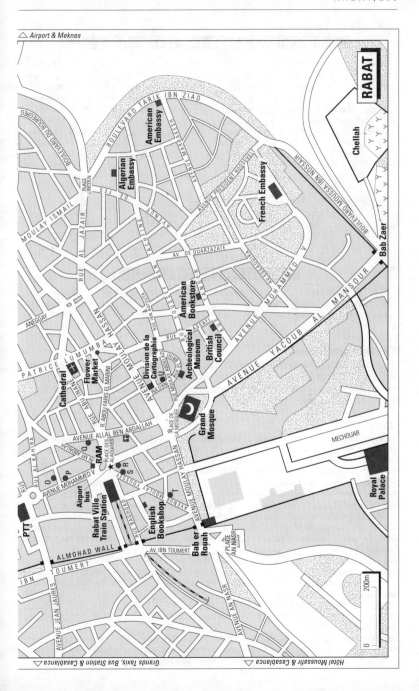

△ Airport & Meknes

RABAT

Chellah

BOULEVARD DU BOURREG

BOULEVARD TARIK IBN ZIAD

American Embassy

Algerian Embassy

PLACE LINCOLN

MOULAY ISMAIL

RUE AL JAZAIR

DE FES

AVENUE LACHFINE

AVENUE PRESIDENT ROSEVELT

AV. DE OUARAZATE

French Embassy

BOULEVARD MOUSSA IBN MOSSOR

Bab Zaer

ANEGGAY

RUE MOULAY HASSAN

AVENUE PATRICE LUMUMBA

AVENUE MOULAY ABDALLAH

RUE YOUSSEF

RUE IBN BATOUTA

American Bookstore

Archeological Museum

ANGEL

ALISSAOUA

AVENUE MOHAMMED V

AVENUE YACOUB AL MANSOUR

Cathedral

Flower Market

RUE ABOU INANE

RUE ABOU FARIS EL MARINI

Division de la Cartographie

RUE DEM

RUE MOULAY ISMAIL

RUE THIBET

British Council

ASSAFI

AVENUE

Grand Mosque

PLACE DE LA MOSQUEE

AVENUE ALLAL BEN ABDALLAH

RAM

RUE AV ABDALLAH

AVENUE MOHAMMED V

S R

PLACE DES ALAOUITES

RUE BAGHDAD

AVENUE MOULAY YOUSSEF

AVENUE MOULAY HASSAN

MECHOUAR

RUE AL KAHIRA

Airport bus

Rabat Ville Train Station

English Bookshop

Bab er Rouah

Royal Palace

PTT

ALMOHAD WALL

AV. IBN TOUMERT

PLACE AN NASR

IBN TOUMERT

AVENUE JEAN JAURES

AVENUE AN NASR

200m

0

▽ Grands Taxis, Bus Station & Casablanca

▽ Casablanca

▽ Hotel Moussafir & Casablanca

HOTEL PRICE CODES AND STAR RATINGS

Hotels are no longer obliged to charge according to the official star-ratings (from 1* to 5* luxury), as had long been the custom. Nevertheless, **prices** continue to reflect the star-ratings acquired. The basis of our own **hotel price codes**, set out below and keyed throughout the guide, is the price currently quoted for the cheapest double room in high season (June–September) – and is thus more reliable than quoting notional prices according to star-rating.

Note that cheaper prices in the lower categories are generally for rooms with just a washbasin – you always pay extra for **en-suite** shower and WC – and that double rooms can generally be converted into **triples/family rooms**, with extra beds, for a modest extra charge. Note also that the prices quoted by all hotels are subject to various local and regional **taxes**, which can add 15 to 20 percent to the bill.

Our code	Classification	Single room price	Double room price
⓪	Unclassified	25–60dh	50–99dh
①	1*A/1*B	60–105dh	100–149dh
②	2*B/2*A	105–145dh	150–199dh
③	3*B/3*A	145–225dh	200–299dh
④	4*B/4*A	225–400dh	300–599dh
⑤	5*luxury	Upwards of 400dh	Upwards of 600dh

TELEPHONE CODES

All telephone numbers in the Rabat/Kenitra region are prefixed **07**. When making a call within the region you omit this prefix. For more explanation of phone codes and making calls within (or to) Morocco, see pp.45–46.

Ville Nouvelle Hotels

Most of the Ville Nouvelle hotels are modest, French-built places. If your budget is limited, go for one of these as the four- and five-star hotels are mostly standard chain efforts, and there are better splurges elsewhere. All recommendations below are keyed on the main Rabat map (pp.254–255).

CHEAP

Auberge de Jeunesse (Youth Hostel) [A], 43 Bd. Marrassa (☎07/72.57.69). Conveniently sited, just west of the Almohad walls of the Medina and to the north of Bd. Hassan II. It is pleasant, clean and well furnished. IYHF card preferred and strict opening hours: 8–10am, noon–3pm and 6–10.30pm. Despite the 'cook pot' symbol in the IYHF guide, there are no self-catering facilities.

Hôtel Berlin [I], 261 Av. Mohammed V (☎07/72.34.35). A small nine-room establishment, with hot showers; located above the Chinese *Restaurant Hong Kong*. Central, and value for money. ①

Hôtel Central [O], 2 Rue Al Basra (☎07/70.73.56). Not to be confused with the *Hôtel du Centre* in the Medina (which is not recommended), this is one of the best cheapies in the city, located alongside the (prominent) *Hôtel Balima* on Av. Mohammed V – and thus convenient for restaurants, banks, the train station, and a nightcap at the *Balima* bar. There's also a pleasant café for breakfast, right next door. ①

Hôtel Gaulois [H], corner of Rue Hims and Av. Mohammed V (☎07/72.30.22). One of a cluster of budget hotels around the bottom end of Av. Mohammed V. The rooms do not live up to the spacious grand entrance, but are value for money, and you can pay a little more for a shower en suite. ①

Hôtel Majestic [G], 121 Av. Hassan II (☎07/72.29.97). This is a friendly old hotel with a faded charm, facing the Medina; it's often full, though, and you'll be lucky to find a room much after midday. There are good eating places nearby, including the next door *Café Restaurant Shahrazade*. ①

Hôtel Velleda [Q], 106 Av. Allal Ben Abdallah (☎07/76.95.31). A decent hotel near the train station, though not very easy to find, being tucked away on the fourth floor (there is a lift) above a dry cleaners/laundry. All rooms have showers and some have toilets as well. ①

MODERATE

Grand Hôtel [N], 19 Rue Patrice Lumumba (☎07/72.72.85). On the corner with Rue Moulay Rachid and almost opposite the Tourist Information Office which is always closed. The hotel is quiet and well established, with en-suite rooms, but the restaurant and the bar are nothing special. ③

Hôtel d'Orsay [S], 11 Av. Moulay Youssef, on Place de la Gare (☎07/70.13.19). The top choice in this budget – friendly, helpful and efficient, and convenient for the train station and numerous café-restaurants. It's very popular with Moroccan (and overseas) businessmen, so book ahead. ③

Hôtel de la Paix [K], 2 Rue Ghazza, on corner with Av. Allal Ben Abdallah (☎07/72.29.26). A reasonably pleasant downtown standby; en-suite showers; breakfasts extra. ②

Royal Hôtel [L], 1 Rue Amman, on corner with Av. Allal Ben Abdallah (☎07/72.11.71). Across the road from the *Royal Cinema*; comfortable and reasonable rooms, the best of which overlook the attractive Parc du Triangle de Vue. ③

Splendid Hôtel [J], 8 Rue Ghazza (☎07/72.32.83). This nice old hotel has a sense of better days; the best rooms overlook a courtyard which the owner plans to landscape. Opposite, the *Café-Restaurant Ghazza* is good for breakfast and snacks. ②

Hôtel Terminus [R] 384, Av. Mohammed V (☎07/70.06.16), Round the corner from *the Hôtel d'Orsay* and a possible alternative if it is full. It's a large, featureless block, but the interior has been recently updated and it's now reasonable. ③

EXPENSIVE

Hôtel Balima [P], corner of Rue Jakarta and Av. Mohammed V (☎07/70.86.25). This was once Rabat's top hotel and, though long overtaken, retains an Art Deco grandeur. It has been refurbished in recent years but still has quite reasonable prices, not least for its suites. Thami El Glaoui, Pasha of Marrakesh, (see p.338 and 384) stayed in one of these on his visits to the city in the early 1950s. The open-air café between the hotel and the avenue is shaded and popular; the bar has a rather shadier clientele – but is no less popular! ④

Hôtel Bélère [T], 33 Av. Moulay Youssef (☎07/70.98.01). Comfortable, air-conditioned tour-group hotel, well positioned for the train station. Rooms are OK but somewhat overpriced. ④

Hôtel Chellah [U], 2 Rue d'Ifni (☎07/70.10.51). An upmarket tour-group hotel with comfortable rooms in a rather characterless block, some way out from the centre and sights. On the plus side, it has a good grill-restaurant, *Le Kanoun*. ④

Medina hotels

These are the pick of the Medina's dozen or so hotels (again see main map for key).

CHEAP

Hôtel Dorhmi [F], 313 Av. Mohammed V (☎07/72.38.98). The best Medina choice – refurbished to a decent standard, and nicely positioned, just inside Bab El Djedid and above the pleasant *Café Essalam*. Competitive prices, though hot showers are extra. ①

France Hôtel [B], 46 Souk Semarine (☎07/72.34.57). At the far western side of the street by the market. Has a bit of character, with a banana tree patio and terrace. Basic facilities, but friendly – and there are excellent public showers in the next street. ①

Hôtel Al Maghrib Al Jadid [D], 2 Rue Sebbahi (☎07/73.22.07). Corner hotel on a side road off Av. Mohammed V. A reasonable pension, with hot and cold showers extra. ①

Hôtel Marrakesh [E], 10 Rue Sebbahi (☎07/72.77.03). Another decent if basic pension, with cold showers, but good-sized rooms, and friendly staff. ①

Hôtel les Voyageurs [C], 8 Rue Souk Semara – just off Av. Mohanmed V (☎07/72.37.20). The cheapest hotel in town – and often full. There are no showers, but it's otherwise satisfactory. ①

The Medina and souks

Rabat's **Medina** – all that there was of the city until the French arrived in 1912 – is a compact quarter, wedged on two sides by the sea and the river, on the others by the twelfth-century Almohad and seventeenth-century Andalucian walls. It is not the most interesting Medina in the country – open and orderly in comparison to those of Fes or

Marrakesh, for example – but coming here from the adjacent avenues of the modern capital it remains a surprise. In appearance, the quarter is still essentially the town created by Andalucian Muslim refugees from Badajoz in Spain, and with these external features intact, its way of life seems remarkably at odds with the government business and cosmopolitanism of the Ville Nouvelle.

That this is possible – here and throughout the old cities of Morocco – is largely due to **Marshal Lyautey**, the first, and certainly the most sympathetic to the indigenous culture, of France's Resident Generals. Colonizing Algeria over the previous century, the French had destroyed most of the Arab towns, replacing their traditional structures (evolved through the needs of Islamic customs) with completely European plans. In Rabat, Lyautey found this system already under way, the builders tearing down parts of the Medina for the construction of a new town and administrative quarters. Realizing the aesthetic loss – and the inappropriateness of wholesale "Europeanization" – he ordered work to be halted and the Ville Nouvelle built outside the walls.

It was a precedent accepted throughout the French and Spanish zones of the colony, a policy which inevitably created "native quarters", but one which also preserved continuity, maintained the nation's past and, at least so Lyautey believed, showed the special relationship of the Protectorate. Lyautey himself resigned and left Morocco in 1925 but when he died in 1934 he was returned to Morocco and buried in a Moorish monument in Rabat. Symbolism was reversed when, in 1961, his body was 'repatriated' and entombed in Les Invalides, the soldiers' church, in Paris.

Into the Medina

The basic grid-like regularity of its Medina, cut by a number of long main streets, makes Rabat a good place to get to grips with the feel and lay-out of a Moroccan city. Its plan is typical, with a main market street – **Rue Souika** and its continuation **Souk Es Sebbat** – running beside the Grand Mosque, and behind it a residential area scattered with smaller *souks* and "parish" mosques. The buildings, characteristically Andalucian, in the style of Tetouan or Chaouen, are part stone and part whitewash, with splashes of yellow and turquoise and great, dark-wood studded doors.

From **Bd. Hassan II**, half a dozen gates and a series of streets give access to the Medina, all leading more or less directly through the quarter, to emerge near the Kasbah and the hillside cemetery. On the west side, the two main streets – **Av. Mohammed V** and **Rue Sidi Fatah** – are really continuations of Ville Nouvelle avenues, though, flanked by working-class café-restaurants and cell-like hotels, their character is immediately different. Entering along either street, past a lively, modern food market and a handful of stalls selling fruit, juice and snacks, you can turn very shortly to the right and come out on the cubicle shops of **Rue Souika**. Dominated by textiles and silverware along the initial stretch, these give way to a concentration of *babouche* and other shoe stalls as you approach the Grand Mosque. They are all fairly everyday – though quite high quality – shops, not for the most part geared to tourists.

Stalls selling cheaper goods, and the *joutia* (flea market), are off towards the river, round the old Jewish quarter of the Mellah (see below). Along the way are few buildings of particular interest, as most of the medieval city – which predated that of the Andalucians on this site – was destroyed by Portuguese raids in the sixteenth century.

The **Grand Mosque**, founded by the Merenids in the fourteenth century, is a partial exception, though it has been considerably rebuilt – its minaret, for example, was only completed in 1939. Entry to the mosque is, as throughout Morocco, forbidden to non-Muslims. Opposite, there is a small example of Merenid decoration in the stone facade of a public **fountain**, which now forms the front of an Arabic bookshop.

The Mellah and Joutia

The most direct approach from Bd. Hassan II to the Grand Mosque section of the Medina is through **Bab Chellah**, which gives way onto a broad, tree-lined, pedestrian way. Alternatively, continuing a couple of blocks (past the old *Hôtel Bou Regreg*), you can go in by the **Bab El Mellah**, which gives onto Rue Oukassa.

To the east of this street is the **Mellah**, the old Jewish quarter, and still the poorest and most run-down area of the city. It was designated as a Jewish quarter only in 1808 – Jews previously owned several properties on Rue des Consuls, to the north – and no longer has a significant Jewish population. If you can find a local guide, you may be able to look into some of its seventeen former **synagogues**. None of these function: the only active synagogue in the city is a modern building, one block from here, at the bottom end of Rue Moulay Ismail.

With its meat and produce markets, the Mellah looks a somewhat uninviting and impenetrable area, but it is worth a wander through towards the river. A **Joutia**, or **flea market**, spreads out along the streets below Souk Es Sebbat, down to Bab El Bahr. There are clothes, pieces of machinery, and vendors touting wonderful old movie posters, garishly illustrating titles like *Police Militaire* and *La Fille du Désert*.

Towards the Kasbah: Rue des Consuls

Beyond the Mellah, heading towards the Kasbah, you can walk out by **Bab El Bahr** and follow an avenue near the riverside up to the Oudaïa Gate; to the left of this busy main road is the *Musée National de l'Artisanat* (National Craft Museum) currently being rehoused and refurbished; directly opposite is a lively, above-average **Ensemble Artisanal** (Mon–Sat: 9am–6pm). Here you can watch, and buy, a range of crafts: embroidery, silk belts, small carpets, leather, copper and wood.

Rue des Consuls, a block inland is not so busy and is a more interesting approach; like the Mellah, this, too, used to be a reserved quarter – the only street of the nineteenth-century city where European consuls were permitted to live. Many of the residency buildings survive, as do a number of impressive merchants' *fondouks* – most in the alleys off to the left. The main street, particularly at its upper end, is largely a centre for **rug and carpet shops** and on Monday and Thursday mornings becomes a **souk**, with locals bringing carpets – new and old – to sell.

Rabat carpets, woven with very bright dyes (which, if vegetable-based, will fade), are a traditional cottage industry in the Medina, though they're now often made in workshops, one of which you can see on the Kasbah's *platforme* (see below). Some of the traditional carpets on sale, particularly in the shops, will have come from further afield. They are officially 'graded' (superior, extra superior, etc) at a special centre just off Rue des Consuls – to the right as you climb towards the Kasbah.

The Kasbah des Oudaïas

The site of the original *ribat* and citadel of the Almohad, Merenid and Andalucian towns, the **Kasbah des Oudaïas** is a striking and evocative quarter. Its principal gateway, the **Bab Oudaïa**, is perhaps the most beautiful in the Moorish world, and within the Kasbah walls is the **Museum of Moroccan Arts**, housed in a seventeenth-century palace, and a perfect **Andalucian garden**.

The Bab Oudaïa

The **Bab Oudaïa**, like so many of the great external monuments of Morocco, is of Almohad foundation. Built around 1195, concurrently with the Hassan Tower, it was inserted by Yacoub El Mansour within a line of walls already built by his grandfather, Abd El Moumen. The walls in fact extended well to its west, leading down to the sea

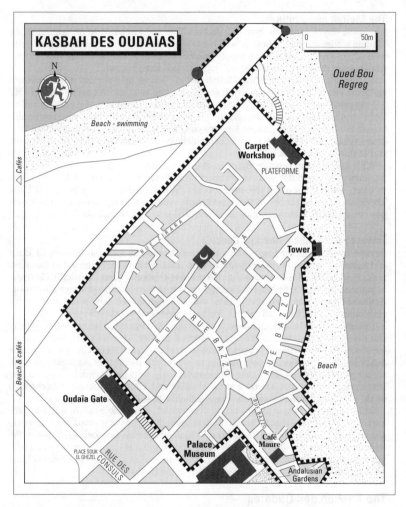

KASBAH DES OUDAÏAS

N

0   50m

Oued Bou Regreg

Beach - swimming

△ *Cafés*

Carpet Workshop

PLATEFORME

RUE ZRARA

RUE DJEMAA

Tower

△ *Beach & cafés*

RUE

RUE BAZZO

RUE BAZZO

RUE BAZZO

Beach

Oudaïa Gate

RUE BAZZO

PLACE SOUK EL GHEZEL

RUE DES CONSULS

Palace Museum

Café Maure

Andalusian Gardens

at the edge of the Medina, and the gate cannot have been designed for any real defensive purpose – its function and importance must have been purely ceremonial. It was to be the heart of the Kasbah, its chambers acting as a courthouse and staterooms, with everything of importance taking place nearby. The **Souk El Ghezel** – the main commercial centre of the medieval town, including its wool and slave markets – was located just outside the gate, while the original sultanate's palace stood immediately inside it.

The gate itself doesn't impress so much by its size, which is not unusual for an Almohad structure, as by the visual strength and simplicity of its decoration. This is based on a typically Islamic rhythm, establishing a tension between the exuberant, outward expansion of the arches and the heavy, enclosing rectangle of the gate itself. Looking at the two for a few minutes, you begin to sense a kind of optical illusion –

the shapes appear suspended by the great rush of movement from the centre of the arch. The basic feature is, of course, the arch, which here is a sequence of three, progressively more elaborate: first, the basic horseshoe; then, two "filled" or decorated ones, the latter with the distinctive Almohad *darj w ktarf* patterning, a cheek-and-shoulder design somewhat like a fleur-de-lis. At the top, framing the design, is a band of geometric ornamentation, cut off in what seems to be an arbitrary manner but which again creates the impression of movement and continuation outside the gate.

The dominant motifs – scallop-shell-looking palm fronds – are also characteristically Almohad, though without any symbolic importance; in fact, there's very little that's symbolic in the European sense in any Islamic decoration, the object being merely to distract the eye sufficiently to allow contemplation.

Around the Kasbah

You can enter the **Kasbah** proper through the Oudaïa Gate (or, if it's closed, through the small gateway on its right), or by a lower, horseshoe arch at the base of the ceremonial stairway. This latter approach leads directly to the **Andalucian gardens** and **palace museum**, which can also be reached fairly easily after a short loop through the Kasbah, along Rue Djemaa and, then right, down Rue Bazzo.

An airy, village-like part of the city, the Kasbah is a pleasant quarter in which to wander – and not remotely dangerous or "closed to visitors" as the hustlers round the gate may try to suggest. Hardly more than 150m from one end to the other, it's not a place where you really need a guide; but if you're approached, talk to the hustlers, be easygoing and explain you're only wandering down to *la plateforme*.

Once inside the Oudaïa Gate, it would actually be hard not to find the way down to the *plateforme* since the single main street, **Rue Djemaa** (Street of the Mosque), runs straight down to a broad belvedere/terrace commanding views of the river and sea. Along the way, you pass by the **Kasbah Mosque**, the city's oldest, founded in 1050, though rebuilt in the eighteenth century by an English renegade known as Ahmed El Inglisi – one of a number of European pirates who joined up with the Sallee Rovers.

El Inglisi was also responsible for several of the forts built below and round the seventeenth-century **Plateforme**, originally a semaphore station, on which was built an eighteenth-century warehouse, now housing a carpet co-operative workshop. The guns of the forts and the *plateforme* regularly echoed across the estuary in Salé. The Bou Regreg ("Father of Reflection") River is quite open at this point and it would appear to have left the corsair fleets vulnerable, harboured a little downstream, where the fishing boats today ferry people across to Salé. In fact, a long sandbank lies submerged across the mouth of the estuary – a feature much exploited by the shallow-keeled pirate ships, which would draw the merchant ships in pursuit, only to leave them stranded within the sights of the city's cannon. This is action which you can imagine, up here amid the low-lying alleys and the sea towers, though, as so often in Morocco, it is hard to come to terms with just how recent a past it is.

At the same time, the long sandbank, which contributed to the prosperity of Rabat/Salé until the mid-nineteenth century, proved a handicap in the early twentieth century and diverted commercial trade to the better endowed Casablanca.

From the *plateforme*, it is possible to climb down towards the *Restaurant Caravelle* (see p.267) – a good lunch stop – and the **beach**, crowded with locals throughout the summer, as is the Salé strip across the water. Neither of these beaches is very inviting, in fact, and if you're more interested in swimming than in keeping your head above the polluted water, you'd be better off at the more relaxed (and less exclusively male) sands at the Plage des Nations or Temara Plage (see p.250 and 274).

The Palace Museum and Gardens

Getting down to the **Palace Museum** and gardens is fairly straightforward: from Rue Djemaa, the main Kasbah street, Rue Bazzo zigzags down towards them.

Depending on which fork you take, you'll come out either by the entrance to the palace or at the **Café Maure** – beside the gardens. Oddly enough, the café is not at all "Moorish" but it's a fine place to retreat: high on a terrace overlooking the river, serving mint tea, brewed up on an ancient brazier, and trays of pastries. It is used as much by Moroccans as tourists, and is ordinarily priced.

The **Palace** itself is seventeenth century, one of many built by Moulay Ismail, the first sultan since Almohad times to force a unified control over the country. Ismail, whose base was at Meknes, gave Rabat – or New Salé, as it was then known – a relatively high priority. Having subdued the pirates' republic, he took over the Kasbah as a garrison for the Oudaïas – Saharan tribesmen who accepted military service in return for tax exemption, and who formed an important part of his mercenary army. This move was in part because they proved uncontrollable in Fes or Meknes, but it was also an effective way of ensuring that the pirates kept up their tribute with a constant supply of slaves and booty.

An interesting building in its own right, the palace and adjacent buildings now house the fine **Museum of Moroccan Arts** (9am–noon and 3–5.30pm; closed Tues; 10dh admits to all buildings). At any time, some exhibits are being restored or loaned elsewhere. Thus some collections, described in current publicity, are sometimes – and often inexplicably – missing. The lack of explanation, and occasionally disinterest, of those on duty can be frustrating.

In this case, the buildings themselves compensate for any disappointment about the contents, however. The design of the main building is classic: a series of reception rooms grouped round a central court, giving access to the private quarters where you can take a look at the small *hammam* – a feature of all noble mansions. Within the main building, there are usually displays of Berber and Arab jewellery from most of the regions of Morocco, while the main reception hall has been furnished in the styles of nineteenth-century Rabat and Fes. A room just off to the left as you leave is often kept shut, though opened on request; once the palace mosque, it usually houses a display of local carpets.

In a nearby building, against the Kasbah wall, there is a display of traditional Berber costumes from the Rif to the Tafilalt, with some of the best examples coming from the Zemmour region around Khémisset. Back in the main building, you should ask after the display of Berber musical instruments currently being restored. These particular items, together with the carpets and costumes, again reveal the startling closeness of a medieval Andalucian past.

The beautiful **Andalucian Gardens** occupy the old palace grounds. What you see today was actually constructed by the French in the present century – though true to Spanish-Andalucian tradition, with deep, sunken beds of shrubs and flowering annuals. If you're familiar with Granada, it is illuminating to compare the authentic Moorish concept here with the neat box hedges with which the Alhambra has been restored. But historical authenticity aside, it is a delightful place, full of the scent of datura, bougainvillea and a multitude of herbs and flowers. It has a definite modern role, too, as a meeting place for women, who gather here in dozens of small groups on a Friday or Sunday afternoon.

The Hassan Mosque and Mohammed V Mausoleum

The most ambitious of all Almohad buildings, the **Hassan Mosque** and its vast minaret dominates almost every view of the capital – a majestic sight from the Kasbah, from Salé, or glimpsed as you arrive across the river by train. If it had been completed, it would (in its time) have been the second largest mosque in the Islamic world, outflanked only by the one in Smarra, Iraq. Even today its size seems a novelty.

There is also the poignancy of its ruin. Designed by El Mansour as the centrepiece of the new capital and as a celebration of his great victory over the Spanish kings at Alarcos, the mosque's construction seems to have been more or less abandoned at his death in 1199. The tower was probably left much as it appears today; the mosque's hall, roofed in cedar, was used until the Great Earthquake of 1755 (which destroyed central Lisbon) brought down its central columns. Its extent, however, must always have seemed an elaborate folly. Morocco's most important mosque, the Kairaouine in Fes, is less than half the Hassan's size, but served a much greater population, with adequate space for 20,000 worshippers. Bearing in mind that it is only men who gather for the weekly Friday prayer – when a town traditionally comes together in its Grand Mosque – Rabat would have needed a population of well over 100,000 to make adequate use of the Hassan's capacity. As it was, the city never really took off under the later Almohads and Merenids, and when Leo Africanus came here in 1600, he found no more than a hundred households, gathered for security within the Kasbah.

The **tower**, or minaret, was begun by Yacoub El Mansour in 1195 – at the same time as the Koutoubia in Marrakesh and the Giralda in Seville – and it is one of the few Moroccan buildings which approach the European idea of monumentality. This is due in part to its site, on a level above the river and most of the city, but perhaps equally to its unfinished solidity. The other great Moroccan minarets, perfectly balanced by their platform decoration and lanterns, are left "hanging" as if with no particular weight or height. The Hassan Tower, with no such movement, stands firmly rooted in the ground.

The minaret is unusually positioned at the centre rather than the northern corner of the rear of the mosque. Some 50m tall in its present state, it would probably have been around 80m if finished to normal proportions – a third again the height of Marrakesh's Koutoubia. Despite its apparent simplicity, it is perhaps the most complex of all Almohad structures. Each facade is different, with a distinct combination of patterning, yet the whole intricacy of blind arcades and interlacing curves is based on just two formal designs. On the south and west faces these are the *darj w ktarf* of the Oudaïa Gate; on the north and east is the *shabka* (net) motif, an extremely popular form adapted by the Almohads from the lobed arches of the Cordoba Grand Mosque – and still in contemporary use.

The Mohammed V Mausoleum

Facing the tower – in an assertion of Morocco's historical independence and continuity – are the **Mosque and Mausoleum of Mohammed V**, begun on the king's death in 1961 and inaugurated six years later. The **Mosque**, extending between a stark pair of pavilions, gives a somewhat foreshortened idea of how the Hassan Mosque must once have appeared, roofed in its traditional green tiles.

The **Mausoleum**, designed by a Vietnamese architect, Vo Toan, was one of the great prestige projects of modern Morocco. Its brilliantly surfaced marbles and spiralling designs, however, seem to pay homage to traditional Moroccan techniques, while failing to capture their rhythms and unity. It is, nevertheless, an important shrine for Moroccans – and one which, unusually, non-Muslims are permitted to visit. You file past fabulously costumed royal guards to an interior balcony; the tomb, carved from white onyx, lies below, groups of old men squatting beside it, reading from the Koran.

Around the Ville Nouvelle

French in construction, style and feel, the **Ville Nouvelle** provides the main focus of Rabat's life, above all in the cafés and promenades of the broad, tree-lined Av. Mohammed V, and in the pleasant **Parque du Triangle de Vue**, opposite the south wall of the Medina – popular afternoon meeting places; the park closes around 6pm). Another attractive and colourful spot is the **Flower Market**, held in a sunken garden just to the north of Av. Moulay Hassan.

There's a certain grandeur in some of the old, *Mauresque* public buildings around the main boulevards, too, which were built with as much desire to impress as any earlier epoch. However, it is the **Almohad walls and gates**, the **citadel of Chellah** (see the next section) and the excellent **Archeological Museum** which hold most of interest in the quarter.

The walls and gates

More-or-less complete sections of the **Almohad walls** run right down from the Kasbah to the Royal Palace and beyond – an extraordinary monument to Yacoub El Mansour's vision. Along their course four of the original **gates** survive. Three – **Bab El Alou, Bab El Had** and **Bab Zaer** – are very modest. The fourth, **Bab Er Rouah** (Gate of the Wind), is on an entirely different scale, recalling and in many ways rivalling the Oudaïa.

Contained within a massive stone bastion, **Bab Er Rouah** again achieves the tension of movement – with its sunlike arches contained within a square of Koranic inscription – and a similar balance between simplicity and ornament. The east side, approached from outside the walls, is the main facade, and must have been designed as a monumental approach to the city; the shallow-cut, floral relief between arch and square is arguably the finest anywhere in Morocco. Inside, you can appreciate the gate's archetypal defensive structure – the three domed chambers aligned to force a sharp double turn. They are used for exhibitions and usually open.

From Bab Er Rouah, it's a fifteen-minute walk down towards the last Almohad gate, the much-restored **Bab Zaer**, and the entrance to the **Necropolis of Chellah.** On the way, you pass a series of modern gates leading off to the vast enclosures of the **Royal Palace** – which is really more a collection of palaces, built mainly in the nineteenth century and decidedly off-limits to casual visitors – and, off to the left (opposite the *Hôtel Chellah*), the Archeological Museum.

The Archeological Museum

Rabat's Archeological Museum on Rue Brihi (9–11.30am and 2.30–5.30pm; closed Tues; 10dh) is the most important in Morocco. Although small – surprisingly so in a country which saw substantial Phoenician and Carthaginian settlement and three centuries of Roman rule – it houses an exceptional collection of Roman era bronzes.

The bronzes are displayed in a special annexe with a separate entrance; if it is closed, seek entry (at no extra cost). They date from the first and second centuries AD and were found mainly at the provincial capital of Volubilis (near Meknes), together with a few pieces from Chellah and the colonies of Banasa and Thamusida. Highlights include superb figures of a guard dog and a rider, and two magnificent portrait heads, reputedly those of Cato the Younger (Caton d'Utique) and Juba II – the last significant ruler of the Romanized Berber kingdoms of Mauretania and Numidia before the assertion of direct imperial rule. Both of these busts were found in the House of Venus at Volubilis.

Back in the main building, there are showcases on two floors; each contains finds from different digs, of little interest unless you have already visited the area – or plan to do so. Captions are in French and, if you ask, you may be provided with a guide to the museum – also in French.

The Chellah Necropolis

The most beautiful of Moroccan ruins, **Chellah** (open daily; 8.30am–6.30pm; 10dh) is a startling sight as you emerge from the long avenues of the Ville Nouvelle. Walled and towered, it seems a much larger enclosure than the map suggests, and it feels for a

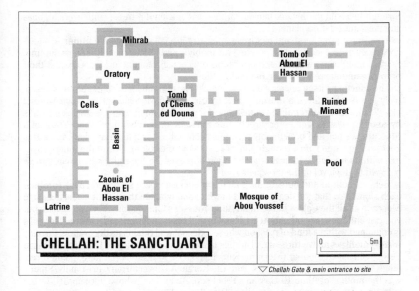

CHELLAH: THE SANCTUARY

Mihrab

Oratory

Cells

Tomb of Chems ed Douna

Basin

Zaouia of Abou El Hassan

Latrine

Tomb of Abou El Hassan

Ruined Minaret

Pool

Mosque of Abou Youssef

0   5m

▽ Chellah Gate & main entrance to site

moment as if you've come upon a second Medina. The site is, in fact, long uninhabited – since 1154, when it was abandoned in favour of Salé across the Bou Regreg. But for almost a thousand years prior to that, Chellah (or *Sala Colonia*, as it was known) had been a thriving city and port, one of the last to sever links with the Roman Empire and the first to proclaim Moulay Idriss founder of Morocco's original Arab dynasty. An apocryphal local tradition maintains that the Prophet himself also prayed at a shrine here.

Under the Almohads, the site was already a royal burial ground, but most of what you see today, including the gates and enclosing wall, is the legacy of the Merenid sultan, **Abou El Hassan** (1331–51). The greatest of Merenid rulers, conquering and controlling the Maghreb as far east as Tunis, Abou El Hassan, "The Black Sultan", was also their most prolific builder. In addition to Chellah, he was responsible for important mosques in Fes and Tlemcen, as well as the beautiful *medersas* of Salé and Meknes.

The **main gate** here is the most surprising of Merenid monuments, its turreted bastions creating an almost Gothic appearance. Its base is recognizably Almohad, but each element has become inflated, and the combination of simplicity and solidity has gone. In its original state, with bright-coloured marble and tile decoration, the effect must have been incredibly gaudy – a bit like the nineteenth-century palaces you see today in Fes and Marrakesh. An interesting technical innovation, however, are the stalactite (or "honeycomb") corbels which form the transition from the bastion's semi-octagonal towers to their square platforms; these were to become a feature of Merenid building. The Kufic inscription above the gate is from the Koran and begins with the invocation: "I take refuge in Allah, against Satan."

The Sanctuary

There are usually a number of guides hanging around the gate, but hiring them is not mandatory – once inside, things are clear enough. Off to your left, in a state of long-suspended excavation, are the main **Roman ruins** (closed off for many years), including the visible outlines of a forum, temple and craftsmen's quarter. The **Islamic ruins** are down to the right, within a second inner sanctuary approached along a broad path through half-wild gardens of banana, orange and ancient fig trees, sunflowers, dahlias and poisonous datura plants.

Their most prominent and picturesque feature is a tall stone-and-tile **minaret**, a ludicrously oversized stork's nest perched invariably – and photogenically – on its summit. Storks, along with swallows and crows, have a certain sanctity in Morocco, and their presence on minarets is a sign of good fortune.

The sanctuary itself appears a confusing cluster of tombs and ruins, but it is essentially just two buildings: a mosque, built by the second Merenid sultan, Abou Youssef (1258–86), and a *zaouia*, or mosque-monastery, added along with the enclosure walls by Abou El Hassan. You enter directly into the *sahn*, or courtyard, of **Abou Youssef's Mosque**, a small and presumably private structure built as a funerary dedication. It is now very much in ruins, though you can make out the colonnades of the inner prayer hall with its *mihrab* to indicate the direction of prayer. To the right is its minaret, now reduced to the level of the mosque's roof.

Behind, both in and outside the sanctuary enclosure, are scattered **royal tombs** – each aligned so that the dead, dressed in white and lying on their right sides, may face Mecca to await the Call of Judgement. Abou Youssef's tomb has not been identified, but you can find those of both **Abou El Hassan** and his wife **Shams ed Douna**. Hassan's is contained within a kind of pavilion whose external wall retains its decoration, the *darj w ktarf* motif set above three small arches in a design very similar to that of the Hassan Tower. Shams ed Douna, (Morning Sun) has only a tombstone – a long, pointed rectangle covered in a mass of verses from the Koran. A convert from Christianity, Shams was the mother of Abou El Hassan's rebel son, Abou Inan, whose uprising led to the sultan's death as a fugitive in the High Atlas during the winter of 1352.

The **Zaouia** is in a much better state of preservation, its structure, like Abou El Hassan's *medersas,* that of a long, central court enclosed by cells, with a smaller oratory or prayer hall at the end. Each of these features is quite recognizable, along with those of the ablutions, preceding the main court, for the worshippers' purification. There are fragments of *zellij* (mosaic tilework) on some of the colonnades and on the minaret, which again give an idea of its original brightness, and there are traces, too, of the *mihrab's* elaborate stucco decoration. Five-sided, the **mihrab** has a narrow passageway (now blocked with brambles) leading to the rear – built so that pilgrims might make seven circuits round it. This was once believed to give the equivalent merit of the *hadj*, the trip to Mecca: a tradition, with that of Muhammad's visit, probably invented and propagated by the *zaouia's* keepers to increase their revenue.

Off to the right and above the sanctuary enclosure are a group of **koubbas** – the domed tombs of local saints or *marabouts* – and beyond them a **spring pool**, enclosed by low, vaulted buildings. This is held sacred, along with the eels which swim in its waters, and women bring hard-boiled eggs for the fish to invoke assistance in fertility and childbirth. If you're here in spring, you'll get additional wildlife, with the storks nesting and the herons roosting.

At the far end of the sactuary, you can look down a side-valley to the Bou Regreg estuary. From here, you can appreciate that this site was destined, from early times, to be settled and fortified. It was hidden from the sea by low hills and a bend in the Bou Regreg river. At the same time, once navigated, access from the river was easy and safe. The fertile low land by the river was ideal for crops and grazing animals. Pliny said that the meadows were invaded by herds of elephants, which were slaughtered for their ivory, and that nomad tribes, intent on pillage, fared no better. The site itself was easy to defend and the springs provided water in times of siege.

Nowadays, you can also appreciate from here the steady expansion inland of Salé – with its sprawling suburb, Betana. Salé is also expanding, ribbon-like, either side of the main road north towards Kenitra.

Eating and drinking

For a capital city, Rabat is pretty quiet. By 9.30 at night, the restaurants are closing up and most of the population home. Nonetheless, the city's café life is pleasant, and it has one of the country's best collections of restaurants – many of them inexpensive.

Medina café-restaurants

As ever, the cheapest places to eat are to be found in the **Medina**. Just on the edge of the quarter, down Av. Mohammed V and along Rue Souika, there are a string of good everyday **café-restaurants** – clean enough and serving regular Moroccan fare. They are excellent value, especially at lunchtime, when many have fixed-price meals for the office and shop workers. Alternatively, for only a few dirhams, you can pick up a range of snacks and juices just inside the Medina walls, by the market shown on our main city map. Elsewhere, facing the *Hôtel Al Maghrib Al Jadid* (keyed D on our map), there are the popular *Restaurant de l'Union* and *Restaurant de la Libération* on Av. Mohammed V. Both are cheap.

Ville Nouvelle restaurants

In the **Ville Nouvelle** you can pick from a fine selection of Moroccan and French restaurants, plus a few Oriental places for a change of cuisine. Worthwhile choices include:

Café-Restaurant El Bahia, Bd. Hassan II, built into the Andalucian wall, near the junction with Av. Mohammed V. Reasonably priced *tajines*, kebabs and salads, served in a pleasant courtyard, upstairs or on the pavement outside. Service can be slow and helpings modest, but ambience compensates. Cheap to moderate.

Hôtel Balima, Av. Mohammed V. Inexpensive dishes in the snack bar all day; pricier ones in the main restaurant, open in the evening only; but they're nothing special – the indoor bar and outdoor café under the trees are the thing here. Moderate.

Restaurant La Bamba, 3 Rue Tanta – a small sidestreet behind the *Hôtel Balima*. Mainly Moroccan dishes, but there's paella to promote the Spanish theme. There are several other eating places on this street so there are alternatives if *La Bamba* doesn't suit, including *La Mamma* opposite (see below). Moderate.

Restaurant Caravelle, below the Kasbah (see p.261) on the seaward side, with fine views of the beaches either side. A nice place for lunch with, as you'd hope, fish on offer. Moderate.

La Clef, Rue Hatim – a narrow sidestreet just off Av. Moulay Youssef, and near the *Hôtel d'Orsay*. There's serious drinking in the bar downstairs, but the restaurant upstairs is quiet and serves good French and Moroccan dishes. Try *tajines, brochettes* and the excellent *pastilla*. Moderate.

Restaurant Fouquet's, 285 Av. Mohammed V. It changed hands recently – which is good news because the previous regime let standards slip. It still specializes in fish dishes, has renewed its drinks licence, and promises well. Open 10am–3pm and 6–11pm; closed Sundays. Expensive.

Café-Restaurant Français, 3 Av. Moulay Youssef, just off Place de la Gare and alongside the *Hôtel D'Orsay*. Another downstairs bar with upstairs restaurant like *La Clef* nearby. Arguably the best and most consistent around the train station. Moderate.

Restaurant Hong Kong, 261 Av. Mohammed V on the first floor. Good Chinese cuisine and value for money. Closed Mondays. Moderate.

Restaurant Koutoubia, 10 Rue Pierre Pavent (☎07/72.01.25). Off Rue Moulay Abdelaziz, facing RTM (radio and TV station) and near the *Hôtel* Chellah. There's an upmarket bar and, with a separate entrance through a quaint wood and glass extension, an old-style restaurant. It claims King Hassan among past clientele, and an elderly patron who knew his father, Mohammed V. Excellent cooking. Expensive (but not cripplingly so). An evening to dine out on.

Pizza La Mamma, 6 Rue Tanta. It's opposite *La Bamba* and is its Italian-style rival, providing an excuse for pizza and pasta. *La Dolce Vita*, next door to *La Mamma*, is owned by the same patron and so takes care of the sweet course. Moderate.

Le Mandarin, 100 Av. Abdel Krim Al Kattabi (☎07/72.46.99; closed Wed). Popular business restaurant in L'Océan quarter, southwest of the Bab Oudaïa. The best oriental food in the city. Moderate to expensive.

Pizzeria Napoli, 8 rue Moulay Abdelaziz, between the *Hôtel Chellah* and *Restaurant Koutoubia* – and facing RTM. Pizzas cooked over a wood fire – to eat in or take away.

Restaurant La Pagode, 13 Rue Baghdad – parallel to (and south of) the train station. Small restaurant serving Vietnamese and Chinese dishes. Moderate.

Café-Restaurant de la Paix, 1 Av. Moulay Youssef, just off Place de la Gare. Again, as with the nearby *La Clef* and *Français*, there's some heavy drinking in the ground floor bar, but you can eat well outside (in an old French-style glass corridor) or upstairs. Moderate.

Café-Restaurant Saadi, 81 bis Av. Allal Ben Abdallah, on the corner with Rue El Kahira. The café is on the street, with a restaurant part in the arcade at the side. Fine *couscous* and *tajines*; beer and wine. Moderate.

Restaurant Saïdoune, in the mall at 467 Av. Mohammed V, opposite the *Hôtel Terminus*. A good Lebanese restaurant run by an Iraqi; also a bar. Moderate.

Café-Restaurant Shahrazade, 119 Bd. Hassan II, nxt to the *Hôtel Majestic*. Quick, friendly service, in or out of doors. Park now given over to a useful *téléboutique*. Cheap to moderate.

Taki Fried Chicken, in an arcade on Av. Mohammed V across from the Parliament building. *McDonald's* has now arrived in Rabat (across from the train station) and there's a *Pizza Hot* (on Rue Tanta), but the first of that ilk was *Taki Fried Chicken* which still does good fast food. Cheap.

Cafés, bars and nightlife

Avenues Mohammed V and Allal Ben Abdallah have some excellent **cafés**, for coffee, soft drinks and pastries. Particularly pleasant spots include the **Hôtel Balima** outdoor café (very popular with locals – and a bit cruisy), the **Café Maure** in the Kasbah, and the café in the shady **Parc du Triangle de Vue**, just south of Bd. Hassan II, which is usually full of students working or arguing over a mint tea.

Bars – outside the main hotels – are few and far between. The one inside the *Hôtel Balima* is as good as any; it tends to stay open as late as there are customers and attracts an interesting crowd of Moroccan drinkers. Other bars are to be found at the restaurants *La Clef, de la Paix, Saïdoune* and *Koutoubia* (see above). There is also the *Baghdad Bar* on Rue Tanta, behind the *Hôtel Balima,* and the *Bar Le Grillon*, at the bottom end of Av. Allal Ben Abdallah.

After these have closed, the city's **late-night options** are a handful of **disco-bars** around Place de Melilla (east of the Parc du Triangle de Vue), and on Rue Patrice Lumumba – where you'll find the *Biba* and *Jefferson* discos. Another popular danceclub is *5th Avenue*, near the Moulay Youssef Sport complex, in the Agdal quarter, south of the centre, easiest reached by *petit taxi*. If you went early, you could eat first at the *Pizza Reggio* in the complex; the prices are reasonable and there's a good atmosphere.

Finally, and back in the Ville Nouvelle, the *Jour et Nuit* nightclub, at the junction of Av. Abderrahman Neggay and Rue Moulay Rachid, attracts a young crowd until the early hours.

Listings

In addition to listings below, you may want to consult *Telecontact*, an annual directory with yellow pages style listings for businesses and services in the Rabat/Casablanca/Kenitra region. It is available from newsstands.

Airlines *Royal Air Maroc* is just across from the train station on Av. Mohammed V (☎07/70.97.66) and *Air France* (☎07/70.70.66) is on the same avenue just below the *Hôtel Balima* at no. 281. Neither *British Airways*, nor *Iberia* has an office in Rabat; the nearest are in Casablanca (☎02/30.76.07 and ☎02/29.40.03 respectively).

American Express has no agent in Rabat; their nearest office is in Casablanca (☎02/22.29.47).

Animal Welfare *SPANA* (Society for the Protection of Animals Abroad) has a small refuge in Rabat at 1 Bd. de l'Océan (☎07/69.00.43). Albeit small, the treatment of working animals and domestic pets is interesting and Mr A Khoubane welcomes visitors. It's some way out of town on the coastal road – near the wholesale market (*marché en gros*) and by the *Shell* petrol station; a *petit taxi* is the best bet.

Banks Most are along Av. Allal Ben Abdallah and Av. Mohammed V. The *BMCE* exchange counter at 260 Av. Mohammed V is open Mon–Fri 8am–noon and 2–7pm, Sat & Sun 10am–2pm and 4–7pm, and at the train station Mon–Fri 8am–noon and 3–7pm, Sat–Sun 9am–noon and 3–6pm; they handle *VISA/Mastercard*, travellers' cheques and cash.

Beaches Nearest options are the Kasbah and Salé beaches, with the latter best reached by one of the ferryboats which cross from below the Mellah. For clearer waters, head by bus to either Plage des Nations (see p.250) or Temara Plage (see p.274).

Books The *American Bookstore*, Rue Tangier (marked on our map) has a good selection of Penguin novels, etc, along with an enterprising shelf on Moroccan architecture, Islam and some of Paul Bowles's translations of Moroccan fiction. The *English Bookshop*, 7 Rue Alyamama (again marked on our map), stocks new titles; it also has a wide selection of secondhand paperbacks (Mon–Sat 9am–noon and 3–7pm). You can get coffee-table books on Morocco and phrasebooks from several of the bookshops along Av. Mohammed V. Look for *Kalila Wa Dimna* at no. 334, or Av. Allal Ben Abdallah.

Car rental Cheaper deals tend to be available in Casablanca, but if you want a car in Rabat, there are twenty or so rental agencies to choose from. Main companies include: *Avis*, 7 Rue Abou Faris Al Mairini (☎07/76.97.59); *Budget*, at the train station (☎07/70.57.89: Mon–Sat 8.30am–noon and 2.30–7pm); *Citer*, corner of Rue du Caire/Rue Ghandi (☎07/73.09.87); *Europcar/InterRent*, 25 bis Rue Patrice Lumumba (☎07/72.23.28); *Hertz*, 467 Av. Mohammed V (☎07/70.92.27); *Hassan I* (☎07/72.62.31) and *Visa Car*, 9 Rue Baït Lahm (☎07/70.13.58).

Car repairs Try *Concorde*, 6 Av. Allal Ben Abdallah or, particularly for Renaults, the garage at 14 Av. Misr.

Cinemas There are several cinemas on or near Av. Mohammed V; *Cinema Martignan*, below *Le Fouquet's* restaurant has the latest US and French films. Near the *Hotel Royal*, is the *Cinema Royal*, more given to Kung Fu and Asian romances. More of an arts cinema is the smaller *Salle de 7ème Art* on Av. Allal Ben Abdallah; advance booking advisable.

Culture The *Théâtre National Mohammed V* on Rue Cairo (south of Bd. Hassan II – see map) puts on a range of concerts (Arabic and Western classical music) and films. There are a number of cultural centres: *American*, 41 Av. Allal Ben Abdallah; *British*, 6 Av. Moulay Youssef; *German*, 10 Rue Jebli; *Spanish*, Rue Mohammed El Fakir; and *French*, Rue Gandhi.

Embassies include: **Britain**, 17 Bd. Saomaât Hassan (☎07/72.09.05 or 07/73.14.03); **Canada**, 13 bis Rue Jaâfar As-Saddik (☎07/67.28.80); **Denmark**, 4 Rue Khémisset (☎07/73.92.93); **Netherlands**, 40 Rue Tunis (☎07/73.35.12); **Sweden**, 159 Av. John Kennedy (☎07/75.93.13); **USA**, 2 Av. Marrakesh – near the far end of Av. Allal Ben Abdallah (☎07/76.22.65). Standard hours are 8.30–11.30am, Mon–Fri, though you can phone at any time in an emergency. **Irish** citizens are represented by the British Embassy; **Australians** by the Canadians; **Norwegians** by the Norwegian Consul in Casablanca (10am–noon; ☎02/30.59.61). Israelis by the Bureau de Liaison d'Israel, 52 Bd. Mehdi Ben Barka Souissi (☎07/65.76.81).

Galleries Unusually for Morocco, Rabat has a number of worthwhile art galleries, showing works by contemporary artists. *L'Atelier*, 16 Rue Annaba, is the major dealer; try also *Galerie Marsam*, 6 Rue Osquofiah (opposite *Restaurant l'Oasis*); and *Galerie Le Mamoir*, 7 Rue Baït Lahm (near *Hôtel Bélère* and *Visa Car*).

Golf The *Royal Dar Es Salaam* golfcourse, on the outskirts of Rabat, is the country's finest – featuring two 18-hole and one 9-hole course designed by Robert Trent-Jones.

Hiking maps Division de la Cartographie, Ministère de l'Agriculture et de la Réforme Agraire (MARA), 31 Av. Moulay Hassan; Mon–Thur 8.30am–11am and 2.30–5.30pm. Hiking maps to the Toubkal area are sold over the counter; other topographic maps of the main hiking areas in the High and Middle Atlas, which can be selected from the official index, have to be ordered and collected 48hr later, discounting Sat and Sun, but only if officially sanctioned. There's no postal service. These are good maps, at up to 1:50,000, but the policy and the service make it virtually impossible to buy them.

Libraries/cultural associations The *British Council*, 36 Rue Tangier (☎07/76.08.36; marked on our map) operates a small library, with UK papers available for browsing, and puts on various films and events in English. It is also a possible source of information if you want to stay on in Morocco and teach English; open Mon–Fri 9.30am–noon and 2.30–5.45; closed Mon am. The *George Washington Library*, 35 Av. de Fes, has American newspapers. The *American Women's Association Library*, 22 bis Al Jazair (Mon and Wed 10am–noon, Thur 5.30—7.30pm, Fri 2–4pm, Sat 10am–noon; (liable to change, check beforehand) has a one-for-one paperback exchange, open to all. These libraries can also put you in touch with people if you want to take lessons in Moroccan Arabic.

Library research Rabat, as the capital, houses the major national libraries. Access is restricted to serious researchers, authenticated by their home university and/or embassy (see above). The five most important institutions are *La Bibliothèque de la Source*, 26 Av. Chellah (Mon–Fri 2.30–6.30pm and Sat 9am–noon and 2.30–6.30 pm); *Institut de Recherche sur le Maghreb Contemporain* (IRMC) 1 Rue Annaba; *La Bibliothèque Generale et Archives*, Av. Ibn Batouta, (the largest collection in Morocco); *Hassaniya Library*, Royal Palace (official archives of the Alaouite dynasty and as far back as the eighth century*); Centre National de Documentation*, Av. Maa Al Ainain (excellent for computerized searches and microfiche material).

Police The main office is in Rue Soekarno, a couple of blocks from Av. Mohammed V; a central police post is manned at Bab El Jdid. In emergency ☎19.

Post office The central *PTT* (open 24hr for phones and there are call boxes outside) is halfway down Av. Mohammed V; its *poste restante* section is across the road from the main building. The *PTT* also has a small **Postal Museum**, with displays of Moroccan stamps; pride of place is given to Morocco's first official stamp, dated May 12, 1912, showing the Grand Mosque in Tangier.

Religious services The **Synagogue** Talmud Torah is at 9 Rue Moulay Ismail and the Jewish Community Centre is at 3 Rue Moulay Ismail (☎07/72.45.04); the **Catholic Cathédral** Saint Pierre is on Place Al Katidraliya at the top end of rue Abou Inane, Mass is occasionally celebrated in English (☎07/72.23.01); the **Protestant Church** is at 44 Av. Allal Ben Abdallah, there are services on Sunday mornings (☎07.72.38.48).

Supermarkets One of the best shops for provisions (including beer and wine) was *Maxi Marché* on Rue Baghdad, a sidestreet just to the south of the train station, but it has closed temporarily – worth checking out. Otherwise, there are two supermarkets facing the Cathedral (see above). Or, if you have transport, there is the *Centre Commercial Marjane*, between Rabat and Salé, where there is a bona fide *Pizza Hut*!

Tourist offices The most helpful tourist office is in Agdal: on the corner of Av. Al Abtal and Rue Oued Fes (☎07/77.51.71); bus #3 drops you opposite the tourist office, which has had a crashed car sitting on its front lawn for some years. The receptionist at the side entrance has brochures and maps; outside and to the right is the underground car park; ask at the office on the left about free posters to take home; a mixture of charm and perseverance, particularly at month end, is said to succeed.

Salé

Although it is now essentially a suburb of Rabat, **SALÉ** was the pre-eminent of the two right through the Middle Ages, from the decline of the Almohads to the uneasy alliance in the pirate republic of Bou Regreg (see p.252). Under the Merenids, in particular, it was a port of some stature, and endowed as such, the most notable survival of these times being its superb **Medersa Bou Inan** – a monument to rival the best of those of Rabat.

In this century, following the French creation of a capital in Rabat, and the emergence of Casablanca as Morocco's great port, Salé passed into a backwater role. The original Ville Nouvelle, as developed during the Protectorate, was restricted to a small area around the bus station and the northern gates. But, more recently, Salé has spread inland and alongside the main road north towards Kenitra. The increased Salé-Rabat traffic has called for an additional road bridge over the Bou Regreg.

Nevertheless, Salé still looks and feels very distinct from Rabat, particularly within its medieval walls where the *souks* and life remain surprisingly traditional.

Access and orientation

From Rabat you can cross the river to Salé by **rowing boat** (see the map), or take a **bus** (#6 or #12) from Bd. Hassan II. The boats charge 5dh per person and drop you close to the Salé beach; from here it's a steep walk up to **Bab Bou Haja**, one of the main town gates. Both buses drop you at an open terminal just outside the town's principal gate, **Bab Mrisa**.

Salé has a basic but well-managed **campsite**: *Camping de la Plage* (☎07/78.23.68; open all year), near the beach, and a small, but adequate **hotel**, the *Saadiens* (☎07/78.36.45; ①). Place du Marché. But unless you want to use the campsite as a base for Rabat, there seems little reason to stay. In the evenings, you can eat reasonably at one of the many workers' **cafés** along Rue Kechachin, but the streets empty even earlier than Rabat's.

The Medina

The most interesting point to enter Salé's Medina is through **Bab Mrisa**, near the *grand taxi* terminal. Its name – "of the small harbour" – recalls the marine arsenal which used to be sited within the walls, and explains the gate's unusual height. A channel running here from the Bou Regreg has long silted up, but in medieval times it allowed merchant ships to sail right into town, a device that must have been useful during the years of the pirate republic. Robinson Crusoe was brought into captivity through this gate in Daniel Defoe's novel. The gate itself is a very early Merenid structure of the 1270s, its design and motifs (palmettes enclosed by floral decoration; bands of Kufic inscription and *darj w ktarf*, etc) still inherently Almohad in tone.

The souks

Inside Bab Mrisa you'll find yourself in a small square, at the bottom of the old **Mellah** (Jewish) quarter. Turning to the left and continuing close to the walls, you come out after around 350m at another gate, **Bab Bou Haja**, beside a small park. If you want to explore the *souks* – the route outlined below – take the road along the left-hand side of the park. If not, continue on just inside the walls to a long open area; as this starts to narrow into a lane (about 40m further down) veer to your right into the town. This should bring you out more or less at the **Grand Mosque,** opposite which is the **Medersa of Abou El Hassan.**

The park-side street from Bab Bou Haja is **Rue Bab El Khabaz** (Street of the Bakers' Gate), a busy little lane which emerges at the heart of the **souks** by a small **kissaria** (covered market) devoted mainly to textiles. Most of the alleys here are grouped round specific crafts, a particular speciality being the pattern-weave mats produced for the sides and floors of mosques – to be found in the **Souk El Merzouk**. There is also a wool *souk*, the **Souk El Ghezel**, while wood, leather, iron ware, carpets and household items are to be found in the **Souk El Kebir** – the grand *souk*.

Close by the *kissaria* is a fourteenth-century hospice, the **Fondouk Askour**, with a notable gateway (built by Abou Inan – see the Medersa below), and beyond this the Medina's main street, **Rue de la Grande Mosque** leads uphill through the middle of town to the Grand Mosque. This is the simplest approach, but you can take in more of the *souks* by following **Rue Kechachin**, parallel. Along here are located the carpenters and stone-carvers, as well as other craftsmen. In **Rue Haddadin**, a fairly major intersection which leads off to its right up towards Bab Sebta, you'll come upon gold- and coppersmiths.

The Grand Mosque and Medersa

As far as buildings go, the **Grand Mosque** marks the most interesting part of town, its surrounding lanes fronting a concentration of aristocratic mansions and religious *zaouia* foundations. Almohad in origin, the mosque is one of the largest and earliest in Morocco, though what you can see as a non-Muslim (the gateway and minaret) are recent additions.

You can, however, visit its **Medersa** (10dh admission; you will probably need to ask in shops nearby for the caretaker or *gardien*), opposite the mosque's monumental, stepped main entrance. Salé's main monument and recently restored, it was founded in 1341 by Sultan Abou El Hassan (see Chellah, in Rabat), and is thus more or less contemporary with the Bou Inania *medersas* in Meknes and Fes. Like them, it follows the basic Merenid plan of a central courtyard opening onto a prayer hall, with a series of cells for the students – for whom these "university halls" were endowed – round its upper floors. If this is the first example you've seen, it will come as a surprise after the sparse Almohad economy of the monuments in Rabat. The great Merenid *medersas* are all intensely decorated – in carved wood, stucco and *zellij* – and this is no exception. Within the entrance gate, there is hardly an inch of space which doesn't draw the eye away into a web of intricacy.

What is remarkable, despite a certain heaviness which the great Merenid *medersas* manage to avoid, is the way in which each aspect of the workmanship succeeds in forging a unity with the others, echoing and repeating the standard patterns in endless variations. The patterns, for the most part, derive from Almohad models, with their stylized geometric and floral motifs, but in the latter there is a much more naturalistic, less abstracted approach. There is also a new stress on calligraphy, with monumental inscriptions carved in great bands on the dark cedarwood and incorporated within the stucco and *zellij*. Almost invariably these are in the elaborate cursive script, and they are generally passages from the Koran. There are occasional poems, however, such as the beautiful foundation inscription, set in marble against a green background, on the rear wall of the court, which begins:

Mosquée Hassan II, Casablanca

The walls, Essaouira

Camels near Essaouira

Essaouira

Safi pottery

Thuya workshop, Essaouira

Cité Portugaise, El Jadida

Marrakesh souk

Locksmith, Marrakesh

Dyers' souk, Marrakesh

Djemaa El Fna, Marrakesh

Craft school, Marrakesh

Djebel Oujdad, High Atlas

Lakes below Anhroner, High Atlas

Imlil, High Atlas

l of the cemetery (again forbidden to non-Muslims), which spreads
r, is a third revered site, the white *koubba* and associated buildings of
of **Sidi Ben Achir**. Sometimes known as "Al Tabib" (The Doctor), Ben
urteenth-century ascetic from Andalucia. His shrine, said to have the abil-
shipwrecks and quell storms – good pirate virtues – reputedly effects
indness, paralysis and madness. Enclosed by nineteenth-century pilgrim
, too, has a considerable annual *moussem* on the eve of Mouloud.

h towards Casablanca

ttle over an hour by *grand taxi* from Rabat to Casa (under an hour by express
and, if you're making a quick tour of Morocco, there's little to delay your
press. The landscape, wooded in parts, is a low, flat plain, punctuated inland by a
ser of scruffy light industrial towns.

the coast, things are slightly more promising: **Mohammedia** has a fine beach
and good restaurants, and is, with the smaller resorts of **Temara** and **Skhirat**, a popular seaside escape for the affluent of Rabat and Casablanca. For visitors, however,
there's a lot more to get excited about on the coast south from Casa towards Agadir.

Rabat to Mohammedia

Temara Plage, some 14km to the south of Rabat, is (along with Plage des Nations, see
p.250), the capital's closest beach resort. If you are planning a day-trip, you could take
a *grand taxi* direct to the beach from Rabat (around 20min), or local bus #17 to **Temara
Ville** (4km inland); both leave Rabat from Av. Hassan II.

If you're driving, the **coast road** is preferable. Leaving Rabat, take Bd. Misr alongside the Medina wall, then bear left onto Av. Al Moukaouma and its continuation Av.
Sidi Mohammed Ben Abdallah. The route is built up almost the whole way from Rabat
to Temara. Along the way, you pass by the **National Zoo**; a vast **Complexe
Olympique**, built for the 1983 Mediterranean games; and a small but impressive **royal
palace** belonging to the heir of Hassan II, Sidi Mohammed.

Temara Zoo
Temara Zoo (Mon–Fri: 10am–6pm; Sat and Sun: 9.30am–6pm) is an unexpected
delight. Most "zoos" in Morocco are scrubby little enclosures with a few sad-looking
Barbary apes. This one, however, is positively palatial, as you might expect from what
was formerly King Hassan's private menagerie. Amid the imaginatively laid-out
grounds there are lions, elephants, gazelles, jackals, desert foxes, giraffes and monkeys; there is a lake, too, with pelicans and wading birds.

Temara Ville and Plage
TEMARA VILLE has an old **Kasbah**, dating from Moulay Ismail's reign, which is now
home to the Royal Cavalry School; other than that, there's little else to delay you, unless
ou want to stock up for picnics on the beach or the campsites further south. **TEMARA
LAGE** consists of several sandy strips, plus a cluster of discos that provide a summer
ternative to the lack of action in Rabat. Few people stay here overnight, other than the
ll-heeled of Rabat, who maintain summer villas. However, if you want a beach base
Rabat, there are three **hotels**. The *Hôtel La Felouque* (☎07/74.43.88; ④), by the main
ch, known locally as Plage Les Sables d'Or, has a swimming pool, tennis courts and
ll-regarded **restaurant**, *Les Sables d'Or*. Better value for money is the *Hôtel
rama* (☎07/74.42.89; ③), whoe terrace overlooks the beach; the staff are friendly,

> Look at my admirable portal!
> Rejoice in my chosen company,
> In the remarkable style of my construction
> And my marvellous interior!
> The workers here have accomplished an
> Creation with the beauty of youth. . . .

(Translation from Richard B. Parke

The *medersa* is only sporadically visited and yo
(except for the sparrows and the caretaker) – a quiet,
entrance there is a stairway up to the old, windowless ce
roof, where, looking out across the river to Rabat, you s
Hassan Tower.

Zaouias, moussems and marabouts

Round the Grand Mosque, and over to the northwest, you can view (but
unless you are Muslim) a trio of interesting buildings.

The first of these is the **Zaouia Sidi Ahmed El Tijani**, whose elaborate portal
the Grand Mosque and Medersa. *Zaouias* are a mix of shrine and charitable establishment, maintained by their followers, who once or more each year hold a *moussem*, a pilgrimage-festival, in the saint-founder's honour.

The most important of Salé's *moussems* is that of its patron saint, **Sidi Abdallah Ben
Hassoun**, whose *zaouia* stands at the end of the Rue de la Grande Mosquée, a few
steps before the cemetery. The saint, who for Muslim travellers plays a role similar to
St Christopher, lived in Salé during the sixteenth century, though the origins and significance of his *moussem* are unclear. Taking place each year on the eve of *Mouloud* –
the Prophet's birthday – it involves a spectacular procession through the streets of the
town with local boatmen, dressed in corsair costumes, carrying huge and elaborate
wax lanterns mounted on giant poles. It is by all acounts a lively occasion, much of
which can be witnessed away from the forbidden precincts.

OULJA: THE COMPLEXE DES POTIERS

On the Salé side of the estuary, 3km out from the town, the suburb of **Oulja** houses one
of Morocco's finest **potteries**. It has been open only since 1989, established around
rich vein of clay, so its techniques and kilns are modern. For instance, while just thr
out of the 180 kilns at Safi (Morocco's largest potting town) are fired by gas or electr
ty, here the ratio is almost exactly the reverse, with just a few specialist kilns u
tamarisk wood fuel. Nevertheless, despite different techniques, lovely and wonde
imaginative objects are produced at both Oulja and Salé.

The complex also has a major craft/exhibition centre, an area specializing in
work and a friendly café. Visitors are made welcome at the twenty-odd potterie
complex and you could pick interesting potteries at random. Good ones,
include:

Poterie Demnate (#12). The patron, Bennami Abdelaziz came here after
Demnate. Wares are enhanced by striking hand-painted flowers.

Poterie Hariky (#10). Superb Islamic designs.

Poterie Tarfaya (#9). Traditional tea sets and mugs – and a flourishing
wall plates of Hassan II.

Oulja can be reached by *grand taxi* from Rabat or Salé. If you want a t
for it to return; otherwise you'll have to walk. If so, head east to cros
you can then cut up to the high ground towards the Tour Hassan.

and there is some attempt to maintain lawns and gardens. A third, more upmarket option is the *Hôtel St Germain en Laye* (☎07/74.42.30; ④); it's dearer than *La Felouque*, but there are discounts out of season.

Back on the coastal road, there is a good **restaurant** the *San Francisco*, built by a Moroccan returned from thirty years in California, and decorated with a full-size Ford Mustang bursting through the bar mirror.

Ech Chiana

ECH CHIANA, also known as Rose Marie Plage, is 9km south from Temara and a slightly plusher resort, with a luxury beachside **hotel**, *La Kasbah* (☎07/74.91.16; ④), popular with French package tourists. A little back from the beach there is also the cheaper *Hôtel Les Gambusias* (☎07/74.91.49; ③), which does good meals, especially fish dishes, and has a swimming pool and a seasonal **campsite**. A second campsite (Jul–Sep) is attached to the restaurant-bar, *Plage Johara* (☎07/74.92.51).

Skhirat Plage

The **Royal Palace** at **SKHIRAT PLAGE** was the site of a notorious coup attempt by senior Moroccan generals during King Hassan's birthday celebrations in July 1971. The coup was mounted using a force of Berber cadets, who took over the palace, imprisoned the king and massacred a number of his guests. It came within hours of being success-ful, being thwarted by the apparently accidental shooting of the cadets' leader, General Mohammed Medbuh, and by the strength of personality of Hassan, who re-asserted con-trol over his captors. Among the guests who survived was Malcolm Forbes (see p.81).

The palace still stands, though it has understandably fallen from royal favour, and there are a good many luxurious French-style villas in the vicinity – some old, some new, many unfinished. There are also two **hotels** on the beach to the south of the main resort. *La Potinière* (☎07/74.22.04; ②), is a French-style auberge, run by a French cou-ple; it is open in July and August only. *Hôtel Amphitrite* (☎07/74.25.71; ⑤) is a luxury resort, with private beach, swimming pool, sauna, tennis and bungalows.

Getting to the resort by public transport, take any of the slow **trains** on the Rabat–Casa line to SKHIRAT VILLE, a small (and uninteresting) farming town, on the hillside, a couple of kilometres up from the beach.

Bouznika and Mansouria

If you have transport, there are further turn-offs to beaches, prior to Mohammedia. The coastal plain here is increasingly barren and the beaches are less developed, indeed isolated, and in places reached only by sandy tracks from the main road. At **BOUZNIKA PLAGE** and **DAHOMEY PLAGE**, around 20km before Mohammedia, there are primitive summer **campsites**. Further south, 6km before Mohammedia, **MANSOURIA** has two more campsites, the *Oubaha* (Jun-Sep) and the rather better *Mimosa* (☎03/32.33.25; open all year).

The last place of note before Mohammedia is **PORT BLONDIN**, at the mouth of the Oued Nefifikh and the beginning of the Mohammedia sands. It is flanked by a couple of seasonal campsites and the *Hôtel La Madrague* (☎03/32.20.20; ③), a rambling build-ing, but well maintained and friendly.

From here, it's a straight run into Mohammedia, its approach heralded by bright new villas either side of the road (now S222).

Mohammedia

The port of **MOHAMMEDIA** has a dual identity. As the site of Morocco's main oil refineries, and the base of its petrochemical industry, it is an important industrial and commercial city, with a population of some 130,000. Yet it is also a big-name resort – a holiday playground for Casablanca – with one of the best beaches on the Atlantic, a racecourse, the new *Ibn Batouta* yacht marina and a state-of-the-art 18-hole golf course. King Hassan has a little palace by the links; his presence is signalled by exceptional police activity in the rough ground off the fairways.

These two faces of the city – tourism and industry – are kept quite distinct, with the latter contained in a zone to the southwest of the city centre and beach. In summer, the city's population is given a huge boost by Moroccan tourists, mainly from Casa, who camp by the beach in what is called *Mohammedia-Est*: a sequence of tented villages that stretch northeast towards Port Blondin and Mansouria. For foreign visitors, there is perhaps less to tempt a stay. Despite a longish history as a trading port, this was still a small village at the turn of the century and the city has little to speak of in the way of monuments of "old Morocco". The only sight to speak of is a modern building, the **Erradouane Mosque**, which with its elegant minaret has become a landmark of Mohammedia since it was inaugurated in March, 1991.

Still, Mohammedia makes a very pleasant stopover, with its friendly, easy-going atmosphere, and a fine selection of restaurants. If you are flying in or out of Casablanca, you could do a lot worse than spend a first or last night here; it's only 20 minutes by train from Casa and there are a dozen or so trains a day each way. In July, it may be worth a special trip, too, for the week-long **Mohammedia Festival**, which encompasses all kinds of cultural activities, craft exhibitions, a *fantasia*, cycling races and a marathon.

Orientation and accommodation

Orientation is not difficult as "downtown" Mohammedia is quite a small town. Between the **rail station** and the **Ville Nouvelle**, there is a small **Kasbah/Medina** area, built in a period of Portuguese occupation and still preserving their gateways. To the west of the Kasbah, a sequence of boulevards lead down to the beach. **Buses** and **grands taxis** operate beside a small park on Rue de Baghdad, just in front of the train station; local bus #1 runs from here, too, down to the beach.

There are, at time of writing four **hotels**. A fifth, the luxury *Miramar* is in the throes of building work, possibly for conversion into a royal palace, although it may reopen as an exclusive resort.

HOTELS

Hôtel Castel [D], Av. Abderrahmane Serghini (☎03/32.25.33). The closest hotel to the train station and the cheapest in town. Rooms off a first-floor central hall and on the roof terrace. Simple, with cold showers only, but there is a *douche publique* off Av. des F.A.R. ①

Hôtel La Falaise [A], Rue Farhat Hachad (☎03/32.48.28). Run by an energetic French lady and closer to the beach than the *Castel*. Ten reasonable rooms, but only one en suite. Located off a central courtyard, with a café/snack bar. ②

Hôtel Sabah [B], 42 Av. des F.A.R. (☎03/32.14.51). A new hotel, halfway between the Kasbah and the port. Expensive and catering more for businessmen than tourists. ④

Hôtel Samir [C], 34 Bd. Moulay Youssef (☎03/32.40.05). A once-smart, beachside hotel, with swimming pool and tennis court – and with a range of cafés and restaurants on the promenade alongside. A little cheaper than the new *Hôtel Sabah*. ④

CAMPSITE

Camping Loran, 2km north of Mohammedia, on the Rabat road (☎03/32.49.46 or 57). A well-established campsite with a restaurant, bar, small shop, bungalows, swimming pool – and direct access to the beach.

Practicalities, restaurants and nightlife

Mohammedia has most facilities you'll need. There is a branch of the *BMCI* **bank** at the top end of Av. des F.A.R., facing the small roundabout in front of the main entrance

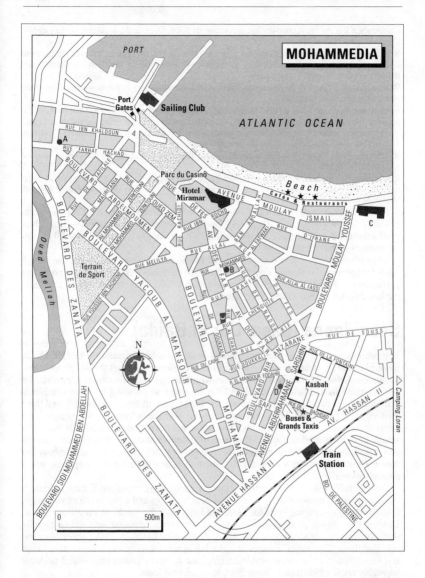

to the Kasbah, and a branch of the *BMCE* on Rue Rachidi, one block to the west of Rue de Fes. The *PTT* is on Av. Mohammed Zerktouni, also one block to the west of Rue de Fes – and facing the Parc du Casino. The **travel agency** *Fedala Voyages* at 35 Av. des F.A.R. (☎03/32.73.90) is helpful for confirming flights, arranging car rental, etc.

For its size, Mohammedia's choice of **restaurants** is impressive. Pick from:

Restaurant au Bec Fin, Rue Cheikh Chouaib Doukali, near the port gates. A small, but highly recommended restaurant with a truly Spanish flavour. Moderate.

Chaplin's, 8 Rue du Rif. A good choice, just off Av. de F.A.R. Once again, small; try the fish dishes. Cheap to moderate.

Restaurant La Frégate, Rue Oued Zem, near the *Hôtel La Falaise*. Lobster, prawns, shrimps and all manner of seafish. Generous helpings, particularly of shellfish paella. And there's a takeaway and delivery service. Moderate to expensive.

Restaurant du Parc, Rue de Fes, facing the Parc du Casino and next to the *Ranch Club*. Excellent, with fish specialities. Moderate.

Restaurant du Port, 1 Rue du Port, next to the port gates. Previously known as *Chez Iréne*, this is possibly the town's best-known restaurant, renowned for its charcoal grills, served in a flower-strewn garden. Indoors, there's a strongly nautical décor. Same patron as *La Brasserie Bavaroise*, 133/139 Rue Allal Ben Abdallah, Casablanca. Moderate to expensive.

Restaurant Sans Pareil, Rue Farhat Hachad – near the *Hôtel La Falaise*. French cuisine, seafood and paella. Moderate.

Restaurant des Sports, Rue Farhat Hachad. Large and classy, with 'folkloric spectacles' at week-ends in the season. The owners trained at Cornell University – and it shows. Excellent seafood. Moderate to expensive.

For **breakfast and snacks**, there are several pavement cafés facing the main entrance to the Kasbah: the *Tiznit* and *Tarfaya*, both serve grills and *brochettes*. Just inside the main gate of the Kasbah, on the right, there are a number of similar café-restaurants worth a trial or two.

Mohammedia has a few **bars** additional to the restaurants and hotels: the *Ranch Club*, for instance, on Rue de Fes, facing the Parc du Casino. But the old Casino is now permanently closed. If it's nightlife you crave, it would be better to stay in Casa and explore the Aïn Diab corniche (see following).

Casablanca (Casa, Dar El Baida)

The principal city of Morocco, and capital in all but administration, **CASABLANCA** (*Dar El Baida* in its literal Arabic form) is now the largest port of the Maghreb – and busier even than Marseilles, the city on which it was modelled by the French. Its development, from a town of 20,000 in 1906, has been astonishing but it was ruthlessly deliberate. When the French landed their forces here in 1907, and established their Protectorate five years later, Fes which was Morocco's commercial centre, and Tangier its main port. Had Tangier not been in international hands, this probably would have remained the case. However, the demands of an independent colonial administration forced the French to seek an entirely new base. Casa, at the heart of *Maroc Utile*, the country's most fertile zone and centre of its mineral deposits, was a natural choice.

Superficially, Casa is today much like any other large southern European city: a familiarity which makes it fairly easy to get your bearings and a revelation as you begin to understand something of its life. Arriving here from the south, or even from Fes or Tangier, most of the preconceptions you've been travelling round with will be happily shattered by the city's cosmopolitan beach clubs or by the almost total absence of the veil. But these "European" images shield what is substantially a first-generation city – and one still attracting considerable immigration from the countryside – and perhaps inevitably some of Morocco's most intense social problems.

Alongside its show of wealth and its prestige developments – most notably the vast **Mosquée Hassan II**, on a promontory looking out to the Atlantic – the city has had since its formation a reputation for extreme poverty, prostitution, crime, social unrest and the *bidonvilles* (shanty towns) which you will see both sides of the rail track as you approach Casablanca. The *bidonville* problem resulted partly from the sheer extent of population increases – which exceeded one million in the 1960s – and partly because few of the earlier migrants intended to stay permanently. Most of them sent back their

NEW NAMES AND NEW AVENUES

The names of Casa's chief squares – **Place Mohammed V** and **Place des Nations Unies** - are a source of enduring confusion. In 1991, Hassan II declared that the old Place des Nations Unies (around which are grouped the city's main public buildings) be known as Place Mohammed V, while the old Place Mohammed V (the square beside the Medina) became renamed Place des Nations Unies.

Note also that, as elsewhere in Morocco, many of the **old French street names** have been revised to bear Moroccan names; older people and many *petit taxi* drivers still use the old names – as do some street maps still on sale. Significant conversions include:

Rue Branly – Rue Sharif Amziane

Rue Claude – Rue Mohammed El Qorri

Rue Colbert – Rue Chaouia

Rue Foucauld – Rue Araibi Jilali

Rue de l'Horloge – Rue Allal Ben Abdallah

Further map confusion is likely to be caused around the millennium by the proposed remodelling of avenues to create a ceremonial approach from the (new) Place des Nations Unies to the Mosquée Hassan II. The planned route – the so-called **Mosquée–Théâtre axis** – will mean a fair amount of demolition southwest of the Old Medina.

earnings to their families in the country, intending to rejoin them permanently as soon as they had raised sufficient funds for a business at home.

The pattern is now much more towards permanent settlement, and this, together with a strict control of migration and a limited number of self-help programmes, has eased and cleared many of the worst slums. Also, *bidonville* dwellers have been accorded increasing respect during recent years. They cannot be evicted if they have lived in a property over two years, and after ten years they acquire title to the land and building, which can be used as collateral at the bank for loans. The dread of every *bidonville* family is to be evicted and put in a high-rise block, which is regarded as the lowest of the low on the housing ladder.

The problem of a concentrated urban poor, however, is more enduring and represents, as it did for the French, an intermittent threat to government stability. Casa, through the 1940s and 1950s, was the main centre of anti-French rioting, and post-independence it was the city's working class which formed the base of Ben Barka's Socialist Party. There have been strikes here sporadically in subsequent decades, and on several occasions, most violently in the food strikes of 1982, they have precipitated rioting. Whether Casa's development can be sustained, and the lot of its new migrants improved, must decide much of Morocco's future.

Orientation

Casa is a large city by any standards and it can be a bewildering place in which to arrive, especially if you come in on one of the trains that terminate at the main **Gare des Voyageurs** (2km from the centre) rather than continuing on to the better-situated **Gare du Port** (see "Points of Arrival", on p.282).

Once you're in the city centre, however, orientation is relatively straightforward. The city centre is focused on a large public square, **Place Mohammed V** (but note box above), and most of the places to stay, eat, or (in a rather limited way) see, are located in and around the avenues that radiate from it. A few blocks to the north, still partially walled, is the **Old Medina**, which was all there was of Casablanca until around 1907.

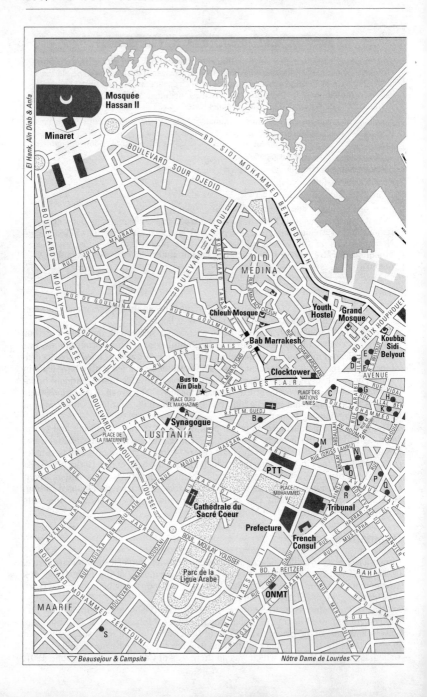

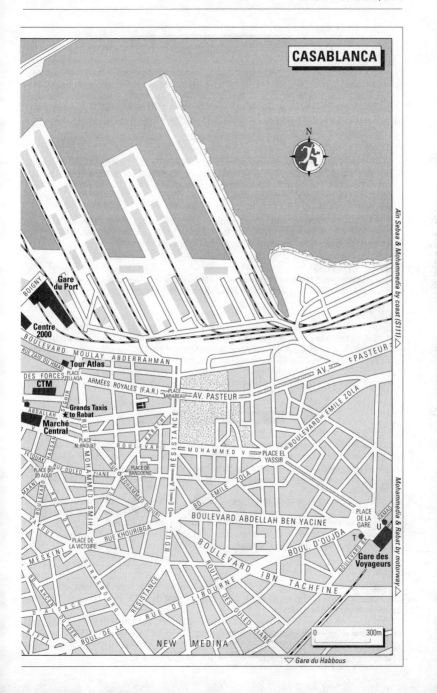

CASABLANCA

N

Aïn Sebaa & Mohammedia by coast (S111) ▷

Mohammedia & Rabat by motorway ▷

Gare du Port

Centre 2000

BOULEVARD MOULAY ABDERRAHMAN

RUE ZAID OU HMAD

BOIGNY

Tour Atlas

PLACE ZELLAQA

DES FORCES

CTM

ARMÉES ROYALES (F.A.R.)

PLACE MIRABEAU

AV. PASTEUR

AV. = E PASTEUR

RUE SEGHIR

ABDALLAH

Grands Taxis ★ to Rabat

Marché Central

PLACE N. PAQUET

RUE KARACHI

BOULEVARD

RUE HASSAN

FETOUAK

RUE OULED

PLACE DU 20 AOÛT

RUE MOHAMMED SMIHA

RUE MOHAMMED DIOURI

PLACE DE BANDOENG

BOULEVARD

MOHAMMED V

DE LA RÉSISTANCE

BOULEVARD EMILE ZOLA

PLACE EL YASSIR

BD EMILE ZOLA

MAAN

TAKDOUT

RUE DE

PLACE DE LA VICTOIRE

RUE KHOURIBGA

BOULEVARD ABDELLAH BEN YACINE

PLACE DE LA GARE

U

NAMAH

BOULEVARD

MESKIN

STRASBOURG

RESISTANCE

BOULEVARD

ROUTE DE LIBOURNE

BOULEVARD IBN TACHFINE

BOUL. D'OUJDA

BOULEVARD

T

Gare des Voyageurs

D'ALSACE

D'ALGER

BOUL. DE LA

RUE DE LIBOURNE

RUE DES OULED ZIANE

0   300m

NEW MEDINA

▽ Gare du Habbous

POINTS OF ARRIVAL

BY TRAIN

All the **trains** from Marrakesh run to the **Gare des Voyageurs**, at the far end of Bd. Mohammed V. Here, you can wait for a train from the airport which passes through Gare des Voyageurs and terminates at the central **Gare du Port**, 150m from Place des Nations Unies. From Rabat (and Fes/Tangier), trains either terminate at Gard du Port or, if carrying on to Marrakesh, pass through Gare des Voyageurs, from where you could wait for the train from the airport.

If you don't care to wait for a train from the airport and if you are quick and very determined, you might just get a place on bus #30, which runs into town from the square in front of the **Gare des Voyageurs**; otherwise, reckon on a twenty-minute walk or a *petit taxi* ride. Bd. Mohammed V runs straight ahead from the square in front of the station, curving slightly to the left as you come to the next main square (Place El Yassir).

BY BUS

Bus stations are more central and straightforward. All the CTM buses arrive at the CTM *Gare Routière* on Rue Léon l'Africain (off Av. des F.A.R. and behind the *Hôtel Safir*). Private line buses use a terminal south of the Place de la Victoire.

BY GRAND TAXI

Grands taxis usually stop just behind the CTM *Gare Routière* (see buses, above), near the *Hôtel Safir* and the *Complex Culturel Sidi Belyout* at 28 Rue Léon l'Africain.

BY AIR

Coming from the **Aéroport Mohammed V**, used by all international and most domestic flights, there is a train service to Casablanca, calling at both the Voyageurs (20 min) and Port (30 min) stations; it runs roughly every hour from 7.25am to 10.30pm and costs 35dh. There is also a shuttle bus between the airport and the CTM Gare Routière.

For flights at odd hours you would need to charter a *grand taxi* to get from Casa to the airport. These are available from behind the CTM (see above) and should cost around 200dh.

CITY TRANSPORT

Getting around the city, **petits taxis** are easy to find along the main avenues and are invariably metered – as long as the meter is switched on you will rarely pay more than 6dh per taxi for a trip round town. For Aïn Diab the fare is currently 18dh (4dh extra if you get the driver to detour en route round the Mosquée Hassan II). There is a 20 percent surcharge at night.

You are unlikely to need to make use of **city bus** services, other than those from the airport or Gare des Voyageurs (see above), and, if headed for the seaside, the #9 service from Bd. de Paris to Aïn Diab. They get very crowded at rush hours.

Traffic is a nightmare in Casa: if you can avoid **driving**, try to do so. If you have a car, the larger hotels at Aïn Diab offer more security than those in the city centre.

Much further out to the south is the **Habous** quarter – the **New Medina**, created by the French, while to the west, along the corniche past the Mosquée Hassan II, lies the beach suburb of **Aïn Diab**.

Our **map** on the previous page covers the city centre, but not Habous and Aïn Diab; to see how these relate, take a look at the map in the Casablanca ONMT pamphlet. Along with other information, this is available at the city's **ONMT** office at 55 Rue Omar Slaoui , or the **Syndicat d'Initiative** at 98 Bd. Mohammed V.

Accommodation

Although there is a large number of hotels in Casa, they operate at near capacity for much of the year and can fill unexpectedly (and sometimes at short notice) for conferences. If possible, phone ahead for a room, or at least arrive fairly early in the day. Even if you have a reservation, it's wise to phone ahead the day before to confirm. If there is a royal-patronage event on, your hotel may well be commandeered.

City centre

The recommendations listed below are in the main, central area of the city. No hotels in the Old Medina have been included, as most overcharge for miserable rooms; in the "new city", by contrast, many of the cheaper classified places are quite stylish Art Deco buildings.

CHEAP

Auberge de Jeunesse (Youth Hostel) [labelled], 6 Place Amiral Philibert (☎02/22.05.51). A friendly, airy place, nicely sited just inside the Medina, and well maintained. To reach it from Gare du Port, walk up Bd. Houphouet Boigny, then turn right along Bd. des Almohades and take the second opening in the Medina walls: the hostel is on your right, at the near side of a small square. IYHF card not required but, if you are a member, it's cheaper (30dh per person, otherwise 40dh: includes breakfast and shower). Despite being more expensive than most, it's value for money – and popular; reservations are advisable June–Sept. Open 8–10am and noon–11pm. On the leafy square, there's a good café, small *PTT* and a *hammam*. YHA card obligatory.

Hôtel Colbert [J], 38 Rue Chaouia (☎02/31.42.41). Useful location if you arrive by bus; it's one block from the CTM. The hotel sign is difficult to see, but it is across the street from the daily flower stalls against the outer wall of the Marché Central. A bit gloomy, but clean and friendly. Rooms with showers cost more. ①

Hôtel de Foucauld [G], 52 Rue Araibi Jilalali (☎02/22.26.66). An old French hotel and perhaps the best of the cheapies. In summer it runs a restaurant and there are many good eating places around, starting with snacks at the *Glacier Alaska* next door. ①

Hôtel Kon-Tiki [K], 88 Rue Allal Ben Abdallah (☎02/31.49.27). Ordinary but satisfactory. The presence of a bar, *Cintra*, next door might (or might not) appeal. ⑩

Hôtel Mon Rêve [I], 7 Rue Chaouia (☎02/31.14.39). One of the best in a cluster of cheap hotels in this area. Showers on the corridor. ⑩

Hôtel Rialto [L], 9 Rue Mohammed El Qorri (☎02/27.51.22). Nothing special, though the location is handy, facing the *Hot Dog* snack bar, and near the Cinema Rialto. Showers in the rooms, toilets on the corridor. ①

Hôtel Terminus [T], 184 Bd. Ba Hamad (☎02/24.00.25). Close to the Gare des Voyageurs, so quite convenient: clean, decent rooms with hot showers on the corridor. It's not in the same league as the nearby *Hôtel Ibis* (see "Expensive") but then it's less than one third of the cost. ⑩

Hôtel Touring [H], 87 Rue Allal Ben Abdallah (☎02/31.02.16). Another old French hotel that gets rather mixed reports from readers. A fall-back, really. ⑩

Hôtel Volubilis [P], 20 Rue Abdelkrim Diouri (☎02/20.77.89). Another fall-back choice – nothing special, nothing terrible. ⑩

MODERATE

Hôtel Aviatic [S], 197 Bd. Brahim Roudani (☎02/25.78.55). Well maintained and popular, but a little way out, by the Parc de la Ligue Arabe. Rooms on the courtyard are quieter. ②

Hôtel du Centre [F], 1 Rue Sidi Belyout/corner Av. des F.A.R. (☎02/44.61.80). A golden oldie, once called the *Georges V*, with an antique lift and dicey wiring in some rooms, but central and cheerful. Breakfast included. ③

Hôtel Excelsior [C], 2 Rue El Amraoui Brahim, off Place des Nations Unies (☎02/20.02.63). Another once-grand hotel, opened in 1915 and thus Casa's oldest surviving hotel. Although outclassed these days by the big chain hotels on Av. des F.A.R. Central, it retains an elegance and a very convenient location, near the Gare du Port. ③

Hôtel Lausanne [M], 24 Rue Tata – aka Rue Poincaré (☎02/26.86.90). Not easy to find; it's opposite the *Cinema Lutetia* which most locals know well. The owner has lived in Switzerland where, according to Bernard Shaw, they know all about hotels. The *Hôtel Lausanne* illustrates his point; it's comfortable and well managed – and there is to be a *salon de thé* next door. ③

Majestic Hôtel [Q], 55 Av. Lalla Yacout (☎02/31.09.51). Built in 1945, this hotel, with extravagant Moorish decor, has class. All mod cons, including TV in the rooms. Comfortable and good value. Restaurant. ③

Hotel de Noailles [R], 22 Bd. du 11 Janvier (☎02/26.05.83) just off Av. Lalla Yacout. Immaculate and tasteful with a salon de thé: a touch of class, but friendly with it. ③

Hôtel de Paris [O], 2 Rue Sharif Amzian (☎02/27.38.71), on the corner with the pedestrianized length of Rue Prince Moulay Abdallah. In the centre of town and highly recommended; it's often full, so book or arrive early. ③

Hôtel Plaza [D], 18 Bd. Houphouet Boigny (☎02/22.02.26). A short walk up from the Gare du Port. Another old hotel with big gloomy rooms, some en suite. However, it's in the throes of refurbishment and is still reasonable value. ③

Hôtel Windsor [A], 93 Place Oued El Makhazine (☎02/20.03.52). Another nice hotel; large rooms with showers or bathrooms. The long-term plans, following the completion of the Mosquée Hassan II, include a metro system with a station – and the proposed new theatre – on Place Oued El Makhazine. This could lead to the hotel's demolition – or enhance its value. ③

EXPENSIVE

Hôtel Basma [B], 35 Av. Moulay Hassan I, just off Place des Nations Unies (☎02/22.33.23). A newish business hotel, with a first floor restaurant. Views over the Medina and towards the Mosquée Hassan II. ④

Hôtel Guynemer [N], 2 Rue Mohammed Belloul (☎02/27.57.64). A 1920s hotel: in 1993, the new owner refurbished the hotel – and a restaurant is promised. Currently, it's pretty good value. ④

Hôtel Ibis [U], Bd. Ba Hamad, Place de la Gare (☎02/40.19.84). As with all hotels in this popular chain (formely Moussafir), the site is by the train station; in this case Casa-Voyageurs, so it's hard-

---

HOTEL PRICE CODES AND STAR RATINGS

Hotels are no longer obliged to charge according to the official star-ratings (from 1* to 5* luxury), as had long been the custom. Nevertheless, **prices** continue to reflect the star-ratings acquired. The basis of our own **hotel price codes**, set out below and keyed throughout the guide, is the price currently quoted for the cheapest double room in high season (June–September) – and is thus more reliable than quoting notional prices according to star-rating.

Note that cheaper prices in the lower categories are generally for rooms with just a wash-basin – you always pay extra for **en-suite** shower and WC – and that double rooms can generally be converted into **triples/family rooms**, with extra beds, for a modest extra charge. Note also that the prices quoted by all hotels are subject to various local and regional **taxes**, which can add 15 to 20 percent to the bill.

Our code	Classification	Single room price	Double room price
⑩	Unclassified	25–60dh	50–99dh
①	1*A/1*B	60–105dh	100–149dh
②	2*B/2*A	105–145dh	150–199dh
③	3*B/3*A	145–225dh	200–299dh
④	4*B/4*A	225–400dh	300–599dh
⑤	5*luxury	Upwards of 400dh	Upwards of 600dh

TELEPHONE CODES

All telephone numbers in the Greater Casablanca region are prefixed **02**. When making a call within the region you omit this prefix. For more explanation of phone codes and making calls within (or to) Morocco, see pp.45–46.

ly central, though convenient for a late arrival (book in advance) or early departure. Restaurant, (sometimes noisy) bar, and small swimming pool. ④

Hôtel Toubkal [E], 9 Rue Sidi Belyout – off Av. des F.A.R. (☎02/31.14.14). An upmarket location, near the chic shops on Bd. Mohammed V, and luxurious, air-conditioned rooms. Nonetheless, it's nothing very special for the price. ⑤

Aïn Diab

The seaside suburb of Aïn Diab (12dh by *petit taxi*) provides an alternative base if you can afford any of the trio of hotels below; all are comfortable business/tourist places, close by the beach. There are also a few unclassified hotels in the area but these cater exclusively for Moroccan guests, and tourists are unlikely to find rooms on offer.

Azur Hôtel, 41 Bd. de la Corniche (☎02/39.13.64). Previously the *Hôtel Tarik*, there's been a change of name but not of owner, and the hotel is much the same as before. It's on the landward side of the coast road, so does not have ready access to the beach, but it has a swimming pool. The rooms are simple, but elegantly finished. ④

Hôtel Bellerive, 38 Bd. de la Corniche (☎02/39.14.09). Overlooks the beach so the absence of a swimming pool is no great drawback, and the restaurant, albeit a touch expensive, compensates. ③

Hôtel de la Corniche, Bd. de la Corniche (☎02/36.27.82). Old, well-established hotel on the beach and with a swimming pool. A little careworn but still comfortable. ④

Camping

Camping Oasis, Av. Jean Mermoz, Beausejour (☎02/25.33.67). This is the nearest site, 8km out on the P8 road to Azemmour and El Jadida. It is frequented mainly by campervans. If driving, follow Bd. Brahim Roudani out from the centre; this eventually becomes Av. Jean Mermoz. Hereabouts, ask for Marché Beausejour; the campsite, which is poorly signposted, is on the left at the end of this street market. There's no camp shop, but the local street market is more than sufficient. Bus #19 and #35 run past the site.

For details of **other accessible campsites**, see the Rabat to Mohammedia coast (pp.274–275), or the coast southwest to El Jadida (pp.294–296).

The City

Guidebooks used to declare, with some amazement, that Casa had not a single "real" monument. Given the scale and success of the 1930s **Art Deco** landmarks of the city centre – including the ensemble of public buildings on **Place Mohammed V** designed by the French architect d'Henri Prost – this was never quite true. However, the city did undoubtedly lack any one single, great building: a situation that, in part, prompted King Hassan II's decision to construct the **Mosquée Hassan II** on a truly epic scale.

The King first spoke of the Mosque on July 9, 1980 (his birthday and Youth Day) saying: 'I wish Casablanca to be endowed with a large, fine building of which it can be proud until the end of time ... I want to build this mosque on the water, because God's throne was on the water. Therefore, the faithful who go there to pray, to praise the creator on firm soil, can contemplate God's sky and ocean.' Thus the Mosque now stands beside the sea on the road to Aïn Diab – and, if curiosity leads no further in this city, it must be seen – indeed, it cannot be missed.

The Mosquée Hassan II

Work on the huge complex of the **Mosquée Hassan II** was launched in 1980 and the mosque was inaugurated on August 30, 1993. The whole complex, however, and the proposed remodelling of the avenues leading towards it from Place des Nations Unies, is unlikely to be completed before the Millennium. Raised on a rocky platform reclaimed from the ocean, it represents the present monarch's most ambitious building project and will surely be his legacy to Moroccan architecture. And, despite the Moroccan tradition of refusing non-Muslims access to religious sites and buildings, it is open to all on accompanied one-hour visits (9am, 10am, 11am and 2pm; closed Fridays; adults 100dh, students 50dh, children 25dh).

Designed by the French architect, Michel Pinseau, the mosque-complex is a phenomenal undertaking. Looking out towards it from the city centre, its huge size tricks you into thinking it is far nearer than it is. Its minaret is actually two hundred metres high, making it by far the tallest structure in the country – as well as the tallest minaret in the world; a laser on its summit projects a beam towards Mecca – to 'point out the way to Allah'. The mosque itself provides space for 20,000 worshippers within, where a glass floor reveals the ocean below, and a further 80,000 in its courtyard. Statisticians note that it is thus second only to Mecca in the mosque-size league – and that St Peter's in Rome could fit comfortably inside. In order that the faithful can 'contemplate God's sky', the enormous roof of the Mosque rolls open on occasions. Eventually, the complex will include a *medersa*, museum and a library. The *medersa* has been completed; the other two were started in 1987, and due for completion in August 1993, but are not yet finished. It's not possible for non-Muslims to visit the *medersa*, but it's assumed that, when completed, visitors will be welcome in the museum, if not the library.

The facts of the mosque's construction are almost as startling as its size. During the early 1990s, when it was being readied for opening, 1400 men worked by day and a further 1100 by night. Most were master-craftsmen, working marble from Agadir, cedar from the Middle Atlas, granite from Tafraoute, and (the only import) glass from Murano near Venice. Equally extraordinary was its cost – which is reckoned to have exceeded £500m/$750m – and the fact that this was raised entirely by public subscription. Press reports outside Morocco have alleged resentment of an over-enthusiastic sponsoring operation which generated donations through non-voluntary deductions from wages, as well as door to door collections – including approaches to expatriate Moroccan workers everywhere from Germany to Saudi Arabia. However, in Morocco there is a genuine pride in the project, and pictures of the mosque (in effect, illustrated receipts) are displayed in homes and cafés throughout the land. The mosque had a knock-on effect on the economy, too; at one stage the level of donations was so high that it temporarily reduced Morocco's money supply and brought down inflation.

That the mosque bears King Hassan's name has inspired rumours that it is designed in part as his mausoleum, along the lines of that of his father, Mohammed V, in Rabat. But it is important to add that in addition to his secular position, Hassan is also "Commander of the Faithful", the spiritual leader of Moroccan Muslims. And the building's site, in addition to reflecting his wish to give the city a heart and a memorable symbol, is designed to represent God's creation of earth, sea and sky.

Mauresque: Place Mohammed V and around

The French city centre and its formal colonial buildings already seem to belong to a different and distant age. Grouped round **Place Mohammed V** (the former Place des Nations Unies), they served as models for administrative architecture throughout Morocco, and to an extent still do. Their style, heavily influenced by Art Deco, is known as *Mauresque* – a French idealization and "improvement" on Moorish design. The effect of the central ensemble is actually very impressive, the only feature out of place being a clocktower in the *préfecture* – an irresistible French colonial addition. Three times a week the fountain is lit from within by changing coloured lights, to taped music.

Other fine Mauresque and Art Deco buildings are to be seen along Boulevard Mohammed V, including a couple of the older hotels. They are begining to be appreciated by the local authorities and there are, apparently, plans to establish an Art Deco historic district. Trademarks of the style on these private buildings are wrought-iron windows, staircases and balconies, and floral, animal and geometric designs on stuccoed pediments and friezes.

The Cathedral and Quartier Habous

More European in style, though again adopting traditional Moroccan forms, is the old **Cathedral of Sacre Cœur** at the far end of the **Parc de la Ligue Arabe**. It was built to a wonderfully balanced and airy design, paying genuine homage to its Moroccan setting. But it has fallen on hard times. After independence, it was used as a school and then as a theatre and cultural centre; now it is empty and, although the exterior is still magnificent, the interior is desecrated by neglect. Its future is uncertain; entry is forbidden – and may even be dangerous.

About a kilometre to the southwest, at the end of Av. Mers Sultan, is the **New Medina** – or **Quartier Habous** – which displays a somewhat more bizarre extension of *Mauresque*. Built in the 1930s as a response to the first *bidonville* crisis, it was intended as a model quarter, and after half a century it still has a kind of Lego-land look, with its neat little rows of streets. What's most unreal, perhaps, is the neighbourhood mosque, flanked by a tidy stretch of green just as if it were a provincial French church.

South again from the New Medina, at the junction of Av. Mers Sultan and Av. 2 mars, alongside the Rond-point de l'Europe, is a last sight in these parts – the **Church of Notre-Dame de Lourdes**. Completed in the 1950s, it is smaller than the cathedral and still in use. Its pride and joy are its beautiful stained-glass windows, the work of Gabriel Loire, a master craftsman from Chartres.

The Jewish Community

Today, more than 60 percent of Morocco's 6000 to 7000 Jews live in Casablanca, mainly in the **Lusitania district** – on and around Rue Ibn Rochd, formerly Rue Lusitania. The city's principal synagogue, **Benarroch**, stands at the junction of Rue Ibn Rochd and Rue J.J. Rousseau; another, **Em Habanime**, is to be found on Rue Ibn Rochd. In the same area, there are two Jewish **schools**, one primary and the other secondary, on Bd. Moulay Youssef near its intersection with Bd. d'Anfa at Place de la Fraternité; up to 350 children attend these schools, though other Jewish children attend Moroccan state schools. A Jewish museum is planned in a nearby building that served as a *yeshita* (rabbinical college for Orthodox students) until 1990.

For further information on Jewish affairs in Casablanca, visit the ICF business school at 73 Bd. Mohammed V and ask to speak with the director: M Abergel (☎02/22.17.59 or ☎02/36.22.68).

The Old Medina and the port

The **Old Medina**, lapsing into dilapidation above the port, is largely the product of the late nineteenth century, when Casa began its modest growth as a commercial centre. Before that, it was little more than a group of village huts, half-heartedly settled by local tribes after the site was abandoned by the Portuguese in 1755. *Casa Branca*, the town the Portuguese founded here in the fifteenth century after the expulsion of the pirates, had been virtually levelled by the great earthquake of that year (which also destroyed Lisbon). Only its name ("The White House"; *Casablanca* in Spanish; *Dar El Baida* in Arabic) survives.

Now relatively underpopulated, the Medina has a slightly disreputable, if also fairly affluent, air. It is said to be the place to go to look for any stolen goods you might want to buy back – a character well in keeping with many of the stalls. There's nothing sinister though, and it can be a good source for cheap snacks and general goods. A single main street, which starts from the top end of Bd. Houphouet Boigny by the restored clocktower as **Rue Chakib Arsalane**, becomes **Rue Jemaa Ach Chleuh** halfway

---

YOU MUST REMEMBER THIS . . .

Probably the best-known fact about Casablanca is that it wasn't the location for the movie – all of which was shot in Hollywood. In fact, Warner Bros, upset by the Marx Brothers filming *A Night in Casablanca*, attempted to copyright the very name Casablanca – which could have been inconvenient for the city.

The film of course owes its enduring success to H. Bogart, I. Bergman and Sam's songs, but at the time of its release it received a major publicity boost by the appearance of Casablanca and Morocco in the news. As the film was being completed, in November 1942, the Allies launched **Operation Torch**, landing 25,000 troops on the coast north and south of Casablanca, at Kenitra, Mohammedia and Safi. The troops were commanded by General Eisenhower and consisted principally of Americans, whom Roosevelt believed were less likely than the British to be fired on by the Vichy French government in Morocco. An infinitely more fortunate coincidence, however, took place in the week of the film's première in Los Angeles in January 1943. Churchill and Roosevelt had arranged an Allied Leaders' summit, and the newsreels revealed its location: the **Casablanca Conference**, held in a hotel (long since gone) in the affluent suburb of Anfa, out beyond Aïn Diab.

Such events – and the movie – are not, it has to be said, evoked by modern-day Casa. Film buffs with a strong sense of irony, however, might check out **Rick's Bar** (open from 10pm) in the *Hôtel Hyatt Regency* on Place des Nations Unies, where the waiters take your (very expensive) drinks orders dressed in trenchcoats and fedoras. And for a glimpse of True Brit Expat life, as it used to be lived, there is always the **Churchill Club** on Rue Pessac in Aïn Diab. Established in 1922, as the "British Bank Club", its one condition of membership is that "the English language only should be spoken on the premises". One of the social highlights of the week is still the post-church and pre-Sunday lunch drinks.

---

along. This street edges its way right through the quarter, past most of the market stalls and the principal mosque from which it takes its second name. At the far end, a small eighteenth-century bastion,: the **Skala**, has been restored, with some old cannons. The walls on the west side of the Medina, starting with a restored Ottoman-style clock tower, have also been renovated.

While in the Medina area, you might also take the time to wander down to the **Centre 2000** complex, by the Gare du Port. Built in the mid-1980s, it encompasses twenty or so shops and five restaurants (see p.290), and all in all is quite an eye-opener into modern Casa life.

The one other building of interest hereabouts is the **Koubba of Sidi Belyout**, on the left as you walk up Bd. Houphouet Boigny from the Gare du Port and Centre 2000. There's a high wall round a small enclosure (which is forbiden to non-Muslims) but through the open door you can see the white domed tomb. Sidi Belyout is the patron saint of Casablanca and he has lent his name to the district southeast of the port. Legend has it that he despaired of mankind, blinded himself and went to live with animals who took care of him.

Aïn Diab: the beach

You can get out to the beach suburb of **Aïn Diab** by bus (#9 from Bd. de Paris; see our map), by *petit taxi* (easily engaged around Place des Nations Unies) or on foot. The beach starts around 3km out from the port and Old Medina, past the Mosquée Hassan II, and continues for about the same distance.

A beach right within Casa may not sound alluring – and it's certainly not the cleanest and clearest stretch of the country's waters. But Aïn Diab's big attraction is not so much the sea – in whose shallow waters Moroccans gather in phalanx formations, wary of the currents – as the **beach clubs** along its front. Each of these has one or more pools, usually filled with filtered seawater, a restaurant and a couple of snack bars; in the fancier ones there'll also be additional sports facilities like tennis or volleyball and perhaps even a disco. The novelty of coming upon this in a Moroccan city is quite amazing, and it's a strange sight to see women veiled from head to toe looking down onto the cosmopolitan intensity unfolding beneath them.

The prices and quality of the **beach clubs** vary enormously and it's worth wandering round a while to check out what's available. Most locals have annual membership and for outsiders a day or weekend ticket can work out surprisingly expensive (£5–10 a day). But there's quite often one place which has thrown its doors open for free in an attempt to boost its café business. If you are taking a *petit* taxi from the Mosquée Hassan II or the city centre, ask to be set down at any one of *Le Tonga, Miami, Tahiti* or *Plage Anfa;* then reconnoitre and make your choice..

Out beyond Aïn Diab, along the corniche and inland from it, is the suburb of **Anfa**, where the city's wealthy have their villas, and companies their corporate headquarters – including the striking **OCP** (*Office Chérifien des Phosphates*) shiny black block alongside the Old Casablanca airport, now known as Aeroport Casa Anfa and used for private and business internal flights. Here, too, are the villas of rich Saudis, and overlooking the corniche, the wealthy **Ibn Saud Foundation** and its beautiful mosque.

Restaurants, bars and nightlife

Casa has the reputation of being the best place to eat in Morocco, and if you can afford the fancier restaurant prices, this is certainly true. There are fine seafood restaurants along the corniche at Aïn Diab and the bays beyond, and some stylish old French colonial ones round the central boulevards. On a budget, too, there's little problem in finding good-value meals or snacks.

Restaurants

Good restaurants in three areas – **downtown Casa**, inside the **Centre 2000** (the shopping complex by the port) and around the **Corniche/Aïn Diab** – are suggested below. In addition, there are inexpensive hole-in-the-wall eateries in the **Old Medina**, and if you're putting together a picnic, the **Marché Central** (6am–2pm) on Rue Chaouia groans under the weight of the freshest and best produce in Morocco.

DOWNTOWN: AROUND THE MAIN BOULEVARDS

Snack Bouli de Nega, 72 Rue Araibi Jilali. Convenient for *Hôtel Foucauld*; open all hours. Tasty and cheap snacks.

Le Buffet, 99 Bd. Mohammed V. Quick and bright, and very popular. Good value *menu du jour*. Unlicensed. Cheap to moderate.

Le Caféteria, corner of Rue Abdelkrim Diouri and Rue Chaouia, near *Hôtel Volubilis*. Casa's answer to the American drugstore; popular with the city's youth. Unlicensed. Cheap to moderate.

Restaurant Le Cardinal, 11 Bd. Mohammed (☎02/22.15.60). Traditional French restaurant on the first floor. Moderate

Restaurant La Corrida, 35 Rue El Avaar – parallel to Rue Mustata Al Maani (☎02/27.81.55). Informal tapas-style Spanish restaurant run by a Spanish-French couple. In summer, eat in the garden. Closed Sundays and for the month of September. Moderate.

Taverne du Dauphin, 115 Bd. Houphouet Boigny (☎02/22.12.00). Long-established and very popular fish restaurant. You may need to queue, or you might try making a reservation. Moderate to expensive.

L'Entrecôte, 78 Av. Mers Sultan (☎02/27.26.74), next to a RAM office. French cuisine in a relaxed setting. Moderate to expensive.

Restaurant l'Étoile Marocaine, 107 Rue Allal Ben Abdallah (☎02/31/41/00). Ambitious, with specialities like *pastilla* and *mechoui*. A good atmosphere and convenient for the CTM bus station and Marché Central. Unlicensed. Evenings only. Cheap to moderate.

Restaurant des Fleurs, 42 Av. des F.A.R (☎02/31.27.35). The snack bar downstairs is good for breakfast; upstairs, there is a more formal restaurant serving French and Moroccan dishes. Cheap to moderate.

Café l'Intissar, 14 Rue Chaouia, corner with Rue Allal Ben Abdallah. Excellent-value dishes – with a reliable plat du jour – served up by a young enthusiastic team. Unlicensed. Cheap to moderate.

Le Marignan, 69 Bd. Mohammed V, corner with Rue Mohammed Smiha (☎02/30.98.17). Basement restaurant with excellent Korean food, some cooked at the tables. Moderate to expensive.

Al Mounia, 95 Rue du Prince Moulay Abdallah (☎02/22/26.69). Traditional Moroccan cuisine served in a salon or out in the garden. You can eat well for 150dh. Closed Sundays.

Restaurant La Pagode, 95 Rue Ferhat Hachad (☎02/27.71.55). A good Chinese restaurant, a little out from the city centre, near *Hôtel du Palais*. Moderate.

Restaurant au Petit Poucet, 86 Bd. Mohammed V (☎02/27.54.20). A slice of old Casablanca style, this French restaurant is dressed up like a 1920s Parisian salon (which is really what it was). It was here that the French aviator and writer Saint-Exupéry used to recuperate between his mail-flights south to the Sahara; a couple of framed sketches by him grace the walls. You come for the decor rather than the food – which is OK but nothing more. Prices are moderate and there is a (much cheaper) snack bar next door.

Restaurant Le Tonkin, 34 Rue Prince Moulay Abdallach (☎02/22.19.13). On the pedestrianized length of the street and on the first floor. Chinese and Vietnamese dishes in a 'cadre exotique'. Moderate.

Restaurant La Tuffe Blanche, 57 Tahar Sebti (☎02/27.72.63). One of the few remaining Jewish eating places and serving halal dishes. Convenient for the *Hôtel Guynemer* and *Hôtel de Paris*. Cheap to moderate.

CENTRE 2000

There are five restaurants in this shopping complex, which is down by the Gare du Port; all of them are good value, albeit on the pricey side, and open form 8pm.

Le Chalutier (☎02/20.34.55; closed Sun). A busy Spanish-run fish restaurant. Moderate.

La Gondole (☎02/27.74.88). Despite the name, it's French-run – Toulousian to be precise. But it serves a range of European dishes from crêpes to pizzas. Moderate.

Le Mekong (☎02/27.65.36; closed Mon). Asiatic, mainly Chinese, cuisine. So successful it has expanded into part of *La Gondole*. Moderate.

Le Retro 1900 (☎02/20.58.28; closed Sun). The most upmarket Centre 2000 choice, serving French cuisine with flair, supervised by chef Jacky Rolling. Popular with businessmen at noon and *bon viveurs* in the evenings. Expensive.

Le Tajine (☎02/27.64.00). Well-prepared Moroccan specialities. Moderate to expensive.

ON THE COAST

Listings below are from east to west along the Corniche to Aïn Diab and beyond.

Le Cabestan, El Hank (☎02/39.11.90; closed Sun). French cuisine, overseen by a highly competent patronne. Nice views of the El Hank lighthouse. Moderate to expensive.

La Mer, El Hank (☎02/36.33.15). Almost next door to *Le Cabestan*; specializes in seafood and fish. Expensive.

Orient Express, 41 Bd. de la Corniche (☎02/36.70.73). An eccentric bar-restaurant, alongside the *Azur Hôtel*, in a coach from the Orient Express. Now more drinking than eating, but still fun.

Notre Alsace, 59 Bd. de la Corniche (☎02/36.71.91). A very pleasant bar-restaurant-brasserie; also has a few rooms to let. Moderate.

Restaurant La Mamma, corner of Bd. de la Corniche and Bd. de Biarritz (☎02/39.15.58). A wide range of pasta and standard Italian dishes. Moderate.

Restaurant Sijilmassa, Bd. de Biarritz (☎02/36.13.50). Classic Moroccan dishes, including *pastilla*, served in gardens overlooking the sea. Fantastic view, but you may be discouraged by the restrictions. Women and children must be accompanied; cheques and credit cards are not accepted; and photography is forbidden! Moderate.

A Ma Bretagne, Sidi Abderrahmane, 2km west of Aïn Diab (☎02/36.21.12; closed Sun and throughout Aug). French gastronomes visit Casablanca purely to eat at this restaurant, which is run by

André Halbert, one of just three *Maître Cuisiniers de France* working in Africa and recipient of an award for the best French cooking in the continent. All the certificates and awards are displayed in the foyer. Specialities include *huîtres au Champagne* and *salade de l'océan au foie gras*; the site is delightful, close to the little island *marabout* of Sidi Abderrahmane (see p.294). Naturally, it's not cheap and you should anticipate upwards of 300dh a head.

Ice cream and pâtisseries

Casa has a reputation for its **ice cream parlours** and **pâtisseries**, too.

Oliver's, Av. Hassan II; **L'Igloo**, Bd. du Janvier (south of Place Mohammed V). The two best ice cream parlours in the city.

Gâteaux Bennis, 2 Rue Fkih El Gabbas. A rival in the Quartier Habous.

Bars and nightclubs

Casa has a surprisingly elusive **nightlife**, at least in the centre, where the clubs tend to be 1960s-themepark-stripjoints. More happens out at Aïn Diab, though none are much recommended to Western women out for a hassle-free drink. Hotel bars provide a fall-back – see the hotel listings for suggestions.

CENTRAL CASA

Au Petit Poucet, 86 Bd. Mohammed V. A bar attached to the famous restaurant; one of the more pleasant downtown serious drinking holes.

American Bar, 49 Bd. Houphouet Boigny. Similar, if perhaps noisier.

La Cage, Centre 2000. Attracts a young crowd.

Club 84, Bd. El Mouahadine, near Gare du Port. Much the same as *La Cage* – and they are near enough to try both.

Don Quichote, 6 Bd. Houphouet Boigny at the junction with Av. des F.A.R. A real late-night dive, where you'll likely meet some Casa low-life.

La Arizona, across Av. des F.A.R. (from the *Don Quichotte*) on Rue El Amraoui Brahim, near the *Hôtel Excelsior*. Dancing of all sorts, a lot of noise and occasional shows.

La Fontaine, 133 Bd. Houphouet Boigny. Worse still: an ill-lit strip joint, with a band, belly dancing, and obligatory drinks for the women bar-staff.

Hôtel Safir, Av. des F.A.R in front of the CTM bus station. The hotel has an expensive, very swish (and pretty tasteful) bar – as well as a disco. Relaxed – especially by comparison with all the above.

Hôtel Hyatt Regency, Place des Nations Unies. The hotel houses *Rick's Bar* (see boxed feature "You must remember this . . ." on p.288), another expensive bar, and a nightclub, the *Black House*.

ON THE COAST

Le Balcon 33, 33 Bd. de la Corniche. Lively regular disco.

Le Tube, Bd. de la Corniche. Another popular disco.

Palm Beach Club, Aïn Diab. If you want to live a little more dangerously, try this beerhall, with its belly dancers, heavy-drinking crowd and police on the door to prevent trouble.

Metropolis, in the *Hôtel Suisse*; **La Notte** and **Calypso** are also on the Corniche and can be fun. Or maybe the driver of your *petit taxi* will tell you which bars and nightclubs are suited to your taste.

Listings

In addition to listings below, you may want to consult *Telecontact*, an annual directory with yellow pages style listings for businesses and services in the Rabat/Casablanca/Kenitra region. It is available from newsstands.

Airline offices include: *Royal Air Maroc*, 44 Av. des F.A.R. (☎02/31.11.22); *Air France*, 15 Av. des F.A.R. (☎02/29.30.30); *Iberia*, 17 Av. des F.A.R. (☎02/29.40.03); *British Airways/GB Airways*, c/o *Menara Tours*, Tour Atlas (6th floor), 57 Place Zellaqa (☎02/30.76.29).

American Express c/o *Voyages Schwarz*, 112 Rue Prince Moulay Abdallah (☎02/22.29.47); open Mon–Fri 8.30am–noon & 2.00–6.00pm, Sat 8.30am–noon.

Banks *SGMB,* 84 Bd. Mohammed V; *Crédit du Maroc,* 48–58 Bd. Mohammed V; many others along the same boulevard; *BMCE,* 140 Av. Hassan II, has ATM. Most of the larger hotels will change money outside banking hours. Central ones include the *Royal El Mansour* at 27 Av. des F.A.R., *Hôtel Safir* at 160 Av. des F.A.R. and the *Hyatt Regency* on Place des Nations Unies.

Books/Newspapers For English-language **books** try English Forum, 27 Rue Mouftaker Abdelkader, or the American Language Centre Bookstore, 1 Place de la Fraternité (just off Bd. Moulay Youssef), both of which have a good range of paperbacks and fair sections on Morocco. Librairie Farairie, 43 Rue Araibi Jilali, and Librairie Nationale, 2 Av. de Mers Sultan, are also good for a browse. British **newspapers** and the *International Herald Tribune* are available from stands around Place des Nations Unies (and in the *Hyatt Regency* on the *place*) and at the Gare du Port.

Car rental *Telecontact* (see previous page) lists 65 car rental firms in Casa. Competition is stiff and deals are generally the best in the country, if you spend a while phoning around, or call in at the offices grouped along the Av. des F.A.R. A shortlist might include: *Afric Cars,* 33 Rue Omar Slaoui (☎02/24.21.81); *Avis,* 19 Av. des F.A.R. (☎02/31.24.24); *Budget,* 50 Av. des F.A.R. (☎02/31.41.09); *Citer,* Hôtel Hyatt Regency (☎02/26.13.34); *Europ-Car/InterRent,* 144 Av. des F.A.R. (☎02/31.40.69); *Goldcar,* 5 Av. des F.A.R. (☎02/20.25.10); *Golden Tours,* 117 Rue Mustapha El Maani (☎02/44.74.34); *Hertz,* 25 Rue Araibi Jilali (☎02/31.22.23); *Tourist Cars,* 53 Rue Allal Ben Abdallah (☎02/31.19.35); *Visacar,* Hôtel Washington, 26 Bd. Rahal El Meskini (☎02/29.46.76); and *Week-end Cars,* 3 Rue du Thann, off Bd. Rahal El Miskini (☎02/44.22.53).

Car repairs Garages include Renault (☎02/30.05.91) Place de Bandoeng; Leyland and Fiat, Afric Auto (☎02/27.92.85), 147 Rue Mustapha El Maoui; Ford, AutoHall (☎02/31.90.56), 44 Av. Lalla Yacout; Peugeot, Siara (☎02/30.17.62), 193 Av. des F.A.R.; and Volvo, Saidia StarAuto (☎02.31.90.03), 88 Av. Lalla Yacout.

Consulates There are far fewer consuls than in Rabat. They include: **Britain**, 43 Bd. d'Anfa (☎02/20.33.16); **USA**, 8 Bd. Moulay Youssef (☎02/26.45.50); **Denmark**, 30 Rue Sidi Belyout (☎02/22.07.52). The **French Consulate** on Rue Prince Moulay Abdallah is worth visiting for the equestrian statue of Marshal Lyautey in the couryard; it is by François Gognué and was unveiled in 1933 – a year before Lyautey's death.

Cultural events The new *Complex Cultural Sidi Belyout,* 28 Rue Léon l'Africain (☎02/30.37.60), behind the CTM bus station, has a programme of music, drama and dance. The older *communal theatre* is nearby on Av. des F.A.R. and hosts visiting groups. The *Centre Culturel Français,* 121/3 Bd. Mohammed Zerktouni (☎02/25.90/77) has an extensive programme, particularly in winter: films, concerts, recitals, exhibitions, and library. Details of these, and other events are to be found in the local press, occasionally in the fortnightly *La Quinzaine du Maroc,* from the venues, from the tourist offices and in the major hotels.

Ferry agent *Comanav Voyages,* 43 Av. des F.A.R. (☎02/31.20.50), will give details and sell tickets for most ferry departures from Morocco.

Films Casa is well served by cinemas. The Dawliz chain has two cinemas: *Dawliz Habous* (two screens) in the city near the *Restaurant des Fleurs* (and the Cinema Rif) and *Dawliz Corniche* (three screens) near McDonalds on the Corniche. Besides the *Cinema Rif* on Av. des F.A.R. (see above), there are the *Empire* on Av. Mohammed V, the *Lusitania* opposite the *Hôtel Lausanne* on Rue Tata and, said to be the best, the *Lynx* on Av Mers Sultan.

Hammams Every neighbourhood has several; one of the best is said to be the new 'Turkish' *hammam,* Rue Gerra in the Maarif area – ask a *petit taxi* to take you there.

Medical aid Dial ☎15 for emergency servicesor call *SOS Médecins* (☎02/20.20.20). Addresses of doctors from the larger hotels. Details of pharmacies open out of hours are to be found in the local press, or, out of hours, consult lists displayed by all pharmacies.

Police Phone ☎19. Main station is on Bd. Brahim Roudani.

Post office The main *PTT* (for phones/*poste restante*) is on Place Mohammed V (Mon–Fri 8.00am–6.30pm and Sat 8am–noon). Use separate entrance (open 24hr a day) for international calls and *poste restante.* The building is *Mauresque* in style (see p.286) and was opened in 1919 by Marshal Lyautey.

Religious services At St John the Evangelist, rue Felix et Max Guedj, services in English: 9.30 and 11.15am (to confirm ☎02/25.31.71) and at the Church of Notre-Dame de Lourdes Mass in French: 11am.

Shopping Alpha *55,* Av. de Mers Sultan, is a useful **department store**, with a good, 7th-floor restaurant. For **Moroccan crafts**, there are many shops on both sides of Bd. Houphouet Boigny;

here you might gain extra by bargaining but, at the upmarket boutiques at the Centre 2000, you can expect to pay more. **Supermarkets** are mainly out of the town centre; there are two on Route Bouskara, in L'Oasis district: Macro and, with a *Pizza Hut* as an added attraction, Marjane. There is another Macro in Aïn Sebaa.

Sports Casa is the best place in Morocco to see **football**; the city's rivals, RAJA and WYDAD both have grounds in the Beausejour district; check the local press for fixtures. The city also boasts a **racecourse**, the Hippodrome, at Anfa (active some Sundays) and, beside it, a 9-hole **golfcourse** (☎02/36.53.55); there is another golfcourse with 18 holes at Mohammedia to the northeast (☎03/32.46.56). As well as the beach clubs on the Corniche, you can **swim** in the open-air *Piscine Oceanic* in Aïn Sebaa. In the Maarif district, there is the *Stade d'Honneur*, a sports complex (☎02/36.23.72) with a lot to offer. Finally, and not strictly sporting but, if you have children to entertain, there is the *Sindibad* **amusement park** beyond the hotels on the Corniche, with a huge cut-out of Sinbad: pedalos, dodgems, roundabouts, slides, etc.

Tourist Offices The Délégation du Tourisme (formerly ONMT), 55 Rue Omar Slaoui (☎02/27.11.77; Mon-Fri 8.30am–noon and 2.30–6.30pm) has little to offer; the Syndicat d'Iniative, 98 Bd. Mohammed V (☎02/22.15.24; Mon–Sat 8.30am–noon and 3–6.30pm: Sat 8.30am–noon) is more helpful and has regular exhibitions of local artists' work.

Tours If you want to book onto a tour of Morocco, *KTI Voyages*, based in Casa, are a very reliable operator, used by British companies like Hayes & Jarvis and Kuoni; their head office is at 161 Av. Hassan II (☎02/27.62.44). If you want to see a lot in a short time, and are rich, you could fly from Casa Anfa with *Privair* (☎02/13.86.39) à la destination de votre choix!

MOVING ON FROM CASA

Moving on from Casa, CTM run **buses** to just about everywhere, including Safi (6 daily), Essaouira (1), Agadir (2), Tiznit (1) and various European destinations; tickets and times from the terminal on Rue Léon l'Africain (see map). If you are heading south for Essaouira, the best service is the "Mumtaz Express", which leaves at 5.00pm, arriving 9.30pm at Essaouira; most other services run via El Jadida and/or Safi. **Grands taxis** also run to Rabat, from the main stand.

You'll probably prefer to go by **train** to Rabat (15 daily), Tangier (4), Meknes (7), Fes (7) or Marrakesh (7). These departures are mainly (but not exclusively) from the *Gare des Voyageurs* but every train from *Gare du Port* to the airport passes through *Gare des Voyageurs* so it's not hard to make a connection.

Casa to Marrakesh: Settat

The road and railway speed south across the plains from **Casa to Marrakesh** – and few people think of stopping along the way. To the east lies the phosphate-mining region, the Plateau des Phosphates, while along the road you pass scarcely more than a handful of local market centres for the (initially quite fertile) agricultural villages, watered by Morocco's greatest river, the Oum Er Rbia.

If you are driving, the one detour to consider is to the **Kasbah de Boulaouane**, 50km west of the region's main town, Settat. The Kasbah was one of Moulay Ismail's grandest and most strategic, protected on three sides by a loop in the Oum Er Rbia. It has a well, preserved gateway and, within, remains of a palace, vaulted underground chambers and a *hammam*. Boulaouane gives its name to the rosé, *Gris de Boulaoune,* produced from the extensive vineyards to be found around the Kasbah and village.

SETTAT itself is a sizeable town and still growing. The bulk of new investment is inevitably in the Casablanca area; but Kenitra and Settat are joint second to Casablanca, whereas the Rabat-Salé area represents a small percentage of new investment. Already, Settat is the centre of the Moroccan **cotton industry**: spinning, weaving and ready-made clothes. In 1992, the Spanish company Tavex, a leading European producer of denim cloth, built a factory here. It now produces half the denim needed for Morocco's clothing industry and has a contract with Wrangler in the US. The town's two-star **hotel** has accordingly been replaced by the five-star business complex, *Hôtel du Parc* (☎03/40.39.51); ④), 3km out on the Marrakesh road.

South to El Jadida

Buses and trains cover the ninety-odd kilometres from **Casablanca to El Jadida** on swift inland routes, of no great interest save for the town of **Azemmour**, an old Portuguese fortress-town at the estuary of the Oum Er Rbia – Morocco's greatest river. Using public transport, Azemmour is easiest visited as an excursion from El Jadida, which is only 16km further southwest.

If you have transport of your own, the old **S130 road** is an enjoyable alternative, trailing the coast the whole way from **Casa to Azzemmour**. As you clear the urban area, the beaches are increasingly enticing and, as yet, virtually undeveloped.

Sidi Abderrahmane and beyond

En route to Azemmour, the most attractive spot is the beach facing the picturesque little island **Marabout of Sidi Abderrahmane**, 10km from central Casa, in the first bay that you come to after passing through Aïn Diab. The island itself is a tiny outcrop of rock, under fifty metres from the rock shore, from which it is possible to walk across at low tide. Non-Muslims, however, may not enter the shrine, which is entirely occupied by the *marabout* – or pilgrim centre – laid out around the shrine of Sidi Abderrahmane, a Muslim Sufi from Baghdad. The pilgrims are, for the most part, the mentally ill and their families, for whom the saint has supposedly curative powers.

Nearby, overlooking the beach, is *A Ma Bretagne* (see p.290), the finest – and most expensive – **restaurant** in the Casablanca area. If you can afford it, and read this in time to make an advance booking, this is likely to be the best meal you ever have in Morocco, or anywhere else come to that.

Further along towards Azzemour, there's little beyond a couple of **campsites**, fronting onto stretches of beach. First of these, 16km from Casa, is *Camping Desserte des Plages*, reached by turning right off the S130, 5km before Dar Bouzza. It's a modest family affair, with no phone and a summer-only café. The other site, *Camping des Tamaris* (☎02/32.00.02), is at Hajra Khala; 20km from Casablanca turn right and it's then a further 5km to the coast and campsite. This takes its name from the surrounding tamarisk bushes whose combustible branches fuel the pottery kilns of Safi. It is a well-run site with aged waiters in faded red dinner jackets serving in the bar.

Azemmour

AZEMMOUR has an oddly remote feel – and history, considering its strategic site on the great Oum Er Rbia River. It has long been outside the mainstream of events. When the Portuguese controlled El Jadida, Safi and Essaouira, they stayed here for under thirty years; later, when the European traders moved in on this coast, the town remained a "closed" port. Little bothered by the French, it remains today very much a backwater and sees possibly fewer tourists than any other Moroccan coastal town.

A short visit, nonetheless, is worthwhile, and the town is easily reached by **bus** or **grand taxi** from El Jadida. It's also on a branch line which runs from the Casablanca–Marrakesh main line but there is only one **train** a day and the station is 2km out of town, on the far side of the P8.

THE EMBROIDERY OF AZEMMOUR

The **embroidery** of Azemmour is distinctive and attractive, but it is more likely to be seen on display in Tangier's Kasbah Museum, or in Rabat's Oudaïas Museum than locally.

Its appeal lies in its design and technique. The designs reflect Renaissance Italy, filtered through Iberia. They depict stylized women, possibly godesses, with upraised arms and full, triangular skirts. There are mythological animals – dragons, griffins and other fabulous beasts. The trees are stylized like a Jewish menorah, the candlestick with seven branches and the ancient symbol of Judaism: surely no coincidence. The technique is often to fill the background with small cross-stiches, revealing the subject in silhouette, reminiscent of embroidery from Assisi.

Once in town, getting your bearings is pretty straightforward. Buses and *grands taxis* stop on **Av. Mohammed V**, the main thoroughfare of the new town, where drivers will also emerge. At the street's end is a garden square, the **Place du Souk**, with the **Medina** straight ahead. If you want to stay, there's just one **hotel**, the basic but friendly *La Victorie* at 308 Av. Mohammed V (☎03/34.71.57; ⑪). The town also has several café-restaurants, best of which is the *Café El Manzah* on Place du Souk, with an active card school upstairs. There's another café-restaurant down at the beach (see below).

The Medina

The Portuguese remained in Azemmour long enough to build a circuit of walls, which are stacked directly above the banks of the river and dramatically extended by the white, cubist line of the **Medina**. The best view of all this – and it is impressive – is from across the river, on the way out of town towards Casablanca.

To look round the Medina, make your way to the Place du Souk, on the landward side of the ramparts, where you will see a sixteenth-century **gate** with an unusual 'European' semi-circular arch. Through it extends the old **Kasbah** – largely in ruins but safe enough to visit. If you wait around, the local *gardien* will probably arrive, open things up and show you round; if he doesn't turn up, you might find him by asking at the cafés. Once inside the ruins, you can follow the parapet wall round the ramparts, with views of the river and the gardens, including henna orchards, along its edge. You'll also be shown **Dar El Baroud** (The House of Powder), a large tower built over the ruins of an old gunpowder store; note also the ruined Gothic window.

The old **Mellah** – Azzemour had a substantial Jewish population until the 1960s – lies beyond the Kasbah at the northern end of the Medina. Here, beside ramparts overlooking the Oum Er Ribia, you will be shown the old town synagogue which is still well maintained and visited occasionally by practising Jews from Casablanca and El Jadida. It's cared for by a local family and you can – for an additional tip – see inside, where rests the tomb of Rabbi Abrahim Moul Niss – still a shrine for Jewish pilgrims and the focus of an August *moussem*.

These sights might not sound like much on paper, and you'll have to negotiate the final tip with the *gardien*, but all in all it's an interesting and enjoyable break from El Jadida, or a stop en route to the town, and easily combined with a swim.

The beach – and birds

The river currents at Azemmour are notoriously dangerous, but there's a nice stretch of **beach** half an hour's walk through the eucalyptus trees beyond the town. If you go by road, it's signposted to the "Balneaire du Haouzia", a small, cabins and camping complex occupying part of the sands. There is a **restaurant** here, *La Perle* (☎03/34.79.05), which is expensive but good (around 110dh per person), serving paella and other fish dishes; it is open all year. In summer, you can camp in the private complex; and, in winter, you can safely camp alongside the restaurant.

For **bird-watchers**, the scrub dunes around the mouth of the river should prove rewarding territory.

Golf and Mehioula

The coast between Azemmour and El Jadida is showing signs of development, the most ambitious of which is the **El Jadida Royal Golf Club** (☎03/35.22.51), beside the sea, 10km from Azemmour and 6km from El Jadida. The eighteen-hole golf course was designed by the American Cabell B. Robinson. Alongside is *Le Royal Golf Hôtel* (☎03/35.41.41; ⑤) managed by *Club Med* and *Sogatur*. The publicity promises "a haven of luxury and conviviality"; the "romantic swimming-pool is heart-shaped"; and all is designed to satisfy "les golfeurs-gourmets et les amateurs de confort!"

If you want a break from the coast, an alternative possible excursion is to **Mehioula**, 14km from Azemmour on the S1318. The road follows the southern banks of the Oum Er Ribia through groves of oranges to a gorge. The small hotel here, famous in French days, has alas long closed its doors.

El Jadida (Mazagan)

EL JADIDA is a stylish and beautiful town, retaining the lanes and ramparts of an old Portuguese Medina. It was known as *Mazagan* under the Portuguese who held it from 1506 until 1769 when it was taken by Sultan Sidi Mohammed Ben Abdallah. Moroccan *Mazagan* was renamed *El Jadida* – "The New" – after being resettled, partly with Jews from Azemmour, by the nineteenth-century Sultan Abd Er Rahman. Under the French, it grew into a quite sizeable administrative centre and a popular beach resort.

Today it's the beach that is undeniably the focal point. Moroccans from Casablanca and Marrakesh, even Tangier or Fes, come here in droves in summer, and, alongside this cosmopolitan mix, there's an unusual feeling of openness. The bars are crowded (a rare feature in itself), there's an almost frenetic evening promenade and – as in Casa – Moroccan women are visible and active participants.

Orientation and accommodation

Once you realize that the beach faces northeast, not southwest as you would expect, orientation is straightforward, with the old **Portuguese Medina**, walled and looking out over the port, and the **Ville Nouvelle** spreading to its south along the seafront.

By bus, you will almost certainly arrive at the **bus station** at the southern end of town (bottom-centre on our map), from where it's a twenty-minute walk to the Medina or to most hotels. Coming by train (there is one daily service to and from Rabat/Casa) you arrive at a station 1500m out of town along the Marrakesh road (P8); *petits taxis* are usually available. In summer, leaving El Jadida, bus tickets for Marrakesh or Casablanca should be bought a day ahead.

Orientation and accommodation

In summer you'd also be well advised to make a **hotel** booking – rooms can be very hard to find. In fact, at all times you may prefer to make some phone calls before pacing the streets, as the town extends for some distance along the seafront. Bear in mind also that, in summer, prices get hiked up to match demand.

If you have problems, the very helpful **Délégation du Tourisme**, Immeuble Chambre de Commerce, Av. Ibn Khaldoun (☎03/34.47.88) or the less helpful **Syndicat**

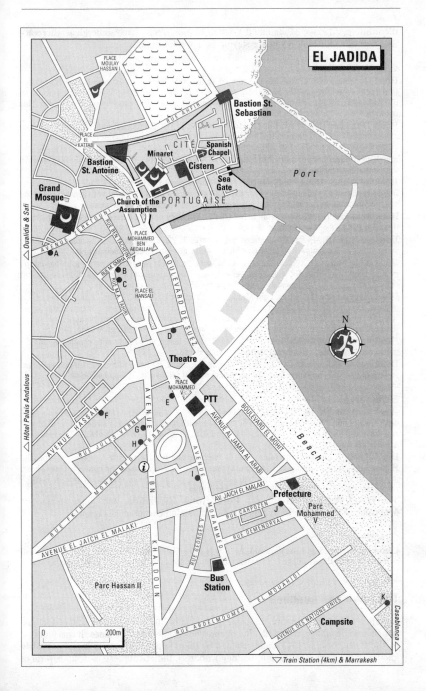

d'Initiative, 33 Place Mohammed V (☎03/37.06.56), may have some ideas; there are flats and villas for rent, if you are staying for a week or more.

CHEAP TO MODERATE

Hôtel Bordeaux [C], 47 Rue Moulay Ahmed Tahiri (☎03/35.41.17). Not easy to find; it's off Rue Ben Tachfine and beyond the signposted *Restaurant Tchikito*. An old hotel – the oldest in town, so the patron claims. Attractively refurbished and well maintained. Hot showers on the corridor. This is the best value for money in town. ①

Hôtel Bruxelles [G], 40 Av. Ibn Khaldoun (☎03/34.20.72). Bright and cheerful, with pleasant, clean rooms – with balconies at the front; despite the address, it's next to the *Hôtel Royal*. ①

Hôtel Cristour [E], 7 Av. Mohammed V (☎03/32.26.43) opposite the theatre and behind the prominent *Café Français*. Small rooms off a courtyard. Adequate, but noisy. A useful fall-back at the bottom end of the market. ①

Hôtel de France/Hôtel Maghreb [D], 12/16 Rue Lescoul (☎03/34.21.81). This is in reality one hotel – though with two entrances, stairways and names. It's old and roomy, with great views of the sea, hot showers on the landing, and a ground floor café. Highly recommended. ①

Hôtel Moderne [F], 27 Av. Hassan II (☎03/34.31.33). Very much a family hotel, with a small garden. Hot showers on the corridor. ①

Hôtel de Nice [B], 15 Rue Mohammed Smiha (☎03/35.22.72). Off Rue Ben Tachfine and on the same street as the *Restaurant Tchikito,* which is well signposted. An OK fallback. ①

Hôtel de la Plage [J], 3 Av. Al Jamia Al Arabi (☎03/34.26.48). Despite the rather grim bar on the ground floor, this is friendly, with clean, perfectly adequate rooms and separate facilities on the corridor. Convenient for the bus station and the *patron* also owns the campsite. ①

Hôtel de Provence [H], 42 Av. Fqih Mohammed Errafi (☎03/34.23.47). The English owner of this popular hotel has died; his Moroccan partner has taken over and has pledged to maintain standards. It's clean, central, with a good restaurant, a garden for breakfast, and covered parking nearby. Still the best budget choice, so be sure to reserve ahead, particularly in the high season. ②

Hôtel Royal [I], 108 Av. Mohammed V (☎03/34.00.11). Large, airy rooms with erratic plumbing, a garden and lively bar. Convenient for the bus station. ①

Hôtel Suisse [A], 145 Av. Zerktouni (☎03/34.28.16). Small, friendly, with a garden and patio; en-suite facilities and pleasant café next door (same owner) for breakfast. Good value. ①

EXPENSIVE

Hôtel Doukkala [K], Av. Al Jamia Al Arabi (☎03/34.37.37). This was the *Hôtel-Club Salam* – a modern package hotel on the beach south of the town, with tennis courts and swimming pool. It was run-down and had a bad press. Privatized in April, 1995, it is now the *Hôtel Doukkala*. The new team is keen and it could come good. ④

Hôtel Palais Andalous [off map], Rue de la Nouie aka Bd. Docteur de Lanouy – it's opposite Hôpital Mohammed V (☎03/34.37.45). Built in the 1930s for a local pasha and converted into a hotel in 1980, this remains quite an attractive place – and, out of season, reasonably priced. But the restaurant has closed of late, which may herald decline. ④

The **Hôtel Agudeal**, **Hôtel du Port**, **Hôtel El Jadida**, and (once upmarket) **Marrahôtel** are at time of writing not recommended except as last resorts.

CAMPING

Camping Caravaning International, Av. des Nations Unies (☎03/34.27.55). Lots of shade and popular; the only disadvantage is its distance from town: 15min to the bus station and another 20min to town.

The town and beaches

El Jadida's **Medina** is the most European-looking in Morocco: a quiet, walled and bastioned seaside village, with a handful of churches scattered on its lanes. It was founded by the Portuguese in 1513 – and retained by them until 1769 – and it is still popularly known as the **Cité Portugaise**. As they withdrew, the Portuguese blew up several of the churches and other important buildings. The Moors who settled here after the Portuguese withdrawal tended to live outside the walls. Budgett Meakin, writing in the 1890s, found an "extensive native settlement of beehive huts, or *nouallahs*" spreading back from the harbour, while European merchants had re-established themselves in the "clean, prosperous and well-lighted streets" of the Medina. As in all the "open ports" on this coast, there was also an important Jewish community handling the trade with Marrakesh; uniquely, old Mazagan had no separate Jewish quarter, or *Mellah*.

The Cité Portugaise

The **Cité Portugaise** is steadily being restored, and a walk round its newly spruced-up ramparts is not to be missed. Nor, above all, is a visit to the beautiful old **Portuguese Cistern** (Mon–Fri 9am–noon and 2–6pm; June–Sept 7pm; 10dh which also entitles you to visit the ramparts), a subterranean vault that mirrors its roof and pillars in a shallow film of water covering the floor. It is entered midway along the Medina's main street, on the left walking down, opposite a small souvenir shop.

The cistern was used to startling effect in Orson Welles's great film of *Othello*; he staged a riot here, provoked by Iago to discredit Cassio, and filmed it from within and above. It currently features in a Moroccan TV ad for *Samar* coffee and locals associate it with that, rather than Orson Welles. If the idea of competing with either appeals, you'll need a fast film for the refracted light.

At the entrance to the cistern there is a useful model of the *Cité Portuguese*, and if you continue up the street you'll come to its most prominent feature – the **Porte de la Mer**, the original sea gate which opened onto the port. The churches and chapels, long converted to secular use, are generally closed; but, if you have time, you can look for the small Spanish chapel (see map p.297) and the even smaller synagogue nearby, closed and bricked-up. More impressive is the seventeenth-century Portuguese Church of the Assumption by the entrance to the Cité Portuguese; it is now a cultural centre and is being restored. The minaret of the **Grand Mosque** here was once a five-sided watchtower or lighthouse, and is said to be the only pentagonal minaret in Islam.

The beaches

El Jadida's town **beach** spreads southeast from the *cité* and port, well beyond the length of the town. It's a popular strip, though from time to time polluted by the ships in port. If it doesn't look too good, or you feel like a change, take a *petit taxi* 3km north-west along the coastal road past the **Phare Sidi Ouafi** (lighthouse), a broader strip of sand where dozens of Moroccan families set up tents for the summer. Good swimming is to be had and there are makeshift beach cafés.

Plage Sidi Bouzid, 2km further southwest, is more developed, flanked by some fancy villas; a chic restaurant-bar, *Le Requin Bleu*, renowned for its fish; the less expensive *Restaurant Beausejour*; and makeshift summer camping. The beach can be reached on bus #2 from alongside Place Mohammed Ben Abdallah, or by *grand taxi*.

Practicalities

For its size, El Jadida is well served by **restaurants**, and has most other facilities you might want to make use of.

Restaurants

Restaurant La Broche, 46 Place El Hansali. In keen competition with the neighbouring *Restaurant Cherazad*. Open 11.30am–3.30pm and 6.30–11pm; menu of the day 45dh. Cheap to moderate.

Restaurant Le Caporal, 40 Bd. de Suez. Newly opened in 1995 and offering good dishes with minimum delay. Open noon–11pm. Cheap to moderate.

Restaurant Charazad, 38 Place El Hansali. Separated from *La Broche*, its nearest competitor, by the *Cinema le Paris;* the menu is similar, but sometimes dishes are not available. Nevertheless, marginally cheaper. Cheap to moderate.

Café Cherazad, Rue Fkih Mohammed Errafi, near the *Hôtel de Provence* and *Bruxelles* and good for breakfast and midday snacks. Not to be confused with the restaurant on Place El Hansali. Cheap.

Restaurant Clair du Lune, 1km from the centre, past Parc Mohammed V, on the road to Casablanca. Café and pizzeria on the ground floor and a restaurant above, looking out to sea. Good but allow enough time. The menu is hardly *rapide!* Moderate.

Restaurant El Khaima, Av. des Nations Unies, opposite the campsite. Good-value Moroccan and Italian dishes. Well worth the walk. Moderate.

Hôtel-Restaurant de Provence, 42 Av. Fqih Mohammed Errafi. Well-prepared, French-inspired meals, open to non-residents, and licensed. Worth making a reservation (☎03/34.23.47).

Restaurant Tchikito, Rue Mohammed Smiha. A memorable fish restaurant, with generous helpings and Koranic decorations. Unlicensed, of course, but the atmosphere is intoxicating. Moderate.

Restaurant Le Tit, 2 Av. Al Jamia El Arabi, by the *PTT*. Classy cooking and good service. Moderate.

In high season, there are many more eateries. Before deciding where to eat, stroll through Place El Hansali and Place Mohammed Ben Abdallah or along Bd. El Mohit towards Parc Mohammed V – until something catches your eye.

Bars

Bars are to be found mainly in the hotels – try the *Hôtel de la Plage* (lively), *de Provence* (pleasant) and *Palais Andalous* (more upmarket).

Listings

Banks include *Credit du Maroc*, *BMCI* and *WAFA* on Av. Al Jamia El Arabi, and *BMCE,* with ATM, on the corner of Av. Ibn Khaldoun and Av. Fqih Mohammed Errafi.

Cinemas The *Cinema de Paris* and *Cinema Rif* are both on Place El Hansali.

Post office The main *PTT* is on Place Mohammed V.

Souk A Wednesday *souk* takes place by the lighthouse northwest of town.

Theatre El Jadida is the only Moroccan town to boast a pre-independence theatre still in use – a fine building facing the townhall in the centre of town.

El Jadida to Safi

Once again, the main road (and express buses) south, from **El Jadida to Safi**, take an inland road, across the plains. The coast road, however, is almost as direct, and a very pleasant drive, with little development, lovely stretches of beach, and major **bird habitats** around the low-key resort of **Oualidia**. It's not much frequented by tourists, who seem to visit either El Jadida from Casa or Essaouira from Marrakesh – rarely both.

El Jadida to Oualidia

The main sights along this strip of coast come from **bird-watching**, though there is a minor ancient ruin at **Moulay Abdallah** and fine beaches once you are beyond Cap Blanc and the industrial **Port de Jorf-Lasar** (17km from El Jadida), the terminal for the *OCP* phosphate plants on the plains inland.

Moulay Abdallah and the ruins of Tit

MOULAY ABDALLAH, 11km from El Jadida, is a tiny fishing village, dominated by a large *zaouia* complex and partially enclosed by a circuit of walls in ruins. At the *zaouia* an important **moussem** is held towards the end of August, attracting tens of thousands of devotees – and almost as many horses in the parades and *fantasias*.

BIRD HABITATS AROUND OUALIDIA

The 70km of coast between SIDI MOUSSA (36km south of El Jadida) and CAP BED-DOUZA (34km south of Oualidia) is one of the richest **birdlife habitats** in Morocco. The coastal wetlands, sands and saltpans, the jagged reefs, and the lagoons of Sidi Moussa and Oualidia, shelter a huge range of species – flamingoes, avocets, stilts, godwits, storks, waders, terns, egrets, warblers and many small waders. Numerous countryside species come in, too; golden oriole and hoopoe have been recorded, and flocks of shearwaters are often to be seen not far offshore.

The best watching locations are the two **lagoons** and the rocky headland at **Cap Beddouza**.

The village walls span the site of a twelfth-century **ribat**, or fortified monastery, known as **Tit** ("eyes" or "spring" in the local Berber dialect) and built, so it is thought, in preparation for a Norman invasion: a real threat at the time – the Normans having launched attacks on Tunisia – but one which never materialized. Today, there is little to see, though the minaret of the modern **zaouia** (prominent and whitewashed) is Almohad in origin; behind it, up through the graveyard, you can walk to a second, isolated minaret, which is thought to be even older. If it is, then it is perhaps the only one surviving from the Almoravid era – a claim considerably more impressive than its simple, block-like appearance might suggest.

Sidi Abed and Sidi Moussa

The first good beach beyond Cap Blanc is at **SIDI ABED**, a small village with a café-restaurant and a scattering of villas, 27km from El Jadida. A couple of kilometres before the village, and on the right travelling towards it, is *Le Relais* (☎03/34.54.98; ③) in summer it has **accommodation**, with showers in the rooms and toilets on the corridor, and year round, except for Ramadan, it is a restaurant: worth a stopover if you have time.

The coast hereabouts is an alternation of sandy beach and rocky outcrops, and past **SIDI MOUSSA**, 37km from El Jadida, it's backed by huge dunes, then, towards Oualidia, cut off by a long expanse of salt marshland. From here on south, for the next 70km or so, bird-watchers are in for a treat (see box above) but Sidi Moussa is attractive to non-twitchers, too, with its estuary-like lagoon, its beach, and a very pleasant **hotel**, the *Villa la Brise* (☎03/34.69.17; ①), with French cooking, a bar, and a swimming pool that's sometimes full. It's a popular base for fishing parties.

South of Sidi Moussa, the roadside is flanked by saltpans and by extensive plastic hothouses, for intensive cultivation of tomatoes and other vegetables; 63km from El Jadida, there's a Friday *souk* at **SOUK EL DJEMAA**, as the name suggests.

Oualidia and beyond

OUALIDIA, 78km from El Jadida, is a stunningly picturesque little resort – a fishing port and lagoon beach, flanked by a Kasbah and a royal villa. The **Kasbah** is seventeenth century, built by the Saadian Sultan El Oualid (after whom the village is named) as a counterweight and alternative to El Jadida then held by the Portuguese. Until Sultan Sidi Mohammed took El Jadida, the extensive lagoon made an excellent harbour and, as late as 1875, a French geographer thought that 'by a little dredging the place would again become the safest shipping station on the whole Moroccan seaboard.' The **royal** villa, which now stands empty, was built by Hassan II's father, Mohammed V, who celebrated many birthdays and other family events here.

Today, most Moroccans know Oualidia for its **Japanese oysters**; Morocco's first oyster farm was launched here in 1957 and nowadays it harvests some 200 tons a year, most of which are sold locally. But the town really deserves to be better known as a resort: its beach is excellent for surfing and windsurfing, the atmosphere is relaxed, and swimming is safe and easy.

Practicalities

Most visitors to Oualidia are Moroccan families, who settle into tent-colonies in and around the **campsite**, *Camping Oualidia*, which is pleasantly laid out in a garden behind the sand dunes. The **hotels** are all very good, too, and offer seafood meals to residents and non-residents alike. Choices are:

Motel-Restaurant à L'Araignée Gourmande (☎03/36.61.44). This stands alongside the lagoon beach. Good-value rooms and a wide range of *prix-fixe* menus, starting at 65dh. ②

Complexe Touristique Chems (☎03/36.64.78). Also alongside the beach – and under the same management as nearby *L'Araignée Gourmande*. There are cabins of various sizes, from singles to fully-equipped bungalows for up to five people; all with hot showers. It offers half-board for around 300dh a head, which is not bad value as the restaurant is pretty good. ④

Hôtel Hippocampe (☎03/36.61.08). A delightful place, halfway up the slope from the lagoon up to the village on the top. Rooms off a flower-filled courtyard and steps down to a 'private' beach; also has a pool. Once again, half-board is preferred – at around 500dh. ④

Auberge de la Lagune aka *Complexe Touristique La Lagune* (☎03/36.64.77). At the top of the hill, with a stunning view from the terrace at any hour of the day or night. Accommodation is limited to five old rooms and five new rooms; advance booking in high season is essential; 200dh for a double room, 350dh half-board. ③

Inland from Oualidia: Kasbah Gharbia

The Doukkala plains, inland from the El Jadida–Safi coast have long been a fertile and fought-over region, and there are scattered forts and Kasbahs at several villages. One of the most interesting and accessible is at **GHARBIA**, 20km from Oualidia on the S1336 across an undulating limestone plateau. The **Kasbah** here is a vast enclosure, four kilometres long on each side, bastioned at intervals, and with a gate at each point of the compass, giving onto roads to Oualidia, Safi, El Jadida and Marrakesh: a strategic site. Within, a few houses remain in use and there's a large white house in the centre, occupied by the *caid* in the days of the Protectorate. If you visit – the trip is only really feasible if you have transport – you will be shown round by a charming bunch of locals, intent on pointing out the various features.

Cap Beddouza and Lalla Fatna

Continuing south from Oualidia, the road climbs a little inland and above the sea, which is hidden from view by sand dunes. It's a pretty stretch and the more so as you approach **Cap Beddouza**, where the rocky headland gives way intermittently to sandy beaches, sheltered by cliffs. At the cape there is a lighthouse and an **auberge**, the *Cap Beddouza* (Safi ☎04 via the operator; ⑩), with a restaurant, bar and basic, rather overpriced cabins on the cliff top.

The best of the cliff-sheltered beaches is known as **Lalla Fatna**, 51km from Oualidia and just 15km short of Safi (with which it's connected by local bus #10 or #15). It is totally undeveloped, with nothing more than a **koubba** and in summer a few Moroccan tents, sometimes a café. If you are intending to stay, you'll need your own transport and to take provisions. The beach is a steep two-kilometre descent from the road; camping on the beach, make sure you've pitched your tent far enough back from the tides. There is a **moussem** at the *koubba* on the thirteenth day of Chaâbane (the month before Ramadan).

Finally, beyond Cap Safi, you pass the *marabout* of Sidi Bouzid, overlooking Safi with its Medina, port and industry. Down below is **Sidi Bouzid beach** – Safi's local strand – where on November 8, 1942, American troops uner Gerneal Patton landed as the

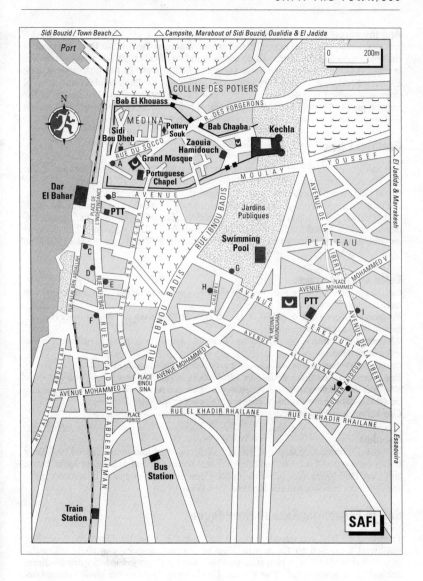

Sidi Bouzid / Town Beach △   △ Campsite, Marabout of Sidi Bouzid, Oualidia & El Jadida

Port

0   200m

COLLINE DÈS POTIERS

Bab El Khouass

R. DES FORGERONS

MEDINA

Sidi Bou Dheb

Pottery Souk

Bab Chaaba

Kechla

Zaouia Hamidouch

RUE DU SOCCO

Grand Mosque

Portuguese Chapel

A

Dar El Bahar

AVENUE

RUE DE L'INDÉPENDANCE

B

PTT

RUE IBNOU BADIS

MOULAY YOUSSEF

Jardins Publiques

RUE BEN NACEUR

C

Swimming Pool

PLATEAU

AVENUE DE LA LIBERTE

RUE IDRISS

AVENUE MOHAMMED V

D

E

RUE DU RBAT

G

H

R. CHAWI

AVENUE

PLACE MOHAMMED V

PTT

I

AVENUE DE LA LIBERTE

RUE ALLAL BEN ABDALLAH

F

RUE DU CAID

RUE IBNOU BADIS

MEDINA MOUNOUARA

AVENUE

ZERKTOUNI

RUE IBN ZAIDOUN

AVENUE MOHAMMED V

PLACE IBNOU SINA

ALLAL LIAN

J J

RUE SIDI ABDERRAHMAN

PLACE IDRISS

RUE EL KHADIR RHAILANE

RUE EL KHADIR RHAILANE

Bus Station

Train Station

SAFI

△ El Jadida & Marrakesh

△ Essaouira

have made scarcely an inroad on the tamarisk-fired kilns – and the quarter is worth at least the time it takes to wander up the new concrete steps and pathways. At the foot of the hillside is a 'street' of showrooms. The products on display are of interest, but the colour dyes and garish designs are hardly comparable to the beautiful old pieces that can be seen around the country's crafts museums. Indeed, you are as likely to see U-bends for toilets being fired, as anything else.

And the sardines?

Safi's famed sardines are caught in the deeper waters of the Atlantic from Boujdour in the south to Safi in the north. There are around five hundred 50/60ft wooden trawlers in the town fleet and you can still see them being made in the boatyards at Safi, Essaouira and Agadir. The fleet lands 350,000 tons of sardines annually and most of them are canned in Safi. Increasingly, those caught further south are landed at the nearest port and brought to Safi in refrigerated trucks. Most of the tins get sold abroad – Morocco being the world's largest exporter of sardines.

Practicalities

Safi has a fair selection of restaurants, plus all the usual city facilities, grouped round the Place Mohammed V, Place de l'Indépendance (the main *PTT* is here) and Place Ibnou Sina (where you'll find most of the banks).

For a town which is not well endowed with historic monuments, beaches , or memorable vistas, Safi also has an unusually helpful **tourist office**, located near the bus station at 26 Rue Imam Malik (☎04/62.24.96; Mon–Fri 8.30am–noon and 2.30–6.30pm) and there's an additional information kiosk behind the *PTT* and near the *Hôtel Assif* (no phone, same hours).

Cafés and restaurants

Café-Restaurant El Bahia, Place de l'Indépendance. Café downstairs and restaurant above, with more fancy Moroccan dishes. Moderate.

Restaurant Gégéne, Rue de la Marine, just off Place de l'Indépendance. A lively restaurant with limited, but satisfying menu. Moderate.

Restaurant de la Poste, Place de l'Indépendance. The upstairs restaurant is good: French cuisine and seafood. Moderate.

Restaurant de Safi, Rue de la Marine, next to Gégéne. Grills. Cheap to moderate.

Restaurant La Trattoria, 2 Route de l'Aouinate (☎04/62.09.59; closed Sun) near the École Maritime, towards the port; follow the signs. Upmarket and very pleasant Italian restaurant. Live music: Thu–Sat evenings. Yvette Morone is a fine *patronne*. Moderate to expensive.

Café M'Zoughan, Place de l'Indépendance. Café-pâtisserie, good for breakfast.

Beaches

The coast immediately south of Safi is heavily polluted and industrialized, and for a beach escape you'll want to head north. Local buses #10 and #15 run to **Lalla Fatna** and **Cap Beddouza** (see p.302) from the Place de l'Indépendance. In summer there are also local buses to **Souira Kedima** (see below).

Safi to Essaouria: Kasbah Hamidouch

Travelling by bus, you usually have no option but to take the inland P8, if heading southwest from **Safi to Essaouria**. With your own transport, you could follow the minor road S6531/6537, which runs past the canning plants towards **Souira Kedima**, around 30km south of Safi. This is a fine beach fronted by a rather bleak holiday-bungalow complex, used by people from Safi and Marrakesh on their summer holidays; nearby, on a windswept headland, there is an old Portuguese fortress known as **Agouz**.

A little beyond Souria Kedima, a new bridge allows you to cross the Oued Tensift to reach, along a stretch of good but sandy piste, the large and isolated fortress of **Kasbah Hamidouch**. This was built by the ever-industrious Moulay Ismail to control the mouth of the Tensift – one of the most active Moroccan rivers, which here finishes its course from Marrakesh. You can reach its ramparts across the fields.

South of the Kasbah, a **new road** – still marked tentatively on some current maps – heads off along the coast towards Essaouira via **Cap Hadid**; it joins the Marrakesh-Essaouira road (P10) 4km outside Essaouira.

Djebel Hadid was once mined for iron ore and, indeed, in the nineteenth century, this coast was known as the Iron Coast.

Essaouira (Mogador)

ESSAOUIRA is by popular acclaim Morocco's most likeable resort: an eighteenth-century town, enclosed by medieval-looking battlements, facing a cluster of rocky offshore islands, and trailed by a vast expanse of empty sands and dunes. Its whitewashed and blue-shuttered houses and colonnades, its wood workshops and art galleries, its boat-builders and sardine fishermen, its feathery Norfolk Island pines which only thrive in a pollution-free atmosphere: all provide a colourful and very pleasant backdrop to the beach. The life of the resort, too, is easy and uncomplicated, and very much in the image of the predominantly youthful Europeans and Marrakchis who come here on holiday; unlike Agadir, few of the visitors who stay here are on package tours.

Essaouira features in none but the most trendy brochures and upmarket TV travel programmes; and you will only be aware of packaged tourism at lunch-time when hungry coachloads from the four-star hotels in Marrakesh arrive. The seafront restaurants are best reserved for the evening meal.

Many of the foreign tourists, making their own way, are drawn by the wind, known locally as the *alizee*, which can be a bit remorseless for sunbathing but creates much sought-after waves for **surfing** and **windsurfing**. In recent years, Essaouria has gained quite a reputation in this respect, promoting itself as "Wind City, Afrika" and hosting national and international surfing contests. This burgeoning popularity is, inevitably, changing the town's character, with villas springing up along the corniche, but as yet it's very far from spoilt, and remains a thoroughly enjoyable base to rest up after the big-city tensions of Casa or Marrakesh.

Some history

With its dramatic sea bastions and fortifications, Essaouira seems a lot older than it is. Although a series of forts had been built here from the fifteenth century on, it was only in the 1760s that the town was established and the present circuit of walls constructed. It was known to European sailors and then traders – as **Mogador**, said to be a reference to the prominent *koubba* of Sidi Mgdoul, used for navigating entry to the bay. Less likely is the legend that the town's patron saint was a Scotsman named McDougal who was shipwrecked here in the fourteenth century. To the Moroccans it was known as *Seurah*, from the Berber 'little picture'.

The work on the town's walls, which was completed in 1770, was ordered by the Sultan **Sidi Mohammed Ben Abdallah**, and carried out by a French captive architect, Theodore Cornut, which explains the town's unique blend of Moroccan Medina and French grid layout. The sultan's original intention was to provide a military port, as Agadir was in revolt at the time and Sultan Mohammed Ben Abdallah needed a local base. It lent itself superbly to the purpose, as its series of forts ensured complete protection for the bay. Soon, however, commercial concerns gained pre-eminence. During the nineteenth century, Mogador was the only Moroccan port south of Tangier that was open to European trade, and it prospered greatly on the privilege. Drawn by protected trade status, and a harbour free from customs duties, British merchants settled in the Kasbah quarter, and a large Jewish community in the Mellah, within the northeast ramparts.

Decline set in during the French Protectorate, with Marshal Lyautey's promotion of Casablanca. Anecdote has it that he arrived in Essaouira on a Saturday when the Jewish

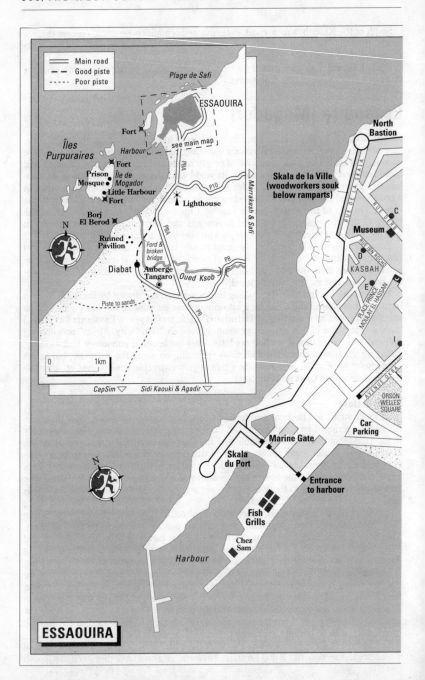

ESSAOUIRA

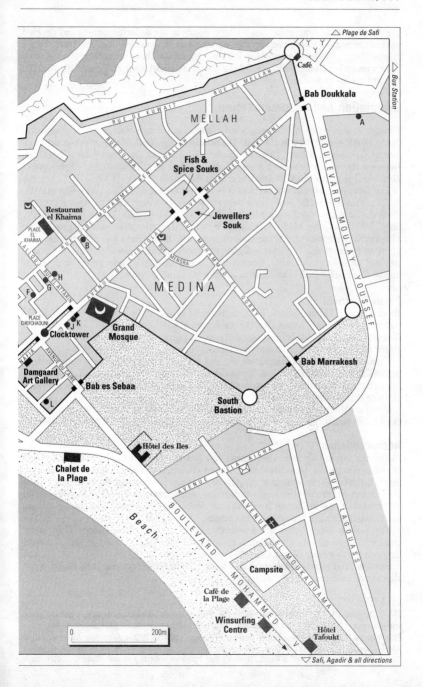

△ Plage de Safi

▷ Bus Station

Café

Bab Doukkala

A

RUE EL MELLAH

BOULEVARD MOULAY YOUSSEF

RUE DE KUWAIT

MELLAH

RUE OUJDA

RUE SIDI MOHAMMED BEN ABDALLAH

MOHAMMED ZERKTOUNI

Fish & Spice Souks

Restaurant el Khaima

PLACE EL KHAIMA

B

AVENUE DE L'ISTIQLAL

RUE MOHAMMED EL QORRY

RUE MENSRA

Jewellers' Souk

MEDINA

RUE EL ATTARIN

H

G

F

PLACE CHEFCHAOUNI

J K

Clocktower

Grand Mosque

Damgaard Art Gallery

AVENUE OUKACHA

Bab es Sebaa

L

Bab Marrakesh

South Bastion

Hôtel des Iles

Chalet de la Plage

AVENUE ALLA AICHA

RUE LAGOUASS

Beach

BOULEVARD MOHAMMED

AVENUE EL MOUKAOUAMA

Campsite

Café de la Plage

Winsurfing Centre

Hôtel Tafoukt

V

0   200m

▽ Safi, Agadir & all directions

community was at prayer; he cast a single glance at the deserted streets and decided to shift the port of Casablanca further up the coast! The decline was accelerated after independence, by the exodus of the Jewish community. These days, however, the town is very much back on its feet, as a fishing port and market town, and especially with the recent impetus of tourism.

Orientation and accommodation

Though long overflowing its ramparts, Essaouira is a simple place to get to grips with. At the north end of town is the **Bab Doukkala**; at the south is the town's pedestrianized main square, **Place Prince Moulay El Hassan**, and the fishing **harbour**. Between them run two main parallel streets: **Av. de l'Istiqlal/Av. Mohammed Zerktouni** and **Rue Sidi Mohammed Ben Abdallah**.

The town has recently acquired its own **tourist office**, on Av. du Caire opposite the police station, having for years been "served" by Safi. However, it has hardly felt the lack, since the long-standing **Jack's Kiosk**, 1 Place Prince Moulay El Hassan (☎04/47.55.38, fax 47.69.01) has long fulfilled just about every useful function you could imagine, acting as information booth, and accommodation agency. It currently lets apartments, runs horse and camel trips, reconfirms flights, serves as an international phone and fax centre, and sells English books (secondhand books upstairs), newspapers and tourist goods. It is run by Jack Oswald, who, despite his name, is Swiss.

Points of arrival

Buses (both CTM and private lines) arrive at a bus station, inconveniently sited on the outskirts of the town, about 1km (fifteen minutes' walk) north of Bab Doukkala in the Quartier Industrielle. It is unsignposted and, especially at night, it's well worth taking a *petit taxi* into or out from town; the charge is around 7dh (10dh at night).

Grands taxis also operate from the bus station, though they will normally drop arrivals at Bab Doukkala or, less likely, close to Place Prince Moulay El Hassan. There is a **petit taxi rank** by the clocktower on Av. Oqba Ibn Nafia (once the *mechouar*) east of Place Prince Moulay El Hassan.

If you are driving, it's worth making use of the **car parking** space, manned round the clock (10dh for 24hr) in front of the harbour offices, south of Place Prince Moulay El Hassan.

Accommodation

At holiday times (summer, Christmas/New Year), you need to arrive early or book ahead to ensure the accommodation of your choice; if you plan to stay for a week or more, it can be worth renting an apartment or a villa, for example, through *Jack's Kiosk* (see above) or through the local windsurfing centre, housed in a white building about 100m south along the beach from the Café de la Plage (see map). Season by season, more apartments are available, so ask around.

The **hotels** listed below are a selective list of recommended places. If by some chance, they're all full, a half-dozen basic hotels (eg *Agadir, Amis*) in the alleyways between the two main Medina streets provide last resorts.

Surfers and windsurfers may also want to consider the coast around Diabat as an alternative base (see p.317).

CHEAP

Hôtel Argana [A], Av. 2 Mars (☎04/47.59.75). Facing the Bab Doukkala square, a market place and occasional funfare, this is a reasonable, fairly new hotel; some rooms have showers. ①

Hôtel Beau Rivage [E], Place Prince Moulay El Hassan (☎04/47.59.25). Attractive, old-established hotel, above a popular café. Rooms, some with showers, look out onto the main square; there's a "terrasse panoramique" and a kiosk/shop by the entrance where you can change money, cash cheques or use credit cards. The enterprising *patron* owns the next door *Opera* pâtisserie and the new *Hôtel Riad Al Madina*. ①

Hôtel Chakib [B], 2 Rue Sidi Abdesmih (☎04/47.22.91). Midway between the two main Medina streets. Fairly modern, with cold showers on the corridor; a useful fall-back. ①

Hôtel Majestic [C], 40 Rue Derb Laâlouj (☎04/47.54.98). No sign, but not difficult to find; look for it opposite the museum. Good, clean rooms and hot showers on the corridor, if a bit cheerless. ①

Hôtel du Mechouar [K], Av. Okba Ibn Nafia (☎04/47.28.28). Reasonable rooms with cold showers, and hot showers on the corridor. Currently closed for restoration. ①

Hôtel des Remparts [D], 18 Rue Ibn Rochd (☎04/47.61.66). As the name suggests, the *Remparts* overlooks the sea walls. A typical three-storey, courtyard building, recently re-decorated and welcoming. Rooftop café offers a town/sea panorama and sunbathing out of the wind. There's a modish boutique for browsing on the ground floor. ①

Hôtel Tafraout [G], 7 Rue de Marrakesh (☎04/47.21.20). Modernish hotel in the heart of the Medina; comfortable rooms, some with showers. ①

Hôtel du Tourisme [L], Rue Mohammed Ben Messaoud (☎04/47.50.75). Located in an old house in the Kasbah quarter, near the southeast corner of the ramparts; from outside the walls, you can see the blue-on-white sign high on the side of the hotel; decent, clean rooms, but charges extra for cold showers. ①

MODERATE

Hôtel Kasbah [F], 4 Rue Tetouan (☎04/47.56.05). Well signposted off Place Prince Moulay El Hassan/Place Chefchaouni, this is a vast old house with arts and crafts on sale in open-air courtyard. Some pleasant rooms to let with splendid rooftop views. ②

Hôtel Riad Al Madina [H], 3 Rue Attarine (☎04/47.27.27). Opened in 1996, this is a stylish conversion of a substantial, town-house, with thirty en-suite rooms off the three-storey central courtyard and a sauna promised. The old house has a local notoriety from the 60s hippies who lived in the old building here – Jimi Hendrix slept here, so it is said! ③

Hôtel Sahara [J], Av. Okba Ibn Nafia (☎04/47.52.92). Big rooms around a central well, and hot showers most of the time. Recently re-decorated and breakfasts in an attractive salon. ②

EXPENSIVE

Hôtel des Iles [labelled], Bd. Mohammed V (☎04/47.53.29). Outside, but close to, the Medina. Comfortable, but a bit dull with rooms in a main block and chalet rooms round the swimming pool. Non-residents can use the pool for 35dh a day. Overpriced, but discounts out-of-season. ④

Villa Maroc [I], 10 Rue Abdallah Ben Yassin near the clocktower (☎04/47.61.47). Accessible on foot only along a newly paved passage just inside the Medina wall, though the hotel will carry your luggage from its car park. This unique hotel is straight out of a *World of Interiors* magazine feature: two old houses converted into a dozen or so rooms and suites – heated in winter and decorated with the finest Moroccan materials. Non-residents can dine if they reserve before 4pm. ④

Hôtel Tafoukt [labelled], Bd. Mohammed V (☎04/47.75.05). 1km south of the old town, facing the beach, this is a comfortable modern block, with a good restaurant, *La Petite Algue*, open to non-residents. Demi-pension available, but not obligatory. ④

CAMPING

Camping d'Essaouira, Bd. Mohammed V (☎04/47.51.00). The small town campsite is just 300m out from the walls, past the *Hôtel des Iles*. It is open year round and convenient for the beach, town and Catholic church; its high walls, topped with broken glass, ensure security. But it's smaller than the previous campsite which was further along the beach and is now occupied by a large hotel – still unfinished. The present site is more suitable for campervans, caravans and cars than for tents. Reasonable toilets and cold showers.

The Town

There are few formal "sights" in Essaouria, but it's a great place just to walk around, exploring the **ramparts**, the **harbour** and the **souks** – above all the **thuya wood workshops** – or wandering along the immense wind-swept **beach**.

The Skala de la Ville, thuya wood workshops and galleries

The ramparts are the obvious place to start a tour of Essaouira. If you head north along the lane at the end of Place Prince Moulay El Hassan, you can gain access to the **Skala de la Ville**, the great sea bastion which runs along the northern cliffs. Along the top of it are a collection of European cannon, presented to Sultan Sidi Mohammed Ben Abdallah by ambitious nineteenth-century merchants, and at its end is the circular **North Bastion**, with panoramic views across the Medina, Kasbah and Mellah quarters, and out to sea.

Along the Rue de Skala, built into the ramparts, are a group of **marquetry and wood-carving workshops**, long established in Essaouira. These artesans produce amazingly painstaking and beautiful marquetry work from the local **thuya** (or *thuja*, or *arar* in Arabic), a mahogany-like hardwood from a local coniferous tree, from which they adapt both the trunk and the roots (or *loupe*). With total justice, they claim that their produce is the best in the country. If you see good examples elsewhere they've probably come from here, and if you're thinking of buying – boxes and chess sets are for sale, as well as traditional furniture – this is the best place to do it.

Also of interest for the local craft content is the **Musée Sidi Mohammed Ben Abdallah** (8.30am–noon & 2.30–6pm; closed Tues) on Rue Derb Laâlouj. This again features excellent displays of marquetry, past and present. There are also displays of carpets, costumes, jewellery and musical instruments decorated with marquetry and still used by the *gnawa* musicians locally and on tour overseas; and don't miss the gallery of old pictures of Essaouira. It is housed in a nineteenth-century mansion which served as the town hall during the Protectorate; it's been restored recently and the central courtyard is now glassed over.

CRAFTS IN ESSAOUIRA

The quality of the marquetry and carving in Essaouira is so high that it seems invidious to pick out individual workshops from the forty or so along the Skala. However, there are certain outlets elsewhere in the town that are worth visiting; some of them also display the work of local artists, many of whom are well-known in Morocco and in Europe. These include:

Afalkay Art, 9 Place Prince Moulay El Hassan. A vast and somewhat impersonal emporium, but useful for guaging quality and prices elsewhere.

Jamal and Noureddine Hajhouj, 7 Place Chefchaouni. The brothers Hajhouj now have a couple of outlets here; the main one is in an old Jewish house, and with the ultimate thuya artefact – an inlaid lavatory seat.

Jiska, 11 Rue Derb Laâlouj, near the museum. A popular *boutique* which includes Alain Delon amongst its regular customers: old and new carpets, ceramics from Fes and Safi, original thuya sculptures and many leather jackets.

Hotel La Kasbah, 4 Rue Tetouan. There is usually a good show of arts and crafts in the open-air courtyard.

Maroc Art, Chez Mounaim, 3 Rue El Hajjali, between Place Chefchaouni and Place Prince Moulay El Hassan. Abdulmounaim Bendahhan once worked here with the Hajhouj brothers, but now he has his own place with some of his own sculptures on show.

Galerie d'Art Frederic Damgaard on Av. Oqba Ibn Nafia (daily 9am–1pm & 3–7pm). It is more a gallery for paintings than thuya creations, regularly exhibiting twenty or so locally based artists. However, it is run by a Danish furniture designer, who uses the traditional thuya techniques in a highly imaginative, modern context – and these pieces are well worth seeing.

Espace Othello, 9 Rue Mohammed Layachi, behind the *Hôtel Sahara*. This art gallery was opened in 1993 and displays the work of local artists; most of which is for sale. The owner is the *patron* of the nearby *Restaurant El Minzah*.

ORSON WELLES' OTHELLO

Orson Welles filmed much of his **Othello** in Essaouira, returning the Moor (played by Welles himself) to his homeland. The film opens with a tremendous panning shot of the Essaouira ramparts, where Welles placed a scene-setting "punishment" of Iago, suspended above the sea and rocks in a metal cage. Later locations included a local *hammam* for the murder of Rodrigo – the costumes Welles had ordered from Jewish tailors in the Mellah were not ready, so he had to shoot a scene with minimal clothing – and the Portuguese cistern in El Jadida (see p.299).

The film was something of a personal crusade for Welles, who financed it himself, leaving the cast at intervals to try and borrow money off friends in Italy and France. During the course of the filming, he got through at least four – and perhaps six – Desdemonas, beginning with his fiancée Lea Padovani, until she soured relations by beginning an affair with one of the crew. In the end they were all dubbed, as indeed were many other of the characters – Welles performing most himself.

On its release in 1952, *Othello* was panned by the critics, and at Welles's death it was the only one of his dozen films to which he owned the rights. Forty years on, however, it was restored by his daughter for its anniversary, and shown at film festivals worldwide, and to huge acclaim. Even Essaouira had an open-air showing, in the presence of King Hassan's heir, Sidi Mohammed; this event was accompanied by the official naming of a park area on the front **Orson Welles' Square**, complete with a thuya wood memorial made by Samir Mustapha, one of the town's most talented young craftsmen.

Spice and jewellery souks and the Mellah

The town's **other souks** spread around and to the south of two arcades, on either side of Rue Mohammed Zerktouni, and up towards the Mellah. Worth particular attention are the **Marché d'Épices** (spice market) and **Souk des Bijoutiers** (jewellers' market). Stallholders in the spice *souk* will extol the virtues of their their wares, including exotic remedies for baldness, infertility and so on.

The jewellery business was one of the traditional trades of Essaouira's Jewish community, who have long since deserted the **Mellah**, in the northwest corner of the ramparts. A gloomy-looking part of the town, it was locked at night up until the end of the nineteenth century.

There have been various estimates as to the size of the **Jewish community** in the last quarter of the nineteenth century, ranging from 4000 to 9000 – the likelihood being at the top end of the scale. It is also probable that they comprised around half of the total population. Trade was carried out mainly with Marseilles and London, but there were never more than 300 Europeans living in the Mellah, engaged primarily in trade. The principal exports were almonds, goatskins, olive oil and ostrich feathers; and the principal imports were cotton goods (half the total value) and tea. The philanthropist **Moses Montefiore** was born here.

Today, the old Jewish quarter is noticeably in decline, with many of its houses deserted and in a dangerous condition. A dozen or so Jews currently live in Essaouira, but not necessarily in the old Mellah.

The port

At some point, perhaps around lunchtime or early evening, make your way down to the **harbour,** where fresh sardines (and all variety of other fish) are cooked on the quays. There is also an impressive sea bastion here, the **Skala du Port**, and in addition to the fishing activities – Essaouria is the country's third fishing port, after Agadir and Safi – a busy boatbuilding and repairs industry. Almost all the local craft, even the biggest fishing vessels, are still almost entirely wooden.

The port is entered by a small gate to the left of its main **Marine Gate**.

The beach

Essaouira has beaches to north and south. The **northern** one, known as the Plage de Safi, is good in hot weather and with a calm sea, but it's less attractive and can be dangerous if the winds are up. It is reached from the end of the town by skirting left through a malodorous area, but the miles of sand are often delightfully empty.

The **southern beach** extends for miles from the town, often backed by dunes, out towards Cap Sim. On its early reaches, the main activity, as ever in Morocco, is football. There's virtually always a game in progress and at weekends a full-scale local league, with a dozen matches side by side and kick-offs timed by the tides. If you're a player, you'll be encouraged to join in, but the weekend games are fun just to watch, and on occasions half the town seems to turn out.

Bordj El Berod and Diabat

Walking further along the beach, past the football and the crowds, you pass the riverbed of the Oued Ksob and come upon the ruins of an old fort, the **Bordj El Berod**, which is surrounded by the sea at high tide. Inland can be seen the ruins of a royal summer pavilion and a broken bridge. This spot provided the inspiration for Jimi Hendrix's song *Castles in the Sand*; the guitarist once spent a long, drug-happy summer in the town, as hotel-keepers still like to remind their clients – all claim to have let rooms to the man. The fort is an excellent viewing spot for the Iles Purpuraires, offshore, and their birdlife (see box opposite).

A little further south, inland through the scrub, is the little Berber village of **Diabat**. This was once a legendary hippie hangout, and mythology again suggests that Jimi Hendrix spent time in the colony. These days, it has reverted to an ordinary Berber farming village.

Few venture beyond the *Oued Ksob*, from which an aqueduct once carried water to Essaouira, but a walk to Cap Sim and back is an all-day challenge. Take plenty of water and visit the *Auberge Tangaro* on the way back. (see p.317)

Practicalities

With its fishing fleet and market, Essaouira offers a good range of cafés and restaurants. It also has most services you might need during a stay, including post, phones, banks, etc.

Cafés and restaurants

For an informal lunch, or early evening meal, you can do no better than eat at the line of **grills down at the port**, an Essaouira institution, and cooking fish as fresh as it is possible to be; prices are highly negotiable.

Also quite pleasant, if you want to eat Moroccan style, are a series of **"Berber Cafés"**, off to the right (if you're walking up from the harbour) of the *souks* on Avenue Zerktouni. Amounting to little more than a street of tiny rooms covered with matting, these serve soup, tea and a variety of *tajines* – or anything you present to be cooked. Some of them are a bit of a tourist trap (and a few are haunted by hustlers peddling dope), but they are frequented also by local fishermen and workers.

Finally, there are several snack bars and food stalls on, and near, the Place Prince Moulay El Hassan: locally the *'place'*.

Among the more mainstream restaurants, pick from:

Café-Restaurant El Ayoune, Rue Hajjali. A new eaterie just off the *place*. Breakfast: 12/15dh; lunch/dinner: 30/40dh. Swift service, but you're not rushed.

Dar Baba, 2 Rue de Marrakesh, on corner with Rue Sidi Mohammed Ben Abdallah. Italian dishes: spaghetti, pasta, pizza; around 20dh a dish.

Café-Restaurant Bab Laâchour, on the *place*. A café favoured by locals downstairs, with a more tourist-orientated restaurant on the floor above. Menu includes fish dishes and rival *Chez Sam*; 60/70dh, wine/beer extra.

Restaurant La Calèche Bleue, Av. Okba Ibn Nafia, to one side of Galerie d'Art Frederic Damgaard; the *Restaurant El Minzah* is on the other side of the gallery. The two restaurants have much in common, but if you are looking for something simpler and cheaper, the *La Calèche Bleue* is better. There are a few calèches in Essaouira which operate from Bab Doukkala, but they aren't blue!

Chez Driss, 10 Rue Hajjali, just off the *place*. Well-established and one of the town's most popular meeting places. Delicious fresh pastries and coffee in a quiet leafy courtyard. Ideal for leisurely breakfast.

Café-Restaurant Essalam, on the *place*. Mohammed El Ouajibi is in charge and he ensures the best-value set meals in town. He also has three delightful apartments for rent. You can eat well for 35/45dh. It's very popular with locals and tourists alike. On the walls, you will see small watercolours by **Charles Kérival** who visits and paints Essaouira often. Born in Brittany, he discovered Morocco when the oil-tanker on which he was working visited Casablanca in 1956. He exhibits frequently in Morocco.

Restaurant L'Horloge, Place Chefchaouni; moderately priced Moroccan meals: 25dh to 45dh. Standard and lacking imagination, but value for money. Housed in one-time synagogue.

Restaurant El Khaima, Rue Derb Laâlouj/Place El Khaima. Rather overpriced meals (70/160dh) in a modern building, surrounded by a traditional tent (hence *Khaima*) and far back from the street, almost opposite the museum and on a square which it shares with lock-up workshops. It goes out for the tour-group trade but on the plus side is licensed, takes cards, and stays open late.

Dar Loubane, 24 Rue du Rif, a stone's throw from Place Chefchaouni. A new upmarket restaurant on the ground floor patio of an attractive eighteenth-century mansion. Moroccan and French cuisine (25/60dh); friendly service, interesting semi-kitsch decor and exhibits which are of interest. Live *gnawa* music Saturday evenings.

Café Marrakesh, on the *place*. Open all day, but especially good for breakfast. Popular with locals who will want to chat.

Restaurant El Minzah, Av. Okba Ibn Nafia, alongside the Galerie d'Art Frederic Damgaard, and housed in a converted almond store. Pleasant atmosphere; set menus (60/75dh) and à la carte.

THE ILE DE MOGADOR AND ELEONORA'S FALCON

Out across the bay from Essaouira lie the **Iles Purpuraires**, named from the dyes for purple imperial cloth that the Romans once produced here. Here also, Sir Francis Drake ate his Christmas lunch in 1577, commenting on the "verie ugly fish". The largest of the islands, known as the **Ile de Mogador**, is flanked on each side by a fort which, together with the fort on the islet just off the town harbour, and the Borj El Berod on the beach, covers all possible approaches to the bay. It also has a small harbour, a mosque, a few rusting cannons and a nineteenth-century prison used for political exiles, but long closed.

It is of most interest these days, however, as a nature reserve, for this is the only non-Mediterranean breeding site of **Eleonora's falcon** – Morocco's most dramatic bird. They are not hard to see, with binoculars, from the beach. The best time is the early evening half-light, when you might spot as many as two or three dozen of these magnificent birds, gliding in low over the sea to hawk for insects. The falcons are summer visitors to Morocco, staying between May and October before making the long return journey south to Madagascar for the winter. The nearby river course also has many **waders** and **egrets** and occasional rarities such as gull-billed tern and Mediterranean gull.

The island has no inhabitants, save for a *gardien* who keeps an eye on the falcons. If you want to visit – and this is strongly discouraged when the birds are resident – you'll first have to get a *permit d'autorisation* from the *Province*, signposted inland from Bd. Mohammed V after the *Hôtel Tafkout* and then the approval of the harbour-master in his office before the Marine Gate; the latter's say-so depends on the state of the tide and the weather forecast. Then, and only then, can you negotiate for a boat ride. Don't pay for the ride until you've been collected and returned to the town!

A visit such as this is problematic, time-consuming and calls for perseverance – but it is possible! Allow a couple of days at least for due processes.

Café-Restaurant Mogadur, Bd. Mohammed V, on the seafront on the same side as, and just before the *Hôtel Tafoukt*. The aroma of the nearby baker is tempting – to supplement the *Mogadur* breakfas, or buy for a picnic lunch.

Chalet de la Plage, Bd. Mohammed V – on the seafront, just above the high-tide mark. Built entirely of wood by the Ferraud family in 1893, the building is now a little gloomy and barnacled with marine mementos, but the seafood and sea views are truly memorable. Menus range from 80dh to 150dh. Avoid lunchtime when day-trippers overwhelm the kitchen. Licensed.

Chez Sam – Restaurant du Port, at the seaward end of the harbour. Another fine seafood restaurant and bar, serving huge portions of fish and (at a price) lobster. Occasional off days, but cat-lovers will enjoy the feline company.

Bars

You can get a beer or a bottle of wine at *Chez Sam's* or the *Chalet de la Plage*, though both prefer customers to take a meal, and at the *Café Mogador* on the seafront. Alternatives are basically down to the hotels *Tafoukt* and *des Iles*; at the latter, Moroccans gather to drink beer and play chess and draughts.

If you want to buy your own beer or wine, at very much lower prices, there are a number of small supermarkets.

Listings

Banks There are four banks in or near Place Prince Moulay El Hassan: a *BMCE, BCM, Banque Populaire* and *Credit du Maroc.*

Car rental You are unlikely to want to rent a car in Essaouira (any more than in Venice), but, if so, try *Hamza Car,* based at the *Hôtel Kasbah.*

Festivals A dozen or so local *moussems*, fairs and festivals are held between March and October. The main event is the *Festival d'Essaouira* in July. In October, the air rally commemorating the *Aéropostale Service* of the 1920's passes through Essaouira.

Post office The *PTT* is just outside the ramparts on Av. Lalla Aicha; it is open 8am-6pm daily; the phone section is a lot less reliable than *Jack's Kiosk* (see p.310), or the recently installed *téléboutiques.*

Religious services Mass is celebrated in the Catholic church near the campsite: Sundays at 10am.

Shopping Despite its size, Essaouira rivals Marrakesh and Fes as a centre for attractive items of lasting value (see box and text). and it's relatively hassle-free. For a worthy cause, you may choose to look for the little exhibition of the *Association des Parents et Amis des Handicapés* at 11 Rue El Fatouaki, open every afternoon; there are home-made items for sale.

Leaving Essaouira

Leaving Essaouira for **Marrakesh**, there is a non-stop *Supratours* bus which leaves from Av. Lalla Aicha and arrives in Marrakesh at the train station; tickets for this should be bought from the nearby kiosk the day before; departures are currently at 5.50am, arriving at Marrakesh at 8.20am, in time for the 8.30am train to Casa, arriving (11.36am) and Rabat, arriving (12.39pm); coming the other way, it leaves Marrakesh at 6.30pm, arriving at Essaouira at 9pm.

The best buses direct to **Casablanca** are the CTM "Mumtaz Express" (leaves Essaouira bus station daily at midnight, arriving Casa at 5am) and the night Pullman du Sud; they cost around 10dh more than other departures – money that you will, in any case, save on baggage loading. There's also a SATAS bus leaving Essaouira bus station at 9.30am, which travels via Safi and El Jadida, arriving at Casa at 3pm.

South to Agadir

The main road south from Essaouira to Agadir (P8) runs inland for the first 100km or so, with just the occasional piste leading down to a beach or fishing hamlet scattered

---

WINDSURFING AROUND ESSAOUIRA

Essaouira and its nearby beaches are Morocco's prime windsurfing centre, drawing enthusiasts almost year-round. There is a windsurfing centre in Essaouira, and the hotels south of Essaouira at Diabat and Sidi Kaouiki (see below) have become major gathering points.The trade wind at Essaouira is northwesterly and blows year-round; it is stronger in summer but the swell is bigger in winter. The winds are strong (sails required are 5.03.5) and the water is cool enough at any time of year to make a wetsuit essential.

---

along the rugged, cliff-lined coast. Along this stretch there is just one resort, Sidi Kaouki, which has the reputation of being Morocco's best windsurfing beach.

The region **inland** is known as the **Haha**, populated by Tashelhaït-speaking Berbers, and actually the westernmost range of the High Atlas. Its slopes are covered in **argan trees** (see p.464) which are often to be seen with a goat halfway up, nibbling away at the fruit. A handful of very rough pistes head into the hills, struggling over the mountains to meet the Tizi Machou road from Marrakesh to Agadir.

Sidi Kaouki and Cap Sim

The old road south from Essaouira used to go via **Diabat**, but since the bridge over the Oued Ksob was broken and replaced by a tricky ford, the main road (P8A leading to P8) crosses the river upstream before joining the P8 to Agadir. A turning to the right just before this junction takes you to Diabat by a metalled side road (see inset map on p.308).

En route to Diabat and signposted from the main road is the *Auberge Tangaro* (☎04/78.57.35 or 78.47.84; ④), a rather chic, Italian-owned place that provides a tempting alternative to staying in Essaouira, if you have transport of your own. Little used except at weekends, when groups of French and German windsurfers arrive from Casablanca and Marrakesh, the *auberge* has a number of **chalet rooms**, and it serves excellent meals. Demi-pension is obligatory. Next door is a small **campsite** with hot showers and youth hostel prices (20dh per person). The beach is a half-hour hike.

Back on the P8, a further 7km brings you to a sideroad signposted to **SIDI KAOUKI**. The beach here attracts **windsurfers** virtually year round, and looks set for mainstream development. Currently, the choice of accommodation is limited to two possibilities. The *Residence Kaouki Beach* has ten comfortable rooms; it's run by the *Villa Maroc* in Essaouira (bookings through it: ☎04/47.31.47; ②). Demi-pension is available and much cheaper than the *Auberge Tangaro;* the restaurant is fine and open – on reservation – to non-residents in the evening. The newer *Auberge de la Plage* (☎04/47.33.83; ②) is a little cheaper. It's managed by a German/Italian couple who have a small stable and horses to hire for trekking along the beach. To supplement the hotel restaurants, there is one beach café, *Chez Omar.*

Near the beach is the original **Marabout of Sidi Kaouki**, which has a reputation for curing sterility in women, and beyond that is **Cap Sim**, backed by long expanses of dunes.

On towards Agadir

The piste south of Sidi Kaouki, marked on the Michelin map, requires a four-wheel-drive vehicle, but back on the inland P8 there is little of interest. **SMIMOU** is a tiny roadside stop with a filling station and a couple of café-restaurants; to the east, one of the better roads leads into the hills to SOUK TNINE IMI N TLIT, where a large **Monday souk** takes place. **TAMANAR** has a petrol station and a reasonable roadside **hotel-restaurant**, the *Étoile du Sud* (☎04/78.81.84; ③).

Fifteen kilometres south of Tamanar, a metalled road, much damaged in the winter 1995/96 storms, cuts down to the coast at **POINTE IMESSOUANE**, a picturesque little harbour with a few fishermen's cottages. Just to the east is a bay and beach known as **Imoucha**, which, like Sidi Kaouki, is popular with **windsurfers** – and, to a lesser degree, surfers. The cliff top is a favourite site for campervans and caravans. It's possible to stay overnight in one of the huts by the harbour and there's a little shop. Fish is sold in the small *crieé* in the centre of things.

A few kilometres beyond the roadside settlement of **TAMRI** (117km), the road rejoins the coast, passing a lagoon, which might detain bird-watchers, and the fishing village of TARHAZOUTE (see Chapter Seven) before the final run to Agadir. Honey and bananas are on sale by the roadside, the latter to boost your sense of arrival in the south.

travel details

Trains

Rabat–Casablanca More or less hourly departures (50min–1hr 30min). Most run to/from *Casa-Port,* though a few exclusively to/from *Voyageurs.*

Casablanca–Tangier 4 daily, via Mohammedia, Rabat, Salé, Kenitra, Asilah and Tangier. (6hr).

Casablanca–El Jadida 1 daily (2hr).

Casablanca–Safi 1 daily via Benguerir on the Casablanca/Marrakesh line (5hr).

Buses

From Rabat Casablanca (10 daily; 1hr 40min); Fes (6 daily; 5hr 30min); Larache (4 daily: 3hr 30min); Meknes (3 daily; 4hr); Salé (frequent; 15min); Tangier (2 daily; 5hr).

From Casa CTM operates on a national scale; to Agadir (2 daily; 9hr 30min); to Al Hoceima (1 daily; 10hr 15min); to Beni Mellal (2 daily; 4hr); to Chaouen (1 daily; 8hr); to Er Rachidia (1 daily; 10hr 15min); to Fes (8 daily; 5hr 15min); to Marrakesh (4 daily; 4hr 15min); to Nador (1 daily; 11hr 45min); to Ouarzazate (1 daily; 8hr 20 min); to Oujda (1 daily; 11hr 30 min); to Safi (6 daily; 4hr 45min); to Tangier (5 daily; 6hr 30 min); to Taza (1 daily; 7hr 30 min); to Tetouan (3 daily; 7hr); and to

Tiznit (1 daily; 11hr 30min). *Other lines* are cheaper, but usually slower and are most useful for shorter journeys, including Tangier (2 daily; 7hr); Rabat (10 daily; 1hr 40min); El Jadida (3 daily; 2hr); Essaouira (3 daily; 5–7hr; best is the *SATAS*); Agadir (1 daily; 10hr); Marrakesh (4 daily; 45hr).

From El Jadida Casablanca (3 daily; 2hr 30min); Oualidia (2 daily; 1hr 30min); Rabat (2 daily; 4hr).

From Safi Oualidia/El Jadida (3 daily; 1hr 25min/2hr 30min).

From Essaouira Agadir (6 daily; 3hr 30min); Casablanca (4 daily; 5–9hr); El Jadida (2 daily; 8hr); Marrakesh (6 daily; 3hr–4hr 30 min); Safi (2 daily; 6hr); Tiznit (1 daily; 7hr).

Grands Taxis

Rabat–Casablanca Regular route, 1hr 20min.

From El Jadida Negotiable to Casablanca.

Flights

Rabat/Casa Mohammed V Airport: RAM direct international flights to destinations from Abidjan to Zurich and domestic flights to all major cities in Morocco from Agadir to Tetouan.

CHAPTER FIVE

MARRAKESH

Marrakesh – "Morocco City", as early travellers called it – has always been something of a pleasure city, a marketplace where the southern tribesmen and Berber villagers bring in their goods, spend their money and find entertainment. For visitors it's an enduring fantasy – a city of immense beauty, low, red and tentlike before a great shaft of mountains – and immediately exciting. At the heart of it all is a square, **Djemaa El Fna**, really no more than an open space in the centre of the city, but the stage for a long-established ritual in which shifting circles of onlookers gather round groups of acrobats, drummers, pipe musicians, dancers, storytellers and comedians. However many times you return there, it remains compelling. So, too, do the city's architectural attractions: the immense, still basins of the **Agdal** and **Menara** gardens, the delicate Granada-style carving of the **Saadian Tombs** and, above all, the **Koutoubia Minaret**, the most perfect Islamic monument in North Africa.

Unlike Fes, for so long its rival as the nation's capital, the city exists very much in the present. After Casablanca, Marrakesh is Morocco's second largest city and its population continues to rise. It has a thriving industrial area which reflects the rich farmlands of the **Haouz** plain which surround it: notably flour mills, breweries and canning factories. And it remains the most important market and administrative centre of southern Morocco. None of this is to suggest an easy prosperity – there is heavy unemployment here, as throughout the country, and intense poverty, too – but a stay in Marrakesh leaves you with a vivid impression of life and activity. And for once this doesn't apply exclusively to the new city, **Gueliz**; the **Medina**, substantially in ruins at the beginning of this century, was rebuilt and expanded during the years of French rule and retains no less significant a role in the modern city.

The Koutoubia excepted, Marrakesh is not a place of great monuments. Its beauty and attraction lie in the general atmosphere and spectacular location – with the magnificent peaks of the Atlas rising right up behind the city, towering through the heat haze of summer or shimmering white of winter. The feel, as much as anything, is a product of this. Marrakesh has **Berber** rather than Arab origins, having developed as the metropolis of Atlas tribes – Maghrebis from the plains, Saharan nomads and former slaves from Africa beyond the desert, Sudan, Senegal and the ancient kingdom of Timbuktu. All of these strands shaped the city's *souks* and its way of life, and in the crowds and performers in Djemaa El Fna, they can still occasionally seem distinct.

For most travellers, Marrakesh is the first experience of the south and – despite the inevitable 'false' guides and hustlers – of its generally more relaxed atmosphere and attitudes. **Marrakchis** are renowned for their warmth and sociability, their humour and directness – all qualities that (superficially, at least) can seem absent among the Fassis. There is, at any rate, a conspicuously more laid-back feel than anywhere in the north, with women, for example, having a greater degree of freedom and public presence, often riding mopeds around on the streets. And compared to Fes, Marrakesh is much less homogenous and cohesive. The city is more a conglomeration of villages than an urban community, with quarters formed and maintained by successive generations of migrants from the countryside.

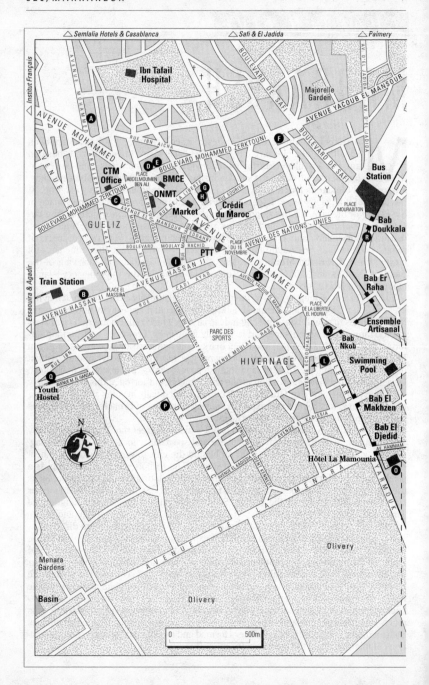

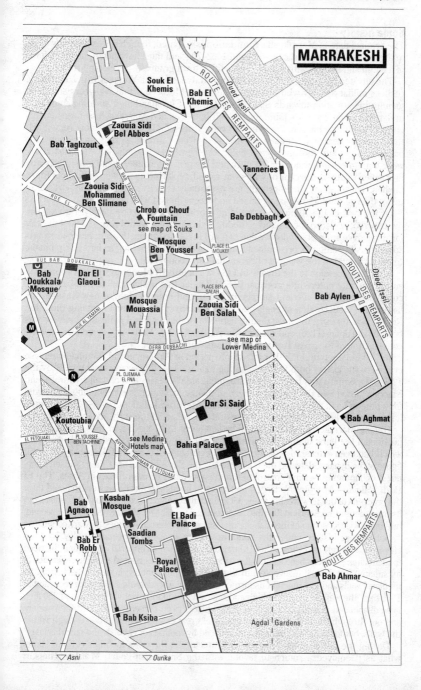

Some history

The original date of Marrakesh's **foundation** is disputed, though it was certainly close to the onset of **Almoravid** rule – around 1062–70 – and must have taken the initial form of a camp and market with a *ksour*, or fortified town gradually developing round it.

The city's founder (as that of the Almoravid dynasty) was **Youssef bin Tachfine**, a restless military leader who conquered northern Morocco within two years and then, turning his attention towards Spain, defeated the Christian kings, to bring Andalucia under Moroccan rule. Tachfine maintained both Fes and Marrakesh as bases for his empire, but under his son, the pious **Ali ben Youssef**, Marrakesh became very much the dominant centre. Craftsmen and architects from Córdoba worked on the new city: palaces, baths and mosques were built; underground channels, known as *khettara*, were built to provide water for the town and the growing palmery; and, in 1126–27, the first seven-kilometre **circuit of walls** was raised, replacing an earlier stockade of thorn bushes. These, many times rebuilt, are essentially the city's present walls – made of *tabia*, the red mud of the plains, mixed and strengthened with lime.

Of the rest of the Almoravid's building works, there remains hardly a trace. The dynasty that replaced them – the orthodox and reforming **Almohads** – sacked the city for three days after taking possession of it in 1147. Once again, though, Marrakesh was adopted as the empire's pre-eminent capital, its domain stretching as far as Tripolitania (modern Libya) in the wake of phenomenal early conquests.

With the accession to the throne in 1184 of **Yacoub El Mansour**, the third Almohad sultan, the city entered its greatest period. Under this prolific builder, *kissarias* were constructed for the sale and storage of Italian and oriental cloth, a new Kasbah was begun, and a succession of poets and scholars arrived at the court – among them Ibn Rochd, aka *Averroes*, the most distinguished of Arabic medieval philosophers, who was born in Córdoba (1126) and died in Marrakesh (1198). Mansour's reign also saw the construction of the great **Koutoubia Mosque** and minaret.

It is astonishing to think that this whole period of Almoravid and Almohad rule – so crucial to the rise of both the city and the nation – lasted barely two centuries. By the 1220s, the empire was beginning to fragment amid a series of factional civil wars, and Marrakesh fell into the familiar pattern of pillage, ruination and rebuilding. It revived for a time to form the basis of an independent **Merenid** kingdom (1374–86) but overall it gave way to Fes until the emergence of the Saadians in the early sixteenth century.

Taking Marrakesh, then devastated by famine, in 1521, and Fes in 1546, the **Saadians** provided a last burst of imperial splendour. Their first sultans regained the Atlantic coast, which had been extensively colonized by the Portuguese; **Ahmed El Mansour**, the great figure of the dynasty, defeated the Portuguese at the Battle of the Three Kings and led a conquest of Timbuktu, seizing control of the most lucrative caravan routes in Africa. The **El Badi Palace** – Marrakesh's largest and greatest building project – was constructed from the proceeds of this new wealth, though it again fell victim to dynastic rivalry and, apart from its mausoleum (the **Saadian Tombs**), was reduced to ruins by **Moulay Ismail,** the second, but first effective, sultan of the Alaouite dynasty, who preferred Meknes to Marrakesh.

Subsequent history under the **Alaouites** – the dynasty perpetuated today by King Hassan – is largely undistinguished. Marrakesh remained an imperial capital, and the need to maintain a southern base against the tribes ensured the regular, alternating residence of its sultans. But from the seventeenth to the nineteenth century, it shrank back from its medieval walls and lost much of its former trade. The *Encyclopedia Britannica* recorded in 1875 that "the wall, 25 or 30 feet high and relieved by square towers at intervals of 360 feet, is so dilapidated that foot-passengers, and in places even horsemen, can find their way in and out through the breaches. Open spaces of great extent are numerous enough within the walls, but for the most part they are defaced by mounds of rubbish and putrid refuse."

During the last decades prior to the Protectorate, the city's fortunes revived somewhat as it enjoyed a return to favour with the Shereefian court. **Moulay Hassan**

(1873–94) and **Moulay Abd El Aziz** (1894–1908) both ran their governments from here in a bizarre closing epoch of the old ways, accompanied by a final bout of frantic palace building. On the arrival of **the French**, Marrakesh gave rise to a short-lived pretender, the religious leader El Hiba, and for most of the colonial period it was run as a virtual fiefdom of its pasha, **T'hami El Glaoui** – the most powerful, autocratic and extraordinary character of his age (see p.338).

Since **independence**, the city has undergone considerable change, with rural emigration from the Atlas and beyond, new methods of cultivation on the Haouz plain and the development of a sizeable tourist industry. The impressive **Palais des Congrès**, opened in 1989, has given Marrakesh international prestige, hosting such events as the 1994 ratification of the GATT accord. All of these factors combine to make Marrakesh Morocco's best-known city and, after Casablanca, the country's largest trading base and population centre – 1,425,000 at the last estimate.

Orientation

Despite its size – and the maze of its *souks* – Marrakesh is not too hard to navigate. The broad, open space of **Djemaa El Fna** lies right at the heart of the **Medina**, and almost everything of interest is concentrated in the web of alleyways north and south of the square. Just to the west of the Djemaa El Fna is the unmistakeable landmark of the **Koutoubia** minaret – in the shadow of which begins **Avenue Mohammed V**, leading out through the Medina walls at Bab Nkob and up the length of the French-built new city, **Gueliz**.

POINTS OF ARRIVAL

BY TRAIN

The **train station** is at the edge of the new town, Gueliz. Keep your wits about you as you emerge, or you'll immediately find yourself engaged with a guide or taxi driver. A regular *petit taxi* (beware unofficial taxis) is a good idea in general, since it's quite a walk to hotels in Gueliz – and a long way to the Medina; the taxi fare should be no more than 10dh to the Medina, less to hotels in Gueliz. The #3 and #8 buses run from the station to the Place de Foucauld, alongside Place Djemaa El Fna.

However, if you plan to stay at the youth hostel, you should, luggage permitting, be able to walk there from the train station in five minutes or so.

BY BUS

The **gare routière** (for all long-distance bus services) is just outside the walls of the Medina by Bab Doukkala. You can walk into the centre of Gueliz from here in around ten minutes by following Av. des Nations Unies; to the Place Djemaa El Fna it's around twenty to twenty-five minutes, most easily accomplished by following the Medina walls down to Av. Mohammed V. Alternatively, catch the #3 or #8 bus, which run in one direction to the Koutoubia, in the other to Gueliz; or save yourself trouble by taking a *petit taxi* (about 10dh).

BY AIR

The city's **airport** is 5km to the southwest. The #11 bus is supposed to run every half hour to the Place Djemaa El Fna, but it is very erratic. *Petits taxis* or *grands taxis* are a better option, though you will have to watch that you pay a reasonable fare. The *grands taxis* currently display a price of 50dh (day) and 60dh (night) for the trip from the airport to Gueliz; try not to pay a lot more.

Arriving at the airport before 8am or after about 6pm any day of the week, you won't always find the *BMCE* or *Banque Populaire* kiosk open to change money or travellers' cheques; taxis, however, will accept pounds or dollars, at more or less the equivalent dirham rate.

LOCAL BUS ROUTES

The following buses leave from Av. El Mouahidine alongside Place de Foucauld, opposite *Hôtel de Foucauld*:

#1 to Gueliz, along Av. Mohammed V.

#2 to Riad El Arous and Bab Doukkala (for the bus station).

#3 to Douar Laskar by Av. Mohammed V/Av. Hassan II, via the train station and passing close to the youth hostel.

#4 to Daoudiat (a northern suburb), by Av. Mohammed V/Av. d'El Jadida, passing close to the Jardin Majorelle.

#8 to Douar Laskar by Av. Mohammed V/Av. Moulay El Hassan, via the train station and close to the youth hostel.

#10 to Bd. de Safi, by Bab Doukkala, via the bus station.

#11 to the airport by Av. Menara.

#14 to the train station.

Only in the **souks** might you want to consider taking a guide, though you'll have plenty of offers; moped-riding guides, driving dangerously alongside new arrivals, are also unfortunately in evidence.

City transport

It is a fairly long walk between Gueliz and the Medina, but there are plenty of **petits taxis** and **grands taxis**, which will take you between the two for around 10dh. There are taxi ranks at most intersections in Gueliz and in the Medina at the Place Djemaa El Fna, outside the *Grand Hôtel Tazi* and at the Place des Ferblantiers end of Av. Houman El Fetouaki. **Bus** #1 also runs between the main Gueliz squares and the Koutoubia/Place de Foucauld in the Medina. (For more bus routes, see the box above).

Note that very few of the *petits taxis* are **metered** (or admit to a functioning meter); you either have to fix a price in advance, haggle on arrival, or just decide on what you're paying and hand it over at the end of the trip; most trips should cost around 10dh, or 15dh in the evening. *Grands taxis* and *calèches* have by law to display prices for specified trips; these prices are per trip and not per person, as drivers often claim.

In addition to taxis, there are **calèches**, horse-drawn cabs which line up near the Koutoubia, the Badi Palace and some of the fancier hotels. These can take up to five people and are not much more expensive than *petits taxis* – though be sure to fix the price in advance, particularly if you want a tour of the town.

An alternative, for exploring the more scattered city sights such as the Agdal and Menara gardens, or the palmery, the ideal transport is a **bike** or **moped**. You can rent them from the outlets listed in the "Listings" at the end of the chapter (see p.354); they will cost up to 100dh a day. **Grands taxis** can also be chartered by the day for around 150dh, which works out very reasonable if you split it between four people (the taxis take a maximum six passengers – but four is comfortable). Negotiate at the ranks in Djemaa El Fna or by the *PTT* in Gueliz.

Accommodation

As always, there is a choice between staying in the Medina or the Ville Nouvelle (Gueliz), and further options in the hotel-dominated quarters of Hivernage or Semlalia, out out on the Casablanca road.

HOTEL PRICE CODES AND STAR RATINGS

Hotels are no longer obliged to charge according to the official star-ratings (from 1* to 5* luxury), as had long been the custom. Nevertheless, **prices** continue to reflect the star-ratings acquired. The basis of our own **hotel price codes**, set out below and keyed throughout the guide, is the price currently quoted for the cheapest double room in high season (June–September) – and is thus more reliable than quoting notional prices according to star-rating.

Note that cheaper prices in the lower categories are generally for rooms with just a washbasin – you always pay extra for **en-suite** shower and WC – and that double rooms can generally be converted into **triples/family rooms**, with extra beds, for a modest extra charge. Note also that the prices quoted by all hotels are subject to various local and regional **taxes**, which can add 15 to 20 percent to the bill.

Our code	Classification	Single room price	Double room price
⑩	Unclassified	25–60dh	50–99dh
①	1*A/1*B	60–105dh	100–149dh
②	2*B/2*A	105–145dh	150–199dh
③	3*B/3*A	145–225dh	200–299dh
④	4*B/4*A	225–400dh	300–599dh
⑤	5*luxury	Upwards of 400dh	Upwards of 600dh

TELEPHONE CODES

All telephone numbers in the Marrakesh region are prefixed **04**. When making a call within the region you omit this prefix. For more explanation of phone codes and making calls within (or to) Morocco, see pp.45–46.

The **Medina**, as usual, has the main concentration of cheap, unclassified hotels, most of which are quite pleasant (though they can be cold in winter), along with a few more expensive places on its periphery. Given the attractions of the Place Djemaa El Fna and the *souks*, these have to be the first choice.

The main advantages of **Gueliz** hotels are their convenience if you are arriving late at night, particularly at the train station, and, in the more upmarket ones, the presence of a swimming pool. Hotels in **Hivernage** and **Semlalia** are all upmarket, modern buildings, consistently comfortable and sometimes with wonderful pools and design. Semlalia, however, is a bit remote, and Hivernage, while not too far from the Djemaa El Fna, lacks any city-life of its own.

Advance bookings for hotels are a wise idea, especially for the classified places in the Medina. The worst times are the **Easter** and **Christmas/New Year** holiday periods, when you may arrive and find virtually every decent hotel full to capacity – often with the entourage who travel with King Hassan, who likes to stay in Marrakesh, particularly over the New Year period.

Note that there is **no city campsite**; the municipal site (still on many maps) closed in 1995.

Medina hotels

Most of the Medina hotels are grouped about a compact, easily walkable area just south of the Place Djemaa El Fna (see map below). It's best to book rooms in advance – and essential if you are hoping to stay in one of the pricier, **classified** places. The **unclassified (cheap) hotels** detailed below are the best of those available; there are many others in the same grid of streets, some of which are keyed on our map for reference, finding your way around, but are not recommendations. At time of writing, most unclassified places charge between 50–100dh afor a double room.

△ *Hôtel Oukaïmeden (across square)*

MARRAKESH: MEDINA HOTELS

D J E M A A   E L   F N A

Banque Populaire
Bureau de Change

PTT

Banque du Maroc

Crédit du Maroc

Hammam (men & women)

Wafa Bank

Place de Foucauld

BMCE

Cinema Mabrouka

Hammam (men only)

RUE DE LA RECETTE

Banque Populaire

AVENUE EL MOUAHIDINE

BMCI

AVENUE HOUMAN EL FETOUAKI

0   100m

△ *Hôtels Islane & les Almoravides*
△ Horse & Carriage Stand
◁ Local Buses
RUE MOULAY ISMAIL
RUE MARINE
RUE BANI
RUE BAB AGNAOU
RUE BAB
RUE DU DISPENSAIRE
RIAD ZIIOUN KADEM
▽ *Hôtel La Mamounia*

CLASSIFIED

1 Hôtel Ali
2 Hôtel Arset el Bilk
3 Hôtel CTM
4 Hôtel de Foucauld
5 Hôtel Gallia
6 Hôtel Ichbilia
7 Hôtel Oukaïmeden (off map)
8 Grand Hôtel Tazi

UNCLASSIFIED

9 Hôtel Afriquia
10 Hôtel el Amal
11 Hôtel des Amis

12 Hôtel el Atlal
13 Hôtel el Azhar
14 Hôtel Cecil
15 Hôtel Central
16 Hôtel Challa
17 Hôtel Charaf
18 Hôtel Eddakhla
19 Hôtel Essaouira
20 Hôtel el Farah
21 Hôtel de France
22 Hôtel la Gazelle
23 Hôtel Hassan
24 Hôtel Hillal
25 Hôtel de la Jeunesse

26 Hôtel Kawabib
27 Hôtel Mabrouka
28 Hôtel Mauretania
29 Hôtel Medina
30 Hôtel Nouzha
31 Hôtel de la Paix
32 Hôtel Provence
33 Hôtel Sahara
34 Hôtel Smara
35 Hôtel Souria
36 Hôtel de Tourisme
37 Hôtel el Ward
38 Hôtel Zagora

Note: This map is intended for reference only and not all hotels included are recommended.

UNCLASSIFIED: CHEAP

Hôtel Afriquia [9], 45 Derb Sidi Bouloukat (☎04/44.24.03). Decent rooms off a pleasant courtyard with orange trees. Clean, well-maintained and excellent value. ①

Hôtel El Amal [10], 93 Derb Sidi Bouloukat (☎04/44.50.43). Newly converted house with eleven rooms on two floors. Clean, modern facilities which work. ①

Hôtel Essaouira [19], 3 Derb Sidi Bouloukat (☎04/44.38.05). One of the most popular cheapies in Marrakesh – and with good reason. It's a well run, safe place, with 30 rooms, hot showers for 5dh, a laundry service and rooftop café. ①

Hôtel de France [21], 197 Rue Zitoun El Kadem (☎04/44.30.67). Not to be confused with the dire *Hôtel du Café de France* on the Djemaa El Fna, this is one of the oldest and best of the cheapies, attracting a wide age range. Cash and travellers' cheques changed. ①

Hôtel la Gazelle [22], 12 Rue Bani Marine (☎04/44.11.12). Well-kept hotel with bright, airy rooms, and free hot showers, on a street with a row of outdoor foodstalls and small grill cafés; price-wise it is at the top end of the unclassified Medina scale, but well worth it. ③

Hôtel Medina [29], 1 Derb Sidi Bouloukat (☎04/44.29.97). Marvellous; a real gem – small, clean, laid-back and friendly. Showers extra (5dh hot) and breakfast (7dh each) on the terrace. ①

Hôtel Souria [35], 17 Rue de la Recette (☎04/44.59.70). Deservedly popular hotel which rivals the *Medina* as the best in these listings. The grand old *patronnne* has died, alas, but her heirs are maintaining a fine tradition: small, clean and family run. ①

Medina hotels not greatly recommended at time of writing include: *Hôtel des Amis*; *Hôtel Central*; *Hôtel du Café de France*; *Hôtel Mauretania*; *Hôtel de la Paix*; *Hôtel Sahara*; *Hôtel de Tourisme*; *Hôtel El Ward*.

CLASSIFIED: CHEAP

Hôtel Ali [1], Rue Moulay Ismail (☎04/44.49.79). A deservedly popular small hotel with reliable showers in most rooms, heating in winter, air-conditioning in summer – and a rooftop terrace for sunbathing. The restaurant serves à la carte lunch and, in the evening, an excellent (and modest-priced) buffet with ten or more dishes, steaming *tajine*-style. The hotel is used as an assembly point for various groups heading to the High Atlas and so is a good source of trekking (and other) information. It also changes money and rents bikes. ①

Hôtel Arset El Bilk [2], Rue Bani Marine (☎04/42.64.30). A relatively new hotel, opened in 1996, almost opposite the well-established *Hôtel Gazelle*. With showers and toilets en suite in all rooms, it is an attractive alternative to the *Gazelle* (see above) and nearby *Ichbilia* (see below). ①

Hôtel CTM [3], Place Djemaa El Fna (☎04/44.23.35). Decent-sized rooms, as clean and as cheap as many of the unclassified places. Rooms with showers, albeit cold, are a little dearer but, even then, just under 100dh. The hotel is above the old bus station (hence its name) and has a useful underground garage, if you have a car to look after. ①

Hôtel Ichbilia [6], 1 Rue Bani Marine (☎04/32.04.86). Near the Mabrouka cinema. Quite new and wearing well, with comfortable rooms off a courtyard and gallery, but separate toilet and showers. Don't be confused if locals refer to it as *Hôtel Sevilla;* Ichbilia is the Arabic for Seville. ①

CLASSIFIED: MODERATE

Hôtel de Foucauld [4], Av. El Mouahidine – facing Place de Foucauld (☎04/44.54.99). Rooms are on the small side, but this is a generally reliable choice, with friendly staff, bicycles for rent, help with local information and a licensed restaurant. Like the *Ali* across the *place,* some High Atlas guides hang out here. ③

Hôtel Gallia [5], 30 Rue de la Recette (☎04/44.59.13). A pleasant building in a quiet cul-de-sac. Airy and spotless rooms off two tiled courtyards, one with fountain, palm tree and caged birds. Central heating in winter and air-conditioning in summer. Good breakfasts. A long-term favourite and highly recommended. Booking is advisable, but not always reliable. ②

Grand Hôtel Tazi [8], corner of pedestrianized Rue Bab Agnaou/Av. Houman El Fetouaki (☎04/44.21.52). A once quite grand hotel that has seen better days. It is managed by an extended family which leads to some disorder, but the rooms are generally comfortable and most have TV, en-suite toilet and bath/shower. There's a bar open to non-residents and a restaurant (with 20 per-cent discount for residents, but you would be better advised to eat elsewhere). The swimming pool, however, is a real plus – and can be used by non-residents. ②

Medina/Hivernage periphery

The three hotels below are located on the periphery of the Medina, over towards the Hivernage quarter. They are more upmarket (and the *Mamounia* is as pricey as Morocco gets) but, if you can afford them, all offer excellent locations. They are keyed on the main map of Marrakesh on pp.320–321.

MODERATE

Hôtel Islane [N], 279 Av. Mohammed V (☎04/44.00.81). A very central location, only a short walk from the Djemaa El Fna, facing the Koutoubia. The views compensate for the traffic noise from rooms at the front – and there is a rooftop restaurant. ③

Hôtel Yasmine [K], Bd. El Yarmouk (☎04/44.62.00). A small hotel that does not look too attractive, but the staff are helpful and the rooms adequate. ③

EXPENSIVE

Hôtel Les Almoravides [M], Arset Djenan Lakhdor (☎04/44.51.42). This is a quiet location, just behind the *Ensemble Artisanal*, not far from the Medina's sights. It has a swimming pool, good restaurant, and impeccable service. ④

La Maison Arabe [R], 1 Derb Assebbe Bab Doukkala – opposite the Doukkala mosque (☎04/39.12.33). A classy addition to the hotel scene, this is a gorgeous nineteenth-century mansion, newly restored as a series of luxurious suites, each with its own private terrace. At 1700dh and up, the prices rival the Mamounia, but if money's no object. . . ⑤

Hôtel La Mamounia [O], Av. Bab Jdid (☎04/44.89.81). Set within its own palace grounds, this is – alongside the *Palais Jamai* in Fes – the most beautiful hotel in Morocco. It is also the most expensive, with doubles from 2500dh if you book independently. Room prices drop a bit during the low season, or if you book as part of a holiday package – but they are still pretty astronomical. For a description of the gardens, see p.349. ⑤

Gueliz hotels

This is a selection of the better-value and best hotels in these areas – and a review of a few others that are used by package tour operators. All are keyed on the main map of Marrakesh on pp.320–321.

CHEAP

Auberge de Jeunesse (Youth Hostel) [Q], Rue El Jahid (☎04/43.28.31). Quiet, clean, friendly and family run, with small garden, scented by orange trees. It is a useful first-night standby if you arrive late by train , being just five minutes' walk from the station (and its buses to the Medina). Open 8–9am, noon–2pm and 6–10pm (winter), 6pm–midnight (summer); IYHF cards compulsory.

Hôtel Farouk [I], 66 Av. Hassan II (☎04/43.19.89). This is highly recommended, being owned by the same family as the *Ali* in the Medina. Warm welcome, hot showers in all rooms, excellent restaurant – and convenient for the train station. ①

Hôtel Franco-Belge [E], 62 Bd. Mohammed Zerktouni (☎04/44.84.72). Old hotel built for officers during the Protectorate. The best rooms are off an open courtyard; those facing the street are noisy. The entrance, lost in a row of shops, is not easy to see. ①

Hôtel Toulousain [H], 44 Rue Tariq Ben Ziad (☎04/43.00.33). Behind the municipal market; set back off the street. Friendly and known locally as the *Peace Corps* hotel after its regular clientele over the years. Some rooms have showers; breakfast extra. ①

Hôtel des Voyageurs [D], 40 Bd. Mohammed Zerktouni (☎04/44.72.18). Old, respectable hotel; unexciting, but inexpensive. Rooms with showers extra. ①

MODERATE

Hôtel Ezzahia [off map], Av. Mohammed Abdelkrim El Kattabi (☎04/44.62.44). Built in the late 1980s, well furnished and with a pool. It is a little way out on the Casablanca road, but bicycles, mopeds and motor bikes can be rented opposite. ③

Hôtel du Pacha [G], 33 rue de la Liberté (☎04/43.13.26). An old-style hotel with a courtyard, but with some modern rooms as well – and a good restaurant. ③

EXPENSIVE

Hôtel Agdal [C], 1 Bd. Mohammed Zerktouni (☎04/43.71.18). One of the best hotels in Gueliz, with a pool, bar and restaurant; it is also well placed for the other restaurants around Place Abdelmoumen Ben Ali. ④

Residence El Hamra [A], 26 Av. Mohammed V (☎04/44.84.23). Self-catering apartments which are not terribly exciting, but would suit a family or a group of three or four. ④

Hôtel Ibn Batouta [J], Av. Yacoub El Marini (☎04/43.41.45). Newish hotel with good rooms; used by French and Spanish tour groups and convenient for a small shopping centre – but service is sometimes lax and falls short of its rating. ④

Kenza Hôtel [F], Av. Yacoub El Mansour (☎04/44.83.30). A fine hotel with tastefully luxurious rooms and furnishings, an enticing pool, two bars and two restaurants. Not very central, but close to the Jardin Majorelle. ④

Ibis Hôtel [B], Av. Hassan II/Place de la Gare (☎04/43.59.29). Tasteful (ex-Moussafir) chain hotel by the train station, with a swimming pool, bar and restaurant. ④

Hivernage hotels

Hivernage has a concentration of upmarket hotels and if you're on a package, you're likely to find yourself here. The two below are the pick of the bunch if you are looking to book independently.

EXPENSIVE

Hôtel Atlas Asni [P], Av. de France (☎04/44.70.51). One of the largest and best known of the Hivernage 4-star hotels. Outwardly bleak and barrack-like, but reportedly friendly and helpful with good restaurant. ⑤

Hôtel Le Grand Imilchil [L], Av. Echouhada (☎04/44.76.53). On a fine avenue, near to Place de la Liberté and not too far from the Medina. The swimming pool may be small but the hotel is good value for the price. ④

Semlalia hotels

Semlalia might suit you if you have a car, or if you want to spend a good part of your time in Marrakesh lazing by the pool, with trips into the Medina by taxi.

EXPENSIVE

Hôtel Tichka [off map], Triangle d'Or, B.P. 894, 3km out of town on the Route de Casablanca (☎04/44.87.10). State-of-the-art hotel, with fine architecture and internal decor by Bill Willis, renowned American *décorateur*. On Saturday evenings, there's a pool-side Moroccan buffet, but otherwise the restaurant can disappoint. ⑤

Hôtel Tropicana [off map], alongside *Hôtel Tichka*, but no B.P. (☎04/44.74.50). Lively and, at half the cost of the Tichka, good value for money. It's currently managed by *Nouvelles Frontières*; hence, its competitive pricing. ④

The Djemaa El Fna

There's nowhere in Morocco like the **Djemaa El Fna** – no place that so effortlessly involves you and keeps you coming back. By day it's basically a market, with a few snake charmers, storytellers and an occasional troupe of acrobats. In the evening it becomes a whole carnival of musicians, clowns and street entertainers. When you arrive in Marrakesh, and after you've found a room, come out here and you'll soon be immersed in the ritual: wandering round, squatting amid the circles of onlookers, giving a dirham or two as your contribution. If you want a respite, you can move over to the rooftop terraces of the *Café de France* or the *Restaurant Argana* to gaze over the square and admire the frame of the Koutoubia.

What you are part of is a strange process. Some say that tourism is now vital to the Djemaa's survival, yet apart from the snake charmers, monkey handlers and water vendors (all of whom live by posing for photographs), there's little that has compromised

THE DEVELOPMENT OF THE DJEMMA EL FNA

Nobody is entirely sure when or how Djemaa El Fna came into being – nor even what its name means. The usual translation is "assembly of the dead", a suitably epic title that seems to refer to the public display here of the heads of rebels and criminals. This is certainly possible, since the Djemaa was a place of execution well into the last century; the phrase, though, might only mean "the mosque of nothing" (*djemaa* means both "mosque" and "assembly" – interchangeable terms in Islamic society, as is *synagogue* in Jewry), recalling an abandoned Saadian plan to build a new grand mosque on this site.

Whichever is the case, as an open area between the original Kasbah and the *souks*, the *place* has probably played its present role since the city's earliest days. It has often been the focal point for rioting – even within the last decade – and every few years there are plans to close it down and to move its activities outside the city walls. This, in fact, happened briefly after independence in 1956, when the new "modernist" government built a corn market on part of the square and tried to turn the rest into a car park. The plan, however, lasted for only a year. Tourism was falling off and it was clearly an unpopular move – it took away one of the people's basic psychological needs, as well as eliminating a perhaps necessary expression of the past. As Paul Bowles has said, without the Djemaa El Fna, Marrakesh would become just another Moroccan city.

itself for the West. In many ways it actually seems the opposite. Most of the people gathered into circles round the performers are Moroccans – Berbers from the villages and lots of kids. There is no way that any tourist is going to have a tooth pulled by one of the dentists here, no matter how neat the piles of molars displayed on their square of carpet. Nor are you likely to use the scribes or street barbers or, above all, understand the convoluted tales of the storytellers, round whom are gathered perhaps the most animated, all-male crowds in the square.

Nothing of this, though, matters very much. There is a fascination in the remedies of the herb doctors, with their bizarre concoctions spread out before them. There are **performers**, too, whose appeal is universal. The square's acrobats, itinerants from Tazeroualt, have for years supplied the European circuses – though they are perhaps never so spectacular as here, thrust forward into multiple somersaults and contortions in the late afternoon heat. There are child boxers and sad-looking trained monkeys, clowns and Chleuh boy dancers – their routines, to the climactic jarring of cymbals, totally sexual (and traditionally an invitation to clients).

And finally, the Djemaa's enduring sound – the dozens of **musicians** playing all kinds of instruments. Late at night, when only a few people are left in the square, you encounter individual players, plucking away at their *ginbris,* the skin-covered two- or three-string guitars. Earlier in the evening, there are full groups: the *Aissaoua,* playing oboe-like *ghaitahs* next to the snake charmers; the Andalucian-style groups, with their *ouds* and violins; and the black *Gnaoua,* trance-healers who beat out hour-long hypnotic rhythms with iron clanging hammers and pound tall drums with long curved sticks.

If you get interested in the music there are two small sections on opposite sides of the square where stalls sell recorded **cassetttes**: one is near the entrance to the *souks* and the other is on the corner with the recently pedestrianized Rue Bab Agnaou. Most of these are by Egyptian or Algerian Raï bands, the pop music that dominates Moroccan radio, but if you ask they'll play you Berber music from the Atlas, classic Fassi pieces, or even Gnaoua music – which sounds even stranger on tape, cut off only by the end of the one side and starting off almost identically on the other. These stalls

---

As a foreigner in the Djemaa El Fna, you can feel something of an interloper – your presence accepted, though not wholly welcomed. Sometimes the storyteller or musician will pick on you to take part or contribute generously to the end-of-show collection. Entering into the spectacle, it's best to go denuded of the usual tourist trappings – watches, belt-wallets, etc; **pickpockets** do very well out of the square. Beware, also, of being duped by women selling "silver" jewellery; if you decline to buy, they may give you a "present" – and as you move on, large male friends will arrive to accuse you of stealing the trinket.

---

apart, and those of the nut roasters, whose massive braziers line the immediate entrance to the potters' *souk,* the **market** activities of the Djemaa are mostly pretty mundane.

Eating in the square

Not to be missed, even if you lack the stomach to eat at any of them, are the rows of makeshift **restaurants** that come into their own towards early evening. Lit by butane and paraffin lanterns, their tables piled high with massive bowls of cooked food, each vendor extols his own range of specialities. If you're wary, head for the orange vendors on the far side from the *Hôtel CTM,* or go for a handful of cactus fruit, peeled in a couple of seconds at the stalls nearby. For details on more substantial eating in the Djemaa El Fna and elsewhere, (see pp.350–353).

The Koutoubia

The absence of any architectural feature on Djemaa El Fna – which even today seems like a haphazard clearing – serves to emphasize the drama of the **Koutoubia Minaret**, the focus of any approach to the city. Nearly seventy metres high and visible for miles on a clear morning, this is the oldest of the three great Almohad towers (the others remaining are the Tour Hassan in Rabat and the Giralda in Seville) and the most complete. Its proportions – a 1:5 ratio of width to height – established the classic Moroccan design. Its scale, rising from the low city buildings and the plains to the north, is extraordinary, the more so the longer you stay and the more familiar its sight becomes.

Completed by Sultan Yacoub El Mansour (1184–99), work on the minaret probably began shortly after the Almohad conquest of the city, around 1150. It displays many of the features that were to become widespread in Moroccan architecture – the wide band of ceramic inlay near the top, the pyramid-shaped, castellated *merlons* rising above it, the use of *darj w ktarf* and other motifs – and it also established the alternation of patterning on different faces. Here, the top floor is similar on each of the sides but the lower two are almost eccentric in their variety; the most interesting is perhaps the middle niche on the southeast face, a semicircle of small lobed arches, which was to become the dominant decorative feature of Almohad gates.

If you look hard, you will notice that at around this point, the stones of the main body of the tower become slightly smaller. This seems odd today but originally the whole minaret would have been covered with plaster and its tiers of decoration painted. To see just how much this can change the whole effect – and, to most tastes, lessen much of its beauty – take a look at the Kasbah mosque (by the Saadian Tombs) which has been carefully but completely restored in this manner.

There have been plans over the years to do the same with the Koutoubia and the local press have recently been running a number of articles on various schemes, possibly involving a restoration of the whole mosque area. To date, however, the only parts of the structure that have been renovated are the three gilt balls made of copper at the summit. These are the subject of numerous legends, mostly of supernatural interventions to keep away the thieves. They are thought originally to have been made of gold and were possibly the gift of the wife of Yacoub El Mansour, presented as a penance for breaking her fast for three hours during Ramadan.

Currently, the tower itself is encased in scaffolding, the purpose of which is not yet clear. At the same time, archeologists are excavating the precincts of the mosque, possibly to verify that the original mosque, which predates the tower, had to be rebuilt to correct its alignment with Mecca.

Alongside the mosque, and close to Av. Mohammed V, is the tomb of Fatima Zohra, now in a white *koubba*. She was the daughter of a seventeenth-century religious leader and tradition has it that she was a woman by day and a white dove by night; consequently children dedicated to her, even today, never eat pigeons.

The souks and northern Medina

It is spicy in the souks, and cool and colourful. The smell, always pleasant, changes gradually with the nature of the merchandise. There are no names or signs; there is no glass . . . . You find everything – but you always find it many times over.

Elias Canetti: *The Voices of Marrakesh*

The **souks** of Marrakesh sprawl immediately north of Djemaa El Fna. They seem vast the first time you venture in, and almost impossible to navigate, though, in fact, the area that they cover is pretty compact. A long, covered street, **Rue Souk Smarine**, runs for half their length and then splits into two lanes – **Souk El Attarin** and **Souk El Kebir**. Off these are virtually all the individual *souks:* alleys and small squares devoted to specific crafts, where you can often watch part of the production process. At the top of the main area of *souks*, too, you can visit the Saadian **Ben Youssef Medersa** – the most important monument in the northern half of the Medina and arguably the finest building in the city after the Koutoubia Minaret.

If you are staying for some days, you'll probably return often to the *souks* – and this is a good way of taking them in, singling out a couple of specific crafts or products to see, rather than being swamped by the whole. To come to grips with the general layout, though, you might find it useful to walk round the whole area once with a **guide** (see below). Despite the pressure of offers on Djemaa El Fna, don't feel that one is essential, but until the hustlers begin to recognize you (seeing that you've been in the *souks* before), they'll probably follow you in; if and when this happens, try to be easygoing, polite and confident – the qualities that force most hustlers to look elsewhere.

The most interesting **times** to visit are in early morning (between 6.30 and 8am if you can make it) and late afternoon, at around 4 to 5pm, when some of the *souks* auction off goods to local traders. Later in the evening, most of the stalls are closed, but you can wander unharassed to take a look at the elaborate decoration of their doorways and arches; those stalls that stay open, until 7 or 8pm, are often more amenable to bargaining at the end of the day.

Towards Ben Youssef: the main souks

On the corner of Djemaa El Fna itself there is a small potters' *souk,* but the main market area begins a little further beyond this. Its **entrance** is initially confusing. Standing at the

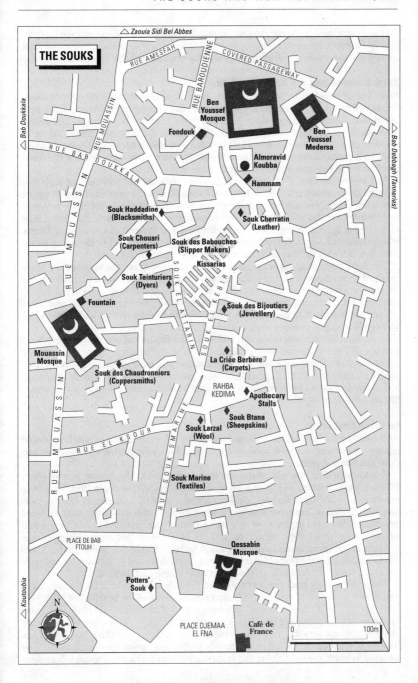

THE SOUKS

△ *Zaouia Sidi Bel Abbes*

△ *Bab Doukkala*

△ *Bab Debbagh (Tanneries)*

RUE AMESFAH

RUE BAROUDIENNE

COVERED PASSAGEWAY

RUE BAB DOUKKALA

RUE MOUASSIN

Ben Youssef Mosque

Fondouk

Ben Youssef Medersa

Almoravid Koubba

Hammam

Souk Haddadine (Blacksmiths)

Souk Cherratin (Leather)

Souk Chouari (Carpenters)

Souk des Babouches (Slipper Makers)

Kissarias

Souk Teinturiers (Dyers)

SOUK EL ATTARIN

SOUK EL KEBIR

Souk des Bijoutiers (Jewellery)

Fountain

Mouassin Mosque

La Criée Berbère (Carpets)

Souk des Chaudronniers (Coppersmiths)

RAHBA KEDIMA

Apothecary Stalls

RUE MOUASSIN

RUE SOUK SMARINE

Souk Larzal (Wool)

Souk Btana (Sheepskins)

RUE EL KSOUR

Souk Marine (Textiles)

PLACE DE BAB FTOUH

Qessabin Mosque

△ *Koutoubia*

N

Potters' Souk

PLACE DJEMAA EL FNA

Café de France

0   100m

Café de France (and facing the mosque opposite), look across the street and you'll see the *Café El Fath* and, beside it, a building with the sign "Tailleur de la Place" – the lane sandwiched in between them will bring you out at the beginning of Rue Souk Smarine.

Souk Smarine and the Rahba Kedima

Busy and crowded, **Rue Souk Smarine** is an important thoroughfare, traditionally dominated by the sale of textiles and clothing. Today, classier tourist "bazaars" are moving in, with *American Express* signs displayed in the windows, but there are still dozens of shops in the arcades selling and tailoring traditional shirts and caftans. Along its whole course, the street is covered by a broad, iron trellis that restricts the sun to shafts of light; it replaces the old rush (*smar*) roofing, which along with many of the *souks'* more beautiful features was destroyed by a fire in the 1960s.

Just before the fork at its end, Souk Smarine narrows and you can get a glimpse through the passageways to its right of the **Rahba Kedima**, a small ramshackle square with a few vegetable stalls set up in the middle of it. Immediately to the right, as you go in, is **Souk Larzal**, a wool market feverishly active in the dawn hours, but closed most of the rest of the day. Alongside it, easily distinguished by smell alone, is **Souk Btana,** which deals with whole sheepskins – the pelts laid out to dry and be displayed on the roof. You can walk up here and take a look at how the skins are treated.

The most interesting aspect of Rahba Kedima, however, are the **apothecary stalls** grouped round the near corner of the square. These sell all the standard traditional cosmetics – earthenware saucers of cochineal (*kashiniah*) for rouge, powdered *kohl* or antimony for darkening the edges of the eyes, *henna* (the only cosmetic unmarried women are supposed to use) and the sticks of *suak* (walnut root or bark) with which you see Moroccans cleaning their teeth.

In addition to such essentials, the stalls also sell the herbal and animal ingredients that are still in widespread use for manipulation, or spellbinding. There are roots and tablets used as aphrodisiacs, and there are stranger and more specialized goods – dried pieces of lizard and stork, fragments of beaks, talons and gazelle horns. Magic, white and black, has always been very much a part of Moroccan life, and there are dozens of stories relating to its effects.

La Criée Berbère

At the end of Rahba Kedima, a passageway to the left gives access to another, smaller square – a bustling, carpet-draped area known as **La Criée Berbère** (the Berber auction) aka **Souk Zrabia**.

It was here that the old **slave auctions** were held, just before sunset every Wednesday, Thursday and Friday, until the French occupied the city in 1912. They were conducted, according to Budgett Meakin's account in 1900, "precisely as those of cows and mules, often on the same spot by the same men . . . with the human chattels being personally examined in the most disgusting manner, and paraded in lots by the auctioneers, who shout their attractions and the bids". Most had been kidnapped and brought in by the caravans from Guinea and Sudan; Meakin saw two small boys sold for £5 apiece, an eight-year-old girl for £3 and 10 shillings and a "stalwart negro" went for £14; a beauty, he was told, might exceptionally fetch £130 to £150.

These days, **rugs and carpets** are about the only things sold in the square, and if you have a good deal of time and willpower you could spend the best part of a day here while endless (and often identical) stacks are unfolded and displayed before you. Some of the most interesting are the Berber rugs from the High Atlas – bright, geometric designs that look very different after being laid out on the roof and bleached by the sun. The dark, often black, backgrounds usually signify rugs from the Glaoui country, up towards Telouet; the reddish-backed carpets are from Chichaoua, a small village near-

CRAFTS, "GUIDES", THE SOUKS AND SHOPS

Like Fes, Marrakesh can be an expensive place to **buy craft goods** – though if you have anything to barter (designer T-shirts, trainers, rock music cassettes, etc), you'll find people eager enough to arrange an exchange. Before setting out into the *souks* in search of rugs, blankets, or whatever, check out the classic designs in the **Dar Si Said** museum and take a look at the more or less fixed prices in the well-run **Ensemble Artisanal** (daily 9am–1pm and 3–7pm), on Av. Mohammed V, midway between the Koutoubia and the ramparts at Bab Nkob.

Behind the Ensemble Artisanal, but part of the same complex, there are a dozen or so active workshops with young people learning a range of crafts – and, if you need cash, there's a branch of the *Banque Populaire* too.

Official **guides** (50dh for a half day) can be arranged at the *ONMT* or large hotels; unofficial ones in Djemaa El Fna and almost anywhere you're seen looking perplexed. Some of the latter can be fine, others a struggle, as you are escorted into shop after shop; fix a price in advance. A favourite recommendation of the hustlers is the so-called Berber market – "only today", they'll tell you, with great urgency. In fact, all the main **souks** are open every day, though they're quiet on Friday mornings. Even the big Souk El Khemis (the Thursday Market, held outside Bab Debbagh) now operates most days of the week.

If you prefer to buy from a more **conventional shop**, there are many in Gueliz and, possibly cheaper, in the Medina. Try, for example, two shops next to the *Stylia* restaurant in the Medina: *Artisanal Dar Essalam*, 26 Rue Ksour (☎04/44.38.65) sells pottery, leather goods, marquetry and wood-carving – some of it from Essaouira. The shop is housed in an old mansion, and the ceiling is worth a free look. *Dar El Ksour*, 28 Rue Ksour (☎04/44.28.13) sells old and modern carpets and rugs. Both take cash or cards.

However, or wherever you shop, tourists are free to consult the **Price Control Service** (☎04/30.84.30 ext 360), although it is not clear what a phone call would lead to.

ly half way to Essaouira, and are also pretty common. There is usually a small **auction** in the *criée* at around 4pm – an interesting sight with the auctioneers wandering round the square shouting out the latest bids, but it's not the best place to buy a rug – it's devoted mainly to heavy, brown woollen *djellabas*.

Around the Kissarias

Cutting back to **Souk El Kebir**, which by now has taken over from the Smarine, you emerge at the **kissarias**, the covered markets at the heart of the *souks*. The goods here, apart from the many and sometimes imaginative *couvertures* (blankets), aren't that interesting; the *kissarias* traditionally sell the more expensive products, which today means a sad predominance of Western designs and imports. Off to their right, at the southern end of the *kissarias*, is **Souk des Bijoutiers**, a modest jewellers' lane, which is much less varied than the one established in the Mellah (see "The Lower Medina") by Jewish craftsmen. At the northern end is a convoluted web of alleys that comprise the **Souk Cherratin**, essentially a leather workers' *souk* (with dozens of purse makers and sandal cobblers), though it's interspersed with smaller alleys and *souks* of carpenters, sieve makers and even a few tourist shops. If you bear left through this area and then turn right, you should arrive at the open space in front of the Ben Youssef Mosque; the *medersa* (see the section overleaf) is off to its right.

The Dyers' Souk and a loop back to the Djemaa El Fna

Had you earlier taken the left fork along **Souk El Attarin** – the spice and perfume *souk* – you would have come out on the other side of the **kissarias** and the long lane of the **Souk des Babouches** (slipper makers) aka **Souk Smata**.

The main attraction in this area is the little **Souk des Teinturiers** – the dyers' *souk*. To reach it, turn left along the first alley you come to after the Souk des Babouches. Working your way down this lane (which comes out in a square by the Mouassin Mosque), look to your right and you'll see the entrance to the *souk* about halfway down – its lanes rhythmically flash with bright skeins of wool, hung from above. If you have trouble finding it, just follow the first tour group you see.

There is a reasonably straightforward alternative route back to Djemaa El Fna from here, following the main street down to the **Mouassin Mosque** (which is almost entirely concealed from public view, built at an angle to the square beside it) and then turning left on to Rue Mouassin. As you approach the mosque, the street widens very slightly opposite an elaborate triple-bayed **fountain**. Built in the mid-sixteenth century by the prolific Saadian builder, Abdallah El-Ghalib, this is one of many such fountains in Marrakesh with a basin for humans set next to two larger troughs for animals; its installation was a pious act, directly sanctioned by the Koran in its charitable provision of water for men and beasts.

Below the Mouassin Mosque is an area of coppersmiths, **Souk des Chaudronniers**. Above it sprawls the main section of **carpenters'** workshops, **Souk Chouari** – with their beautiful smell of cedar – and beyond them the **Souk Haddadine** of blacksmiths – whose sounds you'll hear long before arriving.

The Ben Youssef Medersa

One of the largest buildings in the Medina, and preceded by a rare open space, the **Ben Youssef Mosque** is quite easy to locate. Its **medersa** – the old student annexe, and their home until they had learnt the Koran by rote – stands off a side street just to the east, distinguishable by a series of small, grilled windows. The entrance porch is a short way down the side street, covering the whole lane at this point. Recently restored, it is open from 9am to 5pm every day; admission is the standard 10dh.

Like most of the Fes *medersas* (see p.200 for a description of their development and function), the Ben Youssef was a Merenid foundation, established by Sultan Abou El Hassan in the fourteenth century. It was, however, almost completely rebuilt under the Saadians, and it is this dynasty's intricate, Andalucian-influenced art that has left its mark. As with the slightly later Saadian Tombs, no surface is left undecorated, and the overall quality of its craftsmanship, whether in carved wood, stuccowork or *zellij*, is startling. That this was possible in sixteenth-century Marrakesh, after a period in which the city was reduced to near ruin and the country to tribal anarchy, is remarkable. Revealingly, parts have exact parallels in the Alhambra Palace in Granada, and it seems likely that Muslim Spanish architects were employed in its construction.

Inside the *medersa*, you reach the main court by means of a long outer **corridor** and a small entry **vestibule**. To the side of this are stairs to **student cells**, arranged round smaller internal courtyards on the upper floors, an **ablutions hall** and **latrine,** still in evil-smelling use. Until very recently, a remarkable tenth-century Ommayad marble basin – decorated with eagles and griffins – completed the ensemble, though it has now been removed to the Dar Si Said museum.

The **central courtyard**, weathered almost flat on its most exposed side, is unusually large. Along two sides run wide, sturdy, columned arcades, which were probably used to supplement the space for teaching in the neighbouring mosque. Above them are some of the windows of the **dormitory quarters**, from which you can get an interesting perspective – and attempt to fathom how over eight hundred students were once housed in the building.

At its far end, the court opens onto a **prayer hall,** where the decoration, mellowed on the outside with the city's familiar pink tone, is at its best preserved and most elaborate. Notable here, as in the court's cedar carving, is a predominance of pinecone and palm motifs; around the *mihrab* (the horseshoe-arched prayer niche) they've been applied so as to give the frieze a highly three-dimensional appearance. This is rare in Moorish stuccowork, though the inscriptions themselves, picked out in the curling, vegetative arabesques, are from familiar Koranic texts. The most common, as in all Moroccan stucco and *zellij* decoration, is the ceremonial *bismillah* invocation: "In the name of Allah, the Compassionate, the Merciful . . . ".

The Almoravid Koubba

Even though it is signposted opposite the entrance to the Ben Youssef *medersa*, the **Almoravid Koubba** (aka **Koubba Ba'adiyn**) is easy to pass by – a small, two-storey kiosk, which at first seems little more than a grey dome and a handful of variously shaped doors and windows. Look closer, though, and you may begin to understand its significance and even fascination. For this is the only intact surviving Almoravid building, and it is at the root of all Moroccan architecture. The motifs you've just seen in the *medersa* – the pinecones, palms and acanthus leaves – were all carved here for the first time. The windows on each of the different sides became the classic shapes of Almohad and Merenid design – as did the *merlons*, the Christmas tree-like battlements; the complex "ribs" on the outside of the dome; and the dome's interior support, a sophisticated device of a square and star-shaped octagon, which is itself repeated at each of its corners. Once you see all this, you're only a step away from the eulogies of Islamic art historians who sense in this building, which was probably a small ablutions annexe to the original Ben Youssef Mosque, a powerful and novel expression of form.

Excavated only in 1952 – having been covered over amid the many rebuildings of the Ben Youssef *medersa* – the *koubba* lies just to the south of the present (mainly nineteenth-century) Ben Youssef Mosque. It is mostly below today's ground level, though standing with your back to the mosque you can make out the top of its dome behind the long, low brick wall. There is an entrance gate down a few steps, opposite the Ben Youssef Mosque, where a *gardien* will emerge to escort you round and sell you a ticket (10dh), and may also show you the huge, old water conduits nearby, which brought water from the Atlas.

If the *koubba* is closed, you can get almost as good a view from the roof of a very ancient (but still active) *hammam* down to the right; the attendants will give you access for a small tip.

The tanneries and northern gates

The main *souks* – and the tourist route – stop abruptly at the Ben Youssef *medersa*. Beyond them, in all directions, you'll find yourself in the ordinary **residential quarters** of the Medina. There are few particular "sights" to be found here, but if you've got the time, there's an interest of its own in following the crowds, and a relief in getting away from the central shopping district of Marrakesh, where you are expected to come in, look round and buy.

Probably the most interesting targets are **Bab Debbagh** and **Souk El Khemis**. From Ben Youssef you can reach these quite easily: it's about a fifteen-minute walk to the first, another fifteen to twenty minutes round the ramparts to the second. As you pass the entrance porch to the *medersa,* you'll quickly reach a fork in the side street. To the left, a covered passageway leads around behind the mosque to join Rue Amesfah (see below). Head instead to your right, and then keep going as straight as possible until you emerge at the ramparts by Bab Debbagh; on the way you'll cross a small square and intersection, **Place El Moukef**, where a busy and sizeable lane goes off to the left – a more direct approach to Bab El Khemis.

If you were to turn right, not left, from Place El Moukef, you would arrive within ten minutes at Place Ben Salah and the **Zaouia of Sidi Ben Salah** with a very fine, and prominent minaret built by a fourteenth-century Merenid sultan.

Bab Debbagh and the tanneries

Bab Debbagh is supposedly Almoravid in design, though over the years it must have been almost totally rebuilt. Passing through the gate, you become aware of its very real defensive purpose: three internal rooms are placed in such a manner as to force anyone attempting to storm it to make several turns. The leather goods shop, on the right-hand side of Bab Debbagh, gives good views from its roof (for a small fee) over the quarter.

Looking down, you have an excellent view over the **tanneries**, built here at the edge of the city for access to water (the summer-dry Oued Issil runs just outside the walls) and for the obvious reason of the smell. If you want to take a closer look at the processes, come in the morning, when the co-operatives are at work; any of the kids standing around will take you in. As at Fes, a tour is an ambivalent experience. There's a beauty about the proceedings, but the traditional dyes have been in large part replaced by modern chemicals, which can cause sciatica, malignant melanoma and other internal cancers.

Bab El Khemis

Following the road from Bab Debbagh, outside the ramparts, is the simplest approach to **Bab El Khemis** (Gate of the Thursday Market) another reconstructed Almoravid gate, built at an angle in the walls. The Thursday market now seems to take place more or less daily, around 400m to the north, above a cemetery and *marabout's* tomb. It is really a local produce market, though odd handicraft items do occasionally surface.

North of the Ben Youssef Mosque

The area immediately **north of the Ben Youssef Mosque** is cut by two main streets: Rue Assouel (which leads up to Bab El Khemis) and Rue Bab Taghzout, which runs up to the gate of the same name and to the Zaouia of Sidi Bel Abbes. These were, with Bab Doukkala, the principal approaches to the city until the present century and along them you find many of the old **fondouks** used for storage and lodging by merchants visiting the *souks*.

One of these *fondouks* is sited just south of the mosque and a whole series can be found along Rue Amesfah – the continuation of Baroudienne – to the north and west.

EL GLAOUI: THE PASHA OF MARRAKESH

El Glaoui, the famous Pasha of Marrakesh during the French Protectorate, was the last of the great southern tribal leaders, an active and shrewd supporter of colonial rule and a personal friend of Winston Churchill. Cruel and magnificent in equal measure (see p.384), he was also one of the most spectacular partygivers around – in an age where rivals were not lacking. At the extraordinary *difas* or banquets held at his Marrakesh palace, the Dar El Glaoui, "nothing", as Gavin Maxwell wrote, "was impossible" – hashish and opium were freely available for the Europeans and Americans to experiment with, and "to his guests T'hami gave whatever they wanted, whether it might be a diamond ring, a present of money in gold, or a Berber girl or boy from the High Atlas".

Not surprisingly, there was little enthusiasm for showing off the palace since El Glaoui's death in 1956, an event that led to a mob looting the palace, destroying its fittings and even the cars in the garages, and then lynching any of Glaoui's henchmen to be found.

However, passions have burnt out over the years, and the family has been rehabilitated – one of Thami's sons, Glaoui Abdelssadak, is high up in the Moroccan civil service and vice president of Gulf Oil.

Most are still used in some commercial capacity, as workshops or warehouses, and the doors to their courtyards often stand open. Some date from Saadian times and have fine details of wood carving or stuccowork. If you are interested, nobody seems to mind if you wander in.

The Zaouia of Sidi Bel Abbes

Rue Amesfah runs for around 150m north of the intersection with Rue Baroudienne before reaching the junction of Rue Assouel (to the east) and **Rue Bab Taghzout** (to the west). Following Rue Bab Taghzout, you pass another *fondouk*, opposite a small recessed fountain known as **Chrob ou Chouf** ("drink and admire"), and around 500m further down, the old city gate of **Bab Taghzout**. This marked the limits of the original Almoravid Medina, and continued to do so into the eighteenth century, when Sultan Mohammed Abdallah extended the walls to enclose the quarter and the **Zaouia of Sidi Bel Abbes**.

Sidi Bel Abbes was born in Ceuta in 1130. As a *marabout* and a prolific performer of miracles, particularly giving sight to the blind, he is the most important of Marrakesh's seven saints, and his **zaouia**, a kind of monastic cult centre, has traditionally wielded very great influence and power, often at odds with that of the sultan and providing a refuge for political dissidents.

The present buildings, entry to which is strictly forbidden to non-Muslims, date largely from a reconstruction by Moulay Ismail, an act that was probably inspired more by political motivation than piety. You can see something of the complex and its activities from outside the official boundary – do not, however, try to pass through the long central corridor. The *zaouia* has prospered over the centuries; in 1875, it was said to possess 'property to the value of £200,000 and serves as a great almshouse and asylum'. It still owns much of the quarter to the north and continues its educational and charitable work, distributing food each evening to the blind.

The tomb of Sidi Bel Abbes is in the nearby Sidi Marouk cemetery and can, for a small fee, be visited by non-Muslims; look for the white *koubba* with the light green dome. A couple of blocks to the southwest, there is a smaller, though again significant **zaouia** dedicated to **Sidi Mohammed ben Slimane,** a Saadian *marabout* and another of Marrakesh's seven saints.

West to Bab Doukkala: Dar El Glaoui

A third alternative from Ben Youssef is to head west **towards Bab Doukkala.** This route, once you've found your way down through Souk Haddadine to **Rue Bab Doukkala,** is a sizeable thoroughfare and very straightforward to follow. Midway, you pass the **Dar El Glaoui**, the old palace of the Pasha of Marrakesh (see box opposite) and a place of legendary exoticism throughout the first half of this century. Part of it is nowadays occupied by the Ministry of Culture; visitors are allowed in at the discretion of the caretaker, but there's little to see. The main section of the palace remains private.

The Lower Medina: the Royal Palace, Saadian Tombs and Mellah

Staying in Marrakesh even for a few days, you begin to sense the different appearance and life of its various Medina quarters, and nowhere more so than in the shift from north to south, from the area to the north of Djemaa El Fna and that to the south of it. At the southern extremity (a kind of stem to the mushroom shape of the city walls) is **Dar El Makhzen**, the royal palace. To its west stretches the old inner citadel of the **Kasbah**; to the east, the **Mellah**, once the largest Jewish ghetto in Morocco; while rambling to the north of it is a series of mansions and palaces built for the nineteenth-century elite.

All in all, it's an interesting area to wander round, though you inevitably spend time trying to figure out the sudden and apparently arbitrary appearance of ramparts and enclosures. And there are two obvious focal points, not to be missed: the **Saadian Tombs**, preserved in the shadow of the Kasbah mosque, and **El Badi**, the ruined palace of Ahmed El Mansour.

The Saadian Tombs

Sealed up by Moulay Ismail after he had destroyed the adjoining Badi Palace, the **Saadian Tombs** lay half-ruined and half-forgotten at the beginning of this century. In 1917, however, they were rediscovered on a French aerial map and a passageway was built to give access from the side of the Kasbah mosque. Restored, they are today the city's main "sight" – over-lavish, maybe, in their exhaustive decoration, but dazzling nonetheless. They are open daily from 9am to 5pm; go late afternoon, if possible. As a national monument, admission is the usual 10dh; there is no longer a compulsory guided tour, however – you are left to look round on your own or even just to sit and gaze. A quiet, high-walled enclosure, shaded with shrubs and palms and dotted with bright *zellij*-covered tombs, it seems as much a pleasure garden as a cemetery.

Some form of burial ground behind the royal palace probably predated the Saadian period, though the earliest of the tombs here dates from 1557, and all the principal structures were built by Sultan Ahmed El Mansour. This makes them virtual contemporaries of the Ben Youssef Medersa – with which there are obvious parallels – and allows a revealing insight into just how rich and extravagant the El Badi must once have been. Their escape from Moulay Ismail's systematic plundering was probably due to superstition – Ismail had to content himself with blocking all but an obscure entrance from the Kasbah mosque. Despite this, a few prominent *Marrakchis* continued to be buried in the mausoleums; the last, in 1792, was the "mad sultan", Moulay Yazid, whose 22-month reign was probably the most violent and sadistic in the nation's history.

The mausoleums

There are two main **mausoleums** in the enclosure. The finest is on the left as you come in – a beautiful group of three rooms, built to house El Mansour's own tomb and completed within his lifetime. Continuing round from the courtyard entrance, the first hall is a **prayer oratory**, a room probably not intended for burial, though now almost littered with the thin marble stones of Saadian princes. It is here that Moulay Yazid was laid out, perhaps in purposeful obscurity, certainly in ironic contrast to the cursive inscription round the band of black and white *zellij*: "And the works of peace they have accomplished", it reads amid the interlocking circles, "will make them enter the holy gardens."

Architecturally, the most important feature of this mausoleum is the *mihrab*, its pointed horseshoe arch supported by an incredibly delicate arrangement of columns. Opposite this is another elaborate arch, leading to the domed **central chamber** and **El Mansour's tomb**, which you can glimpse through the next door in the court. The tomb, slightly larger than those surrounding it, lies right in the middle, flanked on either side by those of the sultan's sons and successors. The room itself is spectacular, faint light filtering onto the tombs from an interior lantern in a tremendous vaulted roof, the *zellij* full of colour and motion and the undefined richness of a third chamber almost hidden from view. Throughout, there are echoes of the Alhambra in Granada, built two centuries previously, and from which its style is clearly derived.

The **other mausoleum**, older and less impressive, was built by Ahmed in place of an existing pavilion above the tombs of his mother, Lalla Messaouda, and of

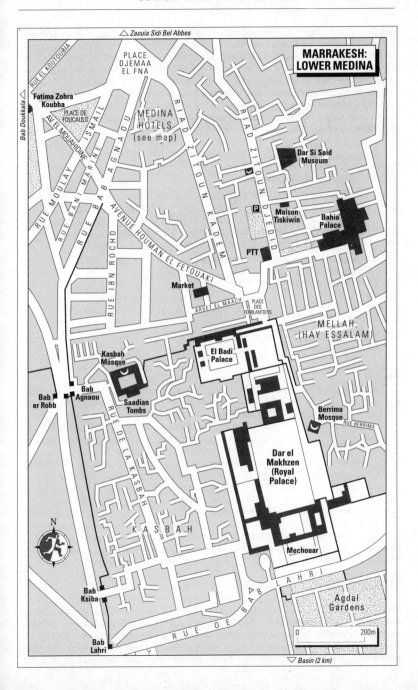

△ *Zaouia Sidi Bel Abbes*

**MARRAKESH:
LOWER MEDINA**

RUE EL KOUTOUBIA

PLACE
DJEMAA
EL FNA

Bab Doukkala ◁

**Fatima Zohra
Koubba**

PLACE DE
FOUCAULD

AV EL MOUAHIDINE

RUE MOULAY ISMAIL

RUE BAN MARINE

RUE BAB AGNAOU

MEDINA
HOTELS
(see map)

RIAD ZITOUN KADEM

RIAD ZITOUN DJEDID

**Dar Si Said
(Museum)**

**Maison
Tiskiwin**

P

**Bahia
Palace**

PTT

RUE IBN ROCHD

AVENUE HOUMAN EL FETOUAKI

Market

ARSET EL MAACH

PLACE
DES
FERBLANTIERS

**MELLAH
(HAY ESSALAM)**

**Kasbah
Mosque**

**El Badi
Palace**

**Bab
er Robb**

**Bab
Agnaou**

**Saadian
Tombs**

RUE DE LA KASBAH

**Berrima
Mosque**

RUE BERRIMA

**Dar el
Makhzen
(Royal
Palace)**

N

K A S B A H

Mechouar

**Bab
Ksiba**

RUE DE BAB LAHRI

**Agdal
Gardens**

0   200m

**Bab
Lahri**

▽ *Basin (2 km)*

Mohammed ech Sheikh, the founder of the Saadian dynasty. It is again a series of three rooms, though two are hardly more than loggias. Messaouda's tomb is the niche below the dome in the outer chamber. Mohammed esh Sheikh is buried in the inner one – or at least his torso is, since he was murdered in the Atlas by Turkish mercenaries, who salted his head and took it back for public display on the walls of Istanbul.

Outside, **round the garden and courtyard**, are scattered the tombs of over a hundred more Saadian princes and members of the royal household. Like the privileged 66 given space within the mausoleums, their gravestones are brilliantly tiled and often elaborately inscribed. The most usual inscription reads quite simply:

> There is no God but God.
> Muhammad is God's envoy.
> Praise Be to God.
> The occupant of this tomb died on . . . .

But there are others – epitaphs and extracts from the Koran – that seem to express the turbulence of the age to a greater degree, which, with Ahmed's death in 1603, was to disintegrate into nearly seventy years of constant civil war. "Every soul shall know death", reads one tombstone; "Death will find you wherever you are, even in fortified towers", another. And, carved in gypsum on the walls, there is a poem:

> O mausoleum, built out of mercy, thou whose
> walls are the shadow of heaven.
> The breath of asceticism is wafted from thy tombs
> like a fragrance.
> Through thy death
> the light of faith has been dimmed,
> the seven spheres are fraught with darkness
> and the columns of glory
> broken with pain.

Access

Getting to the Saadian Tombs, the simplest route from Djemaa El Fna is to follow **Rue Bab Agnaou** outside the ramparts. At its end you come to a small square flanked by two gates. Directly ahead is **Bab Er Robb** – outside of which the *grands taxis* and private-line buses leave for Ourika and other local destinations. To the left, somewhat battered and eroded, is the city's only surviving Almohad gateway, **Bab Agnaou** (Gate of the Gnaoua [the blacks]). This is an impressive structure, smaller than the monumental gates of Rabat, but sharing much of their force and apparent simplicity. Notice how the semicircular frieze above its arch creates a strong, three-dimensional effect without any actual depth of carving. At the time of its construction, it was the only stone building in Marrakesh apart from the Koutoubia Minaret.

Passing through the gate, the **Kasbah mosque** is in front of you: its minaret looks gaudy and modern but is, in fact, contemporary with both the Koutoubia and Hassan towers – it was restored to its exact original state in the 1960s. Work is still going on to clear and make good the space alongside the mosque. The narrow passageway to the Saadian Tombs is well signposted, at the near right-hand corner of the mosque.

El Badi Palace

To reach the ruins of the **El Badi Palace** – which seems originally to have sprawled across the whole area east of the Kasbah mosque – you have to backtrack slightly from the Saadian Tombs. At Bab Agnaou, follow the ramparts up again, this time taking the road just inside them, until you come to a reasonably sized street on your right (just before the walls temporarily give out). Turn into this street, keep more or less straight,

AHMED EL MANSOUR

The El Badi Palace was begun shortly after Ahmed El Mansour's accession, its initial finance came from the enormous ransom paid out by the Portuguese after the Battle of the Three Kings at Ksar El Kebir. Fought in the summer of 1578, this was one of the most disastrous battles in Christian medieval history; ostensibly in support of a rival Saadian claimant, but to all intents a Portuguese crusade, it was led by the young king, Dom Sebastião, and supported by almost his entire nobility. Few escaped death or Moorish capture. Sebastião himself was killed, as were both the Saadian claimant and the ruling sultan.

As a result, Ahmed – dubbed *El Mansour* (The Victorious) – came to the throne, undisputed and commanding immediate wealth from the ransoms paid for the captured Portuguese nobles. He reigned for 25 years, trading in sugar and slaves with Britain, Spain and Italy; seized the gold route across the Sahara with the resultant capture of Timbuktu, which earned him the additional epithet *El Eddahbi* (The Golden); and maintained peace in Morocco through a loose confederation of tribes. It was the most prosperous period in the country's history since the time of the Almohads – a cultural and political renaissance reflected in the coining of a new title, the Shereefian Empire, the country's official name until independence in 1956.

and in about 550m, you'll emerge at **Place des Ferblantiers** – a major intersection. On the south side of the *place* is a gate known as **Bab Berrima**, which opens onto a long rectangular enclosure, flanked on either side by walls; go through it, and on your right you'll come to the Badi's entrance. Hours are generally 9am to 5pm; admission 10dh; a guided tour is touted but far from essential.

The Incomparable palace

Though substantially in ruins, and reduced throughout to its red *pisé* walls, enough remains of **El Badi** to suggest that its name – "The Incomparable" – was not entirely immodest. It took the sultan Moulay Ismail over ten years of systematic work to strip the palace of everything moveable or of value, but even so, there's a lingering sense of luxury and grandeur. The scale, with its sunken gardens and vast, ninety-metre-long pool, is certainly unrivalled, and the odd traces of *zellij* and plaster still left evoke a decor that was probably as rich as that of the Saadian Tombs.

What you see today is essentially the ceremonial part of the **palace complex**, planned on a grand scale for the reception of ambassadors, and not meant for everyday living. It seems likely that El Mansour and the multiple members of his court each had private palaces – smaller, though built to a similar ground plan – to the west and south, covering much of the area occupied by the Dar El Makhzen, the present Royal Palace.

The **entrance** in current use was probably not the main approach. Going through, you find yourself at the side of a **mosque**, like everything else within this complex, of enormous height. To the rear extends the great **central court**, over 130m long and nearly as wide, and constructed on a substructure of vaults in order to allow the circulation of water through the pools and gardens. When the pools are filled – as during the June folklore festival which takes place here – they are an incredibly majestic sight, especially the main one, with an island that was originally surmounted by an elaborate double fountain.

On each side of the pools were summer pavilions, traces of which survive. The most prominent is at the far end, a monumental hall that was used by the sultan on occasions of state and known as the **Koubba El Hamsiniya** (The Fifty Pavilion), for the number of its columns. Strangely enough, their size and splendour were documented by an observer far removed from the Arab chroniclers who extolled their beauty. The French philosopher Montaigne, while travelling through Italy, saw craftsmen preparing the columns – "each of an extreme height . . . for the king of Fes and Barbary".

South of the courtyard are ruins of the palace **stables**, and beyond them, leading towards the intriguing walls of the present royal palace, a series of **dungeons**, used into the present century as a state prison. You can explore part of these and could easily spend a whole afternoon wandering round the various inner courts above, with their fragments of marble and *zellij* and their water conduits for the fountains and *hammams*. Like the Saadian Tombs, the Badi inspired contemporary poets, and there is an account, too, by the chronicler El Ifrani, of its construction:

> *El Mansour made workmen come from all the different countries . . . . He paid for the marble sent from Italy in sugar, pound for pound awarded his workers very generously . . . and paid attention even to the entertainment of their children, so that the artisans might devote themselves entirely to their work without being distracted by any other preoccupation.*

If this is even half true, there could be no greater contrast with the next great Moroccan builder, and dismantler of the El Badi Palace, Moulay Ismail, whose palace workmen in Meknes were beaten up, starved and abused, and then buried in the walls where they fell. But sixteenth-century crèches aside, the most enduring account of the palace concerns its state opening, a fabulous occasion attended by ambassadors from several European powers and by all the sheikhs and *caids* of the kingdom. Surveying the effect, Ahmed turned to his court jester for an opinion on the new palace. "Sidi," the man replied, "this will make a magnificent ruin."

The Mellah

It was in 1558 – five years before Ahmed's accession – that the Marrakesh **Mellah**, the separate Jewish quarter in Morocco, was created. There is no exact record of why this was done at this particular time. Possibly it was the result of a pogrom, with the sultan moving the Jews to his protected Kasbah – and they, in turn, forming a useful buffer zone (and scapegoat) between his palace and the populace in times of social unrest. But, as likely as not, it was simply brought about to make taxation easier. The Jews of Marrakesh were an important financial resource – they controlled most of the Saadian sugar trade, and comprised practically all of the city's bankers, metalworkers, jewellers and tailors. In the sixteenth century, at least, their quarter was almost a town in itself, supervised by rabbis, and with its own *souks,* gardens, fountains and synagogues.

THE MARRAKESH FESTIVAL

Marrakesh utilizes the Badi Palace – and other venues in the city – for an annual two-week **Festival National des Art Populaires**. This is the country's biggest and best folklore and music festival, and is currently held in June. If you are interested in Moroccan music, it would be worth planning your trip around it – were you to be able to establish the precise dates, which vary year by year.

The festival comprises a series of totally authentic and unusual performances, with groups of musicians and dancers coming in from all regions of Morocco. A typical programme will span the range of Moroccan music – from the Gnaoua drummers and the panpipers of Jajouka, to Berber *ahouaches* from the Atlas and southern oases, to classical Andalucian music from Fes.

The shows are held each evening from around 9pm to midnight (tickets are 50dh); before they start, towards sunset, there is a **fantasia** at Bab El Djedid – a spectacle by any standard, with dozens of Berber horsemen firing their guns in the air at full gallop.

The present Mellah, which is now known officially as the **Hay Essalam** quarter and is much smaller in extent, is now almost entirely Muslim – most of the *Marrakchi* Jews left long ago for Casablanca (where some 6000 still live) or emigrated to France or Israel. The few who remain, outwardly distinguishable only by the men's small black skullcaps, are mostly poor or old or both. Their quarter, however, is immediately distinct: its houses are taller than elsewhere, the streets are more enclosed, and even the shop cubicles are smaller. Until the Protectorate, Jews were not permitted to own land or property – nor even to ride or walk, except barefoot – outside the Mellah; a situation that was greatly exploited by their landlords, who resisted all attempts to expand the walls. Today its air of neglect and poverty – since this is not a prized neighbourhood in which to live – is probably less than at any time during the past three centuries.

Around the quarter

The main entrance to the Mellah, which is still a largely walled district, is at **Place des Ferblantiers** – the tinsmiths' square. Formerly called Place du Mellah, this was itself part of the old Jewish *souk*, and an archway (to your right, standing at Bab Berrima) leads into it. Near the upper end is a **jewellers' souk**, one of the traditional Jewish trades now more or less taken over by Muslim craftsmen; further down are some good spice and textile *souks*. Right at the centre – and situated very much as the goal of a maze – is a small square with a fountain in the middle, **Place Souweka**. You will almost certainly find yourself back here if you wander round for a short while and manage to avoid the blind alleys.

To the east, some 200m away, is the **Jewish cemetery**, the **Miâara**, reckoned to date from the early seventeenth century. It is well-tended and boasts eleven Jewish *marabout* (*tsadikim* in Hebrew) shrines. Nearby are two **synagogues**. The **Lazama**, on Rue Talmud Torah is still in use. The smaller **El Fassiines** may, with American help, become a museum. Neither is easy to find, but a local guide could show you.

Just outside the Mellah, on Arset El Maach, are two further synagogues. The **Bitoun** has a leaking roof and is being restored. The **Rabbi Pinhas** is smaller and still in use – to find it, walk from Place des Ferblantiers eastwards along Arset El Maach and after 100m look for a brown wooden door on the left (it's the only wooden door of this length). If you have a problem finding it, or want to know when it might be open, ask at 4 Arset El Maach, which is further along and on the right, facing the municipal compound for trucks.

You may well be directed to other synagogues (*s'noga*) which look more like lived-in houses (and indeed often are lived-in houses). This should not surprise you because, even when in active use, many of the Moroccan synagogues were as much private houses as temples – " . . . serving also as places in which to eat, sleep and to kill chickens", according to Budgett Meakin.

North of the Mellah: the Bahia Palace

Heading north from the Mellah – back towards Djemaa El Fna – there are three direct and fairly simple routes. To the left of Place des Ferblantiers, **Avenue Houman El Fetouaki** will bring you out by the Koutoubia. North of the *place*, two parallel streets, **Riad Zitoun Kadem** and **Riad Zitoun Djedid** lead up to the Djemaa El Fna.

Zitoun Kadem is basically a shopping street, lined with grocers, barbershops and, at the far end, a couple of *hammams* (open all day; one each for men and women). Zitoun Djedid is more residential, and it is here that you find the concentration of **palaces and mansions** built in those strange, closing decades of the last century, and the first few years of our own, when the sultans Moulay Hassan and Moulay Abd El Aziz held court in the city. Several of these are now upmarket restaurants, notably *Restaurant Douirya* and *Palais Gharnatta*. You may not want to pay for a meal and the 'tourist spectacle' in these (though see p.353 for recommendations) but it's worth looking into one or two of them on your way just to see the turn-of-the-century decor.

The Bahia

By far the most ambitious and costly of these mansions was the **Bahia Palace**, built by the grand vizier, Si Ahmed Ben Moussa. Shrewd, wilful and cruel, as was the tradition of his age, **Bou Ahmed** (as he was better known) was a Black slave who rose to hold massive power in the Shereefian kingdom and, for the last six years of his life, exercised virtually autocratic control. He was first chamberlain to Moulay Hassan, whose death while returning home from a *harka* he managed to conceal until the proclamation of Abd El Aziz in Rabat (see "Writers on Morocco", in *Contexts*, for the dramatic account). Under Abd El Aziz (who was just twelve when he acceded to the throne), Bou Ahmed usurped the position of vizier from the ill-fated Jamai brothers (see p.209), and then proceeded to rule.

He began building the Bahia in 1894, later enlarging it by acquiring the surrounding land and property. He died in 1900. The name of the building means "The Effulgence" or "Brilliance", but after the **guided tour** round various sections of the rambling palace courts and apartments you might feel this to be a somewhat tall claim. There is reasonable craftsmanship in the main **reception halls**, and a pleasant arrangement of rooms in the **harem quarter,** but for the most part it is all fabulously vulgar and hasn't aged too well. Perhaps this is the main reason for a visit: you come away realizing just how much mastery and sophistication went into the Saadian *medersa* and tombs, and how corrupted and dull these traditions had become.

But there is also a certain pathos to the empty, echoing chambers – and the inevitable passing of Bou Ahmed's influence and glory. Walter Harris, who knew the vizier, described his demise and the clearing of his palace in *Morocco That Was*, published just twenty years after the events, by which time Bou Ahmed's name had already become "only a memory of the past":

> For several days as the Vizier lay expiring, guards were stationed outside his palace waiting in silence for the end. And then one morning the wail of the women within the house told that death had come. Every gateway of the great building was seized, and no one was allowed to enter or come out, while within there was pandemonium. His slaves pillaged wherever they could lay their hands. His women fought and stole to get possession of the jewels. Safes were broken open, documents and title-deeds were extracted, precious stones were torn from their settings, the more easily to be concealed, and even murder took place . . . A few days later nothing remained but the great building – all the rest had disappeared into space. His family were driven out to starvation and ruin, and his vast properties passed into the possession of the State. It was the custom of the country.

Access

For some years during the Protectorate, the palace was used to house the Resident-General, and it is still called into use when the royal family is in the city. This is usually during the winter months, at which times there is no public admission. Its normal **opening hours** are daily from 8.30 to 11.45am and 2.30 to 5.45pm; it costs 10dh, but the guided tour is obligatory and you are expected to tip a further 10dh or more.

Finding your way to the palace is easy enough: from Rue Zitoun follow the signs to the *Palais Gharnatta* restaurant, keeping straight when they suddenly direct you to the right under an arch.

The Dar Si Said Museum

Also worth your while in this area is the **Dar Si Said**, a smaller version of the Bahia, built by a brother of Bou Ahmed, who, being something of a simpleton, nonetheless gained the post of royal chamberlain. It's a pleasurable building, with beautiful pooled courtyards, scented with lemons, palms and flowers, and it houses an impressive **Museum of Moroccan Arts**.

The museum is particularly strong on its collection of **Berber jewellery** and daggers, swords and other weapons – boldly designed objects of great beauty. There are also fine displays of eighteenth- and nineteenth-century **woodwork**, some of it from the Glaoui Kasbahs and most of it in cedar wood. Besides the furniture, there are Berber doors, window frames and wonderful painted ceilings. There are also a number of traditional **wedding chairs** – once widely used for carrying the bride, veiled and hidden, to her new home. Today, such chairs are still made in the *souks* and used, albeit symbolically, to carry the bride from her womenfolk in one room to the groom's menfolk in the next room. Indeed, the video of the marriage of King Hassan's eldest daughter shows this ceremony in full.

Near the entrance is the museum's most important exhibit, recently brought here from the Ben Youssef medersa. It is a marble **basin**, rectangular in shape and decorated along one side with what seem to be heraldic eagles and griffins. An inscription amid the floral decorations records its origin in tenth-century Córdoba, then the centre of the western Muslim world; the Ommayad caliphs, for whom it was constructed, had few reservations about representational art. What is surprising is that it was brought over to Morocco by the highly puritan Almoravid sultan Ali Ben Youssef and, placed in his mosque, was left untouched by the dynasty's equally iconoclastic successors, the Almohads.

Also near the entrance, do not miss the **fairground swings**, shaped like a wooden Ferris wheel, and used at *mousseums* until the early 1960s.

Access

Dar Si Said is is open every day except Tuesdays from 9–11.45am and 2.30–5.45 pm; on Fridays the lunch break is longer – from 11.30am–3pm; 10dh admission. It is to be found a block to the west of Riad Zitoun Djedid. You can either turn right opposite a mosque, midway along Riad Zitoun Djedid walking from Place des Ferblantiers; or you can turn right 100m before the mosque and from the car park there, take the gate to the right of the *Prefecture de Marrakesh Medina* as you face it with your back to the car park. This latter route passes the **Maison Tiskiwin** (see below), which is 30m inside the gate.

Maison Tiskiwin

A further, superb collection of Moroccan art and artefacts is housed in the **Maison Tiskiwin**, which lies between the Bahia and Dar Si Said palaces at 8 Rue de la Bahia. It is not easy to find: start out from the Bahia car park and look out for the name in wrought iron, above a heavy wooden door. It is easy to find from the Dar Si Said car park (see above); look for the yellow sign, with white lettering, above a heavy wooden door. It's open every day from 9.30am–12.30pm and 3–6pm.

Behind the wooden door is a beautiful town house, built at the turn of the century in Spanish-Moroccan style, and furnished from the collection of a Dutch anthropologist, Bert Flint, who has been resident in Morocco since the 1950s. Each of the rooms features carpets, fabrics, clothes and jewellery from a different region or town – Tangier, Chaouen, the Rif, Meknes, Fes, Middle Atlas, Khenifra, Beni Mellal and Azilal – and backed by informative notes (in French).

Flint's collection of southern and Saharan exhibits are displayed in Agadir.

The gardens

With summer temperatures of 90 to 100°F – and peaks well above that – it seems best to devote at least the middle of a Marrakesh day to total inactivity. A good place to do so is one of the city's gardens. There are two – the **Agdal** and **Menara** – designed for just this purpose. Each begins near the edge of the Medina, rambles through acres of orchards and olive groves and has, near its centre, an immense, lake-size pool of water. This is all – they are not flower gardens, but, cool and completely still, they seem both satisfying and luxurious, and in perfect contrast to the close city streets. Other, smaller gardens of note include the gorgeous **Jardin Majorelle**, which should on no account be missed, and those of the fabled **Hôtel La Mamounia**.

With the exception of the *Hôtel Mamounia*, you will want **transport** to get to any of these gardens – either a *petit taxi* or *calèche*. If you are considering a *calèche* trip at any stage, the Agdal or Menara are the perfect destinations. Alternatively, to take in both gardens and tour the ramparts and palmery, you could hire a **bike** or charter a *grand taxi* for the day.

Jardin Agdal

The **Agdal** is a confusingly large expanse – some 3km in extent and with half a dozen smaller irrigation pools in addition to its *grand bassin*. Beginning just south of the Mellah and Royal Palace, it is a logical continuation of a tour of the Lower Medina. Take the road outside the ramparts below Bab Agnaou/Bab Er Robb, and then turn left as you are about to leave the city at Bab Irhli; this route will take you through a *mechouar* (parade ground) by the Royal Palace and to the corner gate of the garden. The garden is often closed during the winter months, if the king is in residence in Marrakesh.

The garden is watered by an incredible system of wells and underground channels, known as *khettera,* that go as far as the base of the Atlas in the Ourika Valley and that date, in part, from the earliest founding of the city. Over the centuries, the channels have at times fallen into disrepair and the gardens been abandoned, but the present nineteenth-century layout probably differs little from any of its predecessors. It is surrounded by walls, with gates at each of the near corners, while inside, the orange, fig, lemon, apricot and pomegranate orchards are divided into square, irrigated plots by endless raised walkways and broad avenues of olive trees.

If you walk out here, it is around 4km from Djemaa El Fna, and a further 2km of unsignposted paths to the main series of pools at its heart. The largest of these is the **Sahraj El Hana** (Tank of Health), which was probably dug by the Almohads and is flanked by a ramshackle old *menzeh*, or summer pavilion, where the last few precolonial sultans held picnics and boating parties. You can climb up on its roof for a fabulous view over the park and across to the Koutoubia and Atlas, and if the caretaker's around, you'll be shown the steam-powered launch which capsized in 1873, bringing Sultan Sidi Mohammed to his death – or, as his epitaph rather more elegantly put it, he "departed this life, in a water tank, in the hope of something better to come". The launch is in a wooden shed and, failing the caretaker, you could peep between the warped planks.

Nowadays, probably the most dangerous thing you could do here would be to swim in the algae-ridden waters, though the kids do it and it does look unbelievably tempting. It's perhaps better just to pick up some food beforehand – and perhaps a bottle of wine from the Gueliz – and spread out a picnic in local fashion on the paved, shaded pathway round the water's edge.

Jardin Menara

The **Menara** is in a similar vein to the Agdal, though it has just the one central basin, and it is more olive grove than orchard, with lines of trees rather than groves and walks. It is also much more visited: a popular picnic spot for local families, as well as tourists drawn by its postcard image *bassin* and *menzeh*, with its backdrop of the High Atlas mountains. If you just want to gaze upon one of these still sheets of water, then come out here; it's a lot easier to get to than the Agdal (and a cheaper ride too). The garden couldn't be simpler to find: just follow Av. de la Menara from Bab Djedid, by the *Hôtel La Mamounia*. In summer, it has several drinks stalls.

Like the Agdal, the Menara was restored and its pavilions rebuilt in the mid-nineteenth century. The poolside *menzeh* (5dh admission) is said to have replaced an original Saadian structure.

Jardin Majorelle

The subtropical **Jardin Majorelle** (or Jardin Bou Saf) is one of the most delightful spots in Marrakesh: a small, meticulously planned botanical garden, created from the 1920s on by the French painter, Jacques Majorelle (1886–1962). Now superbly mature, it is owned and splendidly maintained by fashion designer Yves Saint Laurent, and is open daily to visitors (8am–noon and 2–5pm winter; 8am–noon and 3–7pm summer; 15dh; no children or animals allowed). The entrance is on a small side street off the jacaranda-lined Av. Yacoub El Mansour.

The garden – twelve acres in extent – has an amazing feeling of tranquillity, an atmosphere enhanced by the verdant groves of bamboo, dwarf palm and agave, and the various lily-covered pools. Its keynote colour, used as a wash on the walls, is a striking mauvish-blue – the colour of French workmen's overalls, so Majorelle claimed, though it seems to have improved in the Moroccan light. This brilliantly offsets both the plants – multicoloured bougainvillea, rows of bright orange nasturtiums and pink geraniums – and also the strong colours of the pergolas and concrete paths – pinks, lemon-yellows and apple-greens that look straight out of Yves Saint Laurent's collections. The garden's enduring sound is the chatter of the common bulbuls, flitting among the leaves of the date palms. The pools also attract bird residents such as turtle doves and house buntings.

In Majorelle's former **studio**, a **Museum of Islamic Arts** (a further 15dh; closed Mon) exhibits Saint Laurent's fine personal collection of North African carpets, pottery, furniture and doors; Saint Laurent was himself born in Algeria. It also has one room devoted to Jacques Majorelle's engravings and paintings – mainly of interest for the local scenes (fifty years ago), which include the fortified village of Anemiter and the Kasbah of Aït Benhaddou, near Ouarzazate.

Hôtel La Mamounia

Finally – and much closer – you might consider spending an hour or two looking round the gardens of the luxurious **Hôtel La Mamounia**. Walled from the outside world, yet only five minutes' walk from the Djemaa El Fna, these were once royal grounds, laid out by the Saadians with a succession of pavilions. Today they're slightly Europeanized in style but have retained the traditional elements of shrubs and walkways.

For the cost of a drink or some tea on the terrace – the latter not cripplingly exorbitant – you can sit and admire the surroundings. Be prepared, though, to resist the swimming pool, since it is strictly reserved for residents, and dress up: visitors are not allowed in wearing shorts or jeans.

If you ask at the desk, and the staff aren't too busy, someone may be prepared to give you a quick tour of the old part of the hotel – where the **Winston Churchill suite** is preserved as visited by its namesake. There are editions of Churchill's books on the shelves, a truly sultan-like bed (and smaller sleeping quarters for his manservant) and photographs of him painting in the gardens. Churchill was a frequent visitor to Marrakesh from the 1930s to the 1950s, and the Mamounia gardens were, as he remarked when he was there with Franklin D Roosevelt in 1943, the loveliest spot in the whole world. Signifcantly, it was here that Churchill painted his only picture during World War. II

Even though the hotel has been rebuilt and enlarged since Churchill's day, it's not hard to understand the lasting appeal. Decoratively, it is of most interest for the 1920s Art Deco touches of **Jacques Majorelle** (see previous page), and their enhancements, in 1986, by King Hassan's then-favourite designer, **André Paccard**. The collective result is a splendid fantasy of **public rooms** – including a **casino**, where you might want to gamble your all on the prospect of a stay.

Eating, drinking and nightlife

Marrakesh **eating and entertainment options** break down less rigidly than usual between the Ville Nouvelle, in this case Gueliz, and the Medina. **Gueliz**, naturally enough, is where you'll find most of the city's French-style cafés, bistros and restaurants, and virtually all the bars. In the **Medina**, however, there's plenty of choice for meals, including the spectacle of the Djemaa El Fna food stalls, many inexpensive café-restaurants, and a number of upmarket palace-restaurants (a couple of which offer Morocco's traditional cuisine at its very best).

Medina cafés and restaurants

Recommendations for the Medina span the range: from 30dh to 550dh a head: from a bench in the Djemaa El Fna to the most sumptuous palace decor. Only the places listed under "Moderate" or "Expensive" are licensed to sell alcohol.

Note that many of the **palace-restaurants** are well-hidden in the Medina and often difficult to find, especially at night; if in doubt, phone in advance and ask for directions – sometimes the restaurant will send someone to meet you. Be wary of palace-restaurants that aren't listed below; they tend to be geared towards tour groups, with kitsch belly-dancing entertainment, and uninteresting food.

Cheap café-restaurants

Terrace Café El Badi, by Bab Berrima, on a rooftop overlooking Place des Ferblantiers and towards the Mellah. This is a fine viewpoint, level with nesting storks on the palace walls; the café serves a limited range of hot and soft drinks, but will send out for sandwiches and more substantial cold fare. On the far side of the *place*, the tinsmiths still work and the entrance to the Mellah is lined with gold and jewellery boutiques.

Rue Bani Marine. This narrow street which runs south from the *PTT* and *Banque du Maroc* on Djemaa El Fna, between and parallel to Rue Bab Agnaou and Rue Moulay Ismail, has about ten excellent-value café-restaurants and several mobile grill-bars. Look for *Casse-Croûte des Amis* (aka Chez Elghassi) and, alongside the *Hôtel Gazelle*, *El Bahja*, with its *hadj* patron.

Chez Chegrouni, Place Djemaa El Fna. Look for the small café, with its orange plastic sign, 10m north of the *Café de France* and alongside the *Café Montréal*. It serves breakfast, *harita* soup and eggs cooked several ways; there is also a great vegetarian *tajine*.

Restaurant Diamant Rouge, beyond *Chez Chegrouni* and just off Djemaa El Fna, opposite *Hôtel Panorama*. A small, bright, lively café serving salads, sandwiches, cakes and fruit juices.

Café Restaurant El Fatha. Another small café, with balcony terrace, on the northern side of the *place*. It's quiet and doesn't get too crowded; usual range of snacks and drinks.

Mik Mak, Place de Foucauld, by *Hôtel Ali*. A well-established pâtisserie, for pastries and a range of breads; useful for takeaway breakfasts and picnics, but it doesn't have tables and chairs.

Pâtisserie des Princes, 32 Rue Bab Agnaou. A sparkling new pâtisserie which rivals *Mik Mak* – and has a back room for breakfasts, morning coffee and afternoon tea.

Laiterie et Pâtisserie Toubkal, in the far corner of Djemaa El Fna, beyond *Hôtel CTM* and best recognized by its backdrop of a dozen colourful carpets for sale. As well as fruit juices, yoghurts and pâtisseries, there's soup and *brochettes*.

DJEMMA EL FNA FOODSTALLS

Even if you don't eat at one of them, at some stage you should at least wander down the makeshift lane of food stalls at the north end of the Djemaa El Fna. They look great in the evening, lit by lanterns, and have boundless variety. To partake, just take a seat on one of the benches, ask the price of a plate of food and order all you like; if you want a soft drink or mineral water, the owners will send a boy to get it for you. Guides often suggest that the stalls aren't very healthy, but, as the cooking is so visible, standards of cleanliness are doubtless higher than in many hidden kitchens.

Moderate restaurants

Hôtel Ali, Rue Moulay Ismail. Justifiably popular restaurant in this highly recommended hotel, with à la carte lunches from 60dh, and a marvellous buffet every evening, featuring, *harira*, salads, *cous-cous* and ten or more *tajine*-style dishes – you can eat what you like, and as much as you wish, for (at time of writing) a bargain 60dh.

Restaurant Argana, Place Djemaa El Fna. This is possibly the best Djemaa El Fna vantage point – opposite the *Banque du Maroc*. There's a limited choice of French-Moroccan dishes and the service can be slow – better to time your visit for sunset! Allow 70dh per person.

Café Etoile de Marrakesh, on Rue Bab Agnaou (not to be confused with the simpler *Café Etoile* nearer Place Djemaa El Fna). Very popular with the locals, especially at midday; you can eat upstairs on the balcony for around 50dh.

Hôtel de Foucauld, Av. El Mouahidine. The restaurant is attached to the hotel; it may be small, but the welcome is warm, the food is good and the helpings generous – second helpings of fine *harira* soup are the order of the day; menu 90dh to 110dh.

Hôtel du Café de France, Place Djemaa El Fna. Another superb viewpoint. The hotel itself is wretched but the restaurant and café are acceptable; nothing special, but reliable.

Café Restaurant Iceberg, Av. El Mouahidine. Although it's central and popular with the locals, this pleasant eating place is largely ignored by tourists. At street level, it's unattractive, but upstairs there's a comfortable restaurant and you can eat well for around 70dh. The present owner has been in charge for 35 years – before that it was an ice-cream parlour – hence its name.

Hôtel Islane, 279 Av. Mohammed V. The rooftop restaurant was originally known as *Pizzeria Venetia*, but poor management gave it a bad name. Changes have improved things and traditional Moroccan dishes are now good and well-served at around 100dh a head. And the view of the Koutoubia remains unparallelled.

Expensive: palace restaurants

Restaurant Al Baraka, 1 Place Djemaa El Fna, by the Commisariat de Police (☎04/44.23.41). French-Moroccan restaurant open for lunch (11.30am–2pm) and dinner (8pm–late) in a beautiful fountain courtyard. Around 350dh a head.

Restaurant Doüirya, 14 Derb Djedid, Hay Essalam/Mellah, near Place des Ferblantiers (☎04/40.30.30). *Doüirya* may mean small house, but this is on a grand scale with a remarkable ceiling. Open daily for lunch (150dh–200dh) and dinner with Andalous music (350dh). Easy to find.

Palais Gharnatta, 5/6 Derb El Arsa, off Riad Zitoun Djedid (☎04/44.06.15). From the car park of the Dar Si Said Museum, take the gate to the right of the *Prefecture de Marrakesh Medina* and, after passing the *Maison Tiskiwin* on your right, look for signs to the restaurant. The sixteenth-century decor is magnificent and note the central alabaster fountain, also sixteenth century and from Italy. The food and music are also fine. According to the vistors' book, Jacqueline Kennedy and the Agha Khan have eaten here and, according to the publicity, some of 'The Return of the Pink Panther' was filmed here. Cost 350dh per head.

Dar Hadj Idder, 1 Derb El Hajra, (☎04/44.53.75). Leave Place Djemaa El Fna by Derb Debbachi, between the *Pharmacie Menara* and the Qessabin Mosque; the restaurant is on a side street to the right (with a sports shop on the corner). The original building and garden were a gift from El Glaoui, Pasha of Marrakesh, to Hadj Idder, his chamberlain. Thus, the building is in the grand style, but not very old. Traditional feasts at midday and in the evenings; 200dh to 350dh.

Dar Marjana, 15 Derb Ettir, off Rue Bab Doukkala (☎04/44.57.73). Look for the sign above the entrance to a passageway diagonally across the street from the corner of the Dar El Glaoui; take the passage and look for the green door facing you before a right turn. This is an early nineteenth-century palace, said by some to be the most beautiful palace in the Medina, while the food is rightly praised by Michelin. Open evenings only, but closed on Tuesdays; it will cost you about 550dh.

Restaurant Le Marrakechi, 52 Rue des Banques (☎04/44.33.77). The entrance is just off Place Djemaa El Fna by the *Café de France* and *Chez Chegrouni*, but with a fine view of the *place* from the first-floor restaurant. Imperial, but intimate decor, impeccable service and indescribably delicious *pastilla*. There are three menus from which to choose: 250dh, 350dh and 450dh. Open seven days a week, at midday and (with fewer tour groups) in the evenings.

Le Pavillon, 47 Derb Zaouia (☎04/39.12.40). Despite signs at Bab Doukkala, which lead to 9 Derb Hanah (the back entrance to Le Pavillon's kitchen), this is best approached from the Bab Doukkala Mosque alongside the defunct cinema *El Fath*. The tasteful brass plates labelling both doors are letter-box-slot size but then this is a restaurant owned by a star professional decorator, Gerrard. He has beautifully restored this middle-class house, which is best seen in evening light. The restaurant is open every evening, save Tuesday. The menu is always value for money: 250dh–300dh.

Restaurant Yacout, 79 Sidi Ahmed Soussi (☎04/31.01.04). Another gorgeous old palace in the heart of the Medina, and another restaurant that gets Michelin plaudits. You must book ahead (it opens every evening, save Monday, from 8pm onwards) and take a *petit taxi* – the driver will usually walk with you to the plain door – there is no sign of course! Five-course meals are served round an Andalucian courtyard with pool, and there's a terrace with views over the Medina for coffee: 500dh a head.

Gueliz restaurants

Although Gueliz is not so picturesque a setting for a meal, it would be a mistake to dismiss it entirely as modern and French. It is, after all, the city's main centre and its restaurants are generally good value, while the pricier ones are licensed. If you want to menu-browse, the main concentration of places is around Place Abdelmoumen Ben Ali.

Cheap

Café Agdal, 86 Av. Mohammed V, facing *Hôtel Amalay*. Good for breakfast and snacks; open 'til late.

Boule de Neige, 20 Rue de Yugoslavie, close to Place Abdelmoumen Ben Ali. A lively pâtisserie which serves breakfast and all-day snacks.

Restaurant Snack Chawarma, 23 Rue Mauritania. A *chawarma* is best described as a 'doner kebab sandwich', besides which the snack bar also specializes in crepes of several types. Open from 6am to midnight. Again, good for breakfast and all-day snacks.

Cafeteria Le Jet d'Eau, Place de la Liberté. Open all day: breakfast from 20dh and menu of the day for 60dh.

Brasserie du Régent, 34 Av. Mohammed V. Menu of the day is good value at 50dh; there is also a fairly serious bar.

Café Snack Le Sindibad. A new ground floor and pavement café in front of the new *Résidence Elite* and shopping mall on Av. Mohammed V. *Harira* soup with hard-boiled eggs and dates followed by a *tajine kefta* for 32dh.

Café Le Siroua, 20 Bd. Mohammed Zerktouni, next to the cinema *Colisée*. A small, friendly café, open long hours. Good for breakfast: orange juice and coffee.

Moderate

Bagatelle Restaurant, 101 Rue de Yugoslavie (☎04/43.02.74). A pleasant place run by a French couple – and in summer meals are served outside in the shady garden. You can eat well for under 100dh. Closed Wed and Sept.

Le Cantanzaro, Rue Tarik Ibn Ziad (☎04/43.37.31). Behind the municipal maket, near the *Hôtel Toulousain*. One of the city's most popular Italian restaurants, crowded at lunchtime with locals, expats and tourists. The low ceiling with beams may be *ersatz*, but the Italian dishes are genuine and generous. 110dh per head, and there's a takeaway service as well. Closed Sun.

Le Dragon d'Or, 10 bis Bd. Mohammed Zerktouni (☎04.43.06.17). Vietnamese and Chinese cuisine. The decor is bright and cheerful; it's popular with local families and there's a takeaway service. Prices are reasonable if a group 'pick 'n mix'. Open lunchtime and evenings.

Restaurant L'Entrecôte, 55 Bd. Mohammed Zerktouni (☎04/44.94.28). On the ground floor of a new speculative block. The menu is truly international: pizzas, paella and hamburgers; but the speciality is 'Wild West' steaks. The 'express' menu of two courses and coffee is 70dh and there's a children's menu at 50dh. Closed Sundays.

Hôtel Farouk, 66 Av. Hassan II (☎04/43.19.89). The restaurant, and hotel, may not be as well known as the *Ali*, which is its better-half in the Medina, but it is equally good and value for money.

Chez Jack'Line, 63 Av. Mohammed V, near Place Abdelmoumen Ben Ali (☎04/44.75.47). French, Italian and Moroccan dishes, directed by the indefatigable Jack'Line Pinguet and supervised by *Ulysses*, her silent and elderly green parrot. You can eat splendidly for 75dh to 100dh.

Restaurant Le Jardin, Rue Oum Rabia, on a side road off Av. Mohammed V; look for the *Pizza Hut* on the opposite side of the avenue (☎04/43.31.92). Modern decor, with pink walls and little lamps on each table. The speciality is crepes, both savoury and sweet – and there's always a choice of good grills. Up to 150dh per head.

Rotisserie de la Paix, 68 Rue Yugoslavie, opposite the Bagatelle Restaurant and alongside the closed cinema Lux-Palace (☎04/43.31.18). Established in 1949, this continues to offer fine French and Moroccan dishes, served in a salon with a roaring fire in winter, in a shaded garden in summer. Specialities include *boeuf bourguignon* on Wednesdays and *couscous* on Thursdays.

Restaurant Puerto Banus, Rue Ibn Hanbal, opposite the Police Headquarters on the Royal Tennis Club (☎04/44.65.34). French management and Spanish dishes: *gazpacho* soup and a generous paella cost 120dh.

Expensive

Al Fassia, 232 Av. Mohammed V (☎04/43.40.60). At the junction with Rue Sebou, this restaurant is truly Moroccan, both in decor and cuisine. Lunch is around 120dh but, in the evening, dinner will cost twice that. The ambiance and service are superb.

Le Jacaranda, 32 Bd. Mohammed Zerktouni – on Place Abdelmoumen Ben Ali, (☎04/44.72.15). French auberge with beams and a fireplace. The menu is extensive and tempting; with self-discipline and modest bottle of wine, it will cost around 250dh a head. Closed all day Tues and midday Wed. There is usually an interesting exhibition of work by local artists.

La Trattoria, 179 Rue Mohammed El Bekal (☎04/43.26.41). Decor by the acclaimed Bill Willis (as in the *Hôtel Tichka*) while the owner and cuisine are Italian. The service is friendly and the cooking excellent. Open evenings, Tuesday through Sunday. Cost 275dh to 325dh.

Villa Rosa, 64 Av. Hassan II, next to the *Hôtel Farouk* (☎04/43.08.32). Once managed by an Italian, the restaurant is now in French hands. Light wood, pastel shades and silk drapes decor; French menu and faultless dishes. There's also a 'jazz bar' and a courtyard of citrus trees. You will eat well for 250dh a head.

Bars and nightlife

Entertainment and nightlife in the **Medina** revolve around Djemaa El Fna and its cafés, though sometimes there might be a music group playing in an enclosure behind the Koutoubia on Av. Mohammed V. The only bars in easy reach are in the hotels *Tazi* and *Foucauld* (on the roof), or, for those on expense accounts, the *Mamounia*; see hotel listings for addresses. In **Gueliz**, there's more variety. Some of the hotels have **discos**, and many have **bars**, in which you are more likely to have Moroccans for company.

Gueliz bars

Hôtel Amalay, 87 Av. Mohammed V. Next to the *Shell* petrol station close to Place Abdelmoumen Ben Ali. Fairly relaxed.

Café-Bar de l'Escale, Rue Mauretania, just off Av. Mohammed V.

Hôtel Oasis, 50 Av. Mohammed V. Beyond Place Abdelmoumen Ben Ali, going towards Route de Casablanca. Enter by a door beside the hotel.

Brasserie du Petit Poucet, corner of Av. Mohammed V/Rue Mohammed El Bequal. This drinkers' bar is along a corridor by the restaurant (which itself is long past its 'sell-by' date).

Brasserie du Regent, 34 Av. Mohammed V (see restaurant listings).

Hôtel La Renaissance, on Place Abdelmoumen Ben Ali. The hotel is closed but the café on the ground floor and pavement still functions, as does the rooftop terrace bar, known as the *Mirador,* which offers beers and great views up Av. Mohammed V to the Koutoubia and the High Atlas beyond. Take the lift from the café to the terrace.

Café Oued El Had, 100 Av. Casablanca – a *petit taxi* ride to the outskirts of town. A complex of three bars – the best of them upstairs. Open to 2am.

Discos

Currently spots include:

Le Byblos, *Hôtel N'Fis*, Av. de France.
Cotton Club, *Hôtel Tropicana*, Semlalia.
Le Diamant Noir, *Hôtel le Marrakech*, Place de la Liberté.
Paradise, *Hôtel Mansour Eddahbi*, alongside Palais des Congrès, Av. de France.

Casino

Grand Casino, in the *Hôtel La Mamounia*, Av. Bab Djedid. This feels pretty unreal, walking in from the Medina. Roulette, craps and blackjack, and lots of slots. Entrance is free, but men need a tie and jacket. Open 8pm 'and stays open until you run out of money'.

Listings

Airlines *British Airways* and *GB Airways* are represented by *Menara Tours* (see Travel Agencies, below). RAM, 197 Av. Mohammed V (☎04/43.62.05; Reservations ☎04/44.64.44). *RAM* and *Air France* have desks at the *Hôtel Atlas Asni* (see main map). For **airport information** ☎04/44.78.62.

American Express c/o *Voyages Schwarz*, Immeuble Moutoukil, 1 Rue Mauretania (☎04/43.66.00). Business hours Mon–Fri 9am–12.30pm and 3–4pm (open until 7pm for mail).

American Language Center 3 Impasse du Moulin, off Bd. Mohammed Zerktouni, Gueliz (☎04/44.72.59). The center is mainly for locals to learn English – there are no Arabic classes. But you can study in the library or become a subscriber and borrow books.

Animal welfare The British animal charity SPANA maintain a Centre Hospitalier pour Animaux (☎04/30.31.10) at Cité Mohammedia, in the Daoudiat quarter. This was their first Moroccan centre and remains the biggest. Visitors are welcome to come and see its work with pets and working animals. Take a *petit taxi* or bus #6 or #9, and ask for El Morsli Abdellatif.

Banks Most banks have branches in both Gueliz and the Medina; many have a *bureau de change* alongside and these stay open longer in the late afternoon/early evening; an increasing number also have cashpoints/cash dispensers, aka ATMs (automated teller machines). As elsewhere, the *BMCE* is the best bet for exchange – accepting VISA/Mastercard, travellers' cheques, Eurocheques and most currencies; it has branches in Gueliz (144 Av. Mohammed V) and in the Medina (Place Foucauld/Rue Moulay Ismail – back entrance for exchange), open 10am–2pm and 4–8pm every day and both have ATMs. *Banque Populaire* has a useful *bureau de change* just off Place Djemaa El Fna, on Rue Bab Agnaou (Mon–Sat 9am–7pm). *Crédit du Maroc* has a *guichet* for exchange (no Eurocheques) at 215/217 Av. Mohammed V and another new one on Rue Bab Agnaon (in both cases Mon–Sat 9.30am–2pm and 3.30–7pm); both branches have ATMs. There is a new *BCM bureau de change* next to the *Hôtel Imperial Borj*, on Av. Echouhada in the Hivernage quarter (Tue–Fri: 9am–12noon and 2–4pm, closed Sat afternoon and all day Sun). Most 3- and 4-star hotels will change travellers' cheques and most currencies.

Bicycles, mopeds and motor bikes Bikes can be rented from *Hôtel de Foucauld* and *Hôtel Ali* in the Medina; and there's a small repair shop near *Hôtel Atlal*, Rue de la Recette, from which you can also hire bikes. Elsewhere, bikes can be rented from *Hôtel Imperial Borj*, Av. Echouhada, Hivernage, and from 76 Av. Mohammed Abdelkrim El Kattabi opposite *Résidence Ezzahia*. Mopeds and motor bikes can be rented from Marrakech Moros, aka Chez Jamal Boucetta, at 31 Av. Mohammed Abdelkrim El Kattabi (☎04/44.83.59), near the Goodyear garage.

Bookshops Two good bookshops (stocking mainly French titles) face each other across Av. Mohammed V in Gueliz: *Librairie Chatr* at no. 19 and *Librairie Gilot* at no. 44. In the new *Résidence Taib*, 55 Bd. Mohammed Zerktouni, Gueliz, there is *Librairie d'Art* which stocks the beautiful ACR range of French art and coffee-table books, including 'La Vie et l'Oeuvre de Jacques Majorelle' and 'Marrakech: Demeures et Jardins secrets'. In the Medina, there's a small bookshop which sells French books and a range of stationery: *Librairie Ghizlane*, 51 Rue Bab Agnaou.

Car rental Marrakesh rates are generally the most competitive after Casablanca. The best value deals are usually from local agencies, with whom you can bargain for discounts; try *Concorde Cars*, 154 Av. Mohammed V (☎04/43.99.73); *Fathi Cars*, 183 Av. Mohammed V (☎04/43.17.63); *Najm Car*, 21 Rue Loubnane (☎04/43.78.91) or *Hôtel du Pacha*; *Nomade Car*, 112 Av. Mohammed V (☎04/44.71.26), or *Tansift Car*, 72 Av. Mohammed Abdelkrim El Kattabi (☎04/44.91.45). National/international agencies include *Avis*, 137 Av. Mohammed V (☎04/43.37.27); *Budget*, *Hôtel Al Bustan*, 66 Bd. Mohammed Zerktouni (☎04/43.46.04); *Citer*, 1 Rue de la Liberté (☎04/43.06.83); *Europcar/InterRent*, 63 Bd. Mohammed Zerktouni (☎04/43.12.28); *Golden Tours*, 113 Av. Mohammed V (☎04/44.91.61); *Hertz*, 154 Av. Mohammed V (☎04/43.99.84) and *Tourist Cars*, 64 Bd. Mohammed Zerktouni (☎04/44.84.57). Of the national/international agencies, all but *Golden Tours* have desks at the airport.

Car repairs *Garage Ourika*, 66 Av. Mohammed V (☎04/44.82.66), deals with Hondas, Fiats, Toyotas and BMWs (look for the large Honda sign). *Garage Renault*, Route de Casablanca, after the Safi crossroads (☎04/44.80.82) deals with Renaults; and *Thoniel*, 68 Rue Tarik Ibn Ziad (☎04/43.13.59) deals with Peugeots, Citroens, Talbots and Mercedes. For spare parts, try the following which are close to one another: *Sud Transmission*, 8/10 Bd. Moulay Rachid (☎04/43.34.34); *Société-Jihad Pièces Autos*, 18 Bd. Moulay Rachid (☎04/43.40.98); and *Union Pièces Autos*, 18 Av. El Mansour Eddahbi (☎04/43.17.90).

Churches, The Roman Catholic *Eglise des Saints Martyrs* is on Rue El Imam Ali, near the *Hôtel Ibn Batouta* in Gueliz (☎04/43.05.85); mass from Oct to June: Sun 10.30am and 7pm, Mon–Sat 6.30pm; from July to Sept: Sun 9.30am, Mon–Sat 7.30pm. The *Eglise Reformée Protestante* is at 89 Bd. Moulay Rachid, Gueliz; for details of its monthly services ring ☎04/43.14.79.

Cinemas In Gueliz, the *Colisée,* alongside the *Café Le Siroua* on Bd. Mohammed Zerktouni, is one of the best. It shows general releases and has enjoyed a recent face-lift. In the Medina, the *Cinéma Mabrouka* on Rue Bab Agnaou and the *Cinéma Eden*, off Derb Dabbachi, have a certain curiosity value, but watch your wallet.

Consulates The only consulate in Marrakesh is the *Consulat de France*, on Rue Ibn Khaldoun in the shadow of the Koutoubia (☎04/44.40.06).

Dentist Dr Bennani, 112 Av. Mohammed V (first floor), opposite the ONMT office, Gueliz, is recommended (☎04/43.11.45). He speaks some English.

Doctor Dr Abdelmajid Bentbib, 171 Av. Mohammed V, Gueliz (☎04/43.10.30), is recommended and speaks English.

Ferry tickets *Comanav Voyages,* Kawkab Centre, 16–17 Rue Imam Chafi (☎04/43.66.02).

Festivals Local *moussems* include: *Asni* (beginning Aug); *Setti Fatma* (Ourika; around 15 Aug, see p.362); *Sidi Bouatmane* (near Amizmiz; Sept); and *Moulay Brahim* (near Asni; ten days after Mouloud; see p.365).

Food shopping Putting together a picnic lunch, or supplies for the Atlas, the muncipal market on Av. Mohammed V, in Gueliz, is convenient, as is the covered market between Av. Houmane El Fetouaki and Arset El Maach in the Medina.

French Culture The *Institut Français* (Djebel Gueliz, BP566) is to be found on the edge of Gueliz alongside the *Lycée Français Victor Hugo* and the *École Française Renoir* with which it shares beautiful grounds (☎04/44.69.30). The monthly programme includes theatre, cinema, lectures and exhibitions, and there is a good library. Bus #7 from the Medina or Gueliz.

Golf There are two golf courses: the *Royal Golf Club*, 6km out on the road to Ouarzazate (☎04/44.43.31), and the *Golf de la Palmeraie*, 4km out on the road to Tizi n'Tichka (☎04/30.10.10 which is also the number of the five-star *Palmeraie Golf Palace*). Both courses are open to non-members: green fees around 150dh.

Jewish Community The *Communauté Israélite de Marrakech* (☎04/44.87.54) is on Impasse du Moulin, opposite the American Language Center. Here there is the Synagogue Beth Habad. For other synagogues and the Jewish community in general, see p p.344–345.

Laundry and dry-cleaning In Gueliz, *Blanchisserie Oasis*, 44 Rue Tarik Ibn Zaid, behind the muncipal market (☎04/43.45.78); in the Medina, *Blanchisserie du Sud*, 10 Rue Bab Agnaou (☎04/44.33.31).

Marathon The Marrakesh international marathon takes place each second Sunday in January. It starts on Place Djemaa El Fna, passes through the Hivernage, encircles the Palmeraie and finishes a couple of hours later back at the Djemaa El Fna.

Markets The most interesting **weekly souks** in the Marrakesh region include: Asni (Sat); Amizmiz (Tues); Aït Ourir (Tues); and Ourika (Mon at Souk Tnine de l'Ourika – and a smaller Sunday market further up the valley at Setti Fatma, see Chapter Six for coverage).

Newspapers The most reliable newstand for American and British newspapers is outside the ONMT office on Av. Mohammed V; you can buy *The International Herald Tribune, Time, Newsweek,* plus British publications *The Guardian, Independent, Times, Weekly Telegraph* and *Economist.*

Pharmacies There are several along Av. Mohammed V, including a good one just off Place de la Liberté: *Pharmacie de la Liberté,* which will call a doctor for you. In the Medina, try *Pharmacie Menara* on Place Djemaa El Fna. There's an all-night pharmacy by the Comisariat de Police on Place Djemaa El Fna and another on Rue Khalid Ben Oualid near the fire station in Gueliz. Other all-night and weekend outlets are listed in pharmacy windows and the local press, for example, *Le Message de Marrakech.*

Photography Photographic equipment, film, batteries, etc can be obtained from W*rédé*, 142 Av. Mohammed V (☎04/43.57.39).

Post office The main *PTT*, which receives all **poste restante** mail, is on Place 16 Novembre, midway down Av. Mohammed V in Gueliz; it is open Mon–Sat 8am–2pm. The **telephone** section, with its own entrance, stays open until 9pm, and operators will place a call for you. There is also a separate office, round the side, for sending parcels. The Medina *PTT* in Place Djemaa El Fna stays open until 7pm. With so many **téléboutiques** around town, including one opposite the main *PTT*, the telephone section is of less use – except for reversed-charge (collect) calls.

Swimming pools There's a large municipal pool on Rue Abou El Abbes Sebti – the first main road to the left off Av. Mohammed V as you walk past the Koutoubia towards Gueliz; it's very popular and 99 percent male. Many hotels (but, alas, not the *Mamounia*) allow non-residents to use their pools if you have a meal, or for a fee. A useful one, if you're staying in the Medina, is the pool at the *Grand Hôtel Tazi*, a short walk from the Place Djemma El Fna. The municipal pool in the Daoudiaf quarter is very popular with the locals.

Tourist offices The ONMT, now referred to as the *Délégué Régional du Tourisme*, is on Place Abdelmoumen Ben Ali (☎04/43.62.39) and the *Syndicat d'Initiative*, now referred to as APOTM (*Association Provinciale des Operateurs de Tourisme de Marrakech*) is at 170 Av. Mohammed V (no phone). Both are open Mon–Fri 9am–12 noon and 3–6.30pm; Sat 9am–12 noon. The ONMT occasionally houses an exhibition of local art, otherwise it is, in the words of the Travel Editor of the *Daily Telegraph*, 'a waste of time'; the *Syndicat* is no better.

Travel agencies *Menara Tours*, 41 Rue de Yougoslavie (☎04/44.66.54), near the ONMT office in Gueliz, are agents for *British Airways* and run good tours of the south. The *Best of Morocco* (see "Basics", p.6), 3rd floor, Apartment 15, 92 Bd. Mohammed Zerktouni (☎04/43.98.42) offers a comparable service – land rover desert safaris of the south.

Weather ☎04/43.04.09; Telex 04/43.05.66.

travel details

Trains

Trains are the most comfortable way of getting to Casa and Rabat. If you're heading back to **Tangier** it's possible to do the trip in one, most easily by booking (in advance) a couchette on the night train (10–12hrs); this must be done on the morning of the day of travel.

Marrakesh-Casablanca Voyageurs (7 daily; 4hr).

Marrakesh-Fes, via Casablanca (2 daily; 8-10hr).

The train company, **ONCF** also operates **Supratours** express buses, leaving from the train station, to **Essaouira** (1pm), **Agadir** (12.58pm, 10.37pm), and **Laayoune** (10.37pm), though they only sell tickets if there is space after the allocation for train passengers from Casablanca/Rabat. *Grands taxis* are generally on hand to pick up the overflow at these times and are good value, a place to Agadir costing around 80dh.

Buses

Buses to all **long-distance destinations** leave from the main terminal at **Bab Doukkala**. Buy tickets a day in advance – or turn up early – for the more popular destinations such as Fes, El Jadida, Taroudannt or Zagora, and note that CTM and all the private companies have their own individual ticket windows – choices can be more extensive than at first appears. **CTM** also have an office on Bd. Mohammed Zerktouni in Gueliz, near the ONMT office, where you can buy tickets, and where some of the buses make a secondary call.

Recommended lines/departures, at time of writing, include:

Agadir Best are *Supratours* (see "Trains" above) and CTM (3hr 30min).

Essaouira Best are *Supratours* (see "Trains" above). (3hr 30min)

Fes CTM at 6.30am and 9pm (9hr 15min)

Ouarzazate (over the Tizi n'Tichka) CTM at 5.30am, 7.30am, 11am and 5.30pm (4–5hr).

Taroudannt (over the Tizi n'Test route) SATAS bus at 5am (8hr 30min).

Tafraoute (best on CTM via Agadir)

Zagora CTM at 7am (arrives 4.30pm).

Buses to **local destinations**, including **Ourika**, **Asni** (the trailhead for Djebel Toubkal; 1hr 30min), and **Moulay Brahim**, leave from just outside **Bab Er Robb**. (Some buses also run to Asni from the Bab Doukkala bus station).

Grands Taxis

Grands taxis can also be useful for getting to **Ourika** or to **Asni** – negotiate for these by Bab Er Robb (12.5dh is the local rate for a place to Asni).

Taxis run less frequently to other destinations but you could try asking some of the drivers at the stands in Djemaa El Fna and by Bab Er Raha (between Av. Mohammed V and Bab Doukkala). **Essaouira** and **Agadir** (see "Trains", above) are both possible.

Flights

Royal Air Maroc operates domestic flights to Casa (with onward connections to Tangier and Fes), Ouarzazate (taking just 25–30 minutes), and in summer Agadir. *GB Airways* fly weekly to Gibraltar. See "Listings" for addresses/phone numbers.

CHAPTER SIX

THE HIGH ATLAS

The **High Atlas**, North Africa's greatest mountain range, contains some of the most intriguing and most beautiful regions of Morocco. A historical and physical barrier between the northern plains and the pre-Sahara, its Berber-populated valleys feel – and indeed are – very remote from the country's mainstream or urban life. For visitors, it is, above all, trekking country, with walks to suit all levels of ability and commitment, from casual day-hikes to week-long (or more) expedition routes combining a series of peaks (*djebels*) and passes (*tizis* or, in French, *cols*). **Rock-climbing** and **ski mountaineering** also offer fine sport, while **mountain-biking**, too,

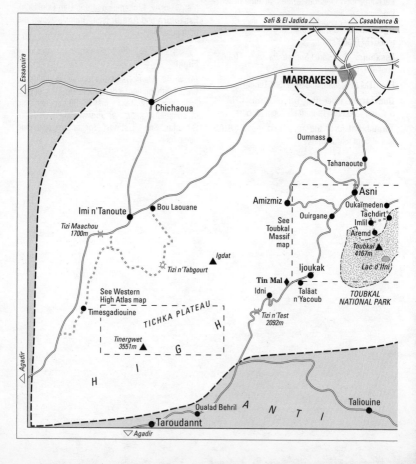

is increasingly popular on the dirt tracks (pistes) and mule paths. You could also **ride**. There are horses for hire at Ouirgane for organized local treks while the adventurous might consider buying (and reselling) a mule at one of the local souks; those who have done it claim there is no better way to experience the mountain culture.

Despite the forbidding appearance of its peaks, these are surprisingly populated mountains; their slopes drop away to valleys and streams, with Berber villages terraced into their sides. At many of the **villages** – particularly in the two main hiking centres of **Djebel Toubkal** (Morocco's highest peak) and the less known **Bou Goumez valley** – gîte-style accommodation is offered in local houses, and there is an established infrastructure of guides and mules for trekking. It must be stressed, though, that part of the attraction of Atlas trekking is that it remains so undeveloped in comparison with, say, the Pyrenees or Alps. The network of pistes and paths is there because it remains in everyday local use, and you enter a mountain life which has hardly altered in centuries.

This chapter – although entitled "The High Atlas" actually covers only the **Western part of the range**; for more on **easterly peaks and routes**, which offer four-wheel drive or travel on local Berber trucks, as well as trekking, see the following chapter.

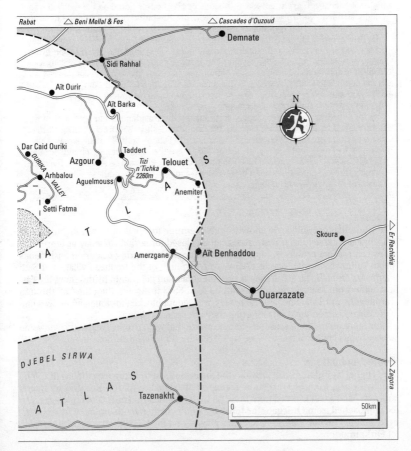

HIGH ATLAS BERBERS

Until recent decades, the High Atlas region – and its **Berber inhabitants** – was almost completely isolated. When the French began their "pacification" in the 1920s, the way of life here was essentially feudal, based upon the control of the three main passes (tizis) by a trio of "clan" families, "the Lords of the Atlas". Even after the French negotiated the co-operation of these warrior chiefs, it was not until the spring of 1933 – 21 years after the establishment of the Protectorate – that they were able to subdue them and control their tribal land, and only then with the co-operation of the main feudal chief, **T'hami El Glaoui**, who continued to control the region as Pasha of Marrakesh (see p.384).

These days, the region is under official government control through a system of local *caids*, but in many villages the role of the state remains largely irrelevant, and if you go trekking you soon become aware of the mountains' highly distinctive culture and traditions. The longest established inhabitants of Morocco, the Atlas Berbers never adopted a totally orthodox version of Islam (see Contexts) and the Arabic language has, even today, made little impression on their indigenous **Tachelhaït** dialects. Their **music** and **ahouache** dances (in which women and men join together in broad circles) are unique, too, as is the village **architecture**, with stone or clay houses tiered on the rocky slopes, craggy fortified **agadirs** (collective granaries), and **Kasbahs**, which continued to serve as feudal castles for the community's defence right into the present century.

Berber women in the Atlas go about unveiled and have a much higher profile than their rural counterparts in the plains and the north. They perform much of the heavy labour – working in the fields, herding and grazing cattle and goats and carrying vast loads of brushwood and provisions. Whether they have any greater status or power within the family and village, however, is questionable. The men retain the "important" tasks of buying and selling goods and the evening/night-time irrigation of the crops, ploughing and do all the building and craftwork.

As an outsider, you'll be constantly surprised by the friendliness and openness of the Berbers, and by their amazing capacity for languages – there's scarcely a village where you won't find someone who speaks French or English, or both. The only areas where you may feel exploited – and pestered by kids – are the main trekking circuits around Djebel Toubkal, where tourism has become an all-important source of income. Even the hustling, however, is gentler than in the cities – and, given the harshness of life up here, its presence is hardly surprising.

Seasons

The High Atlas are subject to **snow** from **November to April**, and even the major Tizi n'Tichka and lesser Tizi n'Test passes can be closed for periods of a day or more. The **thaw** can present problems, too, when the snows melt in spring or during flash floods (from summer storms); one in 1995 destroyed much of the trailhead villages of Setti Fatma and Imlil. If you are driving across the Atlas, and get caught by the snow, the easiest route from Marrakesh to the south is road 6543 to Agadir, then the P32 through Taroudannt and Taliouine, but the passes are seldom blocked for long and notices outside Marrakesh on the roads inform if they are open or closed.

For more on trekking seasons – and be aware that winter routes above the snow line are a serious endeavour here – see the "Trekking Practicalities" box, on pp.366–7.

Routes and passes

The **Djebel Toubkal** massif provides the focus for most trekking expeditions. It can be reached easily from Marrakesh by taking a bus or taxi to **Asni** – just over an hour's journey – and a truck or taxi from there on to the trailhead at **Imlil**. The region can also be approached from **Ouirgane** or **Ijoukak**, a little further south, or, more energetically, from the **Ourika Valley** – a summer playground for Marrakesh – or the ski resort of **Oukaïmeden**.

FLASH FLOODS

The possibility of flash floods, when the snow thaws, or from summer storms, must be taken seriously. They erupt suddenly and violently and they are extremely dangerous. In August 1995, summer storms caused devastating flooding in the Atlas – and in particular the Ourika valley, where the Setti Fatma festival was in full swing. Dozens of buildings and bridges were washed away in the valley and over 300 lives lost, mainly young visitors camping for the festivities.

It is wise, at almost any time of year, to **camp on high ground**, avoiding any spot where water can lie or that might become a course for the torrents when they descend. This includes, most obviously (although it's hard to believe in summer), dried up and apparently terminally inactive river beds.

Asni, Ouirgane and Ijoukak all lie on the dramatic **Tizi n'Test road**, which runs over the highest Atlas pass to connect Marrakesh with Taroudannt: a switchback of almost continuous hairpin curves to be driven with care. As well as its scenic appeal and trekking possibilities, the route has an easily accessible historic attraction in the ruins of the twelfth-century mosque of **Tin Mal**, the base from which the Almohads swept down to conquer Morocco and Spain.

To the east is the **Tizi n'Tichka**, a more substantial road pass, which cuts across to Ouarzazate and today bears most of the traffic across the Atlas. It was built to replace the old caravan route to Tafilalt, which was controlled over the last century and for much of the present by the legendary **Glaoui family**, "the Lords of the Atlas" (see p.384). Their Kasbah, a bizarre cluster of crumbling towers and kitschy-looking 1930s reception halls, is still to be seen at **Telouet**, just an hour from the main road.

The third main Atlas pass, the **Tizi Maachou**, has less drama, unless you leave the main road behind to get into the hills for some trekking in the Western Atlas, the least-known part of the range. For most travellers it simply offers a fast and convenient route between Marrakesh and Agadir.

The Ourika Valley and Oukaïmeden

The **Ourika Valley** is a pleasant prelude to the Atlas and an enjoyable escape from the summer heat of Marrakesh. It's a weekend resort for young *Marrakchis* who ride out here on their mopeds to lie around beside the streams and waterfalls.

The road through the valley has been wiped out by floods countless times over the centuries, most recently (and catastrophically) in 1995. At time of writing, it's in good shape as far as Dar Caid Ouriki, and being widened and improved from there to Setti Fatma, the end of the tarmac. **Setti Fatma** is the place to head for, with its series of waterfalls in the hills above, and one of the country's biggest *moussems* (festivals) in mid-August. Poised above the valley to the west is the ski resort of **Oukaïmeden**.

Getting to the Ourika Valley

Weather permitting, access to Ourika is fairly simple. **Grands taxis**, **buses** and a fast **minibus** service leave Marrakesh's Bab Er Robb regularly through the morning, from around 6am to noon, running down to Setti Fatma (if the road is clear of repair work) and returning in the late afternoon/early evening. If buses can't get through, minibuses generally take over. The valley is also an easy destination if you rent a moped from Marrakesh, and most of the road presents little problem to a rental car.

Setti Fatma (67km from Marrakesh) is about two hours from Marrakesh by bus or taxi. Try to get transport headed there, or at least to **Asgaour** (63km), the last village before Setti Fatma, and not just to the near end of the valley at **Dar Caid Ouriki** (33km) or **Arhbalou** (50km). Returning from Setti Fatma, you might have to walk to Asgaour to pick up a bus or taxi.

Into the valley

The Ourika Valley really begins at **SOUK TNINE DE L'OURIKA** (30km from Marrakesh), a small roadside village, which, as its name proclaims, hosts a Monday **souk** – an excursion offered by many of the tour hotels in Marrakesh. Just beyond it, across the river, is **DAR CAID OURIKI**, with a picturesque *zaouia* set back in the rocks, near the ruins of an old caidal **Kasbah**.

Beyond here, scattered at intervals over the next forty kilometres, are a series of tiny hamlets, interspersed by a few summer homes and the occasional hotel or café-restaurant. The one sizeable settlement is **ARHBALOU** (43km from Marrakesh), where most of the local people on the buses get off. The village has a "palace-restaurant", *Le Lion d'Ourika* (☎04/44.53.22), which has plans to open as a hotel, as well as basic rooms to let in the village. There is good walking in the surrounding hills; as well as the possibility of some serious trekking in Djebel Yagour (see "Treks from Setti Fetma"). A road west into the mountains leads to the trekking trailhead and ski resort of Oukaïmeden.

Moving on through the valley **towards Setti Fatma**, those with transport might want to stop at the **antiques/crafts shop**, *Le Musée d'Arhbalou*, 4km south of Arhbalou, which often has interesting stock. A further 2km on, there are pleasant **rooms** at the *Hôtel Amnougar* (☎04/44.53.28; ③).

Setti Fatma

SETTI FATMA, a straggly riverside village largely rebuilt after the 1995 devastation, is the most compelling Ourika destination. The setting, with its grassy terraces, feels like a real oasis after the dry plains around Marrakesh.

In the rocky foothills above the village are a series of six (at times, seven) **waterfalls**. To reach them, you first have to cross the stream, by whatever bridge has been thrown up after the last floods; near the beginning of the climb are several cafés, where you can order a *tajine* for your return. The first waterfall is a fairly straightforward clamber over the rocks, flanked by another café, the *Immouzer*. The higher ones are a lot more strenuous, and quite tricky when descending, requiring a head for heights and solid footwear. Returning, from the first of the falls you can loop back to Setti Fatma via the village's twin, ZAOUIA MOHAMMED, a few hundred metres further down the valley.

Staying

Setti Fatma has several **accommodation** options. Best are those at the modern *Hôtel Tafoukt* (with en-suite shower and toilet; ③), at the beginning of the village, or the rooms at the *Café-Restaurant Asgaour* (⑩) in the village proper, which are a little more basic but spotless and overlooking the river; the *Asgaour* patron, Chebob Lahcen, also cooks excellent meals. The *Café des Cascades* (the first on the route to the falls) also has decent if basic rooms, and the *Café Atlas*, at the north end of the village, has roof space. The *Hôtel Azrou* (⑩) is a bit of a last resort.

Alternatively, try the excellent *Auberge Bella* (③), a little way back up the valley towards Arhbalou. This is excellent, provides good food and has a shop.

Setti Fatma Moussem

The Setti Fatma Moussem – one of the three most important festivals in the country – takes place for four days around the middle of August, centred on the **Koubba of**

Setti Fatma, a little upstream from the Café des Cascades. Entry to the *koubba* is forbidden to non-Muslims, but the festival itself is as much a fair and market as religious festival and well worth trying to coincide with on your travels.

Treks from Setti Fatma

Ourika cuts right into the **High Atlas**, whose peaks begin to dominate as soon as you leave Marrakesh. At Setti Fatma they rise on three sides to 3658m: a startling backdrop which, to the southwest, takes in the main **trekking/climbing zone of Toubkal**. The usual approach to this is from Asni – see p.365 – but it is possible to set out from Setti Fatma, or from Oukaïmeden (see below).

If you are thinking of approaching Toubkal from Setti Fatma, one route is to trek via **Timichi** and **Oukaïmeden** and take the trail from there to Tachdirt. It is around six hours' walk from Setti Fatma to Timichi (see p.376), and a similar figure on to Oukaïmeden (see below), including a steep ascent to the Tizi n'Ouhattar. The ridge connecting this tizi with the Tizi n'Itbir, under Argour, gives pleasant rock scrambling (3100m). The two-to-three-day trek direct from **Timichi to Tachdirt** is perhaps best done in the opposite direction – and is so described on p.375.

Other adventurous treks from Setti Fatma include the **Djebel Yagour**, with its many prehistoric rock carvings; **Adrat Meltzen**, via **Tourcht** (one bivouac) or the secretive **Oued Zat** region reached by the demanding Tizi n'Tilst. The **Taska n'Zat–Arjoût peaks** require scrambling (up gorges and on the crests) while the way down the Oued Zat offers some days of gorges to reach the piste out. An ancient route climbs to the **Tizi Tazarzit** and reachs the P31 at **Agouim** south of the range. These are some of the hardest options in the range which may partly account for their neglect. One of the guides from Imlil would be useful, or you could ask for Hosain Izahan at the *Café Azapza* in Setti Fatma.

Oukaïmeden

The village and ski centre of **OUKAÏMEDEN** is a much easier trekking base from which to set out towards Toubkal – and a good target in its own right, even if you don't have anything that ambitious in mind. "Ouka", as it's known, is reached via a good modern road which veers off from Ourika just before Arhbalou. **Grands taxis** sometime go up from Marrakesh in the winter for the skiers or you have to charter a taxi for *la course*. The resort has a 10dh entrance fee. A snowplough keeps the road open in the ski season.

Accommodation

There are several **hotels**, including the excellent *Chalet-Hôtel Chez Juju* (☎04/45.90.05; ②), which has solid French food and a bar (also open in summer).

The *Club Alpine Chalet* (CAF) is well equipped, with a bar and restaurant and is cheaper, especially for members of Alpine Clubs. They sell Atlas guidebooks.

Rock carvings

There is an indispensible guidebook (on sale in the CAF chalet and in Marrakesh bookshops), *Gravures Rupestres du Haut Atlas*, which details the sites of the fascinating **prehistoric rock carvings**, showing animals, weapons, battle scenes and puzzling symbols. For a few dirhams a local will guide you to the better sites.

Skiing

Ouka has the best **skiing** in Morocco – on the slopes of **Djebel Oukaïmeden** – and up until the war it could boast the highest ski lift in the world, which remains impres-

HIGH ATLAS WILDLIFE

The High Atlas has unique flora and fauna, which are accessible even to the most reluctant rambler if you base yourself at **Oukaïmeden**, **Imlil** or **Ouirgane**.

The spring bloom on the lower slopes comprises aromatic thyme and thorny caper, interspersed with golden spreads of broom. Higher slopes are covered by more resilient species, such as the blue tussocks of hedgehog broom. The passes ring to the chorus of the painted frog and the North African race of the green toad during their spring breeding seasons, while some species of reptile have become adapted to the specific environment of the stony walls that form the towns and villages of the Atlas mountains, such as the **Moorish gecko**. **Butterflies** which brave these heights include the Moroccan copper and desert orange tip. Other inhabitants range from the almost-invisible praying mantis to the scampering ground squirrel and rare elephant shrew.

Birds to be found among the sparse vegetation include Moussier's redstart and the crimson-winged finch, which prefers the grassy slopes where it feeds in flocks; both birds are unique to North African mountains. The rocky outcrops provide shelter for both chough and alpine chough, the mountain rivers are frequented by dippers who swim underwater in their search for food. Overhead, darting Lanner falcon or flocks of brilliantly coloured bee-eater add to the feeling of abundance which permeates the slopes of the High Atlas. In the cultivated valleys look out for the magpie which, uniquely, has a sky-blue eye mark; there are, too, storks galore. Other High Atlas birds, as the snow melts, include shore larks, rock bunting, alpine accentor, redstarts and wheatears.

Flora is impressive, too. The wet meadows produce a fantastic spread of hooped-petticoat daffodils, *romulea* and other bulbs. Oukaimeden in May/June has acres of orchids.

sive at 3273m. It gives access to good piste and off-piste skiing, too, with several nursery and intermediate runs on the lower slopes.

Snowfall and snow cover can be erratic but February to April is fairly reliable. Slopes are sometimes icy early and wet by afternoon, but not having to queue in the mornings lets you get in plenty of sport. Equipment can be hired from several shops next to *Chez Juju* (one offers gear a reasonable 100dh a day), ski-passes cost just 30dh, and lessons are available from local instructors. The lifts close at the end of April (even if there is perfect conditions for skiing!).

Several other summits are accessible for **ski-mountaineering** sorties, and cross-country enthusiasts often ski across to Tachdirt.

Oukaïmeden to Tachdirt

For casual walkers, the trails from Oukaïmeden are strictly summer only: routes can be heavily snow-covered even late into spring. However, weather conditions allowing, the **trail to Tachdirt** (3hr) is pretty clear and easy-going. It begins a short distance beyond the ski lift, veering off to the right of the dirt road that continues for a while beyond this point. The pass, **Tizi n'Eddi**, is reached in about two hours; on the descent, the trail divides in two, either of which branch will lead you down into Tachdirt. For more details of this route, described in reverse, and routes on from Tachdirt, see pp.375–376.

The Djebel Toubkal Massif

The **Toubkal Massif**, a more or less roadless area enclosing the High Atlas's highest peaks, is the goal of almost everyone who goes trekking in Morocco. It is easy to get to from Marrakesh – Asni, the "first base", is just over an hour by bus or, simpler, by *grand taxi* (from Bab Er Robb) – and its main routes are reasonably well charted.

Walking even fairly short distances, you feel very much a visitor in a rigidly individual world. The villages look amazing, their houses stacked one on top of another in apparently organic growth from the rocks, and, even while working in the fields, the women dress in brilliantly-coloured costumes.

From late spring to late autumn (see note on "Seasons" on p.366), the region's trails are accessible for anyone reasonably fit. Mule tracks round the mountain valleys are well contoured and kept in excellent condition, and there's a network of village gîtes, unofficial houses and refuge huts for accommodation.

In summer, **Djebel Toubkal**, at 4167m the highest peak in North Africa, is walkable right up to the summit; if you're pushed for time, you could trek it, and be back in Marrakesh, in three days – though at the risk of altitude sickness. Further away, over a demanding pass, and much less visited, is **Lac d'Ifni**, tucked in a hollow in the mountains, while infinite variations on **longer treks** could lead you into the mountains for a week, two weeks, or more. For anyone really short on time, or who feels unable to tackle an ascent of Toubkal, it's possible to get a genuine taste of the mountains by spending time exploring the beautiful valleys and lower passes of the range. Options head east and west over tizis to neighbouring villages and valleys which can be followed down to the Tizi n'Test road or one can go over passes to Ijoukak or down valleys such as the Ourika or Agoundis, all areas happily free of organized trekking groups. If heading on over the Tizi n' Test afterwards, there is a splendid view to the Toubhad range from the final bends of the ascent.

Moulay Brahim

MOULAY BRAHIM is a picturesque village, just off the main Marrakesh–Asni road and dominating the gorges leading up from the plains. The **Kik Plateau** and its escarpment, which runs above the main road towards Ouirgane, is rich botanically and offers perhaps the best panorama of the Atlas mountains. It can be reached from the top end of the town, on a piste past marble quarries (see p.368).

The village is a popular weekend spot for *Marrakchis* and an alternative base for a first night in the Atlas, with several **hotels** – mostly cheapies ⑩plus the better equipped *Star's Hôtel* and *Haut Rocher* (①) – and **cafés**, and regular **buses** and **taxis** to/from Asni/Marrakesh. It hosts a large **moussem** two weeks after the Mouloud.

Asni

The end of the line for the Toubkal bus and Marrakesh *grands taxis*, **ASNI** is little more than a roadside village and marketplace, and many trekkers pass straight through to get up into the mountains. If you're in a hurry, this is good reasoning, though it's no disaster if you have to stay overnight. The village can feel a bit overcommercialized on arrival, with locals hawking meals and jewellery, but this doesn't last long, and between buses the village drifts back to its usual farming existence.

The most interesting time to be here before heading on to Toubkal is for the **Saturday souk**, when the enclosure behind the row of shop cubicles is filled with produce and livestock stalls, plus the odd storyteller or entertainer. An advantage of arriving on Saturday morning (or Friday night) is that you can stock up with cheap supplies, before heading into the mountains.

Rooms and meals

Asni has a **hotel and youth hostel**, either of which will store luggage if you want to go off trekking unencumbered. Touts may also offer rooms but you should be wary of accepting, especially if alone, or female. The choices are:

TOUBKAL TREKKING PRACTICALITIES

EQUIPMENT AND EXPERIENCE

Unless you're undertaking a particularly long or ambitious trek – or are here in winter conditions – there are no technical problems to hold anyone back from trekking in the Toubkal area, or making the peak itself. However, the mountain needs to be taken seriously and taken slowly until you are acclimatized. You really should have decent **footwear and clothing** – it's possible to be caught out by summer storms as well as bad winter conditions – and must also be prepared to camp out if neccessary, as the Toubkal refuge is often full.

The main physical problems are the high altitudes (3000–4000m throughout the Toubkal region), the midday heat and the tiring process of walking over long sections of rough boulders or loose scree. All of these can combine to make casual ascents by the inexperienced an unhappy and perhaps foolhardy experience.

SEASONS

Toubkal is usually under snow from November until mid-June. If you have some experience of winter trekking and conditions, it is feasible to climb the peak, and trek the low-level routes, year round, though for Toubkal you may need to wait around a couple of days for clear weather, and carry and know how to use ice axe and crampons (which can usually be rented in Imlil). For beginners, trekking is better limited to below the snow line. And only those with winter climbing experience should try anything more ambitious than Toubkal, or going much beyond hut level, from November to May; ice axe, crampons, good rain gear and winter competence are required, as several fatalities have recently shown. Full rivers and flash floods in spring and high summer can pose additional problems.

ALTITUDE

Toubkal is 4167m above sea level and much of the surrounding region is above 3000m, so it's possible that you might get altitude sickness and/or headaches. Aspirins can help, but just sucking on a sweet or swallowing often is as good as anything. If you experience more than slight breathlessness and really feel like vomiting, go down straight away. Take your time too, hurrying is a major cause of altitude sickness.

ACCOMMODATION

At most Atlas villages, it is usually possible to arrange a room in a local house; just turn up and ask. At some of the villages on more established routes, there are official gîtes, often the homes of mountain guides, who can provide mules and assistance – as well as food, showers, toilets and sometimes *hammams*. All gîtes have to be of recognized quality for inclusion in the ONMT *GTAM* pamphlet (see "Guidebooks", opposite). Most charge around 30–40dh per person for a night and can provide meals.

There are also three *refuge* **huts**, Toubkal (formerly known as Neltner), Tazarhart (formerly known as Lepiney) and Tachdirt, run by the *Club Alpin*; they charge 30dh per person for a bed on average (less for members of Alpine Clubs, more for casual visitors); Toubkal is often fully booked – especially at Easter – and is always crowded in March/April and July/August.

If you are doing anything remotely ambitious, however, you'll need to be prepared to **camp**, for which you will need a tent and warm sleeping bag – nights can be cold, even in summer.

GUIDES AND MULES

Guides can be engaged at Imlil and at a number of the larger villages in the Toubkal region; **mules**, too, can be hired, usually in association with a guide or porter. Rates are around 150dh a day for a guide, 70dh for a mule. One mule can usually be shared among several people – and if you're setting out from Imlil, say, for Lac d'Ifni, or the Toubkal or Tazarhart refuges, it can be a worthwhile investment. Two extras are to be added to the price – a fee to the car park supervisor in Imlil and a tip to the porter at the end. (Payment to all parties, incidentally, is best made at the end of a trip.)

Note that guides are more reluctant – and reasonably so – to work during the month of **Ramadan** (see p.47).

WATER
There are *Giardia* **bacteria** in many of the streams and rivers downriver from human habitation – including the Toubkal trailhead, Imlil. Purification tablets are advisable, as, of course, is boiling the water.

CLOTHES
Even in the summer months you'll need a warm sweater or jacket and preferably a wind-breaker, but tents at this time aren't necessary if you're just ascending Toubkal, so long as you have a good sleeping bag and bivibag/groundsheet. Hiking boots are ideal though you can get by with a decent pair of trainers or jogging shoes. Some kind of hat is essential and sunglasses are helpful.

OTHER THINGS WORTH BRINGING
You can buy **food** in Asni, Imlil and some of the other villages – or negotiate meals – though it gets increasingly expensive the higher and the more remote you get. Taking along a variety of canned food, plus tea or coffee, is a good idea. A quart bottle of **water** is enough because you can refill it regularly; water purification tablets are worthwhile on longer trips, as are stomach pills and insect repellent.

Children are constantly asking you for cigarettes, bon-bons and cadeaux – but it's per-haps better for everyone if you don't give in, and limit **gifts** to those who offer genuine assistance. A worthwhile contribution trekkers can make to the local economy is to trade or give away some of your gear – always welcomed by the guides, who need it.

GUIDEBOOKS/INFORMATION
There are almost limitless Atlas trekking routes, only a selection of which are detailed in these pages. For other ideas, either engage a guide at Imlil, or invest in the Atlas Mountain trekking guidebooks by **Michael Peyron** (West Col) – pick of the bunch, **Robin Collomb** (West Col), or **Karl Smith** (Cicerone Press); you may well find one or other of these books on sale at Imlil or the CAF at Oukaimeden. The booklet *La Grande Traversée des Atlas Marocains*, published by the ONMT, is also useful, listing all the qual-ified guides, *muletiers* and *gîtes*, along with their tarifs. This can be obtained from the London Tourist Office and the English-language guidebooks are also available in Britain (see p.23).

MAPS
Survey-type maps are best obtained in advance – see p.23 – though at Imlil you can usu-ally obtain the 1:50,000 and/or 1:100,000 government-survey sheets covering the Toubkal area. They can also be consulted in the *refuges*.

SKI-TOURING
The Toubkal Massif is popular with **ski-mountaineering** groups from February to April. Most of the *tizis* (cols), and Djebel Toubkal and other peaks, can be ascended, and a *Haute Route* linking the huts is possible. Toubkal summit to Sidi Chamarouch must rank as fine a descent on ski as you'll ever find.

The Toubkal refuge can get pretty crowded at these times, and the Tachdirt refuge (or, for a serious approach in winter, Tazarart refuge) can make better bases.

Auberge de Jeunesse/Youth Hostel, at the far end of the village. Open all year and to all comers, with slightly higher charges for non-IYHF members. There are no cooking facilities and you'll need your own sleeping bag, though blankets can be hired; the location by the river can be very cold in winter. Nonetheless, a friendly place and good meeting point.

Grand Hôtel du Toubkal, on the roadside (☎04/48.45.84). A last chance of luxury before the mountains, this recently refurbished hotel has a bar, swimming pool (filled from June to September) and good meals. It is beautifully decorated and offers magnificent balcony views.

For **meals**, most of the café-stalls will fix you a *tajine* or *harira*, if you don't want to splash out at the *Grand Hôtel*.

Transport

Getting from Asni **to Imlil** is pretty straightforward, with minibuses, pick-ups (*camionettes*) and taxis shuttling back and forth along the 17km of road, along with larger lorries on Saturdays for the *souk*. All normally wait until they fill their passenger quota, though the latter can be chartered; a place is currently 15dh for tourists.

Buses from Asni run to Marrakesh, Moulay Brahim or Ijoukak and – at around 6am – over the Tizi n'Test to Taroudannt (see p.377). A place in a **grand taxi** can be negotiated to Marrakesh (12.5dh), Moulay Brahim (3dh) or Ouirgane (12dh). Buses and taxis leave from the *souk* entrance area.

Walks around Asni and Moulay Brahim

With time to spare, there are many local walks in the fruit-growing areas around Asni and Moulay Brahim, which will get you acclimatized for the higher peaks. They are not much explored and so have a charm of their own. Here are some ideas.

The Kik plateau

The forested slopes above Asni and Moulay Brahim are dominated by a rocky scarp which is the edge of the hidden limestone **Kik plateau**. In spring a walk up here is a delight, with a marvellous spread of alpine flowers and incomparable views. To get the best from it, set off early in the day and carry water; six to eight hours' walking will bring you over the plateau and onto Moulay Brahim or Ouirgane.

Leaving Asni, walk up the Test road to where it swings out of sight (past the red conical hill). Just past a souvenir stall a mule track breaks off and can be seen rising up the hillside. Take this, then fork right to gain the first pass. Turn right again, through fields, and you eventually join the plateau edge, which you can follow to **Moulay Brahim**; leave the crest to join a piste down to the left, which passes big marble quarries just before the village (see p.365). You can also cut down to Asni by a path leaving the route midway along.

An alternative day's trek on the plateau is to make for **Ouirgane**, further south on the Tizi n'Test road (see p.378). On the rise to the plateau keep on, forking left, to the pass/village of TIZI OUADU and then follow the dip where a rough piste crosses. Take this down to the road at TIZI OUZLA and follow the road down, with salt mines apparent below. Turn off right to work through paths to join the Nfis River and follow this to Ouirgane.

Valley approaches

The valleys between Asni/Ouirgane and Imlil (Mizane), Tachdirt (Imenane) and Tizi Oussem (Azzadene) offer fine walks, which you might do to acclimatize yourself prior to tackling Toubkal or other mountains. They are all much easier-going if you walk them downhill – back to Asni/Ouirgane, from which it is easy enough to return to Imlil.

Imlil to Asni. This is a pleasant half-day walk. From Imlil, walk back down the road, then, after about an hour, swap over to the old mule track on the east side of the valley.

Take this path up eventually to a pass and along the trackless crest to the prow that looks to Asni and back to the hills. Descend from here and follow down along the east side of the valley to Asni.

Tachdirt to Asni. There is a long but straightforward trail from Tachdirt downvalley to Asni, taking around seven to nine hours. It's an enjoyable route, through a fine valley with no road or electricity – a good (and neglected) exit from the mountains. You could also do this route from Imlil, heading off towards the trail at the Tizi n'Tamatert (1hr from Imlil), then dropping down to the bottom of the valley at Tinhourine. If you want to camp out a night, en route, there are possible places to pitch a tent below Ikiss or Arg. There are also rooms and soft drinks available at Ikiss and Amsakrou. A fine pass rises opposite Ikiss to cross a tizi to Aguer sioual and so back to Imlil, an excellent round.

Imlil

The trip from Asni to **IMLIL** is a startling transition. Almost as soon as it leaves Asni, the road begins to climb, while below it the valley of the Oued Rhirhaia unfolds before you, heaped with boulders from the terrible flash flood of 1995 (the worst on record). Small villages crowd onto the rocky slopes above.

At Imlil the air feels quite different – silent and rarefied at 1740m – and paths and streams head off in all directions. If you want to make an early start for the Toubkal (Neltner) hut and the ascent of Toubkal, the village – now more or less rebuilt after the flash flood – is a better trailhead than Asni, as is Aroumd (the next village on towards Toubkal – see p.372). It is not advisable to try and reach the Toubkal Hut from Asni in one day.

Accommodation

Imlil comprises a small cluster of houses, along with many provisions shops, a CAF *refuge* and several cafés. There is a fair choice of accommodation.

CAF Refuge. Old-established French Alpine Club *refuge*, rebuilt after the flash flood. It provides bunk beds, camping mattresses and blankets, as well as kitchen and washing facilities and luggage storage; rates (due to rise shortly) are 20dh for a dormitory bed (15dh with IYHF card; 10dh with Alpine Club membership). Open all year round.

Hôtel-Café Soleil, on the square by the river; **Hôtel-Café Aksoual**, facing the *refuge*. Both offer decent rooms and the former does superb *tajines*. ⓪

Hôtel Étoile de Toubkal. As fancy as Imlil gets – and expensive. ②

Kasbah du Toubkal. This tastefully restored Kasbah above Imlil is essentially a field study centre but at most times of year offers traditional accommodation to individuals – and it can be used by campers. Rooms can be booked through the *Hôtel Foucauld* in Marrakesh (☎04/44.54.99) or through the British company *Discover Ltd* (☎01883/744 392). ②

Gîtes. Several houses offer rooms. Among the best are those offered by the guide Aït Idir Mohammed (contact him at the shop behind the concrete route indicator) at his house in Targa Imoule, an eyrie overlooking Imlil; he will take care of your baggage while you go trekking.

Trekking resources and guides

Lahcen Esquary of the "Shopping Centre" is an experienced Atlas guide who speaks English well. The *Ribat Tours* agency also organizes activities. Both shop and agency sell maps and guides, when available. Also helpful is the *Hôtel-Café Soleil* owner, Aziam Brahim, who works for part of the year for a French trekking company, and his brother Ibelaid Brahim. Another source of **information** is the CAF *refuge*, its noticeboard, book and *gardiens* (wardens).

Lahcen Esquary, Aziam and Ibelaid Brahim and Aït Idir Mohammed, are among the most experienced of the **qualified guides** listed in the guides office in the corner of

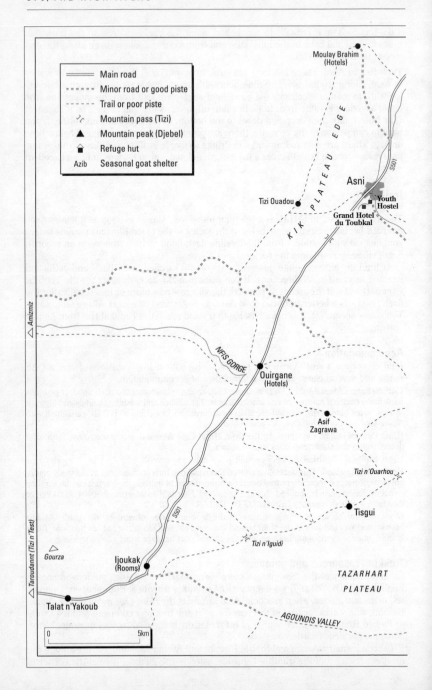

Main road
Minor road or good piste
Trail or poor piste
Mountain pass (Tizi)
Mountain peak (Djebel)
Refuge hut
Azib   Seasonal goat shelter

Moulay Brahim
(Hotels)

KIK PLATEAU EDGE

S501

Asni
Youth
Hostel

Tizi Ouadou

Grand Hotel
du Toubkal

Amizmiz

NFIS GORGE

Ouirgane
(Hotels)

Asif
Zagrawa

Tizi n'Ouarhou

Tisgui

S501

Tizi n'Iguidi

Gourza

Taroudannt (Tizi n'Test)

Ijoukak
(Rooms)

TAZARHART

PLATEAU

Talat n'Yakoub

AGOUNDIS VALLEY

0   5km

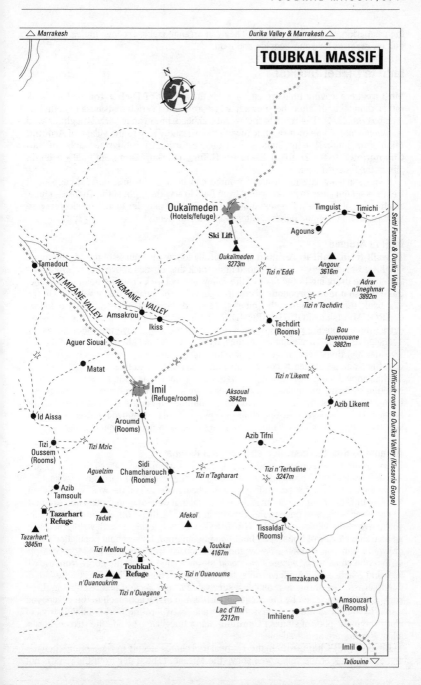

TOUBKAL MASSIF

N

Oukaïmeden
(Hotels/fefuge)

Ski Lift

Oukaïmeden
3273m

Timguist Timichi

Agouns

Angour
3616m

Adrar
n'Ineghmar
3892m

Tamadout

AÏT MIZANE VALLEY

INEMANE VALLEY

Amsakrou

Ikiss

Tizi n'Eddi

Tizi n'Tachdirt

Tachdirt
(Rooms)

Bou
Iguenouane
3882m

Aguer Sioual

Matat

Imil
(Refuge/rooms)

Aksoual
3842m

Tizi n'Likemt

Azib Likemt

Id Aissa

Aroumd
(Rooms)

Azib Tifni

Tizi
Oussem
(Rooms)

Tizi Mzic

Aguelzim

Sidi
Chamcharouch
(Rooms)

Tizi n'Tagharart

Tizi n'Terhaline
3247m

Azib
Tamsoult

Tazarhart
Refuge

Tadat

Afekoï

Tazarhart
3845m

Tizi Melloul

Toubkal
4167m

Tissaldaï
(Rooms)

Toubkal
Refuge

Ras
n'Ouanoukrim

Tizi n'Ouagane

Tizi n'Ouanoums

Timzakane

Lac d'Ifni
2312m

Amsouzart
(Rooms)

Imhilene

Imlil

△ Setti Fatma & Ourika Valley

△ Difficult route to Ourika Valley (Kissaria Gorge)

the car park near the CAF Refuge. They can arrange treks, ascents, mules, camping, guides, *gardiens* for your baggage and food.

Imlil to Djebel Toubkal

Most trekkers leaving Imlil are en route for the **ascent of Djebel Toubkal** – a walk rather than a climb, after the snows have cleared, but a serious business nonetheless (see box on p.374). The route to the ascent trailhead, however, is fairly straightforward – and enjoyable in its own right, following the Mizane Valley to the village of **Aroumd** (4km from Imlil; 1hr–1hr 30mins) and thence through the pilgrim hamlet of **Sidi Chamarouch** to the **Toubkal (Neltner) Refuge** (3200m; 12km from Imlil – 5–6hr in all), at the foot of Toubkal.

If you start out late in the day, Aroumd can be a useful first base, though most trekkers set out early to mid-morning from Imlil to stay the night at the Toubkal refuge, starting out at first light the next morning for Toubkal in order to get the clearest possible panorama from its heights. Afternoons can be cloudy.

Imlil to Aroumd

To **walk from Imlil to Aroumd**, you basically follow the course of the Mizane river. On the west side there's a well-defined mule track that zigzags above the river for about 2km before dropping to the floor of the valley, just before a crossing point to Aroumd; there is also a more circuitous piste, driveable in a reasonably hardy vehicle. On the east bank, there's a rough path – much the same distance but slightly harder to follow.

AROUMD (aka AROUND, AREMD) is the largest village of the Mizane Valley, an extraordinary-looking place, built on a huge moraine spur above the valley at 1840m. Terraced fields of corn, potatoes, onions, barley and various kinds of fruit line the valley sides and there is some grazing, too; the village streets are often blocked by goats or cattle – and permanently covered in animal excrement and flies.

This notwithstanding, Aroumd is very much on the trekking circuit. A British trekking company maintains a base in the village and there is a now a café and **guest-house/campsites** by the river, and quite a number of **rooms** for rent in the village houses. There is as yet only one shop – despite a population of five hundred – so if you lack the energy to arrange a meal, take along food from Asni or Imlil.

Aroumd to Sidi Chamarouch and Toubkal Refuge

From Aroumd, the **Toubkal trail** goes up the flood plain then follows the east (ie the Aroumd) side of the Mizane, climbing and zigzagging round the hard, grey rocks, high above the river. If you have been following the main mule trail on the west side of the valley from Imlil to Aroumd, you can join the Toubkal trail without going round into Aroumd.

The river is crossed once more, 1hr 30min to 2hr further from Aroumd, just before you arrive at the village of **SIDI CHAMAROUCH**. Set beside a small waterfall, this is an anarchic cluster of houses, all built one into another. Its seasonal population of ten or twelve run soft drinks/grocery shops for tourist trekkers and for Moroccan pilgrims, who come to the village's *marabout* shrine – sited across the gorge from the village and reached by a modern concrete bridge which non-Muslims are strictly forbidden to cross. The shrine is probably a survival of a very ancient nature cult – in these parts often thinly veiled by the trappings of Islam. (On the approach to the village you might have noticed a tree, sacred to local tradition, where the Berbers hang strips of cloth and make piles of stones.) **Camping** below the village, beside the stream, is possible. **Rooms** are also available.

Beyond Sidi Chamarouch, the Toubkal trail climbs steeply in zigzags and then traverses the flank of the valley well above the Mizane. (The water from the river is not safe to drink untreated until you get above the Toubkal hut, though the smaller streams and springs by the path are said to be safe.) The trail, however, is pretty clear the whole way to the **Toubkal Refuge**, which, at 3207m, marks the spring snow line. In winter the snow line can drop to Sidi Chamarouch and mules have to be replaced by porters if one wants assistance to the Toubkal Hut.

The Toubkal Refuge

Even in mid-August it gets pretty cold up at the **Toubkal Refuge** (formely *Refuge Neltner*) once the sun has disappeared behind the ridge. You will probably, therefore, want to take advantage of its shelter. The hut is open all year and charges 30dh per person for a bed (22.50dh with IYHF card; 10dh with Alpine Club membership). The *gardien* is usually prepared to cook meat or vegetable *tajine* for guests (about 25dh per person), though beware that the hut can be very busy – and crowded. It is badly in need of extension.

Another reason for staying at the *refuge* is that the area around is covered in rubbish (human waste, too), so if you plan on **camping** nearby, you'll want to go some way upstream or use the meadows a bit down from the hut.

Climbing Toubkal

At the Toubkal *refuge* you're almost bound to meet people who have just come down from **Djebel Toubkal** – and you should certainly take advantage of talking to them (and/or the *refuge gardien*) for an up-to-the-minute description of the routes and the state of the South Cirque trail to the summit. If you don't feel too confident about going it alone, take a guide – they are usually available at the *refuge* – but don't let them try and rush you up the mountain.

THE SOUTH CIRQUE

The **South Cirque** (*Ikkibi Sud*) is the most popular and straightforward ascent of Toubkal and, depending on your fitness, should take between 2hr 30min and 3hr 30min hours (2–2hr 30min coming down). It is now a well-worn route and with reasonable instructions on the spot is easy enough to follow without a guide. More of a problem – and something you should be careful about at any time of the year – is finding the right track down. It is easy to find yourself in fields of loose scree.

The **trail** begins above the Toubkal hut, dropping down to cross the stream and then climbing over a short stretch of grass and rock to reach the first of Toubkal's innumerable fields of boulders and scree. These – often needing three steps to gain one – are the most tiring (and memorable) feature of the trek up, and gruelling for inexperienced walkers. The summit, a triangular plateau of stones marked by a tripod, is eventually reached after a lot of zigzagging up out of the cirque.

It should be reiterated that **in winter even this ascent is a snow climb** and not for walkers.

THE NORTH CIRQUE

Robin Collomb, in his *Atlas Mountains* guide, recommends the **North Cirque** (*Ikkibi Nord*) as an alternative – though longer (4hr 30min) and more ambitious – ascent. En route you will pass the remains of an aircraft (it crashed while flying arms to Biafra) and the small peak of Tibherine has its engine as a cairn. The final ridge to the summit area calls for some scrambling and in general the route calls for experience.

The Toubkal Refuge to Lac d'Ifni and beyond

Lac d'Ifni is one of the largest mountain lakes in the Atlas – and the only one of any size in the Toubkal region. From the *refuge* it's about 4–5hr trek, again involving long, tedious stretches over loose rock and scree, and with odd stretches of snow remaining

> ## CLIMBING TOUBKAL AND OTHER SUMMITS
>
> **Toubkal** and the other **major summits** should always be treated as serious efforts. In winter they are only for properly equipped and experienced mountaineers and strictly out-of-bounds for walkers. Even in late spring, if the icy snow has lingered on, they may need ice axe and crampons to justify proceeding. There have been fatalities among inexperienced, ill-equipped walkers going out onto steep snow and slipping, so this is not an alarmist warning. If in doubt, turn back. There are trained guides at Imlil who can rent equipment and lead ascents (and show their qualifications/ID card); do not use casual "guides" encountered along the way, who will often not know the route themselves.
>
> All the area up behind Toubkal – **Lac d'Ifni and beyond** – needs to be treated as a proper expedition, too, and hiring a local guide is strongly recommended.

into July. On the way back, the scree scrambling is even more pronounced. To make the trip worthwhile, take along enough food for a couple of days' camping; there are no facilities of any kind en route.

Toubkal to Lac d'Ifni

The **Lac d'Ifni trail** begins at the Toubkal hut, climbing up a rough, stony slope and then winding round to the head of the Mizane Valley towards the imposing *tizi* (or pass) of **Tizi n'Ouanoums**. The pass is reached in about an hour and the path is reasonably easy to follow. The trail up the pass itself is a good, gravel path, zigzagging continually until you reach the summit (3664m), a narrow platform between two shafts of rock.

The views from the *tizi* are superb, taking in the whole route that you've covered and, in the distance to the south, the hazy green outline of the lake (which disappears from view as you descend). At this point the hard work seems over – but this is a totally false impression! The path down the valley to Lac d'Ifni is slow, steep progress, the scree slopes are apparently endless, and the lake doesn't come back into sight until you are almost there. It is, in fact, virtually enclosed by the mountains, and by what look like demolished hills – great heaps of rubble and boulders.

Lac d'Ifni is a fine sight, its only human habitations a few shepherds' huts, and the only sound that of water idly lapping on the shore; it is exceptionally deep – up to 50m over much of its area. It makes a poor campsite, however, with scrubby terraces, somewhat fly-ridden by day, and no drinking water source (the lake waters are polluted). You can camp much more enjoyably by carrying on for another hour until you reach the first patches of irrigated valley, high above the village of Imhilene.

On from Lac d'Ifni: a loop to Tachdirt or Imlil

Most people return from Lac d'Ifni to the Toubkal *refuge* by the same route but it's quite feasible to make a longer, anticlockwise, loop towards **Tachdirt** or **Imlil**.

LAC D'IFNI TO SIDI CHAMAROUCH

From the lake, you can strike east to the valley above IMHILENE, and beyond it to the Kasbah-like village of AMSOUZART, reached in around three hours. There is a café/campsite here and gîte accommodation and meals at Omar's house; ask for him at the café or shop, which is your last chance of supplies on this route.

At Amsouzart, the path to the north follows the west bank for the river, reaching the village of TISSALDAÏ in about four hours; camping is possible in the valley above. From here, it is at least four hours of strenuous trekking to get up the **Tizi n'Terhaline** (3247m). It is worth all the effort, as you descend into a beautiful valley. After about two hours' walking from the pass, you will reach AZIB TIFNI, a collection of shepherds' huts, none more than a metre high.

You can then follow the valley west over another high pass, Tizi n'Tagharat to descend steeply to **Sidi Chamarouch**.

THE LOOP TO TACHDIRT
An alternative route from AZIB TIFNI (see opposite) is to follow the valley to the east, into one of the magnificent gorges of this region. Crossing the first pass, you can camp easily near AZIB LIKEMT (2hr from Azib Tifni), beyond which another more demanding pass, the high **Tizi n'Likemt** (3555m) leads to Tachdirt CAF refuge; also good camping on the Tizi Likemt side of the valley by springs. From the beginning of October, these *azibs* are empty as the valley becomes completely cut off in winter.

The country east of Azib Likemt, The Kissaria Gorges, is wild in the extreme (too hard even for mules!), so it is inadvisable to try and reach the Ourika Valley that way.

If making this loop and including Toubkal it is strongly advisable to go in the other direction to gain acclimatization and fitness before climbing the mountain.

Tachdirt and beyond

Tachdirt (3000m), 8km east of Imlil, is an alternative and in many ways more attractive base for trekking expeditions. As at Imlil, there is a CAF *refuge*, and a fine range of local treks and onward routes. But despite its comparatively easy access – a pleasant mule track up the valley over Tizi n'Tamatert (more direct than the tortuously winding piste) – the village sees only a handful of the trekkers who make it up to Toubkal.

You can walk the **mulepath from Imlil** in three to four hours, or on Saturdays there is a Berber **lorry** (for the Asni *souk*) along the piste. There is only one small shop in the village (soft drinks are sold at the refuge), so take along your own food. The **CAF refuge** (20dh a bed; cooking facilities and some supplies available through the *gardien*) is just above the trail on the left-hand side as you enter the village; it's kept locked, but the *gardien* should soon appear. He can arrange a guide and mules. There is also a gîte in the village.

Tachdirt to Setti Fatma
This is one of the more obvious routes for anyone contemplating anything beyond a simple day-trip into the hills. Taken at a reasonably human pace, the route can be accomplished in two days' walking from Tachdirt. There is a well-defined trail all the way, used by locals (who take mules along the whole length), so no particular skills are demanded beyond general fitness and a head for heights. Several sections of the trail are quite exposed and steep.

You'll probably want to carry some food supplies with you. However, meals are offered at the village of Timichi, so cooking gear and provisions are not essential. If you are carrying gear, you might want to hire mules at Tachdirt.

TACHDIRT TO TIMICHI
Tachdirt to Timichi is a superb day's walk. The first three hours or so are spent climbing up to the Tizi n'Tachdirt (3616m), with ever more spectacular views. The character of the valley changes abruptly after the pass, green terraced fields giving way to rough and craggy mountain slopes. The path down is one of the more exposed sections of the route. As you approach Timichi the valley again becomes more green and vegetated.

TIMICHI's gîte is a welcoming place, with a very helpful *gardien*, who offers a tempting range of meals. If you arrive reasonably early in the day, you can explore up the main valley to Agounns, dominated by Angour. There is a spectacular pass over to Oukaïmeden.

TIMICHI TO SETTI FATMA
Timichi to Setti Fatma is another beautiful trek, taking about half a day. At first you follow the river fairly closely but soon the track climbs upward, to about 1000 or 1500ft above the riverbed. There is little water available for several miles, and the track is perched on the side of the extremely steep valley. You finally join up with a piste that zigzags down into the Ourika Valley about 2km north of Setti Fatma. An adventurous option is to abandon the piste as soon as it is reached and keep down by (and occasionally in) the stream, an easy but impressive introduction to a Moroccan speciality of gorge-travelling.

Tachdirt to Oukaïmeden
This is a fairly straightforward route – a three- to four-hour walk over a reasonable mule track by way of the 2960m **Tizi n'Eddi**.

The Angour Traverse
Hiking along the ridge of Angour is pretty demanding, taking a full day from Tachdirt and (if the weather turns on you) demanding a night's bivouac. It requires basic climbing skills.

From Tachdirt, the trail zigzags up the left-hand side of the **Imenane Valley** up towards **Tizi n'Tachdirt** (which remains visible the whole way). At the pass (a three-and-a-half-hour steep walk, taking you up to 3616m), a path climbs due north up a rough, grassy slope, to break through crags onto the sloping **plateau**, which can be followed to the **summit of Angour**. This plateau is an unusual feature on a peak with such dramatic cliffs. It is split by a valley. With care, you can follow a ridge down from here to **Tizi n'Eddi** (to pick up the Oukaïmeden trail), or break away straight down to Tachdirt. A guide would be useful.

Tachdirt to Imlil via Tizi n'Aguersioual
An alternative route back from **Tachdirt to Imlil** is by way of **Tizi n'Aguersioual**. This takes you down-valley to the hamlets of TINERHOURHINE (1hr) and IKISS (15min further down; soft drinks/rooms). From Ikiss a good path on the other side of the valley (ask someone to point it out) leads up to the Aguersioual pass and then zigzags down to the village of AGUERSIOUAL, from where you can follow the Asni road back up to Imlil.

West of Imlil: Tizi Oussem and the Tazarhart Refuge

The area west of Imlil and the Djebel Toubkal trail offers a good acclimatization trek to **Tizi Oussem**, harder treks to the south to the **Tazarhart Refuge** (accessible also, from the Toubkal refuge), and the possibility of one- or two-day treks **out to Ouirgane or Ijoukak** on the Tizi n'Test road, or back to the Asni–Imlil road at **Tamadout**.

Tizi Oussem and on to Ouirgane
The village of **TIZI OUSSEM** is in the next valley west of Imlil and is reached in about four hours over the Tizi Mzic; the track is not that easy to find and has suffered badly from the 1995 flood, so ask for initial directions. The most interesting section is the path down from the pass to the village. If you are heading for the Tazarhart refuge, another path from the pass follows round the hillside to Azib Tamsoult, and then to the gorge for the Tazarhart hut. The valley itself offers a long day's trek **down to Ouirgane** on the Tizi n'Test road. At its foot it becomes a piste, but this wanders off to the right and you should abandon it in order to go left and, with luck, arrive at the *Au Sanglier Qui Fume* in Ouirgane (see p.378). Experienced walkers can make a three-day expedition

to reach **Ijoukak**, with two camps en route, one just below the Tizi Ouarhou (2672 height on 100,000 map) and the second before the Tizi n' Iguidi.

The **route to Ouirgane** has been made more difficult because of the flood damage (the valley bed is utterly destroyed). From Tizi Oussen you need to keep to the east bank initially and then drop onto the flood plain to ensure facing the west bank at a narrowing (Aït Ouissàdene on map). The path keeps high then zigzags down to cross the river to gain height on the east side, passing the walled farm of Azerfsane. The path swings west and drops to the river where the piste used to end. A mule track on the left bank helps them cross to pull up to a spur with a commanding view to the rich Ourigane (Wirgane) valley. When the piste veers off cut down and follow cultivation paths on the left bank (or use the bare valley bottom) to reach the main road and the accommodation options.

One can also reach Asni by keeping to the east bank and a rising path, then piste, over the **Tizi n'Tacht** to reach the Asni-Imlil piste at Tamadout.

The Tazarhart Refuge and around

The **Tazarhart Refuge** (formely known as the *Refuge Lepiney*) is some 6hr 30min to 7hr 30min from Imlil and essentially a rock-climbing base for the fine cliffs of **Tazaghârt**. To get access, you (or a porter) may have to go down to the village of Tizi Oussem to get the hut *gardien*, Omar Abdallah, who is also a very good (and extremely pleasant) guide; he can arrange a room in the village, too. Details of a number of climbs from the *refuge* are given in the Collomb guide, but be warned that in winter they require crampons and ice axes – and climbing experience; there was a fatal accident here in 1989, involving an organized trekking party.

Tizi Melloul (3–4hr from the Tazarhart refuge) allows trekking access to Tazarghârt (3843m), an extraordinary plateau and fine vantage point. You can also cross Tizi Melloul and, with one camp or bivouac, walk **down the Agoundis Valley to Ijoukak**. The Agoundia Valley can also be reached over the Tizi n'Ouagane at the head of the Neltner Valley.

Tizi n'Test: Ijoukak, Ouirgane and Tin Mal

The **Tizi n'Test**, the road that extends beyond Asni to Taroudant or Taliouine, is unbelievably impressive. Cutting right through the heart of the Atlas, it was blasted out of the mountains by the French from 1926 to 1932 – the first modern route to link Marrakesh with the Souss plain and the desert, and an extraordinary feat of pioneer-spirit engineering. Until then, it had been considered impracticable without local protection and knowledge: an important pass for trade and for the control and subjugation of the south, but one that few sultans were able to make their own.

Through much of the last century – and the beginning of the twentieth – the pass was the personal fief of the **Goundafi** clan, whose huge Kasbahs still dominate many of the crags and strategic turns along the way. Much earlier it had served as the refuge and power base of the Almohads, and it was from the holy city of **Tin Mal**, up towards the pass, that they launched their attack on the Almoravid dynasty. As remote and evocative a mountain stronghold as could be imagined, Tin Mal is an excursion well worth making for the chance to see the carefully restored ruins of the twelfth-century mosque, a building close in spirit to the Koutoubia, and for once accessible to non-Muslims.

Practicalities

If you are setting out by **bus from Marrakesh,** you should have three choices, leaving at either 5am (sometimes 6am), 2pm or 6pm. The 5am/6am bus is the only direct one to Taroudannt (7hr 30min), but the others go as far as Ijoukak (4hr); the 2pm bus stops there, and the 6pm one goes on to Taliouine (arriving, after a scary night descent, at around 1–2am). It's important to turn up at least half an hour early if you want tickets on the morning bus. If you're **coming from Asni**, you can pick up any of these buses a little over an hour after they leave Marrakesh.

For anyone **driving**, some experience of mountain roads is essential. The route is well contoured and paved, but between the pass and the intersection with the P32, the Taliouine–Taroudannt road, it is extremely narrow (one and half times a car's width) with almost continuous hairpin bends and blind corners. Since you can actually see for some distance ahead, this isn't as dangerous as it sounds – but you still need a lot of confidence and have to watch out for suicidal local drivers bearing down on you without any intention of stopping or slowing down. Bus and lorry drivers are, fortunately, more considerate. If you are driving a hire car, which is liable to overheat, try to avoid driving the route at midday in the summer months.

From November to the end of April, the pass is occasionally blocked with **snow**. When this occurs, a sign is put up on the roadside at the point where the Asni–Test road leaves Marrakesh and on the roadside past Tahanoute.

The road to the pass

Heading out on the dawn bus from Marrakesh, you have the least interesting part of the Taroudannt journey to catch up on lost sleep. The landscape over the first hour of the Haouz plain to TAHANOUTE (Tuesday souk) is fairly monotonous up until the gorges of the Moulay Brahim up to Asni. There is some 'Badlands' scenery (forested to stop erosion) and you can see salt leaking from the soil before a rich basin and a second watershed leads to the bigger Ouirgane basin. If you are driving, the road off to the right to the *Residence Ourigane* (see below) is worth following for the view alone.

Ouirgane and the Nfis gorges

OUIRGANE is a tiny place, long touted by French guidebooks as a beautiful valley and *étape gastronomique*. In the early hours of an Atlas morning, coming from Marrakesh, this might not be much of an attraction, but after trekking around Toubkal, it is a wonderful place – with a dash of luxury – to lie around and recover. It is also a very pleasant base in itself for day walks, mountain-bike forays or horse riding. It hosts a Thursday *souk*.

There are three **hotels**. The *Résidence de la Roseraie* (☎4 through the operator; ④), is a grand four-star place, with a swimming pool, sauna, tennis and prices to match. It offers horse riding: 250dh for a half day, 3500dh for a week's package, including two nights at the hotel. You should bring your own helmet. A lot cheaper is *Au Sanglier Qui Fume* (☎9 through the operator; ③), across the river. This has a series of cool chalet-type rooms, scattered round a garden and small pool. Mules for local treks can be arranged here and there's good food. Evidence of the 1995 floods is still to be seen, with the garden piled with huge boulders. There are also simple, pleasant rooms at the *Café Badaoui*. Lastly, high on a viewpoint hill is the new *Residence Ourigane* (☎02/11.74.47), built in traditional style in superb gardens.

Trekking up behind Ouirgane, one rewarding route is to head for **Tizi Ouadou** and the **Kik plateau** – and then down to Asni and back by taxi. Rather more ambitiously, you could strike northwest to Amizmiz, by way of the Nfis gorges.

OUIRGANE TO AMIZMIZ: THE NFIS GORGES

From Ouirgane, a seven-hour walk by the **Nfis gorges** leads to **AMIZMIZ**, which has regular bus and *grand taxi* connections with Marrakesh along the S507 (to/from the

Bab Er Robb). It is also the site of a long-established **Tuesday souk**, one of the largest Berber markets of the Atlas, and not on the tourist trail. The town itself comprises several quite distinct quarters – including a *zaouia,* Kasbah and former Mellah – separated by a small ravine. **Accommodation** is available at the basic (but licensed) *Hôtel de France.*

Ijoukak

Moving on, a good trailhead for exploring the Tizi n'Test area is **IJOUKAK**. The village has a few basic shops and four small **cafés**, but unfortunately nowhere decent to stay. *Guide Collomb* indicates a CAF-supervised hut at Ijoukak, but it is actually the state forestry house and does not welcome guests.

Walking out from Ijoukak, you can easily explore Tin Mal and Talâat n'Yacoub (see pp.381–3) or try some more prolonged **trekking in the Nfis and Agoundis valleys** – see below. The Agoundis can also be enjoyable just as a day's wandering, if you have nothing more ambitious in mind, or you can take the winding forestry road up the hill dominating the village for its commanding view.

Trekking around Ijoukak

Ijoukak gives access to some of the most enjoyable trekking in the High Atlas – all much less developed than the main Toubkal area. Starting from the village, you can trek east up the **Agoundis Valley towards Toubkal**, or west up the long **Ogdemt Valley**. The region to the **west of the Tizi n'Test road** is wilder still; for details – in reverse – of the trek to Afensou and Imi n'Tanoute (on the Marrakesh–Agadir road), see the "Tichka Plateau treks" section at the end of this chapter.

The **survey map** for the area (if you can get hold of it) is *Tizi n'Test* (1.100,000).

Agoundis Valley

East from Ijoukak winds the **Agoundis River Valley**. It offers alternative access to Toubkal, but is seldom used. To reach the Toubkal Refuge would take two days of serious trekking. However, if "peak bagging" is not part of your plan, you could still enjoy a day's trek or an overnight trip up this way.

From Ijoukak walk back down the road towards Marrakesh until you cross the river (200m). A dirt road leads off to your right. A small sign there warns you not to fish for trout in the river. This road continues along the valley for about 10km. It's used by lorries hauling ore from the mines. If you're in a hurry, you could hitch a lift; otherwise, the walk is a pleasant one. There are several villages strung out along the valley making use of the year-round water to farm small patches in the river bottom and on the terraced hillsides. About 2km down the road there is a small square hut below the road on the right. It's a **watermill** which is fascinating to watch if you happen to catch someone inside. Another 3km further and you'll pass an abandoned **rock-crushing factory**, its huge tin and timber structure half falling down. In the house just beyond it, to the west, Ibrahim and Abdallah Jhouliyine offer **rooms** and **meals**. Just beyond is the village of **TAGHBART**.

The road splits after 8km, the right fork descending to the river, crossing and continuing on into the mountains to the south. Take the left fork (get off the lorry if you've hitched this far) and follow it as it curves round to the left, to the northeast. At the curve is another village, **EL MAKHZEN**. The road has now been extended a couple of kilometres to **TIJRHICHT**. Along this last section is an ingeniously constructed irrigation ditch hugging the cliffside beneath the road. Here the road ends and a mule trail begins. If you've hitched up here, it probably will have taken you no more than half an hour; on foot it's about two to three hours.

The **trail towards Toubkal refuge** begins to climb into a narrowing limestone gorge with the river a great distance below. Tiny Berber villages are perched on rocky outcrops every 2–3km. Good views in both directions. Toubkal finally appears, rising above the upper reaches of the valley.

At **AÏT YOUB** (8km from the end of the road), you will have reached the last and highest cultivated areas (1900m). *Guide Collomb* estimates 3hr 30min to arrive this far, with the help of the occasional lift. Figure on six to eight hours' walking, depending on your fitness.

Toubkal refuge and **Djebel Toubkal** are another long day's trek from here. It's possible to hire a mule and a muleteer, who acts as a guide simply because he knows the way. However, this is not as straightforward and organized as in more frequented places like Imlil. This far into the mountains it is unlikely that you will find anyone who speaks English, but with simple French or Arabic phrases you should be understood.

If you wish to continue on foot alone, *Guide Collomb* is helpful from here. Keep in mind that snow can impede your crossing the pass until midsummer. In any case, you'll need to stay overnight in Aït Youb. Camping should be no problem. It's usually best to ask permission for politeness' sake. When you ask, be prepared for an offer of hospitality and a night's stay in the village. You're in no way imposing by accepting it, but it is understood in all but a few cases that you'll offer something in return when you leave. It will customarily be turned down at least once but usually accepted with persistence on your part. In winter/spring it is perhaps best to descend the Agoendis. It is easier to retreat from the Neltuer side of the Tizi n'Ouagane is deemed impassable.

Ougdemt Valley

West from Ijoukak and the Agoundis Valley lies the **Ougdemt**, a long, pleasant valley filled with Berber villages surrounded by walnut groves.

A dirt road for lorries now stretches for several kilometres up the valley from **MZOUZITE** (3km beyond Tin Mal and 8km from Ijoukak). Beyond this, a trail continues winding up along the river to **ARG** at the head of the valley (6–7hr walking). From Arg you could go for **Djebel Erdouz** (3579m) to the north of Tizi n'Tighfist (2895m), or the higher **Djebel Igdat** to the south (3616m), by way of Tizi n'Oumslama. Both are fairly straightforward when following the mule paths to the passes and can be reached in five to six hours from Arg. Be sure to take your own water in summer as the lower elevations can be dry. A two to three-day traverse of these peaks on to Djebel Gourza (3280m) and down to Tinmal is a challenging adventure. The east ridge of Erdouz gives serious scrambling.

For the very adventurous, a further expedition could be undertaken **all the way to the Tichka plateau** – summer grazing pastures at the headwaters of the Nfis River – and across the other side to the Marrakesh–Agadir road. This would take at least six days from the Tizi n'Test road and require you to carry provisions (and water in summer) for several days at a time.

For a detailed route description, see Peyron's *Great Atlas Traverse*. A brief summary of this trail, taken from the opposite direction, follows in the "Tichka Plateau treks" section on p.387.

Idni and the pass

At **IDNI**, well up on the pass, the small *Café Igdet* has very basic rooms (with bed mats), as well as preparing hot meals and tea. The old *Hôtel Alpina* has long ago closed. From the hamlet, a path zigzags down to the Nfis which can then be followed out to the main road again.

The **Tizi n'Test** (2093m) lies 18km south of Idni. There's a **café-restaurant**, the *Cassecroute*, just to the south of the pass, where you can normally get buses either to drop you off or pick you up. From the summit of the pass a piste rises up towards a platform mounted by a TV relay station. The views down to the Souss Valley and back towards Toubkal can be stunning. There is also a piste (path direct for the tizi to join it) leading down to Souk Sebt on the Nfis. Descending this and following the Nfis east is a good trip; one bivouac.

Over the pass, the **descent towards Taroudannt/Taliouine** is hideously dramatic: a drop of some 1600m in little over 30km. Throughout, there are stark, fabulous vistas of the peaks, and occasionally, hundreds of feet below, a mountain valley and cluster of villages. Taroudannt is reached in around 2hr 30min to 3hr Taliouine in a little more; coming up, needless to say, it all takes a good deal longer. For details on Taroudannt and Taliouine, see Chapter Eight.

Tin Mal Mosque

The **Tin Mal Mosque**, quite apart from its historic and architectural importance, is a beautiful ruin – isolated above a lush reach of river valley, with stack upon stack of pink

IBN TOUMERT AND THE ALMOHADS

Tin Mal's site seems now so remote that it is difficult to imagine a town ever existing in this valley. In some form, though, it did. It was here that **Ibn Toumert** and his lieutenant, **Abd El Moumen**, preached to the Berber tribes and welded them into the **Almohad** ("unitarian") movement; here that they set out on the campaigns which culminated in the conquest of all Morocco and southern Spain; and here, too, a century and a half later, that they made their last stand against the incoming Merenid dynasty.

This history – so decisive in the development of the medieval Shereefian empire – is outlined in "The Historical Framework" in *Contexts*. More particular to Tin Mal are the circumstances of Ibn Toumert's arrival and the appeal of his puritan, reforming teaching to the local tribes. Known to his followers as the *Mahdi* – "The Chosen One", whose coming is prophesied in the Koran – Toumert was himself born in the High Atlas, a member of the Berber-speaking Masmouda tribe, who held the desert-born Almoravids, the ruling dynasty, in traditional contempt. He was an accomplished theologian and studied at the centres of eastern Islam, a period in which he formulated the strict Almohad doctrines, based on the assertion of the unity of God and on a verse of the Koran in which Muhammad set out the role of religious reform: "to reprove what is disapproved and enjoy what is good". For Toumert, Almoravid Morocco contained much to disapprove of and, returning from the East with a small group of disciples, he began to preach against all manifestations of luxury – above all, wine and performance of music – and against women mixing in male society.

In 1121, Toumert and his group arrived in Marrakesh, the Almoravid capital, where they began to provoke the sultan. Ironically, this was not an easy task – Ali Ben Youssef, one of the most pious rulers in Moroccan history, accepted many of Toumert's charges and forgave his insults. It was only in 1124, when the reformer struck Ali's sister from her horse for riding unveiled (as was desert tradition), that the Almohads were finally banished from the city and took refuge in the mountain stronghold of Tin Mal.

From the beginning in this exiled residence, Ibn Toumert and Abd El Moumen set out to mould the Atlas Berbers into a religious and military force. They taught prayers in Arabic by giving each follower as his name a word from the Koran and then lining them all up to recite it. They also stressed the significance of the "second coming" and Toumert's role as *Mahdi*. More significant, perhaps, was the savage military emphasis of the new order. Hesitant tribes were branded "hypocrites" and massacred – most notoriously in the Forty-Day Purge of the mountains – and within eight years none remained outside Almohad control. In the 1130s, after Ibn Toumert had died, Abd El Moumen began to attack and "convert" the plains. In 1145, he was able to take Fes and, in 1149, just 25 years after the march of exile, his armies entered and sacked Marrakesh.

Atlas peaks towering beyond its arches. It has recently been restored and re-opened and is a highly worthwhile stop if you're driving the Tizi n'Test. If you're staying at Ijoukak, it's an easy eight-kilometre walk, passing en route the old Goundafi Kasbah in Talaat n' Yacoub (see below). You can return on the opposite side of the Nfis.

The mosque is set a little way above the modern village of TIN MAL (or IFOURIREN) and reached by wandering uphill, across a roadbridge. It is kept locked, but the *gardien* will soon spot you, open it up and let you look round undisturbed (10dh admission – and a tip is expected by the *gardien*). It is used by villages for the Friday service and closed to non-Muslims on that day.

The mosque

The **Tin Mal Mosque** was built by Abd El Moumen around 1153–54, partly as a memorial and cult centre for Ibn Toumert and partly as his own family mausoleum. Obviously fortified, it probably served also as a section of the town's defences, since in the early period of Almohad rule, Tin Mal was entrusted with the state treasury. Today, it is the only part of the fortifications – indeed, of the entire Almohad city – that you can make out with any clarity. The rest was sacked and largely destroyed in the Merenid conquest of 1276 – a curiously late event, since all of the main Moroccan cities had already been in the new dynasty's hands for some thirty years.

That Tin Mal remained standing for that long, and that its mosque was maintained, says a lot about the power Toumert's teaching must have continued to exercise over the local Berbers. Even two centuries later the historian Ibn Khaldun found Koranic readers employed at the tombs, and when the French began restoration in the 1930s they found the site littered with the shrines of *marabouts*.

Architecturally, Tin Mal presents a unique opportunity for non-Muslims to take a look at the interior of a traditional Almohad mosque. It is roofless, for the most part, and two of the corner pavilion towers have disappeared, but the *mihrab* (or prayer niche) and the complex pattern of internal arches are substantially intact.

The arrangement is in a classic Almohad design – the T-shaped plan with a central aisle leading towards the *mihrab* – and is virtually identical to that of the Koutoubia in Marrakesh, more or less its contemporary. The one element of eccentricity is in the placing of the **minaret** (which you can climb for a view of the general layout) over the *mihrab*: a weakness of engineering design that meant it could never have been much taller than it is today.

In terms of decoration, the most striking feature is the variety and intricacy of the **arches** – above all those leading into the *mihrab*, which have been sculpted with a stalactite vaulting. In the **corner domes** and the **mihrab vault,** this technique is extended with impressive effect. Elsewhere, and on the face of the *mihrab*, it is the slightly austere geometric patterns and familiar motifs (the palmette, rosette, scallop, etc), of Almohad decorative gates that are predominant.

The Goundafi Kasbahs

The **Goundafi Kasbahs** don't really compare with Tin Mal – nor with the Glaoui Kasbah in Telouet (detailed in the following Tizi n'Tichka section). But, as so often in Morocco, they provide an extraordinary assertion of just how recent is the country's feudal past. Despite their medieval appearance, the buildings are all nineteenth- or even twentieth-century creations.

Talâat n'Yacoub and other Kasbahs

The more important of the Kasbahs is the former Goundafi stronghold and headquarters near the village of **TALÂAT N'YACOUB**. Coming from Ijoukak, this is reached off to the right of the main road, down a very French-looking, tree-lined country lane; it is 6km south of Ijoukak, 3km north of Tin Mal.

The **Kasbah**, decaying, partially ruined and probably pretty unsafe, lies at the far end of the village. Nobody seems to mind if you take a look inside, though you need to avoid the dogs near its entrance. The inner part of the palace-fortress, though blackened from a fire, is reasonably complete and retains traces of its decoration.

It is difficult to establish the exact facts with these old tribal Kasbahs, but it seems that it was constructed late in the nineteenth century for the next-to-last Goundafi chieftain. A feudal warrior in the old tradition, he was constantly at war with the sultan during the 1860s and 1870s, and a bitter rival of the neighbouring Glaoui clan. His son, Tayeb El Goundafi, also spent most of his life in tribal campaigning, though he finally threw in his lot with Sultan Moulay Hassan, and later with the French. At the turn of the century, he could still raise some 5000 armed tribesmen with a day or two's notice, but his power and fief eventually collapsed in 1924 – the result of El Glaoui's manoeuvring. The Kasbah here at Talâat must have already been in decay then; today, it seems no more linked to the village than any castle in Europe.

An interesting mountain **souk** takes place in the village on Wednesdays.

Agadir n'Gouj and Tagoundaft

Another dramatic-looking Goundafi Kasbah is to be seen to the left of the road, a couple of kilometres south of Tin Mal. This one, **Agadir n'Gouj** is set on a hilltop, and is now privately owned. It is well preserved – as indeed it should be, having been constructed only in 1907.

When the road begins to turn up and away from the river another stark ruin may be noticed perched, up to the left. This is the **Tagoundaft**, the most imposing but seldom visited of the Goundafi Kasbahs.

Telouet and the Tizi n'Tichka

The **Tizi n'Tichka** – the direct route from Marrakesh to Ouarzazate – is not so remote or spectacular as the Tizi n'Test pass. As an important military (and tourist) approach to the south, the road is modern, well constructed and relatively fast. At **Telouet**, however, only a short distance off the modern highway, such mundane current roles are underpinned by an earlier political history, scarcely three decades old and unimaginably bizarre. For this pass and the mountains to the east of it were the stamping ground of the extraordinary Glaoui brothers, the greatest and the most ambitious of all the Berber tribal leaders. Their Kasbah-headquarters, a vast complex of buildings abandoned only in 1956, are a rewarding detour (44km from the main road).

For trekkers, bikers or four-wheel-drivers, Telouet has an additional and powerful attraction, offering an alternative and superb piste to the south, following the old tribal **route to Aït Benhaddou**.

Telouet: the Glaoui Kasbah

The **Glaoui Kasbah** at TELOUET is one of the most extraordinary sights of the Atlas – fast crumbling into the dark red earth, but visitable, and offering a peculiar glimpse of the style and melodrama of recent Moroccan political government and power. The village itself is tiny, though it holds a small **souk** on Thursdays and has several **cafés**, which serve meals. There are two small **hotels**, the *Auberge Onez Ahemd* (run by an ex-*gartien* of the kasbah) and the nicer and newer *Chez Bennouri*, run by Mohammed Benouri (a trekking guide) and his father, in part of an old ksar.

The Glaoui

The extent and speed of **Madani** (1866–1918) and **T'Hami** (1879–1956) **El Glaoui's** rise to power is remarkable enough. In the mid-nineteenth century, their family were simply local clan leaders, controlling an important Atlas pass – a long-established trade route from Marrakesh to the Drâa and Dades valleys – but lacking influence outside of it. Their entrance into national politics began dramatically in 1893. In that year's terrible winter, **Sultan Moulay Hassan**, on returning from a disastrous *harka* (subjugation/burning raid) of the Tafilalt region, found himself at the mercy of the brothers for food, shelter and safe passage. With shrewd political judgement, they rode out to meet the sultan, feting him with every detail of protocol and, miraculously, producing enough food to feed the entire 3000-strong force for the duration of their stay.

The extravagance was well rewarded. By the time Moulay Hassan began his return to Marrakesh, he had given *caid*-ship of all the lands between the High Atlas and the Sahara to the Glaouis and, most important of all, saw fit to abandon vast amounts of the royal armoury (including the first cannon to be seen in the Atlas) in Telouet. By 1901, the brothers had eliminated all opposition in the region, and when **the French** arrived in Morocco in 1912, the Glaouis were able to dictate the form of government for virtually all the south, putting down the attempted nationalist rebellion of El Hiba, pledging loyalty throughout World War I, and having themselves appointed **pashas of Marrakesh**, with their family becoming *caids* in all the main Atlas and desert cities. The French were content to concur, arming them, as Gavin Maxwell wrote, "to rule as despots, [and] perpetuating the corruption and oppression that the Europeans had nominally come to purge".

The strange events of this age – and the legendary personal style of T'Hami El Glaoui – are beautifully evoked in Gavin Maxwell's *Lords of the Atlas*, the brooding romanticism of which almost compels a visit to Telouet:

> *At an altitude of more than 8,000 feet in the High Atlas, [the castle] and its scattered predecessors occupy the corner of a desert plateau, circled by the giant peaks of the Central Massif.... When in the spring the snows begin to thaw and the river below the castle, the Oued Mellah, becomes a torrent of ice-grey and white, the mountains reveal their fantastic colours, each distinct and contrasting with its neighbour. The hues are for the most part the range of colours to be found upon fan shells – reds, vivid pinks, violets, yellows, but among these are peaks of cold mineral green or of dull blue. Nearer at hand, where the Oued Mellah turns to flow though the Valley of Salt, a cluster of ghostly spires, hundreds of feet high and needle-pointed at their summits, cluster below the face of a precipice; vultures wheel and turn upon the air currents between them ....*
>
> *Even in this setting the castle does not seem insignificant. It is neither beautiful nor gracious, but its sheer size, as if in competition with the scale of the mountains, compels attention as much as the fact that its pretension somehow falls short of the ridiculous. The castle, or Kasbah, of Telouet is a tower of tragedy that leaves no room for laughter.*

And that's about how it is. If you've read the book, or if you've just picked up on the fascination, it's certainly a journey worth making, though it has to be said that there's little of aesthetic value, many of the rooms have fallen into complete ruin (restoration is "planned"), and without a car, it can be a tricky and time-consuming trip. Nevertheless, even after thirty years of decay, there's still vast drama in this weird and remote eyrie, and in the painted salon walls, often roofless and open to the wind. The sumptuous heart of the building has however been made safe.

The Kasbah

Driving through Telouet village you bear off to the right, on a signposted track, to the **Kasbah**. The road twists round some ruins to a roughly paved courtyard facing massive double doors. Wait a while and you'll be joined by a caretaker-guide (tours 20dh

Berber women collecting wood, near Tata

Aït Benhaddou kasbahs

Agadir

Tata

Argan trees near Taroudannt

Sidi Ifni: Spanish Art Deco

Dadès valley hairpins

ït Benhaddou

onstruction of the Tichka road, the **pass from Telouet to Aït** was the main route over the Atlas. It was the presence in the Telouet Hami's xenophobic and intransigent cousin, Hammou ("The Vulture"), e French to construct a road along the more difficult route to the west. four-wheel drive (or a mountain bike), or want a good two-day walk, it is llow the old pass, heading south from Telouet along the 6803 piste. This s far as Anemiter but pretty rough beyond there, and requires fording at s – most precariously just north of Aït Benhaddou, where a bridge col-ods in 1989 and has not (at time of writing) been repaired.

t is 35km from Telouet to Aït Benhaddou. If you are walking or biking, the u tranquillity and unparalleled views of green valleys, a river that splashes hole course and remarkable coloured scree slopes amid the high, parched lespite the absence of settlements on most of the maps, much of the **valley** ased communities, all making abundant use of the narrow but fertile valley. his a wealth of dark red and crumbling **Kasbahs**, collections of homes nong patchworks of wheatfields, terraced orchards, olive trees, date palms nd everywhere children calling to each other from the fields, the river or le. You will need to take provisions for the trip.

Anemiter

shared taxis (and the daily bus) between Telouet and **ANEMITER** (12km), one largest and best-preserved fortified villages in Morocco. It has a basic au (☎04/89.07.80), run by Elyazid Mohammed, who will take groups (or indi-vidu **trekking tours** into the Atlas hereabouts. He speaks French and some Er

head of the Oued Ounila on which Anemiter stands lies the huge sprawl of Ar (3607m) and the smaller Zarzamt. Between them lie the turquoise **akes**. Beyond here, crossing the Tizi n'Fedrahate, a piste from the south er to the splendid **Tessaout valley** and, from Ait Timlil, climbs north to North of this area lies a magnificent and almost unknown trekking area, g when it has such notable entry routes. The **Bou Guemez/Mgoun** area st is second only to Toubkal in popularity. Trekking right through on long t links is highly recommended (and detailed in Peyron's guide).

to Aït Benhaddou

occasional truck-taxis (*camionettes*) south of Anemiter, along the piste, but if ng out without transport it would be best to accept that you'll walk most of Tamdaght, where the tarmac resumes; it takes around ten hours.

Anemiter, the main mule track clings to the valley side, alternately climb-scending, but with a general downhill trend as you make your way south. kilometres you cross a sturdy bridge. Beyond here the piste follows the the river to the hamlet of ASSAKO (two and a half hour's walk from where it climbs to the left round some spectacular gorges and then drops

ould aim to get beyond this exposed high ground before camping. At ound six or seven hours from Anemiter, you might be able to find a room ome. Another three hours south of Tourhat, the trail brings you to a scattered collection of buildings with a classic **Kasbah**. This was used an MGM epic, and retains some of its authentic Hollywood decor, along rickety storks' nests on the battlements.

Ameln valley, Tafraoute

Carpets for the King

The famous sign at Zagora

The dunes at Merzouga

per group), necessary in this case since the building
locked doors and connecting passages; it is said that n
their way around the complex. Sadly, these days you're
reception rooms. You can ask to see more – the harem, t
the usual reply is "*dangereux*", and so it most likely is: if y
is generally allowed) you can look down upon some of th
bright *zellij* and stucco enclosing great gaping holes in the

The **reception rooms** – "the outward and visible signs
tion", in Maxwell's phrase – at least give a sense of the quan
ration, still in progress when the Glaouis died and the old regir
They have delicate iron window grilles and fine carved ceili
result is once again the late nineteenth- and early twentieth-cent
sitive imitation of the past and out-and-out vulgarity. There is
affectation, too, perfectly demonstrated by the use of green Salé t
ally reserved for mosques and royal palaces.

The really enduring impression, though, is the wonder of how a
to be built at all, since, wrote Gavin Maxwell:

> It was not a medieval survival, as are the few European castles still
> descendants of feudal barons, but a deliberate recreation of the Middle
> their blatant extremes of beauty and ugliness, good and evil, elegance
> power and fear – by those who had full access to the inventions of conte
> ence. No part of the Kasbah is more than a hundred years old; no part
> predecessors goes back further than another fifty. Part of the castle is built o
> tinguishing it sharply from the other Kasbahs that are made of pisé or sun-d
> for no matter to what heights of beauty or fantasy these might aspire, they
> the final analysis, soluble in water.

Approaches to Telouet: Irherm, Taddert and Aït Ourir

Getting to Telouet is easy enough if you have transport: it is a straigh
drive from the Tizi n'Tichka (P31) road, along the paved 6802. Using pu
there is a daily **bus** from Marrakesh, departing from Bab Rhemat (d
2–3pm), to Telouet and on to Anemiter (see below); it returns from A
(7am from Telouet). Alternatively, there are shared **grands taxis**
Anemiter, via Aït Durir and Telouet.

Irherm and Taddert
IRHERM, 10km beyond the Tichka mountain pass, has a
Chez Mimi – a reasonable place to stay if you get stuck. **TA**
side of the pass, has a dishevelled, rather gloomy and
Noyers (☎3 through operator; ⓪), though with some co
region's beautiful mountain stream, holm oaks and
half-hour walk to the village of TAMGUEMEMT, abo

The Tizi at the head of this valley offers green
through to the old Glaoui pass via Titoula and the

Aït Ourir
An alternative stopping point, if you are followi
and don't want to carry on to Marrakesh, is **A**
side the village, is an attractive **hotel**, *Le Coq*
a bar, restaurant, swimming pool (not always
so book ahead for a room. The *Hermitage*,

From **Tamdaght to Aït Benhaddou** the road is again paved to AÏT BENHADDOU (see p.401), where there are cafés and three simple hotels where you can pick up a taxi (or usually hitch a lift) on to Ouarzazate.

Marrakesh to Agadir: the Tizi Maachou

The direct route from **Marrakesh to Agadir** – the **Imi n'Tanoute**, or **Tizi Maachou**, pass – is, in itself, the least spectacular of the Atlas roads but if you are in a hurry to get south it is a reasonably fast trip (4hr drive to Agadir) and when the Test and Tichka passes are closed through snow, it normally remains open. Its hinterland also offers some exciting trekking, well off the beaten track, for more on which see the section below ("Tichka Plateau treks").

Chichaoua, Imi n'Tanoute and the pass

Leaving Marrakesh, most of the buses follow the Essaouira road (P10) as far as **CHICHAOUA**, a small village and administrative centre with several cafés and **hotels** (all unclassified), and a makeshift campsite, with no facilities or security. The village is set at the entrance to the mountains, and is famed in a small way for its carpets. Brightly coloured and often using stylized animal forms, they are sold at the local **Centre Coopératif** and also at the **Thursday market**. The village is the most pleasant stop along the road to break your journey. Beyond Chichaoua, the **road to Essaouira** continues across the drab Chiadma plains. SIDI MOKHTAR, 25km on from Chichaoua, has a **Wednesday souk** with an attractive array of carpets.

For **Agadir**, you begin a slow climb towards **IMI N'TANOUTE**, another administrative centre, with a **Monday souk**, and then cut through the last outlying peaks of the High Atlas. Imi n'Tanoute is of little interest, though if you need to stay before setting out on a trek (see below), there are **rooms** at a couple of the cafés and provisions. There is a minor tarred road, the 6403, which breaks off the Marrakesh–Essaouira road just west of the Pont du Nfis and goes direct to Imi n'Tanoute. It is probably no faster but pleasantly unbusy.

A few kilometres further along from Imi n'Tanoute on the Agadir road, the phrase "Allah – Nation – King" (Alla–al-Watan–al-Malik) is picked out in painted stone letters, over 50ft high, on the hillside. Beyond it is the pass, **Tizi Maachou**, at 1700m. Over it, along the roadside, you often have locals selling bottles of golden argan oil (see p.464), which makes a change from fossils. The road passes the **dams of Tanizaourt** and descends to the fertile **Souss Valley**, with its intensive greenhouse cultivation. If you are planning to trek into the Atlas from TIMESGADIOUINE or ARGANA (see pp.389–390), make sure you get dropped at the appropriate turnoff.

Western High Atlas: Tichka Plateau treks

Exploring the **Tichka Plateau** and the **western fringes of the Atlas**, you move well away from the tourist routes, miles away from any organized refuge, and pass through Berber villages which see scarcely a foreigner from one year to the next. You'll need to carry provisions, and be prepared to camp or possibly stay in a Berber village home if you get the invitation – as you almost certainly will. Sanitation is poor in the villages and it's not a bad idea to bring water purification tablets if you plan to take water from mountain streams – unless you're higher than all habitation. Eating and drinking in mountain village homes, though, is surprisingly safe as the food (mainly *tajines*) is cooked slowly and the drink is invariably mint tea.

Getting into these mountains, there are approaches from both north and south: **Imi n'Tanoute**, **Timesgadiouine** and **Argana**, on the main Marrakesh–Agadir bus route (north), and **Taroudannt–Oualed Behril** (south). From the north approaches, rides on trucks bound for mines or markets at trailheads have to be used; from the south, *camionettes* ply up daily to Imoulas, the Medlawa Valley, Tigouga, etc.

The *IGN* 1:100,000 maps for the area are *Tizi n'Test* and *Igli*.

Imi n'Tanoute to the Tichka Plateau

A dirt road leads up into the mountains from Imi n'Tanoute to **Afensou**, nearby where a Thursday market (Al Khemis) is held, making your best chance of a lift up on Wednesday with one of the lorries. This trip takes several hours, so don't arrive late in Imi n'Tanoute or you might get stranded. The road (possible for ordinary passenger cars) crosses the **Tizi n'Tabghourt** pass at 2666m, from where you have an excellent panorama of the entire area, which includes some peaks reaching 3350m.

At Afensou you are in the **Haut Seksawa** with some of the highest mountain walks in the Atlas lying to the south and holding the romantic **Tichka Plateau** in their midst. **Moulay Ali** (3349m) dominates and the ridge from it to the main chain remains unclimbed. The **Tizi Asdim** gives the easiest access to the Tichka Plateau, passing under **Djebel Ikkis** and other climbing peaks. A few other tizis offer routes across the range and the traversing of the main ridge offers an exceptionally good multi-day trip with plenty scrambling.

Afensou can also be reached on a new, better piste from **Timesgadiouine** (serving the mines above the village) which makes a spectacular crest-route in to the Seksawa (see below).

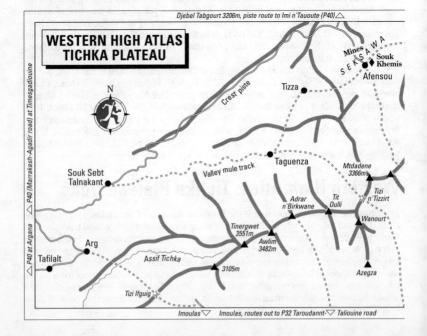

WESTERN HIGH ATLAS
TICHKA PLATEAU

Djebel Tabgourt 3206m, piste route to Imi n'Tauoute (P40)

Mines

S E K S A W A

Souk Khemis

Afensou

Crest piste

Tizza

N

P40 (Marrakesh-Agadir road) at Timesgadiouine

Souk Sebt Talnakant

Valley mule track

Taguenza

Mtdadene 3366m

Tizi n'Tizzirt

P40 at Argana

Adrar n'Birkwane

Tit Oulli

Wanourt

Tinergwet 3551m

Arg

Awlim 3482m

Tafilalt

Assif Tichka

3105m

Azegza

Tizi Ifguig

Imoulas   Imoulas, routes out to P32 Taroudannt   Taliouine road

Timesgadiouine and the Aït Driss

The second access point to the mountains along the Marrakesh–Agadir road is **TIMESGADIOUINE**, about 50km south of Imi n'Tanoute. A small sign indicates Timesgadiouine: get off the bus here, where you'll see a dirt road, a small building and perhaps a few people who, like yourself, are waiting for lifts – nothing else identifies this as an entrance to the mountains. The actual village is 3–4km along the dirt road.

Souk Sebt

Your destination is **SOUK SEBT TALMAKENT**. Lorries will be driving up on Friday afternoon for the Saturday *souk*, but others go up during the week to the mines above AFENSOU and they all pass through Souk Sebt. Be prepared for a wait and a long dusty ride. If you ride up on Friday afternoon, you can camp overnight. Basic food items can be bought here. There are no cafés and no rooms, although the government workers posted to this nowhere place might offer you a room in their offices.

The Aït Driss

The **Aït Driss River** winds its way just below Souk Sebt. It's a pretty valley that narrows to a gorge for a kilometre or two before spreading out and filling up with walnut trees and Berber villages. As you trek up, several other tributaries come down on your right from the main ridge. The two most conspicuous peaks, **Tinerghwet** (3551m) and **Awlim** (3482m), are the same two you can see from Taroudannt, which lies in the Souss plain on their far side. Turn up any of these tributaries for an interesting day's trek. For camping, you're better off in the Aït Driss Valley, where the ground is flatter.

In August you'll see entire families out for the **walnut harvest**. The men climb high into the trees to beat the branches with long poles. Underneath, the women and chil-

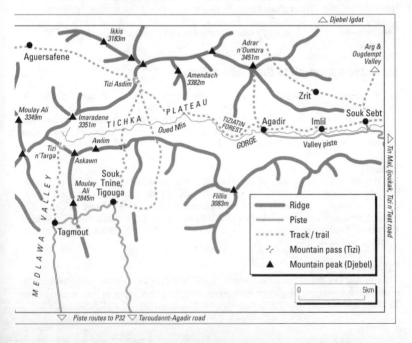

dren gather the nuts, staining their hands black for weeks from the outer shells. In this part of the Atlas, the women often wear their hair in bunches that hang down the sides of their faces.

To the head of the Aït Driss

You can reach the **head of the Aït Driss** at TAMJLOCHT in a day's trekking from Souk Sebt. From there a steep climb over the **Tizi n'Wannas** pass (2367m) takes you to TIZZA, a small village at the head of the parallel valley, the Warguiwn. Tizza is not a big market town nor does any road reach it, yet somehow it merits a place on most Moroccan road maps.

From Tizza trek east up a small valley 2–3km, then climb up **Tizi n'Timirout** (2280m) – which is not named on the survey map. There's a dramatic view of the main ridge from this pass, its rugged peaks stretching to the northeast. The most prominent one is Moulay Ali at 3349m. Afensou (see p.388) awaits you after a long descent, from where you can hitch back out to Souk Sebt or Imi n'Tanoute or continue trekking to the Tizi n'Test road.

Argana to Djebel Tichka

ARGANA, the third access point, lies off on a signposted road to the left some kilometres on down the Agadir road, a large town but virtually abandoned since the new road bypassed it. In a film it could pass for a frontier town in the wild west. An old kasbah above points to its one-time importance.

Careful questioning and a long walk will lead you to **Tafilatt** and **Arg**, villages under the high wall of **Djebel Tichka**, gained by brutally steep tracks. A little below the crest on the other side lies the Oued Tichka, which breaks out to the south (a notable water channel leads its waters to the north side). Following up this river to reach the peaks of **Tinergharet** and **Awlim** is one of the most rewarding ventures of its kind. Both peaks demand some scrambling and route-finding abilities and Awlim has acres of unclimbed cliffs. Passes southwards can round off a visit to this little-visited area.

Southern approach to the Tichka Plateau

In the last few years the potential for mountain exploration in the Western High Atlas and "lost world" of the Tichka Plateau (and the beautiful valleys leading up to the heights) has been realized. Going it your own way, *camionettes* from Taroudannt (see p.467) and Ouled Behril ply up to **Imoulas**, **Tagmout** and **Souk Tnine Tigouga**, from whence mule trails lead over the crests. The main routes are outlined below.

Imoulas

IMOULAS is the main town of the foothills, with a Sunday *souk*. From here a piste extends for about 6km northwest to TINIGHAS, whence there is a dramatic route through a gorge to high *azibs* and a hard ascent to **Djebel Tinerghwet** (3551m), the highest peak in the area, and **Awlim** (3481m). East of Awlim extends the "**Ridge of a Hundred Peaks**", running on to the distant Tichka Plateau. Awlim's east face has climbing potential.

Tagmout

You can stay in a delightful local house at **TAGMOUT**, before following the mule track north, up the stunning **Medlawa Valley** and over the Tizi n'Targa to the top end of the Tichka Plateau.

Souk Tnine Tigouga

As the name suggests, **SOUK TNINE TIGOUGA** has a **Monday souk**, the easiest time to get a lift up (or out of) here. Mule tracks north of the village offer a more direct approach to the central area of the Tichka Plateau, and lead over to Aguersaffen and Afensou (see p.388).

Down the Oued Nfis

However you approach it, the **Tichka Plateau** is a delight. Grazing is controlled so the meadows are a mass of early daffodils and spring flowers. **Imaradene** (3351m) and **Amendach** (338m – 3882 by error on the 1:100,000 map) are the highest summits, west and east, and are superlative viewpoints. The plateau is drained by the Oued Nfis, first through the Tiziatin oak forest, using or bypassing gorges, then undergoing a series of villages, one, another Imlil, is a shrine to the Toumert, the founder of the Tinmal/Almohad dynasty.

A two-day trek from the plateau will take you to **SOUK SEBT TANAMMERT**. From this Saturday market, a lorry road climbs up to the Test road, not far from the pass itself. You can hitch out here or continue trekking for two more days to MZOUZITE, near Tin Mal: one day north to ARG via Tizi n'Aghbar (2653m) and Tizi n'Tiddi (2744m), and the second day east along the long Ougdemt Valley to Mzouzite, as described under the Tizi n'Test section (see p.379). An excellent trail also descends the Oued Nfis Valley from Souk Sebt, going through beautiful gorges and forested countryside. What the trekking expert Hamish Brown describes as a "Wonder Walk" has been worked out linking the Tichka Plateau to Djebel Toubkal, using guides/mules from Taroudannt and Imlil for successive sections. Details are available from Hamish Brown's company, *AMIS* (see p.23).

travel details

Buses

From Marrakesh, buses run from the main terminal at **Bab Doukkala** to:

Agadir Best are *Supratours* and CTM (3hr 30min).

Ouarzazate (over the Tizi n'Tichka) CTM at 5.30am, 7.30am, 11am and 5.30pm (4–5hr).

Taroudannt (over the Tizi n'Test route) SATAS bus at 5am (8hr 30min).

Buses to **Ourika**, **Asni** (the trailhead for Djebel Toubkal; 1hr 30min), and **Moulay Brahim**, leave from just outside **Bab Er Robb**. (Some buses also run to Asni from the Bab Doukkala bus station).

Grands Taxis

Grands taxis run from Marrakesh to **Ourika** and **Asni** – negotiate for these by Bab Er Robb (12.5dh is the local rate for a place to Asni).

See the main text for all other travel details.

CHAPTER SEVEN

THE GREAT SOUTHERN OASIS ROUTES

Immediately when you arrive in the Sahara, for the first or the tenth time, you notice the stillness. An incredible, absolute silence prevails outside the towns; and within, even in busy places like the markets, there is a hushed quality in the air, as if the quiet were a constant force which, resenting the intrusion of sound, minimizes and disperses it straightaway. Then there is the sky, compared to which all other skies seem faint-hearted efforts. Solid and luminous, it is always the focal point of the landscape. At sunset, the precise, curved shadow of the earth rises into it swiftly from the horizon, cutting it into light section and dark section. When all daylight has gone, and the space is thick with stars, it is still of an intense and burning blue, darkest directly overhead and paling toward the earth, so that the night never really grows dark.

Paul Bowles: *The Baptism of Solitude*

The **Moroccan pre-Sahara** begins as soon as you cross the Atlas to the south. It is not sand for the most part – more a wasteland of rock and scrub – but it is powerfully impressive. The quote from Paul Bowles may sound over the top, but staying at M'hamid or Merzouga, or just stopping a car on a desert road between towns, somehow has this effect.

There is, too, an irresistible sense of wonder as you catch a first glimpse of the great southern river valleys – the **Drâa**, **Dadès**, **Todra**, **Ziz** and **Tafilalt**. Long belts of date palm oases, scattered with the fabulous mud architecture of Kasbahs and fortified *ksour* villages, these are the old caravan routes that reached back to Marrakesh and Fes and out across the Sahara to Timbuktu, Niger and old Sudan, carrying gold, slaves and salt well into the nineteenth century. They are beautiful routes, even today, tamed by modern roads and with the oases in decline, and if you're travelling in Morocco for any length of time, they are a must. The simplest circuits – **Marrakesh–Zagora–Marrakesh**, or **Marrakesh–Tinerhir–Midelt** – can be covered in around five days, though to do them any degree of justice you need a lot longer.

The **southern oases** were long a mainstay of the precolonial economy. Their wealth, and the arrival of tribes from the desert, provided the impetus for two of the great royal dynasties: the Saadians (1154–1669) from the Drâa Valley, and the present ruling family, the Alaouites (1669–) from the Tafilalt. By the nineteenth century, however, the advance of the Sahara and the uncertain upkeep of the water channels had reduced life to bare subsistence even in the most fertile strips. Under the French, with the creation of modern industry in the north and the exploitation of phosphates and minerals, they became less and less significant, while the old caravan routes were dealt a final death blow by the closure of the Algerian border after independence. The pattern of the last twenty-five years has been one of steady emigration to the northern cities.

Today, there are a few urban centres in the south; **Ouarzazate** and **Er Rachidia** are the largest and both were created by the French to 'pacify' the south; they seem only

SOUTHERN PRACTICALITIES

TRANSPORT

All the main road routes in this chapter are covered by regular **buses**, and often *grands taxis*. On many of the others, local **Berber trucks** (*camionettes*) or **landrover and transit taxis** (detailed in the text) run a bus-type service, charging standard fares for their trips, which are usually timed to coincide with the network of *souks* or markets in villages en route. The trucks cover a number of adventurous desert pistes – such as the direct routes from Zagora to Foum Zguid and Tata or to Rissani – and some very rough roads over the Atlas behind the Dadès or Todra gorges. If you plan to **drive** on these, you'll need to have a decent vehicle (4x4s are essential for some routes) and be able to do basic mechanical repairs.

Travelling by bus in the desert, in summer, the main disadvantage is the sheer physical exhaustion involved: most trips tend to begin at dawn to avoid the worst of the heat and, for the rest of the day, it can be difficult to summon up the energy to do anything. If you can afford to **rent a car** – even for just two or three days – you'll be able to to take in a lot more, with a lot less frustration, in a reasonably short period of time. There are numerous rental outlets in Ouarzazate, most of which allow you to return their vehicles to Agadir, Marrakesh, Fes, or even Casablanca if you enjoy driving.

Filling **stations** can be found along all the main routes, but they're not exactly plentiful. Fill the tank whenever and wherever you have the opportunity. It's wise to carry **water**, too, in case of overheating, and, above all, be sure you've got a good **spare tyre** – punctures tend to be frequent on all southern roads. As throughout the country, however, local **mechanics** are excellent (Er Rachidia has an especially good reputation) and most minor – and routine – problems can be quickly dealt with.

CLIMATE AND SEASONS

Temperatures can climb well above 120°F (50°C) in midsummer and you'll find the middle of the day is best spent being totally inactive. If you have the option, spring is by far the most enjoyable time to travel – particularly if you're heading for Zagora (reckoned to be the hottest town in the country), or Rissani-Merzouga. Autumn, with the date harvests, is also good. In winter, the days remain hot, though it can get fairly cool at night, and further south into the desert, it can actually freeze. Some kind of light hat or cap, and sunglasses, are pretty much essential.

Be aware, too, that the Drâa, in particular, is subject to **flash floods** in spring, as the snow melts in the Atlas and forges the river currents. Passes across the Atlas at this time, and even trips such as Ouarzazate to Aït Benhaddou or Skoura, can be difficult or impossible.

HEALTH

Rivers in the south are reputed to contain bilharzia, a parasite that can enter your skin, including the soles of your feet so, even when walking by streams in the oases, take care to avoid contact.

---

to underline the end of an age. Although the date harvests in October, centred on **Erfoud** can still give employment to the *ksour* communities, the rest of the year sees only the modest production of a handful of crops – henna, barley, citrus fruits and uniquely roses – the latter developed by the French around **El Kelâa des Mgouna** for the production of rose-water and perfume in May. And to make matters worse, in recent years the seasonal rains have frequently failed. Perhaps as much as half the male population of the *ksour* now seeks work in the north for at least part of the year.

Tourism brings in a little money, particularly to Ouarzazate and Zagora – once the Gate of the Desert (fifty-two days to Timbuktu) but it too has declined in the 1990s, leaving many hotels empty or, in the case of Ouarzazate, unfinished.

OUARZAZATE AND THE DRÂA

Ouarzazate – easily reached from Marrakesh (6hr by bus) – is the main access point and crossroads of the south. East of the town stretches the Dadès River, the "Valley of the Thousand Kasbahs", as promoted by the Ministry of Tourism. South, on the other side of a tremendous ridge of the Anti-Atlas, begins the **Drâa Valley** – 125km of date palm oases, which eventually merge into the Sahara near the village of M'hamid.

It is possible to complete a circuit through and out from the Drâa, heading from the valley's main town, **Zagora**, across piste roads west through Foum Zguid and Tata to the Anti-Atlas, or north into the Djebel Sarhro (an October to April trekking area – see pp.417–20 for details), or east across to Rissani in the Tafilalt. However, most visitors content themselves with a return trip along the main **P31** between Ouarzazate and Zagora: a great route, taking you well south of anywhere in the Tafilalt, and flanked by an amazing series of turreted and cream-pink-coloured *ksour*.

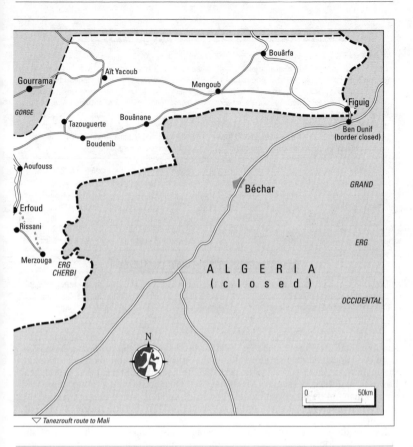

▽ *Tanezrouft route to Mali*

Ouarzazate

At some stage, you're almost bound to spend a night in **OUARZAZATE** and it can be a useful base from which to visit the *ksour* and Kasbahs of Aït Benhaddou or Skoura. It is not exactly compelling in itself, however. Like most of the new Saharan towns, it was created as a garrison and administrative centre by the French in the late 1920s and remains pretty much the same today: a deliberate line of functional buildings, together with an array of modern hotels, set along the main highway and lent an odd sort of permanence by the use of concrete in place of the pisé of the *ksour*.

During the 1980s, Ouarzazate was a bit of a boomtown. The tourist industry embarked on a wildly optimistic building programme of luxury hotels, based on Ouarzazate's marketability as a staging point for the "Saharan Adventure", and the town was given an additional boost from the attentions of movie makers. The region first came to prominence in the film world nearly thirty years ago, when David Lean shot *Lawrence of Arabia* at nearby Aït Benhaddou and in the Tafilalt, and in the last decade, numerous directors – most famously Bernardo Bertolucci,

HOTEL PRICE CODES AND STAR RATINGS

Hotels are no longer obliged to charge according to the official star-ratings (from 1* to 5* luxury), as had long been the custom. Nevertheless, **prices** continue to reflect the star-ratings acquired. The basis of our own **hotel price codes**, set out below and keyed throughout the guide, is the price currently quoted for the cheapest double room in high season (June–September) – and is thus more reliable than quoting notional prices according to star-rating.

Note that cheaper prices in the lower categories are generally for rooms with just a wash-basin – you always pay extra for **en–suite** shower and WC – and that double rooms can generally be converted into **triples/family rooms**, with extra beds, for a modest extra charge. Note also that the prices quoted by all hotels are subject to various local and regional **taxes**, which can add 15 to 20 percent to the bill.

Our code	Classification	Single room price	Double room price
⑩	Unclassified	25–60dh	50–99dh
①	1*A/1*B	60–105dh	100–149dh
②	2*B/2*A	105–145dh	150–199dh
③	3*B/3*A	145–225dh	200–299dh
④	4*B/4*A	225–400dh	300–599dh
⑤	5*luxury	Upwards of 400dh	Upwards of 600dh

TELEPHONE CODES

Telephone numbers in **Ouarzazate, Zagora and Tinerhir** regions are prefixed 04; **Er Rachidia/Erfoud** numbers are prefixed 05. When making a call within a region you omit the prefix. For more explanation of phone codes and making calls within (or to) Morocco, see pp.45–46.

shooting Paul Bowles's novel, *The Sheltering Sky* – used the town as a base. The town even spawned its own film studios, the Atlas Corporation, 6km northwest on the main road (P31) towards Marrakesh. The Gulf War interruption to tourism, however, and the recessionary 1990s have left Ouarzazate with a rather depressed air and many of its hotels unfinished or vacant. In anticipation of more traffic, the authorities built a new bypass to the north of the town, but the traffic, at present, isn't here.

Despite these developments and disappointments, Ouarzazate still has a mystic attraction for Moroccans – similar to the resonance of Timbuktu for Europeans. Indeed, many urban Moroccans respond to any mention of Ouarzazate with the odd rejoinder: 'see Ouarzazate and die'. Maybe this dates from the adventures of the Foreign Legion in the 1930s. If so, the only echo today is the early morning bugle sounding reveille behind the walls of the barracks.

Orientation and accommodation

Orientation is simply a matter of getting your bearings along the old highway and main road, **Av. Mohammed V**. The **CTM** bus station more or less marks the centre, with the *PTT* alongside, and a **tourist office** across the road. **Private line buses** and **grands taxis** operate out of the central Place Mouahidine, a block to the west of the CTM and off the main road; and at the east end of Av. Mohammed V is the town's main sight, Kasbah Taorirt. Ouarzazate's **airport** is just 1km north of town and served by local taxis.

There is a (not especially useful) **tourist office** on Av. Mohammed V, just across from the *PTT* (☎04/88.24.85).

Accommodation

Finding a hotel room should present few problems. Most of the cheaper and unclassified places are grouped in the centre of town, near the bus stations; the more upmarket ones are mainly set back on the plateau to the north. A rather more romantic alternative would be to stay at Aït Benhaddou (see following section).

CHEAP

Hôtel Amlal [C], 24 Rue du Marché, near junction with Av. Prince Heretier Sidi Mohammed (☎04/88.40.30). A newish hotel which is reasonably comfortable and decent value for money, though the restaurant functions only for breakfast, and the area is a bit desolate – but safe enough and with a *gardien* to look after parked cars. ①

Hôtel Atlas, [D], 13 Rue du Marché (☎04/88.23.07) Adequate; some rooms have showers, others use showers on the corridor; in both cases hot water in the evenings. A possible fall-back if the nearby *Hôtel Royal* is full. ①

Hôtel Bab Sahara [F], Place Mouahidine (☎04/88.47.22). Another 1990s-built hotel, convenient for buses and shops. The restaurant serves breakfast, and there's a menu du jour for 40dh. The only drawback is that it is in the noisiest quarter of town. ①

Hôtel Es Saada [G], 12 Rue de la Poste (☎04/88.32.31). Next to the Cinema Atlas and convenient for cafés and buses. Despite some re-decoration, still a little gloomy. ①

Hôtel Royal [E], 24 Av. Mohammed V (☎04/88.24.75). This is the best of the real cheapies, with a variety of rooms, priced accordingly; it is central and can be noisy. ①

Hôtel Saghro [off the map], 1km south of the town in the Tabount district and on the Zagora road (☎02/88.43.05). A modern hotel and a bargain, although it's some distance from the centre. There are a few shops and a petrol station nearby. ①

Hôtel La Vallée [off the map], also in the Tabount district (☎04/88.26.68). Older and more lively than the *Hôtel Saghro* accross the road. After a bad patch, it has a new owner and things have improved. Two pluses: a swimming pool and fine views from the terrace. Used for overnights by trekking groups, including Exodus and Explore. ①

MODERATE

Hôtel La Gazelle [A], Av. Mohammed V (☎04/88.21.51). Set back on the left as you enter town from Marrakesh. An attractive garden courtyard full of birdlife hardly compensates for the run-down rooms, erratic restaurant and noisy bar. Useful for late arrivals or early departures, particularly if you have your own transport; otherwise you would be better off in the town centre. ②

Hôtel Residence Al Warda [B], Av. Mohammed V on corner with Place du 3 Mars (☎04/88.23.44). On first sight these well-equipped studios and apartments are an attractive option, but they have not been well-maintained. A fall-back option. ②

EXPENSIVE

Hôtel Azghor [I], Bd. Prince Moulay Rachid (☎04/88.26.12). This established 4-star hotel has fabulous views to the south and a good-sized swimming pool. It was privatized in 1995, and is probably the best in Ouarzazate – if you can afford it. ④

Hôtel Bélère [J], Bd. Prince Moulay Rachid (☎04/88.28.03). A little more fancy than the *Hôtel Azghour* and consequently dearer; once again it has a fine swimming pool. ④

Hôtel Berber Palace [H], Bd. Prince Moulay Rachid (☎04/88.30.77). A new state-of-the-art hotel that looks like a film set for The Arabian Nights. ⑤

CAMPING

Camping Municipal, 4km east of the centre, just past the Kasbah Taorirt (☎04/88.46.36). A well-maintained site, with clean toilets and showers, but limited shade. Meals are available: breakfast (12.50dh), midday (40dh) and evening (40dh) best ordered in advance. Alongside is the municipal swimming pool, now incorporated in the Complex Le Ouarzazate (see Listings p.400).

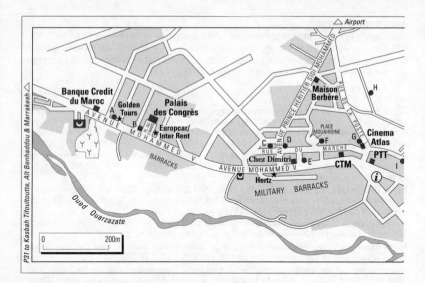

The Town and Kasbahs

Aside from the local Glaoui Kasbah of **Taorirt**, and that of **Tifoultoutte**, 10km out on the old southern bypass, Ouarzazate has little in the way of sights. If it's not too hot, a good walk is to the **Barrage El Mansour Eddahbi** (northeast of the town), quite a sight in spring after heavy rains. If you follow the bank round to the east of the lake you come to the semi-ruined **Tazrout Kasbah**, or "Kasbah des Cigognes", with its storks nesting in the battlements.

There is little else in – or to – Ouarzazate, and really the most interesting option is to get out for the day, either to Aït Benhaddou (see p.401) or a little along the Dadès to Skoura – a beautiful and rambling oasis (see p.412), easily accessible as a day-trip using the Boumalne/Tinerhir buses.

Kasbah Taorirt

The **Kasbah Taorirt** (8am–6.30pm) stands to the right of Av. Mohammed V, at the east (Tinerhir direction) end of town. It's a dusty, twenty-minute walk from the bus stations.

Although built by the Glaoui, the Kasbah was never an actual residence of its chiefs. However, located at this strategic junction of the southern trading routes, it was always controlled by a close relative. In the 1930s, when the Glaoui were the undisputed masters of the south, it was perhaps the largest of all Moroccan Kasbahs – an enormous family domain housing numerous sons and cousins of the dynasty, along with several hundred of their servants and labourers, builders and craftsmen, even semi-itinerant Jewish tailors and moneylenders.

Since then, and especially since being taken over by the government after independence, the Kasbah has fallen into drastic decline. In 1994, the government announced plans to 'rehabilitate' the Kasbah – and also those at Aït Benhaddou (see p.401) but at time of writing the work had not started and parts of the structure had disappeared, washed away by heavy rains; others are completely unsafe; and it is only a small section of the original, a kind of village within the Kasbah, that remains occupied today. That part is towards the rear of the rambling complex of rooms, courtyards and alleyways. What you are shown is just the main reception courtyard and a handful of prin-

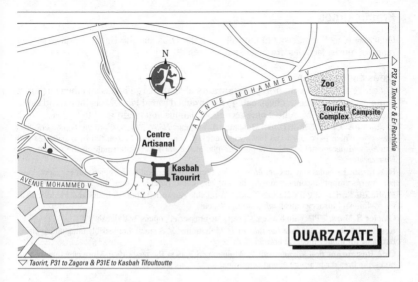

Taorirt, P31 to Zagora & P31E to Kasbah Tifoultoutte

cipal rooms, lavishly decorated but not especially significant or representative of the old order of things. With an eye, perhaps, to tourism, they are known as "the harem".

Crafts

Opposite the Kasbah Taorirt is the **Centre Artisanal** (Mon–Fri 8.30am–noon and 3–6.30pm; Sat 8.30am–noon), a complex of half a dozen or so little shops with good quality items at fixed (but not cheap) prices. Besides stone carvings and pottery, look for two local specialities: the geometrically patterned, silky woollen carpets of the region's *Ouzguita* Berbers, and the silver jewellery – necklaces and earrings incorporating *tazras* (chunky orange copal beads). There are also musical instruments used for the *ahouach*, a dance usually performed in the light of great fires until the first rays of light. Finally, look in at Rachid Maatallah's minerals shop no. 6; and no. 7, where Mohammed Ouirghare has stone carvings and pottery.

There are many shops on Av. Mohammed V and, after studying the items at the **Centre Artisanal**, you may choose to try your bargaining skills there. Better still, but more difficult to find, is the *Maison Berbère*, on Av. Prince Heritier Sidi Mohammed; this is a branch of the Alaoui family chain selling high quality carpets and rugs in towns south of Ouarzazate: Zagora, Tinerhir and Rissani.

Kasbah Tifoultoutte

Nearby Ouarzazate is the **Glaoui Kasbah of Tifoultoutte**. It stands majestically on the banks of the Oued Tifoultoutte, though it is rather more impressive from a distance than on entry. To reach it, follow the old southern bypass (P31E) which runs from Zagora through the Tabount district of Ouarzazate towards Marrakesh; it is on the right, 2km before the junction of the P31E with the P31 to Marrakesh.

In the 1960s, the Kasbah was converted to a hotel for the cast of *Lawrence of Arabia*. Today it functions mainly as a 'traditional entertainment annexe' for hotel tour groups. It no longer has accommodation on offer, even for film stars. Nevertheless, it is open most daylight hours, most days, and the view from the roof is worth the entry fee (10dh); you can also dine there most evenings by arrangement (☎04/88.58.99).

Practicalities

Ouarzazate, as the gateway to the valleys of the Drâa and the Dadès, ensures a good range of tourist facilities, from banks to car rental.

Cafés and restaurants

There are reasonable but pricey **restaurants** at all the large hotels and the two tourist complexes (see listings), cheap **café-grills** grouped round Place Mouahidine and along the nearby Rue du Marché. Some recommendations you might want to try are:

Restaurant Chez Dimitri, Av. Mohammed V (near *Hôtel Royal*). Foreign Legion-era bar-brasserie, which is licensed and has a wide-ranging menu (80dh). Patronized by expatriates and tourists and occasional locals. The photographs of the early days contribute to the mystique of Ouarzazate.

Restaurant Es Salam, (aka *Chez Moulay*) Av. Prince Heritier Sidi Mohammed. An excellent, inexpensive restaurant, unconnected with the (not very good) hotel next door: menu du jour 50dh.

Étoile du Sud, facing the Kasbah Taorirt. A reliable restaurant open all hours and friendly. 40dh for traditional Moroccan meal: *tajine, brochette*, etc.

Glacier 3 Mars, 7 Place du 3 Mars. Cheap café-brasserie, popular with locals.

Restaurant Royal (aka *Chez Boussalem*) 24 Mohammed V. A small, not terribly imaginative place, but value for money meals at around 45dh.

Café Restaurant des Voyageurs, Av. Mohammed V, near the post office. More café than restaurant – the breakfasts are good and convenient for the bus stations.

Tourist complexes – and pools

Complexe Le Ouarzazate (☎04/88.31.10) in the Sidi Daoud district (alongside the campsite) incorporates the municipal swimming pool. Entry to the complex and use of all its facilities costs 30dh. The restaurants seat 600 and, most evenings, there are displays of song, music and dance. Opposite is a small *Parc Zoologique* (9am–noon and 3–6.30pm) with local small animals.

Ksar El Farrah (aka *Fantasia*), also in the Sidi Daoud district. This specializes in *fantasias* (horse riding displays) and serves lunches in the shade of tents (☎04/88.55.55).

Listings

Airport The *Aeroport Taorirt* is 2km north of town, and served by *petits taxis*. There are direct *RAM* flights to Agadir (2 a week), Casablanca (3), Marrakesh (3) and, jointly with *Air France*, to Paris (2); there's a *Club Med* in Ouarzazate! *RAM* have an office near *Chez Dimitri* on Av. Mohammed V (☎04/88.50.80).

Banks All the banks are on the north side of Av. Mohammed V. They include (moving west to east): *Crédit du Maroc*, *Wafabank*, *BMCE*, *BCM* and *Banque Populaire*.

Bicycles – including mountain bikes – can be hired out from Ksour Voyages, 11 Place du 3 Mars.

Buses There are CTM services, leaving from their station near the *PTT*, to Agadir (via Taliouine, Taroudannt and Inezgane – for connections to Agadir) at noon; to Casablanca at 9pm; to Er Rachidia at 10.30am, to Marrakesh at 8.30, 11am, 12.30 and 9pm; and to Zagora and M'Hamid at 12.30. SATAS and other buses go from Place Mouahidine; they are cheaper, but take longer. Between them they run as – or more – frequently than CTM, but timings change frequently.

Car rental Agencies include: *Avis*, Place du 3 Mars (☎04/88.48.70); *Budget*, Av. Mohammed V, alongside *Hôtel Residence Al Warda* (☎04/88.35.65); *Citer*, Place du 3 Mars (☎04/88.52.38); *Europcar/InterRent*, Place du 3 Mars (☎04/88.20.35); *Golden Tours*, Av. Mohammed V, near *Hôtel La Gazelle* (☎04/88.58.58); *Hertz*, 33 Av. Mohammed V (☎04/88.20.84); and *Weekend Cars*, Av. Mohammed V (☎04/88.28.80). *Avis, Citer* and *Europcar/InterRent* have desks at the airport.

Car repairs *Garage Raquiq El Habib*, Quartier Industriel No. 99 (☎04/88.49.33) is recommended.

Cinema *Cinéma Atlas*, Rue de la Poste, next to *Hôtel Es Saada*.

Grands taxis leave from the Place Mouahidine on regular runs along the Dadès to Boumalne (30dh a place; connections on towards Tinerhir and Er Rachidia), and can be negotiated for Marrakesh or Zagora.

Post office The *PTT* on Av. Mohammed V has *poste restante* facilities, plus a direct-dialling international phone section; it is open Mon–Sat 8.30am–noon & 2.30–6pm.

Shopping *The Super Marché*, 73 Av. Mohammed V, opposite *Chez Dimitri* (☎04/88.26.53) is well-stocked, including beer and wine, and is open until 10pm; just the place to stock up for picnics.

Aït Benhaddou

The first thing you hear from the guides on arrival at **AÏT BENHADDOU** is a list of its movie credits. This is a feature of much of the Moroccan south – where landscapes are routinely fantastic and cheap, exotic-looking extras are in plentiful supply – but, even so, the Benhaddou Kasbahs have a definite edge over the competition. *Lawrence* was filmed here, of course; Orson Welles used it as a location for *Sodom and Gomorrah*; and for *Jesus of Nazareth* the whole lower part of the village was rebuilt. In recent years, more controlled restoration has been carried out under UNESCO auspices and, in 1994 the government announced plans to 'rehabilitate' Aït Benhaddou in order to conserve the national and cultural heritage.

Aït Benhaddou is not really the place to catch a glimpse of fading Kasbah life but it is one of the most spectacular sights of the Atlas, piled upon a dark shaft of rock above a shallow, reed-strewn river. Its collection of Kasbahs are among the most elaborately decorated and best preserved; they are less fortified than is usually the case along the Drâa or the Dadès but, towered and crenellated, and with high, sheer walls of dark red pisé, they must have been near impregnable in this remote, hillside site.

As ever, it's impossible to determine exactly how old the Kasbahs are, though there seem to have been buildings here since at least the sixteenth century. The importance of the site, which commands the area for miles around, was its position on the route from Marrakesh through Telouet to Ouarzazate and the south: the caravans passing through it carried salt across the Sahara and returned with gold, ivory and slaves. In time, this trade diminished, largely because the coast of West Africa was opened up: hence the colonial 'Ivory Coast' and 'Gold Coast' and the trans-Atlantic slave trade. In this century, the significance of this route disappeared with the creation of the new French road over the Tichka pass, which has led to severe depopulation over the last thirty years. There are now only half a dozen families living in the Kasbahs, earning a sparse living from the valley's agriculture and rather more from the steady trickle of tourists.

Looking around

Arriving at Aït Benhaddou is somewhat confusing. When you reach the "new village", on the west bank of the river, the road comes to an end. There's a **café** here and usually a few guides around, who will escort you across the river (in winter you have to wade across, though it is usually only knee-deep) up to the **Kasbahs**. They are bisected by an incredibly confusing network of lanes, so a guide is useful – and if you ask, it should be possible to see one or two Kasbah interiors. At the top of the hill are the ruins of a vast and imposing **agadir**, or fortified granary.

Accommodation

The "new village" has three rival **auberges**, catering mainly for tour group lunches but offering basic meals in the evening, and a handful of rooms.

Al Baraka (Aït Benhaddou ☎5, through the operator; or the *patron* ☎04/88.22.58), on the road to the village. There are nine en-suite rooms, all with hot showers You can sleep in the salon and/or tent for less, and on the roof for even less. Music accompanies the meals. ⑩

La Kasbah (Aït Benhaddou ☎2, through the operator), poised on a terrace above the village. The *patron*, Mohammed Tebou, is a friendly source of information. There are six double rooms, with half or full board. If you propose to eat, but not to stay, advance notice helps. ②

Ksour (*ksar* in the singular), or Kasbahs, are to be found throughout the southern valleys and, to an extent, in the Atlas. They are essentially fortified tribal villages, massive but transitory structures, built in the absence of other available materials out of the mud-clay pisé of the riverbanks and lasting only as long as the seasonal rains allow. A unique and probably indigenous development of the Berber populations, they are often monumental in design and fabulously decorated, with bold geometric patterns incised or painted on the exterior walls and slanted towers.

The **Kasbah**, in its southern form, is similar to the *ksar*, though instead of sheltering a mixed village community, it is traditionally the domain of a single family and its dependants. **Agadirs** and **tighremts**, also variants of the *ksar* structure, used to serve as a combination of tribal fortress and communal granary or storehouse in the villages.

THE DADÈS KASBAHS

Ksour line the route more or less continuously from Agdz to Zagora; most of the larger and older ones are grouped a little way from the road, up above the terraces of date palms. Few that are still in use can be more than a hundred years old, though you frequently see the ruins and walls of earlier *ksour* abandoned just a short distance from their modern counterparts. Most are populated by **Berbers**, but there are also Arab villages here, and even a few scattered communities of **Jews**, still living in their Mellahs. All of the southern valleys, too, have groups of **Haratin**, Blacks descended from the west Sudanese slaves brought into Morocco along these caravan routes. Inevitably, these populations have mixed to some extent – and the Jews here are almost certainly converted Berbers – though it is interesting to see just how distinct many of the *ksour* still appear, both in their architecture and customs. There is, for example, a great difference from one village to the next as regards women's costumes, above all in the wearing and extent of veils.

Visiting the region, bear in mind that all of the Drâa **ksour** and **Kasbahs** tend to be further from the road than they look: it's possible to walk for several hours without reaching the edge of the oasis and the upper terraced levels.

El Ouidane *(*Aït Benhaddou ☎12, through the operator). This is the newest auberge and has fabulous views of the 'old' village. There are eleven rooms, nine of them en suite, but electricity can be unreliable and hot water limited. The hotel also does meals. ①

Transport

Getting to Aït Benhaddou is simple enough by car. Leaving Ouarzazate on the P31 (Tizi n'Tichka) road, you turn right after 18km – along a new, surfaced road (the old piste road runs 4km north). Without a car, the best solution is to get together with others and charter a *grand taxi* from Ouarzazate. Otherwise, you'll need to get a bus to the turn-off and walk from there; coming back, if you don't get a lift from fellow visitors, you would have to try and flag down one of the Marrakesh–Ouarzazate buses (which may not be inclined to stop).

If you're into trekking, mountain biking, or very rough piste-driving, the **jeep track** beyond Aït Benhaddou continues to **Tamdaght**, and from there mule paths climb over the old pass to **Telouet** (see p.386).

South to Zagora: the Drâa oases

The road from **Ouarzazate to Zagora** is wide and well maintained, though it does seem to take its toll on tyres. As in the rest of the south, if you're driving make sure you have a good spare and the tools to change it with. If you're on the bus, get yourself a seat on the left-hand side, for the most spectacular views.

BIRDS AND THE BARRAGE EL MANSOUR EDDAHBI

For bird-watchers, the shore line of the Barrage El Mansour Eddahbi is likely to attract migrants at the appropriate times of the year; ruddy shellduck, other waterfowl and waders are possible. Hereabouts, there have also been sightings of mourning wheatear, trumpeter finch, blackbellied sandgrouse, thick-billed lark (and other larks) and raptors, including lanner falcon.

Although Zagora is the ostensible goal and destination, the valley is the real attraction. Driving the route, try to resist the impulse to burn down to the desert, and take the opportunity to walk out to one or another of the *ksour* or Kasbahs. Using local transport, you might consider hiring a *grand taxi* for the day – or half-day – from Ouarzazate, stopping to explore some of the Kasbahs en route; if you intend to do this, however, be very clear to the driver about your plans.

The lake and over the Tizi n'Tinififft

The route begins unpromisingly: the course of the Drâa lies initially some way to the east and the road runs across bleak, stony flatlands of semi-desert. After 15km a side road, the P31F, leads down to the **El Mansour Eddahbi dam and reservoir** – which you can see from part of Ouarzazate. In 1989 freak rains flooded the reservoir, and the Drâa, for the first time in recent memory, ran its course to the sea beyond Tan Tan.

On the main road, the first interest comes just beyond AÏT SAOUN, one of the few roadside villages along this stretch, where a dramatic change takes place. Leaving the plains behind, the road climbs, twists and turns its way up into the mountains, before breaking through the scarp at the pass of **Tizi n'Tinififft** (1660m). From the summit of the pass there are fine views to the north, with the main Atlas mountains framing the horizon.

The pass is just 4km beyond Aït Saoun. Beyond it the road swings down through a landscape of layered strata, until finally, some 20km from the pass, you catch a first glimpse of the valley and the oases – a thick line of palms reaching out into the haze – and the first sign of the Drâa Kasbahs, rising as if from the land where the green gives way to desert.

Agdz and beyond

You descend into the Drâa Valley at **AGDZ** (pronounced Ag–a–dèz; 68km from Ouarzazate), a stopping point for many of the buses and a minor administrative centre for the region. The village consists of just one long street, blood-red coloured, save for the columns of its arcade of shops, picked out in flashes of white and blue. Many of these sell carpets and pottery – and in the few minutes before the bus leaves, prices can drop surprisingly. If you stop here – travelling in either direction – it is unlikely that you'll get a place back on the Zagora/Ouarzazate bus; however, there are **grands taxis** (to either destination), which, like the buses, leave from from the "Grande Place", and it is possible to stay, too.

It is certainly worth a stop, for just to the north of the village begins a beautiful **palmery**. If the river here is low enough (take care to avoid the bilharzia-infested water) you can get across to view a few **Kasbahs** on the far side, in the shadow of **Djebel Kissane** which, as you approach Agdz from the north – and in certain lights – looks more like Djebel Tajine. Geologically speaking, however, it's an outcrop of the **Djebel Sarhro** (see p.417).

The village has a trio of **hotels** which could provide an attractive and low-key introduction to the valley. The *Hôtel Drâa* (☎04/84.30.24; ①) and *Hôtel des Palmiers* (☎04/84.31.27; ①) are both clean and adequate, and on the Grande Place; the former, given advance warning, will arrange excursions and picnics. By the ceremonial archway at the northern entry to the town is the pricier *Hôtel Kissane* (☎04/84.30.44; ②), a new and very pleasant place with obliging staff, a panoramic café and a good salon **restaurant**. The *Hôtel Drâa* also has a restaurant (lunch or dinner: 48dh) and the *Restaurant En Nahda*, next to the *Hôtel des Palmiers*, does inexpensive grills.

There is also a **campsite**, *Camping Kasbah Palmerie* (☎04/84.30.80) alongside the Caïd Ali Kasbah in Aslim village; to get to it turn left off the main street, just after the Grande Place on the right. The signpost says 2km to the campsite, but it's possibly twice that. The site has plenty of shade, with clean and simple sanitation, and you can also have a room in the Kasbah (①).

At the campsite, you can meet Abdelilah Aït El Caid who is a qualified **mountain guide**.

Tamnougalt and Timiderte

The *ksour* at **TAMNOUGALT** – off to the left of the road, about 6km past Agdz – are perhaps the most dramatic and extravagant of any in the Drâa. A wild cluster of buildings, each is fabulously decorated with pockmarked walls and tapering towers. The village was once the capital of the region, and its assembly of families (the *djemaa*) administered what was virtually an independent republic. It is populated by a Berber tribe, the *Mezguita*.

A further 8km south is the more palace-like Glaoui Kasbah of **TIMIDERTE**, built by Brahim, the eldest son of the one-time Pasha of Marrakesh, T'hami El Glaoui. A kilometre to the south, across stepping stones in the river, is another superb Kasbah, the **Aït Hammousaid**. There are also rock carvings to be seen 7km to the west of Timiderte, signposted from the main road.

Tinzouline

Another striking group of *ksour*, dominated by a beautiful and imposing *caïd*'s Kasbah, stands back from the road at **TINZOULINE**, 57km beyond Timiderte (37km north of Zagora). There is a large and very worthwhile **Monday souk** held here and, if you're travelling by bus, the village is one of the better places to break the journey for a while.

Zagora

ZAGORA seems unpromising at first sight: a street-village with a few modern hotels and government buildings. Two things, however, redeem it. The first is its location: this is the most productive stretch of the Drâa – indeed, of all the southern valleys – and you only have to walk a mile or so out of the town (really little more than a big village) to find yourself amid the palms and oasis cultivation. The second is a distinct air of unreality. Directly behind the town rises a bizarre Hollywood-sunset mountain, and at the end of the main street is a mock-serious roadsign to Timbuktu ("*52 jours*" – by camel – if the border were open).

Another draw for Zagora is its festivals. The Drâa's big event, the **Moussem of Moulay Abdelkader Jilali**, is celebrated here during the Mouloud, and like other national festivals here, such as the **Fête du Trône**, is always entertaining.

Orientation and accommodation

Though it can seem a bit of a hassle on arrival, and in summer the oven-dry heat is staggering (as are the *frigidaire* nights in winter), Zagora is an easy place to get oriented. Almost everything of note is on the main street, **Bd. Mohammed V**, or the lower – and lesser – **Av. Hassan II**. Across the river, to the southeast, is the palmery and hamlet of **Amazrou**, a good alternative base, with a couple of hotels and two campsites.

Accommodation

There is a good choice of hotels – in Zagora and Amazrou – and some nicely located campsites, especially for those with transport.

CHEAP

Hôtel des Amis, Bd. Mohammed V (☎04/84.79.24). The cheapest rooms in Zagora; some are en suite and some have a balcony overlooking the street; showers are sometimes hot, and the *Hammam Naceur* is nearby. In summer the hotel rents out (slightly cooler) space on its *terrasse*. There's a reasonable restaurant (menu du jour 50dh) on the ground floor. ⓪

Hôtel La Fibule/Hôtel Kebir (☎04/84.73.18), 200m beyond the bridge over the Oued Drâa, out towards Amazrou – and located in its palmery. A restaurant with rooms round a rooftop terrace; next door is the *Hôtel Ksar* (see overleaf). ①

Hôtel de la Palmeraie, Bd. Mohammed V (☎04/84.70.08). At the far end of the main street, this is a popular hotel, recently expanded from a dozen to close on sixty rooms. Consequently, there is a range of prices: the dearest are en suite with showers. It caters for budget groups and offers good half-board prices. The restaurant does a 60dh menu du jour and there's a bar open to non-residents. Occasionally a little frenzied, but a good choice. ①

Hôtel Valleé Drâa, Bd. Mohammed V (☎04/84.72.10). This is about 50 percent pricier than the *Hôtel des Amis* next door – and that's about right for the extra comfort. Very welcoming and clean, with hot showers. The restaurant has a menu du jour at 40dh. ⓪

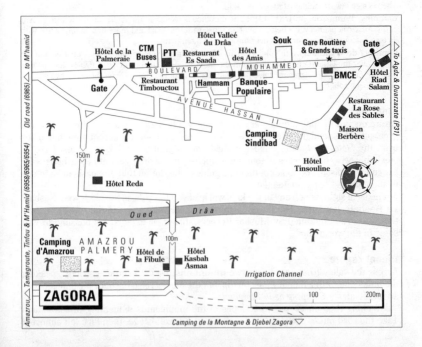

MODERATE

Hôtel Kasbah Asmâa (☎04/84.72.41), 150m beyond the bridge (over the Oued Drâa) at Amazrou. A Kasbah-style hotel, set in a beautiful garden, with a swimming pool and excellent restaurant. It's smaller, has better decor and a warmer welcome than the rival *Hôtel La Fibule*. The Alaoui family also own the new *Hôtel Kasbah Asmâa* outside Rissani (see p.444), and are building a third hotel at Tinerhir. ③

Hôtel La Fibule/Hôtel Ksar(☎04/84.73.18), towards Amazrou – see below. The pricier wing of the Hôtel La Fibule offers more comfort, a swimming pool and a reasonable if limited restaurant. It's used by tour groups, which can mean a raw deal for independent travellers, as well as a rather loud *folklorique* show in the evening. The hotel also arranges camel rides and 4x4 trips.

EXPENSIVE

Hôtel Riad Salam Bd. Mohammed V (☎04/84.74.00). Opened in 1993, this 4-star hotel is on the left as you enter the town and just before the entrance gateway. From outside, it's featureless, but inside it's better – albeit the reception is a little off-hand. It has two swimming pools, three tennis courts, two restaurants and a 'hotel bar'; the 150 spacious rooms are the height of luxury at de luxe prices. ④

Hôtel Reda (☎04/84.72.49), on the road from Zagora down to the Oued Drâa. Another relatively new tour-group hotel which has the edge on the *Hôtel Tinsouline* and possibly the *Hôtel Riad Salem* but, costing at least 50 percent more than the *Tinsouline* and 15 percent more than the *Riad Salem*, it's not such a bargain. ⑤

Hôtel Tinsouline, Av. Hassan II(☎04/84.72.52). Zagora's original "grand hotel" owned by ONMT and managed by KTH, but due to be privatized. It is showing its age, but the rooms are OK, service is good, and there's a pool. The restaurant is not up to much, however. ⑤

CAMPING

Camping Sindibad, Av. Hassan II – five minutes' walk from the town centre (☎04/84.75.53). A small, pleasant site, with lots of shade and a swimming pool. Hot showers and a few rooms for rent. There's a café with traditional meals for 50dh.

Camping d'Amazrou (☎04/84.74.19). The entrance is alongside the *Hôtel La Fibule* (see above) in the Amazrou palmery. It's better suited to those with transport and more of a 'family' site – with its own camels available for rides over towards the mountain.

Camping de la Montagne (no phone). This site is alongside the irrigation canal, upstream of the bridge over the Oued Drâa, and 3km from the main Zagora-Tamegroute road (6958). It's cheaper than the *Sindibad* and *Amazrou* sites, but it's bleak and not too clean. Given the other two sites, it offers no advantages.

Amazrou

Amazrou is a hamlet and palmery just to the south of Zagora, across the Drâa, and a great place to spend the afternoon, wandering (or biking – you can rent mountain bikes from the *Hôtel La Fibule*) amid the shade of its gardens and *ksour*. The village is, inevitably, wise to the ways of tourism – children try to drag you into their houses for tea and will hassle you to adopt them as guides – but for all that, the oasis life and cultivation are still fairly unaffected.

The local sight, which any of the kids will lead you towards, is the old Jewish Kasbah, **La Kasbah des Juifs**. The Jewish community here were active in the silver jewellery trade – a craft continued by Muslim Berbers after their exodus. It's possible to visit some of the workshops.

Djebel Zagora

Across the valley from Zagora are two **mountains**. Djebel Zagora is strictly speaking the bulky one, with a military post on top, but the name is also used for the smaller, sugarloaf hill above *Camping de la Montagne*.

Watching the sunset from the slopes of the mountain is something of a tradition. Take the road out to the *Hôtel La Fibule/Hôtel Kasbah Asmâa*, then turn left almost at once at the river to follow the road/irrigation channel to *Camping de la Montagne*. Here, swing right on the rough track which leads to a pass between the two peaks, then bends back, rising across the hillside to make an elbow bend on a spur. This is the popular viewpoint – and just feasible by a Renault 4 or, preferably, a 4x4. The views are startling: you look out across the palmery to further *ksour*, to the Djebel Sarhro (see pp.417–21), and even to a stretch of sand dunes to the south.

There are ruins a little downhill of an eleventh-century Almoravid fort, built as an outpost against the powerful rulers of Tafilalt; later it was used to protect the caravans passing below, to and from Timbuktu. The road subsequently goes on to the military fort on the summit (entry forbidden) but the view gains little; from the spur a footpath runs across and down the hillside and can be followed back down to the road just opposite *La Fibule*.

On foot you can climb the mountain more directly on an old zigzag footpath up from near the *Hôtel Kasbah Asmâa*.

Meals

There are **meals** to be had at most of the Zagora/Amazrou hotels; *La Fibule* and *Kasbah Asmâa* are especially good. In addition, the *Restaurant Timbouctou* and *Restaurant Es Saada*, both on Av. Mohammed V, do inexpensive Moroccan staples, and are as popular with locals as tourists. Finally, it's worth checking out the *Restaurant La Rose des Sables*, next to the Maison Berbère carpet/crafts shop on Av. Hassan II.

The **dates** of the Zagora oasis are some of the finest in Morocco and stallholders at the market sell dozens of varieties: among them, the sweet *boufeggou*, which will last for up to four years if stored properly; the small, black *bousthami*; and the light, olive-coloured *bouzekri*.

Listings

Banks There are two banks: *BMCE* is opposite the *gare routiére/grand taxi* park and the *Banque Populaire* is on the same side, but midway down Bd. Mohammed V.

Bikes – new mountain ones – are available for hire at the *Hôtel La Fibule*; they are a good way to explore the palmery and Kasbahs of Amazrou; rates are negotiable.

Buses CTM departures are from their office on Bd. Mohammed V; private lines leave from the *gare routière/grand taxi* park further along the street. For Ouarzazate, the most convenient departure is the CTM at 7am; arriving at Ouarzazate at 11am and Marrakesh at 4pm; in the other direction, the CTM leaves Zagora at 4pm and arrives at M'Hamid at 7pm. There are two private-line departures later in the day.

Camel trips There are three camel owners in Zagora, based at the *Kasbah Asmâa, Camping d'Amazrou* (which can be arranged through *Hôtel La Fibule*) and *Camping de la Montagne* (see opposite). All offer standard trips at the same prices: for an hour, an afternoon or morning (including lunch), or a full day (with three meals). They are open to negotiation for longer trips.

Grands taxis There are regular runs to Ouarzazate, from the rank by the *gare routière*. *Grands taxis* can also be negotiated for a trip south to Tamegroute and M'hamid (see pp.408–410).

Petrol There is an Agip filling station by the *Banque Populaire*, and others by the exit from town on the Agdz/Ouarzazate road.

Post office The *PTT* on Bd. Mohammed V offers *poste restante* and phones.

Shops There is a branch of the Maison Berbère carpet/crafts shop on Av. Hassan II. This is one of the best-quality outlets in the south, with other Alaoui family branches at Ouarzazate, Tinerhir and Rissani.

Souk Markets take place on Wednesdays and Sundays; with dates in autumn. There are daily stalls at the entrance for fresh vegetables and fruit.

Swimming pool There is no public pool but the *Hôtel Tinsouline* allows non-residents to swim for a steep 50dh a day.

Tours Most of the hotels offer tours or expeditions to Kasbahs in the Drâa Valley and/or into the desert: it's worth shopping around, and comparing prices. Camel rides – or longer expeditions – are offered by the *Hôtel La Fibule* and *Camping de la Montagne*.

South to M'hamid

The **Zagora oasis** stretches for some 30km south of the town, when the Drâa dries up for a while, to resurface in a final fertile belt before the desert. You can follow this route all the way down: the road (6958/6965/6954) is now paved over the full 98km from **Zagora to M'hamid**, and with a car it's a fine trip, and with the option of a night's stop near the dunes at Tinfou, or beyond.

If you don't have transport, it's a bit of an effort; there are buses to Tamegroute and further south to M'hamid, but times are inconvenient: the CTM leaves Zagora at 4pm, and arrives at M'hamid at 7pm, and there are local buses which leave Zagora later for Tamegroute only. It is possible to charter a *grand taxi* for an early morning departure, however, which would not be too expensive if you can find a group to share costs, and limit your sights to a day visit to **Tamegroute** and the **sand dunes** near Tinfou.

Tamegroute and Tinfou

Tamegroute (19km from Zagora) is reached by a good asphalt road (6958) down the left/east bank of the Drâa, just past the *Hôtel La Fibule*. Take care that you get onto this, and not the old road (6965) to M'hamid on the right/west bank of the river. **Tinfou** lies 10km on from Tamegroute at a point marked on the Michelin map as **"Dunes"**.

Tamegroute

TAMEGROUTE is an interesting and unusual village. At first sight, it is basically a group of *ksour* and Kasbahs, wedged tightly together and divided by low, covered passageways with an unremarkable Saturday *souk* and small potters' co-operative. Despite appearances, it was once the most important settlement in the Drâa valley; it appears on nineteenth-century maps – produced in Europe – as *Tamgrat* or *Tamagrut,* surrounded by lesser places whose names have little or no resonance today.

It owes its importance to its ancient and highly prestigious *zaouia*, which was a seat of learning from the eleventh century and, from the seventeenth century, the base of the Naciri Brotherhood. Founded by Abou Abdallah Mohammed Ben Naceur (an inveterate traveller and revered scholar), this exercised great influence over the Drâa tribes until recent decades. Its sheikhs (or holy leaders) were known as the "peacemakers of the desert" and it was they who settled disputes among the *ksour* and among the caravan traders converging on Zagora from the Sudan. They were missionaries, too, and as late as the 1750s sent envoys to preach to and convert the wilder, animist-minded Berber tribes of the Atlas and Rif.

Arriving in the village, you'll likely be "adopted" by a guide and taken off to see the **Zaouia Naciri** (8am–12.30pm and 2–6pm daily; donations expected), the entrance to which is on a side-street to the left of the main road (coming from Zagora). If you are not 'adopted' or prefer to explore unaided, look for the tall white minaret to the left of the main road.

The *zaouia* consists of a *marabout* (the tomb of Naceur, closed to non-Muslims), a *medersa* (theological college – still used by up to 80 students, preparing for university) and a small library, which welcomes non-Muslim visitors and where you will see illuminated korans, some on animal hides, as well as twelfth-century works on mathematics, medicine and history. The sanctuary, as for centuries past, is a refuge for the sick and mentally ill, whom you'll see sitting round in the courtyard; they come in the hope of miraculous cures and/or to be supported by the charity of the brotherhood and other benevolent visitors.

The **library** was once the richest in Morocco, containing 40,000 volumes. Most have been dispersed to Koranic schools round the country, but Tamegroute preserves a number of very early editions of the Koran printed on gazelle hide, and some interesting books, including a thirteenth-century algebra primer featuring Western Arabic numerals, which, although subsequently dropped in the Arab world, formed the basis of the West's numbers, through the influence of the universities of Moorish Spain.

The **potters' cooperative** is on the left as you leave Tamegroute travelling towards Tinfou. Visitors are welcome (Mon–Fri, 7am–7pm) and there is no pressure to buy. If you want to see the production of pottery in its simplest form, you will find this an ideal opportunity. Do not be surprised to find the green glaze, on finished items, reminiscent of Fes pottery. This is no accident; the founders of the Naciri Brotherhood wanted to develop Tamegroute – to city status, they hoped. Thus, they invited merchants and craftsmen from Fes to settle in Tamegroute. Two families, still working in the pottery, claim Fes forebears.

More recently, in 1995, the pottery enjoyed further patronage, in the form of a state grant to purchase two gas-fired kilns. This is part of a project to revive the fortunes of the Drâa valley. You will see elegant bowls thrown from the local clay on a foot-operated wheel and then the sun-dried 'biscuit' stacked in seven traditional kilns built into the slope. Spinifex (known locally as jujube) and sagebrush raise the temperature to 1000°C, producing the green-glazed ware in a single firing. The minerals for the glaze colour are found locally (copper) and near Tata (manganese).

The village **hotel**, the *Riad Dar Naciri* (☎6 through the operator; ①), used to be popular with tourists travelling to Tamegroute and beyond, but it is no longer reliable.

Tinfou

The tiny hamlet of **TINFOU** stands at the edge of an impressive line of sand dunes – a good substitute for Merzouga if you want to see a real Moroccan sand desert. It is home to an idiosyncratic **hotel**, the *Auberge Repos du Sable* (☎04/84.85.66; ①), an old Kasbah building, with a medieval room key system, a wonderfully ramshackle pool, a private *hammam*, and a restaurant. The *auberge* has long been a favourite of readers of this book. What made it special was the Farouj family who run it. The parents, Hassan and Fatima, are both artists, who have exhibited widely in Morocco and Europe. One of their sons, Mourad, manages the *auberge*, while a second son, Majid, is a camel driver, and arranges trips out to the sand dunes. Unfortunately, it seems to have dropped its standards recently and has had mixed reports. Take a look anyway, and make up your own mind – it's not to everyone's taste.

Competition, in the form of *Porte au Sahara*, aka *Bivouac Sahara* (☎04/84.70.02; ③), may well spur the Farouj family into action. This venture, set up by Germans in 1991 is to be found just before the *auberge* (coming from Zagora), also on the left. It has ten comfortable and well equipped rooms, and also offers camping in a tent, or on the roof terrace (mattresses provided). It has a rather pricey restaurant and, again, offers camel trips to the dunes, through Abdallah Aabi, who will be touting custom before you have downed your first cool drink on the veranda.

Besides the local dunes, the best **camel expeditions** will take you east to the Djebel Tadrant or south towards the Djebel Bani.

Tinfou to M'hamid

About 4km south of Tinfou, you cross the Oued Drâa, and shortly after that are joined by the old road from Zagora to M'hamid (6965). Ahead, apparently blocking the route, rises the great mass of the **Djebel Bani** (1095m), through which the road winds up and over a high-level pass. Once across, you enter a picturesque stretch of palmery; 6km before Tagounite. Signs to the left will direct you to the *Kasbah Aït Isfoul*, which has **rooms and camping** (☎2 through the operator; ②).

The sand dunes hereabouts may not be as high as around Tinfou, but they are spread over a larger area, with a fringe of surrounding palm trees, a distant mountain range and, close by, a village of pisé buildings. A Norwegian correspondent writes: 'this beautiful and placid place will give a much better fulfilment of the images of a desert than the Tinfou dunes (which besides are more crowded with tourists). During my visit in Aït Isfoul, I was the only tourist there and could really sense a 'true' desert landscape – the only element I missed was the camel ...'

Moving on, **TAGOUNITE** (74km from Zagora) has a **Thursday souk**, and a **café-restaurant**, the *Es Saada*, with nine **rooms**, or space on its terrace, if you want to stay overnight ⑩. A piste to the west – suitable for 4x4 vehicles only – leads off to Foum Zguid (see Chapter Eight).

Continuing south, the road crosses another pass of the Djebel Bani, the **Tizi Beni Slimane**, to reach the last fertile belt of the Drâa, the **M'hamid El Gouzlane** – Plain of the Gazelles. A few kilometres on, at the palmery/village of **OULAD DRISS**, the Drâa turns sharply towards the west and the Atlantic; there are some well-preserved *ksour* to explore here, and a small **campsite:** *Carrefour des Caravanes* (☎4 through the operator). There's also the promise of an auberge with ten rooms, but not open yet.

A signpost, echoing that of Zagora, tells you that it is *50 jours à Timbuktu*; the two days' camel ride thus far from from Zagora takes around an hour and a half to full day by car – though only a little further south of here a camel would come into its own. On the final approach to M'hamid, sand has often drifted across the road, despite being lined with woven palm-leaf shields.

M'hamid

M'HAMID El DJEDID (new M'hamid) is just a small administrative centre, the end rather than climax of this trip. It was once an important market place for nomadic and trans-Saharan trade, but of this role only a rather mundane **Monday souk** remains; there is no sign of any camel traders or Blue Men, as the tourist literature suggests. Of rather more interest, however, are the **sand dunes** about 4km away from the village, and the *ksour* of **M'hamid El Bali** (old M'hamid), the village across the Drâa that existed prior to a Polisario attack in the 1970s.

The best **place to stay** in new M'hamid is undoubtedly the *Hôtel Sahara* (☎9 through the operator; ⑩). This was once a primitive place, but now the village has electricity and piped water and its rooms are clean, well blanketed and cheap; a café behind serves decent meals. It has a rival in the *Hôtel Iriqui* (☎23 through the operator; ⑩), across the village square, while over the riverbed, along an avenue of tamarisk shrubs, alternative accommodation is offered at the basic *Auberge El Khaima*; this again has inexpensive rooms, plus couches in a Berber tent, or **camping**.

M'Barek Naâmani, the *patron* of the *Hôtel Sahara*, a tall Tuareg, will be delighted to arrange for overnight, or longer, **expeditions**. If you have the time and get this far, and very much further south than Merzouga, it would be a pity not to taste the real Sahara.

The **bus** back from M'hamid leaves at 6am, passes Tinfou around 7.15am and arrives in Zagora at 9am. A second bus usually leaves M'hamid at 3.30pm.

Desert pistes east and west from Zagora

Most people return from Zagora to Ouarzazate, which is the only road covered by bus, and in some ways the most interesting route, allowing you to continue east along the Dadès Valley towards Boumalne and the Dadès Gorge and then to Tinerhir and the Todra Gorge. For the adventurous, however, there are pistes **east to Rissani** or **west** to **Foum Zguid** (and beyond to Tata). The Rissani route is possible by landrover taxi, or the occasional *grand taxi* and the Foum Zguid route by lorry or landrover taxi if you coincide with the markets. With your own vehicle, you'll generally have no difficulty, except for the stretch of piste between Zagora and Foum Zguid, as long as you keep to the recently surfaced roads. Bear in mind, however, that sudden storms cause flooding which can wash the road away particularly where the road runs close to mountain streams or, indeed, crosses them by ford or bridge. Such hazards are more dangerous at night – and driving in the dark is best avoided.

East: Zagora to Rissani

The long route east from **Zagora to Rissani**, in the Tafilalt, is covered by **taxi** (landrover and occasionally *grand*) regularly, but particularly on Wednesdays, and sometimes on Saturdays, to serve weekly *souks*. Ask your hotel for information and help in booking a place if that's thought advisable. The usual route is to backtrack 66km along the Drâa to **Tansikht**, before heading 233km east to Rissani, via Nkob, Tazzarine and Alnif. The more direct route from Zagora, over the **Tizi n'Tafilalt**, has partially disappeared and is very hard to follow.

Conveniently sited midway between Zagora and Rissani is **TAZZARINE,** set in a grassy oasis surrounded by bare mountains. The modern *Hôtel Restaurant Bougafer* (☎04/83.80.10; ②) has simple, but handsome **rooms** with constant hot water and showers (electricity is available from 6pm–6am only). The licensed restaurant is good; menu du jour 50dh. There is also a friendly **campsite**, the *Amastton* (☎78 through the operator), a small, shady, well-maintained site watered by a natural spring. It has a couple of rooms for hire or you can sleep in a Berber tent.

At the entrance to the campsite is a **prehistoric rock carving** (*gravure rupestre*) transported from elsewhere; you can see them *in situ* at Nkob (30km distant), Tiouririne (7km) and Aït Ouazik (26km) and one of the camp staff will gladly act as a guide to these or other local sights.

The **rest of the journey** holds less interest. The road crosses a bare plain with distant mountains on both sides and the two passes shown on the map are almost imperceptible. You join the Erfoud/Rissani road alongside the new *Hôtel Kasbah Asmâa* and turn right to reach Rissani in 3km.

Besides its interest as a 'new' route, the road from Zagora to Rissani completes a circuit: from Ouarzazate to Zagora and then anticlockwise to Rissani, Erfoud, Tinerhir for the Todra Gorge, and Boumalne for the Dadès Gorge. Previously visiting them all on one trip called for considerable backtracking. Our **map of the Djebel Sarhro** on p.419 shows these routes, and the accompanying section gives a few details on **trekking possibilities** in the region.

The improved surface of this west/east route should not trick you into assuming that the south/north routes (Nkob to Boumalne Dades or Tinerhir and Alnif to the Tinehir/Tinejdad road) are now surfaced throughout; they are not and a 4x4 vehicle, with sound navigation, is essential.

West to Foum Zguid

West from Zagora the maps indicate a road **direct to Foum Zguid**: a route which extends beyond to Tata and from there on towards Tiznit or Taroudannt. After almost two decades of military restriction, this route has recently been opened to tourists; the first section, from Zagora to Foum Zguid, is still poor piste for which you will need a Renault 4L or, better still, a 4x4. Without a car, you can travel by *camionette* (lorry) taxi which runs regularly, but particularly on Sundays and Wednesdays; the *camionette* taxi costs 50dh. Ask for details from your hotel in Zagora and try to book in advance.

In **FOUM ZGUID**, which has a Thursday *souk* and a café with **rooms**, you can pick up a *camionette* taxi on Mondays and Thursdays to Tata (see p.479); there are also buses (Tues, Thurs & Sat) to Tazenakht (change for Taroudannt/Agadir; see p.476) and Ouarzazate – thus completing another unusual circuit.

Agdz to the Taliouine road

Finally, and again to the west, there is a piste from **Agdz to Tazenakht**, on the road to Taliouine. This is a route for piste enthusiasts – it won't save any time over driving to Tazenakht via Ouarzazate – but it is fairly practicable by car (Renault 4s and certainly 4x4 will be okay), if at times difficult to follow, particularly west of TASLA where you should take the track on the southern side of the valley. It is completed by a paved section, from the cobalt mines at ARHBAR to the S510 Foum Zguid road.

The main settlement en route is AÏT SMEGANE-N-EL GRARA, which has a café; BOU AZZER is just a mine and some workers' accommodation. The first available petrol is at TAZENAKHT, which has a **hotel** and some worthwhile carpet shops (see p.476).

THE DADÈS AND TODRA

The **Dadès**, rambling east from Ouarzazate, is the harshest and most desolate of the southern valleys. Along much of its length, the river is barely visible above ground, and the road and plain are hemmed in between the parallel ranges of the High Atlas and Djebel Sarhro – broken, black-red volcanic rock and limestone pinnacles. This makes the oases, when they appear, all the more astonishing, and there are two here – **Skoura** and **Tinerhir** – among the most beautiful in the country. Each lies along the main bus route from Ouarzazate to Er Rachidia and to Erfoud, offering an easy and excellent opportunity for a close look at a working oasis and, in Skoura, a startling range of Kasbahs.

Impressive though these are, however, it is the two gorges that cut out from the valley into the High Atlas that steal the show. The **Dadès** itself forms the first gorge, carving up a fertile strip of land behind **Boumalne du Dadès**. To its east is the **Todra Gorge**, a classic, narrowing shaft of high rock walls, which you can trail by car or transit lorry from Tinerhir right into the heart of the Atlas. If you're happy with the isolation and uncertainties of the **pistes beyond**, it is possible, too, to continue across the mountains – a wonderful trip which emerges in the Middle Atlas, near Beni Mellal on the road from Marrakesh to Fes.

To the south of the Dadès, the **Djebel Sarhro** also offers exciting options from October to April, either trekking on foot, or exploring its network of rough piste roads in a 4x4 vehicle. Tours and treks can be arranged through British trekking companies (see Basics) or in the "trailhead towns" of El Kelâa des Mgouna, Boumalne du Dadès and Tinerhir.

The Skoura oasis

The **Skoura oasis** begins quite suddenly, around 30km east of Ouarzazate, along a tributary of the Drâa, the **Oued Amerhidl**. It is an extraordinary sight even from the road, which for the most part follows along its edge – a very extensive, very dense palmery, with an incredibly confusing network of tracks winding across fords and through the trees to scattered groups of *ksour* and Kasbahs.

Skoura village

SKOURA village, which lies modestly off the main road, at the east end of the oasis, consists of little more than a *souk* and a small group of administrative buildings, where buses stop. You'll probably want the services of a guide to explore some of the Kasbahs, and possibly visit one or two that are still inhabited.

Don't plan to stay here but, if you have to, there's the *Hôtel Nakhil* (aka *Hôtel Restaurant Palmeraie*; ☎37 through the operator; ⑪), a rather flyblown place, with intermittent running water. Food is available here or at a couple of café-restaurants, *Atlas* and *La Casbah*. There is a **Monday souk**.

Kasbahs in the Skoura oasis

The Skoura oasis comprises a thin line of irrigated, fertile palmery, with dry rocky slopes to either side. Animals are not permitted to graze in the precious, cultivated area and so are kept just on the dry side of the line; to feed them, women constantly struggle up from the valley with huge loads of greenery – a characteristic sight here and throughout the southern valleys.

Southwest of Skoura

The best point to stop and explore the Skoura oasis is 2.5km before you arrive at the village proper, coming from Ouarzazate (see sketch-map). Here, by the roadside, is a ruinous Kasbah, with a more recent single-storey building alongside; tour buses are sometimes parked beside it. This is the **Kasbah de Ben Moro**, which dates from the seventeenth century, and is said to have been built by a Spanish sheikh expelled from Andalucia. It nowadays belongs to the family of Mohammed Sabir, which lived in the old Kasbah until 1970 and now inhabit the house beside it; they use the old part for storage and animals. Mohammed, if at home, will show visitors round, pointing out the living quarters on the first floor, the mill, and kitchens, and he will also guide you through the palmery, along a maze of paths and irrigation channels.

The palmery hereabouts is one of the lushest in Morocco, full of almond, olive and fig trees, vines and date palms, with alfalfa grass planted below for animal feed.

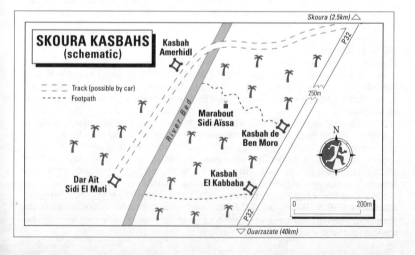

KASBAH MAINTENANCE AND DESTRUCTION

Several of the Skoura Kasbahs date, at least in part, from the seventeenth and eighteenth centuries, though the majority here – and throughout the Dadès oases – are relatively modern. Most of the older fortifications were destroyed in a vicious tribal war in 1893, and many that survived were pulled down in the French "pacification" of the 1920s and 1930s. Once a Kasbah has been left unmaintained, it declines very fast – twenty years is enough to produce a ruinous state, if the pisé walls are not renewed.

The Kasbah walls in the Dadès – higher and flatter than in the Drâa – often seem unscaleable, but in the course of a siege or war there were always other methods of conquest. A favourite means of attack in the 1890s, according to Walter Harris, who journeyed here in disguise, was to divert the water channels of the oasis round a Kasbah and simply wait for its foundations to dissolve.

Following the paths behind the Kasbah de Ben Moro, you pass the half-hidden **Marabout of Sidi Aïssa** (Jesus in his Arabized form), and then the (usually dry) riverbed of the Oued Amerhidl. Straight across is the **Kasbah Amerhidl**, the grandest and most extravagantly decorated in the oasis, and again seventeenth century in origin. The owner's family lives there from time to time and so it is maintained properly. It may well look familiar; it's eminently photogenic and features in travel brochures and coffee table books – and on the back of the current 50 dirham note.

Kasbah Amerhidl can also be reached by car, from a turning further along the Skoura road. If you come this way, you'll be surrounded by any number of boys as soon as you stop, and you really have no option but to pay one to watch your car and another to be your guide.

Beyond Kasbah Amerhidl, a track heads off southwest, past a couple of tumbledown buildings to another impressive-looking Kasbah, the **Dar Aït Sidi El Mati**, and from here it's possible to complete a circuit on foot back to the P32, emerging by the ruinous **Kasbah El Kabbaba**.

Whilst you are here, if you have transport – or a lot of energy – you could search out another Kasbah, the isolated **Kasbah Ben Amar**. This is still lived in and well-maintained. To find it, backtrack along the P32 towards Ouarzazate, and before the bridge over the Oued Amerhidl, look for a track off to the left/southeast; follow the track for a couple of kilometres and you will see the Kasbah ahead. It commands magnificent views of the course of the Oued Dadès.

North of Skoura

There are further impressive Kasbahs to the north of Skoura village, but they are harder to find, and taking a guide along would be invaluable (Mohammed from the Kasbah Ben Moro would be a good choice). To find them, drive through Skoura village and leave it just beyond the *Hôtel Nakhil*, crossing the dry river bed – which is quite wide at this point.

After about 4km, and still well within the palmery, you should come to a pair of Kasbahs, **Dar Aït Sous** and **Dar Lahsoune**; the former, small but once very grand, is in a ruinous state, used only for animals; the latter, once a Glaoui residence, is state-owned, and private. A further 2km drive – and directions from locals – takes you to the magnificent **Kasbah Aït Ben Abou**, which is second in Skoura only to Kasbah Amerhidl. It lies on well-farmed land and is still inhabited.

Finally, on the edge of the palmery, you might follow the trail to the imposing **Marabout Sidi M'Barek ou Ali**. A high wall, broken only by a door, encloses the *marabout*, which doubles as a grain store – a powerful twofold protection on both spiritual and military levels.

El Kelâa des Mgouna

Travelling through the Dadès in spring, you'll find Skoura's fields divided by the bloom of thousands of small, pink Persian roses – cultivated as hedgerows dividing the plots. At **EL KELÂA DES MGOUNA** (also spelt QALAT MGOUNA), 50km east across another shaft of semi-desert plateau, there are still more, along with an immense Kasbah-style **rose-water factory** with two prominent chimneys. Here, the *Capp et Florale* company distil the *eau de rose*. In late May (sometimes early June), a **rose festival** is held in the village to celebrate the new year's crops: a good time to visit, with villagers coming down from the mountains for the market, music and dancing.

The rest of the year, El Kelâa's single, rambling street is less impressive. There's a **Wednesday souk**, worth breaking your journey for, but little else of interest beyond the locked and deserted ruins of a **Glaoui Kasbah**, on a spur above the river. The local shops are always full of *eau de rose*, though, and the factory can be visited, too, for a look at – and an overpowering smell of – the distillation process. A second factory, *Aromag*, alongside the *Mobil* petrol station, 13km out along the Tinerhir road, can also be visited; it is run by a French company, based – of course – at Grasse.

One of a hundred varieties, *Rosa Centifolio* have, as the name implies, hundreds of small leaves on each small bush. Folklore has it that they were brought from Persepolis by the Phoenicians. Aerial photographs testify to there being 4200km of low hedges; each metre yields up to one kilo of petals and it takes ten tons of petals to produce two to three litres of rose-oil. The petals are picked by women who start very early in the morning before the heat dries the bloom.

Practicalities

The town has three **banks** (*Banque Populaire*, as usual in the south; *Credit Agricole*; and *Wafabank*) and two **hotels**. The cheap option, inconspicuously signposted on the main street, is the *Hôtel du Grand Atlas* (☎04/83.62.14; ⑩), a pleasant little place, with a *hammam* and a simple restaurant. It is run by Lahcen Aaddi and his son, Hassan, who can put you in touch, if you wish, with guides for trekking in the Djebel Sarhro (see p.417) and Djebel Mgoun.

The other hotel, up by the Kasbah, is *Les Roses de Dadès* (☎04/88.38.07; ④), an old "Grand Hôtel du Sud", owned by ONMT, with a swimming pool, but little motivation as it awaits privatization.

Vallée des Roses

If you have transport, this "secret valley" of the **Asif M'Goun**, north of El Kelâa, would make a good one-day excursion, or a detour en route to Boumalne. The valley begins due north of the town and is trailed by the minor road 6903 to TOURBIST and BOU THARAR, where the 6904 leads south back to EL GOUMT on the main P32 road; both should be practicable with a Renault 4L. In spring, the route is lined by thousands of roses, and there is a notable Kasbah at **Bou Tharar**.

Boumalne du Dadès

BOUMALNE DU DADÈS is a more interesting stop than El Kelâa. It is again well poised for exploration of the Djebel Sarhro and for the bird-rich Vallée des Oiseaux (guides can be arranged for both through the hotels), and is the gateway to the Dadès Gorge. In addition, it has some charm of its own, with the old town on the eastern bank of the Dadès climbing up the slope to the plateau where a military barracks and trio of hotels command the valley and the entry to the gorge.

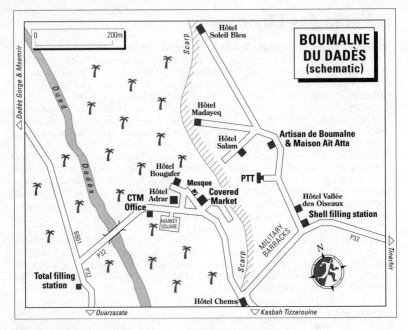

Practicalities

Approaching the town from the Ouarzazate road, you reach a small market square (the *souk* takes place on Wednesday) and the old *Hôtel Adrar*, above which is a mosque and a covered market open daily. **Grands taxis** and local buses go from the market square or from the front of the covered market; the CTM office is downhill of the market square. Uphill from here, on the plateau, are several hotels, a *Shell* petrol station, a *PTT* (there is no bank), and two **shops**. Both of the shops – the *Artisanale de Boumalne* and *Maison Aït Atta* – are worth looking round for a range of carpets and carvings, on sale without great pressure.

Grands taxis make regular runs to Ouarzazate and Tinerhir. For Msemrir and the Dadès Gorge, you can usually get a landrover taxi, transit or lorry; a transit/minibus leaves for Msemrir daily between noon and 2pm, returning at dawn the next morning.

For details of **guides for trekking and bird-watching**, see the listings below for the hotels *Salam*, *Soleil Bleu* and *Kasbah Tizzarouine*.

Accommodation and meals

There is a decent selection of hotels, all of which have **restaurants** – though a few hours' notice may be required for meals. In addition, for simple Moroccan fare, try the *Restaurant Ossikis* on the market square or the *Restaurant Place de la Mosquée*, half way up the hill by the grand mosque.

Hotels comprise:

CHEAP

Hôtel Adrar (☎04/83.43.55). An adequate hotel with 26 rooms on three floors; it's handy for the buses, taxis and market square, and there's a terrace café from which to watch the day go by. ①

HAMMADA BIRDS AND THE VALLÉE DES OISEAUX

Boumalne offers some exceptional bird-watching and wildlife possibilities – as can be seen from the logbook at the *Hôtel Soleil Bleu* (see hotel listings). To the south of the town are abundant and accessible areas of **hammada** or desert fringe, and a grassy valley. The hammada provides an austere environment, whose dry, sunny conditions are ideal for cold-blooded reptiles and are frequented by Montpelier snake, Atlas agama and fringe-toed lizard. The **grassy plains** provide food for small herds of Edmi gazelle and Addax antelope and shelter for a variety of specialist bird species such as **cream-coloured courser**, **red-rumped wheatear** and **thick-billed lark**. Predatory **lanner falcon** patrol the skies and the rare and elusive **Houbara bustard** makes an occasional appearance.

The most rewarding birding trip in the region is to the so-called **Vallée des Oiseaux**, which heads off the 6907 from Boumalne to Iknioun in the Djebel Sarhro. This is the 'Tagdilt track' and well known to birdwatchers; it is marked by a line of green (picturesque) shading on the Michelin map. Here, you will find **Temmink's horned lark**, **bar-tailed desert lark**, **eagle owl** and several **sandgrouse**: pin-tailed, crowned and black bellied. And, for extra measure, they make traditional pottery at Tagdilt.

Hôtel Bougafer (☎04/83.07.68). Behind the *Hôtel Adrar*, this was once only a restaurant/café, but now has six rooms which are, considering that the tariff is half that of the *Adrar*, good value. Like the *Adrar*, it has hot showers separate from the rooms. ⓪

Hôtel Chems (☎04/83.00.41). An attractive hotel, with a good restaurant and a new Moroccan salon. Built on the hillside, the rooms overlooking the valley have spectacular views; and all the rooms are en suite. ①

Hôtel Salam (☎04/83.07.62). This is a small hotel on the plateau now managed by Daoud Ochatou and, an Englishman, Martin Sutton. There are nine rooms, with separate facilities, and simple catering (40dh for main meals). They are keen to help those who want to trek or ski. ①

Hôtel Soleil Bleu (☎04/83.41.63). Reached along a piste, 300m beyond the *Hôtel Madayeq*, this has stunning views of the valley, and good, simple rooms with hot showers. It is run by the Najim brothers, who specialize in tours and treks, particularly for bird-watchers; day visits to the Vallée des Oiseaux and other promising locations (see box feature) are possible, and the hotel maintains an excellent bird-watching log. ①

Hôtel Vallée des Oiseaux (☎04/83.07.64). A motel-style place with a pleasant garden but, away from the edge of the plateau, no views; some en-suite rooms. ①

MODERATE

Kasbah Tizzarouine (☎04/83.06.90). More of a compound than a Kasbah, but with an impressive gatehouse, this relatively new venture is half a kilometre beyond the *Hôtel Chems*, along a side road and with some impressive views from the scarp edge. Within the compound, you can camp or park a campervan, sleep in a Berber tent, rent well-equipped rooms or (the pièce de résistance) occupy a *chambre troglodytique*. There are five caves on the cliff edge; two of them were originally occupied by nomads twice a year as they moved their animals from the valleys to the Djebel Sarhro and back. In addition, Dahni Mohammed Lamnaouar, who works at the *Tizzarouine*, is a qualified mountain guide and can be contracted here for a range of trips. ②

EXPENSIVE

Hôtel Madayeq (☎04/83.07.63). A chain hotel owned by ONMT and awaiting privatization; from the outside it looks like a drunken Kasbah, made up of huge up-ended bricks. Indoors, the decor and service evoke memories of *Intourist* hotels. ④

The Djebel Sarhro

The **Djebel Sarhro** (or Saghro) lies south of the road from Ouarzazate to Tinerhir and east of that from Ouarzazate to Zagora. It is a starkly beautiful jumble of volcanic peaks, quite unlike the High Atlas or Anti-Atlas, and punctuated by gorges, ruined Kasbahs, occasional villages, and the black tents of the semi-nomadic **Aït Atta** tribe. Fiercely independent through the centuries, and never subdued by any sultan, the Aït Atta were the last bulwark of resistance against the French, making their final stand on the slopes of Djebel Bou Gafer in 1933 (see box feature).

Until recently, the Djebel Sarhro had seen few visitors but it is becoming better known and more accessible through **trekking** operators like Explore and Sherpa Expeditions. They operate here from October to April, when the High Atlas is too cold and snow-covered for walking; in the summer, Sarhro itself is impracticable, being too hot and exposed, and with water, always scarce, quite impossible to find. In fact, Djebel Sarhro means 'dry mountain' in Berber.

Independent exploration of the range is possible by **car** (all roads on our map are passable by Renault 4L in reasonable weather). However, bear in mind that road signs are rare and that flash floods often lead to diversions or worse; navigation is not easy and taking along a local guide would be useful.

A **guide** is certainly recommended for trekking. They can be contacted through the *Hôtel Soleil Bleu* and the *Kasbah Tizzaarouine* in Boumalne Dadès and the *Hôtel Tomboctou* in Tinerhir. Alternatively, if you are approaching the Djebel Sarhro from the southwest, you could discuss your plans and hire a guide at the campsite at Agdz; qualified guides are also based at Nkob. The bureau for guides, based at El Kelâa des Magouna, no longer functions – despite its inclusion in current ONMT literature.

Treks and routes

When planning a trek in the Sarhro, bear in mind the harshness of the terrain and the considerable distances involved. With the exception of the **Vallée des Oiseaux**, off the Boumalne–Iknioun road (see wildlife box on p.417), this is not an area for short treks, and nor does it have much infrastructure; you will need to be prepared to camp.

Given ten days, you could set out from El Kelâa des Mgouna, explore the area west of the **Tizi n'Tazazert** and loop back to El Kelâa or Boumalne. Alternatively, with about five days free, you could travel by local taxi from Boumalne du Dadès or Tinerhir to **Iknioun** and then walk south, by **Djebel Bou Gafer**, to **Imi n'Site** and **Nkob**, taking local transport from there either back to Boumalne or Tinerhir or across to Tansikht on the Ouarzazate–Zagora road.

You could also do the latter trip in the opposite direction from the Drâa Valley, arranging a guide at Nkob.

Iknioun to Nekob

The easiest access to the range for **trekkers** is a transit taxi from Boumalne to **IKNIOUN**; this runs most days, but Wednesday, after the Boumalne *souk*, is the most reliable. There are **rooms** in Iknioun, if you wish to stay. Alternatively, you can ask to be dropped at the junction of the piste 7km before Iknioun (there is a large sign here, so you shouldn't miss it), which you could follow in two or three days' **walk to Nkob** (35km). The people at the village 1km along the Nkob road will provide rooms for a first night's stop, though walkers should be prepared to camp, beyond here. The Nkob *souk* is on a Sunday, so if you walk slowly, you can pick up a ride on the Saturday.

Following this route – which is also practicable with a four-wheel-drive vehicle – it takes about an hour's walk to reach a junction (at 2014m) to Tiouft: turn left here and climb steadily for an hour to a faux col, and then across an easy plateau for half an hour to the true col, **Tizi n'Tazazert** (2283m). From here, it's downhill, through rocky scenery, with table-top mesas and volcanic cones visible to the west; there are traces of underground water, with palm trees in gullies, and camels grazing almost to the winter snow line. The piste zigzags down in two hours' walking (there are a lot of shortcuts

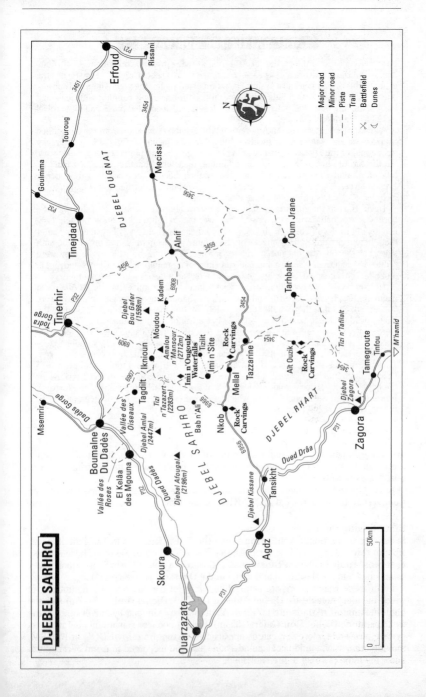

THE BATTLE FOR BOU GAFER

For three centuries or more, the **Aït Atta** tribe were the great warriors of the south, dominating the Djebel Sarhro and its eastern extension, the Djebel Ougnat. At the turn of the century, the British journalist Walter Harris reported seeing the young men at Touroug, one of their tribal strongholds (see map on p.419), practising running with galloping horses, holding onto their tails – a breakneck skill which enabled those on foot to travel as fast as the riders.

As guerrilla fighters, the Aït Atta resisted the French occupation from the outset. Led by **Hassou Ba Salem**, they finally retreated, at the beginning of 1933, to the rocky stronghold of the **Djebel Bou Gafer**, a chaos of gorges and pinnacles. Estimates vary, but the Aït Atta had at least a thousand fighting men, who, together with their families, totalled around 7000 people, accompanied by their flocks. They faced vastly superior French forces. Ali, the son of Hassou Ba Salem, says that, according to his father, these included 83,000 troops and four aircraft squadrons.

David Hart in the *Aït Atta of Southern Morocco* (1984) concluded that this was 'the hardest single battle which the French had ever had to fight in the course of their 'pacification of Morocco'. The French first attacked the stronghold on 21 February and, after that, there were almost daily attacks on the ground and from the air. Many died on both sides but the Aït Atta did not surrender for over a month, by which time they were reduced to half their strength and had run short of ammunition. The victors, moving in on 25 March, occupied, according to one of them, "an indescribable charnel house".

Hassou Ba Salem's conditions on surrender included a promise that the Aït Atta could maintain their tribal structures and customs, particularly insofar as law and order were concerned, and that they would not be "ruled" by the infamous T'Hami El Glaoui , the Pasha of Marrakesh, whom they regarded as a traitor to their homeland. The French were content to accept, the battle meaning that their "pacification" was virtually complete, and giving them access to the valuable silver and copper mines at Moudou.

Hassou Ba Salem died in 1960 and was buried at Tagia, his birthplace, 5km from Tinerhir. Ali, his son, succeeded him as leader of the tribe, and took part in the 1975 Green March into the Western Sahara. He died in 1992 and is also buried at Tagia. As for the battlefield itself, local guides will show you the sites, including ruins of the fortress. It is still littered with spent bullets, which are covered in spring by colourful clumps of thyme, rockroses and broom.

for walkers), running due south down the main valley to Nkob. If you have energy, there's an interesting excursion off to the west, up a side valley, to the striking **mountain** "gate" **of Bab n'Ali**.

At **NKOB** there is a café with basic **rooms**, and nearby rock carvings. Transits run from here to the main road at **TANSIKHT**, on the Drâa.

Other driving routes

In addition to the **north–south route over** the **Tizi n'Tazazert** to Tansikht, it is possible to drive over a much lower pass, the **Tizi n'Tafilalt**, to Zagora. There are also **east–west routes** between **Tansikht** and **Rissani** (in Tafilalt), which are much better established and are described at the end of the Drâa section (see p.411).

From these roads, there are astonishing views of the surrounding mountains, of which the most notable are **Djebel Afougal** (2196m), **Djebel Amlal** (2447m) and, the highest, **Amalou n'Mansour** (2712m). All of them are climbed by one or other of the trek operators. **Djebel Bou Gafer** (1598m) is lower and less remarkable but its history (see box) adds interest; it can be approached on foot from MOUDOU or KADEM, though either way a guide is again advisable and you may need to camp overnight to make the most of a visit to the battlefield.

Other less demanding attractions include the **Imi n'Ougoulz waterfalls** and **pre-historic rock carvings** near Nkob, Mellal and Tazzarine (local guides are essential for all of these).

The Dadès Gorge

The **Dadès Gorge**, with its high cliffs of limestone and weirdly shaped erosions, begins almost immediately north of Boumalne. Leaving the P32, you follow the 6901 road, signposted "Mserhir" (Msemrir). Most travellers cover the first 25km or so by car or taxi, then turn back, which makes for a fine day's trip. If you have a 4x4, however, you could **loop over to the Todra Gorge** or continue **up and across the High Atlas** to the Beni Mellal–Marrakesh road. Alternatively, a couple of days' walking along the gorge from Boumalne will reward you with superb scenery, and plenty of Kasbahs and pisé architecture to admire; there are rooms in several of the villages en route to Msemrir.

The gorge is accessible by local transport from Boumalne, with Peugeot taxis, transit vans and Berber pick-ups (*camionettes*) and lorries (*camions)* leaving regularly from the market square for Aït Ali (25km) and less often to Msemrir (63km). Pick-ups run occasionally to Atlas villages beyond but they do so more often on the Todra gorge (see p.428) route, which would make an easier access point if you plan to cross the Atlas on local transport. Returning to Boumalne, a transit/minibus leaves Msemrir daily at 4am.

See our **map** "Over the Atlas: Beyond Todra and Dades" on p.429 for routes.

Into the gorge: Boumalne to Msemir

For the first 15–20km, the **Dadès Gorge** is pretty wide and the valley carved out of it is green and well populated. There are *ksour* and Kasbahs clustered all along this stretch, many of them flanked by more modern houses, though even these usually retain some feature of the decorative traditional architecture.

Boumalne to Aït Oudinar

About three kilometres along the road (6901) into the gorge from Boumalne, you pass an old **Glaoui Kasbah**, strategically sited as always to control all passage. Four kilometres further in, where the road begins to turn into a hairpin corniche, there is a superb group of **ksour** at **AÏT ARBI**, built against a fabulous volcanic twist of the rocks. The Kasbahs seem like natural extensions of their setting – tinged with the colour of the earth and fabulously varied, ranging from bleak lime-white to dark reds and greenish blacks.

Four kilometres on from here is a region known as **Tamnalt**, which is also known by the locals as the "Hills of Human Bodies" after its strange formations which, in fact, look mostly like feet. Geologically the rock is a weathered conglomerate of pebbles which probably lay where a great river entered a primordial sea. Hereabouts, you climb over a little pass, flanked by the *Café-Restaurant Meguirne,* 13km from Boumalne. The views make this a fine place to stop for lunch (as tour groups do) and it also has seven basic **rooms** for rent (no phone; ⓪). Nearby there is a hidden side-valley, entered by a narrow gorge: the owners of the *Meguirne* take a proprietary interest in this patch of nature and will try to involve you in *le camping sauvage.* A kilometre north of the *Meguirne* there are further rooms – clean and quite reasonable – at the *Hôtel-Restaurant Kasba* (no phone; ⓪), which again caters for tour groups by day, laying on "Berber Weddings" in its courtyard.

On from here, the valley floor is less fertile and the hills gentler. The road continues through the hamlet of AÏT ALI (25km from Boumalne) to a spot known as **Aït**

Oudinar, where a bridge spans the river, and the gorge narrows quite dramatically. There is a little **hotel**, the *Auberge des Gorges du Dadès* (☎04/83.07.62; ⑩), by the bridge, an attractive place to stay, offering a choice between cheap, basic **rooms** or pricier ones with en-suite hot showers; **bivouac tents** on the terrace, or **camping** alongside the river where the few poplar trees provide some shade. The *auberge* serves meals, and arranges **mule** and **4x4 trips** into the gorge and Atlas. It has a tie-up with the *Hôtel de Foucauld* in Marrakesh.

There is further accommodation 2km further along the road (which deteriorates into a poor piste) from the bridge, on the east bank of the river. This consists of a row of small, fairly basic **hotels**, hemmed in by slabs of cliff; they are, in order of appearance: the *Auberge des Peupliers* (⑩), *Hôtel La Gazelle du Dadès* (⑩), *Hôtel La Kasbah de la Vallée* (①), and *Auberge Tisadrine* (⑩), beyond which a more upmarket hotel is being built. The best rooms, with en-suite showers, are at *La Gazelle* and *La Kasbah*. All of the group offer riverside camping.

The gorge at this point has narrowed to a canyon, and there are some good walks to be had, stream hopping and wading; the hotels will help with advice and, if you want, fix you up with a guide.

Aït Oudinar to Msemrir

The road north of Aït Oudinar is a bone-shaking piste, and in a rental car you may decide to go no further than the canyon mouth described above – and even then you may decide to walk the last 2km from the bridge. After passing the cluster of hotels, the road climbs by a coil of hairpin bends above the gorge, before sqeezing through a tight, narrow gap to reach **Taghia n'Dadès** where there is the small and basic *Café-Hôtel Taghia* (⑩ no electricity and limited toilet facilities). Walking from here, you can scramble up the hill east to a cave with stalactites, or go north to a small but impressive gorge, with views down over the Dadès Gorge.

Spring floods permitting, it is usually possible to drive on to Msemrir (63km in all from Boumalne). For a distance, the east side of the gorge is dominated by the **Isk n'Isladene** cliffs and then the road follows a canyon to **Tidrit** where the road snakes up and crosses the face of one of the huge canyon loops before the final run to Msemrir. Two kilometres before Msemrir, the **Oussikis** valley, to the left, can be visited by an even rougher piste.

On from Msemrir

At **MSEMRIR** there is **accommodation** and meals to be had at the *Café Agdal* ⑩; and the newer *Hôtel Aït Atta* (both ⑩) Beyond here, is a choice of piste routes: east to join the Todra Gorge at Tamtatoucht (6–8hrs by landrover), or north across the High Atlas. People drive Renault 4Ls across both these routes in summer but they are not really suitable transport – and will break rental conditions. There are frequent wash-outs, bare slabs to cross and other hazards, and really best left for lorries or landrovers with four-wheel drive.

Over the Atlas

Heading over the High Atlas, the most direct route is to join the road from Todra at Agoudal: 60km or so of very rough driving, over the **Tizi n'Ouano**. Some details of the route beyond is included in the Todra Gorge section (see p.426).

If you are looking for local transport, you may strike lucky with a lorry from Msemrir to Agoudal, but the route isn't driven nearly as regularly as that from Todra, so be prepared for a long wait at Msemrir – and winter often closes this road completely.

Across to Tamtatoucht

If you are intent on **crossing to the Todra Gorges** to Tamtatoucht, there is virtually no chance of a local lorry, though you might just find a lift with fellow tourists. It should be added, too, that, if you are driving, you'd find it considerably easier to go in the other direction. Coming from the Dadès it's a long, uphill haul, and the seventy-odd kilometres of piste, often in a shocking state, can take a full day to travel.

About a kilometre out from Msemrir, the **Imilchil piste** swings off across the valley; the Tamtatoucht track (not always worthy of the name) keeps on up the valley to reach **Tizi n'Uguent Zegsaoun** (2639m). The piste then sweeps down to follow the **Tizgui n'Ouaddou** valley and next climbs to a smaller pass where the view opens out to the plains stretching to Aït Hani. A very rough descent over limestone joins the plain and crosses it to hit the Tamtatoucht/Aït Hani piste (see pp.428–430 including map).

Tinerhir (Tinghir)

TINERHIR is largely a base for the trip up into the **Todra Gorge** – but it is also a much more interesting place than other administrative centres along this route. It is overlooked by a ruinous but ornamental Glaoui Kasbah, and just east of the modern town is an extensive palmery, which feels a world apart, with its groups of *ksour* built at intervals into the rocky hills above. Don't be in too much of a hurry to catch the first lorry up to the Todra Gorge – the Tinerhir and, to the northeast, the Todra **palmeries** – are major attractions in themselves.

The palmeries seem all the more special after the **journey from Boumalne**: a bleak drive across desolate plains, interrupted by the sudden oases of IMITER (with several fine Kasbahs) and TIMADRIOUINE. The **Djebel Sarhro** (see p.417) looms to the south for the latter part of the trip, dry barren outlines of mountains, like something from the Central Asia steppes; the drama of this part of the range was another big backdrop in David Lean's *Lawrence of Arabia*.

South of Imiter, in the foothills of the Djebel Sarhro, you will see – from the Boumalne-Tinerhir road (P32) – the spoil and silver mines of the *Société Métallurgique*

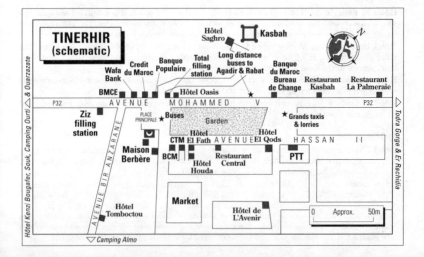

d'Imiter (SMI). Outside interest is not encouraged and rumours abound locally about other mining enterprises, possibly including gold mining; as you enter Tinerhir, you pass alongside the SMI company houses, signposted *Cité de Personnel*.

Orientation – and transport

Orientation is straightforward. The centre of Tinerhir is a long **garden square**, flanked by hotels, café-restaurants and the **PTT**; here are to be found the **grands taxis** for standard runs to Boumalne, Er Rachidia and Erfoud and the **lorries** which go up the Todra Gorge to Tamtatoucht and Imilchil. In the **Place Principale** to the southwest of the garden square are the local **buses** and **CTM** office; long-distance buses, passing through Tinerhir en route for Agadir and Rabat, call here or stop on Av. Mohammed V facing the central garden.

There are regular **buses** from Tinerhir to Ouarzazate (the 6am goes on to Marrakesh), to Fes and Meknes (leaving at 7pm), and to Er Rachidia, and **grands taxis** in both directions (places available for Ourzazate/Boumalne/Er Rachidia/occasionally Erfoud). The Berber lorries (*camionettes*) make regular runs to villages in the **Todra Gorge and beyond**; on Mondays, from around noon (following the *souk*), numerous lorries set out for Atlas villages, including one that goes right over the mountains to Arhbala, driving through the night. Note that you can also arrange transport (and/or trips) for the **Todra gorge** (or beyond) through the *Hôtel Tombouctou* or *Camping Ourti* (see below).

Four **banks** (*Banque Populaire, Crédit du Maroc, Wafabank* and *BMCE*) are on the northwest side of Av. Mohammed V as it leaves the Place Principale towards Boumalne; *BCM* is on the Place Principale, alongside the CTM office; and *Banque du Maroc* has a useful bureau de change on Av. Mohammed V facing the *grands taxis* and lorries.

Accommodation

Most of the cheaper **hotels** line Av. Hassan II, facing the central garden; the dearer ones are a bit more scattered, but all walkable from the set-down points of taxis and buses – with the possible exception of the *Hôtel Kenzi Bougafer* out on the Boumalne road opposite the *souk*.

CHEAP

Hôtel El Fath, 56 Av. Hassan II (☎04/83.48.06). By the CTM office, this self-styled *résidence* has smart, clean rooms (some on the small side) with hot showers on the corridor. The café-restaurant on the ground floor serves good standards – on the rooftop terrace if you wish. ①

Hôtel Houda, 11 Rue Moulay Ismail (no phone). On a side street, off Av. Hassan II, close to the CTM office and the *Hôtel Raha* and *Hôtel Salam* (neither of which is recommended), this small hotel opened in 1995 and is a good cheap choice. ①

Hôtel L'Oasis, Av. Mohammed V (☎04/83.36.70). Another promising, central choice, recently remodelled to include ten en-suite rooms. ①

Hôtel Al Qods, 8 Av. Hassan II (☎04/83.46.05). A small, clean and very reasonable hotel with hot showers, and a restaurant. ①

MODERATE

Hôtel l'Avenir, near the central market (☎04/83.45.99). This excellent budget hotel was set up by a Spaniard, Roger Mimó (see below), and has been taken over by a Basque, Mercedes Garayoa. Standards remain high and her paella is quite a treat. ②

Hôtel Tombouctou, Av. Bir Anzarane (☎04/83.46.04). On a side road, opposite BMCE and to the left of Av. Mohammed V (direction Boumalne). A 1940s Kasbah, tastefully converted by Roger Mimó, who established the *Hôtel L'Avenir* and has a reputation as an authority hereabouts. The place is a delight – one of the memorable small hotels of Morocco – and Roger (who is author of an excellent Spanish trekking guide on Morocco) is a great source of knowledge. He can help with your plans, hire guides and vehicles for you, and rents out bikes for exploring the Tinerhir/Todra oases. ③

EXPENSIVE

Hôtel Kenzi Bougafer, Av. Mohammed V (☎04/83.32.80). A modern hotel (opened 1993), located opposite the Monday *souk*. It's a luxurious place, already promoted from three to four stars, with very comfortable suites, rooms, a restaurant, bar and swimming pool. ④

Hôtel Saghro, on a hill to the north of the town centre (☎04/83.41.81). Another of the 'Grands Hôtels du Sud', owned by ONMT, and rather drifting along awaiting privatization. Still, it has a swimming pool, restaurant and bar (residents only), and the views of the palmeries are stunning. ④

CAMPSITES

Camping Ourti, Av. Mohammed V (☎04/83.32.05), on the Boumalne road, beyond the *souk*. A new site, enthusiastically managed by a young crowd. It is open year round and has a good range of facilities – including hot showers and a swimming pool (April–October) There's a restaurant (50dh) and a few bungalows, which sleep up to three people (35dh per head). The site can also arrange 4x4 transport, driver and guide for the gorge, or other expeditions.

Camping Almo, off Av. Bir Anzarane (☎04/83.43.14). Beyond the new *Hôtel Tomboctou* on the opposite side of the road. A longer established site and consequently a little more shaded. It has hot showers, a small shop, and a swimming pool.

Meals and carpets

There are **restaurants** at the hotels *L'Avenir, Kenzi Bougafer, Al Qods, Saghro* and *Tomboctou*; the *Kenzi Bougafer* and *Saghro* are expensive and the latter is overpriced; otherwise all are recommended. The restaurants *Central*, in the centre, and *Kasbah* and *La Palmeraie*, on the road out to Er Rachidia, are all good, too – the (relatively upmarket) *Kasbah*, especially.

If you're interested in buying **crafts**, Tinerhir has a branch of the excellent **Maison Berbère** chain (run by the Alaoui family like those in Ouarzazate, Zagora and Rissani), which usually has high-quality rugs, carpets and especially silver; there are now two shops, both near the Place Principale: one by the mosque and the other by the *Café de la Gazelle* – find one and they will take you to the other so you can buy at both!

The Tinerhir and Todra palmeries

There are **palmeries** to the southeast and northeast of Tinerhir, lining both sides of the Todra River. For an overview, the *Hôtel Saghro* has the town's best viewing point. To explore, you're best off renting a **bike** from Roger Mimó at the *Hôtel Tomboctou*, and discussing a route with him; our map was based upon his sketches. Alternatively, you could hire a mule – and arrange a guide – in one of the oasis villages.

The palmeries follow the usual pattern in these valleys: date palms at the edge, terraces of olive, pomegranate, almond and fruit trees further in, with grain and vegetable crops planted beneath them. The **ksour** (family compounds) each originally controlled one section of the oasis, and there were frequent disputes over territory and, above all, over access to the mountain streams for each *ksour*'s network of water channels. Even in this century, their fortifications were built in earnest, and, as Walter Harris wrote (melodramatically, but probably with little exaggeration): "The whole life was one of warfare and gloom. Every tribe had its enemies, every family had its blood feuds, and every man his would-be murderer."

Our map indicates several good viewing points, or **miradors**; don't miss the length of road between Taorirt and Ichmarirne – which is breathtaking in the hour before sunset. The map also names the most picturesque villages – many of which have **ksour and Kasbahs** with extraordinarily complex patterns incised on the walls. Some include former Jewish quarters – mellahs – though today the populations are almost entirely Berber and Muslim, mainly from the Aït Todra tribe north of Tinerhir and the Aït Atta tribe to the south.

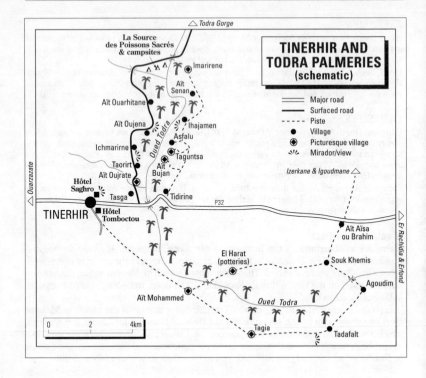

Southeast of Tinerhir there are potteries at **El Harat**, while at nearby **Tagia** are the tombs of the Aït Atta's chiefs, Hassou Ba Salam, and his son, Ali Ba Salam (see p.420). there's a *marabout* near El Harat which is the focus of a June/July *moussem*; this area was originally settled by black slaves who were known as Haratin. For more on the **Todra palmery** – and the approach to the gorge – see below.

The Todra Gorge

Whatever else you do in the south, spend at least a night in the **Todra Gorge**. You don't need your own transport, nor any great expeditionary zeal to get up there, and yet it seems remote from the routes through the main valleys – still and splendid in the fading evening light when the day visitors have gone.

The deepest, narrowest and most spectacular part of the gorge is only 15km from Tinerhir, and there are three hotels where you can get a meal and stay the night. These can be reached by *grand taxi* or minibus from Tinerhir; they leave frequently and charge 6/8dh a place. Returning to Tinerhir, you stand a better chance of a taxi if you walk back to the **Zaouïa Sidi Abdelâli**, 3km before the gorge, or hitch a lift with day visitors or other tourists.

Beyond the cluster of hotels, the road turns into a piste, providing an adventurous route right **over the Atlas via the village of Imilchil** (famed for its wedding market), as well as a possible loop over to the Dadès gorge. You can arrange transport along the Imilchil route, either by chartering it at Tinerhir, or by paying for a place on a series of

---

TODRA WILDLIFE AND BIRDS

The **Todra Gorge** offers excellent wildlife and bird-watching opportunities. Along the **riverbeds** are colonies of marsh frog and green toad, while the rocky slopes provide shelter for small numbers of ground squirrel. The **scrubby areas** ring to the calls of common bulbul and the **rocky outcrops** provide occasional glimpses of black wheatear, blue rock thrush and rock dove. There are also good numbers of pale crag martin wheeling overhead and soaring above the gorge crest and, if you strike lucky, it is possible to observe the pair of **Bonelli's eagles** which nest in the gorge.

Berber lorries, which shuttle across for village *souks*. If you plan to drive the route, you will need a suitable (preferably 4x4) vehicle.

Tinerhir to the gorge

En route to the gorge proper, the road climbs along the Todra palmery (see palmery map on previous page), a last, fertile shaft of land, narrowing at points to a ribbon of palms between the cliffs. There are more or less continuous villages, all of them the pink-grey colour of the local rock, and the ruins of Kasbahs and *ksour* up above or on the other side.

Around 9km from Tinerhir, you cross a tributary of the Todra, and come to three **campsites**, flanking a particularly luxuriant stretch of the palmery. The first of these, *Camping Atlas*, is the largest and best equipped, with a shop, restaurant and, across the road, the *Auberge de l'Atlas* (☎04/83.42.09; ➀) with simple rooms to rent. Next along are the well-shaded *Camping du Lac* (☎04/83.42.15; ➀), with rooms and a restaurant, and *Auberge Camping de la Source des Poissons Sacrés* (☎04/83.42.04; ➀), again also with rooms. The latter is set beside a pool known as **La Source des Poissons Sacrés**, where women come to bathe (on three successive Fridays) as a cure for sterility.

Anywhere else, a stay in one of these campsites would be a major recommendation. But if time is at all limited, you might as well continue to the beginning of the gorge. If you're on local transport, and it's not too hot, you could get yourself set down here, have a snack and walk the final 6km. The valley narrows to a thin strip of green on this final approach, until finally the surfaced road gives out and you arrive at a mini-gorge, leading into an amphitheatre of cliffs, prefacing the **gorge** proper – a wonderful sight, with canyon walls rising 300m on both sides.

The mouth of the gorge

The really enclosed section of **the gorge** extends for just a few hundred metres; it should certainly be walked, even if you're not going any further, for the drama of the scenery. If you are interested in **birds**, this is also one of the best bird-watching locations in the south (see box above).

If at all possible, take the time to stay the night here, as the beauty of the place unfolds in the evening light. Just at the end of the surfaced road, is the *Hôtel El Mansour* (☎04/83.42.13; ➀) an attractively ramshackle place with a pair of palm trees growing out through the roof, excellent and copious meals, and a choice of sleeping in one of four rooms, on the roof (the best option in summer), or on matresses in the downstairs salon. Through the mini-gorge in the "amphitheatre" of cliffs are two slightly fancier hotels, the *Les Roches* (☎04/83.48.14; ➀) and *Yasmina* (☎04/83.42.07; ➁). These each have restaurants, sometimes under pressure from tour groups, but the food is good and the set lunches are a bargain. Again, they offer a choice of accommodation, including en-suite rooms, or cheaper beds in the salon or tent dining rooms, or out on the terrace. Prices fluctuate according to season and thus demand.

All three hotels are very friendly and relaxed – and all are very cold in winter, when the sun leaves the gorge early in the afternoon. If you wanted to camp, you would do better walking four or five kilometres up the gorge, to reach a more open section, though be sure to pitch your tent on reasonably high ground, in case of flash floods.

Climbing

The Todra Gorge is increasingly being recognized for its climbing potential. There are now many bolted routes, French Grade 5 and above. The *Hôtel El Mansour* keeps an excellent French topo-guide for reference; it includes 150 routes, the pitches being mainly French Grades 6 and 7 (UK Grades 5 and 6).

Beyond Todra: over the Atlas

It is possible to continue on piste routes beyond the Todra Gorge to **Tamtatoucht**, and from there across the High and Middle Atlas ranges, to emerge on either the P24 (Azrou–Beni Mellal), or the P21 (Midelt–Er Rachidia). In between, you are travelling on isolated and at times very rough tracks, for which four-wheel-drive vehicles (or mountain bikes) are highly desirable, though people make it across in Renaults or Citroens in summer. If you don't have transport, you can travel on a succession of **Berber lorry-taxis** (*camionettes*), timed to coincide with local village *souks*. The attractions of this journey are considerable, offering a real experience of Berber mountain life – the villagers are generally very open and friendly – and some of the most exciting scenery in Morocco, in a succession of passes, mountains, rivers and gorges.

It is also possible to cross from the Todra Gorge to the **Dadès Gorge**, on a rough piste from Tamtatoucht (see p.430).

Some practicalities

There are no **banks** between Tinerhir and Khenifra/Kasba Tadla/Rich, so you'll need to have enough cash for the journey. Don't underestimate the expense of buying **food** in the mountains (30–100 percent above normal rates), nor the prices charged for rides in the **Berber lorries**; as a very general guideline, reckon on about 20dh for every 50km. There are police stations at Aït Hani and Imilchil if you need serious help or advice on the state of the pistes.

Setting out on the **lorries** from Todra, the managers of the hotels at the mouth of the gorge usually have an idea of when the next *camionette* will pass through – and will help arrange your first ride. Promising days to start out are **Wednesday** (to coincide with Aït Hani's Thursday *souk*) and **Friday** (for Imilchil's Saturday *souk*), but it is all a bit pot luck, and you should be prepared for the odd day's wait in a village for a ride, or to walk one or other of the stages of the route. Eventually, everyone seems to get across to **Arhbala** or **Naour** (where there are buses down to Kasba Tadla/Khenifra) or to **Rich** (on the Midelt–Er Rachidia road and bus route); heading for Rich, the most used route is the 3443 from Bouzmou.

Travelling from the **north or east**, the same pattern applies, with lorries up from Arhbala/Rich for the Imilchil *souk*, and down to Todra/Tinerhir after it.

Driving, it would be unwise to attempt the route, without a four-wheel-drive vehicle, outside the midsummer period of **June to September**.

Tamtatoucht and beyond: some routes

The road up the Todra Gorge (from the hotels) is the worst section of the route; the track crosses or uses the river beds, or jolts along rough embankments. A *marabout*

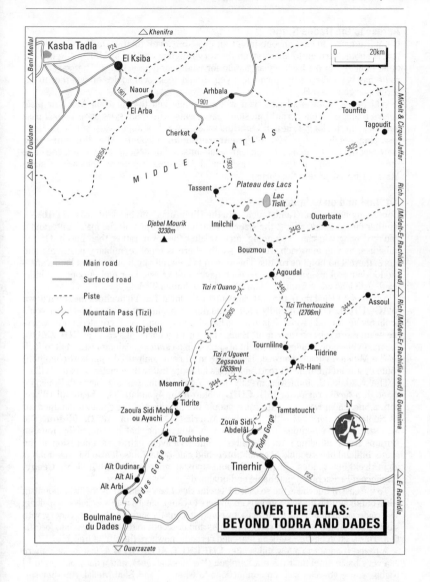

marks the top end of the gorge and a delightful shady walk; and then, 17km from the entrance to the gorge, you reach **TAMATOUCHT**: a sizeable sprawl with a few basic hotels and cafés. At the entrance is the new and friendly *Auberge Baddou* (①), with clean rooms, hot showers, good food and *terasse panormamique*. You can also camp alongside. Beyond this point, the road improves considerably, though it is still unsurfaced and slow, difficult mountain driving.

Across to the Dadès Gorge

It's at Tamtatoucht that anyone intent on **crossing over to the Dadès Gorge** (see p.421) should turn off to the west, on the very rough piste 3444 to MSEMRIR; lifts are most unlikely, so it's basically an option for landrover-type vehicles. The start of this route has been altered by storms and you should seek local advice on whether to cut across, or go via Aït Hani.

Whichever route is advised, you will eventually join the Aït Hani–Msemrir piste before a tough ascent across limestone pavements. The track goes over a small pass and then up the long **Tizgui n'Ouadda** valley towards a huge scarp before the final sweeping bends to the **Tizi n'Uguent Zegsaoun** (2639m). The difficulties then increase; the road is in a bad state with wash-outs and diversions. Only when you edge the final plain and join the Msemrir-Agoudal piste does it improve – by which stage Msemrir is just around the corner.

Aït Hani and on to Imilchil

Continuing north from Tamtatoucht into the High Atlas, you head towards **AÏT HANI**, another large village, almost the size of Tamtatoucht. It's just off the main route, and if you're driving you can keep going, turning after the town, rather than into it. On the outskirts, as you approach from the south, there is a police/military post, café and store; there's no hotel or rooms. This region is generally high and barren landscape – the locals travel amazing distances each day to collect wood for fuel. A poor and little-used piste leads east from Aït Hani towards Goulmima/Rich.

North of Aït Hani there is a stiff climb up to 2700m at **Tizi Tirherhouzine**, then down to **AGOUDAL**. This is a friendly village, and though again there is no official hotel, you'll probably be offered a room. It is in a less harsh setting, too, better irrigated, and the people seem more relaxed than at Aït Hani. There is the chance of a room at **BOUZMOU**, the next village on, where you might also pick up a *camionette* along piste 3443 to Rich on the Midelt–Er Rachidia road. This is the most commonly used (and best condition) route east from the Imilchil road and sees a lot more traffic than pistes 3444 or 34425.

The road north improves greatly from Agoudal on, passing beyond Bouzmou through a fertile region to **IMILCHIL** (45km from Agoudal). This beautiful village, with a fine caidal Kasbah, is for most people the highlight of the route. It is famed for its September *moussem* – the so-called **Marriage Market of Aït Haddidou**. The *moussem*, once a genuine tribal function, is now somewhat corrupted by tourism (groups are shuttled up from Marrakesh), but it's a lively, extravagant occasion all the same. Imilchil has a couple of small **hotels** and café-restaurants. It also has several resident trekking guides; Bassou Chabout (postal address: 51930 Imilchil Centre, Province d'Er Rachidia) is reliable and qualified.

To the east of Imilchil is the so-called **Plateau des Lacs** – flanked by the twin mountain lakes of **Isli** and **Tislit**. Some groups go up here to camp, but it's not especially compelling. The route north of Imilchil to Arhbala, by contrast, runs through spectacular scenery, with steep drops off the road side, constant climbs and descents, and a slow move into forestation. This section has few settlements – and certainly nowhere the size of Imilchil.

A paved road starts a few miles after **CHERKET**. At **ARHBALA** (see p.238), there is a very basic hotel near the marketplace (Wednesday *souk*), and a daily bus on to El Ksiba, where you can pick up connections to Khenifra and Beni Mellal. Another surfaced road heads off to join the Khenifra–Midelt road (P33).

Tinerhir to Er Rachidia and Erfoud

East from Tinerhir, there is little to delay your progress to **Erfoud/Er Rachidia** and the Tafilalt. The more attractive route is the minor road (3451) from **Tinejdad to**

ROCKS, FOSSILS AND MINERALS: WHAT TO LOOK FOR

Along roadsides in the High and Anti-Atlas and down into the southeast, boys bound into the paths of oncoming cars to offer crystalline mementos of Morocco, and rocks, fossils and minerals are staples of most tourist shops in the south. Before purchasing, you might want to read these notes:

● **Geode** Tennis-ball sized specimens of crystals in a hollow geode cost around £12/$20 in Britain or the US; on the Moroccan hard-shoulder, they may cost more. Brilliant orange and red *geodes* and slices of rock crystal (quartz) look attractive but are unknown to natural science, as are the quartz *geodes* given an irredescent metal coating by vendors.

● **Ammonites** Attractive spirals of ammonites (from Carboniferous to Jurassic) are common in the limestone areas of Britain but in Morocco they can be bought sliced and polished as well as 'raw'. Do not rely on the species name you are given by the shopkeeper – look at the centre of the spiral of the ammomite and at the ridge around its shell to check how far natural features have been 'enhanced' by a chisel.

● **Trilobites** Slightly older than ammonites, trilobites often appear in shops as identical beige coloured fossils on grey slate. In nature, they are rarely so perfect – beware plaster casts. The early trilobite *paradoxides* is about the size of a hand, with long whisker-like spines. A deep-sea inhabitant, it is often found looking rather squashed sideways, where the silts on which it lived have been sheared by pressure. The *Calymene* and *Phacops* types of trilobites are about 200 million years younger than *Paradoxides*. They measure about two inches long, with a crab-like outer skeleton. The half-rounded shield-like skull, often found separated from the exo-skeleton, can appear in a shop with the rest of the skeleton carved around it as a tribute to modern Moroccan craftsmanship!

● In the black limestone regions near Erfoud, the white crystalline shapes of **belemnoids, ammonites** and **nautilus** are cross-sectioned and polished to emphasise the internal structure before being formed into ash-trays and even coffee tables, which can of course be transported for you at a cost. They don't always look so good back home . . .

Erfoud; the **Er Rachidia road** (P32) is a fast but dull highway; neither presents any problems for drivers.

Using local transport, you can get buses or *grands taxis* along the P32 to Er Rachidia; the taxis involve changes at **Tinejdad** (buses and taxis leave from the east end of the town) and **Goulmima**. Alternatively, a private-line bus leaves Tinejdad (from the square used by the *grands taxis*, on the main road) daily at 9.30am along the 3451 **to Erfoud and Rissani**, arriving at Rissani about four hours later; to make the connection, get a *grand taxi* from Tinerhir to Tinejdad.

To Er Rachidia via Goulmima

This is a straightforward and largely barren route, broken only by the oases of Tinejdad and Goulmima.

GOULMIMA, a long, straggling palmery, is made up of some twenty or so scattered **ksour**. If you have transport, and are interested in exploring, ask directions along the complex network of tracks to the *ksour* known as **Gheris de Charis**, the grandest in the palmery. Modern Goulmima, beside the highway, is signalled by the usual "triumphal" entrance and exit arches of the south, and has little more within. There is, however, a *Banque Populaire*, and a smal hotel, the *Gheris* (☎05/78.31.67; ①), 2 Rue Saadian, off Bd. Hassan II and facing the *souk*. For meals, the *Restaurant Elle et Lui* is recommended. **Buses** leave from the street to the left of the eastern archway exit (coming from Tinerhir), **grands taxis** from further up this street.

To Erfoud via Tinejdad

This alternative route – **direct to Erfoud** – is, in parts, eerily impressive. It is well-paved all the way to Erfoud, though sections are sometimes covered over with sand, the result of small, spiralling sandstorms that can suddenly blow across the region and, for twenty or thirty seconds, cut visibility to zero.

The road branches off from the P32 to Er Rachidia at **TINEJDAD**; at the junction itself, there is the useful and welcoming *Café Restaurant Oued Ed-Dahab*. From here the road follows a course of lush oases – populated by the Aït Atta tribe, traditional warriors of the south who used to control land and exact tribute as far afield as the Drâa, 175 km to the southwest and on the far edge of the Djebel Sarhro (see p.417). There are some impressive Kasbahs – ask directions to the **Kasbah Asrir** – and, in the modern, one-street village, numerous cafés and a couple of filling stations; if needs must, there are rooms at the *Café-Restaurant Al Fath*.

You leave the oasis at **MELLAB**, which has another fine **ksar**, and from then on it's more or less continuous desert *hammada* until the beginning of the vast palmery of **EL JORF** – the Tafilalt's largest *ksar* (6000 population) – on the approach to Erfoud. There are a few cafés in the modern village, a post office and a filling station, but no hotel. Beside the road, over much of the distance from Mellab to Erfoud, the land is pock-marked by parallel lines of strange, volcanic-shaped humps – actually man-made entries to the old underground **irrigation channels** or *khettara*. Another curiosity, notable here and elsewhere along the oasis routes, are the Berber **cemeteries** walled off from the desert at the edge of the *ksour*. These consist of long fields of pointed stones thrust into the ground and the occasional cactus and thorn bush, but otherwise unidentified: a wholly practical measure to prevent jackals from unearthing bodies – and in so doing, frustrating their entry to paradise.

ER RACHIDIA, THE ZIZ VALLEY AND THE TAFILALT

The great date-palm oases of the **Oued Ziz** and **Tafilalt** come as near as anywhere in Morocco to fulfilling Western fantasies about the Sahara. They do so by occupying the last desert stretches of the **Ziz** Valley: a route shot through with lush and amazingly cinematic scenes, from its fertile beginnings at the *Source Bleu* (springwater pool) oasis meeting point of **Meski**, to a climax amid the rolling sand dunes of **Merzouga**. Along the way, once again, are an impressive succession of *ksour*, and an extraordinarily rich palmery – historically the most important territory this side of the Atlas.

Strictly speaking, the Tafilalt (or Tafilalet) comprises the oases south of **Erfoud**, its principal town and gateway. Nowadays, however, the provinical capital is the French-built garrison town and administrative centre of **Er Rachidia**. If you're making a circuit of the south, you will pass through here, from or en route to Midelt – a journey through the great canyon of the **Ziz Gorges** (see p.236). Er Rachidia is also a crossroads for the route east to Figuig – which used to be an important crossing point into Algeria when the frontier was open.

Er Rachidia

ER RACHIDIA was established by the French as a regional capital – when it was known as *Ksar Es Souk*, after their Foreign Legion fort. Today, it represents more than anywhere else the new face of the Moroccan south: a shift away from the old desert

markets and trading routes to a modern urban centre. The town's role as a military out-post, originally against tribal dissidence, particularly from the Aït Atta (see p.420), was maintained after independence by the threat of territorial claims from Algeria, and there is still a significant garrison here, even though Morocco's military focus has long been hundreds of miles distant, in the Western Sahara.

The town is, in fact, quite a pleasant and relaxed place to stay, with an air of relative prosperity, and a large student population, at the lycée and university. In the evenings, the streets come alive, with groups strolling along the main street and packing into the café-restaurants.

Orientation

Er Rachidia has a functional grid layout, with most facilities – banks, cafés and restau-rants, a covered market and tourist office – strung along the highway/main street, **Av. Moulay Ali Cherif**. This runs all the way through town, between the familiar southern ceremonial roadside arches, turning into **Av. El Massira** after crossing the bridge over the Oued Ziz.

All **buses** arrive at the main bus station, on the Place Principale, just south of Av. Moulay Ali Cherif. **Grands taxis** leave both from here and from Place Hassan II to the north: check on your destination before setting out with baggage.

Hotels

Despite its size, Er Rachidia has a limited choice of decent **hotels** and if you want to camp, the position is no better: the Municipal site, still signposted just across the bridge, is closed and the *Source Bleu* at Meski, 18km south of Er Rachidia (see p.435), is the nearest possibility. Fortunately, the tourist complex at Meski has now improved beyond measure and it's a recommended alternative.

CHEAP

Hôtel Ansar [off map], 34 Rue Ibn Batouta (☎05/57.39.19). A friendly, new hotel in a back street, convenient for the bus station; fourteen clean and simple rooms. ①

Hôtel Renaissance, 19 Rue Moulay Youssef (☎05/57.26.33). This is very much the best budget choice, offering cheap, simple rooms, some with showers, and a decent restaurant; again,close to the bus station. ①

Hôtel Royal, 8 Rue Mohammed Zerktouni (☎05/57.30.68). This is the best of the three hotels near Place Hassan II, convenient for *grands taxis*, 100m uphill from the bus station. The nearby *Hôtel Marhaba* and *Hôtel Oliviers* (aka *Zitoun*) are both cheaper, but not recommended. ①

MODERATE

Hôtel M'Daghra [off map], 92 Rue Madaghra (☎05/57.40.87). Opened in 1994, this is an OK place, a block south of the bus station. En-suite rooms and a reasonable restuarant. ②

Hôtel Meski [off map], Av. Moulay Ali Cherif (☎05/57.20.65). 400m out of town, on the right as you come in from Midelt or Goulmima. Car parking is assured, but it's not convenient for public transport. There are rooms with and without showers; the restaurant is alcohol-free. All in all, best kept in reserve in case other hotels are full. ②

Hôtel de l'Oasis, 4 Rue Sidi Bou Abdallah (☎05/57.25.19). There has been a change of management and this hotel, still conveniently central, is no longer value for money – except for the restaurant which continues to prosper. ②

EXPENSIVE

Hôtel Kenzi Rissani, Av. Al Massira (☎05/57.21.86). Just across the bridge, on the right-hand side travelling towards Meski. This was privatized in 1994, and is now one of the Kenzi chain. It's considerably improved and has some sparkle and energy; the rooms have been refurbished and TV installed – and the restaurant functions; evening meal 140dh. ④

Restaurants and bars

You can eat well at the hotels *Kenzi, Rissani, M'Daghra, Oasis* and *Renaissance*. Alternatively, there are any number of cafés and restaurants, of which the following, all on Av. Moulay Ali Cherif, are recommended:

Restaurant Imilchil. Excellent food and an attractive setting, opposite the covered market and *petits taxis*; roadside and terrace.

Restaurant Lipton. Small, but reasonable, and good for breakfast; near the bus station.

Café Terminus. Much like the *Lipton* and worth checking out.

There's also a nameless place by the entrance to the bus station which serves good *harira* soup and there's a reasonable **bar**, cheaper than that in the *Hôtel L'Oasis*, facing the *PTT*.

Listings

Banks There are four banks – *Banque Populaire, BMC, BMCE* and *BMCI* – all shown on the map. If you're going on to Figuig and possibly Algeria you'll need to change travellers' cheques here.

Buses leave at least four times a day for Erfoud/Rissani, and a similar number head north to Midelt and Fes or Meknes, via the dramatic Ziz Gorge. The CTM bus to Ouarzazate goes on to Marrakesh. Note that the only bus to Figuig leaves at 5am (passing the turn-off for Meski about 25 minutes later – where you could flag it down).

Car repairs/spare parts There is a Renault agent on Place Hassan II, which carries a large supply of parts and will order others efficiently from Fes.

Filling stations The Shell filling station is shown on the map. There is also a Ziz station on the Midelt road, and a Somepi station on the Erfoud road.

Grands taxis It is usually no problem to get a seat in a *grand taxi* to Erfoud or, paying the same price, to the Meski turning; these leave from opposite the bus station, as do *grands taxis* to Tinerhir. *Grands taxis* from Place Hassan II run to other destinations.

Petits taxis leave from outside the covered market on Av. Moulay Ali Cherif.

Post office The *PTT* on Av. Mohammed V – see map – has all usual services.

Religious Services There is a small Catholic church, one of the oldest buildings in town, on Rue Begue, off the map. On leaving town towards Midelt/Tinerhir, turn right after the *Hôtel Meski* on the left, and look for a metal blue door; if in doubt and/or you want to know times of Mass, ask at *Hôtel Meski*.

Shops The covered market is a reliable source of fresh food. There's a good craft shop, 6 Rue Sidi Ben Abdellah, by the *Hôtel L'Oasis*, for once, the invitation to 'just look' is sincere and there's no hassle. The *Ensemble Artisanal* (8.30am–noon and 2.30–6.30pm) is on Av. Moulay Ali Cherif, opposite the Banque Populaire, on the way out of town towards the *Hôtel Kenzi Rissani*; it has a good display of local goods: pottery, brass, wood and, truly indigenous, basket ware made of palm leaves. Once again, there's no hassle and the staff are knowledgeable and helpful.

Tourist office The *Syndicat d'Initiative* on Av. Moulay Ali Cherif is very closed. However, there's a helpful *Délégation du Tourisme*, alongside the *Hôtel Meski*, if you want detailed information or guidance on anything in the Province (☎05/57.09.44: open Mon–Fri: summer 7am–2pm; winter 8.30am–noon and 2.30–6.30pm).

Tours The *Hôtel Renaissance* offers landrover expeditions.

Meski and the Ziz valley

The small palm grove of **MESKI** is watered by a natural springwater pool – the famous **source bleue**, extended by the French Foreign Legion and long a postcard image and favourite campsite for travellers. It is set on the riverbank, below a huge ruined *ksar* on the opposite bank and, with several of the springs channelled into a **swimming pool**, it is as romantic a spot as any in the south. Outside midsummer, you might also consider walking part of the way downstream in the valley bottom, southeast of Meski. The superb four-hour **trek** along the Oued Ziz will bring you to **Oulad Aïssa**, a *ksar* with fabulous views over the upper Tafilalt.

In recent years, the **campsite** was poorly maintained but it has now been taken over by the local commune of M'Daghra which seems to have got a grip on the place and it is, once again, highly recommended. The pool is enticing; it is moving springwater, so said to be safe from bilharzia. The toilets are also flushed by springwater; and the camping areas are shaded by bamboo, palms and tamarisks. The site is inexpensive, too, charging just 8dh per person, 8dh per small tent, 10dh per car, or 20dh for a campervan. The **café** is modest, but meals are usually available, given a little notice.

The *source* is somewhat insignificantly signposted, to the south of the Erfoud road, 18km south of Er Rachidia. Coming by bus, ask to get out by the turn-off: from here it's only 400m down to the pool and campsite. **Going on** to Erfoud or back to Er Rachidia from Meski can be tricky, since most of the buses pass by full and don't stop. However, this is an easy place to hitch a lift from other tourists.

South from Meski: the Ziz palmery

Heading south from Er Rachidia and Meski, **towards Erfoud**, the P21 trails the final section of the **Oued Ziz**: make sure you travel this in daylight, for it's one of the most pleasing of all the southern routes: a dry red belt of desert just beyond Meski, and then, suddenly, a drop into the valley and the great **Tizimi palmery** – a prelude of the Tafilalt, leading into Erfoud. Away from the road, **ksour** are almost continuous – glimpsed through the trees and high walls enclosing gardens and plots of farming land.

If you want to stop and take a closer look at the *ksour*, **AOUFOUSS**, midway to Erfoud, and the site of a **Thursday souk**, is perhaps the most accessible. **MAADID**, too, off to the left of the road as you approach Erfoud, is interesting – a really massive **ksar**, which is considered to be the start of the Tafilalt proper.

Between Aoufouss and Maadid, 15km from Erfoud and to the west of the road near the one remaining tower of Borj Yerdi, you will see a couple of spectacular **chalybeate geysers** shooting aerated iron-bearing water up to five metres into the air: a photo-opportunity, if nothing else – and not a hustler in sight!

THE TAFILAT: PAST AND PRESENT

The Tafilalt was for centuries the Moroccan terminus of the **caravan routes** – the famous **Salt Road** to the south across the Sahara to West Africa, by way of Timbuktu. Merchants travelling south carried with them weapons, cloth and spices, part of which they traded en route at Taghaza (in modern-day Mali) for local **salt**, the most-sought after commodity in West Africa. They would continue south and then make the return trip from the old Kingdom of Ghana, to the west of Timbuktu, loaded with **gold** (one ounce of gold was exchanged for one pound of salt at the beginning of the nine-teenth century) and, until European colonists brought an end to the trade, with **slaves**.

These were long journeys: Taghaza was twenty days by camel from Tafilalt, Timbuktu sixty, and merchants might be away for up to a year if they made a circuit via southern Libya (where slaves were still sold until the Italian occupation in 1911). They also, of course, brought an unusual degree of contact with other cultures, which ensured the Tafilalt a reputation as one of the most unstable parts of the Moroccan empire, frequently riven by religious dissent and separatism.

The separatism had a long history, dating back to the eighth century, when the region prospered as the independent kingdom of **Sijilmassa** (see p.443); the dissent began when the *Filalis* – as Tafilalt's predominantly Berber population is known – adopted the **Kharijisite heresy**, a movement which used a Berber version of the Koran (orthodox Islam forbids any translation of God's direct Arabic revelation to Muhammad). Then in the fifteenth century it again emerged as a source of trouble, fostering the Marabout uprising that toppled the Saadian dynasty.

It is with the establishment of the **Alaouite** (or, after their birthplace, *Filali*) dynasty that the Tafilalt is most closely associated. Mounted from a *zaouia* in Rissani, by Moulay Rachid, and secured by his successor, Moualy Ismail, this is the dynasty which still holds power in Morocco, through Hassan II, the fourteenth sultan in the line. The Alaouites were also the source of the wealth of many of the old Kasbahs and *ksour*, from the time of Moulay Ismail, through to this century, the sultans exiled princes and unruly relatives out here to the edge of the desert.

The Tafilalt was a major centre of resistance to the French, who were limited to their garrison at Erfoud and an outpost of the Foreign Legion at Ouled Zohra until 1931.

THE TAFILALT TODAY – AND BAYOUD DISEASE

The Tafilalt today, deprived of its contacts to the south, is something of a backwater, with a population estimated at around 80,000 and declining, as the effects of drought and Bayoud disease have taken hold on the palms. Most of the population are smallhold farm-ers, with thirty or so palms for each family, from which they could hope to produce around a thousand kilos of dates in a reasonable year. With the market price of dates around 6dh a kilo there are no fortunes to be made.

It is reckoned that two-thirds of Moroccan palmeries are infected with **Bayoud dis-ease**. First detected in the Drâa at the beginning of this century, this is a kind of fungus, which is spread from root to root and possibly by transmission of spores. Palms die with-in a year of an attack, creating a secondary problem by leaving a gap in the wedge of trees, which allows the winds to blow through. The disease cannot be treated economi-cally – the most that farmers can do is to isolate trees by digging a ditch round them – and the only real hope seems to lie in the development of resistant species of palms. Moroccan and French scientists, in collaboration with the Total oil company, are at pre-sent working on new methods of propagation and cross-breeding. A resistant species has already, in fact, been developed in France, but there's one problem: the dates, so far, taste awful . . .

Erfoud

ERFOUD, like Er Rachidia, is largely a French-built administrative centre, and its desultory frontier-town atmosphere fulfils little of the promise of the Tafilalt. Arriving from Er Rachidia, however, you get a first, powerful sense of proximity to the desert, with frequent sandblasts ripping through the streets, and total darkness in the event of a (not uncommon) electrical black-out. This desert position is best appreciated from the vantage point of the **Borj Est**, the hill-fort 3km across the river, from where you can get a glimpse of the sands to the south; the fort itself is still used by the military but you can drive up to the public car park, by *petit taxi* or rental car, and then walk the last 200 metres for the all-round views.

Views apart, for most travellers Erfoud functions very much as a staging post for the sand dunes near **Merzouga**, and/or the last oasis village of **Rissani**. Its only other point of interest, aside from its **date festival** (see box overleaf), is the local **marble industry**, which produces a unique, high quality black marble which, like all marbles, is metamorphosed limestone, in this case containing fascinating fossils. When polished, it is attractive and is to be seen locally on every bar top and reception desk.

You can visit the marble works on the Tinerhir road; ask – or look for – the *Usine de Marmar* (see map). A German sculptor, Fred Jansen, and his *Arts Natura* group, pioneered carving the marble so that the fossils are revealed in 3D and, at its best, this is most impres-

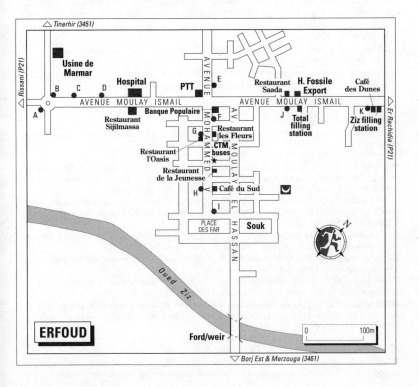

THE FESTIVAL OF THE DATES

Erfoud's **Festival of Dates** is held over three days in October and you will be richly rewarded if you can visit at that time. As with all such events, it's a mixture of symbolism, sacred rites and entertainment. Traditionally, dates bring good luck: tied to a baby's arm they ensure a sweet nature, thrown at a bride they encourage fertility, and offered to strangers they signify friendship.

On the first morning of the festival, prayers are said at the mausoleum of Moulay Ali Shereef at Rissani and, the same evening, there is a fashion show of traditional costumes: a pride of embroidered silk, silver and gold head-dresses, sequins and elaborate jewellery. Then there are processions, athletics and, on the last night, traditional music and spiritual songs.

---

sive. But the process has been developed locally without taste so that the contrived artifacts are pure kitsch. The better-class work can be seen in the showroom at the marble works or the more central *H. Fossile Export* opposite the *Hôtel Saada* on Av. Moulay Ismail.

Accommodation and meals

Erfoud has an impressive range of **hotels**, at all price levels, although its finest – the old Kasbah-like four-star *Hotel Sijilmassa* – has departed from the lists of late and been converted into a residence for King Hassan II (his first palace in the Province). In picking a hotel, you may want to go for one that offers transport to the dunes at Merzouga in order to see the desert dawn. Or you may prefer to stay at or en route to Merzouga (see following section).

Most of the hotels have **restaurants**. In addition, the *Restaurant les Fleurs, Restaurant de la Jeunesse, Restaurant l'Oasis* and *Café du Sud*, all on Av. Mohammed V serve modestly priced meals, as do the *Café des Dunes*, near the *Hôtel Tafilalet*, and the *Restaurant Sijilmassa*, opposite the hospital on Av. Moulay Ismail.

Hotel options include:

CHEAP

Hôtel Atlas [D], 5 Av. Moulay Ismail (no phone). A small hotel with café on ground floor and rooms upstairs. Showers, sometimes hot, on corridor. The hotel is not easy to spot: it's near, and on the same side of the street as, the hospital. ⑩

Hôtel El Filalia [H], 36 Av. Mohammed V (☎05/57.60.33). This was previously the *Hôtel Les Palmiers*, but it now has a new owner and name. There are showers in the rooms, and toilets in the corridors; and redecoration, including the downstairs café, is promising. ⑩

Hôtel La Gazelle [E], Av. Mohammed V (☎05/57.60.28). By the *Gendarmerie Royale* and opposite the *PTT*. Pleasant and cheerful nine-room hotel with en-suite rooms and constant hot water. There's a new restaurant in the basement; menu du jour: 55dh. ①

Hôtel Lahmada [C], Av. Mohammed V (☎05/57.69.80). A modern hotel, opened in 1994. En-suite rooms with quality furniture and the corridors are tiled. Value for money. ①

Hôtel Merzouga [G], 114 Av. Mohammed V (☎05/57.65.32). En-suite rooms with hot showers; or you can sleep on the terrace for 25dh a head. ⑩

Hôtel Saada [J], 50 Av. Moulay Ismail (☎05/57.63.17). Under new ownership, things are looking up with en-suite facilities promised for all rooms. But it is still noisy. ⑩

Hôtel Sable d'Or [F], 141 Av. Mohammed V (☎05/57.63.48), near the junction with Av. Moulay Ismail and the Banque Populaire. Good on most counts: clean, comfortable, en suite, hot showers, views from terrace. ①

MODERATE

Hôtel Farah Zouar [B], Av. Moulay Ismail (☎05/57.62.30). On the roundabout where roads to Rissani and to Tinerhir part. An elegant new hotel, whose *terrasse panoramique* looks over the palmery and towards Borj Est. It is a friendly place and caters for individuals rather than groups. Restaurant, but no bar. ③

Hôtel Tafilalet [K], Av. Moulay Ismail (☎05/57.65.35). The top choice if you have a little money to spare. It rivals the much more expensive *Hôtel Salam* (see below), with a swimming pool, attractive decor and friendly staff. The hotel also runs a useful shuttle to Merzouga and owns the *Hôtel Merzouga* there. ③

Hôtel Ziz [I], 3 Av. Mohammed V (☎05/57.61.45), at the bottom end of the main street and nearest to the Sunday *souk*. Well-furnished en-suite rooms, air-conditioned and around a small courtyard. The owner, quite an entrepreneur, runs the wholesale warehouse next door, and again has a couple of landrovers available for the sunrise shuttle to Merzouga. ②

EXPENSIVE

Hôtel Salam [A], Av. Moulay Ismail (☎05/57.66.65). A pricey tour group hotel with an old and (more expensive) new wing. Swimming pool and restaurant. ④–⑤

Listings

Bank There is a branch of the *Banque Populaire* (see map).

Buses CTM buses leave from Av. Mohammed V (see map); others from the Place des F.A.R. There is a daily private-line service to Tinejdad, which allows you to make a connection to Tinerhir, avoiding the need to backtrack via Er Rachidia.

Car repairs Try Madkouri Abid at 114 Av. Mohammed V, next door to the *Hôtel Merzouga*.

Petrol There are Total and Ziz filling stations on the Er Rachidia road.

Post office The *PTT* has **poste restante** and other standard services.

The dunes of Merzouga

The **Erg Chebbi** – the sand dunes at **Merzouga** – are one of the great sights of Morocco. They are reached most directly along the 3461 road south of Erfoud, which is surfaced for the first 16km, then gives way to 35km of piste. It is along this road that the landrover tours are offered by the *Hôtel Ziz* and *Hôtel Tafilalet*, to catch sunrise at the dunes. If you can't afford these, it may be possible to join up with other tourists doing the trip – try asking round at the *Hôtel Salam* or *Hôtel Tafilalet*, either the night before or at dawn. Your presence may be welcome as an extra shoulder to push the car if it gets trapped in the sand.

You can, alternatively, reach Merzouga by way of **Rissani** – or complete a circuit by travelling back this way. The Merzouga–Rissani route is covered in a southeast to northwest direction on p.442; it is served by local transit and landrover taxis.

Erfoud to Merzouga

The road from Erfoud to Merzouga is practicable by Renault 4L. It takes around an hour and a quarter, and is reasonably easy to follow, with a line of telephone poles running parallel almost the whole way. A guide isn't necessary, though, if you're travelling alone, an extra person to push, when you get stuck in the sandy tracks, would be wise.

Leaving Erfoud, you cross the Oued Ziz by a ford-cum-weir and drive past the road which goes up to the Borj Est (3km). At around the 15km mark, the surfaced road gives way to piste. Not far beyond is the little *Auberge Kasbah Derkaoua* (aka *Chez Michel*; ☎05/57.71.40; demi-pension ④), an attractive, French-run **hotel**, which offers charming rooms and superb meals; it closes January, June and July and booking is advisable in March and April when groups of ornithologists fly in – hotel transport will meet *RAM* flights at Er Rachidia (twice a week via Casablanca)

From this point on, the line of telephone poles becomes useful, as the road splays into numerous parallel tracks carved out by cars, landrovers and motorbikes, in the sandy

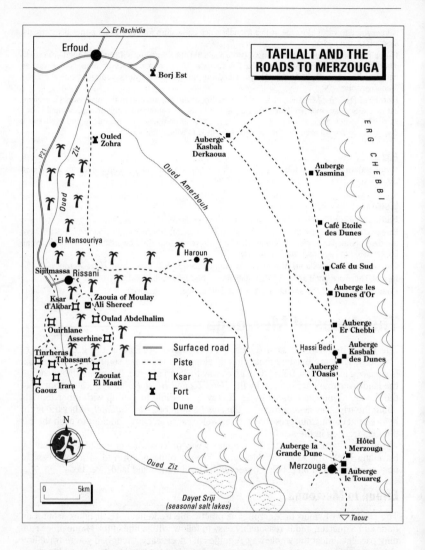

TAFILALT AND THE ROADS TO MERZOUGA

crust. The dunes, clearly visible by this stage, provide further orientation, aligned almost perfectly north–south. On the hammada/dune line is a 20km string of little **auberges**, offering rooms, meals and camping. Of those shown on our map, the best are:

Yasmina A small, basic place but the setting is fabulous; you can camp amongst a few trees and, in winter/spring there's sometimes a small lake nearby, with flamingoes. ⑩

Les Dunes d'Or A larger place with rooms around a courtyard, hot showers, good cooking, pleasant staff. Parked outside is the ageing plywood plane used in a film of Antoine de Saint-Exupéry's fable, *Le Petit Prince*: 'une panne dans le désert du Sahara'.

Kasbah des Dunes Another small, basic hotel – and as it's near the hamlet of Hassi Bedi ("white well"), there's the opportunity to meet the locals; quite an experience. ⑩

L'Oasis A cheerful place with hot showers and the possibility of camping and camel rides; it's also near Hassi Bedi. ⓓ

Finally, just one kilometre before you arrive at Merzouga village, and overlooked by the highest of the sand dunes, is:

Hôtel Merzouga This is an outpost of the *Hôtel Tafilalet* in Erfoud and can be booked through them (☎05/57.65.35). It's well managed and has now taken over the next-door *Hôtel Salam*: together they offer a range of accommodation and, as in most of the auberges, you can choose to sleep in a tent or on the terrace/roof if you prefer. ⓶

Merzouga village – and camel trips

Merzouga village is no great shakes, but if you want to stay, there are half a dozen **café-hotels** scattered in and round the village, most of them pretty basic, with no electricity and outside toilets and showers. The best of these cheapies is the *Café des Amis* but, having come this distance, it's a shame not to stay alongside the dunes (in one or other of the options above).

Any visitor to Merzouga will receive no end of offers of **camel trips** – anything from a couple of hours' climb up the dunes to two or three days' trekking. It is best to seek the advice of the staff at one of the auberges recommended above if you want to be assured of your money's worth. For the uncommitted, two hours at sunset should be sufficient to get a taste of the dunes and avoid getting saddle-sore. The prices are highly negotiable: 75dh per person is perhaps about right for a two-hour ride.

The dunes

The **dune** beside the *Hôtel Merzouga* is said to be the highest in Morocco – and, so locals would have it, the world. It is undeniably impressive and it may look familiar, for it was used in a Renault advert, with a car driving down its slope. Cars, incidentally, seem to have an uncontrollable passion for dunes, for Merzouga is a post in the **North African Rally** (held in January); the drivers' stickers add a slightly surreal tone to the

---

DESERT WILDLIFE AND THE LAKE

Merzouga makes an excellent centre for the exploration of Morocco's sandy (or "true") desert, whose flora and fauna show ingenious adaptations to these least hospitable of living conditions. Bird-watchers will find most of interest. In early spring a lake, **Dayet Srji**, usually forms just to the west of Merzouga village, and it regularly attracts scores of pink flamingoes – a wonderful sight out here in the wilds.

During the spring migration, the lake and the bushes thereabouts attract many birds which have just crossed the desert; look particularly for the ruddy sheldrake and note that the first Moroccan sighting of Kittllitz's plover was recorded here. More unusual sightings, if you strike lucky, might include the desert sparrow (best seen at the Café Yasmina, Tristram's desert warbler, Egyptian nightjar and Arabian bustard.

The desert is also an ideal environment for **reptiles**, including the Algerian sand lizard and Berber skink, and typical **desert mammals** – more often located by their giveaway tracks in the morning sand than by nocturnal sightings – include the jerboa, desert hedgehog and fennec (desert fox).

Plant life is limited because of the extreme scarcity of water; the only survivors include the lichens and algae which can take up sufficient water from the condensation of dew which forms on the undersurfaces of rocks and stones, although even the desert has an all-too-brief **spring bloom** when the rains do come – dominated by pink aspho-dels and mauve statice.

village. A more appropriate transport on the dunes is demonstrated by local kids, who sandsurf on plastic bags down the slopes of an evening.

The desert of dunes fascinates Moroccans and foreigners alike. Mention 'Merzouga' anywhere in Morocco and people will tell you of the power of the sands to cure rheumatics who come here to be buried up to the neck in the sand. Widely believed, but never seen! The dunes also have a wide-ranging aesthetic appeal; witness the film directors, writers, artists and photographers who struggle to convey their beauty. An extraordinary book of photographs by Michel Teuler illustrates this and one critic, Gérard Lanux, visiting the dunes has put into words their dramatic appeal: 'Here there isn't a single trace of man's presence, of his appetite for conquest or destruction. The real master is invisible. The wind shapes the landscape as it likes. It is an unchanging landscape which is constantly changing. There is something both derisory and magnificent to want to grasp something imperceptible, to want to fix for eternity lights and shapes which no longer exist. This is perhaps the real mystery and real lesson of the desert: to make us believe that death is possible while telling us that there is only life and perpetual transformation.'

Merzouga to Rissani

Landrover taxis leave Merzouga for Rissani at around 7am; passenger **lorries** at a similar time on the morning after a *souk*. The piste route is not that easy to follow, and if you are driving, it would be wise to join a party with one of these vehicles, or arrange a local guide; as with the Erfoud route, you will certainly need two or more people to push the car when you get stuck in the sand. More seriously, if you were caught in high winds you could easily get lost in a sandstorm, and recent rains would present problems to all but four-wheel-drive vehicles. Assuming you're not stuck or lost too often, or too long, the trip should take around two hours.

The route (or a route) is essentially this: leave Merzouga past the post office (on your left); keep the telephone poles on your right for a while; follow the pistes off to the left; skirt the (dry) salt lake and you'll eventually hit asphalt road somewhere in Rissani's palmery. You then bear left to reach Rissani.

Rissani

RISSANI stands at the last visible point of the Ziz River; beyond it, steadily encroaching on the present town and its ancient *ksour* ruins, begins the desert. From the eighth to the fourteenth centuries, this was the site of the first independent kingdom of the south, Sijilmassa (see box). It was the first capital of the Tafilalt, and served as the last stop on the great caravan routes south. The British journalist Walter Harris reported thriving gold and slave auctions in Rissani as late as the 1890s.

Rissani has a special place in modern Moroccan lore. It was from the *zaouia* here – which is still an important national shrine – that the ruling **Alaouite dynasty** launched its bid for power, conquering first the oases of the south, then the vital Taza Gap, before triumphing finally in Fes and Marrakesh. Its main interest lies in the scenic approaches to the village, from Erfoud or Merzouga; in its surrounding **ksour**; and its three-times weekly **souks**.

The village

A quarter of Rissani's population still live in a large seventeenth-century **ksar**, in addition to which there is just the Place al Massira and one street, lined by the usual administrative buildings. It's a quiet place, which comes to life three times a week for the

SIJILMASSA: THE BERBER KINGDOM

Sijilmassa was founded in 757 by Berber dissidents, who had broken away from orthodox Islam, and for five centuries, until its collapse under civil unrest in 1393, it dominated southern Morocco. The early dominance and wealth of Sijilmassa was due to the fertility of the **oases** south of Erfoud. These are watered by parallel rivers, the Oued Rheris and Oued Ziz, which led to Sijilmassa's description as the "Mesopotamia of Morocco". Harvests were further improved by diverting the Ziz, just south of modern Erfoud, to the west of its natural channel, thus bringing it closer to the Rheris and raising the water table. Such natural wealth was reinforced by Sijilmassa's trading role on the **Salt Road** to West Africa (see box on p.436), which persisted until the west coast of Africa was opened up to sea trade, particularly by the Portuguese, in the fifteenth century. Coins from Sijilmassa, in this period, have been found as far as Aqaba, Jordan.

Historians disagree about the extent and pattern of Sijilmassa at its height. Some see it as a divided city, comprising several dispersed *ksour*, much as it was after the civil war at the end of the fourteenth century. Others view it as a single, elongated city, spread along the banks of the rivers: 14km from end to end, or half a day's walk.

There is still a gate to be seen on the east side of the Oued Ziz, at the ancient city's northern extremity, just south of El Mansouriya. This is known locally as the **Bab Errih** and may date from the Merenid period (1248–1465), although it has certainly undergone restoration since then. The Alaouites, who brought Sijilmassa to renewed prominence as the provincial capital of the Tafilalt in the seventeenth century, did a major restoration of the garrison. The southernmost point of the ancient city was near the *ksar* of Gaouz, on the "Circuit Touristique".

The (mainly Alaouite) central area is under excavation by a joint team from the Moroccan Institute of Archaeology and the Middle Tennessee State University, under the direction of Dr Ronald Messier. The most accessible and visible remains are to be found a little to the west of Rissani, on the east bank of the Oued Ziz, and within the right angle formed by the north–south main road (P21) as it turns east into Rissani. Here can be traced the walls of a mosque with an early *mihrab* facing south, an adjoining *Medersa* and the walls of the citadel with towers on the length by the river. In Rissani, there is a small museum and study centre where you may get help to explore the site.
With thanks to Dr Ron Messier.

souk – held on Sunday, Tuesday and Thursday. This is more for locals than tourists but often turns up a good selection of Berber jewellery – including the crude, almost iconographic designs of the desert. Some of the basic products (dried fruits, farming implements and so on) are interestingly distinct from those of the richer north. Don't expect camels, as some guides promise: apart from the caravans, these were never very common in Tafilalt, the Berbers preferring more economical mules. They are still very much in evidence.

The *souk* aside, you might care to visit the modest **museum** in the central *ksar*; it is signposted the *Centre d'Etudes et de Recherches Alaouites* (open Mon–Fri 8.30am–noon and 2.30–6.30pm; free). There's interesting material about the Alaouite dynasty, but not much on Sijilmassa nor the excavations there (see box above) and most of the captions are in Arabic. Nevertheless, the staff are enthusiastic and will let you browse in the library where, as you would expect, the texts are mainly in French. Here, for example, there is a catalogue of rock carvings in southern Morocco. There are plans to move the museum and library to the nineteenth-century Ksar Al Fida; if it's moved, you would need to take a *petit taxi* from the town centre to find it.

Two permanent **craft shops** might also draw you into an hour or two's browsing: the **Maison Touareg** (☎05/57.54.93), on the left of the road out to Merzouga, and **Maison Berbère** (☎05/57.50.54), more difficult to find – across the open area alongside the

Centre de la Jeunesse. The Maison Berbère is part of the Alaoui family chain which has a reputation for quality rugs – and no hassle.

Ksour around Rissani

Rissani's older monuments are well into the process of erosion – both through crumbling material and the slow progress of the sands. **Sijilmassa**, whose ruins were clearly visible at the beginning of this century, has more or less vanished (though see the box feature). The various Kasbahs and reminders of the Alaouite presence are also mostly in an advanced stage of decay, though there is just enough remaining to warrant a battle with the morning heat.

From the village's administrative street/bus terminal you can head towards a collection of *ksour* on the signposted "Circuit Touristique". The first you encounter, about 2.5km to the southeast, houses the **Zaouia of Moulay Ali Shereef**, the original Alaouite stronghold and mausoleum of the dynasty's founder. Many times rebuilt – the last following floods in 1955 – the shrine is forbidden to non-Muslims.

Beside it, dominating this group of buildings, is the nineteenth-century **Ksar d'Akbar**, an awesomely grandiose ruin which was once a palace in exile, housing the unwanted members of the Alaouite family and the wives of the dead sultans. Most of the structure, which still bears considerable traces of its former decoration, dates from the beginning of the nineteenth century. A third royal *ksar*, the **Ksar Oualad Abdelhalim**, stands around 1500m further down the road. Notable for its huge ramparts and the elaborate decorative effects of its blind arches and unplastered brick patterning, this is one of the few really impressive imperial buildings completed in this century. It was constructed around 1900 for Sultan Moulay Hassan's elder brother, whom he had appointed governor of the Tafilalt.

You can complete the circuit by passing a further group of *ksour* – **Asserehine**, **Zaouiet El Maati**, **Irara**, **Gaouz**, **Tabassant**, **Tinrheras** and **Ouirhlane** – and then looping back into town past a section of **Sijilmassa**. Tinrheras, a ruined *ksar* on a knoll, has fine views over Tafilalt.

Rissani hotels – and transport

Rissani offers a choice of three **hotels**, all of which have restaurants. In the village, you'll find the *Hôtel El Filalia* (☎05/57.50.96; ①) with cheap rooms, and space on its roof terrace, and the *Hôtel Sijilmassa* (☎05/57.50.42; ②), which is new, enthusiastic and much better quality and value. Out of town, 3km north at the junction of the P21 and 3454, is the three-star *Hôtel Kasbah Asmâa* (☎05/57.54.94; ③), a promising new venture run by the Alaoui family of carpet store fame. The village also has a **bank** (*Banque Populaire*), **post office**, several **filling stations**, and a men's **hammam**.

Leaving Rissani, you can get landrover or transit taxis to **Merzouga** (see p.442 for the route), or, on market days, lorries (*camionettes*) laden to the hilt with Berbers; travelling by taxi, it's best to specify a particular hotel in or around Merzouga. To secure a ride in one of the *camionettes*, head down the main street, past the bank and taxi stand, to the filling station and *Café Panorama*.

Heading **west** from Rissani, the 10am bus to **Er Rachidia** connects with the 1pm bus to Tinerhir (arriving around 4.30pm) and Ouarzazate. *Grands taxis* also run direct from Rissani to **Tinerhir** (45dh).

An alternative route out from Rissani is the **piste west to Zagora, via Alnif**. This is detailed in reverse on p.411 and is possible in a Renault 4L or, if you can coincide with the market days, by a local landrover taxi. The taxi usually leaves the *Hôtel El Filalia* on Thursdays and Sundays, after the Rissani market, arriving in Zagora around ten hours later; it's possible to arrange a place through the hotel.

EAST TO FIGUIG AND BOUARFA

The six- to eight-hour desert journey from **Er Rachidia to Figuig** (pronounced F'geeg) is spectacular in its isolation and physically extraordinary: the real outlands of Morocco, dominated by huge empty landscapes and blank red mountains. It used to be quite a common route for travellers intent on entering Algeria, in the south, but the civil war there has ended such traffic and the border is closed. It is thus a somewhat perverse route to take – a lot of travelling in order to complete a loop round to northern Morocco at Oujda. You can, however, make the journey easily enough by car or bus.

It is 400km from **Er Rachidia** to Figuig via **Mengoub** and **Bouarfa**, and a further 270km from **Figuig to Oujda**. A new road (P19a), however, which runs directly east from Mengoub to Figuig, allows you to bypass Bouarfa and cuts around 100km off. If you want to stay en route, you are best off in **BOUARFA**, a friendly place with a Shell filling station and two **hotels**. The *Hôtel Haut Plateau* (no phone; ①) has cool rooms on a first floor terrace and is convenient for the bus lot opposite; 200m down Rue de la Marche Verte is its rival, the *Hôtel Tamalt* (☎06/79.87.99; ①), entered through a ground floor café. ①

Figuig

The southern oases are traditionally measured by the number of their palms, rather than in terms of area or population. **FIGUIG**, with something like 200,000 trees, has long been one of the largest – an importance enhanced by its strategic border position. At least twice it has been lost by Morocco – in the seventeenth-century wars, and again at the end of Moulay Ismail's reign – and as recently as 1975 there was fighting in the streets here between Moroccan and Algerian troops.

In recent decades the settlement reverted to a quiet existence, with a modest trade from its frontier position – including a trickle of tourists crossing into southern Algeria. Since the Algerian civil war erupted in the mid-1990s, however, and the border was effectively sealed, Figuig's economy has virtually collapsed. If you do visit, you'll likely be the first foreigner in weeks, if not months.

Orientation, hotels, food and transport

The oasis has even less of an administrative town than usual, still basically consisting of its seven distinct *ksour* villages – which in the past feuded almost continuously over water and grazing rights.

Orientation is relatively simple, with almost everything on the road by which you enter the town. The *Hôtel El Meliasse* (no phone; ①), the only **hotel** still functioning (and barely so), is on the right, above the *Shell* service station. It's pretty grim. Buses sometimes stop here – there is no bus terminal as such in Figuig – and then again outside the (closed) *Hôtel Sahara*. Beyond lie various shops and cafés, and a branch of the *Banque Populaire*. For **snacks**, try the *Café de la Paix*, opposite the bank, or the *Café Oasis* in a little park. Beyond that, there is nowhere else to eat.

If you're getting a bus out, the **ticket office for buses** is to be found by walking north from the old *Hôtel Sahara* and turning left at the fountain/junction. The office is to the right, under the arcades. A mercifully early 6am departure goes direct to Oujda with a breakfast stop at Bouarfa. Heading for Er Rachidia, there are just two buses a day from Bouarfa (at 8am and 2pm); you will need to catch the 5am bus from Figuig if you want to avoid a long wait.

Exploring the ksour

Figuig's **ksour** are signposted off the main road and are spread out round the base of the hill – each enclosing its own palmery within high turreted walls. Although sporadically organized into a loose confederation, they were until this century fiercely independent – and their relations with each other were peppered with long and bitter blood feuds and, above all, disputes over the limited water supply. Their strange, archaic shape – with watchtowers rising above the snaking feggaguir (or irrigation channels) – evolved as much from this internal tension as from any need to protect themselves from the nomadic tribes of the desert. Likewise, within each of the *ksour*, the elaborate tunnel-like networks of alleys are deliberate (and successful) attempts to prevent any sudden or easy progress.

Your best chance of getting an overview of it all is to head for the platforme, poised above the *ksar* of **Zenaga**. The view from here spans a large part of the palmery and its pink-tinged *ksour*, and you can gaze at the weird, multicoloured layers of the enclosing mountains. If you can find the energy – Figuig in summer feels a little like sitting inside a fan-heater – head down into Zenaga, the largest and richest of the seven villages. Going to your left, you should reach its centre, more developed than most in this area, with a couple of cubicle shops and a café in addition to a mosque. For a look at the other *ksour*, it is possible to loop to the right of the main administrative road, past the *ksour* of **El Maiz** to **El Hammam El Foukanni**.

El Maiz is the prettiest quarter, with small vaulted lanes and houses with broad verandas. In El Hammam, as the name suggests, there is a **hot spring**, used by the people for their ablutions. Anyone offering their services as a guide will take you to it. Back on the other side of the administrative road is the **Ksar El-Oudarhir**, which also has some natural springs (one hot, one salty), as well as terraces similar to the ones in El Maiz.

All of the *ksour* have exclusively Berber populations, though up until the 1950s and 1960s there was also a considerable Jewish population. Until the beginning of the twentieth century, Figuig was also the final Moroccan staging point on the overland journey to Mecca.

Figuig to Oujda

Unless you have a strange fascination for very small town life, there is really nowhere else on this eastern plateau between Figuig and Oujda which offers much temptation. **TENDRARA** (Tuesday market) and **AÏT BENIMATHAR** both have basic café-hotels, if you need to stay overnight. Aït Benimathar is the better choice – a quiet little **hot water oasis**, full of tortoises and snakes. Even if you don't want to stay, it's not a bad place to spend the middle of an afternoon, which you can do by taking the early morning bus from Figuig, then catching a later one for the final 50km to Oujda.

To the west of Bouarfa, the towns are all fairly bleak. If you're into piste driving, there are said to be troglodyte (cave) dwellings up in the hills behind BOUDENIB, towards GOUMARRA.

travel details

Buses

From Ouarzazate CTM to Agadir (1 daily; 8hr 30min); to Casablanca (1 daily; 8hr 20min); and to Marrakesh (1 daily; 3hr 30min). Other lines, Marrakesh (4 daily; 5hr); Zagora (3 daily; 5hr 30min); Tailiouine/Taroudannt (2 daily; 3hr 30 min/5hr); Tinerhir (3 daily; 5hr).

From Zagora Ouarzazate (4 daily; 4–5hr); Marrakesh (2 daily; 9–11hr).

From Tinerhir Er Rachidia (2 daily; 3hr); Ouarzazate (3; 5hr).

From Er Rachidia CTM to Casablanca (1 daily; 10hr 15min); and to Marrakesh (1 daily; 9hr 45min). Other lines, Erfoud/Rissani (4 daily; 1hr 30 min/3hr); Tinerhir (2 daily; 3hr); Figuig (1 daily via Bouarfa, currently at 5am; 10hr); Midelt (5 daily; 3hr 30 min); Fes (3 daily; 8hr 30min); Meknes (1 daily; 8hr).

From Erfoud Rissani (4 daily; 1hr 30min); Er Rachidia (4; 1hr 30min); Fes (daily; 11hr).

From Rissani CTM to Meknes (1 daily; 8hr 30min). Other lines, Tinejdad/Goulmima (daily; 3hr 30 min/4hr).

From Figuig Oujda (4 daily; 7hr); Er Rachidia (via Bouarfa; 1 daily; 10hr).

Grands Taxis

From Ouarzazate Regularly to Zagora (3hr). Negotiable for Skoura (1hr) and Aït Benhaddou (1hr 45min, but expensive private trip).

From Zagora Regularly to Ouarzazate (3hr); lorries to Rissani (10hr) and Foum Zguid (8hr).

From Boumalne Landrover taxi at least daily to Msemrir (3hr). Regular run to Tinerhir (50min).

From Tinerhir Regular runs to Boumalne (50 min) and Tinejdad (1hr; from there on to Er Rachidia).

From Er Rachidia Fairly frequent runs to Erfoud (along the route you can negotiate a ticket to Meski) and to Tinejdad (2hr).

From Erfoud Fairly frequent runs to Rissani (1hr 30min) and Erfoud (2hr). Landrover trips direct to Merzouga (1hr; relatively expensive).

Trains

There is a night train from Bouarfa to Oujda (8hr), but this carries mainly freight, and is a distinctly eccentric alternative to the bus from Figuig.

CHAPTER EIGHT

AGADIR, THE SOUSS AND ANTI-ATLAS

S outhern Morocco's major tourist destination is **Agadir**, a city that was rebuilt specifically as a resort following its destruction by an earthquake in 1960. It became something of a showpiece for the "new nation", and these days is an established beach city, with some fine hotels around its great sweep of sand. If you are travelling around Morocco, however, you are unlikely to want to stay for long, for Agadir is very deliberately developed – mainly as a winter resort for Europeans – and feels rather sanitised of local, Moroccan culture.

You don't have to travel far to find a very different country. Just north of Agadir is a series of small fishing villages and cove-beaches without a hotel in sight, while a short way inland is **"Paradise Valley"**, a beautiful and exotic palm gorge, from which a mountain road trails up to the seasonal waterfalls of **Immouzer des Ida Outanane** – a superb one- or two-day trip. To the south of Agadir, too, the beaches are scarcely developed, ranging from solitary campsites at **Sidi Rbat** – one of Morocco's best locations for bird-watching – and **Sidi Moussa d'Aglou**, down to the old port of **Sidi Ifni** – only relinquished by Spain in 1969 and full of splendid Art Deco colonial architecture.

Inland and to the south of Agadir are the **Souss** and the **Anti-Atlas**, easy-going regions whose Chleuh Berber populations share the distinction of having together cornered the country's grocery trade. **Taroudannt**, capital of the fertile Souss plain, has massive walls, animated *souks* and good hotels – a natural place to stay on your way to Marrakesh (which can be reached over the spectacular **Tizi n'Test** pass) or Ouarzazate. Further south, into the Anti-Atlas mountains, **Tafraoute** and its valley are even more compelling – the stone-built villages and villas set amid a stunning landscape of pink granite and vast rock formations.

For those with more time, a number of adventurous piste and desert trips can be made in the region. One of the best is the **Tata loop**, a surfaced but little-travelled road across the southern Anti-Atlas to the pre-Sahara, comprising a string of true desert **oases**. The route is most easily covered from Tiznit, but it is feasible to do it east to west from Taroudannt. It's well off the usual (or even unusual) tourist trails and is highly recommended.

A more well-trodden route is down to **Goulimine**, the most accessible "desert town" in this part of Morocco, and promoted by the tourist trade for its camel market – the traditional meeting place of the "Blue Men" (Touareg tribesmen, whose faces are tinged blue by their masks and robes). Alas, it is now more frequented by tourists than anyone else. Nonetheless, it is quite a drive, and with your own vehicle you can explore several oases nearby. Going further, you begin to need real commitment to reach towns in the Deep South, like Tan Tan or Laayoune. These are covered in the following chapter, along with the rest of Morocco's Western Saharan province.

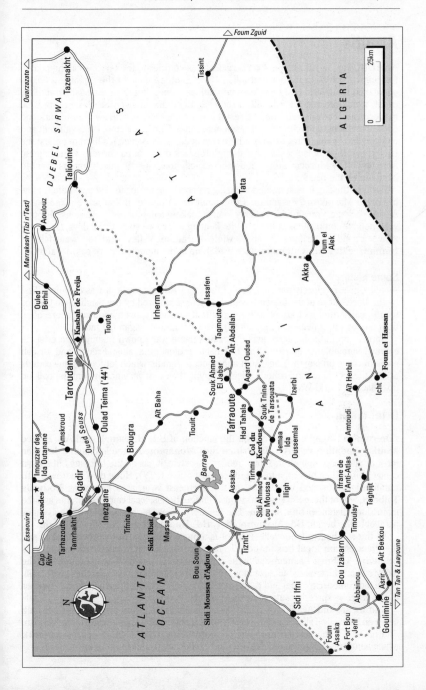

Agadir

AGADIR was, by all accounts, a characterful port, prior to the terrible earthquake of February 29, 1960: a tremor that killed 15,000 and left most of the remaining 50,000 population homeless. Just four years into independence, it was an especially traumatic event, which created a great will to recreate a city that showed Morocco in its best, modern face. Four decades on, the result is quite impressive, with swathes of park and garden breaking up the hotel and residential zones. The beach, too, is magnificent and untramelled by Spanish Costa-style high-rise building. However, it's hard to escape the feeling that the city lacks soul, and though the lack of bustle has novelty value coming from any other Moroccan town, it doesn't exactly merit a stay unless you just want to hang out on the beach.

Perhaps the city is best treated as a staging post – or a place to rest up – before moving on to Marrakesh, Essaouira, Taroudannt or Tafraoute. If you are booked on an Agadir package, you should certainly look at making a number of excursions, through your holiday company or going it alone. Renting a car for two or three days, the towns above are all in striking distance, while **Paradise Valley** and the waterfalls of **Immouzer des Ida Outanane** (see p.465), up in the mountains, are easy local trips.

Some history

Agadir's history closely parallels that of the other Atlantic ports. It was colonized first by the Portuguese in the fifteenth century, then, recaptured by the Saadians in the sixteenth, carried on its trading with intermittent prosperity, overshadowed, more often than not, by the activities of Mogador (Essaouira) and Mazagan (El Jadida).

Abroad, up until the earthquake, Agadir's name was known mainly for a crisis in colonial squabblings in 1911. The Germans, protesting against French and British plans to carve up North Africa, sent a gunboat to Agadir, which let loose a few rounds across the bay. Like the Fashoda crisis in Egypt, the event very nearly sent the balloon up to launch World War I.

Orientation

"Downtown" Agadir is centred on the junction of **Bd. Hassan II** and **Av. Prince Moulay Abdallah** with **Av. du Prince Sidi Mohammed** – the left-hand side of the inset on our map. Rebuilt in 1960s "modernist" style, it has all the trappings of a town centre, with office blocks, a tourist office, post office (*PTT*), Hôtel de Ville (townhall), municipal market and banks. Just to the northeast is an area known as **Nouvelle Talborjt**, where there is a concentration of budget hotels, local café-restaurants and the main (long-distance) **bus station**. The fancier hotels are grouped along the avenues parallel to the beach: **Bd. Mohammed V, Bd. Hassan II** and **Bd. du 20 Août**.

To the southeast of Nouvelle Talborjt is a more working-class residential area and the **Place Salam local bus station**. To the northeast is a hilly, grassed area known as **Ancienne Talborjt** – a memorial to the earthquake, under which lie the remains of the old Medina, which were bulldozed for fear of typhoid breaking out. Further north, still, is the old **Kasbah**, and beyond it, the new industrial port and suburb of **Anza**. Another industrial zone spreads south towards Inezgane.

Getting around Agadir, you might want to make use of **petits taxis**, as it's a fair walk between Nouvelle Talborjt and the beach, for instance, and a long haul up to the Kasbah. Alternatively, you can rent **mopeds** or **motorbikes** (see "Listings" on pp.460–461), which would also allow you to explore the beaches north and south of town.

Arriving by air

Agadir's **Al Massira airport** is 25km east of the city. It is well equipped and stays open all night, though the café and restaurant are closed from around 7pm, and the banks and car rental offices open only during normal office hours and are closed on Sundays. Taxis, however, will accept foreign currency.

Holiday companies run their own buses to meet flights and shuttle passengers to their hotels, and if you've bought a flight-only deal it's worth tagging along with fellow passengers. If you don't get one of these, airport officials will direct you to the **grands taxis** outside, which charge a standard 150dh fare to central Agadir, which covers up to six passengers. If you plan to share a fare, arrange this *inside* the terminal. There is no bus to downtown Agadir.

If you are planning to move straight on from Agadir, you might do best to take a taxi or bus to **Inezgane** (13km southeast of Agadir; see p.462). Taxis charge around 60dh for the run (again for up to six people). The white *GAT* #22 bus (every 40min; 6am–7pm) charges 3dh per person. It leaves from outside the airport building. If money is tight, you could take this to Inezgane and a bus or taxi from there to Agadir.

Driving from the airport, you are well positioned for a first night at Agadir (half an hour's drive), Taroudannt (45min), or even Marrakesh (about 4hr). **Driving to the airport** from Agadir, you have a choice of routes. The easiest is to leave Agadir by way of Aït Melloul and the Taroudannt (P32) road, turning right at the signposted junction. Alternatively, you can approach from the north, leaving Agadir on the Marrakesh (P40) road, then turning off (left) just after Tikiouine.

Arriving by bus or grand taxi

All Agadir long-distance buses operate from the **Talborjt bus station** (*gare routière*) behind Place Lahcen Tamri (see map inset).

If you're coming in by **bus** from the south, however, you might find yourself dropped in **Inezgane**, 13km southeast (see p.462). Getting into Agadir from here, take local buses #5 or #6, or a **grand taxi** (3dh a place); either of these will drop you at the local bus terminal in **Place Salam** (aka Place de l'Abattoir).

For details of leaving Agadir, see p.459.

Getting around

Agadir is for the most part a walkable city, though you may want to use **petits taxis** for transport between the Talborjt bus station and the beach hotels, or for getting to the grand taxi terminal at Place Salam. There are also a few useful **city buses**:

#1	Place Salam – Av. Prince Monlay Abdallah – Port-Anza
#5,6	Place Salam – Inezgane
#12	Place Salem – Av. Mohammed V – Taghazoute
#13	Place Salem – Tamrarht (Banana Village) – Iminiki
#14	Place Salem – Taghazoule – Tamri
#22	Inezgane – Agadir Airport

Fares for most of these bus trips are 3dh.

Accommodation

Agadir has a vast number of hotels, tourist apartments and "holiday villages", though in high-season periods – Christmas/New Year, Easter, July and August – it is still worth booking ahead. Out of season, you can often get discounts at the large, four-star hotels.If you plan to move out of Agadir more or less immediately, you might be better off staying at **Inezgane** (see p.462), where long-distance buses leave for the south.

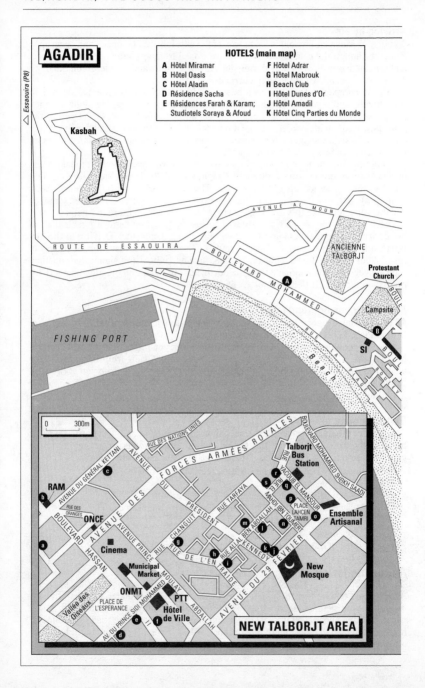

AGADIR

△ Essaouira (P8)

HOTELS (main map)

A Hôtel Miramar
B Hôtel Oasis
C Hôtel Aladin
D Résidence Sacha
E Résidences Farah & Karam;
   Studiotels Soraya & Afoud

F Hôtel Adrar
G Hôtel Mabrouk
H Beach Club
I Hôtel Dunes d'Or
J Hôtel Amadil
K Hôtel Cinq Parties du Monde

Kasbah

AVENUE AL MOUN

ANCIENNE
TALBORJT

Protestant
Church

ROUTE DE ESSAOUIRA

BOULEVARD MOHAMMED V

Campsite

FISHING PORT

Beach

SI

NEW TALBORJT AREA

0   300m

RUE DES NATIONS UNIES

BOULEVARD MOHAMMED SHEIKH SAADI

FORCES ARMÉES ROYALES

AVENUE DU GÉNÉRAL KETTANI

Talborjt
Bus
Station

RAM

RUE DES
ORANGES

AVENUE DES

RUE YACOUB EL MANSOUR

ONCF

AVENUE DU PRÉSIDENT

RUE TARFAYA

RUE CHANGUIT

RUE EL FELAH

RUE MAHDI IBN TOUMERI

PLACE
LAHCEN
TAMRI

Ensemble
Artisanal

Cinema

BOULEVARD HASSAN

RUE ALLAL BEN ABDALLAH

RUE DE L'ENTRAIDE

RUE ALLAL KENNEDY

Municipal
Market

AVENUE DU 29 FÉVRIER

New
Mosque

ONMT

Vallée des
Oiseaux

PLACE DE
L'ESPERANCE

MOULAY ABDALLAH

PTT

Hôtel
de Ville

AV. DU PRINCE SIDI MOHAMMED

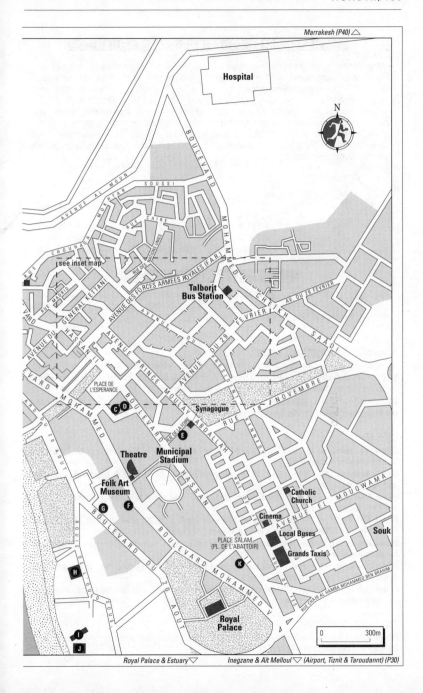

Marrakesh (P40) △

Hospital

N

BOULEVARD MOHAMMED

SOUSSI

AVENUE AL MOUN

AVENUE MOKHTAR

RUE CAIRE

CHOUHADA

RUE DES NATIONS UNIES

see inset map

RUE DES FORCES ARMEES ROYALES (FAR)

Talborjt
Bus Station

RUE MADRID

RUE GENERAL KETTAN

AVENUE DU HASSAN I

AVENUE

AVENUE PRINCE MOULAY ABDALLAH

AVENUE DU 29 FEVRIER

CHEIKH SAADI

AV DU 29 FEVRIER

BOULEVARD

PLACE DE
L'ESPERANCE

C D

E

Synagogue

RUE 18 NOVEMBRE

RUE DE LA TOUR

BOULEVARD

RUE KENNEDY

Theatre

Municipal
Stadium

HASSAN I

Folk Art
Museum

G

F

Catholic
Church

Cinema

AVENUE EL MOUDAWAMA

Souk

AVENUE EL

BOULEVARD DU 20 AOUT

BOULEVARD DU 20 AOUT

PLACE SALAM
(PL. DE L'ABATTOIR)

Local Buses

Grands Taxis

ROUTE D'OUED SOUS

H

BOULEVARD MOHAMMED V

RUE CHAIR AL HAMRA MOHAMMED BEN BRAHIM

K

I

J

Royal
Palace

0   300m

Royal Palace & Estuary ▽   Inegzane & Aït Melloul ▽ (Airport, Tiznit & Taroudannt) (P30)

Nouvelle Talborjt/City Centre

Most of the budget-priced hotels are to be found in **Nouvelle Talborjt**, in the grid of streets around the **bus station**. They, are all small, indepently run places, frequented to an extent by Moroccans on holiday, as well as tourists. Down towards the city centre are a few more upmarket places. The following are recommended and are **keyed on the map inset (with lower case letters)**:

CHEAP

Hôtel Aït Laayoune [q], Rue Yacoub El Mansour (☎08/82.43.75). The former *Hôtel Tifawt*, refurbished and well managed. ①

Hôtel Amenou [o], 1 Rue Yacoub El Mansour (☎08/82.30.26). A newish hotel with smart decor and hot showers. ①

Hôtel Diaf [l], Rue Allal Ben Abdallah (☎08/82.58.52). One of the best cheapies around – reliable, welcoming and comfortable. ①

Hôtel Excelsior [r], 19 Rue Yacoub El Mansour (☎08/82.10.28). Favoured by Moroccans; fair rooms but a bit noisy, by the bus station and next to a couple of grill-cafés. ①

Hôtel Itrane [h], 23 Rue de l'Entraide (☎08/82.14.07). Quiet, welcoming, and one of the cheapest hotels in town. ①

Hôtel Moderne [s], Rue El Mahdi Ibn Toumert (☎08/82.33.73). Tucked away in a quiet location. Rooms with and without showers en suite. ①

Hôtel Select [m], 38 Rue Allal Ben Abdallah (no phone). Aong with the *Itrane*, this has Agadir's cheapest rooms – a little basic, but there's a convenient public *douche* (showers) alongside. ⓤ

MODERATE

Hôtel Aferni [c], Av. Général Kettani (☎08/84.07.30). A large and rather prison-like building, but friendly and flexible, and with a pool. ③

Atlantic Hôtel [f], Bd. Hassan II (☎08/84.36.61). A good-value, comfortable hotel with a small garden; over towards the city centre. ②

Hôtel Ayour [i], 4 Rue de l'Entraide (☎08/82.49.76). Another decent mid-budget choice; friendly and offering a bit more privacy than usual. ②

Hôtel El Bahia [n], Rue El Mahdi Ibn Toumert (☎08/82.27.24). A fine little hotel – beautifully modernized and with friendly, English-speaking staff. ②

Hôtel Kamal [e], Bd. Hassan II (☎08/84.28.17). Rooms and self-catering studios, set round a small swimming pool. ③

Hôtel les Palmiers [d], Av. du Prince Sidi Mohammed (☎08/84.37.19). Clean, well-kept rooms, a bar and an excellent restaurant. ②

Hôtel de Paris [k], Av. Kennedy (☎08/82.26.94). Rooms round a fountain courtyard; hot showers are a bit unreliable. ②

Hôtel Petit Suede [b], Bd. Hassan II (☎08/84.07.79). A very pleasant, small hotel – one of the first built after the earthquake, so with a bit of character. Does car rental. ②

Hôtel Sindibad [p], Place Lahcen Tamri (☎08/82.34.77). Comfortable and popular budget hotel with a restaurant and bar. ②

Hôtel Talborjt [g], Rue de l'Entraide (☎08/84.03.86). Popular modern hotel. ③

Hôtel le Tour Eiffel [j], 25 Rue 29 Fevrier (☎08/82.37.12). Another pleasant, newish place with a café-restaurant. ④

EXPENSIVE

Hôtel Sud Bahia [a], Rue des Administrations Publics (☎08/84.07.82). Large but welcoming, 1960s-style package tour hotel, with a good-sized swimming pool, restaurant, bar and nightclub; also exchange and car rental. ④

Main boulevards – towards the beach

The hotels along the main boulevards, and particularly towards the beach, are rather fancier places; they are **keyed in capital letters on the main map**.

CHEAP

Hôtel les Cinq Parties du Monde [K], Bd. Hassan II (☎08/84.54.81). A friendly hotel with modern, clean rooms off a tiled courtyard, plus a decent set-menu restaurant. ①

MODERATE

Hôtel Aladin [C], Rue de la Jeunesse (☎08/84.32.28). Small hotel in a quiet back street, with a small pool, a coffee bar and restaurant. ③

Hôtel Mabrouk [G], Bd. du 20 Août (☎08/84.06.06). Another small hotel, with an attractive garden. ③

Hôtel Miramar [A], Bd. Mohammed V (☎08/84.07.70). This was the only hotel that survived the earthquake. It's a homely, twelve-room place, elegantly redesigned by André Paccard, doyen of the *Hôtel La Mamounia* in Marrakesh and several of King Hassan's palaces. It has a bar and Italian restaurant, but no pool, which makes it fine value. ③

EXPENSIVE

Hôtel Adrar [F], Bd. Mohammed V (☎08/84.04.17). Not a very promising building but has a good reputation for service and facilities. ④

Hôtel Amadil [J], Route de l'Oued Souss – south of the *Beach Club* (☎08/84.06.20). A huge complex, with a trio of pools and everything from sauna to pétanque; beach-trikes are rented nearby, too. ④

Beach Club [H], Route de l'Oued Souss (☎08/84.43.43). At the southern end of the beach, this is a tasteful new hotel with all facilities. ④

Hôtel Oasis [B], Bd. Mohammed V (☎08/84.33.13). Brand-new, Swiss–run luxury hotel. Very efficient and everything works – as you'd expect. ④

Studios and apartments (résidences)

At the mid-range of the price scale, **studios and apartments** are as popular as hotels in Agadir. All of those listed below are in the city centre/main avenue-beach area and have self-catering facilities and in some cases good restaurants, too; many of them discount prices by 40 percent out of season. Again, they are **keyed on the main map**.

MODERATE

Résidence Farah [V] (☎08/84.39.33), **Hôtel-Résidence Karam** [V] (☎08/84.42.49), **Studiotel Soraya** [V] (☎08/82.38.05), **Studiotel Afoud** [V] (☎08/84.39.99), all on Rue de la Foire, off Bd. Hassan II. The *Farah* and *Afoud* have highly regarded Moroccan restaurants. All except the *Farah* have (small) swimming pools. ③

Résidence Sacha [D], Place de la Jeunesse (☎08/82.55.68). Just off the town centre in a quiet square. French managed, good-sized studios (some with private gardens), and a small swimming pool. ③

Out of town beach hotels – and the youth hostel

There are several hotels (and a new youth hostel) off the road south of town towards Inezgane and the airport, with access to stretches of the beach. The recommendations below are, for convenience, listed in order of appearance driving from Agadir on the Inezgane road, and detailed as being on the left or right of the road.

Auberge de Jeunesse/Youth hostel, off Route de Inezgane, 5km from Agadir, right (☎08/232754). The location is tricky unless you have transport, but it's clean and quiet. *HI* cards compulsory, and not available here.

Hôtel Pyramid, Chemin de l'Oued Souss, off route Inezgane – 6km from Agadir, right (☎08/83.47.05). An attractive hotel with a swimming pool and stable, where you can hire horses to go trekking along the dunes and over to the bird-rich estuary. ③

Hôtel-Club Hacienda, Chemin de l'Oued Souss, off route Inezgane – 6km from Agadir, right (☎08/83.01.76). A top-category *Village de Vacances* rather closer to the beach, offering golf, swimming, stables and all the facilities. ⑤

Hôtel-Restaurante La Pergola, Route de Inezgane – 8km from Agadir, left (☎08/33.08.41). Characterful French-run hotel with a restaurant which, when on form, is memorable. ②

Hôtel Provençal, Route de Inezgane – 9km from Agadir, right (☎08/83.26.12). Another French-style *auberge*, with a decent restaurant, plus a bar and a swimming pool. ③

Camping

Camping Agadir [labelled], Bd. Mohammed V (☎08/84.66.83). This is reasonably well located, within easy walking distance of the centre and beach, and is reasonably secure, but there's little shade and campervans dominate. It has a snack bar and other facilities. Open all year.

The beach and town

More than most resorts, Agadir's life revolves round its beach. The town itself, being modern and very much a resort, has few sights of any note with the exception of its excellent **folk art museum**. If you have kids to amuse, you might consider a ride on the **"tourist real train"**, which does a thirty-minute run (10dh)around town every hour or two (listen for the whistle and bell), starting out from Bd. 20 Août opposite the end of rue de la Plage.

Along the beach

Agadir's **beach** is as good as they come: a wide expanse of fine sand which extends an impressive distance to the south of the town, is swept each morning and, being patrolled by mounted police, is almost devoid of hustlers. Along its course are a number of cafés which sell drinks and rent out sunbeds and umbrellas – the *Oasis Bar* is

THE SOUSS ESTUARY: BIRDS AND THE PALACE

For anyone with an interest in **bird-watching**, the **Oued Souss estuary** should prove rewarding. The northern banks of the river have good views of a variety of waders and wildfowl including greater flamingo (most evident in August and September), spoonbill, ruddy shelduck, avocet, greenshank and curlew, while the surrounding scrubby banks also have large numbers of migrant warblers and Barbary partridge.

An additional sight, of a rather different nature, is Hassan II's **Royal Palace**, built in the 1980s in an imaginative blend of traditional and modern forms, which can be glimpsed from the riverbank. It cannot, of course, be visited.

To reach the estuary, you could walk along the beach – if you're energetic – from Agadir. If you do this, however, be warned that we have had reports of robbery at knife-point along the way, so leave your valuables behind. Alternatively, you can go by road, taking the Inezgane road out of town and turning off to the right at the signpost to the **Hôtel Pyramid** (see Agadir hotels – "Out of Town beach hotels", opposite). If your main interest is wildlife, you might want to stay out here, as the hotel hires out horses, with which you can trek through the woods, and along the dunes to the estuary.

one of the nicest, very clean and with good service. There is a municipal **swimming pool** (summer only) at the north end if you don't care for the ocean, which – it should be stressed – has a **very strong Atlantic undertow** and is definitely not suitable for children unless closely supervised.

At the south end of the beach, **wet-biking** (200dh for 20min) is available near the *Hôtel Amadil*. Beyond it, a firm called *Locafun* (☎08/824595 – ask for Martine) rent out **beach-trikes and buggies**, and some of their employers do a sideline in **horse and camel rides**. All of these can be rented for a ride along the sands, up on the dunes, and over to the estuary (see box above). This is reached past an area known as **Founty**, quite a pleasant place, where a hundred or so villas are scattered behind the sand dunes and eucalyptus forest.

The fishing port

To the north of the beach, the **fishing port** is worth a stroll. You can haggle for fish yourself, at very low prices, if you're doing your own cooking, or have it cooked for you at grills in the *Marché du Port* by the entrance. Most of these operate until 11pm in summer, 7pm in winter, and prices are very reasonable.

The Valley of the Birds and Folk Art Museum

As a break from the beach, you might wander into the **"Valley of the Birds"** (Wed–Sun 9.30am–12.30pm & 3–7pm; 5dh), a dry river valley which runs down from Bd. Hassan II, under Bd. Mohammed V, to Bd. du 20 Août. It's basically a narrow strip of parkland, with a little aviary and zoo, a waterfall and a children's playground: all very pleasant, and the lush vegetation draws a rich variety of birds throughout the year.

A few blocks to the south is an outdoor theatre – built along Roman odeon lines – underneath the south side of which is the new **Agadir Folk Art Museum** (Mon–Sat 9.30am–1pm & 2.30–6pm; ☎08/87.07.84; 10dh). This has been set up by Bert Flint, a Dutch anthropologist, and serves as a sister museum to his Maison Tiskiwin in Marrakesh, housing his extensive collections of southern Moroccan crafts and arte-facts, with special attention to Saharan nomadic art. The exhibits are superb and are eventually to be supplemented with slides, videos and photographs to illustrate their expression of traditional and contemporary daily life.

Just along the path from the folk museum is Agadir's new **Municipal Museum**, with no permanent exhibits as yet, but showing occasional art exhibitions.

Markets

Agadir has two main markets, both containing stalls selling normal Moroccan goods, as well as tourist souvenirs.

The **Marché Municipal**, a two-storey concrete block, stands in the centre of town between Av. des F.A.R. and Av. Prince Sidi Mohammed, with a display of wet fish downstairs cheek by jowl with fossils and handicrafts. Upstairs, it's almost all tourist shops selling goods from around the region, and indeed the country. Starting prices are very high, and you can certainly get some of the same things cheaper elsewhere, but there are some interesting goods here and it's worth a look around.

Much more Moroccan in style is the **souk**, in a massive walled enclosure on Rue Chai-al Hamra Mohammedben Ben Brahim; here the tourist stalls are in a minority, albeit a significant one.

Ancienne Talborjt and the old Kasbah

The raised plateau of **Ancienne Talborjt**, which entombs the town demolished in the 1960 earthquake, stands to the west of the city centre. It is marked by a small mosque and unfinished memorial garden. Relatives of the 15,000 dead come to this park area to walk, remember and pray: a moving sight, after so many years.

For visitors, a more tangible sight of old Agadir is the **Kasbah**, on the hill to the north of the port. This is an eight-kilometre trip, worth making if you have transport, or by *petit taxi*, for a marvellous view of Agadir and the coast. You can see the Kasbah quite clearly from central Agadir – and more particularly a vast "Allah–Nation–King" slogan, picked out in Arabic, in white stones, on the slopes below.

Athough it survived the quake, the Kasbah is little more than a bare outline of walls and an entrance arch – the latter with an inscription in Dutch and Arabic recording that the Netherlands began trading here in 1746 (capitalizing on the rich sugar plantations of the Souss plain). It's not much, but it is one of the few reminders that the city has any past at all, so complete was the destruction of the 1960 earthquake.

Eating, drinking and nightlife

For an international resort, Agadir is a bit staid, with little in the way of bars, clubs or discos, outside of the large hotels. However, there are plenty of cafés and restaurants, for all budgets, including a few "ethnic" choices if you feel like a break from Moroccan or French-style food.

Restaurants

As with hotels, there's a concentration of inexpensive café-restaurants in **Nouvelle Talborjt**, where you can get regular Moroccan meals (including some bargain set menus) at pretty much regular Moroccan prices. There are a scattering of cafés and mid-price restaurants on or near the **beach**, too, including two that stay open 24 hours, along with a fair range of more sophisticated places – a few of which almost justify a stopover in themselves.

NOUVELLE TALBORJT/CITY CENTRE

L'Amirante, 19 Rue des Orange. Value for money if you stick to the local dishes – which are in any case better than the international offerings. Moderate.

Restaurant Caverne, Bd. Hassan II. In front of the *Atlantic Hotel*. Friendly and good value. Moderate.

Restaurant l'Étoile de Marrakech, on the ground floor of the *Studiotel Afoud*, Rue de la Foire (☎08/84.39.99). Renowned for its traditional Moroccan dishes. Moderate.

Café-Restaurant Maouid Chabab, Place Lahcen Tamri. This usually has a good and inexpensive menu du jour and it's understanding of the needs of vegetarians (especially those with their own stock cubes). Open to midnight. Cheap.

Mille et Une Nuits, Place Lahcen Tamri. Serves a range of Moroccan staples – *couscous*, *tajine*, *brochettes* and *harira*; always fresh, busy and good value. Set menu available. Cheap.

Restaurant Select, 38 Rue Allal Ben Abdallah. Beneath the hotel of the same name. Food varies from mediocre to delicious, but always good for the price. Set menu available.

Café-Restaurant Tamount, 47 Av. President Kennedy. Copious helpings of well-prepared Moroccan dishes. Moderate.

La Tonkinoise, ground floor of *Residence Tislit*, Av. du Prince Sidi Mohammed (☎08/84.25.27). Chinese and Vietnamese cooking, some of the latter very good. The Soupe Tonkinoise is highly recommended. Moderate.

Tour de Paris, Av. Hassan II (☎08/84.09.01). A pricier but high quality place, with enticing menus. Moderate.

Via Veneto, Bd. Hassan II (☎08/84.14.67). The best Italian food in town.

MAIN BOULEVARDS/TOWARDS THE BEACH

Restaurant Don Vito, on the beach. Good for pizza and pasta, snacks and soft drinks, though the wall-to-wall Roger Whittaker is a bit much to take. Moderate.

Restaurant Jour et Nuit, on the beach; **Restaurant Tente**, "under" the municipal swimming pool. French-style dishes and snacks. Both are open 24hr. Moderate.

Le Miramar, in the *Hôtel Miramar*, Bd. Mohammed V (☎08/84.07.70). This is the city's most chic restaurant – a beautifully decorated place overlooking the fishing port. Fine Italian cooking, particularly fish and seafood. Fairly expensive.

Residence Tafoukt, Bd. du 20 Août. This tourist complex has a number of moderate to expensive restaurants, with French, Moroccan, Italian and seafood menus. Also tucked away inside, the *Eis Bar* has the best ice creams in Agadir, served up in waffle cones, and cakes to kill for. Across the street, in the *El Madina Centre*, you'll find moderately priced Lebanese food, and even a *Tex-Mex*.

Yacht Club Restaurant du Port, Port d'Agadir (☎08/84.37.08) – near the campsite. Fish and seafood – as you'd expect from the location inside the fishing port. Take your passport, as you have to go through customs. Open noon–3pm & 7–11pm. Moderate.

PÂTISSERIES

Yacht Traiteur, Av. 20 Fevrier between Rue de l'Entraide and Prince Monlay Abdallah. Agadir's best pâtisserie produces Lebanese specialities such as *baklava* as well as top-whack versions of Moroccan favourites.

Bars and nightlife

Both the *Jour et Nuit* and *Tente* restaurants (see above) have bars open 24 hours, while clubs and hotel discos tend to stay open as long as there are people upright on the dance floor – as late as 4 or 5am in summer, but often only till 2am off season. Promising options include:

Disco Tan Tan, in the *Hôtel Almohades*. (☎08/84.02.33). Perhaps the best of the hotel discos.

Bylbos Disco, in the *Hôtel Les Dunes d'Or*. (☎08/84.01.50). This can be lively, too, though admission and drinks are expensive.

Leaving Agadir

Agadir is a reasonable transport terminal, with efficient **buses** to a range of destinatons, and regular **grand taxi** (collective taxi) runs to Taroudannt and Tiznit. If you are going somewhere out of the way, you may need to connect with a bus or *grand taxi* at **Inezgane**. This can be reached most easily by *grands taxis*; they leave throughout the day from Place Salam, charging 3dh a place.

For details of **car rental** companies, see the "Listings" following.

By bus

Leaving Agadir **by bus**, the best services are operated by **ONCF/Supratours** (the train company; ticket office is at 10 Rue des Oranges; ☎08/841207), **CTM** and **SATAS**, though you may need to use other private lines for a few minor destinations, or travel via Inezgane. All the services except ONCF's leave from the **Talborjt terminal**, most of which depart from **Rue des Oranges** (off Bd. Hasian II near the junction with Av. Gen Kettani); these fluctuate, though, so check in advance.

Useful departures include:

ONCF: Marrakesh (4.15am, 7.30am, 2.15pm, 8pm; all 4hr express service 7.30am departs from Talborjt); Laayonne (11hr 15min) via Goulimine (3hr 30min) and Tan Tan (5hr 30min); 8pm, 2am; the 8pm departure continues to Dachla, arriving 4pm); Laayoune (8.30pm; arriving 5am).

CTM: Marrakesh (4pm, 7.30pm); Casablanca (7.30am, 10pm, 10.30pm, 11pm); Fes (7.30pm); Essaouira & Safi (7.30am & 7pm); Rabat & Tangier (10.30pm); Taroudannt & Ouarzazate (9.30am); Trenit (6.30am, 3.30pm); Laayonne (11pm, also 8pm Dakhla via Laayonne).

SATAS: Marrakesh (8am, 10am, noon, 8pm, 9.30pm, 10.30pm); Casablanca (6am, 9.30pm, 10.30pm); Essaouira (6am, 9am, 12.30pm, 2.30pm (all except 2.30pm continue to Safi)); Taroudannt (6am, 9.30pm); Tata (6am, 7.30am); Tafraoute (1.45pm); Tiznit (6am, 7.30am, 2pm); Goulimine & Tan Tan (6am, 2pm); Goulimine and Assa Zag (9am).

Grands taxis

Agadir's **grands taxis** gather at a rank a block south of the local bus station at **Place Salam**. They run direct to Tiznit, Taroudannt and sometimes to other southern destinations, but it is often easier to take one to Inezgane and get a connection there.

Listings

Airlines *Royal Air Maroc* have an office on Av. du Général Kettani, opposite the junction with Bd. Hassan II (☎08/84.07.93). They fly from Agadir to Clasablanca (3 or 4 daily), Layoune (5 weekly), Tangier (1–2 weekly), Marrakesh (weekly), and Ouarzazate (weekly in winter). Also twice weekly to Las Palmas in the Canary Islands, and direct scheduled flights to major European cities. *Air France*, who run some of these services in co-operation with *RAM*, have an office on Av. Prince Sidi Mohammed behind the *Hôtel Kamal*.

American Express c/o *Voyages Schwartz*, opposite the municipal market, behind the *Via Veneto* restaurant (☎08/84.29.69); open Mon–Fri 9am–noon & 3–6pm; closed weekends.

Banks There are over a dozen banks in the downtown area; regular summer hours are Mon–Fri 8am–noon & 2.30–5pm; in winter Mon–Thurs 8.15–11.30am and 2.15–4.30pm, Fri 8.15–11.15am & 2.45–4.45pm. *Banque Populaire* on Bd. Hassan II is helpful – and will guide you through the motions of opening an account if you decide to stay on in Morocco; they also have a little *bureau de change*, next to *Hôtel Kamal* on Bd. Hassan II, which is open on Saturdays. *ABM* on Av. du Prince Sidi Mohammed (opposite the *PTT*), *BMCE* on Av. du Général Kéttani and *Crédit du Maroc* on Av. des F.A.R. are useful for VISA/Access transactions. There is now a proliferation of cash-point machines that accept VISA debit cards. Most large hotels also change money.

Books and newspapers A small selection of paperbacks and coffee table books on Morocco are sold at *Al Mougar* on Av. Prince Moulay Abdallah opposite the end of Av. 29 Fevrier, and the odd one or two at *Atlas Bureau*, 16/18 Av. Prince Moulay Abdallah, and *Debit Pilote*, 65 Bd. Hassan II. British daily papers, as well as *Time, Newsweek, USA Today* and the *International Herald Tribune* can be found at stands on Bd. Hassan II between Av. des F.A.R. and Av. du Prince Sidi Mohammed, and at the foot of the latter, as well as at larger hotels. The *Crown English Bookshop* by the tourist office has now re-opened and sells mostly secondhand books.

Car rental If you're heading for the Anti-Atlas or southern oases, renting a car from Agadir makes a lot of sense. It's also very competitive, with fifty or so companies competing for your custom. Shopping around, check that you are being offered an all-inclusive price (insurance, etc), and whether you can return the car to another city, or to Agadir airport. A good place to start looking is the *Bungalow Marhaba* on Bd. Mohammed (see map), where you'll find *Hertz* (☎08/84.09.39),

Budget (☎08/84.46.00), *Europcar/InterRent* (☎08/84.03.37) and *Tourist Cars* (☎08/84.02.00), together with the local operators *Weekend Cars* (☎08/84.06.67), *Lotus Cars* (☎08/84.05.88) and *Afric Cars* (☎08/84.09.22; highly recommended by our resident Agadir correspondent). *Avis* (☎08/84.17.55), the only other major company, are on Bd. Hassan II at the corner with Rue Madrid. Also personally recommended are three other local companies: *Amoudou Cars*, Bd. Hassan II, corner of Av. Mouqaouama (☎08/84.37.72); *Golden Tours*, Bd. Mohammed V opposite the campsite (☎08/84.03.62); and *Méditerranée Cars*, Immeuble Dolador, Rue El Massira (☎08/84.19.68).

Car repairs Some recommendations: for Renaults, *Castano*, Rue Kadi Aïad; for Citroëns/Peugeots, *Garage Citroën*, Bd. 2 Mars, corner of Av. Mouqaouama (☎08/82.06.19); for Fiats, *Auto-Hall*, Rue de la Foire (☎08/84.39.73). There are many others, doubtless equally good.

Cinemas The town has three: the *Sahara* on Pl Lahcen Tamri in Talborjt; the *Salam*, on Av. Mouqaouama opposite the city bus station; and *Rialto*, the newest, off Av. des F.A.R., behind the municipal market.

Consulates An honorary British consul is based at the *Beach Club* hotel on the beach (☎08/84.43.43); there are also consuls for Norway (☎08/82.34.47) and Sweden, Rue de l'Entrade near the corner with Av. 29 Fevrier (☎08/82.30.48). Other consulates include Belguim, France, Finland, Italy, Peru, Spain. There is no US, Canadian, Australian or Dutch consular representation.

Craft shops Good first stops are *Adrar*, on Av. Prince Moulay Abdallah, through the passageway behind the Crown English Bookshop, and the *Uniprix* shop at the corner of Bd. Hassan II and Av. du Prince Sidi Mohammed and *Sud Galeries*, further along Bd. Hassan II in front of the *Hotel Atlantic*, as they sell goods at fixed prices. So, too, does the chaotic *Ensemble Artisanal* (Mon–Sat 9am–1pm & 3–7.30pm) on Rue 29 Fevrier, just north of Place Lahcen Tamri. If you buy anything elsewhere in Agadir – rugs, carpets, *babouches*, etc – you will have to do some very heavy bargaining indeed. You would do better (and have more fun) visiting the *souks* at Taroudannt for the day.

Food and drink shops The *Uniprix* shop (see above) also sells the cheapest spirits, beer and wine (along with general provisions). The best supermarket is *Sawma Supermarket*, 1 Rue de Hôtel de Ville, just off Av. Hassan II near Rue de la Foire.

Ferries For Tangier ferries, book at *COMANAV*, Bd Mohammed V, opposite the campsite (☎08/84.04.53). The ferry from Agadir to Las Palmas (Canary Islands) has been discontinued.

Medical care Most of the big hotels can provide addresses for English-speaking doctors. Current recommendations include: doctors: Dr Martinez Espinoza (☎08/82.06.31) and Dr Tarik Ljubuncic (☎08/84.10.79); and dentists: Dr Noureddine Touhami, Immeuble MZ – Apt. 4 (near the *PTT*), Av. Prince Moulay Abdallah (☎08/84.26.48). Alternatively, take a taxi to the Polyclinique (☎08/82.49.56) or the Clinique Massira, a few blocks down from the *PTT* on Av. Prince Moulay Abdallah (☎08/84.32.38).

Moped/motorbike/bike rental Various outfits rent out Yamaha 125s (useful for day-trips to Immouzer and beyond) at around 250dh a day, with lower rates for the week, and also cheaper mopeds (200dh a day) which are intended for local use but handy for shuttling to Banana Village and the beach at Taghazoute. They can be found along Bd. 20 Août, on the stretch between *Résidence Tafoulet* and a little way beyond the *Hôtel Mabroule*, as well as just off there on Route de l'Oued Souss. It pays to deal with a decent firm, since a number of cowboy outfits operate, renting unserviced bikes with inadequate insurance cover and no redress in the event of a breakdown. A reliable renter will have several, usually identical vehicles on display, will rent for 24hr rather than just until nightfall (when they'll need their bike back to get home), and will be able to show you full paperwork (rather than just a receipt) proving that the insurance, minimal though it might be, covers you (and passenger if necessary) and detailing help in the event of a breakdown.

Post office The main *PTT* is right in the middle of town at the top of Av. Sidi Mohammed; hours are Mon–Fri 8.30am–6.45pm, Sat 8.30am–noon only; the efficient telephone section is open 8am–9pm daily.

Religious services The Catholic *Église Sainte-Anne* in Rue de Marrakesh (☎08/82.22.51) celebrates daily Mass in French at 6.30pm and in various languages on Sundays at 10am and 7pm; its priests are French, Dutch and Indian. There is also a Protestant church at 2 Rue Chouada, near the campsite (☎08/84.00.92), and a synagogue on the corner of Av. Prince Moulay Abdallah and Rue de la Foire.

Tourist offices The ONMT is on the balcony level of Immeuble A, entered off Av. Sidi Mohammed along the raised walkway opposite the post office (Mon–Thurs 8.30am–noon & 2.30–6pm, Fri 8.30–11.30am & 3–6.30pm). There is a Syndicat d'Initiative on Bd. Mohammed V, opposite the campsite (Mon–Fri 9am–noon & 3–6pm, also occasionally at weekends; ☎08/84.03.07).

Travel agents *Menara Tours*, 1st floor, 341 Bd. Hassan II opposite the *Hotel Cinq Parties du Monde* (☎08/82.54.69), are agents for *British Airways* and *GB Airways* and offer all usual services, including car rental.

Inezgane

INEZGANE, on the north bank of the Oued Souss, is almost a suburb of Agadir, just 13km distant. The two could hardly be more different, though, for Inezgane is wholly Moroccan, and is a major transport hub for the region – much more so than Agadir – with buses and *grands taxis* going to most southern destinations.

Orientation and transport
Inezgane is connected with Agadir by local bus #5 and #6 bus (very frequent) and by frequent *grands taxi* (2.5dh a place, arriving/leaving Agadir at Place Salam). Long distance CTM and SATAS buses stop on Av. Mokhtar Soussi, a wide street running from the central Place Al Massira to the main Agadir road (where you'll find local buses). Parallel with it is the main street, Bd. Mohammed V with the market and, behind that, the **grand taxi** rank in between the two. To find the bus station for private bus operators, head uphill for 100m on Bd. Mohammed V and take a left down Av. Gsima.

Useful **bus and grand taxi departures** from Inezgane include Taroudannt, Essaouira and Marrakesh. Note that *grands taxis* from Inezgane to Taroudannt sometimes cover the route in two stages: the first taxi takes you to OULAD TEIMA (or "44" as it's known after the kilometre-marker from Agadir), where your driver will arrange a connection on to Taroudannt.

Accommodation
If you arrive late at Agadir airport, and want to head straight on south, you could do a lot worse than stay here, rather than Agadir; you may be able to negotiate a slightly cheaper taxi from the airport, too. Rooms are usually no problem, with dozens of hotels on and around the central Place Al Massira, and near the bus station. Good choices would be:

Hôtel de Paris, 30 Bd. Mohammed V . Cheap and basic, with an inexpensive restaurant. ①
Hôtel Issafen, 179 Bd. Moulay Abdallah, opposite the Total station (☎08/33.04.13). A bit more comfort, with en-suite rooms. ①
Hôtel Hagounia, 9 Av. Mokhtar Soussi (☎08/83.27.83). A slightly more upmarket choice, again with a good inexpensive restaurant. ②

North of Agadir: the coast to Cap Rhir

Along the **coast north of Agadir**, tourist development rapidly begins to fade, and the beach at **Tarhazoute** (19km from Agadir) belongs to a different world, with entirely local accommodation and not a "proper" hotel in sight. This – and the coast towards Cap Rhir – is popular surfing territory, and Essaouira (see p.317) is of course a major surfing resort. The route is also a good one for bird-watchers – as is the coastline south of Agadir.

Public transport is pretty straightforward. From Agadir, city buses #12 and #14 run more or less on the hour up the coast to Taghazoute, while Essaouira buses take the route beyond, via Cap Rhir. The coast is a good target, too, if you rent mopeds or motorbikes in Agadir.

Agadir to Tarhazoute

The coast road north of Agadir begins unpromisingly, passing through the city's industrial sector, a strip known as CITÉ ANZA. You can see and smell the petrol, butane, cement and fish, and may wonder why you left Agadir bay.

At 11km from Agadir, however, things improve, as you reach **TAMRAGHT**, which is universally known as "**Banana Village**" after its thriving banana grove and roadside stalls. You can eat extremely well at the roadside **café-restaurants** here, which are a weekend favourite of the wealthier Agadiris; the ones to look for are the last three on the left, heading north, best of which is the *Baraka* and, a few km further, *Aourir*. At the north end of the village is "**Banana Beach**", a sandy strip, broken by the Oued Tamraht. To the east, a kilometre before you reach Tamraht proper, a road heads inland through "**Paradise Valley**", a beautiful palm-lined gorge, and up into the mountains to **Immouzer des Ida Outanane** (see p.465).

Around 2km out of Tamrarht, a prominent rocky headland, **Les Roches du Diable**, is flanked by further good beaches on either side. The southern one is used by fishermen who stay in bamboo huts here in the summer. Shortly beyond here (16km from Agadir but opposite a beach which calls itself 'Km 17'), a signposted piste leads to *Ranch R.E.H.A.*, where you can go **horse trekking** into the mountains; you can book by phone (☎08/84.75.49) or through many of the larger Agadir hotels.

Tarhazoute

Eighteen kilometres from Agadir is the fishing village of **TARHAZOUTE** (or TAGHAGANT, as it appears on some maps), a ramshackle cluster of compact, colourwashed houses. It is flanked on either side – indeed, from way north of Cap Rhir down to Agadir – by a great swathe of beach, interrupted here and there by headlands and for the most part deserted. The village has no running water and inevitably attracts a rather different clientele from Agadir. Twenty and even ten years ago, it was Morocco's hippy resort *par excellence*, and things haven't changed all that much. International hippydom has been replaced by surfers and young Moroccans – plus an added campervan community of elderly Europeans in the winter – and in summer, the café-managers still belt out non-stop rock music and play cool.

Accommodation is mainly in private rooms, all pretty basic, which give you buckets to fetch water for washing from the spring beside the mosque (there are *hammams* for both sexes in Tamrahrt/Banana Village). Most people rent rooms by the week and rates are therefore highly negotiable – try 250dh a week for two people. There is also a **campsite**, *Camping Tarhazoute*, set just back from the beach, south of the village (☎08/31.44.34), run by a British-Hungarian woman, with full facilities including a go-kart track.

For **meals**, *Restaurant Les Sables d'Or* (08/31.44.40), on the cliff top at the south end of the village, is highly recommended specializing in seafood, and not as pricey as it looks. It's a café and bar, as well, with steps down to the beach. Otherwise, small restaurants in the village serve up grilled fresh fish at very reasonable prices indeed. The *Café Restaurant Florida* on the main road is the best value, and the *Panorama* on the beach also has excellent fish dishes.

Tarhazoute can be reached from Agadir by **local bus** #12 or #14 (from Place Salam or Bd. Mohammed V).

On to Cap Rhir: beaches and bird-watching

North of Tarhazoute is a beach known, somewhat literally, as **25km-Plage** (its distance from Agadir). This is an attractive spot, defined by a rocky headland, and offering good surfing. A further 5km brings you to – yes, **30km-Plage**, flanked by smart

---

ARGAN TREES

One of the stranger sights of the Souss is goats clambering about the trunks of spiny, knotted **argan trees** – a tree, similar to the olive, that is found only in this region. The argan nuts are harvested from late May onwards, depending on the height above sea level, and often have to be recovered from the goat dung (having passed through their gut).

Unappetizing though that might sound, **argan oil** has a sweet and rich taste, and is used in many Moroccan dishes and salads, or for dunking bread. It is quite a delicacy, and not easily extracted: whilst one olive tree provides around five litres of olive oil, it takes the nuts from thirty argan trees to make just one litre of argan oil. Plastic bottles of argan oil are commonly sold at the roadside in the Agadir area.

---

summer villas, and the little village of AGHOUT. From here on to Cap Rhir, there are many little beaches, with caves on the rocky outcrops. The stretch is also known as **Paradis Plage**, and so marked on some maps. At the spot known as Amesnaz (not a village as such), 33km from Agadir, there's a really superb strand.

Cap Rhir (41km from Agadir) is distinguished by its lighthouse, one of the country's first, built by the French in 1926; the keepers welcome visits – and tips. This area, together with **TAMRI** village and **lagoon**, 3km north, is particularly good for **bird-watching**. A report in *Bird Watching* magazine claimed some notable seabird sightings at the cape in recent years, among them Madeiran and Bulwer's petrels, "though you are more likely to see Cory's or Manx Shearwaters, Gannet and Common Scoter". At the lagoon, Audouin's gulls come in to bathe. This is the most reliable site to see the **bald ibis**, one of the world's rarest birds, which roosts on the cliffs north of Tamri and feeds in the lagoon and on the surrounding hillsides. There are a couple of forlorn-looking **cafés** at Tamri for sustenance.

For the continuation of this route along the P8, see pp.316–318, where it is covered in a north–south direction from Essaouira. For much of the distance the road runs some way inland, with just the occasional piste leading down to the sea.

Inland to "Paradise Valley" and Immouzer

The trip up to **Immouzer des Ida Outanane** and its waterfalls – via **"Paradise Valley"**, a beautiful palm-lined gorge – is a superb excursion from Agadir. It is feasible in a day (Immouzer is 62km from Agadir) but much more enjoyable if you stay the night at one or other of the superb *auberges* (30km up the valley or at Immouzer) or take time to explore and camp in the valley.

The road to Immouzer is surfaced the whole way; it leaves the P8 coast road at AORIRE, 11km north of Agadir (make sure you take the right-hand fork in the village – the left-hand one is a dead-end, up a palmery). A daily bus leaves Agadir at 2pm (from 47 Rue El Mahdi Ibn Toumert, just around the corner from the autogare), arriving in Immouzer around 6pm; it returns each morning at 8am. There is an additional bus Thursdays at 5am, returning at 2pm. Minibus taxis also run to Immouzer for the Thursday market (a trip that can be booked at any Agadir travel agent or through most of the larger hotels).

"Paradise Valley"

"Paradise Valley" begins around 10km east of Aorire, as the road suddenly turns a bend into a deep, palm-lined gorge, with a river snaking along the base. The best stretch starts just after the turn-off for Immouzer. You can hire a mule to explore the valley's numerous Berber villages, and it's a glorious place to **camp**, though pitch your tent well away from the riverbed in case of flash floods.

Continuing along the "main road" (7002), at around the 30km mark from Tamrarht, you pass a small new **auberge**, the *Hôtel Tifrit* (no phone; ③). Set in a beautiful little palmery, with a river winding through, this is a rival for the famous *Immouzer Hôtel* – and about half the price. It is run by a charming family, has a swimming pool and provides fine Moroccan meals.

After a further 20km of winding mountain road, you reach the village of **Immouzer des Ida Outanane**, tucked away in a westerly outcrop of the Atlas.

Immouzer des Ida Outanane

IMMOUZER DES IDA OUTANANE is a minor regional and market centre (of the Ida Outanane, as its full name suggests). The **waterfalls**, for which the village is renowned, roll down from the hills 4km to the northwest: follow the road down through the main square and off to the left. They can be spectacular in spring, when the waters reach flood levels and almond blossoms are everywhere, but tight control of irrigation reduces the cascade on most occasions to a trickle, with the villagers "turning on" the falls for special events only. However, the petrified canopy of the falls is of interest in its own right, and there's a full **plunge pool**, and also a second waterfall, nearby, which is still allowed to flow its natural course (ask directions to "Le Deuxieme Cascade").

However, what is really appealing here is the overall feel of things. There's a hamlet just across the stream from the falls, and a **café** (*Café de Miel*) with basic food, near which you can camp out in the olive groves. The whole area is perfect for walkers. You can follow any of the paths with enjoyment – a good one, near the village, cuts up across the cliffs to the *Hôtel des Cascades* – or even trek off to the Marrakesh road (see below). The **birdlife** adds an exciting dimension, with birds of prey commonplace; Bonelli's eagle is a good bet, and you might well spot golden eagles or crag martins.

In Immouzer village, there's a **souk** every Thursday. The local speciality is honey, and the bees are said to feed from wild marijuana and other herbs in the mountains.

Staying in Immouzer

Hôtel des Cascades (☎08/84.26.71 or 82.60.16; ③) is on the edge of Immouzer and signposted from its main square. It is a really delightful place, set amid gardens of vines, apple and olive trees, and hollyhocks, with a huge and placid panorama of the mountains rolling down to the coast, and a spectacular path down to the foot of the falls. The food, too, is memorable and there's a swimming pool (full in summer) and tennis court, and pony-trekking. It is slightly pricey, perhaps, but can be open to bargaining on half-board rates.

If at all possible, book ahead, as the only alternative accommodation is basic rooms at the café just on the right as you enter the village, or at the *Hôtel Tifrit*, 30km distant on the road up from "Paradise Valley" (see above).

East from Immouzer: treks and pistes

A very rough piste road breaks off from the Immouzer–Agadir road, 5km south of Immouzer, and leads to the Agadir–Marrakesh road (P40): it makes for a varied and interesting full day's hike and you can catch a bus or taxi back from the S511 to Agadir. The *Hôtel des Cascades* will run walkers to the end of the initial valley (or you could walk there the night before and sleep out on the pass beyond; carry water), from which the road winds up to cross a high limestone plateau. It then drops to circuit a huge hollow in the hills and descends to a (seasonal) river before climbing up to a pass through to the P40.

If you have a sturdy vehicle, there's a better road which runs east through Immouzer village and over to the P40 at ARGANA, by way of ISK. This is a high route – often snow-bound in winter and perilous in spring after the thaw – and quite spectacular in parts, blasted out of sheer rock face, before descending amid Martian-red hills.

South of Agadir: the Massa lagoon

The **Massa lagoon**, around 40km south of Agadir, is possibly Morocco's most important **bird habitat** (see box below), attracting unusual desert visitors and often packed with flamingoes, avocets and ducks. The immediate area of the lagoon is a protected zone, closed to visitors, but you can get in some rewarding bird-watching if you base yourself at the nearby campsite and chalet complex of **Sidi Rbat**, set beside a long, wild beach and rolling sand dunes. The best **times to visit** are March to April or October to November.

Transport of your own is a considerable advantage for exploring the lagoon area. The best approach from Agadir is to turn west off the P30 Tiznit road at Aït Belfa; from the south you can turn west along the 7053 towards Tassila, shortly after reaching the Oued Massa. Either route will bring you to a T-junction in the centre of MASSA, a long, straggling village with a small **hotel**, the *Tassila* (②), which is sometimes used by bird-watching groups. From here, 8km of sandy road lead alongside the coast and north of the lagoon to a *marabout's* tomb, **Sidi Rbat**, and, nearby, beside the sea, a **campsite/chalet compex**, *La Complexe et Balnéaire Sidi R'bat* (☎ 08/25.50.96). This rather scruffy site was closed at last check, following a drugs bust in 1996.

If you don't have transport, you could charter a taxi in Agadir or Inezgane for the day. Alternatively, you could take a local bus/*grand taxi* from Agadir to Inezgane, and a *grand taxi* from there to Massa, and then walk/hitch on from there. On the return journey, you would need to try to get a lift with fellow tourists as few of the taxis stop in Massa on their way north to Agadir.

The **beach** at Sidi Rbat itself can often be misty and overcast – even when Agadir is basking in the sun – but on a clear day, it's as good as anywhere else and the walks, at any rate, are enjoyable.

THE MASSA LAGOON: BIRD-WATCHING

The protected reserve of **Oued Massa** has perhaps the richest habitat mix in Morocco, drawing in a fabulous array of birds. The **sandbars** are visited in the early morning by flocks of sandgrouse (black-bellied and spotted species) and often shelter large numbers of cranes; the **ponds** and **reedbed** margins conceal various waders, such as black-tailed godwit, turnstone, dunlin, snipe, as well as the black-headed bush shrike (tschagra) and little crake; the deeper **open waters** provide feeding grounds for greater flamingo, spoonbill, white stork and black-winged stilt; and overhead the skies are patrolled by marsh harrier and osprey.

The surrounding **scrubby areas** also hold black-headed bush shrike and a variety of nocturnal mammals such as Egyptian mongoose, cape hare and jackal, while the Sidi R'bat *complexe* offers its own wildlife highlights – a local population of Mauritanian toad in the shower block at night and a café terrace.

Enthusiasts with transport might also like to follow the Oued Massa inland, 20km to the east, to the **Barrage Youssef Ben Tachfine**, an enormous freshwater reservoir, edged by the Anti-Atlas. Possible sightings include black wheatear and rock dove. By the lake is a car park, where campervans sometimes overnight.

Tifnite

The stretch of coast south of Agadir, and north of Massa, is virtually undeveloped, once you clear the sprawl at the edge of Inezgane. It is accessible at a couple of points from the P30, but there is little to go out of the way for. **TIFNITE**, the name that appears most prominently on most maps, is a little collection of fishing huts, strange to come upon so close to "international" Agadir. It attracts a few campervan travellers in summer.

At the hamlet of **Sidi Bibi**, (20km south of Agadir, and marked on the Michelin map), the site of a proposed entrepôt for vegetables, those with their own transport might be tempted to take a break at the wonderful open-air *tajine* restaurant under the trees just off the main road.

Taroudannt

With its majestic, red-ochre circuit of walls, **TAROUDANNT** is one of the most elegant towns in Morocco and an excellent "first base" if you arrive in the country at Agadir. The walls, the *souks* and the stark, often heat-hazed backdrop of the High Atlas to the north, are the town's chief attractions – though none of them is powerful enough to bring in the Agadir tour groups in any great number. It is consequently a very friendly, laid-back sort of place, with all the good-natured bustle of a Berber market town. In addition, the town forms a useful base for trekking into the Western High Atlas or on to the Djebel Sirwa to the east, while for anyone into great road journeys, it stands at the beginning of two superb road routes – north over the **Tizi n'Test** to Marrakesh (see pp.364–365), and south to the oases of **Tata** and Foum El Hassan (see p.478).

Taroudannt's position at the head of the fertile Souss Valley has always given it a commercial and political importance – it was often the first major conquest of new imperial dynasties. It never became a "great city", however. Even the Saadians, who made Taroudannt their capital in the sixteenth century (and built most of its circuit of walls), moved on to Marrakesh. The town's present status, as a major market centre, but with a population of only around 30,000, is probably much as it always has been.

Orientation and accommodation

On arrival, the town can seem highly confusing, with ramparts heading off for miles in every direction and large tracks of open space and derelict building areas – some due to flash flooding, others under cultivation.

In fact, the central town, with its *souks* and workshops, is quite compact, and within the walled "inner city" there are just two main squares – **Place Assarag** (officially renamed Place Alaouyine) and **Place Talmoklate** (officially Place en Nasr) – with the **souk** area between them to the north. Place Assarag, with its low arcaded front and its many cafés, is very much the centre of activity. Over to the east is a further walled enclosure, the old **Kasbah** area, in one corner of which is the *Hôtel Palais Salam*. If you arrive by **bus**, you may be dropped at Place Assarag or Place Talmoklate but more likely at the new **Gare routière** outside the walls to the south. *Grands taxis* operate from outside the Bab Zorgane (see "Listings" for details of departures).

Getting round town, there are **petits taxis** (usually to be found in Place Talmoklate) and, with similar tariffs, a few **calèches** – horse-drawn cabs. You can also rent **bikes** (again, see "Listings" for details).

Hotels

All the cheaper **hotels** are on or around Place Assarag or Place Talmoklate, while dotted round town are a few rather fancier places, including a fine splurge, the *Hôtel Palais*

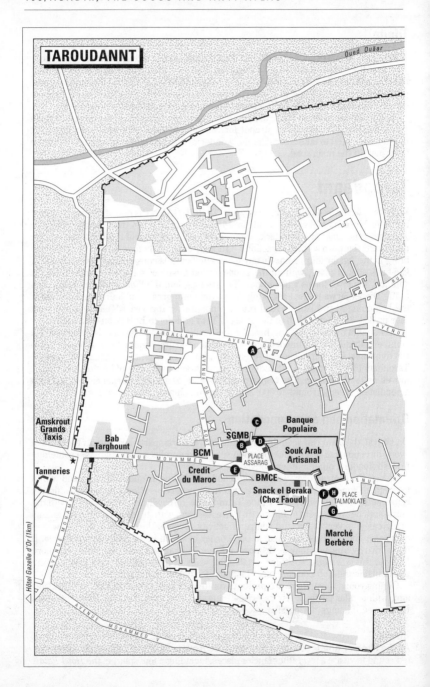

TAROUDANNT

Oued Ouäar

Amskrout
Grands
Taxis

Bab
Targhount

Tanneries

△ Hôtel Gazelle d'Or (1km)

**Banque
Populaire**

SGMB

BCM

PLACE
ASSARAG

Credit
du Maroc

**Souk Arab
Artisanal**

BMCE

Snack el Beraka
(Chez Faoud)

PLACE
TALMOKLATE

**Marché
Berbère**

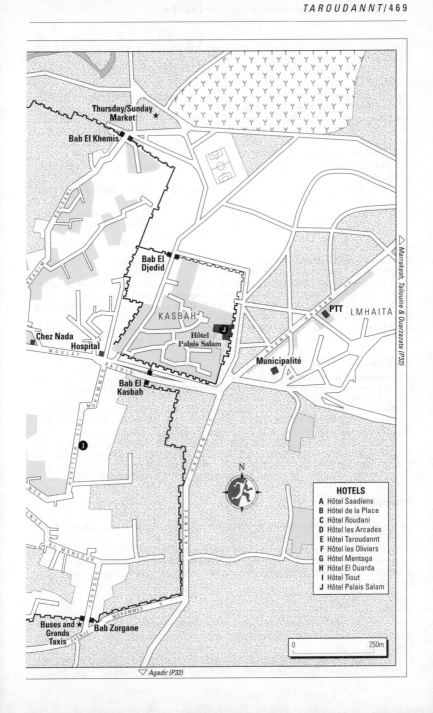

Thursday/Sunday Market ★

Bab El Khemis

Bab El Djedid

KASBAH

Chez Nada
Hospital

Hôtel
Palais Salam

J

PTT

LMHAITA

Municipalité

Bab El Kasbah

I

N

Buses and ★ Bab Zorgane
Grands
Taxis

△ *Marrakesh, Taliouine & Ouarzazate (P32)*

HOTELS
A Hôtel Saadiens
B Hôtel de la Place
C Hôtel Roudani
D Hôtel les Arcades
E Hôtel Taroudannt
F Hôtel les Oliviers
G Hôtel Mentaga
H Hôtel El Ouarda
I Hôtel Tiout
J Hôtel Palais Salam

0   250m

▽ *Agadir (P32)*

Salam. Recommendations (the less salubrious and poor-value hotels around the two main squares aren't listed) include:

CHEAP

Hôtel les Arcades [D], Place Assarag (☎08/85.23.73). Better known for its restaurant, but it has four decent enough rooms and very friendly staff. ①

Hôtel Mentaga [G], Place Talmoklate (☎08/85.23.83). Four rooms round each of the six landings; unusually for Morocco, it is run by a woman, who was widowed but has kept the hotel going. ①

Hôtel les Oliviers [F], Av. du Prince Heritier Sidi Mohammed (☎08/85.20.21). Small, pretty basic rooms – but cheap, clean and friendly with a rather better 'salon' for up to five people. ①

Hôtel El Ouarda [H], Place Talmoklate (☎08/85.27.63). Front rooms have balconies over the square. ①

Hôtel de la Place [B], Place Assarag (no phone). Slightly grubby and rather basic rooms, but okay for the price with friendly staff and a roof terrace. ①

Hôtel Roudani [C], overlooking Place Assarag (☎08/85.22.19). Marginally better rooms, a relaxed and welcoming atmosphere, meals on the square, and a fine rooftop terrace for breakfast. ①

MODERATE

Hôtel Saadiens [A], Bordj Oumansour (☎08/85.25.89). A pleasant modern hotel, north of the squares, with a restaurant, a pâtisserie, hot showers and swimming pool. ②

Hôtel Taroudannt [E], Place Assarag (☎08/85.24.16). A Taroudannt institution and the oldest hotel in town, this was run by a grand old French *patronne* up until her death in 1988, and retains her influence (and amazing poster collection). It is well worth the money for its patio garden, cool air and bar. The cooking is variable but good if you strike lucky. ②

Hôtel Tiout [I], Av. Prince Heritier Sidi Mohammed (☎08/85.03.41). A new place whose spotless, airy rooms (each with en-suite shower and most with a balcony) face out back to avoid noise. ②

EXPENSIVE

Hôtel Gazelle d'Or [off map], 1km out of town to the southwest (☎08/85.20.39). This is an extraordinary place, worth seeing even if you have no possibility of staying: a hunting lodge created by a French baron in the 1920s, in a Morocco-meets-Provence style. It was converted to a hotel after the war and guests (mostly well-heeled Brits) stay in bungalows in the lush gardens. Rates are astronomical – quite possibly the highest in North Africa. Facilities include horse riding and croquet. ⑤

Hôtel Palais Salam [J] (☎08/85.21.30 or 85.23.12). Located in a nineteenth-century palace, just inside the ramparts of the Kasbah (entrance outside the walls), this is a bit of a gem – probably one of the best four-star splurges in the country. It's worth paying more (you may not need to in winter) to get the rooms or suites in the towers or garden pavilions, rather than on the new modern floor. There is a small swimming pool, cocktail bar, tennis court, and two excellent restaurants. ④

Around the town

Taroudannt's twin attractions are its **ramparts** – best toured by bike – and its **souks**. The latter are not large by Moroccan city standards, but are varied and authentic and much of the work you find here is of outstanding quality. On Thursdays and Sundays there is a **regional souk**, which brings in Chleuh Berbers from the villages to sell farm produce and a few odd pieces of craftwork; this takes place out by the northeast gate, **Bab El Khemis**.

The souks

There are two principal *souks*: the **Souk Arab Artisanal**, immediately east of Place Assarag (and north of Place Talmoklate), and the **Marché Berbère**, south of Place Talmoklate.

The **"Arab" souk** – easiest approached along the lane by the BMCE bank (you will probably emerge in Place Talmoklate – it's a tiny area) – is good for rugs, carpets, leather goods and other traditional crafts, but most especially **jewellery**. This comes mainly from the Anti-Atlas villages nowadays (little of it is as "antique" as the sellers would have you believe), though until the 1960s there was an active artisan quarter here of predominantly Jewish craftsmen. Some stalls also sell striking limestone **sculptures**, similar to the ones found in the north at Chaouen and an obvious oddity – often figurative in design and more African than Islamic. For good-quality wares, the *Antiquaire Haut Atlas*, run by Licher El Houcine at 36 Souk Smara, is recommended, while the shop at #120 does superb hand-embroidered kaftans for women, and *gandoura* (short-sleeve) and *foukia* (long-sleeve) robes for men.

The **Marché Berbère** is a more everyday *souk*, with spices and vegetables, as well as clothing and pottery, and again jewellery and carpets. It is most easily entered alongside the *Hôtel Mentaga* in Place Talmoklate. Interesting shops include the *Cadeaux de Taroudannt*, 35 Av. Nasr (next door to the *Hôtel Mentaga*), run by Benjeddi Ahmed.

The tanneries

The leather **tanneries**, as ever, are located some distance from the main *souks* – placed outside the town walls on account of their smell – leather is cured in cattle urine and pigeon droppings – and for the proximity to a ready supply of water. In comparison to Marrakesh, or particularly Fes, the tanneries here are small, but, sadly, they display a rare variety of skins for sale – not just the ubiquitous sheep and cows, but silver foxes, racoons and mountain cats. Many of these furs are illegal imports into Europe or North America and we urge no participation in the process. If you want to visit the tanneries all the same, follow the continuation of the main street past the *Hôtel Taroudannt* to the ramparts; turn left there and, after 100m, take the first turning to the right.

The walls and Kasbah

The town's various **walls and bastions** can hardly be ignored, and, outside the height of summer, they make an enjoyable circuit to explore. They total around five kilometres in extent and you can walk along stretches of them – sometimes dropping down to the foot of collapsed stretches and always with an eye to avoiding excrement. On balance, it is probably more enjoyable to cycle (see "Listings") round the outside perimeter.

TREKKING FROM TAROUDANNT

The Western High Atlas – routes across which are covered on pp.387–391 – are easily accessible from Taroudannt, the peaks of Tinergwet (3551m) and Awlim (3481m) west of the Tichka Plateau looking temptingly close as you look out to the mountains from a roof terrace at dawn or dusk. One of the very best trekking routes in Morocco – "The Wonder Walk" as it is called by some trekking companies – is to make a two-week trip up to the plateau and on to Djebel Toubkal (see p.372), Morocco's highest peak. The Djebel Sirwa (see p.474) is also within easy reach of the town.

If you are interested in a guided trek, contact **El Aouad Ali** (BP127, Taroudannt, Souss, Morocco; fax 212/08/85.36.44; or through the *Hôtel Roudani* or *Hôtel Taroudannt*). He is a highly knowledgeable, English-speaking mountain guide, and has planned out a number of magnificent routes with the Scottish mountain writer, Hamish Brown; he has also worked with BBC TV film crews. Ali's possible itineraries include the "Wonder Walk" above, though he is happy to take you on one- or two-day treks if you prefer. He provides real experience of Berber life on his treks, staying and eating in local houses or camping on the plateau or by the spectacular Nfis River (bread baked on the spot, muleteers singing round a bonfire – it's a world of magic). Independent trekkers can also use his services to get established before going on to trek, climb or (increasingly popular on the Tichka Plateau) ski-tour.

On your way round, take a good look at the old **Kasbah quarter** round the *Hôtel Palais Salam*. Now a kind of village within the town, this was once a winter palace complex for the Saadians and contains the ruins of a fortress built by Moulay Ismail. Outside the walls here are a couple of palm-shaded **parks** popular for an evening stroll – and keep in mind that non-residents can use the swimming pool at the *Palais Salam* for a daily fee of 40dh.

Beyond the walls to the south, signs point to the **Hôtel Gazelle d'Or** (see "Hotels"), a pleasant cycle ride. A mint tea on its terrace is just about affordable and worthwhile for a look at the gardens, especially in spring, but it may be worth calling in advance as they sometimes refuse admittance to non-residents.

Eating and drinking

Basic but inexpensive **café-restaurants** can be found along the street between the two main squares – you could pick from any one of these hole-in-the-wall stalls, most of which have just a couple of tables outside. Listed below are some of the places large enough to have a name, along with the better hotel restaurants.

CHEAP TO MODERATE

Chez Nada, Av. Moulay Rachid. Excellent *tajines*, and also *pastilla* if ordered in advance.

Hôtel Roudani and **Hôtel les Arcades**, Place Assarag. Both hotel restaurants serve good-value *tajines* and sometimes *couscous*.

Hôtel Saadiens, Bordj Oumansour. Top-floor licensed restaurant, with a view of the High Atlas from its terrace.

Snack El Beraka (Chez Fouad), Av. Sidi Mohammed – between the two squares. Best of a group of cheap, hole-in-the-wall, fried fish cafés. The nearest you will get to fish and chips in the Souss – and very good they are, too.

Hôtel Taroudannt, Place Assarag. Fine French and Moroccan meals – and a bar.

EXPENSIVE

Hôtel Gazelle d'Or, 1km out of town. The tented dining room here is quite a sight – and a major extravagance for dinner, when reservation is compulsory and men are required to wear jackets and ties. Lunch by the pool is less costly (though, again, best reserved in advance) – and nobody would be likely to object to your swimming afterwards.

Hôtel Palais Salam, Kasbah. French and Moroccan restaurants – both superb in the evening (lunches cater for groups), though fairly expensive. Also has a pleasant terrace bar.

Leaving Taroudannt: buses and grands taxis

The most reliable **bus services** are those operated by CTM (whose office is in the *Hôtel les Arcades* in Place Assarag) and SATAS (on the south side of Place Assarag), both of which have departures from the new **Gare routière**. However, the CTM and SATAS buses do not originate in Taroudannt and may already be full on arrival, sometimes even by-passing the town completely as a result.

In theory, at least, **CTM** have departures for Ouarzazate at 1.30pm, Agadir at 8pm, and Casa via Agadir and Marrakesh at 9pm. **SATAS** serve Marrakesh via Agadir (5am; arrives 11.30am), Tata (8am – tickets when the bus arrives at 7.30am; arrives 1pm), Ouarzazate via Taliouine (10.30pm; arrives 4am), and Agadir (10.30pm). Two other companies have departures to Casa via Agadir and Essaouira, while others serve Casa and Rabat. (Two companies share the 5am bus over the Tizi 'n'Test to Marrakesh – and, confusingly, departures alternate the gare routiere, between Place Assarag and Place Talmoklate. Ask around the night before and get there early!)

THE TIZI N'TEST

The Tizi n'Test route from Taroudannt to Marrakesh (S501) is one of the most exciting mountain roads in Morocco: a series of hairpin bends cutting across the High Atlas. It is covered, in the opposite direction. As detailed opposite, it is covered by just one bus a day and has no regular *grands taxis*. If driving, be aware of what's in store . . .

Grands taxis operate from a rank outside Bab Zorgane on regular runs to and from Inezgane/Agadir, (often with a change of cars midway at Ouled Teima – see p.462), with less frequent departures for Marrakesh, Ouled Berhil (on the road to Taliouine), and Igherm (on the way to Tata). They can also be chartered for Taliouine, or at considerable expense, Asni or Marrakesh (over the Tizi n'Test road). For Amskroute, they leave from just outside Bab Targhount.

Listings

Banks There are seven: the *BMCE, SGMB* and *Banque Populaire* on Place Assarag, *Crédit du Maroc* and *BCM* just off it on Av. Mohammed V, and the *BMC* on Place Talmoklate and the *BCMI* just off that in Av. Bir Zaran. All have exchange facilities.

Bicycles can be hired by the hour, half- or full-day from a little shop on Av. Mohammed V just off Place Assarag between *Credit du Maroc* and *BCM* (40dh a day).

Car repairs There's a garage for Citroens and Peugeots just inside Bab Targhount (☎08/85.25.22).

Hammam There is a *hammam* located on Av. Mohammed V 30m along from the *Hôtel Taroudannt* – it is signposted only in Arabic (a green tiled entrance, no. 30, next to a butcher's), so you may need to ask someone. Women can steam from noon to 6pm; men 4–11am and 6pm–midnight; 4dh admission (massage extra).

Trekking See box on p.471.

Around Taroudannt: Freija and Tioute

East of Taroudannt, the oases and Kasbahs of **Freija** and **Tioute** are close enough to explore in a half-day's trip by car (or an energetic day by rented bike). Freija lies 11km east of Taroudannt, on the south bank of the Oued Souss; Tioute is a further 26km.

    Bird-watchers may find they don't actually reach either site, due to the attractions of the **Oued Souss** itself (see box overleaf).

Freija

The shortest **route to Freija** is to turn south from the Ouarzazate road (P32) at Aït Iazza, 8km out from Taroudannt. After a further kilometre ford the riverbed (this may be impossible in spring if the river is in flood) and follow an abandoned causeway.

    FREIJA is interesting for two features. First, it is an ancient, fortified village, standing on a low hill above (and safe from flooding by) the Souss. In the past it was easy to defend; today, it affords sweeping views of the river, the fertile plains beyond, and the High Atlas. Second are the remains of an old **Kasbah**, a little further to the south, alongside the road in from the 7027. Built of *pisé* (mud and gravel), this is now crumbling in parts but the guest section (fronting the road) remains in good condition, and families still occupy the resident wings, along with their domestic animals. If you enter the courtyard and show an interest, you are likely to be invited in to look round.

Tioute

TIOUTE can be reached directly from Freija on the minor 7024 road, or – more easily – by turning right off the 7025 Igherm road 16km beyond Aït Iazza. Either way, you

---

THE OUED SOUSS: BIRD-WATCHING

The **Oued Souss** is another key Moroccan bird habitat, with a rich array of winter residents, and a huge range of migrants in the spring.

Using Taroudannt as your base, the bridge or causeway north of **Freija** (see below) would be good points to spend a day bird-watching. Hoopoe, woodchat shrike, orphean, sub-Alpine and Bonelli's warbler, bee-eater and nightingale are all likely sightings in the spring, while stone curlew, great grey shrike and serin are common in winter. Raptors are also likely to be evident: black and black-shouldered kite, griffon vulture and tawny eagle among them. In the evening, you might spot black-bellied sandgrouse and red-necked nightjar (a Souss speciality).

Another site, more scenic and likely to be even more rewarding for birds, is the **Aoulouz Gorge**, 90km east of Taroudannt (just off the P32 Taroudannt–Taliouine road). The gorge is home to a small colony of bald ibis; spring migrants include everything from booted eagle and black kite to white stork; and Barbary falcon, Moussier's and black redstart, blue rock thrush and rock bunting all winter here.

Over **Taroudannt** itself, you can usually see little and pallid swift in the evenings, while serin and Spanish swallow are common in scrubby areas.

---

should arrive at one of the seven straggling villages which form Tioute palmery, with a hill before you, capped by a large, stone-built Glaoui **Kasbah**.

A rough track leads up to the Kasbah, which is one of the grandest in the south and still owned by the local *caid*. It has been renovated and operates as a **restaurant** (☎08/85.10.48), catering mainly for tour groups. If you just turn up, you may be able to see part of the interior – including water tanks, a vault (for valuables), a prison (for hostages), and an open space for festivities. Profiled against the first foothills of the Anti-Atlas, it is a highly romantic sight – a location for *Ali Baba and the Forty Thieves*, starring Fernandel and Yul Brynner. Equally impressive are its fabulous views over the luxuriant palmery, with the High Atlas peaks beyond.

Taliouine and the Djebel Sirwa

The roads east from **Taroudann to Taliouine** lack the drama of Tizi n'Test – the great route from Taroudannt to Marrakesh – but they are efficient approaches to the southern oases. There are some scenic stretches, too, particularly the Taliouine–Ouarzazate section, which changes gradually to semi-desert and offers views of the weirdly shaped mountains of the Anti-Atlas.

For trekkers, the **Djebel Sirwa** (or Siroua), north of Taliouine, is one of the finest mountain sections of the Anti-Atlas. It is scarcely less impressive than the more established High Atlas trekking areas, and a great deal less frequented.

Taroudannt to Taliouine – and an approach to Toubkal

The new 7027 road follows the **Oued Souss** from Taroudannt, shortening the approach to Taliouine for drivers but it's a narrow tarmac strip, with horrendous verges. Better to stick to the old P32, which the new road meets just south of the village of AOULOUZ.

Buses and *grands taxis* run along the P32, with a major halt (and taxi stage) at **OULED BERHIL**, 43km east of Taroudannt. **Grands taxis** from here serve three destinations: Taroudannt, Aoulouz, and Tajingont (15km on the road to Tizi n'Test – but no onward connections). An old **Kasbah** 800m south of the main road (signposted from the centre of the village) has been turned into a sumptuous **restaurant,** the *Riad Hida*, with half a dozen **rooms** (☎08/53.01.13; ①). The house formerly belonged to a Dane, who scrupulously restored its traditional and highly ornate ceilings and architecture. The garden is also magnificent and both the rooms and the meals are very good value indeed. The only other place to stay is the *Hotel Nasr* (⑩), very basic but very cheap, just off the main road on the way to the *Riad Hida*.

AOULOUZ gives onto a **gorge**, rich in bird-watching opportunities (see box opposite). If you decide to stay, there is a small **hotel**, the *Vallée de Souss* (⑩) on the main road, with a restaurant, and a café with a few further rooms. The village hosts *souks* on Wednesdays and Sundays. Aoulouz is a regular **grand taxi** stage, with runs back to Ouled Berhil (for Taroudannt) and Taliouine.

Towards Toubkal; the Assif n'Tifnout

To the east of Aoulouz, piste P32b leads to TAÏSSA, at the southern end of the **Assif n'Tifnout** valley, which is trailed north by a rough piste to Amsouzart, just east of **Lac d'Ifni** and **Djebel Toubkal** (see map on p.370). It is possible to drive this in a sturdy vehicle and you can make a two-day tour, returning to Taliouine (or doing it in the opposite direction – see overpage). Alternatively, you could walk it. From Aoulouz there are minibuses to ASSARAG, where you'll find rooms, and whence a few hours' walk north will take you to **AMSOUZART** (see p.374) where you can find rooms; from there you can reach **Lac d'Ifni** and Djebel Toubkal.

Taliouine

TALIOUINE lies at a pass, its land gathered into a bowl, with a scattering of buildings on and above the roadside. More village than town, its dominant feature is a magnificent **Kasbah** (east of the village) built by the Glaoui, though in a much-decayed state. It is nowadays used mainly to house farm animals, though the best-preserved section is still inhabited by a few families, who might offer to show you round. The Kasbah's decoration is intricately patterned, its windows moulded with palm fronds (some still showing their original paint), and the towers (climb very much at your own risk) are built round squat, downward-tapering pillars.

With your own vehicle, you can set out from Taroudannt, visit the Kasbah and move on easily enough to Ouarzazate the same day. Relying on public transport, you should reckon on staying, which, in any case, is an attractive proposition. Few tourists do, despite the presence of **hotels** in all price ranges, and there are other Kasbahs in the hills round the village, if you have time to explore them.

Taliouine practicalities

Taliouine has a choice of four **hotels**, with a clear winner, the *Souktana*. Travelling by bus, ask to be dropped outside it, if possible.

Auberge Souktana (☎08/53.40.75), by the Kasbah and prominent *Ibn Toumert* hotel (just before it, coming from Taroudannt). This is a wonderful little place, run by Ahmed Jadid (who is an experienced mountain guide – see overleaf) and his French wife Michelle. In winter, try to turn up early in the day as they have only four rooms; it doesn't matter so much in summer, when you can sleep out on their roof terrace or camp in the garden (at other times it's too cold). Travelling by bus, ask to be dropped at one or other hotel. ①

Grand Hôtel Ibn Toumert (☎08/85.12.31), right next to the Kasbah. A comfortable place but nothing very special for the price. ④

Hôtel Rennaissance, in the centre, and **Auberge Askaoun** (☎08/53.40.17), just east of town. These are the fall-back choices, if you can't get a room at the *Souktana*. The Askaoun is the better of the two and also has space for campers. ⑩

The village also a **hammam** (the *Souktana* will give you directions), and a Monday **souk** is held across the valley behind the Kasbah.

Heading on by **bus** from Taliouine can be tricky as many arrive – and leave – full for Taroudannt or Ouarzazate; it pays to go to the main bus stop, as buses can pass the *Souktana* full and then leave half empty from the bus stop. In all, seven buses a day (in each direction) pass through Taliouine en route to Agadir (via Taroudannt) or Ouazazate (via Tazenalcht), including one each way operated by CTM and one each way by SATAS. The 10pm Ouarzazate bus continues to Tinerhir, and there's a 7am departure from the town centre for Marrakesh, and one every two days for Zagora.

Grands taxis from Taliouine make the run west to Aoulouz (change for Ouled Berhil and again there for Taroudannt). There are, frustratingly, no shared **grands taxis** to Tazenakht/Ouarzazate, though you could try chartering one to take you to Tazenakht (see below).

Another approach to Djebel Toubkal

A classic piste route north of Taliouine (piste 6386) skirts the edge of the Djebel Sirwa to reach **Amsouzart**, just east of Lac d'Ifni and Djebel Toubkal. There, you could trek in the Toubkal area, or alternatively make a loop back down to Aoulouz via the Assif n'Tifnout (see previous page). This route is shown on the "Région de Marrakech" inset on the Michelin map (Amsouzart is unmarked but is just north of Mezguemnat), and Ahmed Jadid at the *Souktana* has a detailed route-map, as he offers it as a **two-day landrover expedition**. In summer it is just about practicable in an ordinary car; from Taliouine the road is tarmac halfway to Askaoun.

Tazenakht and on to Ouarzazate

TAZENAKHT, at the junction of the Ouarzazate and Foum Zguid roads, is quite a transport hub, with regular buses and *grands taxis* to Ouarzazate, plus buses to Foum Zguid and Arhbar (from where you might be able to get a lorry across to Agdz in the Drâa Valley – see p.403). There are seven daily buses (but no *grands taxis*) westward to Taliouine, Taroudannt and Agadir.

The village offers decent if basic **rooms** and meals at the *Hôtel Zenaga* (☎04/84.10.32; ⓪), or less enticing ones at the *Café-Restaurant Étoile* (⓪), and has a *Banque Populaire* and filling station. Alongside the *Café-Restaurant Étoile* is a large courtyard with a magnificent display of **carpets**, blankets and clothes, including many of the bold geometric designs of the Ouzguita tribe. If you have time on your hands, you could also visit the carpet co-operative.

The road beyond Tazenakht **to Ouarzazate** is unexciting, running well to the east of Djebel Sirwa.

The Djebel Sirwa (Siroua)

The **Djebel Sirwa** (or Siroua) is an isolated volcanic peak, rising from a high area (3000m-plus, so take it easy!) to the south of the High Atlas. It offers as good trekking as you can find anywhere – rewarded by magnificent views, a cliff village and dramatic gorges. It is best in spring; winter is extremely cold.

A week-long circuit, taking in Sirwa, is outlined on our map, the numbers being the overnight halts. Mules to carry gear, as well as tent rental, can be arranged by **Jadid Ahmed** at the *Auberge Souktana* or by **El Aouad Ali** in Taroudannt (see box on p.471), though neither operate in the Sirwa in winter. Mules would be a worthwhile investment

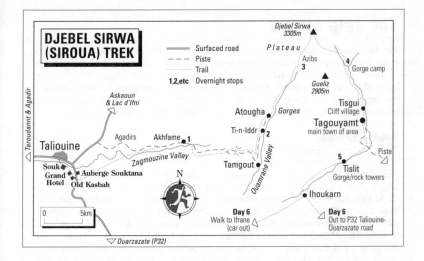

to ensure enjoyment – and accurate navigation. Having Ali or Ahmed along, however, is the best guarantee of success. Both are great characters – and cooks, and both speak fluent French and English.

If you are going it alone, the relevant survey maps are the 1:100,000 *Taliwine* and 1:50,000 *Sirwa*. Jadid Ahmed can show you these, and he dispenses advice whether or not you engage his guiding services.

The circuit

The initial day is a gentle valley ascent along a piste to **AKHFAME** where there are rooms and a Kasbah. The piste actually reaches west of here as far as Atougha but, *souk* days apart, transport is non-existent and the walk is a pleasant introduction. Beyond Akhfame the piste climbs over a pass to another valley at **TAMGOUT** and up it to **ATOUGHA**, before contouring round into the upper valley, where you can stay at *azibs* (goat shelters) or bivouac.

Djebel Sirwa (3304m) can be climbed from Atougha in five to six hours: a pull up from the southern cirque onto a plateau, crowned with rock towers; the nervous may want to be roped for one section of the final scramble. The sub-peak of **Guliz** is worth ascending, too, and a bivouac in the gorge below is recommended.

Beyond Guliz, you should keep to the lower paths to reach **TISGUI** – and don't fail to visit the unique **cliff village** just outside: its houses, ranked like swallows' nests on a 1000ft precipice, are now used as grain stores. Continuing the circuit, past fields of saffron, you reach **TAGOUYAMT**, the biggest village of the Sirwa area and connected by piste to the Taliouine road. Trails, however, leave it to pass through a couple of villages before reaching the river, which is followed to the extraordinary conglomerate features of the **Tislit gorges**. This natural sculpture park is amazing; you can camp or get rooms at the village.

On the last day, you can follow the valley to **IHOUKARN** and then to **IFRANE**, where it's possible to get a vehicle out; alternatively, a three-hour trek to the southeast leads to the Taliouine–Ouarzazate road, near its highest point, from where transport back to Taliouine is easier. Ahmed can arrange transport at either point to meet unaccompanied parties.

The Tata circuit

Heading **south** across the **Anti-Atlas** from Taroudannt, or east from Tiznit, you can drive, or travel by bus, or a combination of *grands taxis* and trucks, to the **desert oases** of **Tata**, **Akka** and **Foum El Hassan**. This is one of the great Moroccan routes, increasingly popular since it was surfaced, though still very much a world apart, with its camel herds and lonely, weatherbeaten villages. As throughout southern Morocco, **bilharzia** is prevalent in the oases, so avoid contact with pool and river water.

Roads and buses

The paved roads along the Taroudannt–Tata–Tiznit circuit are not clearly marked on all maps (the Michelin has them right), so are worth setting out here. They are: the 7027/7025 from Taroudannt to Igherm; then the 7085 to Imitek; and finally the 7111, which joins the Akka–Tata road (7084) 5km south of Tata.

By **bus**, the route can be covered in either direction. From **Taroudannt**, SATAS buses run to Tata daily (8am departure, arriving around 1pm), with a further bus every other day (departing 5am). From **Tiznit**, buses leave for Tata daily at 5am and 9.30am. The 9.30am bus (run by SATAS) starts at Agadir, however, and may be full by the time it reaches Tiznit; if it is, you could probably catch it at BOU IZAKARN (or BOUIZAKARNE), where it lets off passengers, by taking a *grand taxi* there from Tiznit.

Taroudannt to Tata

Leaving the P32 Taroudannt–Taliouine road after 8km at Aït Iazza, the Tata road skirts through the edge of the oasis of **Freija**, and past the turning to **Tioute** (for both of which, see p.473), before winding its way up into the stark Anti-Atlas mountains.

At **IGHERM** (93km from Taroudannt) there's a **Wednesday souk**, where the bus will stop for a long break. This is also where your *grand taxi* will drop you if coming from Taroudannt. The region is said to be known for its silver daggers and inlaid rifle butts, though more than likely you'll just find an assortment of hand-made copper pots and water urns. Igherm itself, now an administrative centre and with some new buildings to prove it, was a copper town for centuries, carrying on trade with the Saharan caravans. The *souk* apart, it is today a drab, sluggish town – not a place to get caught between buses. If by chance you do find yourself stranded, there are a couple of **rooms** at the *Restaurant Atlas* on the way into the village from Taroudannt.

For the dedicated driver, pistes lead from Igherm to **Tafraoute** and **Taliouine**. Both are in pretty terrible condition, and few vehicles use them. If you want to enquire about trucks along them (or conditions), try asking around the main square (where there's a petrol station), or in the café-restaurant just off it, where the truck drivers hang out and play cards. The very rough piste 7160/7086 heads south to Tata, though it has seen little traffic since the paving of the 7085.

Leaving Igherm, the paved road (7085) crosses the **Tizi Touzlimt** and then descends to ISSAFEN, also called KHEMIS ISSAFEN for its Thursday *souk*. You may need to change vehicles here; again, if stranded, there's a *Café-Restaurant Atlas*, on the main road, with two rooms available. Beyond here, you enter the **Akka Valley**, lined by a palmery over the next thirty kilometres. It's a wonderful trip, with, to the east, the amazing contours of the Anti-Atlas mountains, which twirl and twist from pink to grey-green, their sharply defined bands of rock varying from horizontal to vertical.

At IMITEK, the last oasis before Tata, the surfaced road becomes the 7111 for Tata (35km). The 7085 deteriorates to piste for a 34km stretch to Akka.

Tata

TATA is a small administrative and garrison town, flanking a large oasis. Its tiled and colonnaded streets are laid out in a rigid grid below a steep-sided hill – known as **La Montagne** (largely occupied by the military) – and flanked by the predictable duo of **Av. des F.A.R.** and **Av. Mohammed V**. Just off Av. Mohammed V in the centre of town is the main square, **Place Marche Verte**, which **buses** run in and out of.

The town is a leisurely place with a friendly (if early-to-bed) air, and distinct desert influences in the darker complexion of the people, the black turbans of the men and the colourful sari-like coverings of the women (who wear black in the Anti-Atlas). It makes for a good overnight stop along this circuit.

Accommodation

Tata has four recommendable **hotels** (plus three rock bottom ones) and a small campsite. There are separate **hammams**: one for women down by the oued; another for men on Av. des F.A.R. (opposite the bottom end of Av. Hassan II).

CHEAP

Hôtel Essalam, 41 Av. Mohammed V (☎08/80.21.24). The staff are friendly but rooms are basic and not all that clean. ⓪

Hôtel Sahara, 81 Av. Mohammed V (☎08/80.21.61). The rooms here are marginally better. ⓪

Not recommended: *Hôtel Marche Verte* (by the bus station), *Hôtel Bir Inzran* and, especially, *Jema's* (both by the hospital).

MODERATE

Les Relais des Sables, Av. des F.A.R. (☎08/80.23.01). A smart new hotel with comfortable rooms built round a succession of little gardens – and a swimming pool, bar and restaurant. ③

Hôtel de la Renaissance, 9 Av. des F.A.R. (☎08/80.20.42). On both sides of the road – an older cheaper section on one side and a new, more comfortable barrack-like block on the other. The restaurant is good – and licensed. A double room in the old block costs very little more than in the unclassified hotels. ②

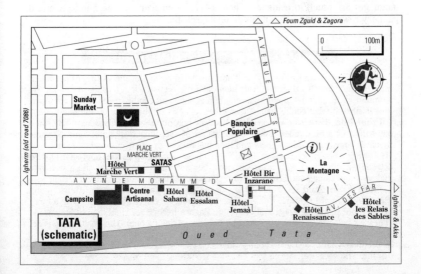

CAMPING

Camping Municipal, by the municipal swimming pool on Av. Mohammed V. A small site, with shade, and for tents, real grass.

Food, banks, shops

For meals, you'll find several **grill-cafés** under the colonnades on Av. Mohammed V, plus a pâtisserie. The café-restaurant right next to the pâtisserie serves a fine t*ajine*. For something more fancy (and/or a drink), your only choices are the restaurants in the *Relais des Sables* and *Rennaissance* hotels – at the latter it's best to order meals a few hours in advance, if possible.

Tata also has a **bank** (*Banque Populaire*), a **post office**, two **petrol stations**, a **Centre Artisanal**, which was closed recently, but should reopen, and a good souvenir shop, *Maison des Nomades*. There's a **Sunday market** in town and very lively **Thursday souk** held at an enclosure – or, more accurately a series of pisé courtyards – known as **El Khemis**, 6km out on the Akka road (7084); the mainstay is dates.

Transport

SATAS have **buses** departing at 3am for Agadir via Akka and Tiznit, and at 6am for Agadir via Igherm and Taroudannt, supplemented every two days by a private firm on the latter route. Other private lines run to Ouarzazate via Foum Zguid, and Goulimine via Tiznit, both currently departing at 2pm. For all these, if possible, book a seat.

There are routine **grand taxi** runs to Akka, Tissint and Foum Zguid, as well as **taxi-trucks** to Foum Zguid (especially on Sunday night and Monday morning for Foum Zguid's Monday *souk*).

Akka and its oasis

Continuing along the circuit towards Tiznit, the 7084 passes through **AKKA**, a roadside town with a large palmery extending to the north. It is said to have been one of the northern depots of the ancient caravan routes and still hosts an important weekly **souk**, on Thursdays, where the oasis dates (Akka means "dates" in the local Berber language) are much in evidence. There is also a smaller *souk* on Sundays, and the palmery rewards a visit, with its traditional oasis life.

EAST TO THE DRÂA: FOUM ZGUID

The route from **Tata to Foum Zguid** and, for the intrepid, beyond to **Zagora** is a much more remote journey than the "Tata loop", and the second leg at least is strictly for the committed. At the time of writing, though, it is open and can be travelled without a permit (a situation that could change at any time: check with the police post in Tata).

From Tata, there is now a paved road, a daily bus, and regular *grands taxis*. The route runs through a wide valley, following the course of a seasonal river, amid some extremely bleak landscape, which is now and then punctuated by the occasional oasis and *ksar*. There are passport controls at TISSINT (halfway) and again as you approach **FOUM ZGUID**, a tiny place with a café (rooms, but not much to eat) opposite a welcome palmery and some *ksour*. There are also campsites at both Foum Zguid and Tissint.

From Foum Zguid, there are SATAS **buses** three times a week (Tuesday, Thursday and Saturday at 7am) to **Ouarzazate** – and on to Marrakesh. Alternatively, a ride with a **lorry** along more very rough piste will get you to **Zagora** in seven or eight hours (Sunday and Tuesday, being local *souks*, offer your best chance of finding one). This road, again, is not suitable for light vehicles and the transport is a bit haphazard; it also lacks most of the redeeming features of Tata to Foum, with no oases or villages to break the tedium.

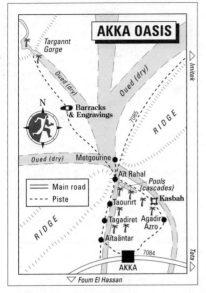

At present, unfortunately, the town has just one **café-hotel**, the *Tamdoult* (☎08/80.80.30; ⑪), an unwelcoming place with poor rooms, though decent food, and a rough and ill-equipped **campsite** on the main road.

Around the palmery

It's worth taking a morning to explore Akka's palmery. You will probably need to do so on foot, as most of the oasis pistes are impossible in a two-wheel drive vehicle. Its local sights include a **Kasbah** and an **agadir** (fortified granary), southeast of the village of Aït Rahal, and **Les Cascades** – a series of shallow, dammed irrigation pools, enclosed by palms. Local people bathe in these pools, but they are reputed to harbour bilharzia, so be careful to avoid contact with the water – both here and in the irrigation canals. To reach them on foot, you leave Akka by crossing the dry river bed by a concrete barrage and then follow a path through the almost continuous palmery villages of Aït Aäntar, Tagadiret and Taouriret.

A three-hour trek to the northwest of Aït Rahal is the **Targannt Gorge**, in which a cluster of oases are tucked between the cliffs. There are ruins of houses, though the place is deserted nowadays, save for the occasional nomadic camel herder. The route is across desert, passable to landrover-type vehicles, though the track is poorly defined. En route (and an aid to navigation) is a small hill on which the French built a barracks. There are **rock engravings** of oxen at the eastern end of the hill – some modern, others perhaps up to two thousand years old. Approaching the gorge, a lone palm tempts you to its mouth. A guide from the village would be helpful, while bringing food and a tent would reward you with a gorgeous camping spot.

Oum El Alek

There are more **rock carvings**, said to be prehistoric, near the village of **OUM EL ALEK** (or OUM EL AÄLAGUE), 7km southeast of Akka, off the Tata road. Anyone with a particular interest is best advised to get in touch with the official *guardien*, Mouloud Taârabet who lives in Oum El Alek and can be contacted in the village, or through the *Hôtel Rennaissance* in Tata or the *Café Hôtel Tamdoult* in Akka. Mouloud knows all the rock carvings in the region, and should be able to take you to any of them you want to see, if you have a car or are prepared to charter a taxi. (See also Aït Herbil, below).

West to Foum El Hassan and Aït Herbil: rock carvings

The next major oasis beyond Akka is **FOUM EL HASSAN** (FAM EL HISN on the Michelin map), 90km to the west – and 6km off the main road. This is basically a military post on the edge of an oasis. Some fighting with Polisario took place here several years ago, but everything's quiet now; there is, however, passport control. If you need a **room**, the only possibility is at the café on the right-hand side of the square. Besides a couple of shops, there's very little else.

Prehistoric rock carvings at Tircht . . .

There are countless **prehistoric rock carvings** in this region, and engaging a guide you will probably be shown the local favourites. Those at **Tircht** can be reached by foot from Foum El Hassan by following the oued through the 'V' in the mountains behind the town (bear right after 2km where it splits). Tircht is a peaked mountain to the left about 5km from town, but neither it nor the carvings are easy to find: you are best advised to employ someone from town as a guide. The best require a little climbing to get to, but they are

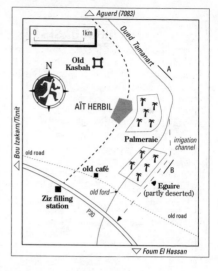

among the finest in Morocco – elephants and rhinoceros, 15–30cm high, dating roughly from 2000–500 BC, a time when the Sahara was full of lakes and swamps. Camping is possible here in the valley and preferable to staying in the town.

. . . and more rock carvings around Aït Herbil

Less renowned are the rock carvings at the village of **AÏT HERBIL**, 2km off the P30, around 15km west of Foum El Hassan. The junction is easy to recognize, as it's right opposite a Ziz filling station. You can get there by *grand taxi* from Foum El Hassan or Bou Izakarn/Tiznit. There are two series of rock carvings, marked as "A" and "B" on our sketchmap above, both easily accessible on foot.

To reach "A" walk northeast from Aït Herbil village, across the dry riverbed. On the opposite bank is a steep rock fall, and to the right of a patch of distinctive grey rocks are perhaps as many as a hundred small carvings, depicting gazelles, bison, a giraffe and a bird or two. The rock fall looks recent but clearly, with the carvings all in the same plane, it has not shifted for centuries, even millennia.

For "B" leave the village to the southeast, walking through the palmery, and again across the dry riverbed, to find a concrete irrigation channel which at this point runs high above the level of the river. Before reaching the partly deserted village of Eguire, high on the left, look for carvings on the rocks to the left. Alternatively, follow the irrigation channel from the main road. There are fewer examples here but they are larger.

West to Bou Izakarn

Beyond Aït Herbil, the P30 continues across a barren patch of *hammada* to the oasis and roadside village of **TAGHJICHT** (or **TARHJIJT**), where a road heads off north of to Amtoudi (see opposite). If you need to stop the night, en route, Taghjicht has a good new **hotel**, the *Taghjijt* (☎08/87.30.53; ②). The village also has regular *grand taxi* runs to Bou Izakarn; in the other direction you might be lucky and pick one up on its way to Foum El Hassan. At **TIMOULAY**, 26km further west, it is usually possible to get a *grand taxi* to Ifrane de l'Anti-Atlas (see opposite). You should also be able to get a taxi for the final 14km stretch to Bou Izakarn, on the main Tiznit–Goulimine road.

BOU IZAKARN is a larger village with a Friday **souk**, a *PTT*, *Banque Populaire*, municipal swimming pool (summer only), and a basic **hotel**, the *Anti-Atlas*, (☎08/87.41.34; ②), which does little to deserve its two-star status. A place across the street and about fifty metres towards Goulimine does very good, and cheap, fried fish. There are regular **buses** and **grands taxis**. Taxi runs include Goulimine (these leave from a rank on the Goulimine road at the south end of the village), and Tiznit (for Tafraoute), Ifrane, Inezgane (for Agadir), and Foum El Hassan (all these leave from the main taxi rank in the town centre).

Amtoudi (Id Aïssa)

If you have transport, it's worth making an excursion from the Bou Izakarn/Tiznit road to visit **AMTOUDI** (or ID AÏSSA, as it appears on most maps). This can be reached by either of two roads north of the P30 (at around 55km and 70km from Foum El Hassan); they join at SOUK TNINE D'ADAÏ, where the last 10km of road to Amtoudi become rougher and less distinct. Using local transport, you might be able to negotiate a *grand taxi* at TAGHJIJT, the second junction, especially on a Monday, when there is a market at Souk Tnine d'Adaï. If you intend to stay, be sure to have enough provisions, since Amtoudi has just one small shop and a lunch-only restaurant for visiting tour groups.

The sight that brings tour groups to Amtoudi is its **agadir**, which is one of the most spectacular and best preserved in North Africa. *Agadirs* are collective, fortified store-houses, where grain, dates, gunpowder and other valuables were kept safe from marauding tribes. This one is built impressively on a pinnacle of rock. You can climb (or ride a mule) up a winding track and walk around the site, providing the *gardien* is there. If by chance you find the place overrun by tourists, you can escape the crowds with a walk down the palm-filled **gorge**; here another imposing but decaying *agadir* is perched on top of the cliff and, after about 3km, you'll come to a spring and waterfall. It is possible to **camp** near the river.

Ifrane de l'Anti-Atlas

IFRANE DE L'ANTI-ATLAS is one of the most rewarding oasis detours on the Tata loop. A small Berber settlement, it comprises three surrounding *douar* (each with its own Kasbah and endless walls), together with **Souk Ifrane**, an administrative and market centre (Sunday *souk*), with a pink, fort-like barracks. The place is particularly out of the way and visitors can expect to be the object of attention and followed everywhere by kids, but it's worth braving them: there are beautiful walks among the *douar*, springs, and ingenious water channels.

If you have a car, you may want to just stop a few hours, but there are basic **rooms** available at the *Café de la Paix* with a roof terrace looking out across the valley and distant oasis; this is also the best place to eat.

The Oasis and Mellah

The Ifrane **oasis** is the centre of one of the oldest settled regions in Morocco – and was one of the last places in the south to convert to Islam. Across the dry riverbed stand the ruins of the old **Jewish Kasbah**, or **Mellah**. Legend holds that Ifrane's Jews settled here in the sixth century BC, fleeing persecution from King Nebuchadnezzar of Babylon; this has yet to be substantiated but it is certain that the Jewish community goes back to pre-Islamic days. It endured up until the 1950s, when, as elsewhere in the south, there was a mass exodus to Israel and, to an extent, Casablanca and Rabat. A

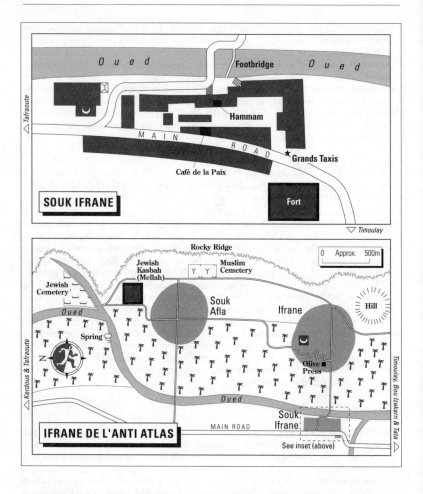

Berber family has since moved into one of the inhabitable Kasbahs, and a few of the other buildings remain partially intact; the rest is a mass of crumbling walls. Locals recall their former Jewish neighbours as "good people" who kept mainly to themselves.

Around the next bend in the stony riverbed, and up the hill on the right, lies the Jewish **cemetery**. Broken tombstones, inscribed in Hebrew, lie strewn about. It's said that relatives still come here to visit the graves and burn candles in memory of the deceased. The Muslim past of Ifrane is evident as well, with white-domed tombs of saints and *marabouts* dotting the surrounding countryside.

Tiznit

Despite its solid circuit of walls, **TIZNIT** was founded as late as 1882, when Sultan Moulay Hassan (Hassan I) was undertaking a *harka* – a subjugation or (literally) "burning" raid – in the Souss and Anti-Atlas. It still seems to signal a shift towards a desert, frontier-town mentality and past: to the west the Chleuh Berbers of the Anti-Atlas suffered their first true occupation only with the bitter French "pacification" of the early 1930s, and Tiznit itself was the base of **El Hiba**, who declared himself sultan here in 1912 after learning of Moulay Hafid's surrender to the French under the Treaty of Fes. The so-called "Blue Sultan" – a name given on account of his blue desert robes – El Hiba led a considerable force of Berbers to Marrakesh, which acknowledged his authority, before advancing on Fes in the spring of 1913. Here they were defeated, though El Hiba's resistance continued, first in Taroudannt, later into the Anti-Atlas, until his death, near Tafraoute, in 1919.

The town bears the stamp of its military history – huge *pisé* walls, neat administrative streets and a considerable garrison – but it's not a bad staging point en route to Tafraoute, Sidi Ifni or Tata. It is easily reached by bus from Agadir or *grand taxi* from Inezgane and has an exhilarating **beach** at **Sidi Moussa d'Aglou**, 17km distant, where the surf and the fierce Atlantic currents have warded off development.

Orientation, rooms and food

Orientation is straightforward. Tiznit has five kilometres of walls and eight major gates, the most important of which are **Bab Oulad Jarrar** and **Les Trois Portes**. Most of the traffic in and out of the walls passes through these gates – the latter of which (as its name suggests) was a French addition. Quite why it is called *Les Trois Portes* ('the three gates') is not clear, since there are in fact four.

Arriving by **bus** you will find yourself set down in the **Mechouar** – the old parade ground, now the main square – just inside the town walls. Coming by **grand taxi**, you will probably be dropped outside the walls, at one of the locations detailed on our map. Around the Mechouar and along the adjacent **Av. 20 Août** you'll find banks, the post office, bus offices, a market area and a Centre Artisanal – and all of the cheap **hotels**. A few more upmarket hotels are outside the walls on the Goulimine road.

Hotels

There are a dozen or more unclassified hotels in the walled city, the best of which are listed below; none can guarantee hot water, but in a cul-de-sac off Rue du Bain Maure there is a public showerhouse, *Douche Atlas* (men and women 5am–9pm; 4.5dh; sign in Arabic only). Also listed below are all three classified options.

CHEAP

Hôtel des Amis [C], Mechouar (☎08/86.21.29). Spartan but clean and good value, with friendly staff and a roof terrace overlooking the square. ①

Hôtel Atlas [D], Mechouar (☎08/86.20.60). This popular hotel is one of the best of the cheapies, and there is also quite a decent restaurant. ①

Hôtel Belle Vue [B], Rue du Bain Maure (☎08/86.21.09). An old and well-maintained hotel. ①

Hôtel CTM [F], opposite the *grands taxis* park (☎08/86.22.11). This just pips the Atlas as the best of the cheapies – a friendly place with a little English spoken, and clean showers. There's also a café-restaurant on the first floor. ①

Hôtel Al Mourabatine [A], Rue du Bain Maure (no phone). A bit of a fall-back – but OK. ①

Hôtel Sahara [E], Rue de l'Hôpital (☎08/86.24.98). Still more of a fall-back. ①

MODERATE

Hôtel Mauretanie [I], Rue Bir Anzarane (☎08/86.20.72). This is quite good value, with decent rooms, easy parking, a restaurant and bar, and several cafés and shops nearby. ②

Hôtel de Paris [G], Av. Hassan II (☎08/86.28.65). A new, friendly and modestly priced hotel, with a deservedly popular local restaurant. (A new three-star place is being built opposite). ②

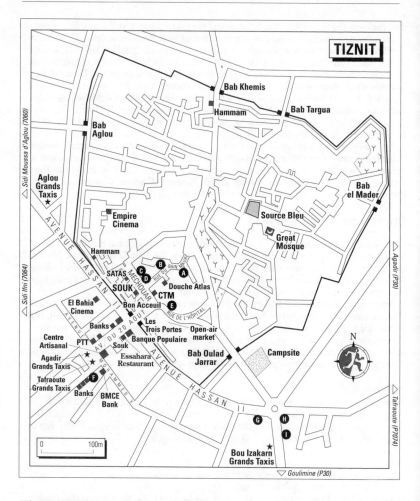

Hôtel de Tiznit [H], Rue Bir Anzarane (☎08/86.24.11). A classier alternative, with a bar, nightclub in summer and swimming pool. ③

CAMPING

Camping Municipal, just outside Bab Oulad Jarrar. A secure but unshaded site.

The Town

The promise of Tiznit's walls turns out to be a little empty, with large areas, as at Taroudannt, occupied by gardens or nothingness. There is, however, a certain fascination in realizing just how recent the place is – a traditional walled town built only a century ago – and in seeing how the builders simply enclosed a number of existing *ksour* within their new grid. These are the large angled enclosures, clearly visible on our map.

Taking a brief loop through the town, start out at the **jewellery souk** (*Souk des Bijoutiers*), still an active crafts industry despite the loss to Israel of the town's large number of Jewish craftsmen. The jewellers occupy the northern part of the **main souk**, which can be entered from the Mechouar. Over to the south, across Av. du 20 Août, is a larger **open-air market**, mainly selling food and produce. The town's main weekly *souk* (Thursdays) is held out on the Tafraoute road.

North of the Mechouar, Rue de l'Hôpital winds round, past the hospital, to join the main road from Bab Ouled Jarrar which then heads towards an arcade of shops and a mosque (at the top of Rue du Bain Maure). Taking a left just before the arcade of shops, bearing left at the T-junction and right at the next fork, brings you to the **Great Mosque**, which has an unusual minaret, punctuated by a series of perches. These are said to be an aid to the dead in climbing up to paradise, though are more commonly found south of the Sahara in Mali and Niger. Alongside the mosque is the **Source Bleu**, dedicated to the town's patroness, Lalla Tiznit, a saint and former prostitute martyred on this spot (whereupon water miraculously appeared). These days, more or less devoid of water, the spring is profoundly unflattering to her.

Following the street on north of the *source*, you reach the north gate, **Bab Targua**. Inside the gate, a hole in the wall allows you to climb the bastion, though it can't really be described as safe. If you ascend, you can look over the town and, outside the walls, to the rather mournful olive groves and abandoned palmery.

If you were to head north-east from the source, you would emerge from the town at another gate, **Bab El Mader**, beside which is a large Muslim cemetery with a white *marabout*'s tomb, its corners picked out in green. This may look familiar to users of the last edition of this book: it was pictured on the cover.

Practicalities

Tiznit has most facilities you'll need – and if you're setting off for the south, you'd do well to change travellers' cheques or make VISA transactions here. There are four **banks** on Av. du 20 Août, with others nearby, and you'll find the **PTT** and a reasonable **Centre Artisanal** facing each other across the same street.

Restaurants

There are numerous **café-restaurants** in and around the Mechouar, the best of which is the *Bon Acceuil*, directly opposite the *Atlas*. The *Essahan* next to the *Banque Populaire* in Av. 20 Août also does excellent and inexpensive *tajines*.

For a more upmarket meal, or a drink, your best bets are the restaurants of the hotels *Mauretanie, Paris* or *Tiznit*.

Cinemas, hammams and pools

As to entertainments, Tiznit also has a couple of **cinemas** – the *El Bahià* just off Av. Hassan II opposite Bab El Aouina, and the *Empire* inside the Medina near the south-western corner.

There are traditional **hammans** just outside the walls at Bab El Khemis and between Bab El Aouina and the nameless pedestrian-only gate at the Medina's south-western corner. Should you prefer a swim, non-residents can use the *Hôtel Tiznit's* pool for a 25dh daily charge.

Moving on: transport

All the **buses** leave from the Mechouar. CTM have three departures: 5am for Goulimine [arriving 8.30] via Bou Izakarn; 5.30am for Casa via Agadir, Essaouira and Safi; and 9pm for Tangier via Agadir, Marrakesh, Casa, Rabat and Kenitra. Their office is to the right of the exit to Rue du Bain Maure as you look at it. SATAS have their office diagonally across the Mechouar, with services to Agadir (9.30am, 9.45am, 10am, 11am, 7.30pm and 8pm), Marrakesh and Casa (8pm), Goulimine and Tan Tan (8am, 11am and 4pm) (the 11am one continues to Assa-Zag), Essaouira and Safi (11am), Akka and Tata (9.30am), and Tafraoute (4pm). Various private firms also operate, mainly to Agadir, Marrakesh, Casa and Rabat.

Grands Taxis operate from the far end of Av. du 20 Août, opposite the *Hôtel CTM*, to Inezgane, Agadir, Tafraoute, Mihrleft and Sidi Ifni. From opposite the *Hôtel Mauretanie* on Rue Bir Anzarane near the roundabout, they go to Bou Izakarn, Goulimine and, less frequently, Tan Tan and even Laayoune. For Sidi Moussa d'Aglou, they leave from Av. Hassan II near the southwestern corner of the Medina.

Sidi Moussa d'Aglou

The beach at **SIDI MOUSSA D'AGLOU** is 17km from Tiznit, along a barren, scrub-lined road. **Grands taxis** make routine runs from Tiznit (leaving from Av. Hassan II by the southwestern corner of the Medina), though some only go to Aglou village, 3km short of the beach. What awaits you is an isolated expanse of sand, with a wild, body-breaking Atlantic surf. It has a dangerous undertow, and the beach is watched over in summer by military police coastguards, who only allow swimming if conditions are safe – if in doubt, ask them. **Surfing** can be good but you have to pick the right spots.

Quite a few Moroccans (many of them migrant workers from France) come down here in the middle of summer, and there's a trickle of Europeans in winter. Between times, however, the place is very quiet. If you want to stay, you'll find a **campsite** about 500m before you get to the beach, on the right if coming from Tiznit. Alternatively, by the beach, at the end of the road, the *Motel Aglou* (☎08/86.61.63; ⑩) has fifteen **cabins** to rent, allows camping in its grounds, and has a café and restaurant. Across the road, the *Café-Restaurant Ameragh* offers fish *tajines*, and has plans to open up as a hotel in the near future.

There are a couple of *marabout* tombs on the beach and, about 1500m to the north, a tiny (and rather pretty) **troglodyte fishing village**, with a hundred or so primitive cave-huts dug into the rocks.

Tafraoute

Approached by beautiful scenic roads through the Anti-Atlas – either from Tiznit (the best approach) or Agadir – **Tafraoute** is worth all the effort and time it takes to reach. The town is the centre for a group of stone-built villages on the strange, wind-eroded slopes of the **Ameln Valley**, shot through with pink- and mauve-tinged thumbs of granite and enclosed by a jagged panorama of mountains – "like the badlands of South Dakota", as Paul Bowles put it, "writ on a grand scale".

The best time for a visit to Tafraoute is early spring, in order to see the almond trees in full blossom, or in autumn, after the intense heat is subdued. In midsummer, it can be stunningly hot here, destroying almost all incentive to wander round the villages.

The routes from Tiznit and Agadir

Both approaches to Tafraoute are rewarding and, if you're driving, you may well want to take advantage of this by coming in from Tiznit and leaving for Agadir, or vice versa. If you're doing just one, the Tiznit approach has a distinct edge, winding through a succession of gorges and a grand mountain valley.

Buses and **grands taxis** cover the route from Tiznit several times daily, but there is no public transport along the road from Agadir via Aït Baha – though you could of course charter a taxi at Agadir or Tafraoute.

Tiznit to Tafraoute

The Tiznit–Tafraoute road (7074) passes a succession of oasis-like villages, almost all of them named after the *souk* that they are host to (see p.53 for the Arabic name-days). In winter and spring the road is sometimes crossed by streams but it is generally passable enough; the drive takes around two hours, but leave plenty of time to see (and navigate) the mountains before dusk.

At **ASSAKA** (20km from Tiznit), a substantial new bridge has been built over the Oued Tazeroualt – the river that causes most difficulty in winter and spring. Around 19km further on, just before Tirhmi, a road heads south into the Anti-Atlas to the **Zaouia of Sidi Ahmed ou Moussa** (10km), which for a while in the seventeenth century controlled its own local state, the Tazeroualt, whose capital was at nearby (and now deserted) **Illigh**. The *zaouia* remains active and hosts a **moussem** during the second or third week of August, which would be worth trying to attend. Sidi Ahmed is the patron of Morocco's acrobats – most of whom come from this region of Morocco – and return to perform.

Just beyond **TIRHMI** (aka TIGHMI; 42km from Tiznit), the road begins its ascent of the **Col du Kerdous** (1100m). At the top of the pass is a **hotel**, the *Kerdous* (☎08/86.20.63; ④), created from an old fortress and recently re-opened after a long restoration. It is worth at least a stop for a tea and breathtaking views. This area is also a hot-spot for paragliding – Ibrahim at the *Hôtel Tafraout* in Tafraoute has details.

At the end of the descent is the village of **JEMAA IDA OUSSEMLAL** (64km from Tiznit), which offers basic rooms at the *Hôtel de la Victoire* (⑩), and the last filling station before Tafraoute. The **road divides** as you enter the village. The left fork, which runs downhill through the village (and past the hotel), is the **"old road"**, which continues to Tafraoute as the 7074 – a picturesque route that drops into the Ameln Valley via HAD TAHALA (once a Jewish village). The right fork (7146), skirting the village, is a **"new road"** to Tafraoute, via IZERBI, where the Minister of Housing has a Disney-style chateau. It is a longer route but well surfaced, flatter and faster going, arriving in Tafraoute through a grand spectacle of mountains and the lunar landscape around Agard Oudad (see p.494).

Agadir/Inezgane to Tafraoute via Aït Baha

The S509 road runs from Agadir to Tafraoute via Aït Baha. It is a bit drab between Agadir and Aït Baha, but the section from there on to Tafraoute is a highly scenic (and slow and winding) mountain ride past a series of fortified Kasbah-villages. Two daily **buses** run to Agadir along this route, together with **grands taxis**.

AÏT BAHA is the largest village en route, a characterless roadside halt with two basic **hotels,** the *Tafraoute* and the *El Massira* (both ⑩), two cafés and very little shade. It hosts a **Wednesday souk**.

Beyond, the most spectacular Kasbah to be seen is **TIOULIT**, off to the left of the road, around 35km from Aït Baha. Another 25km brings you to a junction of roads, with the left fork heading off to Irherm on the Tata loop (a very rough piste once you pass the village of AÏT ABDALLAH), the right to Tafraoute. Around 5km beyond this junction is the village of **SIDI ABDALLAH EL JABAR**, scene of a small, but lively *moussem* around its *zaouia*, celebrated annually between October 20–22.

GROUND SQUIRRELS

Along the road from Tiznit to Tafraoute, you may notice children holding little furry animals for sale – live, on a piece of string – by the roadside. These are ground squirrels, which are known locally as *anzid* or *sibsib*, and are destined for the *tajine* dish, in which they are considered quite a delicacy. Recognizable by the prominent stripes down their side, and long tails, ground squirrels are common in the tropics but unknown in Europe. They have long been ascribed medicinal properties – which makes them licit. You will not get *Anzid tajine* in any restaurant, however, unless perhaps you provide the squirrels yourself.

Tafraoute

TAFRAOUTE stands at the edge of a rambling palmery – quite unexpected after a rather barren approach over the last few kilometres from both Tiznit and Agadir. It is a small place, created as an administrative centre by the French, and little expanded since, as *Tafraoutis* prefer to stick to their villages, or at least return to them after working elsewhere or abroad (see box opposite). It is a pleasant place and most visitors – women as well as men – find it one of the most relaxed destinations in Morocco. **Getting around** the Ameln villages, you can use a combination of taxis and walking, or rent **mountain bikes** from an outlet opposite the **PTT**.

Accommodation and meals

The town has a campsite and five hotels, so it's wise to arrive early or book ahead to be sure of a room.

CHEAP

Hôtel Redouane, by the bridge (☎08/80.00.66). A bit seedy with basic and not very clean rooms at erratic prices. Has a terrace restaurant on the first floor. ⑪

Hôtel Tanger, across the road (☎08/80.00.33). Slightly better rooms, cheaper for singles, with friendly staff and quite a good restaurant where you can eat outside. ⑪

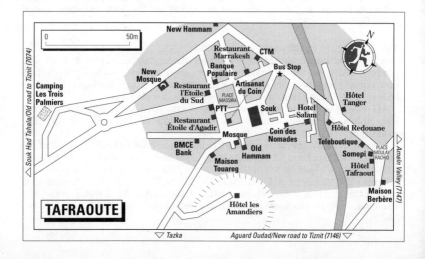

Hôtel Tafraout, Place Moulay Rachid – by the filling station (☎08/80.01.21). Much better than the *Redouane* and *Tanger*, with well-decorated rooms, hot showers on the corridor, a decent restaurant, and a very welcoming manager. This hotel is often used as a base by paragliding groups, and Ibrahim who works here keeps details of local sites. ①

MODERATE

Hôtel Salama (☎08/80.00.26), across the river from the *Redouane*. A large new hotel with good en-suite bathrooms and a roof terrace. ②

EXPENSIVE

Hôtel Les Amandiers, on the hill above the town – ten minutes' walk (☎08/80.00.08). Kasbah-style building offering comfortable if unexciting rooms, a dull restaurant (cheaper for residents), but great views from the terrace, and the town's only swimming pool (very pleasant) and bar. ④

CAMPING

Camping Les Trois Palmiers, ten minutes' walk from the centre (☎08/80.00.38). A small, secure enclosure, with hot showers. Also four rooms for rent.

Meals

In addition to the hotels, there are a three **restaurants** in the town:

Café-Restaurant Étoile d'Agadir. A good little place, serving classic *tajines* (lamb with prunes and almonds, chicken with lemon and olives) at moderate cost.

Restaurant l'Étoile du Sud. The has a tent done up for tourists and an embarrassing cabaret of music and belly-dancing, but the food can be worthwhile if you hit a good day and there's a nice indoor salon for winter evenings.

Restaurant Marrakesh. A family-run place with excellent-value meals and friendly service.

Listings

Banks The *Banque Populaire* is open only on Wednesdays for the town's *souk*, but there's an inconspicuous *BMCE* behind the *PTT*, with standard opening hours.

Buses leave from the main street where CTM and a firm called El Hilal have their offices. There are five departures for Tiznit, Agadir and Casa, leaving at 8.30am, 2pm, 3pm, 5pm and 7pm. The first and last (which is CTM's) go via Marrakesh the others via Essaouira.

Guides Recommended trekking guides for the region include Mohammed Ouakrim (contact through the *Restaurant lÉtoile du Sud*), and Mohammed Ouhammou, who lives in the village of

---

TAFRAOUTE VILLAGE ECONOMICS

Among Tafraoute villagers, **emigration** to work in the grocery and hotel trade – all over Morocco and France – is a determining aspect of life. The men always return home to retire, however, building European-looking villas amid the rocks, and most of the younger ones manage to come back for a month's holiday each year – whether it be from Casablanca, Tangier, Paris or Marseilles.

But for much of the year, it is the women who run things in the valley, and the only men to be found are the old, the family-supported or the affluent. It is a system that seems to work well enough: enormously industrious, and very community-minded, the *Tafraoutis* have managed to maintain their villages in spite of adverse economic conditions, importing all their foodstuffs except for a little barley, the famed Tafraoute almonds and the bitter oil of the argan tree.

Oddly enough, this way of life has exact parallels in Tunisia, with the people of Djerba; less surprisingly, both social structures developed through crisis and necessity. Between 1880 and 1882, this whole region was devastated by famine.

Tiouada but can be contacted through his friend who runs the Coin des Nomades shop, or by phone ☎08/80.05.47; he usually only gives guided treks at weekends.

Hammam The old *hammam* is down a side street by the central mosque, and there's a new one near the bend in the main street (behind the bakery, turn left and it's 100m further, under the arch). Both *hammams* have entrances for men and women, open from around 5am, but the women's side closes at around 5pm, the men's stays open till about 7.30pm.

Market/shops There is a Wednesday **souk**, held in the centre of town. Worthwhile permanent **crafts shops** include the *Coin des Nomades* and *Artisanat du Coin*, both unpressurized, and *La Maison Touareg*, only marginally more so, for carpets. Also recommended is the *Maison Berbère* near Place Moulay Rachid. Tafraoute is well known for its *babouches*, and a narrow street of *cordonniers* sell quality slipperwear just below the Place Marche Verte.

Post Office The *PTT* is open 8.30am–noon & 2–6.30pm Mon–Fri and Sat morning; when it is closed, phone calls can be made from the *Téléboutique* by Place Moulay Rachid.

Swimming pool You can usually use the one at the *Amandiers* (despite the sign) for a small fee, which varies with the season.

Taxis Shared *grands taxis* and landrover taxis leave from opposite the CTM office. The only regular *grand taxi* destination is Tiznit.

The Ameln Valley

You could spend days, if not weeks, wandering round the 26 villages of the **Ameln Valley**. Set against the backdrop of the rocks, they are all beautiful both from afar and close up – with springs, irrigation systems, brightly painted houses, and mosques. On no account, either, should you miss out on a walk to see the **painted rocks** in their albeit faded glory.

Starting out from Tafraoute, **Oumesnat**, 6km to the northeast, is a good first objective, as you can usually get a lift there, or charter a taxi at modest cost; taxis could also be arranged to pick you up from a village at the end of the day. From Oumesnat, you could walk the length of the valley from village to village: the walk to Anemeur, for example, is around 10–12km. More serious walkers might consider making an ascent of the **Djebel El Kest** (2359m) or, best of all, **Adrar Mkorn** (2344m), an isolated peak to the southeast with spectacular twin tops (this involves some hard scrambling).

The **Ameln villages** are built on the lower slopes of the Djebel El Kest, between the "spring line" and the valley floor, allowing gravity to take the water through the village and on to the arable land below. Tracks link the villages, following the contour lines – and frequently the irrigation channels – and most are accessible from the road only by crossing an intricate network of these irrigation canals, orchards and allotments. Many of the villages have basic shops where you can buy drinks, if little else.

Oumesnat to Anameur – and a loop back to Tafraoute

OUMESNAT, like most Ameln settlements, emerges out of a startling green and purple rockscape, crouched against the steep rock walls of the valley – on which locals point out the face of a lion. From a distance, its houses, perched on the rocks, seem to have a solidity to them – sensible blocks of stone, often three storeys high, with parallel sets of windows. Close up, they reveal themselves as bizarre constructions, often built on top of older houses deserted when they had become too small or decrepit; a few of them, with rooms jutting out over the cliffs, are held up by enormous stilts and have raised doorways entered by short (and retractable) ladders.

One of the houses, known as **La Maison Traditionelle**, is owned by a blind Berber and his son, who will show visitors round (*gratuité* expected). They give an interesting tour, explaining the domestic equipment – grindstones, water-holders, cooking equipment – and the layout of the house with its guest room with separate entrance, animals' quarters, and summer terrace for sleeping out. To get the most from a visit, you may need to engage an interpreter.

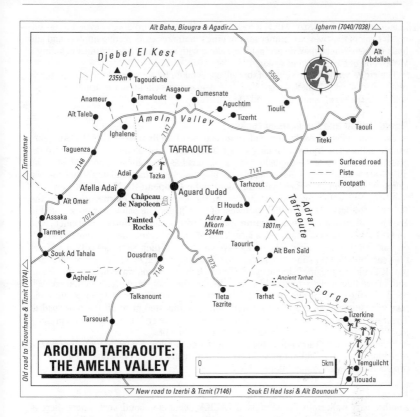

From Oumesnat, you can walk through or above a series of villages to **ANAMEUR**, where there is a *source bleu*, or natural springwater pool, a meandering hike of around three hours.

The Ameln's highest village, **TAGOUDICHE** (TAGDICHTE on the road sign), where the trail up the **Djebel El Kest** (or Lekst) begins, is accessible by landrover along a rough piste. There is a shop, and a floor can usually be found if you want to stay overnight, for an early morning ascent. The Djebel El Kest is a rough and rocky scramble – there's no actual climbing involved – over a mountain of amethyst quartzite. There is a black igneous dyke below the summit pyramid, and a few goatherd shelters (*azibs*) on the top.

Returning to Tafraoute from the Ameln Valley, you can walk over a pass back from the 7148 road near IGHALENE in around three hours. The path isn't particularly easy to find but it's a lovely walk, taking you past flocks of sheep and goats tended by their child-shepherds. The route begins as a piste (east of the one to Tagoudiche), then you follow a dry riverbed off to the right, up a side-valley, where the zigzags of an old track can be seen. Cross to go up here – not straight on – and, once over the pass, keep circling left till you can see Tafraoute below.

Tirnmatmat

To the west of Tafraoute, the road (7148) along the Ameln Valley crosses an almost imperceptible watershed into a valley to the west. At AÏT OMAR (see map), a piste heads north to **TIRNMATMAT**, a welcoming village. Around 200m beyond it, on the north bank of the river, are numerous **carvings** in the rocks, depicting hunters and animals (some of these may be prehistoric), along with more modern graffiti (including a VW Beetle of clearly recent vintage).

The **ridge walk** to the south of this village is taken by some trekking parties and is really special, with Bonelli's eagles circling below, goats climbing the argan trees, and wild boar (beware!) snuffling round the bushes.

Agard Oudad and the painted rocks

A short but enjoyable walk from Tafraoute is to head south to **AGARD OUDAD** (3km from Tafraoute), a dramatic-looking village built under a particularly bizarre outcrop of granite. Like many of the rocks in this region, this has been given a name. Most of the others are named for animals – people will point out their shapes to you – but this one is known (in good French-colonial tradition) as **Le Chapeau de Napoléon**.

A stranger sight, however, awaits you in the form of "Les Pierres Bleues" – the **Painted Rocks** – 1500m to the southwest of the village. The painting was executed in 1984 by a Belgian artist, **Jean Verame**, together with a team of Moroccan firemen, who hosed some 18 tons of paint over a large area of rocks; Verame had previously executed a similar project in Sinaï. The rocks have lost some of their sharpness of colour over the years but they remain weird and wonderful: blue and red hills, clusters of black and purple boulders, mesmerising in effect. To reach them on foot, walk through the village and follow the flat piste round to the right, behind the Chapeau de Napoléon, then walk parallel to the oued for one and a half kilometres – if you're in doubt a young guide will take you. In a car, you can go part way along a signposted piste off the new road to Tiznit – a longer 5km route with a ten-minute walk at the end. But, unless you prefer a longer route, don't follow the road sign if you are on foot.

Verame stayed in Tafraoute at the *Hôtel Redouane* while completing his work and the reception there will (without great interest!) show you a coffee-table book detailing the project in its newly painted glory.

Tazka

Another easy walk from Tafraoute is to **TAZKA**, about 2km southwest, where there is a **prehistoric carving** of a gazelle. To get there, follow a path through the palmery, just beyond the *souk* enclosure marked on our Tafraoute map. When you emerge, past the remains of an old Kasbah, you will see on your left the houses of Tazka at the foot of a high granite bluff. Take the lesser path to the right of the bluff and the carvings – a modern one on the rockface and an old one on the tilted surface of a fallen rock – are on your left after around 200m.

A southern circuit from Tafraoute

A beautiful day-trip from Tafraoute is to drive southeast towards **Souk El Had Issi**, a route that takes in some of the most beautiful country of the Anti-Atlas, including a fabulous gorge and palmery. If you have a sturdy vehicle and a taste for bone-shaking pistes, you can make a loop of it, returning to Tafraoute on the "new road" from Tiznit via Izerbi. The route is also offered as a **landrover trip** by the local guide Ouhammou Mohammed (see Tafraoute "Listings"), who has family at Souk El Had Issi; he can also arrange accommodation in the village, if you fancy staying out there for a day or two.

Leaving Tafraoute, follow the "new road" out past Agard Oudad, turning left around 3km south of the village. This road climbs over the hills, with superb panoramas back across Tafraoute and the Ameln Valley, to reach **TLETA TAZRITE** (15km from Tafraoute), which has a *souk* on Friday – not Tuesday as its name implies.

The paved road is quite broken beyond here. Past the modern village of **TARHAT** (TAGHAOUT) you enter a canyon, which the piste follows for the next 46km, and just a little beyond here, high on your left, are the twelfth-century remains of **ancient Tarhat**, a fortified village and agadir perched on the lip of a sheer rock wall. A footpath leads up to it from the modern village.

At **TIZERKINE**, a lovely oasis snaking along the canyon, all semblance of paved road comes to an end. A passable piste continues (be sure to take the right fork, 5km from Tizerkine) to the village of **TEMGUILCHT**, dominated by the very large and impressive **Zaouia Sidi Ahmed ou Mohammed** (no entrance to non-Muslims); on to **SOUK EL HADD ISSI** (SOUK EL HAD ARFALLAH IHRIR on the Michelin map), with a Sunday *souk*; then past a fine agadir (5km on); and finally to **AÏT BOUNOUH** at the end of the canyon.

A piste climbs over the hills from Aït Bounouh to bring you out on the "**new road**" from **Tiznit** to **Tafraoute** near IZERBI. At Izerbi, pistes also continue south towards Amtoudi and the Bou Izakarn–Tata road.

Tiznit to Goulimine – and Sidi Ifni

Heading **south from Tiznit to Goulimine**, you have a choice of routes: a fast inland road across scrubby desert via **Bou Izakarn** (see p.483), or a more circuitous journey along the coast, by way of the splendid old Spanish colonial port of **Sidi Ifni**. Most people will probably choose to do one route down and the other back, which is sound enough. On no account, however, dismiss the Sidi Ifni route as an unneccessary detour: it turns out an unexpected highlight for many visitors.

Tiznit to Sidi Ifni: Mirhleft

The route down the coast from Tiznit to Sidi Ifni passes, around the midway point, the roadside village of **MIRHLEFT**, a friendly, bustling little place, overlooked by a ruined French fort and set back a kilometre from a good beach. Buses and *grands taxis* from Tiznit could drop you here – or you could use Sidi Ifni as a base. The beach itself is a beautiful, totally undeveloped curve of sand, with crashing waves and strong currents; it attracts surfers and campervans.

The village has several cafés and five basic **hotels**. Four of them are on the village's main street, the best being the *Hôtel Farah* (☎08/71.90.76; ⑩) with a friendly, English-speaking proprietor. The *Hôtel du Sud* (☎08/71.90.24; ⑩) and the *Hôtel Tafoukt* (☎08/71.90.77; ⑩) are also clean and bright. Prices vary with demand. For campervans there is an accepted parking area, along a track leading from the waterstand to the beach. The village also hosts a Monday **souk**, devoted mainly to secondhand items.

To the south are further **beaches**, of which the best are **Plage du Marabout** (3km from Mirhleft, by a prominent *marabout* tomb) and **Plage Aftas**.

Sidi Ifni

SIDI IFNI is uniquely interesting: a town that was relinquished by Spain only in 1969, after the Moroccan government closed off landward access to the colonial enclave. Thirty years on, it still preserves an outpost air and, if the mood takes you, can seem rather wonderful. Built in the 1930s, on a cliff-top site, it is full of sweeping architectural lines and elaborate ironwork: all in all, a bizarre memorial to colonialist purpose (or perhaps the lack of it), and surely the finest and most romantic Art Deco military town ever built. It is a very relaxed place and of late has a rather more prosperous air, with

renovation and patches of gardens turning round its old decayed film-set atmosphere. It has easy connections with Tiznit and Goulimine by bus and *grand taxi*. On Sundays a large **souk** – complete with musicians and storytellers – takes place out near the abandoned airfield; taxis shuttle out from town. On June 30 every year there is a **festival** to celebrate Ifni's 1969 reincorporation into Morocco.

The town, or more accurately the site then known as Santa Cruz del Mar Pequeño, 'Holy Cross of the Small Sea', was Spanish from 1476 to 1524, when the Saadians threw them out. In 1860, the Treaty of Tetouan – the culmination of Morocco's first military defeat by a European power in 200 years – gave it back to them, though they didn't re-occupy it until 1934, after they (and the French) had "pacified" the interior.

Orientation and accommodation

Approaching Sidi Ifni from Tiznit, you pass through a modern and nondescript Moroccan suburb, then the road swings down, across the Oued Ifni, and into Sidi Ifni proper (stay on the bus!). Once you've arrived in town, you should have no orientation problems: it's a straightforward grid, with steps leading down to the sea.

Finding **accommodation** is easy enough also, with seven hotels, all moderately priced, and a campsite. The choices are:

Hôtel Aire Nouvelle, Av. Sidi Mohammed Abdallah (☎08/87.52.98). **Hôtel Houria** (aka *Hôtel Liberté*), off Av. Mohammed V; **Hôtel Ifni**, Av. Mohammed V. All of these have small, clean rooms catering mainly for a Moroccan clientele, in town for the market. ⑩

Hôtel Aït Ba Hamram, Rue de la Plage – at the bottom of the steps (☎08/87.52.67). A grand building, with decent rooms, a good restaurant (order in advance – especially fish), and a bar. ③

Hôtel Bellevue, Place Hassan II (☎08/87.50.72). Another fine building, also good value, with a new wing, sweeping views over the beach, a noisy bar and a slow restaurant. ③

Hôtel Suerte Loca, Rue Moulay Youssef (☎08/87.53.50). A characterful place – the name ("Crazy Luck") and a *bodega*-style bar with table football and pinball reveals its small-town Spanish origins – which has been well renovated and is run by a very welcoming (and English-speaking) family. It has cheap rooms in the old Spanish wing, slightly pricier en-suite ones in a new wing, and is deservedly popular. It also has a good café-restaurant, local music most nights, a fixed rate crafts shop, and a terrace overlooking the town and sea. ③

Camping Sidi Ifni, Av. Sidi Mohammed. A rather spartan site with little shade.

Apart from the hotels mentioned above, there is not a vast choice of places to eat, though you'll find a few cheap restaurants around the *souk* and post office, notably the **Restaurant le Marine** on Av. Mohammed V.

The Town

It is the Spanish feel – and the **Art Deco architecture** – that is most attractive about Sidi Ifni. The town beach, with a *marabout* tomb at its northern end, is not that great (Mirhleft, see preceding section, is better) and is prone to long sea mists.

The obvious place to start out is the **Place Hassan II**, formerly *Plaza de España*. It stands at the heart of the town and immediately sets a tone for the place. Its centrepiece is an Andalucian garden with Spanish tiled benches and a Moroccan tiled fountain, flanking a plinth which once bore the statue of General Capaz, who took Ifni for Spain in 1934. At one end of this square stands a **Spanish consulate** – a building straight out of García Márquez, now it seems, terminally closed. Next to it, a **church** in Moorish-Art Deco style has now been adopted for use as the law courts. At the other end of the plaza, by a **town hall** complete with town clock, the former governor-general's residence is now the **royal palace**. Many of these buildings are in immaculate condition, with their stunning pastel shades picked out.

More Art Deco splendour is to be seen off the square and along Av. Hassan II, as well as around the **post office** which was also rather splendid before the top storey was demolished, and whence those mystifying stamps of the 1950s emerged, as any (ex-) collector will recall. Next to the *Hôtel Suerte Loca* and alas sadly dilapidated nowadays, a building in the shape of a ship once housed the **naval secretariat** – its two forward portholes being windows of cells where miscreant sailors were held. And there are a whole sequence of monumental **stairways**, rambling down towards the port and beach, and a magnificent deco **lighthouse**. Lovers of **mazes** will also be pleased to find a small one (perhaps the only one in Morocco) in Av. Jardin Houria on Av. El Houria. It won't, however, take you long to find your way out.

To the south of the town is the **old port**, built by the Spanish, and out to sea is an odd little concrete island, where ships used to dock. It was connected to the mainland by a unique cablecar, which hauled goods as well as passengers. There's a **new port** further south, with big new sardine- and anchovy- processing factories. On the way to the latter is the former Spanish prison, now disused, and an airfield, also disused, whose last landing was an American locust-spraying plane, forced down here on one engine after being shot at by Polisario guerillas in 1988. The airport building is now a meteorological station.

If you have a special interest in Ifni's past, you may care to call in on the barber's shop at 25. Av. Mohammed V, where Hassan Anzag, the barber, will be glad to show you his collection of all photos of the town and to chat about its history.

Surfing and paragliding

Sidi Ifni has become something of a base for **surfing and paragliding**. Favourite spots for the former are on the main beach, just in front of the tennis courts, and another beach 100m south of the new port. Favourite paragliding spots are **Legzira**, a beach 11km north of Ifni overlooked by a Spanish fort, where there's a basic hotel (⓪), though without electricity, and the hills behind Ifni (though be careful not to fly over the town). Ahmed at the *Hôtel Suerte Loca* can provide details for those interested.

Moving on

CTM **bus** services to/from Sidi Ifni are currently pending widening of the main road, which leaves three daily departures, all early morning, leaving from Av. Mohammed V, opposite the *Banque Populaire*. They are 5am for Tiznit, Inezgane and Marrakesh; 7am for Tiznit and Agadir; and 6.30am for Goulimine. **Grands taxis** run to Tiznit and Goulimine, leaving from a street in the northwest of the grid (see map).

There is little of note on the route south from **Sidi Ifni to Goulimine**, though the route itself is a pleasant one, especially in spring, when the slopes are green with a mass of euphorbia.

Tiznit to Goulimine via Bou Izakarn

Moussems apart, it is **the route down** to Goulimine that is the main attraction. It is best taken, at least in one direction, with a detour to Sidi Ifni (see above).

Travelling on the inland route, the only place of any size that you pass is the palmery and village of BOU IZAKARN, where the road to Ifrane de l'Anti-Atlas and the Tata oasis (see p.478) heads off east into the Anti-Atlas. *Grands taxis* can be negotiated here for Ifrane de l'Anti-Atlas and Amtoudi (see p.483).

Goulimine

GOULIMINE (also spelt GUELMIM or GULIMIME) sounds pretty exciting in the brochures: "The Gateway to the Sahara", with its nomadic "blue men" and traditional **camel market**. The truth, sadly, is considerably more mundane. Though the scenery is indeed impressively bleak, you're still a long way short of seeing any Saharan dunes, and the camel market itself is a rather depressing sham, maintained largely for tour groups bussed in from Agadir. Even the locals have begun to indulge in theatrical cons, ferrying people out to see "genuine *hommes bleus*" in tents outside town. For a more convincing and exciting sense of the desert, you would do a lot better to make for M'hamid in the Drâa (see p.410) or Merzouga in the Tafilalt (see p.441).

The one time that a visit to Goulimine would be worthwhile in itself is if you could coincide with one of the region's annual **moussems** – when you really are likely to see Touareg nomads. It's difficult to get information about the exact dates of the *moussems* – they vary considerably from year to year – but there is usually a large one held in June at Asrir, 10km southeast of Goulimine.

Moussems and markets aside, the nearest thing Goulimine has to a tourist sight is the remains of **Caid Dahman Takni's palace**, in the back streets behind the *Hôtel la Jeunesse*, very ruined now, but barely a hundred years old.

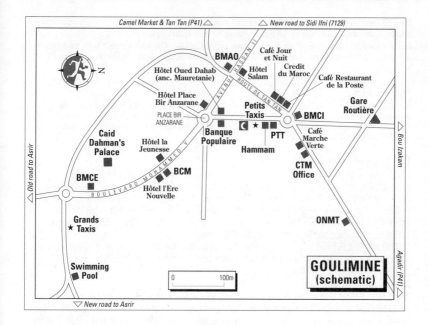

Map labels:
- Camel Market & Tan Tan (P41)
- New road to Sidi Ifni (7129)
- BMAO
- Café Jour et Nuit
- Hôtel Oued Dahab (anc. Mauretanie)
- Hôtel Salam
- Credit du Maroc
- Café Restaurant de la Poste
- AVENUE HASSAN II
- ROUTE DE TAN TAN
- Hôtel Place Bir Anzarane
- Petits Taxis
- Gare Routière
- PLACE BIR ANZARANE
- BMCI
- Caid Dahman's Palace
- Hôtel la Jeunesse
- Banque Populaire
- PTT
- Hammam
- Café Marche Verte
- Bou Izakam
- Old road to Asrir
- BOULEVARD MOHAMMED V
- BCM
- BMCE
- Hôtel l'Ere Nouvelle
- CTM Office
- Grands Taxis
- ONMT
- Swimming Pool
- Agadir (P41)
- 0   100m
- **GOULIMINE (schematic)**
- New road to Asrir

Orientation

Goulimine is a fairly standard administrative town but with a distinctly frontier feel to it, and with a couple of small, fairly animated *souks*. At its heart is the **Place Bir Anzarane**, with the main cluster of hotels and café-restaurants to its north.

If you arrive by **bus**, you'll probably be dropped to the north of this area (top of our map), while **grands taxis** run to a square a similar distance to the south.

There is a **tourist office** at 3 Residence Sahara out on the Agadir road (☎08/87.31.85; Mon–Fri 8.30am–noon & 2.30–6.30pm). In addition, the town has five **banks** – all marked on our map – and numerous **shops**, several of which specialize in Saharan "antiques" – mainly carpets and jewellery, but also leather goods, silver ware, knives, stones and old money. The town **hammam**, with showers as well as steam, is currently being refurbished but should soon be open for both sexes 6am–midnight. It is right in the centre of town, by the **post office.** If you prefer full immersion, there is a municipal **swimming pool** (open summer only) out on the new Asrir road.

Accommodation

Accommodation is very limited and prices at hotels are hiked up every Friday night as tourists come into town for the camel market. All but one are unclassified. A trio of more interesting alternatives to a night in Goulimine are detailed in the "Around Goulimine" section, overleaf.

The better choices in town include:

CHEAP

Hôtel l'Ere Nouvelle, Bd. Mohammed V (☎08/87.21.18). Not too bad, with friendly staff and hot showers on request. ⓪

Hôtel la Jeunesse, Bd. Mohammed V – opposite (☎08/87.22.21). A tolerable second choice, if the above is full. Located up a steep flight of steps. ⓪

Hôtel Oued Ed Dahab, Place Bir Anzarene (☎08/87.28.07). No showers but there's a *hammam* nearby. Downstairs rooms are a bit dingy – upstairs ones rather better. ①

Hôtel Place Bir Anzarane, Place Bir Anzarane (☎08/87.26.02). OK, with a café. There are no showers but again the *hammam* is nearby (diagonally across the square, between the mosque and *PTT)*. ①

MODERATE

Hôtel Salam, Route de Tan Tan (☎08/87.20.57). You might decide it's worth paying the extra money for a room here at the town's finest hotel. It offers reasonably large rooms round an open patio, a decent restaurant and Goulimine's only bar. The hotel displays 3-D paintings by an excellent local artist, Hamid Kahlaoui. ②

The "Camel Market"

Goulimine's **Saturday souk** serves a regular local purpose, with all the usual Moroccan goods on sale: grain, vegetables, meat, clothes, silver, jewellery, sheep and goats. What it doesn't have in very great measure are camels, as the beasts have steadily fallen from favour over the years in the wake of lorries and transit vehicles, and the caravan routes are more or less extinct. The few you do see here have either been brought in just for show or to be sold off for meat.

The market is held a kilometre out of town on the road to Tan Tan; it starts around 6am and a couple of hours later the first tour buses arrive from Agadir.

Meals and shows

The *Hôtel Salam* has the best **meals**, as well as rooms. Other places worth considering include *Café Marche Verte*, *Café de la Poste* and *Café Jour et Nuit*, up near the *PTT*; the latter is usually open night and day, as it promises. The *Hôtel Salam* has a bar, but its atmosphere is rather all male.

Several of the hotels and cafés put on shows of **Guedra dancing** on Friday and Saturday nights and Saturday lunchtimes. Much has been written about this traditional, seductive women's dance of the desert – performed, from a kneeling position (developed for the low tents) to a slow, repetitive rhythm. The shows here, however, are a bit of a travesty.

Moving on: buses and grands taxis

Moving on, daytime **bus departures** are from the Gare Routière on the Bou Izakam road. These include eight departures for Agadir (of which four continue to Marrakesh and Casa, one to Rabat), four for Tan Tan, and one for Assa-Zag. Only one CTM bus leaves from there (8pm to Casa): all later departures, as well as the ONCF services, leave from outside the **CTM office** by the *Café Marche Verte* on the Agadir road: they run to Laayoune at 12.30am (continuing to Dakhla), 12.45am (via Smara), 2am and 6.30am; to Marrakesh at 9.30pm, midnight and 12.30am; to Agadir at 3.30am and 4am.

Grands taxis also hang out around the CTM office at night (betwen around 10pm and 6am); in the daytime they leave from the gare routière for Ifni, Bou Izakarn, Tiznit, Inezgane, Agadir, Tan Tan, Laayoune and Smara, and from stations on the new Asrir road for Asrir, Aït Bekkon and Assa-Zag.

Around Goulimine: springs, oases and Plage Blanche

There are good little trips out from Goulimine to the hot springs of **Abbainou**, 15km northeast, and to the oasis of **Aït Boukha**, 17km southeast; both offer pleasant alternative **accommodation** to a night in Goulimine. So, too, does the recently established auberge-campsite at **Fort Bou-Jerif**, an old French Foreign Legion post, inland from **Plage Blanche** – the "White Beach" that stretches for sixty or so kilometres along the coast southwest of Goulimine.

Abbainou

ABBAINOU is a tiny oasis, with a *koubba* and hot springs, channelled into two bath enclosures – divided according to sex – where you can soak the afternoon away. The women's enclosure (28°C) is very welcoming, though the men's is 10°C hotter! There is mixed bathing in the evenings.

Located 15km northeast of Goulimine, the oasis is an easy excursion if you have transport; if you don't, you could negotiate a *grand taxi* (from the main rank by the *souk*). The French-run *Auberge Abainou* at the oasis has **rooms** round a courtyard, cold showers, a restaurant and a bar. There is also a **campsite**, *Camping Abainou*, and several café-restaurants.

Aït Bekkou

The largest and most spectacular oasis in the Goulimine area is **AÏT BEKKOU** (or Aït Boukka), 10km southeast along the road to ASRIR, then a further 7km on piste. To get there again requires either your own transport or chartering a *grand taxi*. Alongside the palmery is an impressive new **hotel**, the *Tighmert* (③), built in mock-Kasbah style and decorated, like the *Hôtel Salam* in Goulimine, with paintings by Hamid Kahlaoui.

Aït Bekkou is a thriving agricultural community, with an especially lush strip of cultivation along a canal, irrigated from the old riverbed and emerging from a flat expanse of sand. You might even see the odd herd of camels being grazed out here. To reach the canal, head for the thicket of palms about 2km behind the oasis (or pick up a guide on the way).

Fort Bou-Jerif and Plage Blanche

Fort Bou-Jerif is a truely romantic spot, set beside the Oued Assaka, 13km from the sea. It is marked on the Michelin map by a little fort symbol (with the words *O. Noun* to the left). The **auberge-campsite** here is run by a young French couple, Guy and Evy Dreumont. If the attractions of staying at an old French Foreign Legion camp in the middle of nowhere are not enough to entice you, consider that there is also good French cooking (camel *tajine*, no less), and that the Dreumonts offer some superb **four-wheel-drive excursions** in the area, including, of course, trips to the Plage Blanche. They offer rooms as well as camping, power points for caravans, and rows of very clean showers (hot water) and toilets. To book ahead, write to them at: Fort Bou Jerif, BP 504 Guelmin, Morocco.

The route to the fort from Goulimine involves 20km of paved road (to TISSÉGUEMANE), then 18km of piste, passable by car or campervan; it can, alternatively be approached by landrover along the coast from Sidi Ifni. Without your own transport, you might be able to get a lift from Guy, who comes into town three times a week to pick up groceries from a store at the end of Av. Hassan II (over the oued from the town but it's the last grocery store on the left, with a tabac sign); otherwise there's a collective landrover taxi that passes the store around 3pm daily.

travel details

Buses

From Agadir to Marrakesh (12 daily; 4–5hr); Laayoune (3 daily; 11hr); Dakhla (1 daily; 20hr 30min); Smara (1 daily; 9hr); Fes (1 daily; 12hr 30min); Tan Tan (8 daily; 7hr 30min); Ouarzazate (7 daily; 7hr 30min); Tiznit (10 daily; 2hr); Casablanca (7daily; 9hr); Essaouira (6 daily; 3hr 30min), Safi (5daily; 5hr 30min), Rabat (1 daily; 11hr); Tangier (1 daily; 6hr);

Goulimine (10 daily; 4hr 30min); Taroudannt (8 daily; 2hr 30min); Tata (2 daily; 9hr); Tafraoute (5 daily; 5hr); Immouzer (1 daily; 2hr 30min).

From Taroudannt to Ouarzazate (7 daily; 5hr) via Taliouine (2hr) and Tazenakht (3hr); Tata (1–2 daily; 5hr); Casablanca (8 daily; 10hr); Rabat (3 daily; 13hr); Marrakesh (5 daily; 6hr 30min); Agadir (8 daily; 2hr 30min).

From Taliouine to Agadir (7 daily; 4hr 30min) via Taroudannt (2hr); Ouarzazate (7 daily; 3hr) via Tazenakht (1hr); Tinerhir (1 daily, 8hr); Marrakesh (1 daily; 9hr).

From Tata to Agadir (2 daily; 9hr); Taroudannt (1–2 daily; 5hr) via Igherm (2hr 30min); Tiznit (2 daily; 7hr); Goulimine (1 daily; 9hr 30min); Ouarzazate (1 daily; 5hr) via Foum Zguid (2hr 30min).

From Tiznit to Agadir (10 daily; 2hr), Goulimine (4 daily; 2hr 30min); Tata (2 daily; 7hr); Marrakesh (10 daily; 7hr); Casablanca (8 daily; 11hr); Rabat (6 daily; 13hr); Tangier (1 daily; 18hr); Tafraoute (5 daily; 3hr).

From Tafraoute to Casablanca (5 daily; 14hr) via Tiznit (3hr); Agadir (5hr); Marrakesh (2 daily; 10hr); Essaouira (3 daily; 9hr 30min).

Sidi Ifni to Marrakesh (1 daily; 8hr 30min); Agadir (1 daily; 3hr 30min); Tiznit (2 daily; 2hr 30min); Goulimine (1 daily; 1hr 30min).

From Goulimine to Agadir (10 daily; 4hr 30min); Tan Tan (8 daily; 3hr); Marrakesh (6 daily; 9hr 30min); Laayoune (3 daily; 7hr); Dakhla (1 daily; 15hr 30min); Smara (1 daily; 6hr); Sidi Ifni (1 daily; 1hr 30min); Tiznit (4 daily; 2hr 30min); Casablanca (4 daily; 14hr); Rabat (1 daily; 16hr).

Grands Taxis

From Agadir to Tiznit (2hr 15min); Taroudannt (1hr 30min); Inezgane (15min). Change to Inezgane for most southern destinations.

From Inezgane to Agadir (15min); Marrakesh (3hr); Taroudannt (1hr 15min); Tiznit (2hr); Sidi Ifni (3hr 30min); Goulimine (4hr 30min); Essaouira (2hr 30min); Bou Izakarn (3hr 30min).

From Taroudannt to Inezgane (1hr 15min); Agadir (1hr 30min); Marrakesh (4hr); Igherm (1hr); Ouled Berhil (40min).

From Berhil to Aoulouz (40min); Aoulouz to Taliouine (40min).

From Tata to Akka (1hr); Tissint (1hr).

From Bou Izakarn to Goulimine (1hr); Tiznit (1hr 30min); Inezgane (3hr 30min); Ifrane de l'Anti-Atlas (20min); Foum El Hassan (1hr 30min).

From Tiznit to Agadir (1hr 15min); Inezgane (1hr); Tafraoute (2hr); Mirhleft (45min); Sidi Ifri (1hr 30min); Bou Izakarn (1hr 30min); Goulimine (2hr 30min); Sidi Moussa d'Aglou (15min).

From Sidi Ifni to Mirhleft (45min); Tiznit (1hr 30min); Goulimine (1hr).

From Goulimine to Sidi Ifni (1hr); Bou Izakara (1hr); Tiznit (2hr 30min); Inezgane (4hr 30min); Agadir (4hr 45min); Tan Tan (2hr 30min); Lauyoune (5hr); Smara (4hr 30min).

Flights

From Agadir to Casablanca (3–4 daily); Laayoune (5 weekly); Tangier (1–2 weekly); Ouarzazate (1 weekly in winter); Las Palmas (2 weekly); Amsterdam; Brussels; Copenhagen; Frankfurt; Geneva; Paris; Vienna; Zurich.

CHAPTER NINE

THE DEEP SOUTH: WESTERN SAHARA

F ew travellers venture south of Goulimine – and on the surface there is little enough to commend the trip. The towns – **Tan Tan**, **Tarfaya**, **Laayoune** and **Dakhla** – are modern administrative centres, with no great intrinsic interest. The route, however, across vast tracts of *hammada* – bleak, stony desert – is another matter. The odd line of dunes unfolds on the horizon to the east, the ocean parallels much of the road to the west, and there is no mistaking that you have reached the **Sahara** proper. Returning, if you don't fancy a repeat of the journey, there are flights from Ad Dakhla and Laayoune to Agadir, or from Laayoune to the **Canary Islands** (also accessible from Agadir).

An additional point of interest, now that the war with Polisario seems to be at an end, is the attention being lavished on the region by the Moroccan authorities. The **Western Saharan Provinces** (the old Spanish Saharan colony, claimed by Morocco with the 1975 Green March) begin just to the south of Tarfaya. **Laayoune**, never greatly regarded by the Spanish, has been transformed into a showcase capital for the new provinces; there are industrial plans for **Tarfaya**; and, with an eye to the traditional nomadic dwellers, the Moroccan authorities have also been assisting in building up the local camel herds.

The region's economic importance was long thought to centre on the phosphate mines at **Boukra**, southeast of Laayoune. However, these have not been very productive in recent years, and the deposits are not especially rich by the standards of the Plateau des Phosphates east of Casablanca. In the long term, the rich deep-water fishing grounds offshore are likely to prove a much better earner. This potential is gradually being realized with the construction of a new port at Laayoune, together with industrial plant for fish storage and processing.

Throughout the Western Sahara and the former Spanish protectorate nowadays, Spanish is fast being replaced by French as the dominant second language. Some older residents still speak Spanish, but younger people, officials and administrators, as well as migrants into the Western Sahara from Morocco proper, are much more likely to understand French.

Goulimine to Tan Tan

The approach from **Goulimine to Tan Tan** runs along 125km of straight desert road, across a bleak area of scrub and *hammada*. There are few features to speak of en route: a café and filling station (55km from Goulimine); a small pass (85km); and finally a crossing of the **Oued Drâa** (109km), invariably dry at this point.

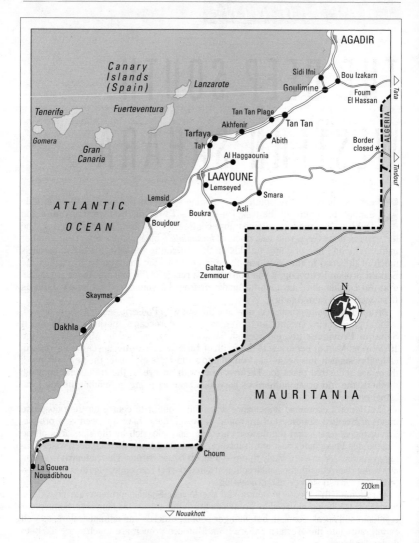

In colonial times, the Drâa was the border between the French and Spanish protectorates and a piste heads west to a last French **fort** at its mouth. Somewhat confusingly, although this was the border of the Protectorate, the land to the south was not actually part of the Spanish Saharan colonies: the northernmost of these, Seguiat El Hamra, began at the 27°40' N line just south of Tarfaya, and the southern one at the 26th parallel, just south of Boujdour. After independence in 1958, the Spanish gave back to Morocco the strip of territory north of 27°40', keeping the two Saharan colonies until November 1975 (see box on p.508).

Tan Tan

Arriving at **TAN TAN**, under an archway of kissing camels, you might just find yourself wondering why. A drab administrative centre, it survives in a low-key way through its status as a duty-free zone (the shops are full of radios and electric razors) and rather more so by its fishing port (25km distant), which is responsible for a large percentage of Morocco's sardine exports. Its one claim to fame is that it was a departure point for the famous **Green March** (*La Marche Verte* – see p.508), an event commemorated on postcards throughout the south.

The town has around 50,000 inhabitants, many of them former nomads, who retain their distinctive pale blue robes. This clothing is much in evidence in the **souks** – the most animated part of a hot, sleepy town – as are a variety of *lithams*, strips of cotton that are wrapped round the head. The latter are a wise investment as sun protection if you are heading further south.

Orientation

Tan Tan's main artery is the inevitable **Av. Mohammed V**, and most of the town is spread out along it. Although the avenue is lined with buildings for the whole of its length, you can still catch glimpses down side streets of a parallel ridge, and to the west the riverbed of Oued Ben Khlil, overgrown with thorn apples, which 'flows' north to join Oued Drâa.

Just off the bottom end of Av. Mohammed V is the **Place de la Marche Verte**, with the **bus** and **grand taxi** rank, and several hotels. At the other end, a smaller square with several cafés and an arcade of shops down one side is referred to locally as **La Poste de la Police** because of the small police post in the middle of it. **Petits taxis** can be found here, along with more cheap hotels, and **grands taxis** for Tan Tan plage. Beyond the square, the street continues up to meet **Bd. Hassan II**, the main road in and out of town, which enters from Goulimine through from a kissing camel archway and heads out, across the riverbed, towards Tan Tan plage, the airport and Laayoune.

Most of the administrative buildings are at this (north) end of town: the main **PTT** is on Bd. Hassan II, with a branch office in Place de la Marche Verte, and there are two **banks**: *BMCE* on Bd. Hassan II at the junction with Av. Mohammed V, and *Banque Populaire* down near la Poste de la Police. Should you need a **hammam**, there's one for both sexes just behind the southern end of Place de la Marche Verte.

Hotels

There are a number of unclassified hotels on and around Place de la Marche Verte and La Poste de la Police, most of them grotty if very cheap. Rather better hotels, all fairly basic and inexpensive, include:

Hôtel Aoubour [B], junction of Av. Mohammed V and Bd. Hassan II (no phone). Basic but acceptable, and cheap. Its "draw" is that it's handy for CTM and ONCF bus departures. ⓪

Hôtel Bit Anzarane [A], 154 Bd. Hassan II (☎08/87.78.34). Across the oued on the edge of town, this is a good-value place, with decent rooms (though with shared bathrooms, and not all rooms have outside windows), and low prices. Its main drawback is its distance from the centre. ①

Hôtel Dakar [G], Place Marche Verte (☎08/87.71.86). Slightly cheaper than the *Tafoukt* (see below) and almost as good. ⓪

Hôtel Royal [C], Av. Mohammed V – up past la Poste de la Police (☎08/87.71.86). The best hotel in town, with comfortable, carpeted rooms and en-suite bathrooms throughout. It is in fact a military officers' mess, but they'll take tourists if they have room. ①

Hôtel Tafoukt [F], 98 Pl Marche Verte (☎08/87.70.31). The best of the Place Marche Verte hotels, new and clean, and not a lot pricier than the competition. ①

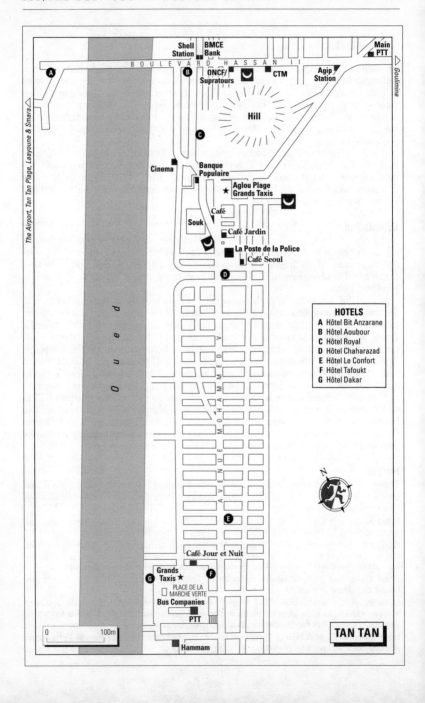

Shell Station
BMCE Bank
Main PTT
BOULEVARD HASSAN II
ONCF/Supratours
CTM
Agip Station
Goulimine
A
B
Hill
C
Cinema
Banque Populaire
Aglou Plage Grands Taxis
★
Café
Souk
Café Jardin
La Poste de la Police
Café Seoul
D

The Airport, Tan Tan Plage, Laayoune & Smara

O u e d

AVENUE MOHAMMED V

HOTELS
A Hôtel Bit Anzarane
B Hôtel Aoubour
C Hôtel Royal
D Hôtel Chaharazad
E Hôtel Le Confort
F Hôtel Tafoukt
G Hôtel Dakar

E

Café Jour et Nuit
Grands Taxis ★
F
G
PLACE DE LA MARCHE VERTE
Bus Companies
PTT

0   100m

Hammam

N

TAN TAN

Should you find all these full, the better fall-back options (both cheap) are:
Hôtel Chaharazad [D], La Poste de la Police (no phone). ⑩
Hôtel Le Confort [E], 315 Av. Mohammed V, close by Pl de la Marche Verte (☎08/87.80.74). ⑪

Meals and entertainment

For a **meal**, there are cafés around Place de la Marche Verte, best of which is the *Jour et Nuit* which, true to its name, can produce you a *tajine* at any hour of the day or night. The best place to sip a mint tea and watch the world go by is in one of the cafés at la Poste de la Police, in particular, the *Café le Jardin* with its big open shelter, and slightly dilapidated garden behind. The *Snack Seoul* on the same square offers snacks, but nothing Korean in fact.

There is no licensed bar in town, and entertainment is limited to the *Renaissance* **cinema** between the Poste de la Police and the oued. It has a café, *Le Glacier*, attached.

Moving on

Most **buses** leave from Place de la Marche Verte, the south side of which has a row of ticket offices. SATAS have departures for Agadir at 5am and 3pm and there are currently seven other daily buses to Agadir, one of which (at 5.30pm) continues to Marrakesh and Casa, another (at 7pm) to Essaouira and Safi. Etoile de Sahara have a single 10pm departure for Tarfaya and Laayonne.

CTM and ONCF buses stop outside their offices on Bd. Hassan II near the main post office. CTM's single departure is at 6pm for Marrakesh. ONCF buses leave for Agadir and Marrakesh at 9.50pm, 10pm, 1.40am and 3am. The 9.50pm departure is your surest bet as it actually starts in Tan Tan. Heading south, there are departures for Laayonne at 8.15am, 1.25am (continuing to Dakhla) and 1.50am (via Smara).

Grand taxi runs include Goulimine, Inezgane, Agadir, Smara and Laayoune; if you strike lucky, you may also find direct taxis for Tarfaya and Tiznit. They leave from Place de la Marche Verte except for taxis to Tan Tan Plage, which run from just north of La Poste de la Police.

Tan Tan's **airport** (☎08/87.41.43) is 9km out of town off the Smara road, with one weekly flight to Casa, and one to Laayonne, both currently on Friday. To get there, you'll need to take a *petit taxi*. The *RAM* office is in Av. de la Ligne Arabe (☎08/87.72.59).

Tan Tan Plage

TAN TAN PLAGE, 28km from town on the coastal route to Laayoune, has been theoretically earmarked for development as a resort, though in the past ten years the ambitious four-star *Hôtel Ayoub* has failed to get much beyond its foundations. At present, therefore, there is very little to see (a scattering of houses, shops, banks and a couple of mosques), even less to do, and nowhere to stay. There are, however, two **cafés**, the better of which, *Étoile de l'Océan*, serves good fish.

The **beach** itself is unenticing – littered with broken glass, not too clean due to the proximity of a large sardine port nearby, and often swamped in seaweed.

A loop through Smara

It is possible to make a loop **from Tan Tan along the new road to Smara**, returning by way of the P44 to Laayoune, and from there across to Tan Tan via Tarfaya – a circuit of some 800km. There are **buses** along each section (though not every day). If you're driving, you will find **filling stations** in Tan Tan, Smara and Laayoune – petrol, incidentally, is subsidized throughout the Western Sahara – so if you embark on the trip be sure to fill up, and to carry good water supplies.

THE SAHARAN PROVINCES

Until 1988 any trip **south of Tan Tan**, into the **former Spanish Sahara**, involved getting permission from the military authorities. The routes are today open quite routinely – indeed the Moroccan authorities are actively encouraging tourists to explore the region. The French *Club Med* is already established at Laayoune.

THE GREEN MARCH, WAR AND POLITICAL CLAIMS

The politics of the Saharan Provinces are a highly sensitive matter in Morocco: so much so, that all maps and guides of the country must have the territory included (and labelled as part of the Moroccan kingdom). Some background to this is included in *Contexts*. The essential facts are that the old Spanish colonies of **Rio de Oro** and **Seguiat El Hamra**, sometimes referred to as the **Western Sahara**, were occupied by Morocco on Spanish withdrawal in 1975. These claims were based on historic Moroccan control of the area, including the presence of a fort said to have been built by Moulay Ismail in the 1670s near Laayoune, and the activities here of Hassan I.

Whatever their legitimacy, King Hassan II enjoyed enormous acclaim with his tactical occupation of the territory – the so-called **Green March** (*La Marche Verte*) of November 1975, when 300,000 unarmed civilians walked across the old frontier and "returned" the territories to the Alaouite Kingdom of Morocco. Territorial counterclaims, however, came almost immediately from Mauritania and from various groups among the indigenous Sahrawis.

Through the next two decades, a war raged on and off in the desert between the Moroccan military (who administer the entire former Spanish colony) and Algerian-backed **Polisario** guerrilla fighters, operating from bases round Tindouf, across the border in Algeria. The war, which for a time affected areas within Morocco's "former" boundaries, was, by the end of the 1980s, largely contained by the creation of an extraordinary **"desert wall"** (see *Contexts*). In the meantime Polisario increasingly turned to diplomacy to gather support.

In 1988 a UN-sponsored ceasefire, with a **referendum** on "incorporation" or independence, was accepted in principal by both sides, and it seemed a settlement was at last in sight. However, the years since have seen frustration of the UN aims, with arguments over the voting list leading to repeated postponement of the referendum. In theory, it will still take place, but observers are sceptical. Having invested so much in the territory – not only in military terms, as subsidies, tax concessions and infrastructure building have all been a heavy drain on the economy – it seems inconceivable that Morocco would relinquish its claims. Polisario have threatened renewed military action if the referendum fails to take place, but at time of writing the stalemate and truce seem entrenched.

VISITING THE PROVINCES

Given the factors above, travellers are advised to get **up-to-date information** before attempting anything too ambitious in the region. Visiting **Laayoune** and **Smara** is nowadays pretty routine, though it does involve answering a series of questions (name, age, profession, parents' names, passport number and date of issue, etc) at numerous police checkpoints along the way. This is all usually very amicable, but time-consuming, and taxi drivers may, as a result, be unwilling to carry foreigners. Apart from this, the only obstacle here would be for visitors who admit to being a 'writer' or 'journalist': a profession not welcome in the region, unless under the aegis of an official press tour.

A more practical problem, however, is **accommodation**, with UN supervisors occupying virtually all of the better hotels in Laayoune, Boujdour, Dakhla and Smara. It would be wise to phone a few places in these towns in advance of a visit, unless you are prepared to camp.

As for continuing south, the **border with Mauritania** is, at present, open and functional, although all traffic must form part of a convoy. If this forms part of your planning, however, you would be wise to get reports from recent travellers. The regulations and procedures have changed several times over the past decade.

Tan Tan to Smara

The ONMT literature on the Deep South extols the P44 between Tan Tan and Smara as "the new Saharan road". It is indeed impressive, in the sheer absence of habitation and features: there are grand vistas of hills and valleys to the east for the first 20km, then for the next 200km to Smara it is perfectly flat.

At 75km from Tan Tan is the route's single roadside hamlet, **ABITH** (or ABBATIH), where there are a couple of flyblown cafés and a flagpole. Another 36km and you cross into the Western Saharan provinces; just over the border is a service station where you can take advantage of the lower fuel prices. There is nothing else of interest before Smara, although the desert does get perceptibly darker in colour, due to the presence of black basalt.

Smara

SMARA (ES SEMARA) developed as an important caravan route across the Sahara, but today it is basically a military garrison town. The only link with its past are the remains of the Palace and Great Mosque of **Ma El Aïnin**, the "Blue Sultan", who controlled the region at the turn of the century. If you do come to the town you should certainly see them.

The military presence in Smara includes both the Moroccan army and the UN, here to supervise the ceasefire and referendum. The difficulties of this are apparent even from a cursory look at the town, for there is a huge tented city outside of former residents of Western Sahara returned from the north; Polisario, inevitably, contest their origins and right to vote. Nonetheless, Smara manages quite an ambience, in spite of itself. The area around the *souk* in particular gets very lively of an evening with grills in action along the street, traders selling their wares, and even the odd medicine man and snake charmer in attendance.

Accommodation

None of Smara's eight **hotels** offer much in the way of luxury, and the best of them are occupied by UN personnel at present, so don't expect to find anything more than a basic room. The options are:

Hotel Atlas, Av. Hassan II, entrance round the side (no phone). Unusually, managed by a woman. No showers but a *hammam* is close by. ①

Hotel El Azhar, Rue de Figuig (no phone). A very cheap, basic place with paint-splattered concrete floors and an unfinished look about it. ①

Hotel Chabab Sakia El Hamra, Av. Hassan II (☎08/89.25.24). A little more expensive but worth the extra if you can get a room. The reception is on the first floor, above the CTM/ONCF office. ②

Hotel Erraha, 16 Av. Hassan II (☎08/89.92.27). A friendly hotel with small rooms, cold showers, and a roof terrace. There are grill-cafés on either side. ①

Hôtel les Fleurs (aka Hôtel Zouhaur), 70 Bd. de Stade (☎08/89.95.58). Same management as the *Azhar*, same price, much better. Clean rooms and toilets, and cold showers if working. ①

Hôtel Café Restaurant les Holes, Rue l'Hôpital, by the hospital (☎08/89.97.72). A new hotel with upstairs single rooms rather better than the dingy downstairs doubles. ①

Hotel Maghrib El Arbi, Av. Hassan II (☎08/89.51.91). This modern hotel is Smara's top offering, but currently block-booked by the UN. ②

Hotel Sable d'Or, Av. Hassan II (☎08/89.94.52). Another basic but adequate place. ①

Around town

Ma El Aïnin's Palace is fairly well preserved. It stands near the oued and comprises the distinct residences of Ma El Aïnin's four main wives, one of which is now occupied by the *gardien* and his family. If you knock on the door, someone will open up and show you around. Inside you can see the domed *zaouia*. Though plastered over, it is, like the

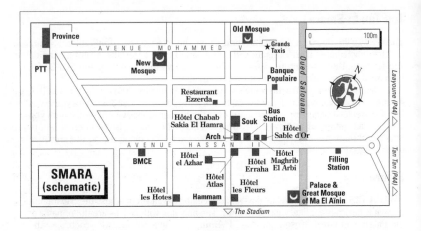

rest of the palace, built of black basalt from the local hills. You can also see the palace's original armoured doors. What's left of the **Great Mosque**, a separate building further away from the river, is less well preserved, but you can still see the *mihrab*, and rows of basalt arches.

The '**old mosque**' marked on our map is also made of local basalt, with a rather pretty stone minaret. This stands in the part of town built under Spanish rule, roughly bounded by the two arches and the *Hôtel Sable d'Or*. A distinctive aspect of the houses here (and elsewhere in the region) is the eggshell-like domes which serve as roofs, a device said to keep the interior cooler. Behind the mosque, you'll also find some of the strange tubular barracks put up by the Spanish to house their troops, now private homes. Like most buildings in Smara, they are painted a deep red ochre.

Other practicalities

Getting a **meal** is no problem. There are numerous café-restaurants and open-air grill-cafés along Av. Hassan II. The top choice is *Restaurant Ezzerda* near the souk.

The town **hammam** is slightly hidden away, near the *Hôtel les Fleurs*. Coming up Bd. de Stade from Av. Hassan II, take the next right and you'll see a small grocer at the first corner on the left. Women turn left – your entrance is the first (tiled) doorway on the right; men go straight on instead – your entrance is the third (tiled and signposted) doorway on the left (the second is for wood to heat the water).

As elsewhere in the Western Sahara, **international phone calls** can only be made from the **post office** which is by the *Province* at the western end of Av. Mohammed V. The town also has a couple of **banks** (*BMCE* and *Banque Populaire*), a **filling station**, and several garage-workshops for **car repairs**.

Transport

The only **buses** are run by ONCF/Supratours, who have an office between the entrances to the *Hôtel Charab Sakia El Hamra* and the *Hôtel Maghrib El Arbi*. They have a grand total of two daily departures: 6am to Laayonne, and 10pm to Agadir (connecting for Marrakesh).

Grands taxis leave from a large square near the *Hôtel Sable d'Or* (with tiled shopfronts all around it). Runs are to Laayonne, Tan Tan, Agadir and Marrakesh.

Note that the **road east from the town**, towards the Algerian town of TINDOUF (where the Polisario have their main base), is firmly closed.

Smara to Laayoune

West from Smara, heading towards Laayoune, you pass through slightly more featured landscape than the route from Tan Tan to Smara. For the first 5km the desert remains black-ish from the basalt, before resuming its customary lighter hue for the rest of the route.

A new road is under construction, beginning at the 19km mark, which will follow a much straighter trajectory and should, when completed, reduce mileage and travelling time considerably. The old road cuts from time to time across the pre-existing piste, which is still marked by lines of cairns and poles. On the north side of the road, 31km from Smara stands a large brown flat-topped hill called **Gor El Bered** ('Hill of the Wind'). At the foot of its west side is a small brown cupola-domed building resembling a *marabout* but is in fact a structure built by the Spanish in the 1930s to extract chalk from the calcium-rich rock of the hill. A genuine *marabout* is to be found at **Sidi Khatari**, to the north of the road 91km from Smara. A couple of kilometres beyond, a water-processing plant desalinates the brackish water of the local well, before pumping it through recently laid pipes to Smara. Opposite is a **filling station** and **café**. More intrepid travellers might try to locate the prehistoric rock carvings nearby at Asli.

There is little of any note to be seen for the next 70-odd kilometres before the **turn-off to Boukra**, a mining town with a large garrison 25km to the south-east. Thereafter, however, you become aware of the **Boukra-Laayonne conveyor belt** snaking its way south of the road, bearing phosphates seaward for export. The vast region south of Boukra is a restricted military zone, and inaccessible to casual visitors.

As the road swings west for the last 50km before Laayonne its surface markedly improves and the canyon of the **Seguiat El Hamra** comes into view on the northern side. Seguiat El Hamra means 'Red River' and, though there is no water in it for most of the year, the local clay turns it red when it does flow. The canyon is pretty impressive, but if you stop to take a snapshot be sure you are out of range of anything military. Meanwhile, signs along the road warn of animals crossing; the animal depicted, naturally, is a camel.

The oasis of **LEMSEYED**, 12km before Laayoune, is a local beauty spot offering fine views over the canyon. Across the Oued, the **Fort of Dchira** was built by the Spanish in the very early days of their rule. It is currently occupied by the Moroccan army.

Tan Tan to Laayoune

The route between **Tan Tan Plage and Laayoune** is the most memorable stretch of the journey in the Deep South, cutting as it does between desert and ocean. The coast, somewhat defying expectations, is mainly cliff – the desert dropping directly away to the sea, with only the occasional stretch of beach.

Tan Tan to Tarfaya

Between Tan Tan and Tarfaya there is little more than the roadside settlement of **AKHFENIR** (about 150km south of Tan Tan) with its 24–hour filling station and six cafés, of which the *Café Paris* serves the best fresh fish in the area, while the *Café Puerto Cansado*, with its brightly painted cartoon characters and English-speaking owner, has one of the few pool tables in the Western Sahara. The *Puerto Cansado* can also arrange accommodation, as well as trips to **PUERTO CANSADO**, 27km south (permit required) where you can see flamingoes. Just beyond here is a rare stretch of accessible beach, with reputedly wonderful fishing.

Tarfaya

TARFAYA is a small town (population 7000) with a fishing port and a large monument to the Green March. It may be in line for greater things if an oil shale development, currently under consideration by Shell, goes ahead, but for the moment it's a quiet place, probably not far different from its years as a staging post for the *Aéropostale Service* – when aviators such as **Antoine de Saint-Exupéry** (author of *Night Flight* and *The Little Prince*) used to rest up on their way down to West Africa.

The air service is commemorated annually in October by a **"Rallye Aérien"**, with small planes flying south from Toulouse to Dakar in Senegal; Tarfaya is a night's stop. A monument to Saint-Exupéry in the form of a plane stands at the northern end of the beach. Oddly enough, Tarfaya was actually founded, at the end of the last century, by a Scottish trader, named Donald Mackenzie, and was originally known as Port Victoria. Mackenzie's original fort, now known as **Casa Mar** lies just offshore – a few metres' swim at low tide. During the Spanish occupation, the town was called Villa Bens and served as a very low-key capital for the "Southern Protectorate"; they abandoned it in 1958, leaving a church and a handful of villas.

These days Tarfaya has been overshadowed by Laayoune, though it has two **hotels**, the *Tarfaya* (no phone; ⓤ), and the *Elmassira Elkhadra* (☎08/89.50.45; ⓤ), which are both pretty basic but can get quite busy during the fishing season (Dec–Mar). For **meals** try the *Embiric Restaurant*, with fish and *tajine*, or one of the cafés on the main street to the harbour.

South to Laayoune

South of Tarfaya you cross the old border of Spanish Sahara at Tah, and traverse real sand desert – the **Erg Lakhbayta**. The effect, however, is lighter than that implies, for along the way are a series of enormous **lagoons**, their water prevented from reaching the sea by long spits of sand, and **salt pans**, still being worked. These are important migratory sites, which should provide rewards for **bird-watchers**.

Laayoune

With a population of 100,000, **LAAYOUNE** (AL AYOUN) is the largest and the most interesting town of Western Sahara. Its development as a provincial capital is almost immediately obvious – and impressive, as you survey its building programmes like the 30,000-seat stadium, with real grass, maintained for the area's handful of football teams. The city has the highest per capita government spending in Morocco and soldiers, billeted here for the conflict with Polisario, have been employed in many of the projects.

The population growth – from little more than a village when the Moroccans took over – has been aided by massive subsidies, which apply throughout Western Sahara, and by an agreement that settlers should initially pay no taxes. They are a mix of Saharawis, many of them driven here by the drought of the last few years, and Moroccan immigrants from the north in search of work.

Orientation and accommodation

The first sight of Laayoune, coming from Tarfaya, is across the steep-sided valley of the **Seguiat El Hamra**, which has been dammed to make another, shallow lagoon. The old "**lower**" **town**, built by the Spanish, lies on the southern slope of the valley, with the new "**upper**" **town**, developed since the Green March, on the high plateau beyond. Our map opposite is somewhat diagrammatic.

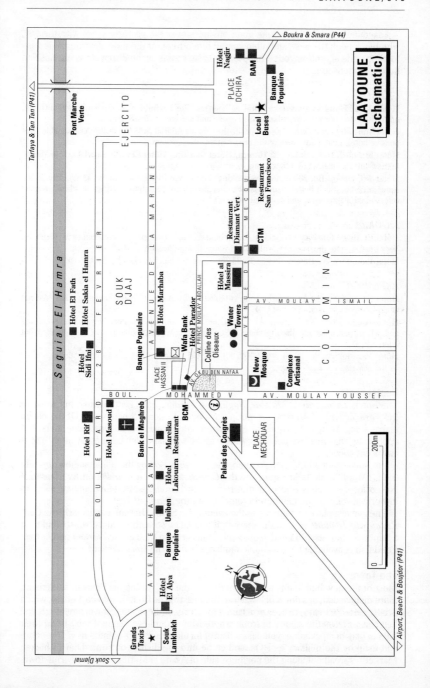

LAAYOUNE (schematic)

Laayoune's **hotels** have done good business over the past few years with the UN, who block-book the best, and often spread into others. At the time of writing, it is wise to phone ahead, unless you're happy with basic rooms at the dozen or so unclassified hotels. Options are:

CHEAP

Hôtel Atlas, **Hôtel Victoire** (aka **Hôtel El Nasr**), **Hôtel Errimal**, all in the Souk Djemal (Jmal), off to the left of our map. Very basic, very cheap and unused to Westerners. ⓪

Hôtel Marhaba, Av. de la Marine – opposite the Cinema Adgrad (☎08/89.32.49). A reasonable inexpensive hotel, a cut above most of the others in this category. ⓪

Hôtel Masoud, Hôtel Sakira El Hamra, Hôtel Sidi Ifni, Hôtel El Fath, all off Av. de la Marine in the Souk Djaj district. Another group of very basic cheapies. ⓪

Hôtel Rif, just off Bd. 28 Fevrier, overlooking the Seguiat El Hamra (☎08/89.43.69). This is the same price but much better value than the cheapies mentioned above – a friendly place, recently refurbished. Inexpensive and excellent value. ⓪

MODERATE

Hôtel El Alya, 1 Rue Kadi El Ghalaoui, just behind the Goulimine *grand taxi* station (☎08/89.19.55). Very poor, despite the category, with no hot water, though friendly staff. ③

Hôtel Lakouara, Av. Hassan II (☎08/89.33.78). Good but block-booked by the UN. ③

EXPENSIVE

Hôtel Al Massira, 12 Av. de la Mecque (☎08/89.42.25). A quality hotel owned by *Club Med* but again UN block-booked at present. ⑤

Hôtel Nagjir, Place Bir Anzarane (☎08/89.41.68). New and very comfortable, with a restaurant, and, when open, a bar and disco (perhaps the only disco in Western Sahara). Not block-booked, but often full. ④

Hôtel Parador, Av. de l'Islam (☎08/89.45.00). The old Spanish grand hotel, once again taken over by the UN. ④

Restaurants

The hotels *Lakouara, Al Massira, Nagjir* and *Parador* have **restaurants**, but those at the *Parador* and *Al Massira* are not always open to non-UN personnel. Of the cheap places along Av. de la Mecque, the *Restaurant San Francisco* is the best value, clean and appetizing, with massive helpings. A hole-in-the-wall sandwich bar nearby at no. 126 is also a cut above.

For something a little more refined, the *Diamant Vert* by the filling station opposite the CTM on Av. de la Mecque, and the *Café-Restaurant La Marelka* on Av. Hassan II both offer moderately priced food in relaxed surroundings. Fast-food addicts will find low-priced relief at the hamburger joint behind the *Diamant Vert*.

The liveliest place to hang out in the evenings is **Souk Djemal**, particularly the *Café-Restaurant Tagadite* next to the market; if you fancy something more substantial than a mint tea, they also do good soup, while stalls around the café sell *meloni* and *harseh*. Fried fish is available from a couple of places behind the *Hôtel Victoire*.

The Town

Most of the new building is in the upper town; the bulk of the old Spanish settlement, more dishevelled, lies down below, stretching eastwards from the old **cathedral**, which is now closed (rusting notices proclaim it 'property of the Spanish government'). If you head east across the square in front, where Mums (and even some Dads) bring their kids to play of an evening, you pass a pair of fort-like buildings painted in yellow ochre and used by the military as HQs, and come into the district of **Souk Djaj** ('Chicken Market'), spread out along the northern side of Av. de la Marine. Pleasantly run-down, with a smattering of cheap hotels, its houses are typified by the eggshell-domed roofs said to cool the interior. A few tiled Spanish street signs are still in evidence, though most have been replaced by blue metal plaques painted in Arabic and French.

East of Souk Djaj, the district of **Ejercito** (Spanish for 'army') houses Moroccan troops as it did their Spanish predecessors. South of Av. de la Marine, some of the tubular barracks are now private houses, hemmed in by more modern, box-like, blocks of flats. The other district left from Spanish days is **Colomina**, to the south of Avenue de la Mecque. It is referred to popularly as Colomina Tarduss ('Kick') because, when the Spanish left, local people kicked in the doors to squat their houses. Nowadays, most of the quarter has been rebuilt.

A more workaday, working-class area is **Souk Djemal**, west of the Goulimine *grand taxi* station. This is where the **main market** is located and it is the most animated part of town, especially around dusk. It also shows perhaps a truer face of the new Laayoune than the grandiose monuments in the centre.

Most striking of the modern developments is the **Place Mechouar**, which is flanked by the new **Great Mosque**. Lining one side of the square is a series of tent-like canopies for shade and at each corner are towers to floodlight the square at night. There is also an ambitious **Palais des Congrès**, designed by King Hassan's then-favourite architect, French-born André Paccard. Across the way is the new **stadium**, which, if the Moroccans have their way, and FIFA decide to "go for Africa", will be a venue for World Cup football before very long.

In addition to such public statements, there are a few pleasant corners, like the landscaped gardens of the **Colline des Oiseaux**, with their cages of exotic birds – with blinds to be drawn down over the cages in the event of sandstorms. Of some interest, too, is the **Complexe Artisanal**, behind the Great Mosque, where twenty little workshops, capped with cupolas, provide space for metal, wood and jewellery craftsmen.

Listings

Banks are located at the foot of Bd. Mohammed V, near Place Hassan II. They include: *BMCE, Banque Populaire, BCM, Wafabank* and *Banque Al Maghrib*. *BMCE* and *Banque Populaire* also have branches in Place Dchira, as do *Banque Populaire* and *Unibon* in Av. Hasan II.

Buses CTM departures are from outside their office at 80 Av. de la Mecque. There are four daily: 8am to Dakhla, 8.30am to Agadir (these two are through services, often full, especially in summer or holiday time), 3pm to Marrakesh direct and 6pm to Agadir. ONCF buses run from Supratours office on Av. Oum Saad at the southern end of Av. Moulay Ismail. They leave for Dakhla at 7.15am, and for Agadir and Marrakesh at 5pm, 6pm (via Smara) and 9pm. The only other bus service from Laayoune is *Etoile du Sahara's* noon departure for Tan Tan leaving from Place Bir Anzarane in front of the *Hôtel Nagjir*.

Car rental No major firms are represented and there is a rapid turnover of small operators due to shortage of punters, so it's best to phone ahead if you intend to rent a car. At present two companies rent out vehicles: *Souabi* (☎08/89.36.61), and *Laayoune Cars* (☎08/89.47.44); both have offices near Place Dchira.

Cinema The *Palace Cinema* is in Rue Moulay Abdelaziz, off Av. Hassan II by no. 62.

Hammams There's one just off Av. de la Marine (southside) between Pl. Hassan II and *Hôtel Marhaba*, but more renowned is the *Hammam Samir* next to a mosque in the Ha'i El Kacem districts not far from Souk Djemal.

Flights *RAM*, 7 Place Bir Anzarane by the *Hôtel Nagjir* (☎08/89.40.77), operate flights from the town airport (a short taxi ride or long walk east of town; ☎08/89.40.77) to Agadir (5 weekly), Casablanca (5 weekly), Dakhla (3 weekly), Tan Tan (1 weekly), and Las Palmas (2 weekly).

International Phone Calls Only at present possible from the post office.

Post office The main office is on Av. de la Mecque, on the first bend coming from the *Hôtel El Massira* towards Place Dchira. There is no sign, but look for the Moroccan flag fluttering above it. Opening hours are 8.30am–noon and 2.30–6.30pm except Fridays when lunch break is 11.30am–3pm. Only the phone section is open Saturday afternoons and Sundays. The old post office is on Pl. Hassan II, complete with its original weighing machine marked 'Correos' in Spanish.

Supermarket Try the Baida at 111 Av. de la Maque.

Taxis There are four *grand taxi* stations, as follows: for Goulimine, Agadir, Inezgane and occasionally Marrakesh, they leave from Soule Lamkhaleh at the western end of Av. Hassan II; for Boujdor and Dakhla they leave from a rank out near the airport; for Smara and Tan Tan, they leave from Rue Djekelama off the Smara road; while for Laayoune Plage, there is a rank in Colomina. Landrover taxis can be chartered in Av. Mazouir, again just off the Smara road.

Tourist office There may be no tourists in town but there's a tourist delegation and information office on Av. de l'Islam, opposite the *Parador* (☎08/89.22.33).

Laayoune Plage

LAAYOUNE PLAGE is 20km distant: leave town on the P41 to Boujdor, then, past the airport, turn right off the main road and quickly left at a sign to *Camping Touristique*. At the beach – which is very windy, year round, with big Atlantic breakers – there is a sporadically open café-restaurant. If you want to camp, you'll find the site 2km north beyond the beach settlement, reached along a rough piste; it is a large compound with cold showers, electricity and a little shop, open all year. In July and August, reputedly, it can get very full with Moroccans from Smara and Tan Tan. The nearby *Club Med* annex has been requisitioned by the government and is unlikely to reopen for tourism in the foreseeable future.

South from Laayoune to Dakhla

Continuing **south of Laayoune** down to Dakhla is pretty routine now, and you no longer need special permission. There are daily CTM/ONCF buses along this route (they start out from Agadir) and *grand taxi* runs; the bus is often full, so you'll have to push your way on if you want to pick it up en route. The road is reasonably good, though drivers should beware of occasional sand-drifts, and camels grazing by or on the road. Foreigners will need to form-fill at numerous checkpoints along the way.

Laayoune to Dakhla

The first habitation along the road is **LEMSID**, 110km from Laayoune, which, if you're not into travel for travel's sake, or heading towards Mauritania, is perhaps the place to turn round. A small **café-shop** provides basic meals for the route's lorry drivers.

South of Lemsid, the sea is guarded by cliffs most of the way to the newly developed fishing port of **BOUJDOR**. The landscape here is a little more mellow, with a long beach to the north. Rocks, however, make the sea dangerous for swimming and surfing. The village has a filling station, various cafés and a **hotel**, the *Boughraz* (no water; ⑩); a large tent encampment is on the outskirts. The hotel lobby doubles up as a cinema, which is the main excitement going, though the old Portuguese lighthouse can be visited if you find yourself stuck for something to do. A three-star hotel is planned for Boujdor in the future.

South again from Boujdor the road runs inland, rejoining the coast at the tiny settlement of SKAYMAT – less of an oasis than it looks on the map.

Dakhla

Some 544km from Laayoune, you reach the town of **DAKHLA** (or AD DAKHLA) on a long spit of land. This was a Spanish outpost, known as Villa Cisneros in the colonial days, when it served as a minor administrative centre for the Rio de Oro, though the only remains are a church and the odd manhole cover. It remains military in character, and once you have explained your presence, you should be prepared to mix largely with soldiers.

Dakhla is small, compact and easy to find your way around, but should you need any help, the **tourist office** is at 1 rue Tiris (☎08/89.83.89). There are half a dozen basic **hotels**, the best of which are the *Hôtel Doubs* (⓪), to the left on entering the town, near a large barracks, and the *Hôtel Bahia* (⓪), close to the bus depot. There's also a **campsite**. It's not the most compelling resort, but there are lovely beaches nearby, superb fishing, and there's even a **bar** in town, *Bar Juan*, which conjures up real beers. The Garage Mechanique Général on the seafront are **landrover experts** who you may wish to visit for a last minute pit stop before the long journey south – or north.

The road to Mauritania

If you are travelling south from **Dakhla to the Mauritanian border** you will have to obtain a *laisser-passer* from the *Suretée*, for which you must apply at least a day in advance. These are becoming little more than a formality, but you will need a **Mauritanian visa** and all the relevant documents for your vehicle; if you are without a vehicle, you will first have to find one to take you; the campsite is the best place to ask around. Armed with your *laisser-passer*, you can join one of the **twice-weekly convoys** (Thursday and Friday) with Moroccan military protection down to **LA GOUÈRA**, the Moroccan frontier post, and then with Mauritanian troops from **NOUADHIBOU**.

The route, it scarcely needs to be said, is quite an adventure: 464km of mixed piste and tarmac down to Nouadibhou, crossing the tropic just south of Dakhla. Tsetse fly are said to be a problem in La Gouèra, so be sure to carry some repellant.

Coming the other way, your big problem is that the Mauritanian authorities do not allow exit by land via Nouadibhou-La Gouèra, on the grounds that the border area is mined and dangerous. It would be unwise to try and dodge the Mauritanian border post, as there are genuinely minefields. If you find the Mauretanians are letting vehicles through, the Moroccan authorities will not give you any problems on entry, and you should be able to travel up to Dakhla with the next convoy.

travel details

Buses

From Laayoune to Dakhla (1 daily, 9hr); Agadir (3 daily, 11hr 30min) via Goulimine (7hr); Marrakesh (4 daily, 15hr); Smara (1 daily, 3hr); Tan Tan (4 daily, 3hr 30min).

From Smara to Laayoune (1 daily, 3hr); Marrakesh (1 daily, 13hr 15min) via Tan Tan (2hr) and Agadir (9hr).

From Dakhla to Agadir (1 daily, 20hr 30min) via Laayoune (9hr); Tan Tan (12hr 30min); Goulimine (16hr).

From Tan Tan to Laayoune (4 daily, 4hr); Smara (1 daily, 3hr); Dakhla (1 daily, 12hr); Agadir (8 daily, 7hr 30min) via Goulimine (3hr); Marrakesh (6 daily, 12hr); Casablanca (1 daily, 16hr); Safi (1 daily, 13hr) via Essaouira (11hr).

Grands Taxis

From Laayoune to Smara (3hr); Tan Tan (3hr 30min); Dakhla (6hr); Goulimine (5hr).

From Smara to Laayoune (3hr); Tan Tan (2hr); Agadir (9hr); Marrakesh (12hr); Goulimine (4hr 30min).

From Tan Tan to Goulimine (2hr 30 min); Inezgane (6hr); Agadir (6hr 15min); Smara (3hr); Laayoune (3hr 30min); Tan Tan Plage (20min).

Flights

From Tan Tan to Laayoune (1 weekly); Casablanca (1 weekly).

From Laayoune to Agadir (5 weekly); Casablanca (5 weekly); Dakhla (3 weekly); Las Palmas (2 weekly); Tan Tan (1 weekly).

From Dhakla to Laayoune (3 weekly).

PART THREE

THE

CONTEXTS

THE HISTORICAL FRAMEWORK

Morocco's emergence as a nation-state is astonishingly recent, dating from the occupation of the country by the French and Spanish at the turn of this century, and its independence in 1956. Prior to this, it is best seen as a kind of patchwork of tribal groups, whose shifting alliances and sporadic bids for power defined the nature of government.

With a handful of exceptions, the country's ruling sultans controlled only the plains, the coastal ports and the regions around the imperial capitals of Fes, Marrakesh, Rabat and Meknes. These were known as *Bled El Makhzen* – the governed lands, or, more literally, "Lands of the Storehouse". The rest of the Moroccan territories – the Rif, the three Atlas ranges and the outlying deserts – comprised *Bled es Siba*, "Lands of the Dissidents". Populated almost exclusively by Berbers, the region's original (pre-Arab) inhabitants, they were rarely recognized as being under anything more than local tribal authority.

The balance between government control and tribal independence is one of the two enduring themes of Moroccan history. The other is the emergence, expansion and eventual replacement of the various **sultanate dynasties**. These at first seem dauntingly complicated – a succession of short-lived tribal movements and confusingly similar-named sultans – but there are actually just seven main groups.

The first of them, the **Idrissids**, became the model by founding the city of Fes towards the end of the eighth century and bringing a coalition of Berber and Arab forces under a central *makhzen* (government) authority. The last, the **Alaouites**, emerged in the mid-seventeenth century from the great palm oasis of Tafilalt and, continuing with the current king, Hassan II, still hold constitutional power. It is around these groups – together with the medieval dynasties of the **Almoravids, Almohads, Merenids, Wattasids** and **Saadians** – that the bulk of the following sections are organized.

PREHISTORY

The first inhabitants of the **Maghreb** – the Arab term for the countries of North Africa – probably occupied the **Sahara**, for thousands of years a great savannah fertile enough to support elephants, zebras and a whole range of other game and wildlife. Little is known about these ancestors of the human species, although it seems likely that there were groups of hunter-and-gatherer hominids here as early as 1,000,000 BC.

Around 15,000 BC there seem to have been **Paleolithic** settlements, and before the Sahara went into decline (from 3000 BC), primitive pastoral and agricultural systems had begun to develop. It is possible also to trace the arrival of two independent Stone-Age cultures in the Maghreb: the Neolithic **Capsian Man** (circa 10,000–5000 BC), probably emerging from Egypt, and, slightly later, **Mouillian Man**. From these people, fair-skinned and speaking a remote "Libyan" language, stem the cave and rock drawings of the pre-Sahara and High Atlas, the earliest archeological sites in Morocco.

PHOENICIANS AND CARTHAGINIANS

The recorded history of the area begins about 1100 BC with a series of trading settlements established by the **Phoenicians**. These were small, isolated colonies, most of them built on defensible headlands round the coast, and there was probably little initial contact between them and the inhabitants of the interior, whom they knew as Libyans and Ethiopians – or collectively as *Barbaroi*, or **Berbers**.

As the emphasis shifted away from the Phoenicians, and their African trading routes were taken over by the former colony of **Carthage** (modern Tunis), some of the ports grew into considerable cities, exporting grain and grapes, and minting their own coinage. On the "Moroccan" coast, the most important colonies were at **Lixus** (near Larache), **Tingis** (Tangier) and **Chellah** (near Rabat), but they spread as far east as Melilla; in the south a flourishing dye factory was also maintained on an island off Essaouira.

Officially, the Carthaginian Empire collapsed with its defeat in the **Punic Wars** (196 BC) against Rome, but in these provincial outposts, life seems to have been little affected. If anything, the colonies grew in stature and prosperity, absorbing hundreds of Punic refugees after the Roman sacking of Carthage. It was a first sign of Morocco's intrinsic historic and geographic isolation in what was to become known as *Maghreb El-Aska* (Land of the Farthest West). Even after the Romans had annexed and then abandoned the country, Punic was still widely spoken along the coast.

BERBER KINGDOMS AND ROMAN RULE

Prior to total Roman annexation, and the imposition of direct imperial rule in 24 AD, the "civilized" Moroccan territories for a while formed the **Berber kingdom of Mauritania**. This was probably little more than a confederation of local tribes, centred round **Volubilis** (near Meknes) and **Tangier**, but it gained a certain influence through alliance and occasional joint rule with the adjoining Berber state of **Numidia** (essentially modern Algeria).

The most important of the Berber rulers, and the only ones of which any substantial records survive, were **Juba II** (25 BC–23 AD) and his son **Ptolemy**. Both were heavily Romanized: Juba, an Algerian Berber by birth, was brought up and educated in Rome, where he married the daughter of Antony and Cleopatra. His reign, if limited in its extent, seems to have been orderly and prosperous, and under his son the pattern might well have continued. In 42 AD, however, Emperor Caligula summoned Ptolemy to an audience in Lyons and had him assassinated – so the story goes, for appearing in a more brilliant cloak than his own. Whatever the truth, and Rome may just have been eager for direct rule, it proved an inauspicious beginning.

ROMAN RULE

The early years of Rome's new imperial province were taken up with near-constant **rebellions** – the first one alone needing three years and over 20,000 troops to subdue.

Perhaps discouraged by this unexpected resistance, the **Romans** never attempted to colonize Morocco-Mauritania beyond its old limits. The Rif and Atlas mountains were left unpenetrated, and, of the interior, it was only **Volubilis** – already a city of sorts, and at the heart of the north's fertile vineyards and grain fields – that was in any way exploited. In this the Romans were establishing an enduring precedent: not just in their failure to subdue *Bled Es Siba*, which also defied the later sultans, but also in their treatment of Morocco as a useful "corridor" to the greater agricultural wealth of Algeria, Tunisia and Spain.

When the Roman legions were withdrawn in 253 AD, and the **Vandals** took power in southern Spain, the latter were interested only in taking Tangier and Ceuta for use as staging posts en route to northern Tunisia. Similarly, the **Byzantine General Belisarius**, who defeated the Vandals and laid claim to the Maghreb for Justinian's Eastern Empire, did little more than replace the Ceuta garrison.

It was understandable, of course. Any attempt to control Morocco would need manpower far in excess of these armies, and the only overland route through the country – across the Taza gap – was scarcely practicable even in peacetime. Not until the tenth century, and the great northward expansion of the desert nomads, was Morocco to become a land worthy of substantial exploitation in its own right, and even then only through the unifying and evangelizing impetus of Islam.

THE COMING OF ISLAM

The irruption of **Islam** into the world began in 622 AD, when the Prophet Muhammad moved with his followers from Mecca to Medina. Within thirty years they had reached the borders of India, to the east; were threatening Byzantine Constantinople, to the north; and had established themselves in the Maghreb at Kairouan in present-day Tunisia.

After this initial thrust, however, sweeping across the old provinces of the Roman world, the progress of the new religion was temporarily slowed. The Berbers of Algeria – mainly pagans but including communities of Christians and Jews – put up a strong and unusually unified resistance to Arab control. It was only in 680 that the governor of Kairouan, **Oqba Ibn Nafi**, made an initial foray into Morocco, taking in the process the territory's last Byzantine stronghold at Ceuta.

What happened afterwards is unclear. There is a story, perhaps apocryphal, that Oqba embarked on a 5000-kilometre **march through Morocco**, raiding and subjugating all in his path, and preaching Islam all the way to the west – the Atlantic Ocean. But whether this expedition had any real Islamicizing influence on the Moroccan Berbers is questionable. Oqba left no garrison forces and was himself killed in Algeria on his way back to Kairouan.

Islam may, however, have taken root among some of the tribes. In the early part of the eighth century the new Arab governor of the West, **Moussa Ibn Nasr**, returned to Morocco and managed to establish Arab control (and carry out mass conversions to Islam) in both the northern plains and the pre-Sahara. However, like the Romans and Byzantines before him, his main thrust was towards **Spain**. In 711, the first Muslim forces crossed over from Tangier to Tarifa and defeated the Visigoths in a single battle; within a decade the Moors had taken control of all but the remote Spanish mountains in northern Asturias; and their advance into Europe was only halted at the Pyrenees by the victory of Charles Martel at Poitiers in 732.

The bulk of this invading and occupying force were almost certainly **Berber converts** to Islam, and the sheer scale of their military success must have had enormous influence in turning Morocco itself into a largely Muslim nation. It was not at this stage, however, in any way an Arab one. The extent of the Islamic Empire – from Persia to Morocco, and ancient Ghana to Spain – was simply too great for Arab numbers. Early attempts to impose taxes on the Moroccan Berbers led to a rebellion and, once again outside the political mainstream, the Maghreb fragmented into a series of small, independent **principalities**.

THE IDRISSIDS (8TH–11TH CENTURIES)

The Maghreb's fragmentation found an echo in the wider events of the Muslim world, which was undergoing its first – and most drastic – dissension, with the split into **Sunni** and **Shia** sects. In Damascus the Sunni Ummayad dynasty took power, the Shi'ites dispersing and seeking refuge to both the east and west.

One of them, arriving in Morocco around 787, was **Moulay Idriss**, an evidently charismatic leader and a direct descendant (great-grandson, in fact) of the Prophet Muhammad. He seems to have been adopted almost at once by the citizens of Volubilis – then still a vaguely Romanized city – and by the Aouraba Berber tribe. He was to survive for three more years, before being poisoned by order of the Sunni caliph, but in this time he managed to set up the infrastructure of an essentially Arab court and kingdom – the basis of what was to become the Moroccan nation. Its most important feature, enduring to the present with Hassan II, was his being recognized as *Imam*. To the Moroccans this meant that he was both spiritual and political leader, "Commander of the Faithful" in every aspect of their lives.

Despite the brevity of Moulay Idriss's reign, and his sudden death in 791 or 792, his successors, the **Idrissids**, were to become the first recognizable Moroccan dynasty. Moulay Idriss himself left a son, born posthumously to a Berber woman, and in 807, after a period of an apparently orderly regency, **Moulay Idriss II** was declared sultan and *imam*. He ruled for a little over twenty years – something of a golden age for the emerging Moroccan state, with the extension of a central, Arabized authority throughout the north and even to the oases beyond the Atlas.

Idriss's most important achievement, however, was the establishment (if perhaps not the foundation) of the city of **Fes**. Here, he set up the apparatus of court government, and here he also welcomed large contingents of Shi'ite **refugees**. Most prominent among these were groups from Córdoba and Kairouan, then the two great cities of Western Islam. In incorporating them, Fes (and, by extension, Morocco) became increasingly Arabized, and was suddenly transformed into a major Arab centre in its own right. The **Kairaouine University** was established, becoming one of the three most important in Islam (and far ahead of those in Europe); a strong crafts tradition took root; and Fes became a vital link in the trade between Spain and the East, and between the Maghreb and Africa south of the Sahara.

Fes was to remain the major Moroccan city, and the country's Arab spiritual heart, right up until the present century. The Idrissid state, however, split once more into **principalities**, most of which returned to their old isolation, until, at the turn of the tenth century, the context began to change. In Al-Andalus – the Muslim territories of Spain – the Western Caliphate collapsed and itself splintered into small rival states. Meanwhile in Tunisia, the well-established Fatimid dynasty moved their capital to Egypt, clashed with their nominated governors, the Zirids, and unleashed upon them the hostile nomadic tribe of the Banu Hilal.

It was a move which was to have devastating effects on the Maghreb's entire lifestyle and ecological balance, as the **Hilali** nomads swept westwards, destroying all in their path, laying to ruin the irrigation systems and devastating the agricultural lands with their goats and other flocks. The medieval Maghrebi historian, **Ibn Khaldun**, described their progress as being like a swarm of locusts: "the very earth seems to have changed its nature", he wrote, "all the lands that the Arabs have conquered in the last few centuries, civilisation and population have departed from them".

THE ALMORAVIDS (1062–1145)

Morocco was to some extent cushioned from the Hilali, and by the time they reached its southern oases (where they settled), the worst was probably over. But with the shattered social order of the Maghreb, and complex power struggles in Moorish Spain, came an obvious vacuum of authority.

It was this which created the opportunity for the two great Berber dynasties of the Middle Ages – the **Almoravids** and the **Almohads**. Both were to emerge from the south, and in each case their motivating force was religious: a purifying zeal to **reform** or destroy the decadent ways which had reached Morocco from the wealthy Andalucian Muslims of Spain. The two dynasties together lasted only a century and a half, but in this period Morocco was the pre-eminent power of Western Islam, maintaining an **empire** that at its peak stretched right across the Maghreb to Libya, south to Senegal and ancient Ghana and north into Spain. Subsequent history and achievements never matched up to this imperial dream, though even today its memories are part of the Moroccan concept of nation.

"**Greater Morocco**", the nationalist goal of the late 1950s, sketched out areas that took in Mauritania, Algeria, Tunisia and Libya, while even the present war in the Sahara looks back to the reality of the medieval empires.

The **Almoravids** began as a reforming movement among the Sanhaja Berbers in Koumbi Saleh, capital of ancient Ghana, in what is now Mauritania. A nomadic desert tribe – similar to the Touaregs who occupy the area today – they had been converted to Islam in the ninth century, but perhaps only to nominal effect. The founders of the Almoravid movement, a local sheikh who had returned from the pilgrimage to Mecca and a *fakir* from the Souss plain, found widespread abuse of orthodox practice. In particular, they preached against drinking palm wine, playing licentious music and taking more than four wives. It held an appeal for this already ascetic, tent-dwelling people, and rapidly took hold.

Founding a *ribat* – a kind of warrior monastery similar to the Templar castles of Europe – the Almoravids soon became a considerable military force. In 1054, they set out from the *ribat* (from which the movement derived its name) to spread the message through a *jihad* (holy war), and within four years they had captured and destroyed the ancient empire of Ghana to the south. Turning towards Morocco, they established themselves in Marrakesh by 1062, and under the leadership of **Youssef bin Tachfine** went on to extend their rule throughout the north of Morocco and, to the east, as far as Algiers.

At no time before had any one leader exercised such strong control over these territories; nor had the tribes before been united under a single religious doctrine – a simple, rigorous and puritanical form of Sunni orthodoxy. And so it remained, at least as long as the impetus of *jihad* was sustained. In 1085, Youssef undertook his first, and possibly reluctant, expedition to **Spain**, invited by the Muslim princes of **Al-Andalus** after the fall of Toledo to the Christians. He crossed over the straits again in 1090, this time to take control of Spain himself. In this he was successful, and before his death in 1107, he had restored Muslim control to Valencia and other territories lost in the first wave of the Christian Reconquest.

The new Spanish territories had two decisive effects. The first was to reorientate Moroccan culture towards the far more sophisticated and affluent Andalucian civilization; the second to stretch the Almoravid forces too thin. Both were to contribute to the dynasty's decline. Youssef, disgusted by Andalucian decadence, had ruled largely from **Marrakesh**, leaving governors in Seville and other cities. After his death, the Andalucians proved disinclined to accept these foreign overlords, while the Moroccans themselves became vulnerable to charges of being corrupt and departing from their puritan ideals.

Youssef's son **Ali** was himself, in fact, extraordinarily pious, but he was unprepared for (nor interested in) ceaseless military activity; in Spain he turned to Christian mercenaries to maintain control. His reign, and that of the Almoravids, was effectively finished by the early 1140s, as a new movement, the Almohads, seized control of the main Moroccan cities one after another.

THE ALMOHADS (1145–1248)

Ironically, the **Almohads** shared much in common with their predecessors. Again, they were forged from the Berber tribes – this time in the High Atlas – and again, they based their bid for power on an intense puritanism. Their founder **Ibn Toumert,** attacked the Almoravids for allowing their women to ride horses (a tradition in the desert), for wearing extravagant clothes, and for being subject to what may have been Andalucian corruptions – the revived use of music and wine.

He also provoked a **theological crisis**, claiming that the Almoravids did not recognize the essential unitary and unknowable nature of God: the basis of Almohad belief, and the source of their name – the "unitarians". Banished from Marrakesh by Ali, Ibn Toumert set up a *ribat* in the Atlas at **Tin Mal**. Here he waged war on local tribes until they accepted his authority, and he eventually revealed himself to them as the Mahdi – "the chosen one" and the final prophet promised in the Koran.

Charismatic and brutal in his methods, Toumert was aided by a shrewd assistant and brilliant military leader, **Abd El Moumen**, who took over the movement after Toumert's death and extended the radius of their raids. In 1145, he was strong enough to displace the Almoravids from Fes, and two years later he drove them from their stronghold in Marrakesh. With the two cities subdued, he was now effectively sultan.

Resistance subsided and once again a Moroccan dynasty moved **towards Spain** – this time finally secured by the third Almohad sultan, **Yacoub El Mansour** (The Victorious), who in 1195 defeated the Christians at Alarcos. El Mansour also pushed the frontiers of the empire east to Tripoli, and for the first time, there was one single rule across the entire **Maghreb**, although it did not stretch as far south as under the Almoravids. With the ensuing wealth and prestige, Yacoub launched a great building programme – the first and most ambitious in Moroccan history – which included a new capital in **Rabat** and the magnificent (and in large part still surviving) gateways and minarets of Marrakesh and Seville.

Once more, though, imperial expansion precipitated disintegration. In 1212, Yacoub's successor, **Mohammed en Nasr**, attempted to drive the Spanish Christians as far back as the Pyrenees and met with decisive defeat at the battle of **Las Navas de Tolosa**. The balance of power in Spain was changing, and within four decades only the Kingdom of Granada remained in Muslim hands. In the Maghreb, meanwhile, the eastern provinces had declared independence from Almohad rule and Morocco itself was returning to the authority of local tribes. In 1248, one of these, the **Merenids** (or Beni Merin), took the northern capital of Fes and turned towards Marrakesh.

THE MERENIDS AND WATTASIDS (1248–1554)

This last (300-year) period of Berber rule in Morocco is very much a tailpiece to the Almoravid and Almohad empires – marked by increasing domestic **instability** and economic stagnation, and signalling also the beginning of Morocco's **isolation** from both the European and Muslim worlds. Under the Merenids, the Spanish territories were not regained, and Granada, the last Moorish city, fell to Ferdinand and Isabella in 1492. Portuguese sea power saw to it that foreign seaports were established on the Atlantic and Mediterranean coasts. To the east, the rest of the Maghreb fell under Turkish domination, as part of the Ottoman Empire. The Portuguese ability to navigate beyond Mauretania also meant the eventual end of the trans-Sahara caravan route.

In Morocco itself, the main development was a centralized administrative system – the **Makhzen** – which was maintained without tribal support by standing armies of Arab and Christian mercenaries. It is to this age that the real distinction of *Bled El Makhzen* and *Bled Es Siba* belongs – the latter coming to mean everything outside the immediate vicinities of the imperial cities.

THE MERENIDS

Perhaps with this background it is not surprising that few of the twenty-one **Merenid sultans** – or their cousins and successors, the Wattasids – made any great impression. The early sultans were occupied mainly with Spain, at first in trying to regain a foothold on the coast, later with shoring up the Kingdom of Granada. There were minor successes in the fourteenth century under the "Black Sultan", **Abou El Hassan**, who for a time occupied Tunis, but he was to die before being able to launch a planned major invasion of Al-Andalus, and his son, **Abou Inan**, himself fell victim to the power struggles within the mercenary army.

The thirteenth and fourteenth centuries, however, did leave a considerable **legacy of building**, perhaps in defiance of the lack of political progress (and certainly a product of the move towards government by forced taxation). In 1279, the garrison town of **Fes El Djedid** was established, to be followed by a series of brilliantly endowed colleges, or **medersas**, which are among the finest surviving Moorish monuments. Culture, too, saw a final flourish. The historians **Ibn Khaldun** and **Leo Africanus**, and the travelling chronicler **Ibn Battuta**, all studied in Fes under Merenid patronage.

THE WATTASIDS

The **Wattasids**, who usurped Merenid power in 1465, had ruled in effect for 45 years previously as a line of hereditary viziers. After their coup, they maintained a semblance of control for a little under a century, though the extent of the Makhzen lands was by now minimal.

The **Portuguese** had annexed and colonized the seaports of Tetouan, Ceuta, Tangier, Asilah, Agadir and Safi, while large tracts of the interior lay in the hands of religious warrior brotherhoods, or **marabouts**, on whose alliances the sultans had increasingly to depend.

THE SAADIANS AND CIVIL WAR (1554–1669)

The rise and fall of the **Saadians** was in some respects a replay of all of the dynasties that had come before them. They were the most important of the *marabouts* to emerge in the early years of the sixteenth century, rising to power on the strength of their religious positions (they were *Shereefs* – descendants of the Prophet), climaxing in a single, particularly distinguished reign, and declining amid a chaos of political assassinations, bitter factional strife and, in the end, civil war.

As the first **Arab dynasty** since the Idrissids, they marked the end of Moroccan Berber rule, though this was probably less significant at the time than the fact that theirs was a government with no tribal basis. The *Makhzen* had to be even further extended than under the Merenids, and Turkish guards – a new point of intrigue – were added to the imperial armies.

Slower to establish themselves than the preceding dynasties, the Saadians began by setting up a small principality in the **Souss**, where they established their first capital in **Taroudannt**. Normally, this would have formed a regular part of *Bled El Makhzen*, but the absence of government in the south allowed them to extend their power to **Marrakesh** around 1520, with the Wattasids for a time retaining Fes and ruling the north.

In the following decades the Saadians made breakthroughs along the coast, capturing Agadir in 1540 and driving the Portuguese from Safi and Essaouira. When the Wattasids fell into bankruptcy and invited the Turks into Fes, the Saadians were ready to consolidate their power. This proved harder, and more confusing, than anyone might have expected. **Mohammed esh Sheikh**, the first Saadian sultan to control both the southern and northern kingdoms, was himself soon using Turkish troops, and was subsequently assassinated by a group of them in 1557. His death unleashed an incredibly convoluted sequence of factional murder and power politics, which was only resolved, somewhat fortuitously, by a battle with the Portuguese twenty years later.

THE BATTLE OF THE THREE KINGS

This event, **The Battle of the Three Kings**, was essentially a Portuguese crusade, led by the youthful King Sebastião on the nominal behalf of a deposed Saadian king against his uncle and rival. At the end of the day all three were to perish on the battlefield, the Portuguese having suffered a crushing defeat, and a little-known Saadian prince emerged as the sole acknowledged ruler of Morocco.

His name was **Ahmed** "**El Mansour**" (The Victorious, following this momentous victory), and he was easily the most impressive sultan of the dynasty. Not only did he begin his reign clear of the intrigue and rivalry that had dogged his predecessors, but he was immensely wealthy as well. Portuguese ransoms paid for the remnants of their nobility after the battle had been enormous, causing Portugal to go bankrupt – the country, with its remaining Moroccan enclaves, then passed into the control of Habsburg Spain.

Breaking with tradition, Ahmed himself became actively involved in European politics, generally supporting the Protestant north against the Spanish and encouraging Dutch and British trade. Within Morocco he was able to maintain a reasonable level of order and peace, and diverted criticism of his use of Turkish troops (and his own Turkish-educated ways) by embarking on an **invasion of Timbuktu** and the south. This secured control of the Saharan salt mines and the gold and slave routes from Senegal, each sources of phenomenal wealth, which won him the additional epithet of *El Dhahabi* (The Golden One). It also reduced his need to tax Moroccans, which made him a popular man.

CIVIL WAR AND PIRACY

Ahmed's death in 1603 caused abrupt and lasting chaos. He left three sons, none of whom could gain authority, and, split by **civil war**, the country once again broke into a number of principalities. A succession of **Saadian rulers** retained power in the Souss and in Marrakesh (where their tombs remain testimony to the opulence and turbulence of the age); another *marabout* force, the **Djila**, gained control of Fes; while around Salé and Rabat arose the bizarre **Republic of the Bou Regreg**.

The Bou Regreg depended almost entirely on **piracy**, a new development in Morocco, though well established along the Mediterranean coasts of Algeria and Tunisia. Its practitioners were the last Moors to be expelled from Spain – mainly from Granada and Badajoz – and they conducted a looting war primarily against Spanish ships. For a time they had astounding success, raiding as far away as the Irish coast, dealing in arms with the British and the French, and even accrediting foreign consuls.

MOULAY ISMAIL AND THE EARLY ALAQUITES (1665–1822)

Like the Saadians, the **Alaouites** were *Shereefs*, first establishing themselves as religious leaders – this time in Rissani in the **Tafilalt**. Their struggle to establish power also followed a similar pattern, spreading first to Taza and Fes and finally, under Sultan **Moulay Rashid**, reaching Marrakesh in 1669. Rashid, however, was unable to enjoy the fruits of his labour, since he was assassinated in a particularly bloody palace coup in 1672. It was only with Moulay Ismail, the ablest of his rival sons, that an Alaouite leader gained real control over the country.

MOULAY ISMAIL

The reign of **Moulay Ismail**, perhaps the most notorious in all of Morocco's history, stretched over 55 years (1672–1727) and was to be the country's last stab at imperial glory. In Morocco, where his shrine in Meknes is still a place of pilgrimage, he is remembered as a great and just, if unusually ruthless, ruler; to contemporary Europeans – and in subsequent historical accounts – he is noted for extravagant cruelty. His rule certainly was tyrannical, with arbitrary killings and an appalling treatment of his slaves, but it was not much worse than that of the European nations of the day; the seventeenth century was the age of the witch trials in Protestant Europe, and of the Catholic Inquisition.

Nevertheless, Moulay Ismail stands out among the Alaouites because of the grandness of the scale on which he acted. At **Meknes**, which he made his new imperial capital, he garrisoned a permanent army of some 140,000 Black troops, a legendary guard he had built up personally through slaving expeditions in Mauritania and the south, as well as by starting a human breeding programme. The army kept order throughout the kingdom – Morocco is today still littered with their Kasbah garrisons – and were able to raise taxes as required. The Bou Regreg pirates, too (the so-called Sallee Rovers), were brought under the control of the state, along with their increasingly lucrative revenues.

With all this, Ismail was able to build a palace in Meknes that was the rival of its contemporary, Versailles, and he negotiated on equal terms with the **Europeans**. Indeed, it was probably the reputation he established for Morocco that allowed the country to remain free for another century and a half before the European colonial powers began carving it up.

SIDI MOHAMMED AND MOULAY SLIMANE

Like all the great, long-reigning Moroccan sultans, Moulay Ismail left innumerable sons and a terminal dispute for the throne, with the powerful standing army supporting and dropping heirs at will.

Remarkably, a capable ruler emerged fairly soon – Sultan **Sidi Mohammed** – and for a while it appeared that the Shereefian empire was moving back into the mainstream of European and world events. Mohammed recaptured the port of El Jadida from the Portuguese, founded the port of Essaouira, traded and conducted treaties with the Europeans, and even recognized the **United States of America** – the first ruler to do so.

At his death in 1790, however, the state collapsed once more into civil war, the two capitals of Fes and Marrakesh in turn promoting claimants to the throne. When this period drew to some kind of a close, with **Moulay Slimane** (1792–1822) asserting his authority in both cities, there was little left to govern. The army had dispersed; the *Bled Es Siba* reasserted its old limits; and in Europe, with the ending of the Napoleonic wars, Britain, France, Spain and Germany were all looking to establish themselves in Africa.

Moulay Slimane's rule was increasingly isolated from the new realities outside Morocco. An intensely orthodox Muslim, he concentrated the efforts of government on eliminating the power and influence of the **Sufi brotherhoods** – a power he underestimated. In 1818 Berber tribes loyal to the Derakaoui brotherhood rebelled and, temporarily, captured the Sultan. Subsequently, the sultans had no choice but to govern with the co-operation of local sheikhs and brotherhood leaders.

Even more serious, at least in its long-term effects, was Moulay Slimane's isolationist attitude towards **Europe**, and in particular to Napoleonic France. Exports were banned; European consuls banished to Tangier; and contacts which might have helped maintain Moroccan independence were lost.

MOULAY HASSAN AND EUROPE DOMINATION

Once started, the European domination of Moroccan affairs took an inevitable course – with an outdated, medieval form of government, virtual bankruptcy and armies press-ganged from the tribes to secure taxes, there was little that could be done to resist it.

The first pressures came from the **French**, who defeated the Ottomans in 1830 and occupied Algiers. Called to defend his fellow Muslims, Sultan **Abd Er Rahman** (1822–59) mustered a force but was severely defeated at Isly. In the following reign of **Mohammed III** (1859–73), **Spanish** aspirations were also realized with the occupation of Tetouan – regained by the Moroccans only after the offer to pay Spain massive indemnities and provide them with an Atlantic port (which the Spanish later claimed in Sidi Ifni).

MOULAY HASSAN

Outright occupation and colonization were by the end of the nineteenth century proving more difficult to justify, but both the French and the Spanish had learned to use every opportunity to step in and "protect" their own nationals. Complaints by **Moulay Hassan**, the last precolonial sultan to have any real power, actually led to a debate on this issue at the 1880 **Madrid Conference**, but the effect was only to regularize the practice on a wider scale, beginning with the setting up of an "international administration" in Tangier.

Moulay Hassan could, in other circumstances, have proved an effective and possibly inspired sultan. Acceding to the throne in 1873, he embarked on an ambitious series of modernizing **reforms**, including attempts to stabilize the currency by minting the *rial* in Paris, to bring in more rational forms of taxation, and to retrain the army under the instruction of Turkish and Egyptian officers. The times, however, were against him. He found the social and monetary reforms obstructed by foreign merchants and local *caids*, while the European powers forced him to abandon plans for other Muslim states' involvement in the army.

Moulay Hassan played off the Europeans as best he could, employing a British military chief of staff, **Caid MacClean**, a French military mission and German arms manufacturers. On the frontiers, he built Kasbahs to strengthen the defences at Tiznit, Saïdia and Selouane. But the government had few modern means of raising money to pay for these developments. Moulay Hassan was thrown back on the traditional means of taxation, the *harka*, setting out across the country to subdue the tribes and to collect tribute. In 1894, returning across the Atlas on just such a campaign, he died.

SULTANS

The last years of independence under Moulay Hassan's sons, Moulay Abd El Aziz and Moulay Hafid, were increasingly dominated by Europe.

The reign of **Abd El Aziz** (1894–1907), in particular, signalled an end to the possibilities of a modern, independent state raised by his reforming father. The sultan was just a boy of ten at his accession, but for the first six years of his rule the country was kept in at least a semblance of order by his father's vizier, **Bou Ahmed**. In 1900, however, Bou Ahmed died, and Abd El Aziz was left to govern alone – surrounded by an assembly of Europeans, preying on the remaining wealth of the court.

The first years of twentieth-century Morocco were marked by a return to the old ways. In the Atlas mountains, the tribal chiefs established ever-increasing powers, outside the government domain. In the Rif, a pretender to the throne, **Bou Hamra**, led a five-year revolt, coming close to taking control of Fes and the northern seat of government.

European manipulation during this period was remorselessly cynical. In 1904, the French negotiated agreements on "spheres of influence" with the British (who were to hold Egypt and Cyprus), and with the Italians (who got Tripolitana, or Libya). The following year saw the German Kaiser Wilhelm visiting Tangier and swearing to protect Morocco's integrity, but he was later bought off with the chance to "develop" the Congo. France and Spain, meanwhile, had reached a secret arrangement on how they were going to divide Morocco and were simply waiting for the critical moment.

In 1907, the French moved troops into **Oujda**, on the Algerian border and, after a mob attack on French construction workers, into Casablanca.

Abd El Aziz was eventually deposed by his brother, **Moulay Hafid** (1907–12), in a last attempt to resist the European advance. His reign began with a coalition with the principal Atlas chieftain, **Madani El Glaoui**, and intentions to take military action against the French. The new sultan, however, was at first preoccupied with putting down the revolt of Bou Hamra – whom he succeeded in capturing in 1909. By this time the moment for defence against European entrenchment, if indeed it had ever been possible, had passed. Claiming to protect their nationals – this time in the mineral mines of the Rif – the Spanish brought over 90,000 men to garrison their established port in Melilla. Colonial occupation, in effect, had begun.

THE TREATY OF FES

Finally, in 1910, the two strands of Moroccan dissidence and European aggression came together. Moulay Hafid was driven into the hands of the French by the appearance of a new pretender in Meknes – one of a number during that period – and, with Berber tribesmen under the walls of his capital in Fes, was forced to accept their terms.

These were ratified and signed as the **Treaty of Fes** in 1912, and gave the French the right to defend Morocco, represent it abroad and conquer the *Bled Es Siba*. A similar document was also signed with the Spanish, who were to take control of a strip of territory along the northern coast, with its capital in Tetouan and another thinner strip of land in the south, running eastwards from Tarfaya. In between, with the exception of a small Spanish enclave in Sidi Ifni, was to be French Morocco. A separate agreement gave Spain colonial rights to the Sahara, stretching south from Tarfaya to the borders of French Mauritania.

The arbitrary way in which these boundaries were drawn was to have a profound effect on modern Moroccan history. When Moroccan nationalists laid claim to the Sahara in the 1950s – and to large stretches of Mauritania, Algeria and even Mali – they based their case on the obvious artificiality of colonial divisions.

THE FRENCH AND SPANISH PROTECTORATES (1912–56)

The fates of **Spanish and French Morocco** under colonial rule were to be very different. When **France** signed its Protectorate agreement with the sultan in 1912, its sense of **colonial mission** was running high. The colonial lobby in France argued that the colonies were vital not only as markets for French goods but because they fulfilled France's "mission civilisatrice" – to bring the benefits of French culture and language to all corners of the globe.

There may have been Spaniards who had similar conceptions of their role in North Africa, but reality was very different. **Spain** showed no interest in developing the Sahara until the 1960s; in the north the Spanish saw themselves more as conquerors than colonists. Its government there, described by one contemporary as a mixture of "battlefield, tavern and brothel", did much to provoke the Rif rebellions of the 1920s.

LYAUTEY AND "PACIFICATION"

France's first resident-general in Morocco was **General Hubert Lyautey**, often held up as the ideal of French colonialism with his stated policy: "Do not offend a single tradition, do not change a single habit." Lyautey recommended respect for the terms of the Protectorate agreement, which placed strict limits on French interference in Moroccan affairs. He recognized the existence of a functioning Moroccan bureaucracy based on the sultan's court with which the French could co-operate – a hierarchy of officials, with diplomatic representation abroad, and with its own social institutions.

But there were other forces at work: French soldiers were busy unifying the country, ending tribal rebellion; in their wake came a system of roads and railways that opened the country to further colonial exploitation. For the first time in Moroccan history, the central government exerted permanent control over the mountain regions. The "**pacification**" of the country brought a flood of French settlers and administrators.

In France these developments were presented as echoing the history of the opening up of the American Wild West. Innumerable articles celebrated "the transformation taking place, the stupendous development of Casablanca port, the birth of new towns, the construction of roads and dams . . . The image of the virgin lands in Morocco is contrasted often with metropolitan France, wrapped up in its history and its routines. . .".

Naturally, the interests of the natives were submerged in this rapid economic development,

and the restrictions of the Protectorate agreement were increasingly ignored.

SPAIN AND REVOLT IN THE RIF

The early history of the **Spanish zone** was strikingly different. Before 1920 Spanish influence outside the main cities of Ceuta, Melilla and Tetouan was minimal. When the Spanish tried to extend their control into the Rif mountains of the interior, they ran into the fiercely independent Berber tribes of the region.

Normally, the various tribes remained divided, but faced with the Spanish troops they united under the leadership of **Abd El-Krim**, later to become a hero of the Moroccan nationalists. In the summer of 1921, he inflicted a series of crushing defeats on the Spanish army, culminating in the massacre of at least 13,000 soldiers at **Annoual**. The scale of the defeat, at the hands of tribal fighters armed only with rifles, outraged the Spanish public and worried the French, who had Berber tribes of their own to deal with in the Atlas mountains. As the war began to spread into the French zone, the two colonial powers combined to crush the rebellion. It took a combined force of around 360,000 colonial troops to do so.

It was the last of the great tribal rebellions. Abd El-Krim had fought for an independent **Rifian state**. An educated man, he had seen the potential wealth that could result from exploiting the mineral deposits of the Rif. After the rebellion was crushed, the route to Moroccan independence changed from armed revolt to the evolving middle-class resistance to the colonial rulers.

NATIONALISM AND INDEPENDENCE

The French had hoped that by educating a middle-class elite they would find native allies in the task of binding Morocco permanently to France. It had the opposite effect. The educated classes of Rabat and Fes were the first to demand reforms from the French that would give greater rights to the Moroccans. When the government failed to respond, the demand for reforms escalated into demands for total independence.

Religion also played an important part in the development of a nationalist movement. France's first inkling of the depth of nationalist feeling came in 1930, when the colonial government tried to bring in a **Berber dahir** – a law setting up a separate legal system for the Berber areas. This was an obvious breach of the Protectorate agreement, which prevented the French from changing the Islamic nature of government. Popular agitation forced the French to back down.

It was a classic attempt to "divide and rule", and as the nationalists gained strength, the French resorted more and more to threatening to "unleash" the Berber hill tribes against the Arab city dwellers. They hoped that by spreading Christianity and setting up French schools in Berber areas, the tribes would become more "Europeanized" and, as such, useful allies against the Muslim Arabs.

Up until World War II, Morocco's **nationalists** were weak and their demands aimed at reforming the existing system, not independence. After riots in 1937, the government was able to round up the entire executive committee of the small nationalist party. But with French capitulation in the war, the climate changed. In 1943, the party took the name of **Istiqlal** (Independence); the call for complete separation from France grew more insistent.

The loyal performance of Moroccan troops during the war had raised hopes of a fairer treatment for nationalist demands, but post-war France continued to ignore Istiqlal, exiling its leaders and banning its publications. During the postwar period, it steadily developed into a mass party – growing from 10,000 members in 1947 to 100,000 by 1951.

To some extent, the developments of the 1950s, culminating in Moroccan independence in 1956, resemble events in Algeria and Tunisia. The French first underestimated the strength of local independence movements, then tried to resist them and finally had to concede defeat. In Algeria and Tunisia, the independence parties gained power and consolidated their positions once the French had left. But in Morocco, Istiqlal was never uncontested after 1956 and the party soon began to fragment – becoming by the 1970s a marginal force in politics.

The decline and fall of Istiqlal was due mainly to the astute way in which Sultan (later King) **Mohammed V** associated himself with the independence movement. Despite threats from the French government, Mohammed became more and more outspoken in his support for independence, paralysing government opera-

tions by refusing to sign legislation. Serious rioting in 1951 persuaded the French to act: after a period of house arrest, the sultan was sent into exile in 1953.

This only increased his popularity. After a brief attempt to rule in alliance with **Thami El-Glaoui**, the Berber pasha of Marrakesh who saw the sultan's absence as an opportunity to expand his power base in the south, the French capitulated in 1955, allowing the sultan to return. The government in Paris could see no way out of the spiralling violence of the nationalist guerrillas and the counterviolence of the French settlers. Perhaps equally significant, they could not sustain a simultaneous defence of three North African colonies – and economic interests dictated that they concentrate on holding Algeria. In 1956, Morocco was given full **independence** by France and Spain.

On independence, Sultan Mohammed V changed his title to that of king, foreshadowing a move towards a **constitutional monarchy**.

MOHAMMED V

Unlike his ancestor sultans, **Mohammed V** had inherited a united country with a well-developed industrial sector, an extensive system of irrigation and a network of roads and railways. But years of French administration had left little legacy of trained Moroccan administrators. Nor was there an obvious party base or bureaucracy for the king to operate within.

In 1956, Istiqlal party members held key posts in the first **government**. The regime instituted a series of reforms across the range of social issues. Schools and universities were created, a level of regional government was introduced and ambitious public works schemes launched. There were moves, also, against European "decadence", with a wholesale cleanup of Tangier, and against the unorthodox religious brotherhoods – both long-time targets of the Istiqlal.

Mohammed V, as **leader of the Muslim faith** in Morocco and the figurehead of independence, commanded huge support and influence in Morocco as a whole. In government, however, he did not perceive the Istiqlal as natural allies. The king bided his time, building links with the army – with the help of Crown Prince Hassan, whose period as commander-in-chief was a defining moment in his political development – and with the police.

Mohammed's influence on the army would prove a decisive factor in the Moroccan state withstanding a series of **rebellions** against its authority. The most serious of these were in the Rif, in 1958–59, but there were challenges, too, in the Middle Atlas and Sahara. The king's standing and the army's efficiency stood the test. Crown Prince Hassan, meanwhile, as the army commander, helped to translate internal pressures into renewed nationalism. The army began a quasi-siege in the south, exerting pressure on the Spanish to give up their claims to the port of **Sidi Ifni**.

In party politics, Mohammed's principal act was to lend his support to the **Mouvement Populaire** (MP), a moderate party set up to represent the Berbers, and for the king a useful counterweight to Istiqlal. In 1959, the strategy paid its first dividend. Istiqlal was seriously weakened by a split which hived off the more left-wing members into a separate party, the **Union Nationale des Forces Populaires** (UNFP) under Mehdi Ben Barka. There had always been a certain tension within Istiqlal between the moderates and those favouring a more radical policy, in association with the unions. A tendency towards parties dividing within and among themselves has been apparent in Moroccan politics ever since, helping to maintain the primal role of the Palace in the political arena.

MODERN MOROCCO: HASSAN II (1961–)

The death of Mohammed V in 1961 led to the accession of **King Hassan II**, the current monarch. Now, towards the end of its fourth decade, his reign represents perhaps the longest period of stability – albeit with some uncertain episodes – in the country's troubled history.

In many respects the nation's **development since independence** has been remarkable. The French had built an administrative capital in Rabat and a relatively sophisticated infrastructure in Casablanca and other economically useful zones, but most other regions were left without adequate roads, health and education facilities or other trappings of a modernizing state. In the kingdom's northern and southern extremities, Spanish colonial rule left even less on which the new state could base its policy of creating viable development. At independence, there was an almost total absence of doctors or graduates in the Spanish zones.

Despite the poverty still apparent in so much of the country, it should be remembered that in less than four decades much has been done to bring the whole kingdom into the twentieth century. It is an achievement in the face of a huge **population explosion** which means there are now more than 30 million Moroccans. They form a predominantly youthful population – more than 40 percent are aged under 14 – and are clamouring for the sort of jobs and education of which their parents and grandparents were routinely deprived. Indeed, a critical problem for governments at the turn of the century is that these sorts of jobs are in very short supply, and graduate unemployment is perhaps as high as 70 or 80 percent.

VALUES AND TRADITIONAL ROLES

While the quest for modernization has been one theme running through post-independence Morocco, **traditional values** – as perceived by the Palace – are another important factor in understanding the contemporary kingdom.

In many respects Hassan is a very modern monarch, regularly pictured playing golf, flying a jet fighter, or meeting fellow heads of state. As a power politician he has few peers. But he is also careful to maintain his status as a traditional ruler – one of the very few left in the Afro-Arab world. When in his flowing robes at a state occasion or religious festival, Hassan is *Al-Amir Al-Muminin* (Commander of the Faithful), **Morocco's religious leader** as well as its temporal ruler.

This role is of great political significance as it adds to Hassan's prestige in the country and gives his monarchy the sort of deep-rooted legitimacy so lacking in other developing countries. Presiding over a complex system of traditional loyalties, ethnic and regional divisions, Hassan has used traditions based in the days of the Sultanate to underpin his modern monarchy – and so far they have served him well.

This is one reason why the Palace remains at the centre of the Moroccan political universe and why one word from the king carries more weight than all the debates in a parliamentary session, the decisions of his most powerful ministers or even international opinion. Hassan himself has stated that it would be an abnegation of his religious role as king if he were not to play a central role in government.

Critics say that for the system to evolve Hassan must genuinely devolve power. Through the promotion of multi-party politics – which in early 1998 saw a coalition led by opposition politicians form the government – and of more responsive local authorities (*collectivités locales*) a form of **devolution** is under way. Hassan has even talked of dividing the country along federal lines, with the German *länder* as a model. Also pointing to the emergence of a new Morocco in the 1990s has been the emergence of literally thousands of **non-governmental organizations** (NGOs) and other associations.

The continued postponement of general elections in the period 1989–97 was explained in part by the political system's inability to develop a new configuration in which the Throne would remain dominant with increased input from a wider **body of opinion**. Those pushing to be heard include a growing younger generation of professionals who feel alienated from the traditional political parties, which are mostly still run by men who emerged during the independence struggle and Hassan's first years as monarch.

Riots in Fes in December 1990 showed that there was a large urban underclass whose voice must also be heard, but perhaps surprisingly, such incidents have been rare in recent years. Far more common – and underlining tensions within the kingdom – have been strikes by workers for improved living conditions, protests by unemployed graduates, and sometimes violent incidents in the kingdom's universities, where the student movement linked to Morocco's biggest opposition party, the **Union Socialiste des Forces Populaires** (USFP) has been in retreat as a growing Islamist movement has taken control of student unions.

The **rise of radical Islam** across the Arab world, and notably in neighbouring Algeria which has been torn apart by civil conflict since 1991-92, has not left Morocco unaffected. However, King Hassan feels confident in his unique blend of religious authority – moulded by listening to the mosque as well as to more Westernized opinion – and the efficiency of his security forces. The security forces monitor dissident sentiment closely, especially in such Islamist recruiting grounds as local mosques, and have undoubtedly played a part in avoiding the emergence of a mass Islamist movement such as the *Front Islamique du Salut* (FIS) across the border in Algeria.

Islamist sentiments, though, retain the potential to provoke popular rebellions against established regimes throughout the Arab world, and other challenges must be faced. The Palace has understood that the political system must evolve to meet the demands of a fast-liberalizing economy and an increasingly literate, urbanized population. And Hassan, who will turn seventy in 2001, must retain all his finely developed political faculties to be sure of handing over a peaceful kingdom to **Crown Prince Sidi Mohammed**, his heir apparent.

CONSTITUTION AND ELECTIONS

Domestic politics since independence have centred on a battle of wills between the dominant political forces in the kingdom: the Palace and its allies; a legalized opposition which has at times succumbed to the temptation to enter government; and underground movements such as the Marxist-Leninist Ilal Amam (which has all but disappeared) and, more recently, groups of Islamist radicals.

Even before independence, in a 1955 speech, Mohammed V had promised to set up "democratic institutions resulting from the holding of free elections". The country's first constitution was not ready until after his death, however. It was only in 1962, under Hassan II, that it was put to, and approved by, a popular referendum.

The constitution was drafted in such a way as to favour the pro-monarchy parties of the centre. In the **1963 elections** that followed, a coalition of loyalist parties, the *Front pour la Défense des Institutions Constitutionelles* (FDIC), won a majority of seats, though with a strong showing still by the Istiqlal, whose powerbase was in Fes and the agricultural belt of the north, and by the UNFP, who held much support in the Souss and in Casablanca.

In the political struggles which followed, an increasingly radicalized UNFP criticized not just the government (which was possible) but also the king (which was not). It was no great surprise when in 1963 the authorities "discovered" a plot against Hassan's life in which UNFP leaders were implicated. There followed the **Ben Barka affair**, one of the most notorious episodes in modern Moroccan (and French) history. Ben Barka, the UNFP leader, seeking exile in France, was assassinated there – an incident whose political ramifications have endured into the 1990s.

The UNFP subsequently split, with the largest element going on to form the *Union Socialiste des Forces Populaire* (USFP), led by Abderrahim Bouabid until his death in 1992. Party politics were not allowed to develop as the opposition would have liked and Hassan was able to rule without democratic institutions. Despite the increasingly strident attacks on what it called a "feudal" and "paternalistic" regime, the UNFP never managed to develop a coherent platform from which it could oppose the king and build real popular support.

The weakness of the parties was further revealed in 1970, when Hassan announced a new constitution, to bring an end to emergency rule. Its terms gave the king greater control over parliament, but events in 1971–72 were to show the real nature of the threat to the monarchy. In July 1971, a group of soldiers led by an army general broke into the royal palace in Skhirat in an attempt to stage a **coup**; more than 100 people were killed, but in the confusion Hassan escaped. The following year another attempt was launched, as the king's private jet was attacked by fighters of the Moroccan Air Force. Again, he had a very narrow escape – his pilot was able to convince the attacking aircraft by radio that the king had already died. The former interior minister, General Mohamed Oufkir, seems to have been behind the 1972 coup attempt and it was followed by a major shake-up in the armed forces. Oufkir died soon after; his family remained imprisoned and incommunicado until 1991.

THE GREEN MARCH AND SAHARAN WAR

The king's real problem was to give a sense of destiny to the country, a cause similar to the struggle for independence that had brought such prestige to his father.

That cause was provided in 1975, when the Spanish finally decided to pull out of their colony in the **Western Sahara**. In the 1950s Istiqlal had laid claim to the Sahara, as well as parts of Mauritania, Algeria and Mali, as part of its quest for a "greater Morocco". By 1975, Hassan had patched up the border dispute with Algeria and recognized the independent government in Mauritania; it turned out this was only a prelude to a more realistic design – Moroccan control of the Western Sahara.

The discovery of **phosphate reserves** in the Sahara during the 1960s brought about Spain's first real attempt to develop its Saharan colony. Before then it had been content merely to garrison the small coastal forts in Dakhla (then known as Villa Cisneros) and La Guera, with occasional forays into the interior to pacify the tribes. With increased investment in the region during the 1960s, the nomads began to settle in the newly created towns along the coast, particularly the new capital in Laayoune. As education became more widespread, the Spanish were confronted with the same problem the French had faced in Morocco thirty years earlier – the **rise of nationalism**.

Pressure began to mount on General Franco's government to decolonize one of the last colonies in Africa. In 1966, he promised the UN that Spain would hold a referendum "as soon as the country was ready for it". Economic interests kept Spain from fulfilling its promise, and in 1969 work began on opening the phosphate mines in Boukraa. Meanwhile, the Saharans began to press the case for independence themselves. In 1973, they formed the *Frente Popular para la Liberación de Saguia El-Hamra y Rio de Oro*, or **Polisario**, which began guerrilla operations against the Spanish. Polisario gained in strength as Spain began to signal it would pull out of the Sahara and as the threat to Saharan independence from Morocco and Mauritania grew more obvious.

Spanish withdrawal in 1975 coincided with General Franco's final illness. King Hassan timed his move perfectly, sending some 350,000 Moroccan civilians southward on **Al Massira** – the "Green March" or **La Marche Verte** – to the Sahara. Spain could either go to war with Morocco by attacking the advancing Moroccans or take the easy way out and withdraw without holding the promised referendum. Hassan's bluff worked, and the popular unrest of the 1960s and the coup attempts of 1971–72 were forgotten under a wave of patriotism. Without shedding any blood, Morocco had "recaptured" part of its former empire.

In November 1975 a secret agreement was reached in Madrid to divide the Spanish Sahara between Morocco and Mauritania as soon as Spanish troops had withdrawn. But both parties had underestimated the native Sahrawis' determination to fight for an independent Sahara, their Saharan Arab Democratic Republic (SADR). Nearly 40,000 of them fled the Moroccan advance, taking refuge in Mauritania and Algeria.

In an unprecedented move, Algeria ceded an area of its territory in the desolate *Hamada* region southeast of **Tindouf** to Polisario. Sahrawi refugees – along with a number of Moroccan-born dissidents – settled in camps run by Polisario. According to the best estimates there were about 165,000 people living in five tented and increasingly unhygienic camps by 1989. Polisario, however, had managed to set up schools and hospitals in these most unpromising circumstances – winning many friends abroad in the process, much to Morocco's displeasure.

The camps also formed a base for the movement's government-in-exile, the SADR, and a launch pad for a classic guerrilla campaign against Morocco and Mauritania, until Sahrawi pressure proved too much for Nouakchott and it withdrew from its alliance with Morocco in 1979. By the early 1980s Polisario had succeeded in closing the territory's mines and had pinned the Moroccan *Forces Armées Royales* (FAR) into an area round the capital, Laayoune, and Dakhla in the south.

The early success of Polisario's campaign said much for the Sahrawi's prowess as desert guerrilla fighters – a fact Morocco's FAR battle-hardened officers now willingly concede, even if the intensely nationalist local press does not. It also owed much to the high level of military support offered by Algeria, which used Polisario as a stick with which to beat Morocco, its perceived rival for regional dominance.

But beginning in 1981, the FAR built a series of heavily defended **desert walls** that excluded the Polisario from successively larger areas of the desert. By 1985, the phosphate mines were back in use and by 1987 the sixth wall had effectively blocked off Polisario from Mauritania and left only 15 percent of the land area outside Moroccan control. Meanwhile the government was making concerted attempts to win the approval of the Saharan residents, injecting vast sums into creating a model city and capital in Laayoune.

Under United Nations auspices, a **ceasefire** was agreed in the spring of 1989 – and there has been no major military conflict since. Protracted negotiations have continued for a referendum to be held among the Sahrawis to determine their future state. In the early stages of negotiation, King Hassan met with a Polisario deputation in Marrakesh, and promised that if

the Sahrawis voted for independence, Morocco would be the first nation to open an embassy in Laayoune.

Such talk reflected a new confidence in the situation, and a conviction, seemingly shared among all parties, that the conflict had burned itself out – but eight years after the UN announced its ceasefire, the path to a referendum remains apparently blocked, although a vote was promised for 1998-99 – after the perennial issue of voting lists was resolved.

A resolution to the dispute is essential. With Algeria in turmoil, the Saharan dispute remains a potential point of conflict in a volatile region. A lasting settlement would also help efforts to promote regional unity. These had seemed promising when in February 1989 Algerian, Libyan, Mauritanian, Moroccan and Tunisian leaders met in Marrakesh and agreed to form the long-awaited regional grouping, the **Arab Maghreb Union** (known by its evocative acronym UMA, from the French *Union de Maghreb Arabe* but sounding like the Arabic word *'umma*, or community). However, this initiative has been stalled in recent years by disputes, and by civil war in Algeria.

ECONOMIC AND SOCIAL PROBLEMS

The attention and budget demanded by the Saharan war compounded economic problems for Morocco. By 1981, an estimated 60 percent of the population were living below the poverty level, unemployment ran at approximately 20 percent (40 percent among the young) and perhaps 20 percent of the urban population lived in shantytowns, or *bidonvilles.*

Official figures for **unemployment** and even gross domestic product (GDP) are often approximate. The young "student" operating as a guide in Fes or Marrakesh may well not appear in national employment figures. The shopkeeper he leads you to could also be in the informal economy, outside the tax net and compass of official data. And despite sometimes strenuous efforts to modernize and rationalize economic behaviour in the 1970s and 1980s, the "**informal sector**" remains enormous – perhaps equal in size to GDP, fuelled by farmers and traders who exist outside the tax net, and by the cannabis trade in northern Morocco.

Informal economic activity and the family network (for many still the only effective system of social services they know) have acted as a safety-valve for a hard-pressed population. The informal economy also finances some of Morocco's richest citizens, whose huge wealth – reflected in the opulent villas, discreetly hidden in the most upmarket quarters of major cities, such as Casablanca's "California" suburb – may also not appear in official data.

Throughout much of the 1980s, the government, preoccupied by the war, seemed to neglect its pressing **social problems**; indeed, an austerity campaign to please international creditors, including a wage freeze and a cut in subsidies for basic foodstuffs, appeared to increase the problems even more for the poor. In June 1981 a one-day **protest strike** in Casablanca led to at least 100 deaths and the jailing of demonstrators – including the USFP leader Bouabid and fourteen socialist members of parliament.

Local **elections** were held in June 1983, and appeared to be a resounding royalist victory, providing the government with a mandate to continue with its austerity measures. But the opposition parties, including Istiqlal, complained of electoral fraud, and the failure to proceed with parliamentary elections in October showed that all was not well. Using Article 19 of the constitution, Hassan assumed all executive and legislative power, **governing by decree** in the absence of an elected government. It was a brave move on his part. The government was facing bankruptcy and if the IMF was to reschedule Morocco's massive debts, the **austerity campaign** would have to become even harsher. Hassan announced a 12.5 percent cut in government expenditure and massive cuts in subsidies, and then stood alone to face the backlash.

Demonstrations against the cuts began in Marrakesh in early January 1984, and within a week had spread north to Nador and Al Hoceima. Later, **"bread riots"** broke out in Oudja and Tetouan. By the end of the month between 100 and 600 people had died. Hassan announced on television that further cuts in subsidies would be postponed, but a massive campaign of arrests and long prison terms also followed.

THE IMF AND EU

Despite the pessimistic assessments of many analysts, the 1984 bread riots were not repeated later in the decade and the 1980s will be remembered as a period of relative social peace, economic hard times and consolidations in the Western Sahara after several years of setbacks. In September 1984 Hassan went to the polls once more and was rewarded with the re-election of a centrist-royalist coalition.

Following the mid-1980s economic crisis – which was compounded by a build-up of international debt, contracted in the over-optimistic mood of the previous decade when Morocco hoped that rising phosphate prices (which then did not hold) would do for it what rising oil prices did for the OPEC states – relations with the **IMF** and the World Bank have been a constant factor in Moroccan life. The struggle to mobilize sufficient funds to finance essential imports and schemes in priority sectors like agriculture, power and water is ever present. Without international support, achieving sustainable economic growth would have proved impossible – although Moroccans also place much store in their native entrepreneurial talents. In sectors ranging from vehicle assembly to marketing, Morocco has developed domestic industries to a relatively high level, and the opening up of a more liberal economy in the 1990s has created one of the Arab world's most vibrant private sectors.

Substantial international support remains essential, however, and has forced Morocco to depart from its nineteenth-century image as "the China of the West" and seek closer ties with a wide range of countries. Relations with the IMF, World Bank and bilateral supporters have prompted moves towards liberalizing the economy in the period since Morocco's first rescheduling in 1984. In 1989 Hassan called for all non-strategic public companies and holdings to be privatized. A **privatisation** minister was appointed, and many public companies and services have passed into the private sector, a trend which has increased their efficiency.

Meanwhile, with the king firmly nailing his colours to the mast of economic liberalization, new efforts were made to encourage foreign investment in technologically advanced manufacturing industries, **textiles** and, an increasingly important earner, **tourism**. Modern management skills have begun to take hold with the emergence of a new managerial class independent of the old social loyalties.

Morocco's controversial application to join the **European Union**, made in the 1980s, was rejected. But Brussels has pushed European governments to develop closer relations with the kingdom and in 1996 Morocco's became only the second Arab government (after Tunisia) to sign one of the European Union's new **Euro-Mediterranean Partnership** agreements, an accord which opens the way for the kingdom to join a free trade zone planned for the region in the early 2000s.

Greater access to European markets and closer ties with the EU back Morocco's claims to be an ideal base for investment by multinationals and smaller companies on the flank of the Mediterranean – a region now promoting itself as a manufacturing and services centre for Europe's **southern sunbelt**, the projected focus for EU growth over the next few decades. If this strategy succeeds, Morocco hopes to achieve the high levels of economic growth enjoyed by the "new dragons" of the Pacific Rim. At a more sobering level, this is essential if it is to meet the demands of its fast-growing, youthful and increasingly well-educated population.

CHANGE AND ELECTIONS

The opposition, which had been quiet through much of the 1980s, started to reassert itself in the new decade. In May 1990, the **Chamber of Representatives** (parliament) debated the first ever motion of censure against a Moroccan government, criticizing its economic management. This failed, but pointed to changing attitudes. Traditional opposition parties showed revived enthusiasm for challenging the government – though not the king – with the knowledge that if their opposition failed, younger Moroccans may be tempted to follow Islamist and other illegal political trends. King Hassan, for his part, also seems aware of the need for change.

Despite delays to parliamentary elections, major changes were achieved in the mid-1990s, most notably through Morocco cleaning up its previously appalling **human rights** record. It was finally understood that a bad press abroad could damage international relations. In 1992, the leading dissident, Abraham Serfaty, was one of many well-known figures in a **release of political prisoners** that included many soldiers held since the 1972 failed coup in a dungeon prison at Tazmamart in the High Atlas.

Former student radicals, who may have been imprisoned in the 1970s and 1980s, now hold positions of responsibility in the local press,

universities and even government departments. As a new **civil society** has begun to emerge – especially in the liberalized commercial capital of Casablanca. Serious weekly newspapers such as the Casablanca-based *L'Economiste* have taken root, as has a woman's magazine *La Citidine*, which challenges social taboos, and a more vibrant local press.

In 1996 Hassan judged there to be sufficient consensus on the direction of Moroccan politics to hold a referendum on constitutional reforms, opening the way for a new bi-cameral parliamentary system. Local and national elections were held in 1997 and for the first time there seemed the prospect of bringing the opposition into government, with genuine power.

Disappointingly, the elections produced a lacklustre campaign and much voter apathy, as a three-way split gave right-wing, centrist and left-wing/nationalist groupings a similar number of seats in the lower house of parliament. This meant that, once again, the nation's dominant figures, King Hassan and his powerful Interior Minister **Driss Basri**, would act as arbiters between rival groups. After a long period of power-broking, King Hassan appointed the USFP leader **Abderrahmane Youssoufi** prime minister. He, in turn, appointed Morocco's first government of "alternance", including USFP and Istiqlal ministers.

These moves – and indeed the polls themselves – represent a cautious move towards wider democracy, and may have given those at the centre of power more time to reshape and modernize the political system ahead of the eventual succession of **Crown Prince Sidi Mohammed**. The election campaign and polling were seen as the fairest and freest of Morocco's elections to date.

ISLAMIST POLITICS

While leftists dominated the opposition in the first three decades of independence, **radical Islam** poses the greatest challenge in the 1990s – especially given Hassan's status as *Al Amir al Muminin* (Commander of the Faithful). However, Morocco has not followed neighbouring Algeria on a path of violence, despite incidents between rival student groups and an isolated armed attack – for which Algerian-French radicals were charged – on a hotel in Marrakesh in 1994.

One notable factor in the 1997 general election was that Islamist deputies were voted into parliament for the first time, under the **Mouvement Populaire Constitutionnel et Démocratique (MPCD)** banner. An entryist move into the MPCS by members of Abdelilah Benkirane's **Attajdid wal Islah** (Renewal and Reform) movement had revived the small, inactive party led by veteran nationalist Abdelkrim Khatib, and was rewarded with nine seats from 142 candidates. This was welcomed by the new prime minister, Youssoufi, as a move "reinforcing the ranks of the opposition".

This parliamentary debut for the Islamists came at a time when their calls for a change in views on public morality and private sector development were gaining appeal among those most alienated by increasing social tensions and allegations of corruption. A growing number of Moroccans wear modern urban Islamist fashions, and small neighbourhood mosques and Islamic charitable organizations are in vogue. Whether this leads to greater public support for more radical parties remains a key question. The future success of the Islamists – who are already the biggest political force in universities – could hinge on whether further liberalization in a society already regarded as the most liberal in North Africa will enrich people sufficiently to woo them away from thoughts of radicalism.

The rise of the Islamicists provides an urgency to such moves, as does the question of King Hassan's succession. Whether parliament can deliver is anyone's guess. There is at least a genuine parliamentary mix, and when the opposition entered government after the 1998 elections, they did so on the promise of social and legal reforms, as well as the maintenance of economic liberalization. It is imperative that solutions are found to these pressing issues for Morocco to remain at peace with itself.

CHRONOLOGY: MONUMENTS

10,000–5000 BC	**Capsian** and **Mouillian Man** spread across the Maghreb Neolithic cultures	**Rock carvings** in Oukaïmeden, Foum El Hassan and other less accessible sites
1100 BC	**Phoenician** settlements	Bronze Age. First trading port in **Lixus** (near Larache)
500 BC	**Carthaginians** take over Phoenician settlements and greatly expand them	Remains in Lixus, and in Rabat Archaeological Museum
146 BC	Fall of Carthage at end of the Third Punic War; Roman influence spreads into **Berber kingdoms** of Mauritania-Numidia	Bust of Juba II (Rabat)
27 BC	Direct **Roman** rule under Emperor Caligula	**Volubilis** developed as provincial capital; other minor sites at Lixus and Tangier Mosaics in Tetouan and Rabat museums
253 AD	Roman legions withdrawn	
429	**Vandals** pass through	
535	**Byzantines** occupy Ceuta	

ISLAM

622	Muhammad and followers move from Mecca to Medina and start spread of Islam	
ca. 705	**Moussa Ibn Nasr** establishes Arab rule in north and pre-Sahara, and in 711 leads Berber invasion of Spain	

IDRISSID DYNASTY (788–923)

788	**Moulay Idriss** establishes first Moroccan Arab dynasty	Founding of Moulay Idriss and Fes
807	Moulay Idriss II (807–836)	**Fes** developed with Kairouan and Andalucian refugee quarters, and establishment of Kairaouine Mosque
10th–11th c.	Hilali tribes wreak havoc on Maghrebi infrastructure	

ALMORAVID DYNASTY (1062–1145)

1062	**Youssef bin Tachfine** establishes capital in Marrakesh; first great Berber dynasty	**Koubba** in **Marrakesh** is only surviving monument, except for walls and possibly a minaret in **Tit** (near El Jadida)
1090	Almoravid invasion of **Spain**	

ALMOHAD DYNASTY (1147–1248)

1120s	**Ibn Toumert** sets up a ribat in Tin Mal in the High Atlas	Ruined mosque of **Tin Mal**
1145–1147	**Abd El Moumen** takes first Fes and then Marrakesh	Extensive building of walls, gates and **minarets**, including the Koutoubia in **Marrakesh**
1195	**Yacoub El Mansour** (1184–99) extends rule to Spain, and east to Tripoli	New capital begun in **Rabat**: Hassan Tower, Oudaia Gate
1212	Defeat in Spain at Las Navas de Tolosa	

MERENID DYNASTY (1248–1465)

Abou Youssef Yacoub (1258–86) establishes effective power

Zaouia and mausoleum in **Chellah** (Rabat); new city (El Djedid) built in **Fes**

Abou El Hassan (1331–51) and **Abou Inan** (1351–58), two of the most successful Merenids, extend rule briefly to Tunis

Medersas in Fes (Bou Inania, Attarin, etc), Meknes and Salé

Portuguese begin attacks on Moroccan coast, taking Ceuta and later other cities

Portuguese cistern in El Jadida; walls and remains in Azzemour, Asilah and Safi

WATTASID DYNASTY (1465–1554)

Wattasids – Merenid viziers – usurp power
Fall of **Granada**, last Muslim kingdom in Spain; Jewish and Muslim refugees settle in Morocco over next 100 years or so

Chaouen built and **Tetouan** founded again by refugees

Marabouts establish *zaouias*, controlling parts of the country

SAADIAN DYNASTY (1554–1669)

Mohammed esh Sheikh (d. 1557) founds dynasty in Marrakesh

Saadian Tombs and **Ben Youssef medersa** (Marrakesh); pavilion extensions to **Kairaouine** Mosque (Fes)

Battle of Three Kings leads to accession of **Ahmed El Mansour** (1578–1603), who goes on to conquer Timbuktu and the gold and slave routes to the south

El Badi palace (Marrakesh)

Pirate **Republic of Bou Regreg** set up by Andalucian refugees

Rabat Medina

ALAOUITE DYNASTY (1669–)

Moulay Ismail imposes the Alaouite dynasty on Morocco

New imperial capital in **Meknes** (Ismail's mausoleum, etc); **Kasbahs** and **forts** built; **palaces** in Tangier and Rabat

Sidi Mohammed (1757–90)

Ismail and his successors rebuild **grand mosques**, etc, especially in **Marrakesh,** where many later Alaouites make their capital – many of the city's **pavilions** and **gardens** date from the early eighteenth century

Moulay Suleiman (1792–1822)

Final burst of **palace** building – El Badi (Marrakesh), Palais Jamai (Fes)

Treaty of Fes brings into being French and Spanish **"Protectorates" (1912–56)**

European **Villes Nouvelles** built outside the Moroccan Medinas; **"Mauresque"** architecture developed for administrative buildings

T'Hami El Glaoui becomes Pasha of Marrakesh **(1907)**. French use T'Hami El Glaoui to conquer the southern tribes **(1912)**

Glaoui palaces in Telouet and Marrakesh; **Kasbah** fortresses throughout the south

Riffian revolt under Abd El Krim **(1921)**

Nationalist **Istiqlal** party formed in Fes **(1943)**

Independence (1956)

Accession of **Hassan II (1961)**

Green March into Western Sahara (1975)

New royal **palaces** in all major cities – most recently and spectacularly in Agadir
Hassan II Mosque in Casablanca

Democratic elections (1997)

ISLAM IN MOROCCO

It's difficult to get any grasp of Morocco, and even more so of Moroccan history, without first knowing something of Islam. What follows is a very basic background: some theory, some history and an idea of Morocco's place in the modern Islamic world. For more depth on each of these subjects, see the book listings on p.582.

BEGINNINGS: PRACTICE AND BELIEF

Islam was a new religion born of the wreckage of the Greco-Roman world beyond the Mediterranean. Its founder, a merchant named **Muhammad*** from the wealthy city of Mecca (now in Saudi Arabia), was chosen as God's Prophet: in about 609 AD, he began to receive divine messages which he transcribed directly into the **Koran** (*Qu'ran*), Islam's Bible. This was the same God worshipped by Jews and Christians – Jesus *(Aïssa* in Arabic) is one of the major prophets in Islam – but Muslims claim that he had been misunderstood by both earlier religions.

The distinctive feature of this new faith was directness – a reaction to the increasing complexity of established religions and an obvious attraction. In Islam there is no intermediary between man and God in the form of an institutionalized priesthood or complicated liturgy, as in Christianity; and worship, in the form of prayer, is a direct and personal communication with God. Believers face five essential requirements, the so-called **"Pillars of faith":** prayer five times daily (*salat*); the pilgrimage (*hadj*) to Mecca; the Ramadan fast (*sanm*); almsgiving (*zakat*); and, most fundamental of all, the acceptance that "There is no God but God and Muhammad is His Prophet" (*shahada*).

---

*"Muhammad" is the standard spelling today of the Prophet's name – and a more accurate transcription from the Arabic. In Morocco there is some cause for confusion in that the name of the former king, Mohammed V, is still spelled that way on maps and street signs and in most Western histories.

THE PILLARS OF FAITH

The Pillars of Faith are still central to Muslim life, articulating and informing daily existence. Ritual **prayers** are the most visible. Bearing in mind that the Islamic day begins at sunset, the five daily times are sunset, after dark, dawn, noon and afternoon. Prayers can be performed anywhere, but preferably in a mosque, or in Arabic, a *djemaa*. In the past, and even today in some places, a *muezzin* would climb his minaret each time and summon the faithful.

Nowadays, the call is likely to be less frequent, and prerecorded; even so, this most distinctive of Islamic sounds has a beauty all its own, especially when neighbouring *muezzins* are audible simultaneously. Their message is simplicity itself: "God is most great (*Allah Akhbar*). I testify that there is no God but Allah. I testify that Muhammad is His Prophet. Come to prayer, come to security. God is great." Another phrase is added in the morning: "Prayer is better than sleep".

Prayers are preceded by ritual washing and are recited with the feet bare. Facing Mecca (the direction indicated in a mosque by the *mihrab*), the worshipper recites the Fatina, the first chapter of the Koran: "Praise be to God, Lord of the worlds, the Compassionate, the Merciful, King of the Day of Judgement. We worship you and seek your aid. Guide us on the straight path, the path of those on whom you have bestowed your Grace, not the path of those who incur your anger nor of those who go astray." The same words are then repeated twice in the prostrate position, with some interjections of *Allah Akhbar*. It is a highly ritualized procedure, the prostrate position symbolic of the worshipper's role as servant (Islam literally means "obedience"), and the sight of thousands of people going through the same motions simultaneously in a mosque is a powerful one. On Islam's holy day, Friday, all believers are expected to attend prayers in their local grand mosque. Here the whole community comes together in worship led by an *imam*, who may also deliver the *khutba*, or sermon.

Ramadan is the name of the ninth month in the lunar Islamic calendar, the month in which the Koran was revealed to Muhammad. For the whole of the month, believers must obey a rigorous fast (the custom was originally modelled on Jewish and Christian practice), forsaking all forms of consumption between sunrise and sundown; this includes food, drink, cigarettes and any form of sexual contact. Only a few categories of people are exempted: travellers, children, pregnant women and warriors engaged in a *jihad*, or holy war. Given the climates in which many Muslims live, the fast is a formidable undertaking, but in practice it becomes a time of intense celebration.

The pilgrimage, or **hadj**, to Mecca is an annual event, with millions flocking to Muhammad's birthplace from all over the world. Here they go through several days of rituals, the central one being a sevenfold circumambulation of the Kaba, before kissing a black stone set in its wall. Islam requires that all believers go on a *hadj* as often as is practically possible, but for the poor it may well be a once-in-a-lifetime occasion, and is sometimes replaced by a series of visits to lesser, local shrines – in Morocco, for instance, to Fes and Moulay Idriss.

Based on these central articles, the new Islamic faith proved to be inspirational. Muhammad's own Arab nation was soon converted, and the Arabs then proceeded to carry their religion far and wide in an extraordinarily rapid territorial expansion. Many peoples of the Middle East and North Africa, who for centuries had only grudgingly accepted Roman paganism or Christianity, embraced Islam almost immediately.

DEVELOPMENT IN MOROCCO

Islam made a particularly spectacular arrival in Morocco. **Oqba Ibn Nafi**, the crusading general who had already expelled the Byzantines from Tunisia, marked his subjugation of the far west by riding fully armed into the waves of the Atlantic. "O God," he is said to have exclaimed, "I call you to witness that there is no ford here. If there was, I would cross it".

This compulsory appreciation of Morocco's remoteness was prophetic in a way, because over the succeeding centuries Moroccan Islam was to acquire and retain a highly distinctive character. Where mainstream Islamic history is concerned, its development has been relatively straightforward – it was virtually untouched, for instance, by the Sunni–Shia conflict that split the Muslim world – but the country's unusual geographical and social circumstances have conspired to tip the balance away from official orthodoxy.

Orthodoxy, by its very nature, has to be an urban-based tradition. Learned men – lawyers,

Koranic scholars and others – could only congregate in the cities where, gathered together and known collectively as the *ulema*, they regulated the faith. In Islam, this included both law and education. Teaching was at first based entirely in the mosques; later, it was conducted through a system of colleges, or *medersas*, in which students would live while studying at the often adjoining mosque. In most parts of the Islamic world, this very learned and sophisticated urban hierarchy was dominant. But Morocco also developed a powerful tradition of **popular religion**, first manifested in the eighth-century Kharijite rebellion – which effectively divided the country into separate Berber kingdoms – and endures to this day in the mountains and countryside.

MARABOUTS

There are three main strands of this popular religion, all of them deriving from the worship of saints. Everywhere in Morocco, as well as elsewhere in North Africa, the countryside is dotted with small domed **marabouts**: the tombs of holy men, which became centres of worship and pilgrimage. This elevation of individuals goes against strict Islamic teaching, but probably derives from the Berbers' pre-Islamic tendency to focus worship round individual holy men. At its simplest local level, these saint cults attracted the loyalty of the Moroccan villages and the more remote regions.

More prosperous cults would also endow educational institutions attached to the *marabout*, known as **zaouias**, which provided an alternative to the official education given in urban *medersas*. These inevitably posed a threat to the authority of the urban hierarchy, and as rural cults extended their influence, some became so popular that they endowed their saints with genealogies traced back to the Prophet. The title accorded to these men and their descendents was *shereef*, and many grew into strong political forces. The classic example in Morocco is the tomb of Moulay Idriss – in the eighth century just a local *marabout*, but eventually, the base of the Idrissid clan, a centre of enormous influence that reached far beyond its rural origins.

Loyalty to a particular family – religiously sanctified, but essentially political – was at the centre of the shereefian movements. In the third strand of popular devotion, the focus was more narrowly religious. Again, the origins lay in small, localized cults of individuals, but these were individuals worshipped for their magical and mystical powers. Taken up and developed by subsequent followers, their rituals became the focal point of **brotherhoods** of initiates.

THE AISSAOUA

Perhaps the most famous Moroccan brotherhood is that of Sidi Mohammed Bin Aissa. Born in Souss in the fifteenth century, he travelled in northern Morocco before settling down as a teacher in Meknes and founding a *zaouia*. His powers of mystical healing became famous there, and he provoked enough official suspicion to be exiled briefly to the desert – where he again revealed his exceptional powers by proving himself immune to scorpions, snakes, live flames and other hostile manifestations. His followers tried to achieve the same state of grace. Six hundred were said to have attained perfection – and during the saint's lifetime, *zaouias* devoted to his teachings were founded in Figuig and elsewhere in the Maghreb.

Bound by its practice of a common source of ritual, the Aissaoua brotherhood made itself notorious with displays of eating scorpions, walking on hot coals and other ecstatic practices designed to bring union with God. It was perhaps the most flamboyant of these brotherhoods, but most at any rate used some kind of dancing or music, and indeed continued to do so well into this century. The more extreme and fanatical of these rites are now outlawed, though the attainment of trance is still an important part of the *moussems*, or festivals, of the various confraternities.

TOWARD CRISIS

With all its different forms, Islam permeated every aspect of the country's pre-twentieth-century life. Unlike Christianity, at least Protestant Christianity, which to some extent has accepted the separation of church and state, Islam sees no such distinction. **Civil law** was provided by the *sharia*, the religious law contained in the Koran, and **intellectual life** by the *msids* (Koranic primary schools where the 6200 verses were learned by heart) and by the great medieval mosque universities, of which the Kairaouine in Fes (together with the Zitoura in Tunis and the Al Azhar in Cairo) was the most important in the Arab world.

The religious basis of Arab study and intellectual life did not prevent its scholars and scientists from producing work that was hundreds of years ahead of contemporary "Dark Age" Europe. The remains of a monumental water clock in Fes and the work of the historian Ibn Khaldun, are just two Moroccan examples. Arab work in developing and transmitting multi-cultural influences (Greco-Roman, Persian, Indian and Chinese) was also vital to the whole development of the European Renaissance. By this time, however, the Islamic world – and isolated Morocco in particular – was beginning to move away from the West. The Crusades had been one enduring influence promoting division. Another was the Islamic authorities themselves, increasingly suspicious (like the Western church) of any challenge and actively discouraging of innovation. At first it did not matter in political terms that Islamic culture became static. But by the end of the eighteenth century, Europe was ready to take advantage. Napoleon's expedition to Egypt in 1798 marked the beginning of a century in which virtually every Islamic country came under the control of a **European power**.

Islam cannot, of course, be held solely responsible for the Muslim world's material decline. But because it influences every part of its believers' lives, and because East–West rivalry had always been viewed in primarily religious terms, the nineteenth and twentieth centuries saw something of a **crisis in religious confidence**. Why had Islam's former power now passed to infidel foreigners?

REACTIONS

Reactions and answers veered between two extremes. There were those who felt that Islam should try to incorporate some of the West's materialism; on the other side, there were movements holding that Islam should turn its back on the West, purify itself of all corrupt additions and thus rediscover its former power. While they were colonies of European powers, however, Muslim nations had little chance of putting any such ideas into effective practice. These could only emerge in the form of co-operation with, or rebellion against, the ruling power. But the postwar era of **decolonization**, and the simultaneous acquisition through oil of relative economic independence, brought the Islamic world suddenly face to face with the question of its own spiritual identity. How should it deal with Western values and influence, now that it could afford — both politically and economically — almost total rejection? A return to the totality of Islam — **fundamentalism** — is a conscious choice of one consistent spiritual identity, one that is deeply embedded in the consciousness of a culture already unusually aware of tradition. It is also a rejection of the West and its colonial and exploitative values. Traditional Islam, at least in some interpretations, offers a positivist brand of freedom that is clearly opposed to the negative freedoms of Western materialism. The most vehement Islamic fundamentalists, in Morocco as elsewhere, are not passive reactionaries dwelling in the past, but young radicals — often students — eager to assert their "anti-imperialist" religion.

MODERN MOROCCO

There are two basic reasons why only a few Islamic countries have embraced a rigidly traditional or fundamentalist stance. The first is an ethical one: however undesirable Western materialism may appear, the rejection of all Western values involves rejecting also what the West sees as the "benefits" of development. Perhaps it is begging the question in strictly Islamic terms to say that the emancipation of women, for example, is a "benefit". But the leaders of many countries feel that such steps are both desirable and reconcilable with a more liberal brand of Islam, which will retain its place in the national identity. The other argument against militant Islam is a more pragmatic, economic one. Morocco is only one of many countries which would suffer severe economic hardship if they cut themselves off from the West: they have to tread a narrow line that allows them to maintain good relations both with the West and with the Islamic world.

ISLAM AND THE STATE

In Morocco today, Islam is the official state religion, and King Hassan's secular status is interwoven with his role as "Commander of the Faithful". Internationally, too, he plays a leading role. Meetings of the Islamic Conference Organisation are frequently held in Morocco and, in one of the most unlikely exchanges, students from Tashkent in Uzbekistan have come to study at Fes University. For all these indications of Islamic solidarity, though, **state policy** remains distinctly moderate — sometimes in the face of extremist pressure.

RURAL RELIGION

Not surprisingly, all of this has had more effect on urban than on rural life — a difference accentuated by the gap between them that has always existed in Morocco. Polarization in religious attitudes is far greater in the **cities**, where there is tension between those for and against secularization, as well as a large body of urban poor, for whom Islamic fundamentalism can seem to offer solutions.

Away from the cities, religious attitudes have changed less over the past two generations. Religious brotherhoods such as the Aissaoua have declined since the beginning of the century, when they were still very powerful, and the influence of mystics generally has fallen. As the official histories put it, popular credulity in Morocco provided an ideal setting for charlatans as well as saviours, and much of this has now passed. All the same, the rhythms of **rural life** still revolve around local *marabouts*, and the annual *moussems*, or festivals-cum-pilgrimages, are still vital and impressive displays.

WILDLIFE

Few countries in the Mediterranean region can match the variety and quality of the wildlife habitats to be found in Morocco. Whether you are an expert botanist, a dedicated bird-watcher or simply a visitor with an interest in a totally different environment, the wildlife experience of your travels should be extremely rewarding.

HABITATS

There are three main **vegetation zones** which can be distinguished as you travel through the country.

● The most northerly and westerly zone – the **Mediterranean** and **northern Atlantic coastal strips** – is typical of the European Med region, encompassing semi-arid pastoral lands of olive groves and cultivated fields.

● Further inland lie the barren **Rif mountains** (the home of *kif* or marijuana plants) and the more fertile **Middle Atlas range**, where the montane flora is dominated by cedar forest which, despite its reduction in more recent times, provides a unique mosaic of forest and grassland. The **High Atlas**, beyond, is more arid but has its own montane flora.

● Finally, there is the most southerly zone of the desert fringe or **Sahel**, a harsh environment characterized by pebbly *hammada*, tussock grass, the occasional acacia tree and a number of sand dunes, or *ergs*.

These zones provide a wide variety of **habitat types**, from coastal cliffs, sand dunes and estuarine marshlands to subalpine forests and grasslands, to the semi-arid and true desert

areas of the South. The **climate** is similarly diverse, being warm and humid along the coastal zones, relatively cooler at altitude within the Atlas ranges and distinctly hotter and drier south of the High Atlas, where midday temperatures will often climb higher than 40°C during the summer months. Not surprisingly, the plant and animal life in Morocco is accordingly parochial, species distributions being closely related to the habitat and climate types to which they are specifically adapted.

Many of these habitats are currently under threat from land reclamation, tourist development and the inevitable process of **desertification**, and the resulting habitat loss is endangering the existence of several of the more sensitive species of plants and animals to be found in Morocco. Human persecution of wildlife, however, is limited, as the tribes are largely disarmed and hunting is more the preserve of French tourists.

On the positive side, the *International Committee for Bird Preservation* (I.C.B.P.) and the *Eaux de Forêt* of the Moroccan Agriculture Ministry have been involved in the designation of protected status to several **wetland sites** along the Atlantic coast; at Merdja Zerga and Lac de Sidi Bourhaba, education centres have been set up with resident wardens and interpretive materials. The government has also done some good work on the problems of erosion and desertification and has implemented extensive and impressive schemes of **afforestation and reclamation**.

BIRDS

In addition to a unique range of **resident bird species**, distributed throughout the country on the basis of vegetation and climatic zonation, the periods of late March/April and September/October provide the additional sight of vast **bird migrations**.

Large numbers of birds which have overwintered south of the Sahara migrate northwards in the spring to breed in Europe, completing their return passage through Morocco in the autumn. Similarly, some of the more familiar northern European species choose Morocco for their overwintering grounds to avoid the harshness of our winter clime. These movements can form a dramatic spectacle in the skies, dense flocks of birds moving in procession through bottleneck areas such as Tangier and Ceuta where sea crossings are at their shortest.

RESIDENT SPECIES

The **resident species** can be subdivided on the basis of their preferred habitat type:

● **Coastal/marine species**. These include the familiar moorhen and less familiar **crested coot**, an incongruous bird which, when breeding, resembles its northern European relation but with an additional pair of bright red knobs on either side of its white facial shield. Other species include the diminutive **little ringed plover** and **rock dove**.

● **South of the High Atlas**. Among these are some of the true desert specialities, such as the **sandgrouse** (spotted, crowned, pin-tailed and black-bellied varieties), **stone curlew, cream-coloured courser** and **Houbara bustard** – the latter standing over two feet in height. Other well-represented groups include **wheatears** (4 varieties), **larks** (7 varieties) and **finches, buntings, warblers, corvids** (crow family), **jays, magpies, choughs** and **ravens**, **tits** (primarily blue, great and coal) and **owls** (barn, eagle, tawny and little). Although many of these species can be found in northern Europe, subtle variations in colour and pattern can be misleading and a closer look is often worthwhile.

Raptors (birds of prey) provide a mouth-watering roll call of resident species, including **red-** and **black-shouldered kite, long-legged buzzard, Bonelli's, golden and tawny eagles, Barbary, lanner and pere-grine falcons** and more familiar **kestrel**.

MIGRANT SPECIES

Migrant species can be subdivided into three categories: summer visitors, winter visitors and passage migrants.

● **Summer visitors**. The number of species vis-iting Morocco during the summer months may be low but includes some particularly interest-ing varieties. Among the **marine/coastal types** are the **manx shearwater, Eleonora's falcon** and **bald ibis** – in one of its few remaining breeding colonies in the world.

The **mountain species** include the small **Egyptian vulture** and several of the **hirundines** (swallows and martins) and their close relatives, the **swifts**, such as **little swift, red-rumped swallow** and the more familiar **house martin**.

A particularly colourful addition at this time of year in the **Sahel regions** is the **blue-cheeked bee-eater**, a vibrant blend of red, yellow, blue and green, unmistakeable if seen close up.

● **Winter visitors.** The list of winter visitors is more extensive but composed primarily of the marine or coastal/estuarine varieties. The most common of the truly marine (*pelagic*) flocks include **cory's shearwater, storm petrel, gannet, razorbill** and **puffin**. These are often found congregated on the sea surface, along with any combination of **skuas** (great, arctic and pomarine varieties), **terns** (predominantly sandwich) and **gulls** (including black-headed, Mediterranean, little, herring and the rarer Audouin's) flying overhead.

A variety of coastal/estuarine species also arrive during this period, forming large mixed flocks of **grebes** (great-crested, little and black-necked), **avocet, cattle egret, spoonbill, greater flamingo,** and wildfowl such as **shel-duck, wigeon, teal, pintail, shoveler, tufted duck, pochard** and **coot**.

Migrant **birds of prey** during the winter months include the **common buzzard** (actually a rarity in Morocco), **dashing merlin** and both **marsh** and **hen harriers**.

● **Passage migrants**. There are many birds which simply pass through Morocco en route to other areas, and are thus known as passage migrants. Well-represented groups include **petrels** (5 varieties) and **terns** (6 varieties) along coastal areas, and **herons** (4 varieties), **bitterns, cranes, white and black stork** and **crake** (spotted, little, Baillon's and corncrake) in the marshland/estuarine habitats.

Further inland, flocks of multicoloured **roller**, **bee-eater** and **hoopoe** mix with various **larks, wagtails** and **warblers** (13 varieties), forming large "windfall" flocks when climatic conditions worsen abruptly. Individual species of note include the aptly named **black-winged stilt**, an elegant black and white wader, with long, vibrant red legs, often found among the disused saltpans; and the nocturnal **nightjars** (both common and red-necked), which are most easi-ly seen by the reflection of their eyes in the headlamps of passing cars.

Birds of prey can also form dense passage flocks, often mixed and including large numbers of **black kite, short-toed eagle** and **honey**

THE SHAPE OF MOROCCO

For geologists, Morocco is a place of pilgrimage, a country where the structure of the land lies exposed to view, quite unlike other more temperate parts of Europe where it is hidden by grass, soil and cities.

Long after the layers of rock forming Morocco were laid down at the bottom of some early sea or river estuary, an ocean formed between Europe and Africa at a time when Africa was still attached to Brazil. The rocks forming the Anti-Atlas and Tafilalt region are therefore very old indeed (in places Precambrian) whilst the High Atlas on the other side of a long fault-line are quite young (Jurassic). It was not until quite recent geological times that the whole of Africa swung round anti-clockwise, more or less, to its present position. About the time the chalk Downs of southern England were being laid down, Spain was moving westwards along the Moroccan coast.

When you travel through the landscape of Morocco, bear in mind that these rocks were formed when Europe and America were in a different position to where they are now and that the dry rock surfaces you will encounter were not caused by the tiny streams, flash floods and winds of the present, but by climates many millenia past.

buzzard. Over open water spaces, the majestic **osprey** may be seen demonstrating its mastery of the art of fishing.

● **"Vagrant" species**. Finally, Morocco has its share of occasional or "vagrant" species, so classified on the unusual or rare nature of their appearances. These include such exotic varieties as **glossy ibis**, **pale-chanting goshawk**, **arabian bustard** and **lappet-faced vulture**. Inevitably, they provide few, if any, opportunities for viewing.

FLORA

In the light of its climatic harshness and unreliable rains, the flora of Morocco is remarkably diverse. Plant species have adapted strategies to cope with the Moroccan climate, becoming either specifically adapted to one particular part of the environment (a habitat type), or evolving multiple structural and/or biochemical means of surviving the more demanding seasons. Others have adopted the proverbial "ostrich" philosophy of burying their heads (or rather their seeds in this case) in the sand and waiting for climatic conditions to become favourable – often an extremely patient process!

The type of flowers that you see will obviously depend entirely on where and when you decide to visit. Some parts of the country have very short flowering seasons because of high temperatures or lack of available water, but generally the best times of year for flowering plants are either just before or just after the main temperature extremes of the North African summer.

The best time to visit is **spring** (late March to mid-May), when most flowers are in bloom. Typical spring flowers include purple **barbary nut iris**, deep blue **germander** and the aromatic **claret thyme**, all of which frequent the slopes of the Atlas ranges. Among the **woodland flora** at this time of year are the red **pheasant's eye**, pink **virburnum**, violet **calamint** and purple **campanula**, which form a resplendent carpet beneath the cedar forests. By late spring, huge tracts of the High Atlas slopes are aglow with the golden hues of **broom** and secluded among the lowland cereal crops, splashes of magenta reveal the presence of **wild gladioli**.

By **midsummer** the climate is at its most extreme and the main concern of plants is to avoid desiccation in the hot, arid conditions. Two areas of exception to these conditions are the **Atlantic coastal zones**, where sea mists produce a slightly more humid environment, and the upper reaches of the **Atlas ranges** which remain cool and moist at altitude throughout the year. Spring comes later in these loftier places and one can find many of the more familiar garden rock plants, such as the **saxifrages** and **anemones** in flower well into late July and August.

Once the hottest part of the summer is past (September onwards), then a second, **autumn** bloom begins with later varieties such as **cyclamens** and **autumn crocus**.

HABITAT VARIETIES

The range of plants you are likely to encounter is similarly influenced by specific habitats:

● **Seashores**. These include a variety of sand-tolerant species, with their adaptations for coping with water-loss, such as **sea holly** and **sea stocks**. The dune areas contrast starkly with the Salicornia-dominated salt marshes – monotonous landscapes broken only by the occasional dead **tamarisk** tree.

● **Arable land.** Often dominated by cereal crops – particularly in the more humid Atlantic and Mediterranean coastal belts – or **olive and eucalyptus groves**, which extend over large areas. The general lack of use of herbicides allows the co-existence of many **"wild flowers"**, especially in the fallow hay meadows which are ablaze with the colours of **wild poppy**, **ox-eye daisy**, **muscali** (borage) and various yellow composites.

● **Lowland hills**. These form a fascinating mosaic of dense, shrubby species, known as *maquis*, lower-lying, more grazed areas, known as *garrigue*, and more open areas with abundant aromatic herbs and shrubs.

Maquis vegetation is dominated by **cistaceae** (**rock roses**) and the endemic **argan** tree. The lower-lying *garrigue* is more typically composed of aromatic herbs such as **rosemary**, **thyme** and **golden milfoil**. Among these shrubs, within the more open areas, you may find an abundance of other species such as **anemones, grape hyacinths** and **orchids**.

The orchids are particularly outstanding, including several of the *Ophrys* group, which use the strategy of insect imitation to entice pollinators and as such have an intricate arrangement of flowers.

● **Mountain slopes**. Flowering later in the year, the slopes of the **Atlas ranges** are dominated by the blue-mauve **pitch trefoil** and golden drifts of **broom**. As you travel south through the Middle Atlas, the verdant **ash, oak**, **atlantic cedar** and **juniper forest** dominates the landscape. Watered by the depressions that sweep across from the Atlantic, these slopes form a luxurious spectacle, ablaze with colour in spring.

Among the glades beneath the **giant cedars** of the Middle Atlas, a unique flora may be found, dominated by the vibrant **pink paeony**. Other plants which form this spectacular carpet include **geranium, anchusa, pink verburnum, saffron mulleins, mauve cupidanes, violet calamint, purple campanula**, the diminutive **scarlet dianthus** and a wealth of **golden composites** and **orchids**.

Further south, the **Toubkal National Park** boasts its own varieties and spring bloom; the thyme and thorny caper are interspersed with the blue-mauve **pit trefoil, pink convulvulus**, the silver-blue and pinks of everlasting flowers of **cupidane** and **phagnalon** and golden spreads of **broom**. At the highest altitudes, the limestone Atlas slopes form a bleak environment, either covered by winter snows or scorched by the summer sun. However, some species are capable of surviving even under these conditions, the most conspicuous of these being the widespread purple tussocks of the **hedgehog broom**.

● **Steppeland**. South of the Atlas, temperatures rise sharply and the effect on flora is dramatic; the extensive cedar forests and their multicoloured carpets are replaced by sparse grass plains where the horizon is broken only by the occasional stunted **holm oak, juniper** or **acacia**. Commonly known as wattle trees, the acacia were introduced into North Africa from Australia and their large yellow flowers add a welcome splash of colour to this barren landscape. One of the few crop plants grown in this area is the **date palm**, which is particularly resistant to drought. The steppeland is characterized by the presence of **esparto grass**, which exudes toxins to prevent the growth of competing species. These halfa grass plains are only broken by the flowering of **broom** in May. Within rocky outcrops, this spring bloom can become a mini-explosion of colour, blending the hues of **cistus** and **chrysanthemum** with the pink of **rock rose**, yellow of **milfoil** and mauve of **rosemary**.

● **Desert fringe (*hammada*)**. Even the desert areas provide short-lived blooms of colour during the infrequent spring showers; dwarf varieties such as pink **asphodels**, yellow **daisies** and mauve **statice** thrive briefly while conditions are favourable. Under the flat stones of the hammada, colonies of lichens and microscopic algae eke out an existance; their shade tolerance and ability to obtain sufficient water from the occasional condensation which takes place under these stones allows them to survive in this harshest of environs. No matter how inhospitable the environment or extreme the climate, somewhere, somehow, there are plants surviving – if you take time to look for them.

AMPHIBIANS

There are very few remaining amphibians in Morocco – relics of a bygone, more fertile era, now restricted to scarce watery havens. They are more apparent by sound than sight, forming a resonant chorus during the night and early morning. One of the more common varieties is the **green frog**, typically immersed up to its eyes in water, releasing the odd giveaway croak. Another widespread individual, most abundant in the regions round Marrakesh, is the **western marsh frog**.

The toads are represented by the **Berber toad**, another nocturnal baritone, and the **Mauritanian toad** whose large size and characteristic yellow and brown-spotted colouration make it quite unmistakeable.

Some Moroccan amphibians are capable of survival at surprisingly **high altitudes**. The **painted frog** is a common participant in the chorus that emanates from the *oueds* (riverbeds) of the High Atlas, while the wide-ranging whistle of the North African race of the **green toad**, famed for its ability to change its colour with the surrounding environment, can be heard at altitudes in excess of 2000m.

REPTILES

Reptiles are far more widespread in their distribution than their amphibious cousins. Their range extends from the Mediterranean coastal strip – where the few remaining **tortoises** (sadly depleted through "craft items" sold to the tourist trade) are to be seen – to the *hammada* itself.

The forested slopes of the Middle Atlas are frequented by the **blue and green-eyed lizard** and the **chameleon**; the former uses its size and agility to capture its prey, whereas the latter relies on the more subtle strategy of colour co-ordination, stealth and a quicksilver tongue.

Several species have adapted to the specific environment of the stony **walls** that form the towns and villages. The **Spanish wall lizard** is a common basker on domestic walls, as is the **Moorish gecko**.

Further south, the drier, scrub-covered slopes form an ideal habitat for two of Morocco's largest **snakes**. The **horseshoe snake** (which can exceed 2m in length) and **Montpelier snake** hunt by day, feeding on birds and rats. Also found in this harsh environment are the **Atlas agama** and **fringe-toed lizard**.

Finally, there are the **desert "specialists"**, such as the **Algerian sand lizard** and **Berber skink**. The skinks make a fascinating spectacle; commonly known as "sand fish", they inhabit the ergs and appear to "swim" through the sand, where their yellow-brown coloration provides the perfect camouflage. Of numerous species of lizard that live in the *hammada*, the more obvious include the many colours and varieties of the **spiny-tailed lizard** (*dhub* in Arabic), an omnivore feeding on a mixed diet of insects, fruit and young shoots. The one really poisonous species is the **horned viper**, only half a metre in length, which spends the days buried just below the surface of the sand and feeds by night on jerboas and lizards.

MAMMALS

Larger animal life in Morocco is dominated by the extensive nomadic herds of goats, sheep and camel which use the most inaccessible and barren patches of wilderness as seasonal grazing areas.

One of the most impressive of the wild mammals, however, is the **Barbary ape** – in fact not a true ape but a Macaque monkey. These frequent the cedar forests south of Azrou in the Middle Atlas and can be seen on the ground foraging for food in the glades. Other inhabitants of the cedar forest include **wild boar** and **red fox**.

A speciality of the Oued Souss, outside Agadir, is the **common otter**; this is now a rare species in Morocco and can only be seen with considerable patience and some fortune.

The majority of the smaller mammals in Morocco live south of the Atlas ranges in the *hammada*, where the ever-present problem of water conservation plays a major role in the lifestyle of its inhabitants. Larger herbivores include the **Edmi gazelle** and the smaller, and rarer, **Addax antelope,** which graze the thorn bushes and dried grasses to obtain their moisture.

Many of the desert varieties reduce the problems of body temperature regulation by adopting a nocturnal lifestyle. Typical exponents of this strategy are the **desert hedgehog** and numerous small rodents such as the **jerboa**. A common predator of the jerboa is the **fennec** (desert fox), whose characteristic large ears are used for both directional hearing (invaluable as a nocturnal hunter) and heat radiation to aid body cooling.

An oddity, found in the Djebel Toubkal area of the High Atlas, is the African **elephant shrew** – a fascinating creature, like a little mouse, with an elephantine trunk.

INSECTS

Insect life is widespread throughout Morocco, its variety of form occupying unique, overlapping roles.

BUTTERFLIES

Most colourful are the butterflies, of which over a hundred species have been recorded, predominantly in the Middle and High Atlas ranges. The most obvious, which can be seen from April onwards, are generally the largest and most colourful, such as the brilliant sulphur **Cleopatra**, **large tortoiseshell** and **cardinal**. Located on the grassy slopes within the ranges are less conspicuous varieties: the **hermit**, **Spanish marbled white**, **fritillaries**, **graylings**, **hairstreaks** and **blues** – such as the small **larquin's** and **false baton**.

Later in the year, from about June onwards, the glades and woodland edges of the Middle Atlas cedar forests provide the perfect habitat for **dark green fritillaries**, while in the higher flowery fields, at altitudes of up to 2000m, **knapweed fritillaries**, **large grizzled** and **Barbary skippers** abound. Particularly attractive is the **Amanda's blue**, found at altitudes in excess of 600m through till midsummer if nectar remains available.

On the rocky slopes of Toubkal National Park, south of Marrakesh, the **Morrocan copper butterfly** may be seen flitting through the thyme. In the higher Atlas gorges (1700m or more), the **desert orange tip** is more prevalent, being found on its larval food plant, the thorny caper. The Atlas also sees one of the world's most extraordinary butterfly migrations, when waves of painted ladies and Bath whites pass through, having crossed the Sahara from West Africa, en route across the Bay of Biscay to the west of England.

OTHER INSECTS

Other common groups include **grasshoppers**, **crickets** and **locusts**. In the High Atlas, **praying mantis** may be seen, such as **eremiaphila**, whose brown coloration provides excellent camouflage.

Beetles are another common group, though they tend to avoid the heat of the day, remaining in their burrows and emerging at night to feed. The **darkling beetles** are particularly abundant and voracious scavengers.

Finally there are **arachnids**, of which there are three major groups in Morocco – scorpions, camel spiders and spiders. **Scorpions** are nocturnal, hiding under suitable covered depressions during the day such as rocks and boulders (or rucksacks and shoes!). Some of the six or so species which may be found in Morocco are poisonous but most are harmless and unlikely to sting unless provoked. The **camel spiders** (or wind-scorpions) are unique. They lack a poisonous tail but possess huge jaws with which they catch their main source of prey, scorpions.

Spiders are not common in Morocco, only being found in large numbers within the Atlas ranges. Here, it is possible to see several small species of **tarantula** (not the hairy South American variety!) and the white **orb-web spider** *Argiope lobata*, whose coloration acts as a disruptive pattern against pale backgrounds.

A CHECKLIST OF THE MAIN SITES

Features on key Moroccan wildlife, and especially bird, habitats are to be found throughout the guide; the main entries are boxed. They include:

● **AGADIR/OUED SOUSS** Riverbank attracts waders and wildfowl, migrant warblers and Barbary partridge. → p.457

● **AGUELMAME AZIGZA** Middle Atlas occasional inland lake and forest: hawfinch, diving duck and marbled teal in autumn/winter. → p.230

● **BOUMALNE: DESERT HAMMADA** Atlas agama and fringe-toed lizard; specialist bird species such as cream-coloured courser, red-rumped wheatear and thick-billed lark. **Houbara bustard**. → p.417

● **CEDAR FORESTS SOUTH OF AZROU** Species include green-eyed lizard and chameleon; **butterflies** from April onwards; **Barbary apes**. Moroccan woodpecker and **booted eagle**. → p.230

● **DAYET AAOUA** Another Middle Atlas occasional lake: flocks of grebes, **crested coot**, grey heron and cattle egret; migrant birds of prey include **red kite**. ➡ p.226

● **DJEBEL TAZZEKA NATIONAL PARK** Where the Rif merges with the Middle Atlas: slopes covered in cork oak and woodland; **butterflies** from late May/early June, and **birds** such as the hoopoe. ➡ p.138

● **DJEBEL TOUBKAL NATIONAL PARK** High Atlas mountains: sights include Moorish gecko, rare butterflies; Moussier's redstart and crimson-winged finch, both unique to North African mountains; hooped-petticoat daffodils, *romulea* and various other bulbs in spring. ➡ p.364

● **ESSAOUIRA** Coastal dunes, river and offshore islands attract **waders** and **egrets**; also **Eleanora's falcon** between May and October. ➡ p.315

● **FES** Evening roost of egret and alpine swift; **white stork** on rooftop nests of walls. ➡ p.215

● **LAC DE SIDI BOURHABA** Freshwater lake, with outstanding **birds of prey**. ➡ p.250

● **MARRAKESH: JARDIN MARJORELLE**. Lush garden with turtle doves, house buntings and common bulbuls. ➡ p.349

● **MERDJA ZERGA** Large wetland area guarantees good **bird** numbers at all times of year, especially **gulls and terns** (including the Caspian tern). ➡ p.101

● **MERZOUGA** Sandy (or "true") desert: all-too-brief **spring bloom** of pink asphodels and mauve statice; Algerian sand lizard and Berber skink; **birds** include fulvous babbler, blue-cheeked bee-eater, the rare desert sparrow and even Arabian bustard. ➡ p.441

● **NADOR/KARIET ARKMANE/RAS-EL-MA** Salt marshes and coastal sand dunes, good for waders and gulls. ➡ p.147

● **OUALIDIA** Mix of ragged, rocky coast, sands, lagoon, marshes and salt pans. Good for small waders. ➡ p.301

● **OUED MASSA** Important inland lagoon and reserve that is perhaps the country's number one bird habitat. ➡ p.466

● **OUED MOULOUYA**. Lagoons and sand spits, with outstanding birds.➡ p.147

● **TODRA GORGE** Marsh frog and green toad; ground squirrel; common bulbul, black wheatear, blue rock thrush and rock dove. **Bonelli's eagles** nest in the gorge. ➡ p.427

FIELD GUIDES

There are few publications specifically about Moroccan wildlife, but some field guides to Mediterranean Europe extend coverage to North Africa, and most are in any case reasonably practicable for the area.

● **Butterflies**
Lionel Higgins and Norman Riley *A Field Guide to the Butterflies of Britain and Europe* (Collins, UK/Stephen Green Press, US).

● **Flowers**
Oleg Polunin and Anthony Huxley *Flowers of the Mediterranean* (Oxford UP, UK/US).

● **Mammals**
Theodor Haltenorth and Helmut Diller *A Field Guide to the Mammals of Africa* (Collins, UK/Stephen Green Press, US).

● **Birds**
P and F Bergier *A Birdwatcher's Guide to Morocco* (Prion Press, UK). An excellent practical guidebook which includes site-maps and species lists.

Heinzel, Fitter and Parslow *The Birds of Britain and Europe with North Africa and the Middle East* (Collins, UK/Stephen Green Press, US).

MUSIC

Wherever you go in Morocco you are likely to hear music. It is the basic expression of the country's folk culture – indeed to many of the illiterate country people it is the sole expression – and in its traditions it covers the whole history of the country. There are long and ancient pieces designed for participation by the entire communities of Berber villages; songs and instrumental music brought by the Arabs from the east and Andalucian Spain; and in more recent times, the struggle for independence, too, found celebration in song.

Although the most common musical phenomenon that you will hear is the **muezzin** calling the faithful to prayer, amplified from minarets, most Moroccan music is performed for the sake of entertainment rather than religion. At every weekly **souk,** or market, you will find a band playing in a patch of shade, or a stall blasting out cassettes they have on sale. In the evenings many **cafés** feature musicians, particularly during the long nights of Ramadan. **Television** also plays its part, with two weekly programmes devoted to music, and the **radio stations**, too, broadcast a variety of sounds.

Festivals are perhaps the most rewarding. Every popular or religious festival involves musicians, and the larger **moussems** (see p.48) are always rewarding. Keep an eye out for cultural festivals, too, in particular the summer **Asilah Festival** (see p.91), and the **Festival of Sacred Music** held at the end of May in **Fes** (see p.219).

Below, David Muddyman reviews the breadth and depth of Moroccan music, from the formal repertoire of classical **andalous** to the innovations of electric *chaabi*.

BERBER MUSIC

Berber music is quite distinct from Arab-influenced forms in its rhythms, tunings, instruments and sounds. It is an extremely ancient tradition, probably long predating even the arrival of Arabs in Morocco, and has been passed on orally from generation to generation. There are three main categories: village music, ritual music and the music of professional musicians.

Village music is essentially a collective performance. Men and women of the entire village will assemble on festive occasions to dance and sing together. The best-known dances are the **ahouach**, in the western High Atlas, and the **ahidus**, performed by Chleuh Berbers in the eastern High Atlas. In each, drums (*bendirs*) and flutes (*neys*) are the only instruments used. The dance begins with a chanted prayer, to which the dancers respond in chorus, the men and women gathered in a large ring in the open air, round the musicians. The *ahouach* is normally performed at night in the patio of the Kasbah; the dance is so complicated that the musicians meet to prepare for it in a group called a *laamt* set up specially for the purpose. In the *bumzdi*, a variation on the *ahouach*, one or more soloists perform a series of poetic improvisations.

Ritual music is rarely absent from any rites connected with the agricultural calendar – such as *moussems* – or major events in the life of individuals, such as marriage. It may also be called upon to help deal with *djinn*, or evil spirits, or to encourage rainfall. Flutes and drums are usually the sole instruments, along with much rhythmic hand-clapping, although a community may have engaged professional musicians for certain events.

The **professional musicians**, or *imdyazn*, of the Atlas mountains are itinerant, travelling during the summer, usually in groups of four. The leader of the group is called the *amydaz* or poet. He presents his poems, which are usually improvised and give news of national or world affairs, in the village square. The poet may be accompanied by one or two members of the group on drums and *rabab*, a single-string fiddle, and by a fourth player, known as the *bou oughanim*. This latter is the reed player, throwing out melodies on a double clarinet, and also acts as the group's clown. *Imdyazn* are found in many weekly *souks* in the Atlas.

RWAIS

Groups of **Chleuh Berber** musicians, from the Souss Valley, are known as **rwais**; again they are professional musicians. A *rwai* worthy of the name will not only know all the music for any particular celebration, but have its own repertoire of songs – again commenting on current events – and be able to improvise. A *rwai* ensemble can be made up of a single-string *rabab*, one or two *lotars* (lutes) and sometimes *nakous* (cymbals), together with a number of singers. The leader of the group, the *rayes*, is in charge of the poetry, music and choreography of the performance.

A **rwai performance** will start with the *astara*, an instrumental prelude, played on *rabab*, giving the basic notes of the melodies that follow (this also makes it possible for the other instruments to tune to the *rabab*). The astara is not in any particular rhythm. Then comes the *amarg*, the sung poetry which forms the heart of the piece. This is followed by the *ammussu*, which is a sort of choreographed overture; the *tamssust*, a lively song; the *aberdag*, or dance; and finally the *tabbayt*, a finale characterized by an acceleration in rhythm and an abrupt end. Apart from the astara and tabbayt, the elements of a performance may appear in a different order. The arrangement and duration of the various parts are decided upon freely by the *rwais*.

ANDALOUS MUSIC

Morocco's classical music comes from the **Arab-Andalucían tradition**, and is to be found, with variations, throughout North Africa. It is thought to have evolved, around a thousand years ago, in Córdoba, Spain (then ruled by the Moors), and its invention is usually credited to an outstanding musician from Baghdad called Zyriab). One of his greatest innovations was the founding of the classical suite called **nuba**, which forms what is now known as **andalous music**, or **al-âla**. There are, in addition, two other classical traditions, **milhûn** and **gharnati**, each with a distinctive style and form.

Andalous music, far from being the scholastic relic you might expect, is very much alive,

popular and greatly loved. Television, which plays an important part in the Moroccan music scene, broadcasts nightly programmes of andalous classics during Ramadan, and people who don't have their own TVs congregate at local cafés to watch the shows.

Originally there were twenty-four **nuba** linked with the hours in the day. Only four full and seven fragmentary *nuba* have been preserved in the Moroccan tradition. Complete *nuba* would last between six and seven hours, are rarely performed in one sitting and are usually chosen to fit the time of day or occasion. Each *nuba* is divided into five main parts, or *mizan*, of differing durations. These five parts correspond to the five different rhythms used within a suite. If a whole *nuba* were being performed then these five rhythms would be used in order: the basît rhythm (6/4); *qaum wa nusf* rhythm (8/4); *darj* rhythm (4/4); *btâyhi* rhythm (8/4); and *quddâm* rhythm (3/4 or 6/8).

Traditionally each *mizan* begins with instrumental preludes – *bughya, m'shaliya* and *tuashia* – followed by a number of songs, the *sana'a*. There can be as many as twenty *sana'a* within a given *mizan* although for shorter performances an orchestra may only play three or four before going on to the next rhythm.

The words to many *sana'a* deal, though often obliquely, with subjects generally considered taboo in Islamic society like alcohol and sex – perhaps signifying archaic, pre-Islamic and nomadic roots – although others are religious, glorifying the Prophet and divine laws. The fourteenth *sana'a* of the *basît mizan* in **Al-'Ushshâq** tells of the desire for clarity following an active night entirely given over to the pleasures of sex and wine:

Obscure night steals away
Chased by the light
that sweeps up shadows
The candle wax runs
as if weeping tears of farewell
And then, suddenly and behold,
the birds are singing
and the flowers smile at us.

When the Arabs were driven out of Spain, which they had known as Al-Andalus, the different musical schools were dispersed across Morocco. The school of Valencia was re-established in Fez, that of Granada in Tetuán and Chaouen. The most famous **orchestras** are those of Fes, led by **Abdelkrim Rais**; Tetouan, led by **Abdesadak Chekara**; and Rabat, which was led by the great Moulay Ahmed Loukili until his death in 1988 and is now under **Haj Mohamed Toud**.

Other cities, however, such as **Tangier** and **Meknes**, have their own andalous orchestras and are just as fanatical about the music as the major cities. The **Orchestra of Tangier** have their own clubhouse, in the old city Kasbah, where musicians sit with enthusiasts and play most evenings, in between sucking on their mint tea.

A typical andalous orchestra uses the following instruments: *rabab* (fiddle), *oud* (lute), *kamenjah* (violin-style instrument played vertically on the knee), *kanun* (zither), *darabouka* (metal or pottery goblet drums), and *taarija* (tambourine). Each orchestra has featured unusual instruments from time to time. Clarinets, flutes, banjos and pianos have all been used with varying degrees of success.

MILHÛN AND GHARNATI

Milhûn is a semiclassical form of sung poetry – a definition which sounds a lot drier than it is. Musically it has many links with andalous music, having adopted the same modes as *al-âla* orchestras and, like them, uses string instruments and percussion. But the result can be quite wild and danceable.

The *milhûn* suite comprises two parts: the *taqsim* (overture) and the *qassida* (sung poems). The *taqsim* is played on the *oud* or violin in free rhythm, and introduces the mode in which the piece is set. The *qassida* is divided into three parts: the *al-aqsâm*, being verses sung solo; the *al-harba*, the refrains sung by the chorus; and the *al-drîdka*, a chorus where the rhythm gathers speed and eventually announces the end of the piece. The words of the qassida can be taken from anywhere – folk poetry, mystical poems or nonsense lines used for rhythm.

Al-Thami Lamdaghri, who died in 1856, was one of the greatest *milhûn* composers. He is credited with many well-known songs including "Al-Gnawi" (The Black Slave), "Aliq Al-Masrûh" (The Radiant Beauty) and "Al-'Arsa" (The Garden of Delight):

Open your eyes
Taste the delights and the generous nature
Of this heavenly garden
The branches of the wonderful
   trees intertwine

Like two lovers meeting again
And totter about, heady with happiness
The smile of flowers,
Mingled with the tears of the dew
Recall the melancholic exchange
Of a sad lover and his joyous beloved
Birds sing in the branches
Like as many lutes and rababs.

The **milhûn orchestra** generally consists of *oud*, *kamenjah*, *swisen* (a small, high-pitched folk lute related to the gimbri), the *hadjouj* (a bass version of the swisen), *taarija*, *darabouka* and *handqa* (small brass cymbals). As well as musicians, an orchestra will normally feature a number of **singers**. Some of the best known are **Abdelkrim and Saïd Guennoun** of Fes, **Haj Husseïn** and **Abdallah Ramdani** of Meknes, and **Muhammad Berrahal** and **Muhammad Bensaïd** of Salé.

Gharnati, the third music of Arab-Andalucían tradition, is mainly played in Algeria but there are two important centres in Morocco – the capital, Rabat, and Oujda, near the Algerian border. As with *al-âla*, gharnati music is arranged in suites or nuba, of which there are twelve complete and four unfinished suites.

The *gharnati* orchestra consists of plucked and bowed instruments together with percussion: the usual *ouds* and *kamenjahs* supplemented by the addition of banjo, mandolin and Algerian lute, the *kwîtra*.

SUFI BROTHERHOODS

Music in orthodox Islam is frowned upon unless it is singing God's praises. As well as the chants of the Koran, which are improvised on a uniform beat, the *adhan*, or call to prayer, and the songs about the life of the prophet Muhammad, there is another entire range of prayers and ceremonies belonging to the **Sufi brotherhoods**, or *tarikas*, in which music is seen as a means of getting closer to Allah. These include the music used in processions to the tombs of saints during *moussems*.

The aim is for those present to reach a state of mystical ecstasy, often through **trance**. In a private nocturnal ceremony called the *hadra*, the Sufi brothers attain a trance by chanting the name of Allah or dancing in a ring holding hands. The songs and music are irregular in rhythm, and quicken to an abrupt end. Some brotherhoods play for alms in households that want to gain the favour of their patron saint.

The **Gnaoua brotherhood** (see "Islam in Morocco") is a religious confraternity whose members are descendants of slaves brought from across the Sahara by the Arabs. They have devotees all over Morocco, though the strongest concentrations are in the south, particularly in Marrakesh.

The brotherhood claim spiritual descent from **Sidi Bilal**, an Ethiopian who was the Prophet's first muezzin. Most Gnaoua ceremonies, or *deiceba*, are held to placate spirits, good and evil, who are inhabiting a person or place. They are often called in cases of mental disturbance or to help treat someone stung by a scorpion. These rites have their origins in sub-Saharan Africa, and an African influence is evident in the music itself. The principal instrument, the *gimbri* or *sentir*, is a long-necked lute almost identical to instruments found in West Africa. The other characteristic sound of Gnaoua music is the *garagab*, a pair of metal castanets, which beat out a trance-like rhythm.

Jilala are another brotherhood who are devotees of **Moulay Abdelkader Jilal**. Their music is even more hypnotic and mysterious than that of the Gnaoua and seems to come from a different plane of existence. The plaintive cycling flute (the *qsbah*) and the mesmeric beats of the *bendir* (frame drums) carry you forward unconsciously. While in a trance Jilala devotees can withstand the touch of burning coals or the deep slashes of a Moroccan dagger, afterwards showing no injury or pain.

Nowadays, Gnaoua music can be heard at festivals and in the entertainment squares of Marrakesh and elsewhere. Gnaoua music, featuring the wonderful **Mustapha Baqbou**, has been superbly recorded by Bill Laswell and issued on Axiom.

CHAABI

All of the musical forms mentioned above have had their impact on the most popular music of Morocco – **chaabi**, which means simply "popular" and covers a bewildering mix of styles. The music that takes this name started out as street music performed in the squares and *souks*, but it can now be heard in cafés, at festivals and at weddings. Many towns have café-meeting places where the locals sing songs in the evenings (some cafés keep their own instruments for musicians who can't afford their own) and, at its more basic level, *chaabi* is played by

itinerant musicians, who turn up at a café and bang out a few songs. These songs are usually finished with a *leseb*, which is often twice the speed of the song itself and forms a background for syncopated clapping, shouting and dancing. Early evening during Ramadan is the best time to find music cafés of this kind in full swing.

During the 1970s a more sophisticated version of *chaabi* began to emerge, with groups setting themselves up in competition with the commercial Egyptian and Lebanese music which dominated the market (and the radio) at the time. These groups were usually made up of two stringed instruments – a *hadjuj* (bass gimbri) and a lute – and a *bendir* and *darabouka* or *tam-tam* as percussion. As soon as they could afford it, they updated their sound and image with the addition of congas, buzuks, banjos and even electric guitars. The *hadjuj* and *bendir*, however, remain indispensable.

Their music is a fusion of Arab, African and modern Western influences, combining Berber music with elements taken from the Arab *milhûn* and Sufi rituals, Gnaoua rhythms and the image of European groups. Voices play an important part, with the whole group singing, either in chorus or backing a lead soloist. Lyrics deal with love as well as social issues, and occasionally carry messages which have got their authors into trouble with the authorities – even jailed.

CHAABI GROUPS

The three most popular groups of this kind are Jil Jilala, Lem Chaheb and Nass El Ghiwane, all from Casablanca.

Jil Jilala, which means "Generation of Jilali", was formed in 1972 as a Sufi theatre group devoted to their leader, Jilali. Their music is based on the *milhûn* style, using poetry as a reference (and starting) point. More recently they have worked with Gnaoua rhythms and they occasionally use a *ghaita* in their line-up. The group's central figures are the conga-player and lyricist **Mohammed Darhem**, and **Hassan Mista**, who plays an amplified, fretless *buzuk*. They are rhythmically accompanied by two bendir players – Moulai Tahar and Abdel Krim Al-Kasbaji – and have recorded with a variety of *hadjuj* players, including **Mustapha Baqbou**.

Nass El-Ghiwane, the most politicized of the three chaabi-fusion groups, lays great emphasis on the words of its recitatives and verses and chorus. The band's music, again, combines Sufi and Gnaoua influences while the words may lambast a lazy government official or talk of social injustices. Originally a five-piece band of banjo, *hadjuj*, *bendir*, *tam-tam* and *darabouka*, the band was fronted by lead singer **Boujmia**, a man with a soaring, powerfully melodic voice. He was killed in a car crash in the early 1980s and the rest of the group have continued as a four-piece since. There has been a retrospective cassette from Boujmia's time released in Morocco on the Hassania label, which includes "The Table", the song that made them famous:

Where are they now?
The friends who sat at my table
Where are they now?
All the friends that I loved
Where are the glasses?
Where are the glasses we drank from?
Friendship can be bitter
But it was also sweet to sit at my table

The third major chaabi group, **Lem Chaheb** is probably the Moroccan group best known abroad, through its work with the German band **Dissidenten** (two of whose members play and record with them). Featuring the virtuoso figure of guitarist and *buzuk* player Lamrani Moulay Cherif, they are also the most Westernized of the three big names in electric chaabi.

In the 1980s another generation of groups emerged, combining traditional and modern influences, this time based in Marrakesh but concentrating on Gnaoua rhythms. The most successful of these has been **Muluk El Hwa** (The Demon of Love), a group of Berbers who used to play in the Djemaa El Fna in Marrakesh. Their line-up is totally acoustic: *bendir*, *tam-tam*, *sentir*, *buzuk*, *garagab* and hand claps. The only album available in Europe is "Xara Al-Andalus" (Erde Records, Germany), a collaboration with the Spanish group **Al Tall**. The album features medieval Valencian music and Arabic poetry from Andalucía, which deals with subjects still relevant today – the whims of rulers, exile, love and wine.

Another of their contemporaries, **Nass El Hal**, formed in 1986, offer two shows – one using a traditional acoustic line-up with *buzuk* and violin, the other with drum kit and electric guitar. Their repertoire includes peasant harvest and hunting songs, and religious dances.

Other groups with recordings to their name include **Izanzaren**, of the Casablanca school, and **Shuka**, who do everything from Andalous to Gnaoua.

NAJAT AATABOU

Other *chaabi* artists have remained firmly traditional in their use of instruments, but forward-looking in their musical approach. One such is the sensational singer **Najat Aatabou**. She is proud of her Berber heritage and uses traditional Berber rhythms (though she now sings in Arabic or French) and is very outspoken in her lyrics, which address the inequality between men and women and the injustice of traditional family rules. She is equally capable of writing beautiful love songs. When her ensemble use electric instruments they blend beautifully with more traditional *oud* and *bendir*.

Aatabou's first release, the eye-opening "J'en ai marre" (I am sick of it), sold 450,000 copies. Her second release, "Shouffi Rhirou" (Look for Another Lover), and every subsequent release have sold more than half a million copies, and she is now a huge star throughout the Maghreb and can fill large venues in Europe. A wonderful compilation CD, *The Voice of the Atlas* (which includes "Shouffi Rhirou"), is available on GlobeStyle records.

FUSION

Morocco an ideal starting point for all kinds of fusion experiments. From the 1960s on, such disparate figures as Brian Jones (see box), Robin Williamson, John Renbourn and Pharoah Sanders have been attracted by its rhythms, and in in the 1980s and 1990s collaborations have come thick and fast.

The most successful, perhaps, has been that of the Berlin-based **Dissidenten**. Before their collaboration with Lem Chaheb (see above), they had worked with **Mohammed Zain**, a star player of the nai (flute) from Tangier who belongs to a Sufi sect, and Gnaoua gimbri players Abdellah El Gourd, Abderkader Zefzaf and Abdalla Haroch. Their albums with Lem Chaheb have placed a genuine Moroccan element into a rock context.

A number of Moroccan singers and musicians have also crossed over into 1990s dance

THE MASTER MUSICIANS OF JAJOUKA

During the late 1950s and early 1960s Tangier was as Bohemian a city as any, attracting Beats and, in their wake, rock stars. In 1968 the Rolling Stones paid the first of several visits and their then-guitarist, **Brian Jones** was introduced to the Berber **Master Musicians of Jajouka** in the foothills of the Rif Mountains.

The Master Musicians are essentially trace musicians, producing an awesome sound through a multitude of double-headed drums and the dark drones and melodies of the ghaita, or rhaita, a double-reed pipe or shawm similar in sound to the oboe. They are a kind of brotherhood, and the leadership of the group is passed down from father to son. The present chief, **Bachir Attar**, inherited the post when his father died in the late 1980s.

Jones recorded the Master Musicians with the aid of psychedelic sound trickery and produced his strange "Pipes of Jajouka" album. Its heady con-coction of hypnotic rhythms, wailing pipes and Jones' heavy sound treatments gave what for many was close to a mystical experience – especially when stoned immobile on *kif*. For many years this was the only record available of Moroccan music.

Although the Rolling Stones returned to Morocco in the mid-1980s to use Jajouka on their "Steel Wheels" album, the Master Musicians' next "solo" recording didn't emerge until 1990 when American bassist and composer Bill Laswell, travelled to Morocco. Using the latest digital technology, he produced an album of purity and power. Since then, they have experienced a revival of interest, spurred by the burgeoning World Music scene, appearing at festivals around the world. They have recorded a further CD, and the original Brian Jones album has also been re-released.

---

music. **Yosefa Dahari** is a name to look out for in this respect, with her work (sung in Maghrebi and English) on the Worldly Dance Music label with David Rosenthal and Gil Freeman. **Hassan Hakmoun** is another – a New York-based gnaoua musician who mixes it in the city with all manner of ideas and musicians. Also resident in New York these days is **Bachir Attar**, leader of the **Jajouka** troupe (see box), who has recorded with jazz saxophonist Maceo Parker under the direction of avant garde funk producer Bill Laswell.

Laswell has also been involved in production work with the group **Aisha Kandisha's Jarring Effects** (or AKJE), who mix Moroccan trance sounds with rock, hip hop and techno. They released an amazing debut CD, *Buya*, in 1991 on the Swiss Barbarity label, and followed up with a techno-driven, Laswell-production, *Shabeesation*. They are only known on a subterranean level in Morocco and are yet to perform or release a cassette at home. They have an attitude as radical as their music – akin to, say, Cypress Hill or Ice Cube. Their name refers to a female spirit, whose very mention is taboo, and their lyrics question Moroccan social and religious norms.

The **Barbarity label** has now released about a dozen titles by Aisha Kandisha and other like-minded Moroccan bands seeking to fuse Moroccan music with Western electronic and dance influences. Their catalog includes CDs by the AKJE side project Amira Saqati, and the bands **Ahlam** and **Argan**, both of which feature AKJE musicians.

Elsewhere, expatriate Moroccans have been active in various new treatments. In Britain, **Sidi Seddiki**, Rabat-born but a Londoner since childhod, produced a seductive blend of Moroccan music and Western pop: strong, catchy songs, drawing on *chaabi*, and using a superb classical flautist. Belgium, meanwhile, has provided a base for the blind multi-instrumentalist **Hassan Erraji**, who has released a trio of jazz-flavoured discs with his multicultural groups Belcikal (now disbanded) and Arabesque. He is well worth seeing live, too, with his startling juggling with the *bendir*.

In **Spain** there have been a couple of notable collaborations between flamenco musicians and Andalucían orchestras, such as that of **José Heredia Maya and Enrique Morente** with the **Tetouan Orchestra** (Ariola, Spain), and **Juan Peña Lebrijano** with the **Tangier Orchestra** (GlobeStyle, UK).

The Tetouan orchestra have also collaborated in concert with the British composer **Michael Nyman**.

FOLK INSTRUMENTS

Folk instruments are very rudimentary and fairly easy to make, and this, combined with the fact that many music cafés keep their own, allows for a genuinely amateur development. Many of the instruments mentioned below are also to be found under the same or similar names (and with slight variations) in Algeria, Tunisia, Libya and even Egypt.

Morocco has a great many stringed and percussion instruments, mostly fairly basic in design. There are also a few **wind instruments**. The **Arab flute**, known by different tribes as the *nai, talawat, nira* or *gasba*, is made of a straight piece of cane open at both ends, with no mouthpiece and between five and seven holes, one at the back. It requires a great deal of skill to play it properly, by blowing at a slight angle. The **ghaita** or *rhita*, a type of oboe popular under various names throughout the Muslim world, is a conical pipe made of hardwood, ending in a bell often made of metal. Its double-reeded mouthpiece is encircled by a broad ring on which the player rests his lips in order to produce the circular breathing needed to obtain a continuous note. It has between seven and nine holes, one at the back. The **aghanin** is a double clarinet, identical to the Arab *arghoul*. It consists of two parallel pipes of wood or cane, each with a single-reed mouthpiece, five holes and a horn at the end for amplification. One pipe provides the tune while the other is used for adornments.

The most common **stringed instrument** is the **gimbri**. This is an African lute whose sound box is covered in front by a piece of hide. The rounded, fretless stem has two or three strings. The body of the smaller treble *gimbri* is pear-shaped, that of the bass *gimbri* (*hadjuj* or *sentir*) rectangular. The Gnaouas often put a resonator at the end of the stem to produce the buzz typical of Black African music. The **lotar** is another type of lute, used exclusively by the Chleuh Berbers. It has a circular body, also closed with a piece of skin, and three or four strings which are plucked with a plectrum.

The classic Arab lute, the **oud**, is used in classical orchestras and the traditional Arab orchestras known as *takhts*. Its pear-shaped body is covered by a piece of wood with two or three rosette-shaped openings. It has a short, fretless stem and six strings, five double and one single. The most popular stringed instruments played with a bow are the **kamanjeh** and the **rabab**. The former is an Iranian violin which was adopted by the Arabs. Its present Moroccan character owes a lot to the Western violin, though it is held vertically, supported on the knees. The *rabab* is a spike fiddle, rather like a viol. The bottom half of its long, curved body is covered in hide, the top in wood with a rosette-shaped opening. It has two strings.

The Chleuh Berbers use an archaic single-stringed *rabab* with a square stem and soundbox covered entirely in skin. Lastly, there is the **kanum**, a trapezoidal Arab zither with over seventy strings, grouped in threes and plucked with plectra attached to the fingernails. It is used almost exclusively in classical music.

Rapid hand-clapping and the clashes of bells and cymbals are only part of the vast repertoire of Moroccan **percussion**. Like most Moroccan drums the **darbuka** is made of clay, shaped into a cylinder swelling out slightly at the top. The single skin is beaten with both hands. It is used in both folk and classical music. The **taarija**, a smaller version of the *darbuka*, is held in one hand and beaten with the other. Then there are treble and bass **tan-tan** bongos, and the Moorish **guedra**, a large drum which rests on the ground. There is also a round wooden drum with skins on both sides called a **tabl**, which is beaten with a stick on one side and by hand on the other. This is used only in folk music.

As for **tambourines**, the ever-popular **bendir** is round and wooden, 40 or 50cm across, with two strings stretched under its single skin to produce a buzzing sound. The **tar** is smaller, with two rings of metal discs round the frame and no strings under its skin. The **duff** is a double-sided tambourine, often square in shape, which has to be supported so that it can be beaten with both hands.

Only two percussion instruments are made of metal: **karkabat**, double castanets used by the Gnaouas, and the **nakous**, a small cymbal played with two rods.

RAÏ

Raï – the word means "opinion" – originated in the western Algerian region around the port of Oran. It has traditional roots in Bedouin music, with its distinctive refrain (*ha-ya-rai*), but as a modern phenomenon has more in common with Western music. The backing is now solidly

WHERE TO BUY INSTRUMENTS

FES
Both Talâa Kebira and Talâa Seghira, close to Bab Boujeloud, have stores at intervals. Nearby here, ask for Abdillah Alami in the Kasbah Boujeloud, who sells excellent hand-made drums.

MEKNES
A musical instrument *souk* is under the archway connecting Souk Bezzarin and Rue des Sarraria, on the edge of the Medina – just past Bab El Djedid, if coming from Place El Hedim. Stalls are good value and there is much choice in a small area.

TETOUAN
A couple of good shops to browse and bargain in are to be found in and around the Rue Terrafin and Rue Ahmed Torres area.

AVERAGE PRICES
Oud (£50–100/$80–160); *Ghaïta* (£10–25/$16–40); *Naï* (£5–10/$8–16); *Bendir* (£5–10/$8–16); *Tara* (£5–10/$8–16); *Hadjuj* (£40–60/$65–95); *Darabouka* (£10–15/$16–24); *Qasba* (£10–15/$16–24); *Garageb* (£3–4/$5–7); *Tan-Tan* (£8–20/$13–32); *Gimbri* (£20–40/$32–65).

---

electric, with rhythm guitars, synthesizers and usually a rock drum kit as well as traditional drums. Its lyrics reflect highly contemporary concerns – cars, sex, sometimes alcohol – which have created some friction with the authorities.

Moroccans have taken easily to the music. Algerian *raï* stars such as **Cheb Khaled, Cheb Mami** and **Chaba Fadhela** are to be heard on cassettes in most souks, while home-grown *raï* stars include **Cheb Khader, Cheb Mimoun** and the mysterious **Chaba Zahouania**. The latter is said to be forbidden by her family from being photographed for her recordings.

Raï influence is also to be heard in the folk music of the **Oujda** area, the closest Moroccan town to Oran, in artists like **Rachid Briha** and **Hamid M'Rabati**.

SEPHARDIC MUSIC

Moroccan Jews, many of whom have now emigrated to Israel, left an important legacy in the north of the country, where their songs and ballads continued to be sung in the medieval Spanish, spoken at the time of their expulsion from Spain five centuries ago. Apart from the narrative ballads, these were mainly songs of courtly love, as well as lullabies and biblical songs, usually accompanied on a *tar*.

Moroccan Sephardic traditions and music continue to thrive in Israel. One of the stars of the 1998 Fes Festival of Sacred Music was the Moroccan Jewish singer, **Albert Bouhadanna**, who performed with Mohammed Briouels's Orchestra. Meantime, a rising star in World Music circles is **Emil Zrihan**, now resident in Israel but born in Rabat, whose music mixes Arab and Andalucian influences with the Hebrew liturgy.

DISCOGRAPHY

There has been quite a boom in CDs of Moroccan music in recent years. Most record stores in Britain or the US with a decent world music section should yield at least a few discs of ethnic, folk and Andalous music, or fusion with European groups. In Morocco itself (see overleaf), cassettes are the medium.

COMPILATIONS

ⓓ **Various** *Morocco: Crossroads of Time* (Ellipsis Arts, US). An excellent introduction to

Moroccan music that comes with a well-designed and informative book. The disc includes everything from ambient sounds in the Fes Medina, to powerful Jilala and Gnaoua music, Andalous, Rwai, Berber, and some good contemporary pop from Nouamane Lahlou.

CLASSICAL/ANDALOUS

ⓓ **Juan Peña Lebrijano and the Orquesta Andalusi de Tanger** *Encuentros* (GlobeStyle, UK) and *Casablanca* (Hemisphere, UK). A stunning cross-cultural blend that combines the passion of flamenco with the beauty and grace of andalous music.

⊙ **Orchestre Moulay Ahmed Loukili de Rabat** *Nuba Al-'Ushshâq* (Maison des Cultures du Monde, France). Six-CD set. The only problem with this is the price (£75/$120). It's quite an experience, finely presented and with informative notes.

⊙ **Ustad Massano Tazi** *Musique Classique Andalouse de Fès* (Ocora, France). Again, beautifully recorded and presented. Includes "Nuba Hijaz Al-Kabir" and "Nuba Istihilal".

⊙ **Various** *Maroc:* Anthologie d'Al-Melhûn (Maison des Cultures du Monde, France). A three-CD set containing performances from many of Morocco's finest *milhûn* singers. A good introduction.

CHAABI AND CONTEMPORARY

⊙ **Najat Aatabou** *The Voice of the Atlas* (GlobeStyle, UK). A superb collection of some of Najat's best-loved songs, including "Shouffi Rhirou" which has been covered brilliantly by the 3 Mustaphas 3.

⊙ **Ahlam** *Revolt Against Reason* (Barbarity, Switzerland). A close second to Aisha Kandisha (see below) in the 1990s Moroccan-meets-hip hop stakes, featuring some wonderfully expressive singing.

⊙ **Aisha Kandisha's Jarring Effects** *El Buya* (Barbarity, Switzerland). This intoxicating mix of Moroccan melodies and traditional string instruments with scratching reverb, and rushes of industrial noise is a great, still largely unheralded, early 1990s classic.

⊙ **Hassan Erraji** *Nikriz,* **La Dounia** and **Marhaba** (Riverboat, UK). Erraji is an oud-player, who fuses his classical training with accessible jazz. "Nikriz" is a real showcase for his talents; "la Dounia" has a starker, and more Arabic content; "Marhaba", the latest, is more song-based, upbeat and very listenable.

⊙ **Lem Chaheb** *Lem Chaheb* (Club du Disques Arabe, France). A compilation from the late 1980s. The band's usual line-up of guitar, buzuk, percussion is augmented by trumpets and synthesizers provided by two members of Dissidenten.

⊙ **Sidi Seddiki** *Shouf!* (GlobeStyle, UK). A fine debut album of chaabi meets pop from a London-based musician.

⊙ **Yosefa Dahari** *Yosefa* (Worldly Dance, UK). Just what the label says: dance music with English and Maghrebi songs. A bit of an exotica product but one with promise.

⊙ **Hassan Hakmoun and Zahar** *Trance* (Real World, UK). Gnaoua rhythms meet jazz dance psychedelia.

GNAOUA AND JILALA

⊙ **Various** *Gnawa Night – Music of the Marrakesh Spirit Masters* (Axiom, UK). Gnaoua music at its evocative best, recorded by Bill Laswell.

⊙ **Various** *Moroccan Trance Music* (Sub Rosa, Belgium). Not for the faint hearted, this is intense gnaoua and jilala music, combined on the disc with some of Paul Bowles' personal recordings.

⊙ **Various** *Moroccan Trance 2* (Sub Rosa, Belgium). Good atmospheric selections featuring a Gnaoua Brotherhood from Marrakesh, alongside three tracks of the Master Musicians of Jajouka.

⊙ **Various** *Music of Islam Vol 6: Gnawa* (Celestial Harmonies, US). Clear studio recordings of a gnawa group from marrakesh, with fierce gimbri from Ahmed Baqbou, brother of Jil Jilala's Mustapha Baqbou.

⊙ **Maleem Mahmoud Ghania with Pharoah Sanders** *The Trance of the Seven Colours* (Axiom/island, US). Gnawa-jazz crossover, featuring the great sax player from Coltrane's band.

INSTRUMENTALISTS

⊙ **The Master Musicians of Jajouka** *Apocalypse Across the Sky* (Axiom, UK). Without the electronic trickery of Brian Jones' seminal album, the power and clarity of these remarkable performers stands out all the more on Bill Laswell's outing.

⊙ **Hmaoui Abd El-Hamid** *La Flûte de l'Atlas* (Arion, France). Hypnotic and haunting flute-like ney, backed by percussion, oud and zither.

TOP TEN MOROCCAN CASSETTES

In Morocco, cassettes of all kinds are readily available in any market – and you can buy videos of many artists, too. The following are a personal top ten to ask for (in order of priority).

1. **Nass El-Ghiwane** *Nass El-Ghiwane* (Hassania, Morocco). The only remaining recordings with singer Boujmia. Powerful and hypnotic.

2. **Najat Aatabou** *Najat Aatabou* (Hassania, Morocco). A traditional line-up of oud, violin and drums accompany Najat's magnificent voice.

3. **Jil Jilala** *The Candle* (Disques Gam, Morocco). Poetic introductions to a set of atmospheric songs.

4. **Abdelkrim Rais and the Orchestra of Fez** *Vol 5* (Fassi Disques, Morocco). "Nuba Maya", which is featured on this cassette, has some of the most beautiful melodies in the andalous tradition.

5. **Hamid Zahir** *Hamid Zahir* (Tichkaphone, Morocco). From the old school of chaabi singers. A rich textural orchestra of traditional instruments and vibrant drumming carry Hamid through an uplifting selection of songs and fiery lesebs.

6. **Lem Chaheb** *Lem Chaheb* (Nissim, Morocco). This early tape includes the wonderfully infectious "Nari Nari" which was later covered by Dissidenten as "Radio Arab" – the Moroccan equivalent of the Byrds' jangling guitar sound.

7. **L'Haj L'Houcine Toulali** *L'Haj L'Houcine Toulali* (Tichkaphone, Morocco). Popular milhûn at its best. His orchestration is some of the best and the melodies stay with you for a long time.

8. **Orchestra Faysel** *Orchestra Faysel* (Forkafane, Morocco). A very odd mixture. Synthesizer, drum machine, buzuk and bendir lead the trance dance Berber beats. If the Velvet Underground had been Moroccan, they might have sounded like this.

9. **Mohamed Bajaddoub** *L'Age d'Or de la Musique Andalouse Vol 2* (Disques Gam, Morocco). Beautiful arrangement of andalous suites. Very inspiring stuff.

10. **Nass El Ghiwane** *Chants d'espoir* (Hassania, Morocco). From the late 1980s, a haunting collection of long narratives that draw you in even though you may not understand the lyrics.

MOROCCAN FICTIONS

Storytelling is an age-old Moroccan tradi-tion – and an active one, as any visit to a weekly souk will reveal. The American nov-elist Paul Bowles, a resident in Tangier more or less since the war, became interest-ed in such tales in the early 1950s and began tape recording and transcribing examples told by various Moroccan friends – Ahmed Yacoubi, Larbi Layachi, Abdeslam Boulaich and, in particular, Mohammed Mrabet, with whom he continues to collaborate.

Mrabet's work now amounts to a dozen collections of stories, novels and novellas. The piece included here is in some ways atypical – Mrabet's interests are rooted more in his experience of city life – but it shows his showmanship and masterful handling of a deeply traditional theme of Moroccan storytelling, the casting of spells. Abdeslam Boulaich, better known as a painter, reveals a similar interest in folk humour. Mohamed Choukri, by con-trast, is a more literary figure, with a novel and books on Tennessee Williams and Jean Genet to his name. Alone among the three authors here, he wrote his text (in Classical Arabic), with Bowles translating from an oral reading in Maghrebi.

For details of books by these various authors, see the bibliography on p.579 & pp.583–5.

MOHAMMAD MRABET: *THE LUTE*

A young man named Omar got onto his mare one day and rode over his father's land for many miles, looking for the right place to build a small house of his own. He came to a hill between the forest and the olive groves. This is the spot, he said. Here I can play my lute all day.

Little by little he built a cottage, bringing the materials from his father's house, and doing all the work himself. When it was done he fur-nished it with everything he needed for the pleasant life he intended to lead. His most important possession was his lute, which he had trained so that when anyone was coming it sounded its strings in warning. Then Omar would look into the opening under the strings and watch the person as he approached.

Outside the house he built an arbor of canes where he could lie back and drink his tea. And he would sit out there in the shade of the arbor with the green trees all around him, smoking kif and drinking tea. At length he would take down his lute and begin to play.

Farther down the valley lived two sisters whose father and mother had died, leaving them alone in a big house. The younger sister was still only a girl, and there was a handsome village lad with whom she was friendly. The older sis-ter, who desired the boy for herself, caught sight of him talking to the girl under a tree. Later she questioned her.

Who was that you were talking to?

The boy from the village.

What did he say to you?

The girl smiled and looked very happy. He said beautiful words and wonderful things. Because I love him and he loves me.

What? cried the woman. And you're not ashamed to say such a thing?

Why should I be? We're going to be married.

The older sister jumped up and rushed out. She began to burn powders and to chant, and it was not long before she burst into the room with a scream and flung a handful of black powder over the girl. At that instant her sister no longer stood in front of her – only a camel, which she chained outside.

A few days later the village boy came to see the younger sister. The woman greeted him from the doorway and invited him into the house. He sat down and looked around, and then through the window he saw the camel.

Why have you got that camel chained to the ground with its legs tied together? he asked her.

She's a bad animal, the woman said. I have to keep her chained up so she won't get into trou-ble.

Let the poor thing loose so it can graze, he told her. It has no life at all this way. Unfasten the chain and untie the ropes.

No, no. I can't do that.

The boy waited a moment. Then he said: The girl who lives here. Where is she?

That girl? She's getting married tomorrow.

What? he cried. But she was going to marry me!

No. She never mentioned anything about that to me, she told him. Anyway, that's the way it is.

Then she laughed. And what about me? Don't you like me?

Yes, he said. Of course I like you.

Why don't you and I get married, then?

The boy looked at her, and then he looked out at the camel. All right, he said at length. I'll marry you. But only if you set that camel free.

Without saying anything the woman went outside and undid the chain and ropes, and the camel walked away. Then she came in and said she would see him that evening.

As the boy went along the path to the village he came upon the camel waiting for him. He was horrified to hear it speak with the voice of the girl.

Don't trust my sister, it said. You see what she's done to me. I'm the one you were going to marry. Go as far away from here as you can, and stay away. I've got to try and get back my body somehow.

Then the camel walked away, and the boy was too downcast to call after it. He left the village the same afternoon.

One day not long afterward as Omar lay under his arbor on a mat drinking tea, the cords of his lute suddenly sounded. When he peered inside it he saw a camel. He watched it come nearer, and then he hung up the lute and went out into the orchard. The camel walked straight to him and said: Good afternoon.

Omar was startled. You can speak?

I said good afternoon. Yes, I can speak.

I've never seen a talking camel, he said.

But I'm not a camel. That's the trouble. And she told him what her sister had done to her. Then she said: I have a favor to ask of you. Let me stay here with you for a while.

Omar looked thoughtfully at the animal, and said: Ouakha. You can stay with me.

The camel lay down beside the arbor, and Omar began to play the lute. It was the hour when the birds sang and flew from tree to tree. When the birds became quiet, he glanced at the camel and saw that tears were falling from its eyes. He put the lute aside.

The next day as Omar sat in the arbor talking with the camel, he heard the strings of the lute. When he looked inside, he saw a woman walking through the wilderness, over the rocks and between the trees. He watched for a while, but she did not come any closer. Finally she disappeared. He sat down.

Tell me, he said to the camel. What was your sister doing at the moment you felt yourself becoming a camel?

The camel thought for a while. Then it said: She sprinkled some powder over my head, and she had a piece of green cloth in her hand. I saw her fold it three times and then throw it on top of a chest.

I have a friend who might be able to help, Omar told her. He often comes by around this hour.

As they sat there a large crow came flying over the trees, and alighted on the ground beside the arbor. After they had greeted each other, Omar said: You're an expert thief, aren't you?

The crow was embarrassed. It's true I've stolen things. But all that is in the past.

Omar smiled. Good, he said. But you've still got to steal one more time. Do you know Tchar Flanflani?

Yes.

You've got to get into that big house there and look around until you find a green cloth. Don't unfold it. Bring it to me.

Ouakha, said the crow, and it flew off.

They did not have to wait long for it to return, carrying the green cloth in its claws. As Omar took the cloth in his hands and let it unfold, instead of a camel lying on the ground beside the arbor, it was a girl.

He stared at her first in amazement and then with delight, for she was beautiful. Then she jumped up and threw her arms around him, and he embraced her. Together they went into the house.

The following day when the sister looked to see if the green cloth was safe in its place, she did not find it. She searched for it inside the house and out, but without success. As Omar and the girl sat in the shade of the arbor, the strings of the lute began to vibrate. He peered into it and saw the woman walking in the forest.

Here, he said to the girl. Look in here and see if you know who that is.

She looked inside the lute and drew back. It's my sister! she whispered. She's looking for me.

Omar hung up the lute and walked out to the orchard to meet the woman. When he came up to her she looked at him and said: Who are you?

That's what I want to ask you, he said. Who are you and where have you come from and what do you want here? This is my land you're on, and the edge of it is a long way from here.

I'm looking for a camel, she said. A camel I've lost.

I have your camel, he told her.

What! Where is it? What have you done with it?

It's over there, he said, pointing to the arbor where the girl stood. And she came out and walked toward them.

The woman looked at Omar. You won't win! she cried. Then she turned and went back the way she had come.

A few days after this, Omar put the girl onto the mare and rode with her to his father's house, where they celebrated their marriage with a wedding feast that lasted for three days. Then the married couple rode back to the little house. The two were very happy together, and the days passed swiftly.

But one moonlit night as they lay asleep in bed, the lute hanging on the wall twanged its strings. Omar sprang up and put his eye to the hole. A woman dressed all in white walked in the brilliant moonlight. He pulled the lute down and played softly for a while. The next time he looked in, a dense white cloud had formed around the figure of the woman in the orchard, and the cloud was so thick that she could not move one way or the other. Omar hung the lute on the wall and got back into bed.

What was it?

It was your sister. She's down there in the orchard now, dressed all in white. I've got her shut in. She can't go forward or backward.

Let her go! the girl begged him. We mustn't be cruel to her. I can't bear to think of her suffering.

Omar paid no attention to her pleas, but turned over and went to sleep. In the morning after he had bathed and had his breakfast, he sat down under the arbor, smoked a few pipes of kif, and said to the girl: Come here and look.

Inside the lute she saw the swirling cloud among the olive trees. Omar took the lute and played on it for a moment. Then he handed it back, and she looked again. The cloud had disappeared, and the woman stood there shouting up at them from the orchard.

I'll be back! she screamed.

Another night as they slept, the lute again sounded a warning, and Omar seized it and put his eye to the hole. Seeing the woman, he played a loud fast melody for a while. When he peered in the next time, he saw that once again a cloud had formed around the woman, but this time it had risen high into the air with her, where it remained, as still as a rock. He got into bed and said nothing about it.

But the next morning when the girl looked outside she called to Omar. There's something hanging in the air above the orchard!

It's your sister, he said.

Forgive her this time, and she'll never come back to bother us any more, his wife said, and she went on pleading with him.

Your sister will never change, Omar told her. She ought not to be pardoned and turned loose to do harm in the world.

But the girl sobbed and begged him to let her sister down, and finally he got up and plucked on the lute. The cloud slowly settled onto the ground and blew away. This time the woman did not stay to say anything, but ran off as soon as she felt the earth beneath her feet.

When she got back to her house, she shut herself in and fasted for four days. At the end of this time she had a vision of two trees whose trunks stood very close one to the other. She forced herself between them and knew that something great had happened. When she turned, she saw eight strings of gut stretched from a crosspiece between the tree trunks, and she knew that this was the way to get into Omar's house without alerting the lute. From then on she spent all her time preparing the strips of gut and the other things she would need when she found the two trees. When she had everything ready, she began to go regularly to the forest below the little house, in search of the place she had seen in her vision. She found it one night. It was in a dense part of the woods, just below the house. Quickly she squeezed in between the two tree trunks.

The moment she had pushed through, a wall formed around her body and over her head, so that she was encased in a shell of rock between the two trees. The lute by Omar's bed made a loud sound as though it had been hurled to the floor, and then it began to play a strange, halting melody, a thing Omar had never heard it do before. He waited until it had stopped, and then he took it down and looked into it.

Your sister! he cried. There's nothing I can do! She's dying. The lute did it by itself. I didn't touch it.

The girl seized the lute and held it close to her face. Beyond the strings she saw the two trees and the boulder between them. And then through the casing of the stone she saw her sister's face. Her mouth was open and her eyes rolled from side to side as she gasped

Then the wall of stone around her body became smoke and blew away through the trees, and she fell forward onto the ground.

The next morning Omar and his wife went to the spot and found her body lying there between the two arar trees.

We must bury her, said the girl.

Not on my land, Omar told her. On her own land, if you like, but not here.

And each afternoon when he sat with his wife under the arbor playing the lute, the crow came and sat with them, and listened.

1977

ABDESLAM BOULAICH:
THREE HEKAYAS

Cowardice

A Moslem, a Jew, and a Christian were sitting in a cafe talking about Heaven. They agreed that it was a difficult place to get into, but each one thought he would have a better chance than the others.

You have to have the right clothes, the Christian told them. I always wear a jacket and a tie.

Let's go and see, said the other two.

They started out, and when they got close to Heaven, the Moslem and the Jew stopped walking, and the Christian kept going until he reached the door of Heaven.

Our Lord Solomon, who guards the door, said to him: Where are you going?

Inside, the Nazarene answered.

Who are you?

My name is John.

Stand back, said Our Lord Solomon.

Then the Jew and the Moslem spoke together. The Moslem said: He didn't get in. But we will.

I'll go first, said the Jew.

That's right. You go, the Moslem told him.

So the Jew walked up to the door of Heaven. And Our Lord Solomon said to him: Where are you going?

Inside.

Who are you?

Yaqoub, said the Jew.

Stand back!

The Moslem saw this and said to himself: That's that. Neither one of them got in. Now I'll try.

He walked until he got to the door of Heaven. Then he pulled the hood of his djellaba down over his face. And Our Lord Solomon said to him: Where are you going?

Inside.

Who are you? Our Lord Solomon asked him.

I am the Prophet Mohammed, he said. And he went in. The Jew was watching. He said to himself: If he can get in there, so can I.

And he took a sack and filled it with sticks of wood and slung it over his shoulder. Then he walked up to the door.

Where are you going? asked Our Lord Solomon.

The Jew stuck his foot in the door.

Who are you?

The Prophet Mohammed's manservant, he said. And the Jew went in.

The Christian had been watching. He was afraid to try to get in by lying, and so he went back to his country and told everyone that Heaven did not exist.

Stupidity

In a small mountain village lived a man who could not talk very well because he had no roof to his mouth. When it came time for him to marry, his family chose him a girl who had the same trouble. But since the man had never seen her, nor had the girl seen him, neither one knew how the other one spoke.

The day of the wedding, the man went into the girl's room. The servant brought in the taifor with a pot of couscous on it, and then she went home, leaving the front door unlatched.

The man sat with his hands folded in front of him, and so did the girl. Each one was looking at the other, waiting for the other to speak. She was waiting for the man to say: Eat. And he was waiting for her to say: Eat. He was afraid to speak for fear she would hear his voice and not be able to love him. And the girl was afraid he would hear hers and not want her for a wife. Each one looked at the other, and the door of the house was unlatched.

A beggar was passing through the street, crying: For the love of Allah, a little bread! And no one paid him any attention. When he came to the house of the bridegroom he saw the door ajar, and he pushed it open and walked in. He went through the courtyard and came to the room where the two were sitting. Then he saw the man and the girl looking at one another, with the food in front of them on the taifor, and neither one saying anything. The bridegroom saw the beggar standing there. He wanted to tell him to get out. But he would not speak, and so he shook his head up and down at him. But the beggar thought he meant: Go on and eat. He sat down and began to eat the couscous, and he went on eating until there was only a little left. Then he ate the meat, and when he had finished, he took the bone and hung it around the man's neck on a string, because he thought the man was simple-minded. And he went out.

A dog was running through the street. When it came to the house of the bridegroom it caught the smell of food coming through the open door, and it went into the courtyard. It ran to the door of the room where they were sitting, and went in. The man and the girl sat still and said nothing. The dog put its feet up on the taifor and licked up the rest of the couscous. It was still hungry. Then it saw the bone that hung around the bridegroom's neck, and it seized it between its jaws and tried to run. The man fell over onto the floor, and the dog dragged him to the door. The dog kept pulling, and the man's head hit the wall.

Then the man cried out: Help me untie the string!

The girl heard his words, and she was no longer afraid to speak.

The beggar was right! she said. I can't live with such a man!

But you speak the same way! he cried.

I'm the only one who wouldn't have minded that, she told him. And she went out of the house, and left the man on the floor with the dog pulling at the bone.

Greed

A sickly man who lived in the city married a girl from the country. He was never very hungry, but the girl was healthy and ate a great deal. One day the man went to the market and bought many vegetables and four cow's feet. When he took the food home to his wife, he told her:

Make me a stew so I can have it when I come home for lunch.

Yes, she said.

But wait for me, he said. Don't eat anything until I get back.

I won't, she said.

When he had gone she made the stew. And then she waited. He ought to be here soon, she said to herself. He'll be here any minute.

After he had finished working, the man went to a café and began to play cards. He stayed there in the café a long time, and his wife went on waiting. Soon she was very hungry. She took one of the cow's feet out of the stew and ate it. And she said to herself: It doesn't matter. When he comes I'll make up something to tell him.

The man came home and sat down. Where's the stew? he said. You haven't eaten anything, have you?

Not yet, she told him. She brought the stew and began to ladle it out. Then the man noticed that there were only three feet in the pot. He began to shout: And the other foot? Where is it?

I haven't got it, she said. You brought three and I cooked three. I hate cow's feet anyway.

The man was very unhappy. Do you want to kill me? he cried. Bring me the other foot, or I may die right here.

Die, if that's what you want, she told him. Why are you waiting?

The man rolled over onto the floor and began to moan.

Get up! said his wife. But he only told her to fetch the fqih and make him wash him so he could be buried.

When she came in with the fqih, the girl said to her husband again: Get up off the floor!

Have you got the cow's foot? he asked her.

The fqih began to wash him.

Get up! she said. Don't you want to have your burial clothes put on you?

Have you brought the cow's foot?

She did not answer. The people came in and dressed the man in his kfin, ready to be buried. And then they laid him on the litter.

You're off to the cemetery, his wife told him.

They carried him through the doorway into the street.

Where's the cow's foot? he cried. His wife shut the door.

The people walked through the streets carrying him on the litter. When they passed in front of the market, the butcher saw the procession. Who's that who has died? he asked. They told him.

And to think that only this morning he was here in my shop, the poor man, and he bought four cow's feet!

When the dead man heard this, he sat up on his litter. How many did you say? he called to the butcher.

Four!

Ah, you see? he said. And my wife told me I'd bought only three.

No. It was four, said the butcher.

The man lay down again. And the men carrying him were talking and did not notice anything. They went on their way to the cemetery. When they got there they lifted him off the lit-

ter and started to lower him into the ground. But at that moment he sat up again.

Wait! he told the fqih. I've got three cow's feet at home that I still haven't eaten. It's not good to be hungry when you arrive in Heaven. I'm going to run back and eat them now. If I do get to Heaven then, at least I'll have some food inside me.

The people let go of him, and he ran home. When he went into the house his wife said: You came back? You're still alive?

Give me the three cow's feet, he told her. She gave them to him. He ate one. But then he was no longer hungry, and his wife ate the other two.

1961

MOHAMED CHOUKRI: *THE PROPHET'S SLIPPERS*

More pleasure and fantasy. More money, more ways of getting hold of it. I was tired of enjoying myself, and yet I was not satisfied. Fatin walked toward me, white as snow in the blood-red light of the bar. She took one of my notebooks, looked at it, and grinned.

She muttered something unintelligible and moved away again, disappearing among those who were kicking the air. It was three o'clock in the morning, and I was bored and nervous. Om Kalsoum was singing: "Sleep never made life seem too long, nor long waiting shortened life."

A black man appeared, white on black. He took one of my books and began to read aloud: "This total liberty has its tragic and pessimistic side." He put it down. "What's that book about?" he demanded.

"It's about a man who doesn't understand this world," I said. "He hurts himself and everybody who comes near him."

He nodded, lifted his glass, and drank. When he had finished, he said: "You're crazy."

I saw Fatin writing in a notebook. Meanwhile I smoked, drank, and thought about the matter of the slippers. The lights went off. Women cried out. When they came on again, both men and women murmured. I bought another drink for Khemou, and she gave me a kiss that left a sweet taste in my mouth. Her brown tongue tickled. She was eating chocolate, and her laugh was red in the light from the bar. Khemou

walked off and Fatin came up to me. She handed me a slip of blue paper. On it she had written: Rachid. What do you know about love? You spend more time writing about love than you do making love. The one who has never studied love enjoys it more than the one who knows all about it. Love is not a science. Love is feeling, feeling, feeling.

Miriam Makeba went into "Malaysia." She has a white voice. I began to write on the same piece of blue paper. *Fatin, you are my red bed, and I'm your black blanket. I'm beginning to see it that way.*

I looked around for Fatin. Her mouth was a wound in her face, and a foreign sailor was sucking on it. She had her right arm around him and was pouring her drink onto the floor with her left hand. Khemou came by and offered me her lips, like a mulberry. I bought her another drink. I was so pleased with the effect of her kiss that I began to think once more about selling the slippers. How much ought I to ask for them? A million francs, the Englishman ought to pay, if he wants the Prophet's slippers. He's an idiot in any case, or he couldn't be taken in by such a tale. But how can I tell just how stupid he is? It was he who first brought it up, the black-market story.

Fatin appeared, black, blonde, white. I handed her the slip of blue paper. She looked at me and smiled. I was thinking that girls like her only made trouble. Her little mouth now looked like a scar that had healed. I thought of the Indian poet Mirzah Asad Allah Ghalef:

For those who are thirsty
I am the dry lip.

She wants a kind of love that will make her unhappy. What I like about her is that she still believes the world ought to be changed.

Khemou and Latifa began to scream at each other like two cats fighting, while Miriam Makeba's white voice continued to sing. Khemou pulled Latifa's black hair, knocked her down, and kicked her face. Latifa screamed and the blood ran from her nose. The colors all came together in my head. Leaving the blue paper with me, Fatin ran to separate the two. I read on it: *You're right. I serve them my flesh, but I don't feel it when they eat me.*

Vigon is singing in his white voice. "Outside the Window." Vigon is singing, and I think of the almond trees in flower, and of snow, which I love.

Khemou and Latifa came out of the rest room. They had made up, like two little girls. They began to laugh and dance as if nothing had happened. I sat there smoking, while in my imagination I attacked each man in the bar whose face I didn't like. A kick for this one. a slap in the face for that one, a punch in the jaw for that one over there. Watching myself do as I pleased with them put me into a better frame of mind.

Tomorrow I'll sell the slippers. Fatin came past again, and I asked her why Khemou and Latifa had been quarreling. She said it was because Khemou had told the man Latifa was drinking with that she had tuberculosis.

Is it true? I asked her.

Yes, she said. But she says she's cured now.

The Englishman and I were at my house, eating couscous. He turned to me and said: "This is the best couscous I've ever tasted."

From time to time he looked toward the corner where my grandmother sat, her head bent over. I told him the couscous had been sent from Mecca. "My aunt sends a lot of it each month."

He looked at me with amazement. "It's fantastic!"

So that he would get the idea, I added: "Everything in the house was brought from Mecca. Even that incense burning is sent each month."

We finished the couscous and started on another dish of meat baked with raisins and hot spices. "It's called mrozeya," I told him.

He muttered a few words, and then said: "Ah, nice. Very nice." My grandmother's head was still bent over. I saw that the Englishman was looking at her, sitting there in her white robes. The incense and the silence in the room made her seem more impressive. She was playing her part very well. Our demure little servant brought the tea in a silver teapot. She too was dressed in immaculate white, and she too kept her face hidden. Her fingers were painted with elaborate designs in henna, and her black hair shone above her enormous earrings. She made no false moves. She greeted the Englishman without smiling, as I had instructed her to do. It became her to look grave. I had never seen her so pretty.

The mint tea with ambergris in it seemed to please the Englishman. "Do you like the tea?" I asked him.

"Oh, yes! It's very good!"

There was silence for a while. I thought: The time has come to rub Aladdin's lamp. I got up and went to whisper in my grandmother's ear. I did not even form words; I merely made sounds. She nodded her head slowly, without looking up. Then I lifted the white cushion and removed the piece of gold-embroidered green silk that covered it.

The Englishman looked at the slippers, made colorless by age. His hand slowly advanced to touch the leather. Then he glanced at me, and understood that I did not want him to touch them.

"My God! They're marvelous!"

I covered the slippers as I stood there, in order to let him observe them through the veil of green silk. Slowly and with great care I turned and put the cushion back into its place, as if I were applying a bandage to an injury. He glanced at me, and then stared for a long time in the direction of the slippers. Understanding that it was time to leave, he stood up.

We were sitting at the Café Central. For the third time since we had left the house, he said: "Then it's impossible?"

"A thing like that is so difficult," I said. "I wouldn't know how to do it. It was hard enough to get her to let you even look at them. You can be sure you're the only Christian ever to have seen them. And no other is going to, either."

"I understand," he said. "But perhaps we can come to an agreement."

"I understand too. But what can I do? Those slippers are my grandmother's very life. If she should find them missing, she might lose her mind, or have a heart attack. I'm very fond of her, naturally, and I respect her feelings about the slippers."

"I'll give you time to think about it," he said. "But try and persuade her."

"Yes. But when you think of how hard it was to get her to allow you to look at them, you can see how much harder it would be to persuade her."

"Do what you can," he said.

I said I would, but that I thought it was out of the question. Then I said: "Listen. I have an idea. But only on one condition."

"What's that?"

I hesitated for an instant.

"Tell me. Perhaps we can find a way."

"You'd have to leave Tangier the minute you got the slippers."

"That would be all right," he said, understanding. "It's an excellent tactic."

"And I'd have to get out of Tangier myself and stay somewhere else. And I couldn't come back as long as my grandmother was still alive."

"No."

"I couldn't stay on here once they were gone."

"I quite understand."

"It's those slippers that keep her alive, you might say."

"Yes, yes. How much do you want for them?"

I stared at him, and my voice said: "A million francs."

"Oh!" he cried. "No! That's very high!"

"But you'll have something extremely rare. No museum has anything like them. And I'll regret what I've done for the rest of my life."

"I know, I know. But that's a great deal of money. I'll give you half a million. I can't pay any more than that."

"You'd have to pay more than that," I told him.

"No, no. I can't. I haven't got it."

"You give me your address, and I'll write you from wherever I go, and you can send me the rest later."

We looked at each other for a few seconds. In my mind I was thinking: Go on, say the word, Mister Stewart.

"Very well," he finally said.

Wonderful, Mister Stewart, I thought.

"Where shall we meet tomorrow?" I asked him.

He reflected for a moment, and said: "I'll wait for you in the lobby at the Hotel Minzah."

"No," I said. "Outside the hotel. In the street. And you must have your ticket with you, so you can leave the minute I give you the slippers."

"Of course."

"What time will that be?"

While he hesitated I was thinking: Come on, Mister Stewart. Make up your mind.

"At three o'clock in the afternoon."

I got up, shook hands with him, and said: "Keep it to yourself."

"I shan't breathe a word."

"It's not only my grandmother who's going to be upset, but everybody who knows she has the slippers."

I walked away. A moment later I turned and saw him leaving the café.

I found him waiting for me in front of the hotel. He seemed nervous, and he looked wide-eyed at the bag I was carrying. I saw that he had a packet in his hand. Half a million, I thought. More pleasure, more time to think of other such tricks later. The colors in the bar.

I motioned to him to follow me, and stopped walking only when we were a good distance from the entrance to the hotel. We stood facing one another, and shook hands. He looked down at my bag, and I glanced at the packet he held in his hand.

I opened the bag, and he touched the slippers for a second. Then he took it out of my hands, and I took the packet from him. Pointing to a parked car, he said: "There's the car that's going to take me to the airport."

I thought to myself: And tonight I'll be at the Messalina Bar.

I sat down in the corner the same as always. I smoked, drank, and bought kisses without haggling over their price. I'm fed up with pleasure. Fed up, but not satisfied. One woman is not enough.

"Khemou's in the hospital," Fatin told me. "And Latifa's at the police station. She got drunk and hit Khemou on the head with a bottle."

I asked Fatin who the girls were who were sitting in the corner opposite me. She said they were both from Dar El Beida. She picked up one of my notebooks and walked away with it. I waved at the younger of the two. She spoke for a while with her friend. And I drank and smoked and waited for the first kiss of a girl I had never yet touched.

She got up and came over, and I saw the small face relax. Her mouth was like a strawberry. She began to sip the drink I bought her. Her lips shone. Her mouth opened inside mine. A strawberry soaked in gin and tonic. Eve eating mulberries. Adam approaches her, but she puts the last berry into her mouth before he can get to her. Then he seizes the last berry from between her teeth. The mulberry showed Eve how to kiss. Adam knows all the names of things, but Eve had to teach him how to kiss.

Two men had begun to fight over one of the girls. The shorter of the two lost his balance. The other kicked until someone seized him from behind.

Fatin put a piece of blue paper in front of me. I was drinking, smoking, and eating mulberries from the new small mouth. I read what was written on the piece of blue paper. I'm not the same person I was yesterday. I know it but I can't say it clearly. You must try and understand me.

The new face held up her empty glass. I looked again at the mulberries. The barman was busy drawing squares on a small piece of white paper. "Give her another drink," I told him. The friend who had been sitting with her came over. "Give her a drink too," I said.

I thought: More mulberries and human flesh. More tricks and money. I began to write on Fatin's slip of blue paper: I must not try to understand you.

1973

WRITERS ON MOROCCO

As any glimpse at the book listings following will show, there's a long tradition of
writing on Morocco. The pieces here –
from Budgett Meakin, Walter Harris, Elias
Canetti and Paul Bowles – represent the
best of the genre and much of its range.

BUDGETT MEAKIN: *IN MOORISH GUISE*

To those who have not themselves experienced
what the attempt to see an eastern country in
native guise entails, a few stray notes of what
it has been my lot to encounter in seeking for
knowledge in this style, will no doubt be of
interest. Such an undertaking, like every other
style of adventure, has both its advantages and
disadvantages. To the student of the people the
former are immense, and if he can put up with
whatever comes, he will be well repaid for all
the trials by the way. In no other manner can a
European mix with any freedom with the
natives of this country. When once he has dis-
carded the outward distinguishing features of
what they consider a hostile infidelity, and has
as far as possible adopted their dress and their
mode of life, he has spanned one of the great
gulfs which have hitherto yawned between
them.

Squatted on the floor, one of a circle round a
low table on which is a steaming dish into
which each plunges his fist in search of dainty
morsels, the once distant Moor thaws to an
astonishing extent, becoming really friendly and
communicative, in a manner totally impossible
towards the starchy European who sits uneasily
on a chair, conversing with his host at ease on
the floor. And when the third cup of tea syrup
comes, and each lolls contentedly on the cushions, there is manifested a brotherly feeling not
unknown in Western circles under analogous
circumstances, here fortunately without a suggestion of anything stronger than "gunpowder".

Yes, this style of thing decidedly has its
delights – of which the above must not be taken
as the most elevating specimen and many are
the pleasant memories which come before me
as I mentally review my life "as a Moor". In
doing so I seem to be again transported to

another world, to live another life, as was my
continual feeling at the time. Everything around
me was so different, my very actions and
thoughts so complete a change from what they
were under civilisation, that when the courier
brought the periodical budget of letters and
papers I felt as one in a dream, even my mother
tongue sounding strange after not having heard
it so long.

Often I have had to "put up" in strange quarters; sometimes without any quarters at all. I
have slept in the mansions of Moorish merchants, and rolled up in my cloak in the street. I
have occupied the guest chambers of country
governors and sheikhs, and I have passed the
night on the wheat in a granary, wondering
whether fleas or grains were more numerous. I
have been accommodated in the house of a
Jewish Rabbi, making a somewhat similar
observation and I have been the guest of a
Jewish Consular Agent of a Foreign Power,
where the awful stench from the drains was not
exceeded by that of the worst hovel I ever
entered. I have even succeeded in wooing
Morpheus out on the sea-shore, under the lea of
a rock, and I have found the debris by the side
of a straw rick an excellent couch till it came on
to rain. Yet again, I have been one of half a
dozen on the floor of a windowless and doorless
summer-house in the middle of the rainy season. The tent of the wandering Arab has afford-
ed me shelter, along with calves and chickens
and legions of fleas, and I have actually passed
the night in a village mosque.

When I set out on my travels in Moorish
guise, it was with no thought of penetrating
spots so venerated by the Moors that all non-
Muslims are excluded, but the idea grew upon
me as I journeyed, and the Moors themselves
were the cause. This is how it came about.
Having become acquainted to some extent with
the language and customs of the people during
a residence of several years among them as a
European, when I travelled – with the view of
rendering myself less conspicuous, and mixing
more easily with the natives – I adopted their
dress and followed their style of life, making,
however, no attempt to conceal my nationality.
After a while I found that when I went where I
was not known, all took me for a Moor till they
heard my speech, and recognised the foreign
accent and the blunders which no native could
make. My Moorish friends would often remark

that were it not for this I could enter mosques and saint-houses with impunity.

For convenience' sake I had instructed the one faithful attendant who accompanied me to call me by a Muslim name resembling my own, and I afterwards added a corruption of my surname which sounded well, and soon began to seem quite natural. This prevented the attention of the bystanders being arrested when I was addressed by my man, who was careful also always to refer to me as "Seyyid", Master, a term never applied to Europeans or Jews.

Having got so far, a plan occurred to me to account for my way of speaking. I had seen a lad from Manchester, born there of an English mother, but the son of a Moor, who knew not a word of Arabic when sent to Morocco by his father. Why could I not pass as such a one, who had not yet perfected himself in the Arabic tongue? Happy thought! Was I not born in Europe, and educated there? Of course I was, and here was the whole affair complete. I remember, too, that on one or two occasions I had had quite a difficulty to persuade natives that I was not similarly situated to this lad. On the first occasion I was taken by surprise, as one among a party of English people, the only one dressed in Moorish costume, which I thought under those circumstances would deceive no one. When asked whence I came, I replied "England", and was then asked, "Is there a mosque there?" I answered that I was not aware that there was one, but that I knew a project had been set on foot to build one near London. Other questions followed, as to my family and what my father's occupation was, till I was astonished at the enquiry, "Has your father been to Mekka yet?"

"Why, no", I answered, as it dawned upon me what had been my interrogator's idea – "he's not a Muslim!"

"Don't say that!" said the man.

"But we are not", I reiterated, "we are Christians".

It was not as difficult to persuade him that I was not at least a convert to Christianity from Islam, as I should have thought it would have been to persuade him that I was a Muslim. Bearing this in mind, I had no doubt that by simply telling the strict truth about myself, and allowing them to draw their own conclusions, I should generally pass for the son of a Moorish merchant settled in England, and thus it proved. Once, during a day's ride in Moorish dress, I counted the number of people who saluted by the way, and was gratified to find that although on a European saddle this suggested to the thoughtful that my mother must have been a European, and I heard one or two ask my man whether she was a legal wife or a slave! In conversation, however, I was proud and grateful to proclaim myself a Christian and an Englishman. My native dress meant after all no more than European dress does on an Oriental in England: it brought me in touch with the Moors, and it enabled me to pass among them unobserved.

Another striking instance of this occurred in Fez, where, before entering any house, I paid an unintentional visit to the very shrine I wished to see. Outside the gates I had stopped to change my costume, and passing in apart from my faithful Mohammed, after a stroll to about the centre of the city, I asked at a shop the way to a certain house. The owner called a lad who knew the neighbourhood, to whom I explained what I wanted, and off we started. In a few minutes I paused on the threshold of a finely ornamented building, different from any other I had seen. All unsuspicious, I enquired what it was, and learned that we were in a street as sacred as a mosque, and that my guide was taking me a short cut through the sanctuary of Mulai Idrees!

Some days later, lantern and slippers in one hand, and rosary in the other, I entered with the crowd for sunset prayers. Perspiring freely within, but outwardly with the calmest appearance I could muster, I spread my prayer-cloth and went through the motions prescribed by law, making my observations in the pauses, and concluding by a guarded survey of the place. I need hardly say that I breathed with a feeling of relief when I found myself in the pure air again, and felt better after I had had my supper and sat down to commit my notes to paper. In the Karûeeïn I once caught a suspicious stare at my glasses, so, pausing, I returned the stare with a contemptuous indignation that made my critic slink off abashed. There was nothing to do but to "face it out".

From *The Land of the Moors: A Comprehensive Description*, by Budgett Meakin (London, 1901).

WALTER HARRIS:
THE DEATH OF A SULTAN

In 1893 Mulai Hassen determined to visit the desert regions of Morocco, including far-off Tafilet, the great oasis from which his dynasty had originally sprung, and where, before becoming the ruling branch of the royal family, they had resided ever since their founder, the great-grandson of the Prophet, had settled there, an exile from the East.

Leaving Fez in the summer, the Sultan proceeded south, crossing the Atlas above Kasba-El-Maghzen, and descended to the upper waters of the Wad Ziz. An expedition such as this would have required a system of organisation far in excess of the capabilities of the Moors, great though their resources were. Food was lacking; the desert regions could provide little. The water was bad, the heat very great. Every kind of delay, including rebellion and the consequent punishment of the tribes, hampered the Sultan's movements; and it was only toward winter that he arrived in Tafilet with a fever-stricken army and greatly diminished transport.

Mulai Hassen returned from Tafilet a dying man. The internal complaint from which he was suffering had become acute from the hardships he had undergone, and he was unable to obtain the rest that his state of health required, nor would he place himself under a regimen. For a few months he remained in the southern capital, and in the late spring 1894 set out to suppress a rebellion that had broken out in the Tadla region.

While camping in the enemy country he died. Now, the death of the Sultan under such circumstances was fraught with danger to the State. He was an absolute monarch, and with his disappearance all authority and government lapsed until his successor should have taken up the reins. Again, the expedition was in hostile country, and any inkling of the Sultan's death would have brought the tribes down to pillage and loot the Imperial camp. As long as the Sultan lived, and was present with his expedition, his prestige was sufficient to prevent an attack of the tribes, though even this was not unknown on one or two occasions, and to hold his forces together as a sort of concrete body. But his death, if known, would have meant speedy disorganisation, nor could the troops themselves be trusted not to seize this opportunity to murder and loot.

It was therefore necessary that the Sultan's demise should be kept an absolute secret. He had died in the recesses of his tents, themselves enclosed in a great canvas wall, inside which, except on very special occasions, no one was permitted to penetrate. The knowledge of his death was therefore limited to the personal slaves and to his Chamberlain, Bou Ahmed.

Orders were given that the Sultan would start on his journey at dawn, and before daylight the State palanquin was carried into the Imperial enclosure, the corpse laid within it, and its doors closed and the curtains drawn. At the first pale break of dawn the palanquin was brought out, supported by sturdy mules. Bugles were blown, the band played, and the bowing courtiers and officials poured forth their stentorian cry, "May God protect the life of our Lord". The procession formed up, and, led by flying banners, the dead Sultan set out on his march.

A great distance was covered that day. Only once did the procession stop, when the palanquin was carried into a tent by the roadside, that the Sultan might breakfast. Food was borne in and out; tea, with all the paraphernalia of its brewing, was served: but none but the slaves who knew the secret were permitted to enter. The Chamberlain remained with the corpse, and when a certain time had passed, he emerged to state that His Majesty was rested and had breakfasted, and would proceed on his journey – and once more the procession moved on. Another long march was made to where the great camp was pitched for the night.

The Sultan was tired, the Chamberlain said. He would not come out of his enclosure to transact business as usual in the "Diwan" tent, where he granted audiences. Documents were taken in to the royal quarters by the Chamberlain himself, and, when necessary, they emerged bearing the seal of State, and verbal replies were given to a host of questions.

Then another day of forced marches, for the expedition was still in dangerous country; but Mulai Hassen's death could no longer be concealed. It was summer, and the state of the Sultan's body told its own secret.

Bou Ahmed announced that His Majesty had died two days before, and that by this time his young son, Mulai Abdul Aziz, chosen and nominated by his father, had been proclaimed at Rabat, whither the fleetest of runners had been sent with the news immediately after the death had occurred.

It was a fait accompli. The army was now free of the danger of being attacked by the tribes; and the knowledge that the new Sultan was already reigning, and that tranquillity existed elsewhere, deterred the troops from any excesses. Many took the occasion of a certain disorganisation to desert, but so customary was this practice that it attracted little or no attention.

Two days later the body of the dead Sultan, now in a terrible state of decomposition, arrived at Rabat. It must have been a gruesome procession from the description his son Mulai Abdul Aziz gave me: the hurried arrival of the swaying palanquin bearing its terrible burden, five days dead in the great heat of summer; the escort, who had bound scarves over their faces – but even this precaution could not keep them from constant sickness – and even the mules that bore the palanquin seemed affected by the horrible atmosphere, and tried from time to time to break loose.

No corpse is, by tradition, allowed to enter through the gates into a Moorish city, and even in the case of the Sovereign no exception was made. A hole was excavated in the town wall, through which the procession passed direct into the precincts of the palace, where the burial took place. Immediately after, the wall was restored.

From *Morocco That Was*, by Walter Harris (1921). Reprinted in a paperback edition by Eland Books, London.

ELIAS CANETTI: *THE UNSEEN*

At twilight I went to the great square in the middle of the city, and what I sought there were not its colour and bustle, those I was familiar with, I sought a small, brown bundle on the ground consisting not even of a voice but of a single sound. This was a deep, long-drawn-out, buzzing "e-e-e-e-e-e-e". It did not diminish, it did not increase, it just went on and on; beneath all the thousands of calls and cries in the square it was always audible. It was the most unchanging sound in the Djemaa El Fna, remaining the same all evening and from evening to evening.

While still a long way off I was already listening for it. A restlessness drove me there that I cannot satisfactorily explain. I would have gone to the square in any case, there was so much there to attract me; nor did I ever doubt I would find it each time, with all that went with it. Only for this voice, reduced to a single sound, did I feel something akin to fear. It was at the very edge of the living; the life that engendered it consisted of nothing but that sound. Listening greedily, anxiously, I invariably reached a point in my walk, in exactly the same place, where I suddenly became aware of it like the buzzing of an insect: "e-e-e-e-e-e-e".

I felt a mysterious calm spread through my body, and whereas my steps had been hesitant and uncertain hitherto I now, all of a sudden, made determinedly for the sound. I knew where it came from. I knew the small, brown bundle on the ground, of which I had never seen anything more than a piece of dark, coarse cloth. I had never seen the mouth from which the "e-e-e-e-e" issued; nor the eye; nor the cheek; nor any part of the face. I could not have said whether it was the face of a blind man or whether it could see. The brown, soiled cloth was pulled right down over the head like a hood, concealing everything. The creature – as it must have been – squatted on the ground, its back arched under the material. There was not much of the creature there, it seemed slight and feeble, that was all one could conjecture. I had no idea how tall it was because I had never seen it standing. What there was of it on the ground kept so low that one would have stumbled over it quite unsuspectingly, had the sound ever stopped. I never saw it come, I never saw it go; I do not know whether it was brought and put down there or whether it walked there by itself.

The place it had chosen was by no means sheltered. It was the most open part of the square and there was an incessant coming and going on all sides of the little brown heap. On busy evenings it disappeared completely behind people's legs, and although I knew exactly where it was and could always hear the voice I had difficulty in finding it. But then the people dispersed, and it was still in its place when all around it, far and wide, the square was empty.

Then it lay there in the darkness like an old and very dirty garment that someone had wanted to get rid of and had surreptitiously dropped in the midst of all the people where no one would notice. Now, however, the people had dispersed and only the bundle lay there. I never waited until it got up or was fetched. I slunk away in the darkness with a choking feeling of helplessness and pride.

The helplessness was in regard to myself. I sensed that I would never do anything to discover the bundle's secret. I had a dread of its shape; and since I could give it no other I left it lying there on the ground. When I was getting close I took care not to bump into it, as if I might hurt or endanger it. It was there every evening, and every evening my heart stood still when I first distinguished the sound, and it stood still again when I caught sight of the bundle. How it got there and how it got away again were matters more sacred to me than my own movements. I never spied on it and I do not know where it disappeared to for the rest of the night and the following day. It was something apart, and perhaps it saw itself as such. I was sometimes tempted to touch the brown hood very lightly with one finger – the creature was bound

to notice, and perhaps it had a second sound with which it would have responded. But this temptation always succumbed swiftly to my helplessness.

I have said that another feeling choked me as I slunk away: pride. I was proud of the bundle because it was alive. What it thought to itself as it breathed down there, far below other people, I shall never know. The meaning of its call remained as obscure to me as its whole existence: but it was alive, and every day at the same time, there it was. I never saw it pick up the coins that people threw it; they did not throw many, there were never more than two or three coins lying there. Perhaps it had no arms with which to reach for the coins. Perhaps it had no tongue with which to form the "I" of "Allah" and to it the name of God was abbreviated to "e-e-e-e-e". But it was alive, and with a diligence and persistence that were unparalleled it uttered its one sound, uttered it hour after hour, until it was the only sound in the whole enormous square, the sound that outlived all others.

From *The Voices of Marrakesh*, by Elias Canetti (© Marion Boyars, London, 1978); first published in German in 1967.

PAUL BOWLES: *POINTS IN TIME, X*

The country of the Anjra is almost devoid of paved roads. It is a region of high jagged mountains and wooded valleys, and does not contain a town of any size. During the rainy season there are landslides. Then, until the government sends men to repair the damage, the roads cannot be used. All this is very much on the minds of the people who live in the Anjra, particularly when they are waiting for the highways to be rebuilt so that lorries can move again between the villages. Four or five soldiers had been sent several months earlier to repair the potholes along the road between Ksar Es Seghir and Melloussa. Their tent was beside the road, near a curve in the river.

A peasant named Hattash, whose village lay a few miles up the valley, constantly passed by the place on his way to and from Ksar Es Seghir. Hattash had no fixed work of any sort, but he kept very busy looking for a chance to pick up a

little money one way or another in the market and the cafés. He was the kind of man who prided himself on his cleverness in swindling foreigners, by which he meant men from outside the Anjra. Since his friends shared his dislike of outsiders, they found his exploits amusing, although they were careful to have no dealings with him.

Over the months Hattash had become friendly with the soldiers living in the tent, often stopping to smoke a pipe of kif with them, perhaps squatting down to play a few games of ronda. Thus, when one day the soldiers decided to give a party, it was natural that they should mention it to Hattash, who knew everyone for miles around, and therefore might be able to help them. The soldiers came from the south, and their isolation there by the river kept them from meeting anyone who did not regularly pass their tent.

I can get you whatever you want, Hattash told them. The hens, the vegetables, oil, spices, salad, whatever.

Fine. And we want some girls or boys, they added.

Don't worry about that. You'll have plenty to choose from. What you don't want you can send back.

They discussed the cost of the party for an hour or so, after which the soldiers handed Hattash twenty-five thousand francs. He set off, ostensibly for the market.

Instead of going there, he went to the house of a nearby farmer and bought five of his best hens, with the understanding that if the person for whom he was buying them should not want them, he could return the hens and get his money back.

Soon Hattash was outside the soldiers' tent with the hens. How are they? he said. The men squeezed them and examined them, and pronounced them excellent. Good, said Hattash. I'll take them home now and cook them.

He went back to the farmer with the hens and told him that the buyer had refused them. The farmer shrugged and gave Hattash his money.

This seemed to be the moment to leave Ksar Es Seghir, Hattash decided. He stopped at a café and invited everyone there to the soldiers' tent that evening, telling them there would be food, wine and girls. Then he bought bread, cheese and fruit, and began to walk along the trails that would lead him over the mountains to Khemiss El Anjra.

With the twenty-five thousand francs he was able to live for several weeks there in Khemiss El Anjra. When he had come to the end of them, he began to think of leaving.

In the market one morning he met Hadj Abdallah, a rich farmer from Farsioua, which was a village only a few miles from his own. Hadj Abdallah, a burly, truculent man, always had eyed Hattash with distrust.

Ah, Hattash! What are you doing up here? It's a while since I've seen you.

And you? said Hattash.

Me? I'm on my way to Tetuan. I'm leaving my mule here and taking the bus.

That's where I'm going, said Hattash.

Well, see you in Tetuan, said Hadj Abdallah, and he turned, unhitched his mule, and rode off.

Khemiss dl Anjra is a very small town, so that it was not difficult for Hattash to follow along at some distance, and see the house where Hadj Abdallah tethered his mule and into

which he then disappeared. He walked to the bus station and sat under a tree.

An hour or so later, when the bus was filling up with people, Hadj Abdallah arrived and bought his ticket. Hattash approached him.

Can you lend me a thousand francs? I haven't got enough to buy the ticket.

Hadj Abdallah looked at him. No. I can't, he said. Why don't you stay here? And he went and got into the bus.

Hattash, his eyes very narrow, sat down again under the tree. When the bus had left, and the cloud of smoke and dust had drifted off over the meadows, he walked back to the house where the Hadj had left his mule. She still stood there, so he quietly unhitched her, got astride her, and rode her in the direction of Mgas Tleta. He was still smarting under Hadj Abdallah's insult, and he vowed to give him as much trouble as he could.

Mgas Tleta was a small tchar. He took the mule to the fondaq and left it in charge of the guardian. Being ravenously hungry, he searched in his clothing for a coin or two to buy a piece of bread, and found nothing.

In the road outside the fondaq he caught sight of a peasant carrying a loaf in the hood of his djellaba. Unable to take his eyes from the bread, he walked towards the man and greeted him. Then he asked him if he had work, and was not surprised when the man answered no. He went on, still looking at the bread: If you want to earn a thousand francs, you can take my mule to Mdiq. My father's waiting for her and he'll pay you. Just ask for Si Mohammed Tsuli. Everybody in Mdiq knows him. He always has a lot of men working for him. He'll give you work there too if you want it.

The peasant's eyes lit up. He agreed immediately.

Hattash sighed. It's a long time since I've seen good country bread like that, he said, pointing at the loaf that emerged from the hood of the djellaba. The man took it out and handed it to him. Here. Take it.

In return Hattash presented him with the receipt for the mule. You'll have to pay a hundred francs to get her out of the fondaq, he told him. My father will give it back to you.

That's all right. The man was eager to start out for Mdiq.

Si Mohammed Tsuli. Don't forget.

No, no! Bslemah.

Hattash, well satisfied, watched the man ride off. Then he sat down on a rock and ate the whole loaf of bread. He had no intention of returning home to risk meeting the soldiers or Hadj Abdallah, so he decided to hide himself for a while in Tetuan, where he had friends.

When the peasant arrived at Mdiq the following day, he found that no one could tell him where Si Mohammed Tsuli lived. He wandered back and forth through every street in the town, searching and enquiring. When evening came, he went to the gendarmerie and asked if he might leave the mule there. But they questioned him and accused him of having stolen the animal. His story was ridiculous, they said, and they locked him into a cell.

Not many days later Hadj Abdallah, having finished his business in Tetuan, went back to Khemiss El Anjra to get his mule and ride her home. When he heard that she had disappeared directly after he had taken the bus, he remembered Hattash, and was certain that he was the culprit. The theft had to be reported in Tetuan, and much against his will he returned there.

Your mule is in Mdiq, the police told him.

Hadj Abdallah took another bus up to Mdiq.

Papers, said the gendarmes. Proof of ownership.

The Hadj had no documents of that sort. They told him to go to Tetouan and apply for the forms.

During the days while he waited for the papers to be drawn up, signed and stamped, Hadj Abdallah grew constantly angrier. He went twice a day to talk with the police. I know who took her! he would shout. I know the son of a whore.

If you ever catch sight of him, hold on to him, they told him. We'll take care of him.

Although Tetuan is a big place with many crowded quarters, the unlikely occurred. In a narrow passageway near the Souq El Fouqi late one evening Hadj Abdallah and Hattash came face to face.

The surprise was so great that Hattash remained frozen to the spot, merely staring into Hadj Abdallah's eyes. Then he heard a grunt of rage, and felt himself seized by the other man's strong arm.

Police! Police! roared Hadj Abdallah. Hattash squirmed, but was unable to free himself.

One policeman arrived, and then another. Hadj Abdallah did not release his grip of Hattash for an instant while he delivered his denunciation. Then with an oath he struck his prisoner, knocking him flat on the sidewalk. Hattash lay there in the dark without moving.

Why did you do that? the policemen cried. Now you're the one who's going to be in trouble.

Hadj Abdallah was already frightened. I know. I ought not to have hit him.

It's very bad, said one policeman, bending over Hattash, who lay completely still. You see, there's blood coming out of his head.

A small crowd was collecting in the passageway.

There were only a few drops of blood, but the policeman had seen Hattash open one eye and had heard him whisper: Listen.

He bent over still further, so that his ear was close to Hattash's lips.

He's got money, Hattash whispered.

The policeman rose and went over to Hadj Abdallah. We'll have to call an ambulance, he said, and you'll have to come to the police station. You had no right to hit him.

At that moment Hattash began to groan.

He's alive, at least! cried Hadj Abdallah. Hamdul'lah!

Then the policemen began to speak with him in low tones, advising him to settle the affair immediately by paying cash to the injured man.

Hadj Abdallah was willing. How much do you think? he whispered.

It's a bad cut he has on his head, the same policeman said, going back to Hattash. Come and look.

Hadj Abdallah remained where he was, and Hattash groaned as the man bent over him again. Then he murmured: Twenty thousand. Five for each of you.

When the policeman rejoined Hadj Abdallah, he told him the amount. You're lucky to be out of it.

Hadj Abdallah gave the money to the policeman, who took it over to Hattash and prodded him. Can you hear me? he shouted.

Ouakha, groaned Hattash.

Here. Take this. He held out the banknotes in such a way that Hadj Abdallah and the crowd watching could see them clearly. Hattash stretched up his hand and took them, slipping them into his pocket.

Hadj Abdallah glared at the crowd and pushed his way through, eager to get away from the spot.

After he had gone, Hattash slowly sat up and rubbed his head. The onlookers still stood there watching. This bothered the two policemen, who were intent on getting their share of the money. The recent disclosures of corruption, however, had made the public all too attentive at such moments. The crowd was waiting to see them speak to Hattash or, if he should move, follow him.

Hattash saw the situation and understood. He rose to his feet and quickly walked up the alley.

The policemen looked at each other, waited for a few seconds, and then began to saunter casually in the same direction. Once they were out of sight of the group of onlookers they hurried along, flashing their lights up each alley in their search. But Hattash knew the quarter as well as they, and got safely to the house of his friends.

He decided, however, that with the two policemen on the lookout for him, Tetuan was no longer the right place for him, and that his own tchar in the Anjra would be preferable.

Once he was back there, he made discreet enquiries about the state of the road to Ksar Es Seghir. The repairs were finished, his neighbours told him, and the soldiers had been sent to some other part of the country.

From *Points in Time*, by Paul Bowles (Peter Owen, London, 1982).

BOOKS

I've lost count of the time I have been asked "what one other book would you take on a trip to Morocco?". It depends, obviously, on your interests. If you want fiction, take both Paul Bowles's Fes novel, *The Spider's House*, and Esther Freud's magic evocation of a childhood hippy trip to Marrakesh, *Hideous Kinky*. For twentieth century history that reads like fiction, try Gavin Maxwell's *Lords of the Atlas*, or Walter Harris's *Morocco That Was*. But this is just the tip of a large body of books and literature devoted to (and increasingly coming from) Morocco, the more interesting of which of which are detailed below.

In the reviews following, publishers are listed as "**UK/US**" where two editions exist. Where books are published in one country only, this follows the publisher's name. **O/p** signifies an out-of-print, but still highly recommended, book. University Press is abbreviated as **UP**.

In Britain, there are two useful **specialist booksellers**. The **Maghreb Bookshop**, 45 Burton St, London WC1 (☎0171/388 1840) supplies new, rare and out-of-print books on all aspects of North Africa, both to callers and by worldwide mail order. And for out of print books, an excellent mail order specialist is **Keith Harris Books**, PO Box 207, Twickenham, TW2 5BQ (☎0181/898 7789). In the US, few bookstores keep much Moroccan stock and your best hunting grounds are likely to be the big **Internet bookstores**: *Amazon.com*, *BarnesandNoble.com*, and *Borders.com*.

GENERAL/TRAVEL

ANTHOLOGIES

Margaret and Robin Bidwell (eds), *Morocco: The Traveller's Companion* (IB Tauris,

UK). This fills a much-needed slot, with excerpts from key writers of the past five centuries, including many translated by the editors from the French.

MOROCCO CLASSICS

Paul Bowles, *Points in Time* (Peter Owen, UK), *Their Heads Are Green* (Abacus/Ecco Press). Novelist, poet and composer Paul Bowles has lived in Tangier most of his life and more or less singlehandedly brought translations of local writers (see "Moroccan Fictions" on pp.562–70) to Western attention. *Points* is a remarkable series of tales and short pieces inspired by episodes and sources from earliest times to the present day; the final piece is excerpted in our "Writers on Morocco" section. *Heads* includes a couple of travel essays on Morocco and a terrific piece on the psychology of desert travel.

Elias Canetti, *The Voices of Marrakesh* (Marion Boyars/Farrar Straus and Giroux). Impressions of Marrakesh in the last years of French rule, by the Nobel prize-winning author. The atmosphere of many pieces still holds – see the excerpt printed under "Writers on Morocco".

Walter Harris, *Morocco That Was* (1921; reprinted by Eland Books/Greenwood). Harris, *Times* correspondent in Tangier from the 1890s until his death in 1933, saw the country at probably the strangest ever stage in its history – the last years of "Old Morocco" in its feudal isolation and the first of French occupation. *Morocco That Was* is a masterpiece – alternately sharp, melodramatic and very funny. It incorporates, to some extent, the anecdotes in his earlier *Land of an African Sultan* (1889, o/p) and *Tafilet* (1895, o/p).

Peter Mayne, *A Year in Marrakesh* (Eland Books/Hippocrene Books). Mayne went to Marrakesh in the early 1950s, found a house in an ordinary district of the Medina, and tried to live like a Moroccan. He couldn't, but wrote an unusually perceptive account explaining why.

Budgett Meakin, *The Land of the Moors* (1900; reprinted by Darf/State Mutual Book), *The Moors: A Comprehensive Description* (1902, o/p). These wonderful encyclopedic volumes were the first really detailed books on Morocco and Moroccan life. Many of Meakin's "Comprehensive Descriptions" remain accurate and the sheer breadth of his knowledge – from

"Berber Feuds" to "Specimen Recipes" and musical notations of "Calls to Prayer" – is fascinating in itself. Highly recommended library browsing.

PRE-20TH CENTURY TRAVELS

Leo Africanus, *History and Description of Africa* (no recent edition but available in major libraries). Written in the mid-sixteenth century, this was the book Budgett Meakin (see previous page) followed, "astounded at the confirmation [of its accuracy] received from natives of remote and almost inaccessible districts". Leo, who was Moroccan by birth, was captured as a young man by Christian pirates. He subsequently converted and lived in Italy; the book was suggested to him by the Pope, and so there's more than a hint of propaganda about his accounts. (See also Amin Malouf, under "Western Fiction".)

Edmondo de Amicis, *Morocco: Its People and Places* (1882, reprinted by Darf Publishers, London). Intrepid journeying through Morocco in eras when few Europeans travelled beyond Tangier or the coast. Illustrated with copious line drawings.

R. B. Cunninghame Graham, *Mogreb-El-Acksa: A Journey in Morocco* (1898; reprinted by Marlboro Press, US). And yet more adventuring and anecdotes, most interesting of which is an enforced stay in a caidal Kasbah in the High Atlas (his host did not understand the motive of "curiosity"). The prose, however, is flat.

John Drummond Hay, *Western Barbary: its Wild Tribes and Savage Animals* (1846, o/p). The account is more sympathetic (and less wild) than the title suggests: a fine narrative of a journey from Tangier to Larache, during which Hay (the future British Consul in Tangier) is told fabulous tales of local life.

20TH CENTURY TRAVELS

Nina Epton, *Saints and Sorcerers* (1958, o/p). A very readable – and inquiring – travelogue, concentrating on folk customs and religious sects and confraternities in the 1950s.

John Hopkins, *Tangier Journals 1962–79* (1997; Arcadia/Cadmus Editions). Entertaining journals of Tangier life – and travels across Morocco – from an American novelist, resident in Tangier during the Beat years. Bowles, Burroughs, and the like, figure large in the diary entries.

Sylvia Kennedy, *See Ouarzazate and Die* (Abacus/Scribners). An account of visits to Morocco in 1990–91, both before and during the Gulf War. The narrative is hyperbolic and highly critical – Moroccan officials would not be impressed to find the book in your luggage – but it has some good observations nonetheless.

Rom Landau, *Morocco: Marrakesh, Fez, Rabat* (1967, o/p). Landau wrote numerous books on Morocco, few of them particularly inspiring. This one's redeeming feature is an excellent series of photographs – including rare pictures of mosque interiors.

Wyndham Lewis, *Journey into Barbary* (1932; reprinted by Black Sparrow Press, US). You'll learn more about Lewis than Morocco from this obscure, eccentric and rambling text – but the drawings are wonderful.

Antoine de Saint-Exupéry, *Wind, Sand and Stars and Southern Mail* (various editions, some with *Flight to Arras* and/or *Night Flight*). Accounts by the French aviator (and author of the children's classic, *The Little Prince*) of his postal flights down to West Africa, by way of Cap Juby in the then-Spanish Sahara. **Stacy Shiff**'s biography, *Saint-Exupéry* (Pimlico, UK) is, if anything, even more gripping, taking the story through to Saint-Exupéry's disappearance flying for the Free French in 1944.

Gordon West, *By Bus to the Sahara* (1932; reprinted by Black Swan, UK). This fascinating travelogue describes a journey from Tangier to Rissani, as undertaken by the author and his wife, an amateur artist, coyly referred to as 'the spirit'. As a touristic insight into prewar Morocco, it is unique.

Edith Wharton, *In Morocco* (1920; reprinted by Century/Ecco Press). Wharton dedicated her book to General Lyautey, Resident General of the Protectorate, whose modernizing efforts she greatly admired. By no means a classic, it is nonetheless worth reading for glimpses of harem life in the early part of the century.

PHOTOGRAPHS

Paul Bowles *Photographs* (Scalo, US). Paul Bowles proves himself a talented photographer in this book of images from the 1930s to 1960s. The stunning black and white pictures are complemented by editor Simon Bishoff's recorded conversations with Bowles in Tangier between 1989 and 1991.

Mary Cross, *Morocco: Sahara to the Sea* (Abbeville Press, US). A lavish book of images, with brief text from the photographer, a preface by Paul Bowles, and an introduction by the Moroccan novelist, Tahar Ben Jalloun.

Alan Keohane, *Berbers of the Atlas* (Hamish Hamilton, UK). A marvellous collection of colour photos of daily life in the Atlas.

Owen Logan, *Al Maghrib: Photographs from Morocco* (Polygon, UK). Superb black and white portraits in a beautifully produced monograph.

HISTORY

Neville Barbour, *Morocco* (Thames & Hudson/Walker, o/p). A lucid, straightforward account of Morocco from the Phoenicians to "the present day" (1965).

Roger Le Tourneau, *Fez in the Age of the Marinides* (University of Oklahoma Press, US). Interesting scholarly study of the Merenid capital of Morocco. Tourneau has also written on *The Almohad Movement* (Princeton University Press, 1981, o/p).

Gavin Maxwell, *Lords of the Atlas* (1966, reprinted by Century, UK). Drawing heavily on Walter Harris' accounts of the Moorish court (see "Morocco Classics" on p.579), this is the story of the Glaoui family – literally the "Lords" of the High Atlas, where they exercised almost complete control from the turn of the nineteenth century right through to Moroccan independence in 1956. Not an attractive tale but a compelling one, and superbly told.

Douglas Porch, *The Conquest of Morocco* (Macmillan/Fromm International). Accessible and fascinating account of the extraordinary manoeuvrings and characters of Morocco's turn-of-the-century history.

Susan Raven, *Rome in Africa* (Routledge, UK/US). A new and well-illustrated survey of Roman (and Carthaginian) North Africa.

David Woolman, *Rebels in the Rif* (Stanford University Press, US, o/p). Academic but very readable study of the Riffian war in the 1920s and of the tribes' uprising against the Moroccan government in 1956.

NORTH AFRICA/ARAB WORLD

J.M Abun-Nasr, *History of the Maghreb in the Islamic Period* (Cambridge UP, UK/US). Morocco in the wider context of North Africa by a distinguished Arab historian.

Peter Mansfield, *The Arabs* (Penguin, UK/US). General introduction to the Arab world, from its beginnings through to the 1970s. Short final sections deal with each individual country.

R. Oliver and J. D. Fage, *A History of Africa* (Penguin, UK/US). Morocco within the context of its continent.

ANTHROPOLOGY

Donna Lee Bowen and Evelyn A. Early (**eds**), *Everyday Life in the Muslim Middle East* (Indiana University Press, US). Despite its broad-sweeping title, around a third of this anthology deals with Morocco. It illustrates the experiences of ordinary men, women and children from Afghanistan to Morocco, through essays, short stories and poems. Donna Lee Bowen studied regional development in southern Morocco and Evelyn Early is the US press attaché in Rabat. Highly recommended.

Vincent Crapanzano, *Tuhami: Portrait of a Moroccan* (University of Chicago Press, US). Tuhami is an illiterate Moroccan tilemaker in Meknes: this study is an interesting, if at times slightly impenetrable, mix of ethnography and psychology.

Shlomo Deshen, *The Mellah Society: Jewish Community Life in Sherifian Morocco* (University of Chicago Press, US). Academic study of economic activity and political organization in the Mellahs prior to the Protectorate.

Kevin Dwyer, *Moroccan Dialogues: Anthropology in Question* (Waveland Press, US). A series of recorded conversations with a farmer from near Taroudannt, ranging through attitudes to women, religion and village life to popular Moroccan perceptions of the Jews, the French and even the hippies. Well worth a look.

Elizabeth Fernea, *A Street in Marrakesh* (Waveland Press, US). Highly readable account of a woman anthropologist's period of study and experiences in Marrakesh.

Elizabeth Fernea and Basima Q. Bezirgan, *Middle Eastern Muslim Women Speak Out* (University of Texas Press, US). Straightforward and accessible social anthropology, including interesting transcriptions of Berber women's songs from the High Atlas.

Ernest Gellner and Charles Micaud (eds), *Arabs and Berbers* (Duckworth/Lexington Press, o/p). Authoritative collection of anthropological articles on Berbers and tribalism in Morocco. Interesting, if read on a rather selective basis.

Ernest Gellner, *Saints of the Atlas* (University of Chicago Press, US). The bulk of this book is an in-depth study of a group of *zaouia* villages in the High Atlas, but there are excellent introductory chapters on Morocco's recent past and the concept and origins of Berbers.

David Hart, *The Aït Atta of Southern Morocco: Daily Life and Recent History* (Menas Press, UK). A well written study on the Aït Atta tribe's environment, myths, daily life and material culture. Hart also discusses in detail how the Aït Atta responded to French penetration into southern Morocco at the start of the twentieth century and their struggle against colonial pacification.

Bernard Lewis, *The Jews of Islam* (Routledge/Princeton UP). Morocco had over 30,000 Jews until the mass emigrations to Israel in the 1940s and 1950s. Lewis discusses their position (which was perhaps the most oppressed within the Arab world) and their political and cultural contributions. Disappointingly, he doesn't attempt to cover the period of emigration itself.

Fatima Mernissi, *Beyond the Veil: Male–Female Dynamics in Modern Muslim Society* (Al Saqi Books/Indiana UP). Seminal book by a feminist Moroccan sociologist from the Mohammed V University in Rabat.

Fatima Mernissi, *Doing Daily Battle: Interviews with Moroccan Women* (The Women's Press/Rutgers UP). Eleven women – carpet weavers, rural and factory workers, teachers – talk about all aspects of their lives, from work and housing to marriage. A fascinating insight into a resolutely private world.

Henry Munson, *The House of Si Abd Allah* (Yale University Press, US). A renowned anthropologist records the real life stories behind the social and political tensions in modern Morocco – as told by a traditional Muslim from Tangier and his Westernized cousin, a young Muslim woman living in the US. The word for word record is complicated but the lengthy introduction can stand on its own and its insights into contemporary family life and modern Muslim society are illuminating.

David Seddon, *Moroccan Peasants: A Century of Change in the Eastern Rif* (William Dawson, UK). Covers similar ground to David Woolman (see "History"), though with a more strictly anthropological approach.

Edward Westermarck, *Ritual and Belief in Morocco* (1926); *Wit and Wisdom in Morocco* (1930). *Ritual* is a seminal work on Morocco and remains a fascinating storehouse of social and anthropological detail. *Wit* is entirely a collection of Moroccan proverbs. Both are well worth the effort to track down in libraries.

ISLAM

The Koran (numerous editions). The Word of God as handed down to the Prophet is the basis of all Islam, so essential reading for anyone interested. The Oxford UP edition is the clearest and liveliest translation.

S. H. Nasr, *Ideas and Realities of Islam* (Collins, UK/US). A good general introduction.

Maxime Rodinson, *Muhammad* (Penguin/Pantheon). Challenging account of the Prophet's life and the immediate impact of his ideology.

ART, ARCHITECTURE AND CRAFTS

Jean Besanceon, *Costumes of Morocco* (KPI, UK). Lavish prints, drawn in the 1930s and 1940s when they were still current. Most are now museum pieces.

Michael Brett, *The Moors* (Orbis, o/p). A fine illustrated survey of the Moorish Empire, well thought out and with an understanding text.

Titus Burckhardt, *Fes: City of Islam* (Islamic Texts Society, UK); *Moorish Culture in Spain* (o/p). Burckhardt's *Spain* is a superb study of architecture, history, Islamic city-design and the mystical significance of its art – and as such it's entirely relevant to medieval Morocco. *Fes* is worth dipping into, if only for the photos, as the conceptual approach and respect for tradition can be a bit hard going.

Salma Damluji, *Zillij: the Art of Moroccan Ceramics* (Garnet, UK). An expensive but beautifully illustrated study.

Lisl and Landt Dennis, *Living in Morocco* (Thames & Hudson, UK/US). Fabulous picture studies of Moroccan craft and domestic design, both traditional and modern.

James F Jereb, *Arts and Crafts of Morocco* (Thames & Hudson/Chronicle Books). The arts and crafts of Morocco express the kaleidoscope of influences from Black Africa and Islam to the cultural alliance of the Moors and Spaniards. This book, with over 150 colour photographs, is a fascinating introduction to Moroccan arts and crafts and an excellent guide to the museums of the major cities.

Matisse in Morocco (Thames & Hudson/Abrams). A gorgeous book of the paintings and drawings from the artist's stay in 1912–13.

Andre Paccard, *Traditional Islamic Craft in Moroccan Architecture* (Éditions Atelier, France, 2 vols). The ultimate coffee-table tome by an architect much favoured by King Hassan. The text is poor, but it is massively illustrated and – uniquely – includes photographs of Moroccan Royal Palaces currently in use. Very expensive.

Richard Parker, *A Practical Guide to Islamic Monuments in Morocco* (Baraka Press, Charlottesville, Virginia, US). Exactly what it claims to be – very helpful and well informed, with introductory sections on architectural forms and motifs, and craft traditions. Available at the American Bookstore in Rabat.

Brook Pickering et al, *Moroccan Carpets* (Hali Publications/Near Eastern Research Center). A large format, fully illustrated guide, showing examples of carpets and rugs, region by region. The best book of its kind.

David Talbot Rice, *Islamic Art* (Thames & Hudson, UK/US). Clear, interesting and well-illustrated survey – though only two chapters directly concern Morocco.

Herbert Ypma, *Morocco Modern* (Thames & Hudson/Stewart, Tabori & Chang). This superbly illustrated book traces the origins of the great artisan traditions of Morocco (weavers, woodworkers, potters, *zellij* makers) and looks at the way contemporary designers and architects reinterpret these influences to create suprisingly modern work.

In addition, a number of large, glossy books on Moroccan jewellery, gardens, paintings, manuscripts, carpets, buildings, etc, usually with French texts, are to be found in most of the larger bookshops in Morocco.

FOOD

Robert Carrier, *Taste of Morocco* (Arrow, UK). Robert Carrier lived in Marrakesh for several months of each year and this beautifully illustrated 'cook book' reflects his love of Morocco and its distinctive cuisine – particularly the grand dishes of the south. Carrier considered Morocco to have (with France and China) one of the three greatest cusines in the world.

Zette Guinaudeau, *Traditional Moroccan Cooking: Recipes from Fes* (Serif, UK). Madame Guinaudeau lived in Fes for over thirty years and first published her recipes in French in 1964. Now translated into English, they redress the imbalance of Robert Carrier's focus on Marrakesh cuisine. Some of her recipes echo Mrs Beeton's catering, for at least eight people and sometimes as many as twenty, but they can be adapted.

Claudia Roden, *The Book of Jewish Food* (Viking/Penguin, UK). An interesting and useful book that makes clear the distinctive dishes of the Sephardic Jews (of the Middle East and North Africa), showing that such specialities as *couscous, tajine, harira, kefta* and *mechoui* were to be found in both the Medina and the mellah before the exodus to Israel.

Paula Wolfert, *Good Food from Morocco* (John Murray, UK). Mouthwatering recipes from the largely domestic canon of Moroccan food. Wolfert's book, originally published in the 1960s, has a more rural emphasis than Carrier's tour of the grand kitchens.

MOROCCAN FICTION/BIOGRAPHY

By far the largest body of Moroccan fiction/biography published in English are the translations by the American writer Paul Bowles, who has lived in Tangier since the 1940s.

TRANSLATIONS BY PAUL BOWLES

All of the books below are taped and translated from the Maghrebi by **Paul Bowles**. It's hard to generalize about them, except to say that they are mostly "tales" (even the autobiographies, which seem little different from the fiction), share a common fixation with intrigue and unexpected narrative twists, and are often punctuated by episodes of violence. None have particular characterization, though this hardly seems relevant as they have such a strong, vigorous narrative style – brilliantly matched by Bowles's sharp, economic language.

For a taste of the stories, see "Moroccan Fictions" on pp.562–570.

Mohammed Mrabet, *Love with a Few Hairs* (City Lights, US); *The Boy Who Set the Fire & Other Stories* (City Lights, US); *The Lemon* (Peter Owen/City Lights); *M'Hashish* (City Lights, US); *The Chest* (Tombouctou, US); *Marriage With Papers* (Tombouctou, US); *The Big Mirror* (Black Sparrow Press, US); *Harmless Poisons, Blameless Sins* (Black Sparrow Press, US); *The Beach Café and The Voice* (Black Sparrow Press, US); *Look and Move On: An Autobiography* (Peter Owen/Black Sparrow Press).

Mohammed Mrabet's stories – *The Beach Café* is perhaps his best – are often *kif*-inspired, and this gives them a slightly paranoid quality, as Mrabet himself explained: "Give me twenty or thirty pipes . . . and an empty room can fill up with wonderful things, or terrible things. And the stories come from these things."

Mohamed Choukri, *For Bread Alone* (Al Saqi Books, UK). Now translated into more than ten languages, this first volume of Mohammed Choukri's autobiography speaks for an entire generation of North Africans. Born in the Rif, he moved with his family to Tangier at a time of great famine, spending his childhood in abject poverty. During his adolescence he worked for a time for a French family. He then returned to Tangier, where he experienced the violence of the 1952 independence riots. At the age of 20, and still illiterate, he took the decision to read and write classical Arabic – a decision which transformed his life.

Driss Ben Hamed Charhadi, *A Life Full of Holes* (Grove Press, US). This was Bowles's first Moroccan translation – a direct narrative of streetlife in Tangier. It was published under a pseudonym, the author being **Larbi Layachi** (see below).

Five Eyes, stories by **Mohammed Mrabet, Larbi Layachi, Mohamed Choukri, Ahmed Yacoubi** and **Abdesiam Boulaich** (Black Sparrow Press, US, o/p). An excellent introduction to these writers, sadly out of print.

OTHERS

Margot Badran and Miriam Cooke (eds), *Opening the Gates: A Century of Arab Feminist Writing* (Virago, UK). Includes three Moroccan pieces, including a traditional women's tale, recounted by the Moroccan feminist, Fatima Mernissi.

Mohammed Choukri, *Streetwise* (Al Saqi Books, UK). The second volume of Choukri's autobiography (translated by Ed Emery) spans the 1960s and 70s and ranks among the best works of contemporary Arabic literature. Throughout his adversities, two things shine through: Choukri's determination to use literacy to surmount his desperate circumstances; and his compassion for the normally despised human beings who share this life of 'the lowest of the low'.

Driss Chraibi, *Heirs to the Past* (Heinemann UK/US). A novel concerned with the crisis of Moroccans' post-colonial identity. It is semi-autobiographical as the author-narrator (who has lived in France since the war) returns to Morocco for the funeral of his father. Also available – though in rather over-literal and unspirited translation – are two further Chraibi novels, *The Butts* and *Mother Comes of Age* (Forest Books/Three Continents Press).

Fatima Mernissi, *Dreams of Trespass: Tales of a Harem Girlhood* (Additions Wesley, US). A mix of biographical narrative, tales and fantasies from the renowned Moroccan feminist sociologist, who was born in a harem in Fes in 1940.

Tahar Ben Jelloun, *The Sand Child* (Quartet/Harcourt Brace). Ben Jelloun, resident in Paris, is Morocco's most acclaimed writer – and in the case of this novel, which won the French Prix Goncourt, the reputation is just. An unusually "fictional" tale, its subject, the Sand Child, is a girl whose father brought her up as a boy. Two other novels by Ben Jelloun are available in translation: *Sacred Night* (Quartet/Harcourt Brace) and *With Downcast Eyes* (Little, Brown, US).

Larbi Layachi, *Yesterday and Today* (Black Sparrow Press, US), *The Jealous Lover* (Tombouctou, US). The former is a kind of sequel to *Life Full of Holes* (see above), describing in semi-fictionalized form Layachi's time with Paul and Jane Bowles; the latter is more of a novel and rather less successful.

Anouar Majid, *Si Yussef* (Quarter, UK). An interesting if somewhat tortuous narrative: the author writes as Lamin, a student in Fes, who presents the life story of an old man, born in Tangier in 1908, and his tales of the city.

Brick Ousaïd, *Mountains Forgotten by God* (Forest Books/Three Continents Press). Autobiographical narrative of an Atlas Berber family, which gives an impressive sense of the harshness of mountain life. As the author describes it, it is "not an exercise in literary style [but] a cry from the bottom of my heart, of despair and revolt".

Abdelhak Serhane, *Messaouda* (Carcanet, UK). Adventurous, semi-autobiographical novel about growing up in Azrou during the 1950s. The narrator's development parallels that of his country; his attempts to free himself from the patriarchy and authoritarianism of his father are used as an allegory for the struggle against French colonialism and its aftermath.

WESTERN FICTION

Once again, Paul Bowles is the outstanding fig-ure in Western fiction set in Morocco, so no apologies for splitting this section into "Bowles" and "Others". Though the "Others" incldue a couple of gems.

PAUL BOWLES

NOVELS: *The Sheltering Sky* (Granada/Ecco Press); *Let It Come Down* (Arrow/Black Sparrow Press); *The Spider's House* (Arena/Black Sparrow Press).
STORIES: *Collected Stories of Paul Bowles* 1939–76 (Black Sparrow Press, US) gathers together work from numerous earlier editions. Post-1976 collections include *Midnight Mass* (Peter Owen/Black Sparrow Press), *Call at Corazón* (Peter Owen, UK) and *Unwelcome Words* (Tombouctou, US).

Paul Bowles stands out as the most interest-ing and the most prolific writer using North African themes – and following Bertolucci's film of *The Sheltering Sky* he seems at last to have regained the recognition he was due. Many of his stories are similar in vein to those of Mohammed Mrabet (see above), employing the same sparse forms, bizarre twists and interjections of violence. The novels are something different, exploring both Morocco (or, in *The Sheltering Sky*, Algeria) and the ways in which Europeans and Americans react to and are affected by it. If you read noth-ing else on the country, at least get hold of *The Spider's House* – one of the best political nov-els ever written, its backdrop the traditional daily life of Fes, its theme the conflicts and transformation at the last stages of the French occupation of the country.

The last few years have seen a flurry of **biographies and memoirs of Bowles** and his literary friends and acquaintances in **Tangier**. the best of these are:
Iain Finlayson, *Tangier: City of the Dreams* (Flamingo/HarperCollins, UK). Good on the Moroccans whom Bowles has translated.
Michelle Green, *The Dream at the End of the World: Paul Bowles and the Literary Renegades of Tangier* (Bloomsbury, UK). Strong narrative, compulsively peopled: the best read if you're looking for one book on Tangier literary life.
Bowles's autobiography, *Without Stopping* (Macmillan/Ecco Press), is also of interest for its Moroccan episodes (though William Burroughs wryly dubbed it "Without Telling"), as is his more recent *Two Years Beside the Strait/Days: A Tangier Journal, 1987–89* (Peter Owen/Ecco Press).

In Touch: the Letters of Paul Bowles, edited by **Daniel Halpern** (HarperCollins, UK/US) spans sixty years and reveals a little more, with letters (predominantly from Tangier) to inti-mates such as Burroughs and Aaron Copland.

OTHER FICTION SET IN MOROCCO

Arturo Barea, *The Forging of a Rebel* (Flamingo, UK reprint, 3 volumes, o/p). Autobiographical trilogy dealing with events of the 1930s. Volume two, *The Track*, concerns the war and colonization of the Rif, the Spanish entry into Chaouen and life in Tetouan.

William Burroughs, *Naked Lunch* (Flamingo/Grove Press). This Beat icon was first published in France in 1959 and did not appear in the US until 1962 and in the UK until 1964. Put crudely, the book is about Burrough's addic-tion to hard drugs and young men. Despite plau-dits from the likes of Edmund White and Norman Mailer, it is more talked about than read (which isn't easy).

William Bayer, *Tangier* (Dutton, US, 1971, o/p). Thinly disguised potboiler set amid the Tangier expat life of the 1960s.

Jane Bowles, *Everything is Nice – Collected Stories* (Virago, UK). The title story is a perfect evocation of Moroccan life, rendered in the author's unique and idiosyncratic style. Jane

Bowles was resident in Morocco on and off, with her husband Paul, from the 1940s until her tragic death in 1973. Millicent Dillon's biography, *A Little Original Sin: the Life of Jane Bowles* (Virago, £10.95), includes some fascinating material.

Anthony Burgess, *Earthly Powers* (Penguin, UK/US), *Enderby Anthology* (Penguin, UK/US). Sporadic scenes in 1950s-decadent Tangier.

Aldo Busi, *Sodomies in Eleven Point* (Faber, UK/US). A (highly) picaresque tour of Morocco.

Elisa Chimenti, *Tales and Legends of Morocco* (Astor-Honor, US). Travelling in the 1930s and 1940s with her father, personal physician to Sultan Moulay Hassan, Chimenti learned many of these simple, fable-like tales from Berber tribesmen whose guest she was.

Rafael Chirbes, *Mimoun* (Serpent's Tail, UK/US). Compelling tale of a Spanish teacher, based south of Fes, adrift amid sexual adventures and bizarre local life and antagonisms.

Esther Freud, *Hideous Kinky* (Penguin/Harcourt Brace). An English hippy takes her two daughters to Marrakesh, where they live simply, as locals. A wonderful narrative – funny, sad, and full of informed insights – told through the persona of the five-year-old.

Brion Gysin, *The Process* (Overlook Press, US). Beat novel by ex-Tangier resident and friend of Paul Bowles and William Burroughs. Fun, if a little caught in its zany 1960s epoch.

Richard Hughes, *In the Lap of Atlas* (Chatto, UK, o/p). Traditional Moroccan stories – cunning, humorous and ironical – reworked by the author of *A High Wind In Jamaica*. Also includes a narrative of Hughes' visit to Telouet and the Atlas in 1928.

Jane Kramer, *Honor to the Bride Like the Pigeon that Guards its Grain Under the Clove Tree* (Farrar, Straus & Giroux, US, 1970, o/p). Fictional narrative based on the true story of a Berber woman's kidnap in Meknes.

Amin Malouf, *Leo the African* (Quartet, UK). Superb historical novel, recreating the life of Leo Africanus, the fifteenth-century Moorish geographer, in Granada and Fes and on later travels.

Robin Maugham, *The Wrong People* (Gay Men's Press, UK). Gay tragedy, set in Tangier.

Leonora Peets, *Women of Marrakesh* (C.Hurst, UK). Stories of domestic life in the city from the 1930s to 1970 by a long-term Estonian resident.

GLOSSARY OF MOROCCAN TERMS

ADHAN the call to prayer

AGADIR fortified granary

AGDAL garden or park containing a pool

AGUELMANE lake

AÏN spring

AÏT tribe (literally, "sons of"); also BENI

ALAOUITE ruling Moroccan dynasty from the seventeenth century to the present king, Hassan II

ALMOHAD the greatest of the medieval dynasties, ruled Morocco (and much of Spain) from ca.1147 until the rise to power of the Merenids ca.1224

ALMORAVIDS dynasty that preceded the Almohads, from ca. 1060 to ca. 1147

ANDALOUS Muslim Spain (a territory that centred on modern Andalucía)

ARABESQUE geometrical decoration or calligraphy

ASSIF river (often seasonal) in Berber

BAB gate or door

BABOUCHES slippers (usually yellow)

BALI (or **QDIM**) old

BARAKA sanctity or blessing, obtained through saints or *marab*outs

BARBARY European term for North Africa in the sixteenth to nineteenth centuries

BENI tribe (as Aït)

BERBERS native inhabitants of Morocco, and still the majority of the population

BLED countryside, or, literally "land"; **BLED ES MAKHZEN** – governed lands; **BLED ES SIBA** – land outside government control

BORDJ fort

CAID district administrator; **CADI** is an Islamic judge

CHLEUH southern Berber from the High or Anti-Atlas or plains

COL mountain pass (French)

DAR house or palace; **DAR EL MAKHZEN**, royal palace

DAYA, DEYET lake

DJEBEL mountain peak or ridge; a **DJEBALI** is someone from the mountains; the **DJEBALA** are the main tribe of the Western Rif

DJEDID, JDID new

DJELLABA wool or cotton hooded outer garment

DJEMAA, JAMAA mosque, or Friday (the main day of worship)

DJINN nature spirits (genies)

ERG sand dune

FAKIR Koranic schoolteacher or lawyer, or just an educated man

FANTASIA display of horsemanship performed at larger festivals or *moussems*

FASSI inhabitant of Fes

FILALI alternative name for the Alaouite dynasty – from the southern Tafilalt region

FONDOUK inn and storehouse, known as a caravanserai in the eastern part of the Arab world

GANDOURA man's cotton garment (male equivalent of a kaftan); also known as a FOKIA

GHARB coastal plain between Larache and Kenitra

GNAOUA Moroccan Black person, originally from Guinea; also a sect, or brotherhood, who play drum-based trance music

HABBOUS religious foundation or bequest of property for religious charities

HADJ pilgrimage to Mecca

HAMMADA stony desert of the sub-Sahara

HAMMAM Turkish-style steam bath

HARKA "burning" raid undertaken by sultans in order to raise taxes and assert authority

IDRISSID first Arab dynasty of Morocco – named after its founder, Moulay Idriss

IMAM prayer leader and elder of mosque

ISTIQLAL nationalist party founded during the struggle for independence

JOUTIA flea market

KASBAH palace centre and/or fortress of an Arab town; also used to mean a walled residential quarter around the Medina (eg Fes), or the citadel (eg Tangier and in Tunisia), or the whole medina (eg Algiers). In the south of Morocco, it is a feudal family castle – and it's the root of the Spanish *alcazar*.

KHETTARA underground irrigation canal

KIF marijuana, cannabis

KOUBBA dome; small *marabout* tomb

KSAR, KSOUR (pl.) village or tribal stronghold in the south

LALLA "madam", also a saint.

LITHAM veil

MAGHREB "West" in Arabic, used for Morocco and the North African countries

MAKHZEN government

MARABOUT holy man, and by extension his place of burial. These tombs, usually white-washed domes, play an important (and hetero-dox) role in the religion of country areas

MECHOUAR assembly place, court of judgement

MEDERSA student residence and, in part, a teaching annexe, for the old mosque universities

MEDINA literally, "city", now used for the original Arab part of any Moroccan town.

MELLAH Jewish quarter

MERENIDS dynasty from eastern plains who ruled from the thirteenth to fifteenth centuries

MIHRAB niche indicating the direction of Mecca (and for prayer)

MINARET tower attached to a mosque, used for call to prayer

MINZAH pavilion in a (usually palace) garden

MOULAY descendant of the Prophet Muhammad, a claim and title adopted by most Moroccan sultans

MOULOUD festival and birthday of the Prophet

MOUSSEM pilgrimage-festival

MSALLA prayer area

MUEZZIN, MUEDDIN singer who calls the faithful to prayer

NAZARENE, NSRANI Christian, or, more loosely, a European.

OUED river; can be seasonal or even dry on a permanent basis (a WADI in its anglicized form).

PISÉ mud and rubble building material

PISTE unsurfaced road or track, suitable for 4x4 or Renault 4L.

PROTECTORATE period of French and Spanish colonial occupation (1912–56)

QAHOUAJI café patron

RAMADAN month of fasting

RAS source or head

RAS EL MA water source

RIBAT monastic fortress

SAADIAN southern dynasty from Drâa Valley, who ruled Morocco during the fifteenth century

SEBGHA lake or lagoon

SEGUIA irrigation canal

SHEIKH leader of religious brotherhood

SHEREEF descendant of the Prophet

SIDI, SI respectful title used for any man, like "Sir" or "Mister"

SOUK market, or market quarter

SUFI religious mystic; philosophy behind most of the religious brotherhoods

TABIA mud building material, as pisé

TIGHREMT similar to an agadir – fortified Berber home and storage place

TOUAREG nomadic Berber tribesmen of the disputed Western Sahara, fancifully known as "Blue Men" because of the blue dye of their cloaks (which gives a slight tinge to their skin)

TIZI mountain pass; as COL in French

WATTASID fifteenth-century dynasty who replaced their cousins, the Merenids

ZAOUIA sanctuary established around a *marabout*'s tomb; seminary-type base for religious brotherhood

ZELLIJ geometrical mosaic tilework

GLOSSARY OF MOROCCAN STREET NAMES

Moroccan streets are often named after well-known historical figures, events and dates, and in recent years there has been a concerted drive to replace the old panoply of French and Spanish colonial names. As they're revealing of Moroccan interests and historical figures, a glossary follows of some of the most common.

Transliteration from Arabic into the Roman alphabet means that there are often many variations of the same name.

ABDELKRIM EL KATTABI Leader of the Rif war against the Spanish. In 1921, his Berber warriors defeated a Spanish army of 60,000 at Annoual. He formed the independent republic of the Rif, but was defeated by Spanish/French forces in 1926.

ALLAL BEN ABDALLAH On 11 September, 1953, he tried to kill Sultan Ibn Aaraf who had been appointed by the French to succeed Mohammed V when he was sent into exile. Allal Ben Abdallah crashed an open car into the royal procession on its way to the mosque in Rabat and attacked the Sultan with a knife.

EL FARABI Born in Farab, now in Uzbekistan, he studied in Baghdad and taught as a 'Sufi' in Aleppo, now in Syria. He lived from 870 to 950 and is one of the greatest Islamic philosophers; he harmonized Greek philosophy and Islamic thinking. He studied Aristotle, and was known as second only to him. Thus, he was known as Al Muallim Al Thani ('the second teacher').

FERHAT HACHAD On 7 and 8 December, 1952, there were massive riots in the streets of Casablanca and hundreds were killed. The overt cause of this was the assassination in Tunis of Ferhat Hachad, a Tunisian trade union leader and Arab nationalist.

HASSAN II The reigning monarch and elder son of Mohammed V, whom he succeeded on **3 March, 1961**. He was born on 9 July, 1929, and his birthday is celebrated every year as Youth Day. He launched the Green March (see on p.534) on **6 November, 1975**.

IBN BATOUTA Born in Tangier (1304), he trained as a lawyer, made the pilgrimage to Mecca and was taken with a desire for further travel. He visited China and India, returning to Fes where he dictated his discoveries to a student. At the time, he was regarded as a romancer, but his reports turned out to be true.

IBN KHALDOUN Arab philosopher and historian, born in Tunis (1322) of an aristocratic family long resident in Muslim Spain, which he visited in 1362. He served as ambassador to Castile, Tamerlaine and the court at Fes. Study of North African history led him to his political theories about the natural life of a dynasty which he argued lasted only four generations.

IBN ROCHD Also known as Averroes, another of Islam's greatest philosophers. He was born in Córdoba (1126) and died in Marrakesh (1198). He introduced Christian monks to Aristotle, but worked principally on astronomy, theology, mathematics and, particularly, medicine. Based in Marrakesh, he was doctor to Yacoub El Mansour.

IBN TACHFINE/YOUSSEF IBN TACHFINE A devout Muslim Berber from Adrar, now in Mauritania, and the first Sultan of the Almoravid dynasty. He founded Marrakesh in 1060, captured Fes in 1069, fought against Alphonse IV and ruled Muslim Spain and the Maghreb as far east as Algiers.

IBN TOUMERT/MEHDI IBN TOUMERT Learned theologian, radical reformer and revolutionary leader, known as "The Torch". He was born around 1080, travelled to the Middle East in 1107, returned to Marrakesh in 1121, was expelled from there and took refuge with his warrior monks in the mountain stronghold of Tin Mal in 1124, where he died around 1130. He was believed by his followers to be the mahdi – the "sinless one".

IBN ZAIDOUN Leading Andalucian poet of the eleventh century; like others, he followed the traditions of the east.

IBN ZIAD/TARIK BEN ZIAD/TARIK IBN ZIAD Berber chieftain who led the troops of Moussa Ibn Noussar across the Straits of Gibraltar. He defeated the Visigoths, near Tarifa, in 711, to bring seven centuries of civilization when the rest of Europe lived in the Dark Ages. He gave his name to Gibraltar – Djebel (mount) Tarik.

EL MANSOUR EDDAHBI The victory over the Portuguese at the Battle of the Three Kings in 1578 gave great prestige to El Mansour Eddahbi who suceeded his brother (who died in the battle). Mansour means "victorious"; Eddahbi means "golden".

MOHAMMED V Born in Fes in 1909, the third son of Sultan Moulay Youssef, he was chosen by the French to succeed his father on **18 November, 1927**. He was unprepared for his role, but gained strength with experience. He supported the joint manifesto of **11 January, 1944**, arguing for independence; he spoke openly for independence in Tangier, then in the International Zone, on **9 April, 1947**, and was deposed by the French on **20 August, 1953**. He returned from exile on **16 November, 1955**, to a hero's welome and secured independence on **2 March, 1956**. He died in 1961 and was succeeded by his elder son, Hassan II.

MOHAMMED BEN ADDALLAH/SIDI MOHAMMED BEN ABDALLAH Grandson of Moulay Ismail, he gained the throne in 1757, and brought some order out of chaos. He established Essaouira in the 1760s, drove the Portuguese from El Jadida, armed the port of Larache and developed Tangier. Finally he contained the Spanish in their enclaves.

MOHAMMED ZERKTOUNI The most famous Moroccan freedom fighter. On 24 December, 1953, in Casablanca's central market he placed a bomb in a shopping basket which killed twenty people and injured twenty-eight. The choice of Christmas Eve was symbolic: Mohammed V had been exiled on 20 August, 1953 – the eve of Aïd El Kebir.

MOKHTAR SOUSSI Poet and nationalist figure during the French occupation. On independence, he became the government minister of habous (religious foundations which fund mosques, hospitals and schools). He also wrote a twelve-volume history of the Souss, his native province.

MOULAY ABDALLAH/PRINCE MOULAY ABDALLAH Younger son of Mohammed V. He married a Lebanese princess, Lamia Sohl and often deputized for his brother, Hassan II. He died in 1984.

MOULAY EL CHERIF/MOULAY RACHID First Sultan (1666–1672) of the Alaouite dynasty – originally an Arab family which settled in the Tafilalt in the twelfth century, where they lived modestly for centuries before seizing power. Er

Rachidia (and its main street) are named after Moulay Rachid.

MOULAY HASSAN/HASSAN I The last notable Alaouite Sultan (1873–1894) before the French Protectorate. He strived to damp down European-sponsored rebellion, attempting to reform his army with the help of a Scottish clan chieftain, Caid Harry MacLean. He died suddenly and was succeeded by his son, Abd El Aziz, a profligate dreamer.

MOULAY IDRISS/MOULAY IDRISS I/ MOULAY IDRISS II Father and his posthumous son by a Berber mother. Moulay Idriss I (788–91) founded the first orthodox Muslim dynasty, ruling the northern Maghreb from Tlemcen, now in Algeria, to the Atlantic. After a regency, his son, Moulay Idriss II (804–28), came to the throne; he founded Fes and is regarded as the father of the Moroccan state.

MOULAY ISMAIL The second Sultan of the Alaouite dynasty (1672–1727), but the first to establish complete rule over Morocco. His 55-year reign was one of the longest, and said to be the most brutal, in Moroccan history. He chose, and developed, Meknes as his capital. After his death, his sons fought over the succession and chaos ensued.

MOULAY YOUSSEF Appointed by the French as Sultan (1912–27); he was the father of Mohammed V and grandfather of Hassan II.

MOUSSA IBN NOUSSAR Followed Oqba Ibn Nafi (see below) and converted the Berbers again to Islam. He conquered all the territory as far south as the Tafilalt, and launched Tarik Ibn Zaid across the Straits of Gibralter.

OQBA IBN NAFI Military general and missionary who led the first Arab expedition westwards to convert the Berbers to Islam. He left Arabia in 666; founded Kairouan in present-day Tunisia in 670; and moved on into Morocco, reaching the Atlantic in 682. He was ambushed and killed by Berbers in (present- day) Algeria on his return to the east.

PRINCE HERETIER SIDI MOHAMMED/ PRINCE SIDI MOHAMMED Hassan II's elder son and the heir to the throne, born in Rabat on 21 August, 1963. As his father before him, he is being groomed to rule and is increasingly seen with his younger brother, Prince Sidi Rachid, attending national and international events with his father.

SALAH EDDINE EL AYOUBI (1137–90) Better known in the West as Salah Al Din or Saladin. He recaptured Jerusalem (then known, in Arabic, as Al Qods) from the Crusaders in 1187.

YACOUB EL MANSOUR/YACOUB EL MAN-SOUR AL MOUAHIDI Powerful Sultan (1184–99) who created an empire comprising Muslim Spain and most of North Africa. He won the title "Mansour" (Victorious) when he defeated the Christians under Alfonso VIII of Castile at the battle of Alarcos on 18 July, 1195. He was a generous patron of poets and philosophers.

DATES

Numerous dates, particularly those associated with Mohammed V and Hassan II (see their respective entries), have been commemorated as street names. The most common include:

11 January, 1944 Mohammed V backed the nationalist cause when the Istiqlal party issued its manifesto on 11 January, 1944, demanding, for the first time, not just reform but independence.

29 February, 1960 The Agadir earthquake struck thirteen minutes before midnight, lasting fifteen seconds.

2 March, 1956 France renounced the Protectorate and, in a formal treaty, recognized Moroccan independence. It was the 45th anniversary of the entry of French troops into Fes.

3 March, 1961 Aïd El Arch (Feast of the Throne) is celebrated on the anniversary of the accession of the king. Since Hassan II ascended the throne on 3 March, 1961, Aïd El Arch has been celebrated on that date.

16 August, 1953 Over three days (16–18 August, 1953) there were anti-French riots in Casablanca, Rabat, Marrakesh and Oujda. Over 45 people were killed and more than eighty injured in Oujda alone on 16 August.

20 August, 1953 On this day, the eve of Aïd El Kebir, Mohammed V was deposed by the French and was exiled first in Corsica, then Madagascar. Mayhem followed.

6 November, 1975 The date of the Green March – Al Massira Al Khadra (see below).

16 November, 1955 Mohammed V returned from exile to a hero's welcome. He told crowds around the Rabat Palace that the Protectorate was over and independence would follow.

18 November, 1927/18 November, 1955 Mohammed V ascended the throne on 18 November, 1927 and thus, during his reign, this was celebrated as Aïd El Arch (see 3 March, above). In 1955, it was also celebrated as Independence Day and has been celebrated subsequently as such. The three days (16, 17 & 18 November) are taken as a holiday and are known as Les Trois Glorieuses.

EVENTS/ORGANIZATIONS

AL JAMIA AL ARABI The Arab League: formed in Egypt in 1945 and moved to Tunisia in 1979 following the Camp David peace accord between Egypt and Israel.

AL MASSIRA AL KHADRA/MARCHE VERTE The Green March into then-Spanish Sahara was led by Ahmed Osman, Prime Minister at the time and brother-in-law to Hassan II. It began on 6 November, 1975, and on 14 November Spain transferred administration of the territory to Morocco and Mauritania.

BIR ANZARANE Town in the Western Sahara and site of fierce battle between Moroccan and Polisario forces in 1979.

EL HOURIA Houria means freedom/liberté.

F.A.R./FORCES ARMÉES ROYALES After Mohammed V and Hassan II, the Armed Forces is the most popular name for avenues/boulevards, and their motto 'God, the Fatherland and the King' is to be found prominently displayed on many a hillside.

ISTIQLAL Istiqlal means **independence** and was adopted as its name by the nationalist party formed in Fes in 1943, with Allal Al Fasi as its first president. By 1951, the party had 100,000 members.

OUED EL MAKHAZINE Site of the Battle of the Three Kings (see El Mansour Eddahbi, opposite). The Portuguese found themselves trapped in a fork between the river Loukis and its tributary, the Oued El Makhazine. In European histories it is more often referred to as the battle of Ksar El Kebir.

LANGUAGE

Very few people who come to Morocco learn to speak a word of Arabic, let alone anything of the country's three distinct Berber dialects. This is a pity – you'll be treated in a very different way if you make even a small effort to master basic phrases – though not really surprising. Moroccans are superb linguists: much of the country is bilingual in French, and anyone who has significant dealings with tourists will know some English and maybe half-a-dozen other languages, too.

If you can speak French, you'll be able to get by almost anywhere you care to go; it is worth refreshing your knowledge before coming – and, if you're not too confident, bringing a good English–French phrasebook. Spanish is also useful, and widely understood in the old Spanish colonial zones around Tetouan and the Rif, and in the Deep South.

MOROCCAN ARABIC

Moroccan Arabic, the country's "official" language, is substantially different from "classical" Arabic, or from the modern Arabic spoken in Egypt and the Gulf States. If you speak any form of Arabic, however, you will be able to make yourself understood. Egyptian Arabic, in particular, is familiar to most Moroccans, through soap operas on TV, and many will adapt their speech accordingly.

PRONUNCIATION

There are no silent letters – you pronounce everything that's written – including double vowels. Letters and syllables **in bold** should be stressed.
Here are some keys to follow in pronouncing:

kh	like the "ch" in Scottish loch		ay	as in "say"
gh	like the French "r" (a slight gargling sound)		q	like "k" but further back in throat
ai	as in "eye"		j	like "s" in pleasure

BASICS

Yes	Na'**am**, E**ey**eh	(Very) good	Mez**yena** (bz**ef**)
No	La	Bad/"ugly"	**Mes**hee mez**yena**/**khai**b
Please	Min**fad**lik/ Af**ek**	Beautiful	Zween/zweena
Thank you	Shokran/ Baraka**low**fik	Today	Ly**oom**/ lee**oom**
(polite response – **Blej**meel)		Tomorrow	**Gh**edda

GREETINGS AND FAREWELLS

Hello	La **bes**	My name is	Ismee. . .
(informal, to one person)		What's your name?	S**mee**tik?
Response	Be**heer**	See you later.	N'**shoof**ik min bad
Hello	Sal**am** wa**lay**koom	. . . God willing	. . . In**shall**ah
(formal, to a group; response – Wa**lay**koom salam)		(response to "In**shall**ah" is In**shall**ah)	
		Good night	**Leel**a saieeda
Good morning	Sbah l'**khir**	Good-bye	B**slem**ah
Good afternoon	Msa l'**khir**	Bon voyage	Treq sal**ama**

DIRECTIONS, TRAVELLING, AND ACCOMMODATION

Where is . . . ?	Feen **kay**n . . . ?	When is the	Wa**qtash** l'kar/tren?
. . . a (good) hotel?	. . . O**tel** (mizee**yen**)	bus/train?	
. . . a campsite?	. . . Moo**khai**yem	First/last/next	**Loo**wel/L'**akh**er/Lee
. . . a restaurant?	. . . Restaurant		minbad
. . . a bank?	. . . Bank	Write it (please).	Ktib ha (**Af**ek)
. . . the bus station?	. . . **Mah**atat d'l**keer**an	Do you have a room?	Wesh **and**ik wahid
. . . the train station?	. . . l'Gare		beet?
. . . a toilet?	. . . Vaysay/ W.C.	Can I see it?	Wesh yimkin nshoof?
Straight	**Nee**shan/ tol	Is there. . . ?	Wesh kayn . . . ?
(To the) left,	(Al) Leeser,	. . . a (hot) shower?	. . . Doosh (skhoon)
right	Lee**min**	. . . a window?	. . . **Ser**jem
Near, far	Qreeb, Baieed	. . . a key?	. . . **Sar**oot
Junction	Rompwa	Can we camp here?	Wesh yimkin n**khai**moo
Here, there	Hn**na**, Tem**ma**		hanna

BUYING AND NUMBERS

How much (is that)?	Bsh **hal** (hadeek)	I want something. . .	Bgheet shi**haja** . . .
This isn't good	Hadee **mesh**ee mizee**yen**	. . . else	. . . **okh**ra
Too expensive	**Gha**lee bz**ef**	. . . better than this	. . . khir min hadee
. . . (for me)	(**al**iya)	. . . like this	. . . b**hal** hadee
Still too expensive	Mazal **gha**lee bz**ef**	(but)	(walakeen)
Do you have. . . ?	wesh **and**ik. . . ?	. . . larger, smaller	. . . ke**bira**, seg**hira**
Okay	**Wak**ha	. . . cheaper	. . . r**khay**sa

1	wahed	12	tinach	40	arbaeen
2	tneen (Classical)	13	teltach	50	khamseen
	jooj (everyday)	14	arbatach	60	setteen
3	tlata	15	khamstach	70	seba'een
4	arba	16	settach	80	tmaneen
5	khamsa	17	sebatach	90	tsa'een
6	setta	18	tmentach	100	mia
7	sebaa	19	tsatach	200	miateen
8	tmenia	20	achreen	300	telt mia
9	tse'ud	21	wahed u achrin	400	arba mia
10	achra	22	tneen u achrin	1000	alef
11	hadach	30	tlateen		

USEFUL PHRASES/REACTIONS

I have . . .	Andee . . .	. . . baggage	. . . bag**gaj**/how**ayj**
That's all	Sahfee	Help!	A**teqq**/ **Ow**nee!
I don't have any money	Mandeesh floos	How do you say?	Keef t**kool**oo?
I've seen it already.	Shift ha baada	Excuse me	**Smeh** lee
I don't want any.	Mabghee**tsh**	Sorry, I apologise	Asif
I don't understand.	Maf**hem**sh	Never mind, so it goes	**Maa**lesh
Do you understand?	Wesh f**hem**tee?	No problem	Meckee mush**keel**
Get lost!	Seer!	Respect yourself	l**h**tarim na**f**sak
Everything's fine.	**Kool**shee mizee**yen**	(a term of admonition)	
Let's go!	**Yallah!**	Calm down	**Tawil ba**lak
Watch out!	**And**ak/ **Bal**ek!	(literally, "lengthen	
I've lost . . .	Msha leeya . . .	your mind")	
. . . passport	. . . passeport	You honour us	Too-shah-rif-na
. . . ticket	. . . **bee**yay/ warqa	Patience is a virtue	As-**sob**rmin Allah
. . . key	. . . **sar**oot		

BERBER WORDS AND PHRASES IN TASHELHAÏT

There are three **Berber dialects** which encompass roughly geographical areas. They are known by several names, of which these are the most common:

Riffi – The Rif mountains and Northern Morocco
Zaian, Tamazight – The Middle Atlas and Central Morocco
Tashelhaït, Soussi, Chleuh – The High and Anti-Atlas and the South

As the most popular Berber areas for visitors are the High Atlas and South, the following is a very brief guide to **Tashelhaït words and phrases.**

Basics

Yes, no	Eyeh, Oho	Tomorrow	Sbah
Thank you, please	Barakaufik	Yesterday	Eegdam
Good	Eefulkee/Eeshwa	Excuse me	Semhee
Bad	Khaib	Berbers	Shleuh
Today	Ghasad		

Greetings and Farewells (All Arabic greetings understood)

Hello	La bes darik (man)	See you later	Akrawes dah inshallah
(response – la bes)	La bes darim (woman)	Goodbye	Akayaoon Arbee
How are you?	Meneek antgeet?	Say hello to your	Sellum flfamilenik
(response – la bes Imamdulah)		family	

Directions and names on maps

Where is. . . ?	Mani heela . . . ?	I want to go to . . .	Reeh . . .
. . . the road to . . .	. . . aghares s . . .	(literally, "I want")	
. . . the village . . .	. . . doowar . . .		
. . . the river . . .	. . . aseet . . .	**On survey maps you'll find these names:**	
. . the mountain . . .	. . . adrar . . .	Mountain	Adrar, Djebel
. . the pass . . .	. . . tizee . . .	River	Assif, Oued
. . . your house	. . . teegimeenik	Pass (of)	Tizi (n.)
Is it far/close?	Ees yagoog/eeqareb?	Shepherd's hut	Azib
Straight	Neeshan	Hill, small mountain	Aourir
To the right/left	Fofaseenik/fozelmad	Ravine	Talat
Where are you going?	Manee treet? (s.)	Rock	Azrou
	Manee drem? (pl.)	("n" between words indicates the possessive,"of")	

Buying and numbers

1	yen	8	tem	22	Ashreent d seen d mrawet
2	seen	9	tza	30	Ashreent d mrawet
3	krad	10	mrawet	40	Snet id ashreent
4	koz	11	yen d mrawet	50	Snet id ashreent d mrawet
5	smoos	12	seen d mrawet	100	Smoost id ashreent/meeya
6	sddes	20	Ashreent		
7	sa	21	Ashreent d yen d mrawet		

How much is it?	Minshk aysker?	. . . food	. . . teeremt
No good	oor eefulkee	. . . a mule	. . . aserdon
Too expensive	Eeghula bzef	. . . a place to sleep	. . . kra lblast mahengwen
Come down a little (in price)	Nuqs emeek	. . . water	. . . amen
Give me . . .	Feeyee . . .	**Imperatives you may hear**	
I want . . .	Reeh . . .	Sit	Gawer, Skoos
Big/Small	Mqorn/Eemzee	Drink	Soo
A lot/little	Bzef/eemeek	Eat	Shta
Do you have . . . ?	Ees daroon . . . ?	Here	Rede (when handing something to someone)
Is there . . . ?	Ees eela . . . ?		

FRENCH ESSENTIALS

Basics and greetings

Yes/no	Oui/non	Could you?	Pourriez-vous?
Hello, good day	Bonjour	Why?	Pourquoi?
Sorry, excuse me	Pardon	What?	Quoi?
How are you?	Ça va?	Open	Ouvert
Goodbye	Au revoir	Closed	Fermé
Please	S'il vous plaît	Go away!	Va-t-en
Thank you	Merci	Stop messing me about!	Arrête de m'emmerder!
I/you	Je/vous	No confidence!	Pas de confiance!

Directions

Where is the road for . . . ?	Quelle est la route pour . . . ?	Far	Loin
		When?	Quand?
Where is . . . ?	Où est . . . ?	At what time?	A quelle heure?
Do you have . . . ?	Avez vous . . . ?	Write it down, please	Écrivez-le, s'il vous plaît
. . . a room?	. . . une chambre?	Now	Maintenant
Here, there	Ici, là	Later	Plus tard
Right	A droite	Never	Jamais
Left	A gauche	Today	Aujourd'hui
Straight on	Tout droit	Tomorrow	Demain
Near	Proche, près	Yesterday	Hier

Things

Bus	Car, autobus	Key	Clef
Bus station	Gare routière	Roof	Terrasse
Railway	Chemin de fer	Passport	Passeport
Airport	Aéroport	Exchange	Change
Railway station	Gare	Post office	Poste
Ferry	Ferry	Stamps	Timbres
Lorry	Camion	Left luggage	Consigne
Ticket (return)	Billet (de retour)	Visa	Visa
Bank	Banque	Money	Argent

Buying

How much/many?	Combien?	Like this/that	Comme ceci/cela
How much does that cost?	Combien ça coute?	What is it?	Qu'est-ce que c'est?
Too expensive	Trop cher	Enough	Assez
More/less	Plus/moin	Big	Grand
Cheap	Bon marché	Little	Petit

NUMERALS

١	1	١٠	10	١٩	19	٨٠	80
٢	2	١١	11	٢٠	20	٩٠	90
٣	3	١٢	12	٢١	21	١٠٠	100
٤	4	١٣	13	٢٢	22	٢٠٠	200
٥	5	١٤	14	٣٠	30	٣٠٠	300
٦	6	١٥	15	٤٠	40	٤٠٠	400
٧	7	١٦	16	٥٠	50	١٠٠٠	1000
٨	8	١٧	17	٦٠	60		
٩	9	١٨	18	٧٠	70		

ARABIC/BERBER PHRASEBOOKS & LEARNING MATERIALS

Arabic phrasebooks

Moroccan Arabic Phrasebook (Lonely Planet, Australia). The most functional English–Moroccan Arabic phrasebook.

In Moroccan bookshops, you can pick up a *Guide de Conversation/Conversation Guide*, which covers basic phrases of English–French–Moroccan Arabic–Berber.

Arabic coursebooks

Ernest T. Abdel Massih, *An Introduction to Moroccan Arabic*; *Advanced Moroccan Arabic*. Both of these are published by University of Michigan Press, with accompanying tapes.

Richard S. Harris and Mohammed Abn Tald, *Basic Course in Moroccan Arabic* (Georgetown UP).

Berber coursebooks

Ernest T. Abdel Massih, *A Course in Spoken Tamazight: Berber Dialects of the Middle Atlas*; *A Reference Grammar of Tamazight, Plus An Introduction to the Berber Language*. Again, both these are published by University of Michigan Press, with accompanying tapes.

Arabic lessons in Morocco

Contact the American Language Centre (head office: 1 Place de la Fraternité, Casablanca).

University of Michigan Publications

For **books** write to The Publications Secretary, Centre for Near Eastern and North African Studies, 144 Lane Hall, University of Michigan, Ann Arbor, Michigan 48109. For **tapes** write to: Michigan Media Resource Centre (Tape Duplication Service), University of Michigan, 400 S. Fourth Street, Ann Arbor, Michigan 48103.

Bookshops

The following bookshops usually have language reference material:

Librairie des Colonnes, Bd. Pasteur, Tangier.

American Language Centre Bookstore, 1 Place de la Fraternité, just off Bd. Moulay Youssef, Casablanca.

American Bookstore, Rue Tangier, Rabat.

The Maghreb Review and Bookshop, 45 Burton St, London WC1, England.

INDEX

Routes between towns are indicated in small capital letters.

Stay in touch with us!

ROUGH*NEWS* is Rough Guides' free newsletter.
In three issues a year we give you news, travel
issues, music reviews, readers' letters and the
latest dispatches from authors on the road.

I would like to receive ROUGH*NEWS*: please put me on your free mailing list.

NAME . . . .

ADDRESS . . . .

Please clip or photocopy and send to: Rough Guides, 1 Mercer Street, London WC2H 9QJ, England
or Rough Guides, 375 Hudson Street, New York, NY 10014, USA.

direct orders from

		UK	US	CAN
Amsterdam	1-85828-218-7	UK£8.99	US$14.95	CAN$19.99
Andalucia	1-85828-219-5	9.99	16.95	22.99
Antigua Mini Guide	1-85828-346-9	5.99	9.95	12.99
Australia	1-85828-220-9	13.99	21.95	29.99
Austria	1-85828-325-6	10.99	17.95	23.99
Bali & Lombok	1-85828-134-2	8.99	14.95	19.99
Bangkok Mini Guide	1-85828-345-0	5.99	9.95	12.99
Barcelona	1-85828-221-7	8.99	14.95	19.99
Belgium & Luxembourg	1-85828-222-5	10.99	17.95	23.99
Belize	1-85828-351-5	9.99	16.95	22.99
Berlin	1-85828-327-2	9.99	16.95	22.99
Boston Mini Guide	1-85828-321-3	5.99	9.95	12.99
Brazil	1-85828-223-3	13.99	21.95	29.99
Britain	1-85828-312-4	14.99	23.95	31.99
Brittany & Normandy	1-85828-224-1	9.99	16.95	22.99
Bulgaria	1-85828-183-0	9.99	16.95	22.99
California	1-85828-330-2	11.99	18.95	24.99
Canada	1-85828-311-6	12.99	19.95	25.99
Central America	1-85828-335-3	14.99	23.95	31.99
China	1-85828-225-X	15.99	24.95	32.99
Corfu & the Ionian Islands	1-85828-226-8	8.99	14.95	19.99
Corsica	1-85828-227-6	9.99	16.95	22.99
Costa Rica	1-85828-136-9	9.99	15.95	21.99
Crete	1-85828-316-7	9.99	16.95	22.99
Cyprus	1-85828-182-2	9.99	16.95	22.99
Czech & Slovak Republics	1-85828-317-5	11.99	18.95	24.99
Dublin Mini Guide	1-85828-294-2	5.99	9.95	12.99
Edinburgh Mini Guide	1-85828-295-0	5.99	9.95	12.99
Egypt	1-85828-188-1	10.99	17.95	23.99
Europe 1998	1-85828-289-6	14.99	19.95	25.99
England	1-85828-301-9	12.99	19.95	25.99
First Time Asia	1-85828-332-9	7.99	9.95	12.99
First Time Europe	1-85828-270-5	7.99	9.95	12.99
Florida	1-85828-184-4	10.99	16.95	22.99
France	1-85828-228-4	12.99	19.95	25.99
Germany	1-85828-309-4	14.99	23.95	31.99
Goa	1-85828-275-6	8.99	14.95	19.99
Greece	1-85828-300-0	12.99	19.95	25.99
Greek Islands	1-85828-310-8	10.99	17.95	23.99
Guatemala	1-85828-323-X	9.99	16.95	22.99
Hawaii: Big Island	1-85828-158-X	8.99	12.95	16.99
Hawaii	1-85828-206-3	10.99	16.95	22.99
Holland	1-85828-229-2	10.99	17.95	23.99
Hong Kong & Macau	1-85828-187-3	8.99	14.95	19.99
Hotels & Restos de France 1998	1-85828-306-X	12.99	19.95	25.99
Hungary	1-85828-123-7	8.99	14.95	19.99
India	1-85828-200-4	14.99	23.95	31.99
Ireland	1-85828-179-2	10.99	17.95	23.99
Israel & the Palestinian Territories	1-85828-248-9	12.99	19.95	25.99
Italy	1-85828-167-9	12.99	19.95	25.99
Jamaica	1-85828-230-6	9.99	16.95	22.99
Japan	1-85828-340-X	14.99	23.95	31.99
Jordan	1-85828-350-7	10.99	17.95	23.99
Kenya	1-85828-192-X	11.99	18.95	24.99
Lisbon Mini Guide	1-85828-297-7	5.99	9.95	12.99
London	1-85828-231-4	9.99	15.95	21.99
Madrid Mini Guide	1-85828-353-1	5.99	9.95	12.99
Mallorca & Menorca	1-85828-165-2	8.99	14.95	19.99
Malaysia, Singapore & Brunei	1-85828-232-2	11.99	18.95	24.99
Mexico	1-85828-044-3	10.99	16.95	22.99
Morocco	1-85828-169-5	11.99	18.95	24.99
Moscow	1-85828-322-1	9.99	16.95	22.99
Nepal	1-85828-190-3	10.99	17.95	23.99
New York	1-85828-296-9	9.99	15.95	21.99
New Zealand	1-85828-233-0	12.99	19.95	25.99
Norway	1-85828-234-9	10.99	17.95	23.99

UK orders: 0181 899 4036

around the world

Pacific Northwest	1-85828-326-4	UK£12.99	US$19.95	CAN$25.99
Paris	1-85828-235-7	8.99	14.95	19.99
Peru	1-85828-142-3	10.99	17.95	23.99
Poland	1-85828-168-7	10.99	17.95	23.99
Portugal	1-85828-313-2	10.99	17.95	23.99
Prague	1-85828-318-3	8.99	14.95	19.99
Provence & the Cote d'Azur	1-85828-127-X	9.99	16.95	22.99
The Pyrenees	1-85828-308-6	10.99	17.95	23.99
Rhodes & the Dodecanese	1-85828-120-2	8.99	14.95	19.99
Romania	1-85828-305-1	10.99	17.95	23.99
San Francisco	1-85828-299-3	8.99	14.95	19.99
Scandinavia	1-85828-236-5	12.99	20.95	27.99
Scotland	1-85828-302-7	9.99	16.95	22.99
Seattle Mini Guide	1-85828-324-8	5.99	9.95	12.99
Sicily	1-85828-178-4	9.99	16.95	22.99
Singapore	1-85828-237-3	8.99	14.95	19.99
South Africa	1-85828-238-1	12.99	19.95	25.99
Southwest USA	1-85828-239-X	10.99	16.95	22.99
Spain	1-85828-240-3	11.99	18.95	24.99
St Petersburg	1-85828-298-5	9.99	16.95	22.99
Sweden	1-85828-241-1	10.99	17.95	23.99
Syria	1-85828-331-0	11.99	18.95	24.99
Thailand	1-85828-140-7	10.99	17.95	24.99
Tunisia	1-85828-139-3	10.99	17.95	24.99
Turkey	1-85828-242-X	12.99	19.95	25.99
Tuscany & Umbria	1-85828-243-8	10.99	17.95	23.99
USA	1-85828-307-8	14.99	19.95	25.99
Venice	1-85828-170-9	8.99	14.95	19.99
Vienna	1-85828-244-6	8.99	14.95	19.99
Vietnam	1-85828-191-1	9.99	15.95	21.99
Wales	1-85828-245-4	10.99	17.95	23.99
Washington DC	1-85828-246-2	8.99	14.95	19.99
West Africa	1-85828-101-6	15.99	24.95	34.99
Zimbabwe & Botswana	1-85828-186-5	11.99	18.95	24.99
Phrasebooks				
Czech	1-85828-148-2	3.50	5.00	7.00
Egyptian Arabic	1-85828-319-1	4.00	6.00	8.00
French	1-85828-144-X	3.50	5.00	7.00
German	1-85828-146-6	3.50	5.00	7.00
Greek	1-85828-145-8	3.50	5.00	7.00
Hindi & Urdu	1-85828-252-7	4.00	6.00	8.00
Hungarian	1-85828-304-3	4.00	6.00	8.00
Indonesian	1-85828-250-0	4.00	6.00	8.00
Italian	1-85828-143-1	3.50	5.00	7.00
Japanese	1-85828-303-5	4.00	6.00	8.00
Mandarin Chinese	1-85828-249-7	4.00	6.00	8.00
Mexican Spanish	1-85828-176-8	3.50	5.00	7.00
Portuguese	1-85828-175-X	3.50	5.00	7.00
Polish	1-85828-174-1	3.50	5.00	7.00
Russian	1-85828-251-9	4.00	6.00	8.00
Spanish	1-85828-147-4	3.50	5.00	7.00
Swahili	1-85828-320-5	4.00	6.00	8.00
Thai	1-85828-177-6	3.50	5.00	7.00
Turkish	1-85828-173-3	3.50	5.00	7.00
Vietnamese	1-85828-172-5	3.50	5.00	7.00
Reference				
Classical Music	1-85828-113-X	12.99	19.95	25.99
European Football	1-85828-256-X	14.99	23.95	31.99
Internet	1-85828-288-8	5.00	8.00	10.00
Jazz	1-85828-137-7	16.99	24.95	34.99
Millennium	1-85828-314-0	5.00	8.95	11.99
More Women Travel	1-85828-098-2	10.99	16.95	22.99
Opera	1-85828-138-5	16.99	24.95	34.99
Reggae	1-85828-247-0	12.99	19.95	25.99
Rock	1-85828-201-2	17.99	26.95	35.00
World Music	1-85828-017-6	16.99	22.95	29.99

US/International orders: 1-800-253-6476

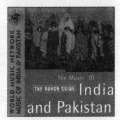

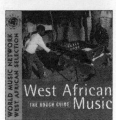

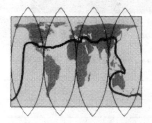

the perfect getaway vehicle

low-price holiday car rental.

rent a car from holiday autos and you'll give yourself real freedom to explore your holiday destination. with great-value, fully-inclusive rates in over 4,000 locations worldwide, wherever you're escaping to, we're there to make sure you get excellent prices and superb service.

what's more, you can book now with complete confidence. our £5 undercut* ensures that you are guaranteed the best value for money in holiday destinations right around the globe.

drive away with a great deal, call holiday autos now on **0990 300 400** and quote ref RG.

holiday autos miles ahead

*in the unlikely event that you should see a cheaper like for like pre-paid rental rate offered by any other independent uk car rental company before or after booking but prior to departure, holiday autos will undercut that price by a full £5. we truly believe we cannot be beaten on price.